Artificial Intelligence and Machine Learning Based Methods and Applications

Artificial Intelligence and Machine Learning Based Methods and Applications

Editors

Adrian Sergiu Darabant
Diana-Laura Borza

MDPI

Basel • Beijing • Wuhan • Barcelona • Belgrade • Novi Sad • Cluj • Manchester

Editors

Adrian Sergiu Darabant
Babes Bolyai University
Cluj-Napoca
Romania

Diana-Laura Borza
Babes Bolyai University
Cluj-Napoca
Romania

Editorial Office
MDPI
St. Alban-Anlage 66
4052 Basel, Switzerland

This is a reprint of articles from the Special Issue published online in the open access journal *Mathematics* (ISSN 2227-7390) (available at: https://www.mdpi.com/si/mathematics/artificial_intelligence_and_machine_learning_based_methods_and_applications).

For citation purposes, cite each article independently as indicated on the article page online and as indicated below:

Lastname, A.A.; Lastname, B.B. Article Title. *Journal Name* **Year**, *Volume Number*, Page Range.

ISBN 978-3-7258-1067-3 (Hbk)
ISBN 978-3-7258-1068-0 (PDF)
doi.org/10.3390/books978-3-7258-1068-0

Contents

About the Editors

Adrian Sergiu Darabant

Adrian Sergiu Darabant received his PhD in 2004 in the field of modeling datasets with complex objects and relations using unsupervised learning. He is currently an Associate Professor at the Babeș Bolyai University of Cluj-Napoca, Romania. He is the author of more than 60 research articles in international peer-reviewed conferences and journals with a focus on modeling distributed systems applied to intelligent and safe transportation and medical care, machine learning theory, and facial analysis.

Diana-Laura Borza

Diana-Laura Borza received her PhD in 2018 in the field of computer vision, with a focus on facial features analysis and movement analysis. Diana Borza is currently a lecturer at the Babeș Bolyai University of Cluj-Napoca, Romania. The application fields of her research are (soft)-biometrics, human behavior understanding, and visual surveillance. In her research work, she successfully applied and combined different paradigms from the field of computer vision: geometrical modeling of objects, probabilistic tracking, motion detection, and deep learning.

Preface

In recent years, significant advancements have been made in the fields of artificial intelligence (AI) and machine learning (ML), and we witnessed their evolution from theoretical concepts and experimental prototypes to powerful technologies that are applied in almost every domain. One of the most notable trends in this evolution is the increasing number of AI and ML practical applications. While theoretical research is important, there has been a significant shift towards applying AI and ML models to address real-world problems. Various domains employ AI and ML to drive innovation, from healthcare and finance to speech recognition and speech and music generation.

Since 2012, the ML methodologies have drastically changed, switching from manually engineered/hand-crafted features to the development of models capable of automatically learning the relevant features from data (convolutional neural networks, recurrent neural networks, and transformers). These approaches enable models to extract meaningful representations directly from the input data without the need for explicit feature engineering. Another observable trend is that different domains, such as computer vision, natural language processing, or structured data processing, adopted similar models. For example, transformers were initially proposed in the field of natural language processing, and over time, they have started to be extensively used in the fields of computer vision (*Vision Transformer, SWIN Transformer, SegFormer,* etc.) and structured data analysis (*TabFormer*). The widespread usage of similar models across various fields proves their effectiveness in capturing complex relationships and extracting representative features from diverse types of data.

The present reprint contains the 26 articles accepted and published in the Special Issue "Artificial Intelligence and Machine Learning Based Methods and Applications, 2023" of the MDPI *Mathematics* journal, which covers a wide range of topics related to the theoretical aspects of artificial intelligence (AI) and machine learning (ML), and their practical applications. The chapters contain theoretical advancements, such as model compression through knowledge distillation, time series analysis, or effective augmentation techniques, but the majority of the works are related to applications of machine learning algorithms. This is proof of the efficiency and power of deep learning models and their potential to drive advancements in various research and application domains. The applications presented in the chapters of this reprint include medical image processing for mammography or lung cancer detection, text analysis for predicting the difficulty of a text or text authorship prediction, speech recognition for young children, and solid deformation resistance analysis.

The compilation of articles in this Special Issue not only shows the amplitude of recent research works in the fields of AI and ML, but it is also a starting point for researchers and AI enthusiasts to understand the landscape of possible real-world AI/ML applications. Moreover, the interdisciplinary nature of the contributions demonstrates the capacity of AI/ML models to go beyond isolated research areas and to foster cross-disciplinary and collaborative research projects.

As Guest Editors of this Special Issue, we express our gratitude to the authors for their high-quality contributions, the reviewers for their insightful comments that helped the authors improve the quality of the submitted manuscripts, and the administrative team at MDPI publications for their assistance in fulfilling this project. Last but not least, a special thank you to Ms. Caitlynn Tong, the Section Managing Editor of the Special Issue, for her exceptional collaboration and invaluable assistance.

Adrian Sergiu Darabant and Diana-Laura Borza
Editors

mathematics

MDPI

Article

Correlation Assessment of the Performance of Associative Classifiers on Credit Datasets Based on Data Complexity Measures

Francisco J. Camacho-Urriolagoitia [1], Yenny Villuendas-Rey [1,*], Itzamá López-Yáñez [1], Oscar Camacho-Nieto [1] and Cornelio Yáñez-Márquez [2,*]

1 Instituto Politécnico Nacional, Centro de Innovación y Desarrollo Tecnológico en Cómputo, Av. Juan de Dios Bátiz s/n, Nueva Industrial Vallejo, GAM, Mexico City 07700, Mexico; fcamachou1300@alumno.ipn.mx (F.J.C.-U.); ilopezy@ipn.mx (I.L.-Y.); ocamacho@ipn.mx (O.C.-N.)
2 Instituto Politécnico Nacional, Centro de Investigación en Computación, Av. Juan de Dios Bátiz s/n, Nueva Industrial Vallejo, GAM, Mexico City 07738, Mexico
* Correspondence: yvilluendasr@ipn.mx (Y.V.-R.); cyanez@cic.ipn.mx (C.Y.-M.)

Abstract: One of the four basic machine learning tasks is pattern classification. The selection of the proper learning algorithm for a given problem is a challenging task, formally known as the algorithm selection problem (ASP). In particular, we are interested in the behavior of the associative classifiers derived from Alpha-Beta models applied to the financial field. In this paper, the behavior of four associative classifiers was studied: the One-Hot version of the Hybrid Associative Classifier with Translation (CHAT-OHM), the Extended Gamma (EG), the Naïve Associative Classifier (NAC), and the Assisted Classification for Imbalanced Datasets (ACID). To establish the performance, we used the area under the curve (AUC), F-score, and geometric mean measures. The four classifiers were applied over 11 datasets from the financial area. Then, the performance of each one was analyzed, considering their correlation with the measures of data complexity, corresponding to six categories based on specific aspects of the datasets: feature, linearity, neighborhood, network, dimensionality, and class imbalance. The correlations that arise between the measures of complexity of the datasets and the measures of performance of the associative classifiers are established; these results are expressed with Spearman's Rho coefficient. The experimental results correctly indicated correlations between data complexity measures and the performance of the associative classifiers.

Keywords: supervised classification; meta-learning; associative classification; finances

MSC: 68T05

Citation: Camacho-Urriolagoitia, F.J.; Villuendas-Rey, Y.; López-Yáñez, I.; Camacho-Nieto, O.; Yáñez-Márquez, C. Correlation Assessment of the Performance of Associative Classifiers on Credit Datasets Based on Data Complexity Measures. *Mathematics* **2022**, *10*, 1460. https://doi.org/10.3390/math10091460

Academic Editors: Anatoliy Swishchuk, Christoph Frei, Catalin Stoean, Diana-Laura Borza and Adrian Sergiu Darabant

Received: 15 February 2022
Accepted: 18 April 2022
Published: 26 April 2022

1. Introduction

Numerous classification models have been developed in the scientific literature, with different theoretical foundations. One of the pioneers is the k-nearest neighbors (kNN) classifier [1], which is based on neighborhood criteria. Other well-known classifiers are based on probabilistic approaches, such as naïve Bayes [2], whereas others use information theory as part of their foundation (for example, ID3 [3] and C4.5 [4]).

From another perspective and focusing on finding hyperspaces where decision classes are separated, support vector machine (SVM) models have been developed [5]. Models of the human nervous system have also been used for classification tasks through the proposal of artificial neural networks (ANN) [6].

On the other hand, in Mexico, the associative approach has been developed, with the Alpha-Beta associative models [7] and their derivatives, for classification tasks. Among these derived models are the Smallest Normalized Distance Associative Memory (SNDAM) method [8] and the Hybrid Associative Classifier with Translation (HACT) method [9], also known as CHAT for its Spanish acronym, and its derivative, the CHAT-OHM classifier [10].

Another classification model within this approach is the Gamma classifier [11], with its versions of weight adjustments with differential evolution (CAG-ED) [12], its version for handling mixed and incomplete data (the Extended Gamma associative classifier, EG) [13], and the version of the latter which uses weight adjustment with differential evolution (Modified Associative Gamma Classifier, CAGM-ED) [14].

In addition to the previous models, the Naïve Associative Classifier (NAC) [15] stands out, with its disambiguation variants (NACe) [16] NACe-kVotes and NACe-kMajority [17] and its variant for the classification of data streams (Naïve Associative Classifier for Online Data, NACOD) [18].

Alpha-Beta associative models and their derivatives have shown satisfactory performance in numerous classification tasks from different fields. Among these, the medical [19], financial [20], social [14], productive [21], educational [22,23], and environmental [24] fields can be highlighted.

However, with so many different models available, how can one know which model will offer the best classification for a specific problem? The focus of our research is on the behavior of associative classifiers in the financial field. Several studies indicate that associative-based classifiers have shown good performance for finance-related datasets, outperforming several of the well-known supervised classifiers such as support vector machines, neural networks, decision trees, statistical-based classifiers, and others [15,16,25,26]. This is where the topic of interest for this paper appears and why we decided to focus on associative-based classifiers.

The algorithm selection problem (ASP) is a challenging learning task, focused on selecting proper classification algorithms for a given problem [27]. ASP has been the focus of various studies in the machine learning community, and for the supervised classification domain, meta-learning has shown ample achievements in solving the ASP. However, even though numerous studies have been conducted using diverse classifiers in the literature, to the knowledge of the authors of this study, there has been no comparative study that critically analyzes, summarizes, and evaluates the performance of associative classifiers derived from Alpha-Beta models, that allows the identification of the measures of data complexity that influence the good or bad performance of these models, considering their correlation with the data complexity measures.

This paper addresses a problem of which the solution would be beneficial for researchers in artificial intelligence, pattern recognition, and related areas: How can we know, in advance, in which dataset(s) a specific classifier will exhibit good (or bad) performance? The innovative and scientific contribution of this paper consists in the analysis of the performance of associative classifiers, considering their correlation with the measures of data complexity, corresponding to six categories based on specific aspects of the datasets.

In this study, we intended to make use of different complexity measures that will help to understand how some of the mentioned associative-based classifiers behave in the financial field, based on the data of the problem to be solved. The experimental results correctly indicate the existing correlations between complexity measures and the performance of the associative classifiers.

2. Background

Ho and Basu attribute the complexity of supervised classification problems to a combination of three main factors: the ambiguity of the classes, the scarcity and dimension of the data, and the complexity of the limit that separates the classes [28].

To determine the presence of such factors, several data descriptors have been introduced, based mainly on the geometric and statistical properties of the data. The data complexity measures proposed by Ho and Basu [28] are dedicated to computing the complexity of the boundary needed to separate binary classification problems (later extended for multiclass problems. Ho and Basu split their measures into three categories: individual feature value overlap measures; class separability measures; and geometry, topology, and density measures of multiple measures.

Ho and Basu's work was instrumental in determining the complexity of a given dataset using data descriptors. Furthermore, Mansilla and Ho [29] studied the competence domains of the XCS classification system (the learning classifier system type) in the area of complexity measures and found that difficult problems for this system are characterized by a large number of samples located in the decision boundaries, the presence of a high number of adherence subsets, a high dispersion of class samples, and a high level of nonlinearity in the shapes of classes and boundaries.

A couple of years later, Sánchez et al. [30] analyzed how the complexity of the training data affects the kNN classifier and showed that the performance of this classifier is very susceptible to class overlapping and class density; in addition, they found that high dimensionality also affects the performance of kNN. Sanchez et al. also pointed out that measures are domain-dependent. That is, the performance of the classifier will depend on the characteristics of the problem.

In their studies, Luengo and Herrera presented two rules that are "simple, interpretable, and precise" to describe the good and bad performance of the FH-GBML method [31]. Two years later, they conducted another study [32]. They computed five data complexity measures and class separability measures to obtain ranges of such metrics for which the method performed significantly well or poorly.

The competence domains of the semi-naïve Bayes network classifiers (BNC) have also been studied by Flores, Gómez and Martínez [33]. They define the general attributes of ideal datasets for classification with BNCs. They also provide an automatic method to find the best BNC (in terms of prediction errors) given a particular dataset.

One year later, Luengo and Herrera [34] proposed a method of automatically extracting the competence domains for classifiers using measures of data complexity. The objective was to recognize whether the classification problem was good or bad for each classifier and obtain intervals of good performance for the classifiers based on data complexity measures. Their results showed that the domains of competence obtained were general enough to find the right datasets for the classifiers.

Years later, Morán-Fernández et al. [35] studied micro-array data, showing that the classification performance can be predicted by complexity measures and observed that attribute selection can reduce the complexity of the data.

In 2018 Barella [36] and collaborators studied data complexity measures for imbalanced classification tasks. They showed that several of the existing data complexity measures do not consider the difficulty of imbalanced classification problems. Therefore, they improved some data complexity measures to assess classes one by one and focus on the minority class. However, they also showed that data complexity measures mainly approximate majority class difficulty, which can be misleading, especially for imbalanced tasks with high class overlap. In addition, Barella suggested evaluating the difficulty of both classes in understanding the full classification problem, although minority class difficulty is often the main challenge in imbalanced tasks.

A year later, Lorena et al. [37] reviewed the main measures of data complexity in the literature and concluded that these measures allow one to characterize the complexity of a classification problem considering a geometrical approach and the distribution of data within or between classes. In 2020 Khan and collaborators [38] produced a survey about meta-learning for classifier selection. Using this approach, they deeply analyzed the problem of recommending a classification algorithm based on meta-learning. Their in-depth analysis showed that meta-learning was successful in the automatic algorithm recommendation process.

A recent study by Maillo et al. [39] analyzed redundancy and complexity measures for big data. The authors emphasized that it is possible to obtain similar or better results in several big data tasks by using a small set of quality data.

Since no classifier can regularly obtain the best performance for each classification problem, an effect proved in the no free lunch theorems [40], the analysis of data complexity measures allows us to understand the situations in which a certain classifier is successful and in which it fails.

3. Materials and Methods

This section describes the most important data complexity measures and some associative classifiers derived from the Alpha-Beta associative models that will be tested against different datasets for the development of this area of research.

3.1. Data Complexity Measures

Some of the most widely used data complexity measures are those proposed by Ho and Basu [28] and later extended in [30,41] to deal with multiclass classification problems. Ho and Basu [28] split the data complexity measures into three groups: (1) individual characteristic value overlap measures; (2) class separability measures; and (3) geometry, topology, and manifold density measurements. Likewise, Sotoca et al. [42] divided complexity measures into the following groups: (1) overlap measures, (2) class separability measures, and (3) geometry and density measurements.

Subsequently, Lorena et al. [37] classified complexity measures into six categories:

1. Feature-based measures;
2. Linearity measures;
3. Neighborhood measures;
4. Network measures;
5. Dimensionality measures; and
6. Class imbalance measures.

In this work, we use five of the six types of measures mentioned above. To compute the measures, we assume that we have a learning dataset "T" that contains pairs of instances (x_i, y_i), where $x_i = (x_{i1}, \ldots, x_{im})$ and $y_i \in \{1, \ldots, n_c\}$. That is, each instance x_i is described by m attributes and also has a class label y_i of one of the n_c classes.

Most data complexity measures assume that the attributes are numeric and complete (no missing values). Categorical values need to be codified into numeric ones, and missing values must be deleted or imputed. An additional assumption is that linearly separable problems are simpler than nonlinear classification problems.

Table 1 presents the data complexity measures used in this study. The measures used consisted of three feature-based measures (F1, F2, and F3), two linearity measures (L1 and L2), four neighborhood-based measures (N1, N2, N3, and N4), one network measure (T1), and one dimensionality measure (T2). We did not consider class-imbalance-related measures in this study. All the data complexity measures used here were presented in a review by Lorena et al. [37].

Table 1. Complexity measures used.

Measure	Equation
Maximum Fisher's Discriminant Ratio (F1)—Complementary formulation [37]	$F1 = \frac{1}{1+\max_{i=1}^{m} r_{fi}}$
Volume of overlap region (F2)	$F2 = \prod_i^m \frac{\text{overlap}(fi)}{\text{range}(fi)} = \prod_i^m \frac{\max\{0, \text{minmax}(fi) - \text{maxmin}(fi)\}}{\text{maxmax}(fi) - \text{minmin}(fi)}$, where $\text{minmax}(fi) = \min(\max(fi^{c1}), \max(fi^{c2}))$, $\text{maxmin}(fi) = \max(\min(fi^{c1}), \min(fi^{c2}))$, $\text{maxmax}(fi) = \max(\max(fi^{c1}), \max(fi^{c2}))$, $\text{minmin}(fi) = \min(\min(fi^{c1}), \min(fi^{c2}))$ and $\max(fi^{cj})$ and $\min(fi^{cj})$ are the maximum and minimum values of each feature in the class $c_j \in \{1, 2\}$, respectively.

Table 1. *Cont.*

Measure	Equation
Maximum Individual Feature Efficiency (F3)—Complementary formulation [37]	$F3 = \min_{i=1}^{m} \frac{n_o(fi)}{n}$, where $n_o(fi) = \sum_{j}^{n} I(x_{ji} > \max\min(fi) \wedge x_{ji} < \min\max(fi))$
Sum of the Error Distance by Linear Programming (L1)	$L1 = 1 - \frac{1}{1 + SumErrorDist} = \frac{SumErrorDist}{1 + SumErrorDist}$, where $SumErrorDist = \frac{1}{n}\sum_{i=1}^{n} \varepsilon_j$. The ε_j values are determined by optimizing an SVM
Error rate of linear classifier (L2)	$L2 = \frac{\sum_{i=1}^{n} I(h(x_i) \neq y_i)}{n}$ where h(x) is the linear classifier.
Nonlinearity of a Linear Classifier (L3)	$L3 = \frac{1}{l}\sum_{i=1}^{l} I(h_T(\acute{x}_i) \neq \acute{y}_i)$ where $h_T(x)$ is the linear classifier induced using the original dataset T, and l in the number of interpolated examples $\acute{x}_i$ and $\acute{y}_i$ are the corresponding labels.
Fraction of Borderline Points (N1)	$N1 = \frac{1}{n}\sum_{i=1}^{n} I((x_i, x_j) \in MST \wedge\ y_i \neq y_j)$, where MST is a Minimum Spanning Tree obtained over the interpolated data.
Ratio of Intra/Extra Class Nearest Neighbor Distance (N2)	$N2 = 1 - \frac{1}{1+intra\_extra} = \frac{intra\_extra}{1+intra\_extra}$, where $intra\_extra = \frac{\sum_{i=1}^{n} d(x_i, NN(x_i) \in y_i)}{\sum_{i=1}^{n} d(x_i, NN(x_i) \in y_j \neq y_i)}$
Error Rate of the Nearest Neighbor Classifier (N3)	$N3 = \frac{\sum_{i=1}^{n} I(NN(x_i) \neq y_i)}{n}$
Nonlinearity of the Nearest Neighbor Classifier (N4)	$N4 = \frac{1}{l}\sum_{i=1}^{l} I(NN_T(x_i') \neq y_i')$
Fraction of Hyperspheres Covering Data (T1)	$T1 = \frac{\#Hyperspheres(T)}{n}$, where #Hyperspheres(T) is the number of hyperspheres needed to cover the dataset, considering that only points of the same class can be inside the same hypersphere.
Average Number of Features per Dimension (T2)	$T2 = \frac{m}{n}$

In addition, the complexity measures presented here are available for computation in KEEL software [43], which is an open software environment designed for experimentation with supervised classification.

3.2. *Associative Classifiers*

3.2.1. CHAT-OHM

The Hybrid Associative Classifier with Translation (HACT or CHAT by its Spanish acronym) is a classification algorithm proposed by Santiago-Montero [9], which has shown good results in supervised classification [25]. It has two phases: association (in which the classifier is trained) and recovery (in which the classes of the instances to be classified are obtained). This classifier assumes that the dataset does not contain absences of information and that all attributes are numeric. Furthermore, it assumes that the class values are consecutive integers.

This classification algorithm was refined in 2014, with the development of a "One-Hot" version (CHAT-OHM) [10]. The first modification arises in the training phase and consists of a new way of coding the classes. In this case, the classes are formed by binary vectors of size p (instead of vectors of size m as in HACT), and the components of said vectors have the form $y_i^{\mu} = \begin{cases} 1 & \text{if } i = \mu \\ 0 & \text{otherwise} \end{cases}$.

The second modification consists of using the majority vote rule in the classification process. To accomplish this, the CHAT-OHM classification phase has three steps:

1. Translate the instance to classify *o*, considering the mean of the training instances, as $\hat{o} \leftarrow o - \hat{x}$.

2. For each class $k \in \{1, 2, \ldots, m\}$, create a masking vector mv^k of size p, of which the components are $mv^k_\mu = \begin{cases} 1 & \text{if } \hat{x}^\mu \in k \\ 0 & \text{otherwise} \end{cases}$ and obtain the output pattern z^o, as $z^o = \left[\alpha \sum_{\mu=1}^{p} y^\mu \left(\hat{x}^{\mu T}\right)\right]\hat{o}$. Then, for each class obtain a counter vector $cv^k = z^o \wedge mv^k$
3. Compute the components of the output vector (class) for the instance to classify $\hat{o}$ as $y^o_i = \begin{cases} 1 & \text{if } \sum_{j=1}^{p} cv^i_j = \max\limits_{h=1..m}\left[\sum_{j=1}^{p} cv^h_j\right] \\ 0 & \text{otherwise} \end{cases}$. Thus, the class of the input instance x^μ will be returned if and only if the obtained vector has a one in the μ-th component and zero in the remaining components.

Although HACT does not handle mixed or incomplete data, it has achieved good performance in the financial field [25].

3.2.2. Extended Gamma

López-Yáñez introduced the Gamma associative classifier as a model designed to predict time series [44]. It has been applied to several supervised classification tasks [11,21,24]. However, the same as HACT, it assumes that the dataset is numeric and complete. To address this drawback, the Extended Gamma (EG) classifier was proposed [13].

Let be X and P the training and test sets, respectively, from a universe of data U, where each instance $x \in X$, $p \in P$ is described by a set of features $A = \{A_1, A_2, \cdots, A_m\}$; and each attribute A_i has associated a definition domain $dom(A_i)$, which can be numeric or categoric. If the value of an attribute A_i in an instance x is missing, it is denoted as x_i = '?'. Extended Gamma considers the data to belong to a set of classes $K = \{K_1, \ldots, K_c\}$.

EG has the same training phase as its predecessor, and for the classification phase, it replaces the gamma similarity operator with the extended gamma similarity operator, γ_{ext}. To determine the class value of an instance, its average similarity with respect to all classes is computed as:

$$c_{k_l} = \frac{\sum_{i=1}^{n}\sum_{j=1}^{m} w_j * \gamma_{ext}\left(x^i_j, p_j\right)}{n} \quad (1)$$

where x^i_j is the value of the j-th attribute in the i-th instance belonging to the class k_l, w_j is the weight associated with the j-th attribute, and n is the number of instances in the training set having k_l as the class value. If there is a unique maximum in the values of c_{k_l}, the process ends. Otherwise, an iterative process is carried out [13].

The definition of the extended gamma similarity operator allows for the handling of mixed continuous and categorical attributes and missing values. When the value of a feature is unknown, it is assumed that the values are similar, and in the case of categorical features, the patterns will only be similar if the values of the features are equal. For the case of continuous attributes, a definition equivalent to the original operator definition is used.

Extended Gamma has been applied effectively to solve problems of a social nature with mixed and incomplete data, such as electoral predictions [14].

3.2.3. Naïve Associative Classifier

Another associative classifier that is able to deal with mixed and incomplete data is the Naïve Associative Classifier (NAC), which has also been applied to solve finance-related problems [15,26]. This classifier has the properties of being transparent and transportable [15].

The training of NAC includes the computation of the standard deviation of each numeric feature. Such values will be used below for classification. To do so, NAC uses a mixed and incomplete similarity operator to compute the similarity between patterns. This operator can deal with both continuous and categorical attribute values and incomplete information in the data. As was the case for Extended Gamma, NAC computes the average similarities to each class k_l for the instance to classify p. If there is a unique maximum, the corresponding class is returned. Otherwise, ties are broken randomly.

NAC has several variants: NACe, which includes a procedure to disambiguate classes [16]; NACe kVotes, and NACe MajoritykVotes [17], which use neighborhoods in the disambiguation process; and NACOD, which allows the handling of data streams [18]. NAC has shown good performance in solving finance-related problems and has been found to be robust to data imbalance [20].

3.2.4. Assisted Classification for Imbalanced Datasets

The Assisted Classification for Imbalanced Datasets (ACID) classifier was also designed [19] for mixed and incomplete classification problems. In the training phase, ACID includes an optional procedure to compute attribute weights via differential evolution. ACID also deals with class disjoints, by performing clustering, and with class imbalance. Additionally, it uses data aggregation to diminish the influence of class overlapping and noisy or mislabeled instances [19].

In this section, we have detailed the most frequently explored data complexity measures in the literature and the associated classifiers. We found no works that analyzed how data complexity, beyond the analysis of data imbalance, affects the performance of the associative classifiers of the Alpha-Beta approach.

4. Results and Discussion

This section describes the datasets used in this study to obtain the complexity measures described in the previous chapter, as well as some of the performance measures obtained from the described classifiers.

4.1. Datasets

Several datasets containing credit data were used. All of these are related to some of the credit process phases: granting, promotion and recovery. Some of the datasets were obtained from the UCI Machine Learning Repository [45]. The datasets that were used in the experiments are:

- Australian credit approval data (Australian, https://archive.ics.uci.edu/ml/datasets/statlog+(australian+credit+approval) accessed on 15 June 2021);
- German credit data (German, https://archive.ics.uci.edu/ml/datasets/statlog+(german+credit+data), accessed on 15 June 2021)
- Japanese credit approval data (Japanese, https://archive.ics.uci.edu/ml/datasets/Credit+Approval, accessed on 15 June 2021);
- Iranian (Iranian), which was introduced in [46] and was shared by Hassan Sabzevari.
- Polish bankruptcy data (Polish_year1 to Polish_year5, https://archive.ics.uci.edu/ml/datasets/Polish+companies+bankruptcy+data, accessed on 15 June 2021);
- The PAKDD 2009 dataset (the PAKDD, https://www.cs.purdue.edu/commugrate/data/credit_card/, accessed on 15 June 2021); and
- Qualitative bankruptcy data (Qualitative, https://archive.ics.uci.edu/ml/datasets/qualitative_bankruptcy, accessed on 15 June 2021).

These datasets (Table 2) included numerical and categorical attributes, and missing data (four mixed and eight with missing values). They also contained class imbalances, due to 8 of the 11 having IR > 1.5. The number of attributes ranged between six and 64 features, whereas the number of instances was between 250 and 20,000. All datasets corresponded to good and default clients; they only contained two classes.

Table 2. Description of the datasets used.

Dataset	Instances	Attributes		Missing Values	Imbalance Ratio
		Continuous	Categorical		
Australian	690	8	6	No	1.25
German	1000	7	13	No	2.33
Iranian	1002	28	0	Yes	19.04

Table 2. *Cont.*

Dataset	Instances	Attributes		Missing Values	Imbalance Ratio
		Continuous	Categorical		
Japanese	690	6	9	Yes	1.21
Polish_year1	7027	64	0	Yes	24.93
Polish_year2	10,173	64	0	Yes	24.43
Polish_year3	10,503	64	0	Yes	20.22
Polish_year4	9792	64	0	Yes	18.01
Polish_year5	5910	64	0	Yes	13.41
Qualitative	250	0	6	No	1.34
The PAKDD	20,000	10	9	Yes	4.12

4.2. Performance Measures

In the following, we address the performance measures [47] we used in this study, which have been proven to be robust for imbalanced problems [48]. The measures were based on a two-class confusion matrix, as shown in Figure 1.

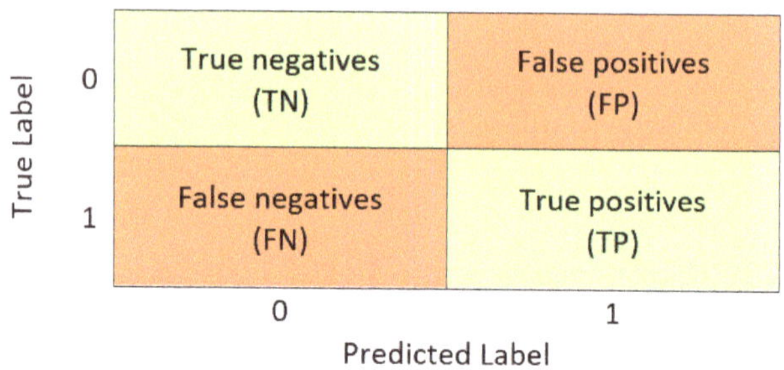

Figure 1. Confusion matrix for a two-class problem.

Three basic performance measures for two-class problems are precision, recall (also known as sensitivity and the true positive rate), and the true negative rate. Other measures, such as the F-score, geometric mean, and the area under the ROC curve, are based on those measures. Table 3 summarizes the performance measures used in this study.

Table 3. Performance measures used.

Measure	Equation
Precision	$P = \frac{TP}{TP + FP}$
Recall	$R = TPR = \frac{TP}{TP + FN}$
True Negative Rate	$TNR = \frac{TN}{TN + FP}$
F-score	$F = 2 * \frac{P * R}{P + R}$
Geometric Mean	$GM = \sqrt{P * R}$
Area under the ROC curve	$AUC = \frac{TPR + TNR}{2}$

In this study, the F-score, the geometric mean, and the area under the ROC curve were considered in order to evaluate the performance of the classifiers.

4.3. Complexity Measures in the Selected Datasets

Table 4 shows the results of the complexity measures computed for the selected datasets. We used KEEL software [43] to obtain these measures. KEEL software automatically stores all data in numeric arrays; therefore, it includes the imputation of the missing values and the conversion of the categorical values of the datasets into numeric values. In addition, KEEL uses the original definition for F1 and F3 measures [28], and therefore, in Table 4, small values of F1 and F3 denote complex problems (inverse relation). Consequently, all remaining complexity measures are proportional to the values; that is, small values correspond to less complex problems.

Table 4. Complexity measure values for the datasets used.

Dataset	F1	F2	F3	L1	L2	L3	N1	N2	N3	N4	T1	T2
Australian	2.28	0.00	0.03	0.30	0.14	0.14	0.32	0.56	0.20	0.16	1.00	39.43
German	2.45	0.01	0.03	0.28	0.14	0.13	0.32	0.57	0.20	0.17	1.00	36.48
Iranian	0.36	0.64	0.01	0.83	0.24	0.33	0.46	0.85	0.31	0.30	1.00	40.00
Japanese	0.35	0.00	0.21	0.10	0.05	0.50	0.12	0.31	0.07	0.37	1.00	28.57
Qualitative	9.51	0.00	0.78	0.60	0.00	0.00	0.03	0.10	0.01	0.00	0.95	33.33
The PAKDD	0.11	0.05	0.00	0.39	0.20	0.50	0.26	0.15	0.06	0.45	1.00	842.11
Polish_year1	0.03	0.00	0.03	0.08	0.04	0.50	0.09	0.57	0.06	0.45	1.00	87.84
Polish_year2	0.01	0.00	0.02	0.08	0.04	0.50	0.11	0.63	0.08	0.47	1.00	127.16
Polish_year3	0.04	0.00	0.03	0.09	0.05	0.50	0.12	0.64	0.08	0.47	1.00	131.29
Polish_year4	0.06	0.00	0.02	0.11	0.05	0.50	0.13	0.63	0.09	0.45	1.00	122.40
Polish_year5	0.18	0.00	0.04	0.14	0.07	0.50	0.15	0.71	0.10	0.39	1.00	73.88

As can be seen, for measure F1 the simplest dataset was the qualitative dataset, and the most difficult ones were the Polish datasets. The F2 measure did not offer much information since it assigned 0.0 to all datasets but the Iranian (0.64), German (0.01), and the PAKDD (0.05) datasets. For measures L1 and L2, the most complex dataset was the German. The L3 measure gave a high complexity to the Japanese, the PAKDD, and the Polish datasets, all of which had values of 0.5.

Regarding measures N1, N2m and N3, again, the German database offered the greatest complexity. According to measure N4, the most complex databases were Polish_year2 and Polish_year3. The T1 measure did not offer much information since it assigned complexities equal to 1.00 for all datasets except the qualitative one. Finally, the T2 measure considered that the most complex dataset was the PKDD09 set.

4.4. Performance of the Classifiers

To establish the performance of the associative classifiers under study, we used a five-fold cross-validation procedure because some datasets were imbalanced. As for performance measures, we used the AUC, F-score, and the geometric mean, as described in Section 4.2. Tables 5–7 present the performance results of each classifier according to the measures mentioned above.

Table 5. Area under the ROC curve of the compared classifiers. The best results are indicated in bold.

Dataset	ACID	CHAT-OHM	EG	NAC
Australian	**0.86**	0.59	0.84	0.83
Japanese	**0.85**	0.66	0.82	0.83
German	0.57	0.64	0.68	**0.69**
Iranian	0.56	0.64	**0.68**	0.50
Qualitative	0.93	0.95	**0.99**	**0.99**
The PAKDD	**0.77**	0.58	0.61	0.61
Polish_year1	0.58	0.52	**0.76**	0.50
Polish_year2	0.56	0.50	**0.71**	0.50
Polish_year3	0.56	0.53	**0.74**	0.50
Polish_year4	0.54	0.55	**0.75**	0.53
Polish_year5	0.65	0.62	**0.79**	0.62

Table 6. F-score of the compared classifiers. The best results are indicated in bold.

Dataset	ACID	CHAT-OHM	EG	NAC
Australian	**0.86**	0.59	0.84	0.83
Japanese	**0.86**	0.66	0.82	0.84
German	0.58	0.63	**0.67**	**0.67**
Iranian	0.60	0.58	**0.63**	0.49
Qualitative	0.93	0.95	**0.99**	**0.99**
The PAKDD	**0.78**	0.57	0.59	0.59
Polish_year1	0.58	0.51	**0.64**	0.50
Polish_year2	0.55	0.50	**0.62**	0.53
Polish_year3	0.57	0.52	**0.64**	0.51
Polish_year4	0.55	0.53	**0.64**	0.54
Polish_year5	0.66	0.57	**0.68**	0.61

Table 7. Geometric mean of the compared classifiers. The best results are indicated in bold.

Dataset	ACID	CHAT-OHM	EG	NAC
Australian	**0.86**	0.59	0.83	0.83
Japanese	**0.85**	0.65	0.82	0.83
German	0.49	0.63	**0.68**	**0.68**
Iranian	0.26	**0.63**	**0.63**	0.00
Qualitative	0.93	0.95	**0.99**	**0.99**
The PAKDD	**0.75**	0.57	0.61	0.61
Polish_year1	0.42	0.51	**0.76**	0.05
Polish_year2	0.39	0.50	**0.71**	0.04
Polish_year3	0.39	0.53	**0.74**	0.10
Polish_year4	0.32	0.55	**0.75**	0.20
Polish_year5	0.57	0.61	**0.79**	0.55

According to the AUC results, the best-performing classifier was EG, which performed the best in seven of the 11 datasets. The ACID and NAC classifiers showed good behavior for the Australian, Japanese, German, and qualitative datasets. Nevertheless, their performance for the remaining datasets was poor, except for the PAKDD dataset, in which ACID showed the best performance. On the other hand, CHAT-OHM demonstrated relatively good performance for the qualitative and German datasets. Equivalent results were shown for the F-score measure.

As for geometric mean, EG was the best in eight of the compared datasets. ACID remained the best in the Australian, Japanese, and PAKDD datasets. In addition, for the qualitative datasets, it displayed satisfactory results. However, the performance was poor for the remaining datasets because the classifier was biased toward one class, with geometric mean values ranging from 0.26 to 0.57.

NAC exhibited a behavior similar to ACID (except for the German dataset, in which NAC performed well), showing bias towards the majority class, with values ranging from 0.0 (Iranian) to 0.55 (Polish_year5). CHAT-OHM obtained average results for most of the compared datasets.

In summary, the ACID classifier showed a good performance for most of the databases, and we observed that it exceeded 0.5 for almost all the measures, except for some databases with a greater number of instances. On the other hand, the CHAT-OHM classifier achieved excellent classification performance for the "qualitative-bankruptcy" database. Nevertheless, in the other datasets it failed to obtain performance percentages greater than 0.7, which made it one of the classifiers with the lowest ranking average for this set of databases.

EG was another classifier with good performance (mostly exceeding percentages of 0.6), making it the classifier with the best results in this study. The EG classifier had an almost perfect classification performance for the qualitative database and relatively good performance for the Australian and Japanese databases.

Finally, in terms of the classification results, the NAC classifier, similarly to the EG, exhibited an almost perfect classification performance with the qualitative-bankruptcy database and a very good performance with the Australian and Japanese databases. However, we can also observe that it showed a certain weakness in the case of databases such as the Polish datasets, in which it classified practically an entire class incorrectly. Moreover, its performance was slightly less efficient compared to the EG classifier.

4.5. Correlation Analysis

Another aim of this study was to analyze in-depth and establish the relationship between complexity measures and associative classifiers. This aspect can be investigated in detail by calculating the correlations that arise between the measures of complexity of the datasets and the measures of performance of the associative classifiers. To accomplish this, intensive use of Spearman's Rho coefficient was made. Spearman's Rho is a nonparametric measure of dependence in which the mean rank of the observations is calculated [49], and the differences are squared and incorporated into the formula. In other words, a classification is assigned to the observations of each variable, and the dependency relationship between two given variables is studied. The interpretation of Spearman's coefficient depends on its values. It ranges between -1 and $+1$, indicating negative or positive associations. Respectively, values close to zero indicate no correlation but not independence. To carry out the correlation tests, two hypotheses were used in all cases:

H0: *There is no correlation between the measures of data complexity and the performance of the analyzed classifiers.*

H1: *There is a correlation between the measures of data complexity and the performance of the analyzed classifiers.*

We set a significance value $\alpha = 0.05$, for a 95% confidence level. Table 8 shows the correlations obtained. In these results, the text "cc" represents the value of the correlation coefficient, whereas "p" is the probability value of the test. If $p \leq \alpha$, we reject the null hypothesis H0 and accept the alternative hypothesis H1; that is, in these scenarios, there is a correlation between the data complexity measures and the performance achieved by the classifiers. These results are shown in bold in the tables. In bold and italics are the results in which the null hypothesis was rejected within a 90% confidence level instead of 95%.

The results obtained for the ACID classifier allowed us to reject the null hypothesis for the measures F1, N2, N4, L1, L3, and T1. The measures F1, N4, and L3 significantly correlated with the performance measures of the F-score, geometric mean, and AUC for the ACID classifier using Spearman's rho coefficient, with 95% confidence. On the other hand, the L1 measure showed a significant correlation with the F-score performance measure, with the geometric mean with 95% confidence, and with the AUC measure with 90%. The N2 measure showed significant correlations with the F-score performance measure with 90% confidence, and T1 showed a significant correlation with the F-score performance measure, with 95% confidence.

The results obtained for the CHAT-OHM classifier allowed us to reject the null hypothesis for the measurements F1, N4, L1, L3, T1, and T2. Furthermore, the measures F1, N4, L1, L3, and T2 significantly correlated with the performance measures of the F-score, geometric mean, and AUC for the CHAT-OHM classifier using Spearman's rho coefficient, with 95% confidence.

On the other hand, the T1 measure showed a significant correlation with the performance measures of the F-score, geometric mean, and AUC with 90% confidence.

The results obtained for the EG allowed us to reject the null hypothesis for the measures F1, F3, N4, L3, and T2. The N4 and L3 measures showed a significant correlation with the F-score, geometric mean, and AUC performance measures for the EG classifier using Spearman's rho coefficient, with 95% confidence. On the other hand, the F1 measure showed a significant correlation with the F-score performance measure with 95% confidence; the F3 measure showed a significant correlation with the geometric mean and AUC measures with 90%, and finally, the T2 measure showed a significant correlation with the F-score measure with 90% confidence

Table 8. Correlation analysis of the data complexity measures and the performance measures.

Complexity Measure	Ro	F-Score				Geometric Mean				AUC			
		ACID	CHAT-OHM	EG	NAC	ACID	CHAT-OHM	EG	NAC	ACID	CHAT-OHM	EG	NAC
F1	cc	0.864	0.991	0.764	0.782	0.682	0.945	0.482	0.800	0.655	0.936	0.482	0.800
	p	**0.001**	**0.000**	**0.006**	**0.004**	**0.021**	**0.000**	0.133	**0.003**	**0.029**	**0.000**	0.133	**0.003**
F2	cc	0.282	0.391	−0.018	0.227	0.164	0.364	−0.364	0.291	0.109	0.327	−0.364	0.245
	p	0.401	0.235	0.958	0.502	0.631	0.272	0.272	0.385	0.750	0.326	0.272	0.467
F3	cc	0.418	0.336	0.436	0.055	0.173	0.400	0.564	0.027	0.291	0.473	0.564	0.064
	p	0.201	0.312	0.180	0.873	0.612	0.223	***0.071***	0.937	0.385	0.142	***0.071***	0.853
N1	cc	0.236	0.364	0.218	0.409	0.273	0.282	−0.109	0.427	0.173	0.218	−0.109	0.427
	p	0.484	0.272	0.519	0.212	0.417	0.401	0.750	0.190	0.612	0.519	0.750	0.190
N2	cc	−0.564	−0.246	0.036	−0.100	−0.345	−0.200	−0.127	−0.173	−0.445	−0.273	−0.127	−0.082
	p	***0.071***	0.467	0.915	0.770	0.298	0.555	0.709	0.612	0.170	0.417	0.709	0.811
N3	cc	−0.036	0.246	0.409	0.309	0.055	0.173	0.145	0.245	−0.045	0.109	0.145	0.318
	p	0.915	0.467	0.212	0.355	0.873	0.612	0.670	0.467	0.894	0.750	0.670	0.340
N4	cc	−0.809	−0.909	−0.818	−0.691	−0.645	−0.845	−0.618	−0.709	−0.645	−0.836	−0.618	−0.700
	p	**0.003**	**0.000**	**0.002**	**0.019**	**0.032**	**0.001**	**0.043**	**0.015**	**0.032**	**0.001**	**0.043**	**0.016**
L1	cc	0.682	0.809	0.509	0.800	0.673	0.755	0.136	0.827	0.573	0.691	0.136	0.809
	p	**0.021**	**0.003**	0.110	**0.003**	**0.023**	**0.007**	0.689	**0.002**	**0.066**	**0.019**	0.689	**0.003**
L2	cc	0.236	0.327	0.045	0.327	0.218	0.273	−0.291	0.355	0.127	0.218	−0.291	0.336
	p	0.484	0.326	0.894	0.326	0.519	0.417	0.385	0.285	0.709	0.519	0.385	0.312
L3	cc	−0.727	−0.853	−0.811	−0.863	−0.769	−0.748	−0.642	−0.863	−0.727	−0.705	−0.642	−0.863
	p	**0.011**	**0.001**	**0.002**	**0.001**	**0.006**	**0.008**	**0.033**	**0.001**	**0.011**	**0.015**	**0.033**	**0.001**
T1	cc	−0.670	−0.563	−0.326	−0.251	−0.363	−0.530	−0.381	−0.326	−0.451	−0.600	−0.381	−0.251
	p	**0.024**	**0.071**	0.328	0.456	0.273	***0.093***	0.247	0.328	0.164	***0.051***	0.247	0.456
T2	cc	−0.573	−0.764	−0.600	−0.355	−0.255	−0.773	−0.436	−0.318	−0.300	−0.809	−0.436	−0.345
	p	0.066	**0.006**	***0.051***	0.285	0.450	**0.005**	0.180	0.340	0.370	**0.003**	0.180	0.298

Finally, the results obtained for the NAC allowed us to reject the null hypothesis for the measures F1, N4, L1, and L3. The measures F1, N4, L1, and L3 showed a significant correlation with the performance measures of the F-score, geometric mean, and AUC for the NAC classifier using Spearman's rho coefficient, with 95% confidence.

It is important to note that F1 showed a stronger correlation than the other feature-based complexity measures. Finding the reasons behind this behavior requires deeper research, including numerical simulations using synthetic data, to be able to bound the factors that may intervene. However, in our opinion, this may be due to the formulation of the feature discriminant ratio. As a result, less complex problems have features that can be used to separate the classes, whereas complex problems are overlapping.

Similarly, N4 and L3 showed a stronger correlation than the other neighborhood-based and network-based measures, respectively. Again, further research is needed to fully understand the reason behind the high correlation between these measures. Our intuition tells us that N4 was again highly correlated because it considers the nonlinearity of the nearest neighbor classifier, focusing on class overlapping, and L3 also uses the notion of nonlinearity for a linear classifier. In our future work, we intend to address this behavior in depth.

The experimental results correctly indicated the existing correlations between complexity measures and the performance of the associative classifiers. The comparison was evaluated and studied, resulting in positive correlation coefficients in regard to different complexity measures for each associative classifier.

The comparative results indicate that our correlation study will depend entirely on the complexity of the problems to be solved and how each associative classifier was created, which leads us to return to the no-free-lunch theorem (NFL), as the ACID, CHAT, and EG classifiers are the ones that presented the highest correlations in terms of performance measures versus complexity measures in the selected datasets. In contrast, the NAC classifier turned out to be the classifier that presented the lowest correlation in its performance against complexity measures.

4.6. Comparison with Other Supervised Classifiers

In this subsection, we present the comparison of the associative-based classifiers with respect to other supervised classifiers in the literature. For this purpose, we again used the area under the ROC curve.

To execute the literature algorithms, with the exception of the nearest neighbor approach, we again used the KEEL environment because it enabled the implementation of naïve Bayes (NB), multilayer perceptron with backpropagation (MLP), and support vector machines (SVM). It is important to mention that all supervised classifiers (associative–based and others) used the same partitions of the five-fold cross-validation procedure, and no algorithm was particularly tuned. No weighing scheme was performed for associative classifiers, and for the literature classifiers, we used the default parameters offered by KEEL. However, those default parameters corresponded to the best values reported in previous studies, and therefore, we can consider the algorithms from the literature to be somewhat optimized. For the nearest neighbor (NN) classifier, we used EPIC software [50,51] with the HEOM dissimilarity function [52]. For the associative-based classifiers, we also used EPIC software. Table 9 shows the results regarding the AUC for the compared algorithms. Best results for each dataset are highlighted in bold.

Table 9. Area under the ROC curve for associative-based and other supervised classifiers.

Dataset	ACID	CHAT-OHM	EG	NAC	NB	NN	MLP	SVM
Australian	**0.86**	0.59	0.84	0.83	0.85	0.71	0.85	0.85
Japanese	0.85	0.66	0.82	0.83	**0.86**	0.72	**0.86**	**0.86**
German	0.57	0.64	0.68	**0.69**	0.68	0.52	0.53	0.66
Iranian	0.56	0.64	**0.68**	0.50	0.61	0.64	0.58	0.50
Polish_year1	0.58	0.52	**0.76**	0.50	0.61	0.54	0.50	0.50
Polish_year2	0.56	0.50	**0.71**	0.50	0.55	0.50	0.50	0.50
Polish_year3	0.56	0.53	**0.74**	0.50	0.61	0.52	0.50	0.50
Polish_year4	0.54	0.55	**0.75**	0.53	0.63	0.54	0.50	0.50
Polish_ year5	0.65	0.62	**0.79**	0.62	0.76	0.55	0.53	0.50
Qualitative	0.93	0.95	0.99	0.99	0.98	1.00	0.99	**1.00**
The PAKDD	**0.77**	0.58	0.61	0.61	0.51	0.53	0.52	0.50
Times Best	2	0	**6**	1	1	0	1	2

We did not include classifier ensembles such as the well-known random forest [53] in the comparison for two main reasons. First, we considered that, since associative classifiers are base (single) classifiers, it would be unfair to compare the algorithms with respect to classifier committees composed of several supervised classifiers. Second, neither KEEL nor EPIC software includes classifier committees in their selection of supervised classifiers.

The results presented in Table 9 showed that the best-performing algorithm was Extended Gamma (EG), which exhibited the best results in five of the datasets, followed by ACID and SVM (which showed the best results in two datasets). The poor results of CHAT-OHM and NN resulted from the class overlapping of the datasets, and those of NAC resulted from the lack of feature weighting. It was shown in [26] that automatic feature weighting improves the performance of NAC. In addition, the ACID classifier also includes an optional feature weighting procedure [19], which was not applied here.

Regarding the interpretability of the supervised classifiers compared in this study, in our opinion, both Extended Gamma (EG) and Naïve Associative Classifier (NAC) was highly interpretable [15]. ACID was also interpretable [19], although it was not as straightforward as EG and NAC. However, these three classifiers were transparent and transportable. On the other hand, the CHAT-OHM classifier obtained an association matrix, which is not easy to interpret. Regarding the other supervised classifiers compared, the nearest neighbor classifier was interpretable, the naïve Bayes was somewhat interpretable, and MLP and SVM were not easy to interpret due to their training process.

5. Conclusions

In this paper, we used meta-learning, in the context of ASP, to analyze the correlations that arise between the measures of complexity of the datasets and the measures of performance of the associative classifiers under study. We observed correlations between complexity measures and the performance of the associative classifiers.

The comparison was evaluated and studied, resulting in positive correlation coefficients in different complexity measures for each associative classifier. The comparative results indicate that our correlation studies will depend entirely on the complexity of the problems to be solved and the way in which each associative classifier was created, which leads us to return to the no-free-lunch theorem (NFL), and the ACID, CHAT, and EG classifiers are the ones that presented the highest correlations in terms of performance measures versus complexity measures in the selected datasets. In contrast, the NAC classifier turned out to be the classifier that presented the lowest correlation in its performance with complexity measures.

In future work, we intend to explore why some complexity measures showed a stronger correlation than others for the compared associative classifiers.

Author Contributions: Conceptualization, Y.V.-R. and C.Y.-M.; methodology, O.C.-N. and I.L.-Y.; software, F.J.C.-U.; validation, Y.V.-R. and C.Y.-M.; formal analysis, Y.V.-R.; investigation, F.J.C.-U.; writing—original draft preparation, F.J.C.-U.; writing—review and editing, Y.V.-R. and O.C.-N.; visualization, I.L.-Y. All authors have read and agreed to the published version of the manuscript.

Funding: This research received no external funding.

Institutional Review Board Statement: Not applicable.

Informed Consent Statement: Not applicable.

Data Availability Statement: All datasets used in this study are available at the Machine Learning Repository of the University of California at https://archive.ics.uci.edu/ml/datasets.php (accessed on 15 June 2021), except for the Iranian dataset, which is available upon request to the authors of [46].

Acknowledgments: The authors would like to thank the Instituto Politécnico Nacional (Secretaría Académica, Comisión de Operación y Fomento de Actividades Académicas, Secretaría de Investigación y Posgrado, Centro de Innovación y Desarrollo Tecnológico en Cómputo and Centro de Investigación en Computación), the Consejo Nacional de Ciencia y Tecnología, and Sistema Nacional de Investigadores for their economic support in developing this work.

Conflicts of Interest: The authors declare no conflict of interest.

References

1. Cover, T.; Hart, P. Nearest neighbor pattern classification. *IEEE Trans. Inf. Theory* **1967**, *13*, 21–27. [CrossRef]
2. John, G.H.; Langley, P. Estimating continuous distributions in Bayesian classifiers. *arXiv* **2013**, arXiv:1302.4964.
3. Quinlan, J.R. Induction of decision trees. *Mach. Learn.* **1986**, *1*, 81–106. [CrossRef]
4. Salzberg, S.L. *C4. 5: Programs for Machine Learning by J. Ross Quinlan. Morgan Kaufmann Publishers, Inc., 1993*; Kluwer Academic Publishers: Dordrecht The Netherlands, 1994.
5. Platt, J. Sequential minimal optimization: A fast algorithm for training support vector machines. *MSRTR* **1998**, *3*, 88–95.
6. Widrow, B.; Lehr, M.A. 30 years of adaptive neural networks: Perceptron, madaline, and backpropagation. *Proc. IEEE* **1990**, *78*, 1415–1442. [CrossRef]

7. Yáñez-Márquez, C.; López-Yáñez, I.; Aldape-Pérez, M.; Camacho-Nieto, O.; Argüelles-Cruz, A.J.; Villuendas-Rey, Y. Theoretical foundations for the alpha-beta associative memories: 10 years of derived extensions, models, and applications. *Neural Process. Lett.* **2018**, *48*, 811–847. [CrossRef]
8. Ramírez-Rubio, R.; Aldape-Pérez, M.; Yáñez-Márquez, C.; López-Yáñez, I.; Camacho-Nieto, O. Pattern classification using smallest normalized difference associative memory. *Pattern Recognit. Lett.* **2017**, *93*, 104–112. [CrossRef]
9. Santiago-Montero, R. Hybrid Associative Pattern Classifier with Translation. Master´s Thesis, Centro de Investigación en Computación, IPN., México City, México, 2003.
10. Uriarte-Arcia, A.V.; López-Yáñez, I.; Yáñez-Márquez, C. One-hot vector hybrid associative classifier for medical data classification. *PLoS ONE* **2014**, *9*, e95715. [CrossRef]
11. López-Yáñez, I.; Argüelles-Cruz, A.J.; Camacho-Nieto, O.; Yáñez-Márquez, C. Pollutants time-series prediction using the Gamma classifier. *Int. J. Comput. Intell. Syst.* **2011**, *4*, 680–711. [CrossRef]
12. Ramirez, A.; Lopez, I.; Villuendas, Y.; Yanez, C. Evolutive improvement of parameters in an associative classifier. *IEEE Lat. Am. Trans.* **2015**, *13*, 1550–1555. [CrossRef]
13. Villuendas-Rey, Y.; Yáñez-Márquez, C.; Anton-Vargas, J.A.; López-Yáñez, I. An extension of the gamma associative classifier for dealing with hybrid data. *IEEE Access* **2019**, *7*, 64198–64205. [CrossRef]
14. Sonia, O.-Á.; Yenny, V.-R.; Cornelio, Y.-M.; Itzamá, L.-Y.; Oscar, C.-N. Determining electoral preferences in Mexican voters by computational intelligence algorithms. *IEEE Lat. Am. Trans.* **2020**, *18*, 704–713. [CrossRef]
15. Villuendas-Rey, Y.; Rey-Benguría, C.F.; Ferreira-Santiago, Á.; Camacho-Nieto, O.; Yáñez-Márquez, C. The naïve associative classifier (NAC): A novel, simple, transparent, and accurate classification model evaluated on financial data. *Neurocomputing* **2017**, *265*, 105–115. [CrossRef]
16. De La Vega, A.R.-D.; Villuendas-Rey, Y.; Yanez-Marquez, C.; Camacho-Nieto, O. The Naïve Associative Classifier with Epsilon Disambiguation. *IEEE Access* **2020**, *8*, 51862–51870. [CrossRef]
17. Camacho-Urriolagoitia, O. Intelligent data science analysis for individual finance. Master's Thesis, Centro de Innovación y Desarrollo Tecnológico en Cómputo, Insituto Politéctnico Nacional, México City, México, 2020.
18. Villuendas-Rey, Y.; Hernández-Castaño, J.A.; Camacho-Nieto, O.; Yáñez-Márquez, C.; López-Yañez, I. NACOD: A naïve associative classifier for online data. *IEEE Access* **2019**, *7*, 117761–117767. [CrossRef]
19. Villuendas-Rey, Y.; Alanis-Tamez, M.D.; Rey-Benguría, C.F.; Yáñez-Márquez, C.; Nieto, O.C. Medical Diagnosis of Chronic Diseases Based on a Novel Computational Intelligence Algorithm. *J. Univers. Comput. Sci.* **2018**, *24*, 775–796.
20. Villuendas-Rey, Y.; Yáñez-Márquez, C.; Camacho-Nieto, O.; López-Yáñez, I. Impact of imbalanced datasets preprocessing in the performance of associative classifiers. *Appl. Sci.* **2020**, *10*, 2779.
21. López-Martın, C.; Lopez-Yanez, I.; Yanez-Marquez, C. Application of Gamma classifier to development effort prediction of software projects. *Appl. Math* **2012**, *6*, 411–418.
22. López-Yáñez, I.; Yáñez-Márquez, C.; Camacho-Nieto, O.; Aldape-Pérez, M.; Argüelles-Cruz, A.-J. Collaborative learning in postgraduate level courses. *Comput. Hum. Behav.* **2015**, *51*, 938–944. [CrossRef]
23. Calvo, H.; Gelbukh, A. Improving prepositional phrase attachment disambiguation using the web as corpus. In Proceedings of the Iberoamerican Congress on Pattern Recognition, Havana, Cuba, 26–29 November 2003; pp. 604–610.
24. López-Yáñez, I.; Sheremetov, L.; Yáñez-Márquez, C. A novel associative model for time series data mining. *Pattern Recognit. Lett.* **2014**, *41*, 23–33. [CrossRef]
25. Cleofas-Sánchez, L.; García, V.; Marqués, A.; Sánchez, J.S. Financial distress prediction using the hybrid associative memory with translation. *Appl. Soft Comput.* **2016**, *44*, 144–152. [CrossRef]
26. Serrano-Silva, Y.O.; Villuendas-Rey, Y.; Yáñez-Márquez, C. Automatic feature weighting for improving financial Decision Support Systems. *Decis. Support Syst.* **2018**, *107*, 78–87. [CrossRef]
27. Rice, J.R. The algorithm selection problem. In *Advances in Computers*; Elsevier: Amsterdam, The Netherlands, 1976; Volume 15, pp. 65–118.
28. Ho, T.K.; Basu, M. Complexity measures of supervised classification problems. *IEEE Trans. Pattern Anal. Mach. Intell.* **2002**, *24*, 289–300.
29. Bernadó-Mansilla, E.; Ho, T.K. Domain of competence of XCS classifier system in complexity measurement space. *IEEE Trans. Evol. Comput.* **2005**, *9*, 82–104. [CrossRef]
30. Sánchez, J.S.; Mollineda, R.A.; Sotoca, J.M. An analysis of how training data complexity affects the nearest neighbor classifiers. *Pattern Anal. Appl.* **2007**, *10*, 189–201. [CrossRef]
31. Luengo, J.; Herrera, F. Domains of competence of fuzzy rule based classification systems with data complexity measures: A case of study using a fuzzy hybrid genetic based machine learning method. *Fuzzy Sets Syst.* **2010**, *161*, 3–19. [CrossRef]
32. Luengo, J.; Herrera, F. Shared domains of competence of approximate learning models using measures of separability of classes. *Inf. Sci.* **2012**, *185*, 43–65. [CrossRef]
33. Flores, M.J.; Gámez, J.A.; Martínez, A.M. Domains of competence of the semi-naive Bayesian network classifiers. *Inf. Sci.* **2014**, *260*, 120–148. [CrossRef]
34. Luengo, J.; Herrera, F. An automatic extraction method of the domains of competence for learning classifiers using data complexity measures. *Knowl. Inf. Syst.* **2015**, *42*, 147–180. [CrossRef]

35. Morán-Fernández, L.; Bolón-Canedo, V.; Alonso-Betanzos, A. Can classification performance be predicted by complexity measures? A study using microarray data. *Knowl. Inf. Syst.* **2017**, *51*, 1067–1090. [CrossRef]
36. Barella, V.H.; Garcia, L.P.; de Souto, M.P.; Lorena, A.C.; de Carvalho, A. Data complexity measures for imbalanced classification tasks. In Proceedings of the 2018 International Joint Conference on Neural Networks (IJCNN), Rio de Janeiro, Brazil, 8–13 July 2018; pp. 1–8.
37. Lorena, A.C.; Garcia, L.P.; Lehmann, J.; Souto, M.C.; Ho, T.K. How Complex is your classification problem? A survey on measuring classification complexity. *ACM Comput. Surv.* **2019**, *52*, 1–34. [CrossRef]
38. Khan, I.; Zhang, X.; Rehman, M.; Ali, R. A literature survey and empirical study of meta-learning for classifier selection. *IEEE Access* **2020**, *8*, 10262–10281. [CrossRef]
39. Maillo, J.; Triguero, I.; Herrera, F. Redundancy and complexity metrics for big data classification: Towards smart data. *IEEE Access* **2020**, *8*, 87918–87928. [CrossRef]
40. Wolpert, D.H. The Supervised Learning No-Free-Lunch Theorems. In *Soft Computing and Industry*; Roy, R., Köppen, M., Ovaska, S., Furuhashi, T., Hoffmann, F., Eds.; Springer: London, UK, 2002.
41. Ho, T.K.; Basu, M.; Law, M.H.C. Measures of geometrical complexity in classification problems. In *Data Complexity in Pattern recognition*; Springer: Berlin/Heidelberg, Germany, 2006; pp. 1–23.
42. Sotoca, J.M.; Sánchez, J.; Mollineda, R.A. A Review of Data Complexity Measures and Their Applicability to Pattern Classification Problems. In *Actas del III Taller Nacional de Minería de Datos y Aprendizaje*; TAMIDA: Granada, Spain, 2005; pp. 77–83.
43. Triguero, I.; González, S.; Moyano, J.M.; García, S.; Alcalá-Fdez, J.; Luengo, J.; Fernández, A.; del Jesús, M.J.; Sánchez, L.; Herrera, F. KEEL 3.0: An open source software for multi-stage analysis in data mining. *Int. J. Comput. Intell. Syst.* **2017**, *10*, 1238–1249. [CrossRef]
44. 44. López-Yáñez., I. Theory and Applications of the Gamma Associative Classifier. Ph.D. Thesis, Centro de Investigación en Computación, Insitituto Politécnico Nacional, México City, México, 2011.
45. Dua, D.; Graff, C. UCI Machine Learning Repository. Available online: http://archive.ics.uci.edu/ml (accessed on 15 June 2021).
46. Sabzevari, H.; Soleymani, M.; Noorbakhsh, E. A comparison between statistical and data mining methods for credit scoring in case of limited available data. In Proceedings of the 3rd CRC Credit Scoring Conference, Edinburgh, UK, 4 November 2007; pp. 1–5.
47. Sokolova, M.; Lapalme, G. A systematic analysis of performance measures for classification tasks. *Inf. Process. Manag.* **2009**, *45*, 427–437. [CrossRef]
48. López, V.; Fernández, A.; García, S.; Palade, V.; Herrera, F. An insight into classification with imbalanced data: Empirical results and current trends on using data intrinsic characteristics. *Inf. Sci.* **2013**, *250*, 113–141. [CrossRef]
49. Spearman, C. "General Intelligence " Objectively Determined and Measured. *J. Psychol.* **1961**, *15*, 201–292. [CrossRef]
50. Hernández-Castaño, J.A.; Villuendas-Rey, Y.; Camacho-Nieto, O.; Yáñez-Márquez, C. Experimental platform for intelligent computing (EPIC). *Comput. Y Sist.* **2018**, *22*, 245–253. [CrossRef]
51. Hernández-Castaño, J.A.; Villuendas-Rey, Y.; Nieto, O.C.; Rey-Benguría, C.F. A New Experimentation Module for the EPIC Software. *Res. Comput. Sci.* **2018**, *147*, 243–252. [CrossRef]
52. Wilson, D.R.; Martinez, T.R. Improved heterogeneous distance functions. *J. Artif. Intell. Res.* **1997**, *6*, 1–34. [CrossRef]
53. Breiman, L. Random forests. *Mach. Learn.* **2001**, *45*, 5–32. [CrossRef]

mathematics

Article

LSTM-Based Broad Learning System for Remaining Useful Life Prediction

Xiaojia Wang [1,*], Ting Huang [1], Keyu Zhu [1] and Xibin Zhao [2]

[1] School of Management, Hefei University of Technology, Hefei 230009, China; 2020170901@mail.hfut.edu.cn (T.H.); zhukeyu@hfut.edu.cn (K.Z.)
[2] School of Software, Tsinghua University, Beijing 100084, China; zxb@tsinghua.edu.cn
* Correspondence: xjwang@hfut.edu.cn

Abstract: Prognostics and health management (PHM) are gradually being applied to production management processes as industrial production is gradually undergoing a transformation, turning into intelligent production and leading to increased demands on the reliability of industrial equipment. Remaining useful life (RUL) prediction plays a pivotal role in this process. Accurate prediction results can effectively provide information about the condition of the equipment on which intelligent maintenance can be based, with many methods applied to this task. However, the current problems of inadequate feature extraction and poor correlation between prediction results and data still affect the prediction accuracy. To overcome these obstacles, we constructed a new fusion model that extracts data features based on a broad learning system (BLS) and embeds long short-term memory (LSTM) to process time-series information, named as the B-LSTM. First, the LSTM controls the transmission of information from the data to the gate mechanism, and the retained information generates the mapped features and forms the feature nodes. Then, the random feature nodes are supplemented by an activation function that generates enhancement nodes with greater expressive power, increasing the nonlinear factor in the network, and eventually the feature nodes and enhancement nodes are jointly connected to the output layer. The B-LSTM was experimentally used with the C-MAPSS dataset and the results of comparison with several mainstream methods showed that the new model achieved significant improvements.

Keywords: remaining useful life (RUL) prediction; broad learning system (BLS); long short-term memory (LSTM); feature extraction

MSC: 68T20

Citation: Wang, X.; Huang, T.; Zhu, K.; Zhao, X. LSTM-Based Broad Learning System for Remaining Useful Life Prediction. *Mathematics* **2022**, *10*, 2066. https://doi.org/10.3390/math10122066

Academic Editors: Adrian Sergiu Darabant and Diana-Laura Borza

Received: 11 May 2022
Accepted: 13 June 2022
Published: 15 June 2022

1. Introduction

Remaining useful life (RUL) is the length of time that an equipment component or system can operate from the current point in time until the point in time at which it is no longer able to perform a specific function [1]. During the operation of equipment, internal and external factors such as high temperature and corrosive working environment, overload operation and illegal operation will cause the performance and health of its components to deteriorate gradually. If appropriate maintenance measures are not taken before components lose their function, not only will the normal operation of the equipment be affected, but there is a risk of damage to the equipment due to damaged components. By continuously monitoring and analyzing the equipment's operating data, RUL prediction helps managers make maintenance or replacement decisions before parts are damaged, ensuring the reliability and safety of system operation and reducing economic losses. Therefore, accurate prediction is essential for maintaining normal production. There are three main types of prediction methods: (1) physics-based methods; (2) data-driven methods; and (3) methods that integrate these two approaches [2,3]. In physics-based methods, a mathematical model is usually constructed to describe the failure mechanism based on a particular piece of equipment and combined with the empirical knowledge of that equipment and the defect growth equation [4,5] to predict the RUL of the equipment. A model-based prognostic method was developed to overcome the influence of the number of sensors on the prediction results. The method is not only an innovation in prediction methods, but also demonstrated the superiority of the approach in reducing the sensor set [6]. Model-based approaches have been shown to be robust in limited sensing scenes. In addition, a method was proposed for online evaluation in cases where little is known about the degradation process and extreme cases are considered: the entire degradation process from start of operation to failure is not observed [7]. El Mejdoubi et al. [8] considered aging conditions in predicting the RUL of supercapacitors where the posterior values of capacitance and resistance are predicted by means of particle filters. Gears are important transmission components and accurate RUL prediction is very important to determine the condition of gearing systems. The accuracy of prediction using the digital twin method was significantly improved due to its comprehensive health indicators [9]. However, physics-based methods require corresponding degradation models based on specific objects and usually are not universal. In addition, as the complexity of the equipment increases, it becomes difficult to model the failure of system objects, limiting the development of RUL prediction methods by model construction.

There are two important branches of data-driven methods, namely, statistical data-driven methods and machine-learning(ML)-based methods, that are the current mainstream methods for RUL prediction [10]. Statistical data-driven approaches are used to predict system status based on monitoring data through statistical models without making assumptions or empirical estimates of physical parameters. Park and Padgett [11] provided a new model of accelerated degeneracy, mainly for faults in geometric Brownian motion or gamma processes, with approximation operations using Birnbaum–Saunders and inverse Gaussian distributions. Chehade and Hussein [12] proposed a multioutput convolutional Gaussian process (MCGP) model that captures the cross-correlation between the capacities of available battery cells and is very effective for long-term capacity prediction of lithium-ion (Li-ion) batteries. Van Noortwijk et al. [13] proposed a method that combines two stochastic processes to assess reliability over time. In [14], a degradation model based on the Wiener process and using recursive filters to update the drift coefficients was developed to predict the RUL. The prediction accuracy of physics-based methods depends on the choice of degradation model, but the degradation models are distinctive for different types of equipment. By contrast, statistical data-driven methods are valid in overcoming the problems associated with model selection.

Recently, ML has matured in applications such as data mining, speech recognition, computer vision, fault diagnosis and RUL prediction due to its powerful data processing capabilities. ML-based prediction methods can overcome the problem of unknown degradation models, as the input is not limited by the type of data but can be many different types of data. ML used to predict RUL can be divided into shallow ML and deep learning (DL) methods. The common shallow ML prediction methods are back-propagation (BP), extreme learning machines (ELMs), support vector machines (SVMs) and relevance vector machines (RVMs). BP-based neural networks have good long-term predictive capabilities. Gebraeel et al. [15] established neural-network-based models to train the vibration data of the bearings to obtain the expected failure time of the bearings. Since a single BP neural network faces the problem of the weights falling into local optima and slow convergence during training, some approaches combining other methods with BP algorithms have been proposed. In [16], Wang et al. predicted the distribution of RUL of cooling fans by building a time-series ARIMA model; the combination with a BP neural network model improved the feature extraction ability of the model and improved the prediction accuracy. ELMs have features such as fast learning speed and high generalization ability, and these advantages are used in RUL prediction to feed the extracted features into ELM models for training, thus improving the prediction accuracy [17]. Maior et al. [18] presented a method combining empirical mode decomposition and SVM for degradation data analysis and

RUL prediction. Improving the accuracy of prediction under uncertainty is a problem that urgently needs to be solved. Wang et al. [19] extended the RVM to the probability manifold to eliminate the negative impact of the RVM evidence approximation and underestimation of hyperparameters on the prediction. Although some studies corroborate the effectiveness of shallow ML in the field of RUL prediction, traditional shallow ML algorithms rely heavily on the prior knowledge of experts and signal processing techniques, making it difficult to automatically process and analyze large amounts of monitoring data.

By contrast, DL models aim to build deep neural network architectures that combine low-dimensional features of the data to form more abstract high-level attributes with strong feature learning capabilities. In 2006, the greedy layer-wise pretraining method was proposed achieved a theoretical breakthrough in DL [20]. Subsequently, DL has had a wide range of applications in several fields, such as image recognition [21], speech recognition [22], fault diagnosis [23] and RUL prediction [24]. Deutsch et al. [25] combined the feature extraction capabilities of DBNs with the superior predictive capabilities of feedforward neural networks (FNNs) in predicting the RUL of rotating equipment. Based on this approach, to obtain the probability distribution of the remaining lifetime, DBN was effectively combined with particle filtering to further improve the prediction accuracy [26]. Deep neural networks (DNNs) have poor long-term prediction accuracy and need to be combined with other methods for better performance. A convolutional neural network (CNN) is a classical feedforward neural network with excellent characteristics such as parameter sharing and spatial pooling. In [27], a deep convolutional neural network (DCNN) and time window approach were utilized for sample preparation and demonstrated the extraction of more efficient features. To facilitate the fusion of comprehensive information, a RUL prediction method was proposed that learns salient features automatically from multiscale convolutional neural networks (MSCNN) and reveals the nonsmoothness of bearing degradation signals through time–frequency representation (TFR) [28]. In contrast to CNNs, recurrent neural networks (RNNs) are feedforward neural networks containing feedforward connections and internal feedback connections. Their special network structure allows the retention of data information of the implicit layer at the previous moment to be preserved and is often used to process monitoring vector sequences with interdependent properties. Heimes [29] realized the prediction of the RUL based on the RNN structure. However, due to the problems of vanishing and exploding gradients, RNNs processing long-term monitoring sequences produce large prediction bias [30]. To effectively address long-term sequence problems, LSTM was used on top of RNN, which made some improvements and allowed the gate structure to determine the information features passed under optimal conditions [31]. Zhao et al. [32] constructed a hybrid model based on the capsule neural network and long short-term memory network (Cap-LSTM) to extract multivariate time-series sensor data, where the model is feature sensitive and feature information is fully utilized resulting in improved prediction accuracy. A number of variants have been proposed based on typical LSTM networks. The attention mechanism can highlight key parts of time-series information and improve accuracy when predicting. The local features of the original signal sequence were extracted by a one-dimensional convolutional neural network, combined with a LSTM network and attention mechanism to analyze sensor signals and predict RUL, improving the robustness of the model and obtaining higher prediction accuracy [33]. DL is widely used for RUL prediction due to its feature representation being stronger than shallow ML and its ability to handle large amounts of data.

In addition, hybrid approaches based on physics-based and data-driven approaches were developed, such as the method of Sunet et al. [34], where empirical model decomposition, Wiener processes and neural networks were combined to take full advantage of both physical models and data-driven approaches. However, it is not easy to design a structure that reflects the advantages of both methods; thus, the use of hybrid methods to predict RUL is uncommon.

Although current ML algorithms perform well in the field of RUL prediction, and in particular LSTM is effective in handling time-series data, there are still some drawbacks to overcome when applying ML to RUL prediction. First of all, the existing methods suffer from inadequate feature representation in RUL prediction, which affects their accuracy. Secondly, the existing prediction models have to reconstruct the whole model and retrain the parameters when a new data input is available, which is less efficient. To address this problem, a new LSTM-based BLS algorithm is proposed. On the one hand, the BLS has powerful feature representation and prediction capabilities and can accurately represent the relationship between data characteristics and predicted outcomes. Meanwhile, compared with DL, the BLS has a simple structure, a high training speed and the advantage of incremental learning. When the network does not reach the expected performance, only incremental learning is required and only the incremental part needs to be computed without rebuilding the entire network. This significantly improves the efficiency of data processing. In addition, LSTM can effectively process time-series data and avoid problems such as parameter setting and single-time prediction randomness. On the other hand, we hope to broaden the theoretical study of BLS networks by constructing a new fusion network and applying it to practical production scenarios to create economic benefits.

We propose a method for predicting RUL that takes into account both feature extraction and time-series information. It is hoped that sufficient feature extraction can improve the prediction performance, and appropriately broaden the theory and application of the BLS. Specifically, the main contributions and innovations of the work we have conducted are listed below:

(1) A new LSTM-based BLS prediction method is proposed to extract the time-series features of the data based on feature extraction, improving the ability of the prediction results to represent the data features and enhancing the RUL prediction accuracy.
(2) The mechanism of model construction represents another innovation. Instead of directly splicing the two methods, the new method is embedded by modifying the internal structure and avoiding the redundancy of the model.
(3) The adaptation on the basis of a BLS enriches the practical significance of the BLS framework, extends the scope of theoretical research and enables the achievement of better results by integrating the BLS with other methods.

The rest of the paper is structured as follows. The constructed B-LSTM model and the required related basics are introduced and presented in Section 2. Section 3 presents the experimental data required and the experimental design. Section 4 applies the dataset for validation of the model performance and comparison with other methods. A summary of the model and possible future research directions are shown in Section 5.

2. Related Work

2.1. Broad Learning System (BLS)

With the continuous development of deep learning, deep networks are widely used in various research fields, but the disadvantages are also more obvious. In order to achieve higher accuracy, the number of network layers has to be gradually increased; however, this consumes more computational resources and causes overfitting to occur in small sample data processing. A BLS is built based on a single hidden layer neural network and uses lateral scaling to improve accuracy and avoid complex hyperparameters. The unique feature node and enhancement node structure also provides a strong guarantee for adequate feature extraction.

The BLS was established by C. L. Philip Chen on the basis of a random vector functional-link neural network (RVFLLNN) and compensated for its shortcomings in handling large-volume and time-varying data [35]. In addition, the multiple variants proposed in the course of subsequent research showed flexibility, stability and remarkable results in classification and regression of semi-supervised and unsupervised tasks [36]. The structure of the BLS is shown in Figure 1. The network structure is constructed using the following steps. First, the mapping of input data to feature nodes is established, and then the enhancement nodes are formed through a nonlinear activation function. Eventually, the feature nodes and the enhancement nodes are combined as outputs, and the output weight can be directly found through pseudo-inverse ridge regression.

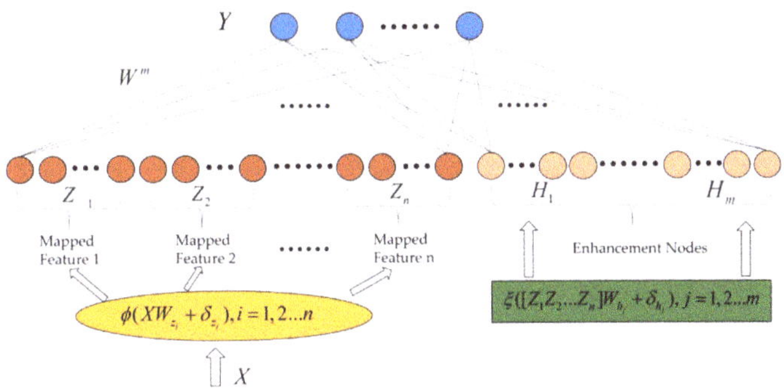

Figure 1. Structure of the BLS network. The Yellow ellipse on the left is the calculation formula for converting input data into feature nodes, the earthy yellow circle on the left is the generated feature nodes, the green rectangle on the right is the calculation formula for converting the left feature nodes into enhancement nodes, the light yellow circle on the right is the generated enhancement nodes, and the blue circle on the top is the output.

The BLS is constructed as follows:

The given data are subjected to a random weight matrix for feature mapping to obtain a feature matrix with the aim of dimensionality reduction and feature extraction. The ith mapped feature is:

$$Z_i = \phi_i(XW_{ei} + \beta_{ei}), i = 1, 2, \ldots, n \tag{1}$$

Here, the parameters W_{ei} and the bias β_{ei} are randomly initialized. We denote $Z^n \triangleq (Z_1, Z_2, \ldots, Z_n)$ as the collection of groups of feature nodes. Then, they are sent to the enhancement nodes.

Similarly, the jth group enhancement nodes are:

$$H_j = \xi_j(Z^n W_{hj} + \beta_{hj}), j = 1, 2, \ldots, m \tag{2}$$

By introducing a nonlinear activation function, the feature nodes are mapped nonlinearly to a higher dimensional subspace and the nonlinear element in the network is enhanced. In addition, the outputs of the enhancement layer are denoted as $H^m \triangleq (H_1, H_2, \ldots, H_m)$.

Finally, the output of the BLS consists of feature nodes and enhancement nodes together, which can be expressed as follows:

$$\begin{aligned} Y &= [Z_1, \ldots, Z_n | \xi(Z^n W_{h1} + \beta_{h1}), \ldots, \xi(Z^n W_{hj} + \beta_{hj})] W_n^m \\ &= [Z_1, \ldots, Z_n | H_1, \ldots, H_m] W_n^m \\ &= [Z^n | H^m] W_n^m \\ &= A_n^m W_n^m \end{aligned} \tag{3}$$

W_n^m are the weights that connect the feature nodes and the enhancement nodes to the output and $W_n^m = [Z^n | H^m]^+ Y$, where the pseudo-inverse $[Z^n | H^m]^+$ can be directly calculated by ridge regression.

2.2. Long Short-Term Memory (LSTM)

The LSTM network structure is built on top of the RNN. The memory cell structure is illustrated in Figure 2. In dealing with the problem of long-term sequences, a cell state is added, which determines whether past and present information can be added through a gating mechanism, overcoming the "gradient vanishing" and "gradient explosion" problems of the RNN. LSTM has three gates to control the flow of information in the network. The forget gate f_t controls how much of the previous state c_{t-1} can be retained. The input gate i_t determines whether to use the current input to update the information of the LSTM. The output gate o_t determines which parts of the current cell state need to be outputted to the next layer for iteration.

$$f_t = \sigma(W^{(f)} x_t + V^{(f)} h_{t-1} + b_f) \tag{4}$$

$$i_t = \sigma(W^{(i)} x_t + V^{(i)} h_{t-1} + b_i) \tag{5}$$

$$o_t = \sigma(W^{(o)} x_t + V^{(o)} h_{t-1} + b_o) \tag{6}$$

$$c_t = f_t \otimes c_{t-1} + i_t \otimes \tanh(W^{(c)} x_t + V^{(c)} h_{t-1} + b_c) \tag{7}$$

$$h_t = o_t \otimes \tanh(c_t) \tag{8}$$

where x_t is the data entered into the memory cell for training and h_t is the output in each cell. In addition, W, V and b are the weight matrix and biases, respectively, σ is the sigmoid activation function used to control the weight of the message passing through and $\otimes$ is the dot product.

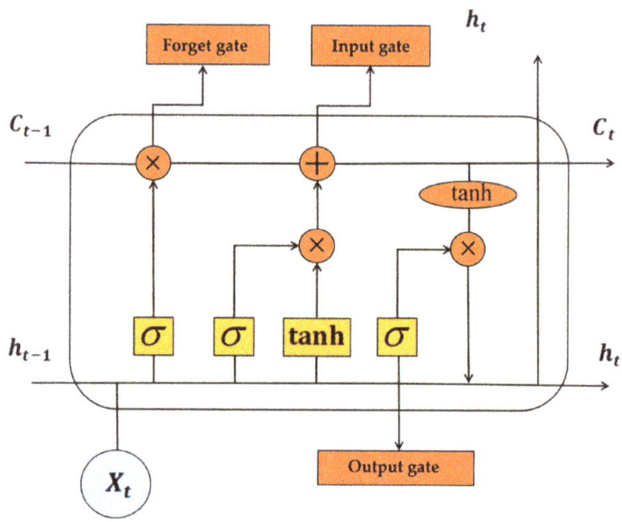

Figure 2. Long short-term cell structure. The blue circle at the bottom is the input data of a cell of the LSTM. The orange rectangular part is the forget gate, input gate and output gate. The yellow part is the calculation formula for generating forget gate, input gate and output gate. The orange circular part is the operator for generating forget gate, input gate and output gate.

Specifically, the update process of a cell state can be divided into the following steps: (1) determine what useless information is discarded from the state of the previous time step; (2) extract the valid information that can be added to the state cell at the current time step; (3) calculate the state unit of the current time step; and (4) calculate the output of the current time step.

Variants of LSTM as part of a prediction model that take full advantage of LSTM in processing time-series information are also a common approaches in current research.

2.3. LSTM-Based Broad Learning System (B-LSTM)

For RUL prediction, more accurate predictions are always obtained by fully learning both the time-series information and feature information of the given data. When performing time-series forecasting, the serial information of the data cannot be learned simply by constructing a framework of mapped features. Therefore, in order to construct a prediction model with comprehensive coverage, a model based on BLS and introducing LSTM is proposed, named B-LSTM. The intuitive idea is to enhance the extraction of time-series information based on the extraction of feature information. The flow is shown in Algorithm 1. In the original BLS framework, each attribute $x_i \in X \in R^D$ must be independent of the others, and due to this independence, each matrix can learn the features through the variation of different weights. The construction mechanism of the B-LSTM is shown in Figure 3. In this figure, unlike the standard BLS, the raw data are first fed into the LSTM to learn the time-series information. The resulting output is then transformed nonlinearly to generate enhancement nodes that extract deeper features and increase the nonlinear fitting capability of the model. Finally, the state output of the LSTM is connected to the output as a feature layer and an enhancement node. The feature matrix and enhancement matrix of the B-LSTM structure are represented as:

$$Z_i = o_i \otimes \tanh(c_i), i = 1, 2, \ldots, n \tag{9}$$

$$H_j = \xi_j(Z^n W_{hj} + \beta_{hj}), j = 1, 2, \ldots, m \tag{10}$$

where $Z^n \triangleq (Z_1, Z_2, \ldots, Z_n)$ is the collection of n groups of feature nodes obtained by the calculation of the LSTM network. Finally, the connections of all of the mapped features and the enhancement nodes are sent to the output layer. The dynamic equation of B-LSTM is shown below:

$$Y = [Z_1, \ldots, Z_n | \xi(Z^n W_{h1} + \beta_{h1}), \ldots, \xi(Z^n W_{hj} + \beta_{hj})] W_n^m \tag{11}$$

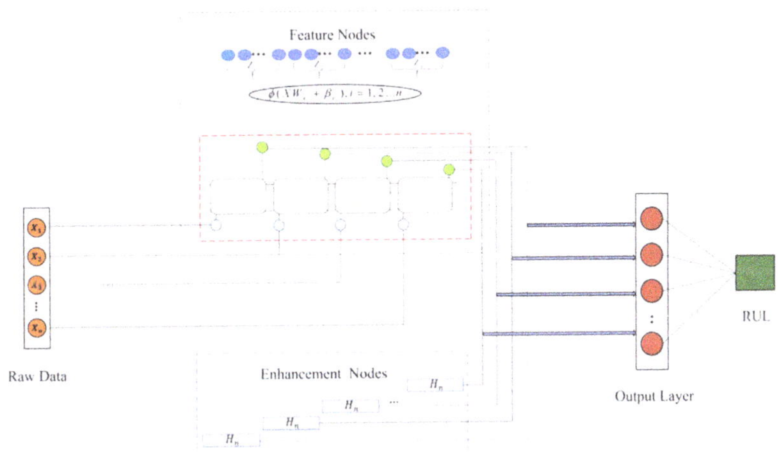

Figure 3. Structure of the B-LSTM network. Multiple orange circles in the left rectangle are the input data. The upper part in the middle indicates that the feature nodes of the new model are replaced by LSTM, the yellow circle in the LSTM part is the input data, the green circle is the feature nodes output by the new model, the lower part in the middle is the enhancement nodes generated by the feature nodes generated by LSTM, the feature nodes and enhancement nodes are connected to the output together, and the red circle on the right is the output of the model.

Algorithm 1: B-LSTM Model

Input: Training data X, Y;
Output: the output weights W;
1: **for** $i = 1; i <= n; i++$ **do**
2: Calculate $c_t = f_t \otimes c_{t-1} + i_t \otimes \tanh(W_c x_t + V_c h_{t-1} + b_c)$;
3: Calculate $Z_i = o_i \otimes \tanh(c_i), i = 1, 2, \ldots, n$;
4: **end for**
5: Set $Z^n \triangleq (Z_1, Z_2, \ldots, Z_n)$;
6: **for** $j = 1; j <= m; j++$ **do**
7: Random W_{hj}, β_{hj};
8: Calculate $H_j = \xi_j(Z^n W_{hj} + \beta_{hj}), j = 1, 2, \ldots, m$;
9: **end for**
10: Set $H^m \triangleq (H_1, H_2, \ldots, H_m)$;
11: Set A_n^m and calculate $(A_n^m)^+$ Equation (11);
12: Calculate W

3. Experimental Procedure and Analysis

3.1. C-MAPSS Dataset

The C-MAPSS dataset contains aircraft turbofan engine degradation simulation data, including simulated sensor data generated by different turbofan engines over time; this dataset was selected for training and evaluation of the effectiveness of the proposed model. Table 1 shows that the dataset consists of four sub-datasets, FD0001, FD0002, FD0003 and FD0004, where both the FD001 and FD003 datasets contain 1 operational condition and contain 1 and 2 fault types, respectively, whereas FD002 and FD004 both contain 6 operational conditions and contain 1 and 2 fault types, respectively. These sub-datasets consist of engine numbers, serial numbers, configuration items and sensor data obtained from 21 sensors, simulating the progressive degradation of the engine from a healthy state to failure for different initial conditions.

Table 1. Parameters of the dataset.

Sub-Dataset	C-MAPSS			
	FD001	FD002	FD003	FD004
Training trajectories	100	260	100	249
Testing trajectories	100	259	100	248
Operating conditions	1	6	1	6
Fault modes	1	1	2	2

Each of the four sub-datasets contains a training set and a test set in which the actual RUL values of the test engine are also included. The training set includes all data from the start of the turbofan engine's operation until its degradation and failure. In the test set, however, the data start from a healthy state and are subsequently arbitrarily truncated; the operating time periods up to the point of system failure were calculated from these data.

3.2. Performance Measures

To quantitatively assess the performance of the model, we compared the prediction results of the new model and the predictions of this model were compared with those of other network structures. Two objective evaluation metrics, namely, RMSE and Score, are introduced in this paper, where $d = R_{pred} - R_{actual}$; when the prediction error d is 0, RMSE and Score are both the minimum values of 0. As the absolute value of d increases, the two evaluation indices are increased. The difference is that when $d > 0$, Score gives different penalty weights for model prediction lag and prediction advance. If the predicted value is smaller than the true value, it means that the prediction is ahead and the penalty coefficient is smaller, and conversely, lagging brings more serious consequences and the penalty coefficient is larger. Predicting the RUL value earlier allows for earlier maintenance planning and avoidance of potential losses.

$$RMSE = \sqrt{\frac{\sum_{i=1}^{n} (d)^2}{n}} \tag{12}$$

$$\text{Score} = \begin{cases} \sum_{i=1}^{n} e^{-\left(\frac{d}{13}\right)} - 1, \; d < 0 \\ \sum_{i=1}^{n} e^{-\left(\frac{d}{10}\right)} - 1, \; d \geq 0 \end{cases} \tag{13}$$

3.3. *Experimental Setup*

Our experimental equipment was a personal computer with an Intel Core i5 CPU, 16GB RAM and NVIDIA GTX 1080ti GPU. The operating system was Windows 10 Professional and the programming platform was MATLAB R2019b.

First, data filtering was performed on the dataset, and in each dataset, a single sampled data sample consisted of 26 variables, of which the first 2 variables represented the engine sequence number and the cycle sequence number, the last 3 variables represented the operation setting items and the remaining 21 variables represented the detection values obtained by the 21 sensors. The third position of the operation setting term and the sensor values with sequence numbers 1, 5, 6, 10, 16, 18 and 19 were unchanged and had no effect on the prediction results, so they were filtered out. Then, since the sensors were of different types and the selected data were of different magnitudes, we made the range of values uniform across the data by data normalization. Finally, we divided the data into training and validation sets proportionally, set the training parameters and inputted the processed training and validation sets into the model for model training.

4. Results and Discussion

4.1. *RUL Prediction*

To verify the performance of the B-LSTM model, we inputted the datasets into the model and roughly determined whether the model can effectively predict based on the fit between the true and predicted values of the RUL. The prediction results are shown in Figure 4. The red solid line indicates the true RUL value, whereas the green scatter plot indicates the predicted value. As can be seen from the figure, the B-LSTM was able to depict the trend of RUL variation for each test set. This shows that the improved structure of extracting time-series information and feature information can be more effective in making predictions. In addition, in the FD001 and FD003 datasets, the B-LSTM model made better predictions compared to the other two datasets because in these two sub-datasets the failure modes and operating conditions were relatively simple. Although the operating conditions and failure modes in the FD002 and FD004 test sets were more complex, they basically described the changing trend of the equipment RUL.

We can see that the true value of RUL in the FD003 sub-dataset in the prediction result plot continued to be constant at the beginning; this is because after our practical verification, due to the smoother operating conditions, the RUL in FD003 remained basically stable at the beginning of the operation and can be considered as constant, and only at a later stage did a linear decline occur as the RUL of the device did not change uniformly with time. In order to make better predictions of RUL, we processed the labels of FD003 training data. The RUL was set to a fixed value when the operating cycle of the device was less than 60, and decreased gradually with the growth of the operating cycle when the operating cycle was greater than 60, as the device gradually declined.

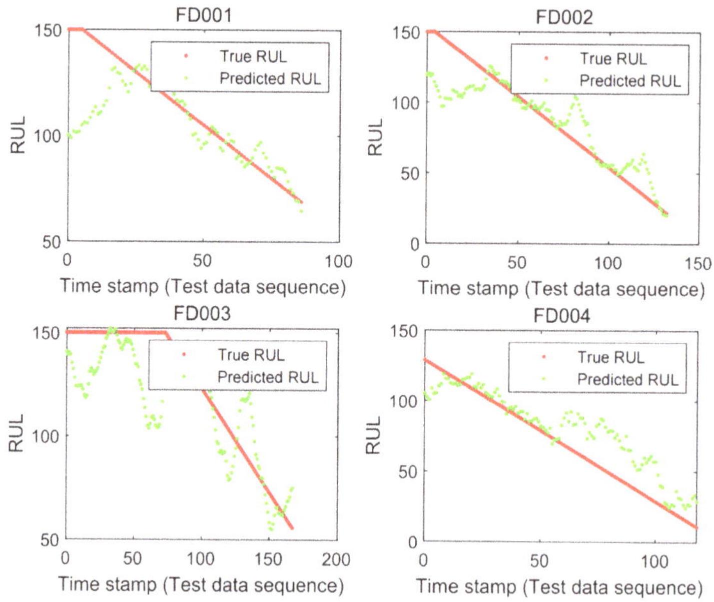

Figure 4. B-LSTM-based prediction results.

4.2. Performance Evaluation

To verify the performance of the model, we compared the proposed method with other existing RUL prediction methods, including MLP [37], SVR [37], CNN [37], LSTM [38], ELM [39], and BiLSTM [40]. The comparison results are shown in Table 2. From Figure 5, we can see that the RMSE of the proposed method was smaller than the other methods in all four sub-datasets, especially in FD001 and FD003, where it achieved good results. Similarly, in Figure 6 it is clear that the Score of the new method improved as compared to the other methods. The comparison results show that the method we constructed can fully extract the features of the data and, thus, obtain more accurate prediction results. In addition, the FD001 and FD003 datasets performed better for each prediction method compared to the other two datasets because the turbine engines in the FD001 and FD003 datasets have fewer operating conditions and can maintain smooth operating conditions during the operating period.

Table 2. Model performance comparison on the C-MAPSS dataset.

Method	RMSE/Score			
	FD001	FD002	FD003	FD004
MLP	37.56/18,000	80.03/7,800,000	37.39/17,400	77.37/5,620,000
SVR	20.96/1380	42.0/590,000	21.05/1600	45.35/371,000
CNN	18.45/1290	30.29/13,600	19.82/1600	29.16/7890
LSTM	16.14/338	24.49/4450	16.18/852	28.17/5550
ELM	17.27/523	37.28/498,000	18.47/574	30.96/121,000
BiLSTM	13.65/295	23.18/41,300	13.74/317	24.86/5430
Proposed method	12.45/279	15.36/4250	13.37/356	16.24/5220

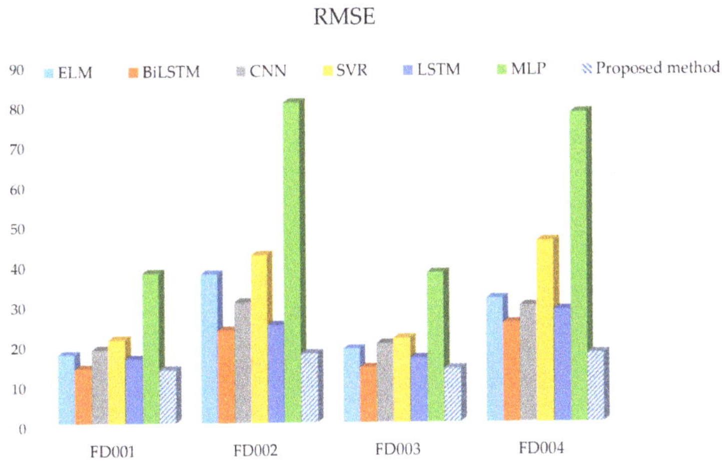

Figure 5. The results of RMSE comparison among different methods.

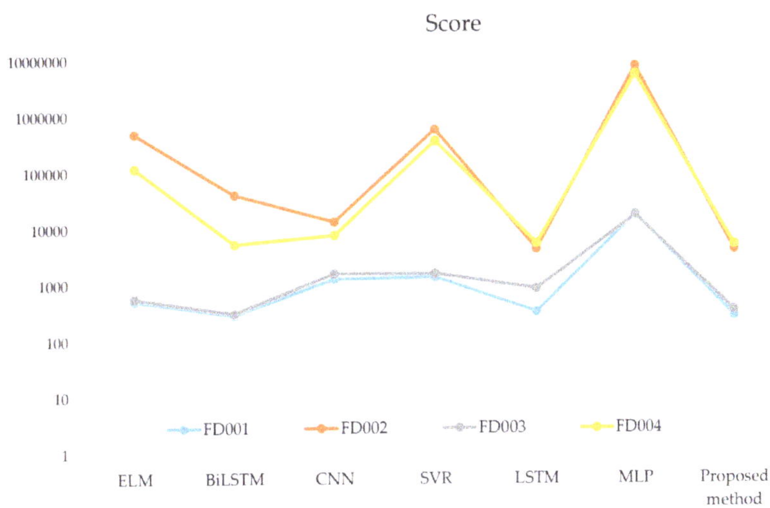

Figure 6. The results of Score comparison among different methods.

5. Conclusions

There are a variety of methods for predicting RUL in the existing research, but these methods can have some problems in actual prediction, such as ignoring time-series features, features not being sufficiently extracted, etc. We proposed a new method for predicting RUL and demonstrated that the method improves prediction performance. Specifically, a new BLS network integrated with LSTM, named B-LSTM, is essential for enriching the theoretical knowledge of RUL prediction.

Theoretically, this network retains the time-series information in the input data while performing sufficient feature extraction so that the output of the model remains strongly correlated with the input data and the interpretability and accuracy of the model is enhanced. In addition, when the model performance was validated using the C-MAPSS dataset, the results obtained were significantly better than other models. Therefore, the B-LSTM performed well in both theoretical construction and data validation. Although this study achieved ideal conclusions, the experimental results of one dataset may be serendipitous; therefore, in the following research, we will use more different datasets to verify the scientificity and generalizability of the proposed model. In addition, this research did not pay too much attention to the training time of the model. In later work, we will focus on further optimizing the model structure to shorten the training time so that the model can be processed quickly and, at the same time, achieve a satisfactory accuracy.

Author Contributions: Conceptualization, X.W.; writing, manuscript preparation, T.H.; review and editing, K.Z.; supervision and project management, X.Z. All authors have read and agreed to the published version of the manuscript.

Funding: This research received no external funding.

Institutional Review Board Statement: Not applicable.

Informed Consent Statement: Not applicable.

Data Availability Statement: The data of this paper came from the NASA Prognostics Center of Excellence, and the data acquisition website was: https://ti.arc.nasa.gov/tech/dash/groups/pcoe/prognostic-data-repository/#turbofan, accessed on 10 February 2022.

Conflicts of Interest: The authors declare no conflict of interest.

References

1. Liu, G. A Study on Remaining Useful Life Prediction for Prognostic Applications. Master's Thesis, University of New Orleans, New Orleans, LA, USA, 2011.
2. Zio, E.; Di Maio, F. A data-driven fuzzy approach for predicting the remaining useful life in dynamic failure scenarios of a nuclear system. *Reliab. Eng. Syst. Saf.* **2010**, *95*, 49–57. [CrossRef]
3. Heng, A.; Zhang, S.; Tan, A.; Mathew, J. Rotating machinery prognostics: State of the art, challenges and opportunities. *Mech. Syst. Signal Process.* **2009**, *23*, 724–739. [CrossRef]
4. Li, C.J.; Lee, H. Gear fatigue crack prognosis using embedded model, gear dynamic model and fracture mechanics. *Mech. Syst. Signal Process.* **2005**, *19*, 836–846. [CrossRef]
5. Fan, J.; Yung, K.C.; Pecht, M.; Pecht, M. Physics-of-Failure-Based Prognostics and Health Management for High-Power White Light-Emitting Diode Lighting. *IEEE Trans. Device Mater. Reliab.* **2011**, *11*, 407–416. [CrossRef]
6. Daigle, M.; Goebel, K. Model-based prognostics under limited sensing. In Proceedings of the IEEE Aerospace Conference, Big Sky, MT, USA, 6–13 March 2010; pp. 1–12.
7. Hu, Y.; Baraldi, P.; Di Maio, F.; Zio, E. Online Performance Assessment Method for a Model-Based Prognostic Approach. *IEEE Trans. Reliab.* **2015**, *65*, 1–18.
8. El Mejdoubi, A.; Chaoui, H.; Sabor, J.; Gualous, H. Remaining useful life prognosis of supercapacitors under temperature and voltage aging conditions. *IEEE Trans. Ind. Electron.* **2017**, *65*, 4357–4367. [CrossRef]
9. He, B.; Liu, L.; Zhang, D. Digital twin-driven remaining useful life prediction for gear performance degradation: A review. *J. Comput. Inf. Sci. Eng.* **2021**, *21*, 030801. [CrossRef]
10. Pei, H.; Hu, C.; Si, X.; Zhang, J.; Pang, Z.; Zhang, P. Review of Machine Learning Based Remaining Useful Life Prediction Methods for Equipment. *J. Mech. Eng.* **2019**, *55*, 1–13. [CrossRef]
11. Park, C.; Padgett, W.J. Accelerated degradation models for failure based on geometric Brownian motion and gamma processes. *Lifetime Data Anal.* **2005**, *11*, 511–527. [CrossRef]
12. Chehade, A.A.; Hussein, A.A. A multi-output convolved Gaussian process model for capacity estimation of electric vehicle li-ion battery cells. In Proceedings of the IEEE Transportation Electrification Conference and Expo (ITEC), Detroit, MI, USA, 19–21 June 2019; pp. 1–4.
13. Van Noortwijk, J.M.; van der Weide, J.A.; Kallen, M.J.; Pandey, M.D. Gamma processes and peaks-over-threshold distributions for time-dependent reliability. *Reliab. Eng. Syst. Saf.* **2007**, *92*, 1651–1658. [CrossRef]
14. Si, X.S.; Wang, W.; Hu, C.H.; Chen, M.Y.; Zhou, D.H. A Wiener-process-based degradation model with a recursive filter algorithm for remaining useful life estimation. *Mech. Syst. Signal Process.* **2013**, *35*, 219–237. [CrossRef]
15. Gebraeel, N.; Lawley, M.; Liu, R.; Parmeshwaran, V. Residual life predictions from vibration-based degradation signals: A neural network approach. *IEEE Trans. Ind. Electron.* **2004**, *51*, 694–700. [CrossRef]
16. Lixin, W.; Zhenhuan, W.; Yudong, F.; Guoan, Y. Remaining life predictions of fan based on time series analysis and BP neural networks. In Proceedings of the IEEE Information Technology, Networking, Electronic and Automation Control Conference, Chongqing, China, 20–22 May 2016; pp. 607–611.
17. Liu, Y.; He, B.; Liu, F.; Lu, S.; Zhao, Y.; Zhao, J. Remaining useful life prediction of rolling bearings using PSR, JADE, and extreme learning machine. *Math. Probl. Eng.* **2016**, *2016*, 1–13. [CrossRef]
18. Maior, C.B.S.; das Chagas Moura, M.; Lins, I.D.; Droguett, E.L.; Diniz, H.H.L. Remaining Useful Life Estimation by Empirical Mode Decomposition and Support Vector Machine. *IEEE Lat. Am. Trans.* **2016**, *14*, 4603–4610. [CrossRef]

19. Wang, X.; Jiang, B.; Ding, S.X.; Lu, N.; Li, Y. *Extended Relevance Vector Machine-Based Remaining Useful Life Prediction for DC-Link Capacitor in High-Speed Train*; IEEE: Piscataway Township, NJ, USA, 1963; pp. 1–10.
20. Hinton, G.E.; Osindero, S.; Teh, Y.W. A Fast Learning Algorithm for Deep Belief Nets. *Neural Comput.* **2006**, *18*, 1527–1554. [CrossRef] [PubMed]
21. Shah, S.A.A.; Bennamoun, M.; Boussaid, F. Iterative deep learning for image set based face and object recognition. *Neurocomputing* **2016**, *174*, 866–874. [CrossRef]
22. Deng, L. Deep learning: From speech recognition to language and multimodal processing. *APSIPA Trans. Signal Inf. Process.* **2016**, *5*, e1. [CrossRef]
23. He, M.; He, D. Deep learning based approach for bearing fault diagnosis. *IEEE Trans. Ind. Appl.* **2017**, *53*, 3057–3065. [CrossRef]
24. Ren, L.; Cui, J.; Sun, Y.; Cheng, X. Multi-bearing remaining useful life collaborative prediction: A deep learning approach. *J. Manuf. Syst.* **2017**, *43*, 248–256. [CrossRef]
25. Deutsch, J.; He, D. Using deep learning based approaches for bearing remaining useful life prediction. In Proceedings of the Annual Conference of the PHM Society 2016, Chengdu, China, 19–21 October 2016.
26. Deutsch, J.; He, M.; He, D. Remaining useful life prediction of hybrid ceramic bearings using an integrated deep learning and particle filter approach. *Appl. Sci.* **2017**, *7*, 649. [CrossRef]
27. Li, X.; Ding, Q.; Sun, J.Q. Remaining useful life estimation in prognostics using deep convolution neural networks. *Reliab. Eng. Syst. Saf.* **2018**, *172*, 1–11. [CrossRef]
28. Zhu, J.; Chen, N.; Peng, W. Estimation of bearing remaining useful life based on multiscale convolutional neural network. *IEEE Trans. Ind. Electron.* **2018**, *66*, 3208–3216. [CrossRef]
29. Heimes, F.O. Recurrent neural networks for remaining useful life estimation. In Proceedings of the International Conference on Prognostics and Health Management, Denver, CO, USA, 6–9 October 2008; pp. 1–6.
30. Pascanu, R.; Mikolov, T.; Bengio, Y. On the difficulty of training recurrent neural networks, In International conference on machine learning. *Proc. Mach. Learn. Res.* **2013**, *23*, 1310–1318.
31. Wu, Y.; Yuan, M.; Dong, S.; Lin, L.; Liu, Y. Remaining useful life estimation of engineered systems using vanilla LSTM neural networks. *Neurocomputing* **2018**, *275*, 167–179. [CrossRef]
32. Zhao, C.; Huang, X.; Li, Y.; Li, S. A Novel Cap-LSTM Model for Remaining Useful Life Prediction. *IEEE Sens. J.* **2021**, *21*, 23498–23509. [CrossRef]
33. Zhang, H.; Zhang, Q.; Shao, S.; Niu, T.; Yang, X. Attention-based LSTM network for rotatory machine remaining useful life prediction. *IEEE Access* **2020**, *8*, 132188–132199. [CrossRef]
34. Sun, H.; Cao, D.; Zhao, Z.; Kang, X. A hybrid approach to cutting tool remaining useful life prediction based on the Wiener process. *IEEE Trans. Reliab.* **2018**, *67*, 1294–1303. [CrossRef]
35. Chen, C.P.; Liu, Z. Broad Learning System: An Effective and Efficient Incremental Learning System without the Need for Deep Architecture. *IEEE Trans. Neural Netw. Learn. Syst.* **2018**, *29*, 10–24. [CrossRef]
36. Gong, X.; Zhang, T.; Chen, C.P.; Liu, Z. *Research Review for Broad Learning System: Algorithms, Theory, and Applications*; IEEE: Piscataway Township, NJ, USA, 1963; pp. 1–29.
37. Sateesh Babu, G.; Zhao, P.; Li, X.L. Deep convolutional neural network based regression approach for estimation of remaining useful life. In *International Conference on Database Systems for Advanced Applications*; Springer: Berlin/Heidelberg, Germany, 2016; pp. 214–228.
38. Zheng, S.; Ristovski, K.; Farahat, A.; Gupta, C. Long short-term memory network for remaining useful life estimation. In Proceedings of the 2017 IEEE International Conference on Prognostics and Health Management (ICPHM), Dallas, TX, USA, 19–21 June 2017; pp. 88–95.
39. Zhang, C.; Lim, P.; Qin, A.K.; Tan, K.C. Multiobjective deep belief networks ensemble for remaining useful life estimation in prognostics. *IEEE Trans. Neural Netw. Learn. Syst.* **2016**, *28*, 2306–2318. [CrossRef]
40. Wang, J.; Wen, G.; Yang, S.; Liu, Y. Remaining useful life estimation in prognostics using deep bidirectional lstm neural network. In Proceedings of the 2018 Prognostics and System Health Management Conference (PHM-Chongqing), Chongqing, China, 26–28 October 2018.

mathematics

Article

Automatic Speech Emotion Recognition of Younger School Age Children

Yuri Matveev [1,*], Anton Matveev [1], Olga Frolova [1], Elena Lyakso [1] and Nersisson Ruban [2]

1 Child Speech Research Group, Department of Higher Nervous Activity and Psychophysiology, St. Petersburg State University, St. Petersburg 199034, Russia; aush.tx@gmail.com (A.M.); olchel@yandex.ru (O.F.); lyakso@gmail.com (E.L.)
2 School of Electrical Engineering, Vellore Institute of Technology, Vellore 632014, India; ruban.ice@gmail.com
* Correspondence: yunmatveev@gmail.com

Abstract: This paper introduces the extended description of a database that contains emotional speech in the Russian language of younger school age (8–12-year-old) children and describes the results of validation of the database based on classical machine learning algorithms, such as Support Vector Machine (SVM) and Multi-Layer Perceptron (MLP). The validation is performed using standard procedures and scenarios of the validation similar to other well-known databases of children's emotional acting speech. Performance evaluation of automatic multiclass recognition on four emotion classes "Neutral (Calm)—Joy—Sadness—Anger" shows the superiority of SVM performance and also MLP performance over the results of perceptual tests. Moreover, the results of automatic recognition on the test dataset which was used in the perceptual test are even better. These results prove that emotions in the database can be reliably recognized both by experts and automatically using classical machine learning algorithms such as SVM and MLP, which can be used as baselines for comparing emotion recognition systems based on more sophisticated modern machine learning methods and deep neural networks. The results also confirm that this database can be a valuable resource for researchers studying affective reactions in speech communication during child-computer interactions in the Russian language and can be used to develop various edutainment, health care, etc. applications.

Keywords: speech emotion recognition; child speech; younger school age

MSC: 68T10

Citation: Matveev, Y.; Matveev, A.; Frolova, O.; Lyakso, E.; Ruban, N. Automatic Speech Emotion Recognition of Younger School Age Children. *Mathematics* **2022**, *10*, 2373. https://doi.org/10.3390/math10142373

Academic Editors: Adrian Sergiu Darabant, Diana-Laura Borza and Jüri Majak

Received: 21 May 2022
Accepted: 4 July 2022
Published: 6 July 2022

1. Introduction

Speech Emotion Recognition (SER) systems are currently being intensively used in a broad range of applications, including security, healthcare, videogaming, mobile communications, etc. [1]. The development of SER systems has been a hot topic of research in the field of human-computer interaction for the past two decades. Most of these studies are focused on emotion recognition from adult speech [2–5], and only a few are from children's speech [6–9]. This follows from the fact that sizable datasets of children's speech with annotated emotion labels are still not publicly available in the research community, which leads most researchers to focus on SER for adults.

The reason is that it is difficult to get a wide range of emotional expressions in children's speech due to the following. Children, especially those of primary school age, find it difficult to pronounce and read long texts, and it is more difficult for children than adults to express emotions in acting speech if a child has not experienced these emotions before. School-age children commonly demonstrate a limited range of emotions when interacting with unfamiliar adults due to differences in social status and with regard to training. Generally, children show vivid emotions when interacting with peers, but this situation is usually accompanied by strong noise and overlapping voices. Due to ethical standards, the provocation of vivid negative emotions, such as fear, sadness and anger should be allowed by an informed consent to be signed by the parents. However, not all of them are ready to provide such consent.

However, children are potentially the largest class of users of educational and entertainment applications with speech-based interfaces.

The characteristics of a child's voice are significantly different from those of an adult's voice. The child's voice's clarity and consistency of speech are low compared to an adult [10], while acoustic and linguistic variability in children's speech is high, which creates challenges for emotion recognition. Another severe problem is the paucity of publicly available transcribed linguistic resources for children's speech. Moreover, research on SER faces the problem that most available speech corpora differ from each other in important ways, such as methods of annotation and scenarios of interaction [11–13]. Inconsistencies in these methods and scenarios make it difficult to build SER systems.

All of the above-mentioned problems make the task of developing automatic emotion recognition in children's speech non-trivial, especially taking into account variations of acoustic features within genders, age groups, languages, and developmental characteristics [14]. For example, the authors of [15] report that the average accuracy of emotional classification is 93.3%, 89.4% and 83.3% for male, female, and child utterances, respectively.

Our analysis of databases of children's emotional speech created over the past 10 years has shown that they cover mainly monolingual emotional speech in such languages as English, Spanish, Mexican Spanish, German, Chinese, and Tamil. The only database of children's emotional speech in Russian is EmoChildRu [16], which was used to study manifestations of the emotional states of three- to seven-year-old children in verbal and non-verbal behavior [17].

Children of three to seven years of age were selected for their ability to maintain a communication with an adult while expressing more pure natural emotions than older children. The socialization of children in accordance with cultural norms and traditions mostly begins with schooling which, in the Russian Federation, starts at six to seven years old. This period characterizes the end of the preschool age.

Nevertheless, other databases we have analyzed consist mostly of children's speech of the younger school age group. The particular qualities of the primary school children are, on the one hand, the partial mastery of accepted cultural norms of emotional manifestations; while on the other hand, they represent the presence of natural spontaneous emotional manifestations characteristic of children of this age.

It is highlighted in [18] that the expansion of existing corpora of child-machine communications is necessary for building more intricate emotional models for advanced speech interactive systems designed for children. These new corpora can include other languages and age groups, more subjects, etc. Therefore, our recent works have included the collecting of children's emotional speech of younger school age (8–12-year-olds) in the Russian language, as studies of children's emotion recognition by voice and speech in Russian are sparse, especially for the younger school age group.

There are several key features of our corpus. Firstly, this is the first large-scale corpus dealing with Russian children's speech emotions, which includes around 30 h of speech. Secondly, there are 95 speakers in this corpus. Such a large number of speakers makes it possible to research techniques for speaker-independent emotion recognition and analysis. To validate the dataset [19,20], a subset of 33 recordings was evaluated by 10 Russian experts [21] who conducted manual tests to understand how well humans identify emotional states in the collected dataset of emotional speech of Russian speaking children. Results of manual evaluation validate the database reliability compared with other databases and the ability of native-speaking experts to recognize emotional states in children's speech in the Russian language with above chance performance.

In this article we report the results of experiments on SER conducted using our proprietary database and state-of-the-art machine learning (ML) algorithms. Such experiments are usually conducted to validate the ability to recognize emotional states in children's speech on specific databases in automatic mode with above chance performance. The article presents the results of the experiments and compares them both with results of SER in manual mode and results of SER in automatic mode from other authors for the same age group and the same ML algorithms.

It is noted in [22] that neural networks and Support Vector Machine (SVM) behave differently, and each have advantages and disadvantages for building a SER; however, both are relevant for the task. Multi-Layer Perceptron (MLP) is the "basic" example of a neural network. Therefore, to get a general impression of our dataset, we conducted baseline speech emotion recognition experiments using two of the state-of-the-art machine learning techniques most popular in emotion recognition, these being SVM and MLP [23,24]. These classifiers have already been used to validate several databases of emotional speech [25] and have shown superior classification accuracy on small-to-medium size databases.

The main contributions of this study are as follows:

1. An extended description of the Russian Younger School Children Emotional Speech (SCES-1) database is provided.
2. Validation of the SCES-1 dataset in automatic mode based on SVM and MLP algorithms to recognize above chance emotional states in the speech of Russian children of the younger school age group (8–12-year-old) is undertaken.

The remainder of this paper is structured as follows. In Section 2, the various existing corpora and both features and classifiers used in the literature for SER are discussed. Section 3 provides a detailed description of our proprietary dataset. In Section 4 we define the experimental setup describing our choice of tools to extract feature sets, tools to implement classifiers and evaluate the results of classification and procedures for training and testing. In Section 5, we provide the experimental results. Finally, Section 6 presents the discussion and conclusions, and topics for future research are discussed.

2. Related Work

There are a lot of studies on emotion manifestations in the voice and other biometric modalities. Recently, attention to research on automatic methods of emotion recognition in speech signals has increased due to the development of new efficient methods of machine learning, the availability of open access corpora of emotional speech and high-performance computing resources.

In the last decade, many SER systems have been proposed in the literature. There are numerous publications and reviews on three traditional SER issues: databases, features, and classifiers. Swain et al. [11] reviewed studies on SER systems in the period from 2000 to 2017 with a strong emphasis on databases and feature extraction. However, only traditional machine learning methods were considered as a classification tool, and the authors missed neural networks and deep learning approaches. The authors of [26] covered all the major deep learning techniques used in SER, from DNNs to LSTMs and attention mechanisms.

In this section, we summarize some of the most relevant recent research on SER, focusing on children's speech. In doing so, we pay special attention to those approaches that use the same feature extraction (FE) and machine learning (ML) methods used in this article.

2.1. Children's Emotion Speech Corpora

Over the past three decades, many emotional datasets and corpora have been created in audio or audiovisual modalities [12,26–28]. Some of them are related to natural emotions (spontaneous emotions from real-life situations), while others are related to acted (simulated, for example, by actors) or elicited (induced/stimulated through emotional movies, stories, and games) emotions. Spontaneous emotions are preferable, but they are difficult to collect. Therefore, most of the available emotional speech corpora contain acted emotional speech. Moreover, the emotional corpora are mainly related to adult speech.

Corpora related to children's speech have also been created over the past three decades [29], but they are not so numerous, and only a few of them are related to children's emotional speech. Most of the corpora are in the English language, but some of them are in the German, French, Spanish, Mandarin, Sesotho, Filipino, and Russian languages. Moreover, these corpora vary not only by language but also by children's age range, different specific groups like specific language impairment [30], autism spectrum disorder [31], etc.

We briefly describe the eight most famous corpora with children's emotional speech in Table 1.

- MESD (Mexican Emotional Speech Database) [15,32], presented in 2021. A part of the MESD with children's speech has been uttered by six non-professional actors with mean age of 9.83 years and a standard deviation of 1.17. The database contains 288 recordings of children's speech with six different emotional categories: Anger, Disgust, Fear, Happiness, Sadness, and Neutral. The results of the evaluation of the database reliability based on machine learning analysis showed the accuracy of 83.3% of emotion recognition on children's voices. An SVM was used as a classifier together with a feature set with prosodic, voice quality and spectral features. MESD is considered a valuable resource for healthcare, as it can be used to improve diagnosis and disease characterization.
- IESC-Child (Interactive Emotional Children's Speech Corpus) [18], presented in 2020. A Wizard of Oz (WoZ) setting was used to induce different emotional reactions in children during speech-based interactions with two Lego Mindstorm robots behaving either collaboratively or non-collaboratively. The IESC-Child corpus consists of recordings of the speech spoken in Mexican Spanish by 174 children (80 girls and 94 boys) between six and 11 years of age (8.62 mean, 1.73 standard deviation). The recordings included 34.88 h of induced speech. In total, eight emotional categories are labeled: Anger, Disgust, Fear, Happiness, Sadness, Surprise, Neutral, and None of the above. The research on building acoustic paralinguistic models and speech communication between a child and a machine in Spanish utilized the IESC-Child dataset with prominent results.
- EmoReact (Multimodal Dataset for Recognizing Emotional Responses in Children) [33], presented in 2016. A multimodal spontaneous emotion dataset of 63 (31 males, 32 females) children ranging between four and 14 years old. It was collected by downloading videos of children who react to different subjects such as food, technology, YouTube videos and gaming devices. The dataset contains 1102 audio-visual clips annotated for 17 different emotional categories: six basic emotions, neutral, valence and nine complex emotions.
- CHEAVD (Chinese Natural Emotional Audio–Visual Database) [34], presented in 2016. A large-scale Chinese natural emotional audio–visual corpus with emotional segments extracted from films, TV plays and talk shows. The corpus contains 238 (125 males, 113 females) speakers from six age groups: child (<13), adolescent/mutation (13–16), youth (16–24), young (25–44), quinquagenarian (45–59), and elder ($\geq$60). Over 141 h of spontaneous speech was recorded. In total, 26 non-prototypical emotional states, including the basic six, are labeled by four native speakers.
- EmoChildRu (Child emotional speech corpus in Russian) [16,17], presented in 2015. This contains audio materials from 100 children ranging between three and seven years old. Recordings were organized in three model situations by creating different emotional states for children: playing with a standard set of toys; repetition of words from a toy-parrot in a game store setting; watching a cartoon and retelling the story, respectively. Over 30 h of spontaneous speech were recorded. The utterances were annotated for four emotional categories: Sadness, Anger, Fear, Happiness (Joy). The data presented in the database are important for assessing the emotional development of children with typical maturation and as controls for studying emotions of children with disabilities.
- ASD-DB (Autism Spectrum Disorder Tamil speech emotion database) [35], presented in 2014. This consists of spontaneous speech samples from 25 (13 males, 12 females) children ranging between five and 12 years old with autism spectrum disorder. The

children's voices were recorded in a special school (open space) using a laptop with a video camera. Recordings were taken in wav format at a sampling rate 16,000 Hz and a quantization of 16 bits. The emotion categories included Anger, Neutral, Fear, Happiness, and Sadness. The database was validated using MFCC features and an SVM classifier.

- EmoWisconsin (Emotional Wisconsin Card Sorting Test) [36], presented in 2011. This contains spontaneous, induced and natural Spanish emotional speech of 28 (17 males, 11 females) children ranging between 7 and 13 years old. The collection was recorded in a small room with little noise using two computers, a desktop microphone and a Sigmatel STAC 9200 sound card. Recordings are mono channel, with 16 bit sample size, 44,100 kHz sample rate and stored in WAV Windows PCM format. We recorded 11.38 h of speech in 56 sessions, two sessions per child over seven days. The total number of utterances was 2040, annotated for seven emotional categories: Annoyed, Confident, Doubtful, Motivated, Nervous, Neutral, and Undetermined. For the database validation based on categorical classification we used an SVM algorithm with 10-fold cross validation. The results of the validation showed a performance above chance level comparable to other publicly available databases of affective speech such as VAM and IEMOCAP.
- FAU-AIBO (Friedrich-Alexander-Universität corpus of spontaneous, emotionally colored speech of children interacting with Sony's pet robot Aibo) [37,38], presented in 2006. The corpus was collected from the recordings of children interacting with Sony's pet robot Aibo. It consists of spontaneous, emotionally colored German/English speech from 51 children (21 males, 30 females) ranging between 10 and 13 years old. The total number of utterances is 4525 with a total duration of 8.90 h. The audio was recorded by using a DAT recorder (16-bit, 16 kHz). Five annotators labeled each word individually as Neutral (default) or using one of the other ten emotions: Angry, Bored, Joyful, Surprised, Emphatic, Helpless, Touchy (=Irritated), Motherese, Reprimanding, Rest (non-Neutral, but not belonging to the other categories). The final label was defined using the majority voting procedure. For the database validation based on classification we used a neural network. The results of validation showed that the performance of speech emotion classification on the FAU-AIBO corpora is above chance level.

Table 1. Corpora of children's emotional speech—main features.

Corpus	Subjects	Language	Age Groups
MESD [15,32]	8	Spanish	8–11
IESC-Child [18]	174	Spanish	6–11
EmoReact [13]	63	English	4–14
CHEAVD [34]	3; 5	Chinese	<13; 13–16
EmoChildRu [16,17]	100	Russian	3–7
ASD-DB [35]	25	Tamil	5–12
EmoWisconsin [36]	28	Spanish	7–13
FAU Aibo [37,38]	51	German	10–13

The results of the analysis of the available children's emotion speech corpora show that they are all monolingual. The corpora contain mainly emotional speech of the school age group, with the exception of EmoChildRu (preschool age group) and CHEAVD (adolescence and adult age groups). All of the corpora were validated using manual perceptual tests and/or automatic SVM/MLP classifiers with different feature sets. The results of validation showed that performance of speech emotion classification on all the corpora is well above chance level.

2.2. Speech Emotion Recognition: Features and Classifiers

The classic pattern recognition task can be defined as the classification of patterns (objects of interest) based on information (features) extracted from patterns and/or their representation [39]. As noted in [40], a selection of suitable feature sets, design of proper classification methods and preparation of appropriate datasets are the key concerns of SER systems.

In the feature-based approach to emotion recognition, we assume that there is a set of objectively measurable parameters in speech that reflect the emotional state of a person. The emotion classifier identifies emotion states by identifying correlations between emotions and features. For SER, many feature extraction and machine learning techniques have been extensively developed in recent times.

2.2.1. Features

Selecting the best feature set powerful enough to distinguish between different emotions is a major problem when building SER systems. The power of the selected feature set has to stay stable in the presence of various languages, speaking styles, speaker's characteristics, etc. Many models for predicting the emotional patterns of speech are trained on the basis of three broad categories of speech features: prosody, voice quality, and spectral features [5].

In emotion recognition the following types of features are found to be important:

- Acoustic features of prosodic: pitch, energy, duration.
- Spectral features: MFCC, GFCC, LPCC, PLP, formants.
- Voice quality features: jitter, shimmer, harmonics to noise ratio, normalized amplitude quotient, quasi-open quotient.

Most of the well-known feature sets include pitch, energy and their statistics, which are widely used in expert practice [21].

For automatic emotion recognition, we have used three publicly available feature sets:

- INTERSPEECH Emotion Challenge set (IS09) [41] with 384 features. It was found that the IS09 feature set provides good performance of children's speech emotion recognition. Nevertheless, we conducted some experiments with other feature sets.
- Geneva Minimalistic Acoustic Parameter Set (GeMAPS) and the extended Geneva Minimalistic Acoustic Parameter Set (eGeMAPS). They are popular in the field of affective computing [42]. The GeMAPS family features include not only prosody but also spectral and other features. The total GeMAPS v2.0.0 feature set contains 62 features and the eGeMAPSv02 feature set contains 26 extra parameters, for a total of 88 parameters.
- DisVoice feature set. This is a popular feature set that has shown good performance in such tasks as recognition of emotions and communication capabilities of people with speech disorders and issues such as depression based on speech patterns [43]. The DisVoice feature set includes glottal, phonation, articulation, prosody, phonological, and features representation learning strategies using autoencoders [43]. It is well known that prosodic and temporal characteristics have often been used previously to identify emotions [5]. Therefore, our next experiments were with the DisVoice prosody feature set.

2.2.2. Classifiers

Many different classification methods are used to recognize emotions in speech. There are a lot of publications on using different classifiers in SER [23,25]. The most popular are classical machine learning (ML) algorithms, such as Support Vector Machines (SVM), Hidden Markov Models (HMM), Gaussian Mixture Models (GMM), Neural Networks (NN), and Multi-Layer Perceptron (MLP) as the "basic" example of NN. Currently, we see the massive application of deep learning (DL) in different fields, including SER. DL techniques that are used to improve SER performance may include Deep Neural Networks

(DNN) of various architectures [26], Generative Adversarial Networks (GAN) [44,45], autoencoders [46,47], Extreme Learning Machines (ELM) [48], multitask learning [49], transfer learning [50], attention mechanisms [26], etc.

The choice of a classification algorithm depends mainly on the properties of the data (e.g., number of classes), as well as the nature and number of features. Taking into account the specifics of children's speech, we must choose a classification algorithm that could be effective in multidimensional spaces on a relatively small-to-medium database size and with low sensitivity to outlier values.

The analysis of the literature shows that the best candidates are SVM and MLP classifiers, where SVM is a deterministic and MLP is a non-deterministic supervised learning algorithm for classification. SVM and MLP are baseline classifiers in numerous studies on emotion speech recognition.

First of all, traditional ML algorithms could provide reliable results in the case of small-to-medium size of training data [51–53]. Second, SVM and MLP classifiers often demonstrate better performance than others [22,23,54]. Some experiments have shown a supercity of SVM and MLP for emotion recognition over classical Random Forest, K-NN, etc. classifiers [54] and also over different deep neural network classifiers [55]. The failure of neural network classifiers in emotion recognition can be explained by the small size of available emotional databases, which are insufficient for training deep neural networks.

We chose to work with an SVM model to evaluate the validity of an emotional database, as it is capable of producing meaningful results with small-to-medium datasets (unlike algorithms such as deep neural networks) and its ability for handling high-dimensional spaces [1]. In [55], it was shown that the SVM classifier outperforms Back Propagation Neural Networks, Extreme Learning Machine and Probabilistic Neural Networks by 11 to 15 percent, reaching 92.4% overall accuracy. In [56] it was also shown that SVM works systematically better than Logistic Regression and LSTM classifiers on the IS09 Emotion dataset.

MLP is the "basic" example of NN. It is stated in [22] that MLP is the most effective speech emotion classifier, with accuracies higher than 90% for single-language approaches, followed closely by SVM. The results show that MLP outperforms SVM in overall emotion classification performance, and even though SVM training is faster compared to MLP, the ultimate accuracy of MLP is higher than that of SVM [57]. SVM has a lower error rate than other algorithms, but it is inefficient if the dataset has some noise [57].

The use of SVM and MLP classifiers allows us to compare the performance of emotion recognition on our database with the performance of the same classifiers on other known databases of children's emotional speech.

Moreover, the results of classification by SVM and MLP can be used as a baseline point for comparison with other models, such as deep neural networks (CNN, RNN, etc.), to see if they provide better performance for SER.

3. Corpus Description

To study emotional speech recognition of Russian typically developing children aged 8–12 years by humans and machines, a language-specific corpus of emotional speech was collected. The corpus contains records of spontaneous speech and acting speech of 95 children with the following information about children: age, place and date of birth, data on hearing thresholds (obtained using automatic tonal audiometry), phonemic hearing and videos with facial expressions and the behavior of children.

3.1. Place and Equipment for Speech Recording

The place for speech recording was the room without special soundproofing.

Recordings of children's speech were made using a Handheld Digital Audio Recorder PMD660 (Marantz Professional, inMusic, Inc., Sagamihara, Japan) with an external handheld cardioid dynamic microphone Sennheiser e835S (Sennheiser electronic GmbH & Co. KG, Beijing, China). In parallel with the speech recording, the behavior and facial expressions of children were recorded using a video camera Sony HDR-CX560E (SONY Corporation, Tokyo, Japan). Video recording was conducted as part of studies on the manifestation of emotions in children's speech [16] and facial expressions [58].

The distance from the child's face to the microphone was in the range of 30–50 cm. All children's speech and video recordings were included in the corpus. All speech files were saved in .wav format, 48,000 Hz, 16 bits per sample. For each child, the recording time was in the range of 30–40 min.

3.2. Speech Recording Procedure

Two types of speech were recorded—natural (spontaneous) speech and acting speech.

Dialogue between the children and the experimenters were used to obtain recordings of the children's natural speech. We hypothesized that semantically different questions could induce different emotional states in children [26]. A standard set of experimenter's questions addressed to the child was used. The experimenter began the dialogue with a request for the child to tell his/her name and age. Further questions included:

- What lessons at school do you like and why?
- Who are your friends at school?
- What do you play at breaks between lessons?
- What are your hobbies?
- What movies and cartoons do you like to watch?
- Can you remember are funny stories?
- Which teachers you don't like and why?
- Do you often fight with other children? Are you swearing?
- Do you often get angry? What makes you angry?
- Do you often get sad? What makes you sad?

Children's acting speech was recorded after dialogue recording sessions. The children had to pronounce speech material—sets of words, words and phrases, as well as meaningless texts demonstrating different emotional states "Neutral (Calm)—Joy—Sadness—Anger". Children were trained to pronounce sets of words, words and phrases, as well as meaningless texts. Before recording the acting speech, each child was asked to pronounce the proposed speech material two to three times depending on the age of the child. Children eight to nine years of age had difficulty pronouncing meaningless texts, so they were instructed to practice to fluently read the whole meaningless text out, rather than articulating individual words.

Two experts estimated how well the children could express different emotional states in their vocal expressions during the training and speech recording sessions. The experts asked a child to repeat the text if the child was distracted, showed an emotion that did not correspond to the given task, or made mistakes in the pronunciation of words.

The selection of this list of emotions was based on the assumption [40] that there is no generally acceptable list of basic emotions, and even though the lists of basic emotions differ, Happiness (Joy, Enjoyment), Sadness, Anger, and Fear appear in most of them. In [59] it was also noted that categories such as Happiness, Sadness, Anger, and Fear are generally recognized with accuracy rates well above chance. In [34] it is noted that regarding the emotion category, there is no unified basic emotion set. Most emotional databases address prototypical emotion categories, such as Happiness, Anger and Sadness.

A number of emotion recognition applications use three categories of speech: emotional speech with positive and negative valence, and neutral speech. In practice, collecting and labeling a dataset with such three speech categories is quite easy, since it can be done by naive speakers and listeners rather than professional actors and experts. As an extension of this approach, some SER [60–63] use four categories of emotional speech, positive (Joy or Happiness), neutral, and negative (Anger and Sadness). In this case it is also quite easy to collect a dataset, but to label the dataset we need experts.

The set of words and set of words and phrases were selected according to the lexical meaning of words /joy, beautiful, cool, super, nothing, normal, sad, hard, scream, break, crush/ and phrases /I love when everything is beautiful, Sad time, I love to beat and break everything/. The meaningless sentences were pseudo-sentences (semantically meaningless sentences resembling real sentences), used e.g., [64] to reduce the influence of linguistic meaning. A fragment of "Jabberwocky", the poem by Lewis Carroll [65] and the meaningless text (sentence) by L.V. Shcherba "Glokaya kuzdra" [66] were used. Children had to utter speech material imitating different emotional states "Joy, Neutral (Calm), Sadness, Anger".

After the completion of the sessions recording the children's speech, two procedures were carried out: audiometry, to assess the hearing threshold, and a phonemic hearing test (repetition of pairs and triple syllables by the child following the speech therapist).

All procedures were approved by the Health and Human Research Ethics Committee of Saint Petersburg State University (Russia), and written informed consent was obtained from parents of the participating children.

Speech recording was conducted according to a standardized protocol. For automatic analysis, only the acting speech of children was taken.

3.3. Process of Speech Data Annotation

After the raw data selection, all speech recordings are split into segments which contain emotions and are manually checked to ensure audio quality. The requirements for the segments are as follows:

a. Segments should not have high background noise or voice overlaps.
b. Each segment should contain only one speaker's speech.
c. Each speech segment should contain a complete utterance. Any segment without an utterance was removed.

The acting speech from the database was annotated according the emotional states manifested by children when speaking: "neutral—joy—sadness—anger". The annotation was made by two experts based on the recording protocol and video recordings. The speech sample is assigned to the determined emotional state if the accordance between two experts is 100%.

2505 samples of acting speech (words, phrases, and meaningless texts) were selected as a result of annotation: 628 for the neutral state, 592 for joy, 646 for sadness, and 639 for anger. In contrast to other existing databases, the distribution of the emotions in our database is approximately uniform.

4. Experimental Setup

4.1. Features and Classifiers

To generate the features vector (eGeMAPS feature set) we have used the openSMILE toolkit v2.0.0 (audEERING GmbH, Gilching, Germany) [67], which is an open-source C++ feature extractor. The code is freely available and well documented.

To implement SVM and MLP classifiers, we have used the Scikit-learn machine learning library. A multiclass version of the SVM model [68] with a linear kernel and default values of all other parameters was chosen. We also used an MLP model that optimizes the log-loss function using LBFGS (Limited-memory Broyden–Fletcher–Goldfarb–Shanno) or stochastic gradient descent algorithms. As it is noted in [69], the stochastic gradient descent solvers work rather well on datasets with thousands of training samples or more in terms of both training time and validation score. However, in our case, we have a small dataset, so we used LBFGS (an optimizer in the family of quasi-Newton methods) because it converges faster and works better for small datasets. To do this we set the parameter solver = 'lbfgs'. After some experiments, we set the parameters alpha = 1×10^{-5}, hidden_layer_sizes = (64,16), max_iter = 500, and the other parameter values are by default.

4.2. Training and Testing Setup

A total of 2505 Russian emotional speech samples were used. We separated the data into 80% (2004 samples) for training and 20% (501 samples) for testing our classification models.

For cross-validation we have used the Stratified K-Folds cross-validator [70]. It provides a greater balance of classes, especially when there are only a few speakers. Due to the small size of the dataset, we used Stratified K-Folds cross-validation with K = 6 (5:1).

4.3. Evaluation Setup

As a tool for evaluation of classification models, we have used a multi-class confusion matrix library PyCM written in Python [71].

In our experiments, we used such evaluation metrics as the per class Accuracy, Precision, Recall, and F1-score. Due to the unequal number of samples in each test class (unequal priors), we have analyzed the results using Unweighted Average Recall (UAR) for multiclass classifiers, closely related to the accuracy as a good or even better metric to optimize when the sample class ratio is imbalanced [72]. UAR is defined as the average across the diagonal of the confusion matrix.

5. Experimental Results

First, we analyzed the results of automatic emotion recognition in children's speech with two state-of-the-art ML classification algorithms, SVM and MLP. Then, following [73], we compared results of manual and automatic speech emotion recognition to understand how well the emotional state in emotional speech is recognized by humans and machines.

5.1. Results of Automatic Emotion Recognition on Extended Feature Set

From Figure 1 and Tables 2 and 3 we can see that performance of SVM and MLP classifiers is approximately the same. For all individual emotions, both classifiers perform noticeably above chance. This is consistent with the results of monolingual emotion recognition in the Russian language [74].

These results are comparable to evaluations in other languages. For example, Sowmya and Rajeswari [75] reported that they achieved an overall accuracy of 0.85 for automatic children's speech emotion recognition in the Tamil language with an SVM classifier on prosodic (energy) and spectral (MFCC) features. Rajan et al. [13] reported that they achieved an Average Recall of 0.61 and Average Precision of 0.60 in the Tamil language using a DNN framework, also on prosodic and spectral features.

Table 2. Per-class scores in multi-class classification, eGeMAPS feature set.

Classifier	SVM				MLP			
Emotion	**Anger**	**Joy**	**Neutral**	**Sad**	**Anger**	**Joy**	**Neutral**	**Sad**
Accuracy	0.929	0.915	0.882	0.888	0.928	0.923	0.894	0.897
Recall	0.875	0.823	0.750	0.780	0.848	0.846	0.796	0.796
Precision	0.851	0.817	0.772	0.785	0.866	0.832	0.784	0.804
F1-score	0.863	0.820	0.761	0.783	0.857	0.839	0.790	0.800

Table 3. Average scores in multi-class classifications, eGeMAPS feature set.

Classifier	SVM	MLP
Overall Accuracy	0.903	0.911
Unweighted Average Recall	0.807	0.822
Unweighted Average Precision	0.806	0.822

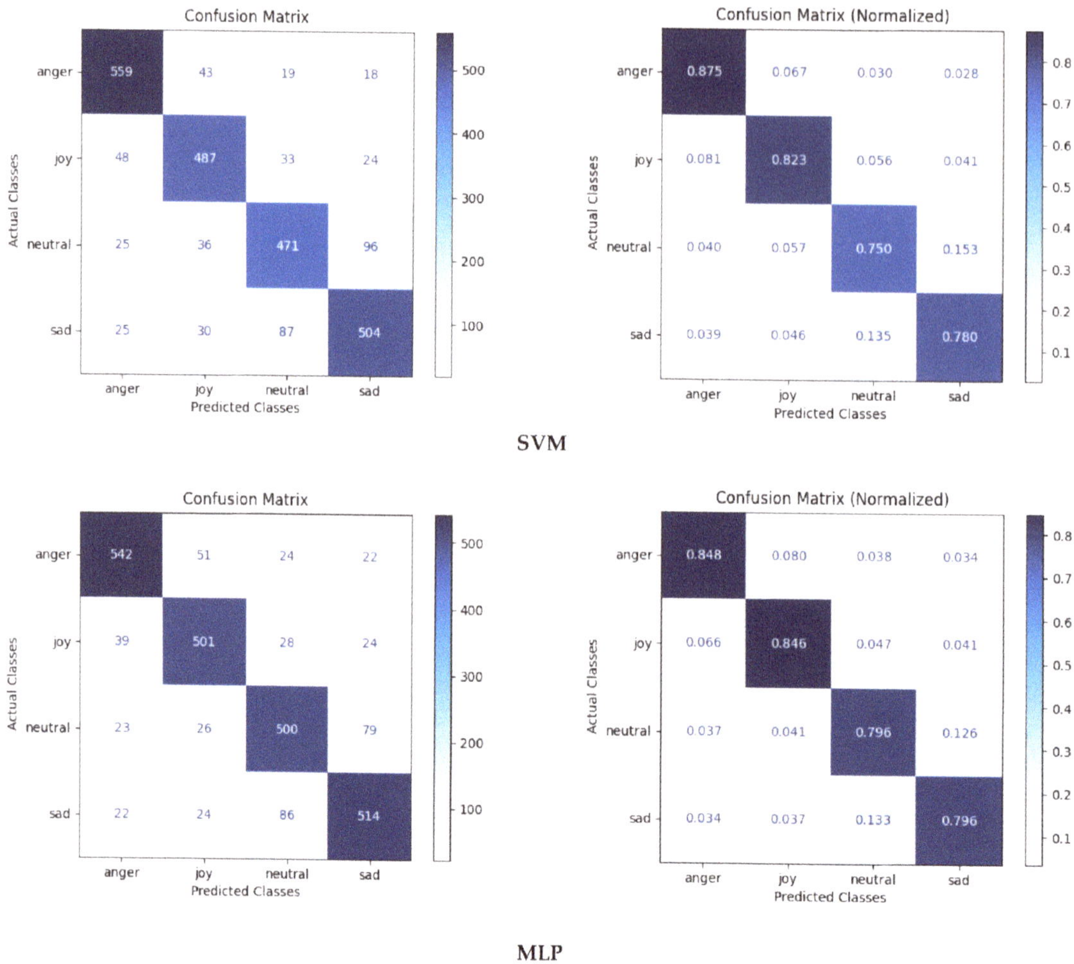

Figure 1. Confusion matrices for SVM and MLP classifiers, eGeMAPS feature set, a dataset of Russian children's emotional speech with 2505 samples for training and testing.

5.2. Results of the Subjective Evaluation of Emotional Speech Recognition

In our first experiment on the subjective evaluation of emotional speech recognition [21], 10 native Russian experts with a mean age of 37.8 years (standard deviation ± 15.4 years) and lengthy (mean ± SD = 14.2 ± 10.3 years) professional experience as experts in the field of speech science manually recognized Happiness/Joy, Anger, Sadness, and Neutral emotional states in children's speech from the dataset consisting of 16 samples of meaningless text from "Jabberwocky" [65] and "Glokaya kuzdra" [66]). There was no preliminary training of experts. The experts were given the task of recognizing emotional states (selected from a list of four emotions) of children while listening to the test sequence. Different utterances were separated by a pause of 7 s, and each utterance was repeated once. This subjective evaluation was conducted to understand how well humans identify emotional states in the acting emotional speech of Russian children. The experts used perceptual evaluation and spectrographic analysis [21] of four samples for each emotional state, with 16 samples in total. The results of this subjective evaluation are shown in Figure 2 and Tables 4 and 5.

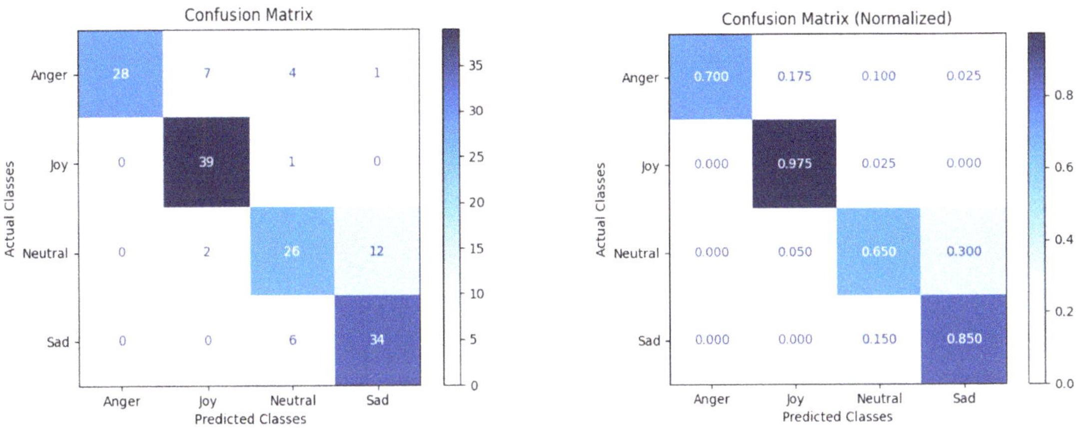

Figure 2. Confusion matrix of subjective evaluation of emotions in acting children's speech in Russian language by Russian experts.

Table 4. Per-class scores in multi-class classification, expert's feature set with 16 samples in total.

Metrics	Emotion			
	Anger	**Joy**	**Neutral**	**Sad**
Accuracy	0.925	0.940	0.845	0.880
Recall	0.700	0.980	0.650	0.850
Precision	1.000	0.817	0.707	0.720
F1-score	0.824	0.891	0.677	0.780

Table 5. Overall scores in multi-class classification, expert's feature set with 16 samples in total.

Metrics	Accuracy
Overall Accuracy	0.898
Unweighted Average Recall	0.795
Unweighted Average Precision	0.811

From Figure 2 and Table 4 we can see that experts recognize all emotions noticeably above chance (0.25 for 4-class classification). This is consistent with the results of perception tests for adult emotion speech. For example, Rajan et al. [13] reported comparable results of subjective evaluation using a perception test with an overall accuracy of 0.846 in recognizing emotional states—happiness, anger, sadness, anxiety, and neutral—from acted emotional speech in the Tamil language.

In this article, we present the results of an extended experiment with the dataset that consists of 16 samples of meaningless text supplemented with 17 samples of words and phrases, for 33 samples in total. The results of this subjective evaluation are shown in Figure 3 and Tables 6 and 7.

Table 6. Per-class scores in multi-class classification, extended expert's feature set with 33 samples in total.

Metrics	Emotion			
	Anger	**Joy**	**Neutral**	**Sad**
Accuracy	0.925	0.938	0.844	0.881
Recall	0.700	0.975	0.650	0.850
Precision	1.000	0.813	0.703	0.723
F1-score	0.824	0.886	0.675	0.782

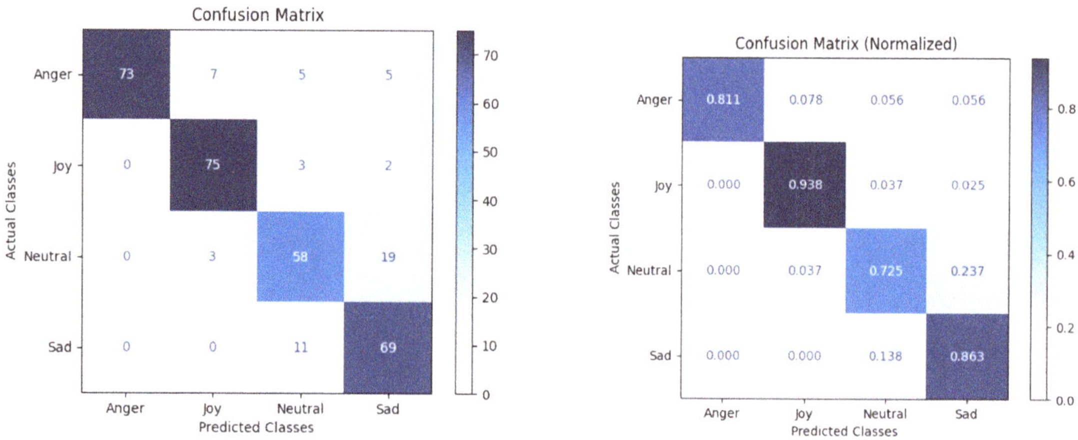

Figure 3. Confusion matrix of subjective evaluation of emotions in acting children's speech in the Russian language by Russian experts on the extended dataset.

Table 7. Overall scores in multi-class classification, extended expert's feature set with 33 samples in total.

Metrics	Accuracy
Overall Accuracy	0.897
Unweighted Average Recall	0.794
Unweighted Average Precision	0.810

From the normalized confusion matrices in Figures 2 and 3 it can be seen that the diagonal values of the matrix in Figure 3 are distributed more evenly than the diagonal values of the matrix in Figure 2, but the overall scores in both cases are approximately the same; see Tables 4–7.

5.3. Comparison of the Subjective Evaluation and Automatic Emotional Speech Recognition

Figure 4 shows the confusion matrices for the SVM and MLP classifiers. The training dataset consists of 2505 samples of the acting emotional speech of Russian children. The test set for automatic evaluation consists of 33 separate samples of acting emotional speech of Russian children used in perception tests [21]. Both classifiers were trained based on the eGeMAPS feature set [72].

The results of automatic classification are shown in Tables 8 and 9. Both SVM and MLP classifiers recognize emotional states with comparable performance, which is noticeably above chance. Their overall accuracy is comparable to the overall accuracy of the subjective evaluation, achieving an overall accuracy of 0.833 in automatic emotion recognition for both SVM and MLP classifiers, and the overall accuracy of 0.898 in the subjective evaluation of Russian children's emotional speech.

Table 8. Per-class scores in automatic multi-class classification, eGeMAPS feature set, testing on 33 samples from subjective evaluations.

Classifier	SVM				MLP			
Emotion	**Anger**	**Joy**	**Neutral**	**Sad**	**Anger**	**Joy**	**Neutral**	**Sad**
Accuracy	0.939	0.939	0.909	0.909	0.939	0.939	0.909	0.909
Recall	0.778	1.000	0.750	0.875	0.889	0.875	0.625	1.000
Precision	1.000	0.800	0.857	0.778	0.889	0.875	1.000	0.727
F1-score	0.875	0.889	0.800	0.824	0.889	0.875	0.769	0.842

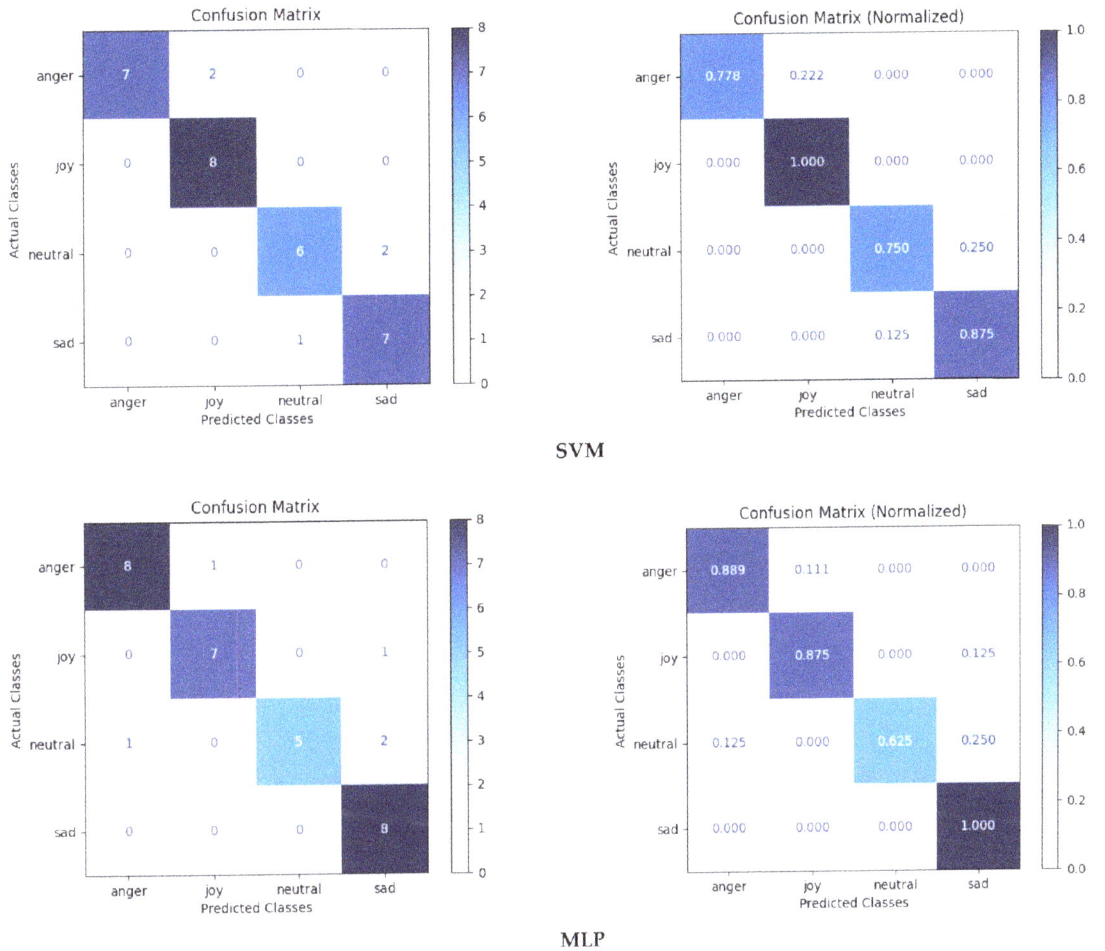

Figure 4. Confusion matrices for SVM and MLP classifiers, a dataset of Russian children's emotional speech with 2505 samples for training, an eGeMAPS feature set, and an additional 33 samples from subjective evaluations for testing.

Table 9. Overall scores in automaticmulti-class classification, eGeMAPS feature set, testing on 33 samples from subjective evaluations.

Metrics	Classifier	
	SVM	**MLP**
Overall Accuracy	0.924	0.924
Unweighted Average Recall	0.851	0.847
Unweighted Average Precision	0.859	0.873

As a result of the comparison of the subjective evaluation and automatic emo-tional speech recognition, we can conclude:

1. Humans are able to identify emotional states in Russian children's emotional speech above chance. Following [13], this ensures the emotional quality and naturalness of the emotions in the collected corpus of Russian children's emotional speech.
2. The performance of automatic emotion recognition using state-of-the-art ML algorithms/classifiers trained on the collected corpus is at least comparable to the perfor-

mance of perception tests. This also proves that the collected corpus can be used to build automatic systems for emotion recognition in Russian children's emotion speech.

6. Discussion and Conclusions

Our experiments were conducted on our proprietary dataset of children's emotional speech in the Russian language of the younger school age group [21]. To our knowledge, this is the only such database.

We have conducted a validation of our dataset based on classical ML algorithms, such as SVM and MLP. The validation was performed using standard procedures and scenarios of the validation similar to other well-known databases of children's emotional speech.

First of all, we demonstrated the following performance of automatic multiclass recognition (four emotion classes): SVM Overall Accuracy = 0.903, UAR = 0.807, and also MLP Overall Accuracy = 0.911, UAR = 0.822 are superior to the results of the perceptual test with Overall Accuracy = 0.898 and UAR = 0.795. Moreover, the results of automatic recognition on the test dataset, which consists of 33 samples used in the perceptual test, are even better: SVM Overall Accuracy = 0.924, UAR = 0.851, and also MLP Overall Accuracy = 0.924, UAR = 0.847. This can be explained by the fact that for the perceptual test we selected samples with clearly expressed emotions.

Second, a comparison with the results of validation of other databases of children's emotional speech on the same and other classifiers showed that our database contains reliable samples of children's emotional speech which can be used to develop various edutainment [76], health care, etc. applications using different types of classifiers.

The above confirms that this database is a valuable resource for researching the affective reactions in speech communication between a child and a computer in Russian.

Nevertheless, there are some aspects of this study that need to be improved.

First, the most important challenge in the applications mentioned above is how to automatically recognize a child's emotions with the highest possible performance. Thus, the accuracy of the speech emotion recognition must be improved. The most prominent way to solve the problem is use deep learning techniques. However, one of the significant issues in deep learning-based SER is the limited size of the datasets. Thus, we need larger datasets of children's speech. One of the suitable solutions we suggest is to study the creation of a fully synthetic dataset using generative techniques trained on available datasets [77]. GAN-based techniques have already shown success for similar problems and would be candidates for solving this problem as well. Moreover, we can use generative models to create noisy samples and try to design a noise-robust model for SER in real-world child communications including various gadgets for atypical children.

Secondly, other sources of information for SER should be considered, such as children's face expression, posture, and motion.

In the future, we intend to improve the accuracy of the automatic SER by

- extending our corpus of children's emotional speech to be able to train deep neural networks of different architectures;
- using multiple modalities such as facial expressions [58], head and body movements, etc.

Author Contributions: Conceptualization, Y.M. and A.M.; methodology, Y.M.; software, A.M.; validation, O.F., E.L. and Y.M.; formal analysis, N.R., O.F. and E.L.; investigation, A.M. and Y.M.; resources, O.F. and E.L.; data curation, N.R., O.F. and E.L.; writing—original draft preparation, Y.M.; writing—review and editing, Y.M., A.M., O.F. and E.L.; visualization, A.M.; supervision, Y.M.; project administration, Y.M. and E.L.; funding acquisition, E.L. All authors have read and agreed to the published version of the manuscript.

Funding: The research was financially supported by the Russian Foundation for Basic Research (projects 19-57-45008–IND) and Russian Science Foundation (project 22-45-02007). Database collection and selection the feature set, powerful to distinguish between different emotions were financially supported by the RFBR project 19-57-45008; automatic emotion speech classification was financially supported by the RSF project 22-45-02007.

Institutional Review Board Statement: Not applicable.

Informed Consent Statement: Informed consent was obtained from all subjects involved in the study.

Data Availability Statement: The publicly available dataset was analyzed in this study. This dataset can be found here: https://github.com/hydra-colab/Emotion-Recognition-of-Younger-School-Age-Children, accessed on 6 May 2022.

Acknowledgments: The study was carried out as part of a joint project with Department of Science and Technology (DST), School of Electrical Engineering, Vellore Institute of Technology, Vellore, India (INTRUSRFBR382).

Conflicts of Interest: The authors declare that they have no conflicts of interest. The funders had no role in the design of the study; in the collection, analyses, or interpretation of data; in the writing of the manuscript, or in the decision to publish the results.

References

1. El Ayadi, M.; Kamel, M.S.; Karray, F. Survey on Speech Emotion Recognition: Features, Classification Schemes, and Databases. *Pattern Recognit.* **2011**, *44*, 572–587. [CrossRef]
2. Lefter, I.; Rothkrantz, L.J.M.; Wiggers, P.; van Leeuwen, D.A. Emotion Recognition from Speech by Combining Databases and Fusion of Classifiers. *Lect. Notes Comput. Sci.* **2010**, *6231*, 353–360. [CrossRef]
3. Schuller, B.W. Speech Emotion Recognition: Two Decades in a Nutshell, Benchmarks, and Ongoing Trends. *Commun. ACM* **2018**, *61*, 90–99. [CrossRef]
4. Ganapathy, A. Speech Emotion Recognition Using Deep Learning Techniques. *ABC J. Adv. Res.* **2016**, *5*, 113–122. [CrossRef]
5. Khalil, R.A.; Jones, E.; Babar, M.I.; Jan, T.; Zafar, M.H.; Alhussain, T. Speech Emotion Recognition Using Deep Learning Techniques: A Review. *IEEE Access.* **2019**, *7*, 117327–117345. [CrossRef]
6. Polzehl, T.; Sundaram, S.; Ketabdar, H.; Wagner, M.; Metze, F. Emotion Classification in Children's Speech Using Fusion of Acoustic and Linguistic Features. In Proceedings of the 10th Annual Conference of the International Speech Communication Association (INTERSPEECH), Brighton, UK, 6–10 September 2009; pp. 340–343. [CrossRef]
7. Lyakso, E.; Ruban, N.; Frolova, O.; Gorodnyi, V.; Matveev, Y. Approbation of a method for studying the reflection of emotional state in children's speech and pilot psychophysiological experimental data. *Int. J. Adv. Trends Comput. Sci. Eng.* **2020**, *9*, 649–656. Available online: http://www.warse.org/IJATCSE/static/pdf/file/ijatcse91912020.pdf (accessed on 20 April 2022). [CrossRef]
8. Cao, G.; Tang, Y.; Sheng, J.; Cao, W. Emotion Recognition from Children Speech Signals Using Attention Based Time Series Deep Learning. In Proceedings of the 2019 IEEE International Conference on Bioinformatics and Biomedicine (BIBM), San Diego, CA, USA, 18–21 November 2019; pp. 1296–1300. [CrossRef]
9. Onwujekwe, D. Using Deep Leaning-Based Framework for Child Speech Emotion Recognition. Ph.D. Thesis, Virginia Commonwealth University, Richmond, VA, USA, 2021. Available online: https://scholarscompass.vcu.edu/cgi/viewcontent.cgi?article=7859&context=etd (accessed on 20 April 2022).
10. Kaur, K.; Singh, P. Punjabi Emotional Speech Database: Design, Recording and Verification. *Int. J. Intell. Syst. Appl. Eng.* **2021**, *9*, 205–208. [CrossRef]
11. Swain, M.; Routray, A.; Kabisatpathy, P. Databases, features and classifiers for speech emotion recognition: A review. *Int. J. Speech Technol.* **2018**, *21*, 93–120. [CrossRef]
12. Akçay, M.B.; Oguz, K. Speech emotion recognition: Emotional models, databases, features, preprocessing methods, supporting modalities, and classifiers. *Speech Commun.* **2020**, *166*, 56–76. [CrossRef]
13. Rajan, R.; Haritha, U.G.; Sujitha, A.C.; Rejisha, T.M. Design and Development of a Multi-Lingual Speech Corpora (TaMaR-EmoDB) for Emotion Analysis. In Proceedings of the 20th Annual Conference of the International Speech Communication Association (INTERSPEECH), Graz, Austria, 15–19 September 2019; pp. 3267–3271. [CrossRef]
14. Tamulevičius, G.; Korvel, G.; Yayak, A.B.; Treigys, P.; Bernatavičienė, J.; Kostek, B. A Study of Cross-Linguistic Speech Emotion Recognition Based on 2D Feature Spaces. *Electronics* **2020**, *9*, 1725. [CrossRef]
15. Duville, M.M.; Alonso-Valerdi, L.M.; Ibarra-Zarate, D.I. Mexican Emotional Speech Database Based on Semantic, Frequency, Familiarity, Concreteness, and Cultural Shaping of Affective Prosody. *Data* **2021**, *6*, 130. [CrossRef]
16. Lyakso, E.; Frolova, O.; Dmitrieva, E.; Grigorev, A.; Kaya, H.; Salah, A.A.; Karpov, A. EmoChildRu: Emotional child Russian speech corpus. *Lect. Notes Comput. Sci.* **2015**, *9319*, 144–152. Available online: https://www.researchgate.net/profile/Heysem-Kaya/publication/281583846_EmoChildRu_Emotional_Child_Russian_Speech_Corpus/links/55ee969208aedecb68fca34c/EmoChildRu-Emotional-Child-Russian-Speech-Corpus.pdf (accessed on 20 April 2022). [CrossRef]

17. Kaya, H.; Ali Salah, A.; Karpov, A.; Frolova, O.; Grigorev, A.; Lyakso, E. Emotion, age, and gender classification in children's speech by humans and machines. *Comput. Speech Lang.* **2017**, *46*, 268–283. [CrossRef]
18. Pérez-Espinosa, H.; Martínez-Miranda, J.; Espinosa-Curiel, I.; Rodríguez-Jacobo, J.; Villaseñor-Pineda, L.; Avila-George, H. IESC-Child: An Interactive Emotional Children's Speech Corpus. *Comput. Speech Lang.* **2020**, *59*, 55–74. [CrossRef]
19. van den Heuvel, H. The art of validation. *ELRA Newsl.* **2000**, *5*, 4–6. Available online: http://www.elra.info/media/filer_public/2013/12/04/elranews_v12-1.pdf (accessed on 20 April 2022).
20. van den Heuvel, H.; Iskra, D.; Sanders, E.; de Vriend, F. Validation of spoken language resources: An overview of basic aspects. *Lang Resour. Eval.* **2008**, *42*, 41–73. [CrossRef]
21. Lyakso, E.; Frolova, O.; Ruban, N.; Mekala, A.M. The Child's Emotional Speech Classification by Human Across Two Languages: Russian & Tamil. *Lect. Notes Comput. Sci.* **2021**, *12997*, 384–396. [CrossRef]
22. Costantini, G.; Parada-Cabaleiro, E.; Casali, D.; Cesarini, V. The Emotion Probe: On the Universality of Cross-Linguistic and Cross-Gender Speech Emotion Recognition via Machine Learning. *Sensors* **2022**, *22*, 2461. [CrossRef]
23. Javaheri, B. Speech & Song Emotion Recognition Using Multilayer Perceptron and Standard Vector Machine. *arXiv* **2021**, arXiv:2105.09406.
24. Zanaty, E.A. Support Vector Machines (SVMs) versus Multilayer Perception (MLP) in data classification. *Egypt. Inform. J.* **2012**, *13*, 177–183. [CrossRef]
25. Farooq, M.; Hussain, F.; Baloch, N.K.; Raja, F.R.; Yu, H.; Zikria, Y.B. Impact of Feature Selection Algorithm on Speech Emotion Recognition Using Deep Convolutional Neural Network. *Sensors* **2020**, *20*, 6008. [CrossRef] [PubMed]
26. Abbaschian, B.J.; Sierra-Sosa, D.; Elmaghraby, A. Deep Learning Techniques for Speech Emotion Recognition, from Databases to Models. *Sensors* **2021**, *21*, 1249. [CrossRef] [PubMed]
27. Emotional Databases. Available online: http://kahlan.eps.surrey.ac.uk/savee/Introduction.html (accessed on 20 April 2022).
28. Devi, S.; Kumbham, V.; Boddu, D. A Survey on Databases and Algorithms used for Speech Emotion Recognition. *Int. J. Adv. Trends Comput. Sci. Eng.* **2020**, *9*, 7032–7039. [CrossRef]
29. List of Children's Speech Corpora. Available online: https://en.wikipedia.org/wiki/List_of_children%27s_speech_corpora (accessed on 20 April 2022).
30. Grill, P.; Tučková, J. Speech Databases of Typical Children and Children with SLI. *PLoS ONE* **2016**, *11*, e0150365. [CrossRef] [PubMed]
31. Matin, R. Developing a Speech Emotion Recognition Solution Using Ensemble Learning for Children with Autism Spectrum Disorder to Help Identify Human Emotions. Unpublished Thesis, Texas State University, San Marcos, TX, USA, 2020. Available online: https://digital.library.txstate.edu/handle/10877/13037 (accessed on 20 April 2022).
32. Duville, M.M.; Alonso-Valerdi, L.M.; Ibarra-Zarate, D.I. Mexican Emotional Speech Database (MESD). *Mendeley Data* **2021**, *V2*, 1644–1647. [CrossRef]
33. Nojavanasghari, B.; Baltrušaitis, T.; Hughes, C.; Morency, L. EmoReact: A Multimodal Approach and Dataset for Recognizing Emotional Responses in Children. In Proceedings of the 18th ACM International Conference on Multimodal Interaction (ICMI), Tokyo, Japan, 12–16 November 2016; pp. 137–144. Available online: http://multicomp.cs.cmu.edu/wp-content/uploads/2017/09/2016_ICMI_Nojavanasghari_Emoreact.pdf (accessed on 20 April 2022). [CrossRef]
34. Li, Y.; Tao, J.; Chao, L.; Bao, W.; Liu, Y. CHEAVD: A Chinese natural emotional audio–visual database. *J. Ambient Intell Hum. Comput* **2017**, *8*, 913–924. Available online: http://www.speakit.cn/Group/file/2016_CHEAVD_AIHC_SCI-Ya%20Li.pdf (accessed on 20 April 2022). [CrossRef]
35. Ram, C.S.; Ponnusamy, R. Recognising and classify Emotion from the speech of Autism Spectrum Disorder children for Tamil language using Support Vector Machine. *Int. J. Appl. Eng. Res.* **2014**, *9*, 25587–25602.
36. Pérez-Espinosa, H.; Reyes-García, C.; Villaseñor-Pineda, L. EmoWisconsin: An Emotional Children Speech Database in Mexican Spanish. In Proceedings of the 4th International Conference on Affective Computing and Intelligent Interaction (ACII), Memphis, TN, USA, 9–12 October 2011; pp. 62–71. [CrossRef]
37. Batliner, A.; Hacker, C.; Steidl, S.; Nöth, E.; D'Arcy, S.; Russell, M.; Wong, M. "You Stupid Tin Box"—Children Interacting with the AIBO Robot: A Cross-linguistic Emotional Speech Corpus. In Proceedings of the Fourth International Conference on Language Resources and Evaluation (LREC), Lisbon, Portugal, 26–28 May 2004; pp. 171–174. Available online: http://www.lrec-conf.org/proceedings/lrec2004/pdf/317.pdf (accessed on 20 April 2022).
38. FAU Aibo Emotion Corpus. Available online: https://www5.cs.fau.de/en/our-team/steidl-stefan/fau-aibo-emotion-corpus/ (accessed on 20 April 2022).
39. Pattern Recognition. Available online: https://www.sciencedirect.com/topics/engineering/pattern-recognition (accessed on 20 April 2022).
40. Basharirad, B.; Moradhaseli, M. Speech Emotion Recognition Methods: A Literature Review. *AIP Conf. Proc.* **2017**, *1891*, 020105-1–020105-7. [CrossRef]
41. Schuller, B.; Steidl, S.; Batliner, A. The INTERSPEECH 2009 Emotion Challenge. In Proceedings of the 10th Annual Conference of the International Speech Communication Association (INTERSPEECH), Brighton, UK, 6–10 September 2009; pp. 312–315. [CrossRef]

42. Eyben, F.; Scherer, K.R.; Schuller, B.W.; Sundberg, J.; Andre, E.; Busso, C.; Devillers, L.Y.; Epps, J.; Laukka, P.; Narayanan, S.S.; et al. The Geneva Minimalistic Acoustic Parameter Set (GeMAPS) for Voice Research and Affective Computing. *IEEE Trans. Affect. Comput.* **2016**, *7*, 190–202. [CrossRef]
43. Disvoice's Documentation. Available online: https://disvoice.readthedocs.io/en/latest/index.html (accessed on 20 April 2022).
44. Chatziagapi, A.; Paraskevopoulos, G.; Sgouropoulos, D.; Pantazopoulos, G.; Nikandrou, M.; Giannakopoulos, T.; Katsamanis, A.; Potamianos, A.; Narayanan, S. Data Augmentation Using GANs for Speech Emotion Recognition. In Proceedings of the 20th Annual Conference of the International Speech Communication Association (INTERSPEECH), Graz, Austria, 15–19 September 2019; pp. 171–175. [CrossRef]
45. Eskimez, S.E.; Dimitriadis, D.; Gmyr, R.; Kumanati, K. GAN-based Data Generation for Speech Emotion Recognition. In Proceedings of the 21th Annual Conference of the International Speech Communication Association (INTERSPEECH), Shanghai, China, 25–29 October 2020; pp. 3446–3450. [CrossRef]
46. Ying, Y.; Tu, Y.; Zhou, H. Unsupervised Feature Learning for Speech Emotion Recognition Based on Autoencoder. *Electronics* **2021**, *10*, 2086. [CrossRef]
47. Andleeb Siddiqui, M.; Hussain, W.; Ali, S.A.; ur-Rehman, D. Performance Evaluation of Deep Autoencoder Network for Speech Emotion Recognition. *Int. J. Adv. Comput. Sci. Appl.* **2020**, *11*, 606–611. [CrossRef]
48. Cai, X.; Yuan, J.; Zheng, R.; Huang, L.; Church, K. Speech Emotion Recognition with Multi-Task Learning. In Proceedings of the 22th Annual Conference of the International Speech Communication Association (INTERSPEECH), Brno, Czechia, 30 August–3 September 2021; pp. 4508–4512. [CrossRef]
49. Han, K.; Yu, D.; Tashev, I. Speech emotion recognition using deep neural network and extreme learning machine. In Proceedings of the 15th Annual Conference of the International Speech Communication Association (INTERSPEECH), Singapore, 14–18 September 2014; pp. 223–227.
50. Padi, S.; Sadjadi, S.O.; Sriram, R.D.; Manocha, D. Improved Speech Emotion Recognition using Transfer Learning and Spectrogram Augmentation. In *Proceedings of the 2021 International Conference on Multimodal Interaction (ICMI)*; Montréal, QC, Canada, 18–22 October 2021, pp. 645–652. Available online: https://tsapps.nist.gov/publication/get_pdf.cfm?pub_id=932172 (accessed on 20 April 2022). [CrossRef]
51. Rumagit, R.Y.; Alexander, G.; Saputra, I.F. Model Comparison in Speech Emotion Recognition for Indonesian Language. *Procedia Comput. Sci.* **2021**, *179*, 789–797. [CrossRef]
52. Ali Alnuaim, A.; Zakariah, M.; Kumar Shukla, P.; Alhadlaq, A.; Hatamleh, W.A.; Tarazi, H.; Sureshbabu, R.; Ratna, R. Human-Computer Interaction for Recognizing Speech Emotions Using Multilayer Perceptron Classifier. *J. Healthc. Eng.* **2022**, *6005446*, 1–12. [CrossRef] [PubMed]
53. Poojary, N.N.; Shivakumar, G.S.; Akshath Kumar, B.H. Speech Emotion Recognition Using MLP Classifier. *Int. J. Sci. Res. Comput. Sci. Eng. Inf. Technol.* **2021**, *7*, 218–222. [CrossRef]
54. Kaur, J.; Kumar, A. Speech Emotion Recognition Using CNN, k-NN, MLP and Random Forest. *Lect. Notes Data Eng. Commun. Technol.* **2021**, *58*, 499–509. [CrossRef]
55. Yang, N.; Dey, N.; Sherratt, R.S.; Shi, F. Recognize Basic Emotional States in Speech by Machine Learning Techniques Using Mel-Frequency Cepstral Coefficient Features. *J. Intell. Fuzzy Syst.* **2020**, *39*, 1925–1936. [CrossRef]
56. Goel, S.; Beigi, H. Cross Lingual Cross Corpus Speech Emotion Recognition. *arXiv* **2020**, arXiv:2003.07996v1.
57. Chugh, V.; Kaw, S.; Soni, S.; Sablan, V.; Hande, R. Speech Emotion Recognition System Using MLP. *J. Emerg. Technol. Innov. Res.* **2021**, *8*, 222–226.
58. Lyakso, E.; Frolova, O.; Matveev, Y. Chapter 14—Facial Expression: Psychophysiological Study. In *Handbook of Research on Deep Learning-Based Image Analysis Under Constrained and Unconstrained Environments*; Raj, A., Mahesh, V., Nersisson, R., Eds.; IGI Global: Pennsylvania, PA, USA, 2021; pp. 266–289. [CrossRef]
59. Laukka, P.; Elfenbein, H.A. Cross-Cultural Emotion Recognition and In-Group Advantage in Vocal Expression: A Meta-Analysis. *Emot. Rev.* **2021**, *13*, 3–11. [CrossRef]
60. Rajoo, R.; Aun, C.C. Influences of languages in speech emotion recognition: A comparative study using malay, english and mandarin languages. In Proceedings of the IEEE Symposium on Computer Applications Industrial Electronics (ISCAIE), Penang, Malaysia, 30–31 May 2016; pp. 35–39. [CrossRef]
61. Heracleous, P.; Yoneyama, A. A comprehensive study on bilingual and multilingual speech emotion recognition using a two-pass classification scheme. *PLoS ONE* **2019**, *14*, e0220386. [CrossRef]
62. Latif, S.; Qadir, J.; Bilal, M. Unsupervised Adversarial Domain Adaptation for Cross-Lingual Speech Emotion Recognition. *arXiv* **2020**, arXiv:1907.06083v4.
63. Latif, S.; Qayyum, A.; Usman, M.U.; Qadir, J. Cross lingual speech emotion recognition: Urdu vs. western languages. *arXiv* **2020**, arXiv:1812.10411.
64. Gilam, G.; Hendler, T. Deconstructing Anger in the Human Brain. *Curr Top Behav Neurosci.* **2017**, *30*, 257–273. [CrossRef]
65. Carrol, L. *Through the Looking-Glass and What Alice Found There*; Macmillan and Co.: London, UK, 1872.
66. GLOKAYA KUZDRA. Available online: http://languagehat.com/glokaya-kuzdr (accessed on 20 April 2022).
67. openSMILE Python. Available online: https://github.com/audeering/opensmile-python (accessed on 20 April 2022).
68. Support Vector Machines. Available online: https://scikit-learn.org/stable/modules/svm.html#svm (accessed on 20 April 2022).

69. Multi-Layer Perceptron Classifier. Available online: https://scikit-learn.org/stable/modules/generated/sklearn.neural_network.MLPClassifier.html (accessed on 20 April 2022).
70. Stratified K-Folds Cross-Validator. Available online: https://scikit-learn.org/stable/modules/generated/sklearn.model_selection.StratifiedKFold.html (accessed on 20 April 2022).
71. Haghighi, S.; Jasemi, M.; Hessabi, S.; Zolanvari, A. PyCM: Multiclass confusion matrix library in Python. *J. Open Source Softw.* **2018**, *3*, 729. [CrossRef]
72. Schuller, B.W.; Weninger, F. Ten recent trends in computational paralinguistics. *Lect. Notes Comput. Sci.* **2012**, *7403*, 35–49. Available online: https://opus.bibliothek.uni-augsburg.de/opus4/frontdoor/deliver/index/docId/72653/file/72653.pdf (accessed on 20 April 2022). [CrossRef]
73. Werner, S.; Petrenko, G.K. A Speech Emotion Recognition: Humans vs Machines. *Discourse* **2019**, *5*, 136–152. [CrossRef]
74. Verkholyak, O.V.; Kaya, H.; Karpov, A.A. Modeling Short-Term and Long-Term Dependencies of the Speech Signal for Paralinguistic Emotion Classification. *Tr. SPIIRAN* **2019**, *18*, 30–56. [CrossRef]
75. Sowmya, V.; Rajeswari, A. Speech emotion recognition for Tamil language speakers. *Adv. Intell. Syst. Comput.* **2020**, *1085*, 125–136. [CrossRef]
76. Guran, A.-M.; Cojocar, G.-S.; Dioşan, L.-S. The Next Generation of Edutainment Applications for Young Children—A Proposal. *Mathematics* **2022**, *10*, 645. [CrossRef]
77. Kaliyev, A.; Zeno, B.; Rybin, S.V.; Matveev, Y.N.; Lyakso, E.E. GAN acoustic model for Kazakh speech synthesis. *Int. J. Speech Technol.* **2021**, *24*, 729–735. [CrossRef]

mathematics

MDPI

Article

Online Support Vector Machine with a Single Pass for Streaming Data

Lisha Hu [1], Chunyu Hu [2,*], Zheng Huo [1], Xinlong Jiang [3] and Suzhen Wang [1]

1 Institute of Information Technology, Hebei University of Economics and Business, Shijiazhuang 050061, China
2 School of Computer Science and Technology, Qilu University of Technology (Shandong Academy of Sciences), Jinan 250353, China
3 Institute of Computing Technology, Chinese Academy of Sciences, Beijing 100190, China
* Correspondence: hcy@qlu.edu.cn

Abstract: In this paper, we focus on training a support vector machine (SVM) online with a single pass over streaming data.Traditional batch-mode SVMs require previously prepared training data; these models may be unsuitable for streaming data circumstances. Online SVMs are effective tools for solving this problem by receiving data streams consistently and updating model weights accordingly. However, most online SVMs require multiple data passes before the updated weights converge to stable solutions, and may be unable to address high-rate data streams. This paper presents OSVM_SP, a new online SVM with a single pass over streaming data, and three budgeted versions to bound the space requirement with support vector removal principles. The experimental results obtained with five public datasets show that OSVM_SP outperforms most state-of-the-art single-pass online algorithms in terms of accuracy and is comparable to batch-mode SVMs. Furthermore, the proposed budgeted algorithms achieve comparable predictive performance with only 1/3 of the space requirement.

Keywords: online learning; support vector machine; minimum enclosing ball

MSC: 68T30

Citation: Hu, L.; Hu, C.; Huo, Z.; Jiang, X.; Wang, S. Online Support Vector Machine with a Single Pass for Streaming Data. *Mathematics* **2022**, *10*, 3113. https://doi.org/10.3390/math10173113

Academic Editors: Adrian Sergiu Darabant and Diana-Laura Borza

Received: 19 July 2022
Accepted: 25 August 2022
Published: 30 August 2022

1. Introduction

Support vector machine (SVMs) is a well-known binary classifier trained offline with supervised datasets [1]. The central idea is to find a hyperplane in the reproducing kernel Hilbert space (RKHS) that splits the data into different classes as well as possible and achieves a maximal margin. Based on the substantial foundations of the Vapnik–Chervonenkis (VC) dimension and the structural risk minimization (SRM) principle [2], SVM has shown its superiority in the literature [3–6].

For traditional batch-mode methods, the data for model training need to be prepared beforehand. This is mainly because once the training process starts, the optimization problem usually requires the cycling of training data many times in order to find the optimal solutions in the data space. In other words, traditional batch-mode models require the data to be prepared beforehand and to be accessible at any time. Traditional batch-mode models usually fail to deal with streaming data that arrive sequentially over time and usually never end. For scenarios in which data arrive in streams individually at a very high rate, every time new data arrive, a batch-mode SVM has to be retrained from scratch to exploit both the previous and new data. Because a batch-mode SVM is typically formulated as a quadratic programming problem with time complexity $O(N^3)$ (where N represents the number of training data points), it is not suitable for streaming data due to the required time efficiency and computational capability [7,8]. Therefore, the training set increases consistently and changes dynamically, and is nearly unusable for learning with batch-mode methods. Fortunately, online SVM is an alternative type of algorithm that directly addresses the streaming data issue.

Thanks to the consistent interest of the online learning community, numerous online SVM algorithms have been proposed in the literature [9–11]. Online SVM algorithms do not initially hold all the data; instead, they receive streams of data one at a time and update the model weights with respect to specified instantaneous objective functions. Most online models adapt the streaming data scenario, in which samples arrive one by one. When one sample arrives as a representative of a new concept, the model can update itself to immediately account for this sample. One benefit of processing singular instead of multiple data is that the model can learn in a timely fashion without the need to wait until a fixed number of samples have been gathered. In addition, if the model is ideally updated in the right direction, a alrge number of samples arriving afterward can be avoided in the online learning process. Many online SVM algorithms [12–14] require multiple passes over the data before the updated weights converge to reasonable solutions. For instance, the algorithm in [12] continues passing through the training data to look for better solutions until a certain stopping criterion is met. In [13], a series of SVM models were trained periodically based on the training set extracted from historical streaming data; all of them needed many passes over the training data to find the appropriate solutions for each model. New data arriving during this period must wait until they can be processed. Therefore, the necessity of multiple passes over the training data hinders these algorithms from being timely and lightweight for fairly high data streaming rates. Recently, a handful of online SVM algorithms have been proposed that require only a single pass over the data [15–18]. Motivated by the work of [16], in this paper, we present a new single-pass online SVM based on the minimum enclosing ball (MEB) problem and three budgeted versions of the proposed algorithm to control the space requirement. We validated our methods on six public datasets, and our experimental results show the effectiveness and superiority of our methods compared to the present state-of-the-art.

The remainder of this paper is organized as follows: In Section 2, we review related works on online SVM algorithms; in Section 3, we provide a brief introduction to the formulation of batch-mode SVMs and MEBs, as well as their equivalence, which is closely related to our methods; in Section 4, we elaborate our proposed methods; in Section 5, we present experimental evaluations and analyses; finally, our conclusions are presented in Section 7.

2. Related Work

There are many online SVM algorithms that can handle streaming training data and achieve good results. Matsushima et al. [12] provided an algorithm for training linear SVMs that utilizes a dual coordinate descent procedure based on blocks of data. Their algorithm performs multiple passes through the training data until a certain stopping criterion is met. Wang et al. [13] presented an online algorithm that automatically extracts one representative set for each class from the historical stream of data and retrains the SVM periodically based on the data from these sets. Zheng et al. [14] provided an online incremental algorithm that learns prototypes and continuously adjusts to the streaming data, and that trains new SVMs periodically based on learned prototypes and old support vectors (SVs). These algorithms suffer from a similar issue in that a series of quadratic optimization problems must be solved in order to obtain intermediate solutions, which requires multiple passes of the chosen training data.

The optimization problem for SVM has several equivalent geometric formulations [19]. Moreover, many of these can be easily adapted to streaming learning scenarios. Several single-pass SVM algorithms have been studied in the literature. Liu et al. [15] presented a single-pass online algorithm based on the polytope distance problem in the computational geometry literature. The central idea of their algorithm is based on an interpretation in which finding the hyperplane with the maximum separating margin is equivalent to finding the shortest distance between two points on the convex hull of two classes of training data, and the latter is equivalent to finding the shortest distance between the origin and a point on the convex hull of the Minkowski difference [20] of two convex hulls. They provided theoretical guarantees regarding the constant time and space requirements of their algorithm. However, their algorithm was proposed for hard margin classification problems, and the data of the two classes ought to be completely separated; this requirement may not always be satisfied. Rai et al. [16] provided another single-pass online algorithm based on a geometric interpretation in which a $\ell 2$-SVM has an equivalent formulation in terms of the MEB problem. Therefore, solving the optimization problem for the $\ell 2$-SVM is equivalent to finding the ball of the minimum radius enclosing the feature vectors mapped by the training data. Their algorithm initializes a ball with radius zero for the first sample. For any incoming point outside of the ball, the algorithm moves the center towards it and simultaneously enlarges the radius in order to cover both the point and the previous ball. However, their algorithm may suffer due to the rapid expansion of the ball leading ti convergence on a suboptimal solution. Motivated by the above, we present a new single-pass online algorithm.

In addition to algorithms based on geometric formulations, Crammer et al. [17] provided an online algorithmic framework that formalizes the trade-off between the correct classification of new data with a sufficiently high margin and the amount of information retained from old data. In light of hard margins and soft margins with $\ell 1$ and $\ell 2$ losses, the authors provide three variants of online algorithms in such frameworks. Our work is compared with all three works in the experimental section, and empirically, our algorithm performs better in most cases.

3. Preliminaries

In this section, we introduce the primal and dual formulations of the batch-mode SVM and MEB, as well as their equivalence, all of which are closely related to our methods.

3.1. Support Vector Machine

Let $\{(x_i, y_i)|x_i \in \mathbb{R}^{d\times 1}, y_i \in \{1, -1\}, i = 1, \cdots, N\}$ be a training set with N labeled samples. The primal optimization problem for unbiased $\ell 2$-regularized $\ell 2$-loss SVMs for binary classification is provided in Equation (1):

$$\min_{\omega,\xi,\rho} \frac{1}{2}\|\omega\|^2 - \rho + \frac{C}{2}\|\xi\|^2 \tag{1a}$$

$$s.t. \quad y_i\omega'\phi(x_i) \geqslant \rho - \xi_i, i = 1, \cdots, N. \tag{1b}$$

Here, $\xi = [\xi_1, \cdots, \xi_N]' \in \mathbb{R}^{N\times 1}$ is a vector consisting of slack variables, C is a penalty parameter used to control the trade-off between $\ell 2$ regularization and $\ell 2$ loss, $\phi(\cdot)$ denotes the kernel mapping function, which maps x into a higher-dimensional feature vector $\phi(x)$ in RKHS, and $\phi(\cdot)$ corresponds to a chosen kernel function $k_\phi : \mathbb{R}^d \times \mathbb{R}^d \to \mathbb{R}$, with $k_\phi(x_i, x_j) = \phi(x_i)'\phi(x_j)$.

Note the variable $\rho \in \mathbb{R}$ in the optimization problem, which means that the boundaries of the margin are $\omega'\phi(x_i) = \pm\rho$. The problem in Equation (1) is denoted as the "primal ρ-SVM" in order to differentiate it from the corresponding batch-mode "SVM" with respect to StreamSVM in [16], which does not contain the variable ρ and has the constant 1 instead. When parameter C is set to $2/N$, ρ-SVM shares a formulation with the unbiased $\ell 2$-regularized $\ell 2$-loss v-SVM [21], with parameter v being equal to 1. Because v can be seen as the lower bound of the ratio of SVs, almost every sample in the training set is recognized as an SV for ρ-SVM.

According to the Karush–Kuhn–Tucker (KKT) theorem [22], solving the primal ρ-SVM is equivalent to solving the dual problem listed in Equation (2), which is denoted as the "dual ρ-SVM".

$$\max_{\alpha} -\sum_{i=1}^{N}\sum_{j=1}^{N} \alpha_i\alpha_j y_i y_j (k_\phi(\boldsymbol{x}_i, \boldsymbol{x}_j) + \frac{\delta_{ij}}{C}) \tag{2a}$$

$$s.t. \quad \boldsymbol{\alpha} \geqslant \boldsymbol{0}, \boldsymbol{\alpha}'\boldsymbol{1} = 1. \tag{2b}$$

Here, $\boldsymbol{\alpha} = [\alpha_1, \cdots, \alpha_N]' \in \mathbb{R}^{N\times 1}$ is a vector consisting of Lagrange multipliers. The transformation of solutions $\boldsymbol{\alpha}$ of the dual ρ-SVM to solutions $\boldsymbol{\omega}$, $\boldsymbol{\xi}$, and ρ of the primal ρ-SVM is provided in the following equation:

$$\boldsymbol{\omega} = \sum_{i=1}^{N} \alpha_i y_i \phi(\boldsymbol{x}_i). \tag{3a}$$

$$\boldsymbol{\xi} = \boldsymbol{\alpha}/C. \tag{3b}$$

$$\rho = y_k \sum_{i=1}^{N} \alpha_i y_i k_\phi(\boldsymbol{x}_i, \boldsymbol{x}_k) + \alpha_k/C, \forall \alpha_k \neq 0. \tag{3c}$$

For a random sample $\boldsymbol{x}$, ρ-SVM predicts its label as follows:

$$y = \mathrm{sig}(\boldsymbol{\omega}'\phi(\boldsymbol{x})) = \mathrm{sig}(\sum_{i=1}^{N} \alpha_i y_i k_\phi(\boldsymbol{x}_i, \boldsymbol{x})). \tag{4}$$

Derivations of Equations (3) and (4) have been listed in Appendix A for reference.

3.2. Minimum Enclosing Ball

An MEB is known as a hard margin support vector data description (SVDD) [23,24], the central idea of which is to find a minimum ball enclosing all the data. Let $\{\boldsymbol{x}_i \in \mathbb{R}^{d\times 1} | i = 1, \cdots, N\}$ be a training set with N samples. The primal optimization problem of the MEB is denoted as the "primal MEB", as follows [25]:

$$\min_{c,r} r^2 \tag{5a}$$

$$s.t. \|\boldsymbol{c} - \varphi(\boldsymbol{x}_i)\|^2 \leqslant r^2, i = 1, \cdots, N. \tag{5b}$$

Here, we utilize $\varphi(\cdot)$ to denote the kernel mapping function employed in the primal MEB. Likewise, $k_\varphi : \mathbb{R}^d \times \mathbb{R}^d \to \mathbb{R}$ denotes the kernel function corresponding to $\varphi(\cdot)$. A hypersphere is represented by $(\boldsymbol{c}, r)$, where the center $\boldsymbol{c}$ is a high-dimensional feature vector in RKHS and $r \in \mathbb{R}^+$ denotes the radius.

According to the KKT theorem, the corresponding dual optimization problem is denoted as the "dual MEB", as follows [25]:

$$\max_{\alpha} \sum_{i=1}^{N} \alpha_i k_\varphi(\boldsymbol{x}_i, \boldsymbol{x}_i) - \sum_{i=1}^{N}\sum_{j=1}^{N} \alpha_i\alpha_j k_\varphi(\boldsymbol{x}_i, \boldsymbol{x}_j) \tag{6a}$$

$$s.t. \quad \boldsymbol{\alpha} \geqslant \boldsymbol{0}, \boldsymbol{\alpha}'\boldsymbol{1} = 1. \tag{6b}$$

The transformation of solutions $\boldsymbol{\alpha} \in \mathbb{R}^{N\times 1}$ of the dual MEB to solutions $\boldsymbol{c}$ and r of the primal MEB is as follows [25]:

$$c = \sum_{i=1}^{N} \alpha_i \varphi(x_i). \tag{7a}$$

$$r = \sqrt{\kappa_\varphi - 2\sum_{i=1}^{N} \alpha_i k_\varphi(x_i, x_k) + \sum_{i=1}^{N}\sum_{j=1}^{N} \alpha_i \alpha_j y_i y_j k_\varphi(x_i, x_j)}, \forall \alpha_k \neq 0. \tag{7b}$$

For a random sample x, the MEB predicts whether it is inside or outside the ball according to the following inequality:

$$\|c - \varphi(x)\|^2 \leqslant r^2. \tag{8}$$

3.3. Equivalence of the SVM and MEB

The supervised ρ-SVM classification problem can be equivalently reformulated as an unsupervised MEB problem by encoding the label y_i of sample x_i in feature vector $\varphi(x_i)$. Specifically, the optimization problems of the dual ρ-SVM in Equation (2) and the dual MEB in Equation (6) are equivalent to each other if the following two conditions are satisfied [16,25]:

1. $\varphi(x_i) = [y_i \phi(x_i); e_i/\sqrt{C}]$
2. $k_\phi(x_i, x_i) = \kappa_\phi, \forall x_i$

Here, e_i denotes the N-dimensional one-hot column vector in which the ith element is 1 and all other elements are 0, while κ_ϕ denotes a constant related to the kernel mapping function $\phi(\cdot)$.

When the kernel utilized by the MEB is k_φ, the center c and radius r of the MEB can be represented by k_φ and the mapping function φ according to Equation (7) in Section 3.2. Moreover, when these two conditions are satisfied, k_φ and φ can be substituted by another kernel k_ϕ and mapping function ϕ. Therefore, the center c and radius r can be represented by k_ϕ and ϕ after substitution, as listed in Equation (9). In other words, for any $\alpha_k \neq 0$, the center c and radius r of the primal MEB can be represented by the solutions α of ρ-SVM. The equivalence of ρ-SVM and the MEB are shown in Figure 1.

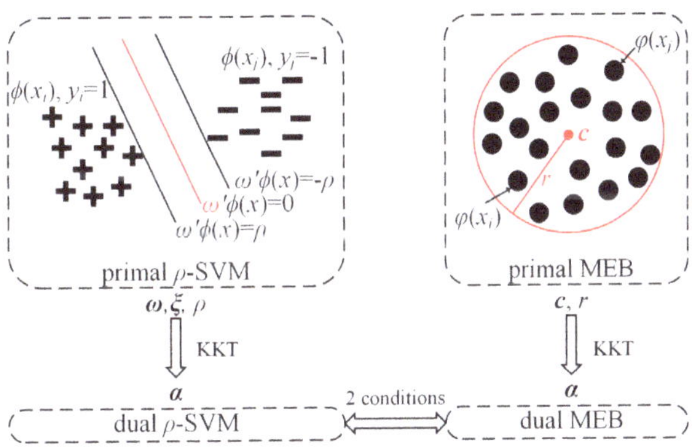

Figure 1. Equivalence of the SVM and MEB.

$$c = [\sum_{i=1}^{N} \alpha_i y_i \phi(\alpha_i); \frac{1}{\sqrt{C}} \sum_{i=1}^{N} \alpha_i e_i]. \tag{9a}$$

$$r = \sqrt{\kappa_\phi + \frac{1}{C} - 2(y_k \sum_{i=1}^{N} \alpha_i y_i k_\phi(x_i, x_k) + \frac{\alpha_k}{C}) + \sum_{i,j=1}^{N} \alpha_i \alpha_j y_i y_j (k_\phi(x_i, x_j) + \frac{\delta_{ij}}{C})}. \tag{9b}$$

4. Methodology

4.1. Motivation

According to Section 3, when the two conditions (see Section 3.3) are satisfied, a batch-mode classifier learned offline by the supervised convex optimization of the SVM can be attained by solving an unsupervised convex optimization of the MEB. In other words, a *classifier* can be equivalently transformed by a minimum enclosing *ball*. In view of such equivalence, a series of online SVM/MEB methods have been proposed in the literature to deal with the data in streams.

Taking the StreamSVM method in [16] as an example, a ball is constructed dynamically by enclosing all the streaming data. When a new sample arrives, StreamSVM learns a minimal ball enclosing both the sample and the current ball. Figure 2 illustrates the ball learned by StreamSVM when the third sample arrives outside. Although the enclosure of the whole current ball (the ball in black) instead of the old data (the first and second samples) prevents multiple passes of the data, it may lead to excessive enlargement of the ball (see the two colored balls for comparison). Because the ball of online methods often grows in an irreversible way, it ought to be enlarged cautiously in order to avoid enclosing any dispensable regions (e.g., the area with vertical lines as the background) as much as possible.

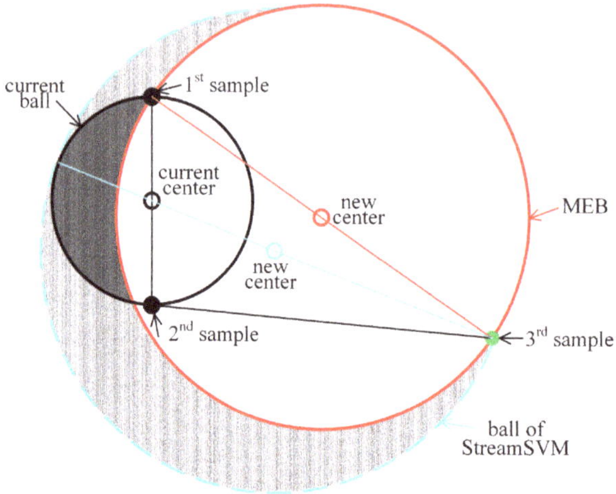

Figure 2. Motivation from StreamSVM [16] in learning the MEB.

Therefore, we attempt to learn a new ball online under the constraint of a minimal radius with a single pass over the streaming data. To achieve this, we choose to relax the constraint of enclosing all data instead of the constraint of the minimal radius utilized by StreamSVM to avoid multiple passes. A new ball is required to enclose both the new sample and majority regions of the current ball, while the minority regions (e.g., the gray area in Figure 2) of the current ball are discarded, which are the regions most dissimilar to the new sample. On this basis, a new online method is proposed in the following section.

4.2. OSVM_SP

In Section 3.3, we introduce the equivalence between the MEB and ρ-SVM and show that the solutions (c, r) of the MEB can be equivalently represented by the solutions $\boldsymbol{\alpha}$ of the ρ-SVM according to Equation (9). In other words, if we can find a way to learn the MEB online, we can obtain its corresponding online classifier. The online learning of a decision hyperplane is equivalently transformed into the online learning of an MEB.

In this section, we present OSVM_SP, a new online SVM algorithm with a single pass over the streaming data. The basic idea of OSVM_SP is as follows: a ball is initialized by taking the first sample to arrive as the center and 0 as the radius; when a new sample arrives that is outside of the current ball, a new ball is learned to enclose both the sample and the majority of the region of the current ball with a radius increment that is as small as possible. To accomplish this, we record the latest sample that leads to the current ball being enlarged. Then, a diameter segment (see Figure 3) that crosses the recorded sample and the center of the current ball can be determined to represent the boundary of the majority of the region that must be enclosed in the new ball. Therefore, the new ball is created to enclose both the new sample and the diameter segment with a minimum radius.

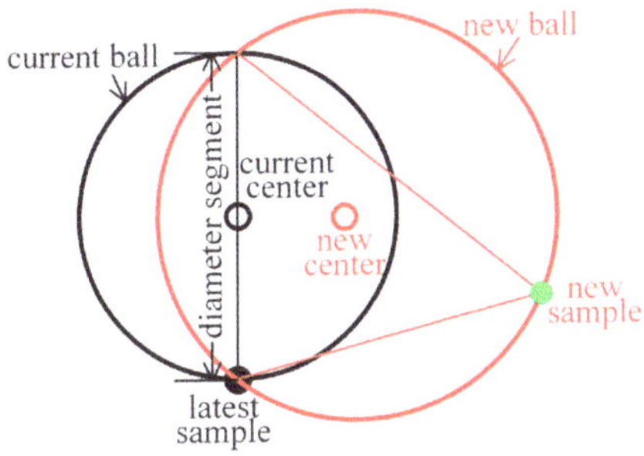

Figure 3. Basic idea of OSVM_SP.

Before we elaborate on OSVM_SP, it is necessary to clarify the variables to be learned and the parameters required during the learning process. When the ith sample $(\boldsymbol{x}_i, y_i)$ arrives, $i = 1, 2, \cdots$ is first mapped into $\boldsymbol{z}_i = \varphi(\boldsymbol{x}_i)$ according to the first condition in Section 3.3. Let the current ball be $(\boldsymbol{c}^{i-1}, r^{i-1})$ and $(\boldsymbol{c}^i, r^i)$ be the new ball to be learned. According to Equation (7a), the center $\boldsymbol{c}^i$ can be represented as $\boldsymbol{c}^i = \sum_{j=1}^{i} \alpha_j^i \boldsymbol{z}_j$ for each i. We use $\boldsymbol{p}^{i-1}$ and $\boldsymbol{q}^{i-1}$ to indicate two endpoints of the diameter segment (see Figure 4c–f), which can be universally expressed as $\boldsymbol{p}^{i-1} = \sum_{j=1}^{i-1} \beta_j^i \boldsymbol{z}_j$ and $\boldsymbol{q}^{i-1} = \sum_{j=1}^{i-1} \gamma_j^i \boldsymbol{z}_j$. Therefore, when the ith sample $(\boldsymbol{x}_i, y_i)$ arrives, online learning of the new ball $(\boldsymbol{c}^i, r^i)$ is equivalent to learning $\boldsymbol{\alpha}^i$, $\boldsymbol{\beta}^i$, $\boldsymbol{\gamma}^i$ and r^i based on $\boldsymbol{\alpha}^{i-1}$, $\boldsymbol{\beta}^{i-1}$, $\boldsymbol{\gamma}^{i-1}$, r^{i-1} and sample $(\boldsymbol{x}_i, y_i)$.

When $i = 1$ and $(\boldsymbol{x}_i, y_i)$ is the first sample to arrive, we can easily initialize the MEB $(\boldsymbol{c}^i, r^i)$ to enclose the sole point $\boldsymbol{z}_i$ by letting the center $\boldsymbol{c}^i$ coincide with $\boldsymbol{z}_i$ and the radius r^i equal 0 (see Figure 4a). In addition, $\boldsymbol{z}_i$ is recorded by considering $\boldsymbol{p}^i$ as the sole end point, and $\boldsymbol{q}^i$ is not available at the moment. See Steps 5–6 in Algorithm 1 for details.

$$d(\boldsymbol{z}_i, \boldsymbol{c}^{i-1}) = \sqrt{\sum_{j,k=1}^{i-1} \alpha_j^{i-1} \alpha_k^{i-1} y_j y_k \left(k_\phi(\boldsymbol{x}_j, \boldsymbol{x}_k) + \frac{\delta_{jk}}{C}\right) - 2y_i \sum_{j=1}^{i-1} \alpha_j^{i-1} y_j k_\phi(\boldsymbol{x}_j, \boldsymbol{x}_i) + \kappa_\phi + \frac{1}{C}}. \quad (10)$$

When the ith sample $(\boldsymbol{x}_i, y_i)$ arrives for $i \geqslant 2$, we first calculate the distance $d(\boldsymbol{z}_i, \boldsymbol{c}^{i-1})$ in Equation (10) and compare it with the radius r^{i-1} to determine whether $\boldsymbol{z}_i$ is inside of the current ball $(\boldsymbol{c}^{i-1}, r^{i-1})$. If it is, neither the ball nor the end points need to be adjusted, and they all inherit from the old ones (see Steps 24–26 in Algorithm 1); if not, a new ball $(\boldsymbol{c}^i, r^i)$ should be learned that encloses sample $\boldsymbol{z}_i$ as well as the current end point(s). Derivations of Equation (10) have been listed in Appendix B for reference.

If $\boldsymbol{z}_i$ is an outsider and the end point $\boldsymbol{q}^{i-1}$ is unavailable, the new ball must enclose two points of end point $\boldsymbol{p}^{i-1}$ and sample $\boldsymbol{z}_i$, which can be easily learned by letting the center $\boldsymbol{c}^i$ be the midpoint of these two points and letting r^i equal half the distance between them (see Figure 4b). Additionally, sample $\boldsymbol{z}_i$ is recorded by $\boldsymbol{q}^i$, and $\boldsymbol{p}^i$ inherits from $\boldsymbol{p}^{i-1}$ in preparation for the next update. In this case, $\boldsymbol{\alpha}^i$, $\boldsymbol{\beta}^i$, $\boldsymbol{\gamma}^i$ and r^i are computed by Equation (11).

$$\alpha_j^i = \begin{cases} \frac{1}{2}\beta_j^{i-1}, & \forall j = 1, \cdots, i-1. \\ \frac{1}{2}, & j = i. \end{cases} \tag{11a}$$

$$\beta_j^i = \begin{cases} \beta_j^{i-1}, & \forall j = 1, \cdots, i-1. \\ 0, & j = i. \end{cases} \tag{11b}$$

$$\gamma_j^i = \begin{cases} 0, & \forall j = 1, \cdots, i-1. \\ 1, & j = i. \end{cases} \tag{11c}$$

$$r^i = \frac{1}{2}d(\boldsymbol{z}_i, \boldsymbol{p}^{i-1}). \tag{11d}$$

Algorithm 1 OSVM_SP

Input: $(\boldsymbol{x}_i, y_i)_{i=1,\cdots,N}$, regularization parameter C, kernel function $k_\phi(\boldsymbol{x}_i, \boldsymbol{x}_j)$ with kernel parameter σ.
Output: *Lagrange* multiplier $\boldsymbol{\alpha} \in \mathrm{R}^{N \times 1}$.
for $i = 1$ to N **do**
  Map sample $(\boldsymbol{x}_i, y_i)$ into $\boldsymbol{z}_i$ according to $\boldsymbol{z}_i = \varphi(\boldsymbol{x}_i) = [y_i\phi(\boldsymbol{x}_i); \boldsymbol{e}_i/\sqrt{C}]$.
  if $i = 1$ **then**
    /*Initialization, see Figure 4a*/
    $\alpha_1^1 \leftarrow 1, \beta_1^1 \leftarrow 1, \gamma^1 \leftarrow NaN, r^1 \leftarrow 0.$
  else if $i \geqslant 2$ **then**
    Compute $d(\boldsymbol{z}_i, \boldsymbol{c}^{i-1})$, the distance of $\boldsymbol{z}_i$ to the center $\boldsymbol{c}^{i-1}$ of the current MEB, according to Equation (10).
    if $d(\boldsymbol{z}_i, \boldsymbol{c}^{i-1}) > r^{i-1}$ **then**
      if $\gamma^{i-1} = NaN$ **then**
        /*See Figure 4b*/
        Compute α_j^i, β_j^i, and γ_j^i, $\forall j = 1, \cdots, i$, and r^i according to Equation (11).
      else if $\gamma^{i-1} \neq NaN$ **then**
        Compute $d(\boldsymbol{z}_i, \boldsymbol{p}^{i-1})$ and $d(\boldsymbol{z}_i, \boldsymbol{q}^{i-1})$, the distances of $\boldsymbol{z}_i$ to the two end points of $\boldsymbol{p}^{i-1}$ and $\boldsymbol{q}^{i-1}$.
        if $d(\boldsymbol{z}_i, \boldsymbol{p}^{i-1}) \leqslant d(\boldsymbol{z}_i, \boldsymbol{q}^{i-1})$ **then**
          /*Exchange $\boldsymbol{\beta}$ and $\boldsymbol{\gamma}$*/
          $\boldsymbol{\beta} \leftrightarrows \boldsymbol{\gamma}$.
        end if
        Compute $\cos\theta$ according to the cosine rule w.r.t. triangle $\boldsymbol{p}^{i-1}\boldsymbol{q}^{i-1}\boldsymbol{z}_i$ with side lengths of $d(\boldsymbol{z}_i, \boldsymbol{p}^{i-1})$, $d(\boldsymbol{z}_i, \boldsymbol{q}^{i-1})$ and $2r^{i-1}$.
        if $\cos\theta \leqslant 0$ **then**
          /*See Figure 4c–e*/
          Compute α_j^i, β_j^i, and γ_j^i, $\forall j = 1, \cdots, i$, and r^i according to Equation (11).
        else if $\cos\theta > 0$ **then**
          /*See Figure 4f*/
          Compute α_j^i, β_j^i, and γ_j^i, $\forall j = 1, \cdots, i$, and r^i according to Equation (12).
        end if
      end if
    else if $d(\boldsymbol{z}_i, \boldsymbol{c}^{i-1}) \leqslant r^{i-1}$ **then**
      $\alpha_i^i \leftarrow 0, \beta_i^i \leftarrow 0, \gamma_i^i \leftarrow 0.$ $\alpha_j^i \leftarrow \alpha_j^{i-1}, \beta_j^i \leftarrow \beta_j^{i-1}, \gamma_j^i \leftarrow \gamma_j^{i-1}, \forall j = 1, \cdots i-1.$
    end if
  end if
end for
return $\boldsymbol{\alpha} = [\alpha_1^N; \cdots; \alpha_N^N]$.

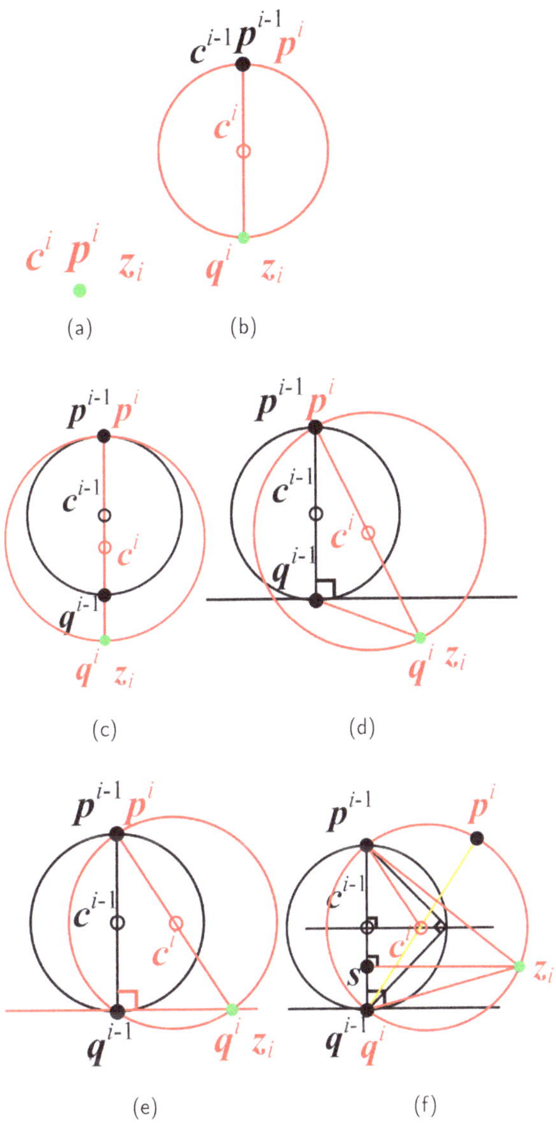

Figure 4. Update of the MEB according to OSVM_SP. A ball is initialized when the first sample comes in (**a**), and enlarged when the second sample comes in (**b**). When the ith sample comes outside later, the ball is enlarged with respect to different values of θ. (**c**) $\theta = \pi$; (**d**) $\theta \in (\pi/2, \pi)$; (**e**) $\theta = \pi/2$; (**f**) $\theta \in (\pi/2, \pi/4)$.

If z_i is an outsider and the end point q^{i-1} is available, the new ball must enclose all three points of p^{i-1}, q^{i-1} and z_i. We assume that p^{i-1} is the end point that is not less near sample z_i than near q^{i-1}. If otherwise, we exchange the values of β^{i-1} and γ^{i-1} to satisfy the assumption. Let θ be $\angle p^{i-1}q^{i-1}z_i$, with $\theta \in (0, \pi]$. According to the value of θ, the construction of a new ball and the update process for the end points are divided into the following four subcases:

1. $\theta = \pi$. The three points are collinear, and q^{i-1} is between them (see Figure 4c). Therefore, the new ball (c^i, r^i) is constructed with the center being the midpoint of

p^{i-1} and z_i, and with the radius being equal to half their distance. Then, sample z_i is recorded by q^i, and p^i inherits from p^{i-1}. All these steps are performed according to Equation (11).

2. $\theta \in (\pi/2, \pi)$. The three points constitute an obtuse triangle (see Figure 4d). A ball that encloses the two points p^{i-1} and z_i can enclose q^{i-1} as well. Therefore, we can replicate the steps in the first subcase to fulfill the task.
3. $\theta = \pi/2$. The three points constitute a right triangle (see Figure 4e). The ball constructed in the first subcase is simply the circumscribed sphere of the right triangle. Therefore, we can replicate the steps in the first subcase to fulfill the task.
4. $\theta = (0, \pi/2)$. The three points constitute an acute triangle (see Figure 4f), and the new ball should be its circumscribed sphere. Therefore, c^i and r^i are set as the circumcenter and circumradius, respectively. Then, sample z_i is recorded by q^i. As c^i must be the midpoint of p^i and q^i, p^i can be obtained accordingly. Therefore, α^i, β^i, γ^i and r^i are computed by Equation (12).

$$\gamma_j^i = \begin{cases} 0, & \forall j = 1, \cdots, i-1. \\ 1, & j = i. \end{cases} \tag{12a}$$

$$r^i = \frac{d(z_i, p^{i-1})}{2\sin\theta}, \beta_j^i = 2\alpha_j^i - \gamma_j^i. \tag{12b}$$

$$\alpha_j^i = \begin{cases} (1 - \frac{\sqrt{(r^i)^2 - (r^{i-1})^2}\cos\theta}{r^{i-1}\sin\theta})\alpha_j^{i-1} \\ + \frac{\sqrt{(r^i)^2 - (r^{i-1})^2}(d(z_i, q^{i-1})\cos\theta - r^{i-1})}{r^{i-1}\sin\theta d(z_i, q^{i-1})}\gamma_j^{i-1}, & \forall j = 1, \cdots, i-1. \\ \frac{\sqrt{(r^i)^2 - (r^{i-1})^2}}{\sin\theta d(z_i, q^{i-1})}, & j = i. \end{cases} \tag{12c}$$

The online learning process of OSVM_SP is provided in Algorithm 1. Whenever there is a label prediction requirement, an optimal hyperplane equivalent to the current ball can be generated accordingly by Equation (4).

The most time-consuming steps in Algorithm 1 are the distance computations in Steps 8 and 13. Among them, the distance to center $d(z_i, c^{i-1})$ in Step 8 must be computed for every upcoming z_i, whereas $d(z_i, p^{i-1})$ and $d(z_i, q^{i-1})$ in Step 13 need to be computed only under certain conditions (see Steps 9 and 12). Note that the space requirement of OSVM_SP grows without limit as the data continue to arrive, which might be infeasible in high-rate data streams.

4.3. Budgeted OSVM_SP

For the aforementioned reason, we propose three budgeted versions of OSVM_SP to decrease the boundless space requirement. Specifically, a budget of fixed size is utilized as the upper bound of the storage space. When this budget is exceeded, it is necessary to remove an SV learned beforehand to make space for the new SV. Therefore, our budgeted algorithms all have constant space complexity. The core of budgeted algorithms is the method of choosing the SV to remove. We employ three widely used SV removal principles [26,27] to remove either a randomly selected SV (-Ran), the oldest SV (-Old), or the least important SV (-Min). Here, the importance of an SV is measured by the value of its corresponding multiplier. Accordingly, the three proposed budgeted versions of OSVM_SP are denoted OSVM_SP-Ran, OSVM_SP-Old, and OSVM_SP-Min.

4.4. Complexity Analysis

The respective time and space complexities of OSVM_SP are $O(N^2)$ and $O(N^2 + Nd)$. Let B be the size of the budget; then, the time complexity of our three budgeted algorithms (OSVM_SP-Ran, OSVM_SP-Old, and OSVM_SP-Min) is $O(NB)$ and the space complexity is $O(B^2 + Bd)$, a constant unrelated to the number of samples N.

Note that when the linear kernel is employed in OSVM_SP, both the center and the two end points can be explicitly computed and stored for computing the distances in Steps 8 and 13. In such a case, OSVM_SP has $O(d)$ space complexity, which is unrelated to the sample number N or time complexity $O(N)$. Table 1 lists the computational complexity of all the methods.

Table 1. Computational complexity of the proposed methods.

Method	Time	Space
OSVM_SP	$O(N^2)$	$O(N^2 + Nd)$
Three Budgeted OSVM_SPs	$O(NB)$	$O(B^2 + Bd)$
OSVM_SP with linear kernel	$O(N)$	$O(d)$

4.5. Comparison of OSVM-SP with StreamSVM

When the first training sample arrives, OSVM-SP and StreamSVM both initialize a ball of $(z_i, 0)$. When the first sample arrives and is outside of the current ball, OSVM-SP and StreamSVM both construct a new ball of (midpoint, distance/2) to replace the current ball. When the third or later sample arrives outside, however, the balls of OSVM-SP and StreamSVM may coincide with each other in certain cases, although most of the time they differ from each other.

Figure 5 illustrates a comparison of OSVM-SP with StreamSVM in the construction of new balls, while z_i denotes the third or later sample coming outside of the current ball (c^{i-1}, r^{i-1}) (the ball in black); hence, $d(z_i, c^{i-1}) > r^{i-1}$. For convenience of analysis, the distance $d(z_i, c^{i-1})$ is equal to a constant d_{const}; therefore, the trajectory of all the possible z_i is a ball denoted (c^{i-1}, d_{const}) (the ball in green). Because the trajectory is bilaterally symmetric, only the left or right half of the trajectory must be considered. Moreover, if we continue to assume that q^{i-1} is the end point closer to sample z_i than p^{i-1}, then only a quarter of the trajectory (the green ball with the gray background) is distinguished for consideration.

Figure 5a–e illustrates five different cases in which the new sample z_i may appear in the trajectory, divided according to the value of angle θ. When $\theta = \pi$ and sample z_i is co-linear to the endpoints (see Figure 5a), new balls of OSVM-SP (the ball in red) and StreamSVM (the ball in dotted blue) coincide with each other; otherwise, these two balls are different (see Figure 5b–d). In particular, when $\theta = \pi/4$ and the distances from sample z_i to those end points are equal (see Figure 5e), the new ball of OSVM-SP is enclosed by the new ball of StreamSVM.

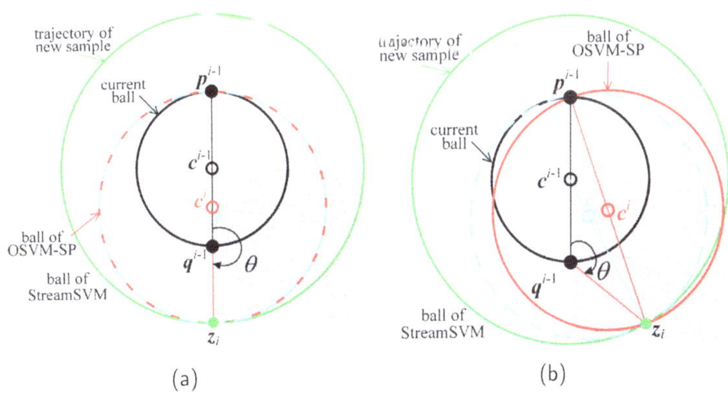

Figure 5. *Cont.*

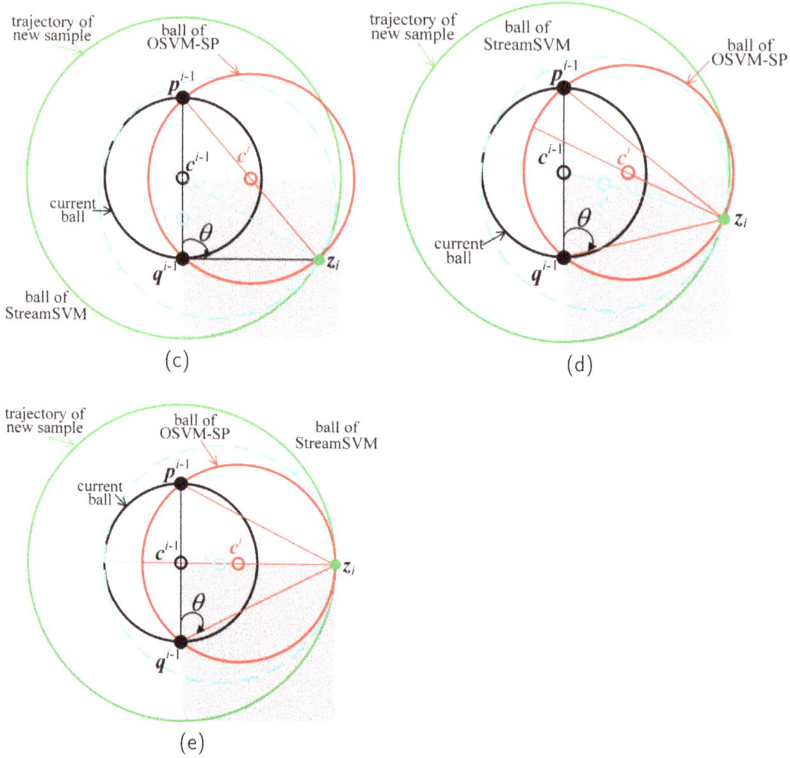

Figure 5. Comparison of OSVM-SP and StreamSVM in the MEB update [16] with respect to different values of θ. (**a**) $\theta = \pi$; (**b**) $\theta \in (\pi/2, \pi)$; (**c**) $\theta = \pi/2$; (**d**) $\theta \in (\pi/2, \pi/4)$; (**e**) $\theta = \pi/4$.

5. Experiments

5.1. Benchmark Datasets

Six binary datasets (*australian*, *fourclass*, *banknote*, *svmguide1*, *EGSSD*, and *occupation*) were employed to validate the performance of our methods; they are all publicly available from the following websites (https://archive.ics.uci.edu/ml/datasets, accessed on 1 January 2022; https://www.csie.ntu.edu.tw/~cjlin/libsvmtools/datasets, accessed on 1 January 2022). Each dataset had already been scaled featurewise to (−1,1) according to min–max normalization. All of the datasets contained only one set of data, except for svmguide1, which contained two sets of training and testing data. We merged these two sets into a single set for unified management during the following experiments, making svmguide1 the same as the remaining datasets. The specifications of the datasets are listed in Table 2, showing the number of features, sample size, and percentage of the majority class contained in each dataset. The missing data issue does not exist in these six datasets as the online methods we focus on in this paper are not able to handle the missing data problem, although this might be an interesting and promising research direction in future work.

Table 2. Specifications of the public datasets.

Dataset	# Features	#Instances	Majority%
australian	14	690	55.51
fourclass	2	862	64.39
banknote	4	1372	55.54
svmguide1	4	7089	56.43
EGSSD	13	10,000	63.80
occupation	5	20,560	76.90

5.2. Baseline Methods

The proposed method is denoted as OSVM_SP, while OSVM_SP-Ran, OSVM_SP-Old, and OSVM_SP-Min are three budgeted versions of OSVM_SP that respectively remove a randomly selected SV, the oldest SV, and the least important SV when the budget is exceeded. The methods for comparison can be divided into three groups: "nonbudgeted online", "budgeted online", and "offline". The nonbudgeted online group consists of five methods (StreamSVM, PA, PA-I, PA-II, and AMM-online), which are mainly compared with the proposed OSVM_SP. Meanwhile, the two budgeted online representatives (BSGD and BPA-S) are compared with OSVM_SP-Ran, OSVM_SP-Old, and OSVM_SP-Min. The two offline batch methods (SVM and ρ-SVM) are listed as the baselines. Nine comparable methods are briefly introduced below.

- *StreamSVM* [16]: StreamSVM is a nonbudgeted online method that leverages the equivalence of SVM and MEB (see Section 3.3), which is similar to our OSVM_SP method. For any incoming point outside of the ball, the StreamSVM algorithm moves the center towards it and simultaneously enlarges the radius to cover both the point and the previous ball. OSVM_SP is different from StreamSVM in that the center moves in different directions and the radius grows according to different strategies; see Figure 4d–f. Taking Figure 4e as an example, the two directions $\boldsymbol{c}^{i-1}$ to z_i (in StreamSVM) and $\boldsymbol{c}^{i-1}$ to $(\boldsymbol{p}^{i-1} + z_i)/2$ (in OSVM_SP) are very different from each other.
- *PA, PA-I, and PA-II* [17]: PA, PA-I, and PA-II are three nonbudgeted online algorithms operating under the same framework provided in [17], which formalizes the trade-off between the correct classification of new data with a sufficiently high margin and the amount of information retained from old data. Among them, PA is a hard margin classifier while PA-I and PA-II are soft margin classifiers with losses of $\ell 1$ and $\ell 2$, respectively.
- *AMM-online* [28]: another nonbudgeted algorithm, AMM-online is an online version of AMM that consists of a set of hyperplanes; each hyperplane is assigned to one class. We employ the implementation of AMM-online in the BudgetedSVM toolbox [29]. Note that the default setting of AMM-online in the toolbox is required to run five training epochs, which deviates from the restriction of single-pass online learning. In fact, we tried to run AMM-online in one epoch; however, its performance declined rapidly. Therefore, the performance of AMM-online with five epochs is listed in all the following experimental results.
- *BSGD* [27]: BSGD is a class of budgeted versions of online SVM algorithms that belong to the SGD family. We employ the implementation of BSGD in the same BudgetedSVM toolbox with two budget maintenance strategies, "-removal" and "-merging", which are based on the removal and merging of support vectors during the training process. The experimental results based on our six datasets show that there is a minor difference between these methods.
- *BPA-S* [26]: BPA-S is a budgeted version of PA-I. When the budget is exceeded, BPA-S removes an SV to make room for the new sample, while the multipliers of the remaining SV remain unchanged.

- *ρ-SVM & SVM*: ρ-SVM is the respective offline batch method corresponding to our OSVM_SP, introduced in Section 3.1. We implemented the dual ρ-SVM in Equation (2) with convex optimization (CVX) [30,31], a package for specifying and solving convex programs. The SVM indicates the corresponding offline model of StreamSVM, which is a transformation of ρ-SVM in which the variable ρ is set to a constant value of 1.

5.3. User-Specified Parameters

For simplicity, we utilize the Gaussian kernel $k(x_i, x_j) = exp(\|x_i - x_j\|^2/\sigma)$ for all the kernelized methods, as it satisfies the 2nd condition in Section 3.3. Therefore, the penalty parameter C and kernel parameter σ must be set for StreamSVM, PA, PA-I, PA-II, SVM, ρ-SVM, and the proposed OSVM_SP, OSVM_SP-Ran, OSVM_SP-Old, and OSVM_SP-Min. As the SVM and ρ-SVM are the corresponding batch versions of StreamSVM and OSVM_SP, they share the same objective functions. Therefore, SVM is utilized to choose the optimal parameter values for StreamSVM as well as itself, and ρ-SVM is utilized both for itself and the proposed four methods. The optimal group (C^*, σ^*) is chosen by performing a grid search with $\{2^{-10}, 2^{-9}, \cdots, 2^9, 2^{10}\} \times \{2^{-10}, 2^{-9}, \cdots, 2^9, 2^{10}\}$. Because there is no explicit batch-mode optimization problem for PA, PA-I, or PA-II, there is no corresponding batch model in the experiments. The values of parameters C and σ within these three methods are set according to the SVM.

The parameter values corresponding to the best performance were chosen as the optimal values, and are listed in Table 3 for each dataset. Each dataset was randomly divided into training and testing sets according to two-fold cross-validation. A series of SVM and ρ-SVM models were learned based on the training set with different parameter values, and their classification accuracies were measured based on the testing set.

Table 3. Optimal parameter values after grid search.

	SVM		ρ-SVM	
	C^*	σ^*	C^*	σ^*
australian	2^{-9}	2^0	2^{-1}	2^1
fourclass	2^{-10}	2^{-8}	2^{-10}	2^{-6}
banknote	2^0	2^{-3}	2^1	2^{-1}
svmguide1	2^6	2^{-3}	2^{-2}	2^{-3}
EGSSD	2^0	2^1	2^{-2}	2^1
occupation	2^{-3}	2^{-5}	2^{-6}	2^{-4}

The experiments in the following subsections were all conducted as follows: each dataset was randomly divided into equal-sized training and testing sets; every method in Section 5.2 was trained with the former set and validated with the latter set; we ran each method five times with randomized permutations, and reported the mean results (along with the standard deviation in several subsections) from the experiments.

5.4. Classification Accuracy

First, we validated the predictive performance of all the methods based on six datasets. This paper focuses on training online models over streaming data, which means that training samples arrive one by one or chunk by chunk. Whenever a new sample arrives, the current model may require a timely update to fit the new sample. Therefore, online models usually change dynamically and frequently during the whole training process. The trend in the performance of an online model is of great importance, as it clearly reflects whether, or even how, the model adapts to the new data. The performance comparison of online models with respect to different sizes of training data is an easy way of displaying the trends, and is widely utilized by many state-of-the-art online learning-related methods [32–35]. Figure 6 shows the classification error with respect to different amounts of training data, while Table 4 lists the classification accuracy attained at the end of the training process.

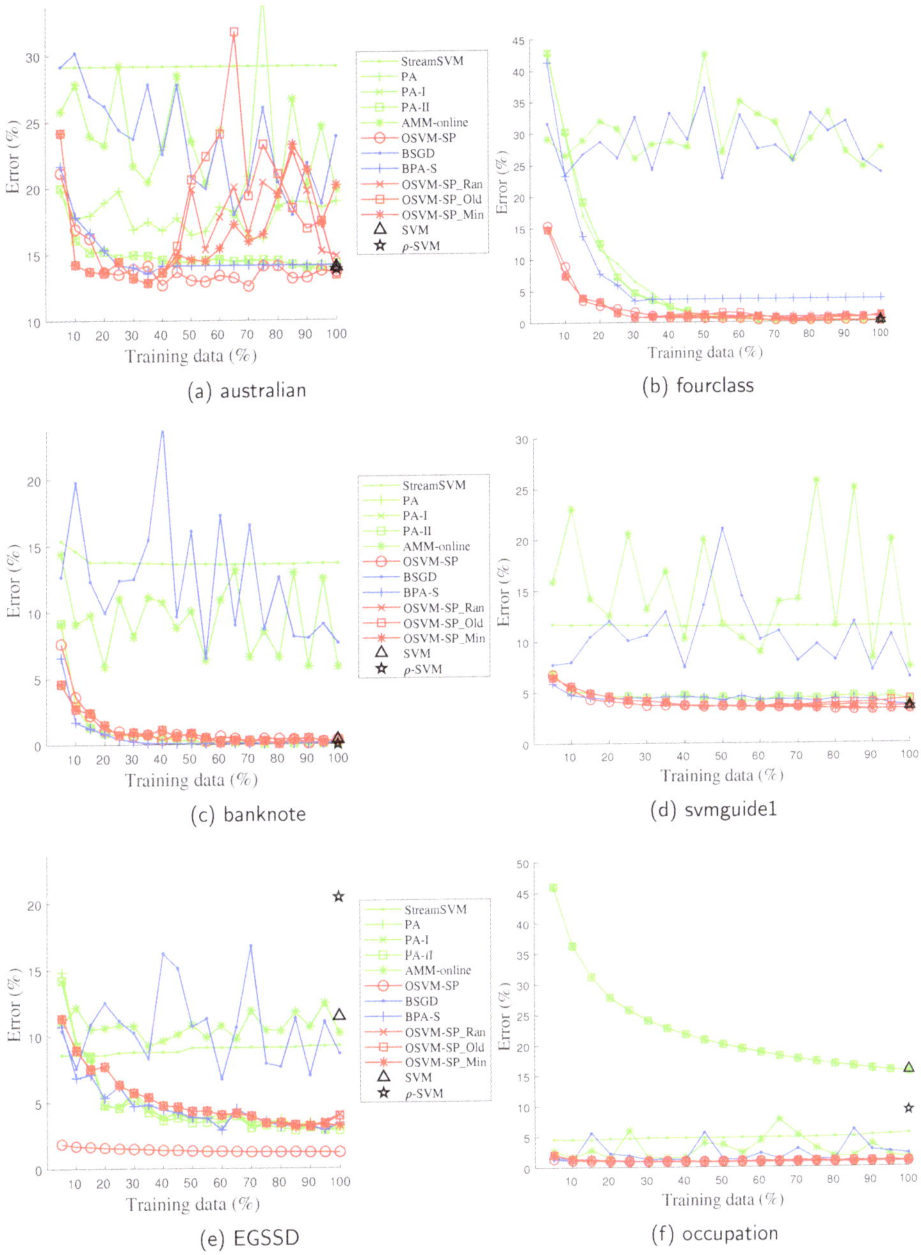

Figure 6. Classification error with varying amounts of training data.

OSVM_SP obtains the highest accuracy among the six nonbudgeted online methods for nearly all the datasets, with the exception of banknote, for which it is surpassed by PA, PA-I, and PA-II with a slight accuracy loss (0.2%). In addition, PA, PA-I, and PA-II share the highest accuracy with OSVM_SP based on the fourclass dataset. The budgeted versions of OSVM_SP, OSVM_SP-Ran, OSVM_SP-Old, and OSVM_SP-Min converge steadily to OSVM_SP in predictive performance for all six datasets. In fact, there is a slight accuracy loss for OSVM_SP-Min based on fourclass and EGSSD compared with OSVM_SP, which seems reasonable as OSVM_SP-Min must occasionally remove SVs in order to make room for the new sample. Despite the accuracy loss, OSVM_SP-Min surpasses the other budgeted online methods (BSGD and BPA-S) most of the time. OSVM_SP-Old beats OSVM_SP-Min and even OSVM_SP based on the australian dataset, achieving the best performance only this once. The superiority of OSVM_SP-Ran does not appear obvious, indicating that an SV removal principle with more explicit intentionality might be more helpful than randomization. The difference in accuracy between the two batch-mode algorithms, the SVM and ρ-SVM, is negligible for most of the datasets. The error of PA increases and then decreases for the australian dataset, while PA-I and PA-II behave much more steadily for all six datasets. PA-I and PA-II are soft margin classifiers that enable misclassification of several training samples, whereas the hard margin classifier, PA, does not. Therefore, we suspect that PA might be sensitive to noise in the data. StreamSVM obtains the best results for fourclass, although it fails for the remaining datasets. Moreover, the performance of StreamSVM remains at a nearly static level, with no further improvement during the training process for the remaining five datasets. This result is analyzed in Section 5.5.

Table 4. Classification accuracy (mean ± STD, %) with best results shown in bold.

	Methods	Datasets					
		Australian	Fourclass	Banknote	Svmguide1	EGSSD	Occupation
non-budgeted online	StreamSVM	70.8 ± 8.0	**99.8** ± 0.2	86.4 ± 11.0	88.6 ± 2.3	90.8 ± 0.8	94.5 ± 1.6
	PA	81.0 ± 2.9	**99.8** ± 0.2	**99.9** ± 0.1	95.8 ± 0.3	96.9 ± 0.4	84.4 ± 0.3
	PA-I	86.0 ± 0.5	**99.8** ± 0.2	**99.9** ± 0.1	95.8 ± 0.3	96.9 ± 0.7	84.4 ± 0.3
	PA-II	85.7 ± 0.7	**99.8** ± 0.2	**99.9** ± 0.1	95.8 ± 0.3	97.1 ± 0.5	84.4 ± 0.3
	AMM-online	80.2 ± 8.3	72.4 ± 7.1	94.2 ± 2.8	92.6 ± 1.5	89.8 ± 2.0	98.5 ± 0.3
	OSVM-SP	**86.4** ± 0.9	**99.8** ± 0.2	99.7 ± 0.2	**96.7** ± 0.1	**98.8** ± 0.1	**99.1** ± 0.0
budgeted online	BSGD	76.2 ± 13.1	76.3 ± 3.0	92.4 ± 3.7	93.6 ± 1.8	91.4 ± 4.8	97.8 ± 2.1
	BPA-S	85.9 ± 2.0	96.3 ± 1.5	**99.9** ± 0.1	96.3 ± 0.2	96.6 ± 1.6	**99.1** ± 0.1
	OSVM-SP_Ran	85.2 ± 2.5	98.8 ± 0.9	99.7 ± 0.3	96.4 ± 0.4	96.0 ± 2.1	99.0 ± 0.1
	OSVM-SP_Old	**86.6** ± 1.4	98.9 ± 0.9	99.7 ± 0.3	95.7 ± 0.5	96.1 ± 1.3	99.0 ± 0.1
	OSVM-SP_Min	79.8 ± 5.3	**99.2** ± 0.7	99.7 ± 0.3	**96.7** ± 0.4	**96.8** ± 0.8	**99.1** ± 0.1
offline	SVM	86.0 ± 1.6	99.8 ± 0.2	99.7 ± 0.3	**96.5** ± 0.3	**88.6** ± 1.1	84.3 ± 0.4
	ρ-SVM	**86.2** ± 1.9	**99.9** ± 0.2	100.0 ± 0.0	**96.5** ± 0.2	79.6 ± 1.5	**90.7** ± 0.3

5.5. Percentage of Support Vectors

Our second experiment examined the computation and memory requirements of each method by counting the percentage of SVs in the training data during the whole training process. As the proposed OSVM_SP and its three budgeted versions along with the majority of the compared methods are kernelized, the number of SVs can be considered one of the most important indicators of computation and memory consumption. Here, an SV is denoted as a training sample with a nonempty Lagrange multiplier. Figure 7 depicts the number of SVs with respect to different amounts of training data.

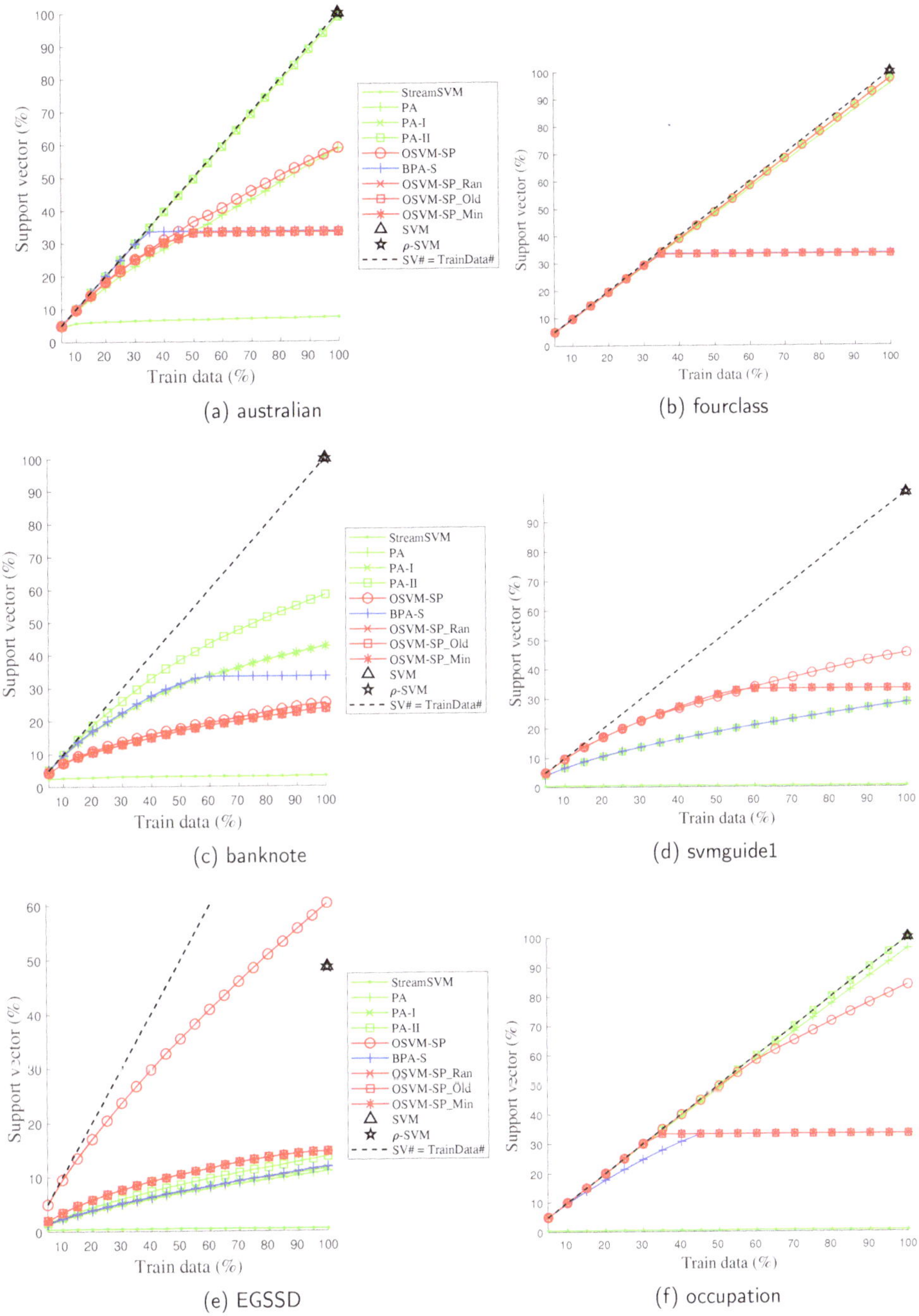

Figure 7. Number of SVs with varying amounts of training data.

For most unbudgeted online methods, the number of SVs increases with the amount of training data. The curve for OSVM-SP varies greatly between different datasets. When the amount of training data approaches 100%, however, the number of SVs for OSVM-SP remains less than (see Figure 7a,c,d,f) or as much as (see Figure 7b) the SV numbers of the SVM and ρ-SVM in most cases. In combination with the accuracy results in Table 4, the effective predictive performance of SVM and ρ-SVM is acquired at a cost of nearly 100% of the training data, as the SVs (see Figure 7a–d) can consume enormous amounts of memory and time latency in both the model training and label prediction processes. Compared with SVM and ρ-SVM, OSVM-SP is more lightweight while attaining a comparable predictive performance. Sometimes, OSVM-SP even achieves higher accuracy (10.2–19.2%, see Table 4) than the batch methods, although at the cost of more SVs (see Figure 7e). PA generates fewer SVs than PA-II and/or PA-I most of the time (see Figure 7a,c,e,f), which is to be expected as the SVs of the hard margin method PA consist of only the misclassified data, while the SVs of the soft margin methods PA-I and PA-II are constructed using both the misclassified data and those that are classified correctly and are within the margin. StreamSVM maintains a small number of SVs based on five datasets, with the exception of fourclass. In combination with the accuracy results of StreamSVM in Table 4, the reason for this might be that the corresponding MEB of StreamSVM expands excessively to cover most of the training data arriving afterwards without triggering any further updates.

For the budgeted online methods, the number of SVs initially increases with the amount of training data. When it grows to the size of the budget (one-third of the training size), it remains constant through the various SV removal principles utilized. The number of SVs for OSVM_SP-Ran, OSVM_SP-Old, and OSVM_SP-Min is controlled in keeping with the size of the budget. Compared with the nonbudgeted OSVM_SP, it can bes observed that decreasing the memory requirement by approximately two-thirds leads to only a 0.6–2.0% loss in accuracy. In other words, OSVM_SP-Ran, OSVM_SP-Old, and OSVM_SP-Min offer great potential for efficiency and effectiveness in budgeted online learning.

5.6. Radius of the Minimum Enclosing Ball

Our third experiment compared the radii of the MEBs corresponding to the proposed nonbudgeted online method (OSVM_SP), the three budgeted online methods (OSVM_SP-Ran, OSVM_SP-Old and OSVM_SP-Min), and the corresponding batch-mode method (ρ-SVM). Figure 8 shows the radii with respect to different amounts of training data.

The methods can be sorted in ascending order of radii, that is, ρ-SVM, OSVM_SP, OSVM_SP-Min, OSVM_SP-Old, and OSVM_SP-Ran, on each dataset. The batch-mode method, ρ-SVM, achieves the minimum radius, as it can iteratively search for the smallest ball among those covering all the training data. OSVM_SP falls between the batch-mode ρ-SVM and the three budgeted online methods. In Figure 4f, the ball with respect to OSVM_SP can be determined by three points represented by two real samples ($\boldsymbol{q}^i$ and $\boldsymbol{z}^i$) and one fake sample ($\boldsymbol{p}^i$), which we believe incurs an expanding radius as well as a loss in accuracy. The budgeted online methods obtain a larger radius than OSVM_SP, as one SV must be removed whenever the budget is exceeded. Because the center of the ball is linearly represented by the SVs, the center drifts away from the location it had after the removal. Therefore, these methods have to enlarge their radii to cover the new data. In addition, the degree of drift varies for different removal principles. Among these budgeted online methods, OSVM_SP-Min achieves the minimal radius mostly by removing the least important SV, while OSVM_SP-Ran or OSVM_SP-Old achieves the maximal radius by removing a randomized SV or the oldest SV. There is occasionally a minor difference in their radius lengths.

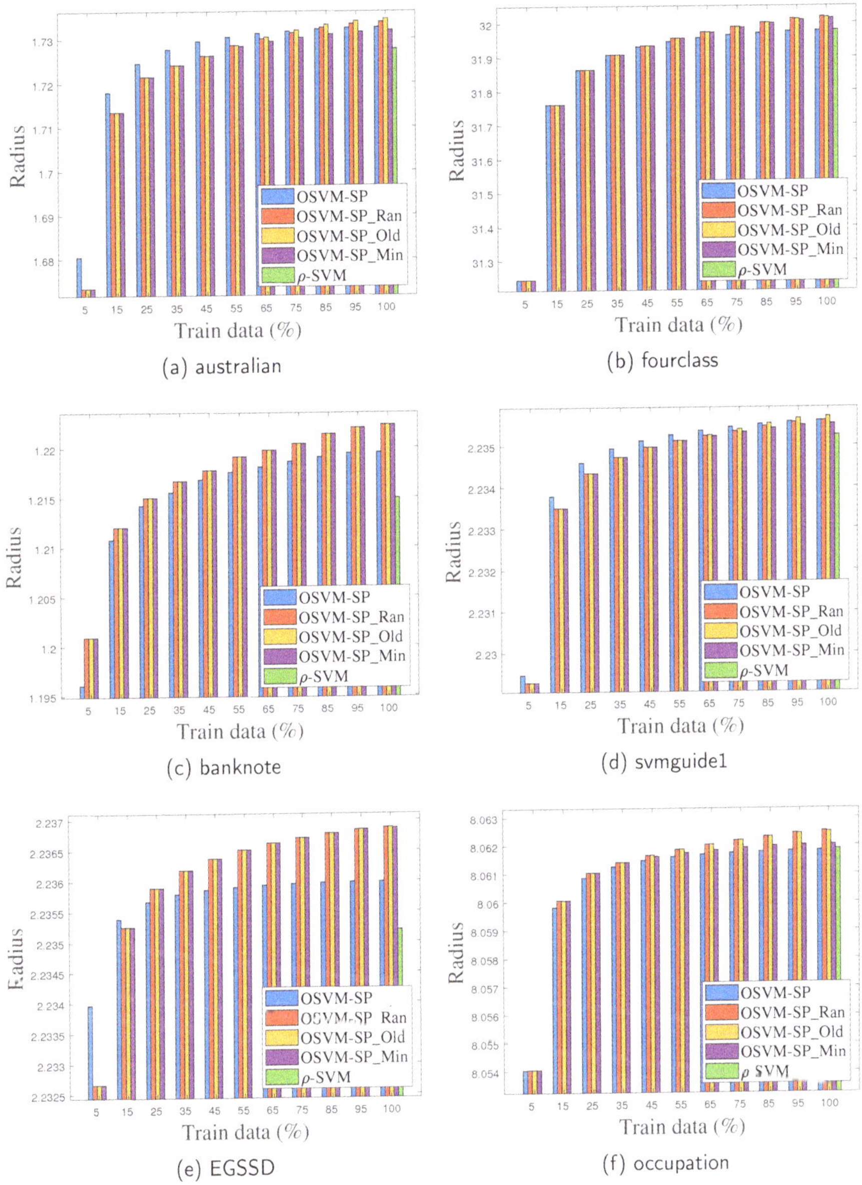

Figure 8. Radius with varying amounts of training data.

5.7. Effect of Budget Size

Our last experiment verified the effect of different budget sizes on the performance of the three proposed budgeted methods, OSVM_SP-Ran, OSVM_SP-Old, and OSVM_SP-Min. The size of the budget was set to be a range of percentages of the training data, with the percentage chosen by a grid search with $(5\%, 10\%, \cdots, 95\%, 100\%)$. Note that when the percentage equals 100%, OSVM_SP-Ran, OSVM_SP-Old, and OSVM_SP-Min are identical to OSVM_SP, which means that the budget is able to store all the training data without any SVs needing to be removed.

Figure 9 depicts the classification error with respect to different budget sizes as well as different amounts of training data. The error decreases with increasing the budget size percentage, and ultimately converges to the error of OSVM_SP. First, the error of the budgeted methods decreases much more quickly when the percentage is small (e.g., less than 20%), which means that a few new data points are not sufficient for learning; the performance of our proposed algorithms can thus be greatly improved by remembering more data. The rate of decrease slows when the percentage is above 40%, which implies that it is not necessary to remember all the old SVs in order to achieve comparable predictive performance. The experimental results in the above section show that when the budget size is set to one-third, the three budgeted algorithms can achieve predictive performance comparable to that of a classifier as well as a radius length comparable to that of the MEB.

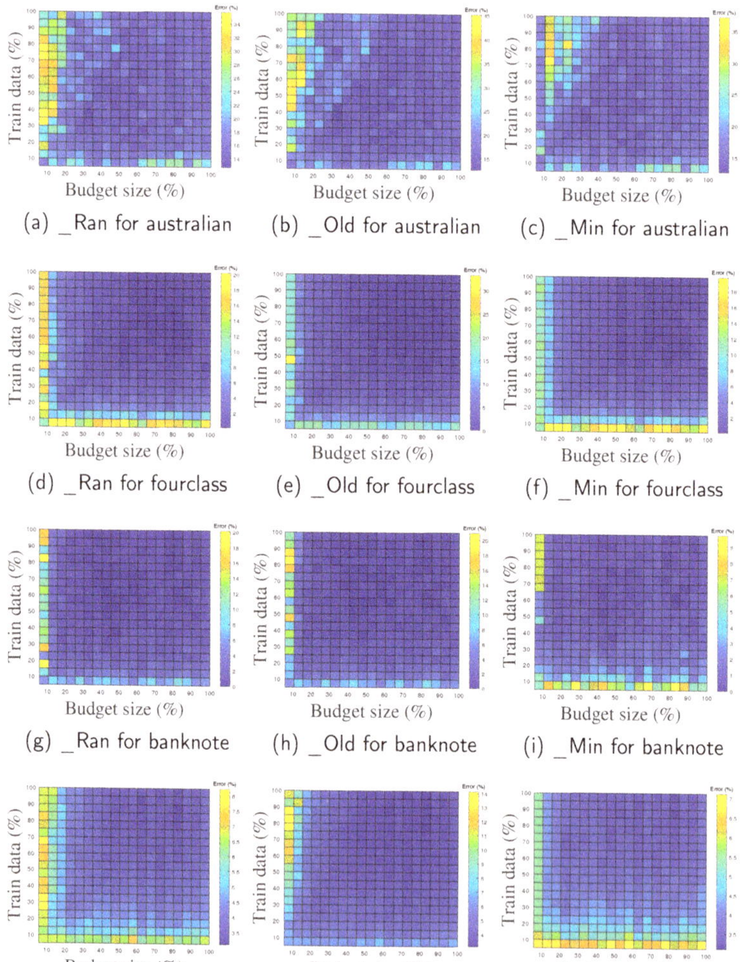

(a) _Ran for australian (b) _Old for australian (c) _Min for australian

(d) _Ran for fourclass (e) _Old for fourclass (f) _Min for fourclass

(g) _Ran for banknote (h) _Old for banknote (i) _Min for banknote

(j) _Ran for svmguide1 (k) _Old for svmguide1 (l) _Min for svmguide1

Figure 9. *Cont.*

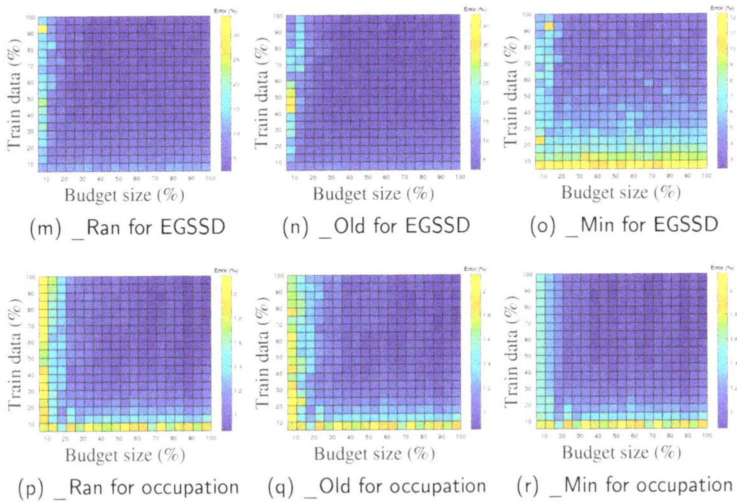

(m) _Ran for EGSSD (n) _Old for EGSSD (o) _Min for EGSSD

(p) _Ran for occupation (q) _Old for occupation (r) _Min for occupation

Figure 9. Error with varying budget size and training data.

6. Discussion

This paper presents OSVM_SP, a single-pass online algorithm for streaming data. Moreover, OSVM_SP-Ran, OSVM_SP-Old, and OSVM_SP-Min are proposed as three budgeted online algorithms to bound the space requirement using support vector removal principles. This section discusses the superiority and limitations of the proposed methods.

The proposed methods are superior in three distinct ways:

1. OSVM_SP has the most effective predictive performance in the family of nonbudgeted online methods and is lightweight compared to batch-mode methods.
2. The budgeted OSVM_SP-Ran, OSVM_SP-Old, and OSVM_SP-Min all converge steadily to the nonbudgeted OSVM_SP in their predictive performance. Compared with OSVM_SP, a decrease in the memory requirement of approximately two-thirds leads to a loss in accuracy of only about 2.0%.
3. For OSVM_SP-Ran, OSVM_SP-Old, and OSVM_SP-Min, the error decreases with the increase in the budget size, and ultimately converges to the error of OSVM_SP. Moreover, the error decreases quickly/slowly when the budget size is small/large; 20–40% of the training size seems to be a proper range for the budget size.

The limitations are three-fold as well:

1. Similar to the other kernelized methods, the proposed OSVM_SP has to save all of the SVs during the whole online learning process, which can become a heavy burden in restricted memory scenarios.
2. OSVM_SP and its three budgeted versions are all proposed for binary classification problems. For multiple classification problems, it is possible to build a series of binary models according to one-versus-one or one-versus-rest techniques. In other words, when new samples arrive, several models have to be learned to maintain updates, which may be computationally burdensome.
3. Class imbalance and missing data issues are not fully considered in this paper. Ways of adapting the proposed methods to streaming data with missing features/labels from imbalanced classes is an interesting and promising direction for future research.

7. Conclusions

In this paper, we present OSVM_SP, a new online SVM algorithm for streaming data, and three budgeted versions of OSVM_SP to bound the space requirement. All of these approaches are based on the online MEB problem and require a single pass over the streaming data. The experimental results obtained for five public datasets show that OSVM_SP outperforms most state-of-the-art single-pass online algorithms in terms of accuracy and is comparable to batch-mode SVMs and MEBs in both accuracy and radius. Our budgeted algorithms reduce the space requirement by two-thirds with only a slight loss in accuracy (0.7–5.7%).

Author Contributions: Conceptualization, L.H.; Methodology, L.H. and C.H.; Validation, L.H. and C.H.; Writing, L.H. and Z.H.; Formal Analysis, X.J.; Supervision, S.W. All authors have read and agreed to the published version of the manuscript.

Funding: This work is supported by the National Natural Science Foundation of China (grant numbers 62002187, 62002098, and 61902379), the Natural Science Foundation of Hebei Province (grant numbers F2020207001, and F2021207005), the Scientific Research and Development Program Fund Project of Hebei University of Economics and Business (grant number 2022ZD10), and Youth Innovation Promotion Association CAS.

Conflicts of Interest: The authors declare that they have no conflict of interest.

Appendix A. Derivation of Equations (3) and (4)

The Lagrange function of Equation (1) is listed as follows:

$$L(\omega, \xi, \rho, \alpha) = \frac{1}{2}\|\omega\|^2 - \rho + \frac{C}{2}\|\xi\|^2 - \sum_{i=1}^{N} \alpha_i(y_i\omega'\phi(x_i) - \rho + \xi_i)$$

According to the KKT Theorem: (a) the partial derivative of the Lagrange function $L(\omega, \xi, \rho, \alpha)$ with respect to all the variables ω, ρ, and $\xi_i, \forall i = 1, \cdots, N$ of Equation (1) is required to be zero; and (b) $\sum_{i=1}^{N} \alpha_i(y_i\omega'\phi(x_i) - \rho + \xi_i) = 0$, which leads to the following solutions.

(a.1) $\partial L/\partial\omega = \omega - \sum_{i=1}^{N} \alpha_i y_i \phi(x_i) = 0 \Leftrightarrow \omega = \sum_{i=1}^{N} \alpha_i y_i \phi(x_i)$; thus, Equation (3a) holds.

(a.2) $\partial L/\partial\xi_i = C\xi_i - \alpha_i = 0, \forall i \Leftrightarrow \xi_i = \alpha_i/C, \forall i \Leftrightarrow \xi = \alpha/C$; thus, Equation (3b) holds.

(a.3) $\partial L/\partial\rho = -1 + \sum_{i=1}^{N} \alpha_i = 0 \Leftrightarrow \sum_{i=1}^{N} \alpha_i = 1 \Leftrightarrow \alpha\mathbf{1} = 1$.

(a.4) $\sum_{i=1}^{N} \alpha_i(y_i\omega'\phi(x_i) - \rho + \xi_i) = 0 \Leftrightarrow \alpha_i(y_i\omega'\phi(x_i) - \rho + \xi_i) = 0, \forall i \Leftrightarrow \rho = y_k\omega'\phi(x_k) + \xi_k, \forall\alpha_k \neq 0$; with Equations (3a) and (3b), $\rho = y_k \sum_{i=1}^{N} \alpha_i y_i k_\phi(x_i, x_k) + \alpha_k/C$, $\forall\alpha_k \neq 0$. Thus, Equation (3c) holds.

Becuase the SVM in this paper indicates the unbiased linear function in RKHS, the classifier learned by SVM can be represented by $y = \text{sig}(\omega'\phi(x))$. In conjunction with Equation (3a), we can find that $y = \text{sig}(\omega'\phi(x)) = \text{sig}(\sum_{i=1}^{N} \alpha_i y_i k_\phi(x_i, x))$, as listed in Equation (4).

Appendix B. Derivation of Equation (10)

$z_i = \varphi(x_i)$, according to the definition of z_i.

$z_i = \left[y_i\phi(x_i); e_i/\sqrt{C}\right]$, according to the first condition in Section 3.2.

$c^{i-1} = \left[\sum_{j=1}^{i-1} \alpha_j^{i-1} y_j\phi(x_j); \sum_{j=1}^{i-1} \alpha_j^{i-1} e_j/\sqrt{C}\right]$, according to Equation (9a).

$d(z_i, c^{i-1}) = \|z_i - c^{i-1}\|$, according to the definition of d.

$$d(z_i, c^{i-1}) = \left\| \left[y_i\phi(x_i) - \sum_{j=1}^{i-1} \alpha_j^{i-1} y_j\phi(x_j); (e_i - \sum_{j=1}^{i-1} \alpha_j^{i-1} e_j)/\sqrt{C}\right] \right\|,$$

$$= \sqrt{\left\|y_i\phi(x_i) - \sum_{j=1}^{i-1} \alpha_j^{i-1} y_j\phi(x_j)\right\|^2 + \left\|e_i - \sum_{j=1}^{i-1} \alpha_j^{i-1} e_j\right\|^2 /C},$$

$$= \sqrt{\|y_i\phi(x_i)\|^2 + \left\|\sum_{j=1}^{i-1} \alpha_j^{i-1} y_j\phi(x_j)\right\|^2 - 2y_i\phi(x_i)' \sum_{j=1}^{i-1} \alpha_j^{i-1} y_j\phi(x_j) + (\|e_i\|^2 + \left\|\sum_{j=1}^{i-1} \alpha_j^{i-1} e_j\right\|^2 - 2\sum_{j=1}^{i-1} \alpha_j^{i-1} e_j' e_i)/C},$$

$$= \sqrt{\kappa_\phi + \sum_{j,k=1}^{i-1} \alpha_j^{i-1} \alpha_k^{i-1} y_j y_k k_\phi(x_j, x_k) - 2y_i \sum_{j=1}^{i-1} \alpha_j^{i-1} y_j k_\phi(x_j, x_i) + (1 + \sum_{j=1}^{i-1} (\alpha_j^{i-1})^2)/C},$$

according to the second condition in Section 3.2.

$= \sqrt{\sum_{j,k=1}^{i-1} \alpha_j^{i-1} \alpha_k^{i-1} y_j y_k (k_\phi(x_j, x_k) + \frac{\delta_{jk}}{C}) - 2y_i \sum_{j=1}^{i-1} \alpha_j^{i-1} y_j k_\phi(x_j, x_i) + \kappa_\phi + 1/C}$.

Thus, Equation (10) holds.

References

1. Cortes, C.; Vapnik, V. Support-vector networks. *Mach. Learn.* **1995**, *20*, 273–297. [CrossRef]
2. Vapnik, V. *The Nature of Statistical Learning Theory*; Springer Science & Business Media: Berlin/Heidelberg, Germany, 2013.
3. Wang, H.; Zhang, L.; Yao, L. Application of genetic algorithm based support vector machine in selection of new EEG rhythms for drowsiness detection. *Expert Syst. Appl.* **2021**, *171*, 114634. [CrossRef]
4. Huang, C.; Zhou, J.; Chen, J.; Yang, J.; Clawson, K.; Peng, Y. A feature weighted support vector machine and artificial neural network algorithm for academic course performance prediction. *Neural Comput. Appl.* **2021**, 1–13. [CrossRef]
5. Ding, C.; Bao, T.Y.; Huang, H.L. Quantum-inspired support vector machine. *IEEE Trans. Neural Netw. Learn. Syst.* **2021**, 1–13. [CrossRef]
6. Che, Z.; Liu, B.; Xiao, Y.; Cai, H. Twin Support Vector Machines with Privileged Information. *Inf. Sci.* **2021**, *573*, 141–153. [CrossRef]
7. Nguyen, H.L.; Woon, Y.K.; Ng, W.K. A survey on data stream clustering and classification. *Knowl. Inf. Syst.* **2015**, *45*, 535–569. [CrossRef]
8. Lawal, I.A. Incremental SVM learning. In *Learning from Data Streams in Evolving Environments*; Springer: Berlin/Heidelberg, Germany, 2019; pp. 279–296.
9. Guo, H.; Zhang, A.; Wang, W. An accelerator for online SVM based on the fixed-size KKT window. *Eng. Appl. Artif. Intell.* **2020**, *92*, 103637. [CrossRef]
10. Mello, A.R.; Stemmer, M.R.; Koerich, A.L. Incremental and decremental fuzzy bounded twin support vector machine. *Inf. Sci.* **2020**, *526*, 20–38. [CrossRef]
11. Soula, A.; Tbarki, K.; Ksantini, R.; Said, S.B.; Lachiri, Z. A novel incremental kernel nonparametric SVM model (iKN-SVM) for data classification: An application to face detection. *Eng. Appl. Artif. Intell.* **2020**, *89*, 103468. [CrossRef]
12. Matsushima, S.; Vishwanathan, S.; Smola, A.J. Linear support vector machines via dual cached loops. In Proceedings of the International Conference on Knowledge Discovery and Data Mining, Beijing, China, 12–16 August 2012; pp. 177–185.
13. Wang, X.; Xing, Y. An online support vector machine for the open-ended environment. *Expert Syst. Appl.* **2019**, *120*, 72–86. [CrossRef]
14. Zheng, J.; Shen, F.; Fan, H.; Zhao, J. An online incremental learning support vector machine for large-scale data. *Neural Comput. Appl.* **2013**, *22*, 1023–1035. [CrossRef]
15. Liu, Y.; Xu, J. One-pass online SVM with extremely small space complexity. In Proceedings of the International Conference on Pattern Recognition, Cancun, Mexico, 4–8 December 2016; IEEE: Piscataway, NJ, USA, 2016; pp. 3482–3487.
16. Rai, P.; Daumé, H.; Venkatasubramanian, S. Streamed learning: One-pass SVMs. In Proceedings of the International Jont Conference on Artifical Intelligence, Hainan Island, China, 25–26 April 2009; pp. 1211–1216.
17. Crammer, K.; Dekel, O.; Keshet, J.; Shalev-Shwartz, S.; Singer, Y. Online passive aggressive algorithms. *J. Mach. Learn. Res.* **2006**, *7*, 551–585.
18. Ñanculef, R.; Allende, H.; Lodi, S.; Sartori, C. Two one-pass algorithms for data stream classification using approximate MEBs. In Proceedings of the International Conference on Adaptive and Natural Computing Algorithms, Ljubljana, Slovenia, 14–16 April 2011; Springer: Berlin/Heidelberg, Germany, 2011, pp. 363–372.
19. Tukan, M.; Baykal, C.; Feldman, D.; Rus, D. On coresets for support vector machines. In Proceedings of the International Conference on Theory and Applications of Models of Computation, Changsha, China, 18–20 October 2020; Springer: Berlin/Heidelberg, Germany, 2020; pp. 287–299.
20. Gärtner, B.; Jaggi, M. Coresets for polytope distance. In Proceedings of the Annual Symposium on Computational Geometry, Aarhus, Denmark, 8–10 June 2009; pp. 33–42.
21. Chang, C.C.; Lin, C.J. Training v-support vector classifiers: Theory and algorithms. *Neural Comput.* **2001**, *13*, 2119–2147. [CrossRef]
22. Kuhn, H.W.; Tucker, A.W. Nonlinear programming. In *Traces and Emergence of Nonlinear Programming*; Springer: Berlin/Heidelberg, Germany, 2014; pp. 247–258.
23. Tax, D.M.; Duin, R.P. Support vector domain description. *Pattern Recognit. Lett.* **1999**, *20*, 1191–1199. [CrossRef]
24. Tax, D.M.; Duin, R.P. Support vector data description. *Mach. Learn.* **2004**, *54*, 45–66. [CrossRef]
25. Tsang, I.W.; Kwok, J.T.; Cheung, P.M.; Cristianini, N. Core vector machines: Fast SVM training on very large data sets. *J. Mach. Learn. Res.* **2005**, *6*, 363–392.
26. Wang, Z.; Vucetic, S. Online passive-aggressive algorithms on a budget. In Proceedings of the International Conference on Artificial Intelligence and Statistics, Sardinia, Italy, 13–15 May 2010; pp. 908–915.
27. Wang, Z.; Crammer, K.; Vucetic, S. Breaking the curse of kernelization: Budgeted stochastic gradient descent for large-scale svm training. *J. Mach. Learn. Res.* **2012**, *13*, 3103–3131.

28. Wang, Z.; Djuric, N.; Crammer, K.; Vucetic, S. Trading representability for scalability: Adaptive multi-hyperplane machine for nonlinear classification. In Proceedings of the 17th ACM SIGKDD International Conference on Knowledge Discovery and Data Mining, San Diego, CA, USA, 21–24 August 2011; pp. 24–32.
29. Djuric, N.; Lan, L.; Vucetic, S.; Wang, Z. Budgetedsvm: A toolbox for scalable svm approximations. *J. Mach. Learn. Res.* **2013**, *14*, 3813–3817.
30. Grant, M.; Boyd, S. *CVX: Matlab Software for Disciplined Convex Programming*, Version 2.1; 2014. Available online: http://cvxr.com/cvx (accessed on 1 January 2022).
31. Grant, M.; Boyd, S. Graph implementations for nonsmooth convex programs. In *Recent Advances in Learning and Control*; Springer: Berlin/Heidelberg, Germany, 2008; pp. 95–110.
32. Zhao, P.; Zhang, Y.; Wu, M.; Hoi, S.C.; Tan, M.; Huang, J. Adaptive cost-sensitive online classification. *IEEE Trans. Knowl. Data Eng.* **2018**, *31*, 214–228. [CrossRef]
33. Sahoo, D.; Pham, Q.; Lu, J.; Hoi, S.C. Online Deep Learning: Learning Deep Neural Networks on the Fly. In Proceedings of the IJCAI, Stockholm, Sweden, 13–19 July 2018.
34. Gözüaçık, Ö.; Can, F. Concept learning using one-class classifiers for implicit drift detection in evolving data streams. *Artif. Intell. Rev.* **2021**, *54*, 3725–3747. [CrossRef]
35. Din, S.U.; Shao, J.; Kumar, J.; Mawuli, C.B.; Mahmud, S.; Zhang, W.; Yang, Q. Data stream classification with novel class detection: A review, comparison and challenges. *Knowl. Inf. Syst.* **2021**, *63*, 2231–2276. [CrossRef]

mathematics MDPI

Article

Co-Occurrence-Based Double Thresholding Method for Research Topic Identification

Christian-Daniel Curiac [1,*], Alex Doboli [2] and Daniel-Ioan Curiac [3,*]

1 Department of Computer and Information Technology, Politehnica University of Timisoara, V. Parvan 2, 300223 Timisoara, Romania
2 Department of Electrical and Computer Engineering, Stony Brook University, State University of New York, Stony Brook, NY 11794-2350, USA
3 Department of Automation and Applied Informatics, Politehnica University of Timisoara, V. Parvan 2, 300223 Timisoara, Romania
* Correspondence: christian.curiac@cs.upt.ro (C.-D.C.); daniel.curiac@aut.upt.ro (D.-I.C.)

Abstract: Identifying possible research gaps is a main step in problem framing, however it is increasingly tedious and expensive considering the continuously growing amount of published material. This situation suggests the critical need for methodologies and tools that can assist researchers in their selection of future research topics. Related work mostly focuses on trend analysis and impact prediction but less on research gap identification. This paper presents our first approach in automated identification of feasible research gaps by using a double-threshold procedure to eliminate the research gaps that are currently difficult to study or offer little novelty. Gaps are then found by extracting subgraphs for the less-frequent co-occurrences and correlations of key terms describing domains. A case study applying the methodology for electronic design automation (EDA) domain is also discussed in the paper.

Keywords: research gap; natural language processing; co-occurrence matrix; double-thresholding method

MSC: 68T50

Citation: Curiac, C.-D.; Doboli, A.; Curiac, D.-I. Co-Occurrence-Based Double Thresholding Method for Research Topic Identification. *Mathematics* **2022**, *10*, 3115. https://doi.org/10.3390/math10173115

Academic Editors: Adrian Sergiu Darabant and Diana-Laura Borza

Received: 29 June 2022
Accepted: 29 August 2022
Published: 30 August 2022

1. Introduction

Identifying potential research gaps is one of the main steps leading toward successful problem framing and then fruitful research achievements. It is rooted in the systematic and comprehensive review of the scientific literature and other related material. With the exponential growth in the number of publications and published work, this activity becomes increasingly laborious and time-consuming, indicating a critical need for automatic tools to assist researchers when selecting their future research themes.

In an effort to automatize research gaps identification, natural language processing (NLP) provides an effective starting point in extracting valuable information from the published body of knowledge, such as by employing term co-occurrence analysis techniques [1]. Such techniques are able to map entire scientific fields to offer cues for identifying unexplored, insufficiently investigated, and mature/well-explored areas [2], hence orienting research towards new and potentially hot topics.

Present NLP research does not directly tackle research gap identification, as it is mainly focused on identifying research trends and fronts. For this, three basic scientometric approaches, as well as their diverse combinations, are employed [3]: (a) *exploring the dynamics of scientific production* in order to model the growth of scientific knowledge within a given domain [4], a representative example in this respect being the identification of the research trends in the field of tourism based on the areas of dispersion and concentration of the scientific information, coupled with the investigation of the scientific influence and productivity of publications [5]; (b) *citation network analysis* that traces the interest and relevance of a topic within the scientific community, based on the evolution and dynamics in the number of citations, including its diverse forms like patent citation analysis [6] or co-citation analysis [7]; (c) *content analysis*. To investigate which scientific areas are rising in popularity using content analysis, a widely used approach is to employ co-word analysis [8,9] and topic modeling to extract the main topics from a relevant scientific document corpus and to explore their time evolution [10–14].

Even though the mentioned research directions have offered unique insights into research domain dynamics, they do not address the discovery of new research gaps and problems. Trend analysis predicts the likely evolution of a research domain and its impact, including the number of citations that a published paper is expected to receive. However, traditional trend analysis does not study the potential connections across different domains and trends, even though many current research needs have a cross-disciplinary nature.

To the best of our knowledge, this work provides the first attempt to automatize the identification of feasible research gaps by analyzing the correlations between a chosen set of key terms (specific to the scientific domain of interest), followed by a double-threshold procedure to discard the research gaps that are difficult to study with the existing knowledge or may offer little novelty. To discover feasible research gaps from a given scientific domain described as an undirected graph of key terms, the method extracts the subgraphs characterized by less-frequent and hence unsolidified links, or, in other words, by key term co-occurrences lying in a particular interval that assures the needed levels of expected novelty and likely success of the research topic.

This paper makes the following contributions:

- A formalization of the feasible research gap identification problem using graph theory and term co-occurrences. Considering that any given scientific domain can be represented as an undirected weighted graph characterized by a finite set of nodes (i.e., key terms) and its corresponding cost adjacency matrix in the form of co-occurrence matrix extracted from publication corpus, this paper is the first that formalizes the feasible research gap discovery process as a subgraph extraction problem driven by novelty and success expectations concepts.
- A NLP methodology to solve this problem by using term co-occurrence analysis and a carefully tailored double-threshold method able to retain only the research gaps that are characterized by adequate novelty and success expectations.
- An illustrative case study on applying the proposed methodology for the electronic design automation (EDA) domain.

The rest of the paper is structured as follows. Section 2 formalizes the feasible research gap discovery problem. Sections 3 and 4 present a new double-threshold method and the proposed methodology to solve this problem, respectively. In Section 5 a case study for extracting feasible research gaps within a specified scientific area from EDA is presented. Finally, conclusions are summarized in Section 6.

2. Problem Formulation

Our goal is to automatically identify research gaps that have the potential to be studied with current theories, methods, and technologies to produce a novel contribution. A set of key terms (e.g., keywords) describes the scientific area where the research gap identification process is focused. We formulated this problem as a graph theoretic problem, as follows.

Let us consider a weighted undirected graph $G = (\mathcal{V}, \mathcal{E}, w)$, where each of the n key terms describing a scientific area is a vertex from the set $\mathcal{V} = \{KT_i \mid i = 1, \ldots, n\}$, $\mathcal{E} \subset \mathcal{V} \times \mathcal{V}$ is the set of edges, and weight $w : \mathcal{E} \to \mathbb{R}$ associates the correlation of a pair of key terms with the corresponding edge. Research gap identification finds all the induced connected subgraphs of a specified order s of graph G that assure a correlation between key terms that can provide sufficient novelty and success expectations.

Co-occurrence is a popular solution in natural language processing (NLP) research to model the correlation between terms [15,16]. It refers to the frequency of the simultaneous presence of two terms in the documents of a corpus [17]. The higher the co-occurrence value, the stronger the expected semantic relationship between terms. Similarly, using term co-occurrences, we described the weighted undirected graph $G = (\mathcal{V}, \mathcal{E}, w)$ by its symmetric cost adjacency matrix in the form of the co-occurrence matrix M of order n, where n is the number of the selected key terms that characterize the scientific domain under investigation. Each element $M(i,j)$ is the number of documents in which both key terms KT_i and KT_j occur, normalized by the total number of documents in the considered corpus. Thus, $M(i,j) \in [0;1]$ and can be interpreted as the average frequency in which the two terms appear in the same document.

Solving research gap identification required the addressing of two related subproblems: (a) finding a suitable condition for the correlation between two key terms to suggest feasibility in the suggested research themes (i.e., sufficient novelty and success expectations); (b) extracting the feasible research gap proposals by finding all the induced connected subgraphs [18], where the feasibility condition, identified by the first subproblem, is met for all edges. The next section proposes a solution to the first subproblem, while an integrated research gap identification methodology is presented in Section 4.

3. Double-Threshold Method to Identify Potential Research Gaps

Since not every research gap is a viable starting point for new research projects, it is important to identify the research gaps that provide enough scientific novelty at a given time moment using the available methods and materials. To address this issue, we proposed a new double-threshold method to identify the feasible research gaps based on the term co-occurrence matrix.

3.1. Modeling

To develop a method for identifying feasible research gaps based on the NLP approach, we first analyzed the underlying information behind the co-occurrence $M(i,j)$ of two key terms, denoted by KT_i and KT_j, in a document corpus. We observed the following two aspects:

1. A very low value for $M(i,j)$ not only indicates that the two terms are hardly encountered in the same document but may also suggest that the current state of knowledge is not well developed to link them or that the two terms may be incompatible. Hence, selecting terms with a co-occurrence lower than threshold α may likely result in an unfeasible research theme, in this sense α playing the role of "critical mass". We denoted this threshold as *success threshold* since $M(i,j) > \alpha$ is expected to offer a more likely successful ratio. Note that the successful integration of the two terms KT_i and KT_j in a new research topic gets higher when raising the $M(i,j)$ co-occurrence value.
2. A very high value of $M(i,j)$ generally indicates that the link between the two terms KT_i and KT_j is strong as the two terms were often encountered together in the same document. This situation may derive from an intensively studied term connection, suggesting that including the two terms in the newly framed research topic might likely be a lesser source of novelty. Thus, selecting terms that have a co-occurrence higher than threshold β may result in a research theme with small novelty. We named β as the *novelty threshold*, where $M(i,j) < \beta$ may provide an acceptable novelty. Note that the potential novelty induced by the two terms KT_i and KT_j inside a new research topic is continuously decreasing for $M(i,j)$ over the $[0;1]$ interval contrary to the success ratio that is continuously increasing over the same interval.

3.2. Double-Threshold Method

We argue that in the co-occurrence matrix for selected terms only the elements $M'(i,j)$ belonging to the interval $[\alpha;\beta]$ must be retained, where α is the indicator for the expected success rate of a research theme and β is the novelty threshold. Table 1 summarizes the procedure to identify feasible research gaps based on the double-threshold method using the co-occurrence matrix for the selected context terms and the key term. For $\beta < M(i,j) \leq 1$, the research gap is valueless since its novelty prospects are reduced, while for $0 \leq M(i,j) < \alpha$, the research gap cannot be likely tackled using existing theories, materials, and methods.

Table 1. Double-threshold approach for identifying feasible research gaps.

	$0 \leq M(i,j) < \alpha$	$\alpha \leq M(i,j) \leq \beta$	$\beta < M(i,j) \leq 1$
Succes	low	high	high
Novelty	high	high	low
Research Gap Type	Unfeasible	**Feasible**	None

Term co-occurrences are corpus-dependant. For example, a document corpus that characterizes a broader scientific domain offers lower $M(i,j)$ co-occurrence values for the same pairs of key terms KT_i and KT_j. Consequently, the selection of the novelty and success thresholds needs to be a result of an exploratory corpus analysis.

3.2.1. Success and Novelty Thresholds Selection

Given a statistically significant document corpus of size $\mathcal{N}$, the novelty and success threshold values can be found using the following three-step procedure:

I. Extract the key term topics from the document corpus using appropriate NLP topic modeling techniques, and then identify the most relevant p key terms within each of the r topics.
II. Compute all $r \times p \times (p-1)/2$ co-occurrences between the most relevant p key terms within each of the r topics. These co-occurrences, denoted by $\mathcal{M}(i,j)$, are calculated in the same way as $M(i,j)$, i.e., the number of documents in which both key terms KT_i and KT_j occur, normalized by the total number of documents in the considered corpus.
III. Select the success threshold α and the novelty threshold β by trimming the ends of the $\mathcal{M}(i,j)$ distribution.

To identify a suitable procedure to select the two thresholds, we analyzed the probability distribution of the $\mathcal{M}$ values within the considered statistically significant document corpus of size $\mathcal{N}$. We found that the terms co-occurrence $\mathcal{M}(i,j)$ values have two important properties: (i) considering the way they are computed, $\mathcal{M}(i,j)$ may take only particular values inside $[0,1]$ interval, namely multiples of $1/\mathcal{N}$; (ii) their distribution is heavily skewed to zero, with no negative values and few observations deviating far from zero. Thus, we can model the distribution of the term co-occurrences $\mathcal{M}(i,j)$ as an exponential-like distribution, where α and β act as two thresholds producing a two-sided trimmed exponential distribution (Figure 1). Neglecting the null values of $\mathcal{M}(i,j)$, we may select α and β such that each of the thresholds filters out approximately 10–30% of the $\mathcal{M}$ values, a practical selection being $\alpha = Q_1$ and $\beta = Q_3$, with Q_1 and Q_3 being the first and third quartiles.

Using the success and novelty thresholds, we retain only the $M(i,j)$ values inside the interval $[\alpha, \beta]$, which are considered in the acceptance range.

It is noteworthy to mention that our double-threshold approach can be tailored to cope with the researcher's risk profile. For this, similar to the definition of financial risk tolerance [19], we could define research risk tolerance as being the maximum amount of uncertainty that a researcher is willing to accept when framing a new research theme. According to the researcher's risk tolerance, we can classify research theme framing in three categories, each of them being characterized by a chosen pair of success and novelty thresholds $\{\alpha;\beta\}$:

1 Conservative framing—low research risk described by $\{\alpha_c;\beta_c\}$;
2 Moderate framing—median research risk described by $\{\alpha_m;\beta_m\}$;
3 Aggressive framing—high research risk described by $\{\alpha_a;\beta_a\}$.

Here, the success threshold values hold $\alpha_a < \alpha_m < \alpha_c$, while the novelty threshold values hold $\beta_a \leq \beta_m \leq \beta_c$. All six threshold values must be selected using the third step of the above thresholds selection procedure.

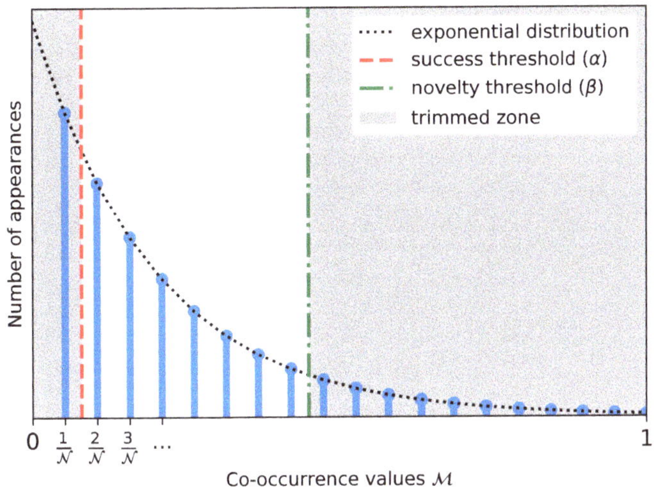

Figure 1. Distribution of terms co-occurrence values $\mathcal{M}(i,j)$ in a corpus of size $\mathcal{N}$.

4. Proposed Methodology

The methodology proposed to automatically recommend feasible research gaps extracted from a given scientific area described by a chosen set of key terms $\mathcal{V}$ is as follows:

1 Select a suitable document corpus $\mathcal{D}$ to identify the research gaps. For this, top-tier journal or conference papers within the scientific domain that encapsulates the given set of key terms $\mathcal{V}$ are suitable options.
2 Calculate the co-occurrence matrix corresponding to the set of key terms $\mathcal{V}$ to describe the weighted undirected graph $G = (\mathcal{V}, \mathcal{E}, w)$. A recent subset of documents from corpus $\mathcal{D}$ can be used, e.g., no older than two years for timely research gaps.
3 Apply the double threshold procedure described in Section 3 to drop all edges from $G = (\mathcal{V}, \mathcal{E}, w)$ for which $M(i,j)$ lays outside the $[\alpha, \beta]$ interval. By this, a new graph $G' = (\mathcal{V}, \mathcal{E}', w')$, with the corresponding adjacency matrix M', is obtained. In order to derive the success threshold α and the novelty threshold β, the entire document corpus $\mathcal{D}$ is used to obtain more statistically significant values.
4 Provide the list of feasible gap recommendations using the double-thresholded version of the co-occurrence matrix M' to extract all induced connected subgraphs [18] of order s from G', where s is the number of key terms considered to adequately depict a feasible research gap.

To help rank the recommendations, for each feasible gap the mean co-occurrence value μ (i.e., average co-occurrence for the induced connected subgraph of order s) is computed using the following formula:

$$\mu = \frac{\sum_{i<j} M'(i,j)}{0.5 \times s \times (s-1)}, \quad (1)$$

where the summation includes only the co-occurrences $M'(i,j)$ for the induced connected subgraph edges that describe the feasible research gap, and the denominator is the number of all possible edges within the subgraph. The higher this metric is, the higher the success is and the lower the novelty.

At the end of this methodology, a set of feasible research gap proposals (i.e., sets of key terms), ranked by corresponding the mean co-occurrence values, is offered to the user, and the researcher is invited to drop all unrealistic gaps (such as gaps with no meaning) and to select one based on his/her goals and expertise.

5. Case Study

We evaluated the proposed methodology for research gap identification for the electronic design automation (EDA) scientific domain. Research in this area can be described by a set of key terms $\mathcal{V}$ containing the following elements: 'machine learning', 'energy efficiency', 'internet of things', 'approximate computing', 'fault tolerant', 'biological neural networks', and 'optimization problem'. Other similar sets can be found as well. Details about each of the four steps of the methodology are presented next.

1 We selected *IEEE Transactions on Computer-Aided Design of Integrated Circuits and Systems (TCAD)*, a top tier EDA journal, to build a suitable document corpus for our methodology. After extracting journal paper metadata from the IEEEXplore database, a *compound abstract* was produced for each journal paper by concatenating its title, keywords, and abstract. All compound abstracts were transformed in sequences of relevant terms (i.e., processed abstracts) by using the TagMe entity linking tool [20] with the link-probability parameter set to 0.1.

2 We computed the co-occurrence matrix M corresponding to the set of seven key terms $\mathcal{V}$ using the processed abstracts of *TCAD* papers from 2019 and 2020. Figure 2 presents the M matrix as a heatmap, while Figure 3 presents the corresponding graph G as a chord diagram.

3 To apply the double threshold procedure described in Section 3, we first derived the success threshold α and the novelty threshold β using the entire document corpus $\mathcal{D}$ (i.e., *TCAD* papers from 2010 to 2020). For this, we performed a latent Dirichlet allocation (LDA) topic modeling [21] for $r = 4$ topics, and selected the most relevant $p = 30$ terms within each of the topics to obtain the $\mathcal{M}(i,j)$ co-occurrences. The histogram of the $\mathcal{M}(i,j)$ co-occurrences and the selection of the $\alpha = 0.000317$ and $\beta = 0.003$ thresholds according to the procedure described in Section 3.2.1 are presented in Figure 4.
Using these threshold values we computed the double-thresholded version M' of the co-occurrence matrix. The matrix M' is presented as a heatmap in Figure 5, while the corresponding graph G' is depicted in Figure 6.

4 Assuming that a set of four key terms are appropriate to characterize a potential research gap, we extracted the following list of feasible research gaps (i.e., all induced connected subgraphs of order s = 4), ranked by their corresponding μ value:
   (a) 'machine learning', 'energy efficiency', 'internet of things', 'approximate computing'; $\mu = 0.00174574$.
   (b) 'machine learning', 'energy efficiency', 'internet of things', 'biological neural networks'; $\mu = 0.00164017$.
   (c) 'machine learning', 'energy efficiency', 'approximate computing', 'biological neural networks'; $\mu = 0.0013756$.
   (d) 'machine learning', 'energy efficiency', 'internet of things', 'optimization problem'; $\mu = 0.0012169$.
   (e) 'machine learning', 'energy efficiency', 'approximate computing', 'optimization problem'; $\mu = 0.0011639$.
   (f) 'energy efficiency', 'internet of things', 'approximate computing', 'biological neural networks'; $\mu = 0.00100549$.
   (g) 'machine learning', 'internet of things', 'approximate computing', 'biological neural networks'; $\mu = 0.00084652$.
   (h) 'energy efficiency', 'internet of things', 'biological neural networks, 'optimization problem'; $\mu = 0.000740740$.
   (i) 'energy efficiency', 'approximate computing', 'biological neural networks', 'optimization problem'; $\mu = 0.0006348836$.

   From these research gap recommendations, we selected two potential research topics, and we offer their textual descriptions in Table 2.

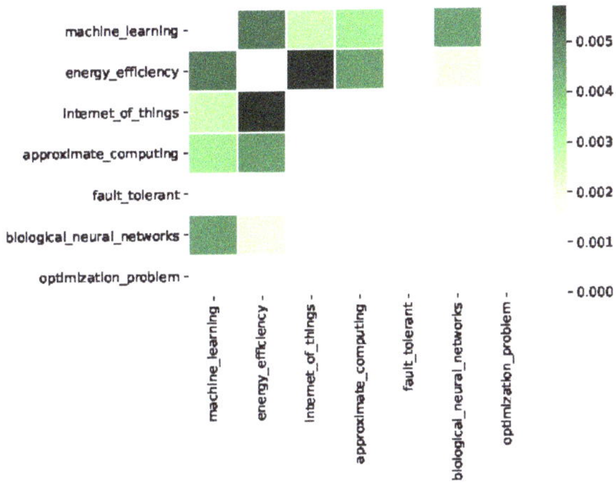

Figure 2. Heatmap visualization of the co-occurrence matrix M.

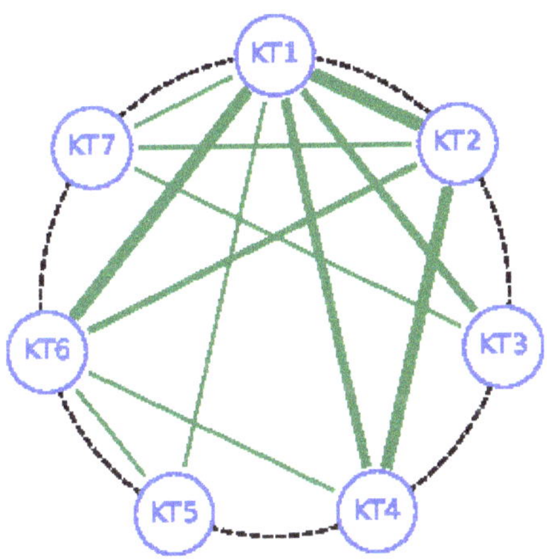

Figure 3. The original graph G of key terms.

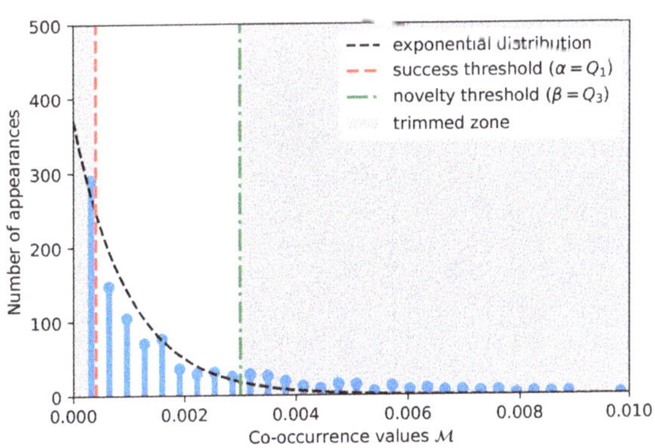

Figure 4. Histogram of the $\mathcal{M}$ co-occurrences and threshold values selection.

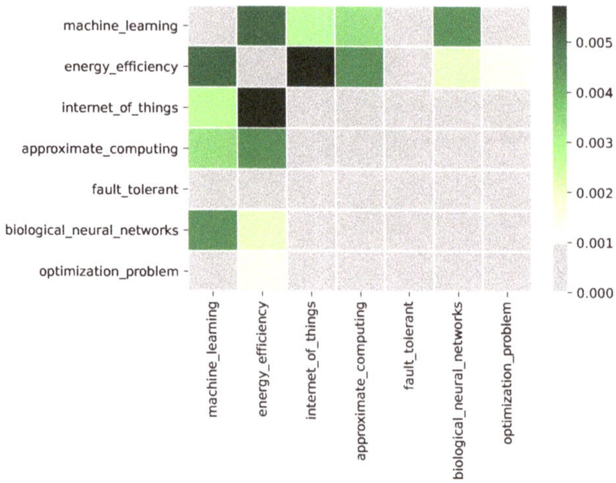

Figure 5. Visualization of feasible research gaps using heatmap.

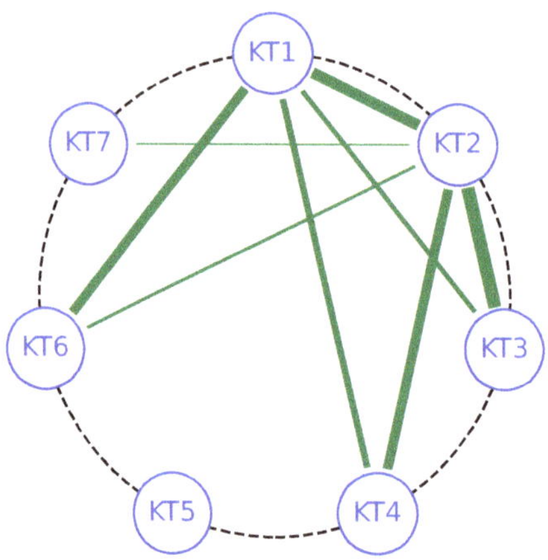

Figure 6. Visualization of feasible research gaps using chord diagram.

Table 2. Potential research topics in the EDA domain.

No.	Feasible Research Gap Terms	Research Theme Description	μ
1.	KT1: machine learning KT3: internet of things KT4: approximate computing KT6: biological neural networks	***Biological neural network*** *inspired algorithms for* ***approximate computing*** *in* ***ML*** *for* ***IoT*** *applications.*	0.00084652
2.	KT1: machine learning KT2: energy efficiency KT3: internet of things KT7: optimization problem	*Design of integrated circuits for* ***IoT*** *applications* ***optimized*** *for* ***energy efficiency*** *by means of* ***ML***.	0.0012169

If we consider the researcher risk categories described in the last paragraph of Section 3.2 (i.e., conservative framing $\{\alpha_c = 0.001; \beta_c = 0.003\}$; moderate framing $\{\alpha_m = 0.0004; \beta_m = 0.003\}$; aggressive framing $\{\alpha_a = 0.0001; \beta_a = 0.003\}$) and the number of terms to characterize possible research gaps $s \in \{3, 4\}$, a sample of recommendations was produced, as presented in Table 3.

Table 3. Research topic examples considering research risk.

No.	Feasible Research Gap Terms	Research Theme Description	Scenario
1.	KT1: machine learning KT2: energy efficiency KT3: internet of things	*Using **ML** for **energy-efficient IoT**.*	conservative
2.	KT1: machine learning KT3: internet of things KT4: approximate computing KT6: biological neural networks	***Biological neural network** inspired algorithms for **approximate computing** in **ML** for **IoT** applications.*	moderate
3.	KT1: machine learning KT2: energy efficiency KT3: internet of things KT7: optimization problem	*Design of integrated circuits for **IoT** applications **optimized** for **energy efficiency** by means of **ML**.*	moderate
4.	KT1: machine learning KT4: approximate computing KT5: fault tolerant KT7: optimization problem	***Approximate computing** for solving **optimization problems** in **fault tolerant ML**.*	aggressive
5.	KT1: machine learning KT2: energy efficiency KT5: fault tolerant KT6: biological neural networks	***Biological neural network** inspired methods for **fault tolerant** and **energy-efficient ML**.*	aggressive

6. Conclusions

Identifying potential research gaps is a main step toward successful problem framing and hence fruitful research achievements. This activity has become very cumbersome due to the increase in the number of publications and published papers. Hence, automatic tools are necessary to assist researchers to select their future research themes. Related techniques can explore research trends by mapping scientific fields' unexplored or insufficiently investigated areas, but do not study potential connections across different domains and trends, even though current research needs are often cross-disciplinary in nature.

This paper discusses a method for automated identification of feasible research gaps by graph-theoretic analysis of the correlations between key terms (specific to the scientific domain of interest), followed by a double-threshold procedure to discard the research gaps that are difficult to study with the existing knowledge or may offer little novelty. The method extracts the subgraphs for the less-frequent graph links to express research key terms that are likely to be part of problem descriptions of expected novelty and likely success. A case study uses the proposed method to find research gaps for the electronic design automation (EDA) domain. Starting from a document corpus based on *IEEE TCAD*, the method extracted subgraphs for less-frequent co-occurring keywords for different researcher risk profiles. The subgraphs were then utilized for research gap description.

Future work will focus on extending the method by devising algorithms to automatically select the parameters of the methods, such as the co-occurrence distributions, and the two threshold values. We also plan to enhance our method by including a citation analysis component and to use other publication corpora for EDA, as well as experiment with different domains.

Author Contributions: Conceptualization, C.-D.C.; methodology, C.-D.C., A.D. and D.-I.C.; software, C.-D.C. and A.D.; validation, C.-D.C. and A.D.; formal analysis, C.-D.C., A.D. and D.-I.C.; investigation, C.-D.C., A.D. and D.-I.C.; resources, A.D. and D.-I.C.; data curation, C.-D.C., A.D. and D.-I.C.; writing—original draft preparation, C.-D.C. and A.D.; writing—review and editing, C.-D.C., A.D. and D.-I.C.; supervision, A.D. and D.-I.C. All authors have read and agreed to the published version of the manuscript.

Funding: This research received no external funding.

Institutional Review Board Statement: Not applicable.

Informed Consent Statement: Not applicable.

Data Availability Statement: Not applicable.

Conflicts of Interest: The authors declare no conflict of interest.

References

1. Manning, C.; Schutze, H. *Foundations of Statistical Natural Language Processing*; MIT Press: Cambridge, MA, USA, 1999.
2. Sedighi, M. Application of word co-occurrence analysis method in mapping of the scientific fields (case study: The field of Informetrics). *Libr. Rev.* **2016**, *65*, 52–64. [CrossRef]
3. Mazov, N.; Gureev, V.; Glinskikh, V. The methodological basis of defining research trends and fronts. *Sci. Tech. Inf. Process.* **2020**, *47*, 221–231.
4. Liu, X.; Jiang, T.; Ma, F. Collective dynamics in knowledge networks: Emerging trends analysis. *J. Inf.* **2013**, *7*, 425–438.
5. Vega-Muñoz, A.; Arjona-Fuentes, J.M.; Ariza-Montes, A.; Han, H.; Law, R. In search of 'a research front' in cruise tourism studies. *Int. J. Hosp. Manag.* **2020**, *85*, 102353.
6. Ge, Y.; Hao, G.; Xiang, L. Technology evolution network model and simulation based on patent citation network. *J. Syst. Simul.* **2021**, *33*, 591.
7. Upham, S.; Small, H. Emerging research fronts in science and technology: Patterns of new knowledge development. *Scientometrics* **2010**, *83*, 15–38. [PubMed]
8. Akimushkin, C.; Amancio, D.R.; Oliveira, O.N., Jr.; On the role of words in the network structure of texts: Application to authorship attribution. *Phys. A Stat. Mech. Appl.* **2018**, *495*, 49–58. [CrossRef]
9. Sulis, E.; Humphreys, L.; Vernero, F.; Amantea, I.A.; Audrito, D.; Di Caro, L. Exploiting co-occurrence networks for classification of implicit inter-relationships in legal texts. *Inf. Syst.* **2022**, *106*, 101821. [CrossRef]
10. Chen, J.; Wei, W.; Guo, C.; Tang, L.; Sun, L. Textual analysis and visualization of research trends in data mining for electronic health records. *Health Policy Technol.* **2017**, *6*, 389–400.
11. Sivanandham, S.; Kumar, A.S.; Pradeep, R.; Sridhar, R. Analysing research trends using Ttopic modelling and trend prediction. In *Soft Computing and Signal Processing*; Springer: Berlin/Heidelberg, Germany, 2021; pp. 157–166.
12. Mohammadi, E.; Karami, A. Exploring research trends in big data across disciplines: A text mining analysis. *J. Inf. Sci.* **2022**, *48*, 44–56. [CrossRef]
13. Muñoz-Leiva, F.; Viedma-del Jesús, M.; Sánchez-Fernández, J.; López-Herrera, A. An application of co-word analysis and bibliometric maps for detecting the most highlighting themes in the consumer behaviour research from a longitudinal perspective. *Qual. Quant.* **2012**, *46*, 1077–1095.
14. Chen, X.; Chen, J.; Wu, D.; Xie, Y.; Li, J. Mapping the research trends by co-word analysis based on keywords from funded project. *Procedia Comput. Sci.* **2016**, *91*, 547–555. [CrossRef]
15. Bird, S.; Klein, E.; Loper, E. *Natural Language Processing with Python: Analyzing Text with the Natural Language Toolkit*; O'Reilly Media, Inc.: Sebastopol, CA, USA, 2009.
16. Hardeniya, N.; Perkins, J.; Chopra, D.; Joshi, N.; Mathur, I. *Natural Language Processing: Python and NLTK*; Packt Publishing Ltd.: Birmingham, UK, 2016.
17. He, Q. Knowledge discovery through co-word analysis. *Libr. Trends* **1999**, *48*, 133–159.
18. Gross, J.L.; Yellen, J. *Handbook of Graph Theory*; CRC Press: Boca Raton, FL, USA, 2003.
19. Grable, J.E. Financial risk tolerance and additional factors that affect risk taking in everyday money matters. *J. Bus. Psychol.* **2000**, *14*, 625–630. [CrossRef]
20. Ferragina, P.; Scaiella, U. TagMe: On-the-fly annotation of short text fragments (by Wikipedia entities). In Proceeding of the International Conference on Information and Knowledge Management, Toronto, ON, Canada, 25–29 October 2010; pp. 1625–1628.
21. Blei, D.; Ng, A.; Jordan, M. Latent Dirichlet Allocation. *J. Mach. Learn. Res.* **2003**, *3*, 993–1022.

mathematics

MDPI

Article

Predicting Subgrade Resistance Value of Hydrated Lime-Activated Rice Husk Ash-Treated Expansive Soil: A Comparison between M5P, Support Vector Machine, and Gaussian Process Regression Algorithms

Mahmood Ahmad [1], Badr T. Alsulami [2], Ramez A. Al-Mansob [3], Saerahany Legori Ibrahim [3,*], Suraparb Keawsawasvong [4,*], Ali Majdi [5] and Feezan Ahmad [6]

1 Department of Civil Engineering, University of Engineering and Technology Peshawar (Bannu Campus), Bannu 28100, Pakistan; ahmadm@uetpeshawar.edu.pk
2 Department of Civil Engineering, College of Engineering and Islamic Architecture, Umm Al-Qura University, Makkah 24382, Saudi Arabia; btsulami@uqu.edu.sa
3 Department of Civil Engineering, Faculty of Engineering, International Islamic University Malaysia, Jalan Gombak 50728, Selangor, Malaysia; ramez@iium.edu.my
4 Department of Civil Engineering, Thammasat School of Engineering, Thammasat University, Pathumthani 12120, Thailand
5 Department of Building and Construction Techniques Engineering, Al-Mustaqbal University College, Hilla 51001, Iraq; alimajdi@mustaqbal-college.edu.iq
6 State Key Laboratory of Coastal and Offshore Engineering, Dalian University of Technology, Dalian 116024, China; ahmadf@mail.dlut.edu.cn
* Correspondence: saerahany@iium.edu.my (S.L.I.); ksurapar@engr.tu.ac.th (S.K.)

Citation: Ahmad, M.; Alsulami, B.T.; Al-Mansob, R.A.; Ibrahim, S.L.; Keawsawasvong, S.; Majdi, A.; Ahmad, F. Predicting Subgrade Resistance Value of Hydrated Lime-Activated Rice Husk Ash-Treated Expansive Soil: A Comparison between M5P, Support Vector Machine, and Gaussian Process Regression Algorithms. *Mathematics* **2022**, *10*, 3432. https://doi.org/10.3390/math10193432

Academic Editors: Adrian Sergiu Darabant and Diana-Laura Borza

Received: 3 August 2022
Accepted: 18 September 2022
Published: 21 September 2022

Abstract: Resistance value (R-value) is one of the basic subgrade stiffness characterizations that express a material's resistance to deformation. In this paper, artificial intelligence (AI)-based models—especially M5P, support vector machine (SVM), and Gaussian process regression (GPR) algorithms—are built for R-value evaluation that meets the high precision and rapidity requirements in highway engineering. The dataset of this study comprises seven parameters: hydrated lime-activated rice husk ash, liquid limit, plastic limit, plasticity index, optimum moisture content, and maximum dry density. The available data are divided into three parts: training set (70%), test set (15%), and validation set (15%). The output (i.e., R-value) of the developed models is evaluated using the performance measures coefficient of determination (R^2), mean absolute error (MAE), relative squared error (RSE), root mean square error (RMSE), relative root mean square error (RRMSE), performance indicator (ρ), and visual framework (Taylor diagram). GPR is concluded to be the best performing model (R^2, MAE, RSE, RMSE, RRMSE, and ρ equal to 0.9996, 0.0258, 0.0032, 0.0012, 0.0012, and 0.0006, respectively, in the validation phase), very closely followed by SVM, and M5P. The application used for the aforementioned approaches for predicting the R-value is also compared with the recently developed artificial neural network model in the literature. The analysis of performance measures for the R-value dataset demonstrates that all the AI-based models achieved comparatively better and reliable results and thus should be encouraged in further research. Sensitivity analysis suggests that all the input parameters have a significant influence on the output, with maximum dry density being the highest.

Keywords: resistance value; M5P; support vector machine; Gaussian process regression; expansive soil; subgrade

MSC: 68T09

1. Introduction

A flexible pavement structure is composed of several layers, the lowest of which is known as the pavement foundation or subgrade. The strength and stiffness of the subgrade are critical for pavement design, construction, and performance. California bearing ratio, resistance value (R-value), and resilient modulus are all terms used to describe subgrade strength and stiffness. In this study, R-value is used to represent subgrade strength and/or weakness. A soil's deformation resistance is expressed as a function of the applied vertical pressure to lateral pressure ratio. The R-value, which ranges from 0 to 100, represents soil strength and stiffness, with 100 representing the highest strength [1]. The resulting pavement may be overdesigned if a low subgrade R-value is used in its design, despite the fact that the actual subgrade is not weak. If a high R-value is utilized in the design while the actual subgrade is weak, the subsequent pavement structure may be too thick to protect the weaker subgrade soil from traffic stresses [2,3]. The R-value is an important parameter in pavement design because the thickness of each layer is determined by the R-value and traffic index (expected level of traffic loading). It can be measured through a particular test called the stabilometer test in the laboratory. This test actually measures the resistance of soil/aggregate sample to the vertically applied load under particular conditions. Usually, foundation material suffers lateral deformation due to subjected vertical loading [4,5]. Rafiqul et al. [6] demonstrated from elastic analysis that increasing subgrade R-values can significantly reduce compressive strain at the top of the subgrade. Subgrade treatment can help to reduce stress and strains in weak subgrade.

This test was first used by Caltron for the purpose of pavement design, replacing the California bearing ratio test. In some areas, R-value testing is used for the road aggregate and subgrade soil. The R-value of a soil stratum can be defined as the ability of a soil medium to resist lateral spreading due to applied vertical load. In the case of pavement, tire load is applied as vertical load. The base course contains well-graded crushed stone with dense gradation bearing R-value of 80+ while silts attain 15–30. For robust pavement design, accurate prediction of the mechanical index of geomaterials is necessary [7]. There are certain parameters on which the pavement design is dependent, one of which is the R-value of the soil [5]. The R-value of a material is determined when the material is saturated to the point where water will be expelled from the compacted test specimen when a 16.8 kN (2.07 MPa) load is applied. Because it is not always possible to prepare a test specimen that will exude water at the specified load, a series of specimens prepared at different moisture contents must be tested [6]. The R-value can be measured using a laboratory stabilometer following the ASTM D 2844, AASHTO T 190, and California Test CT 301 and the following formula [6]:

$$R = 100 - \frac{100}{(2.5/D)[(P_v/P_h) - 1] + 1} \quad (1)$$

where D denotes the displacement of stabilometer fluid required to increase the horizontal pressure from 5 to 100 psi (34.5 to 689.5 kPa), P_v denotes the applied vertical pressure of 160 psi (1103 kPa), P_h denotes the transmitted horizontal pressure of 160 psi (1103 kPa), and R denotes the resistance value. The R-value can also be calculated empirically using soil classification and index properties.

The New Mexico Department of Transportation (NMDOT) uses a field empirical method to estimate the R-value, which involves first determining the American Association of State Highway and Transportation Officials (AASHTO) soil classification and the plasticity index, and then referencing the R-value from a standard estimated table of values [8]. It is a very complex and time-consuming process to determine the R-value in the laboratory [9]. In a similar manner, complications can also occur in the case of expansive soil for strength improvement and needs stabilization [5,9,10]. Onyelowe et al. [11] used 121 data points of expansive soil treated with recycled and activated composites of rice husk ash to predict the behavior of soil-strength parameters, such as R-value using the evolutionary hybrid algorithms of an artificial neural network (ANN). The results demonstrated that the aforementioned model can obtain the measured R-value with acceptable performance.

In the last 10 years, artificial intelligence (AI) techniques have been widely used to solve real-world problems, particularly in civil engineering. AI techniques have been successfully applied to a wide range of real-world scenarios, paving the way for a number of promising opportunities in civil engineering and other fields, such as environmental [12], geotechnical and geological [13–26], and other sciences [27–30] including R-value prediction [11,31]. These studies provided new concepts and ways for predicting R-value. However, this field is still being researched. This paper focuses on the use of AI-based models—especially M5P, support vector machine, and Gaussian process regression—to analyze the prediction of R-value for hydrated lime-activated rice husk ash (HARHA)-treated expansive soil, emphasizing accuracy and efficiency, as well as the ability of each technique to deal with experimental data. This study uses seven input parameters—HARHA, liquid limit (LL), plastic limit (PL), plasticity index (PI), optimum moisture content (OMC), clay activity (A_C), and maximum dry density (MDD)—assessed for the estimation of output R-value. The accuracy of the models was compared with previously developed models in the literature using performance indices of coefficient of determination, mean absolute error, relative squared error, root mean square error, relative root mean square error, and performance indicator.

The first section of this research paper contains the introduction, the second section details about the dataset, Pearson's correlation analysis, and a short literature review on soft computing techniques for estimation of the R-value. The third section has thorough discussion of the results, and the last section summarizes the whole study and presents the conclusions and future prospects.

2. Materials and Methods

2.1. Data Collection

The dataset acquired from Onyelowe et al. [11] was organized into three parts: training, testing, and validation. The total dataset was divided such that the training dataset is 70% (85) of the total dataset and the remaining 30% (36) dataset was equally divided between testing and validation. The complete database is available in Table A1 in Appendix A. In the Onyelowe et al. [11] study, a number of tests were conducted on prepared expansive soil. Both treated and untreated soil specimens were used for determination of the dataset. The seven input parameters—HARHA (X1), LL (X2), PL (X3), PI (X4), OMC (X5), A_C (X6), and MDD (X7)—were assessed for estimation of output R-value (Y). A hybrid geometrical binder called HARHA was prepared from blending of rice husk with 5% hydrated lime $Ca(OH)_2$, and the mix then remained for 24 h for complete activation reaction. The hydrated lime acted as alkali activator, while the rice husk was obtained from rice-processing mills. Basically, rice husk is an agro industrial waste. The rice husk mass was turned into ash by direct combustion to obtain rice husk ash (RHA) [32]. The HARHA was also used to treat the soil in varying proportions ranging from 0.1 to 12. Therefore, in this study, these seven input parameters were used to develop the proposed models for comparison. The descriptive statistics of each input and output are listed in Table 1 and the histograms are presented in Figure 1.

Table 1. Statistical analysis of the input and output parameters.

Dataset	Statistical Parameters	Input and Output Parameters							
		X1 (%)	X2 (%)	X3 (%)	X4	X5 (%)	X6	X7 (g/cm^3)	Y
Training	Minimum	0.00	39.30	14.90	24.30	16.00	1.10	1.25	11.70
	Maximum	8.40	66.00	21.00	45.00	19.00	2.00	1.90	23.50
	Mean	4.20	54.02	18.38	35.65	18.11	1.56	1.57	18.41
	SD	2.47	7.79	1.76	6.07	0.88	0.25	0.19	3.63
	COV	58.77	14.43	9.57	17.03	4.87	16.33	12.01	19.74
Testing	Minimum	8.50	35.50	14.90	20.40	17.84	0.86	1.91	23.60
	Maximum	10.20	39.00	15.20	24.00	18.20	1.00	1.98	25.30
	Mean	9.35	37.06	15.04	22.01	18.07	0.97	1.96	24.37
	SD	0.53	0.96	0.09	0.98	0.14	0.05	0.02	0.50
	COV	5.71	2.60	0.61	4.43	0.77	4.74	1.10	2.04
Validation	Minimum	10.30	27.00	12.80	14.00	17.10	0.60	1.95	25.40
	Maximum	12.00	34.60	14.90	19.70	17.79	0.84	1.99	27.00
	Mean	11.15	30.47	13.61	16.87	17.56	0.72	1.98	26.51
	SD	0.53	2.18	0.55	1.69	0.20	0.07	0.01	0.59
	COV	4.79	7.15	4.07	10.00	1.13	9.19	0.75	2.23

SD = standard deviation, COV = coefficient of variation.

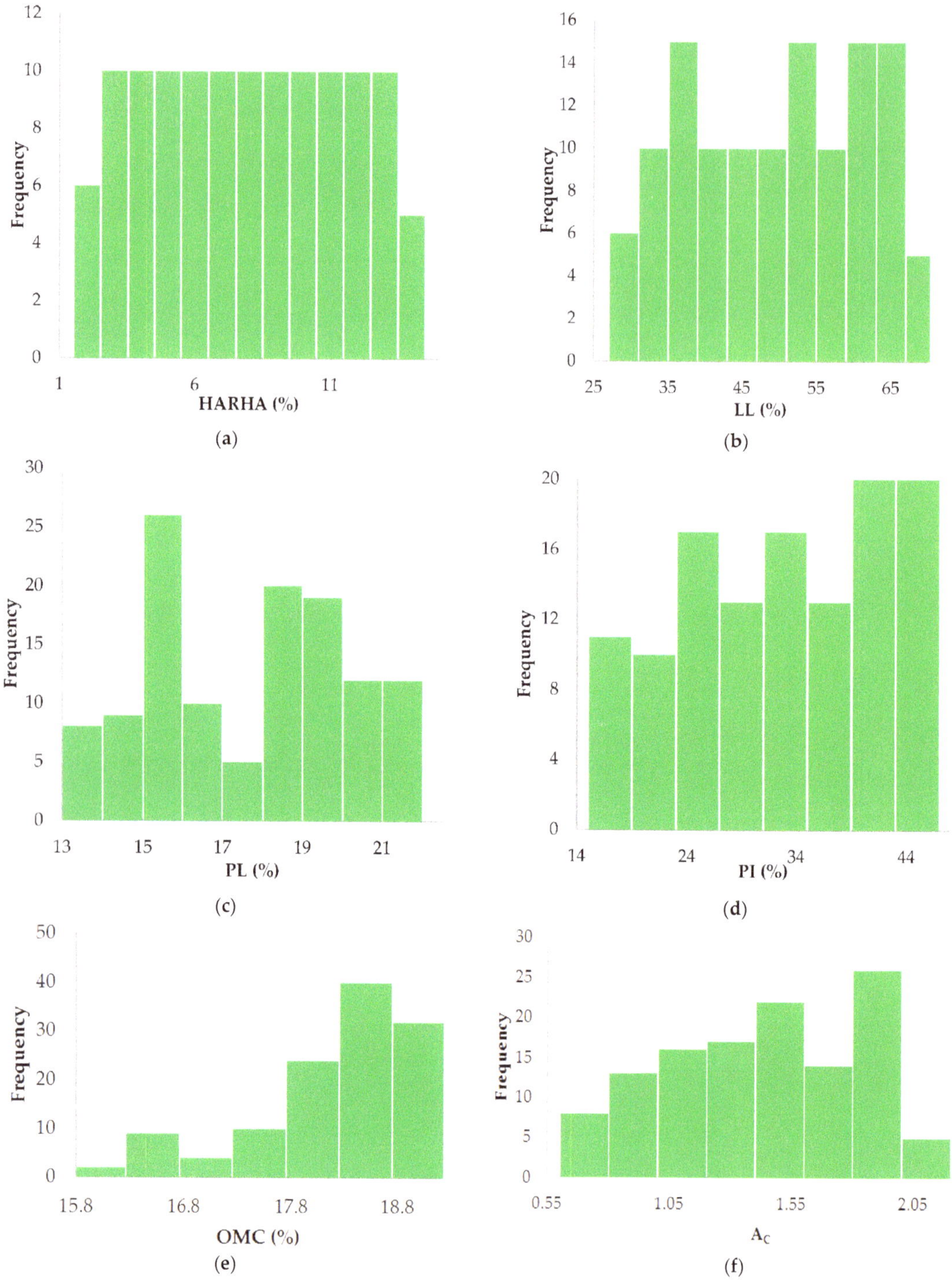

Figure 1. *Cont.*

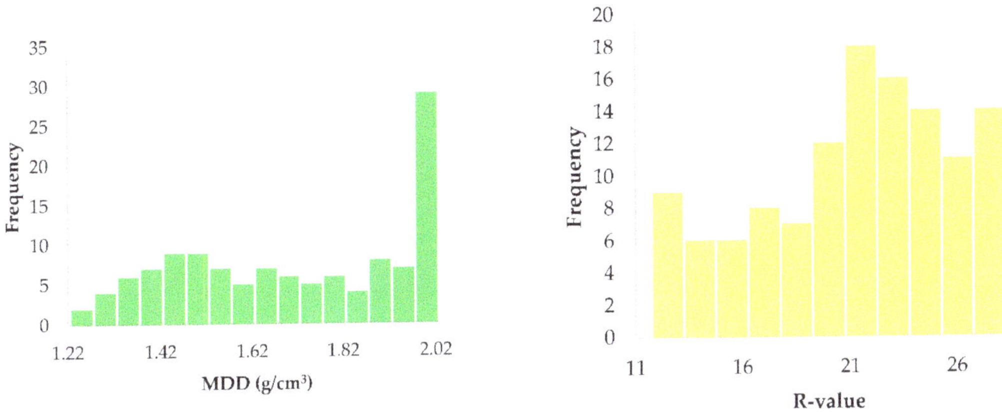

(g) (h)

Figure 1. Histograms of the input (in green) and output (in yellow) variables used in this study.

2.2. Pearson's Correlation Analysis

In order to determine the linear relationship between input and output parameters, this study employed Pearson's correlation coefficient [33]. The Pearson correlation coefficient (ρ) was used to determine the correlations between each pairwise variable. For random variables (p, q), the following equation was used:

$$\rho(p,q) = \frac{\text{cov}(p,q)}{\sigma_p \sigma_q} \tag{2}$$

where σ_p and σ_p are the standard deviations of p and q, respectively, while cov represents the covariance.

Table 2 clearly summarizes the correlation of all parameters according to the ρ (absolute value), where $|\rho| > 0.8$ represents a strong relationship among each pairwise variable, values between 0.3 and 0.8 represent medium relationship, and $|\rho| < 0.30$ represents weak relationship [34]. It can be easily figured out from Table 2 that the HARHA (X1) is strongly correlated with R-value ($|\rho| = 0.9844$), while the optimum moisture content (X5) is slightly correlated with R-value ($|\rho| = 0.3639$).

Table 2. Pearson correlation coefficients for inputs and the target output.

Parameter	X1	X2	X3	X4	X5	X6	X7	Y
X1	1							
X2	−0.9972	1						
X3	−0.9893	0.9915	1					
X4	−0.9965	0.9994	0.9865	1				
X5	0.2014	−0.1435	−0.1749	−0.1348	1			
X6	−0.9939	0.9975	0.9846	0.9981	−0.1204	1		
X7	0.9858	−0.9818	−0.9770	−0.9803	0.2394	−0.9742	1	
Y	0.9844	−0.9721	−0.9695	−0.9700	0.3639	−0.9659	0.9728	1

2.3. Machine-Learning Algorithms

2.3.1. Gaussian Process Regression (GPR)

GPR is a purely probability-based method. It is used for regression and classification problems [35,36]. This method has attracted the interest of many researchers in different scientific areas [37,38]. It gives good results in cases of nonlinear data modeling. Nonlinearity may be due to kernel functions [39]. In addition to regression, it gives a very effective response to input parameters [40].

For the computation and assessment of the training data, the input parameter is assumed as $D = \{(x_i, y_i) | i = 1, \ldots, n\}, X \in R^{D \times n}$ and the output desired parameter is $y \in R^n$. In GPR computation of the output parameter can be calculated from the function $y = f(x) + \varepsilon$, where $\varepsilon \sim N(0, \sigma_n^2) \in R$ is the equal noise variance for all x_i samples [40].

Gaussian process regression number of observations n considered a single point instance in the $y = \{y_1, \ldots, y_n\}$ vector of the Gaussian multivariable distribution. Moreover, it is assumed that this distribution has zero mean value. Covariance is a function that shows the dependence of one observation on another. In GPR, to approximate functions, the square of the covariance determiner is commonly used, which is as follows [35]:

$$k(x, x') = \sigma_f^2 \times \exp\left[-\frac{(x - x')^2}{2l^2}\right] + \sigma_n^2 \delta(x, x') \tag{3}$$

When the values of x and x' are so close to each other, the value of $k(x, x')$ is equal to the maximum allowable covariance. As a result, the values of $f(x)$ and $f(x')$ are approximately the same. l is the length of the kernel function. In addition, $\delta(x, x')$ is called the Kronecker product, which is defined as follows:

$$\delta_{ij} = 1 \text{ if } i = j \text{ and } \delta_{ij} = 0 \text{ if } i \neq j$$

In the case of the training dataset, for a new input pattern, the prediction of y^* as an output value is the final objective. In order to obtain the desired objective, three covariance matrices need to be developed:

$$K = \begin{bmatrix} k(x_1, x_1) & k(x_1, x_2) & \cdots & k(x_1, x_n) \\ k(x_2, x_1) & k(x_2, x_2) & \cdots & k(x_2, x_n) \\ \cdots & \cdots & \cdots & \cdots \\ \cdots & \cdots & \cdots & \cdots \\ k(x_n, x_1) & k(x_n, x_2) & \cdots & k(x_n, x_n) \end{bmatrix} \tag{4}$$

$$\begin{aligned} K_* &= \begin{bmatrix} k(x_*, x_1) & k(x_*, x_2) & \cdots & k(x_*, x_n) \end{bmatrix} \\ K_{**} &= k(x_*, x_*) \end{aligned} \tag{5}$$

Data from Gaussian multivariable distribution are assumed:

$$\begin{bmatrix} y \\ y_* \end{bmatrix} \sim N\left(0, \begin{bmatrix} K & K_*^T \\ K_* & K_{**} \end{bmatrix}\right) \tag{6}$$

From Gaussian multivariable distribution, the approximate average and variance of the predicted output are obtained:

$$\begin{aligned} E(y_*) &= K_* K^{-1} y \\ \text{var}(y_*) &= K_{**} - K^{-1} K_*^T \end{aligned} \tag{7}$$

2.3.2. M5P

Wang and Witten [41] rebuilt and presented the M5P algorithm from the M5 algorithm initially proposed by Quinlan [42], with the addition of a linear regression function to the leaves nodes.

The M5P could perform better on datasets than M5 by trimming the tree size. Typically, M5P consists of the following three steps:

(i) Creating a model tree: Using the dividing criterion, the entered space was divided into numerous subspaces. The predicted error at the node was reduced by applying the standard deviation reduction factor (SDR). The SDR equation is displayed as follows:

$$\text{SDR} = sd(H) - \sum_i \frac{|H_i|}{|H|} \times sd(H_i),$$
$$sd(H) = \sqrt{\sum_1^N \frac{(H_i - \overline{H})^2}{N-1}}, \quad (8)$$
$$\overline{H} = \sum_1^N \frac{H_i}{N}.$$

where H_i is the set that is obtained from a divided node according to a given attribute, sd is the standard deviation of H_i, and H is the instance dataset that stretches the node.

(ii) Pruning tree: In each subspace, a classifying and regression tree is introduced to overfit the problem and improves classification performance. Any errors encountered in the learning data will be removed during the pruning process.

(iii) Smoothing step: The nearby linear models may experience abrupt discontinuities as a result of the pruning tree. Therefore, all of the leaf models will be integrated from the leaf to the root to create the final model in order to tackle this problem. The anticipated value is then filtered all the way back to the root. By combining the current value with the expected value from the linear regression, the final value is smoothed using the following equation:

$$T' = \frac{N_t + KA}{N + K} \quad (9)$$

where T' is the predicted value shift to the higher level of the next node, N_t is the predicted value shifted from the lower node to the present node, N is the total number of training instances that shift to the next lower node, A is the predicted value by the node at this node, and K is a constant value.

2.3.3. Support Vector Machine (SVM)

SVM can be used for regression analysis but is typically employed for classification tasks. SVM exhibits the data points displayed on the plane, resulting in fewer close errors, and describes a hyperplane between groups to assure the maximum difference between the two classes. There would be a nonlinear separation of the training data [43]. Next, a nonlinear separable boundary needs to be constructed. The original space must be mapped to a high dimension to produce a nonlinear border. How to map the space in a specific input space is determined by a kernel function. For the model's optimization, a penalty factor (C) for misclassification was added. By adding up the negative effects of each misclassification, the overall penalty in plotting is calculated. The groundwater and hydrological engineering fields have identified several beneficial applications of the SVM approach [44–46].

2.4. Model Evaluation and Comparison

To validate and compare the models, the six quantitative statistics—coefficient of determination (R^2), mean absolute error (MAE), relative squared error (RSE), root mean square error (RMSE), relative root mean square error (RRMSE), and performance indicator (ρ)—were used. The mathematical expressions of the statistical measures are presented in Equations (9)–(14).

$$R^2 = \left[\frac{\sum_{i=1}^{n} (e_i - \overline{e}_i) \sum_{i=1}^{n} (m_i - \overline{m}_i)}{\sqrt{\sum_{i=1}^{n} (e_i - \overline{e}_i)^2 \sum_{i=1}^{n} (m_i - \overline{m}_i)^2}} \right]^2 \quad (10)$$

$$MAE = \frac{\sum_{i=1}^{n} |e_i - m_i|}{n} \quad (11)$$

$$\text{RSE} = \frac{\sum_{i=1}^{n} (m_i - e_i)^2}{\sum_{i=1}^{n} (\overline{e}_i - e_i)^2} \quad (12)$$

$$RMSE = \sqrt{\frac{\sum_{i=1}^{n}(e_i - m_i)^2}{n}} \quad (13)$$

$$RRMSE = \frac{1}{|\overline{e}|}\sqrt{\frac{\sum_{i=1}^{n}(e_i - m_i)^2}{n}} \quad (14)$$

$$\rho = \frac{RRMSE}{1+r} \quad (15)$$

where e_i and m_i are the nth actual and expected output of the ith sample, respectively. $\overline{e}$ and $\overline{m}_i$ represents the average values of the experimental and expected output, respectively. The number of total datasets is represented by n. The R^2 value ranges from 0 to 1. A higher R^2 value indicates a more efficient model. A model is considered to be effective if its R^2 value is greater than 0.8 and near to 1 [47]. The mean squared difference between the projected output and targets is the criterion of RMSE, and the mean magnitude of the error is the criterion MAE. RRMSE is calculated by dividing RMSE by the average value of the measured data. Model accuracy is considered excellent when RMSE < 10%, good if 10% < RMSE < 20%, fair if 20% < RMSE < 30%, and poor if RMSE > 30% [48]. Relative squared error (RSE) normalizes the total squared error of predicted values by dividing it by the total squared error of measured values. The RSE index ranges from 0 to infinity, with 0 being the ideal. Lower-value RMSE, RRMSE, and RSE indicate better model calibration. A performance indicator (ρ) is proposed to assess the model's performance as a function of both the RRMSE and the coefficient of correlation (r) value [49]. The value of ρ ranges from 0 to positive infinity, with a lower value (close to zero) indicating better model performance. A schematic diagram of the methodology for applying machine learning (ML) algorithms to predict the R-value is illustrated in Figure 2.

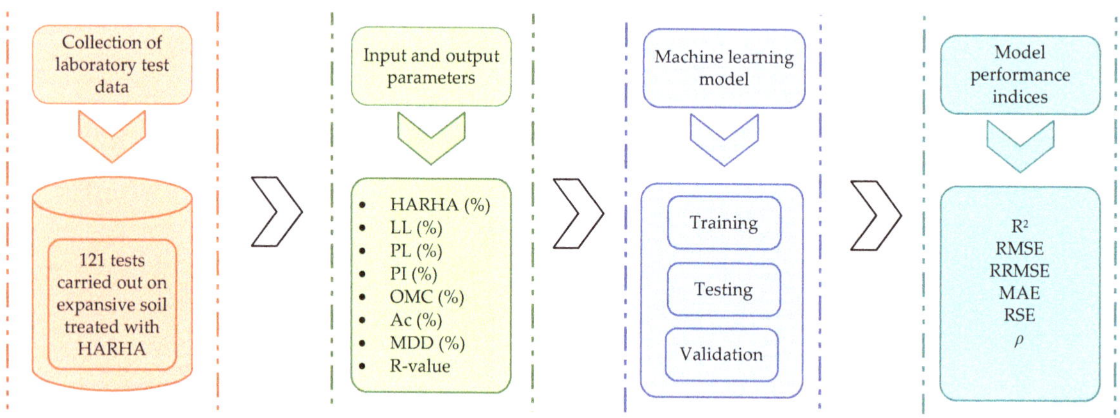

Figure 2. Flowchart for applying ML algorithms to predict the R-value.

3. Results and Analysis

3.1. Hyperparameter Optimization

In the field of ML, hyperparameters control the performance of the model. Multiple runs on training data are used to optimize hyperparameters. Smaller RMSE and MAE values indicate that the modeling methods are closer to the experimental data. Larger R2 values indicate a better match of trends in experimental data by model predictions. This technique tends to point out the optimized setting for the proposed modeling, i.e., GPR, SVM, and M5P, to achieve the best possible prediction. Implementing SVR and GPR techniques requires the selection of an appropriate kernel function that works internally to map the given data to a high-dimension feature space for processing. To achieve a fair comparison in SVM and GPR models, a value of regularization parameter (C = 0.52) in

SVM and Gaussian noise (0.3) in GPR is established and Pearson VII Function kernel (PUK) function is chosen based on modeling performance. The parameter σ controls Pearson width and ω is a tailing factor of the peak in PUK that must be determined based on prediction precision. Both SVM and GPR techniques are used to tune the models for these kernel-specific parameters. Calibration of models in M5P was accomplished by changing the value of the number of instances allowed at each node. The selected primary hyperparameters of the modeling approaches are presented in Table 3.

Table 3. Optimized hyperparameters.

Algorithm	Function	Hyperparameters	Optimal Value
GPR	PUK kernel	Noise	0.3
		σ	0.4
		ω	0.4
SVM	PUK kernel	C	0.52
		σ	1
		ω	1
M5P	-	Instances	4

3.2. Model Performance Evaluation

In the field of ML, models must be evaluated in order to validate the performance of learned models. Different models employ various evaluation methodologies. Following the development of ML models for R-value prediction, the next critical step is to assess the predictive ability of the built ML models. The accuracy of the applied ML models' prediction of R-value was confirmed in this work by comparing the predicted and measured values of R. Figure 3 depicts the comparison of the predicted and measured R-value values in the training, testing, and validation sets. All proposed models demonstrated very good predictive potential ($R^2 > 0.9$) in training, test, and validation stages with less dispersion, with the exception of the ANN model developed in literature displaying a slightly worse result (i.e., $R^2 = 0.87$) in the training stage. Figure 4 shows line graphs of the accuracy of the predicted R-value of different models in the training set, testing set, and validation set. The predicted R-value of the training set, test set, and validation set is in the range of 11.72–26.98, and the predicted value and actual value of the training set, test set, and validation set have a good fitting effect on the whole, with only a few points with large errors in the test set and validation set, e.g., in the test set, the measured value of R-value was about 11.70 and the predicted value was as high as 11.92. However, minor differences in individual data points have no effect on the GPR model's overall predictive ability, i.e., the GPR model can accurately estimate the R-value. The results show that all the models predicted R-value with a high level of accuracy. Table 4 presents performance measures of the developed models and the ANN model. In the training stage, all three models performed equally as well as the SVM model (such as $R^2 = 0.9999$, MAE = 0.0364, RSE = 0.0002, RMSE = 0.0560, RRMSE = 0.0030 and $\rho = 0.0015$) followed by M5P and GPR with parameters (such as $R^2 = 0.9999$, MAE = 0.0453, RSE = 0.0002 and RMSE = 0.05612, RRMSE = 0.0031 and $\rho = 0.0015$) and (such as $R^2 = 0.9999$, MAE = 0.0399, RSE = 0.0003, RMSE = 0.0592, RRMSE = 0.0032 and $\rho = 0.0016$), respectively. Similarly, in the testing stage, the SVM model holds best results (such as $R^2 = 0.9998$, MAE = 0.0056, RSE = 0.0004, RMSE = 0.0100, RRMSE = 0.0004, and $\rho = 0.0002$) and outclassed the GPR (such as $R^2 = 0.9998$, MAE = 0.0221, RSE = 0.0035, RMSE = 0.0287, RRMSE = 0.0012, and $\rho = 0.0006$) followed by M5P (such as $R^2 = 0.9947$, MAE = 0.0374, RMSE = 0.0106, RMSE = 0.0496, RRMSE = 0.0020, and $\rho = 0.0010$). The GPR performance measures had better characteristics: their R^2 value was high, while their MAE value, RSE value, RSME value, RRMSE value, and ρ were low in the validation stage.

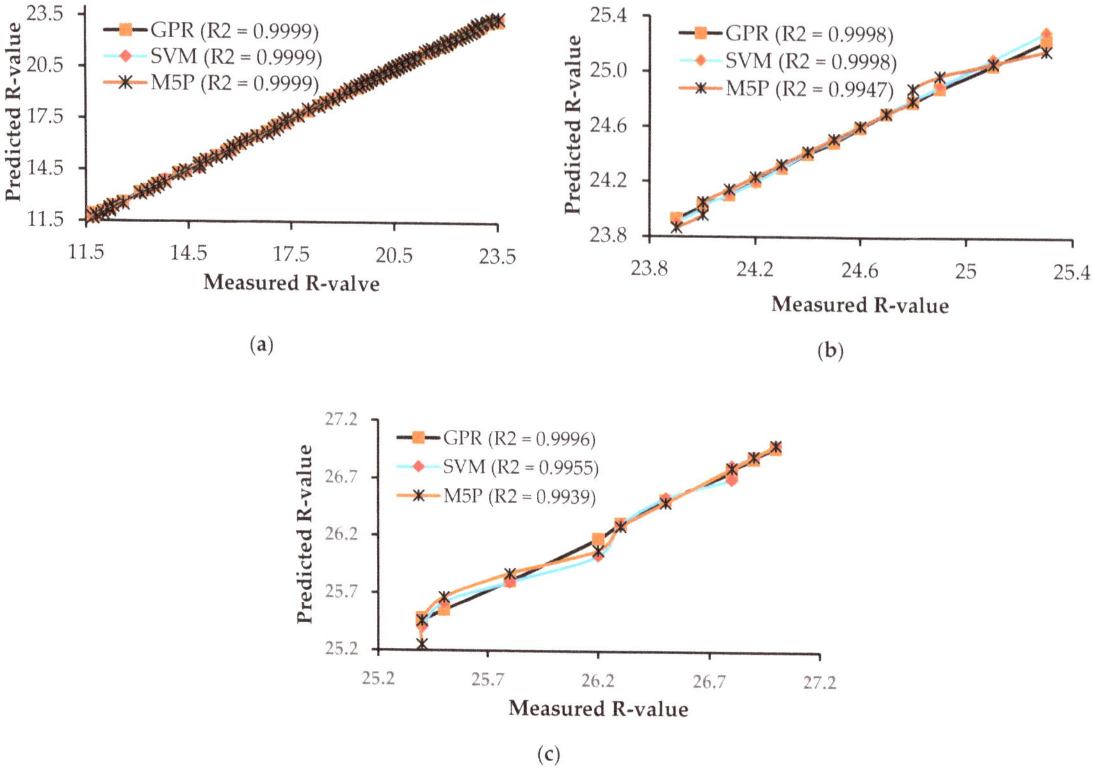

Figure 3. Comparison of measured R-value and predicted R-value in (**a**) training set, (**b**) testing set, and (**c**) validation set.

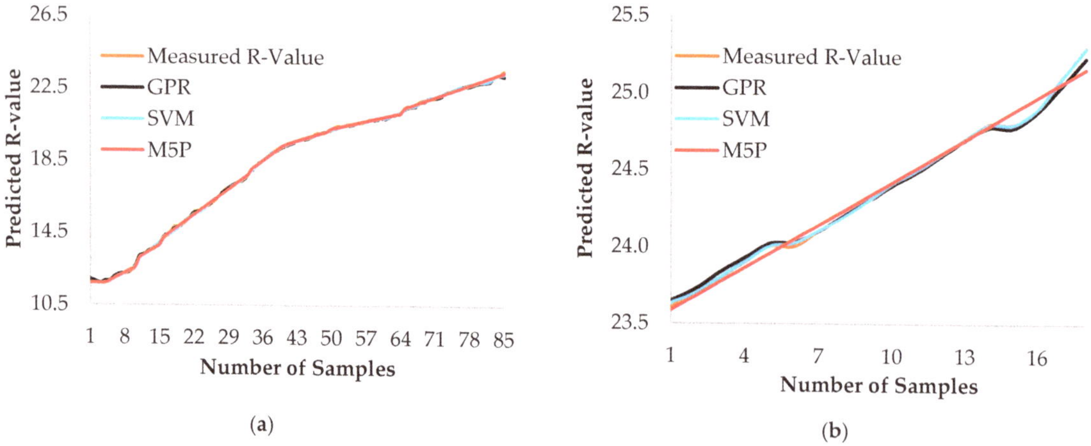

Figure 4. *Cont.*

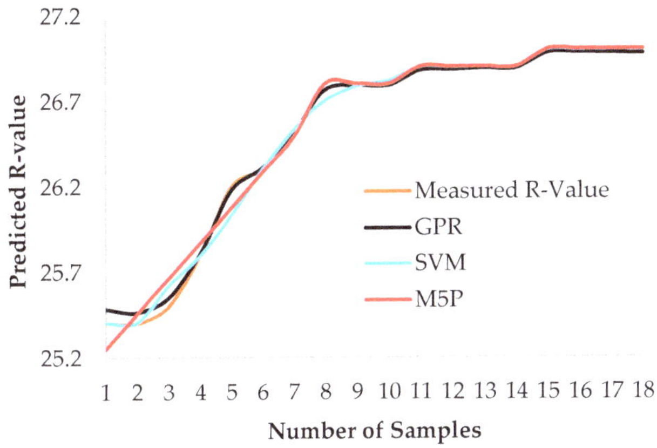

(c)

Figure 4. Line graphs showing accuracy of predicted R-value of different models in (**a**) training set, (**b**) testing set, and (**c**) validation set.

Table 4. Comparison of statistical parameters for performance evaluation of the GPR, SVM, M5P, and ANN models.

Dataset	Model	Statistical Parameters for Performance Evaluation						Reference
		R^2	MAE	RSE	RMSE	RRMSE	ρ	
Training	GPR	0.9999	0.0399	0.0003	0.0592	0.0032	0.0016	Present study
	SVM	0.9999	0.0364	0.0002	0.0560	0.0030	0.0015	
	M5P	0.9999	0.0453	0.0002	0.0562	0.0031	0.0015	
	ANN	0.8700	0.5700	0.0000	4.3200	0.2300	0.1200	[11]
Testing	GPR	0.9998	0.0221	0.0035	0.0287	0.0012	0.0006	Present study
	SVM	0.9998	0.0056	0.0004	0.0100	0.0004	0.0002	
	M5P	0.9947	0.0374	0.0106	0.0496	0.0020	0.0010	
	ANN	0.9900	0.3500	0.0096	4.9300	0.2000	0.1000	[11]
Validation	GPR	0.9996	0.0258	0.0032	0.0325	0.0012	0.0006	Present study
	SVM	0.9955	0.0268	0.0092	0.0551	0.0021	0.0010	
	M5P	0.9939	0.0325	0.0122	0.0636	0.0024	0.0012	
	ANN	0.9900	0.0380	0.0097	1.1900	0.0400	0.0200	[11]

In general, it can be stated that the proposed models are good for the prediction of the R-value, but the GPR model outperforms the SVM, M5P, and ANN models in the validation stage. The advantage of GPR over other models is that it has few parameters to tune and can thus be trained with a small training dataset [50]. The primary benefits of SVM is its ability to deal with overlearning and high dimensionality, which can lead to computational complexity and local extrema [51]. Furthermore, only a few hyperparameters must be tuned or adjusted, giving SVM a simple structure and ease of implementation [52]. However, because SVMs are sensitive to noise, their predictive ability endures when the dataset used is significantly noisy. Pruning in M5P can reduce tree size and the risk of overfitting [53]. Similarly, the ANN is computationally expensive and relies heavily on the capabilities of available hardware [54]. In comparison with previously published ANN model results [11], the results of this modeling study show that some data points are associated with very large model prediction errors (Figure 4), which can be attributed to the large deviations and high correlation between input and output variables of the data used (Table 2). As a result, it is suggested that these models (GPR, SVM, and M5P) be tested and validated on larger datasets with lower variable correlation for improved performance.

3.3. Rank Analysis

The simplest and most popular technique for evaluating the efficacy of constructed models and contrasting their robustness is rank analysis. The ideal values of the statistical parameters, which serve as the benchmark, are used to determine the score value in this study. Using one or more models is appropriate. The outcomes model with the best performance receives the highest score, and vice versa. It is possible that two models with similar results will have similar ranking ratings. The comparison of the testing stage results for the performance measures R^2, MAE, RSE, RMSE, RRMSE, and ρ is shown in Table 5. In addition, in this table, the ranking procedure proposed by Zorlu et al. [55] was used. The ranking system is very easy to understand. The most accurate performance index is ranked first in this system. According to Table 5, the model with the highest accuracy was GPR, which also had the highest rank value (i.e., 24). The SVM was the second most accurate model, with a total rank value of 18, followed by M5P, with a total rank value of 11. The least accurate was the ANN model, with a total rank value of 9.

Table 5. Modeling results for the validation set of GPR, M5P, and SVM, and ANN models.

Model	Performance Measures						Rank							Reference
	R^2	MAE	RSE	RMSE	RRMSE	ρ	R^2	MAE	RSE	RMSE	RRMSE	ρ	Total	
GPR	0.9996	0.0258	0.0032	0.0325	0.0012	0.0006	4	4	4	4	4	4	24	Present study
SVM	0.9955	0.0268	0.0092	0.0551	0.0021	0.0010	3	3	3	3	3	3	18	
M5P	0.9939	0.0325	0.0122	0.0636	0.0024	0.0012	2	2	1	2	2	2	11	
ANN	0.9900	0.038	0.0097	1.1900	0.0400	0.0200	3	1	2	1	1	1	9	[11]

3.4. Sensitivity Analysis

Sensitivity analysis is used to identify each input parameter's individual impact on the output parameter (i.e., R-value). To determine which of the seven input parameters—HARHA (X1), LL (X2), PL (X3), PI (X4), OMC (X5), A_C (X6), and MDD (X7)—had an impact on the anticipated R-value (Y), sensitivity analysis was used in this work. The goal of the sensitivity analysis was to identify the crucial input variable that has the greatest impact on the R-value. In this present study, the cosine amplitude method was used to determine the sensitivity analysis of the problem [56,57]. This method has been utilized in a number of studies [58–63], and it is stated as follows:

$$R_{ij} = \frac{\sum_{t=1}^{n}(y_{it} \times y_{ot})}{\sqrt{\sum_{t=1}^{n} {y_{it}}^2 \sum_{t=1}^{n} {y_{ot}}^2}} \tag{16}$$

where n is the number of data values (this study used 85 data values), y_{it} and y_{ot} are the input and output parameters. The R_{ij} value ranged from zero to one for each input parameter, and the highest R_{ij} values suggested the most efficient output parameter (which was R-value in this study). The findings of the sensitivity analysis, shown in Figure 5, show that the maximum and minimum relative strength effect on the R-value of soil was obtained for X7 (0.9964) and X4 (0.9375), respectively. The remaining input parameters have moderate effect on R-value of the soil. The greater the value of R_{ij}, the greater the effect of that particular input variable on output (i.e., R-value). Hence, the maximum dry density, MDD (X7), has the greatest influence, while the plasticity index, PI (X4), has the least influence in predicting R-value.

Taylor [64] introduced Taylor diagrams to visually demonstrate how closely an estimated output (or set of estimated outputs) matches observations. The correlation and standard deviation of the estimated and observed datasets are used to visualize them. It is particularly helpful when assessing numerous aspects of complex models or comparing the relative skill of numerous models (e.g., [65]). Therefore, a model's efficiency can further be evaluated by constructing a Taylor diagram (see Figure 6). The point (red) is the reference point for all developed models. The loser the developed models to the reference point, the greater will be the performance of the model. In our case, all the models are closer to the reference point, but more significantly, the GPR and SVM models have almost conceded totally to the reference point, indicating best prediction capabilities.

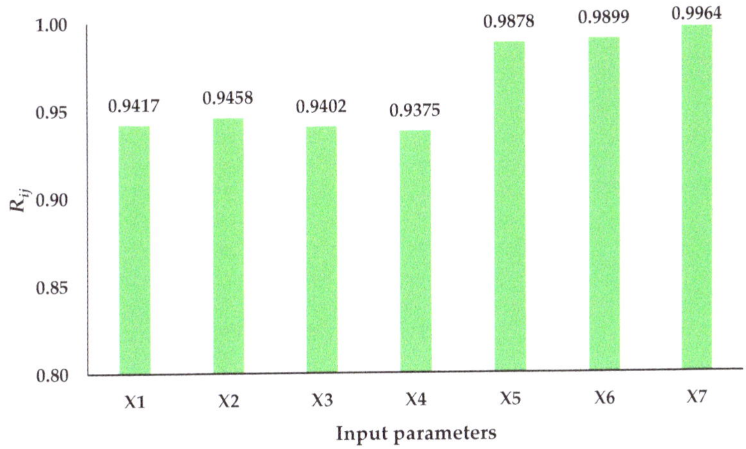

Figure 5. Relative strength effect of input parameters in predicting R-value.

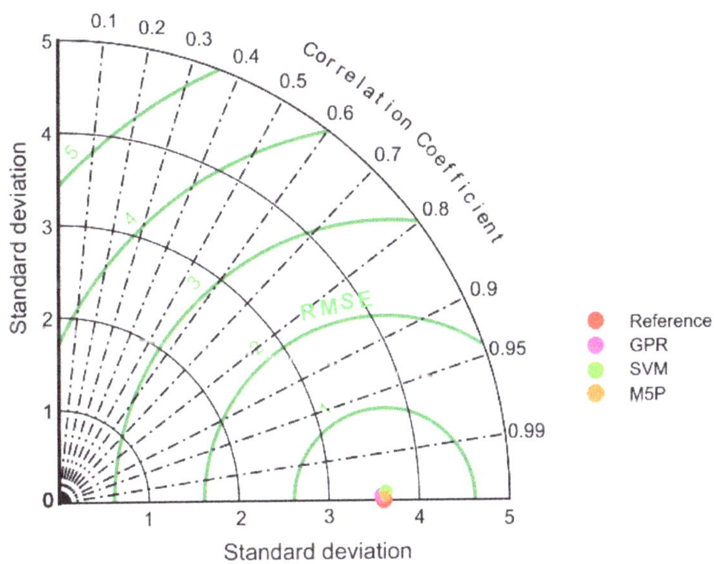

Figure 6. Taylor diagram of GPR, SVM, and M5P predicted models.

The proposed models of GPR, SVM and M5P can efficiently predict the R-value of the subgrade. This is strictly limited to the range of parameter values that was used to train and develop the model. The predicted accuracy of the model is also strictly dependent on the distribution of the parameter values and significantly affected by the parameter values used for training and development. For instance, the provided proportion of HARHA must be limited to 0–12%. In simple words, this provides the accuracy of the particular developed model.

4. Conclusions

In this study, three machine-learning models (i.e., GPR, M5P, and SVM) were used to predict R-value. The predictive capabilities of the aforementioned models were evaluated using statistical measure criteria of R^2, MAE, RSE, RMSE, RRMSE and ρ. In order to assess robustness, the proposed models were also evaluated with an ANN model from the literature. The ML models developed in this research study performed well in the validation stage, but the GPR model (R^2 = 0.9996, MAE = 0.0258, RSE = 0.0032, RMSE = 0.0012, RRMSE = 0.0012, and ρ = 0.0006) was the most viable when compared to other machine-learning models. Statistical analysis revealed that the GPR model shows enhancement in model accuracy by minimizing the error difference between measured and predicted values. Sensitivity analysis revealed that maximum dry density, MDD (X7) has the highest R_{ij} values, showing that this particular input parameter has greater effect in predicting the R-value. It can therefore be inferred that the GPR model is a promising method for predicting R-value, which can be extended to predict other significant basic subgrade stiffness/strength characterizations, such as California bearing ratio or resilient modulus. Thus, the application of GPR in the field of predicting the subgrade physical properties is appropriate, and can be seen as an alternative and suitable approach. For a better understanding and prediction of the R-value, several artificial intelligence techniques, such as fuzzy logic and recurrent neural network response surface methodology, may also be used. Furthermore, more experimental data should be gathered in future studies in order to enhance the performance outcomes of prediction models.

Author Contributions: Conceptualization, M.A., R.A.A.-M. and S.L.I.; Formal analysis, M.A., S.K., A.M. and F.A.; Funding acquisition, S.L.I.; Investigation, M.A., R.A.A.-M., S.K. and A.M.; Methodology, M.A., R.A.A.-M., S.L.I. and S.K.; Project administration, R.A.A.-M. and S.L.I.; Resources, R.A.A.-M. and S.K.; Software, M.A., S.L.I., A.M. and F.A.; Supervision, R.A.A.-M.; Validation, F.A.; Visualization, S.K. and A.M.; Writing—original draft, M.A. and F.A.; Writing—review & editing, B.T.A., S.K. and A.M. All authors have read and agreed to the published version of the manuscript.

Funding: This research received no external funding.

Data Availability Statement: The data used to support the findings of this study are included within the article.

Acknowledgments: The authors wish to express their appreciation to the International Islamic University Malaysia for supporting this study and making it possible. The authors would also like to thank the Deanship of Scientific Research at Umm Al-Qura University for supporting this work by Grant Code: 22UQU4390001DSR05.

Conflicts of Interest: The authors declare no conflict of interest.

Appendix A

Table A1. Data for prediction modeling of R-value.

S. No.	X1 (%)	X2 (%)	X3 (%)	X4 (%)	X5 (%)	X6	X7 (g/cm^3)	R-value	GPR	M5P	SVM
1	0	66	21	45	16	2	1.25	11.7	11.9	11.7	11.7
2	0.1	66	21	45	16	1.98	1.25	11.7	11.8	11.7	11.7
3	0.2	65.7	20.9	44.8	16.1	1.96	1.27	11.7	11.7	11.7	11.7
4	0.3	65.6	20.9	44.7	16.3	1.96	1.27	11.7	11.8	11.7	11.7
5	0.4	65.3	20.8	44.5	16.3	1.93	1.28	11.8	11.9	11.8	11.8
6	0.5	65	21	44	16.4	1.9	1.30	12	12.1	12	12
7	0.6	64.8	20.8	44	16.4	1.88	1.31	12.2	12.2	12.1	12.2
8	0.7	64.5	20.8	43.7	16.45	1.88	1.31	12.2	12.2	12.3	12.2
9	0.8	64.1	20.8	43.3	16.47	1.87	1.33	12.3	12.4	12.4	12.4
10	0.9	63.5	20.9	42.6	16.49	1.85	1.33	12.6	12.6	12.5	12.6
11	1	63	21	42	16.5	1.8	1.35	13.1	13.2	13.1	13.1

Table A1. *Cont.*

S. No.	X1 (%)	X2 (%)	X3 (%)	X4 (%)	X5 (%)	X6	X7 (g/cm^3)	R-value	GPR	M5P	SVM
12	1.1	62.5	20.6	41.9	16.6	1.8	1.35	13.3	13.3	13.3	13.3
13	1.2	62.1	20.3	41.8	16.7	1.81	1.36	13.5	13.5	13.5	13.5
14	1.3	61.9	20.2	41.7	16.8	1.8	1.37	13.6	13.7	13.6	13.7
15	1.4	61.7	20.1	41.6	17	1.81	1.38	13.8	13.9	13.8	13.9
16	1.5	61.5	20	41.5	17.2	1.8	1.38	14.2	14.3	14.2	14.3
17	1.6	61.4	20	41.4	17.2	1.8	1.39	14.4	14.4	14.5	14.4
18	1.7	61.3	20	41.3	17.3	1.79	1.39	14.8	14.7	14.7	14.6
19	1.8	61.3	20.1	41.2	17.5	1.81	1.40	14.8	14.9	14.9	14.8
20	1.9	61.2	20.1	41.1	17.7	1.8	1.41	15	15.1	15.1	15.1
21	2	61	20	41	17.8	1.8	1.41	15.3	15.3	15.3	15.3
22	2.1	60.9	19.9	41	17.9	1.8	1.42	15.6	15.6	15.5	15.5
23	2.2	60.7	19.7	41	17.9	1.8	1.42	15.7	15.7	15.7	15.6
24	2.3	60.6	19.6	41	18	1.8	1.43	15.8	15.8	15.9	15.8
25	2.4	60.4	19.4	41	18.2	1.8	1.43	16	16	16.1	16.1
26	2.5	60	19	41	18.3	1.8	1.43	16.2	16.3	16.3	16.3
27	2.6	59.8	19	40.8	18.35	1.79	1.44	16.5	16.5	16.5	16.5
28	2.7	59.7	19.1	40.6	18.4	1.77	1.45	16.8	16.8	16.7	16.7
29	2.8	59.5	19.1	40.4	18.45	1.75	1.46	17	17	16.9	16.9
30	2.9	59.2	19	40.2	18.5	1.72	1.46	17.1	17.2	17.1	17.1
31	3	59	19	40	18.5	1.7	1.46	17.3	17.3	17.3	17.3
32	3.1	58.8	19.2	39.6	18.55	1.7	1.47	17.4	17.4	17.5	17.5
33	3.2	58.4	18.9	39.5	18.6	1.7	1.48	17.7	17.7	17.7	17.7
34	3.3	57.9	19.1	38.8	18.7	1.71	1.48	18	18	18.1	18
35	3.4	57.4	19	38.4	18.75	1.69	1.48	18.3	18.3	18.3	18.3
36	3.5	57	19	38	18.8	1.7	1.49	18.5	18.5	18.5	18.5
37	3.6	56.8	18.9	37.9	18.85	1.69	1.50	18.7	18.7	18.7	18.7
38	3.7	56.7	19	37.7	18.9	1.65	1.51	18.9	18.9	18.9	18.9
39	3.8	56.5	18.9	37.6	18.93	1.64	1.51	19.1	19.1	19.1	19.1
40	3.9	56.3	19	37.3	18.98	1.61	1.52	19.2	19.2	19.3	19.3
41	4	56	19	37	19	1.6	1.52	19.4	19.4	19.4	19.4
42	4.1	55.7	19	36.7	19	1.59	1.53	19.5	19.5	19.5	19.5
43	4.2	54.9	18.7	36.2	19	1.57	1.54	19.6	19.6	19.6	19.6
44	4.3	54.1	18.5	35.6	19	1.55	1.55	19.7	19.7	19.7	19.7
45	4.4	53.6	18.4	35.2	19	1.52	1.56	19.7	19.7	19.8	19.7
46	4.5	53	18	35	19	1.5	1.57	19.8	19.8	19.8	19.8
47	4.6	52.8	18	34.8	18.98	1.5	1.58	20	19.9	19.9	19.9
48	4.7	52.7	18	34.7	18.96	1.5	1.59	20	20	20	20
49	4.8	52.6	18.1	34.5	18.93	1.5	1.60	20.1	20.1	20.1	20.1
50	4.9	52.3	18	34.3	18.91	1.5	1.61	20.2	20.2	20.3	20.2
51	5	52	18	34	18.9	1.5	1.61	20.4	20.3	20.3	20.3
52	5.1	51.5	17.7	33.8	18.88	1.48	1.62	20.4	20.4	20.4	20.4
53	5.2	51.1	17.7	33.4	18.86	1.46	1.63	20.5	20.5	20.5	20.5
54	5.3	50.8	18.1	32.7	18.84	1.43	1.64	20.5	20.5	20.5	20.5
55	5.4	50.3	18	32.3	18.82	1.41	1.65	20.6	20.6	20.6	20.6
56	5.5	50	18	32	18.8	1.4	1.65	20.6	20.6	20.6	20.6
57	5.6	49.9	18	31.9	18.78	1.4	1.66	20.7	20.7	20.7	20.7
58	5.7	49.6	17.9	31.7	18.75	1.41	1.67	20.8	20.8	20.8	20.8
59	5.8	49.4	17.9	31.5	18.71	1.42	1.67	20.8	20.8	20.8	20.8
60	5.9	49.1	17.7	31.4	18.65	1.41	1.68	20.9	20.9	20.9	20.9
61	6	49	18	31	18.6	1.4	1.69	20.9	20.9	21	20.9
62	6.1	48.6	17.8	30.8	18.55	1.38	1.70	21	21	21	21
63	6.2	48.3	17.6	30.7	18.48	1.37	1.71	21.1	21.1	21.1	21.1
64	6.3	47.7	17.3	30.4	18.6	1.35	1.72	21.2	21.2	21.1	21.2
65	6.4	47.2	17	30.2	18.44	1.33	1.73	21.4	21.4	21.5	21.4
66	6.5	47	17	30	18.4	1.3	1.74	21.5	21.5	21.6	21.5
67	6.6	46.8	17.1	29.7	18.4	1.31	1.75	21.6	21.6	21.7	21.6
68	6.7	46.5	16.8	29.7	18.41	1.31	1.76	21.8	21.7	21.8	21.7
69	6.8	45.6	15.9	29.7	18.4	1.3	1.77	21.9	21.8	21.9	21.9

Table A1. *Cont.*

S. No.	X1 (%)	X2 (%)	X3 (%)	X4 (%)	X5 (%)	X6	X7 (g/cm^3)	R-value	GPR	M5P	SVM
70	6.9	45.2	15.9	29.3	18.41	1.3	1.78	22	22	21.9	22
71	7	45	16	29	18.4	1.3	1.78	22	22	22	22.1
72	7.1	44.8	16.3	28.5	18.39	1.29	1.79	22.1	22.1	22.1	22.2
73	7.2	44.3	16.1	28.2	18.37	1.27	1.80	22.3	22.3	22.2	22.3
74	7.3	43.7	15.9	27.8	18.35	1.26	1.81	22.4	22.4	22.3	22.4
75	7.4	43.4	16	27.4	18.32	1.23	1.83	22.5	22.5	22.4	22.5
76	7.5	43	16	27	18.3	1.2	1.84	22.6	22.6	22.5	22.6
77	7.6	42.8	15.9	26.9	18.29	1.19	1.85	22.7	22.7	22.6	22.7
78	7.7	42.4	16	26.4	18.28	1.18	1.86	22.8	22.7	22.7	22.8
79	7.8	41.8	15.4	26.4	18.26	1.16	1.87	22.8	22.8	22.8	22.8
80	7.9	41.5	15.4	26.1	18.23	1.14	1.87	22.9	22.9	22.9	22.9
81	8	41	15	26	18.2	1.13	1.88	22.9	22.9	23	22.9
82	8.1	40.7	14.9	25.8	18.2	1.12	1.88	23	22.9	23.1	23
83	8.2	40.3	15	25.3	18.2	1.11	1.89	23.2	23.2	23.2	23.2
84	8.3	39.8	15.1	24.7	18.2	1.11	1.90	23.3	23.3	23.3	23.3
85	8.4	39.3	15	24.3	18.21	1.1	1.90	23.5	23.2	23.4	23.4
86	8.5	39	15	24	18.2	1	1.91	23.6	23.6	23.6	23.6
87	8.6	38.8	15	23.8	18.2	1	1.92	23.7	23.7	23.7	23.7
88	8.7	38.3	14.9	23.4	18.2	1	1.93	23.8	23.8	23.8	23.8
89	8.8	37.9	15.2	22.7	18.2	1	1.94	23.9	23.9	23.9	23.9
90	8.9	37.5	15.2	22.3	18.2	1	1.95	24	24	24	24
91	9	37	15	22	18.2	1	1.96	24	24	24	24
92	9.1	37	15	22	18.19	1	1.96	24.1	24.1	24.1	24.1
93	9.2	37	15	22	18.18	1	1.96	24.2	24.2	24.2	24.2
94	9.3	37	15	22	18.16	1	1.97	24.3	24.3	24.3	24.3
95	9.4	37	15	22	18.13	1	1.97	24.4	24.4	24.4	24.4
96	9.5	37	15	22	18.1	1	1.97	24.5	24.5	24.5	24.5
97	9.6	36.8	15.1	21.7	18	0.99	1.97	24.6	24.6	24.6	24.6
98	9.7	36.7	15.1	21.6	17.92	0.98	1.97	24.7	24.7	24.7	24.7
99	9.8	36.5	15.1	21.4	17.93	0.97	1.98	24.8	24.8	24.8	24.8
100	9.9	36.3	15.2	21.1	17.91	0.94	1.98	24.8	24.8	24.9	24.8
101	10	36	15	21	17.9	0.9	1.98	24.9	24.9	25	24.9
102	10.1	35.7	14.9	20.8	17.88	0.88	1.98	25.1	25.1	25.1	25.1
103	10.2	35.5	15.1	20.4	17.84	0.86	1.98	25.3	25.2	25.2	25.3
104	10.3	34.6	14.9	19.7	17.79	0.84	1.98	25.4	25.5	25.3	25.4
105	10.4	33.3	14	19.3	17.73	0.82	1.99	25.4	25.5	25.5	25.4
106	10.5	33	14	19	17.7	0.8	1.99	25.5	25.6	25.7	25.6
107	10.6	32.8	14	18.8	17.7	0.79	1.99	25.8	25.8	25.9	25.8
108	10.7	32.4	13.9	18.5	17.71	0.78	1.99	26.2	26.2	26.1	26
109	10.8	31.5	13.9	17.6	17.71	0.75	1.99	26.3	26.3	26.3	26.3
110	10.9	31.1	14	17.1	17.7	0.72	1.99	26.5	26.5	26.5	26.5
111	11	31	14	17	17.7	0.7	1.99	26.8	26.8	26.8	26.7
112	11.1	30.7	13.9	16.8	17.68	0.7	1.99	26.8	26.8	26.8	26.8
113	11.2	30.3	13.7	16.6	17.63	0.71	1.99	26.8	26.8	26.8	26.8
114	11.3	29.8	13.4	16.4	17.57	0.71	1.99	26.9	26.9	26.9	26.9
115	11.4	29.4	13.2	16.2	17.53	0.71	1.98	26.9	26.9	26.9	26.9
116	11.5	29	13	16	17.5	0.7	1.97	26.9	26.9	26.9	26.9
117	11.6	28.7	12.8	15.9	17.5	0.69	1.97	26.9	26.9	26.9	26.9
118	11.7	28.5	13	15.5	17.4	0.67	1.96	27	27	27	27
119	11.8	27.8	13	14.8	17.3	0.65	1.96	27	27	27	27
120	11.9	27.6	13.2	14.4	17.2	0.62	1.95	27	27	27	27
121	12	27	13	14	17.1	0.6	1.95	27	27	27	27

References

1. American Association of State Highway and Transportation Officials (AASHTO). *Standard Method of Test for Resistance R-Value and Expansion Pressure of Compacted Soils*; Transportation Research Board: Washington, DC, USA, 2002.
2. Bandara, N.; Rowe, G.M. Design subgrade resilient modulus for Florida subgrade soils. In *Resilient Modulus Testing for Pavement Components*; ASTM International: West Conshohocken, PA, USA, 2003.
3. Khazanovich, L.; Celauro, C.; Chadbourn, B.; Zollars, J.; Dai, S. Evaluation of subgrade resilient modulus predictive model for use in mechanistic–empirical pavement design guide. *Transp. Res. Rec.* **2006**, *1947*, 155–166. [CrossRef]
4. Onyelowe, K.C.; Onyia, M.E.; Onyelowe, F.D.A.; Van, D.B.; Salahudeen, A.B.; Eberemu, A.O.; Osinubi, K.J.; Amadi, A.A.; Onukwugha, E.; Odumade, A.O. Critical state desiccation induced shrinkage of biomass treated compacted soil as pavement foundation. *Építöanyag* **2020**, *72*, 40–47. [CrossRef]
5. Onyelowe, K.C.; Bui Van, D.; Ubachukwu, O.; Ezugwu, C.; Salahudeen, B.; Nguyen Van, M.; Ikeagwuani, C.; Amhadi, T.; Sosa, F.; Wu, W. Recycling and reuse of solid wastes; a hub for ecofriendly, ecoefficient and sustainable soil, concrete, wastewater and pavement reengineering. *Int. J. Low-Carbon Technol.* **2019**, *14*, 440–451. [CrossRef]
6. Tarefder, R.A.; Saha, N.; Hall, J.W.; Ng, P.T. Evaluating weak subgrade for pavement design and performance prediction: A case study of US 550. *J. GeoEngineer.* **2008**, *3*, 13–24.
7. Rehman, Z.; Khalid, U.; Farooq, K.; Mujtaba, H. Prediction of CBR value from index properties of different soils. *Technol. J. Univ. Eng. Technol. (UET)* **2017**, *22*, 17–26.
8. Officials, T. *New Mexico Department of Transportation (NMDOT), Standard Specifications for Highway and Bridge Construction. Section 200–600, New Mexico DOT*; Aashto: Washington, DC, USA, 2004.
9. Kişi, Ö.; Uncuoğlu, E. Comparison of three back-propagation training algorithms for two case studies. *Indian J. Eng. Mater. Sci.* **2005**, *12*, 434–442.
10. Van, D.B.; Onyelowe, K.C.; Van-Nguyen, M. Capillary rise, suction (absorption) and the strength development of HBM treated with QD base geopolymer. *Int. J. Pavement Res. Technol.* **2018**, *4*, 759–765.
11. Onyelowe, K.C.; Iqbal, M.; Jalal, F.E.; Onyia, M.E.; Onuoha, I.C. Application of 3-algorithm ANN programming to predict the strength performance of hydrated-lime activated rice husk ash treated soil. *Multiscale Multidiscip. Modeling Exp. Des.* **2021**, *4*, 259–274. [CrossRef]
12. Froemelt, A.; Dürrenmatt, D.J.; Hellweg, S. Using data mining to assess environmental impacts of household consumption behaviors. *Environ. Sci. Technol.* **2018**, *52*, 8467–8478. [CrossRef]
13. Ahmad, M.; Tang, X.-W.; Qiu, J.-N.; Gu, W.-J.; Ahmad, F. A hybrid approach for evaluating CPT-based seismic soil liquefaction potential using Bayesian belief networks. *J. Cent. South Univ.* **2020**, *27*, 500–516.
14. Ahmad, M.; Tang, X.-W.; Qiu, J.-N.; Ahmad, F. Evaluating seismic soil liquefaction potential using bayesian belief network and C4. 5 decision tree approaches. *Appl. Sci.* **2019**, *9*, 4226. [CrossRef]
15. Ahmad, M.; Tang, X.; Qiu, J.; Ahmad, F.; Gu, W. LLDV-a Comprehensive Framework for Assessing the Effects of Liquefaction Land Damage Potential. In Proceedings of the 2019 IEEE 14th International Conference on Intelligent Systems and Knowledge Engineering (ISKE), Dalian, China, 14–16 November 2019; pp. 527–533.
16. Ahmad, M.; Tang, X.-W.; Qiu, J.-N.; Ahmad, F.; Gu, W.-J. A step forward towards a comprehensive framework for assessing liquefaction land damage vulnerability: Exploration from historical data. *Front. Struct. Civ. Eng.* **2020**, *14*, 1476–1491. [CrossRef]
17. Ahmad, M.; Tang, X.; Ahmad, F. Evaluation of Liquefaction-Induced Settlement Using Random Forest and REP Tree Models: Taking Pohang Earthquake as a Case of Illustration. In *Natural Hazards-Impacts, Adjustments & Resilience*; IntechOpen: London, UK, 2020.
18. Ahmad, M.; Al-Shayea, N.A.; Tang, X.-W.; Jamal, A.; M Al-Ahmadi, H.; Ahmad, F. Predicting the Pillar Stability of Underground Mines with Random Trees and C4. 5 Decision Trees. *Appl. Sci.* **2020**, *10*, 6486. [CrossRef]
19. Ahmad, M.; Kamiński, P.; Olczak, P.; Alam, M.; Iqbal, M.J.; Ahmad, F.; Sasui, S.; Khan, B.J. Development of Prediction Models for Shear Strength of Rockfill Material Using Machine Learning Techniques. *Appl. Sci.* **2021**, *11*, 6167. [CrossRef]
20. Noori, A.M.; Mikaeil, R.; Mokhtarian, M.; Haghshenas, S.S.; Foroughi, M. Feasibility of intelligent models for prediction of utilization factor of TBM. *Geotech. Geol. Eng.* **2020**, *38*, 3125–3143. [CrossRef]
21. Dormishi, A.; Ataei, M.; Mikaeil, R.; Khalokakaei, R.; Haghshenas, S.S. Evaluation of gang saws' performance in the carbonate rock cutting process using feasibility of intelligent approaches. *Eng. Sci. Technol. Int. J.* **2019**, *22*, 990–1000. [CrossRef]
22. Mikaeil, R.; Haghshenas, S.S.; Hoseinie, S.H. Rock penetrability classification using artificial bee colony (ABC) algorithm and self-organizing map. *Geotech. Geol. Eng.* **2018**, *36*, 1309–1318. [CrossRef]
23. Mikaeil, R.; Haghshenas, S.S.; Ozcelik, Y.; Gharehgheshlagh, H.H. Performance evaluation of adaptive neuro-fuzzy inference system and group method of data handling-type neural network for estimating wear rate of diamond wire saw. *Geotech. Geol. Eng.* **2018**, *36*, 3779–3791. [CrossRef]
24. Momeni, E.; Nazir, R.; Armaghani, D.J.; Maizir, H. Prediction of pile bearing capacity using a hybrid genetic algorithm-based ANN. *Measurement* **2014**, *57*, 122–131. [CrossRef]
25. Xie, C.; Nguyen, H.; Choi, Y.; Armaghani, D.J. Optimized functional linked neural network for predicting diaphragm wall deflection induced by braced excavations in clays. *Geosci. Front.* **2022**, *13*, 101313. [CrossRef]
26. Armaghani, D.J.; Mohamad, E.T.; Narayanasamy, M.S.; Narita, N.; Yagiz, S. Development of hybrid intelligent models for predicting TBM penetration rate in hard rock condition. *Tunnel. Undergr. Space Technol.* **2017**, *63*, 29–43. [CrossRef]

27. Guido, G.; Haghshenas, S.S.; Haghshenas, S.S.; Vitale, A.; Gallelli, V.; Astarita, V. Development of a binary classification model to assess safety in transportation systems using GMDH-type neural network algorithm. *Sustainability* **2020**, *12*, 6735. [CrossRef]
28. Morosini, A.F.; Haghshenas, S.S.; Haghshenas, S.S.; Choi, D.Y.; Geem, Z.W. Sensitivity Analysis for Performance Evaluation of a Real Water Distribution System by a Pressure Driven Analysis Approach and Artificial Intelligence Method. *Water* **2021**, *13*, 1116. [CrossRef]
29. Asteris, P.G.; Lourenço, P.B.; Roussis, P.C.; Adami, C.E.; Armaghani, D.J.; Cavaleri, L.; Chalioris, C.E.; Hajihassani, M.; Lemonis, M.E.; Mohammed, A.S. Revealing the nature of metakaolin-based concrete materials using artificial intelligence techniques. *Constr. Build. Mater.* **2022**, *322*, 126500. [CrossRef]
30. Hajihassani, M.; Armaghani, D.J.; Sohaei, H.; Mohamad, E.T.; Marto, A. Prediction of airblast-overpressure induced by blasting using a hybrid artificial neural network and particle swarm optimization. *Appl. Acoust.* **2014**, *80*, 57–67. [CrossRef]
31. Onyelowe, K.C.; Jalal, F.E.; Onyia, M.E.; Onuoha, I.C.; Alaneme, G.U. Application of gene expression programming to evaluate strength characteristics of hydrated-lime-activated rice husk ash-treated expansive soil. *Appl. Comput. Intell. Soft Comput.* **2021**, *2021*, 6686347. [CrossRef]
32. Onyelowe, K.; Salahudeen, A.B.; Eberemu, A.; Ezugwu, C.; Amhadi, T.; Alaneme, G. Oxides of carbon entrapment for environmental friendly geomaterials ash derivation. In *International Congress and Exhibition "Sustainable Civil Infrastructures"*; Springer: Berlin/Heidelberg, Germany, 2019; pp. 58–67.
33. Benesty, J.; Chen, J.; Huang, Y.; Cohen, I. Pearson correlation coefficient. In *Noise Reduction in Speech Processing*; Springer: Berlin/Heidelberg, Germany, 2009; pp. 1–4.
34. van Vuren, T. Modeling of transport demand–analyzing, calculating, and forecasting transport demand: By V. A. Profillidis and G. N. Botzoris, Amsterdam, Elsevier, 2018, 472 pp., $125 (paperback and ebook), eBook ISBN: 9780128115145, Paperback ISBN: 9780128115138. *Transp. Rev.* **2019**, *40*, 1–2. [CrossRef]
35. Black, W. A method of estimating the California bearing ratio of cohesive soils from plasticity data. *Geotechnique* **1962**, *12*, 271–282. [CrossRef]
36. Wang, J. An intuitive tutorial to Gaussian processes regression. *arXiv* **2020**, arXiv:2009.10862.
37. Cheng, M.-Y.; Huang, C.-C.; Roy, A.F.V. Predicting project success in construction using an evolutionary Gaussian process inference model. *J. Civ. Eng. Manag.* **2013**, *19*, S202–S211. [CrossRef]
38. Chou, J.-S.; Chiu, C.-K.; Farfoura, M.; Al-Taharwa, I. Optimizing the prediction accuracy of concrete compressive strength based on a comparison of data-mining techniques. *J. Comput. Civ. Eng.* **2011**, *25*, 242–253. [CrossRef]
39. Mahesh, P.; Deswal, S. Modelling pile capacity using gaussian process regression. *Comput. Geotech.* **2010**, *37*, 942–947.
40. Rasmussen, C.E. Gaussian processes in machine learning. In *Summer School on Machine Learning*; Springer: Berlin/Heidelberg, Germany, 2003; pp. 63–71.
41. Wang, Y.; Witten, I.H. *Induction of Model Trees for Predicting Continuous Classes*; University of Waikato, Department of Computer Science: Hamilton, New Zealand, 1996.
42. Quinlan, J.R. Learning with continuous classes. In Proceedings of the 5th Australian Joint Conference on Artificial Intelligence, Ai'92, Hobart, Australia, 16–18 November 1992; World Scientific: Singapore, 1992; pp. 343–348.
43. Tong, S.; Koller, D. Support vector machine active learning with applications to text classification. *J. Mach. Learn. Res.* **2001**, *2*, 45–66.
44. Asefa, T.; Kemblowski, M.; Urroz, G.; McKee, M. Support vector machines (SVMs) for monitoring network design. *Groundwater* **2005**, *43*, 413–422. [CrossRef]
45. Deka, P.C. Support vector machine applications in the field of hydrology: A review. *Appl. Soft Comput.* **2014**, *19*, 372–386.
46. Nguyen, L. Tutorial on support vector machine. *Appl. Comput. Math.* **2017**, *6*, 1–15.
47. Ahmad, M.; Ahmad, F.; Wróblewski, P.; Al-Mansob, R.A.; Olczak, P.; Kamiński, P.; Safdar, M.; Rai, P. Prediction of ultimate bearing capacity of shallow foundations on cohesionless soils: A gaussian process regression approach. *Appl. Sci.* **2021**, *11*, 10317. [CrossRef]
48. Despotovic, M.; Nedic, V.; Despotovic, D.; Cvetanovic, S. Evaluation of empirical models for predicting monthly mean horizontal diffuse solar radiation. *Renew. Sustain. Energy Rev.* **2016**, *56*, 246–260. [CrossRef]
49. Gandomi, A.H.; Roke, D.A. Assessment of artificial neural network and genetic programming as predictive tools. *Adv. Eng. Softw.* **2015**, *88*, 63–72. [CrossRef]
50. Faul, S.; Gregorcic, G.; Boylan, G.; Marnane, W.; Lightbody, G.; Connolly, S. Gaussian process modeling of EEG for the detection of neonatal seizures. *IEEE Trans. Biomed. Eng.* **2007**, *54*, 2151–2162. [CrossRef]
51. Tao, Z.; Huiling, L.; Wenwen, W.; Xia, Y. GA-SVM based feature selection and parameter optimization in hospitalization expense modeling. *Appl. Soft Comput.* **2019**, *75*, 323–332. [CrossRef]
52. Yin, X.; Hou, Y.; Yin, J.; Li, C. A novel SVM parameter tuning method based on advanced whale optimization algorithm. *J. Phys. Conf. Ser.* **2019**, *1237*, 022140. [CrossRef]
53. Ma, J.; Kim, H.M. Continuous preference trend mining for optimal product design with multiple profit cycles. *J. Mech. Des.* **2014**, *136*, 061002. [CrossRef]
54. Mijwel, M.M. Artificial Neural Networks Advantages and Disadvantages. 2018. Available online: https://www.linkedin.com/pulse/artificial-NeuralNetwork (accessed on 15 May 2022).

55. Zorlu, K.; Gokceoglu, C.; Ocakoglu, F.; Nefeslioglu, H.; Acikalin, S. Prediction of uniaxial compressive strength of sandstones using petrography-based models. *Eng. Geol.* **2008**, *96*, 141–158. [CrossRef]
56. Wu, X.; Kumar, V. *The Top Ten Algorithms in Data Mining*; CRC Press: Boca Raton, FL, USA, 2009.
57. Momeni, E.; Armaghani, D.J.; Hajihassani, M.; Amin, M.F.M. Prediction of uniaxial compressive strength of rock samples using hybrid particle swarm optimization-based artificial neural networks. *Measurement* **2015**, *60*, 50–63. [CrossRef]
58. Faradonbeh, R.S.; Armaghani, D.J.; Abd Majid, M.; Tahir, M.M.; Murlidhar, B.R.; Monjezi, M.; Wong, H. Prediction of ground vibration due to quarry blasting based on gene expression programming: A new model for peak particle velocity prediction. *Int. J. Environ. Sci. Technol.* **2016**, *13*, 1453–1464. [CrossRef]
59. Chen, W.; Hasanipanah, M.; Rad, H.N.; Armaghani, D.J.; Tahir, M. A new design of evolutionary hybrid optimization of SVR model in predicting the blast-induced ground vibration. *Eng. Comput.* **2019**, *37*, 1455–1471. [CrossRef]
60. Rad, H.N.; Bakhshayeshi, I.; Jusoh, W.A.W.; Tahir, M.; Foong, L.K. Prediction of flyrock in mine blasting: A new computational intelligence approach. *Nat. Resour. Res.* **2020**, *29*, 609–623.
61. Ahmad, M.H.J.-L.; Ahmad, F.; Tang, X.-W.; Amjad, M.; Iqbal, M.J.; Asim, M.; Farooq, A. Supervised Learning Methods for Modeling Concrete Compressive Strength Prediction at High Temperature. *Materials* **2021**, *14*, 1983. [CrossRef]
62. Ahmad, M.; Amjad, M.; Al-Mansob, R.A.; Kamiński, P.; Olczak, P.; Khan, B.J.; Alguno, A.C. Prediction of Liquefaction-Induced Lateral Displacements Using Gaussian Process Regression. *Appl. Sci.* **2022**, *12*, 1977. [CrossRef]
63. Amjad, M.; Ahmad, I.; Ahmad, M.; Wróblewski, P.; Kamiński, P.; Amjad, U. Prediction of pile bearing capacity using XGBoost algorithm: Modeling and performance evaluation. *Appl. Sci.* **2022**, *12*, 2126. [CrossRef]
64. Taylor, K.E. Summarizing multiple aspects of model performance in a single diagram. *J. Geophys. Res. Atmos.* **2001**, *106*, 7183–7192. [CrossRef]
65. Houghton, J.T.; Ding, Y.; Griggs, D.J.; Noguer, M.; van der Linden, P.J.; Dai, X.; Maskell, K.; Johnson, C. *Climate Change 2001: The Scientific Basis: Contribution of Working Group I to the Third Assessment Report of the Intergovernmental Panel on Climate Change*; Cambridge University Press: Cambridge, UK, 2001.

Σ mathematics

MDPI

Article

Residual Information in Deep Speaker Embedding Architectures

Adriana Stan

Department of Communications, Technical University of Cluj-Napoca, 400114 Cluj-Napoca, Romania; adriana.stan@com.utcluj.ro

Abstract: Speaker embeddings represent a means to extract representative vectorial representations from a speech signal such that the representation pertains to the speaker identity alone. The embeddings are commonly used to classify and discriminate between different speakers. However, there is no objective measure to evaluate the ability of a speaker embedding to disentangle the speaker identity from the other speech characteristics. This means that the embeddings are far from ideal, highly dependent on the training corpus and still include a degree of residual information pertaining to factors such as linguistic content, recording conditions or speaking style of the utterance. This paper introduces an analysis over six sets of speaker embeddings extracted with some of the most recent and high-performing deep neural network (DNN) architectures, and in particular, the degree to which they are able to truly disentangle the speaker identity from the speech signal. To correctly evaluate the architectures, a large multi-speaker parallel speech dataset is used. The dataset includes 46 speakers uttering the same set of prompts, recorded in either a professional studio or their home environments. The analysis looks into the intra- and inter-speaker similarity measures computed over the different embedding sets, as well as if simple classification and regression methods are able to extract several residual information factors from the speaker embeddings. The results show that the discriminative power of the analyzed embeddings is very high, yet across all the analyzed architectures, residual information is still present in the representations in the form of a high correlation to the recording conditions, linguistic contents and utterance duration. However, we show that this correlation, although not ideal, could still be useful in downstream tasks. The low-dimensional projections of the speaker embeddings show similar behavior patterns across the embedding sets with respect to intra-speaker data clustering and utterance outlier detection.

Keywords: speaker embeddings; x-vectors; deep representations; deep embeddings; speaker disentanglement; speaker recognition; residual information; neural architectures; deep learning; artificial intelligence

MSC: 68T01

Citation: Stan, A. Residual Information in Deep Speaker Embedding Architectures. *Mathematics* **2022**, *10*, 3927. https://doi.org/10.3390/math10213927

Academic Editor: Bo-Hao Chen

Received: 16 September 2022
Accepted: 19 October 2022
Published: 23 October 2022

1. Introduction

Recorded speech is an inherently complex signal including information related to the linguistic contents, prosodic or style factors (such as rhythm and intonation), as well as speaker characteristics (such as physiological traits, gender, ethnicity or social background). Humans have the ability to disentangle almost all of these factors and extract their abstractions, being able to reproduce and recognize similar patterns across spoken data from different sources. An essential part of the speech signal with a multitude of downstream applications is related to the disentanglement of the speaker identity. Such an accurate representation of the speaker identity would make it extremely useful in tasks such as speaker recognition and verification applications, text-to-speech synthesis and voice cloning [1], anonymization or generating new, unseen speaker identities [2]. There is already a large number of published works which focus on speaker discrimination, meaning that their task is to estimate if two or more acoustic signals pertain to the same speaker identity. However, in terms of accurately representing the speaker for generative processes (such as text-to-speech or voice cloning), to date, there are no published methods which can accurately solely represent the speaker identity and disregard other factors related to the acoustic signal, such as recording conditions or linguistic contents, although many of these applications use the derived representations as input or conditioning. It is therefore essential to perform an analysis of how well the current speaker representations model the speaker identity.

As a result, in this paper, the focus is on finding out how much *residual information* (i.e., not pertaining to the speaker identity) is present in various deep speaker embeddings. Six open source, easy-to-use, readily available implementations were selected. The implementations report the state-of-the-art results for speaker classification and diarization tasks. A first evaluation carried out in this work aimed at directly comparing the architectures' performances with respect to their intended use, i.e., speaker discrimination. The equal error rates (EER) and inter- and intra-speaker similarity measures were computed over a large multi-speaker parallel dataset. In the second step of the evaluation, the architectures' derived speaker embeddings were analyzed in terms of the amount of residual information present within them, such as the utterance duration, signal-to-noise ratio, linguistic contents and recording conditions. Simple classification and regression algorithms were employed in an attempt to extract this information from the representations. The results show that, to a large extent, the embeddings exhibit a high dependency on these factors, and as such, the speaker identity is not truly disentangled. Based on these initial results, we then attempted to explore if this residual information could still be useful in downstream tasks. The derived speaker embeddings were plotted in a low-dimensional representation to verify if they exhibit similar patterns with respect to clustering different recording sessions and background conditions, as well as to separate utterance outliers and ill-behaved speakers. Such information could be exploited for selecting the appropriate speakers and a set of samples for a text-to-speech synthesis system or data augmentation process in multi-speaker systems.

The **contributions** of this paper can be summarized as follows:

- Six of the most recent speaker embedding deep neural networks are directly compared with respect to their discriminative and generative characteristics;
- The analysis is carried out over a parallel dataset consisting of 46 speakers uttering the same prompts;
- The equal error rates (EER) and inter- and intra-speaker similarity measures for the six architectures are evaluated;
- Decision trees and light gradient boosting machine algorithms are employed to evaluate the amount of residual information present in the embeddings;
- Low-dimensional tSNE-based representations of the embedding space for the six architectures are evaluated in terms of outlier detection and intra-speaker data clustering.

The paper is organized as follows: Section 2 presents some of the previous studies which address the development of accurate speaker embeddings, as well as their use in voice cloning and text-to-speech synthesis systems. Section 3 describes the audio data and speaker embedding architectures adopted in this work. The results of the evaluation are shown in Section 4, while the conclusion and discussions are introduced in Section 5.

2. Related Work

Speaker recognition has been the focus of the research community for quite a long time now, as it is essential for identification, verification and diarization tasks. Speaker identification refers to determining the identity of a spoken utterance from a set of predefined speakers. Speaker verification aims to predict if two utterances pertain to the same speaker or not, while speaker diarization is targeted at separating the different speaker identities present in a larger audio clip and assigning each audio segment to the corresponding speaker. Although these three sub-tasks of speaker recognition seem different in principle, they all share the common component of extracting the numeric representations able to accurately depict individual speaker identities.

Some of the first methods for speaker recognition were based on spectral and template matching, commonly using Mel-Frequency Cepstral Coefficients [3,4], Linear Prediction

Coefficients (LPC) [5,6] or Perceptual Linear Prediction (PLP) Coefficients [7,8]. Starting with the 1990s, Gaussian Mixture Models (GMM) [9,10] became more prevalent. The models estimated the statistics of various speech signal representations for each individual speaker within the dataset. The verification or recognition was performed by computing the distance between the target speaker and each of the probability distribution functions within the GMMs set. With the addition of the Universal Background Model (UBM) [11] and Support Vector Machines (SVM) [12], the performances of speaker recognition methods kept improving. Yet, the evaluations were performed on small, curated, clean datasets and more than often in text-dependent scenarios. Dimensionality reduction techniques were subsequently applied so as to extract the axes of maximum variation among the speakers of interest. Within this area, Principal Component Analysis (PCA) [13] and i-vectors [14] rapidly gained popularity.

The major improvements in speaker recognition, as in many other application fields, came from the introduction of deep learning architectures able to abstractize the information present in the speech signal benefiting from a large amount of spoken data. The first step toward the DNN-based representations was simply to use the deep architecture's posterior probabilities instead of the GMM-based ones [15]. Similar to the PCA technique in traditional speaker recognition models, DNN-based bottleneck features became popular [16], being called d-vectors and extracted at the frame level. D-vectors are part of a larger category of DNN-based representations, called embeddings. X-vectors are also embeddings extracted with Time-Delay Neural Networks (TDNN) [17–19] at the segment level, and they became the standard method for speaker recognition applications. Some other deep architectures employed in speaker recognition are RawNet [20,21] and ResNet [22–24]. These types of embeddings are extracted in an end-to-end manner, meaning that the network is in charge of both finding adequate representations as well as determining the final decision related to the speaker-related task. Previous methods used either the Probabilistic Linear Discriminant Analysis (PLDA) or cosine similarity to estimate the similarities or dissimilarities between the output representations. Some recent studies even attempted to adapt other speech-based neural representations for speaker recognition [25]. An extended overview of the deep learning-based speaker embedding representations can be found in [26,27].

As more and more methods were published, a common evaluation benchmark was required to correctly compare their individual results. Several speaker recognition workshops and challenges have been organized, such as the NIST Speaker Recognition Evaluation (https://www.nist.gov/itl/iad/mig/speaker-recognition, accessed on 18 October 2022), Odyssey (http://www.odyssey2022.org/, accessed on 18 October 2022) or VoxSRC (https://www.robots.ox.ac.uk/~vgg/data/voxceleb/ interspeech2022.html, accessed on 18 October 2022). Within the 2022 VoxSRC challenge, there were two main tracks related to speaker verification (open and closed sets) and speaker diarization. The best performing systems included ResNet and ECAPA-TDNN architectures augmented with self-supervised learned (SSL) representations of the audio signal [28–31].

Although the methods described above are aimed solely at speaker recognition, verification and diarization applications, their findings can be applied to other speech-related tasks. One of the most important and widely used is that of speech synthesis and voice cloning. Speaker embeddings extracted from networks trained on a large number of speakers can be used to condition multi-speaker synthesis models. Using externally learned embeddings enables the models to perform a fast or zero-shot adaptation for unseen speakers [32–36]. And it is for these tasks that a more elaborate analysis of the embeddings' accuracy is extremely important.

3. Experimental Setup

3.1. Speech Data

A problematic part of the speaker embeddings' evaluation is the fact that the spoken data across the speakers may vary. This means that there is a possibility that the number and linguistic content of each speaker's utterance subset may influence the results. Therefore, in this study, we used one of the largest parallel spoken datasets available.

The dataset is the extended version of the SWARA corpus [37]. The initial version of the corpus—which will be referred to as SWARA1.0—includes 18 speakers recorded in a professional studio. Each speaker read aloud between 921 and 1493 utterances. This dataset was recently extended with an additional 28 speakers—we will refer to this subset as SWARA2.0. However, due to the COVID-19 pandemic, the recordings were performed in the speakers' home environments with semi-professional equipment. The speakers read between 1597 and 1797 utterances. As the SWARA2.0 was recorded in home conditions, we expect the background noise and reverberation to affect the performance of the embeddings extracted from this dataset.

In both SWARA1.0 and SWARA2.0 subsets, the speakers were provided with the same text prompts to be read aloud. However, due to the lack of control, especially in the SWARA2.0 scenario, only 712 utterances are truly parallel across all 46 speakers. This means that for the rest of the utterances, the speakers either made deletions, insertions or substitutions with respect to the prompt or did not record some of the prompts at all. There are 24 female speakers and 22 male speakers in the combined datasets, which amount to 32.752 utterances with a total duration of 38 h and 29 min. All data were resampled at 16 kHz and start and end silence segments were trimmed.

3.2. Speaker Embedding Networks

Numerous studies focused on extracting deep learning-based representations for speaker characteristics. Most of these studies are, of course, aimed at discriminating between speakers and performing accurate recognition and diarization tasks. For our evaluation, we targeted the DNN-based architectures which are open source, easily accessible and usable and also provide good pre-trained models. The following architectures were selected:

(1) **Pyannote** (https://github.com/pyannote/pyannote-audio, accessed on 18 October 2022) is an open-source toolkit written in Python for speaker diarization [38,39]. It uses a SincNet [40] architecture, followed by a series of TDNN layers and an average pooling layer. It also includes the implementations for Speech Brain and NeMo Titanet architectures, but we did not use them in this study.

(2) **Speech Brain's** [41] speaker verification network (https://github.com/speechbrain/speechbrain, accessed on 18 October 2022) is based on the ECAPA-TDNN [42] model. It includes a sequence of convolutional and residual blocks, using the additive margin softmax loss as training objective. The speaker embeddings are formed using attentive statistical pooling.

(3) **Clova AI** [22,23] uses a ResNet-like architecture, (https://github.com/clovaai/voxceleb_trainer, accessed on 18 October 2022) and similarly averages the frame-level representations in the final embeddings. The difference is in the change in objective function and the use of training data augmentation.

(4) **NeMo Titanet** (repository for all NeMo architectures is available here: https://github.com/NVIDIA/NeMo/, accessed on 18 October 2022) uses the Titanet architecture [43] which is based on ContextNet [44]. The model uses 1D depth-wise separable convolutions with squeeze-and-excitation layers. The output embeddings are obtained by averaging the statistics of the intermediate variable-length representations.

(5) **NeMo SpeakerNet** uses an ASR architecture's encoder, namely QuartzNet [45], as a high-level feature extractor and averages these features within a pooling layer so as to capture the time-independent speaker features.

(6) **NeMo ECAPA-TDNN** is similar to the Speech Brain architecture and uses the ECAPA-TDNN structure [46]. The difference is that, instead of the residual blocks, the NeMo implementation uses group convolution blocks of single dilation.

Because we aim to use the embeddings in speech synthesis systems, no fine-tuning was performed over the available pre-trained models. Fine-tuning would imply that any time a new dataset is used for synthesis, the embedding networks would need to be re-trained, which would not be feasible. Therefore, we explore the architecture's behavior as is and as their authors made them available for the wide research community.

4. Evaluation

We base our evaluation on a set of analyses which we consider relevant for the use of the speaker embeddings in downstream tasks, outside the speaker recognition or discrimination applications. The following subsections introduce the results of the evaluation scenarios.

4.1. EER, Intra- and Inter-Speaker Similarity

Being derived from neural architectures aimed at speaker recognition, thus in a discriminative-oriented task, the speaker embeddings' performance is commonly evaluated in terms of the equal error rate (EER). The EER is defined as the point on the ROC curve where the false acceptance rate (FAR) is equal to the false rejection rate (FRR). The threshold to compute the EER is generally based on the cosine similarity between pairs of speaker embeddings, defined as:

$$\cos(\mathbf{e}_1, \mathbf{e}_2) = \frac{\mathbf{e}_1\mathbf{e}_2}{\|\mathbf{e}_1\|\|\mathbf{e}_2\|} = \frac{\sum_{i=1}^{n} \mathbf{e}_{1,i}\mathbf{e}_{2,i}}{\sqrt{\sum_{i=1}^{n} (\mathbf{e}_{1,i})^2}\sqrt{\sum_{i=1}^{n} (\mathbf{e}_{2,i})^2}} \tag{1}$$

Because we are using a new speech dataset, it is essential to first evaluate the targeted performance of the selected architectures. Therefore, the first step of our analysis involved the computation of the EER results across the architectures, speakers and sets of speakers. A set of 46,000 random pairs of utterances were selected. The random pairs were chosen such that each speaker is present in 1000 pairs, of which 200 are same-speaker pairs. The EER results are shown in Table 1. We evaluate the results over the entire set of 46,000 pairs and separately for pairs containing only samples for the female speakers, male speakers, speakers from the SWARA1.0 subset and speakers from the SWARA2.0 subset. It can be noticed that all architectures achieve an EER below 1% and that female speakers are better discriminated than male speakers. The same is true for the SWARA1.0 speakers versus the SWARA2.0 speakers. The best results are obtained by the NeMo Titanet architecture.

Table 1. EER values for the different speaker embedding architectures and speaker subsets. Arrows mark the direction of best performance. Best results are highlighted in boldface.

Architecture	All↓	Female↓	Male↓	SWARA1.0↓	SWARA2.0↓
Pyannote	0.040	0.055	0.039	0.024	0.047
Speech Brain	0.025	0.027	0.031	0.011	0.031
Clova AI	0.055	0.060	0.081	0.031	0.073
NeMo Titanet	**0.018**	**0.014**	**0.027**	**0.005**	**0.024**
NeMo SpeakerNet	0.039	0.045	0.051	0.024	0.048
NeMo ECAPA-TDNN	0.032	0.035	0.041	0.023	0.038

NeMo Titanet is also the best performing architecture for each individual speaker (see Figure 1). However, speakers `bvl`, `mgl` and `pbl` have significantly higher EER values than the rest of the speakers. When analyzing these speakers' recordings, we noticed that indeed the background conditions are considerably poorer than for the other speakers and that, in some cases, the segmentation of the waveform is performed after or before the end of the utterance.

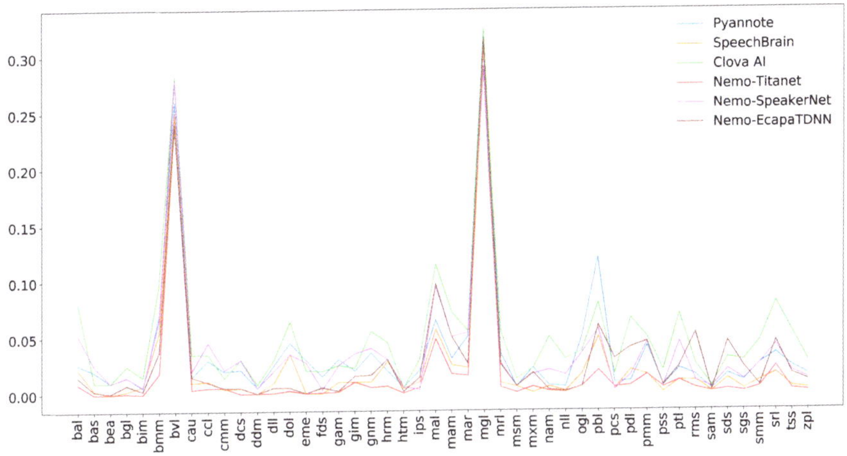

Figure 1. EER values for the individual speakers across the embedding architectures.

The EER gives the optimum threshold for which the FAR is equal to the FRR, but it does not detail the accuracy of the representation. For downstream tasks, the inter- and intra-speaker similarity measures would be more informative. This means that the discrimination between speakers can be translated into high intra-speaker similarity and low inter-speaker similarity, while any intermediate values should ideally represent perceptually similar speakers. The intra-speaker similarity values are presented in Figure 2. The similarity was computed over all pairs of utterances from the same speaker averaged by their number. It can be noticed that the Clova AI architecture exhibits the highest intra-speaker similarity measure, and that again, speakers `bvl`, `mgl` and `pbl` have the lowest intra-speaker similarity. The least performing architecture is Pyannote. In Table 2, we average the above scores at the system-level and also across the different speaker subsets. The Clova AI, Female and SWARA1.0 speakers exhibit the highest intra-speaker similarity measures.

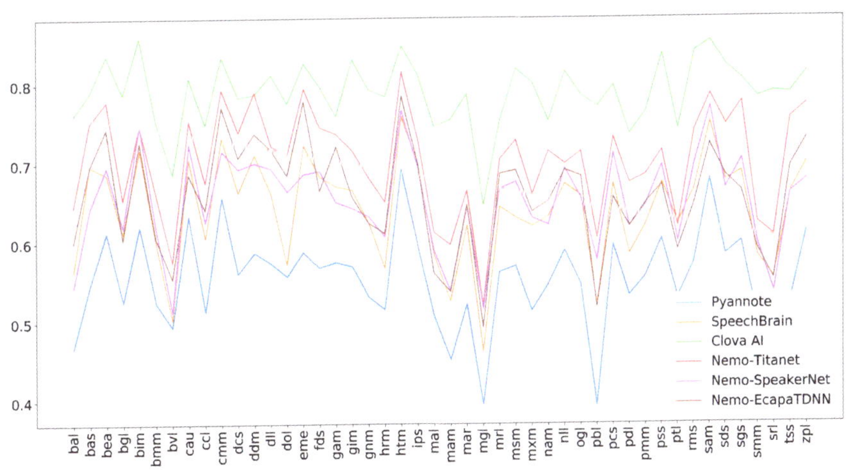

Figure 2. Intra-speaker cosine similarity for each speaker and embedding architecture.

Table 2. Average **intra-speaker** cosine similarity across the different speaker embedding architectures and different speaker subsets. Arrows mark the direction of best performance. Best results are highlighted in boldface.

Architecture	All↑	Female↑	Male↑	Swara1.0↑	Swara2.0↑
Pyannote	0.554	0.557	0.550	0.589	0.531
Speech Brain	0.640	0.651	0.629	0.686	0.610
Clova AI	**0.788**	**0.790**	**0.786**	**0.810**	**0.774**
NeMo Titanet	0.702	0.711	0.695	0.750	0.672
NeMo SpeakerNet	0.651	0.658	0.644	0.693	0.623
NeMo ECAPA-TDNN	0.658	0.670	0.647	0.696	0.635

For the inter-speaker similarity, we use the 46,000 random pairs of utterances used to evaluate the EER and select only those which pertain to different speaker identities. We then compute the average cosine similarities between each pair of speakers. In this scenario, we would expect the architectures to exhibit very low values so as to maximize the discriminative characteristics of the representation. In Table 3, we introduce these results averaged across the architectures and speaker subsets. Although NeMo Titanet seemed to show the best performance in the previous tasks, in terms of discriminative power, NeMo ECAPA-TDNN is the most efficient (with an exception for the inter-male speakers where Pyannote is best). We show the inter-speaker similarity matrix for the NeMo ECAPA-TDNN architecture in Figure 3. The closest speakers based on these scores are `htm` and `mar`, with a similarity of 0.42, followed by `cmm` and `cau` at a 0.40 similarity. These pairs are female speakers and do indeed have perceptually similar voices.

In this section, we looked at common measures to evaluate speaker embedding architectures while aiming to extract additional information that may be useful for downstream tasks. For example, inter-speaker similarity could be used to train speech synthesis systems in limited data scenarios, where data augmentation can be performed by using speech from a different, yet similar sounding speaker.

Table 3. Average **inter-speaker** cosine similarity across the different speaker embedding architectures and different speaker subsets. Arrows mark the direction of best performance. Best results are highlighted in boldface.

Architectures	All↓	Female↓	Male↓	Swara1.0↓	Swara2.0↓
Pyannote	0.127	0.195	**0.129**	0.139	0.127
Speech Brain	0.122	0.188	0.143	0.139	0.118
Clova AI	0.133	0.188	0.157	0.142	0.135
NeMo Titanet	0.132	0.187	0.156	0.143	0.135
NeMo SpeakerNet	0.195	0.272	0.226	0.199	0.198
NeMo ECAPA-TDNN	**0.107**	**0.151**	0.140	**0.136**	**0.110**

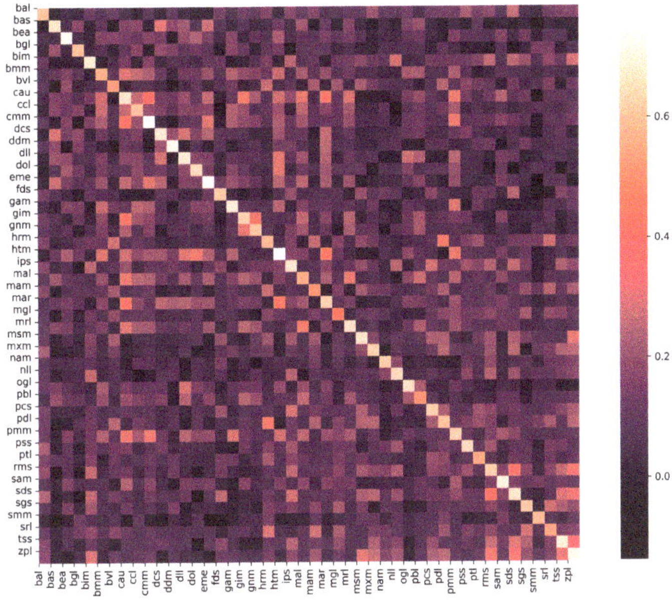

Figure 3. Inter-speaker similarity matrix for the NeMo ECAPA-TDNN architecture.

4.2. Speaker Identity Disentanglement

The previous set of results are definitely aimed at providing the best representation for speaker classification tasks. However, in many downstream applications of the speaker embeddings, this is not enough. And this is true especially in speech synthesis systems, where the embeddings are used as additional input, while information related to the linguistic content and prosodic patterns are the main inputs. Therefore, if information pertaining to other aspects of the speech is present in the embeddings, this can lead to unwanted effects and bias within the training procedure. Starting from the above statement, in this section, we want to explore how much residual information is present within the speaker embeddings, and thus if the speaker identity is truly disentangled from all other speech factors.

A simple method to determine the presence of residual information is to see if simple machine learning algorithms are able to extract this information from the embeddings. We adopt two separate algorithms, depending on the task: a decision tree for the classification tasks and a LightGBM [47] for the regression tasks. The two algorithms were chosen as they are some of the simplest, yet most powerful traditional machine learning methods, and their results are comparable across tasks and datasets. The same parameters were used across the tasks, and the speech dataset was randomly split into 80% training and 20% test sets.

Table 4 shows the results expressed in F1-scores for the classification of speaker gender and speaker identity. For these two targets, the results are supposed to be high, as the embeddings should incorporate this information. Two other targets shown in the table are the text length—expressed in number of characters—and the recording conditions. The recording condition is encoded as a binary classification for the two subsets, SWARA1.0 and SWARA2.0. For these two columns, the accuracy of the predictions should be limited, as information about these two targets should not be easily extracted from the embeddings. For the text length, the results are as expected, and the number of characters present in the utterance cannot be extracted from the embeddings. Yet, an interesting result occurs in the recording conditions column, where the prediction accuracy is rather high. This means that the additional spectral artefacts present in the home recordings are indeed influential for the final embeddings across all embedding architectures.

Table 4. F1-scores for various classification tasks. Arrows mark the direction of best performance. Best results are highlighted in boldface.

Architecture	Speaker ID↑	Gender↑	Utterance Duration↓	Recording Condition↓
Pyannote	0.76	0.94	0.016	**0.87**
Speech Brain	0.84	0.96	0.011	0.90
Clova AI	0.85	0.98	0.015	0.92
NeMo Titanet	**0.90**	**0.97**	**0.010**	0.95
NeMo SpeakerNet	0.85	0.96	0.014	0.91
NeMo ECAPA-TDNN	0.87	0.96	0.015	0.95

For the regression tasks, we look at the utterance duration (measured in seconds), the signal-to-noise ratio (SNR) and the linguistic contents. The SNR was computed with the WADA [48] algorithm. For the text contents, we are only looking at the utterance id, assuming that similar characteristics would be present across speaker embeddings for the same linguistic contents. The accuracy of the LightGBM is measured in terms of the Spearman Rank Correlation Coefficient (SRCC) of the predicted values versus the target values. Table 5 shows the results, and they are not encouraging. All the architectures show a high correlation factor (>0.7) with respect to the evaluated targets. This means that this type of information is not efficiently disentangled from the resulting speaker embedding.

A separate regression task looked into the prediction of the average F0 value at the utterance level (the last column in Table 5). The correlations are rather high and the average mean squared error for the six architectures is 12 Hz.

Table 5. LightGBM-based SRCC results for various regression tasks. Arrows mark the direction of best performance. Best results are highlighted in boldface.

Architecture	Utterance Duration↓	SNR↓	Linguistic Contents↓	F0↑
Pyannote	0.830	0.771	0.723	0.958
Speech Brain	0.734	0.749	0.742	0.959
Clova AI	0.750	0.791	0.734	**0.976**
NeMo Titanet	**0.704**	**0.747**	0.798	0.964
NeMo SpeakerNet	0.796	0.758	**0.709**	0.958
NeMo ECAPA-TDNN	0.862	0.787	0.775	0.962

The results in this section showed that although the task of the embedding architectures is to represent the speaker identity as accurately as possible, residual information is still present within them and that more work should be performed to find a more suitable representation for the downstream tasks. In the following section, we would like to explore how we can use this residual information to the benefit of other tasks by using visual representations of the embeddings.

4.3. Visual Representations

Visually examining high-dimensional data is not feasible. However, in most cases, visual representations of the data are more informative to the developer than just percentages and numbers. As such, we employed a t-SNE dimensionality reduction technique [49] and plotted the speaker embeddings obtained from the six architectures into a two-dimensional space. The algorithm was applied over the entire set of embeddings from each individual architecture, ran over 1000 steps and a perplexity of 30 was used. Figure 4 shows these t-SNE plots for each architecture. It can be noticed that, with some minor exceptions, the speakers are clustered nicely. Moreover, it does not seem that any of the speaker embedding architectures shows a better performance in terms of grouping the speakers. It appears that for some of the speakers, sub-clusters of the embeddings are formed, and in a few cases, outliers are to be observed. By examining the individual speech samples, we noticed that the outliers commonly pertain to the short utterances, reaffirming the previous result of the correlation between the embeddings and the duration of the audio. For the sub-clusters, most speakers recorded the entire set of prompts in at least two recording sessions. Between the sessions, there were differences in the background noise, distance from the microphone, speaking rhythm and vocal effort. The formed t-SNE clusters are indeed consistent with the different recording sessions. It can be noticed that these clusters are more common within the SWARA2.0 subset containing the home recordings. Among the different embedding architectures, it appears that all of them are able to detect these sub-clusters, while NeMo SpeakerNet and Pyannote seem to be more affected by the duration of the audio and present more outliers than the other systems. This means that these two architectures would be more suitable in pre-processing a speaker dataset for downstream applications.

However, when we zoom in on these low-dimension visualizations, we notice some interesting patterns. Figures 5 and 6 show the speaker-level t-SNE representations for the two data subsets, i.e., SWARA1.0 and SWARA2.0, respectively.

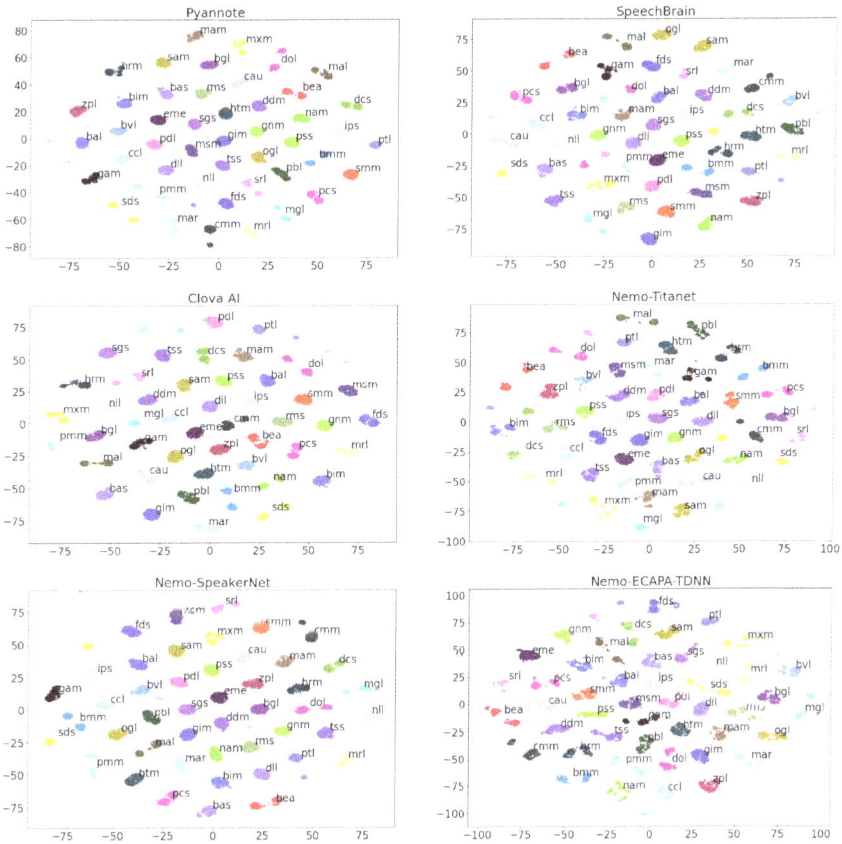

Figure 4. t-SNE representations of the speaker embeddings extracted from the different architectures.

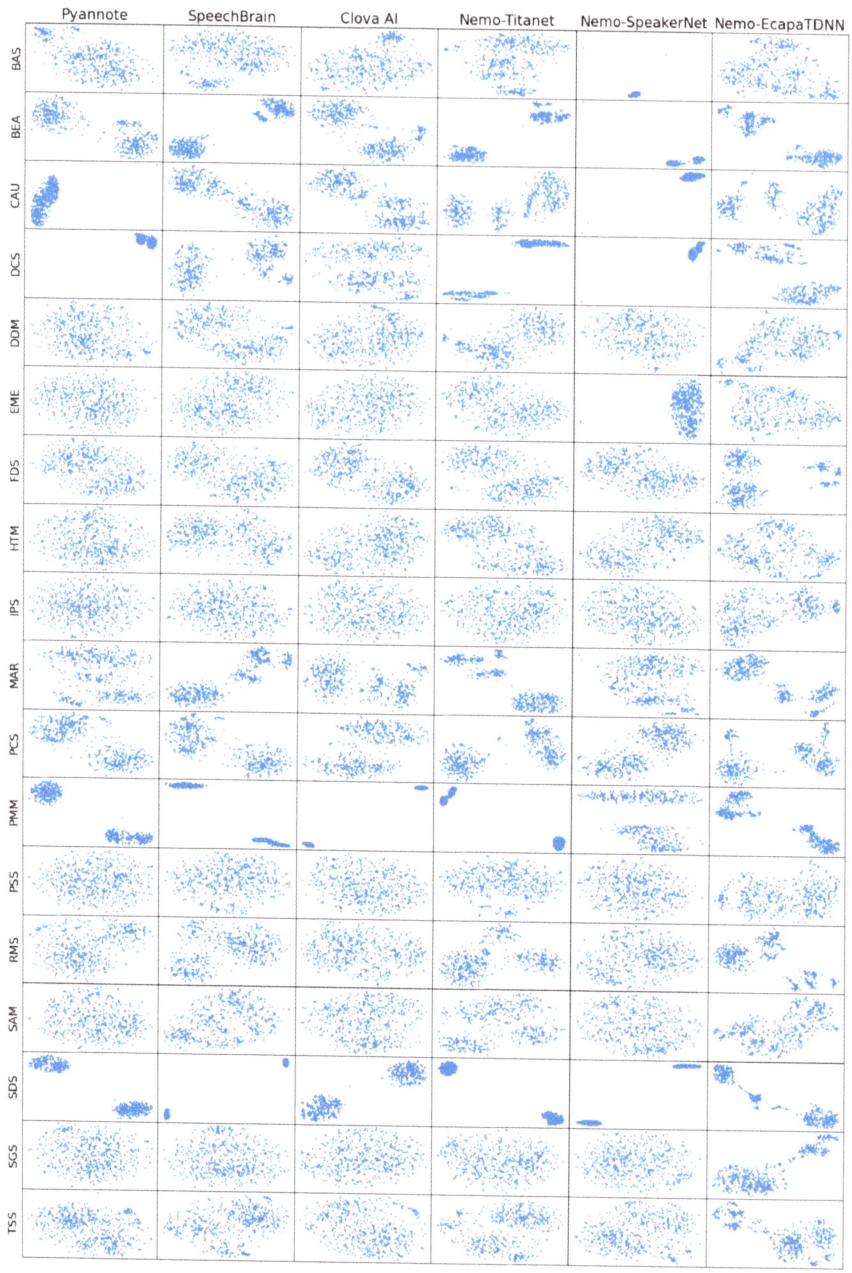

Figure 5. Speaker-level t-SNE plots of the different embedding architectures—**SWARA1.0** subset.

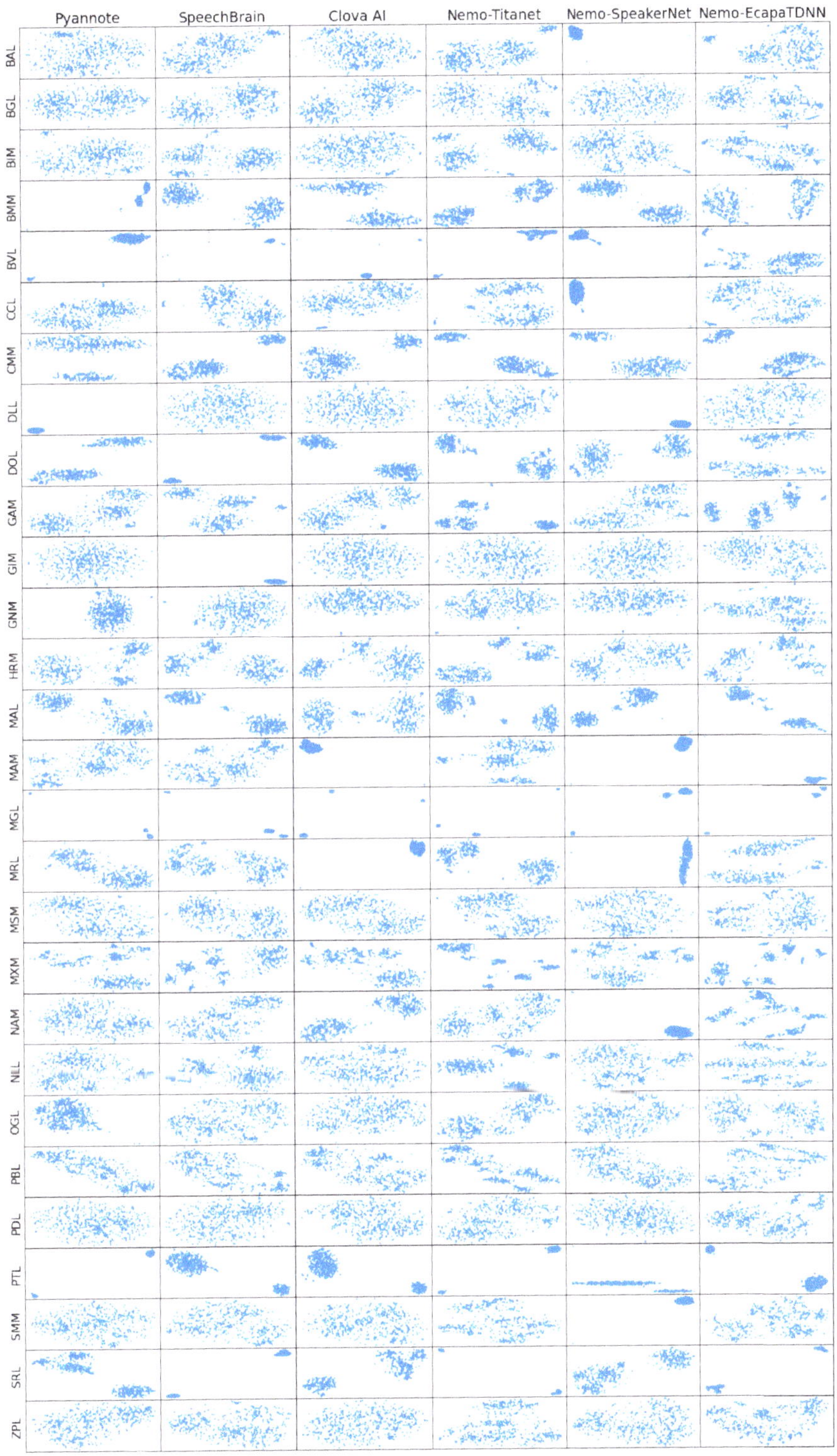

Figure 6. Speaker-level t-SNE plots of the different embedding architectures—**SWARA2.0** subset.

5. Conclusions and Future Work

In this paper, we attempted to evaluate some of the most recent and high-performing deep speaker embeddings with respect to their intended use, i.e., speaker discrimination, as well as with respect to their drawbacks in terms of residual information present in the embeddings. The selected architectures are Pyannote, Speech Brain, Clova AI, NeMo Titanet, NeMo SpeakerNet and NeMo ECAPA-TDNN, and they were evaluated over a large multi-speaker parallel dataset containing over 38 h of spoken data.

In a first set of experiments, the architectures were evaluated in terms of the EER and inter- and intra-speaker similarity measures. With respect to the EER, the best discrimination was obtained by NeMo Titanet. However, in terms of the intra-speaker similarity, the architecture which was able to better cluster the speakers was Clova AI, while NeMo ECAPA-TDNN performed best at maximizing the distance between the speakers' representations. This set of evaluations also looked into the different subsets of the audio data, i.e., the male vs. female and studio recordings vs. home recording subsets. The results showed that the female and studio-recorded speakers achieve lower EER and higher intra-speaker cosine similarity measures. In addition, the male and home-recorded speakers exhibit larger inter-speaker cluster distances.

A second set of experiments measured the amount of residual information present in the six sets of speaker embeddings. Simple classification and regression algorithms were employed. These algorithms were supposed to achieve high accuracy measures when different speech factors were present in the embeddings. The examined factors were: the utterance duration in terms of the number of characters and signal duration, recording conditions, signal-to-noise ratio and linguistic contents. All six architectures showed high correlations to the length of the signal and recording conditions, including the SNR. The least amount of residual information pertaining to the recording conditions was present in the Pyannote architecture. With respect to the utterance duration and SNR, NeMo Titanet-based embeddings were less correlated to these factors, and NeMo SpeakerNet embeddings had the smallest correlation factor with the linguistic contents of the utterance. However, the differences between the six architectures are minimal, and we posit that, to this point, none of them have truly obtained a disentangled speaker representation.

Given the results of the residual information's presence in the embeddings, a third set of experiments looked into how these residual factors could be exploited in further downstream applications of the speaker embeddings. Low-dimensional t-SNE-based representations of the six sets of embeddings were plotted. With respect to global speaker representations, all the architectures showed a similar performance with well-behaved clusters, with the exception of NeMo ECAPA-TDNN for which the clusters had larger distributions. When zooming in on these t-SNE representations at the speaker level, all deep representations exhibited sub-clusters pertaining to different recording sessions, as well as outlier utterances correlated to short utterances. This means that this information present in the embeddings' projections could in fact be used, for example, in the data selection process for text-to-speech or voice cloning applications. Outlier utterances could be removed from the training set, and ill-behaved speaker datasets could be further curated or removed altogether. This is in fact one of the next steps to extend the work presented in this paper. We plan to examine how different text-to-speech architectures are affected by the variability of certain speakers and if removing utterance outliers enhances the performance of the output synthesized speech. Another important result of this work pertains to the use of embedding-based similar speakers for data augmentation in TTS systems, meaning that using the most similar speaker with respect to the target speaker will indeed improve the naturalness and speaker similarity of the resulting system.

Moreover, given the availability of the speaker embedding networks, we are planning to use the findings of this study in a task of multi-speaker text-to-speech synthesis system training and determine the most efficient manner to input these embeddings into the synthesis networks, as well as to verify how the embeddings are affected by the synthetic output and how they can be adjusted to better represent the various speaker identities.

Funding: The work carried out in this paper was partially funded by Zevo Technology under grant agreement no. 21439. The APC was funded by the Technical University of Cluj-Napoca.

Institutional Review Board Statement: Not applicable

Informed Consent Statement: Not applicable.

Data Availability Statement: The processed datasets and experiment flows used in this paper can be obtained from the author.

Conflicts of Interest: The author declares no conflict of interest.

References

1. Jia, Y.; Zhang, Y.; Weiss, R.J.; Wang, Q.; Shen, J.; Ren, F.; Chen, Z.; Nguyen, P.; Pang, R.; Lopez-Moreno, I.; et al. Transfer Learning from Speaker Verification to Multispeaker Text-To-Speech Synthesis. *CoRR* **2018**, Available online: http://xxx.lanl.gov/abs/1806.04558 (accessed on 18 October 2022).
2. Stanton, D.; Shannon, M.; Mariooryad, S.; Skerry-Ryan, R.; Battenberg, E.; Bagby, T.; Kao, D. Speaker Generation. In Proceedings of the ICASSP 2022—2022 IEEE International Conference on Acoustics, Speech and Signal Processing (ICASSP), Singapore, 23–27 May 2022; pp. 7897–7901. [CrossRef]
3. Luck, J.E. Automatic speaker verification using cepstral measurements. *J. Acoust. Soc. Am.* **1969**, *46*, 1026–1032. [CrossRef] [PubMed]
4. Furui, S. Cepstral analysis technique for automatic speaker verification. *IEEE Trans. Acoust. Speech Signal Process.* **1981**, *29*, 254–272. [CrossRef]
5. Ye, W.; Wu, D.; Nucci, A. Experimental Study on GMM-Based Speaker Recognition. In Proceedings of the SPIE—The International Society for Optical Engineering, Orlando, FL, USA, 28 April 2010. [CrossRef]
6. Chandra, M.; Nandi, P.; Kumari, A.; Mishra, S. Spectral-Subtraction Based Features for Speaker Identification. *Adv. Intell. Syst. Comput.* **2015**, *328*, 529–536._58. [CrossRef]
7. McLaren, M.; Scheffer, N.; Graciarena, M.; Ferrer, L.; Lei, Y. Improving speaker identification robustness to highly channel-degraded speech through multiple system fusion. In Proceedings of the 2013 IEEE International Conference on Acoustics, Speech and Signal Processing, Vancouver, BC, Canada, 26–31 May 2013; pp. 6773–6777. [CrossRef]
8. Plchot, O.; Matsoukas, S.; Matejka, P.; Dehak, N.; Ma, J.; Cumani, S.; Glembek, O.; Hermansky, H.; Mallidi, S.; Mesgarani, N.; et al. Developing a speaker identification system for the DARPA RATS project. In Proceedings of the 2013 IEEE International Conference on Acoustics, Speech and Signal Processing, Vancouver, BC, Canada, 26–31 May 2013; pp. 6768–6772. [CrossRef]
9. Reynolds, D.A. A Gaussian Mixture Modeling Approach to Text-Independent Speaker Identification. Ph.D. Thesis, Georgia Institute of Technology, Atlanta, GA, USA, 1992.
10. Reynolds, D.; Rose, R. Robust text-independent speaker identification using Gaussian mixture speaker models. *IEEE Trans. Speech Audio Process.* **1995**, *3*, 72–83. [CrossRef]
11. Reynolds, D.A.; Quatieri, T.F.; Dunn, R.B. Speaker Verification Using Adapted Gaussian Mixture Models. *Digit. Signal Process.* **2000**, *10*, 19–41. [CrossRef]
12. Campbell, W.; Sturim, D.; Reynolds, D. Support vector machines using GMM supervectors for speaker verification. *IEEE Signal Process. Lett.* **2006**, *13*, 308–311. [CrossRef]
13. Zhang, W.; Yang, Y.; Wu, Z. Exploiting PCA classifiers to speaker recognition. In Proceedings of the International Joint Conference on Neural Networks, Portland, OR, USA, 20–24 July 2003, Volume 1, pp. 820–823. [CrossRef]
14. Dehak, N.; Kenny, P.J.; Dehak, R.; Dumouchel, P.; Ouellet, P. Front-End Factor Analysis for Speaker Verification. *IEEE Trans. Audio Speech Lang. Process.* **2011**, *19*, 788–798. [CrossRef]
15. Chen, K.; Salman, A. Learning Speaker-Specific Characteristics with a Deep Neural Architecture. *IEEE Trans. Neural Netw.* **2011**, *22*, 1744–1756. [CrossRef]
16. Hinton, G.E.; Salakhutdinov, R. Reducing the Dimensionality of Data with Neural Networks. *Science* **2006**, *313*, 504–507. [CrossRef]
17. Snyder, D.; Garcia-Romero, D.; Sell, G.; Povey, D.; Khudanpur, S. X-Vectors: Robust DNN Embeddings for Speaker Recognition. In Proceedings of the 2018 IEEE International Conference on Acoustics, Speech and Signal Processing (ICASSP), Calgary, AB, Canada, 15–20 April 2018; pp. 5329–5333. [CrossRef]
18. Garcia-Romero, D.; Snyder, D.; Sell, G.; McCree, A.; Povey, D.; Khudanpur, S. x-Vector DNN Refinement with Full-Length Recordings for Speaker Recognition. In Proceedings of the INTERSPEECH 2019, Graz, Austria, 15–19 September 2019.
19. You, L.; Guo, W.; Dai, L.; Du, J. Multi-Task Learning with High-Order Statistics for x-Vector Based Text-Independent Speaker Verification. *arXiv* **2019**, arXiv:1903.12058.
20. Jung, J.W.; Heo, H.S.; Kim, J.H.; Shim, H.J.; Yu, H.J. RawNet: Advanced End-to-End Deep Neural Network Using Raw Waveforms for Text-Independent Speaker Verification. *arXiv* **2019**, arXiv:1904.08104.
21. Jung, J.W.; Kim, S.B.; Shim, H.J.; Kim, J.H.; Yu, H.J. Improved RawNet with Feature Map Scaling for Text-Independent Speaker Verification Using Raw Waveforms. *arXiv* **2020**, arXiv:2004.00526.
22. Chung, J.S.; Huh, J.; Mun, S.; Lee, M.; Heo, H.S.; Choe, S.; Ham, C.; Jung, S.; Lee, B.J.; Han, I. In defence of metric learning for speaker recognition. *arXiv* **2020**, arXiv:2003.11982.

23. Kwon, Y.; Heo, H.S.; Lee, B.J.; Chung, J.S. The ins and outs of speaker recognition: Lessons from VoxSRC 2020. In Proceedings of the ICASSP 2021—2021 IEEE International Conference on Acoustics, Speech and Signal Processing (ICASSP), Toronto, ON, Canada, 6–11 June 2021.
24. Thienpondt, J.; Desplanques, B.; Demuynck, K. The IDLAB VoxCeleb Speaker Recognition Challenge 2020 System Description. *arXiv* **2020**, arXiv:2010.12468.
25. Vaessen, N.; Van Leeuwen, D.A. Fine-Tuning Wav2Vec2 for Speaker Recognition. In Proceedings of the ICASSP 2022—2022 IEEE International Conference on Acoustics, Speech and Signal Processing (ICASSP), Singapore, 23–27 May 2022; pp. 7967–7971. [CrossRef]
26. Bai, Z.; Zhang, X.L. Speaker recognition based on deep learning: An overview. *Neural Netw.* **2021**, *140*, 65–99. [CrossRef] [PubMed]
27. Ohi, A.Q.; Mridha, M.F.; Hamid, M.A.; Monowar, M.M. Deep Speaker Recognition: Process, Progress, and Challenges. *IEEE Access* **2021**, *9*, 89619–89643. [CrossRef]
28. Makarov, R.; Torgashov, N.; Alenin, A.; Yakovlev, I.; Okhotnikov, A. *ID R&D System Description to VoxCeleb Speaker Recognition Challenge 2022*; ID R&D Inc.: New York, NY, USA, 2022.
29. Cai, Q.; Hong, G.; Ye, Z.; Li, X.; Li, H. The Kriston AI System for the VoxCeleb Speaker Recognition Challenge 2022. *arXiv* **2022**, arXiv:2209.11433.
30. Suh, S.; Park, S. The ReturnZero System for VoxCeleb Speaker Recognition Challenge 2022. *arXiv* **2022**, arXiv:2209.10147.
31. Zhao, Z.; Li, Z.; Wang, W.; Zhang, P. The HCCL system for VoxCeleb Speaker Recognition Challenge 2022. 2022. Available online: https://www.robots.ox.ac.uk/~vgg/data/voxceleb/data_workshop_2022/reports/zzdddz_report.pdf (accessed on 18 October 2022).
32. Casanova, E.; Shulby, C.; Gölge, E.; Müller, N.M.; de Oliveira, F.S.; Junior, A.C.; Soares, A.d.S.; Aluisio, S.M.; Ponti, M.A. SC-GlowTTS: An Efficient Zero-Shot Multi-Speaker Text-To-Speech Model. *arXiv* **2021**, arXiv:2104.05557.
33. Cooper, E.; Lai, C.I.; Yasuda, Y.; Fang, F.; Wang, X.; Chen, N.; Yamagishi, J. Zero-Shot Multi-Speaker Text-To-Speech with State-Of-The-Art Neural Speaker Embeddings. In Proceedings of the ICASSP 2020—2020 IEEE International Conference on Acoustics, Speech and Signal Processing (ICASSP), Barcelona, Spain, 4–8 May 2020; pp. 6184–6188. [CrossRef]
34. Zhou, Y.; Tian, X.; Li, H. Language Agnostic Speaker Embedding for Cross-Lingual Personalized Speech Generation. *IEEE/ACM Trans. Audio Speech Lang. Process.* **2021**, *29*, 3427–3439. [CrossRef]
35. Hu, Q.; Bleisch, T.; Petkov, P.; Raitio, T.; Marchi, E.; Lakshminarasimhan, V. Whispered and Lombard Neural Speech Synthesis. In Proceedings of the 2021 IEEE Spoken Language Technology Workshop (SLT), Shenzhen, China, 19–22 January 2021; pp. 454–461. [CrossRef]
36. Zhang, M.; Zhou, Y.; Zhao, L.; Li, H. Transfer Learning From Speech Synthesis to Voice Conversion with Non-Parallel Training Data. *IEEE/ACM Trans. Audio Speech Lang. Process.* **2021**, *29*, 1290–1302. [CrossRef]
37. Stan, A.; Dinescu, F.; Tiple, C.; Meza, S.; Orza, B.; Chirila, M.; Giurgiu, M. The SWARA Speech Corpus: A Large Parallel Romanian Read Speech Dataset. In Proceedings of the 9th Conference on Speech Technology and Human-Computer Dialogue (SpeD), Bucharest, Romania, 6–9 July 2017.
38. Bredin, H.; Yin, R.; Coria, J.M.; Gelly, G.; Korshunov, P.; Lavechin, M.; Fustes, D.; Titeux, H.; Bouaziz, W.; Gill, M.P. Pyannote.audio: Neural building blocks for speaker diarization. In Proceedings of the ICASSP 2020, IEEE International Conference on Acoustics, Speech, and Signal Processing, Barcelona, Spain, 4–8 May 2020.
39. Bredin, H.; Laurent, A. End-to-end speaker segmentation for overlap-aware resegmentation. *arXiv* **2021**, arXiv:2104.04045.
40. Ravanelli, M.; Bengio, Y. Speaker Recognition from Raw Waveform with SincNet. In Proceedings of the 2018 IEEE Spoken Language Technology Workshop (SLT), Athens, Greece, 18–21 December 2018. [CrossRef]
41. Ravanelli, M.; Parcollet, T.; Plantinga, P.; Rouhe, A.; Cornell, S.; Lugosch, L.; Subakan, C.; Dawalatabad, N.; Heba, A.; Zhong, J.; et al. SpeechBrain: A General-Purpose Speech Toolkit. *arXiv* **2021**, arXiv:2106.04624.
42. Desplanques, B.; Thienpondt, J.; Demuynck, K. ECAPA-TDNN: Emphasized Channel Attention, Propagation and Aggregation in TDNN Based Speaker Verification. In Proceedings of the Interspeech 2020, Shanghai, China, 25–29 October 2020; pp. 3830–3834. [CrossRef]
43. Koluguri, N.R.; Park, T.; Ginsburg, B. TitaNet: Neural Model for speaker representation with 1D Depth-wise separable convolutions and global context. In Proceedings of the ICASSP 2022—2022 IEEE International Conference on Acoustics, Speech and Signal Processing (ICASSP), Singapore, 23–27 May 2022.
44. Han, W.; Zhang, Z.; Zhang, Y.; Yu, J.; Chiu, C.C.; Qin, J.; Gulati, A.; Pang, R.; Wu, Y. ContextNet: Improving Convolutional Neural Networks for Automatic Speech Recognition with Global Context. *arXiv* **2020**, arXiv:2005.03191.
45. Koluguri, N.R.; Li, J.; Lavrukhin, V.; Ginsburg, B. SpeakerNet: 1D Depth-wise Separable Convolutional Network for Text-Independent Speaker Recognition and Verification. *arXiv* **2020**, arXiv:2010.12653.
46. Dawalatabad, N.; Ravanelli, M.; Grondin, F.; Thienpondt, J.; Desplanques, B.; Na, H. ECAPA-TDNN Embeddings for Speaker Diarization. *arXiv* **2021**, arXiv:2104.01466.
47. Ke, G.; Meng, Q.; Finley, T.; Wang, T.; Chen, W.; Ma, W.; Ye, Q.; Liu, T.Y. LightGBM: A Highly Efficient Gradient Boosting Decision Tree. In *Proceedings of the 31st International Conference on Neural Information Processing Systems, NIPS'17, Long Beach, CA, USA, 4–9 December 2017*; Curran Associates Inc.: Red Hook, NY, USA, 2017; pp. 3149–3157.
48. Kim, C.; Stern, R. Robust signal-to-noise ratio estimation based on waveform amplitude distribution analysis. In Proceedings of the Interspeech 2008 Incorporating SST 08, Brisbane Australia, 22–26 September 2008; pp. 2598–2601. [CrossRef]
49. van der Maaten, L.; Hinton, G.E. Visualizing High-Dimensional Data Using t-SNE. *J. Mach. Learn. Res.* **2008**, *9*, 2579–2605.

Σ mathematics

MDPI

Article

An Improved Machine Learning Model with Hybrid Technique in VANET for Robust Communication

Gagan Preet Kour Marwah [1], Anuj Jain [1], Praveen Kumar Malik [1], Manwinder Singh [1], Sudeep Tanwar [2,*], Calin Ovidiu Safirescu [3,*], Traian Candin Mihaltan [4], Ravi Sharma [5] and Ahmed Alkhayyat [6]

1 School of Electronics and Electrical Engineering, Lovely Professional University, Jalandhar 144411, India
2 Department of Computer Science and Engineering, Institute of Technology, Nirma University, Ahmedabad 382481, India
3 Environment Protection Department, Faculty of Agriculture, University of Agricultural Sciences and Veterinary Medicine Cluj-Napoca, Calea Mănăștur 3-5, 400372 Cluj-Napoca, Romania
4 Faculty of Building Services, Technical University of Cluj-Napoca, 400114 Cluj-Napoca, Romania
5 Centre for Inter-Disciplinary Research and Innovation, University of Petroleum and Energy Studies, Dehradun 248001, India
6 College of Technical Engineering, The Islamic University, Najaf 54001, Iraq
* Correspondence: sudeep.tanwar@nirmauni.ac.in (S.T.); calin.safirescu@usamvcluj.ro (C.O.S.)

Abstract: The vehicular ad hoc network, VANET, is one of the most popular and promising technologies in intelligent transportation today. However, VANET is susceptible to several vulnerabilities that result in an intrusion. This intrusion must be solved before VANET technology can be adopted. In this study, we suggest a unique machine learning technique to improve VANET's effectiveness. The proposed method incorporates two phases. Phase I detects the DDoS attack using a novel machine learning technique called SVM-HHO, which provides information about the vehicle. Phase II mitigates the impact of a DDoS attack and allocates bandwidth using a reliable resources management technique based on the hybrid whale dragonfly optimization algorithm (H-WDFOA). This proposed model could be an effective technique predicting and utilizing reliable information that provides effective results in smart vehicles. The novel machine learning-based technique was implemented through MATLAB and NS2 platforms. Network quality measurements included congestion, transit, collision, and QoS awareness cost. Based on the constraints, a different cost framework was designed. In addition, data preprocessing of the QoS factor and total routing costs were considered. Rider integrated cuckoo search (RI-CS) is a novel optimization algorithm that combines the concepts of the rider optimization algorithm (ROA) and cuckoo search (CS) to determine the optimal route with the lowest routing cost. The enhanced hybrid ant colony optimization routing protocol (EHACORP) is a networking technology that increases efficiency by utilizing the shortest route. The shortest path of the proposed protocol had the lowest communication overhead and the fewest number of hops between sending and receiving vehicles. The EHACORP involved two stages. To find the distance between cars in phase 1, EHACORP employed a method for calculating distance. Using starting point ant colony optimization, the ants were guided in phase 2 to develop the shortest route with the least number of connections to send information. The relatively short approach increases protocol efficiency in every way. The pairing of DCM and SBACO at H-WDFOA-VANET accelerated packet processing, reduced ant search time, eliminated blind broadcasting, and prevented stagnation issues. The delivery ratio and throughput of the H-WDFOA-packet VANET benefitted from its use of the shortest channel without stagnation, its rapid packet processing, and its rapid convergence speed. In conclusion, the proposed hybrid whale dragonfly optimization approach (H-WDFOA-VANET) was compared with industry standard models, such as rider integrated cuckoo search (RI-CS) and enhanced hybrid ant colony optimization routing protocol (EHACORP). With the proposed method, throughput could be increased. The proposed system had energy consumption values of 2.00000 mJ, latency values of 15.61668 s, and a drop at node 60 of 0.15759. Additionally, a higher throughput was achieved with the new method. With the suggested method, it is possible to meet the energy consumption targets, delay value, and drop value at node 60. The proposed method reduces the drop value at node 80 to 0.15504, delay time to 15.64318 s, and energy consumption to 2.00000 mJ. These

Citation: Marwah, G.P.K.; Jain, A.; Malik, P.K.; Singh, M.; Tanwar, S.; Safirescu, C.O.; Mihaltan, T.C.; Sharma, R.; Alkhayyat, A. An Improved Machine Learning Model with Hybrid Technique in VANET for Robust Communication. *Mathematics* **2022**, *10*, 4030. https://doi.org/10.3390/math10214030

Academic Editors: Adrian Sergiu Darabant and Diana-Laura Borza

Received: 11 September 2022
Accepted: 25 October 2022
Published: 30 October 2022

outcomes demonstrate the effectiveness of our proposed method. Thus, the proposed system is more efficient than existing systems.

Keywords: VANET; support vector machine; rider optimization algorithm; cuckoo search; whale optimization algorithm; dragonfly; DDoS attack

MSC: 68M10

1. Introduction

In recent years, the vehicular ad-hoc network (VANET) has gained prominence in the networking world. It is a mobile ad hoc network (MANET) primarily utilized for vehicle-to-vehicle and vehicle-to-roadside-unit communication. Data is shared via vehicle-to-vehicle (V2V), vehicle-to-infrastructure (V2I), and vehicle-to-everything (V2X) communications. VANET applies to various areas such as traffic control, traffic congestion monitoring, and driver safety programs [1,2]. However, VANET has its disadvantages, such as in dynamic behavior. This issue is rectified by an effective and efficient routing protocol that broadcasts the data. As cars may not be able to communicate information without an efficient routing method, they will lose all the benefits of sophisticated VANET technology [3].

Recently, many efforts have been made to adapt software-defined network (SDN) ideas to vehicular networks to benefit from the SDN's flexibility and programmability. The ultimate objective of this adaption is to improve VANET performance and make it more suitable for certain services and applications [4]. The software-defined network (SDN) is one of the emerging revolutionary network concepts utilized in data centers and operator networks to satisfy the growing demands of future networks [5]. Network programmability, centralized management control, and interface openness are some features of SDN. It also substantially simplifies network administration and improves networkability [6,7]. SDN is divided into three layers: data, control, and application. Routers, switches, vehicles, and wireless gadgets are all part of the data layer. According to the controller, which would be the SDN's brain and resides in the control plane, devices in the data layer are responsible for packet transmission. It determines how data layer devices send and receive data and how the flow is managed. The network layer consists of software initiatives that manage the network's programming. SDN and VANET techniques are not without their flaws. Despite their numerous advantages and excellent performance, they are subject to attack risk, namely from DoS and DDoS, just as in traditional wireless networks. However, SDN features make it simpler to identify and respond to DoS attacks, and the openness of the data plane creates favorable conditions for additional DoS attacks [8]. A distributed DoS (DDoS) assault occurs when a DoS attack is launched from several vehicles dispersed throughout the network. The targeted system cannot handle any incoming requests due to the breach, and the entire system crashes [9]. In such assaults, the hacker compromises thousands of hosts, including PCs, servers, and IoT devices, and exploits them all at once to overwhelm the victim's resources with traffic. This traffic suspends network users and defending against it is quite difficult [10]. A system administrator can detect a potential threat but cannot handle the simultaneous attacks in real-time. As a result, the SDN controller must be subjected to particular security constraints. Additionally, automatic attack detection systems are required to ensure an optimum level of service quality and to detect suspicious intrusions [11].

The detection of DDoS attacks includes various challenges, including identifying the characteristics of attack traffic; lack of cooperation among the nodes of a coherent network; modification in attack tools; usage of a fake IP address; and short attack duration and limited response time [12]. To deal with these issues, we need a system that can detect intrusions and store data in communication while ensuring data integrity. The ultimate purpose of the intrusion detection method is to identify intrusion before it causes damage to a targeted server and to stop attacks as close to their source as possible [13]. Machine learning (ML) techniques provide a framework frequently employed in VANETs to evaluate large amounts of data and generate efficient rules for attack detection, classification, and prediction [14]. The ML approaches apply not only to intrusion detection but also in fields such as speech recognition, recommendation systems, medical diagnosis, and traffic prediction. It also offers a desirable approach for detecting intrusions in VANETs ahead of time with acceptable speed and accuracy [15].

There are four different forms of communication in VANETs.

- In-vehicle communication: the in-vehicle domain is becoming increasingly crucial in VANET research. Driver and public safety are both improved when in-car communication systems can detect issues such as driver fatigue and drowsiness.
- To better assist drivers, V2V communication can facilitate the exchange of information and warning messages between vehicles.
- Virtual-to-individual (V2I) communication in VANETs is an emerging research area. Through vehicle-to-infrastructure (V2I) communication, drivers can access real-time traffic and weather updates and participate in environmental sensing and monitoring.
- Wireless broadband technology, such as 3G/4G, may be used for vehicle-to-vehicle (V2V) communication. With more traffic data, monitoring information, and entertainment options available in the internet cloud, this type of connectivity will be beneficial for active driver assistance and vehicle tracking.

The primary goal of public safety technology is to improve the overall safety of transportation systems. Real-time traffic conditions, post-crash alerts, traffic monitoring, collision mitigation, and other safety applications are available. Non-public security applications aim to improve driver comfort by offering value-added information, such as nearby petrol stations, hotels, workshops, and restrooms, among other things. It is often advisable to use public safety technology than non-public safety technology. Numerous applications are used in many nations, including Germany, Europe, and Switzerland, to make roads and automobiles safer. Convenience applications are mainly used to handle traffic congestion scenarios, such as available parking spaces, route diversions, and electronic toll collection, among other things. New elements to the services mentioned above that focus on converting traffic jam time into constructive work, such as reading on the internet while waiting in a vehicle for someone, are known as productive activities. Additionally, fuel is saved when the average toll booth wait time is decreased to 1–2 min [16].

The following are the main contributions of the current study:

- The primary objective of this paper was to use a machine learning-hybrid optimization strategy to detect DDoS attacks and allocate bandwidth within the VANET.
- Algorithms and models based on machine learning can support robust communication analysis and resource management, as well as the increasing communication and computation demands of emerging networking applications.
- Security-based modified SVM with HHO technique was utilized to identify DDoS attacks. The SVM-HHO technique demonstrated the most outstanding feature selection and parameter optimization capabilities compared with other well-known metaheuristic algorithms. Using H-WDFOA, the impact of a DDoS attack on the VANET was diminished (H-WDFOA-VANET).
- The combination of DF optimization and WOA increased bandwidth. The condition was repeated until all available bandwidth had been allocated. The H-WDFOA was utilized to achieve effective bandwidth allocation and optimal vehicle routing.
- For the stability of the vehicular network, swift and efficient communication was established once the predicted information had been validated.
- Utilizing performance indicators such as energy consumption, throughput, latency, and packet delivery ratio, the performance of the proposed method was evaluated. The implementation was accomplished using MATLAB software.

2. Literature Review

Poongodi et al. [17] proposed a trust-based methodology for determining the distributed denial of service (DDoS) attack in VANET. The residual energy, trust policy, data factor, statistics, such as frequency value, and true hypothesis were used to create the trust elements. These trust elements were utilized to generate the trust evaluation matrix. The deterrence design of the trust evaluation approach was incorporated with a clustering method to identify the attacker in a proficient manner.

For identifying DDoS assaults on VANET, Adhikary et al. [18] used a hybrid technique. These hybrid approaches were developed using ANOVA Dot and RBF Dot SVM kernel methodology. Features such as collision, jitter, and packet drop were used to replicate a real-time network communication scenario. As a result, the hybrid algorithm-based model was superior at detecting DDoS attacks.

To identify DDoS assaults on VANET, Kolandaisamy et al. [19] devised a multivariant-stream analysis (MVSA) method. The network was protected from distributed denial of service attacks by keeping multiple levels active. This tactic's success hinges on the ability of individual cars to talk to one another through the Road Side Unit.

Using big data technology, Marwah et al. [20] provided a method for detecting DDoS attacks. The real-time network traffic-collecting module and traffic-detection module are two components of the described technique. In addition, spark and HFSA-VANET were also used to speed up data processing and store significant suspicious attacks.

Hind Bangui et al. [21] suggested a machine learning approach that combined traditional methods with more modern ones (IDS) to boost the effectiveness of intrusion detection systems. The IDS was a potential tool for thwarting VANET attacks in advance. Consequently, the coreset was utilized to enhance detection accuracy, and the random forest (RF) was implemented to boost IDS functionality. For VANET, Tang et al. [22] implemented a centralized routing mechanism with mobility prediction (CRS-MP), using a software-defined network (SDN) controller. The Road Side Unit (RSU) or Base Station (BS) determined the average latency and transmission probability of each request from the vehicle based on the mobility forecast. Information was gathered by the SDN controller via RSU, whereas the BS was viewed as mere switches.

Zhang and Zhu [23] presented VANET's PML-CIDS. In this study, the authors used the alternating direction multiplier method (ADMM) to a set of empirical risk minimization (ERM) problems. Differential privacy was used to acquire the PML-CIDS privacy notation, and the NSL-KDD dataset was used for the evaluation. An improved VANET routing model was developed by Gnanasekar and Samiappan [24], which accounted for congestion, travel, collision, and QoS awareness cost. An updated pricing scheme was developed in light of the restrictions. When calculating the optimal route, the authors considered the total cost and quality of service (QoS) component, which was fuzzy-calculated. The optimal routing in VANET was achieved at the lowest possible routing cost by developing a novel RI-CS optimization approach, which was built by fusing the ideas of ROA and CS.

To improve the effectiveness of the routing procedure in VANETs, Ramamoorthyet al.proposed a new routing protocol, EHACORP, which was presented in [25]. At EHACORP, the combination of DCM and SBACO shortened the time it took for ants to find their way around, increased the rate at which they converged, eliminated the need for blind broadcasting packets, expedited packet processing, and prevented bottlenecks. EHACORP increased its packet delivery ratio (PDR) and throughput by avoiding bottlenecks, rapidly processing packets, and quickly converging.

In [26], the authors presented a study on the split delivery vehicle routing problem that arises in the distribution of fresh agricultural products. A mathematical model was developed to find an optimal solution for the problem by considering travel costs, fixed costs, service costs, refrigeration costs, carbon emission costs, and customer satisfaction. This paper added time-varying road network constraints to the model, and multiple time windows were set for each customer. A variable neighborhood search, combined with the non-dominated sorting genetic algorithm II (VNS-NSGA-II), and techniques for order preference by similarity to an ideal solution (TOPSIS) was proposed and applied to solve this problem.

In [27], the authors proposed a scale-adaptive mathematical morphology spectrum entropy (AMMSE) to improve the scale selection. To support the proposed method, two properties of the mathematical morphology spectrum (MMS), namely non-negativity and monotonic decreasing, were shown. It could be concluded from the two properties that feature loss of MMS decreased with the increase in scale. Based on this conclusion, two adaptive scale selection strategies were proposed to automatically determine the scale by reducing the feature loss of MMS. The presented method was applied to identify fault degree on a CWRU-bearing data set and evaluate performance degradation onan IMS-bearing data set. The experiment results showed that AMMSE had better results in both experiments with the same parameters.

3. Proposed Methodology for Robust Communication through Machine Learning Algorithm

The VANET's dynamic condition was developed in this section to select the suitable routing of each node. Furthermore, allocating the bandwidth of each node was obtained for accurate routing. In VANET, the optimization approach SVM-HHO-VANET was developed to select a route based on clustering to provide precise bandwidth allocation for proper routing. Here, the proposed methodology was halved into two phases. Security-based modified SVM was used to find DDoS attacks early on. In the next stage, the HHO optimization approach for the VANET dynamic scenario was used to achieve effective bandwidth allocation. This research included cluster selection, accurate cluster node communication, detecting DDoS attacks, route prediction, bandwidth allocation between the cluster nodes, distance, velocity, speed, bandwidth, number of nearby vehicles, and throughput parameters for QoS analysis. Additionally, evaluation metrics such as energy consumption, delay, and drop were considered for QoS performance analysis. In this work, several nodes in the vehicle were analyzed based on distance, speed, velocity, and bandwidth. The location of the vehicle was determined in each iteration, according to fitness. When the node's position was less than 0.5 and the nearby vehicle was greater than or equal to 1, the best location was updated. If the present iteration was higher than the maximum iteration, the target vehicle's position was considered the best location. To achieve a maximum optimal solution, the DF approach was integrated with WOA.

Furthermore, the dragonfly solution was initialized and determined the bandwidth by QoS value according to the objective function. The maximum iteration was utilized until the process continued to enhance the bandwidth. Finally, energy consumption, delay, and drop were considered based on the QoS parameter for accurate routing. The proposed approach was accurate in allocating bandwidth compared with other existing techniques. This study is robust and fast in predicting DDoS attacks and allocating the bandwidth using the H-WDFOA technique, in the best position after validating for stability in vehicular networks.

4. Background of HHO, SVM, and DDoS Attack

4.1. Harris Hawks Optimization (HHO)

Harris hawks optimization (HHO) is an optimization method that uses a swarm intelligence approach. The primary focus of HHO is on simulating cooperative hunting and successful prey escape strategies employed by hawks in the wild to solve the problem of a single target [28]. Hawks are search agents in HHO, and the best position is that of the prey. The demonstration of the HHO is described in full detail below and depicted in Figure 1.

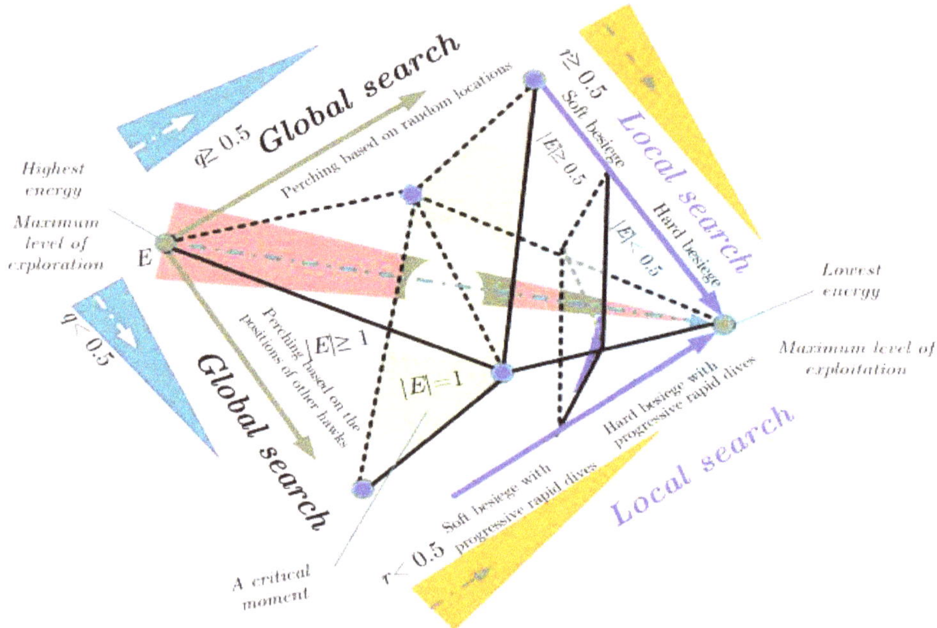

Figure 1. HHO phase [1].

In this approach, hawks locate their prey depending on the positions of the genuine members (the total number of hawks defined by N and represented by Equation (1).

$$X_i(t+1) = \{(X_{prey}(t) - X_m(t) - Y),\ q < 0.5)(X_{rand}(t) - |X_{rand}(t) - 2r_2\ X(t)|, q \geq 0.5) \quad (1)$$

The next iteration shows that the revised position of hawks, t, is represented by $X_i(t+1)$; $X_{rand}(t)$ represents the current location of the hawks; and $r1$, $r2$, $r3$, $r4$, and q denote random numbers inside the collection of hawks (0,1). The position of prey is represented by $X_{prey}(t)$. $X_m(t)$ defines the total average positions of all hawks, which is calculated using Equation (2).

$$X_m(t) = \frac{\sum_{i=1}^{N} X_i(t)}{N} \quad (2)$$

$Y = r_3(LB + r_4\ (UB - LB)$ stands for the gap between the maximum and minimum values of a variable.

4.2. Support Vector Machine (SVM)

The SVM has been validated as a powerful paradigm for classification. SVM provides a crucial mathematical model for use in classification and regression. Twin SVM, Lagrangian SVM, least-square SVM, decision tree SVM, directed acyclic graph SVM, and multi-kernel SVM are only some of the SVM variants that have emerged during the past few decades [29]. In support vector machines (SVM), multi-class categories are typically translated into a large number of binary variants using either OvO (one vs. one) or OvR (one vs. many or one vs. rest) [30]. SVM classifies data by translating it into multidimensional space and creating a higher dimension of hyperplanes. This hyperplane refers to the decision planes in Figure 2.

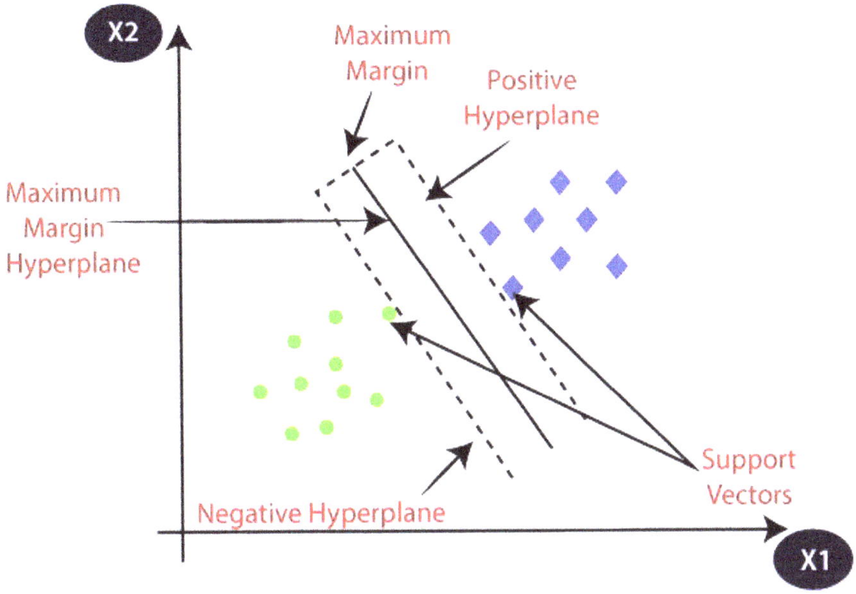

Figure 2. Hyperplane supporter in SVM plan.

4.3. DDoS Attack

As per Figure 3, DDoS attacks are network security threats that aim to overload target networks with malicious traffic. Though several statistical methods exist for DDoS attack detection, the development of a real-time detector that requires minimal processing resources remains to be a fundamental challenge [31]. This paper discusses recent developments in cloud-based DDoS mitigation technologies. In particular, we provide a detailed analysis of the characterization, prevention, detection, and mitigation strategies used in these attacks.

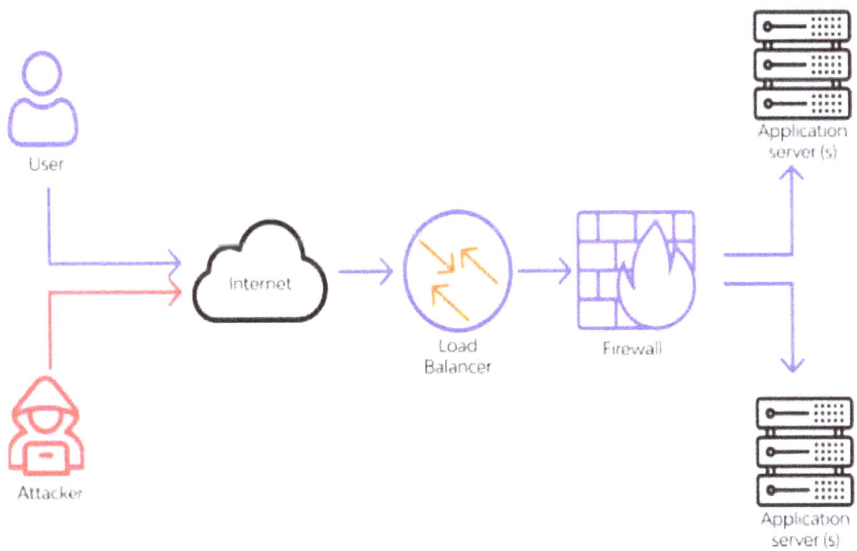

Figure 3. Attack by DDoS.

The flowchart of the proposed methodology is illustrated in Figure 4. First, we initialized the dataset, where 70% of data were utilized in the training phase and 30% in the testing phase. However, the DDoS attack was analyzed and detected by modified SVM. Due to a DDoS attack, node performance was reduced, and bandwidth attracted more attenuation. In addition, based on the number of nodes, hybrid WDFOA was initialized for allocating bandwidth. For allocation, the QoS value was separately analyzed based on bandwidth, distance, speed, and vehicle velocity. The capacity of the node to transfer data was established by running condition assessment if the node's bandwidth is less than a predetermined threshold. To enhance the bandwidth, DF optimization was integrated with WOA. This condition was repeated until the termination of bandwidth was allocated.

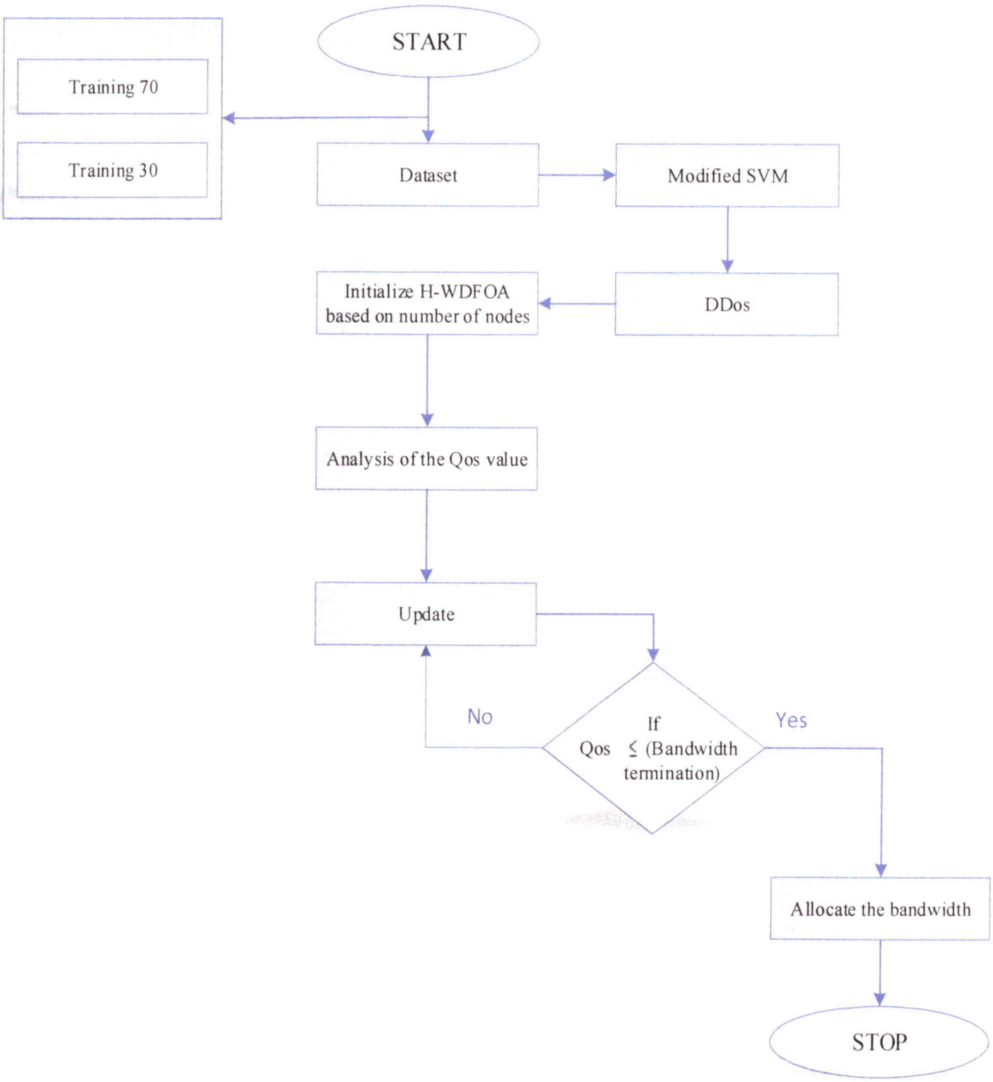

Figure 4. Flowchart for proposed methodology.

5. Simulated Steps for Proposed Methodology

At a fixed location, utilizing 1000 vehicles, VANET was randomly implemented and placed in 1000 × 1000 m. The placement of vehicles is tabulated in Table 1. In a defined area, VANET was randomly placed.

Table 1. Vehicle placement in the VANET.

At Random Places, Vehicles Are Places to Create VANET
➢ $In\ Total - Vehicles,\ For\ each\ x$
➢ $Va(x) = 1000 * run\ if\ (1)$
➢ $Vb(x) = 1000 * run\ if\ (1)$
➢ $Fix\ (V\ a(x),\ V\ b(x))$
➢ $End\ For$

a and *b* are the coordinatesof the vehicle, denoted by *Va* and *Vb*. To randomly position a car at positions a and b, R-studio was used to incorporate the random function run if (1).

5.1. Dataset Production

The data set called the "DDoS attack-based SDN Network Dataset" used deep learning and machine learning techniques that were publicly accessible and used by many researchers. There were 104,345 traffic flows in 23 features in this dataset. The usual attack traffic class label used a dataset comprising UDP, ICMP, and TCP traffic.

5.2. Phase: 1—Security-Based Modified SVM

This study used the modified support vector machine (MSVM) to identify the attack on SDN-based VANETs by DDoS. Here, SVM utilized kernel function to transfer non-linear data to a high-dimensional space based on Harris hawks optimization (HHO). In the SVM classifier, the optimal kernel was selected based on HHO, known as modified SVM. Thus, the kernel-based MSVM was suggested in this paper to identify DDoS attacks.

The architecture of the suggested hybrid detection is shown in Figure 5. The VANET setup consisted of 1000 vehicles in the first module. The second module produced the information needed to develop a training and testing procedure. Finally, a hybrid method was used to make predictions based on data collected during training and testing. Predictions consisted of binary values"0 or 1" for indicating efficient behavior or DDoS attack.

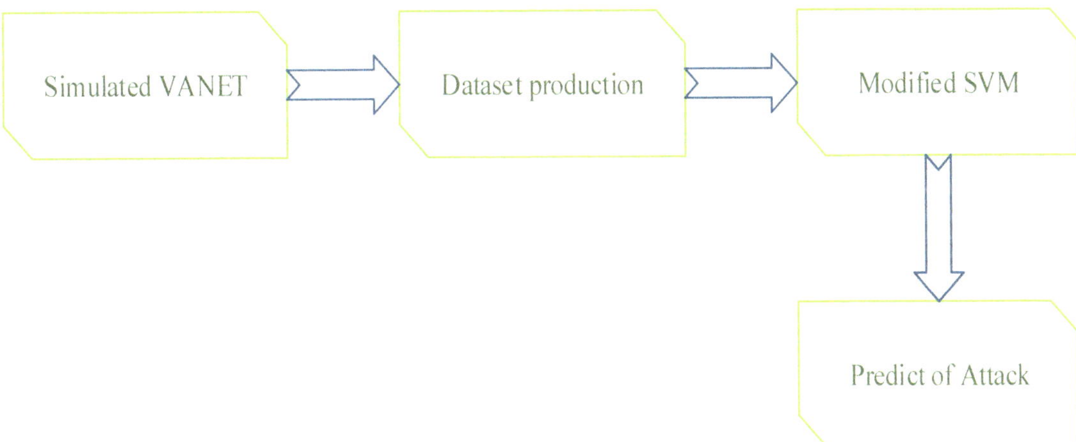

Figure 5. Basic architecture for detection method.

5.2.1. Modified Support-Vector Machine

SVM generalization is the most significant margin classifier and is said to be the best method for categorization difficulties. When comparing two data sets, the margin is the line closest to either set. A flat affine subspace in an x-dimension space forms an x−1 dimension [32] in a hyperplane. In a hyperplane, the following equation determines two dimensions.

$$\alpha_0\alpha_1 y_1 + \alpha_2 y_2 = 0 \quad (3)$$

Here, in the hyperplane, $Y = (Y_1,\ Y_2)^T$ is a point and $\alpha_0,\ \alpha_1,$ and α_2 are the parameters. Equation (1) can be extended, for n-dimensional space.

$$\alpha_0 + \alpha_1 y_1 + \alpha_2 y_2 + \ldots + \alpha_n y_n = 0 \quad (4)$$

If $Y = (Y_1,\ Y_2,\ \ldots Y_n)^T$, Y lies on the hyper plane. The left side of the hyperplane is represented by x in the Equation (3), and is more than zero, whereas if it is on the other side, it is less than zero. A hyperplane reveals which side a point is on in this way.

The SVC can determine which side of the hyperplane an observation from the test space lies on and classify it accordingly. As shown in Figure 6, some data points fell outside of the hyperplane's boundaries. The equation expresses the SVM's working principle,

$$Maximize_{\alpha_0,\alpha_1 \ldots\ldots \alpha_n, \epsilon_1 \ldots\ldots \epsilon_n} \quad (5)$$

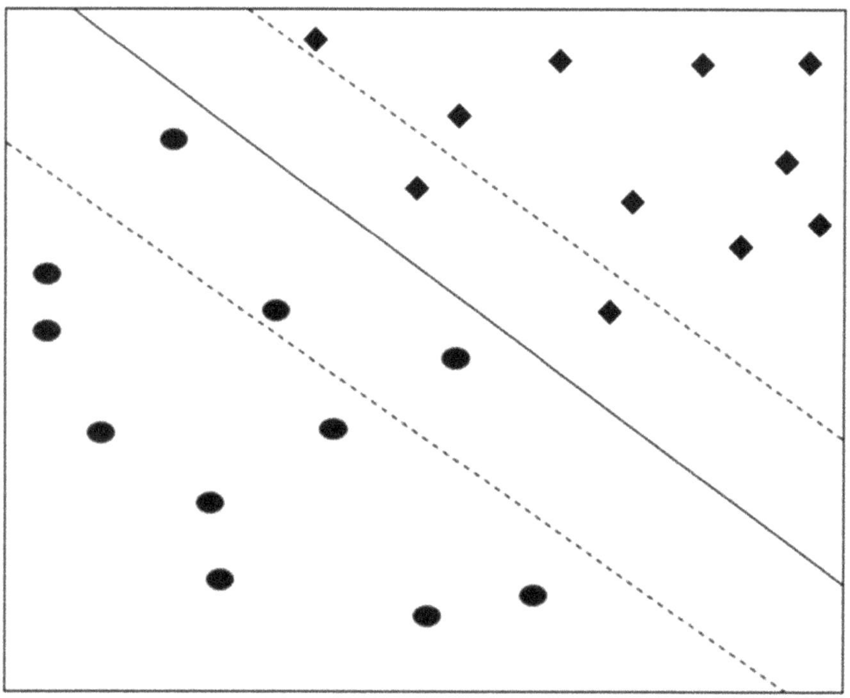

Figure 6. Concept of support vector machine (SVM).

A circumstance where

$$\sum_{i=1}^{n} a_i^2 = 1 \quad (6)$$

$$f_x(\alpha_0 + \alpha_1 y_1 + \alpha_2 y_2 \ldots \ \ldots \ \ldots + \alpha_n y_n) \geq W(1 - \epsilon_x) \quad (7)$$

$$\epsilon_x \geq 0,\ \sum_{x=1}^{n} \in_x \leq T \quad (8)$$

In this case, the positive tuning parameter is denoted by T. The width of the margin is represented by W. A slack variable is ϵ_x, this enables for an observation on the margin's wrong side. The sign of $\alpha_0 + \alpha_1 y_1 + \alpha_2 y_2 \ldots\ldots\ldots + \alpha_n y_n$ is classified as an observation.

To transfer non-linear data, SVM used kernel function based on HHO, known as MSVM. To detect DDoS attacks, MSVM is employed. Hence, the optimal kernel-HHO is detailed in the following section.

5.2.2. Selection of Optimal Kernel Based on Harris Hawks Optimization (HHO)

HHO is defined by a meta-heuristic technique based on a natural population. Harris hawks cooperative hunting behavior is for prey such as rabbits. Exploration, transformation, and exploitation are the three steps included in the HHO optimization technique.

- Initialization Phase

The initial hawk population initializes the solution for this phase. The number of nearest vehicles (n_1, n_2, ..., n_N) encompasses the population. Here, the number of populations are denoted as N. The execution of the technique was done by cluster vehicle (n_{cl}). The cluster and nearby vehicles are denoted as "hawks", whereas the destination vehicle is referred to as prey (rabbit). For all cars, the fitness function was determined in this phase. The fitness of jth vehicle was calculated as follows,

$$f(n_j) = \{\sum D,\ M,\ \delta,\ K\} \tag{9}$$

Here, the fitness function is developed as mobility (M), direction (D), vehicle state (δ), and availability of spectrum (K). Binary values '0' and '1' are described as vehicles' direction. The fitness of the vehicle is enhanced if target and cluster vehicles are in the same direction, so that D = 1 or 0. Furthermore, to enrich the computation fitness, the mobility will be mapped as 0 and 1. When M = 0 or 1, mobility of n_j is higher than average mobility. For data transmission K = 0 or 1, if n_j has an available channel. The function of evaluation metrics is represented as follows:

$$\delta = \frac{P + DR}{D} \tag{10}$$

The throughput function of δ is n_j (P) for n_j, delay (D), and data rate (DR). For data transmission, the optimal path can be achieved by the deciding factor δ of computation fitness with effective channel estimation. In the population, for all vehicles, $f(n_j)$ was computed.

Exploration, transformation, and exploitation are the three phases of HHO. These three phases are described as follows:

- Exploration Phase

During this phase, the process of waiting, searching, and detecting prey is carried out. The following is an example of a hawk's position: The V represents the current iteration and V + 1 represents the next iteration. Hawks can be found at the locations γ_1,γ_2, γ_3, and γ_4, with the range [0, 1] expressing the random integer y. n_{j_a} is the average location of the hawk.

$$n_j\,(V+1) = \left\{ n_{j_{rand}}(V) - \gamma_1 \left| n_{j_{rand}}(V) - 2\, n_j \gamma_2(V) \right| \; if\ m\ \geq 0.5 n_{j_q}\,(V) n_{j_a}\,(V) - \gamma_3\,(l_1 + \gamma_4(v_b - l_1)) \; if\ m < 0.5 \right. \tag{11}$$

$$n_{j_a}\,(V) = \frac{1}{N} \sum_{i=1}^{N} n_j(V) \tag{12}$$

- Transformation Phase

In the exploitation phase, the exploration phase is transformed into the exploitation phase. The energy of the prey degrades from the evading behaviour. Equation (17) defined the transformation phase.

$$\omega_{prey} = 2\omega_0\,(1 - \frac{V}{V_{max}}) \tag{13}$$

where ω_0 shows the initial energy state of prey, V represents the current iteration numbers, and V_{max} represents the maximum number of iterations.

- Phase of Exploitation

The hawk's attack in the previous step serves as a barometer for the quality of the picked prey. In this stage, we tested four distinct approaches: soft besiege, hard besiege, soft besiege with advancing fast dives, and hard besiege with advanced rapid dives. The occurrence of hard and soft relies on the energy level, where $|\omega_{prey}| \geq 0.5$ and $|\omega_{prey}| < 0.5$, respectively.

Attack on a Soft Target:

The attack on a soft target known as a soft besiege and this method may be chosen if $|\omega_{prey}| \geq 0.5$ and $\gamma \geq 0.5$. It is described as:

$$n_j\ (V+1) = \Delta n_j\ (V) - \omega_{prey}\ |\zeta n_j(V - n_j(V))| \tag{14}$$

In this case, the evading method for jump intensity (ζ) is established by $\zeta = 2(1-\gamma_5)$ and $\Delta n_j\ (V) = n_{prey}(V) - n_j(V)$.

Besiege for Hard Target:

If $\gamma \geq 0.5$ and $|\omega_{prey}| < 0.5$, the hard besiege method can be chosen. is the formula is indicated below:

$$n_j\ (V+1) = n_{prey}(V) - \omega_{prey}\ |\ \Delta n_j \cdot (V)\ | \tag{15}$$

Besiege for Soft with High Progressive Dives:

If $\gamma < 0.5$ and $|\omega_{prey}| \geq 0.5$, the soft besiege approach can be chosen. It is determined as follows:

$$\varrho = n_j(M) - \omega_{prey}\ |\ \zeta n_{prey}(V - n_j(V))| \tag{16}$$

The next moving stride (ϱ) of the hawks is calculated. In addition, when hawks dive, the following equation is used to attack the prey.

$$D_n = \varrho + R * LF\ (d) \tag{17}$$

As the dimension d of levy flight is specified as $LF\ (d)$, the random vector is also written as R. The updated location is as follows:

$$n_j\ (V+1) = \{\varrho iff(\varrho) < f(n_j(V)) D_n iff(D_n) < f\ (n_j(V)) \tag{18}$$

Besiege for Hard with High Progressive Dives:

If $\gamma < 0.5$ and $|\omega_{prey}| < 0.5$, the mild besiege strategy may be chosen. It is determined by the updated location:

$$n_j\ (V+1) = \{\varrho iff(\varrho) < f(n_j(V)) D_n iff(D_n) < f\ (n_j(V)) \tag{19}$$

As a result of this, the following equation is derived by ϱ,

$$\varrho = y_{prey}(V) - \omega_{prey} ||\ \zeta n_{prey}(V - n_{j_a}(V))|| \tag{20}$$

The population based on fitness is updated on the location of prey, based on the HHO approach. Thus, the detection of DDoS attacks is effectively classified utilizing MSVM.

5.3. Phase: 2—Reliable Resource Management Using H-WDFOA-VANET

This paper uses hybrid whale–dragonfly optimization-based VANET (H-WDFOA-VANET) for reliable resource management to allocate bandwidth. The proposed H-WDFOA approach is explained, then the background of WOA and DF optimization techniques are individually discussed. In a dynamic VANET scenario, a combination of whale and dragonfly optimization algorithms is represented as H-WDFOA. To achieve bandwidth allocation and obtain routing of the vehicle, the H-WDFOA was employed. Protocol routing also initiated latency and bandwidth utilization to get the designation path. It was difficult during a safety-related and critical time. As a result, to solve this issue, the efficient H-WDFOA technique was utilized to allocate bandwidth and routing protocol.

In a dynamic VANET environment, to see the effect of QoS value, meta-heuristic-based WOA and DF techniques are coupled in this proposed methodology. The hunting behaviour of humpback whales was considered for the whale optimization algorithm

(WOA) generation. The humpback whale's current best strategy is to check its prey's location and encircle it, whereas WOA thinks its prey is a target. After reviewing the current best solution, the best search agent is considered. The different vehicle parameters, such as throughput, number of nearby vehicles, speed, velocity, distance, and speed, were used as the initial population during the start-up phase. The mathematical version of this operation is represented as follows.

$$M = |V \cdot P^*(t) - X(t)| \tag{21}$$

$$P(t+1) = P^*(t) - B \cdot M \tag{22}$$

where t represents iteration, B and V are coefficient vectors, P^* is the position vector of best solution, and P is the position vector

When determining the best solution, P^* of every iteration is periodically updated,

$$B = 2x * r - x \tag{23}$$

$$V = 2 \cdot x \tag{24}$$

Here, r is a random number which range from 0,1.

During the exploitation and exploration phases, the range of the variable is reduced from 2 to 0. At the interval $[-1, 1]$, the phase showed major differences. It was possible for the vehicle to move from its original position to a new position. In the 2D space of the interval $[-1, 1]$, X and Y to X* and Y* were the possible achieved positions. Furthermore, the position was accomplished by updating the procedure, and mathematically represented as:

$$M = |V \cdot P_{rand} - P| \tag{25}$$

$$P(t+1) = P_{rand} - B \cdot M \tag{26}$$

The spiral updating technique can be constructed to analyze the distance of vehicles with one other. This process is determined by the following equation:

$$P(t+1) = M' \cdot e^{sr} \cdot cos\ cos(2\pi r) + P^*(t) \tag{27}$$

Here, M' is the distance of one vehicle $P(t)$ towards another vehicle $P^*(t)$, t is the iteration, s denotes the shape of the logarithmic spiral, and r represents a random number in range $[-1, 1]$.

$$P(t+1) = \{P^*(t) - B \cdot V\ if\ p < 0.5\ M' \cdot e^{sr} \cdot cos\ cos(2\pi r) + P^*(t)\ if\ p > 0.5\} \tag{28}$$

To update vehicle position, 50% probability was chosen for the shrinking encircling mechanism or spiral model. Here, r denoted a random number between the range [0, 1].

To get the maximum optimal solution, the dragonfly optimization approach was hybridized with the whale optimization algorithm to allocate the bandwidth.

The dragonfly's [33] population was initialized in terms of vehicle nodes of $n_j{}'$.

$$n_j{}^* = n_1{}^*, n_2{}', \ldots, n_n{}^* \text{Here, j} = 1, 2, \ldots, \text{n}. \tag{29}$$

In an inquiry space and development reproduction, the dragonfly's artificial position was updated, i.e., position (X) and step (ΔV). The progression vector demonstrates the development of the dragonfly and characters.

$$\Delta X_{t+1} = (wW_i + mA_i + nC_i + pF_i + qE_i) + \overline{w}\,\Delta X_t \tag{30}$$

Here, weight separation is w, weight aliment is m, and n is the cohesion weight, food factor is p, the enemy factor is q, inertia weight is $\overline{w}$, and count iteration is t.

Position vector could be determined as follows:

$$X_{t+1} = X_t + \Delta X_{t+1} \tag{31}$$

In the enhancement phase, various explorative and exploitative processes are accomplished. By Cauchy mutation probability, the dragonfly's situation is refreshed at the point where there is no neighbouring solution. The position vector X is determined by,

$$X_{t+1} = X_t + N_p X_t \tag{32}$$

In the entire swarm at any moment, food source and enemies are determined by the entire arrangement. Thus, the accurate vehicle node is selected, and bandwidth allocation is achieved. A brief flowchart is visualized below.

In Figure 7, the flowchart of the hybrid WDFOA-based VANET is visualized. Initially, the whale optimization parameters were initialized based on the search agent. In this work, several nodes in the vehicle were analyzed based on distance, speed, velocity, and bandwidth. The fitness parameter in each iteration determined the current position of the vehicle. If the node's position was less than 0.5, and the nearby vehicle was equal to or greater than 1, the best location was updated. If the current iteration was higher than the maximum iteration, the target vehicle's position was best. DF was coupled with WOA to obtain optimum optimality.

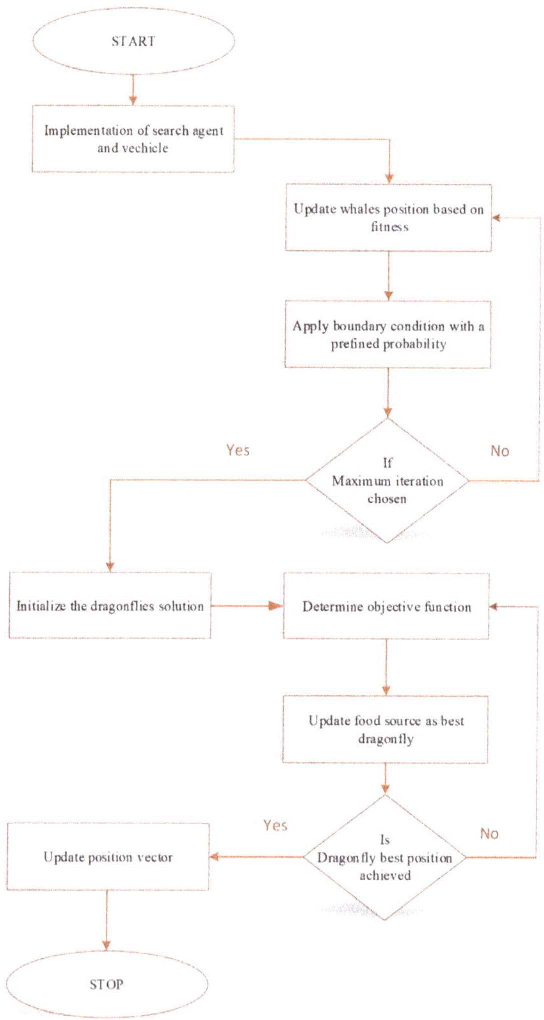

Figure 7. Flowchart for H-WDFOA-VANET.

Furthermore, the dragonfly solution was initialized, and the QoS value determined the bandwidth according to the objective function. The maximum iteration was used until the process is completed and the bandwidth was upgraded. Finally, energy consumption, delay, and drop were considered based on QoS parameters for accurate routing. The proposed approach was valid in allocating bandwidth compared with other existing techniques. This study was robust and fast in predicting DDoS attacks using MSVM and giving the bandwidth using the H-WDFOA technique in the best position after validation for stability in vehicular networks.

6. Results and Discussions

6.1. Dataset Description and Evaluation Metrics

The SDN dataset was created using the Mininet simulator, which was used to classify traffic using machine and deep learning methods [34]. This study began with ten topologies in the Mininet emulator, each of which connected these switches to a single Ryu controller. The network simulators used ICMP, UDP, and TCP traffic, with hostile traffic consisting of a combination of UDP Flood, TCP Sync, and ICMP attacks. The dataset contained a total of 23 features, some of which were collected from switches and others that were estimated. The retrieved features (duration in nan seconds) included Byte count, switch ID, duration, packet count, and duration (in n sec). The sum of duration-sec and duration-nsec was equal to the entire duration. The total number of bytes commuted from the switch port was determined by the destination IP, source IP, port number, and Tx-bytes. Rx-bytes was the total number of bytes received over the switch port. The time and date were transformed into numbers in the dt field, and flow was monitored at 30 s intervals. Furthermore, calculated features such as packet per-flow and byte per-flow counted packets as a single flow. The packet rate was calculated by dividing the total packets per flow by the total number of packets sent per second. Tx-kbps and Rx-kbps were data reception and transmission rates, respectively, and the sums of port bandwidth were Tx-kbps and Rx-kbps. The class labels present in the columns refer to whether the type of traffic was malicious or benign. However, labels 0 and 1 respectively indicate benign and malicious traffic. The duration of the network simulation was 250 min and the row of data possessed was 104,345.

Along with the detailed interval, the simulation of data was authenticated. The dataset was split into two halves for testing and training: 30 and 70%, respectively. The full training process took 42 s to complete [35–37].

The proposed platform was MATLAB 2020a, along with system requirements, which are listed in Table 2.

Table 2. Configuration of Simulation.

System	Requirements
Tool	NS2, MATLAB 2020a
Computer	Windows 10 PRO
Processor	Intel core with high end configuration
RAM	16 GB

6.1.1. Performance Metrics (Ref. [2])

- Efficiency

The efficiency (throughput) parameter defines the total number of packets generated by the sending node in a certain time interval in relation to the quantity of data established via the receiving node in packets. It is represented as:

$$Efficiency(throughput) = number\ of\ received\ data\ packet \times 8/number\ of\ data\ packet\ transmission\ period$$

- Packet Delivery Ratio

This is a method for analyzing incoming and outgoing network data packets in the most efficient way possible. It is calculated based on the ratio of packets generated by the source to data received by the vehicle. The formula utilized to calculate the PDR is:

$$PDR = \frac{ReceivedPackets}{GeneratedPackets} * 100$$

- Drop of packet

During a denial-of-service attack, this parameter tracks the number of packets that were lost because of the malicious behaviour of a single node.

$$Drop\ Ratio = \frac{number\ of\ send\ packet - number\ of\ received\ packet}{number\ of\ send\ packet}$$

- Latency (delay)

It takes time for a package to get from its origin to its destination.

$$delay = \frac{length}{bandwidth}$$

6.1.2. Performance Analysis

The performance of proposed approaches is described in this part using measures such as energy consumption, drop, delay, throughput, packet delivery ratio, and fairness index.

(1) **PHASE 1:**

Phase I detected the DDoS attack using a novel machine learning technique called SVM-HHO, which provided vehicle information. This section describes the analysis, and the proposed performance is detailed below.

Performance measurements were primarily used to assess the model's ability to identify DDoS attacks and allocate bandwidth in VANET situations. From Table 3, it is shown that the proposed modified machine learning-based hybrid optimization technique is more effective compared with existing approaches. In node 60, the proposed methodology attained energy consumption of 0.35 J, delay ratio of 50, and drop ratio of 14.6785. In addition, the suggested approach attained an efficiency of 1710 in comparison with the existing method that attained efficiency of 794.

Table 3. Performance of proposed approach.

Node	Energy Consumption (Joules)	Drop	Delay	Throughput (kilo Bytes/sec)	Network Lifetime	Packet Delivery Ratio (PDR)	Fairness Index (FI)
				Proposed Method			
20	0.25	1.6531	97	1278	339.52	20	4.2477
40	0.32	9.9854	37	1920	664.32	33	2.4125
60	0.35	14.6785	50	1710	524.00	48	1.7961
80	0.43	50.5456	95	1345	370.81	59	1.5752
100	0.51	57.1534	68	1209	307.71	64	1.3947

- Consumption of Energy

The total energy consumption of the proposed approach is shown in Figure 8, based on the data in Table 3. The rate of energy consumption of each node is noted. At node 100, the energy consumption of 0.5 is habited. The increase in nodes is accompanied with an increase in energy consumption.

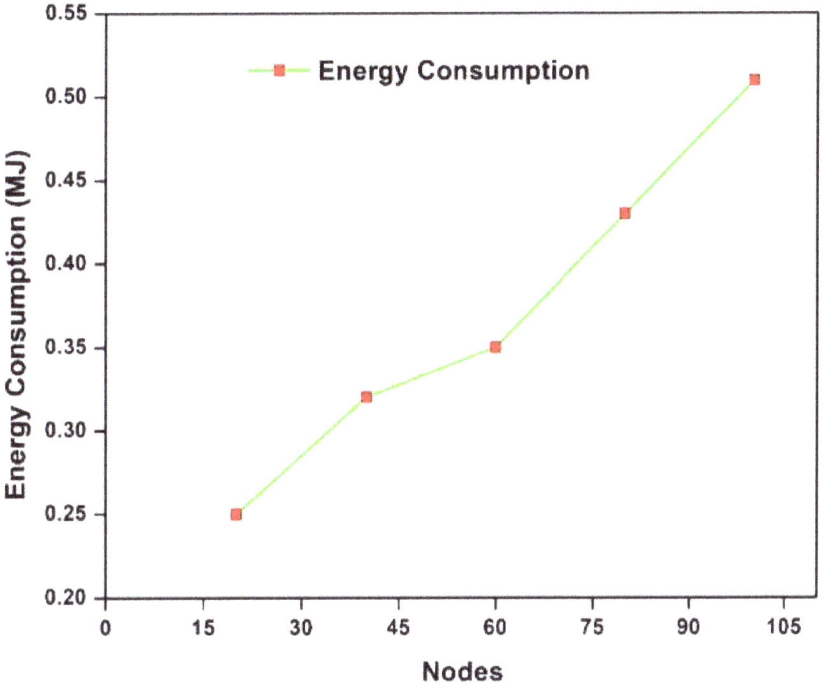

Figure 8. Energy consumption of proposed method.

- Data Rate-Based Energy Consumption

From Table 4, the energy consumption of the proposed method is tabulated at each node with the data set. Nodes with data set values are marked in Table 4.

Table 4. Energy consumption based on data rate.

Node	Data Rate at 4	Data Rate at 6	Data Rate at 8	Date Rate at 10	Data Rate at 12	Data Rate at 14
20	0.8	1.2	1.6	2.1	2.5	2.9
40	0.4	0.6	0.8	1.1	1.2	1.5
60	0.5	0.8	1.0	1.2	1.6	1.8
80	0.7	1.1	1.5	1.9	2.3	2.6
100	0.9	1.3	1.8	2.3	2.7	3.2

Figure 9 shows the data rate-based energy consumption ratio of the suggested approach. If the data packet rates are high, the energy is at a peak; if not, the energy produces lower data rates. From Table 4, we can see that at node 20, energy consumption is 0.8, obtained at a data rate of 4, 1.2 is attained at a data rate of 6, 1.6 is acquired in a data rate of 8, and 2.1 is obtained at a data rate of 10. At a data rate of 12, 2.5 is gained, and at a data rate of 14, energy consumption is 2.9. Similarly, in node 40, energy consumption is 0.4 at a data rate of 4, 0.6 at a data rate of 6, 0.8 at a data rate of 8, 1.1 at a data rate of 10, 1.2 at a data rate of 12, and 1.5 at a data rate of 14. Moreover, at node 60, energy consumption is 0.5 at a data rate of 4, 0.8 at a data rate of 6, 1.0 at a data rate of 8, 1.2 at a data rate of 10, 1.6 at a data rate of 12, and 1.8 at a data rate of 14. In addition, at node 80, energy consumption is 0.7 at a data rate of 4, 1.1 at a data rate of 6, 1.5 at a data rate of 8, 1.9 at a data rate of 10, 2.3 at a data rate of 12, and 2.6 at a data rate of 14. Furthermore, at node 100, energy consumption is 0.9 at a data rate of 4, 1.3 at a data rate of 6, 1.8 at a data rate of 8, 2.3 at a data rate of 10, 2.7 at a data rate of 12, and 3.2 at a data rate of 14.

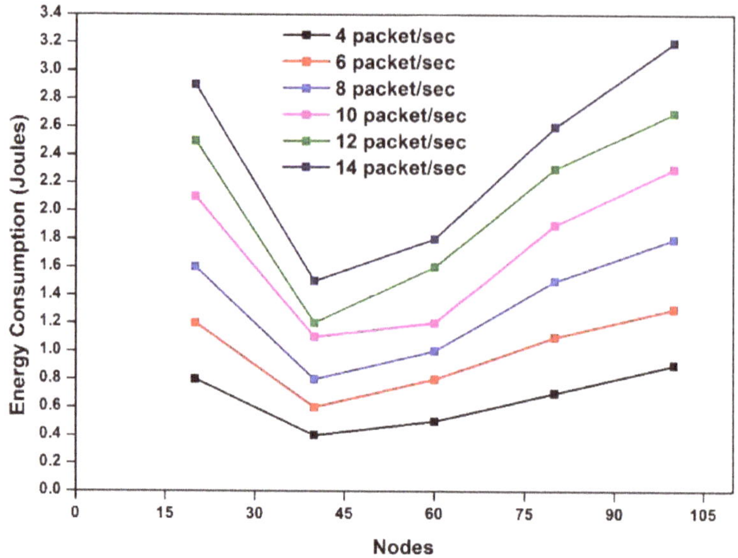

Figure 9. Consumption of energy based on data set.

- Lifetime of the Network

The overall network lifetime of the suggested method from Table 3 is plotted and detailed in Figure 10.

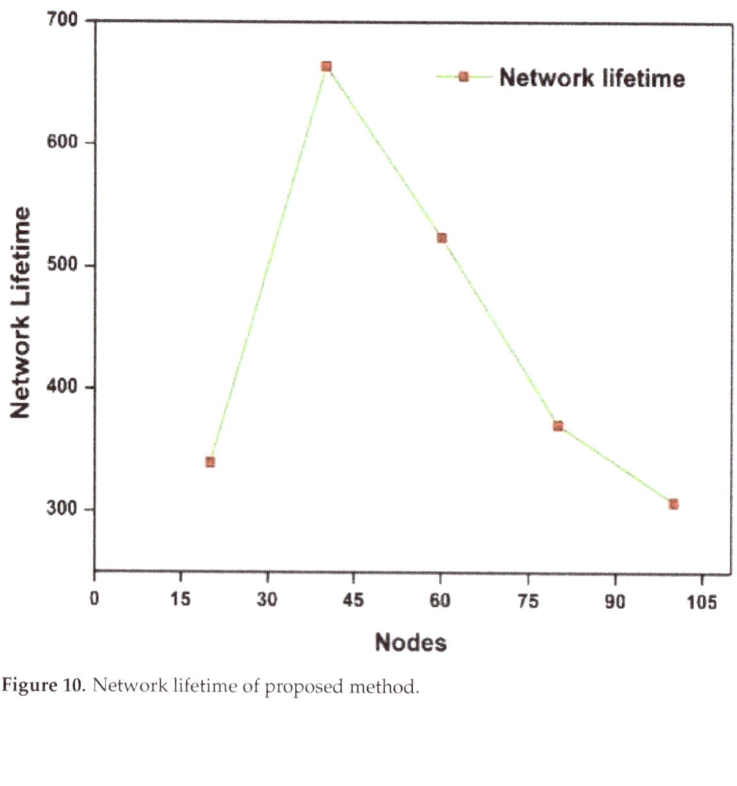

Figure 10. Network lifetime of proposed method.

The lifetime of the network of the suggested approach is shown in Figure 10. The lifetime of the network for each node was noted. At node 100, the network lifetime of 307.71 was habited. The increase in nodes was accompanied with an increase in network lifetime.

- Data Rate-Based Network Lifetime

From Table 5, the network lifetime of the proposed method was tabulated at each node with the data set. Nodes with data set values are marked in the Table 5.

Table 5. Lifetime of network.

Node	Date Rate at 4	Date Rate at 6	Date Rate at 8	Date Rate at 10	Date Rate at 12	Date Rate at 14
20	1339.5	896.1	675.3	500.2	392.2	388
40	2250	1575	1230.1	963	650	600
60	1854.2	1246.5	916.3	669.8	550	500
80	1370.2	932.6	619.1	500.9	400.2	395.4
100	1100	759	530.8	438.5	318	300

Figure 11 demonstrates the proposed system's network lifetime. If the data packet rate is low, the network lifetime appears high. From Table 5, we can see that at node 20, the network lifetime of 1339.5 is obtained at a data rate of 4, 896.1 is attained at a data rate of 6, 675.3 is acquired at a data rate of 8, and 500.2 is accomplished at a data rate of 10. At a data rate of 12, 392.2 is gained, and at a data rate of 14, network lifetime is 388. Similarly, in node 40, the network lifetime is 2250 at a data rate of 4, 1575 at a data rate of 6, 1230.1 at a data rate of 8, 963 at a data rate of 10, 650 at a data rate of 12, and 600 at a data rate of 14. Moreover, at node 60, network lifetime is 1854.2 at a data rate of 4, 1246.5 at a data rate of 6, 916.3 at a data rate of 8, 669.8 at a data rate of 10, 550 at a data rate of 12, and 500 at a data rate of 14. In addition, at node 80, network lifetime is 1370.2 at a data rate of 4, 932.6 at a data rate of 6, 619.1 at a data rate of 8, 500.9 at a data rate of 10, 400.2 at a data rate of 12, and 395.4 at a data rate of 14. Furthermore, at node 100, the network lifetime is 1100 at a data rate of 4, 759 at a data rate of 6, 530.8 at a data rate of 8, 438.5 at a data rate of 10, 318 at a data rate of 12, and 300 at a data rate of 14.

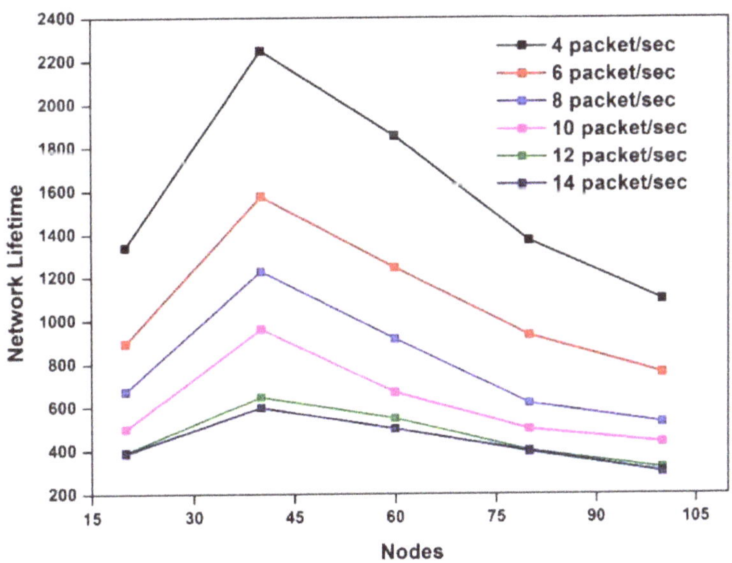

Figure 11. Network lifetime.

- Throughput

The overall efficiency(throughput) of the suggested approach is shown in Figure 12. The rate of throughput of each node is noted. At node 100, a throughput of 1209 was habited. An increase in nodes is accompanied with an increase in throughput.

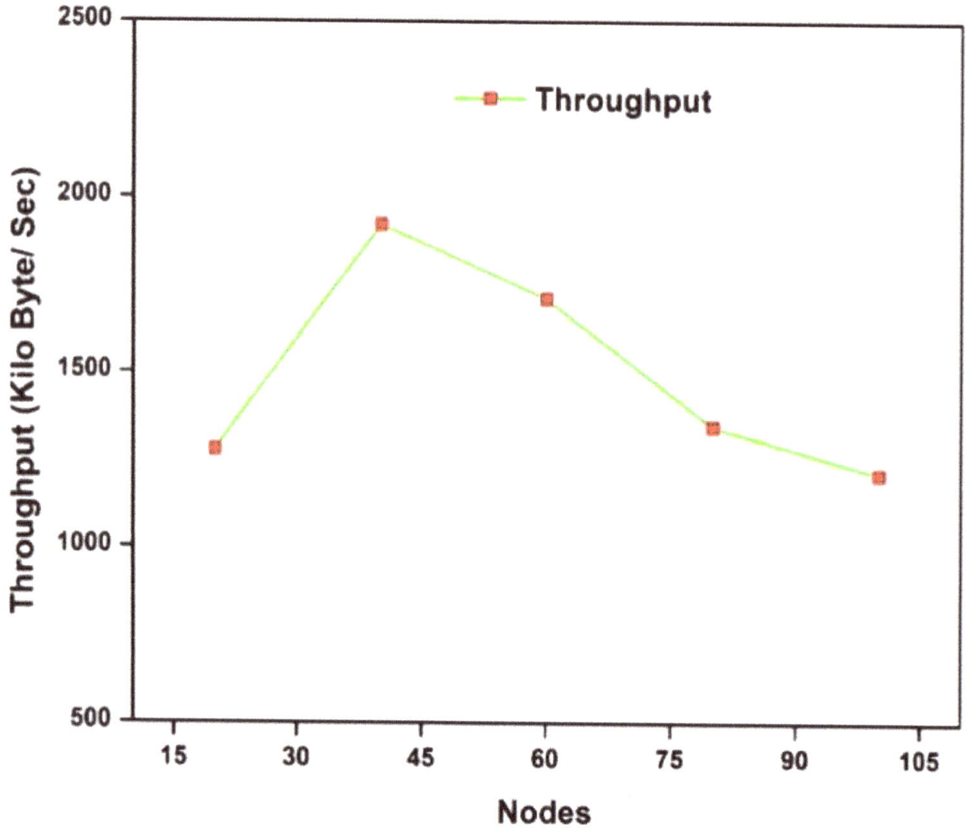

Figure 12. Throughput of the proposed method.

- Data Rate-Based Throughput

In Table 6, the throughput of the suggested approach is tabulated at each node with the data set. Nodes with data set values are marked in Table 6.

Table 6. Throughput based data set.

Node	Data Rate at 4	Data Rate at 6	Data Rate at 8	Data Rate at 10	Data Rate at 12	Data Rate at 14
20	12,700	19,180	25,570	31,960	38,350	44,740
40	19,200	28,800	38,400	48,000	57,600	67,280
60	17,100	25,650	34,200	42,750	51,300	61,700
80	13,450	20,170	26,890	33,620	40,340	47,060
100	12,090	18,140	24,180	30,230	36,280	42,320

Figure 13 demonstrates the throughput ratio of the proposed system. If the data packet rates were low, then the throughput ratio also decreased. The throughput of the proposed technique was reached by 42,320 in node 100 at a data rate of 14 packets/sec. At node

20, 12,700 throughputs were obtained at a data rate of 4. At node 20, 19,180 throughputs were attained at a data rate of 6. At node 20, 25,570 throughputs were acquired at a data rate of 8. At node 20, 31,960 throughputs were accomplished at a data rate of 10. At node 20, 38,350 throughputs were gained at a data rate of 12. At node 20, 44,740 throughputs were fetched at a data rate of 14. Similarly, in node 40, there were 19,200 throughputs at a data rate of 4, 28,800 throughputs at a data rate of 6, 38,400 throughputs at a data rate of 8, 48,000 throughputs at a data rate of 10, 57,600 throughputs at a data rate of 12, and 67,280 throughputs at a data rate of 14. At node 60, there were 17,100 throughputs at a data rate of 4, 25,650 throughputs at a data rate of 6, 34,200 throughputs at a data rate of 8, 42,750 throughputs at a data rate of 10, 51,300 throughputs at a data rate of 12, and 61,700 throughputs at a data rate of 14. In addition, at node 80, there were 13,450 throughputs at a data rate of 4, 20,170 throughputs at a data rate of 6, 26,890 throughputs at a data rate of 8, 33,620 throughputs at a data rate of 10, 40,340 throughputs at a data rate of 12, and 47,060 throughputs at a data rate of 14. Furthermore, at node 100, there were 12,090 throughputs at a data rate of 4, 18,140 throughputs at a data rate of 6, 24,180 throughputs at a data rate of 8, 30,230 throughputs at a data rate of 10, 36,280 throughputs at a data rate of 12, and 42,320 throughputs at a data rate of 14.

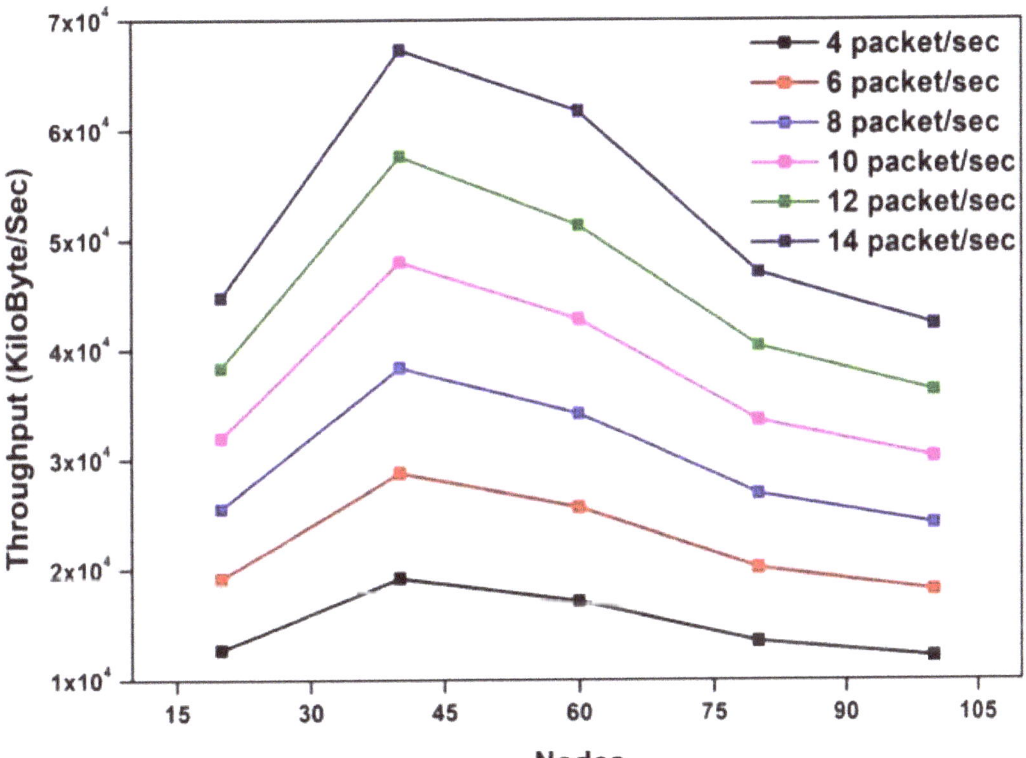

Figure 13. Plot for throughput.

- Packet Delivery Ratio (PDR)

Figure 14 illustrates the packet delivery ratio. To optimize incoming and outgoing network packets, the PDR was evaluated to assess the process. In the VANET scenario, the packet deliver ratio represents the greater presentation of the system.

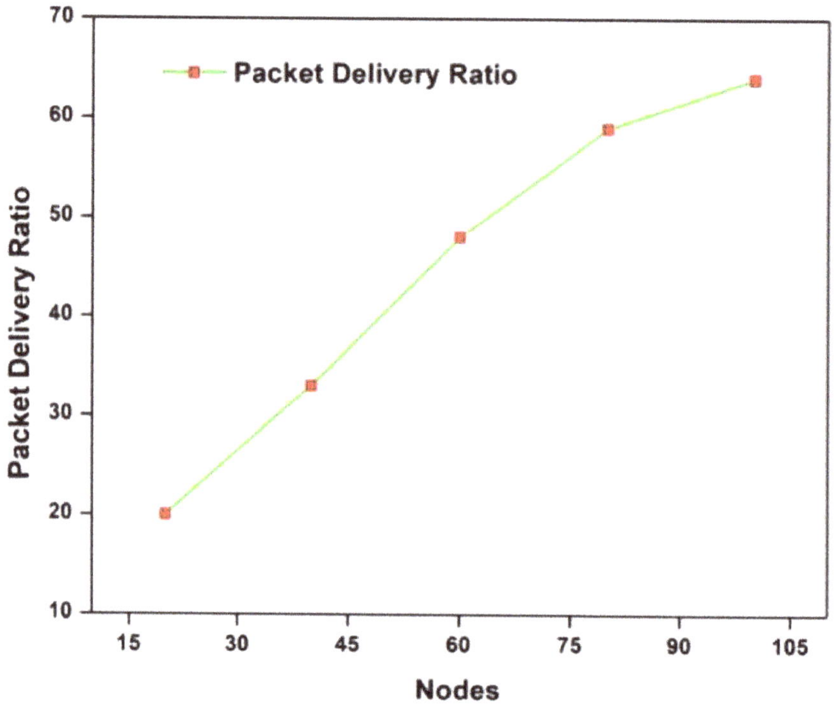

Figure 14. Ratio of packet delivery.

(2) **PHASE 2:**

To better anticipate mobility in VANET, a second phase presented the outcomes of the suggested and implemented approaches for enhancing machine learning with a hybrid optimization strategy. The project's implementation (H-WDFOA-VANET) was analyzed and compared with modern standards (RI-CS, EHACORP). Measured values for the delay, energy consumption, drop, throughput, and fairness index was computed and compared with both proposed (RI-CS) and existing (EHACORP) approaches. In addition, the suggested technique was tested on both the NS2 and MATLAB platforms.

- Results Obtained Through Node

Comparisons were made between the node of the proposed approach and existing techniques in terms of latency, energy consumption, drop, throughput, and fairness index (Figures 15–19). In the table below, we can see the actual values that were measured. Node values for both existing and proposed methods are displayed in Table 7. The major purpose of these performance measures was to evaluate the suggested model's capacity for mobility prediction in VANET. Results from a comparison of the proposed method with state-of-the-art approaches to mobility prediction in VANET are shown in Table 7, which shows that the proposed approach is superior. As such, the performance metrics indicated the proposed model's capacity for mobility prediction in VANET. Table 7 shows that, compared with other methods used to predicting mobility in VANET, the suggested technique, which uses a hybrid optimization strategy to improve machine learning, performs better. Better throughput is achieved using the proposed method. The suggested system achieved 2.00000 mJ of energy consumption, 15.61668 s of latency, and 0.15759 drop in node 60. Furthermore, the throughput attained by the new approach was higher than that of existing methods. There was also a reduction in energy use.

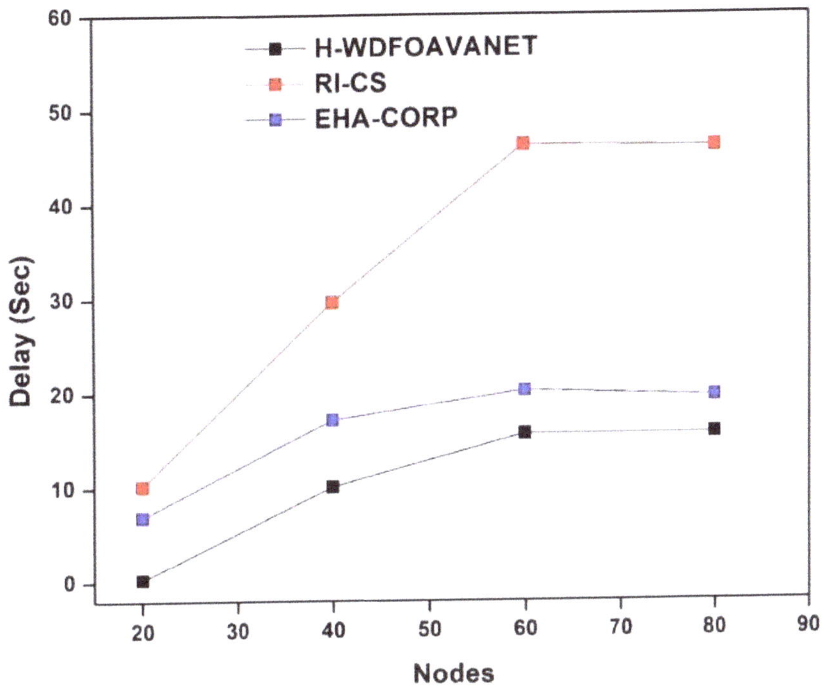

Figure 15. Plots of nodes vs. delays in the suggested approach and existing approaches.

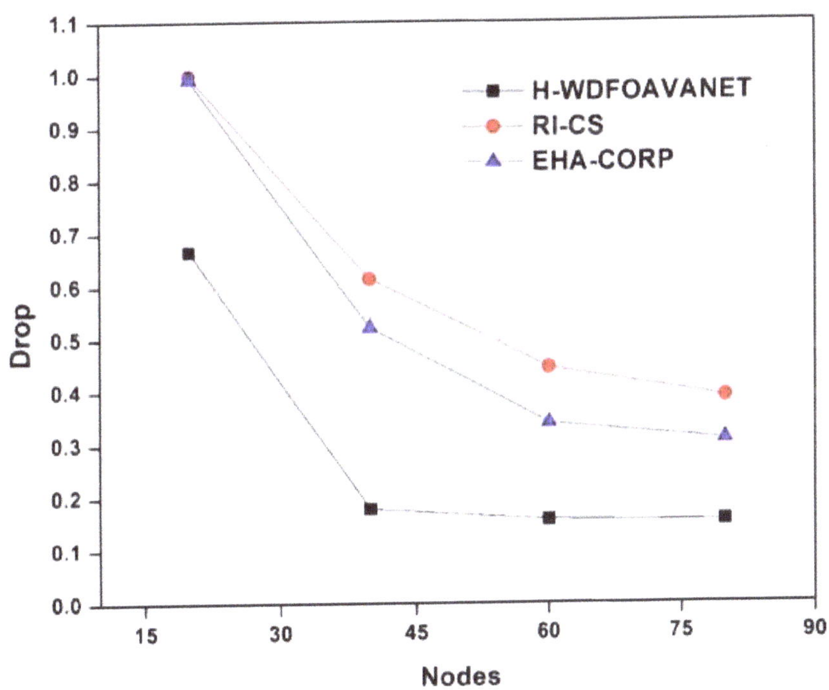

Figure 16. Plots of nodes vs. drop in the suggested approach and existing approaches.

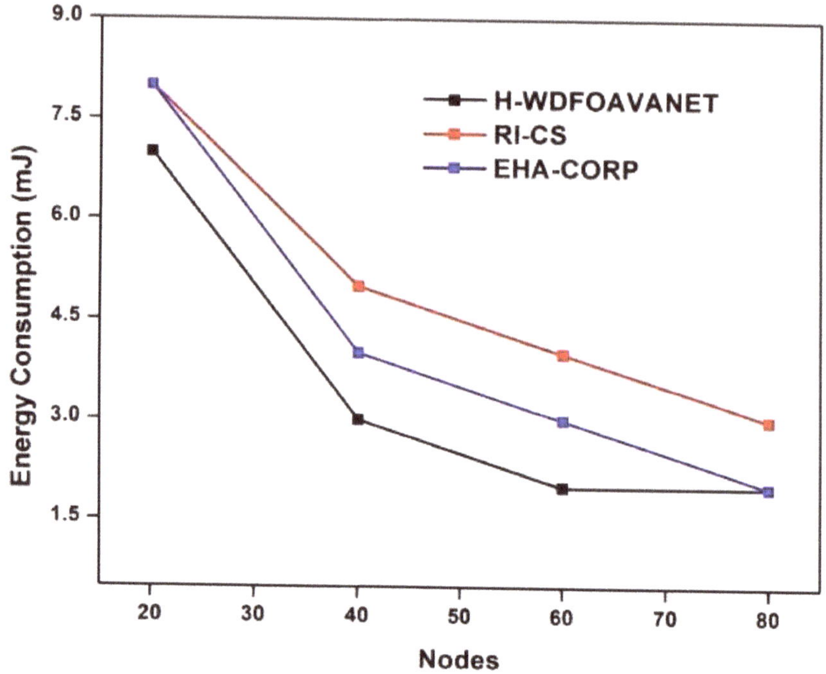

Figure 17. Plots of nodes vs. energy consumption in the suggested approach and existing approaches.

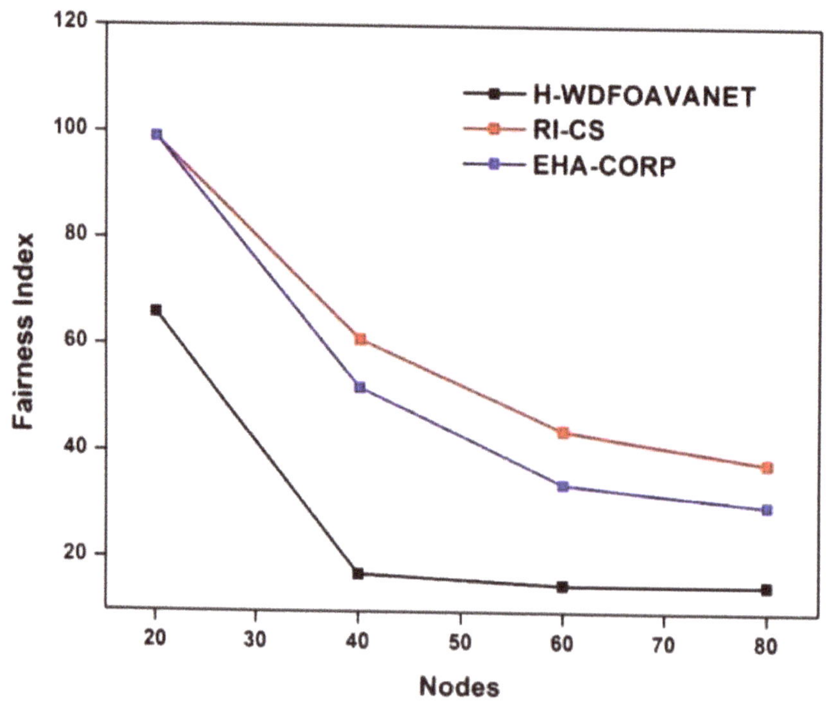

Figure 18. Plots of nodes vs. fairness index in the suggested approach and existing approaches.

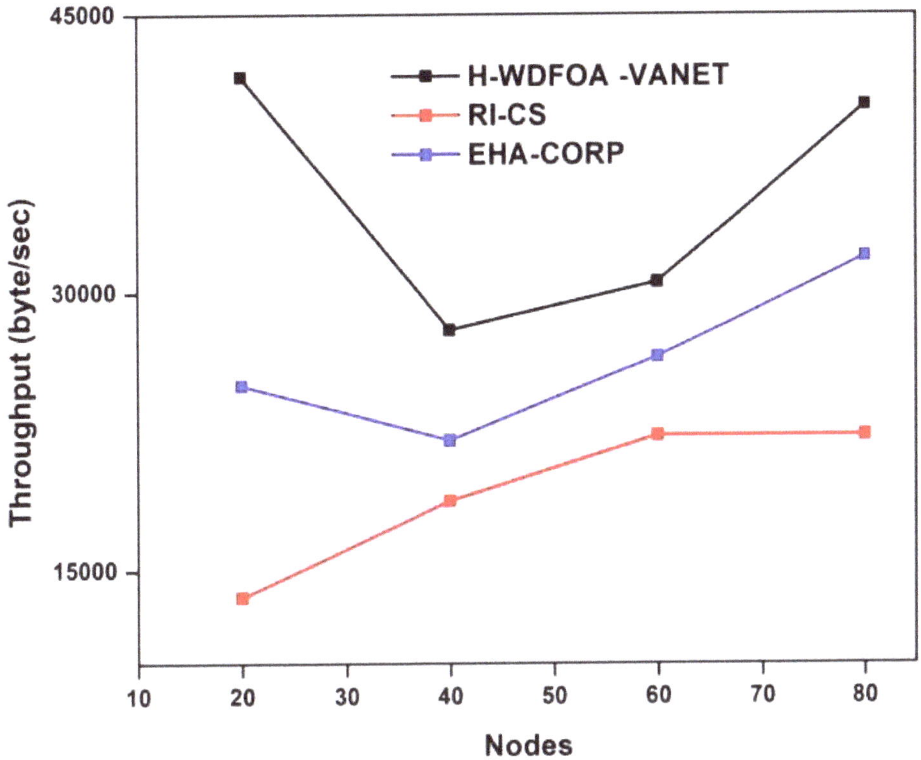

Figure 19. Plots of nodes vs. throughput in the suggested approach and existing approaches.

Table 7. Comparison with existing approaches through nodes.

Performance Parameters	Techniques	Nodes			
		20	40	60	80
Delay (s)	H-WDFOA-VANET	0.299063	10.05305	15.61668	15.64318
	RI-CS	10.22709	29.63915	46.23192	46.03685
	EHA-CORP	6.942181	17.167577	20.178139	19.568945
Energy consumption (mJ)	H-WDFOA-VANET	7	3	2	2
	RI-CS	8	5	4	3
	EHA-CORP	8	4	3	2
Drop	H-WDFOA-VANET	0.66674	0.17871	0.15759	0.15504
	RI-CS	0.99904	0.6142	0.4456	0.3898
	EHA-CORP	0.99293	0.521614	0.340694	0.308867
Throughput (Bps)	H-WDFOA-VANET	41,661	27,995	30,560	40,095
	RI-CS	13,582	18,785	202,302	22,299
	EHA-CORP	25,022	22,043	26,556	31,937
Fairness Index (FI)	H-WDFOA-VANET	66	17	15	15
	RI-CS	99	61	44	38
	EHA-CORP	99	52	34	30

- Results Obtained by Varying the Speed Parameter

The proposed and existing methods were compared and contrasted in terms of speed with delay, energy consumption, drop, throughput, and fairness index (Figures 20–24). The measured values are displayed in Table 8. The estimated speeds of existing and prospective methods are listed in Table 8. Below is a graphical depiction of the speed of other metrics, such as throughput, drop, energy and fairness index, and delay. An evaluation of the suggested method at speed 20 yielded an energy consumption of 1320 mJ, delay of 90.180295 s, and drop value of 13.334678.

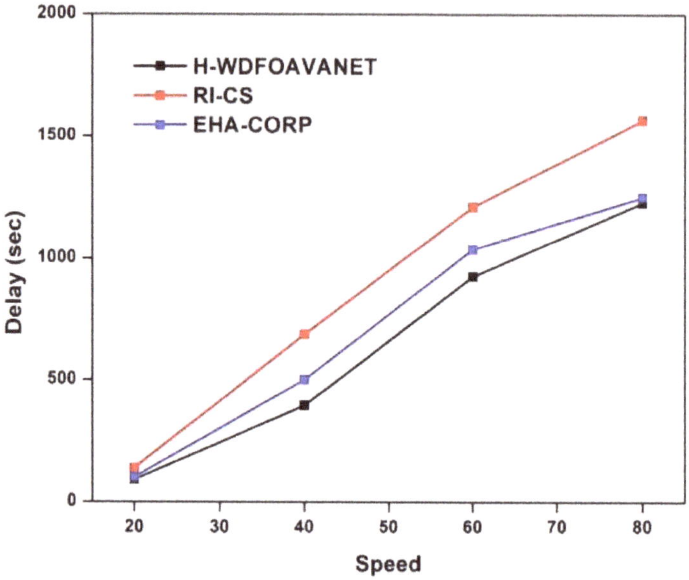

Figure 20. Plots of speed vs. delay in the suggested approach and existing approaches.

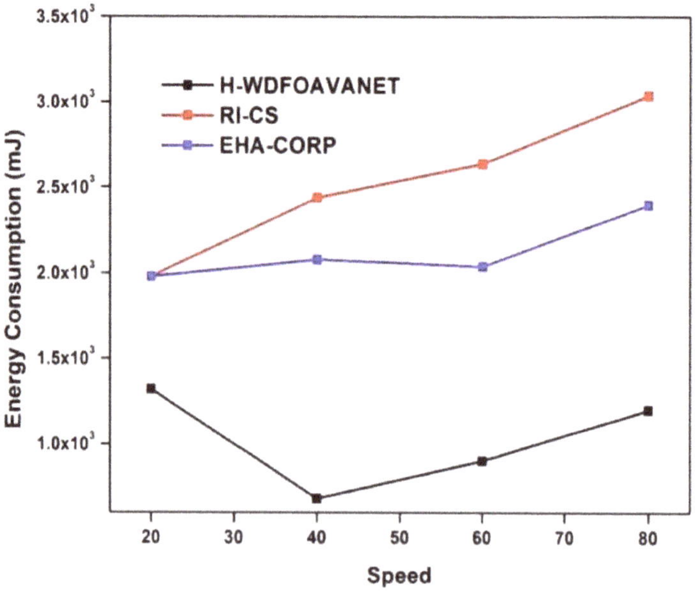

Figure 21. Plots of speed vs. energy consumption in the suggested approach and existing approaches.

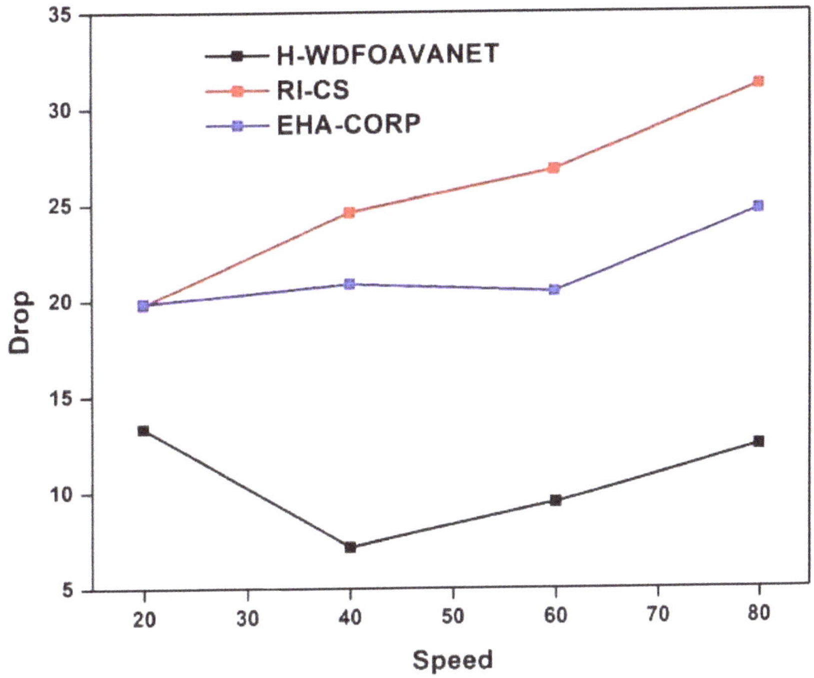

Figure 22. Plots of speed vs. drop in the suggested approach and existing approaches.

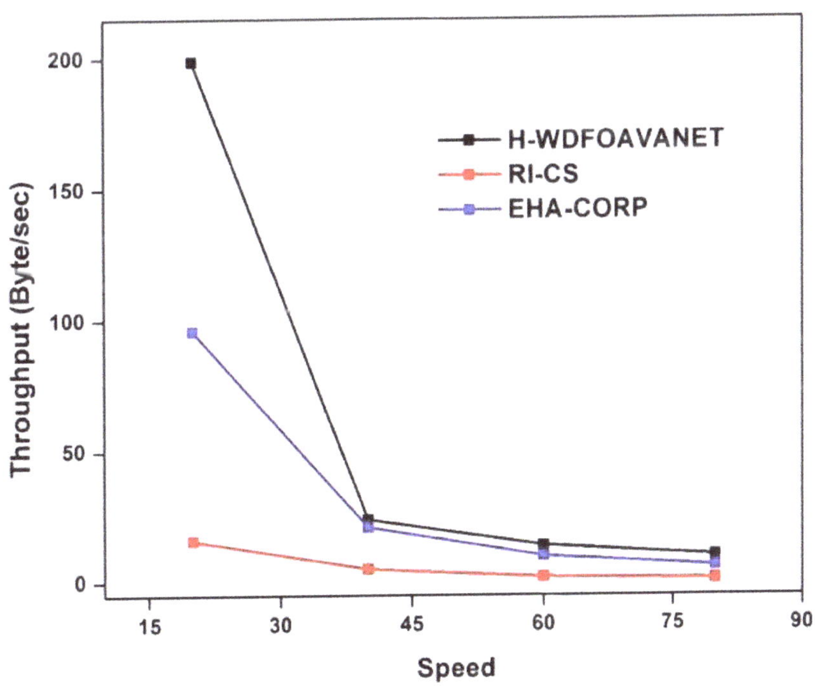

Figure 23. Plots of speed vs. throughput in the suggested approach and existing approaches.

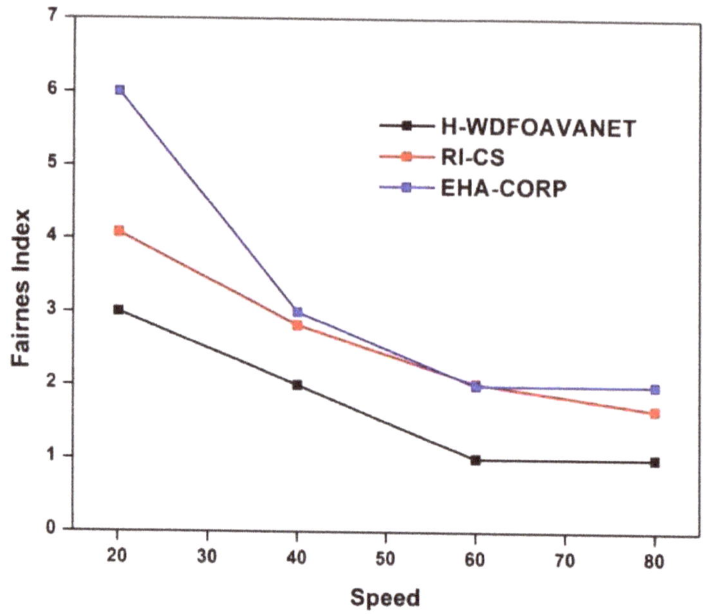

Figure 24. Plots of speed vs. fairness index in the suggested approach and existing approaches.

Table 8. Comparative analysis of suggested approach with existing approaches at different speeds.

Performance Parameters	Techniques	Speed			
		20	40	60	80
Delay (s)	H-WDFOA-VANET	90.180295	395.189005	924.638246	1227.591591
	RI-CS	138.843616	686.703072	1210.68834	1565.515813
	EHA-CORP	100.98126	502.120993	1037.0019	1251.455006
Energy consumption (mJ)	H-WDFOA-VANET	1320	680	900	1200
	RI-CS	1980	2440	2640	3040
	EHA-CORP	1980	2080	2040	2400
Drop	H-WDFOA-VANET	13.334678	7.151254	9.450511	12.405151
	RI-CS	19.80027	24.58287	26.7894	31.195048
	EHA-CORP	19.858595	20.86455	20.441628	24.709388
Throughput (Bps)	H-WDFOA-VANET	199	24	14	10
	RI-CS	16	5	2	1
	EHA-CORP	96	21	10	6
Fairness Index (FI)	H-WDFOA-VANET	3	2	1	1
	RI-CS	4.0746	2.819775	2.0302	1.672425
	EHA-CORP	6	3	2	2

Additionally, the throughput achieved by the new approach is higher than that of the existing approaches. One key difference between the proposed and existing approaches is that the proposed technique includes a fairness score. With the suggested method, the values for energy consumption, delay, and drop at speed 40 were 680 mJ, 395.189005 s, and 7.151254, respectively. In addition, greater throughput could be achieved using the new method than existing methods. The proposed method reduces energy usage to 900 mJ, delay to 924.638246 s, and drop value to 9.450511 when traveling at 60 mph.

7. Conclusions

This study's findings mainly centered on detecting DDoS attacks and allocating bandwidth in the VANET, based on a machine learning-hybrid optimization approach. DDoS attack detection was performed using the SVM-HHO technique, i.e., a modified SVM. Then, the impact of DDoS attacks in the VANET was mitigated using a hybrid whale dragonfly optimization technique (H-WDFOA-VANET). Using a unique optimization method called the hybrid whale dragonfly optimization approach (H-WDOA-VANET), which hybridizes the notion of rider integrated cuckoo search, this study found the best route selection with minimal routing costs (RI-CS). To utilize the predicted information after validation, fast and reliable communication was achieved for stability in vehicular networks. Energy consumption, throughput, latency, and packet delivery ratioswere a few performance indicators used to gauge performance of the suggested approach. To increase the effectiveness of the routing process in VANETs, a new protocol, H-WDFOA-VANET, was introduced.

The DCM and SBACO pairing at H-WDFOA-VANET sped up packet processing, decreased ant search time, and eliminated blind broadcasting packets while preventing stagnation issues. The packet delivery ratio and throughput benefit from H-WDFOA-VANET allowed for the use of the shortest channel without stagnation, due to its rapid processing of packets and fast convergence speed. Finally, the suggested hybrid whale dragonfly optimization approach (H-WDFOA-VANET) was evaluated in comparison with industry standard models, such as rider integrated cuckoo search (RI-CS) and enhanced hybrid ant colony optimization routing protocol (EHACORP). The H-WDFOA-VANET system had values of 2.00000 mJ for energy consumption, 15.61668 s for latency, and 0.15759 for drop at node 60. A higher throughput was achieved using the new approach as well. With the suggested method, the energy consumption target, delay value, and drop value at node 60 may be attained. At node 80, the suggested approach minimized the drop value to 0.15504, delay time to 15.64318 s, and energy consumption to 2.00000 mJ. These results demonstrate the efficacy of the proposed H-WDFOA-VANETapproach. Therefore, the efficiency of the proposed system was greater than that of existing systems.

Author Contributions: Conceptualization: G.P.K.M., S.T. and A.J.; writing—original draft preparation: P.K.M., A.A. and C.O.S.; methodology: M.S., R.S., C.O.S. and T.C.M.; writing—review and editing: P.K.M., R.S. and G.P.K.M.; investigation: C.O.S., A.J. and S.T.; supervision: A.A., M.S. and S.T.; visualization: P.K.M. and T.C.M.; software: T.C.M., R.S. and S.T. All authors have read and agreed to the published version of the manuscript.

Funding: National Research Development Projects to finance excellence (PFE)-14/2022-2024 granted by the Romanian Ministry of Research and Innovation.

Conflicts of Interest: The authors declare no conflict of interest.

Abbreviations

Abbreviations	Full Form
ADMM	Alternating Direction Multiplier Method
AMMSE	Adaptive Mathematical Morphology Spectrum Entropy
ANN	Artificial Neural Network
CRS-MP	Centralized Routing Memechanism with Mobility Prediction
CS	Cuckoo Search
CNN	Convolutional neural network
DCM	Distance Calculation Method
DDoS	Distributed Denial of Service
DF	Dragon Fly
DNS	Domain Name System
EHACORP	Enhanced Hybrid Ant Colony Optimization Routing Proctocal

Abbreviations	Full Form
ERM	Empirical Risk Minimization
GPS	Global Positioning System
HHO	Harris Hwaks Optimization
H-WDFOA	Hybrid Whale Dragonfly Optimization Algorithm
ICMP	Internet Control Messge Protocal l
IDs	Intrusion Detections
MANET	Mobile Adhoc Network
ML	Machine Learning
MMS	Mathematical Morphology Spectrum
MSVM	Multiclass Support Vector Machine
MVSA	MultivariantStream Analysis
NSL-KDD	Network Security Laboratory Knowledge Discovery Dataset
NTP	Network Time Protocal
PML-CIDS	Privacy-preserving Machine-learning BasedCollaborative Intrusion Detection
PPS	Packets Per Second
QoS	Quality of Service e
RI-CS	Rider Intergration Cuckoo Search
ROA	Rider Optimization Algorithm
RPS	Requests per Seconds
RSU	RoadSide unit
SBACO	Source-based Ant Colony Optimization
SDN	SoftwareDefined Networking
SVC	Support Vector Classifier r
SVM	Support Vector Machine
TCP	Transmission Control Protocol
TOPSIS	Technique for Order Performance by Similarity to Ideal Solution
UDP	User Datagram Protocol
V2I	Vehicle to Infrastructure
V2V	Vehicle to Vehicle
V2X	Vehicle to Everything
VANET	Vehicle Adhoc Network
VNS-NSGA	Virtual Network System Nondominated Sorting Genetic Algorithm
WAVE	Waveform Audio File Format
WOA	Whale Optimization Algorithm

References

1. Gao, Y.; Wu, H.; Song, B.; Jin, Y.; Luo, X.; Zeng, X. A Distributed Network Intrusion Detection Systemfor Distributed Denialof Service Attacksin Vehicular Ad Hoc Network. *IEEE Access* **2019**, *7*, 154560–154571. [CrossRef]
2. Cheng, N.; Lyu, F.; Chen, J.; Xu, W.; Zhou, H.; Zhang, S.; Shen, X. Big Data Driven Vehicular Networks. *IEEE Netw.* **2018**, *32*, 160–167. [CrossRef]
3. Khan, Z.; Fan, P.; Fang, S.; Abbas, F. An Unsupervised Cluster-Based VANET-Oriented Evolving Graph (CVo EG) Modeland Associated Reliable Routing Scheme. *IEEE Trans. Intell. Transp. Syst.* **2019**, *20*, 3844–3859. [CrossRef]
4. Correia, S.; Boukerche, A.; Meneguette, R.I. An Architecture for Hierarchical Software-Defined Vehicular Networks. *IEEE Commun. Mag.* **2017**, *55*, 80–86. [CrossRef]
5. Tan, L.; Pan, Y.; Wu, J.; Zhou, J.; Jiang, H.; Deng, Y. A New Framework for DDoS Attack Detectionand Defensein SDN Environment. *IEEE Access* **2020**, *8*, 161908–161919. [CrossRef]
6. Zhijun, W.; Qing, X.; Jingjie, W.; Meng, Y.; Liang, L. Low-Rate DDoS Attack Detection Basedon Factorization Machinein Software Defined Network. *IEEE Access* **2020**, *8*, 17404–17418. [CrossRef]
7. Shu, Z.; Wan, J.; Li, D.; Lin, J.; Vasilakos, A.V.; Imran, M. Securityin Software-Defined Networking: Threatsand Countermeasures. *Mob. Netw. Appl.* **2016**, *21*, 764–776. [CrossRef]
8. Polat, H.; Turkoglu, M.; Polat, O. Deep network approach with stacked sparse autoencoders in detection of DDoS attacks on SDN-based VANET. *IET Commun.* **2020**, *14*, 4089–4100. [CrossRef]
9. Adhikary, K.; Bhushan, S.; Kumar, S.; Dutta, K. Evaluatingthe Impactof DDo SAttacksin Vehicular Ad-Hoc Networks. *Int. J. Secur. Priv. Pervasive Comput.* **2020**, *12*, 1–18. [CrossRef]
10. Sahoo, K.S.; Tripathy, B.K.; Naik, K.; Ramasubbareddy, S.; Balusamy, B.; Khari, M.; Burgos, D. An Evolutionary SVM Modelfor DDOS Attack Detectionin Software Defined Networks. *IEEE Access* **2020**, *8*, 132502–132513. [CrossRef]

11. Bouyeddou, B.; Kadri, B.; Harrou, F.; Sun, Y. DDOS-attacks detection using an efficient measurement-based statistical mechanism. *Eng. Sci. Technol. Int. J.* **2020**, *23*, 870–878. [CrossRef]
12. Ye, J.; Cheng, X.; Zhu, J.; Feng, L.; Song, L. A DDoS Attack Detection Method Based on SVM in Software Defined Network. *Secur. Commun. Netw.* **2018**, *2018*, 9804061. [CrossRef]
13. Hong, K.; Kim, Y.; Choi, H.; Park, J. SDN-Assisted Slow HTTP DDoS Attack Defense Method. *IEEE Commun. Lett.* **2018**, *22*, 688–691. [CrossRef]
14. Kadam, N.; Sekhar, K.R. Machine Learning Approach of Hybrid KSVN Algorithmto Detect DDoS Attackin VANET. *Int. J. Adv. Comput. Sci. Appl. IJACSA* **2021**, *12*, 718–722. [CrossRef]
15. Gad, A.R.; Nashat, A.A.; Barkat, T.M. Intrusion Detection System Using Machine Learning for Vehicular Ad Hoc Networks Based on To N-IoT Dataset. *IEEE Access* **2021**, *9*, 142206–142217. [CrossRef]
16. Wu, D.; Wu, C. Research on the Time-Dependent Split Delivery Green Vehicle Routing Problem for Fresh Agricultural Products with Multiple Time Windows. *Agriculture* **2022**, *12*, 793. [CrossRef]
17. Poongodi, M.; Hamdi, M.; Sharma, A.; Ma, M.; Singh, P.K. DDoS Detection Mechanism Using Trust-Based Evaluation Systemin VANET. *IEEE Access* **2019**, *7*, 183532–183544. [CrossRef]
18. Adhikary, K.; Bhushan, S.; Kumar, S.; Dutta, K. Hybrid Algorithm to Detect DDoS Attacksin VANETs. *Wirel. Pers. Commun.* **2020**, *114*, 3613–3634. [CrossRef]
19. Kolandaisamy, R.; Noor, R.M.; Ahmedy, I.; Ahmad, I.; Z'aba, M.R.; Imran, M.; Alnuem, M. A Multivariant Stream Analysis Approachto Detectand Mitigate DDoS Attacksin Vehicular AdHoc Networks. *Wirel. Commun. Mob. Comput.* **2018**, *2018*, 2874509. [CrossRef]
20. Marwah, G.P.K.; Jain, A. A hybrid optimization with ensemble learning to ensure VANET network stability based on performance analysis. *Sci. Rep.* **2022**, *12*, 10287. [CrossRef]
21. Bangui, H.; Ge, M.; Buhnova, B. A hybrid machine learning model for intrusion detection in VANET. *Computing* **2022**, *104*, 503–531. [CrossRef]
22. Tang, Y.; Cheng, N.; Wu, W.; Wang, M.; Dai, Y.; Shen, X. Delay-Minimization Routing for Heterogeneous VANETs With Machine Learning Based Mobility Prediction. *IEEE Trans. Veh. Technol.* **2019**, *68*, 3967–3979. [CrossRef]
23. Zhang, T.; Zhu, Q. Distributed Privacy-Preserving Collaborative Intrusion Detection Systems for VANETs. *IEEE Trans. Signal Inf. Processing Over Netw.* **2018**, *4*, 148–161. [CrossRef]
24. Gnanasekar, T.S.; Samiappan, D. VANET routing Protocols: Implementation and Analysis Using NS3 and SUMO. *Int. J. Commun. Syst.* **2021**, *34*, e4954. [CrossRef]
25. Ramamoorthy, R.; Thangavelu, M. An enhanced hybrid ant colony optimization routing protocol for vehicular ad-hoc networks. *J. Ambient. Intell. Hum. Comput.* **2022**, *13*, 3837–3868. [CrossRef]
26. Abusitta, A.; Bellaiche, M.; Dagenais, M. An SVM-based framework for detecting DoS attacks in virtualized clouds under changing environment. *J. Cloud Comp.* **2018**, *7*, 9. [CrossRef]
27. Yao, R.; Guo, C.; Deng, W.; Zhao, H. A novel mathematical morphology spectrument ropy based on scale-adaptive techniques. *ISA Trans.* **2022**, *126*, 691–702. [CrossRef]
28. Hossain, M.A.; Noor, R.M.; Yau, K.-L.; Razalli, S.; Zaba, M.; Ahmedy, I.; Jabbarpour, R. Multi-Objective Harris Hawks Optimization Algorithm based 2-Hop Routing Algorithm for CR-VANET. *IEEE Access* **2021**, *9*, 58230–58242. [CrossRef]
29. Prabakeran, S.; Sethukarasi, T. Optimal solution for malicious node detection and prevention using hybrid chaotic particle dragonfly swarm algorithm in VANETs. *Wirel. Netw.* **2020**, *26*, 5897–5917. [CrossRef]
30. Nisha, A.; Gaurav, S. Mukhopadhyay, Debajyoti (2020), "DDOS attack SDN Dataset", Mendeley Data, V1. Available online: https://data.mendeley.com/datasets/jxpfjc64kr/1 (accessed on 10 September 2022).
31. Khalaf, O.I.; Ogudo, K.A.; Singh, M. A Fuzzy-Based Optimization Technique for the Energy and Spectrum Efficiencies Trade-Off in Cognitive Radio-Enabled 5G Network. *Symmetry* **2021**, *13*, 47. [CrossRef]
32. Walia, G.S.; Singh, P.; Singh, M.; Abouhawwash, M.; Park, H.J.; Kang, B.; Mahajan, S.; Pandit, A.K. Three Dimensional Optimum Node Localization in Dynamic Wireless Sensor Networks. *Comput. Mater. Contin.* **2022**, *70*, 305–321.
33. Singh, M.; Kumar, M.; Malhotra, J.; Tiwari, S.; Trivedi, M.; Kohle, M.L. Energy efficient cognitive body area network (CBAN) using lookup table and energy harvesting. *J. Intell. Fuzzy Syst.* **2018**, *35*, 1253–1265. [CrossRef]
34. Majumder, S.; Mathur, A.; Javaid, A.Y. A study on recent applications of blockchain technology in vehicular adhoc network (VANET). In *National Cyber Summit*; Springer: Cham, Switzerland, 2019; pp. 293–308.
35. Wahab, O.A.; Mourad, A.; Otrok, H.; Bentahar, J. CEAP: SVM-based intelligent detection model for clustered vehicular ad hoc networks. *Expert Syst. Appl.* **2016**, *50*, 40–54. [CrossRef]
36. Zhang, C.; Chen, K.; Zeng, X.; Xue, X. Misbehavior detection based on support vector machine and Dempster-Shafer theory of evidence in VANETs. *IEEE Access* **2018**, *6*, 59860–59870. [CrossRef]
37. Thilak, K.D.; Amuthan, A.J.F.G.C.S. Cellular automata-based improved ant colony-based optimization algorithm for mitigating ddos attacks in vanets. *Future Gener. Comput. Syst.* **2018**, *82*, 304–314. [CrossRef]

mathematics

MDPI

Article

Interpretable Deep Learning for Discriminating Pneumonia from Lung Ultrasounds

Mohamed Abdel-Basset [1], Hossam Hawash [1], Khalid Abdulaziz Alnowibet [2], Ali Wagdy Mohamed [3,4,*] and Karam M. Sallam [5]

1 Faculty of Computers and Informatics, Zagazig University, Zagazig 44519, Egypt
2 Statistics and Operations Research Department, College of Science, King Saud University, P.O. Box 2455, Riyadh 11451, Saudi Arabia
3 Operations Research Department, Faculty of Graduate Studies for Statistical Research, Cairo University, Giza 12613, Egypt
4 Department of Mathematics and Actuarial Science School of Sciences Engineering, The American University in Cairo, Cairo 11835, Egypt
5 School of IT and Systems, University of Canberra, Canberra, ACT 2601, Australia
* Correspondence: aliwagdy@staff.cu.edu.eg

Abstract: Lung ultrasound images have shown great promise to be an operative point-of-care test for the diagnosis of COVID-19 because of the ease of procedure with negligible individual protection equipment, together with relaxed disinfection. Deep learning (DL) is a robust tool for modeling infection patterns from medical images; however, the existing COVID-19 detection models are complex and thereby are hard to deploy in frequently used mobile platforms in point-of-care testing. Moreover, most of the COVID-19 detection models in the existing literature on DL are implemented as a black box, hence, they are hard to be interpreted or trusted by the healthcare community. This paper presents a novel interpretable DL framework discriminating COVID-19 infection from other cases of pneumonia and normal cases using ultrasound data of patients. In the proposed framework, novel transformer modules are introduced to model the pathological information from ultrasound frames using an improved window-based multi-head self-attention layer. A convolutional patching module is introduced to transform input frames into latent space rather than partitioning input into patches. A weighted pooling module is presented to score the embeddings of the disease representations obtained from the transformer modules to attend to information that is most valuable for the screening decision. Experimental analysis of the public three-class lung ultrasound dataset (PCUS dataset) demonstrates the discriminative power (Accuracy: 93.4%, F1-score: 93.1%, AUC: 97.5%) of the proposed solution overcoming the competing approaches while maintaining low complexity. The proposed model obtained very promising results in comparison with the rival models. More importantly, it gives explainable outputs therefore, it can serve as a candidate tool for empowering the sustainable diagnosis of COVID-19-like diseases in smart healthcare.

Keywords: explainable artificial intelligence; interpretable deep learning; convolutional networks; vision transformers; COVID-19; ultrasound image

MSC: 68T01; 68T05; 68T07; 68T09; 68T20; 68T30

Citation: Abdel-Basset, M.; Hawash, H.; Alnowibet, K.A.; Mohamed, A.W.; Sallam, K.M. Interpretable Deep Learning for Discriminating Pneumonia from Lung Ultrasounds. *Mathematics* **2022**, *10*, 4153. https://doi.org/10.3390/math10214153

Academic Editors: Adrian Sergiu Darabant and Diana-Laura Borza

Received: 6 October 2022
Accepted: 3 November 2022
Published: 6 November 2022

1. Introduction

By the beginning of 2020, human beings were conquered by the SARS-CoV-2 virus. That virus caused a pandemic infectious disease called COVID-19. The outbreak of COVID-19 has had a catastrophic impact on global health infrastructure, leading to millions of infected cases and thousands of deaths [1]. In clinical practice, real-time reverse transcriptase-polymerase chain reaction (RT-PCR) is used as a standard test to detect COVID-19 infection [2]. However, research studies demonstrated that RT-PCR suffers from high false-positive rates because the clinical practice is strictly impacted by a variety of aspects such as appropriateness of specimen, phase of infection, specimen categories, and specimen conduct, containing sample acquisition time from the inception of COVID-19. Moreover, the fast proliferation of COVID-19 has led to a deficiency of RT-PCR test kits for the discovery of COVID-19. Another obvious shortcoming of this test involves direct interaction between medical staff and patients. This, in turn, made the medical staff more prone to infection, which caused a high death rate in the healthcare community. As a remedy to the above issues, doctors and scholars showed that medical images can be used as an effective tool to detect the presence of COVID-19. X-rays and computed tomography (CT) are broadly used in this respect [3]. Accordingly, the research moved from manual diagnosis of COVID-19 toward computer-aided diagnosis.

Ultrasound imaging is a non-invasive method that has already begun to replace X-rays in pulmonary disease. There has been a surge in demand for point-of-care ultrasound, which is supported by clinical facts and research findings. The advantages of point-of-care ultrasonography (POCUS) include its low cost, ease of mobility, and bedside convenience for patient safety. It is presently underutilized due to a lack of training options and an appreciation of the research supporting this approach. It was discovered that it enhances conventional diagnostic procedures and the technology is rapidly evolving. For wider use, it was also suggested that POCUS be introduced into urgent and core medicine curricula [4]. The latest epidemic of the COVID-19 pandemic forced the healthcare community to utilize ultrasound imaging in emergency departments [5–7]. Discoveries indicated that ultrasound imaging could help in both identifying COVID-19 cases and following up on their states during the hospitalization phase. Nevertheless, lung ultrasound offers just local pathological information on the status of the lung area. Thus, it is critical to thoroughly specify the necessary volume and distribution of lung regions to be scanned. This way, multi-institutional studies are designed to search for an ideal trade-off between a rapid and precise assessment to be performed [8]. For COVID-19 diagnosis, a twelve-area methodology was proposed to signify an optimum trade-off between precision, speed, and exam complication [9]. When it comes to evaluating patients' states from ultrasound data, both pathological information (i.e., pleural line, consolidations, opacities), and sonographic artifacts (i.e., B-lines and A-lines) come to be significant. Nevertheless, identifying this information and appropriately interpreting it demands extremely experienced doctors. Therefore, to date, lung ultrasound data are not broadly accepted, even though their capacity would be somewhat recommended, especially in the face of urgent requirements occurring in screening patients in the COVID-19 pandemic [10].

Deep learning (DL) as a subfield of machine learning (ML) was demonstrated as a key enabler for almost all medical image analysis tasks and computer-aided diagnosis systems. In this regard, convolutional neural networks (CNNs) are showing great capability for extracting valuable representations from medical images [11]. For COVID-19 diagnosis, CNNs are showing great promise in the detection and segmentation of infection and were demonstrated to be very robust tools for achieving many interesting responsibilities, particularly in the realm of image perception. Given an adequate amount of training samples and enough computing power, complex DL could even surpass doctors' performance on particular diagnosis tasks [12]. Research efforts are developing in the way of applying CNNs to ultrasound data. However, training data are difficult to obtain, which is a common issue in medical image analysis and makes it challenging to effectively train these complicated models. Unfortunately, the majority of DL solutions for COVID-19 diagnosis are designed as a black-box model, which means that the model just provides us with the final decision without justifying the reason behind it [13]. In other words, the doctors are unable to interpret the internal working methodology of the DL model, thereby they cannot trust the diagnosis results obtained from the DL model [14]. Generally speaking, the opaque nature of DL models constrains the ability to integrate them into real-world healthcare applications. These constraints come to be more serious in the case of critical or pandemic diseases.

1.1. Research Gaps

When it comes to the diagnosis of COVID-19 from ultrasound images using DL, many research gaps are encountered, making it challenging to do well in combating COVID-19 either in or after the outbreak. By investigating the recent literature, this study considers the following open gaps:

- **Efficiency:** In clinical practice, the task of detecting COVID-19 from lung ultrasound data (either images or videos) necessitates high experience from doctors. Similarly, DL should be able to effectively model the disease representations from the ultrasound data in such a way that enables discriminating between the manifestations of COVID-19 and other kinds of pneumonia with the lowest possible error rate. The healthcare system does not tolerate any errors, especially in the diagnosis of pandemic diseases, making the accuracy of the model an essential requirement [15];
- **Complexity:** Deep models are demonstrated as robust tools for learning inherent features and diagnostic cues from medical image analysis. These models usually have a complicated building structure so that they can model different representations from large-sized and multi-dimensional training datasets. This complexity, in turn, necessitates the model training to be performed on powerful and computationally efficient machines, making it challenging to effectively detect COVID-19 from lung ultrasound data. Another challenge to be considered in this respect is that the complex models are unable to do well when trained on limited training data, which is a typical scenario when dealing with COVID-19 lung data [16,17];
- **Opaqueness:** As stated above, the deep models are characteristically composed of multiple building blocks and layers with several nonlinear interconnected interactions. Even if one is to inspect all these layers and describe their relations, it is unfeasible to fully comprehend how the neural network came to its decision. Therefore, DL is often considered a 'black box'. To properly understand how the model made its choice, one would need to examine all of these constituting layers and define their relationships. This is practically infeasible, leading the community to declare the DL model as a "black box" model. There is growing concern that these black boxes might exhibit some unobserved bias in making their decisions [13,14,18]. This can have far-reaching repercussions, especially in medical applications. When it comes to COVID-19 detection, the same problem exists; however, the dangerousness of the disease even after the outbreak means that doctors have no chance to trust such opaque models. Marginal mistakes in the diagnostic decision may cause catastrophic consequences. Explainable artificial intelligence (XAI) is an evolving subfield to provide a good explanation if it gives insight into how a neural network came to its decision and/or can make the decision understandable.

1.2. Contributions

In response to the above challenges and gaps, this work presents a novel DL solution that affords and is interpretable and efficient in the detection of COVID-19 from ultrasound data. The main contributions of this work are pointed out as follows:

- First, a lightweight convolutional transformer network for flexible and robust modeling of COVID-19 from ultrasound data is designed, while dissipating the nightmare of "data-hungry" models by being able to effectively learn from scratch and attain high screening performance on small-size data.
- Second, two parallel transformer modules are designed with window-based and shifted-window multi-head self-attention layers, respectively, aiming to improve the representational power of the model, while maintaining a few numbers of parameters.
- Third, the convolutional patching module is integrated to empower image tokenization to sustain local spatial representations by encoding relationships between patches.
- Fourth, a weighted pooling module is presented to get rid of the necessity for class tokens and by scoring the sequential embeddings of the disease representations captured by the transformer modules to better relate information across the input frames.

- A gradient activation mapping integrated after-weighted pooling to empower the proposed model visually explains its decided class for a given input frame, which is achieved by highlighting the contribution of different biomarkers in the ultrasound frame.
- Finally, an experimental evaluation of the public lung ultrasound dataset demonstrates the ability of the proposed solution to precisely screen COVID-19, while generating a visual explanation for the generated decisions.

1.3. Organization

The remaining part of this work is systematically organized as follows. Section 2 discusses the literature studies relevant to COVID-19 detection. Section 3 argues the methodology of the proposed solution. In addition, the experimental setting of this study is discussed in Section 4. Then, the results, analysis, and findings are given in Section 5. Finally, Section 6 concludes this work.

2. Related Work

DL was demonstrated to be effective in a variety of imaging tasks spanning semantic segmentation, object detection, etc. Inspired by these achievements, more recently, DL has been progressively applied in medical applications, such as pneumonia detection, localization, and segmentation from chest X-rays. This in turn shows that DL can be used to help and automate preliminary diagnosis, which is of enormous importance to the medical profession.

2.1. Deep Learning for COVID-19 Screening

The literature contains a lot of studies for the screening of COVID-19 from different modalities of medical images, among them the lung ultrasound gains the least research attention despite its demonstrated promise for screening and follow-up diagnosis. For example, Born et al. [19] proposed a convolutional model, called POCOVID-net, which is dedicated to identifying COVID-19, healthy, and bacterial pneumonia from lung ultrasound frames and videos. The POCOVID-net was accompanied by a class activation map (CAM) as an interpretability technique for localizing the spatiotemporal pulmonary manifestations, which are regarded as valuable for human-in-the-loop circumstances in medical studies. Similarly, Diaz-Escobar et al. [20] applied many pre-trained models (i.e., VGG19, InceptionV3, Xception, and ResNet50) to finetune them on lung ultrasound frames to detect COVID-19 and pneumonia patients. Awasthi et al. [21] presented a lightweight convolutional model, termed Mini-COVIDNet [21], for detecting COVID-19 from ultrasound images, where the model can be deployed and used in resource-constrained applications making it ideal for a point-of-care situation. The Mini-COVIDNet was trained to optimize focal loss function to lessen the impact of class imbalance. Moreover, Frank et al. [22] proposed a DL framework that combines domain knowledge into deep networks by feeding anatomical representations and ultrasound artifacts as an extra channel comprising vertical and pleural artifact masks in addition to original lung ultrasonic frames. They claimed that the direct inclusion of this domain knowledge enables the deep networks to achieve different diagnosis tasks using ultrasonic imagery quickly and efficiently. Additionally, the framework was enabled to learn from both convex as well as linear probes and it shows good performance on the COVID-19 severity assessment task, as well as the semantic segmentation model. In addition, Muhammad et al. [17] proposed screening COVID-19 from ultrasound images using a lightweight convolutional model of consisting of five major building convolutional blocks with a small number of trainable parameters. Then, the feature maps from each block are fused to generate a representation vector to be fed into a fully connected layer (FCL), where the final decision is made.

Moreover, Marco et al. [23] presented a DL system for screening COVID-19 from ultrasound data using a pre-trained and residual convolutional model, which is trained (using transfer learning and data augmentation techniques) to quantify the severity of infection as well. In another approach, Xue et al. [24] developed a multimodal approach for assessing the severity of COVID-19 from two types of modality data (ultrasound data and clinical information), where a dual-level supervised multiple-instance learning was applied to combine the zone-associated features and patient-associated representations from heterogeneous training data, hence resulting in discriminatory features. The model aligned the two modalities using a contrastive learning module while maintaining the discriminatory representations of each of them. Furthermore, Roy et al. [15] proposed a spatial transformer network, that concurrently forecasts the degree of severity of COVID-19 in ultrasound frames and localizes pathological artifacts in a weakly supervised manner. The authors also developed a lightweight technique for the efficient aggregation of scores of frames at the video level.

2.2. *Explainable Medical Image Analysis*

With the increased acceptance of DL solutions in medical image diagnosis, explainability becomes an inevitable requirement to effectively use these solutions in real-world healthcare. To this end, many studies have recently emphasized developing explainable models for COVID-19 screening. For example, Wu et al. [25] proposed a multi-task DL framework that jointly classifies COVID-19 and segment infections from a CT scan with the main aim of using the segmentation results to provide an explanation for the screening decisions. In a similar way, Wang et al. [26] proposed a joint learning framework, called DeepSC-COVID, for the screening and segmentation of COVID-19 lesions from 3D CT scans. In particular, the DeepSC-COVID model is composed of three sub-networks, namely the cross-task feature sub-network, segmentation subnetwork for segmenting 3D COVID-19 lesions, and classification subnetwork for identifying COVID-19, pneumonia, and non-pneumonia cases. The latter one contains a multi-layer visualization method to produce evidential masks that include tiny and imprecise lesions for making the task screening of COVID-19 explainable. During the training of DeepSC-COVID, a task-aware loss was developed based on our visualization method for effective collaboration between classification and segmentation. Though the integration of segmentation and classification tasks in the single model help provide an explainable diagnosis, it makes the model very complex and has a very large number of parameters. In addition, Shi et al. [27] presented an explainable attention transfer model network to automatically screen COVID-19 from chest X-ray and CT scans, which consisted of a teacher model and a student model. The former models the global representation and uses a deformable attention module to distill the infection lesions to intensify the reaction to lesions and restrain noise in unrelated areas with an extended reception field. Next, an image fusion unit was proposed to integrate attention knowledge transmitted from teacher to student with the necessary representations in the original input. The student model was designed to concentrate on sporadically formed lesion areas to learn discriminatory features. In [28], the Gradient-weighted CAM (Grad-CAM) algorithm was employed for debugging the convolutional models to provide explainability of its classification decision in chest X-rays.

3. Research Methodology

This section introduces and discusses the proposed framework for screening COVID-19 from lung ultrasound data. To obtain a better interpretation of the proposed framework, an illustration of its structural design is presented in Figure 1. As observed, the proposed framework consists of six main building modules and we are going to dive into the details of each of them in the next subsections.

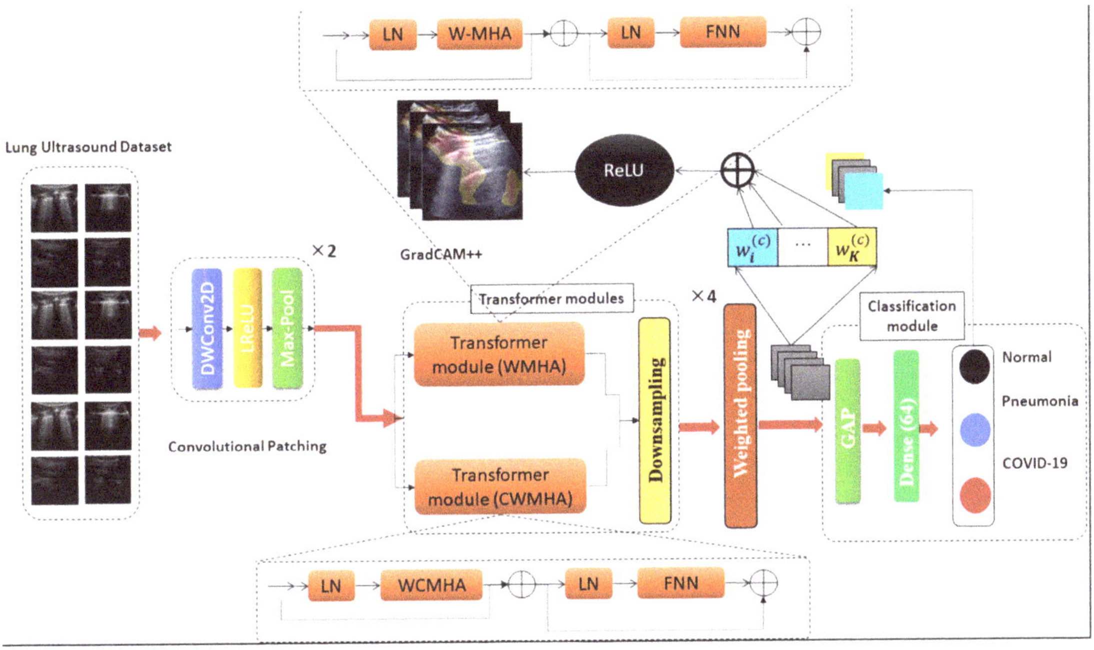

Figure 1. Illustration of the proposed explainable convolutional transformer network for screening pneumonia from lung ultrasound data.

3.1. Convolutional Patching

The conventual language Transformer was designed to accept input in form of a one-dimensional sequence of token embeddings. This seems inappropriate when dealing with 2D ultrasound frames, therefore the input frame $x \in \mathbb{R}^{H\times W\times C}$ is reshaped into a sequence of compressed 2D patches $x_p \in \mathbb{R}^{N\times((p\times p)\cdot C)}$, whereby $H \times W$ represents the spatial dimensions of the original frame, C represents the number of channels, $p \times p$ denotes the spatial dimensions of each patch, and N denotes the number of patches (it is calculated as follows $N = \frac{HW}{p^2}$) , denoting the length of the input sequence of Transformer modules. Each of these modules utilizes a fixed size latent vector D, hence, the generated frame patches are mapped to d dimensions through learnable linear projection, as shown in Equation (1).

$$z_0 = \left[x_{class}, x_p^1 E,\ x_p^2 E,\ \cdots x_p^N E\right] + E_{pos}, E \in \mathbb{R}^{N\times((p\times p)\cdot C)}, E_{pos} \in \mathbb{R}^{(N+1)\times(d)} \tag{1}$$

where the generated output z_0 of this projection can be referred to as patch or token embeddings. The patch embeddings were supplied by one-dimensional position embeddings $E_{pos} \in \mathbb{R}^{(N+1)\times(D)}$ to preserve spatial pathological information in ultrasound frames.

To establish an inductive bias in the proposed model, the standard image patching, as well as token embedding, are replaced with a straightforward convolutional module. The design of a convolutional module consists of a depth-wise convolutional layer $(DWConv2D)$ activated by LeakyReLU ($LReLU$) function and followed by a max-pooling layer. In doing so, the above formula can be formulated as:

$$z_0 = MaxPool(LReLU(DWConv2D(x))) \tag{2}$$

where the $DWConv2D$ layer contains a number of d filters, equal to the embedding dimension in Equation (1). Two convolutional modules are stacked to generate convolutional patching. This convolutional patching makes the model more flexible and simpler than the standard vision transformer. In particular, the convolutional modules are introduced to embed the input ultrasound frames into a latent representation, which is more efficient for modeling pathological information in subsequent layers. Variations in the size of image size do not have an effect on the number of parameters but impact the length of the sequence and consequently the required computing. Even though the standard patching operation necessitates that the dimensions of input frames be dividable by the size of the patch. The convolutional modules enabled the model to accept input of various sizes of data with no requirement for clipping or padding as it alleviates the necessity of uniformly partitioning an image into patches. Another advantage of the proposed model lies in the fact that convolution and max pool layer could be overlapping, enabling the sequence length to become increased but conversely, improving screening performance by infusing inductive bias. Obtaining these convolutional patches enables the model to hold the local spatial pathological information eliminating the need for positional embedding as it achieves a very decent performance.

3.2. *Transformer Modules*

The project sequence of embeddings z_0 are then passed to a stacked transformer module. Each of these modules consists of alternating layers of multiheaded self-attention (MHA) and Feed Forward Network (FNN) blocks.

The traditional self-attention (SA) [29] attention layer is commonly used to calculate the attention score for each head on a global receptive field, leading to quadratic computations in terms of the number of tokens, which makes it inappropriate for ultrasound frames/videos that require a huge set of tokens for modeling pathological information. To address that, window-based or local SA is adopted to calculate SA for local windows, where windows are disposed to uniformly divide the image in a non-overlapping way. Given that the window includes $M \times M$ non-overlapping patches, SA is computed locally within the window.

For each instance in patch embedding $z \in \mathbb{R}^{N \times D}$, a weighted summation is calculated for all values v in the sequence. Then, the attention scores are calculated according to pairwise correspondence between two embedding elements and the corresponding query q_i and key k_j representations.

$$[q, k, v] = zU_{qkv},\ U_{qkv} \in \mathbb{R}^{M^2 \times d_h} \tag{3}$$

$$a = softmax\left(\frac{qk^T}{\sqrt{d_h}} + B\right),\ a \in \mathbb{R}^{N \times N} \tag{4}$$

$$H(z) = a \cdot v \tag{5}$$

where H represents the attention head; $q, k, v \in \mathbb{R}^{M^2 \times d_h}$ represent the query, key, and value matrices; d_h denotes the query/key dimension, M^2 represents the number of window patches and $B \in \mathbb{R}^{M^2 \times M^2}$ represents the relative position bias [16].

The MHA is an expansion of the above calculations by calculating the SA for multiple heads concurrently and then concatenating the output of each of them, and later projecting this concatenation in FFN.

$$MHA(z) = concat\left[H^0, H^1, \cdots, H^{h-1}\right] \tag{6}$$

Layer norm (LN) is applied at the beginning of each module, while the residual connection is applied to the MHA and FNN layers in each module.

By calculating window-based SA, the computational complexity of a global MHA and a window-based MHA (WMHA) over an image containing $h \times w$ patches are formulated as follows:

$$\Omega(MHA) = 4hwC^2 + 2(h \times w)^2 C \tag{7}$$

$$\Omega(WMHA) = 4hwC^2 + 2M^2(h \times w)C \tag{8}$$

where the first formula is quadratic with respect o the number of patches $h \times w$, and the other formula is linear when M is constant. Therefore, the global SA calculation is mostly unreasonable for a large number of patches, while the local SA is usable. However, local SA does not have connections among windows, limiting its representation power [16]. As a remedy, the network requires the application of cross-window connectivity while retaining the effective calculation of non-overlapping windows. This is achieved by designing two parallel transformer modules, one uses WMHA and the other use cross-window-based MHA (CWMHA). Mathematically speaking, the flow of information in the first transformer modules could be formulated as follows:

$$\tilde{z}_l^I = WMHA\left(LayerNormalize\left(z_{l-1}^I\right)\right) + z_{l-1}^I, \quad l = 1 \cdots L \tag{9}$$

$$z_l^I = FFN\left(LayerNormalize\left(\tilde{z}_{l-1}^I\right)\right) + \tilde{z}_{l-1}^I, \quad l = 1 \cdots L \tag{10}$$

In a similar way, the flow of information in the other transformer module is calculated as below:

$$\tilde{z}_l^{II} = CWMHA\left(LayerNormalize\left(z_{l-1}^{II}\right)\right) + z_{l-1}^{II}, \quad l = 1 \cdots L \tag{11}$$

$$z_l^I = FFN\left(LayerNormalize\left(\tilde{z}_{l-1}^{II}\right)\right) + \tilde{z}_{l-1}^{II}, \quad l = 1 \cdots L \tag{12}$$

Like language models [30], a trainable embedding was prepended to the sequence of embedded patches ($z_0 = x_{class}$), whose status at the output of the transformer modules (z_L) serves as the frame/video representation y, as shown in Equation (4).

$$y = LayerNormalize(z_L) \tag{13}$$

During either fine-tuning or pre-training, the classification module accompanies the z_L. The classification module is implemented with FNN composed of a single hidden layer.

3.3. Down-Sampling Module

In order to generate a hierarchical representation, the number of tokens is reduced by down-sampling modules, introduced to reduce the number of tokens as the depth of the network increases. In the earlier patch-merging module, the features of each set of $g \times g$ neighboring patches are concatenated and then passed to a convolutional 1×1 layer. This way, the number of tokens is decreased by a multiple of $g \times g$ (i.e., down-sampling), and the dimension of the output is turned into 2C. The same process is applied after each transformed module and by the end, the stacked modules jointly generate a hierarchical representation with the same dimensions as the feature map generated from standard convolutional networks.

3.4. Weighted Pooling

To encode the sequential outcomes into a singular class index, rather than applying a class token (as commonly performed in common transformer networks), the proposed model presents a weighted pooling layer. Simply, the outputs of the transformer modules are pooled over the whole sequence of data because they include appropriate representation across various sections of the ultrasound frames. Mathematically speaking, the sequential pooling operation can be declared as the mapping function $\mathcal{M} : \mathbb{R}^{b \times n \times d} \rightarrow \mathbb{R}^{b \times d}$ given as:

$$x_L = \mathrm{f}(x_0) \in \mathbb{R}^{b \times n \times d} \tag{14}$$

where x_L represents the feature maps generated from L-th of the transformer module and b, n, d denote the size of the mini-batch, length of the sequence, and embedding dimension. Hence, x_L maps are passed to a linear layer with $SoftMax$ activation to generate the following:

$$x'_L = softmax\left(g(x_L)^T\right) \in \mathbb{R}^{b\times 1\times n} \tag{15}$$

Following this, the obtained probability scores are used to calculate the pooled output as follows:

$$z = x'_L \times x_L = softmax\left(g(x_L)^T\right) \times x_L \tag{16}$$

The design of weighted pooling enables the model to score the sequential embeddings of latent representations generated from transformer modules and robustly relate data throughout the input data. This behavior is similar to the process of attention to sequential data. This pooling layer can be implemented in either trainable or non-trainable manner; however, the latter case is more efficient for the reason that every embedded patch includes a different quantity of entropy. Accordingly, the network is capable of assigning higher scores to input patches that comprise more pathological information valuable for the screening of pneumonia or of COVID-19. Furthermore, the weighted pooling enables the model to improve by using information from heterogeneous sources.

3.5. Classification Module

Given the output of the weighted pooling, the model calculates the final screening decision in the classification module consisting of two fully connected layers, the first with 64 neurons and containing three units corresponding to three classes, i.e., COVID-19, pneumonia, and normal. The last layer is normally activated with SoftMax activation. The parameters of the model-optimized categorical focal loss (SFL) function [31] help lessen the impact of class imbalance on the final classification performance.

$$CFL = -\sum_{i=1}^{n=3} \alpha_i (i - p_i)^{\gamma} \log p_i \tag{17}$$

The hyperparameter γ enables fine-tuning of the weight of various samples. If $\gamma = 0$, this signifies the categorical cross-entropy. Given a higher value of γ, a small set of simply categorized ultrasound frames participate in calculating the training loss, while frames belonging to the minority class are assigned a higher weight. α_i represents a balance factor.

3.6. Explainability Module

When it comes to explaining the DL model, CAM is a popular approach for generating an activation map for every input sample signifying pixel-wise donation to the decision, or disease type in our case. The discriminative ability of CAM stems from the fact that it generates class-aware activation maps offering more analysis at the class level. However, CAM suffers from primary limitations that it adds to the Softmax layer, hence, performing re-training, which might cause the performance to degrade [32]. Grad-CAM++ [18] is integrated to calculate activation maps with no modification to the DL model. They also require a weight matrix to bring together feature maps. This could be accomplished by initially estimating the gradient of a given class with respect to each feature map and then applying global average pooling on the derivatives to obtain a weight matrix. This way, Grad-CAM++ prevents adding up additional layers, thereby eliminating performance degradation and re-training problems. The calculation of weights $w_k^{(c)}$ in Grad-CAM++ can be formulated as follows:

$$w_k^{(c)} = \sum_{i=1}^{H}\sum_{j=1}^{W} \alpha_k^{(c)}(i,\, j).ReLU\left(\frac{\partial Y^{(c)}}{\partial A_k(i,\, j)}\right), \tag{18}$$

where $Y^{(c)}$ represent the model estimated probability for class c immediately prior to the SoftMax layer and $\alpha_k^{(c)}(i, j)$ represent weighting factors for class-specific pixel-wise gradients calculated as follows:

$$\alpha_k^{(c)}(i, j) = \frac{1}{\sum_{i,j} \frac{\partial Y^{(c)}}{\partial A_k(i, j)}} = \frac{\frac{\partial^2 Y^{(c)}}{(\partial A_k(i, j))^2}}{2.\frac{\partial^2 Y^{(c)}}{(\partial A_k(i, j))^2} + \sum_{a,b} A_k(a, b).\frac{\partial^3 Y^{(c)}}{(\partial A_k(i, j))^3}} \quad (19)$$

where (i, j) and (a, b) represent the iterators over the same activation map A_k and were applied to evade disorientation. The final saliency map can be calculated as follows:

$$L_{Grad-CAM++}^{(c)}(x, y) = ReLU\left(\sum_k w_k^{(c)} A_k(x, y)\right) \quad (20)$$

where $A_k(x, y)$ is the activation of node k in the intended network layer at the location (x, y).

4. Experimental Design

This section defines the design settings of proof-of-concept experiments in terms of implementation setup, evaluation metrics, and the dataset adopted for training and evaluations.

4.1. Implementation Setup

To set up the experimentations in this work, a TensorFlow 2.6 running over Python 3.8 virtual environment is employed for implementing the deep models. All experiments are performed on a Dell workstation armed with RAM (256 GB) and CPU (Intel ® Xe®(R) CPU E5-2670 0@ 2.60 GHz). The training of that models was accelerated by NVIDIA Quadro graphical processing unit (GPU). All the experiments are performed using five-fold cross-validations strategies.

4.2. Evaluation Metrics

For evaluating the detection performance of the proposed method and the competing ones, a set of popular multi-class classification metrics calculated as a function of false positive (FB), false negative (FN), true negative (TN), and true positive (TP) samples are opted for and defined as follows:

$$Accuracy\ (A) = \frac{TP + TN}{TP + TN + FP + FN} \times 100, \quad (21)$$

$$Sentivity\ (Se) = \frac{TP}{TP + FN} \times 100, \quad (22)$$

$$Specificity\ (Sp) = \frac{TN}{TN + FP} \times 100, \quad (23)$$

$$F1 - score\ (F1) = \frac{2TP}{2TP + FP + FN} \times 100, \quad (24)$$

Beyond the above metrics, the Area Under the Curve (AUC) is adopted to assess the detection capability of the model.

4.3. Data Description

To train and evaluate the proposed method, a public and open-source LUS dataset is used, which is known as the POCUS dataset. The dataset consists of image and video samples belonging to three classes of infection, namely COVID-19, viral pneumonia, and bacterial pneumonia, in addition to samples from healthy individuals. The dataset contains a total of 261 recordings (202 videos + 59 images) captured from a total of 216 patients with either linear or convex probes. The distribution of samples across different classes is given in more detail in Table 1. Linear probes have high frequency, leading to a superior resolution that enables improved investigation of irregularities near the pleural line [22]. However, the linear probe penetrates the lung tissue less than the convex probe, which could make it hard to tell the difference between B-line artifacts (a major lung artifact) and hidden tissue. The images and videos in the POCUS dataset were aggregated from a variety of sources, such as clinical data obtained from academic ultrasound courses, hospitals, scientific publications, public medical repositories, and health-tech corporations. The complete details of different sources of data in the POCUS dataset can be found in reference [19]. The COVID-19 cases were confirmed by RT-PCR. The dataset is supplemented by a comprehensive metadata file encapsulating the anonymized patient identifier, source URL, source identifier, sex, age, symptoms, pathological manifestations, video frame rate, image resolution, and the total of frames per video. The length and type of videos are a varied (160 ± 144 frames) dataset, whereas they have a frame rate of 25 ± 10 Hz. Outstandingly, all samples in the dataset were reported to be revised and confirmed by one medical expert with more than 10 years of clinical experience and an academic instructor. Figure 2 shows some examples of 2D ultrasound frames for COVID-19, pneumonia, and healthy patients.

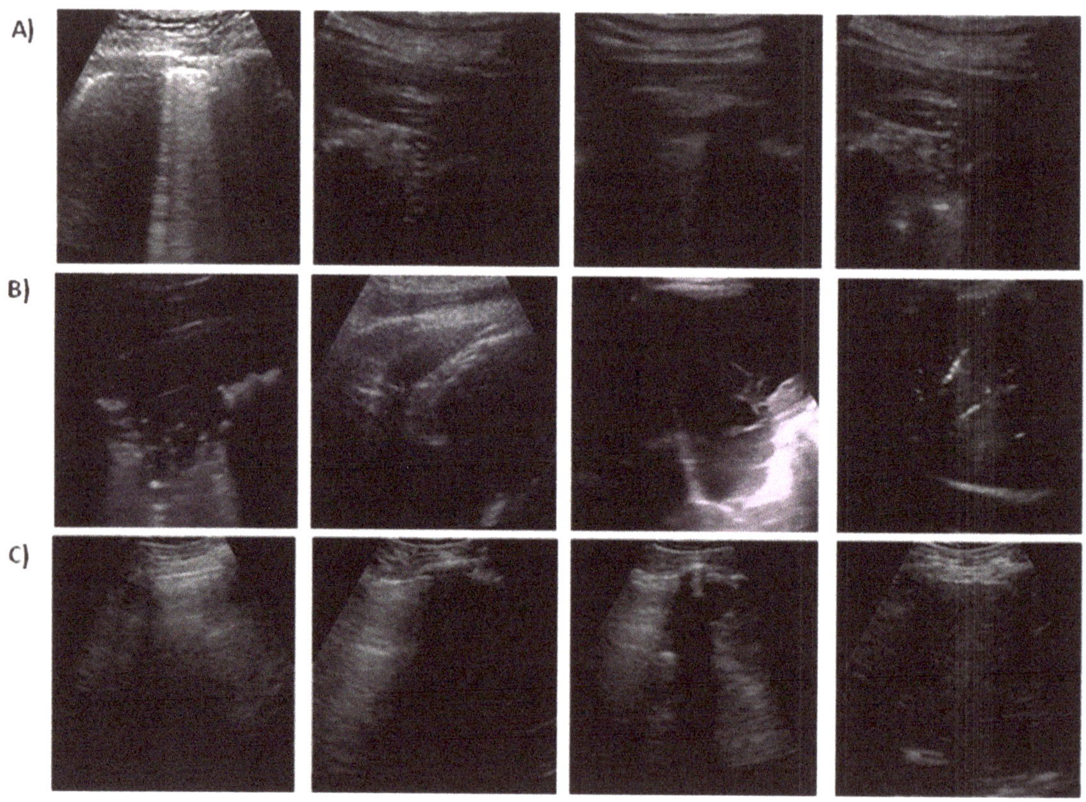

Figure 2. Examples of lung ultrasound images for different pulmonary diseases: (**A**) COVID-19, (**B**) Pneumonia, (**C**) normal case.

Table 1. The class distribution of the POCUS dataset.

		COVID-19	Bacterial Pneumonia	Viral Pneumonia	Healthy	Total
CONVEX	Videos	64	49	3	66	182
	Images	18	20	/	15	53
LINEAR	Videos	6	2	3	9	20
	Images	4	2	/	/	6
Total		92	73	6	90	261

4.4. Data Preparation

As the usual step in developing a DL solution, data need to be pre-processed before going to the training stage. In this regard, the convex ultrasound probes are used for training models in all experimentations. Owing to the small number of samples belonging to the viral pneumonia class (3 convex videos), the data are pre-processed by eliminating the data of that class and the training is performed using only the other three classes. Moreover, all convex ultrasound samples (179 videos and 53 images) were physically pre-processed by dividing the videos into separate images at a 3 Hz frame rate (i.e., maximum of 30 frames per video) resulting in a dataset comprising a total of 1204 COVID-19 images, 704 bacterial pneumonia images, and 1326 images of normal cases. Moreover, the generated image samples are cropped into a quadratic window, eliminating artifacts, ration bars, and text, and then they are resized into 224 × 224 pixels. Different from hold-out testing data, all the presented stated results in this work are attained from five-fold cross-validation stratified by the count of examples in each class. The image samples were divided at the patient level; therefore, it is guaranteed that the frames of one video are existing only per one-fold and that the number of videos per class is almost the same for all folds. All models were trained to classify images as COVID-19, pneumonia, and non-infected. Furthermore, the data were augmented by applying image flipping, rotations $\left[-10^{\circ}, 10^{\circ}\right]$ and translations (up to 10%, which in turn differentiate the data and help avoid overfitting).

5. Results and Analysis

5.1. Comparative Analysis

To evaluate the competitiveness of the proposed model, detection performance is fairly compared against the cutting-edge COVID-19 models, namely CNN [17], POCOVID-Net [19], Mini-COVIDNet [21], Residual Net [23], and Inception [20]. To assure that comparison is very fair, the results of the competing methods are reproduced in the same experimental environment, settings, and training data. During the experiments, an overfitting issue was observed in the case of Mini-COVIDNet, therefore we had to apply some regularization methods to assure the results remain real and representative. Table 2 shows the results obtained from comparative experiments by calculating the mean and standard deviation (std) over different validation folds. Moreover, the comparison also includes the number of parameters of each model to give an intuitive understanding of the model's complexity. It is notable that the pre-trained Residual Net [23] shows the lowest screening performance (accuracy: 71.5%) despite its large number of parameters. Moreover, POCOVID-Net [19] and Mini-COVIDNet [21] show relative improvement in COVID-19 screening performance with an accuracy of 82.1% and 82.7%, respectively. However, they exhibit a large number of parameters. Notably, CNN [17] achieved the most competitive performance across all evaluation metrics, while maintaining a small number of parameters compared with the above methods. More significantly, the proposed model demonstrated robust detection performance across all performance metrics (accuracy: 93.4% F1-score: 93.1%, AUC: 97.5%), overcoming the competing methods with large margins. As observed, the number of parameters of the proposed model is surprisingly smaller than all the competing methods, which can be attributed to the elegant design of building blocks, i.e., convolutional patching and window-based attention. The lightweight nature of the proposed model makes it a time- and space-efficient solution that can be easily integrated into the real-world healthcare system.

Table 2. Comparison of the 5-Fold cross-validation performance (mean ± std) of the proposed methods and competing models for COVID-19 screening from a frame-based lung ultrasound dataset. The Precision, Recall, F1-score, and AUC metrics are reported for each class.

METHOD	ACCURACY (%)	NO. PARAMS	CLASS	PRECISION (%)	RECALL (%)	F1-SCORE (%)	AUC (%)
CNN [17]	90.3 ± 5.13	389,540	COVID-19	93.8 ± 4.75	91.9 ± 2.00	92.8 ±2.8	96.8 ± 3.68
			Pneumonia	95.1 ± 2.90	96.2 ± 1.73	95.6 ± 2.2	97.2 ± 5.59
			Normal	80.1 ± 5.87	75.6 ± 5.2	77.8 ± 5.5	83.1 ± 10.5
POCOVID-NET [19]	82.1 ± 11.6	14,747,971	COVID-19	84.6 ± 6.80	88.1 ± 10.8	86.3 ± 8.3	95.3 ± 1.19
			Pneumonia	93.9 ± 4.20	91.5 ± 2.10	92.7 ± 2.8	97.3 ± 1.57
			Normal	56.2 ± 8.22	51.9 ± 2.90	54.0 ± 4.3	68.2 ± 2.74
MINI-COVIDNET [21]	82.7 ± 10.2	3,361,091	COVID-19	81.9 ± 3.92	91.8 ± 9.65	86.6 ± 5.6	95.3 ± 6.54
			Pneumonia	82.4 ± 4.56	90.3 ± 5.32	86.2 ± 4.9	95.7 ± 9.13
			Normal	62.3 ± 9.50	44.7 ± 11.5	52.1 ± 10.4	63.1 ± 7.63
RESIDUAL NET [23]	71.5 ± 13.5	23,851,011	COVID-19	76.4 ± 8.21	85.2 ± 6.26	80.6 ± 7.1	89.2 ± 5.88
			Pneumonia	89.7 ± 9.76	63.1 ± 9.08	74.1 ± 9.4	82.5 ± 4.82
			Normal	33.2 ± 11.7	37.3 ± 10.7	35.1 ± 11.2	55.6 ± 8.62
INCEPTION [20]	83.3 ± 7.71	20,867,625	COVID-19	**85.6** ± 4.79	80.9 ± 8.27	83.2 ± 6.1	93.1 ± 7.01
			Pneumonia	**80.2** ± 3.43	81.2 ± 3.10	80.7 ± 3.3	91.9 ± 7.33
			Normal	**67.3** ± 15.4	60.7 ± 7.71	63.8 ± 10.3	72.6 ± 4.51
PROPOSED	93.4 ± 3.46	290,891	COVID-19	95.8 ± 2.58	94.5 ± 1.22	95.1 ± 1.7	98.1 ± 2.30
			Pneumonia	95.1 ± 3.84	94.8 ± 1.34	94.9 ± 2.0	98.8 ± 1.68
			Normal	91.2 ± 3.73	87.7 ± 3.43	89.4 ± 3.6	95.7 ± 1.33

5.2. Statistical Analysis

To further investigate whether the achieved results are statistically significant from those obtained from the competing DL methods, the Friedman omnibus test is applied as a common, popular way of contrasting the performance given by ML models. Hence, the Friedman test is applied to the stratified five-fold cross-validation results and the calculated p-values are presented in Table 3. The Python library SciPy is used to implement the Friedman test with threshold $\sigma = 0.05$. It could be noted that all p-values are less than the threshold, implying the rejection of the null hypothesis. This means that the results of the proposed model statistically differ from those of the competing methods across different metrics.

Table 3. The statistical results obtained from the Friedman test with a significance threshold $\sigma = 0.05$.

Method	Accuracy	F1-score	AUC
Proposed vs. CNN [17]	6.25×10^{-3}	5.22×10^{-8}	5.03×10^{-3}
Proposed vs. POCOVID-Net [19]	7.40×10^{-5}	6.98×10^{-3}	9.90×10^{-4}
Proposed vs. Mini-COVIDNet [21]	5.96×10^{-3}	5.96×10^{-6}	7.63×10^{-3}
Proposed vs. Residual Net [23]	2.06×10^{-4}	4.76×10^{-3}	8.89×10^{-7}
Proposed vs. inception [20]	9.84×10^{-6}	5.50×10^{-5}	2.54×10^{-5}

5.3. Ablation Analysis

To deep dive into the building blocks of the proposed model, a group of ablation experiments is performed to analyze the role and the contribution of each building block to the total screening performance. The results of the ablation experiments are presented in Table 4. In these experiments, a shallow version of the standard vision transformer is used as a baseline model and achieved 89.6% accuracy, 89.2% F1-score, and 94.8% AUC. Moving forward, the inclusion of the transformer module with WMHA is shown to be beneficial for improving the COVID-19 screening performance (accuracy: 90.7%, F1-score: 90.8%, AUC: 95.1%). In the same way, the inclusion of the transformer module with SWMHA is observed to lead to similar improvements. More interestingly the parallel integration of the above modules in our model significantly improved the classification performance across all metrics (accuracy: 92.5%, F1-score: 91.9%, AUC: 97.1%). This explains the importance of both features in separate windows and cross-windows being essential to improving the representation power of the model. Finally, the integration of the proposed weighted pooling module is obviously improving the classification performance.

Table 4. Ablation experiments of the proposed model under 5-fold cross-validation.

METHOD	ACCURACY	F1-SCORE	AUC
BASELINE	88.1 ± 2.96	87.3 ± 4.99	94.2 ± 2.45
+CONVOLUTIONAL PATCHING	89.6 ± 1.74	89.2 ± 3.09	94.8 ± 2.68
+WMHA	90.7 ± 3.73	90.8 ± 2.16	95.1 ± 1.08
+SWMHA	90.9 ± 2.35	90.3 ± 2.24	95.6 ± 1.52
+ (WMHA I ISWMHA)	92.5 ± 3.16	91.9 ± 1.93	97.1 ± 2.39
+WIGHTED POOLING	93.4 ± 3.46	93.1 ± 2.43	97.5 ± 1.77

5.4. Explainability Analysis

To understand and interpret the screening decision obtained from the proposed model, the class-related saliency maps for some COVID-19 and pneumonia cases are presented in Figure 3A,B, correspondingly.

It could be seen that the GRAD-CAM++ shades the significant lung areas in the ultrasound frame, contributing to making the prediction of the output classes. It is also observable that the model activates diverse zones in the input frame corresponding to different biomarkers to be learned and considered during the screening. These diverse zones adopted for screening are learned intrinsically in the model. Moreover, it is notable that the regions of activations vary from one frame to another, even though they both belong to the same class of infection, hence, these activations can be further enhanced by using more ultrasound data from the same class. For the pneumonia frame, one may observe the presence of pleural consolidations, which is a common biomarker for that disease [33,34]. On the other hand, COVID-19 was demonstrated to show abnormal pleural lines together with upright artifacts in lung ultrasound frames/videos. Figure 3A highlights the location of the lung infection lesions where it is obvious that our model is considering the area in close proximity to the pleural lines for screening the COVID-19 class. This assessment also establishes that the proposed solution could promptly identify the cases suffering from considerable lung abnormalities displayed as B-lines, which enables improved screening of COVID-19 patients.

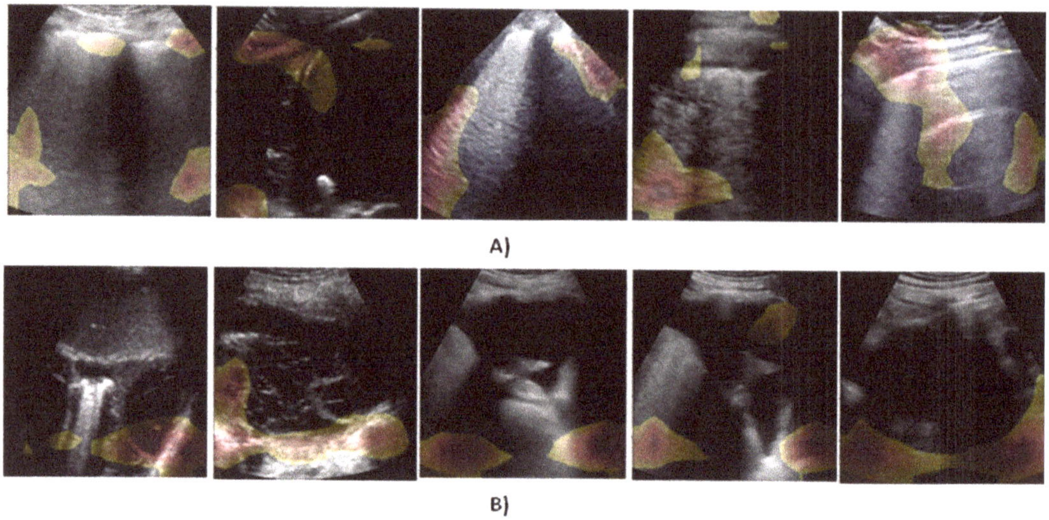

Figure 3. Illustration of visual explanation maps generated by Grad-CAM++ for some of the samples of lung ultrasound frame images after visualization. (**A**) COVID-19-infected lung, (**B**) Pneumonia-infected lung.

6. Conclusions and Future Work

This work presents a lightweight and explainable convolutional transformer model for the efficient screening of COVID-19 from ultrasound data. The representation power of the model is further improved by convolutional patching and parallel window-based transformation modules. The findings demonstrate that the proposed solution considerably improves COVID-19 detection performance with high information compactness, meaning that it achieves both efficiency (high detection accuracy) and effectiveness (a small number of trainable parameters). Beyond and above this, the classification decisions obtained from the proposed solution can be visually explained so they can be easily interpreted and trusted by medical staff. These competitive advantages of the proposed solution render it a candidate for improving the quality of ultrasonic diagnosis in smart healthcare systems during and after the pandemic.

This work can be extended in three ways in the future. First, in coping with the sustainable development strategy in Egyptian Vision 2030, the proposed solution will be extended to be provided as a sustainable diagnosis service/system that can be collaboratively trained using ultrasound data from different Egyptian hospitals. By doing so, the Egyptian Ministry of Healthcare will have great management of COVID-19-like pandemics with automated, efficient, interpretable, and effective tools. Second, the proposed solution will be extended to take advantage of 5G and B5G communication to deliver the patients' data and corresponding diagnosis decisions in real time. This direction will specifically focus on the responsiveness of our system as an essential requirement of the sustainability of the Egyptian healthcare system. Third, the proposed solution will be extended to learn from different modalities of data to improve the quality and functionality of COVID-19 diagnosis in the healthcare system.

Author Contributions: Conceptualization, M.A.-B., H.H. and K.M.S.; methodology, M.A.-B., H.H. and K.M.S.; software, M.A.-B. and H.H.; validation, M.A.-B., H.H., A.W.M., K.A.A. and K.M.S.; formal analysis, M.A.-B., H.H., K.A.A., A.W.M. and K.M.S.; investigation, M.A.-B., H.H., A.W.M. and K.M.S.; data curation, M.A.-B., H.H., A.W.M. and K.M.S.; writing—original draft preparation, M.A.-B. and H.H.; writing—review and editing M.A.-B., H.H., K.A.A., A.W.M. and K.M.S.; visualization, M.A.-B., H.H. and K.M.S.; supervision, M.A.-B.; funding acquisition, K.A.A. All authors have read and agreed to the published version of the manuscript.

Funding: This research is funded by the Researchers Supporting Program at King Saud University, (RSP-2021/305).

Acknowledgments: The authors present their appreciation to King Saud University for funding the publication of this research through the Researchers Supporting Program (RSP-2021/305), King Saud University, Riyadh, Saudi Arabia.

Conflicts of Interest: The authors declare that there are no conflict of interest in the research.

References

1. WHO. WHO Coronavirus Disease. 2020. Available online: WHO.int (accessed on 30 September 2022).
2. Garg, A.; Ghoshal, U.; Patel, S.S.; Singh, D.V.; Arya, A.K.; Vasanth, S.; Pandey, A.; Srivastava, N. Evaluation of seven commercial RT-PCR kits for COVID-19 testing in pooled clinical specimens. *J. Med Virol.* **2020**, *93*, 2281–2286. [CrossRef] [PubMed]
3. Bernheim, A.; Mei, X.; Huang, M.; Yang, Y.; Fayad, Z.A.; Zhang, N.; Diao, K.; Lin, B.; Zhu, X.; Li, K.; et al. Chest CT Findings in Coronavirus Disease-19 (COVID-19): Relationship to Duration of Infection. *Radiology* **2020**, *295*, 200463. [CrossRef] [PubMed]
4. Mischi, M.; Bell, M.A.L.; Van Sloun, R.J.G.; Eldar, Y.C. Deep Learning in Medical Ultrasound—From Image Formation to Image Analysis. *IEEE Trans. Ultrason. Ferroelectr. Freq. Control* **2020**, *67*, 2477–2480. [CrossRef]
5. Bansal, G.; Chamola, V.; Narang, P.; Kumar, S.; Raman, S. Deep3DSCan: Deep residual network and morphological descriptor based framework forlung cancer classification and 3D segmentation. *IET Image Process.* **2020**, *14*, 1240–1247. [CrossRef]
6. Rohmetra, H.; Raghunath, N.; Narang, P.; Chamola, V.; Guizani, M.; Lakkaniga, N.R. AI-enabled remote monitoring of vital signs for COVID-19: Methods, prospects and challenges. *Computing* **2021**, 1–27. [CrossRef]
7. Chamola, V.; Hassija, V.; Gupta, V.; Guizani, M. A Comprehensive Review of the COVID-19 Pandemic and the Role of IoT, Drones, AI, Blockchain, and 5G in Managing its Impact. *IEEE Access* **2020**, *8*, 90225–90265. [CrossRef]
8. Zhang, Y.; He, X.; Tian, Z.; Jeong, J.J.; Lei, Y.; Wang, T.; Zeng, Q.; Jani, A.B.; Curran, W.J.; Patel, P.; et al. Multi-Needle Detection in 3D Ultrasound Images Using Unsupervised Order-Graph Regularized Sparse Dictionary Learning. *IEEE Trans. Med Imaging* **2020**, *39*, 2302–2315. [CrossRef]
9. Mento, F.; Perrone, T.; Fiengo, A.; Tursi, F.; Macioce, V.N.; Smargiassi, A.; Inchingolo, R.; Demi, L. Limiting the areas inspected by lung ultrasound leads to an underestimation of COVID-19 patients' condition. *Intensive Care Med.* **2021**, *47*, 811–812. [CrossRef]
10. McElyea, C.; Do, C.; Killu, K. Lung ultrasound artifacts in COVID-19 patients. *J. Ultrasound* **2020**, *25*, 333–338. [CrossRef]
11. Litjens, G.; Kooi, T.; Bejnordi, B.E.; Setio, A.A.A.; Ciompi, F.; Ghafoorian, M.; van der Laak, J.A.W.M.M.; van Ginneken, B.; Sánchez, C.I. A survey on deep learning in medical image analysis. *Med. Image Anal.* **2017**, *42*, 60–88. [CrossRef]
12. Xie, X.; Niu, J.; Liu, X.; Chen, Z.; Tang, S.; Yu, S. A survey on incorporating domain knowledge into deep learning for medical image analysis. *Med. Image Anal.* **2021**, *69*, 101985. [CrossRef] [PubMed]
13. Tjoa, E.; Guan, C. A Survey on Explainable Artificial Intelligence (XAI): Toward Medical XAI. *IEEE Trans. Neural Networks Learn. Syst.* **2020**, *32*, 4793–4813. [CrossRef] [PubMed]
14. Ahmed, I.; Jeon, G.; Piccialli, F. From Artificial Intelligence to Explainable Artificial Intelligence in Industry 4.0: A Survey on What, How, and Where. *IEEE Trans. Ind. Inform.* **2022**. [CrossRef]
15. Roy, S.; Menapace, W.; Oei, S.; Luijten, B.; Fini, E.; Saltori, C.; Huijben, I.; Chennakeshava, N.; Mento, F.; Sentelli, A.; et al. Deep Learning for Classification and Localization of COVID-19 Markers in Point-of-Care Lung Ultrasound. *IEEE Trans. Med. Imaging* **2020**, *39*, 2676–2687. [CrossRef]
16. Liu, Z.; Lin, Y.; Cao, Y.; Hu, H.; Wei, Y.; Zhang, Z.; Lin, S.; Guo, B. Swin Transformer: Hierarchical Vision Transformer using Shifted Windows. In Proceedings of the IEEE/CVF International Conference on Computer Vision 2021, Montreal, BC, Canada, 11–17 October 2021; pp. 9992–10002. [CrossRef]
17. Muhammad, G.; Hossain, M.S. COVID-19 and Non-COVID-19 Classification using Multi-layers Fusion From Lung Ultrasound Images. *Inf. Fusion* **2021**, *72*, 80–88. [CrossRef] [PubMed]
18. Chattopadhyay, A.; Sarkar, A.; Howlader, P. Grad-CAM ++ : Improved Visual Explanations for Deep Convolutional Networks. In Proceedings of the IEEE Winter Conference on Applications of Computer Vision (WACV), Lake Tahoe, NV, USA, 12–15 March 2018; pp. 839–847. [CrossRef]
19. Born, J.; Wiedemann, N.; Cossio, M.; Buhre, C.; Brändle, G.; Leidermann, K.; Goulet, J.; Aujayeb, A.; Moor, M.; Rieck, B.; et al. Accelerating Detection of Lung Pathologies with Explainable Ultrasound Image Analysis. *Appl. Sci.* **2021**, *11*, 672. [CrossRef]
20. Diaz-Escobar, J.; Ordóñez-Guillén, N.E.; Villarreal-Reyes, S.; Galaviz-Mosqueda, A.; Kober, V.; Rivera-Rodriguez, R.; Rizk, J.E.L. Deep-learning based detection of COVID-19 using lung ultrasound imagery. *PLoS ONE* **2021**, *16*, e0255886. [CrossRef]
21. Awasthi, N.; Dayal, A.; Cenkeramaddi, L.R.; Yalavarthy, P.K. Mini-COVIDNet: Efficient Lightweight Deep Neural Network for Ultrasound Based Point-of-Care Detection of COVID-19. *IEEE Trans. Ultrason. Ferroelectr. Freq. Control* **2021**, *68*, 2023–2037. [CrossRef]
22. Frank, O.; Schipper, N.; Vaturi, M.; Soldati, G.; Smargiassi, A.; Inchingolo, R.; Torri, E.; Perrone, T.; Mento, F.; Demi, L.; et al. Integrating Domain Knowledge Into Deep Networks for Lung Ultrasound With Applications to COVID-19. *IEEE Trans. Med. Imaging* **2021**, *41*, 571–581. [CrossRef]
23. La Salvia, M.; Secco, G.; Torti, E.; Florimbi, G.; Guido, L.; Lago, P.; Salinaro, F.; Perlini, S.; Leporati, F. Deep learning and lung ultrasound for Covid-19 pneumonia detection and severity classification. *Comput. Biol. Med.* **2021**, *136*, 104742. [CrossRef]

24. Xue, W.; Cao, C.; Liu, J.; Duan, Y.; Cao, H.; Wang, J.; Tao, X.; Chen, Z.; Wu, M.; Zhang, J.; et al. Modality alignment contrastive learning for severity assessment of COVID-19 from lung ultrasound and clinical information. *Med Image Anal.* **2021**, *69*, 101975. [CrossRef] [PubMed]
25. Wu, Y.-H.; Gao, S.-H.; Mei, J.; Xu, J.; Fan, D.-P.; Zhang, R.-G.; Cheng, M.-M. JCS: An Explainable COVID-19 Diagnosis System by Joint Classification and Segmentation. *IEEE Trans. Image Process.* **2021**, *30*, 3113–3126. [CrossRef]
26. Wang, X.; Jiang, L.; Li, L.; Xu, M.; Deng, X.; Dai, L.; Xu, X.; Li, T.; Guo, Y.; Wang, Z.; et al. Joint Learning of 3D Lesion Segmentation and Classification for Explainable COVID-19 Diagnosis. *IEEE Trans. Med. Imaging* **2021**, *40*, 2463–2476. [CrossRef] [PubMed]
27. Shi, W.; Tong, L.; Zhu, Y.; Wang, M.D. COVID-19 Automatic Diagnosis with Radiographic Imaging: Explainable Attention Transfer Deep Neural Networks. *IEEE J. Biomed. Health Inform.* **2021**, *25*, 2376–2387. [CrossRef] [PubMed]
28. Brunese, L.; Mercaldo, F.; Reginelli, A.; Santone, A. Explainable Deep Learning for Pulmonary Disease and Coronavirus COVID-19 Detection from X-rays. *Comput. Methods Programs Biomed.* **2020**, *196*, 105608. [CrossRef]
29. Vaswani, A.; Shazeer, N.; Parmar, N.; Uszkoreit, J.; Jones, L.; Gomez, A.N.; Kaiser, Ł.; Polosukhin, I. Attention is all you need. *Adv. Neural Inf. Process. Syst.* **2017**, *2017*, 5999–6009.
30. Ganesh, P.; Chen, Y.; Lou, X.; Khan, M.A.; Yang, Y.; Sajjad, H.; Nakov, P.; Chen, D.; Winslett, M. Compressing large-scale transformer-based models: A case study on bert. *Trans. Assoc. Comput. Linguistics* **2021**, *9*, 1061–1080. [CrossRef]
31. Lin, T.Y.; Goyal, P.; Girshick, R.; He, K.; Dollar, P. Focal loss for dense object detection. *IEEE Trans. Pattern Anal. Mach. Intell.* **2020**, *42*, 318–327. [CrossRef]
32. Selvaraju, R.R.; Cogswell, M.; Das, A.; Vedantam, R.; Parikh, D.; Batra, D. Grad-CAM : Visual Explanations from Deep Networks. *Int. J. Comput. Vis.* **2019**.
33. Boccatonda, A.; Ianniello, E.; D'Ardes, D.; Cocco, G.; Giostra, F.; Borghi, C.; Schiavone, C. Can Lung Ultrasound be Used to Screen for Pulmonary Embolism in Patients with SARS-CoV-2 Pneumonia? *Eur. J. Case Rep. Intern. Med.* **2020**. [CrossRef]
34. Monteiro, R.A.D.A.; Duarte-Neto, A.N.; da Silva, L.F.F.; de Oliveira, E.P.; Nascimento, E.C.T.D.; Mauad, T.; Saldiva, P.H.D.N.; Dolhnikoff, M. Ultrasound assessment of pulmonary fibroproliferative changes in severe COVID-19: A quantitative correlation study with histopathological findings. *Intensive Care Med.* **2021**, *47*, 199–207. [CrossRef] [PubMed]

mathematics

Article

Effective Online Knowledge Distillation via Attention-Based Model Ensembling

Diana-Laura Borza †, Adrian Sergiu Darabant *,†, Tudor Alexandru Ileni † and Alexandru-Ion Marinescu †

Computer Science Department, Babes Bolyai University, 400084 Cluj-Napoca, Romania
* Correspondence: sergiu.darabant@ubbcluj.ro
† These authors contributed equally to this work.

Abstract: Large-scale deep learning models have achieved impressive results on a variety of tasks; however, their deployment on edge or mobile devices is still a challenge due to the limited available memory and computational capability. Knowledge distillation is an effective model compression technique, which can boost the performance of a lightweight student network by transferring the knowledge from a more complex model or an ensemble of models. Due to its reduced size, this lightweight model is more suitable for deployment on edge devices. In this paper, we introduce an online knowledge distillation framework, which relies on an original attention mechanism to effectively combine the predictions of a cohort of lightweight (student) networks into a powerful ensemble, and use this as a distillation signal. The proposed aggregation strategy uses the predictions of the individual students as well as ground truth data to determine a set of weights needed for ensembling these predictions. This mechanism is solely used during system training. When testing or at inference time, a single, lightweight student is extracted and used. The extensive experiments we performed on several image classification benchmarks, both by training models from scratch (on CIFAR-10, CIFAR-100, and Tiny ImageNet datasets) and using transfer learning (on Oxford Pets and Oxford Flowers datasets), showed that the proposed framework always leads to an improvement in the accuracy of knowledge-distilled students and demonstrates the effectiveness of the proposed solution. Moreover, in the case of ResNet architecture, we observed that the knowledge-distilled model achieves a higher accuracy than a deeper, individually trained ResNet model.

Keywords: online knowledge distillation; ensemble learning; attention aggregation; deep learning

MSC: 68T01; 68T07; 68T20; 68T30

Citation: Borza, D.-L.; Darabant, A.S.; Ileni, T.A.; Marinescu, A.-I. Effective Online Knowledge Distillation via Attention-Based Model Ensembling. *Mathematics* **2022**, *10*, 4285. https://doi.org/10.3390/math10224285

Academic Editor: Jakub Nalepa

Received: 11 October 2022
Accepted: 13 November 2022
Published: 16 November 2022

1. Introduction

State-of-the-art machine learning models considerably improve the performance of various image understanding tasks, but they still fail to meet the non-functional requirements necessary for deployment on real-world test scenarios (inference time, latency, performance, throughput). Model compression techniques—such as quantization, pruning, low-rank approximation, knowledge distillation, and neural architecture search—aim to control the inference cost of neural networks [1].

There are numerous situations in which a trained neural network should be deployed on mobile devices (take, for example, the concrete case of an object identification/classification applet, which instead of sending the input to a dedicated server, runs the classification task on the user's device). In order to achieve this, knowledge distillation serves the purpose of a compression tool. By means of KD, the "knowledge" of a large trained model is transferred to a smaller student model. In this way, the lightweight model's accuracy on the test set is boosted, while preserving a low computational and memory footprint.

Knowledge distillation (KD) [2] is an effective technique to boost the accuracy of a lightweight network, by training it under the guidance of a more powerful network or an ensemble of networks. In the context of machine learning, knowledge typically refers to the learned weights of a network. Various distillation techniques have been proposed, in which the student mimics different knowledge sources of the teacher: the decision boundary (logits), intermediate feature maps, or intra-data relationships.

The classical formulation of KD [2,3], offline KD, involves a pre-trained teacher model with fixed weights when distilling knowledge to the student network. Despite its simplicity, this method involves two training steps (one for the teacher and one for the student). A large-capacity model might not always be available, and its training is resource consuming and cumbersome. In addition, the knowledge transfer is one-way (from the teacher to the student), as the teacher's weights are "frozen" during the second training stage. Finally, two-stage KD involves more parameters, which results in higher computational costs.

Online distillation frameworks [4–7] propose an alternative solution to the monolithic, large-capacity teacher, and simplify the training process by simultaneously training several peer students and learning from their combined predictions. One issue with online KD is related to the strategy of building the ensemble based on the students' individual predictions. Simply aggregating the students' logits affects the diversity of the student peers and, therefore, limits the effectiveness of online learning [8].

In this paper, we propose an effective online knowledge distillation framework to improve the generalization and learning capacity of a neural network architecture, while avoiding the increase in inference cost. Our main contribution is an original aggregation strategy inspired by attention mechanisms: The individual predictions of the peer student networks are combined via an attention module that assigns a weight to each network, and the ensemble is computed on the fly as the weighted average of the students' predictions. This ensemble is used throughout the training process as a distillation signal.

The remainder of this manuscript is organized as follows: In Section 2, we discuss other knowledge distillation frameworks, and in Section 3, we present the details of the proposed solution. Next, the experimental results and ablation studies are reported in Sections 4 and 5. Finally, Section 6 concludes this work.

2. Related Work

Knowledge distillation [3] was proposed as an effective and elegant compression technique to derive a lighter and faster network (student) from a more complex one (teacher), by penalizing the difference between their logits. Later, this mechanism was formalized by [2] to distill the "dark-knowledge" from the teacher to the student. The authors noticed that a powerful and confident teacher does not bring more knowledge than ground truth data, as its prediction tends to be a narrow probability distribution with a single peak for the ground truth class. To alleviate this issue, the teacher's logits are "softened" by a *temperature* scaling factor of the softmax activation. In such a manner, the lightweight network can infer what other classes were found similar by the teacher network. More formally, this can be expressed as

$$\zeta_\tau(z_i) = \frac{e^{z_i/\tau}}{\sum_j e^{z_j/\tau}} \tag{1}$$

where τ is the temperature of the softmax function (equation from [2]). When τ is greater than 1, the small probabilities of the softmax function are increased and the output is "softened".

In the classical setup, during training, a Kullback–Libeler divergence loss term is employed to ensure that the student network mimics the teacher's softened predictions. Other methods proposed using the root-mean-square error loss [9] or distilling from hard-labels [10].

2.1. Online KD

Online KD frameworks constitute an effective substitute for classical two-stage offline KD: instead of using a "good" pre-trained teacher network, a cohort of student peers are trained and share their knowledge.

In Deep Mutual Learning (DML) [5], several peer student networks mutually exchange information through a Kullback–Liebler loss term. In this framework, each student plays the role of the teacher for all the other peers. The main drawback of DML is that the predictions of the peer networks can conflict with each other (and even with the ground truth).

On-the-fly Native Ensemble (ONE) [4] is an online KD framework in which an ensemble is formed by adding several auxiliary branches over some shared low-level network layers. A gating component is used to assemble the knowledge of the branches into a more powerful prediction, which is, in turn, distilled back to all branches. This method is applicable only to branches with the same architecture, and the knowledge transfer occurs only at the branch layers.

In [6], the authors proposed a method for collaborative learning based on a hierarchical multiple branch network. The classifier heads provide different views on the data to improve generalization but also act as a regularization term. In addition, backpropagation rescaling was used to avoid gradient explosion and to provide supervision for the shared layers.

A similar approach to the proposed solution is the Knowledge Distillation method via Collaborative Learning (KDCL) [7]; it trains a pool of students together and aggregates their logits to generate soft targets for knowledge distillation. Four methods for assembling the students' predictions were proposed and compared. To ensure the diversity of the peers, each network applied a different set of augmentations to the training data. [11] combined online ensembling and network collaboration into a unified framework. The architecture consists in a multi-branch network, where each branch denotes a *peer*. To improve the quality of the KD, two teachers were computed online: the peer ensemble teacher, which distills knowledge from an online high-capacity teacher to each peer, and the peer mean teacher, which distills knowledge among peers. Random augmentations were performed multiple times on peer inputs.

In [12], Feature Fusion Learning (FFL) was proposed as an online distillation framework for intermediate feature maps. In this framework, several parallel sub-networks are trained together and a fusion module combines their feature maps into a more meaningful one. This is passed to a fused classifier, which performs the overall classification but also delivers its knowledge to each sub-network.

2.2. Attention-Based KD

Inspired by the human visual system, which can effectively focus on salient visual features of complex scenes, attention mechanisms have been integrated into various deep learning architectures, especially in the field of computer vision. The main idea is to redistribute the weights of a feature map according to a computed attention-mask.

SeNets [13] introduced an attention mechanism to perform a channel-wise feature re-calibration process by computing a weight for each channel in the feature maps. Inspired by this mechanism, in [14], the channel attention information is transferred from the teacher to the student. Channel attention weights are computed for the teacher's and student's intermediate feature maps, and the student is guided to learn the attention information of each channel.

In [15], the authors proposed an attention-based feature distillation mechanism, in which a meta-network employs a query-key attention component [16] to identify similarities between the student's and teacher's feature map. The resulting attention vector is used to transfer the teacher's knowledge selectively to student features. The query-key attention mechanism computes the similarities for all possible combinations between the teacher and student networks; so, the training process is computationally expensive.

Online Knowledge Distillation with Diverse peers (OKDDip) [17] applies a two-level KD using multiple auxiliary peers and one group leader. In the first level, group-based learning is achieved via an attention-based mechanism, while in the second level, the knowledge in the ensemble of peers is transferred to the group leader (the model used for inference). The main drawback of this method is that it involves a complex training strategy and more parameters are used during training.

3. Proposed Approach

The following notation will be used throughout this manuscript: N is the number of peer student networks trained within the proposed KD framework, C is the number of categories for the classification problem, $\hat{P}_i^k \in \mathbb{R}^C$ are the non-normalized logits of the ith student network for the kth image, G^k is the one-hot encoding of the ground truth data associated with the kth sample, $\sigma(\cdot)$ is the sigmoid function, $\zeta(\cdot)$ is the softmax function, and $ReLU(\cdot)$ is the Rectified Linear Unit activation function. Table 1 organizes these notations in tabular form.

Table 1. Notations used throughout this manuscript.

Notation	Meaning
N	number of peer students
C	number of categories for the classification problem
$\sigma(\cdot)$	sigmoid function
$\zeta(\cdot)$	softmax function
$ReLU(\cdot)$	Rectified Linear Unit activation function
$\hat{P}_i^k$	non-normalized logits of the ith student network for the kth sample
G^k	one-hot encoding of the ground truth data of kth sample

3.1. Research Methodology

Online KD methods are preferred to classical offline KD frameworks because they involve a simplified one-stage training process, in which all the models are treated as students that gain extra knowledge from each other's predictions or feature representations. This study investigates the problem of online KD and, more specifically, how the students' predictions can be combined to obtain an effective knowledge distillation signal. To this end, we propose a framework in which several student models are trained simultaneously, and an original attention-based aggregation mechanism is employed to combine their predictions into a powerful ensemble. The proposed method was tested on several image classification benchmarks using various network architectures. To demonstrate the effectiveness of the solution, we first train an individual model ("vanilla" model) on a classification benchmark using the classical cross-entropy loss function. Then, using the same training schedule and data processing techniques, we train several models with the same network architecture within the proposed KD framework. Throughout the training process, the predictions of the models are combined using the proposed attention mechanism and the "knowledge" of this ensemble guides the student models via an additional KD loss. For testing, a single knowledge-distilled student is selected—the one with the highest accuracy on the test set. To validate the proposed method, we compare the accuracy of the "vanilla" student with the accuracy of the knowledge-distilled student. The experimental results show that the accuracy of the knowledge-distilled model is always improved, regardless of the network architecture, classification benchmark, or training setup (from scratch or by using transfer learning).

3.2. Solution Outline

The outline of the proposed solution is depicted in Figure 1. A group of lightweight student peers is simultaneously trained into an online distillation framework and their predictions are aggregated into a more powerful ensemble based on an attention mechanism inspired by [18].

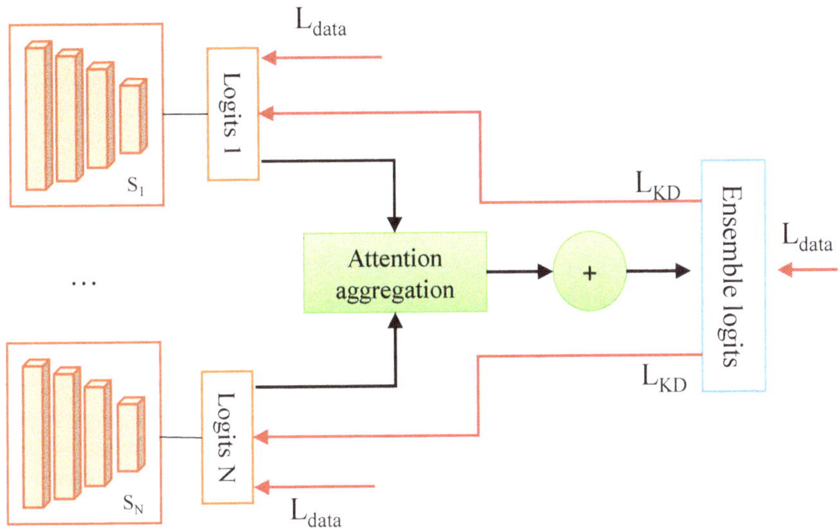

Figure 1. Solution outline. The proposed framework simultaneously trains a group of student peers and learns from the peers' predictions. The red arrows indicate the loss terms applied to each output: L_{data}—the standard cross-entropy loss; L_{KD}—the knowledge distillation loss.

The output of the attention aggregation module is a list of weights w (one for each peer network), used to ensemble the predictions ($\hat{E}$):

$$\hat{E} = \frac{\sum_{i=1}^{N} w_i \cdot P_i}{\sum_{i=1}^{N} w_i}. \tag{2}$$

The ensemble output ($\hat{E}$) will be used as a distillation signal throughout the training process.

All the models are trained in an end-to-end manner, with a multi-task loss function (L):

$$L = L_{data}(G, \hat{E}) + \sum_{i=1}^{N} (L_{data}(G, \hat{P}_i) + \lambda L_{KD}(\hat{E}, \hat{P}_i, \tau)) \tag{3}$$

where λ is the distillation strength and τ is the softmax temperature. The students and the ensemble's output logits are trained with the standard cross-entropy loss [19] (L_{data}):

$$L_{data}(G, \hat{P}) = -\sum_{x \in \chi} G(x) \cdot log(\zeta(\hat{P}(x))). \tag{4}$$

In addition, the ensemble's output is used as a distillation signal for all of the students, through a Kullback–Liebler [20] loss term (L_{KD}):

$$L_{KD}(G, \hat{P}, \tau) = \sum_{x \in \chi} \tau^2 D_{KL}(\zeta_\tau(\hat{E}), \zeta_\tau(\hat{P})), \tag{5}$$

where τ is the softmax temperature parameter; $\hat{E}$ and $\hat{P}$ are the ensemble's and student-softened predictions, respectively; and D_{KL} is the Kullback–Liebler divergence between two distributions p_1 and p_2 defined on the probability space χ:

$$D_{KL}(p_1, p_2) = -\sum_{x \in \chi} p_1(x) \cdot log \frac{p_2(x)}{p_1(x)}. \tag{6}$$

During the inference phase, a single knowledge-distilled student is used; in all the experiments, we report the accuracy of the most accurate student.

3.3. Ensembling Strategy

The question that remains is as follows: *"how could the individual predictions of the student networks be combined into a more powerful ensemble used as a distillation signal?"* To this end, we extract three features based on the predictions of the students, which are then fed to a channel attention mechanism (Figure 2) inspired by [18] to establish the ensembling weights (Equation (2)).

The proposed solution is directly influenced by the attention mechanism proposed in [18]; therefore, it will be described in detail. In [18], the authors proposed the Convolutional Block Attention Module (CBAM), an effective attention mechanism that computes attention maps across the channel and spatial dimensions of intermediate feature maps. The channel attention mechanism is used to ensure the model's focus on relevant features in the input volume; it starts with two pooling operations to aggregate the spatial information of each channel. These pooled features are then forwarded to a shared multi-layer perceptron with a single hidden layer. The output layer uses sigmoid activation to compute the weights for each channel in the input volume. Mathematically speaking, the channel attention mechanism [18] determines the weights w as follows:

$$w = \sigma(MLP(GAP(F)) + MLP(GMP(F))) \tag{7}$$

where MLP denotes the shared multi-layer perceptron, $GAP(\cdot)$ and $GMP(\cdot)$ represent the Global Average and Max pooling operations, F is the input feature map, and σ is the sigmoid activation function.

In the proposed method, the extracted features rely on global pooling operators and are then fed to a multi-layer perceptron, summed together, and passed through a sigmoid activation to determine the attention weights. The aggregation process is also guided by the ground truth data, as it is *solely* used during training. In the beginning, the individual predictions of the students are stacked into a single tensor $P_k \in \mathbb{R}^{N \times C}$. The entire process is detailed in Figure 2.

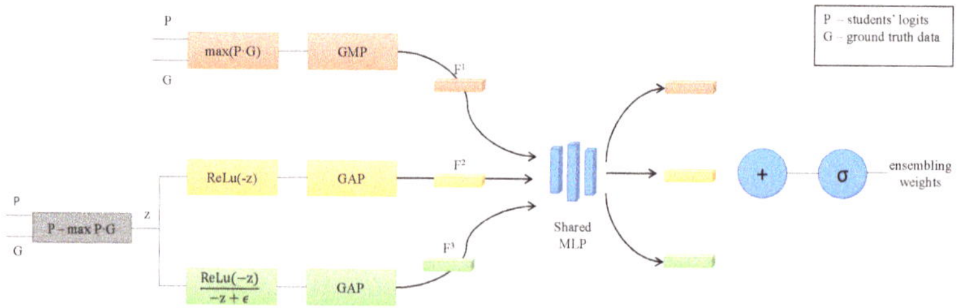

Figure 2. Ensembling strategy. The logits of the peer networks are assembled by an attention mechanism. P are the stacked logits of the sub-networks, and G represents the one-hot encoded ground truth data. Three features (F^1, F^2, and F^3) are computed and then passed through a multi-layer perceptron to compute the assembling weights of the ensemble.

The first extracted feature $F_k^1 \in \mathbb{R}^N$ is related to each student's prediction confidence for the ground truth class:

$$F_k^1 = GMP(P_k \cdot G_k) \tag{8}$$

where *GMP* is the Global Maximum Pooling operator. By multiplying the predictions with the one-hot encoding of ground truth, all except the ground truth class predictions will be set to zero. After applying the global maximum pooling operator, each network will be assigned either a strictly positive value (its confidence on the ground truth class) or a 0 (if its confidence for the ground truth class is less than 0).

The other features account for the students' predictions for the other classes. Let us define $z_k^i = (P_k^i - \max(P_k^i \cdot G_k^i))$ as difference between the ith student's prediction and its prediction for the ground truth class. If the value on position j in z_k^i vector is positive, then the student's prediction for the jth class is larger than for the ground truth class (i.e., the network is more confident on the jth class than on the actual class).

The second feature F_k^2 accounts for the magnitude of the differences between the student's confidence in the actual class versus the other classes. By applying the ReLu activation function on the negative of z_k, all the classes on which the classifier was more confident than on the actual class will be assigned to zero, while for the other classes, the difference between the classifier's confidence in the actual class and the current class will be preserved. More formally, the second feature F_k^2 can be expressed as

$$F_k^2 = GAP(ReLU(-z_k)) \tag{9}$$

where *GMP* is the Global Maximum Pooling operator and $ReLU(\cdot)$ is the Rectified Linear Unit activation function.

Lastly, the third feature F_k^3 is related to the number of classes that have smaller confidence than the actual class. Similarly to F_k^2, we take the ReLU on the negative of z_k but we also divide the result by $-z_k$. In this way, all classes with smaller confidence than the ground truth class will be assigned to one.

$$F_k^3 = GAP\frac{ReLU(-z_k)}{-z_k + \epsilon} \tag{10}$$

where ϵ is a small constant to avoid division by zero.

Finally, as in [18], each of these descriptors (F^1, F^2, and F^3) are forwarded through a multi-layer perceptron with a single hidden layer. Then, to compute the combination weights, the outputs are merged using element-wise summation and passed through a sigmoid function. The ensemble's output is computed as the weighted average of the students' logits and these weights.

4. Experimental Results

In this section, we report the results of a series of experiments conducted to evaluate the proposed knowledge distillation framework on several image classification datasets. We evaluate our method on CIFAR-10, CIFAR-100, and TinyImageNet image classification benchmarks.

As the purpose of this study is to improve the accuracy of a lightweight model via knowledge distillation, without increasing its number of parameters, we employed the following evaluation strategy for a model. We first obtain the "vanilla" version of the model by training independently and evaluate it using the accuracy metric. Then, we train several models with the same architecture within the proposed knowledge distillation framework. For inference/deployment, we select the knowledge-distilled student with the highest accuracy on the test set and evaluate it. As we are interested in the improvement obtained after knowledge distillation, the metric that we are interested in is the gain in accuracy, which we compute as follows:

$$KD\_Gain = ACC_{KD} - ACC_{Vanilla} \tag{11}$$

where ACC_{KD} is the accuracy of the knowledge-distilled student and $ACC_{Vanilla}$ is the accuracy of the "vanilla", independently trained student.

The CIFAR-10, CIFAR-100, and TinyImageNet datasets are generic image classification benchmarks and have balanced testing sets; so, we report only the accuracy metric.

4.1. CIFAR-10 and CIFAR-100 Datasets

CIFAR-10 and CIFAR-100 datasets [21] comprise 60000 RGB-images with 32×32 image resolution, split into training (50,000 images) and validation (10,000 images) subsets. The images of CIFAR-10 are divided into 10 classes, while in CIFAR-100 each image is annotated with a "coarse" label (20 super-classes) and the actual class label (100 categories).

All the models were trained from scratch for 200 epochs, using a batch size of 32, with Adam optimizer and different variants of the ResNet architecture [22]. The initial learning rate was set to 10^{-3} and decayed by 0.1 at epochs 80, 140, and 170. In addition, a learning rate reducer was applied to reduce the learning rate by a factor of $\sqrt{0.1}$ if learning stagnates for 5 epochs. For experiments, $N = 3$ peer networks were trained, the softmax temperature τ was set to 3, and the knowledge distillation strength was set to $\lambda = 1$. (See the ablation studies in Section 5 for more information on varying this hyper-parameter.)

Table 2 reports the results on the CIFAR-10 and CIFAR-100 image classification benchmarks. *Vanilla* refers to the accuracy of the independently trained student and *KD* to the accuracy of the knowledge-distilled student. *MFLOPS* represents the number of mega FLOPS (floating point operations per second) of the model, and *Params.* represents the number of parameters of the model.

Table 2. Results on CIFAR-10 and CIFAR-100 datasets.

Dataset	Model	MFLOPS	Params.	Vanilla	KD	KD Gain
CIFAR-10	ResNet-20	82.298	274,442	92.1%	92.96%	0.86
	ResNet-32	139.325	470,218	92.77%	93.88%	1.11
CIFAR-100	ResNet-20	82.309	280,292	67.54%	69.73%	2.19
	ResNet-32	139.337	476,068	69.60%	72.76%	3.16
	ResNet-50	224.877	769,732	71.35%	73.93%	2.58

The knowledge-distilled network always surpasses an independently trained network. Moreover, the results show that the knowledge-distilled student has a higher accuracy than the immediately larger ResNet version (i.e., a knowledge-distilled ResNet-20 student surpasses an individually trained ResNet-32 network). As a detailed example, in the CIFAR-100 setup, a 0.19 accuracy improvement ($0.19 = 92.96 - 92.77$) is attained with a 41.12% decrease in parameters (from 470,218 to 274,442) and 40.93% decrease in the number of FLOPS (from 139.325 MFLOPS to 82.298 MFLOPS).

4.2. TinyImageNet Dataset

TinyImageNet [23] is a subset of the ImageNet [24] benchmark with 200 class categories; each category has 200 training images, 50 validation images, and 50 test images. In addition, the resolution of the images was reduced to 64×64.

For this setup, the networks were trained from scratch for 100 epochs with Adam optimizer. The initial learning rate was set to 10^{-3} and decayed by 0.1 at epochs 30, 60, and 90. To prevent overfitting, several geometrical augmentation techniques (horizontal flips, width and height shifts, rotations) as well as cutout [25] were applied to the training data. Similar to the CIFAR training setup, the hyper-parameters of the framework were set to $N = 3$, $\tau = 3$ and $\lambda = 1$.

Table 3 reports the results on the TinyImageNet classification benchmark. A 1.43% gain in accuracy is achieved when training the network in the proposed framework.

Table 3. Results on TinyImageNet dataset.

Model	MFLOPS	Params.	Vanilla	KD	KD Gain
ResNet-20	329.277	325,192	52.92%	54.35%	1.43%

4.3. Transfer Learning

Collecting a large-scale dataset required for training an accurate deep model is a challenging and cumbersome task, if not impossible for some tasks for which a limited amount of data are available. Nowadays, as a wide variety of pre-trained models are publicly available, transfer learning is the norm. In this section, we experiment with transfer learning on two classification benchmarks (Oxford Pets and Oxford Flowers datasets) with a limited amount of training data and higher resolution images than CIFAR and TinyImageNet datasets.

Oxford pets [26] contains 37 cat and dog breed categories, with approximately 200 images per class. The images feature large variations in size, lighting, and pose. Oxford flowers [27] is a 102 flower category dataset, and each class contains between 40 and 258 images. Both datasets are already split into training, validation, and test sets. For this experiment, we used the same splits as provided in the datasets. Oxford Flowers comprises 1020 training images, 1020 validation images, and 6149 test images, while Oxford Pets comprises 3680 training images and 3699 test images.

For the transfer learning setup, all peer student networks share the same "frozen" backbone (weights remain fixed during training) initialized with ImageNet weights [24], and only their final classification layers were trained. The weights of the architectures trained on the ImageNet dataset were retrieved from the *tensorflow* machine learning framework https://www.tensorflow.org/api_docs/python/tf/keras/applications, accessed on 25 August 2022. The final trainable classification layers were initialized using Xavier uniform initialization [28]. This process is depicted in Figure 3.

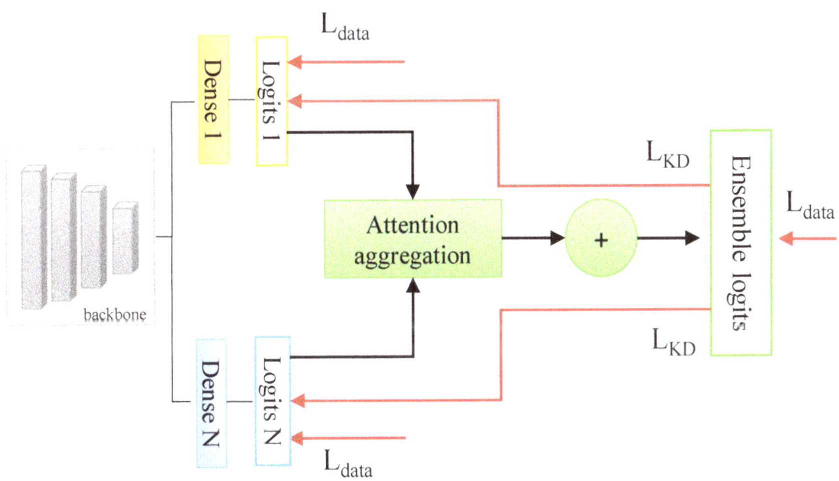

Figure 3. Transfer learning setup: The peer student networks share the same "frozen" backbone, initialized with ImageNet weights.

All the models were trained for 32 epochs, using RMSProp optimizer [29] with a learning rate of 10^{-3}. The data pre-processing step involved padding the images to square shape by duplicating the edge features and then resizing them to 224 × 224. Table 4 reports the results obtained when using transfer learning on Oxford Pets and Oxford Flowers datasets. We experimented with several neural network architectures: DenseNet [30], ResNet [22], NASNet [31], and MobileNet [32]. In this table, the column *Vanilla* indicates the accuracy of an independently trained, "vanilla" student, the column *KD* reports the accuracy of a knowledge-distilled student, and *KD Gain* is the accuracy improvement obtained when training a network in the proposed KD framework.

Table 4. Transfer learning results on Oxford Pets [26] and Oxford Flowers datasets [27].

Model	Oxford Pets			Oxford Flowers		
	Vanilla	KD	KD Gain	Vanilla	KD	KD Gain
DenseNet	90.51	90.89	0.38	85.66	86.11	0.45
ResNet-50	87.66	88.87	1.21	85.31	85.51	0.20
NASNet	87.44	87.63	0.19	69.36	69.85	0.49
MobileNet	88.43	88.98	0.55	82.04	82.68	0.64

The knowledge-distilled student always surpasses the accuracy of the vanilla-trained network; however, in this case, the improvement is lower than by training the networks from scratch. This is expected, as only the final layer benefits from knowledge distillation because the rest of the weights in the peer student networks are frozen.

4.4. Comparison with State of the Art

In this section, we provide a comparison of the proposed KD framework with similar methods for the literature. It is noteworthy that a direct numerical comparison is not always relevant, as other methods use different training schedules, optimizers, and model architectures, all of which have an impact on the networks' performance. However, as we are dealing with the process of KD (in which we want to improve an individually trained model by making it benefit from the knowledge of a more powerful model), we are actually interested in the gain of the knowledge distillation process (i.e., difference between the accuracy of the knowledge-distilled student and the individually trained model). Consequently, when interpreting the results, we rely on the accuracy improvement of a knowledge-distilled student over an independently trained student.

Table 5 compares the results obtained on CIFAR-10 classification benchmark.

Table 5. Comparison with state-of-the-art works on CIFAR-10 database using ResNet-32 [22] as student network.(best gain represented in bold).

Method	Vanilla	KD	KD Gain
ONE [4]	93.07%	94.01%	0.94%
CLCNN [6]	93.17%	94.14%	0.97%
OKDDip net. [17]	93.66%	94.38%	0.72%
OKDDip br. [17]	93.66%	94.42%	0.76%
PCL [11]	93.26%	94.33%	1.07%
Proposed	92.77%	93.88%	**1.11%**

The improvement of the knowledge-distilled students over the independently trained student is marginal (around 1% for all the methods); however, these accuracy levels are close to the reported human accuracy on CIFAR-10 [33].

When compared with other works, the proposed method achieves a higher accuracy gain after knowledge distillation. As opposed to the proposed method, in ONE [4] and CLCNN [6], the low-level layers of the student networks are shared, which could limit the discriminative power and diversity of peer networks.

In Table 6, we compare the proposed solution with other knowledge distillation frameworks on the CIFAR-100 dataset.

Table 6. Comparison with state-of-the-art works for ResNet-32 architecture trained on CIFAR-100 dataset.

Method	Vanilla	KD	KD Gain
DML [5]	68.99%	71.19%	2.20%
KDCL [7]	71.28%	73.76%	2.48%
OKDDip net. [17]	71.24%	74.60%	3.36%
OKDDip br. [17]	71.24%	74.37%	3.13%
SAD [15]	75.32%	77.47%	2.15%
PCL [11]	71.28%	74.14%	2.86%
Proposed	69.6%	72.76%	3.16%

For a fair comparison, the results of KDCL [7] were retrieved from [11], in which the KDCL framework was trained on three parallel peer networks.

The proposed method surpasses DML [5] by almost 0.96% accuracy gain. In DML, a cohort of student networks is trained together with mutual distillation and the parameters of the network are updated in a multi-stage setting. Furthermore, we surpass SAD [15], an offline attention-based KD framework by over 1% accuracy gain. In SAD, a pre-trained teacher network is used together with an attention module that learns the similarities between the teacher's and the student's feature maps, and then applies them to control the distillation intensities of all possible pairs.

Compared with other online KD frameworks [7,11,17], the proposed method attains comparable if not better results. OKDDip [17] can be implemented either in a branch-based setting (the low-level layers of the students are shared)—denoted *br.* in Table 6, or in a network-based setting (each student is an individual network)—denoted *net.* in the table. The OKDDip in-network approach slightly surpassed the proposed method by 0.2%; however, it uses more parameters for training and a more complex training strategy.

5. Ablation Studies

In this section, we perform a series of ablation studies to investigate further properties of the proposed method. All the experiments reported in this section use ResNet-20 [22] as peer student networks trained on the CIFAR-100 dataset. For all studies—except Section 5.1, where N varies from 2 to 5—the number of student networks is set to $N = 3$.

5.1. Number of Student Networks

In the proposed KD framework, the "teacher" is computed on the fly as the weighted average of the N peer student networks. Table 7 reports the impact of this hyper-parameter N over the accuracy of the knowledge-distilled student and the ensemble. The first row from the table accounts for the accuracy of a vanilla-trained student.

Table 7. The effect of the number of students N on the distillation performance.(best results represented in bold).

N	KD	Ensemble	KD Gain
1	67.54%	N/A	N/A
2	69.30%	72.28%	1.76
3	69.73%	73.32%	2.19
4	69.01%	73.61%	1.47
5	**69.9%**	73.69%	**2.36**

It should be noted that the ensemble is used only as a training component (the "teacher" from which the knowledge is distilled) and cannot be used for inference on real-world data because the ground truth data are required when computing the attention features (Section 3.3). Nevertheless, we report its accuracy on the test data to analyze the relationship between the teacher's accuracy and the accuracy of the knowledge-distilled students.

As the number of peer student networks N increases, the accuracy of the ensemble increases as well. The accuracy of the knowledge-distilled students follows the trend, but there is an exception for the case of $N = 4$ students, where we obtained a slightly lower and out-of-order gain in accuracy than the other configurations. Still, in all cases, when training a network in the proposed KD framework we obtain a higher accuracy (with an accuracy boost ranging from 1.47 when $N = 4$ to 2.36 when $N = 5$) than by independently training it. Continuously increasing the number of students would not continually improve the performance of the best student as their knowledge absorption is not boundless.

5.2. Ensembling Features

The main contribution of this paper is the attention-based ensembling strategy that is used to compute the distillation signal across the training process. To compute the ensembling weights, we extracted three features based on the students' logits and the ground truth data (as described in Section 3.3). In Table 8, we analyze the impact of these features on the accuracy of the knowledge-distilled student and the ensemble.

Table 8. Ensembling features.(best results represented in bold).

Features	KD	Ensemble	KD Gain
Vanilla	67.54%	N/A	N/A
F^1	67.89%	71.66%	0.35
F^2	68.76%	72.74%	1.22
F^3	67.29%	71.57%	-0.25
F^1F^2	69.59%	75.5%	2.05
F^1F^3	68.34%	72.39%	0.80
F^2F^3	68.98%	72.64%	1.44
$F^1F^2F^3$	69.73%	73.32%	**2.19**

The first column indicates which features are used by the attention mechanism when computing the ensembling weights. Feature F^2 has the most discriminative power. The experiments show that the best results are obtained when using all the proposed features F^1, F^2, and F^3. The ensemble with the highest accuracy is the one obtained using features (F_1, F_2) at 75.5%. However, this is not the setup yielding the best knowledge-distilled student. Feature F_3 used individually brings a negative gain. However, when combined with either F_1 or F_2, it increases their respective induced gains behaving like a catalyst. When used in combination (F_1, F_2, F_3), F_3 keeps its catalytic effect, helping this combination of features achieve the largest improvement.

5.3. Distillation Strength

Finally, we analyze the impact of the knowledge distillation loss weight λ (Equation (3)) over the accuracy of the knowledge-distilled students (Table 9). The first row from the table represents the accuracy of an independently trained student.

Table 9. Impact of the KD loss weight.(best results represented in bold).

λ	KD	KD Gain
Vanilla	67.54%	N/A
0	68.01%	0.47
0.1	68.69%	1.15
1	69.73%	**2.19**
2	69.41%	1.87
3	68.94%	1.40

Even when the knowledge distillation weight is disabled ($\lambda = 0$), we observe a slight improvement over the independently trained "vanilla" student; so, just by training a model in the proposed framework without any KD loss (Equation (5)), a small boost in accuracy is observed. This is due to the regularizing effect of training the cohort of students together. As we increase the value of λ towards 1, the accuracy of the knowledge-distilled students increases; however, for larger values, the accuracy starts to decrease. Within the proposed framework, the student networks are influenced by two loss functions (Equation (3)): the classification loss L_{data} and the knowledge distillation loss (Kullback–Liebler divergence) L_{KD}. As λ increases, the weight of the latter also increases, while the weight of the classification loss remains the same. These results indicate that the classification loss still plays an important role in the proposed framework and that the students benefit from the ground truth data. Moreover, the classification loss is important because the teacher ensemble relies on the predictions of the individual students.

As future work, we also plan to experiment by varying the λ parameter during the training process.

6. Conclusions and Future Work

This work tackled the problem of knowledge distillation, a teacher–student training setup in which a lightweight student network is guided by the knowledge of a teacher network formed from lightweight students to improve its accuracy while maintaining a low computational cost. As opposed to offline KD, where a pre-trained powerful teacher is required, the proposed method simultaneously trains a group of student models and learns from peers' predictions, which are aggregated into an ensemble via an attention mechanism. The attention mechanism is employed solely throughout the training process and, for inference, a single lightweight network is selected and used. The main advantage of this work is that by training a model in the proposed online KD framework, its accuracy is boosted, without adding any additional parameters. In addition, the learning process is end-to-end, and the teacher's (ensemble) logits are computed on the fly using an original attention-based mechanism.

The proposed method was evaluated on several image classification benchmarks, both by training the networks from scratch and by transfer learning. We proved that the proposed method can be generically used to improve the accuracy of image classification problems. The results show that by training a network in this framework, the performance of the knowledge-distilled student is consistently improved when compared with the vanilla-trained networks. Moreover, for the ResNet architecture, a knowledge-distilled student exceeds the performance of the immediately larger ResNet model trained on the vanilla configuration. Our method was compared with several state-of-the-art works on multiple image classification benchmarks, and the experimental results shows that it attains comparable if not better results. Although the "gain" is not significant in absolute terms, its magnitude is on par with the results from the state of the art. The main contribution is to achieve better accuracy using the same network architectures by slightly changing the training process. Thus, the same known network architectures will obtain better results using KD techniques on the same datasets.

As for all online knowledge distillation methods, one limitation of the present study is the exact mechanism that leads to the accuracy improvement of knowledge distillation over other approaches has not been fully understood [8]. Moreover, the training process has a higher computational resource footprint, as it involves optimizing several peer students at once. However, as opposed to offline KD methods, the training process occurs in a single step.

As future work, we plan to incorporate attention mechanisms to also distill knowledge from intermediate feature maps and to extend the framework for other vision tasks.

Author Contributions: Conceptualization, D.-L.B. and A.S.D.; methodology, D.-L.B.; software, D.-L.B.; validation, D.-L.B., A.S.D., T.A.I. and A.-I.M.; investigation, D.-L.B., A.S.D., T.A.I. and A.-I.M.; resources, D.-L.B. and A.-I.M.; writing—review and editing, T.A.I.; visualization, T.A.I. All authors have read and agreed to the published version of the manuscript.

Funding: This work was supported by a grant of the Romanian Ministry of Education and Research—UEFISCDI, project number PN-III-P2-2.1-PED-2021-3120.

Data Availability Statement: Not applicable.

Conflicts of Interest: The authors declare no conflict of interest.

Abbreviations

The following abbreviations are used in this manuscript:

FLOPS	Floating Point Operations Per Second
GAP	Global Average Pooling
GMP	Global Max Pooling
KD	Knowledge distillation
KL	Kullback–Leibler divergence
ReLU	Rectified Linear Unit

References

1. Cai, H.; Lin, J.; Lin, Y.; Liu, Z.; Tang, H.; Wang, H.; Zhu, L.; Han, S. Enable deep learning on mobile devices: Methods, systems, and applications. *ACM Trans. Des. Autom. Electron. Syst. (TODAES)* **2022**, *27*, 1–50. [CrossRef]
2. Hinton, G.; Vinyals, O.; Dean, J. Distilling the knowledge in a neural network. *arXiv* **2015**, arXiv:1503.02531.
3. Buciluă, C.; Caruana, R.; Niculescu-Mizil, A. Model compression. In Proceedings of the 12th ACM SIGKDD International Conference on Knowledge Discovery and Data Mining, Philadelphia, PE, USA, 20–23 August 2006; pp. 535–541.
4. Lan, X.; Zhu, X.; Gong, S. Knowledge distillation by on-the-fly native ensemble. *arXiv* **2018**, arXiv:1806.04606.
5. Zhang, Y.; Xiang, T.; Hospedales, T.M.; Lu, H. Deep mutual learning. In Proceedings of the IEEE Conference on Computer Vision and Pattern Recognition, Salt Lake City, UT, USA, 18–23 June 2018; pp. 4320–4328.
6. Song, G.; Chai, W. Collaborative learning for deep neural networks. *arXiv* **2021**, arXiv:1805.11761.
7. Guo, Q.; Wang, X.; Wu, Y.; Yu, Z.; Liang, D.; Hu, X.; Luo, P. Online knowledge distillation via collaborative learning. In Proceedings of the IEEE/CVF Conference on Computer Vision and Pattern Recognition, Seattle, WA, USA, 14–19 June 2020; pp. 11020–11029.
8. Wang, L.; Yoon, K.J. Knowledge distillation and student-teacher learning for visual intelligence: A review and new outlooks. *arXiv* **2018**, arXiv:2004.05937.
9. Kim, T.; Oh, J.; Kim, N.; Cho, S.; Yun, S.Y. Comparing kullback-leibler divergence and mean squared error loss in knowledge distillation. *arXiv* **2021**, arXiv:2105.08919.
10. Touvron, H.; Cord, M.; Douze, M.; Massa, F.; Sablayrolles, A.; Jégou, H. Training data-efficient image transformers & distillation through attention. In Proceedings of the International Conference on Machine Learning. PMLR, Virtual, 18–24 July 2021; pp. 10347–10357.
11. Wu, G.; Gong, S. Peer collaborative learning for online knowledge distillation. *Proc. Aaai Conf. Artif. Intell.* **2021**, *35*, 10302–10310. [CrossRef]
12. Kim, J.; Hyun, M.; Chung, I.; Kwak, N. Feature fusion for online mutual knowledge distillation. In Proceedings of the 2020 25th International Conference on Pattern Recognition (ICPR), Milan, Italy, 10–15 January 2021; pp. 4619–4625.
13. Hu, J.; Shen, L.; Sun, G. Squeeze-and-excitation networks. In Proceedings of the IEEE conference on Computer Vision and Pattern Recognition, Salt Lake City, UT, USA, 18–22 June 2018; pp. 7132–7141.
14. Zhou, Z.; Zhuge, C.; Guan, X.; Liu, W. Channel distillation: Channel-wise attention for knowledge distillation. *arXiv* **2020**, arXiv:2006.01683.
15. Ji, M.; Heo, B.; Park, S. Show, attend and distill: Knowledge distillation via attention-based feature matching. *Proc. Aaai Conf. Artif. Intell.* **2021**, *35*, 7945–7952. [CrossRef]
16. Vaswani, A.; Shazeer, N.; Parmar, N.; Uszkoreit, J.; Jones, L.; Gomez, A.N.; Kaiser, Ł.; Polosukhin, I. Attention is all you need. *arXiv* **2017**, arXiv:1706.03762.
17. Chen, D.; Mei, J.P.; Wang, C.; Feng, Y.; Chen, C. Online knowledge distillation with diverse peers. *Proc. Aaai Conf. Artif. Intell.* **2020**, *34*, 3430–3437. [CrossRef]
18. Woo, S.; Park, J.; Lee, J.Y.; Kweon, I.S. CBAM: Convolutional Block Attention Module. In Proceedings of the European Conference on Computer Vision (ECCV), Munich, Germany, 8–14 September 2018.
19. Good, I. Some terminology and notation in information theory. *Proc.-IEE-Part Monogr.* **1956**, *103*, 200–204. [CrossRef]
20. Kullback, S.; Leibler, R.A. On information and sufficiency. *Ann. Math. Stat.* **1951**, *22*, 79–86. [CrossRef]

21. Krizhevsky, A.; Hinton, G. Learning multiple Layers of Features from Tiny Images. Technical Report, University of Toronto, Toronto, ON, Canada. 2009. Available online: https://www.cs.toronto.edu/~kriz/learning-features-2009-TR.pdf (accessed on 1 October 2022).
22. He, K.; Zhang, X.; Ren, S.; Sun, J. Deep residual learning for image recognition. In Proceedings of the IEEE Conference on Computer Vision and Pattern Recognition, Las Vegas, NV, USA, 27–30 June 2016; pp. 770–778.
23. Le, Y.; Yang, X. Tiny imagenet visual recognition challenge. *CS 231N* **2015**, *7*, 3.
24. Deng, J.; Dong, W.; Socher, R.; Li, L.J.; Li, K.; Fei-Fei, L. Imagenet: A large-scale hierarchical image database. In Proceedings of the 2009 IEEE Conference on Computer Vision and Pattern Recognition, Miami, FL, USA, 20–25 June 2009; pp. 248–255.
25. DeVries, T.; Taylor, G.W. Improved regularization of convolutional neural networks with cutout. *arXiv* **2017**, arXiv:1708.04552.
26. Parkhi, O.M.; Vedaldi, A.; Zisserman, A.; Jawahar, C. Cats and dogs. In Proceedings of the 2012 IEEE Conference on Computer Vision and Pattern Recognition, Providence, RI, USA, 16–21 June 2012; pp. 3498–3505.
27. Nilsback, M.E.; Zisserman, A. Automated flower classification over a large number of classes. In Proceedings of the 2008 Sixth Indian Conference on Computer Vision, Graphics & Image Processing, Bhubaneswar, India, 16–19 December 2008; pp. 722–729.
28. Glorot, X.; Bengio, Y. Understanding the difficulty of training deep feedforward neural networks. In Proceedings of the Thirteenth International Conference on Artificial Intelligence and Statistics, Sardinia, Italy, 13–15 May 2010; JMLR Workshop and Conference Proceedings; pp. 249–256.
29. Hinton, G.; Srivastava, N.; Swersky, K. Neural networks for machine learning lecture 6a overview of mini-batch gradient descent. *Cited On* **2012**, *14*, 2.
30. Huang, G.; Liu, Z.; Van Der Maaten, L.; Weinberger, K.Q. Densely connected convolutional networks. In Proceedings of the IEEE Conference on Computer Vision and Pattern Recognition, Honolulu, HI, USA, 21–26 July 2017; pp. 4700–4708.
31. Zoph, B.; Vasudevan, V.; Shlens, J.; Le, Q.V. Learning transferable architectures for scalable image recognition. In Proceedings of the IEEE Conference on Computer Vision and Pattern Recognition, Salt Lake City, UT, USA, 18–23 June 2018; pp. 8697–8710.
32. Howard, A.G.; Zhu, M.; Chen, B.; Kalenichenko, D.; Wang, W.; Weyand, T.; Andreetto, M.; Adam, H. Mobilenets: Efficient convolutional neural networks for mobile vision applications. *arXiv* **2017**, arXiv:1704.04861.
33. Ho-Phuoc, T. CIFAR10 to compare visual recognition performance between deep neural networks and humans. *arXiv* **2018**, arXiv:1811.07270.

mathematics

MDPI

Article

On Methods for Merging Mixture Model Components Suitable for Unsupervised Image Segmentation Tasks

Branislav Panić *, Marko Nagode, Jernej Klemenc and Simon Oman

Faculty of Mechanical Engineering, University of Ljubljana, Aškerčeva Ulica 6, 1000 Ljubljana, Slovenia; marko.nagode@fs.uni-lj.si (M.N.); jernej.klemenc@fs.uni-lj.si (J.K.); simon.oman@fs.uni-lj.si (S.O.)
* Correspondence: branislav.panic@fs.uni-lj.si; Tel.: +386-1-4771-201

Abstract: Unsupervised image segmentation is one of the most important and fundamental tasks in many computer vision systems. Mixture model is a compelling framework for unsupervised image segmentation. A segmented image is obtained by clustering the pixel color values of the image with an estimated mixture model. Problems arise when the selected optimal mixture model contains a large number of mixture components. Then, multiple components of the estimated mixture model are better suited to describe individual segments of the image. We investigate methods for merging the components of the mixture model and their usefulness for unsupervised image segmentation. We define a simple heuristic for optimal segmentation with merging of the components of the mixture model. The experiments were performed with gray-scale and color images. The reported results and the performed comparisons with popular clustering approaches show clear benefits of merging components of the mixture model for unsupervised image segmentation.

Keywords: mixture models; parameter estimation; clustering; unsupervised image segmentation

MSC: 68U10; 94A08; 62H35; 68T45

Citation: Panić, B.; Nagode, M.; Klemenc, J.; Oman, S. On Methods for Merging Mixture Model Components Suitable for Unsupervised Image Segmentation Tasks. *Mathematics* **2022**, *10*, 4301. https://doi.org/10.3390/math10224301

Academic Editors: Marjan Mernik, Adrian Sergiu Darabant and Diana-Laura Borza

Received: 11 October 2022
Accepted: 14 November 2022
Published: 16 November 2022

1. Introduction and Background

Intelligent computer vision systems are becoming increasingly popular. They are very useful tool in many applications that aid the decision making process, for example, agriculture [1], structural health monitoring [2], robotics [3], surveillance [4], product quality and manufacturing [5], self-driving-vehicles [6], medicine [7], and so on.

Image segmentation can be viewed as a useful partitioning of the image. As such, it is a central task in many computer vision systems, and one of most difficult ones [8–11]. It can be supervised or unsupervised, as pointed out by Refs. [12,13]. In supervised image segmentation, we want to partition the image into semantically coherent regions on the image. This can also be referred to as semantic segmentation [3,14]. As such, it is usually based on classification methods [13,15,16]. In unsupervised image segmentation, we are interested in extracting similar segments based on pixel positions and color intensity values with respect to a criterion [17]. As such, clustering algorithms are mostly used [11,12,17,18].

For supervised image segmentation, we usually need very large datasets for training a classification model, e.g., a deep neural network [2,14]. In unsupervised image segmentation, we perform a clustering algorithm directly on the image under consideration [12,17]. Consequently, unsupervised image segmentation based on a clustering algorithm is weaker in performance than classification. However, they do not require large training datasets, are faster, require less computational power, and, most importantly, can be used in conjunction with newer classification methods [3,12,13]. They are also much more useful than their supervised counterparts for certain domain-specific tasks where prior knowledge is lacking, whether due to a lack of plausible training images or other factors [12,13,19,20].

A mixture model is a compelling framework for many pattern recognition tasks [21–24]. Traditionally, it is used in machine learning as a clustering tool and, therefore, in computer vision for unsupervised image segmentation [22,25–27]. Mixture models can be seen as blob detectors, aimed at detecting regions of interest with similar colors or intensities in an image [9,25,28]. In this respect, similar to the fuzzy clustering algorithms [10,12,29], they are very promising for unsupervised image segmentation and as such can be useful for further feature extraction and detection of region of interests [8,19].

Obtaining a useful segmentation with the mixture models is a delicate process. First, the right mixture model must be chosen, i.e., Gaussian, Gamma, Weibul, or another that can capture the detail correctly [11,25,30,31]. Next is the choice of model selection criterion [32]. Finally, the algorithm for estimation can be problematic [9]. All of the above-mentioned can result in either under-segmentation problems (too few regions detected) or over-segmentation (too many segments detected) [9,28,33]. An over-segmented image can be regarded as noisy, while an under-segmented image as incomplete and thus inappropriate for use. To tackle this issue, in this paper, we investigate the usefulness of a clearly over-segmented solution, provided by the estimated mixture model, and the methods for merging different detected regions to obtain a more useful segmentation.

Every component of the estimated mixture model represents a segment of the image, in order to reduce the number of unwanted segments. We are interested in merging different components of the mixture model [33]. By doing so, we are remedying the problems that arose as a result of an inappropriate type of mixture model, the deficiency of model selection criteria, and, to some extent, drawbacks of the estimation algorithm [33–35]. We are investigating if many-to-one mapping as a one-to-one relationship between a mixture model component and a cluster may be insufficient [9,33].

This paper is summarized as follows. We start with an explanation of mixture models and their application in clustering and image segmentation in Section 2. Section 3 is reserved for the derivation of merging procedures and criteria for merging. Section 4 describes the estimation algorithm. Section 5 discuses the optimal segmentation. Section 6 introduces the needed constants for evaluation and in Section 7 we provide the experimental results. In Section 8 we provide some fruitful discussions of the experimental results, and Section 9 finalizes our work and concludes this paper.

2. Mixture Models

Let $\boldsymbol{Y} = \{\boldsymbol{y}_1, \boldsymbol{y}_2, \dots, \boldsymbol{y}_n\}$ be a d-dimensional observed dataset of n continuous observations $\boldsymbol{y}_j = \{y_1, y_2, \dots, y_d\}$. Each observation $\boldsymbol{y}_j$ is assumed to follow the probability density function (PDF):

$$f(\boldsymbol{y}_j|c, \boldsymbol{w}, \boldsymbol{\Theta}) = \sum_{l=1}^{c} w_l f_l(\boldsymbol{y}_j|\boldsymbol{\Theta}_l). \tag{1}$$

Equation (1) gives the PDF of a mixture model. The PDF of a mixture model consists of weighted c components that follow simple parametric probability distribution, such as Gaussian distribution, Weibull distribution, and similar [36,37]. Component distribution PDF is given by the f_l and has the parameters $\boldsymbol{\Theta}_l$. For example, PDF of multivariate Gaussian distribution is

$$f_l(\boldsymbol{y}_j|\boldsymbol{\Theta}_l) = \frac{1}{\sqrt{(2\pi)^d \mathtt{det}(\boldsymbol{\Sigma}_l)}} \exp\left(-\frac{1}{2}(\boldsymbol{y}_j - \boldsymbol{\mu}_l.)\boldsymbol{\Sigma}_l^{-1}(\boldsymbol{y}_j - \boldsymbol{\mu}_l)^T\right). \tag{2}$$

Component parameters $\boldsymbol{\Theta}_l$ are distribution specific. For the Gaussian mixtures, those are the mean vector $\boldsymbol{\mu}_l$ and covariance matrix $\boldsymbol{\Sigma}_l$. Weights w_l have the properties of the convex combination $w_l \geq 0 \wedge \sum_{l=1}^{c} w_l = 1$ [38]. Thus, we can arrange the mixture model parameters in a set Θ

$$\Theta = \{w_1, w_2, \dots, w_c, \Theta_1, \Theta_2, \dots, \Theta_c\}, \tag{3}$$

or concisely and more conveniently

$$\Theta = \{\boldsymbol{w}, \boldsymbol{\Theta}\}. \tag{4}$$

The estimation of the parameters involves estimation of component weights $\boldsymbol{w}$ and component parameters $\boldsymbol{\Theta}$. Usually, we denote the estimations as $\widehat{\Theta}$. The easiest way to estimate the mixture model parameters is via the maximum likelihood. In other words, the parameters $\widehat{\Theta}$ yielding the maximum of

$$L(\boldsymbol{Y}|\Theta = \widehat{\Theta}) = \prod_{j=1}^{n} f(\boldsymbol{y}_j|\widehat{c}, \widehat{\boldsymbol{w}}, \widehat{\boldsymbol{\Theta}}). \tag{5}$$

It is often more convenient to maximize the log-likelihood function

$$\log L(\boldsymbol{Y}|\Theta) = \sum_{j=1}^{n} \log\left(\sum_{l=1}^{c} w_l f_l(\boldsymbol{y}_j|\boldsymbol{\Theta}_l) \right), \tag{6}$$

and, the estimation can be written as

$$\widehat{\Theta} = \underset{\Theta}{\operatorname{argmax}} \log L(\boldsymbol{Y}|\Theta). \tag{7}$$

The maximization problem described with Equation (7) has many inconvenient aspects, mainly because the number of components c in the mixture model is not known in advance. First, it is known that the likelihood value increases with the increase in the number of components due to the overall better fit [28,39]. Second, without knowing the number of components, it is impossible to derive the (6) to obtain the solution to the maximization problem. Lastly, the use of global optimization algorithm is not convenient due to the large number of optimization parameters involved in a mixture model [38]. Thus, some type of model selection procedure is commonly involved in the estimation process [38].

2.1. Model Selection

Usually, we are interested in estimating the number of components $\widehat{c}$ and the accompanying parameters $\widehat{\boldsymbol{\Theta}}$; however, in some cases, the number of components is known [38], in which case the model selection procedure is not needed—this occurs in the minority of cases. In the majority of cases, we are faced with a ubiquitous problem of the maximization of (6) when the number of components is unknown. Nonetheless, to derive Equation (6), we need to know the number of components c. Therefore, it is a common practice to try out different numbers of components and estimate the fit. Thus, it is quite common and justified to denote the mixture model in relation to the number of components c,

$$\Theta(c) = \{\boldsymbol{w}(c), \boldsymbol{\Theta}(c)\}. \tag{8}$$

Additionally, because the likelihood function increases with the increase in the number of components, the selection of the optimal model based solely on maximum likelihood can be misleading. Therefore, there is a need to introduce different model criteria to choose the best fit. Generally, those are called information criteria [38]. We will denote those as IC. The model selection procedure is described with Algorithm 1 [28,39].

In summary, we estimate the optimal mixture model $\widehat{\Theta}$ for different numbers of components c. If the number of components is known, we can solve Equation (7) using, for example, the algorithm EM (expectation–maximization) denoted by the EM function in line 4 of the Algorithm 1. EM is a local optimization algorithm mainly used to estimate the maximum likelihood parameters of mixture models when some initial parameter estimates are known in advance [38]. The optimal model is obtained for each number of components, and the best model is selected from among them. The model giving the optimal selected $\mathrm{IC}_{\mathrm{opt}}$ is thus the best model available. ICF in line 5 of Algorithm 1 represents the generic function for estimating the chosen information criterion.

Algorithm 1: Model selection procedure

Input: dataset $\mathbf{Y}$ and initialize set $C = \{c_1, c_2, \ldots\}$;
Output: optimal mixture model parameters $\boldsymbol{w}_{\text{opt}}, \boldsymbol{\Theta}_{\text{opt}}$;
$\text{IC}_{\text{opt}} = \infty$, $\boldsymbol{w}_{\text{opt}} = \{\}$, $\boldsymbol{\Theta}_{\text{opt}} = \{\}$, $c_{\text{opt}} = 0$;
foreach $c \in C$ **do**:
  Initialize $\boldsymbol{w}_{\text{ini}}(c), \boldsymbol{\Theta}_{\text{ini}}(c)$;
  $\boldsymbol{w}(c), \boldsymbol{\Theta}(c) = \text{EM}(\mathbf{Y}, \boldsymbol{w}_{\text{ini}}(c), \boldsymbol{\Theta}_{\text{ini}}(c))$;
  Estimate criterion $\text{IC} = \text{ICF}(\mathbf{Y}, \boldsymbol{w}(c), \boldsymbol{\Theta}(c))$;
  if $\text{IC} < \text{IC}_{\text{opt}}$:
    $\text{IC}_{\text{opt}} = \text{IC}$, $c_{\text{opt}} = c$, $\boldsymbol{w}_{\text{opt}} = \boldsymbol{w}(c)$, $\boldsymbol{\Theta}_{\text{opt}} = \boldsymbol{\Theta}(c)$;
  end
end

The importance of using a model selection procedure is illustrated in Figure 1. Different models were estimated for different numbers of components c. For each model, a Bayesian information criterion (BIC) was calculated [40]. The BIC is defined as

$$\text{BIC} = -2\log L + M\log n, \tag{9}$$

where M is the number of parameters in the model. It is quite obvious that the term $M\log n$, given that the M increases with the number of components c, is a balance factor to compensate for the increase in log-likelihood value with the increase in number of components c.

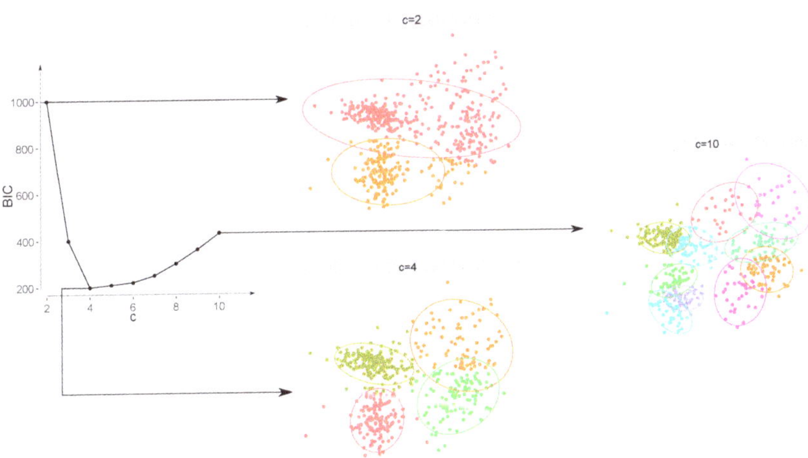

Figure 1. Model selection illustrated.

BIC is also one of the most commonly used information criteria [41]. Choosing the model with the optimal value of BIC should provide the best solution [33,34]. Although every estimated model yields one of the local optima of log-likelihood function from (6), different models provide less or more of the information needed. For example, a model with two components clearly is an under-fit, while a model with ten components gives an over-fit. In contrast, a model with five components seems to be the best selection, at least when the BIC criterion is used.

2.2. Mixture Model-Based Clustering and Image Segmentation

In a mixture model framework, it is generally considered that each component in a model represents one homogeneous unit [42]. In other words, that homogeneous unit represents a sub-population of the whole population. In a clustering sense, that homogeneous unit represents the cluster. A cluster is a group of observations from a dataset that share similar characteristics. Thus, every observation that arose from a certain component in a mixture model is considered to form a cluster. For every observation $\boldsymbol{y}_j$ in dataset $\boldsymbol{Y}$, we can estimate the posterior probability

$$\tau_{jl} = \frac{w_l f_l(\boldsymbol{y}_j|\boldsymbol{\Theta}_l)}{\sum_{\tilde{l}=1}^{c} w_{\tilde{l}} f_{\tilde{l}}(\boldsymbol{y}_j|\boldsymbol{\Theta}_{\tilde{l}})}, \tag{10}$$

that it arose from the lth mixture model component. The cluster assignment is made according to the maximum a posteriori (MAP) rule

$$l_j = \underset{\tilde{l}=1,\ldots,c}{\operatorname{argmax}} \, \tau_{j\tilde{l}} \quad \forall j \in \{1,\ldots,n\}. \tag{11}$$

We are interested in labeling all of the observations in dataset $\boldsymbol{Y}$: ergo, a clustering scheme or simply clustering. Image segmentation is a similar process. We want to identify k partitions of the image, which are coherent in some way. This is illustrated in Figure 2. The original image in Figure 2a comes from the Berkeley dataset [43] and the second image (Figure 2b) is the human segmentation provided by the participants in study.

(**a**) Image. (**b**) Segmentation.

Figure 2. Image segmentation task.

Many clustering algorithms are used for image segmentation [44]. Image segmentation with a mixture model can be conducted using pixel intensity and position; however, using the pixel position values in the estimation of the mixture model often degrades the results, due to their non-random nature. Thus, we are interested only in modeling the PDF of pixel intensity; accordingly, we produce a clustering (scheme). Additionally, for the component distribution, the Gaussian distribution is usually used [9,31]. This is a popular choice because the multivariate extension is straightforward; thus, images with multiple channels (color images opposed to monochrome images) can be segmented. Furthermore, the mixtures of Gaussian distributions are the easiest and most straightforward to estimate. However, using Gaussian distribution as the component distribution brings many problems. The first is that the pixel intensity is bounded, while the Gaussian distribution is not. The second problem arises from the fact that the Gaussian PDF is symmetric around the mode. Because of the non-symetricity of the mode (i.e., the left and right tails are not equal), multiple Gaussian components are estimated to compensate for this. This leads to many clusters, which then leads to many segments, which are not actually present. Although these problems generally arise with the Gaussian mixture model, the problem of estimating too many components in other mixture models is also present, especially when estimating the PDF of an image.

3. Merging of Redundant Components in Mixture Model-Based Clustering

Let us look at the quite famous old faithful geyser dataset [45]. The dataset contains 272 observations on two continuous variables, the first named *eruptions* and the second named *waiting*, as illustrated on plots in Figure 3. The first variable, *eruptions*, gives the geyser eruption time in minutes, whilst the second one, *waiting*, gives the waiting time to next eruption, also in minutes. Figure 3a gives the visualization of the dataset without identified clusters while Figure 3b,c give the clustering solution obtained from the estimated two-component Gaussian mixture model and the three-component Gaussian mixture model.

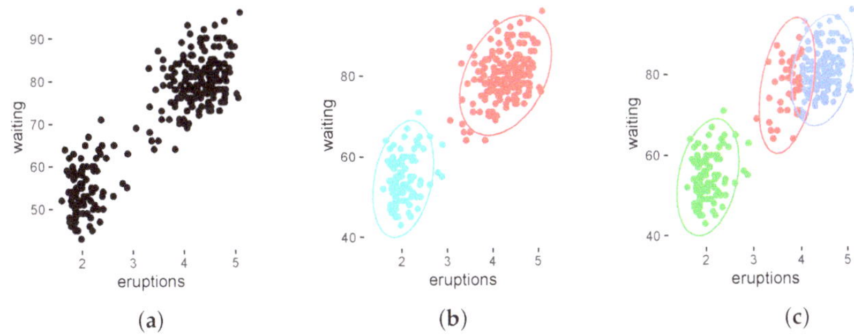

Figure 3. Old faithful dataset with two and three clustering schemes from estimated two- and three component Gaussian mixture models (GMM). (**a**) Old faithful dataset. (**b**) Two-component GMM. (**c**) Three-component GMM.

It occurs quite naturally that the two-component clustering solution is true. Not even by looking at the solution on plot Figure 3b and only by observing non-colored points in plot Figure 3a there is some convincing evidence that there are two groups of points. However, let us examine the obtained values of the IC criteria in Table 1. Even though the difference in IC values is not so dramatic, the three-component solution is the optimal solution judging by two different IC, namely AIC (Akaike information criterion [46]) and BIC. Judging by their value, the three-component solution seems to be a preferred solution. In contrast, the ICL (integrated classification likelihood [42]) criterion had a lower value for the two-component mixture, meaning that this model would be selected as optimal. This is expected because the ICL criterion favors the solution that is more probable to be the optimal clustering solution. The sole reason for the derivation of the ICL criterion is to bypass the somewhat tricky nature of BIC to favor the model that is not an optimal clustering solution.

Table 1. Values of BIC for estimated Gaussian mixture model with different numbers of components.

Gaussian Mixture Model	Two Component Solution	Three Component Solution
AIC	2284	2274
BIC	2320	2314
ICL	2320	2357

3.1. *Entropy-Based Merging*

While the ICL criterion seems to be sufficient for the old geyser dataset and gives an optimal clustering solution, it is far from bulletproof. Mainly, the problem is that it can provide a clustering solution with too few clusters in highly overlapping situations [34]. In image segmentation, such situations are frequent. Another point is provided in [34]. Although the number of components in the mixture model is well met by, e.g., the BIC criterion, the number of components in that scenario is well suited for the underlying PDF of a dataset but not necessarily for clustering. That may well mean that some clusters in the clustering are not well-presented with only one component of the mixture model, meaning that a one-to-one scenario is not practical. This goes hand in hand with many density-based clustering approaches, especially the likes of mean-shift or modal-based EM algorithm [47].

To propose a solution, Baudry et al. [34] developed a merging procedure based on the estimation of entropy of soft clustering: in other words, posterior probabilities. Starting with a number of components c in the mixture model that fits the dataset well and an equal number of clusters $k = c$ as the number of components in the mixture model, the idea is to build a sequence of clusterings with merged pairs of clusters. Thus, the newly created clustering schemes contain $k-1$ clusters. At each stage, merging happens between each and every pair of clusters and the most promising pair for creating the $k-1$ clustering scheme is the one for which the newly obtained $k-1$ clustering scheme maximizes a criterion

$$E_{l\tilde{l}} = -\sum_{j=1}^{n}\left(\tau_{jl}\log\tau_{jl} + \tau_{j\tilde{l}}\log\tau_{j\tilde{l}}\right) + \sum_{j=1}^{n}\tau_{jl\cup\tilde{l}}\log\tau_{jl\cup\tilde{l}}, \quad (12)$$

where the τ_{jl} gives the posterior that the jth observation belongs to lth component/cluster, $\tau_{j\tilde{l}}$ gives the posterior that the jth observation belongs to $\tilde{l}$th component/cluster, and the $\tau_{jl\cup\tilde{l}}$ is the posterior of the merged cluster combined from components/clusters l and $\tilde{l}$. The posterior $\tau_{jl\cup\tilde{l}}$ can be simply calculated as

$$\tau_{jl\cup\tilde{l}} = \tau_{jl} + \tau_{j\tilde{l}}, \quad (13)$$

and obvious condition $l \neq \tilde{l}$ should be met. The number of combinations is therefore equal to

$$\binom{k}{2} = \frac{k!}{2(k-2)!} = \frac{k(k-1)}{2}, \quad (14)$$

when the current number of components/clusters is k.

The final selected merged clustering scheme fits the data as well as the first solution provided by the c mixture model components, since it is based on the same mixture model and the likelihood does not change. Only the number and definition of clusters are different. In contrast, the likelihood of the mixture model selected by the ICL criterion can be worse. The method described above yields just one suggested set of clusters for each k, and the user can choose between them on substantive grounds. For example, the number of clusters in the final clustering scheme can be selected to match the number of components in the mixture model selected with the ICL criterion. Otherwise, because in each merging step we obtain the entropy of merged pair of clusters from the previous clustering scheme, the elbow method can be employed on graphical results of the entropy variation against the number of clusters to select the final number of clusters k [34].

3.2. Merging Based on Directly Estimated Mis-Classification Probabilities

The second method is described by [35]. As the previous method described, this method depends on soft clustering or, in other words, posterior probabilities τ_{lj} and hard clustering or indicator value 1_{lj}. Indicator value 1_{lj} is a binary variable giving the indicator if the observation $\boldsymbol{y}_j$ belongs to lth component/cluster. However, we are not interested in the probability of observation being clustered to the lth component/cluster but the misclassification probability between two components of the mixture model $p_{l\tilde{l}}$. The misclassification probability $p_{l\tilde{l}}$ can be summarized as the distance between two probability distributions, e.g., for two Gaussian distributions, a Bhattacharyya distance [35], but in a more generalized fashion and additionally more focused on clustering application. The misclassification probability can be estimated as

$$\widehat{p}_{l\tilde{l}} = \frac{\sum_{j=1}^{n}\tau_{lj}1(\tilde{l}j)}{\sum_{j=1}^{n}\tau_{lj}}, \quad (15)$$

where the τ_{lj} is the soft clustering for the lth component/cluster and $1(\tilde{l}j)$ is the hard clustering for the $\tilde{l}$th component. It is also important to say that the $\widehat{p}_{l\tilde{l}}$ is not symmetric, meaning that $\widehat{p}_{l\tilde{l}} \neq \widehat{p}_{\tilde{l}l}$; however, this can be violated. Thus, the most optimistic criterion is the

$$q = \max\left(\widehat{p}_{l\tilde{l}}, \widehat{p}_{\tilde{l}l}\right), \quad (16)$$

and should be used to select the merging pair of components/clusters. Again, it is quite obvious that the merged pair will result in equal posterior probabilities $\tau_{jl\cup\tilde{l}}$ as for the previous described method (Equation (13)).

Merely by observing the merging criteria in both methods, it is sufficient to say that both procedures will results in different final clustering schemes. Nonetheless, they share several similarities, given that the $\sum_{l=1}^{k} \tau_{lj} = 1$ must hold for any number of clusters $k \leq c$. The most important similarity, at least for the image segmentation task, is the obvious merging of overlapping components. Namely, two components, not overlapped significantly, will obey the rule of $\tau_{lj} >> \tau_{\tilde{l}j}\ \forall j \in \{1, \ldots, n\}$ or vice versa. In other words, one component will have posterior probabilities close to 1, while the other will have close to 0. Thus, both criteria (Equations (12) and (16)) will be close to 0, suggesting the component should not be merged. Otherwise, if the significant overlap between components exists, both criteria will yield significantly higher values, suggesting that the components should be merged. Simply, the methods will progress to the solution that will minimize the overlap between the posterior probabilities. If the overlap between the mixture model components is not high both methods will yield similar solutions; however, in the presence of high overlap between the components of the mixture model, both methods will give different results.

3.3. *Component Merging Mechanism Inside Mixture Model*

An advantage of both selected merging methods and criteria is in the fact that they can be used for any component distribution in the mixture model, as they both are distribution parameter independent [35]. Instead of recalculating the best possible merging pair based on distribution component parameters, we are calculating the best possible merging pair based on posterior probabilities τ_{lj} and clustering labels (indicator values) 1_{lj}. Thus, both methods have a wider range of application. Furthermore, instead of recalculating new component parameters for new merged pairs, we simply store the merging tree, and only update the posterior probabilities with Equation (13) to reflect the current/desirable number of clusters. Cluster indicator values for new merged clusters can be obtained merely by summing the indicator values of previously merged pair of clusters:

$$1_{jl\cup\tilde{l}} = 1_{jl} + 1_{j\tilde{l}}, \tag{17}$$

and cluster labels by the union of cluster labels of cluster pairs to be merged. Essentially, we are performing a form of hierarchical clustering on mixture model components. By doing so, we maintain the flexibility of a merged cluster being defined by multiple mixture model components.

4. REBMIX Algorithm and Connection with Image Segmentation

This section develops the connection of the REBMIX (Rough-Enhanced-Bayes mixture estimation) algorithm and its usefulness in image segmentation. We will not cover details about the REBMIX algorithm already described in many papers [24,36,37,48,49]. As already indicated by [28], the REBMIX algorithm is a heuristic useful for the estimation of mixture model parameters based on empirical density estimation. The first step in the multi-step procedure employed is the pre-processing step in which the empirical density estimation is carried out. This empirical density estimate can be made with different techniques; however, we are interested in the histogram, which is, in essence, how the pixel density values in an image can be naturally compressed. Given that the digital images are represented by single (gray scale) or multiple channels (color, RGB or otherwise), which are vectors of integers, the input parameter for the REBMIX algorithm pre-processing step is known in advance. For the different bit depths of digital image, this parameter varies; e.g., for 4-bit images this parameter is $K = 2^4 = 16$ and for the 8-bit it is $K = 2^8 = 256$ and so on. Given that the 8-bit digital images are predominantly used, $K = 256$ can be adopted most of the time, because the pixel intensity is an integer value between 0 and 255. However, as pointed out in [28], this parameter can lead to the overflowing of estimated mixture model components, which again emphasizes the merging of components in the mixture model.

5. Optimal Image Segmentation

In revising the merging criteria, we have already given some of the heuristics mentioned in [34,35] that indicate when is optimal to stop merging the mixture components and yield final clustering solution. We will revise them here and propose some more practical ones, especially with respect to image segmentation. As mentioned before, one could aim that the final number of clusters after merging is equal to the number of components of the mixture model selected with the ICL criterion. On the other hand, the merging process could be stopped if the merging criterion is lower than a predetermined lower bound for that specific merging criterion. For example, [35] gives the lower bound for the DEMP merging criterion $q^* = 0.05$ in his experiments. The introduction of new hyperparameters seems, at least to us, somewhat problematic. They might work in one situation and not in another. Their values vary considerably for different examples, leaving a lot of leeway to the user. This can be encouraging and annoying at the same time. We would like to avoid this. In addition, they are usually difficult to automate. The best we can do is to use the elbow method to determine the optimal value. In other words, the heuristic here is the knee of a curve obtained by plotting the values of the merging criterion and the number of clusters. In clustering, we justify this with the notion of loss of explanation due to subsequent merging. We further note that using the elbow method for our purposes leads to the following problem. The digitized nature of the image intensities may result in multiple elbows (or knees), leading to multiple plausible stops, making this heuristic unappealing. Finally, we may also want to use a different metric that does not depend on the mixture model and is more focused on the current application, namely image segmentation.

Measuring entropy has proven to be a useful metric in many artificial intelligence image applications [50–53]. The entropy of an image is simply defined as

$$H = -\sum_{j} p_j \log p_j, \tag{18}$$

where j is the unique color in the image and p_j is the probability of its occurrence. Segmenting the image using the mixture model with c components yields the entropy estimate

$$H = -\sum_{l=1}^{c} w_l \log w_l. \tag{19}$$

It is trivial to see that subsequently merging the mixture components reduces the estimated entropy, since $\widehat{H} \rightarrow 0$ when $c \rightarrow 1$ due to the property of mixture components weights is $\sum_{l=1}^{c} w_l = 1$. Therefore, to approach a practical solution, we propose an average of the image segmentation entropy of the form

$$E(H) = -\sum_{l=1}^{c} w_l^2 \log w_l. \tag{20}$$

Finally, it should be noted that this average of the image segmentation entropy is in no way related to the average entropy of [54], where the goal is the average entropy estimate of a continuous random variable. The optimal image segmentation can therefore be chosen to maximize the average of the image segmentation entropy or max $E(H)$.

6. Experimental Setup

In this section, we further describe the experiments, experimental algorithm settings, different algorithms used, and metrics used for the results evaluation. Experiments are conducted on digital images. Digital images can have multiple channels. Usually, color digital images have three or more channels. Each channel represents one of the primary colors and its intensity. However, monochrome digital images (gray-scale) have only one channel, which contains only the amount of light, i.e., the intensity.

Color digital images carry much more information; thus, they are more demanding for processing. In contrast, monochrome images are easier to process, as they have less information. Some algorithms used for image processing are also only capable of processing gray-scale images. Therefore, color images need to be transformed into gray-scale. A mixture model-based approach is capable of handling color images and, therefore, also gray-scale images. Because gray-scale processing requires fewer parameters to be estimated, it has a better prognosis on gray-scale images. Nonetheless, the results for color images can be promising, as seen in [28].

Thus, the mixture model approach for clustering to both gray-scale and color images will be used to obtain segmentation. For the mixture model, we will use the Gaussian mixture model. For the information criterion, we will use BIC; for the model selection estimation strategy, we will use single REBMX and EM from **rebmix** R package. The strategy is fully described in [39]. In essence, we are combining both REBMIX and EM algorithms to obtain the best possible estimations while keeping the computation overhead minimal, by providing the smoothing parameter K to the REBMIX pre-processing step. The value of parameter $K = 256$ is described in the previous section. The maximum number components to consider in model selection procedure is $c_{\max} = 15$. The merging of mixture model components with the entropy criterion, explained in Section 3.1, is referred to as ENT, and the merging of mixture model components with directly estimated misclassification probabilities, explained in Section 3.2, is referred to as DEMP. In addition, a single REBMX and EM strategy with ICL criterion is used as a baseline approach for optimal image segmentation with Gaussian mixture models. We refer to this as ICL.

We will use several useful external clustering metrics to quantitatively evaluate various image segmentation results.

Remark 1. *For completeness, we reiterate that the terms segmentation and clustering are used interchangeably, as they are equivalent in this context and refer to the same thing. For aesthetic reasons, we use the term segmentation when we want to emphasize the clustering application of image partitioning.*

We use precision P, recall R , Dice score $F1$, Jaccard score, adjusted rand index ARI, and adjusted mutual information AMI. Precision and recall are self-explanatory. The former is the frequency of correctly predicted positives among all predicted positives and the latter is the frequency of correctly predicted positives among all correctly predicted positives. The Dice score is the harmonic mean between Precision and Recall, and the Jaccard score or better known as Intersection over Union is the frequency of correctly predicted positives among all true positives and predicted positives. Formally we define them with following equations

$$P = \frac{TP}{TP + FP} \tag{21}$$

$$R = \frac{TP}{TP + FN} \tag{22}$$

$$F1 = \frac{2 \cdot TP}{2 \cdot TP + FP + FN} \tag{23}$$

$$F = \frac{TP}{TP + FP + FN} \tag{24}$$

where in clustering

- True positives (TP) is the number of pairs of points belonging to the same cluster in predicted and true clustering;
- False positives (FP) is the number of pairs of points belonging to the same cluster in true clustering but they are in different clusters in predicted clustering;

- False negatives (FN) is the number of pairs of points belonging to the same cluster in predicted clustering but they are in different clusters in true clustering;
- True negatives (TN) is the number of pairs of points that do not belong to the same cluster in predicted and true clustering.

These four metrics give several meaningful aspects of segmentation quality with different clustering algorithms compared to ground truth (i.e., perfect or true segmentation). On the other hand, we use ARI and AMI to provide a measure of agreement between two clustering solutions, i.e., predicted and true clustering, that takes into account the randomness of cluster assignments. This is especially important when the number of clusters in the predicted and true clustering is different and when the number of predicted clusters is large. ARI is defined in the range $[-1, 1]$, with values less than 0 indicate that clustering is worse than performing clustering at random, while values greater than zero generally define the degree of agreement between clusters. AMI is defined in the range $[0, 1]$, with values closer to 0 indicating largely independent clusters between the predicted and true clustering, and values closer to 1 indicating stronger agreement between clusters in the predicted and true clustering. The equations for ARI and AMI are somewhat unwieldy, and to avoid further repetition and unnecessary lengthening of the text, we omit them here. Interested readers may wish to consult them in [55], for example.

Finally, a note on clustering algorithms used alongside mixture modeling. There are many clustering algorithms, but the most popular ones, and thus the ones we use for comparison here, are discussed in more detail in the following two groups.

1. EM algorithm with Gaussian mixtures denoted as GMM [38], K-means denoted as KMEANS [56], and Fuzzy C-means denoted as FCMEANS [57],
2. and Meanshift denoted as MS [58], Density-based clustering denoted as DBSCAN [59], and Ordering Points To Identify the Clustering Structure denoted as OPTICS [60].

In the first group of clustering algorithms, the number of clusters must be determined in advance. We will use these algorithms for the experiments if we want to obtain the clustering solution with the desired number of clusters (segments). The second group of clustering algorithms estimates the optimal number of clusters based on internal criteria, providing the optimal clustering. We will use these algorithms for optimal segmentation of images. For their implementation, we use the scikit-learn library for the Python programming language [61]. To use them in the context of image segmentation, we followed the procedure of [44]. First, we used the SEEDS (Superpixels Extracted via Energy-Driven Sampling) superpixel algorithm [62] (from OpenCV library) and reduced the number of pixels in the image. In addition, we tried different values of the required parameters to obtain the best possible segmentation on several images. Once we were satisfied, we kept these values for further evaluation.

7. Experiments

In this section, we further report the results obtained by applying different clustering algorithms to digital images from different datasets. We use these for comparative studies of the discussed merging criteria and the optimal clustering obtained based on the heuristics we proposed in Section 5.

7.1. Crack Image Segmentation

In the first experiment, we will investigate the usefulness of our proposal for the problem of segmenting crack images (see Figure 4). This is a widely known and studied problem in the literature [63]. The goal is to extract the pixels from the digital images that belong to the observed crack on the digital image, essentially a foreground/background segmentation. The images examined are monochromatic (gray-scale) because the crack on the image usually manifests as an area of lower intensity (darker). Many thresholding methods commonly used for this problem fail because the gray density distributions representing the background and foreground are not normal or appear as quasi-unimodal functions [64]. In addition to thresholding methods, a clustering approach is also useful. It can be considered as a two-cluster problem, but may fail because the background and/or foreground object are not optimally estimated with a single distribution and thus require subsequent merging.

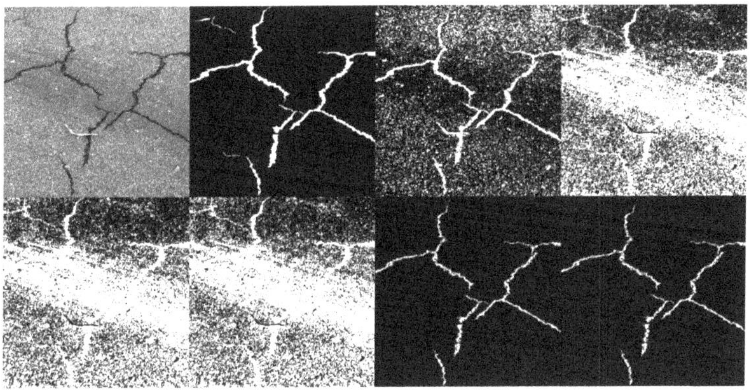

Figure 4. Segmentation of crack images with different clustering algorithms. First row: gray-scale image; true segmentation; GMM; KMEANS. Second row: FCMEANS; OTSU; ENT; DEMP.

For this task, we examined 250 different images that can be found on online dataset repositories. Most of them are from previous studies of crack image segmentation, such as Ref. [63]. The qualitative results can be found in Figure 4. The quantitative results are presented in Figure 5 in the form of boxplots, and the summary average values of the four metrics studied can be found in Table 2. We chose to examine only Precision, Recall, Dice, and Jaccard score because we knew exactly how many segments the optimal segmentation should contain, namely two segments.

Table 2. Averaged metric values obtained on crack segmentation dataset. The best values are in bold.

Metric↓/Algorithm→	GMM	KMEANS	FCMEANS	OTSU	ENT	DEMP
Precision (P)	45.6	39.0	28.2	38.9	**78.4**	70.9
Recall (R)	88.5	92.6	**94.4**	92.6	63.4	73.7
Dice ($F1$)	54.4	45.3	34.8	45.2	61.9	**65.3**
Jaccard (J)	42.6	36.1	26.6	36.0	49.7	**54.1**

From the reported results, it is clear that merging the components with either ENT or DEMP criteria results in much better segmentation than the compared algorithms. For clarity, we have also included the famous Otsu thresholding method (OTSU), although it is not a clustering method. It is also worth noting that we are dealing with an unbalanced problem, which is why the recall value is slightly exaggerated. This is because the cracks only occupy a small portion of the image. Even if the returned segmentation contained only one segment (i.e., no crack was detected), the percentage of correctly returned pixels out of all positively returned segments is still high. On the other hand, the precision is low because the false-positive pixels may exceed the true-positive ones. Judging by the Dice and Jaccard score, the ENT and DEMP algorithms that use mixture merging are far superior.

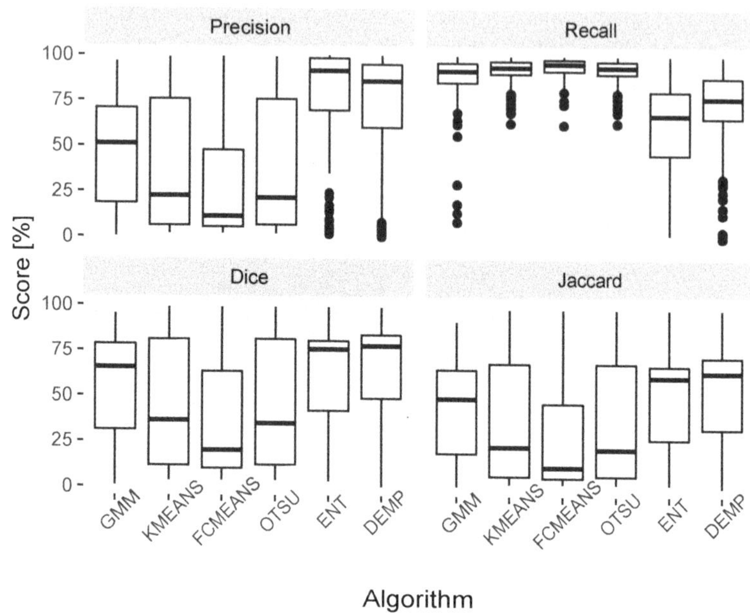

Figure 5. Boxplots of the metric distribution using different clustering algorithms for the crack image segmentation dataset.

7.2. Natural Image Segmentation

The second experiment is natural image segmentation. This is the most common application of image segmentation methods. The goal is to obtain a meaningful segmentation of the image that indicates the different coherent regions in the image. The first experiment is considered a simpler task, so we used only gray-scale variants of the images. The second experiment is much more challenging, as the variations of the different objects on the natural image are harder to distinguish. Therefore, we are forced to use all three RGB channels of a digital color image. All images used are available as a part of the Berkeley image segmentation dataset [43].

7.2.1. Recovering the True Segmentation by Manually Selecting Optimal Number of Segments

We will first present the comparative results of segmentation with merging the components of the mixture model versus estimating one mixture component per segment. In other words, we are interested in whether merging multiple components of the mixture model per segment proves to be better. To extend the comparisons a bit, we added other clustering algorithms from the first group, where we also need to choose the desired number of components (number of clusters in KMEANS and FCMEANS). To make these comparisons more illustrative and also more fair, we selected five simple images from the Berkeley image segmentation dataset and relabeled them so that their true segmentation is more homogeneous in color. This was necessary because first, the true segmentation from the Berkeley image segmentation dataset is more semantically oriented. Second, it lets us know how many segments should be included in the resulting segmentation so that we can specify the desired number of segments for each algorithm to be compared. Selected images are provided in Figure 6.

Figure 6. Selected images from the Berkley image segmentation dataset. Image identifiers are: 35058, 24063, 97033, 353013, 361084.

In the first image, we target two segments, a green background and a red ladybug. In the second image, 24063, we target three segments: house (white), door and balcony (brown), and sky (blue). The third image, 97033, would ideally have four segments, house (brown), snow (white), forest (green), and sky (blue). In the fourth image, 353013, there are five distinguishable colors (table, flowerpot, earth, flower, and background), so five segments, and in the fifth image there are six (earth, elephants, jockeys, blankets, forest, and sky). We summarized all qualitative results in Figure 7 and quantitative results in Table 3. For the quantitative results, we only report Precision P, Recall R, Dice score $F1$, and Jaccard score J because the true segmentation and the predicted segmentation contain the same number of segments. They seem to be sufficiently informative.

Figure 7. Image segmentation with different clustering algorithms. First column: True segmentation; Second column: GMM; Third column: KMEANS; Fourth column: FCMEANS; Fifth column: ENT; Sixth column: DEMP.

From the reported qualitative and quantitative results, it is evident that the merging of the mixture components leads to a better segmentation of the image, both by the highest obtained metric value and by the visual inspection of the segmentation. Moreover, it is clear that the merging of numerous components circumvents the problems caused by the representation of the segment by one component (or cluster for KMEANS and FCMEANS), which are mostly caused by obtaining the locally optimal cluster solution. The algorithms used here would inevitably find a more suitable local clustering solution if we further perturb the initial parameters. However, this could become impractical and computationally infeasible.

Table 3. Quantitative results of segmentation quality of selected images with different clustering algorithms. The best values are in bold.

	Precision score (*P*)				
Algorithm	GMM	KMEANS	FCMEANS	ENT	DEMP
Image					
35058	94	94.2	94.2	**96.8**	**96.8**
24063	91.1	**95.7**	80.3	81.7	96.4
97033	73.4	68.7	67.9	**83.7**	**83.7**
353013	**77.0**	58.4	58.4	65.7	69
361084	76.6	53.1	51.1	**80.9**	75.7
	Recall score (*R*)				
Algorithm	GMM	KMEANS	FCMEANS	ENT	DEMP
Image					
35058	50.4	54.4	54.3	**99.9**	**99.9**
24063	91.1	95.7	80.3	81.7	**96.4**
97033	73.4	68.7	67.9	**83.7**	**83.7**
353013	64.8	63.7	56.8	84.7	**85.1**
361084	73.0	57.0	45.8	**76.5**	69.4
	Dice score (*F1*)				
Algorithm	GMM	KMEANS	FCMEANS	ENT	DEMP
Image					
35058	65.6	69.0	68.9	**98.3**	**98.3**
24063	81.8	93.9	78.9	84.8	**95.7**
97033	55.7	49.4	48.8	**67.0**	**67.0**
353013	70.4	60.9	57.6	74.0	**76.2**
361084	74.7	55.0	48.3	**78.6**	72.4
	Jaccard score (*J*)				
Algorithm	GMM	KMEANS	FCMEANS	ENT	DEMP
Image					
35058	48.8	52.6	52.5	**96.7**	**96.7**
24063	69.3	88.5	65.2	73.6	**91.8**
97033	38.6	32.8	32.3	**50.3**	**50.3**
353013	54.3	43.8	40.4	58.7	**61.6**
361084	59.7	37.9	31.9	**64.8**	56.7

7.2.2. Optimal Segmentation Results on Berkley Image Segmetation Dataset

In the second part of the experiment, we are interested in empirically investigating the optimal segmentation that results from the heuristic described in Section 5. In the first part of the experiment, we manually determined the optimal number of segments based on the image under study. Thus, we limited ourselves to a smaller number of images for comparison. Here, the heuristic selects the optimal segmentation, i.e., the number of segments is determined automatically; therefore, it is plausible to analyze it on the entire dataset. The empirical study was enriched by comparisons with, in addition to the segmentation results obtained with the ICL criterion and the BIC criterion without subsequent merging, the clustering algorithms of the second group (MS, DBSCAN, and OPTICS), which can also provide optimal segmentation.The qualitative results of segmentation by using different algorithms is provided in Figure 8 and Table 4. We have also added some qualitative results in Figure 9 to further illustrate the segmentation of different algorithms. Table 4 shows the averaged metrics for each algorithm over the entire dataset . A better representation is provided by the boxplots for each algorithm and metric in Figure 8, which we can also use to examine scatter.

Table 4. Averaged metrics obtained with the Berkley image segmentation dataset. The best values are in bold.

Metric↓/Algorithm→	BIC	ICL	ENT	DEMP	MS	DBSCAN	OPTICS
Precision (P)	**58.3**	53.6	50.2	51.4	44.4	51.1	41.6
Recall (R)	30.2	50.1	53.8	57.4	**78.9**	66.8	75.7
Dice (F1)	36.1	46.7	47.5	49.8	52.7	**53.7**	49.5
Jaccard (J)	22.9	32.2	32.8	34.9	38.4	**39.5**	35.1
ARI	22	26.8	26.8	29.3	24.7	**31.4**	17.3
AMI	36.9	37.2	37.9	**38.4**	28.1	36.2	25.2

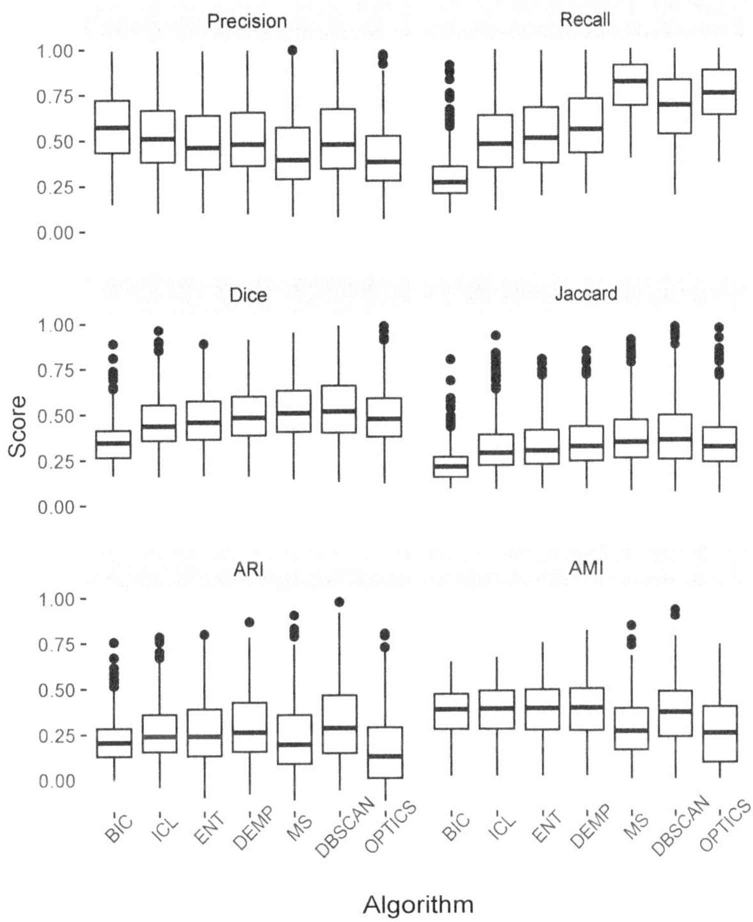

Figure 8. Boxplots of the metric distribution using different clustering algorithms for the Berkley image segmentation dataset.

The results reported here are similar and mostly better than the values in [44]. This could be due to the different setting of the experimental parameters and the different implementation of the algorithm, but we find it interesting. Since the BIC and ICL algorithms returned many segments, and generally more than the other methods studied, which can be further verified in Figure 9, the precision value was high and the recall value was low, as expected. Since the clustering algorithms MS, DBSCAN, and OPTICS preferred a smaller number of segments, the recall value was high and the precision was low. This clustering was also highly dependent on the superpixels obtained. First, the superpixels greatly reduced the number of pixels (we chose about 1000 superpixels), reducing the color variations of small objects while preserving the variations of larger objects. This can also be seen in Figure 9. The ladybugs in Figure 9c or the house in Figure 9b, or rather, their respective segments are missing and were merged with others. The merging algorithms were mostly in the middle, with DEMP consistently better than ENT. The AMI value was the best of all with the DEMP algorithm. ARI's slightly higher scores with the DBSCAN algorithm than with DEMP are due to the fact that many images contain a large portion of the scene with background that was correctly segmented in most cases. Again, both the merging algorithms and the heuristics were inadequate because the optimal segmentation favored more than one segment for the background. Finally, examination of the scatter of the metric values from Figure 8 suggests that the BIC algorithm has the least variation (i.e., the box with the lowest height). This, in turn, could be related to the fact that the BIC algorithm always had the highest number of segments. Therefore, it is expected that the values of the metrics obtained for different images would vary less. On the other hand, with fewer segments, the values may vary greatly from the expected values, resulting in very different metric values for different images.

(a)

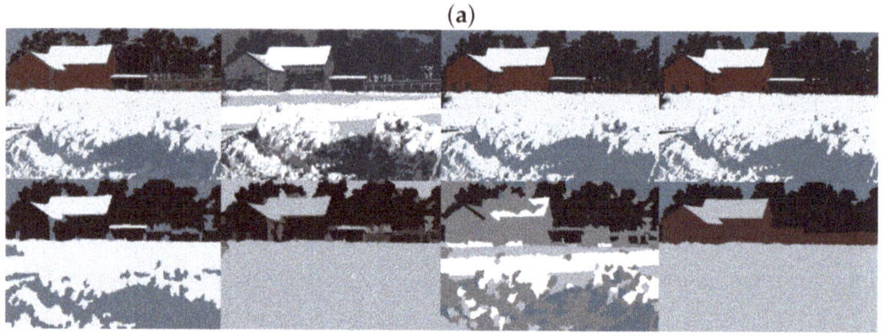

(b)

(c)

Figure 9. Segmentation results on different images from Berkley image segmentation dataset. First row: BIC, ICL, DEMP, and ENT algorithm. Second row: MS, DBSCAN, and OPTICS algorithm. Last image in second row is true segmentation. (**a**) Segmentation results of different algorithms on image 24063. (**b**) Segmentation results of different algorithms on image 97033. (**c**) Segmentation results of different algorithms on image 35008.

7.3. Comparisons of Computational Times

The final reports address the computation time required for each algorithm. Theoretically, the algorithms used here should be evaluated until the maximum number of iterations is exhausted, as noted in Refs. [28,39]. In this case, their time complexity is polynomial. Empirically, however, it turns out that these algorithms perform differently due to their slightly different implementations or approximations used, etc. Here, we focus on the empirical results obtained during runtime. Since the gray-scale images have only one value per pixel and the color images have three, we split the results to obtain a better understanding of the differences.

We provide the results again in the form of boxplots of the computation times for each algorithm and both datasets, one representing the gray-scale images and the other the color images, in Figure 10 and the average computation times over both datasets in Table 5. For the gray-scale images, it can be seen that the single REBMIX and EM strategy with $K = 256$ used for mixture estimation in the R package rebmix yields similarly fast results as the Gaussian mixture implementation of sklearn, although it estimates at least 15 more candidate mixture models, as indicated by the parameter cmax. This is also true for the KMEANS and FCMEANS algorithms used. OTSU was significantly faster, but this was to be expected due to its simple calculations. On the other hand, when comparing the color images, it looks like the mixture model approaches are abundantly exhaustive compared to their counterparts MS, DBSCAN, and OPTICS. It should be noted that the MS, DBSCAN, and OPTICS algorithms ran on largely shrunken data sets with only 1000 values obtained by SEEDS superpixel, as opposed to the mixture approach which ran on the full image resolution. The image resolution was 480×320, giving 153,600 pixel values, which means that the data sets for the mixture model were 150 times larger. One of the main reasons why the superpixels are used at all is that the MS, DBSCAN and OPTICS algorithms would not provide segmentation in an acceptable time to even consider them here. Therefore, the direct comparison of the computation times obtained is somewhat unfair, yet the time performance of the mixture model for color images is definitely not pleasing. Finally, ENT merging seems to be somewhat slower, at least for the gray-scale images. This is somewhat unexpected, since the number of operations is the same for DEMP and ENT merging. The only difference we think is plausible is that ENT merging requires repeated log calculation, which could cause this overhead.

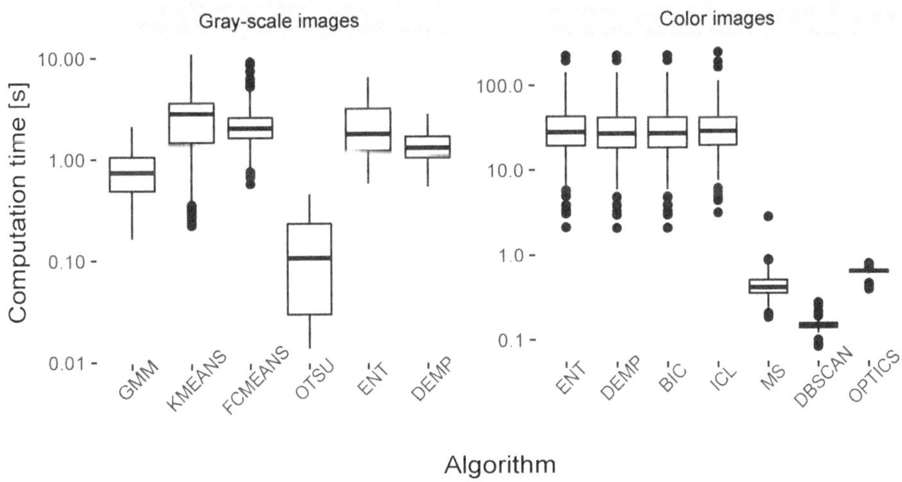

Figure 10. Boxplots of the distribution of computational time using different clustering algorithms for the two datasets used (the dataset for crack segmentation is referred to as gray-scale images and the dataset for Berkley image segmentation is referred to as color images).

Table 5. Average value of computation time over for each algorithm.

Gray-scale images							
Algorithm	GMM	KMEANS	FCMEANS	OTSU	ENT	DEMP	
Computation time (s)	0.786	2.671	2.272	0.139	2.267	1.375	
Color images							
Algorithm	BIC	ICL	ENT	DEMP	MS	DBSCAN	OPTICS
Computation time (s)	32.82	33.75	33.86	32.83	0.429	0.145	0.591

8. Discussion

Merging components of a mixture model based on entropy or misclassification criteria seems to be a very useful approach to quickly improve image segmentation. Indeed, using a model selection procedure and a non-clustering information criterion such as BIC allows greater flexibility in image segmentation than simply using a clustering information criterion, e.g., ICL. The explanation for this lies in the fact that the segment-wise distribution differs from the Gaussian distribution for many images. However, the Gaussian distribution is interesting because of its simple definition and straightforward application. The segment color distribution of a given image may be multimodal or skewed, and the BIC criterion would be sufficient to model the underlying PDF of the image, but the cost is the large number of components. ICL reduces the number of components by penalizing highly overlapping components. The price, however, is that such components may not be well suited for modeling individual segments. We have seen that neither of them is capable of handling image segmentation on its own. Merging components fixes this problem and improves image segmentation and thus the application of the mixture model.

However, upon visual inspection of the segmentation, we noticed that the two merge criteria introduced seem to suffer from the obvious drawback of hierarchical merging of components. More precisely, only one pair of components is merged in each stage of the merging process. In this way, the merge estimation is simplified because in each stage the merge criterion is recalculated for the remaining untouched and merged components. However, this presents an obvious problem when the final clustering solution is not just a few stages away from the original clustering solution. Both criteria clearly focus on merging smaller components with larger ones, and likewise on merging smaller clusters with larger ones. At each stage, they increase the size of the already large cluster, so to speak. For example, if the final merge is 10 stages away from the original solution, the smaller but informative cluster has already been merged because of its size. The smaller cluster will not be merged with the larger one only if its centroid is far apart in the feature space. The optimal segmentation heuristic presented here naively fixes this, as the maximum value of Equation (20) favors more clusters of equal size. However, by using multiple merges in each stage, the problem could be circumvented. This should be considered more critically, however, as it could lead to further undesirable artifacts.

Here we have dealt with unsupervised segmentation of images using only color pixel values. It is also known that using the spatial information, i.e., pixel positions, can enrich the segmentation, especially when the image is contaminated with a lot of noise, see [12] for example. However, including this information as two additional vectors does not lead to better results, since pixel positions are not random variables. They must be explored through well-defined neighborhood systems with spatial interactions. As a starting point, we decided to explore merging only for the color pixel values, since the additional inclusion of the spatial information through a well-defined theory, such as the hidden Markov random fields [38], can only improve the results.

Finally, we would like to discuss the high computational cost of estimating the mixture model. Using the predefined value $K = 256$ for the pre-processing step does not reduce the size of the dataset, but only makes it more compact. We obtained sufficiently fast results for gray-scale images, but the speed was not satisfactory for color images. The value $K = 256$ for three-dimensional space results in 16,777,216 bins. Most of these are empty and we always obtain a smaller number of non-empty bins than the number of pixels in the image. However, most bins contain only one pixel. Decreasing the value of K also decreases the size of the dataset and affects the mixture estimation, especially with the algorithm EM. On the other hand, if we reduce the value of K to $K = 50$, we obtain significantly better computation times than all other algorithms. Nevertheless, the reduction should be critically evaluated and some guidelines need to be given, which we will further focus on in the future.

9. Conclusions

The mixture model is a compelling framework for unsupervised image segmentation. The introduction of merging components of the mixture model further improves segmentation results. Moreover, the introduction of the optimal segmentation heuristic preserves the most relevant segments. We have conducted a series of experiments on gray-scale and color images, which confirm the above statements. Tables 2–4 and the Figures 5 and 8 show that the reported metrics do indeed indicate better image segmentation, which can be further evidenced by looking at the qualitative segmentation in Figures 4, 7 and 9. Further improvements should also be carefully considered in the future. First, the inadequacy of the hierarchical merging process discussed in the previous section could be improved. Second, pixel positions should also be included in the segmentation process in an appropriate framework. Thus, the similarity of two mixture components can be further increased or decreased by introducing spatial relationships, enriching the merging process.

Author Contributions: Conceptualization, B.P., M.N., J.K., S.O.; methodology, B.P., M.N., J.K., S.O.; investigation, B.P., M.N., J.K., S.O.; software, B.P., M.N., J.K., S.O.; writing—original draft preparation, B.P., M.N., J.K., S.O.; writing—review and editing, B.P., M.N., J.K., S.O. All authors have read and agreed to the published version of the manuscript.

Funding: The authors acknowledge financial support from the Slovenian Research Agency (research core funding No. P2-0182 entitled Development Evaluation).

Conflicts of Interest: The authors declare no conflict of interest.

References

1. Bellocchio, E.; Crocetti, F.; Costante, G.; Fravolini, M.L.; Valigi, P. A novel vision-based weakly supervised framework for autonomous yield estimation in agricultural applications. *Eng. Appl. Artif. Intell.* **2022**, *109*, 104615.
2. Alipour, M.; Harris, D.K. Increasing the robustness of material-specific deep learning models for crack detection across different materials. *Eng. Struct.* **2020**, *206*, 110157.
3. Antonello, M.; Chiesurin, S.; Ghidoni, S. Enhancing semantic segmentation with detection priors and iterated graph cuts for robotics. *Eng. Appl. Artif. Intell.* **2020**, *90*, 103467.
4. Fernández-Sanjurjo, M.; Bosquet, B.; Mucientes, M.; Brea, V.M. Real-time visual detection and tracking system for traffic monitoring. *Eng. Appl. Artif. Intell.* **2019**, *85*, 410–420.
5. He, W.; Jiang, Z.; Ming, W.; Zhang, G.; Yuan, J.; Yin, L. A critical review for machining positioning based on computer vision. *Measurement* **2021**, *184*, 109973, https://doi.org/10.1016/j.measurement.2021.109973.
6. Gupta, A.; Anpalagan, A.; Guan, L.; Khwaja, A.S. Deep learning for object detection and scene perception in self-driving cars: Survey, challenges, and open issues. *Array* **2021**, *10*, 100057, https://doi.org/10.1016/j.array.2021.100057.
7. Victória Matias, A.; Atkinson Amorim, J.G.; Buschetto Macarini, L.A.; Cerentini, A.; Casimiro Onofre, A.S.; De Miranda Onofre, F.B.; Daltoé, F.P.; Stemmer, M.R.; von Wangenheim, A. What is the state of the art of computer vision-assisted cytology? A Systematic Literature Review. *Comput. Med Imaging Graph.* **2021**, *91*, 101934, https://doi.org/10.1016/j.compmedimag.2021.101934.
8. Sefidpour, A.; Bouguila, N. Spatial color image segmentation based on finite non-Gaussian mixture models. *Expert Syst. Appl.* **2012**, *39*, 8993–9001.
9. Shi, X.; Li, Y.; Zhao, Q. Flexible Hierarchical Gaussian Mixture Model for High-Resolution Remote Sensing Image Segmentation. *Remote Sens.* **2020**, *12*, 1219, https://doi.org/10.3390/rs12071219.
10. Wei, D.; Wang, Z.; Si, L.; Tan, C.; Lu, X. An image segmentation method based on a modified local-information weighted intuitionistic Fuzzy C-means clustering and Gold-panning Algorithm. *Eng. Appl. Artif. Intell.* **2021**, *101*, 104209.
11. Chen, Y.; Cheng, N.; Cai, M.; Cao, C.; Yang, J.; Zhang, Z. A spatially constrained asymmetric Gaussian mixture model for image segmentation. *Inf. Sci.* **2021**, *575*, 41–65.
12. Wei, T.; Wang, X.; Li, X.; Zhu, S. Fuzzy subspace clustering noisy image segmentation algorithm with adaptive local variance & non-local information and mean membership linking. *Eng. Appl. Artif. Intell.* **2022**, *110*, 104672.

13. Ji, Z.; Huang, Y.; Xia, Y.; Zheng, Y. A robust modified Gaussian mixture model with rough set for image segmentation. *Neurocomputing* **2017**, *266*, 550–565.
14. Long, J.; Shelhamer, E.; Darrell, T. Fully convolutional networks for semantic segmentation. In Proceedings of the IEEE Conference on Computer Vision and Pattern Recognition, Boston, MA, USA, 7–12 June 2015; pp. 3431–3440.
15. Yang, H.Y.; Wang, X.Y.; Zhang, X.Y.; Bu, J. Color texture segmentation based on image pixel classification. *Eng. Appl. Artif. Intell.* **2012**, *25*, 1656–1669.
16. Li, S.; Fevens, T.; Krzyżak, A.; Li, S. Automatic clinical image segmentation using pathological modeling, PCA and SVM. *Eng. Appl. Artif. Intell.* **2006**, *19*, 403–410.
17. Chen, J.; Zheng, H.; Lin, X.; Wu, Y.; Su, M. A novel image segmentation method based on fast density clustering algorithm. *Eng. Appl. Artif. Intell.* **2018**, *73*, 92–110.
18. Kumar, V.; Chhabra, J.K.; Kumar, D. Automatic cluster evolution using gravitational search algorithm and its application on image segmentation. *Eng. Appl. Artif. Intell.* **2014**, *29*, 93–103.
19. Katunin, A.; Nagode, M.; Oman, S.; Cholewa, A.; Dragan, K. Monitoring of Hidden Corrosion Growth in Aircraft Structures Based on D-Sight Inspections and Image Processing. *Sensors* **2022**, *22*, 7616. https://doi.org/10.3390/s22197616.
20. Wronkowicz-Katunin, A.; Katunin, A.; Nagode, M.; Klemenc, J. Classification of Cracks in Composite Structures Subjected to Low-Velocity Impact Using Distribution-Based Segmentation and Wavelet Analysis of X-ray Tomograms. *Sensors* **2021**, *21*, 8342, https://doi.org/10.3390/s21248342.
21. Panić, B.; Klemenc, J.; Nagode, M. Gaussian Mixture Model Based Classification Revisited: Application to the Bearing Fault Classification. *Stroj. Vestnik/J. Mech. Eng.* **2020**, *66*, 215–226.
22. Santos, A.M.; de Carvalho Filho, A.O.; Silva, A.C.; de Paiva, A.C.; Nunes, R.A.; Gattass, M. Automatic detection of small lung nodules in 3D CT data using Gaussian mixture models, Tsallis entropy and SVM. *Eng. Appl. Artif. Intell.* **2014**, *36*, 27–39.
23. Celeux, G.; Govaert, G. Gaussian parsimonious clustering models. *Pattern Recognit.* **1995**, *28*, 781–793.
24. Ye, X.; Xi, P.; Nagode, M. Extension of REBMIX algorithm to von Mises parametric family for modeling joint distribution of wind speed and direction. *Eng. Struct.* **2019**, *183*, 1134–1145.
25. Vacher, J.; Launay, C.; Coen-Cagli, R. Flexibly regularized mixture models and application to image segmentation. *Neural Netw.* **2022**, *149*, 107–123.
26. Cheng, N.; Cao, C.; Yang, J.; Zhang, Z.; Chen, Y. A spatially constrained skew Student'st mixture model for brain MR image segmentation and bias field correction. *Pattern Recognit.* **2022**, *128*, 108658.
27. Nguyen, T.M.; Wu, Q.J. Dirichlet Gaussian mixture model: Application to image segmentation. *Image Vis. Comput.* **2011**, *29*, 818–828.
28. Panić, B.; Klemenc, J.; Nagode, M. Improved initialization of the EM algorithm for mixture model parameter estimation. *Mathematics* **2020**, *8*, 373.
29. Son, L.H.; Tuan, T.M. Dental segmentation from X-ray images using semi-supervised fuzzy clustering with spatial constraints. *Eng. Appl. Artif. Intell.* **2017**, *59*, 186–195.
30. Stosic, D.; Stosic, D.; Ludermir, T.B.; Ren, T.I. Natural image segmentation with non-extensive mixture models. *J. Vis. Commun. Image Represent.* **2019**, *63*, 102598, https://doi.org/10.1016/j.jvcir.2019.102598.
31. Sun, H.; Yang, X.; Gao, H. A spatially constrained shifted asymmetric Laplace mixture model for the grayscale image segmentation. *Neurocomputing* **2019**, *331*, 50–57, https://doi.org/10.1016/j.neucom.2018.10.039.
32. Do, T.M.T.; Artières, T. Learning mixture models with support vector machines for sequence classification and segmentation. *Pattern Recognit.* **2009**, *42*, 3224–3230. https://doi.org/10.1016/j.patcog.2008.12.007.
33. Zeng, S.; Huang, R.; Kang, Z.; Sang, N. Image segmentation using spectral clustering of Gaussian mixture models. *Neurocomputing* **2014**, *144*, 346–356.
34. Baudry, J.P.; Raftery, A.E.; Celeux, G.; Lo, K.; Gottardo, R. Combining Mixture Components for Clustering. *J. Comput. Graph. Stat.* **2010**, *19*, 332–353, https://doi.org/10.1198/jcgs.2010.08111.
35. Hennig, C. Methods for merging Gaussian mixture components. *Adv. Data Anal. Classif.* **2010**, *4*, 3–34.
36. Nagode, M.; Fajdiga, M. The REBMIX Algorithm for the Univariate Finite Mixture Estimation. *Commun. Stat. Theory Methods* **2011**, *40*, 876–892.
37. Nagode, M.; Fajdiga, M. The REBMIX Algorithm for the Multivariate Finite Mixture Estimation. *Commun. Stat. Theory Methods* **2011**, *40*, 2022–2034.
38. McLachlan, G.; Peel, D. *Finite Mixture Models*, 1st ed.; John Wiley & Sons: Hoboken, NJ, USA, 2000.
39. Panić, B.; Klemenc, J.; Nagode, M. Optimizing the Estimation of a Histogram-Bin Width—Application to the Multivariate Mixture-Model Estimation. *Mathematics* **2020**, *8*, 1090.
40. Schwarz, G. Estimating the Dimension of a Model. *Ann. Stat.* **1978**, *6*, 461–464.
41. Zhao, J.; Jin, L.; Shi, L. Mixture model selection via hierarchical BIC. *Comput. Stat. Data Anal.* **2015**, *88*, 139–153, https://doi.org/10.1016/j.csda.2015.01.019.
42. Biernacki, C.; Celeux, G.; Govaert, G. Assessing a mixture model for clustering with the integrated completed likelihood. *IEEE Trans. Pattern Anal. Mach. Intell.* **2000**, *22*, 719–725.

43. Martin, D.; Fowlkes, C.; Tal, D.; Malik, J. A Database of Human Segmented Natural Images and its Application to Evaluating Segmentation Algorithms and Measuring Ecological Statistics. In Proceedings of the 8th Int'l Conference Computer Vision, Vancouver, BC, Canada, 7–14 July 2001; Voume 2, pp. 416–423.
44. Aksac, A.; Özyer, T.; Alhajj, R. CutESC: Cutting edge spatial clustering technique based on proximity graphs. *Pattern Recognit.* **2019**, *96*, 106948.
45. Azzalini, A.; Bowman, A.W. A Look at Some Data on the Old Faithful Geyser. *J. R. Stat. Society. Ser. C (Appl. Stat.)* **1990**, *39*, 357–365.
46. Akaike, H. A new look at the statistical model identification. *IEEE Trans. Autom. Control* **1974**, *19*, 716–723.
47. Scrucca, L. A fast and efficient Modal EM algorithm for Gaussian mixtures. *Stat. Anal. Data Min. ASA Data Sci. J.* **2021**, *14*, 305–314, https://doi.org/10.1002/sam.11527.
48. Nagode, M.; Klemenc, J. Modelling of Load Spectra Containing Clusters of Less Probable Load Cycles. *Int. J. Fatigue* **2021**, *143*, 106006, https://doi.org/10.1016/j.ijfatigue.2020.106006.
49. Nagode, M. Finite Mixture Modeling via REBMIX. *J. Algorithms Optim.* **2015**, *3*, 14–28, https://doi.org/10.5963/JAO0302001.
50. Swain, M.; Tripathy, T.T.; Panda, R.; Agrawal, S.; Abraham, A. Differential exponential entropy-based multilevel threshold selection methodology for colour satellite images using equilibrium-cuckoo search optimizer. *Eng. Appl. Artif. Intell.* **2022**, *109*, 104599, https://doi.org/10.1016/j.engappai.2021.104599.
51. Mamta; Hanmandlu, M. A new entropy function and a classifier for thermal face recognition. *Eng. Appl. Artif. Intell.* **2014**, *36*, 269–286, https://doi.org/10.1016/j.engappai.2014.06.028.
52. Kurban, R.; Durmus, A.; Karakose, E. A comparison of novel metaheuristic algorithms on color aerial image multilevel thresholding. *Eng. Appl. Artif. Intell.* **2021**, *105*, 104410, https://doi.org/10.1016/j.engappai.2021.104410.
53. Robin, S.; Scrucca, L. Mixture-based estimation of entropy. *Comput. Stat. Data Anal.* **2023**, *177*, 107582.
54. Kittaneh, O.A.; Khan, M.A.U.; Akbar, M.; Bayoud, H.A. Average Entropy: A New Uncertainty Measure with Application to Image Segmentation. *Am. Stat.* **2016**, *70*, 18–24, https://doi.org/10.1080/00031305.2015.1089788.
55. Vinh, N.X.; Epps, J.; Bailey, J. Information theoretic measures for clusterings comparison: Variants, properties, normalization and correction for chance. *J. Mach. Learn. Res.* **2010**, *11*, 2837–2854.
56. Franti, P.; Sieranoja, S. How much can k-means be improved by using better initialization and repeats? *Pattern Recognit.* **2019**, *93*, 95–112, https://doi.org/10.1016/j.patcog.2019.04.014.
57. Peizhuang, W. Pattern Recognition with Fuzzy Objective Function Algorithms (James C. Bezdek). *SIAM Rev.* **1983**, *25*, 442–442, https://doi.org/10.1137/1025116.
58. Comaniciu, D.; Meer, P. Mean shift: A robust approach toward feature space analysis. *IEEE Trans. Pattern Anal. Mach. Intell.* **2002**, *24*, 603–619, https://doi.org/10.1109/34.1000236.
59. Schubert, E.; Sander, J.; Ester, M.; Kriegel, H.P.; Xu, X. DBSCAN Revisited, Revisited: Why and How You Should (Still) Use DBSCAN. *Acm Trans. Database Syst. (TODS)* **2017**, *42*, 1–21. https://doi.org/10.1145/3068335.
60. Schubert, E.; Gertz, M. Improving the Cluster Structure Extracted from OPTICS Plots. In Proceedings of the Conference "Lernen, Wissen, Daten, Analysen", LWDA 2018, Mannheim, Germany, 22–24 August 2018; Gemulla, R., Ponzetto, S.P., Bizer, C., Keuper, M., Stuckenschmidt, H., Eds.; 2018; Volume 2191, pp. 318–329.
61. Pedregosa, F.; Varoquaux, G.; Gramfort, A.; Michel, V.; Thirion, B.; Grisel, O.; Blondel, M.; Prettenhofer, P.; Weiss, R.; Dubourg, V.; et al. Scikit-learn: Machine Learning in Python. *J. Mach. Learn. Res.* **2011**, *12*, 2825–2830.
62. Bergh, M.V.d.; Boix, X.; Roig, G.; Capitani, B.d.; Gool, L.V. Seeds: Superpixels extracted via energy-driven sampling. In *European Conference on Computer Vision*; Springer: Berlin/Heidelberg, Germany, 2012; pp. 13–26.
63. Liu, Y.; Yao, J.; Lu, X.; Xie, R.; Li, L. DeepCrack: A deep hierarchical feature learning architecture for crack segmentation. *Neurocomputing* **2019**, *338*, 139–153.
64. Munoz-Minjares, J.; Vite-Chavez, O.; Flores-Troncoso, J.; Cruz-Duarte, J.M. Alternative Thresholding Technique for Image Segmentation Based on Cuckoo Search and Generalized Gaussians. *Mathematics* **2021**, *9*, 2287. https://doi.org/10.3390/math9182287.

Σ mathematics

MDPI

Article

Novel Reinforcement Learning Research Platform for Role-Playing Games

Petra Csereoka, Bogdan-Ionuţ Roman, Mihai Victor Micea and Călin-Adrian Popa *

Department of Computer and Software Engineering, Polytechnic University Timişoara, Blvd. V. Pârvan, No. 2, 300223 Timişoara, Romania
* Correspondence: calin.popa@cs.upt.ro

Abstract: The latest achievements in the field of reinforcement learning have encouraged the development of vision-based learning methods that compete with human-provided results obtained on various games and training environments. Convolutional neural networks together with Q-learning-based approaches have managed to solve and outperform human players in environments such as Atari 2600, Doom or StarCraft II, but the niche of 3D realistic games with a high degree of freedom of movement and rich graphics remains unexplored, despite having the highest resemblance to real-world situations. In this paper, we propose a novel testbed to push the limits of deep learning methods, namely an OpenAI Gym-like environment based on Dark Souls III, a notoriously difficult role-playing game, where even human players have reportedly struggled. We explore two types of architectures, Deep Q-Network and Deep Recurrent Q-Network, providing the results of a first incursion into this new problem class. The source code for the training environment and baselines is made available.

Keywords: Deep Q-Network; Deep Recurrent Q-Network; Dark Souls III; video games; visual-based reinforcement learning; neural networks

MSC: 68T07; 68T40

Citation: Csereoka, P.; Roman, B.-I.; Micea, M.V.; Popa, C.-A. Novel Reinforcement Learning Research Platform for Role-Playing Games. *Mathematics* **2022**, *10*, 4363. https://doi.org/10.3390/math10224363

Academic Editors: Adrian Sergiu Darabant and Diana-Laura Borza

Received: 12 October 2022
Accepted: 17 November 2022
Published: 20 November 2022

1. Introduction

Learning can take various forms, but the primary source of information still remains our interaction with the environment. A significant fraction of the inputs we receive comes in the form of visual signals that are processed and decoded and later reasoned upon. With the latest developments in processing power, computers are now able to process and refine more raw data than before [1], yet humans still have the major advantage of better retaining and organizing the information they accumulate over time, combining it in novel ways to solve problems that arise dynamically [2]. This difference between humans and computer models is even more pronounced when it comes to developing strategies in complex environments that are changing fast and are rich in details. Neural networks have been applied successfully to a wide range of tasks [3,4], making them a potentially strong contender for solving current real-world problems.

Several models have been proposed over time to address this gap; however, the first success story in visual learning is represented by Deep Q-Network (DQN) architectures [5,6] that have managed to achieve human-level performance in several Atari 2600 games. This was made possible by framing the problem as a Markov decision process (MDP) [7] and employing convolutional neural networks (CNNs) to build a control policy using a Q-Learning variant [8]. The neural network thus obtained has managed to learn the mappings between input states and relevant actions and their corresponding values with the help of stochastic gradient descent, experience replay mechanisms and exploration and exploitation techniques.

This breakthrough marked an important milestone, as previous methods assumed complete knowledge about the environment, its rules and states and were fine-tuned for particular scenarios, but the DQN solution was a step towards tackling more generic problems closer to real-world environments. Encouraged by this development, new variants of DQNs appeared, and new test environments were proposed to further push the limits of Q-Learning. An important limitation is related to the problem of observability. Most real world problems involve partial knowledge about the global state of the environment, and, in most cases, the observations that can be recorded are available for a limited time only. Hence, reasoning upon longer sequences of events becomes harder, with detecting recipes that span over longer periods of time being very costly if not impossible.

To mitigate such shortcomings, a new DQN variant was proposed: Deep Recurrent Q-Network (DRQN) [9]. The changes made to the original DQN model were minimal and localized, and the convolutional layers remained unchanged; however, the first fully-connected layer was replaced with a recurrent one containing LSTM cells. This new addition yielded a model able to better integrate information over time, thus making it a more suitable contender for problems that involve longer sequences of actions and a better generalization power for partially observable scenarios. This increase in performance, on the other hand, came with more training time and higher hardware requirements.

Dark Souls III [10] is one of the most notoriously difficult role-playing games even for human players, with statistics collected across the entire user base showing only 83.9% of the players that acquire the game manage to pass the entry zone and only 3.6% finish the game with all the achievements [11]. Their experiences with the challenges vary depending on past encounters with similar games, but nonetheless, all players must familiarize themselves with different warrior classes and enemies with complex movements. The game combines difficult boss battles, layered environments with many hidden secrets and diverse combat strategies that vary with each new enemy encountered.

Our work comes to address the research gap between existing training and testing environments created for deep reinforcement learning. Previously implemented gyms were based on simple games, often with 2D imagery, lacking the challenges agents must face in the real world, which is rich in details and offers a high degree of movement in a refined manner. To the best of our knowledge, this paper provides the first environment created having in mind the main limitations of existing training environments in terms of graphics and degrees of movement for the agents, attempting to boost the work done in problems approaching the real-world level in visual deep learning.

In the next sections, we present our initial results obtained by training an agent to defeat the first major boss, Iudex Gundyr, using DQNs and DRQNs in an OpenAI-type gym. Being a closed-source game, extracting all the necessary information for creating the mission as well as assigning proper rewards requires the implementation of helper programs and scripts to access and modify the data stored in RAM and map the location of each relevant entry. Our results are promising, with the time required to defeat the enemy being comparable to the times obtained by players new to this genre.

This paper makes the following contributions:

- An analysis of existing training and testing environments for deep reinforcement learning in problems that can be modeled with the help of games in a pursuit of reaching lifelong learning;
- A complete training and testing environment, including all the Python source files for the gym, automated RAM address retrieval in the form of Cheat Engine scripts, .dll files needed for a complete interaction between the agent and the game, and documentation on how to use different components and their relationship;
- The implementation of state-of-the-art baselines that match the performance of human newcomers to the game genre, showing that value-based methods can be deployed successfully even for more visually complex problems, and opening the path at the same time for further research using different deep learning approaches.

In the following section, we discuss the state-of-the-art training and testing environments available for researchers pursuing to create agents for reinforcement learning problems. Then, selected baselines are detailed, together with the main components and functional details of the novel proposed gym and mission. These are followed by the initial experimental results obtained for the first mission that players face in normal game mode, and future improvements and conclusions round the analysis. The source code for the training environment and baselines can be found at: https://github.com/Bo-roman/DSIII-RL (accessed on 12 October 2022).

2. Related Work

DQNs have been first applied successfully to Atari 2600 games [5,6] and later similar methods were implemented to solve more complex tasks with good results. To improve on the convergence during training, a series of methods have been applied, such as experience replay mechanisms [12], separating the target network to reduce overestimation of the Q-values, reducing the action space and compressing the input by clipping and conversion to grayscale. However, a large number of the games comprised in this environment ensure total state observability and can be completed within short timespans, rendering it a good starting benchmark [13].

Later, a more realistic training environment was proposed, based on the first-person shooter video game called Doom. Unlike Atari 2600, this platform provided a first-person perspective and more realistic 3D imagery with customizable mechanisms, offering a higher degree of flexibility than previous environments [14]. The agents still had to make decisions based only on the visual information provided by the game, but a series of tasks with various difficulties were proposed over the years, further proving the versatility of DQN approaches: Basic scenarios [14,15], with simple primitive movements and enemy confrontation, Maze navigation [16,17], which requires escaping from custom made complex mazes, Defend the center [18], in which the agent is spawned in the middle of a room and must defend only by performing rotations, DeathMatch scenarios [19–22], which prompted agents to kill as many opponents as possible within a fixed time frame, etc.

Another challenging environment proposed during the same period is represented by the StarCraft family of games [23], providing denser state spaces and a stronger focus on multi-agent tasks. By organizing a high number of bot competitions, the environment gained more popularity, and hence encouraged a constant improvement of the proposed models each year [24]. The full game requires players to gather resources, construct buildings and create an army, and finally eliminate the opponents. The decisions taken at each step influence long term outcomes and the duration of a game can vary. Initial solutions focused on solving either the micro level, namely multi-unit collaboration problems [25], or the macro level, tackling decision-making issues within big state spaces [26]. Later, hierarchical solutions emerged combining the targets previously separated and solved in isolation [27,28].

In recent years, with the creation of the MALMO platform [29], a new horizon has been opened in terms of training and testing environments. Built on top of the open world game called Minecraft, a series of OpenAI Gym-type environments [30] emerged focusing on a variety of tasks, which were not analyzed before, allowing researchers to build agents for long horizon missions, collaborative, and creative problems. The game offers a high degree of freedom in creating missions in an environment which follows the laws of the real world, and with crowd sourced datasets the range of approaches that can be implemented was widened [31,32].

At the same time, a new research direction in the last two years was focused around the topic of coordination in multi-agent scenarios, modeled and experimented with as an instance of the popular card game Hanabi [33]. Games have proved to be important testing and training environments for studying how complex decision making problems can be attempted, and Hanabi forces players to plan ahead, reason at higher levels about beliefs and tactics to achieve a common goal, under time and communication restrictions. The open-source learning environment has gained popularity fast and is now considered a benchmark for machine learning coordination solutions [34,35].

While existing environments enable researchers to test and implement a wide variety of methods for a significant number of missions, starting from simple tasks to scenarios suitable for lifelong learning investigations, they still are strongly anchored in the virtual, and hence cannot model the continuous nature of visual transitions and phenomena from the real world, due to the graphics and movement rules of different entities. The new environment that is proposed comes to address these issues with its 3D immersive graphics and continuous movements, additionally providing starting baselines that can he enhanced in the future.

3. Proposed Methodology

3.1. Mission Description

The first important confrontation within the game is represented by the Cemetery of Ash mission, where the players are facing the entity called Iudex Gundyr. At the start, this enemy has a tall humanoid form with heavy armor and a long halberd; however, after his health is lowered below a certain threshold, the entity will transform into a black monster that is significantly bigger and has a new set of attacks. Initially, the players are confronted with the unique fighting style of the enemy, using a wide range of attacks and combinations that must be dodged or sidestepped in order to survive. During the second phase, the speed and range of the entity are further increased, making it even more difficult to defeat.

Players can choose from 10 warrior classes with various stats, such as endurance, vitality, strength, dexterity, intelligence, faith, defense, resistance, etc., having a great impact on what type of actions the players can take in the first parts of the game. As a starting class, most players recommend either selecting a ranged type, allowing players to attack from farther away and thus avoid the damage caused by most attacks, or the Knight class, as it comes with the most durable armor and shield, as well as a melee weapon in the form of a sword. For our experiments, we have opted for the Knight class, but, to raise the difficulty of the task, we have removed from the list of available actions the parry commands (see Figure 1).

Figure 1. The Knight class warrior battling with Iudex Gundyr in the first phase (**left**) and in the second phase (**right**) [10].

Under normal circumstances, the camera can be pointed in any direction with the help of the mouse, but, to allow the agent to better focus on the mission, we have opted for a Lock Target mechanism which will keep the camera pointed towards the enemy, thus freeing the agent from having to manage that as well.

3.2. Retrieving Attributes for Training

As a first step, to be able to train agents, the relevant parameters from the game must be identified. There are two entities involved: the player or agent and the enemy. In a normal game mode, these classes have a larger set of attributes that are read and updated repeatedly; however, for training purposes, we have opted to reduce these to the bare minimum set that enables us to reinitialize the scenario, grant appropriate rewards, and provide the relevant metrics to the agent.

In order to build the scenario, we need access to:

- The player's health. To start the mission, the health attribute of the player must be reduced to zero to trigger the initialization cycle, which teleports the player to the last checkpoint and resets the map and the attributes of the entities that are present, including the player. This operation is usually performed as part of the environment reset function from the API, and this is the fastest way to achieve it from an operational point of view;
- The player's position along the three axes (X, Y, Z). The last checkpoint is farther than our targeted enemy; hence, by manipulating the coordinates, we can ensure that the agent is moved closer, within the range of the entity. This operation reduces the time wasted between fights, allowing a better use of the available computational resources, and the agent can focus on the actual combat part as opposed to wandering connecting paths with no added bonus;
- The enemy's state: defeated or encountered. In order to trigger the start of the confrontation, the enemy's state must be set to encountered, however, after the initialization cycle, this attribute has a different value, and the player would have to go through numerous interactions to alter it. Therefore, to reduce the time needed to set up the mission, we overwrite this attribute automatically to the desired value.

For awarding the rewards, we have decided to take into account the health points of the player and the enemy, and the player's endurance. For every successful attack, the health of the enemy will be reduced, hence resulting in positive rewards, with the maximum amount when the enemy is killed; if the agent does not retreat to a safe area from attacks, their health attributes are reduced, resulting in negative rewards and ultimately their death scoring the most severe penalty.

These attributes are not directly accessible, as the game does not have an API for parameter and entity manipulations such as existing gyms; hence, they must be extracted and overwritten directly in the RAM memory. Exploring the RAM memory for relevant information is hindered by the protection mechanisms built within the operating system such as Address Space Layout Randomization [36], which makes previously identified memory locations no longer useful at the next training session when we restart the game or the gym. To overcome that, static offsets have to be identified each time, and this can be achieved automatically with the help of the open-source application called Cheat Engine [37].

Cheat Engine provides basic functionalities, such as scanning and modifying the memory zones of running processes within the system, but it also provides more advanced features, such as creating scripts with the help of the integrated Lua interpreter to automate many of the tasks that would otherwise have to be done manually at each run. Previously identified memory zones, offsets, and scripts are stored in a cheat table, and, to identify new locations, methods such as a value scan and a pointer scan can be deployed. The memory locations for certain attributes are easy to find, as their values are shown in the graphical user interface of the game; however, other parameters require extensive search and even interactions with the keys to alter the values and hence aid the search.

3.3. Gym Creation

To build our training environment, we have opted for a standardized formatting; namely, we have extended the `Env` interface from the OpenAI Gym libraries. Most of the methods within the class require a form of interaction with the environment, but, given the nature of the underlying game, in our case, this is only possible via intermediaries, such as Cheat Engine, which functions to retrieve attributes and alter the state of the game, and a community-provided .dll file to allow us to emulate physical key presses from the keyboard with software instructions. The communication between these components is realized with the help of sockets, with the data being structured into JSON bursts in a custom-built formatting.

The list of selected actions for a mission is provided via a configuration file, but definitions within the gym allow users to select from various types of movement, rolls, attacks, and interactions with objects. Within the same configuration file, hyperparameter values, limits, and sizes can be specified, allowing researchers to have full control over the problem and be able to adapt it to their needs (see Figure 2).

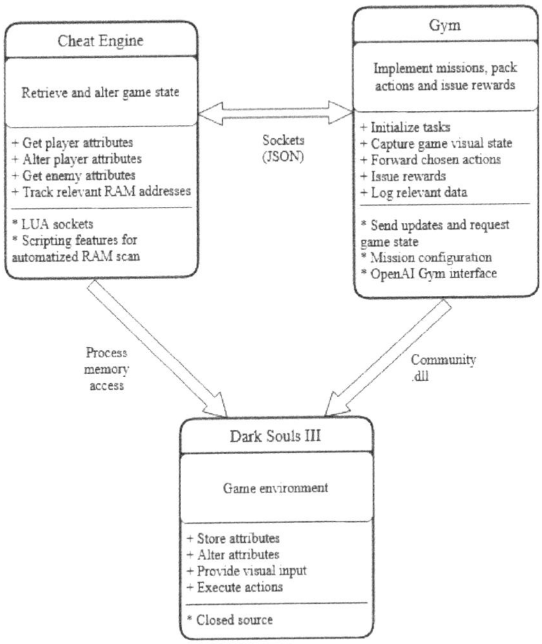

Figure 2. System architecture highlighting main software components for the training and testing environment, as well as main functions and attributes.

3.4. Methods Considered for the Analysis

Given the success of DQN-based architectures in previous training environments, we have considered 2 main approaches for this analysis, namely vanilla and recurrent DQN models. The vanilla network architecture is based on the one proposed by Mnih et al. [5,6] for solving Atari 2600 games, while the recurrent one is closer to the model proposed by Hausknecht et al. [9] (see Figure 3).

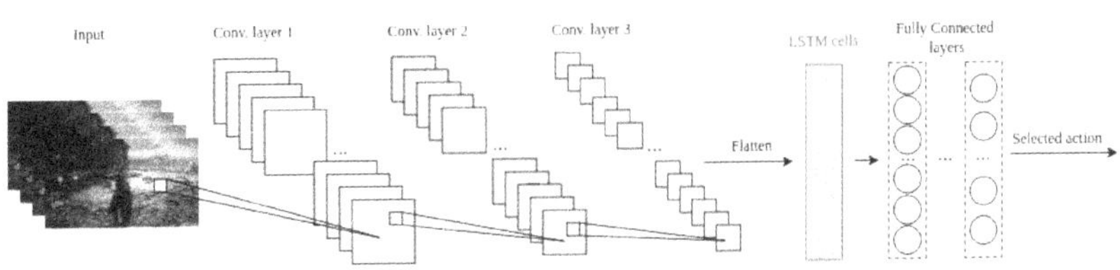

Figure 3. Architectural overview of the models implemented as baselines. The black components are part of both models, while the red LSTM cells are included only in the DRQN variant.

The input images are captured and rescaled to a smaller size while still keeping the main elements visible and distinguishable. Due to the color palette of the game, we have opted to keep the RGB formatting, as after the conversion to grayscale, certain important game elements blended into the background, making it hard to detect them on time.

The feature map extraction was done by 3 consecutive convolutional layers, followed by fully-connected layers to compute the approximation for the Q-values.

To reduce computational costs, gather more system state related information, and build better policies, we have implemented a frame-skipping mechanism with a factor of 4 [38]. To balance exploration and exploitation, we have opted for an ϵ-greedy approach that will prompt the agent to select a random next step with a probability of ϵ and require a deliberate choice otherwise. The starting value was set to 1 and was then annealed to 0.1 to encourage long-term exploration as well.

To ensure convergence, an experience replay memory buffer was used that stores entries as tuples in an SQL Light database. We have opted for this solution as it enables us to store and conveniently load samples of experiences at runtime faster; it offers better control of the training process in case of interruptions.

4. Experiments and Results

As described in previous sections, we have selected the first boss battle from the game that begins in the area called Cemetery of Ash. The player enters the region through a narrow passageway and is confronted by an unmoving entity sitting in the middle of a stone circle. The area is surrounded by impassable large stone remnants of walls and hallways, trees with dense overhanging roots, and parts of an ancient cemetery, except for the western region, which is an open edge over a cliff (see Figure 4).

Figure 4. Mission main battle region.

In order to win, the agent has to defeat the enemy; however, they are at disadvantage, as the entity has much higher health, speed, agility, and attack strength and range, while the agent can also fall over the cliff either by making a wrong choice or getting hit by the entity.

One of the main limiting factors for the player's strategy is represented by the endurance attribute. This stat has a direct impact on the amount of stamina the player has to execute actions, such as dodging and swinging weapons, and it also influences damage resistance. During initial experiments, due to exhausting the endurance attribute in early phases of the mission, the agent overfitted to running away from the entity as opposed to rationing the stamina better by alternating attacks with recharging. Hence, to reduce the difficulty of the task, we have set the endurance to an infinite amount, so the agent can focus more on the combat aspect of the mission.

The rewards and penalties we have considered for this mission can be classified into 2 main categories: primary—they represent the main goal of the agent: every successful attack and the defeat of the enemy will yield a positive reward, while every damage accumulated by the agent, including their death, will be punished with negative rewards, and auxiliary—introduced during training to correct unwanted behaviors: if the agent performs a certain number of consecutive movement/attack actions above a threshold, a small penalty is issued to motivate the agent to perform more attacks/dodge and retreat movements. Defeating the entity in its phase 1 form is an important milestone, as when it morphs into its next evolutionary step, the behavior is changed, and the agent has to learn new tactics.

The models receive 4 input images that were scaled down to 150×93 frames while still keeping the RGB formatting. They are then processed by the 3 consecutive convolutional layers, followed by a variable number of fully connected layers for the DQN architecture and LSTM cells, followed by fully connected layers for the DRQN model.

For the DRQN model, the initial experiments allowed the agent to select from the complete set of actions, and we have implemented a reward-clipping method. The agents trained with this setup have shown a high preference for movement-type actions, resulting in longer episodes with little damage done to the entity and no wins. For the following experiments, we have reduced the action set to movements along the axes, dodges and attacks, increased the training time and changed the reward proportions, obtaining the first win (see Table 1).

Table 1. DRQN model architecture details.

Layer Type	Input Size	Activation	Output Size
Conv1	$150 \times 93 \times 12$	ReLU	$36 \times 22 \times 32$
Conv2	$36 \times 22 \times 32$	ReLU	$17 \times 10 \times 64$
Conv3	$17 \times 10 \times 64$	ReLU	$15 \times 8 \times 64$
LSTM	7680	-	1024
Output	1024	ReLU	No. of actions

For the first model type, we have given a higher reward (double) for attack type actions, as the life of the entity is almost 4 times higher than the one of the agent and to prevent an overfitting on evasive moves, such as those the previous versions did (DRQN-1). This approach resulted in fairly fast wins as opposed to later models; however, they also obtained a lower score, as this aggressive choice also resulted in the agent losing more life points while attacking repeatedly.

The second type was a mirror of the previous model, though this time the evasive moves gained more importance, having in mind that every health unit from the agent is more valuable (DRQN-2); this time the agent had learned combos (chains of actions) that human players also perform in similar scenarios, but it still did not manage to avoid certain type of attacks from the enemy that would have required multiple dodges and putting bigger distance between the agent and Iudex.

The most successful model type (DRQN-3) had 10% more reward for attack moves and had obtained the first victory around the 900-episode milestone, averaging at 10 wins every 500 episodes in the last phases of training (episodes 3000–4500). The agent also managed to reach phase 2 with an increasing tendency, on average in 50 out of every 500 episodes (episodes 1500–4500), see Table 2.

Table 2. Reward table for the DRQN models.

Architecture Type	Frames Trained	Reward for Successful Attack	Reward for Taking Damage from Enemy	Absolute Value for Win/Death
DRQN-1	500,000	+200	−100	2000
DRQN-2	500.000	+100	−200	2000
DRQN-3	500.000	+60	−50	2000

All of these models had 512 LSTM type cells and 2 fully connected layers. The training sessions contained 4500 episodes (training unit lasting from the first state to the ending state), adding up to roughly 500,000 frames for each type.

The DQN model, on the other hand, did not provide such good results. Three architecture types were analyzed: two with a single fully connected layer, but with different sizes, and one with four fully connected layers, mimicking the recurrent model. The first two types managed to reach the second phase in later episodes but never managed to defeat the enemy. The last type succeeded in killing the entity once during episode 1650 in a battle that lasted 50 s and reached the second phase on average 3 times every 500 episodes.

These models were trained on the reduced action set with reward clipping, going through approximately 300,000 frames.

The experiments were performed using an NVIDIA GeForce RTX 2080 Ti GPU and an AMD Ryzen 9 5900X processor, thus marking the hardware requirements at the low-to-medium end of the implementation cost spectrum for machine learning applications. The time complexity of the analyzed models is consistent with the models proposed in the original papers [5,6,9], with an additional ~5% overhead due to frame preprocessing and experience replay storing. The GPU load percentage was monitored during training, and the average time for an inference was 104.985 milliseconds for the DRQN model and 1.001 milliseconds for the DQN model (see Tables 3 and 4).

Table 3. DQN model architecture details.

Layer Type	Input Size	Activation	Output Size
Conv1	150 × 93 × 12	ReLU	36 × 22 × 32
Conv2	36 × 22 × 32	ReLU	17 × 10 × 64
Conv3	17 × 10 × 64	ReLU	15 × 8 × 64
FC1	7680	ReLU	128
FC2	128	ReLU	64
FC3	64	ReLU	32
Output	32	ReLU	No. of actions

Table 4. Highest reward and fastest win for the most successful models.

Architecture	Time until Win (s)	Total Reward	Episode Reached
DRQN-1	31.8	**1500**	1991
	24.9	1450	1867
DRQN-2	37.6	**1670**	1130
	24.3	1450	3031
DRQN-3	63	**1900**	3436
	45	1590	4177
DQN	48.7	1650	2147

With only the game running and the agent in an idle state, the GPU utilization revolves around 6%, with a minimal memory utilization around 3%. Once the episode is reset, both the game and the gym must make several steps to prepare the next session; hence, the utilization will rise above 20%, and the memory is also pushed around 13%. During the inference period (during decision making within the episode), the parameters move to around 37% for the GPU load and 25% for the memory. Given these measurements, we can also conclude that less performant GPUs, such as GTX 1050 Ti, are still able to fulfill the minimal requirements for running our proposed gym and the baseline models (see Figure 5).

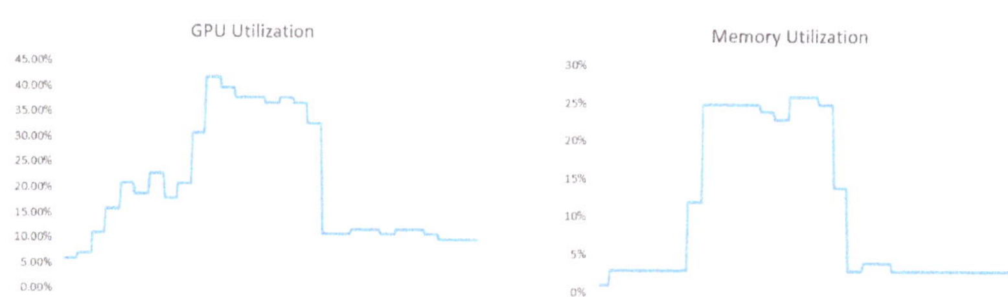

Figure 5. GPU utilization parameters during an episode.

5. Conclusions and Future Work

The currently available training and testing environments for visual learning provide the means for research in specific problem classes, but the niche of more immersive and realistic environments was not yet explored, although they come closer to the way humans perceive visual stimuli. Another important aspect is related to the movement of the agent: in most of the existing environments, actions are performed relative to an existing square grid, which is either hidden by the graphics and existing in the background or revealed, such as in Minecraft, but in the real world, our perception has a more continuous and free nature. The training environment proposed in this paper addresses these two main points, providing the means for a new direction for future research in the field.

The two baselines we have implemented show promising results. During training, both agent types have managed to learn useful combinations of primitive actions that resulted in successful attacks at optimal locations and to avoid many of the long range attacks either by dodging, hiding behind the enemy, or retreating right after a number of successful attacks, thus exploiting weaknesses within the enemy mechanics.

In this paper, we have presented the results obtained by a first incursion into the immersive world of graphically intensive games; however, there are certain aspects to the gym design and models that can be improved in the future.

The player class which we have selected for our experiments has certain advantages and disadvantages compared to the other available options; however, by restricting the list of actions to the basic movements and attacks that all the classes possess, our approach can be easily extended to any of the remaining player types without problems. A more in-depth analysis should be further conducted into the impact of different agent classes on the speed of learning and what attributes impact the success rate the most.

Furthermore, in our current implementation, we have used vanilla ϵ-greedy, but in recent years improved versions for this approach were presented [39], as well as more complex methods to address the problem of exploitation vs. exploration [40]. Similarly, for sampling among gathered experiences, a number of different methods have emerged [41,42] that could aid the training process when the number of available actions is large and the rewards are sparse.

Finally, to automatically point the camera towards the enemy entity, we have employed a target lock mechanism, but this creates certain problems, as Iudex Gundyr in the second phase morphs into a very large entity that is no longer able to fit into the field of view of the agent, which, hence, cannot detect certain attack types in time. Additionally, when the agent is facing the enemy with their back towards the edge of the cliff, choosing an action of the retreat type will inevitably result in the agent dying from falling into the void, as they cannot always see the edge. A better method should be implemented to automatically move the camera to regions of interest.

Author Contributions: Conceptualization: C.-A.P. and M.V.M.; methodology: P.C. and C.-A.P.; software: B.-I.R. and P.C.; validation: P.C., C.-A.P. and M.V.M.; formal analysis: C.-A.P.; investigation: P.C.; resources: C.-A.P. and M.V.M.; data curation: B.-I.R. and P.C.; writing—original draft preparation: P.C.; writing—review and editing: C.-A.P. and M.V.M.; visualization: C.-A.P.; supervision: C.-A.P. and M.V.M.; project administration: P.C. All authors have read and agreed to the published version of the manuscript.

Funding: The APC was funded by Polytechnic University Timişoara, Romania.

Institutional Review Board Statement: Not applicable.

Informed Consent Statement: Not applicable.

Data Availability Statement: Not applicable.

Conflicts of Interest: The authors declare no conflict of interest.

References

1. Zheng, W.; Yin, L. Characterization inference based on joint-optimization of multi-layer semantics and deep fusion matching network. *PeerJ Comput. Sci.* **2022**, *8*, e908. [CrossRef] [PubMed]
2. Zheng, W.; Tian, X.; Yang, B.; Liu, S.; Ding, Y.; Tian, J.; Yin, L. A Few Shot Classification Methods Based on Multiscale Relational Networks. *Appl. Sci.* **2022**, *12*, 4059. [CrossRef]
3. Qin, X.; Liu, Z.; Liu, Y.; Liu, S.; Yang, B.; Yin, L.; Liu, M.; Zheng, W. User OCEAN Personality Model Construction Method Using a BP Neural Network. *Electronics* **2022**, *11*, 3022. [CrossRef]
4. Stai, E.; Kafetzoglou, S.; Tsiropoulou, E.E.; Papavassiliou, S. A holistic approach for personalization, relevance feedback & recommendation in enriched multimedia content. *Multimed. Tools Appl.* **2018**, *77*, 283–326. [CrossRef]
5. Mnih, V.; Kavukcuoglu, K.; Silver, D.; Graves, A.; Antonoglou, I.; Wierstra, D.; Riedmiller, M. Playing Atari with Deep Reinforcement Learning. In Proceedings of the NIPS Deep Learning Workshop, Lake Tahoe, NV, USA, 9 December 2013.
6. Mnih, V.; Kavukcuoglu, K.; Silver, D.; Rusu, A.A.; Veness, J.; Bellemare, M.G.; Graves, A.; Riedmiller, M.; Fidjeland, A.K.; Ostrovski, G.; et al. Human-level control through deep reinforcement learning. *Nature* **2015**, *518*, 529–533. [CrossRef] [PubMed]
7. Bellman, R. A Markovian Decision Process. *J. Math. Mech.* **1957**, *6*, 679–684. [CrossRef]
8. Watkins, C.J.C.H.; Dayan, P. Q-learning. *Mach. Learn.* **1992**, *8*, 279–292. [CrossRef]
9. Hausknecht, M.; Stone, P. Deep Recurrent Q-Learning for Partially Observable MDPs. In Proceedings of the AAAI Fall Symposium on Sequential Decision Making for Intelligent Agents (AAAI-SDMIA15), Arlington, TX, USA, 12–14 November 2015.
10. Available online: https://store.steampowered.com/app/374320/DARK_SOULS_III/ (accessed on 15 August 2022).
11. Available online: https://steamcommunity.com/stats/374320/achievements (accessed on 15 August 2022).
12. Fedus, W.; Ramachandran, P.; Agarwal, R.; Bengio, Y.; Larochelle, H.; Rowland, M.; Dabney, W. Revisiting Fundamentals of Experience Replay. In Proceedings of the International Conference on Machine Learning (ICML), Online, 13–18 July 2020.
13. Fan, J. A Review for Deep Reinforcement Learning in Atari:Benchmarks, Challenges, and Solutions. *arXiv* **2021**, arXiv:2112.04145. https://doi.org/10.48550/ARXIV.2112.04145.
14. Kempka, M.; Wydmuch, M.; Runc, G.; Toczek, J.; Jaskowski, W. ViZDoom: A Doom-based AI research platform for visual reinforcement learning. In Proceedings of the 2016 IEEE Conference on Computational Intelligence and Games (CIG), Santorini, Greece, 20–23 September 2016; IEEE: Piscataway, NJ, USA, 2016. [CrossRef]
15. Adil, K.; Jiang, F.; Liu, S.; Grigorev, A.; Gupta, B.; Rho, S. Training an Agent for FPS Doom Game using Visual Reinforcement Learning and VizDoom. *Int. J. Adv. Comput. Sci. Appl.* **2017**, *8*, 32–41. [CrossRef]
16. Kulkarni, T.D.; Saeedi, A.; Gautam, S.; Gershman, S.J. Deep Successor Reinforcement Learning. *arXiv* **2016**, arXiv:1606.02396. [CrossRef]
17. Woubie, A.; Kanervisto, A.; Karttunen, J.; Hautamaki, V. Do Autonomous Agents Benefit from Hearing? *arXiv* **2019**, arXiv:1905.04192. [CrossRef]
18. Schulze, C.; Schulze, M. ViZDoom: DRQN with Prioritized Experience Replay, Double-Q Learning and Snapshot Ensembling. In Proceedings of the SAI Intelligent Systems Conference, London, UK, 6–7 September 2018; Springer International Publishing: Berlin/Heidelberg, Germany, 2018; pp. 1–17. [CrossRef]
19. Zakharenkov, A.; Makarov, I. Deep Reinforcement Learning with DQN vs. PPO in VizDoom. In Proceedings of the 2021 IEEE 21st International Symposium on Computational Intelligence and Informatics (CINTI), Budapest, Hungary, 18–20 November 2021; IEEE: Piscataway, NJ, USA, 2021. [CrossRef]
20. Lample, G.; Chaplot, D.S. Playing FPS Games with Deep Reinforcement Learning. In Proceedings of the Thirty-First AAAI Conference on Artificial Intelligence, San Francisco, CA, USA, 4–9 February 2017.
21. Bhatti, S.; Desmaison, A.; Miksik, O.; Nardelli, N.; Siddharth, N.; Torr, P.H.S. Playing Doom with SLAM-Augmented Deep Reinforcement Learning. *arXiv* **2016**, arXiv:1612.00380. [CrossRef]
22. Wydmuch, M.; Kempka, M.; Jaskowski, W. ViZDoom Competitions: Playing Doom From Pixels. *IEEE Trans. Games* **2019**, *11*, 248–259. [CrossRef]
23. Vinyals, O.; Ewalds, T.; Bartunov, S.; Georgiev, P.; Vezhnevets, A.S.; Yeo, M.; Makhzani, A.; Küttler, H.; Agapiou, J.; Schrittwieser, J.; et al. StarCraft II: A New Challenge for Reinforcement Learning. *arXiv* **2017**, arXiv:1708.04782. [CrossRef]
24. Certicky, M.; Churchill, D.; Kim, K.J.; Certicky, M.; Kelly, R. StarCraft AI Competitions, Bots, and Tournament Manager Software. *IEEE Trans. Games* **2019**, *11*, 227–237. [CrossRef]
25. Usunier, N.; Synnaeve, G.; Lin, Z.; Chintala, S. Episodic Exploration for Deep Deterministic Policies: An Application to StarCraft Micromanagement Tasks. In Proceedings of the International Conference on Learning Representations (ICLR), Toulon, France, 24–26 April 2017.
26. Xu, S.; Kuang, H.; Zhuang, Z.; Hu, R.; Liu, Y.; Sun, H. Macro action selection with deep reinforcement learning in StarCraft. In Proceedings of the Fifteenth AAAI Conference on Artificial Intelligence and Interactive Digital Entertainment (AIIDE), Atlanta, GA, USA, 8–12 October 2019.
27. Liu, T.; Wu, X.; Luo, D. A Hierarchical Model for StarCraft II Mini-Game. In Proceedings of the 2019 18th IEEE International Conference On Machine Learning And Applications (ICMLA), Boca Raton, FL, USA, 16–19 December 2019; IEEE: Piscataway, NJ, USA, 2019. [CrossRef]

28. Hu, Y.; Li, J.; Li, X.; Pan, G.; Xu, M. Knowledge-Guided Agent-Tactic-Aware Learning for StarCraft Micromanagement. In Proceedings of the Twenty-Seventh International Joint Conference on Artificial Intelligence (IJCAI), Stockholm, Sweden, 13–19 July 2018. [CrossRef]
29. Johnson, M.; Hofmann, K.; Hutton, T.; Bignell, D. The Malmo Platform for Artificial Intelligence Experimentation. In Proceedings of the Twenty-Fifth International Joint Conference on Artificial Intelligence (IJCAI), New York, NY, USA, 9–15 July 2016.
30. Brockman, G.; Cheung, V.; Pettersson, L.; Schneider, J.; Schulman, J.; Tang, J.; Zaremba, W. OpenAI Gym. *arXiv* **2016**, arXiv:1606.01540. [CrossRef]
31. Guss, W.H.; Houghton, B.; Topin, N.; Wang, P.; Codel, C.; Veloso, M.; Salakhutdinov, R. MineRL: A Large-Scale Dataset of Minecraft Demonstrations. In Proceedings of the Twenty-Eighth International Joint Conference on Artificial Intelligence (IJCAI), Macao, China, 10–16 August 2019. [CrossRef]
32. Gray, J.; Srinet, K.; Jernite, Y.; Yu, H.; Chen, Z.; Guo, D.; Goyal, S.; Zitnick, C.L.; Szlam, A. CraftAssist: A Framework for Dialogue-enabled Interactive Agents. *arXiv* **2019**, arXiv:1907.08584. [CrossRef]
33. Bard, N.; Foerster, J.N.; Chandar, S.; Burch, N.; Lanctot, M.; Song, H.F.; Parisotto, E.; Dumoulin, V.; Moitra, S.; Hughes, E.; et al. The Hanabi challenge: A new frontier for AI research. *Artif. Intell.* **2020**, *280*, 103216. [CrossRef]
34. Muglich, D.; de Witt, C.S.; van der Pol, E.; Whiteson, S.; Foerster, J. Equivariant Networks for Zero-Shot Coordination. *arXiv* **2022**, arXiv.2210.12124. [CrossRef]
35. Grooten, B.; Wemmenhove, J.; Poot, M.; Portegies, J. Is Vanilla Policy Gradient Overlooked? Analyzing Deep Reinforcement Learning for Hanabi. In Proceedings of the AAMAS Adaptive and Learning Agents Workshop. *arXiv* **2022**, arXiv:2203.11656. [CrossRef]
36. Jia, X.; Bin, Z.; Chao, F.; Chaojing, T. An Automatic Evaluation Approach for Binary Software Vulnerabilities with Address Space Layout Randomization Enabled. In Proceedings of the 2021 International Conference on Big Data Analysis and Computer Science (BDACS), Kunming, China, 25–27 June 2021; IEEE: Piscataway, NJ, USA, 2021. [CrossRef]
37. Developers, C.E. Cheat Engine. Available online: https://www.cheatengine.org/ (accessed on 15 August 2022).
38. Kalyanakrishnan, S.; Aravindan, S.; Bagdawat, V.; Bhatt, V.; Goka, H.; Gupta, A.; Krishna, K.; Piratla, V. An Analysis of Frame-skipping in Reinforcement Learning. *arXiv* **2021**, arXiv:2102.03718. [CrossRef]
39. Dabney, W.; Ostrovski, G.; Barreto, A. Temporally-Extended ϵ-Greedy Exploration. In Proceedings of the International Conference on Learning Representations (ICLR), Vienna, Austria, 4–8 May 2021.
40. Zhang, W.; Zhou, D.; Li, L.; Gu, Q. Neural Thompson Sampling. In Proceedings of the International Conference on Learning Representations (ICLR), Vienna, Austria, 4–8 May 2021.
41. Schaul, T.; Quan, J.; Antonoglou, I.; Silver, D. Prioritized Experience Replay. In Proceedings of the International Conference on Learning Representations (ICLR), San Juan, Puerto Rico, 2–4 May 2016.
42. Andrychowicz, M.; Wolski, F.; Ray, A.; Schneider, J.; Fong, R.; Welinder, P.; McGrew, B.; Tobin, J.; Abbeel, P.; Zaremba, W. Hindsight Experience Replay. In Proceedings of the Advances in Neural Information Processing Systems (NIPS), Long Beach, CA, USA, 4–9 December 2017.

mathematics

MDPI

Article

Polynomial Fuzzy Information Granule-Based Time Series Prediction

Xiyang Yang [1,2,3,4,5], Shiqing Zhang [1,4], Xinjun Zhang [2] and Fusheng Yu [3,*]

1 Key Laboratory of Intelligent Computing and Information Processing, Quanzhou Normal University, Quanzhou 362000, China
2 Fujian Key Laboratory of Financial Information Processing, Putian University, Putian 351100, China
3 School of Mathematical Science, Beijing Normal University, Beijing 100875, China
4 Fujian Provincial Key Laboratory of Data-Intensive Computing, Quanzhou Normal University, Quanzhou 362000, China
5 Fujian Big Data Research Institute of Intelligent Manufacturing, Quanzhou Normal University, Quanzhou 362000, China
* Correspondence: yufusheng@bnu.edu.cn

Abstract: Fuzzy information granulation transfers the time series analysis from the numerical platform to the granular platform, which enables us to study the time series at a different granularity. In previous studies, each fuzzy information granule in a granular time series can reflect the average, range, and linear trend characteristics of the data in the corresponding time window. In order to get a more general information granule, this paper proposes polynomial fuzzy information granules, each of which can reflect both the linear trend and the nonlinear trend of the data in a time window. The distance metric of the proposed information granules is given theoretically. After studying the distance measure of the polynomial fuzzy information granule and its geometric interpretation, we design a time series prediction method based on the polynomial fuzzy information granules and fuzzy inference system. The experimental results show that the proposed prediction method can achieve a good long-term prediction.

Keywords: polynomial fuzzy information granule; fuzzy inference system; time series prediction

MSC: 68T30; 68T27

Citation: Yang, X.; Zhang, S.; Zhang, X.; Yu, F. Polynomial Fuzzy Information Granule-Based Time Series Prediction. *Mathematics* **2022**, *10*, 4495. https://doi.org/10.3390/math10234495

Academic Editor: Gia Sirbiladze

Received: 12 October 2022
Accepted: 24 November 2022
Published: 28 November 2022

1. Introduction

Time series prediction has been a classic machine learning task widely studied in recent years, and it has been applied to many fields, such as business [1], engineering [2], energy [3], and so on. It is hoped that some prediction methods can be used to find the internal association rules of the time series to predict the future changes.

Popular time series prediction methods include classical time series models, such as linear regression, autoregression, and moving average [4,5], as well as artificial intelligence methods, such as support vector regression (SVR) [6], artificial neural networks (ANNs) [7], nonlinear autoregressive (NAR) [8], recurrent neural networks (RNNs) [9,10], long short-term memory (LSTM) networks [11,12], and so on. The classical time series models usually require the data to be analyzed to meet the ergodicity, stationarity, and other assumptions [13], and these strict conditions may not always hold for real world data. Although many intelligent methods such as SVR and ANNs come with the ability to capture the nonlinear relationship between the input and output variables, and have been applied to solve many real-word problems [14–17], the quality of their prediction depends very much on the data set to be processed [18]. These numerical prediction methods are computationally expensive and more suitable for a short-term prediction. In addition, the lack of interpretability of these numerical methods has become the main barrier in their wide acceptance in time series prediction applications. These methods, as well as their results, are not easy to be understood by humans.

The fuzzy information granulation of the time series [19,20] is one of the feasible methods to solve the above shortcomings. In this method, a time series is firstly divided into some meaningful time windows in the time dimension, and then a fuzzy information granule (FIG) is established on each time window. In this way, a time series is transformed to a sequence of FIGs, each of which is a fuzzy set, and the time series can be now analyzed at the granular level by directly manipulating the FIGs. The combination of an FIG with fuzzy reasoning [21], a support vector machine [22], and other artificial intelligence algorithms for data mining [23–25] has become one of the research hotspots in recent years.

An FIG is usually represented by a fuzzy set, whose membership function is defined on the real number axis. Common forms of the membership functions of FIGs include the interval membership function, triangular membership function, and Gaussian membership function [26–28], and the corresponding FIGs are called Interval FIG(IFIG), Triangular FIG(TFIG), and Gaussian FIG(GFIG) in this paper, respectively. These types of FIGs can reflect the characteristics of the average and range of the temporal data in a time window, but fail to reflect the trend characteristic of the data.

As a modification, the linear fuzzy information granule (LFIG) [29] is represented by a fuzzy set whose membership function is defined both on the real number axis and the time axis. Like the LFIG, the polar fuzzy information granule (polar FIG) [30] defines its membership function in two-dimensional polar coordinates. Compared with the FIG, the added dimension in the membership functions of the LFIG and the polar FIG makes them possible to express the linear changing trends of the samples in the time window. However, both modifications failed to reflect the nonlinear trends of the samples.

In [31], a novel Gaussian-type time-variant FIG, named the generalized zonary time-variant FIG (GZTFIG), was proposed which can reflect the nonlinear trend of data changing. However, the form of the GZTFIG is a bit complex. In addition, GZTFIGs have a lack of specificity [32], that is, their semantics are not so clear.

To solve this problem, based on [29,31], this paper introduces a novel FIG, namely, the polynomial fuzzy information granule (PFIG), which represents the temporal samples in a time window by three kinds of parameters: (1) the length of the time window, (2) a polynomial center line, and (3) the degree of data deviation from the center line. Temporal samples can be reasonably characterized by the polynomial center line with an adjustable order. In the sense of the Hausdorff distance, the distance formula of the PFIG is derived theoretically. In particular, we prove that the distance of the two Gaussian PFIGs has a concise formula expression and intuitive geometric interpretation. Therefore, the PFIG is a well-defined information granule with a good distance property, which is hopeful to become an effective tool in time series granulation and prediction.

The remainder of this paper is organized as follows. Section 2 introduces traditional fuzzy information granules and their distance measure. Section 3 introduces PFIGs as well as their distance measure. It can be proved that the distance of Gaussian PFIGs have a simple formula, which corresponds to a reasonable geometric interpretation. Section 4 presents a long-term prediction method for the time series based on the distance measure of PFIGs and fuzzy inference system with an interpolation scheme. Section 5 describes three experiments to verify the effectiveness and feasibility of the proposed model. Finally, Section 6 provides the conclusions and offers some thoughts on future studies.

2. Fuzzy Information Granules and Their Distance

In this section, we briefly introduce the construction method of some common FIGs along with their distance measurement. These concepts are useful for defining the novel type of granule (PFIG) given in Section 3.

2.1. Fuzzy Numbers and Their Distance Measurement

A fuzzy set (class) A in X is characterized by a membership (characteristic) function $f_A(x)$ which associates with each point in X a real number in the interval [0,1] [33]. Fuzzy numbers are special fuzzy sets. A fuzzy set A is called a fuzzy number if its membership function $A(x)$ satisfies the following conditions [34]:

(a) A is normal: there exists a number $x_0 \in R$, such that $A(x_0) = 1$;
(b) A is convex: $A(\omega x_1 + (1-\omega)x_2) \geq \min\{A(x_1), A(y_2)\}$, $\forall\omega \in [0, 1]$, $\forall x_1,x_2 \in R$;
(c) A is upper semicontinuous: $\forall\varepsilon > 0$, $\exists\delta > 0$, if $x \in \dot{U}(x_0,\delta)$, then $A(x) - A(x_0) < \varepsilon$.
(d) A is compactly supported: the closure of the set $\{x|A(x)\rangle 0\}$ is compact.

Figure 1 shows examples of one-dimensional and two-dimensional fuzzy numbers.

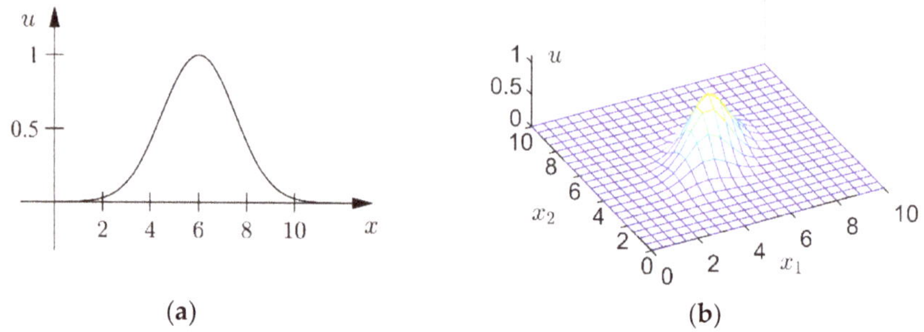

Figure 1. Fuzzy numbers. (**a**) a one-dimensional fuzzy number; (**b**) a two-dimensional fuzzy number.

Fuzzy numbers generalize classical real intervals. Accordingly, the distance of the fuzzy numbers can also be extended from the Hausdorff distance of the real number intervals. Named after Felix Hausdorff, the Hausdorff distance is a generalized metric in the family of closed sets, which measures the maximum distance of a set to the nearest point in the other set [35]. Let $A(\lambda) = \{x \in R|u(x) \geq \lambda\}$ be the λ-level set (or called λ-cut) of fuzzy number A. Since the λ-level sets $A(\lambda)$ and $B(\lambda)$ of fuzzy numbers A and B are classical real intervals, their Hausdorff distance can be written as:

$$d(A(\lambda), B(\lambda)) = \max\left\{\sup_{x\in A(\lambda)}\inf_{y\in B(\lambda)} d(x,y),\ \sup_{y\in B(\lambda)}\inf_{x\in A(\lambda)} d(x,y)\right\}, \tag{1}$$

where $d(x,y)$ represents the distance of real numbers x and y. Based on such a distance for real sets, the Hausdorff distance of fuzzy numbers A and B can be defined as [36]:

$$d(A,B) = \int_0^1 d(A(\lambda), B(\lambda))\mathrm{d}\lambda. \tag{2}$$

2.2. Fuzzy Information Granules and Their Distance

Constructing an FIG A to represent a group of temporal data $\boldsymbol{y} = \{y_1, y_2, \cdots, y_n\}$ should comply with the following two fairly conflicting conditions [32]. The first condition is called representativeness, that is, A should embrace enough data in $\boldsymbol{y}$. In another word, the total membership of $\boldsymbol{y}$ belonging to A, $\sum_{i=1}^{n} A(y_i)$, should be as large as possible, so that A has a good data coverage. The second condition is called specificity, that is, A should be specific enough. This is accomplished by keeping the support of A as compact (small) as possible, so that A has a better semantic clarity [32]. According to the types of membership functions, FIGs can be divided into Interval FIGs (IFIGs), Triangular FIGs (TFIGs), Gaussian FIGs (GFIGs), etc. Denote the membership function of an FIG A as $A(x;\gamma)$, where γ is the parameter set of the membership function of the corresponding type. The optimal value of

γ can be determined by optimizing both the representativeness and the specificity of the FIG $A(\gamma)$ through the optimization methods described below [32].

2.2.1. Interval Fuzzy Information Granules and Their Distance

An IFIG, denoted as $A_I(a,b)$ or $I(a,b)$, comes with the following membership function:

$$A_I(x;a,b) = I(x;a,b) = \begin{cases} 1, & x \in [a,b], \\ 0, & \text{else}. \end{cases} \tag{3}$$

Let $\gamma = \{a,b\}$ be the parameter set of this membership function, a and b are the left and right boundary points of the interval-type membership function, which can be determined by the following optimization model:

$$\max_{a,b} \frac{\sum_{y_i}(2 \cdot I(y_i;a,b) - 1)}{|b-a|}. \tag{4}$$

The numerator part of Equation (4) is related to the number of data $\boldsymbol{y}$ that belong to the IFIG $I(a,b)$. Maximizing the numerator part can make $I(a,b)$ achieve the best data coverage or representativeness. The denominator part of Equation (4) is related to the support of A. Minimizing the denominator part can make $I(a,b)$ achieve the best specificity.

As far as the distance of two IFIGs is concerned, according to Equations (1) and (2), the distance of $I_1(a_1,b_1)$ and $I_2(a_2,b_2)$ can be written as:

$$d(I_1,I_2) = \max\{|a_1-a_2|,|b_1-b_2|\}. \tag{5}$$

2.2.2. Triangular Fuzzy Information Granules and Their Distance

A TFIG, denoted as $A_T(a,m,b)$ or $T(a,m,b)$, comes with the following membership function:

$$A_T(x;a,m,b) = T(x;a,m,b) = \begin{cases} \dfrac{x-a}{m-a}, & a < x < m, \\ \dfrac{x-b}{m-b}, & m \le x < b, \\ 0, & \text{else}. \end{cases} \tag{6}$$

Let $\gamma = \{a,m,b\}$ be the parameter set of $T(a,m,b)$, where a, m, and b are called the "left extreme point", the "normal point", and the "right extreme point", respectively. m can be determined as the median of $\boldsymbol{y}$, and the extreme points a and b can be determined by the following optimization model [37]:

$$\max_{a,b} \frac{\sum_{y_i \le m} \frac{y_i-a}{m-a}}{m-a} + \frac{\sum_{y_i > m} \frac{b-y_i}{b-m}}{b-m}. \tag{7}$$

The numerator part of Equation (7) is related to the total membership degrees of $\boldsymbol{y}$ belonging to A, which reflects the representativeness of $T(a,m,b)$ to $\boldsymbol{y}$. Maximizing the numerator part can make $T(a,m,b)$ achieve the best representativeness. The denominator part of Equation (7) is related to the support of A. Minimizing the denominator part can make $T(a,m,b)$ achieve the best specificity.

As far as the distance of two TFIGs is concerned, according to Equations (1) and (2), the distance of $T_1(a_1,m_1,b_1)$ and $T_2(a_2,m_2,b_2)$ can be written as:

$$d(T_1,T_2) = \frac{1}{2}\max\{|(a_1-a_2)+(m_1-m_2)|,|(b_1-b_2)+(m_1-m_2)|\}. \tag{8}$$

2.2.3. Gaussian Fuzzy Information Granules and Their Distance

A GFIG, denoted as $A_G(\mu, \sigma)$ or $G(\mu, \sigma)$, comes with the following membership function:

$$A_G(x; \mu, \sigma) = G(x; \mu, \sigma) = \exp\left(-\frac{(x-\mu)^2}{2\sigma^2}\right). \tag{9}$$

Let $\gamma = \{\mu, \sigma\}$ be the parameter set of $G(\mu, \sigma)$, where μ and σ can be estimated by the mean value and standard deviation of $\boldsymbol{y}$, respectively. The GFIG has a clear meaning, and compared with the TFIG, the GFIG has less parameters with simpler parameter determination methods. According to the extension principle [38], the linear operation of GFIGs has a concise calculation property. That is:

Theorem 1 ([29]). *For any two GFIGs $G_1(\mu_1, \sigma_1)$, $G_2(\mu_2, \sigma_2)$ and any two real numbers $\omega_1, \omega_2 \in R$, we have*

$$\omega_1 G_1(\mu_1, \sigma_1) + \omega_2 G_2(\mu_2, \sigma_2) = G(\omega_1\mu_1 + \omega_2\mu_2, \omega_1\sigma_1 + \omega_2\sigma_2). \tag{10}$$

Furthermore, the Hausdorff distance of two GFIGs $G_1(\mu_1, \sigma_1)$ and $G_2(\mu_2, \sigma_2)$ can be concisely written as [29]:

$$d(G_1, G_2) = \Delta u + \frac{\sqrt{2\pi}\,\Delta\sigma}{2}, \tag{11}$$

where $\Delta\mu = |\mu_1 - \mu_2|$ and $\Delta\sigma = |\sigma_1 - \sigma_2|$.

3. Polynomial Fuzzy Information Granules and Their Distance Metric

3.1. Polynomial Fuzzy Information Granules

Suppose we are going to granulize a time series $\boldsymbol{y} = \{(t, y_t), t = 1, 2, \cdots, \tau\}$ as shown in Figure 2a. The IFIG, TFIG, and GFIG obtained by the corresponding granulation methods given by Equations (4), (7), and (9) in Section 2 are shown in Figure 2b–d, respectively. Because the membership functions of the IFIG, TFIG, and GFIG (as shown in Equations (3), (6), and (9)) are time-independent, their membership values of (t, y_t) depend only on y_t. As a result, these FIGs can properly reflect the average and range information of $\boldsymbol{y}$. However, they fail to reflect the changing trends of the time series, since the time-varying relationship between y_t and t is ignored.

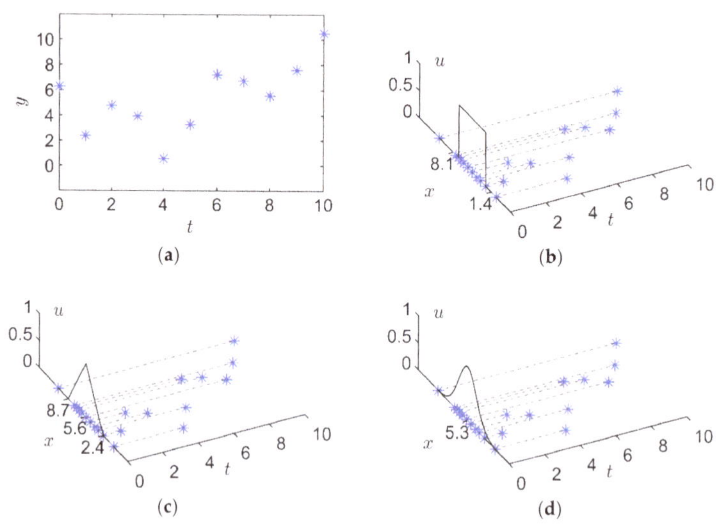

Figure 2. Different types of fuzzy information granules. (**a**) time series data; (**b**) interval fuzzy information granule; (**c**) triangular fuzzy information granule; (**d**) Gaussian fuzzy information granule.

One way to remedy this defect is to add the time variable t to the membership functions of the FIGs. The two-dimensional membership function of an FIG can be obtained by shifting the one-dimensional membership function in Figure 2 along the time axis. Follow this mechanism, the LFIGs [29] accomplish this goal by making the membership function of the GFIG (as shown in Figure 2d) change linearly over time. The two-dimensional membership function of the LFIG is shown in Figure 3.

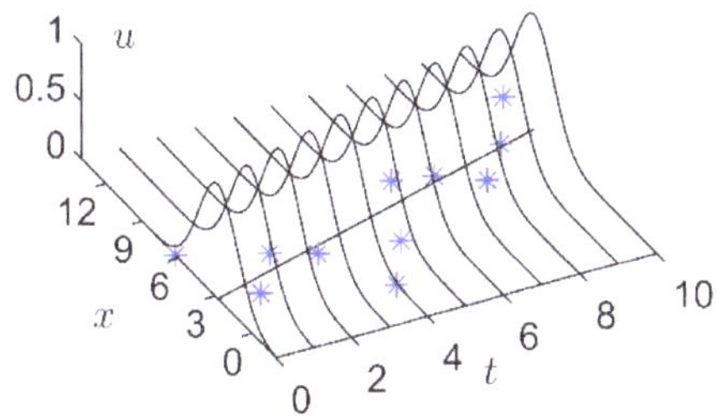

Figure 3. A linear fuzzy information granule.

Motivated by the time variant LFIG, we define a novel class of FIG called polynomial fuzzy information granules (PFIG) in this paper. In order to fully reflect the time-varying characteristics of the data in the time window, a reasonable PFIG should contain three types of parameters:

- The length of the time series $\boldsymbol{y}$, i.e., the size of time window, τ;
- A time-variant p-order center (regression) curve line $y_t = f(t, \boldsymbol{\beta}) = \beta_0 + \beta_1 t + \cdots + \beta_p t^p$ that reflects the changing of the time series;
- The parameters reflecting the deviation degree of the temporal data from the center line.

Definition 1. *(PFIG) For a time series $\boldsymbol{y} = \{(t, y_t), t = 1, 2, \cdots, \tau\}$, a fuzzy information granule $P(\boldsymbol{\beta}, \tau, \gamma)$ representing $\boldsymbol{y}$ is called a PFIG of order p, if its membership function $P((t, x); \boldsymbol{\beta}, \tau, \gamma)$ has a center curve line:*

$$f(t, \boldsymbol{\beta}) = \beta_0 + \beta_1 t + \cdots + \beta_p t^p, \quad t \in [0, \tau], \tag{12}$$

and $P((t, x); \boldsymbol{\beta}, \tau, \gamma)$ can be written as:

$$P((t, x); \boldsymbol{\beta}, \tau, \gamma) = A(f(t, \boldsymbol{\beta}); \gamma), \quad t \in [0, \tau], \tag{13}$$

where A is a fuzzy number, $A(x, \gamma)$ is its membership function, γ is a parameter set of the PFIG that reflects the deviation degree of the data from the center line, and the length of the time series τ is called the granularity of the PFIG.

Recently, Luo proposed a novel generalized zonary time-variant FIG (GZTFIG) in [31], which is able to reflect the nonlinear trends of the time series. The membership function of a GZTFIG is defined as:

$$\begin{aligned} f\left(x; \beta_n, \beta_{n-1}, \cdots \beta_1, \beta_0, \sigma, \underline{\beta}_0, \overline{\beta}_0, \tau\right) &= f\left(x;\ \beta_n t^n + \beta_{n-1} t^{n-1} + \cdots + \beta_1 t + \beta_0, \sigma\right) \\ &= \exp\left(-\frac{\left(x - \left(\beta_n t^n + \beta_{n-1} t^{n-1} + \cdots + \beta_1 t + \beta_0\right)\right)^2}{2\sigma^2}\right), \ \beta_0 \in \left[\underline{\beta}_0, \overline{\beta}_0\right], \end{aligned}$$

where $\left[\underline{\beta}_0, \overline{\beta}_0\right]$ reflects the data fluctuation interval in the current time window. $\left[\underline{\beta}_0, \overline{\beta}_0\right]$ can be determined by making all the data in $\boldsymbol{y}$ locate in the zonary area between the upper boundary $\beta_n t^n + \beta_{n-1} t^{n-1} + \cdots + \beta_1 t + \overline{\beta}_0$, and the lower boundary $\beta_n t^n + \beta_{n-1} t^{n-1} + \cdots + \beta_1 t + \underline{\beta}_0$.

Different from the GZTFIGs proposed in [31], the proposed PFIG no longer restricts its membership function to be Gaussian. Users can choose any appropriate type of membership function to construct a PFIG according to the characteristics of the time series. For the following three reasons, the PFIG uses the center curve line, instead of the zonal central region in the GZTFIG to reflect the changing trends of a time series. First, the width of the zonal region $\overline{\beta}_0 - \underline{\beta}_0$ is to reflect the degree of data deviation from the center line. However, this feature can also be reflected by the parameter γ in the PFIG, which is more concise. Secondarily, compared with GZTFIGs, the process of determining the zonary area is to avoid being in the PFIG. Thus, the construction of the PFIG is simpler. Last but not the least, the central zonary area of a GZTFIG is determined by translating the central line upward and downward, so that all the data are included in the zonary area. This operation increases the representativeness of the GZTFIG but decreases its specificity.

Using the definition of PFIGs, we can give the definitions for three special kinds of PFIGs, namely interval-type PFIGs (IPFIGs), triangular-type PFIGs (TPFIGs), and Gaussian-type PFIGs (GPFIGs).

Definition 2. *(IPFIG). A PFIG $P(\boldsymbol{\beta}, \tau, \gamma) = I_p(\boldsymbol{\beta}, \tau, r)$ is called an IPFIG of order p, if its membership function $P((t, x); \boldsymbol{\beta}, \tau, \gamma)$ can be written as:*

$$I_p((t,x); a(\boldsymbol{\beta},t,r), b(\boldsymbol{\beta},t,r)) = \begin{cases} 1, & x \in [a(\boldsymbol{\beta},t,r), b(\boldsymbol{\beta},t,r)], \\ 0, & \text{else}, \end{cases}$$

where $a(\boldsymbol{\beta},t,r) = f(t,\boldsymbol{\beta}) - r$ and $b(\boldsymbol{\beta},t,r) = f(t,\boldsymbol{\beta}) + r$ are the left and right boundary points of the interval-type membership function at $t \in [0,\tau]$, respectively; $f(t,\boldsymbol{\beta}) = \beta_0 + \beta_1 t + \cdots + \beta_p t^p$ represents the center curve line of PFIG; and r is the radius of this interval.

Definition 3. *(TPFIG): A PFIG $P(\boldsymbol{\beta}, \tau, \gamma) = T_p(\boldsymbol{\beta}, \tau, r_1, r_2)$ is called a TPFIG of order p if its membership function $P((t, x); \boldsymbol{\beta}, \tau, \gamma)$ can be written as:*

$$T_p((t,x); a(\boldsymbol{\beta},t,r_1), m(\boldsymbol{\beta},t), b(\boldsymbol{\beta},t,r_2)) = \begin{cases} \dfrac{x-a}{m-a}, & a(\boldsymbol{\beta},t,r_1) < x < m(\boldsymbol{\beta},t), \\ \dfrac{x-b}{m-b}, & m(\boldsymbol{\beta},t) \le x < b(\boldsymbol{\beta},t,r_2), \\ 0, & \text{else}, \end{cases}$$

where $m(\boldsymbol{\beta},t) = f(t,\boldsymbol{\beta}) = \beta_0 + \beta_1 t + \cdots + \beta_p t^p$ represents the center curve line of the PFIG, and $a(\boldsymbol{\beta},t,r_1) = m(\boldsymbol{\beta},t) - r_1$ and $b(\boldsymbol{\beta},t,r_2) = m(\boldsymbol{\beta},t) + r_2$ are the left and right extreme points of the triangular membership function at $t \in [0,\tau]$, respectively.

Definition 4. *(GPFIG): A PFIG $P(\boldsymbol{\beta}, \tau, \gamma) = G_p(\boldsymbol{\beta}, \tau, \sigma)$ is called a GPFIG of order p if its membership function $P((t, x); \boldsymbol{\beta}, \tau, \gamma)$ can be written as:*

$$G_p((t,x); \boldsymbol{\beta}, \tau, \sigma) = \exp\left(-\frac{(x - \mu(t,\boldsymbol{\beta}))^2}{2\sigma^2}\right), \tag{14}$$

where $\mu(t,\boldsymbol{\beta}) = f(t,\boldsymbol{\beta})$ is the center line of PFIG, and σ is the standard deviation that reflects the degree of data deviation from the center line.

The construction of a GPFIG is straightforward. The center line $\mu(t;\boldsymbol{\beta})$ can be estimated by the polynomial regression of the temporal data $\boldsymbol{y} = \{(t, y_t), t = 1, 2, \cdots, \tau\}$, and σ can be estimated by:

$$\sigma^2 = \frac{1}{\tau} \sum_{t=1}^{\tau} (y_t - \mu(t;\boldsymbol{\beta}))^2. \tag{15}$$

According to the above definitions, the temporal data in Figure 2a can be represented by a second order GPFIG as shown in Figure 4. Compared with the IFIG, TFIG, and GFIG shown in Figure 2b–d, the GPFIG can better reflect the changing trends in the temporal data, as shown in Figure 2a.

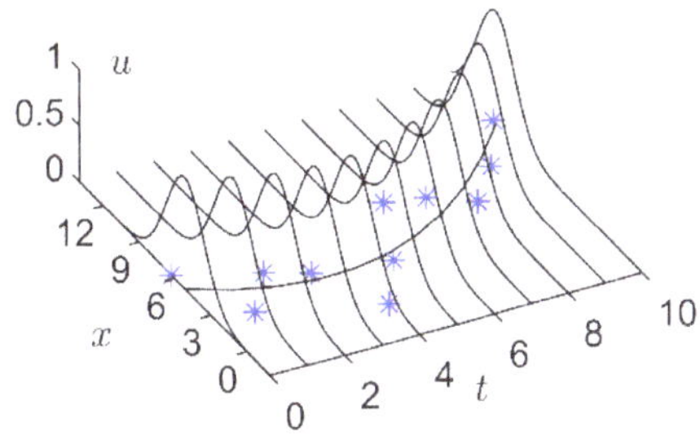

Figure 4. A Gaussian PFIG.

When the order of a PFIG is 0, the PFIG degenerates into the same type of FIGs introduced in Section 1, and when the order of a GPFIG is 1, the center line of the GPFIG becomes a linear function $f(t, \boldsymbol{\beta}) = \beta_0 + \beta_1 t$. Accordingly, the GPFIG degenerates into the LFIG proposed by [29]. Therefore, PFIGs, including GPFIGs, are a generalization of LFIGs.

A GPFIG is an information granule with good properties. From its definition, it can be found that the number of parameters of a GPFIG is small, its meaning is clear, and the Gaussian-type FIG has excellent operation properties, as shown in Theorem 1. In addition, the GPFIG is also easy to understand, given a GPFIG $G_p((t,x); \boldsymbol{\beta}, \tau, \sigma)$, we can imagine a time series of length τ, distributed around a center curve line $f(t, \boldsymbol{\beta}), t \in [0, \tau]$, with σ as the deviation degree of the temporal data from the center line. Therefore, the GPFIG is a good tool to construct the information granule to describe a group of temporal data. For this reason, our experiments in Section 5 will focus only on the GPFIG.

3.2. Distance Metric of Polynomial Fuzzy Information Granules

By comparing Figures 4 and 1b, we can find that the PFIG is a special type of two-dimensional fuzzy set. For a PFIG $P(\boldsymbol{\beta}, \tau, \gamma)$, its membership function is a two-dimensional convex surface. As shown in Figure 5, the λ-level set of $P(\boldsymbol{\beta}, \tau, \gamma)$ is:

$$P(\lambda) = \{(t,x) | P((t,x); \boldsymbol{\beta}, \tau, \gamma) \geq \lambda\}, \tag{16}$$

which can be regarded as a two-dimensional closed interval in the time-number plane (t-x plane).

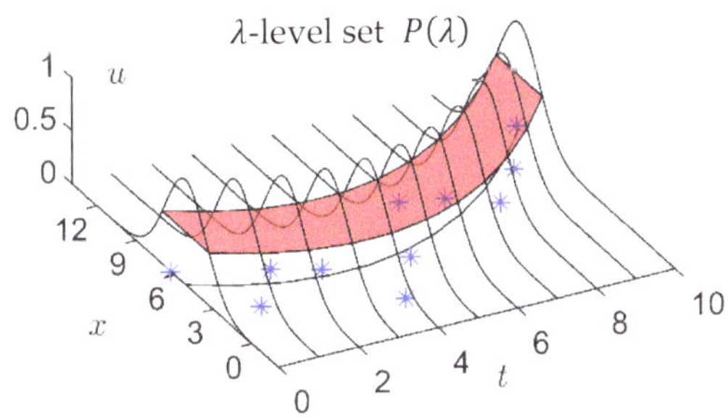

Figure 5. The λ-level set of a PFIG.

Similar to Equation (2), define the distance of two PFIGs $P_1(\boldsymbol{\beta}_1, \tau, \gamma_1)$ and $P_2(\boldsymbol{\beta}_2, \tau, \gamma_2)$ as the sum of all the distances of the λ-level sets [36]:

$$d(P_1, P_2) = \int_0^1 d(P_1(\lambda), P_2(\lambda)) \mathrm{d}\lambda, \tag{17}$$

where $d(P_1(\lambda), P_2(\lambda))$ is the Hausdorff distance of two-dimensional closed intervals $P_1(\lambda)$ and $P_2(\lambda)$, which can be written as:

$$d(P_1(\lambda), P_2(\lambda)) = \max\left\{ \sup_{z_1 \in P_1(\lambda)} \inf_{z_2 \in P_2(\lambda)} d(z_1, z_2),\ \sup_{z_2 \in P_2(\lambda)} \inf_{z_1 \in P_1(\lambda)} d(z_1, z_2) \right\}, \tag{18}$$

where $z_1 = (t_1, x_1) \in P_1(\lambda)$ and $z_2 = (t_2, x_2) \in P_2(\lambda)$.

The calculation of Equation (18) is very complex and is computationally difficult to implement. To solve this problem, we should redefine $d(P_1(\lambda), P_2(\lambda))$ based on the following considerations. The Hausdorff distance is mainly used for the distance measurement of the general multidimensional real intervals, where every dimension is usually independent of the other dimensions. However, since the temporal data $(1, y_1)$, $(2, y_2), \cdots, (\tau, y_\tau)$ are special two-dimensional data, where y_t can be regarded as a function of the time t, these temporal data should have a distance definition different from Equation (18).

As shown in Figure 6, cut the λ-level set $P(\lambda)$ at $t = t_0$, we get a cutting segment $L(\lambda, t_0)$:

$$L(\lambda, t_0) = \{(t, x) | t = t_0, (t, x) \in P(\lambda)\}, \tag{19}$$

which is a one-dimensional closed interval.

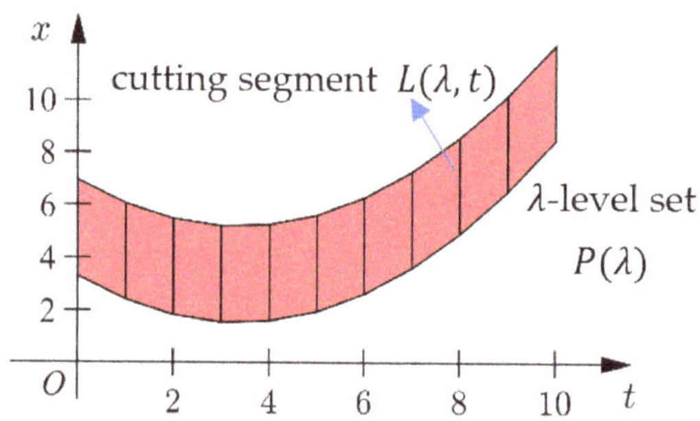

Figure 6. The cutting segment of the λ-level set in a PFIG.

According to Equation (1), the Hausdorff distance of two cutting segments $L_1(\lambda, t)$ and $L_2(\lambda, t)$ at time t is:

$$d(L_1(\lambda, t),\ L_2(\lambda, t)) = \max\left\{ \sup_{x \in L_1} \inf_{y \in L_2} d(x, y),\ \sup_{y \in L_2} \inf_{x \in L_1} d(x, y) \right\}. \tag{20}$$

Then, the distance between $P_1(\lambda)$ and $P_2(\lambda)$ can be regarded as the sum of the distances of all these cutting segment pairs at all t's, that is:

$$d(P_1(\lambda), P_2(\lambda)) = \int_0^\tau d(L_1(\lambda, t),\ L_2(\lambda, t))\mathrm{d}t. \tag{21}$$

In this way, the distance of two PFIGs can be found by substituting Equation (21) to Equation (17). The distance of any different type of PFIGs can be calculated when the corresponding membership function $P((t, x); \boldsymbol{\beta}, \tau, \gamma)$ in Equation (13) is selected. In particular, the distance of two Gaussian PFIGs have the following expression.

Theorem 2. *(Distance of GPFIGs): the Hausdorff distance of two GPFIGs, namely $G_{p1}(\boldsymbol{\beta}_1, \sigma_1, \tau)$ and $G_{p2}(\boldsymbol{\beta}_2, \sigma_2, \tau)$, can be written as the area between their center lines $f_1(t, \boldsymbol{\beta}_1)$ and $f_2(t, \boldsymbol{\beta}_2)$, and a term proportional to the difference of σ_1 and σ_2, that is:*

$$d(G_{p1}, G_{p2}) = \int_0^\tau |\mu_1(t, \boldsymbol{\beta}_1) - \mu_2(t, \boldsymbol{\beta}_2)|\mathrm{d}t + \frac{\sqrt{2\pi}|\sigma_1 - \sigma_2|}{2}\tau, \tag{22}$$

where $\mu(t,\beta) = f(t,\beta)$ is the center line of the GPFIG.

Proof. According to Equation (14), the λ-level set of GPFIG $G_p(\beta,\sigma,\tau)$ can be written as:

$$\begin{aligned} P(\lambda) &= \{(t,x)|P((t,x);\beta,\tau,\gamma) \geq \lambda\} \\ &= \{(t,x)|G_r^- \leq x \leq G_r^+, 0 \leq t \leq \tau\}, \end{aligned}$$

where $G_\lambda^- = \mu(t,\beta) - \sqrt{2\ln(1/\lambda)}\sigma$, and $G_\lambda^+ = \mu(t,\beta) + \sqrt{2\ln(1/\lambda)}\sigma$. By Equation (19), the cutting segment of $P(\lambda)$ at time t can be written as $L(\lambda,t) = [G_\lambda^-, G_\lambda^+]$. Substitute it into Equations (20) and (21) and we can get the following distance metric for λ-level sets $P_1(\lambda)$ and $P_2(\lambda)$.

$$\begin{aligned} d(P_1(\lambda),P_2(\lambda)) &= \int_0^\tau d(L_1(\lambda,t),\ L_2(\lambda,t))dt \\ &= \int_0^\tau \left(|\mu_1(t,\beta_1) - \mu_2(t,\beta_2)| + \left| \sqrt{2\ln\left(\frac{1}{\lambda}\right)}\sigma_1 - \sqrt{2\ln\left(\frac{1}{\lambda}\right)}\sigma_2 \right| \right) \mathrm{d}t \\ &= \int_0^\tau |\mu_1(t,\beta_1) - \mu_2(t,\beta_2)| \mathrm{d}t + \sqrt{2\ln\left(\frac{1}{\lambda}\right)} |\sigma_1 - \sigma_2|\tau. \end{aligned}$$

Substitute it into Equation (17) and the distance between $G_{p1}(\beta_1,\sigma_1,\tau)$ and $G_{p2}(\beta_2,\sigma_2,\tau)$ can be written as:

$$\begin{aligned} d(G_{p1},G_{p2}) &= \int_0^1 d(P_1(\lambda),P_2(\lambda))\mathrm{d}\lambda \\ &= \int_0^1 \left(\int_0^1 |\mu_1(t,\beta_1) - \mu_2(t,\beta_2)| \mathrm{d}t + \sqrt{2\ln\left(\frac{1}{\lambda}\right)} |\sigma_1 - \sigma_2|\tau \right) \mathrm{d}\lambda \\ &= \int_0^1 |\mu_1(t,\beta_1) - \mu_2(t,\beta_2)| dt + \frac{\sqrt{2\pi\tau}}{2} |\sigma_1 - \sigma_2|. \end{aligned}$$

□

Obviously, the first term of Equation (22) is the integral of the distance difference between two center lines $f_1(t,\beta_1)$ and $f_2(t,\beta_2)$ in $[0,\tau]$, which represents the distance caused by the center lines. As illustrated in Figure 7, the geometric meaning of this term is the area between the two center lines. The second term is $\sqrt{2\pi\tau}/2$ times of $|\sigma_1 - \sigma_2|$, which represents the distance caused by data deviations. Therefore, the distance between two GPFIGs is determined by their center lines on the one hand, and the data deviations on the other. This is consistent with our intuition.

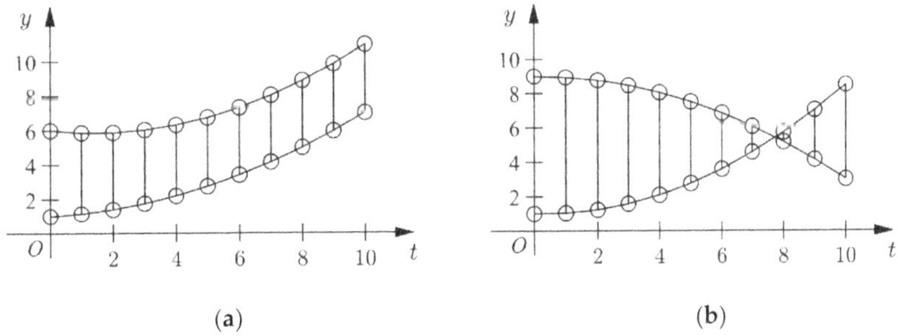

Figure 7. The area between the two center lines. (**a**) The area of two center lines when they have no intersection between $[0,\tau]$, (**b**) the area of two center lines when they have an intersection between $[0,\tau]$.

When PFIGs degenerate into LFIGs, the distance given by Equation (22) is consistent with the distance of LFIGs given in [29], i.e.,

$$d(G_{p1}(\beta_1,\sigma_1,\tau),G_{p2}(\beta_2,\sigma_2,\tau)) = \begin{cases} \frac{1}{2}\tau^2\Delta\beta_1 + \tau\Delta\beta_0 + \frac{\sqrt{2\pi}\tau}{2}\Delta\sigma, & \text{if } t^* < 0, \\ \frac{\Delta\beta_0{}^2}{2\Delta\beta_1} + \frac{(\Delta\beta_0 - \tau\Delta\beta_1)^2}{2\Delta k} + \frac{\sqrt{2\pi}\tau}{2}\Delta\sigma, & \text{if } t^* \in [0,\tau], \\ -\frac{1}{2}\tau^2\Delta\beta_1 + \tau\Delta\beta_0 + \frac{\sqrt{2\pi}\tau}{2}\Delta\sigma, & \text{if } t^* > \tau, \end{cases}$$

where $\boldsymbol{\beta}_1 = (\beta_{10},\beta_{11})$, $\boldsymbol{\beta}_2 = (\beta_{20},\beta_{21})$, and $f(t,\boldsymbol{\beta}_1) = \beta_{10} + \beta_{11}t, f(t,\boldsymbol{\beta}_2) = \beta_{20} + \beta_{21}t$ are the center lines of the two LFIGs, respectively. $\Delta\beta_0 = |\beta_{10} - \beta_{20}|, \Delta\beta_1 = |\beta_{11} - \beta_{21}|$, and $t^* = -(\beta_{10} - \beta_{20})/(\beta_{11} - \beta_{21})$ represents the intersection of the two center lines. $\Delta\sigma = |\sigma_1 - \sigma_2|$ is the difference of two data deviations.

4. Granular Time Series Prediction Method Based on Fuzzy Inference

4.1. Granule Based Fuzzy Inference

Given a time series $\boldsymbol{y} = \{(t,y_t), t = 1,2,\cdots,N\}$, divide it into n consecutive time windows, and then construct an FIG on each time window, and we can obtain a granular time series $\{A_1, A_2, \cdots, A_n\}$. Such a granular time series can induce a fuzzy inference system (FIS) by the following way.

Select $q+1$ consecutive FIGs: $A_t,\ A_{t+1},\ \cdots,\ A_{t+q-1}, A_{t+q}$, and take the first q FIGs as the antecedents of a fuzzy rule, and the last one as the consequent, then these $q+1$ FIGs imply a q-input 1-output fuzzy rule:

$$\text{Rule } t: \ A_t, A_{t+1}, \cdots, A_{t+q-1} \to A_{t+q}.$$

A time series containing n FIGs can form a total of $n-q$ rules. These rules constitute the rule base of the FIS.

As shown in Figure 8, when we use the last q FIGs $A_{n-q+1}, \cdots, A_{n-1}, A_n$ of this granular time series as the inputs, then the output of the FIS, namely $\hat{A}_{n+1}$, can be used to predicted the future values of the original time series. Similar to the process of a Mamdani-type FIS, $\hat{A}_{n+1}$ can be written as a linear combination of all the consequents of the rules, that is:

$$\hat{A}_{n+1} = \sum_{t=1}^{n-q} \omega_t A_{t+q}, \tag{23}$$

where ω_t is the weight of rule t, which can be measured by the Hausdorff distance between the FIS' inputs $A_{n-q+1}, \cdots, A_{n-1}, A_n$, and the antecedents of the t-th rule, $A_t,\ \cdots,\ A_{t+q-2}$, A_{t+q-1}. That is, ω_t can be written as:

$$\omega_t = \frac{1}{D(A_{n-q+1}, A_t)} \frac{1}{D(A_{n-q+2}, A_{t+1})} \cdots \frac{1}{D(A_{n-1}, A_{t+q-1})}, \ t = 1,2,\cdots,n-q.$$

Normalize these weights, then $\hat{A}_{n+1}$ can be computed from the granular time series by Equation (23).

After obtaining a future FIG (data) $\hat{A}_{n+1}$, it is incorporated into the original time series to form a new time series $\{A_1, A_2, \cdots, A_n, \hat{A}_{n+1}\}$ to predict the next FIG (data) $\hat{A}_{n+2}$. Through this closed loop forecasting process, we can predict the values of any length in the future by using the previous predictions as the input. Closed loop forecasting allows us to predict an arbitrary number of time steps, but this can easily lead to large errors because the previous predictions are not the true values during the forecasting process, and the forecasting errors from a previous process can cumulatively affect the subsequent forecasting processes.

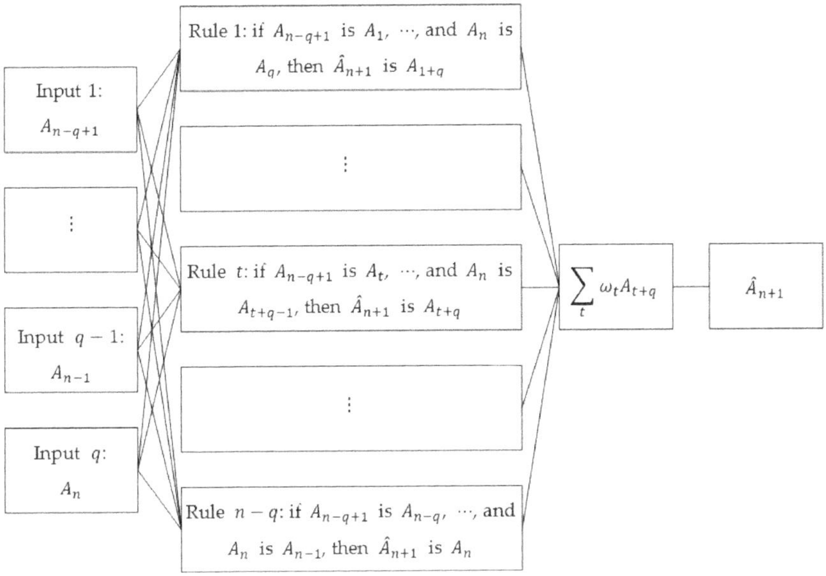

Figure 8. Fuzzy inference system.

4.2. Flow Chart of the Proposed Algorithm

The pseudo-code of the time series prediction algorithm combining FIS and GPFIGs is given in Algorithm 1 as follows:

Algorithm 1: Time series prediction algorithm based on FIS and GPFIGs.

Input: A numerical time series $y = \{(t, y_t), t = 1, 2, \cdots, N\}$ of length N; the granularity (length of time window) τ and the polynomial order p of PFIG. Number of antecedents q of the fuzzy rules in the FIS.
Output: the next FIG $\hat{G}_{p,n+1}$.

(1) Delete the first $N - \text{mod}(N, \tau)$ elements, i.e., let $y = y(N - \text{mod}(N, \tau) : \text{end})$;
(2) Determine the length of granular time series, i.e., let $n = \text{length}(y)/\tau$;
(3) For $i = 1 : n$;
(4) $[\beta_i, \sigma_i] = p\text{th} - \text{OrderPolynomialFitting}(y(i\tau + 1 : (i+1)\tau), p)$;
(5) End
(6) Construct a granular time series $\left\{ \left(i, G_{p,i}(\beta_i, \tau, \sigma_i) \right), i = 1, 2, \cdots, n \right\}$;
(7) For $i = 1 : n - q$;
(8) $\omega_i = \frac{1}{D(G_{p,n-q+1}, G_i)} \cdot \frac{1}{D(G_{p,n-q+2}, G_{i+1})} \cdot \cdots \cdot \frac{1}{D(G_{p,n-1}, G_{i+q-1})}$;
(9) End;
(10) $\hat{G}_{p,n+1} = \sum_{i=1}^{n-q} \left(\frac{\omega_i}{\sum_{t=1}^{n-q} \omega_t} G_{i+q} \right)$.

---

5. Experimental Research

To test the effectiveness of the perdition algorithm combining an FIS and GPFIGs (GPFIG-FIS), the forecasting results of the proposed method are compared with eight competing models in this section.

5.1. Data Description and Experimental Scheme

Three kinds of time series with a pseudo periodicity are selected for the experiment in this section. These data include: (1) the time series of the daily minimum temperature in Melbourne from 1981 to 1990 (this time series is from: https://www.kaggle.com/

datasets/sayedathar11/minimum-daily-temperatures-in-melborne19811990, accessed on 15 August 2022); (2) Tetouan city power consumption time series (this time series is from: https://archive.ics.uci.edu/ml/datasets/Power+consumption+of+Tetouan+city, accessed on 15 August 2022); and (3) American Heart Association electrocardiograms (ECG) time series (this time series dataset is purchased from: https://www.ecri.org/american-heart-association-ecg-database-usb, accessed on 1 June 2020).

Two kinds of indexes, the root mean-square error (*RMSE*) and symmetric mean absolute percentage error (*SMAPE*), are used to measure the effect of the time series prediction methods:

- Root mean-square error:

$$RMSE = \sqrt{\frac{\sum_{t=1}^{n}(\hat{y}(t) - y(t))^2}{n}}.$$

- Symmetric mean absolute percentage error:

$$SMAPE = \frac{1}{n}\sum_{t=1}^{n}\frac{|\hat{y}(t) - y(t)|}{\frac{1}{2}(|\hat{y}(t)| + |y(t)|)} \times 100.$$

where n indicates the number of data to be predicted, and $y(t)$ and $\hat{y}(t)$ indicate the true and predicted values of the time series at time t, respectively.

The following eight prediction methods are selected for a comparison with the GPFIG-FIS method proposed in this paper, among which the first four methods are numerical prediction methods, and the last four methods are methods based on ordinary FIGs and FIS:

- AR(q): Numerical q-order auto regressive model (auto regressive, AR):

$$y(t) = \phi_1 y(t-1) + \phi_2 y(t-2) + \cdots + \phi_q y(t-q) + \epsilon_t,$$

where $\phi_1, \phi_2, \cdots, \phi_q$ can be calculated from the training data by linear regression.

- NAR(q): the q-order NAR is a q-input 1-output feedforward network, whose input is a vector $x_t \stackrel{\text{def}}{=} \{y(t-1), y(t-2), \ldots, y(t-q)\}$ consisting of q data before time t in the given training sequence, and output is the datum in time t, $y_t = y(t)$. The NAR uses a sigmoid transfer function in the hidden layer and a linear transfer function in the output layer. The number of hidden neurons as well as the number of hidden layers is set to 10.
- SVR(q): numerical q-order support vector machine regress model (support vector regress, SVR) [39]:

$$\hat{y}(t) = w_1 y(t-1) + w_2 y(t-2) + \cdots + w_q y(t-q) + b,$$

where parameters $w = (w_1, w_2, \cdots, w_q)$ and b are determined by the following support vector machine regression model:

$$\min_{\mathrm{w}} \frac{1}{2} w^T w + C\frac{1}{l}\sum_{t=1}^{l}(\xi_t + \xi_t^*),$$

$$s.t. \left(w^T x_t + b\right) - y_t \leq \epsilon + \xi_t,$$

$$y_t - \left(w^T x_t + b\right) \leq \epsilon + \xi_t^*,$$

$$\xi_t,\ \xi_t^* \geq 0,$$

where l is the number of training samples, x_t and y_t are the same as in NAR(q);

- LSTM: a sequence-to-sequence regression LSTM network, where the responses are the training sequences with values shifted by one time step. The LSTM updates the cell and hidden states using the hyperbolic tangent function and uses the sigmoid function as the gate activation function. The number of hidden units is set to 128.

- IFIG-FIS: the FIS prediction method based on the IFIG. Equations (4) and (5) are used to granulate the time series, and the FIS with q-input is used for the prediction.
- TFIG-FIS: the FIS prediction method based on the TFIG. Equations (7) and (8) are used to granulate the time series, and the FIS with q-input is used for the prediction.
- GFIG-FIS: the FIS prediction method based on the GFIG. The average and standard deviation of the corresponding window data are used as the parameters in constructing the GFIG, and the FIS with q-input is used for the prediction.
- LIFG-FIS: the FIS prediction method based on the LFIG. The linear regression line and the estimate of the error variance are used as the parameters in constructing the LIFG, and the FIS with q-input is used for the prediction.

5.2. The Experimental Results

5.2.1. Daily Minimum Temperature Dataset

The time series of daily maximum temperature in Melbourne City from 1981 to 1990 is shown in Figure 9. The time series contains a total of 3650 data, and the first 2928 data are selected as the training samples to predict the daily maximum temperature for the next 183, 366, and 549 days (i.e., days after 2928).

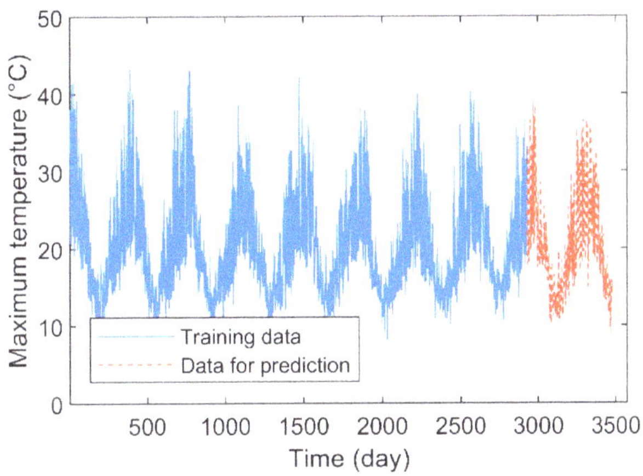

Figure 9. Time series of daily maximum temperature.

For each prediction method, the number of FIS input q is set to three. Since this time series has a natural time cycle, in constructing the granular time series, the size of the time window is set to 183 days, which is about half a year. Additionally, the order of the GPFIG is set as three. Table 1 shows the RMSE and SMAPE indexes by the GPFIG FIS and other methods for a long-term forecasting.

Table 1. Comparison of the prediction indexes of daily minimum temperature.

Index	Time (Day)	AR	NAR	SVR	LSTM	IFIG-FIS	TFIG-FIS	GFIG-FIS	LFIG-FIS	GPFIG-FIS
RMSE	2929–3112	9.83	6.79	6.49	4.30	8.76	6.67	6.45	4.44	**4.19**
	2929–3295	14.76	7.01	6.54	4.25	7.57	6.39	6.18	4.27	**4.14**
	2929–3478	17.23	6.83	6.4	4.25	7.86	6.31	6.11	4.19	**4.04**
SMAPE	2929–3112	42.02	27.58	24.74	14.32	28.14	21.67	22.38	14.66	**14.11**
	2929–3295	62.34	30.63	27.23	15.51	24.48	21.27	21.97	14.71	**14.48**
	2929–3478	74.18	29.9	26.73	14.87	25.85	21.74	22.47	14.66	**14.28**

Note: a value in bold font indicates that the corresponding method achieves the best index among all the methods.

For brevity, Figure 10 shows the predicted values of several prediction methods with better prediction results. It can be found that compared with the numerical prediction methods, the LFIG-FIS and GPFIG-FIG get better prediction results. Because of the length of the time window, which is about half a year, it has a clear meaning in this experiment, the FIGs constructed by the LFIG-FIS and GPFIG-FIG can reflect the main characteristics of the data in each time window very well, which is beneficial to eliminate the influence of random noises in this time series. When these FIGs are regarded as linguistic variables to construct fuzzy inference rules, a reasonable FIS can be obtained. However, since numerical prediction methods are easily disturbed by noise, they cannot get accurate results for a long-term prediction.

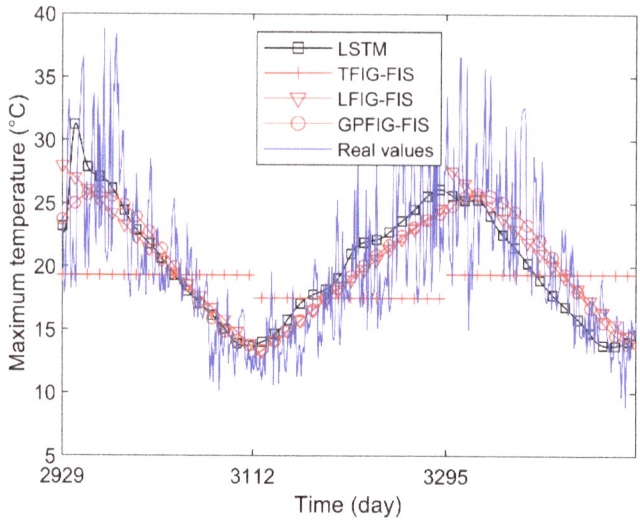

Figure 10. Daily maximum temperature forecast results.

Note that the time series used in this experiment has a clear increasing or decreasing trend in each time window. Because of this, both the LFIG-FIS and GPFIG-FIS that contain trend parameters could accurately reflect these changing trends. Therefore, compared with the other FIG-based prediction methods, the LFIG-FIS and GPFIG-FIS can get better prediction results. Among them, the GPFIG-FIS is slightly better than the LFIG-FIS because it can more accurately reflect the changing trends in each time window.

5.2.2. Power Consumption Time Series

The average power consumption data of the three urban areas every 10 min are collected in the two weeks from 16 to 30 December 2017 in Tetuan, Morocco. As shown in Figure 11, this time series contains 2016 data, and the previous 1920 data are used as the training data set, to predict the last 96 data.

Set the number of FIS input $q = 3$ for the various methods. The length of the time window is set as 16, about one ninth of a day, in constructing various kinds of FIGs. Additionally, the polynomial order of the PFIG is set as three. Table 2 shows the RMSE and SMAPE indexes of various methods in predicting the data in the last six time windows (96 points altogether).

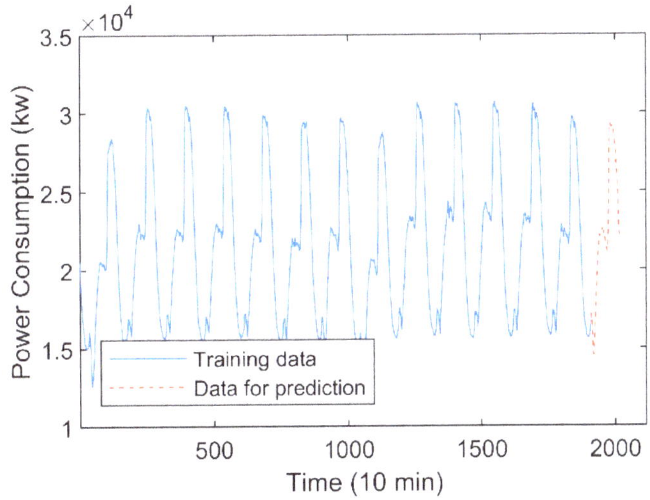

Figure 11. Time series of average power consumption in Tetuan.

Table 2. Comparison of the prediction indexes of electricity consumption in Tetuan.

Index	Time (10 min)	AR	NAR	SVR	LSTM	IFIG-FIS	TFIG-FIS	GFIG-FIS	LFIG-FIS	GPFIG-FIS
RMSE	1909–1926	3479	3128	5556	2934	1630	1155	1033	1087	**692**
	1927–1944	2800	2749	4130	2909	1647	1394	1306	854	**565**
	1945–1962	3030	3896	3415	3522	1394	1146	1077	718	**482**
	1963–1980	3803	4765	3347	3343	1790	1701	1676	1141	**691**
	1981–1998	6020	6815	4504	3755	1687	1603	1547	1101	**744**
	1999–2016	6500	7273	4526	3828	1823	1657	1617	1065	**754**
SMAPE	1909–1926	19.11	16.68	32.89	16.87	8.27	5.55	5.12	5.17	**3.36**
	1927–1944	13.77	13.35	20.14	14.79	7.64	6.22	5.99	3.68	**2.62**
	1945–1962	14.92	18.04	14.94	17.29	6.12	4.42	4.33	2.88	**2.07**
	1963–1980	16.89	21.15	13.29	15.36	7.08	5.48	6.38	4.21	**2.7**
	1981–1998	22.99	27.07	17.05	16.61	6.66	5.33	5.81	4.16	**2.95**
	1999–2016	25.47	29.38	17.38	16.65	6.97	5.68	6.11	4.08	**3.02**

Note: a value in bold font indicates that the corresponding method achieves the best result among all the methods.

For brevity, Figure 12 shows the predicted values of four prediction methods with better prediction results. Figure 12 and Table 2 show that, compared with the numerical prediction methods, the FIG-based prediction methods, namely the IFIG-FIS, TFIG-FIG, LFIG-FIS, and GPFIG-FIG can have more accurate prediction results, among which the LFIG- and GPFIG-based methods can reflect the time-varying trend very well. Therefore, they have better RMSE and SMAPE indexes when dealing with long-term prediction. In predicting the values of different time periods in the future, the GPFIG-FIS always has the best RSME and SMAPE indexes. A reason for this result is that, compared with the previous experiment, the power consumption time series display more complex trend changes in each time window, and the GPFIG with a high-order polynomial center line can better describe these changes. Consequently, the prediction indexes of the GPFIG-FIS are also significantly better than other methods such as the LFIG-FIS.

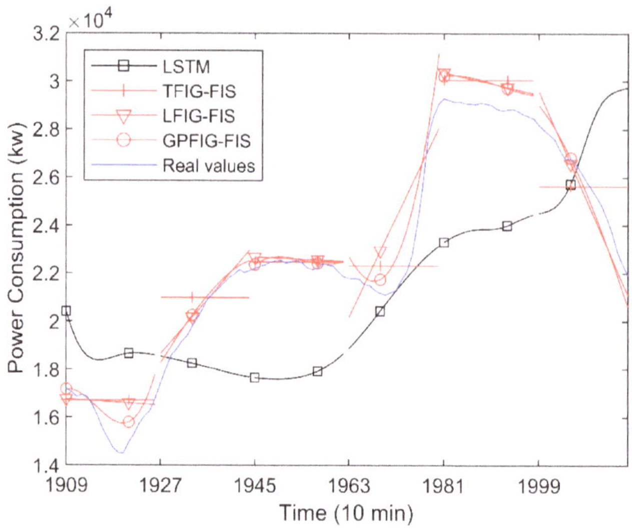

Figure 12. Electricity consumption forecast results of Tetuan city.

5.2.3. American Heart Association Electrocardiogram Time Series

The American Heart Association (AHA) ECG datasets collect voltage values at a sampling rate of 250 Hz. A complete ECG waveform contains about 250 sampling points. So, when constructing various FIGs, the length of the time window is set as 25, which is about one-tenth of a whole waveform. Figure 13 plots a time series containing 4250 sampling points. The first 4000 sampling points (including about 16 waveforms) are used as the training set to predict the last 250 sampling points (about 1 waveform).

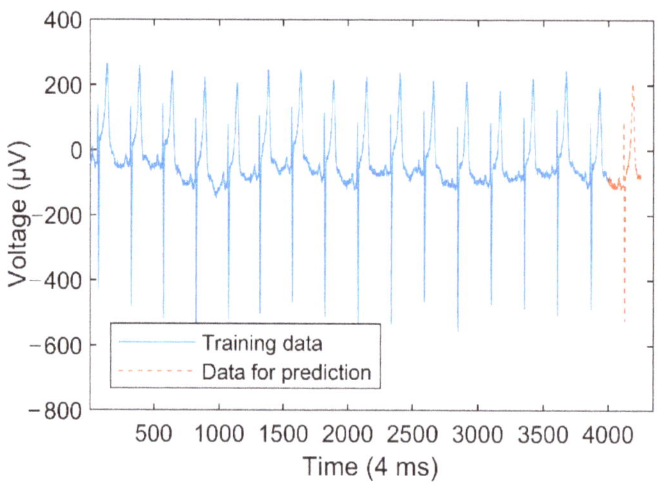

Figure 13. Electrocardiogram time series.

Set the number of the FIS input $q = 10$ for each prediction method. Due to the complexity of the ECG waveform, the polynomial order of the PFIG is set as four. Table 3 shows the RMSE and SMAPE indexes of the various prediction methods.

Table 3. Comparison of the prediction indexes of ECG time series.

Index	Time (4 ms)	AR	NAR	SVR	LSTM	IFIG-FIS	TFIG-FIS	GFIG-FIS	LFIG-FIS	GPFIG-FIS
RMSE	4001–4025	87.91	22.74	41.06	26.83	7.33	7.43	7.7	7.2	7.96
	4026–4050	99.24	40.4	48.48	22.58	**8.61**	10.67	13.03	12.01	11.84
	4051–4075	102.95	52.92	51	94.60	12.23	12.34	13.82	12.93	**12.1**
	4076–4100	102.58	67.47	50.23	85.65	12.68	12.85	14.2	12.27	**11.31**
	4101–4125	124.51	129.95	83.39	114.43	70.03	64.81	64.07	59.72	**30.74**
	4126–4150	131.99	164.89	93.48	130.28	107.32	80.48	76.25	65.06	**29.18**
	4151–4175	122.86	163.78	89.79	139.07	100.47	76.09	72.11	60.88	**28.41**
	4176–4200	127.1	154.01	111.27	157.61	95.37	73.1	69.92	60.01	**28.8**
	4201–4225	121.25	160.38	105.42	149.67	93.44	69.98	66.71	56.75	**27.4**
	4226–4250	117.79	169.45	100.35	142.36	88.9	66.46	63.34	53.9	**26.14**
SMAPE	4001–4025	95.44	22.32	45.72	28.70	6.48	6.75	6.36	**6.31**	7.43
	4026–4050	106.77	39.06	52.28	22.25	**7.59**	9.55	11.5	10.69	10.63
	4051–4075	111.88	52.56	55.11	59.09	**10.77**	11.42	12.75	11.87	11.2
	4076–4100	113.48	67.23	54.62	56.81	11.84	12.38	13.52	11.25	**10.38**
	4101–4125	114.54	91.74	60.64	66.26	25.84	23.55	24.93	27.62	**19.71**
	4126–4150	113.47	127.12	56.93	81.95	70.16	26.25	32.58	33.95	**19.31**
	4151–4175	106.49	164.82	67.18	150.81	71.01	31.95	37.2	35.64	**23.8**
	4176–4200	109.68	149.17	81.82	160.37	67.17	32.85	37.63	36.3	**24.15**
	4201–4225	107.33	174.87	79.45	152.83	73.07	37.05	40.11	35.21	**23.45**
	4226–4250	107.68	190.28	74.94	141.83	68.52	34.43	36.93	32.6	**22.05**

Note: A value in bold font indicates that the corresponding method achieves the best result among all the methods.

For brevity, Figure 14 shows the predicted values of several prediction methods with better results. It can be found from Figure 14 and Table 3 that, compared with numerical prediction methods, the prediction methods based on the FIG and FIS have better prediction results.

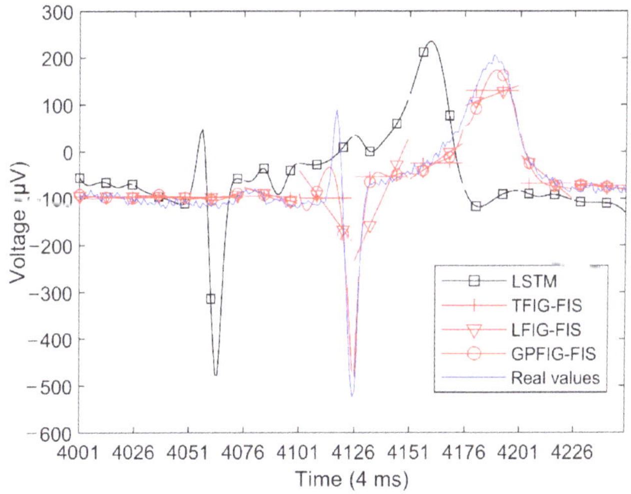

Figure 14. Electrocardiogram prediction results.

The changing trends of the ECG time series are more complex than previous experiments. As is shown in Figure 14, this time series is very stable in the first four time windows, and then there are sharp fluctuations from the fifth time window. Correspondingly, in the first four time windows, the RSME and SMAPE indexes of the GPFIG-FIS are almost the same with those of the other FIS-based methods. However, from the fifth time window, the predictive indexes of the GPFIG-FIS are significantly better than the other prediction methods. The main reason for this result is that GPFIG can accurately describe the changing trends in the ECG data through its high-order polynomial center line. In summary, for the ECG time series with complex changing trends, the GPFIG-FIS method can obtain better long-term prediction results.

6. Summary

The PFIGs can accurately describe the key time-varying nonlinear trends of the time series, and thus are a suitable type of FIGs in granulating a time series. A PFIG has three parameters, namely the length of the time window, the centerline of the adjustable order polynomial, and the degree of the data deviation, which have a good interpretability and are easy to understand.

The distance metric of PFIGs is derived theoretically. It shows that the distance of two Gaussian PFIGs can be reasonably interpreted as the sum of the area between their central polynomial lines, and the difference in their data deviation degrees, which has a good geometric meaning.

This paper also designs a fuzzy inference prediction method based on the GPFIG and their distance metric to verify the effectiveness of the proposed GPFIG. The experiments show that for those time series with pseudo periods, the proposed GPFIG-FIS method can achieve better prediction results compared with some numerical prediction methods such as the AR, NAR, SVR and LSTM, and some fuzzy inference methods based on other types of FIG. This conclusion shows that the proposed GPFIG has a good practicability.

The PFIG time series constructed in this paper is composed of several PFIGs of an equal granularity. A question associated with the granulation method in this paper is how to choose the optimal granularity of these PFIGs. Without sufficient periodic knowledge of the time series to be transformed in advance, it may be difficult to determine the best granularity.

A further generalization of the PFIG can improve the ability of the granular time series in representing the complicated time series. How to use this new PFIG to deal with a real-world prediction problem may be a subject of future research.

Author Contributions: Conceptualization, X.Y. and F.Y.; methodology, X.Y.; software, X.Y. and S.Z.; validation, X.Z. and S.Z.; formal analysis, X.Y. and S.Z.; investigation, X.Y. and F.Y.; resources, X.Y. and S.Z.; data curation, X.Y.; writing—original draft preparation, X.Y. and S.Z.; writing—review and editing, X.Y. and F.Y.; visualization, X.Y.; supervision, F.Y.; project administration, F.Y.; funding acquisition, X.Y. and F.Y. All authors have read and agreed to the published version of the manuscript.

Funding: This research is supported by the National Natural Science Foundation of China (11971065), the Science and Technology Program of Quanzhou (No.2021CT0010), the Fujian Natural Science Foundation Project (2021J01001, 2022N002S), and Fujian Key Laboratory of Financial Information Processing (Putian University).

Data Availability Statement: Not applicable.

Acknowledgments: The authors would like to acknowledge the support by Fujian Provincial Key Laboratory of Data-Intensive Computing, Fujian University Laboratory of Intelligent Computing and Information Processing, Fujian Provincial Big Data Research Institute of Intelligent Manufacturing.

Conflicts of Interest: The authors declare no conflict of interest.

References

1. Zhang, H.; Nguyen, H.; Bui, X.-N.; Biswajeet, P.; Mai, N.-L.; Vu, D.A. Proposing two novel hybrid intelligence models for forecasting copper price based on extreme learning machine and meta-heuristic algorithms. *Resour. Policy* **2021**, *73*, 102195. [CrossRef]
2. Wang, H.; Luo, C.; Wang, X. Synchronization and identification of nonlinear systems by using a novel self-evolving interval type-2 fuzzy LSTM-neural network. *Eng. Appl. Artif. Intell.* **2019**, *81*, 79–93. [CrossRef]
3. Jiang, P.; Yang, H.; Li, H.; Wang, Y. A developed hybrid forecasting system for energy consumption structure forecasting based on fuzzy time series and information granularity. *Energy* **2021**, *219*, 119599. [CrossRef]

4. Box, G.; Jenkins, G.; Reinsel, G. *Forecasting and Control*, 4th ed.; Time Series Analysis; John Wiley & Sons: New York, NY, USA, 2008.
5. Moon, J.; Hossain, M.B.; Chon, K. AR and ARMA model order selection for time-series modeling with ImageNet classification. *Signal Process.* **2021**, *183*, 108026. [CrossRef]
6. Xian, H.; Che, J. Unified whale optimization algorithm based multi-kernel SVR ensemble learning for wind speed forecasting. *Appl. Soft Comput.* **2022**, *130*, 109690. [CrossRef]
7. Yoon, H.; Hyun, Y.; Ha, K.; Lee, K.-K.; Kim, G.-B. A method to improve the stability and accuracy of ANN- and SVM-based time series models for long-term groundwater level predictions. *Comput. Geosci.* **2016**, *90*, 144–155. [CrossRef]
8. Sunayana; Kumar, S.; Kumar, R. Forecasting of municipal solid waste generation using non-linear autoregressive (NAR) neural models. *Waste Manag.* **2021**, *121*, 206–214. [CrossRef] [PubMed]
9. Bandara, K.; Bergmeir, C.; Smyl, S. Forecasting across time series databases using recurrent neural networks on groups of similar series: A clustering approach. *Expert Syst. Appl.* **2020**, *140*, 112896. [CrossRef]
10. Arsov, M.; Zdravevski, E.; Lameski, P.; Corizzo, R.; Koteli, N.; Gramatikov, S.; Mitreski, K.; Trajkovik, V. Multi-Horizon Air Pollution Forecasting with Deep Neural Networks. *Sensors* **2021**, *21*, 1235. [CrossRef]
11. Livieris, I.E.; Pintelas, E.; Pintelas, P. A CNN–LSTM model for gold price time-series forecasting. *Neural Comput. Appl.* **2020**, *32*, 17351–17360. [CrossRef]
12. Jin, X.; Yu, X.; Wang, X.; Bai, Y.; Su, T.; Kong, J. Prediction for Time Series with CNN and LSTM. In Proceedings of the 11th International Conference on Modelling, Identification and Control (ICMIC2019), Tianjin, China, 4 December 2019; Wang, R., Chen, Z., Zhang, W., Zhu, Q., Eds.; Springer: Singapore, 2020; p. 59.
13. Jilani, T.A.; Burney, S.M.A. M-factor high order fuzzy time series forecasting for road accident data: Analysis and design of intelligent systems using soft computing techniques. *Adv. Soft Comput.* **2007**, *41*, 246–254.
14. Wang, L.; Xue, T.; Wang, H.; Liu, Z. Research on stock index forecasting based on recurrent neural network. *J. Zhejiang Univ. Technol.* **2019**, *47*, 186–191.
15. Wang, X.; Wu, J.; Liu, C.; Yang, H.; Niu, W. Exploring LSTM based recurrent neural network for failure time series prediction. *J. Beijing Univ. Aeronaut. Astronaut.* **2018**, *44*, 772–784.
16. Tang, Y.; Yu, F.; Pedrycz, W.; Yang, X.; Wang, J.; Liu, S. Building trend fuzzy granulation based LSTM recurrent neural network for long-term time series forecasting. *IEEE Trans. Fuzzy Syst.* **2022**, *30*, 1599–1613. [CrossRef]
17. Cheng, R.; Yu, J.; Zhang, M.; Feng, C.; Zhang, W. Short-term hybrid forecasting model of ice storage air-conditioning based on improved SVR. *J. Build. Eng.* **2022**, *50*, 104194. [CrossRef]
18. Keogh, E.; Kasetty, S. On the need for time series data mining benchmarks: A survey and empirical demonstration. *Data Min. Knowl. Discov.* **2002**, *7*, 102–111.
19. Zadeh, L. *Advances in Fuzzy Set Theory and Applications*; World Scientific Publishing: Amsterdam, The Netherlands, 1979; pp. 3–18.
20. Pedrycz, W.; Vukovich, G. Abstraction and specialization of information granules. *IEEE Trans. Syst. Man Cybern. Part B* **2001**, *31*, 106–111. [CrossRef]
21. Guo, J.; Lu, W.; Yang, J.; Liu, X. A rule-based granular model development for interval-valued time series. *Int. J. Approx. Reason.* **2021**, *136*, 201–222. [CrossRef]
22. Ruan, J.; Wang, X.; Shi, Y. Developing fast predictors for large-scale time series using fuzzy granular support vector machines. *Appl. Soft Comput.* **2013**, *13*, 3981–4000. [CrossRef]
23. Zhou, Y.; Ren, H.; Li, Z.; Pedrycz, W. Anomaly detection based on a granular Markov model. *Expert Syst. Appl.* **2022**, *187*, 115744. [CrossRef]
24. He, L.; Chen, Y.; Zhong, C.; Wu, K. Granular Elastic Network Regression with Stochastic Gradient Descent. *Mathematics* **2022**, *10*, 2628. [CrossRef]
25. Hu, M.; Wang, C.; Yang, J.; Wu, Y.; Fan, J.; Jing, B. Rain Rendering and Construction of Rain Vehicle Color-24 Dataset. *Mathematics* **2022**, *10*, 3210. [CrossRef]
26. Yu, F.; Pedrycz, W. The design of fuzzy information granules: Tradeoffs between specificity and experimental evidence. *Appl. Soft Comput.* **2009**, *9*, 264–273. [CrossRef]
27. Pedrycz, W.; Wang, X. Designing fuzzy sets with the use of the parametric principle of justifiable granularity. *IEEE Trans. Fuzzy Syst.* **2016**, *24*, 489–496. [CrossRef]
28. Dong, K. *Time Series Information Granulation and Clustering Analysis Based on Granulation*; Beijing Normal University: Beijing, China, 2005.
29. Yang, X.; Yu, F.; Pedrycz, W. Long-term forecasting of time series based on linear fuzzy information granules and fuzzy inference system. *Int. J. Approx. Reason.* **2017**, *81*, 1–27. [CrossRef]
30. Luo, C.; Song, X.; Zheng, Y. A novel forecasting model for the long-term fluctuation of time series based on polar fuzzy information granules. *Inf. Sci.* **2020**, *512*, 760–779. [CrossRef]
31. Luo, C.; Wang, H. Fuzzy forecasting for long-term time series based on time-variant fuzzy information granules. *Appl. Soft Comput.* **2020**, *88*, 106046. [CrossRef]
32. Tang, Y.; Yu, F. Fuzzy information granulation: Review of theory and applications. *J. Beijing Norm. Univ.* **2022**, *58*, 349–361.
33. Zadeh, L.A. Fuzzy sets. *Inf. Control* **1965**, *8*, 338–353. [CrossRef]
34. Shen, Y. Calculus for linearly correlated fuzzy number-valued functions. *Fuzzy Sets Syst.* **2022**, *429*, 101–135. [CrossRef]

35. Rote, G. Computing the minimum Hausdorff distance between two point sets on a line under translation. *Inf. Process. Lett.* **1991**, *38*, 123–127. [CrossRef]
36. Dubois, D.; Prade, H. *Fundamentals of Fuzzy Sets*; Springer: New York, NY, USA, 2000; p. 90.
37. Yu, F.; Dong, K.; Chen, F.; Jiang, Y.; Zeng, W. Clustering Time Series with Granular Dynamic Time Warping Method. In Proceedings of the Clustering Time Series with Granular Dynamic Time Warping Method, Fremont, CA, USA, 2–4 November 2007; p. 393.
38. Luo, C.; Yu, F.; Zeng, W. *Introduction to Fuzzy Sets*; Beijing Normal University Press: Beijing, China, 2019.
39. Fan, R.; Chang, K.; Hsieh, C.; Wang, X.R.; Lin, C.J. LIBLINEAR: A library for large linear classification. *J. Mach. Learn. Res.* **2008**, *9*, 1871–1874.

mathematics

MDPI

Article

A Comparison of Several AI Techniques for Authorship Attribution on Romanian Texts

Sanda-Maria Avram [1,*] and Mihai Oltean [2]

[1] Faculty of Mathematics and Computer Science, Babeș-Bolyai University, 400084 Cluj-Napoca, Romania
[2] Independent Researcher, 515600 Cugir, Romania
* Correspondence: sanda.avram@ubbcluj.ro

Abstract: Determining the author of a text is a difficult task. Here, we compare multiple Artificial Intelligence techniques for classifying literary texts written by multiple authors by taking into account a limited number of speech parts (prepositions, adverbs, and conjunctions). We also introduce a new dataset composed of texts written in the Romanian language on which we have run the algorithms. The compared methods are artificial neural networks, multi-expression programming, k-nearest neighbour, support vector machines, and decision trees with C5.0. Numerical experiments show, first of all, that the problem is difficult, but some algorithms are able to generate acceptable error rates on the test set.

Keywords: authorship attribution; artificial neural networks; multi-expression programming; k-nearest neighbour; support vector machines; decision trees

MSC: 03B65; 62H30; 68T01; 68T05; 68T07; 68T10; 68T20; 68T30; 68T50; 91F20

Citation: Avram, S.-M.; Oltean, M. A Comparison of Several AI Techniques for Authorship Attribution on Romanian Texts. *Mathematics* **2022**, *10*, 4589. https://doi.org/10.3390/math10234589

Academic Editor: Zhao Kang

Received: 9 November 2022
Accepted: 30 November 2022
Published: 3 December 2022

1. Introduction

Automated authorship attribution (AA) is defined in [1] as the task of determining authorship of an unknown text based on the textual characteristics of the text itself. Today the AA is useful in a plethora of fields: from the educational and research domain to detect plagiarism [2] to the justice domain to analyze evidence on forensic cases [3] and cyberbullying [4], to the social media [5,6] to detect compromised accounts [7].

Most approaches in the area of artificial intelligence treat the AA problem by using simple classifiers (e.g., linear SVM or decision tree) that have bag-of-words (character n-grams) as features or other conventional feature sets [8,9]. Although deep neural learning was already used for natural language processing (NLP), the adoption of such strategies for authorship identification occurred later. In recent years, pre-trained language models (such as BERT and GPT-2) have been used for finetuning and accuracy improvements [8,10,11].

The challenges in solving the AA problem can be grouped into three main groups [8]:

1. The lack of large-scale datasets;
2. The lack of methodological diversity;
3. The ad hoc nature of authorship.

The availability of large-scale datasets has improved in recent years as large datasets have become widespread [12,13]. Other issues that relate to the datasets are the language in which the texts are written, the domain, the topic, and the writing environment. Each of these aspects has its own particularities. From the language perspective, the issue is that most available datasets consist of texts written in English. There is PAN18 [9] for English, French, Italian, Polish, and Spanish; or PAN19 [14] for English, French, Italian, and Spanish. However, there are not very many datasets for other languages and this is crucial as there are particularities that pertain to the language [15].

The methodological diversity has also improved in recent years, as it is detailed in [8]. However, the ad hoc nature of authorship is a more difficult issue, as a set of features that differentiates one author from the rest may not work for another author due to the individuality aspect of different writing styles. Even for one author, the writing style can evolve or change over a period of time, or it can differ depending on the context (e.g., the domain, the topic, or the writing environment). Thus, modeling the authorial writing style has to be carefully considered and needs to be tailored to a specific set of authors [8]. Therefore, selecting a distinguishing set of features is a challenging task.

We propose a new dataset named ROST (ROmanian Stories and other Texts) as there are few available datasets that contain texts written in Romanian [16]. The existing datasets are small, on obscure domains, or translated from other languages. Our dataset consists of 400 texts written by 10 authors. We have elements that pertain to the intended heterogeneity of the dataset such as:

- Different text types: stories, short stories, fairy tales, novels, articles, and sketches;
- Different number of texts per author: ranging from 27 to 60;
- Different sources: texts are collected from 4 different websites;
- Different text lengths: ranging from 91 to 39,195 words per text;
- Different periods: the time period in which the considered texts were written spans over 3 centuries, which introduces diachronic developments;
- Different mediums: texts were written with the intention of being read from paper medium (most of the considered authors) to online (two contemporary authors). This aspect considerably changes the writing style, as shorter sentences and shorter words are used online, and they also contain more adjectives and pronouns [17].

As our set is heterogeneous (as described above) from multiple perspectives, the authorship attribution is even more difficult. We investigate this classification problem by using five different techniques from the artificial intelligence area:

1. Artificial neural networks (ANN);
2. Multi-expression programming (MEP);
3. K-nearest neighbor (k-NN);
4. Support vector machine (SVM);
5. Decision trees (DT) with C5.0.

For each of these methods, we investigate different scenarios by varying the number and the type of some features to determine the context in which they obtain the best results. The aim of our investigations is twofold. On one side, the result of this investigation is to determine which method performs best while working on the same data. On another side, we try to find out the proper number and type of features that best classify the authors on this specific dataset.

The paper is organized as follows:

- Section 2 describes the AA state of the art by using methods from artificial intelligence; details the entire prerequisite process to be considered before applying the specific AI algorithms (highlighting possible "stylometric features" to be considered); provides a table with some available datasets; presents a number of AA methods already proposed; describes the steps of the attribution process; presents an overview and a comparison of AA state-of-the-art methods.
- Section 3 details the specific particularities (e.g., in terms of size, sources, time frames, types of writing, and writing environments) of the database we are proposing and we are going to use, and the building and scaling/pruning process of the feature set.
- Section 4 introduces the five methods we are going to use in our investigation.
- Section 5 presents the results and interprets them, making a comparison between the five methods and the different sets of features used; measures the results by using metrics that allow a comparison with the results of other state-of-the-art methods.
- Section 6 concludes with final remarks on the work and provides future possible directions and investigations.

2. Related Work

The AA detection can be modeled as a classification problem. The starting premise is that each author has a stylistic and linguistic "fingerprint" in their work [18]. Therefore, in the realm of AI, this means extracting a set of characteristics, which can be identified in a large-enough writing sample [8].

2.1. Features

Stylometric features are the characteristics that define an author's style. They can be quantified, learned [19], and classified into five groups [20]:

1. Lexical (the text is viewed as a sequence of tokens grouped into sentences, with each token corresponding to a word, number, or punctuation mark):
    - Token-based (e.g., word length, sentence length, etc.);
    - Vocabulary richness (i.e., attempts to quantify the vocabulary diversity of a text);
    - Word frequencies (e.g., the traditional "bag-of-words" representation [21] in which texts become vectors of word frequencies disregarding contextual information, i.e., the word order);
    - Word n-grams (i.e., sequences of n contiguous words also known as *word collocations*);
    - Errors (i.e., intended to capture the idiosyncrasies of an author's style) (requires orthographic spell checker).
2. Character (the text is viewed as a sequence of characters):
    - Character types (e.g., letters, digits, etc.) (requires character dictionary);
    - Character n-grams (i.e., considers all sequences of n consecutive characters in the texts; n can have a variable or fixed length);
    - Compression methods (i.e., the use of a compression model acquired from one text to compress another text; compression models are usually based on repetitions of character sequences).
3. Syntactic (text-representation which considers syntactic information):
    - Part-of-speech (POS) (requires POS tagger—a tool that assigns a tag of morpho-syntactic information to each word-token based on contextual information);
    - Chunks (i.e., phrases);
    - Sentence and phrase structure (i.e., a parse tree of each sentence is produced);
    - Rewrite rules frequencies (these rules express part of the syntactic analysis, helping to determine the syntactic class of each word as the same word can have different syntactic values based on different contexts);
    - Errors (e.g., sentence fragments, run-on sentences, mismatched use of tenses) (requires syntactic spell checker).
4. Semantic (text-representation which considers semantic information):
    - Synonyms (requires thesaurus);
    - Semantic dependencies.
5. Application-specific (the text is viewed from an application-specific perspective to better represent the nuances of style in a given domain):
    - Functional (requires specialized dictionaries);
    - Structural (e.g., the use of greetings and farewells in messages, types of signatures, use of indentation, and paragraph length);
    - Content-specific (e.g., content-specific keywords);
    - Language-specific.

The lexical and character features are simpler because they view the text as a sequence of word-tokens or characters, not requiring any linguistic analysis, in contrast with the syntactic and semantic characteristics, which do. The application-specific characteristics are restricted to certain text domains or languages.

A simple and successful feature selection, based on lexical characteristics, is made by using the top of the N most frequent words from a corpus containing texts of the candidate author. Determining the best value of N was the focus of numerous studies, starting from 100 [22], and reaching 1000 [23], or even all words that appear at least twice in the corpus [24]. It was observed, that depending on the value of N, different types of words (in terms of content specificity) make up the majority. Therefore, when the size of N falls within dozens, the most frequent words of a corpus are closed-class words (i.e., articles, prepositions, etc.), while when N exceeds a few hundred words, open-class words (i.e., nouns, adjectives, verbs) are the majority [20].

Even though the word n-grams approach comes as a solution to keeping the contextual information, i.e., the word order, which is lost in the word frequencies (or "bag-of-words") approach, the classification accuracy is not always better [25,26].

The main advantage of character feature selection is that they pertain to any natural language and corpus. Furthermore, even the simplest in this category (i.e., character types) proved to be useful to quantify the writing style [27].

The character n-grams have the advantages of capturing the nuances of style and being tolerant to noise (e.g., grammatical errors or making strange use of punctuation), and the disadvantage is that they capture redundant information [20].

The syntactic feature selection requires the use of Natural Language Processing (NLP) tools to perform a syntactic analysis of texts, and they are language-dependent. Additionally, being a method that requires complex text processing, noisy datasets may be produced due to unavoidable errors made by the parser [20].

For semantic feature selection an even more detailed text analysis is required for extracting stylometric features. Thus, the measures produced may be less accurate as more noise may be introduced while processing the text. NLP tools are used here for sentence splitting, POS tagging, text chunking, and partial parsing. However, complex tasks, such as full syntactic parsing, semantic analysis, and pragmatic analysis, are hard to be achieved for an unrestricted text [20].

A comprehensive survey of the state of the art in stylometry is conducted in [28].

The most common approach used in AA is to extract features that have a high discriminatory potential [29]. There are multiple aspects that have to be considered in AA for selecting the appropriate set of features. Some of them are the language, the literary style (e.g., poetry, prose), the topic addressed by the text (e.g., sports, politics, storytelling), the length of the text (e.g., novels, tweets), the number of text samples, and the number of considered features. For instance, lexical and character features, although more simple, can considerably increase the dimensionality of the feature set [20]. Therefore, feature selection algorithms can be applied to reduce the dimensionality of such feature sets [30]. This also helps the classification algorithm to avoid overfitting on the training data.

Another prerequisite for the training phase is deciding whether the training texts are processed individually or cumulatively (per author). From this perspective, the following two approaches can be distinguished [20]:

1. *Instance-based approach* (i.e., each training text is individually represented as a separate instance in the training process to create a reliable attribution model);
2. *Profile-based approach* (i.e., a cumulative representation of an author's style, also known as the author's profile, is extracted by concatenating all available training texts of one author into one large file to flatten differences between texts).

Efstathios Stamatatos offers in [20] a comparison between the two aforementioned approaches.

2.2. Datasets

In Table 1, we present a list of datasets used in AA investigations.

There is a large variation between the datasets. In terms of language, there are usually datasets with texts that are written in one language, and there are a few that have texts written in multiple languages. However, most of the available datasets contain texts written in English.

The *Size* column is generally the number of texts and authors that have been used in AA investigations. For example, PAN11 and PAN12 have thousands of texts and hundreds of authors. However, in the referenced paper, only a few were used. The datasets vary in the number of texts from hundreds to hundreds of thousands, and in terms of the number of authors, from tens to tens of thousands.

Table 1. Datasets used for author attribution detection; *Author(s)* are names of individuals who created the dataset (for a group consisting of more than two, only the name of the first person is provided in the list, followed by "et al."); *Paper* is the first paper that introduced that dataset or that is recommended by its creator(s) to be used for citing the dataset; *Language* is the language in which the texts in the database were written; *Size* is the dimension of the dataset; *Features* stands for the types of features that can be or were used on that specific dataset (however, the information here is only indicative and should not be taken literally); *No. of features*, is also more an indicative value for possible feature set dimensions; *Name or link* provides the name by which that specific dataset is known and, when available, links are provided.

Author(s)	Paper	Language	Size	Features	No. of Features	Name or Link
Sanda-Maria Avram	this paper	Romanian	400 texts; 10 authors	conjunctions, prepositions, and adverbs	$27 + 85 + 670 = 782$	ROST
Shlomo Argamon and Patrick Juola	[31]	English	42 literary texts and novels; 14 authors	words, characters, n-grams	>3000	PAN11 https://pan.webis.de/data.html#pan12-attribution [32]
Patrick Juola	[33]	English	42 literary texts and novels; 14 authors	words, characters, n-grams	>3000	PAN12 https://pan.webis.de/data.html#pan12-attribution
Mike Kestemont et al.	[9]	English, French, Italian, Polish, Spanish.	2000 fanfiction texts; 20 authors	char n-gram, word n-gram, stylistic, tokens	>500	PAN18 https://pan.webis.de/data.html#pan18-authorship-attribution [34]
Mike Kestemont et al.	[35]	English, French, Italian, Spanish.	2997 cross-topic fanfiction texts; 36 authors	char n-gram, word n-gram, tokens	>300	PAN19 https://pan.webis.de/data.html#pan19-authorship-attribution [14]
Mike Kestemont et al.	[8]	English	443,000 cross-topic fanfiction texts; 278,000 authors	char n-gram, word n-gram, tokens	>300	PAN20 https://pan.webis.de/data.html#pan20-authorship-verification [36]
Daniel Pavelec et al.	[37]	Portuguese	600 articles; 20 authors	conjunctions and adverbs	$77 + 94 = 171$	–
Paulo Varela et al.	[38]	Portuguese	600 articles; 20 authors	conjunctions, adverbs, verbs and pronouns	$77 + 94 + 50 + 91 = 312$	–
Yanir Seroussi et al.	[39]	English	1342 legal documents; 3 authors	unigrams, n-grams	>2000	Judgment
Yanir Seroussi et al.	[40]	English	79,550 movie reviews; 62 authors	unigrams, n-grams	>200	IMDb62

Table 1. *Cont.*

Author(s)	Paper	Language	Size	Features	No. of Features	Name or Link
Yanir Seroussi et al.	[41]	English	204,809 posts, 66,816 reviews; 22,116 users	unigrams, n-grams	>1000	IMDB1M
Efstathios Stamatatos	[42]	English	5000 newswire documents; 50 authors	unigrams, n-grams	>500	CCAT50
Efstathios Stamatatos	[43]	English	444 articles, book reviews; 13 authors	words, characters, 3-grams	>10,000	Guardian10
Efstathios Stamatatos		English	1000 CCTA industry news; 10 authors	words, characters, 3-grams	>500	C10 https://pan.webis.de/data.html#c10-attribution
Efstathios Stamatatos		English	5000 CCTA industry news; 50 authors	words, characters, n-grams	>500	C50 https://pan.webis.de/data.html#c50-attribution
Jonathan Schler et al.	[44]	English	over 600,000 posts; 19,000 bloggers	tokens, n-grams	>200	Blogs50 https://www.kaggle.com/datasets/rtatman/blog-authorship-corpus
Jade Goldstein et al.	[45]	English	756 documents; 21 authors	tokens, n-grams	> 600	CMCC
Project Gutenberg		English	29,000 books; 4500 authors	tokens, n-grams	>60,000	Gutenberg https://www.gutenberg.org/

2.3. Strategies

According to [46], the entire process of text classification occurs in 6 stages:

1. Data acquisition (from one or multiple sources);
2. Data analysis and labeling;
3. Feature construction and weighting;
4. Feature selection and projection;
5. Training of a classification model;
6. Solution evaluation.

The classification process initiates with data acquisition, which is used to create the dataset. There are two strategies for the analysis and labeling of the dataset [46]: labeling groups of texts (also called *multi-instance learning*) [47], or assigning a label or labels to each text part (by using supervised methods) [48]. To yield the appropriate data representation required by the selected learning method, first, the features are selected and weighted [46] according to the obtained labeled dataset. Then, the number of features is reduced by selecting only the most important features and projected onto a lower dimensionality. There are two different representations of textual data: *vector space representation* [49] where the document is represented as a vector of feature weights, and *graph representation* [50] where the document is modeled as a graph (e.g., nodes represent words, whereas edges represent the relationships between the words). In the next stage, different learning approaches are used to train a classification model. Training algorithms can be grouped into different approaches [46]: *supervised* [48] (i.e., any machine learning process), *semi-supervised* [51] (also known as self-training, co-training, learning from the labeled and unlabeled data, or transductive learning), *ensemble* [52] (i.e., training multiple classifiers and considering them as a "committee" of decision-makers), *active* [53] (i.e., the training algorithm has some role in determining the data it will use for training), *transfer* [54] (i.e., the ability of a learning mechanism to improve the performance for a current task after having learned a different but related concept or skill from a previous task; also known as *inductive transfer* or *transfer of knowledge across domains*), or *multi-view learning* [55] (also known as *data fusion* or *data integration* from multiple feature sets, multiple feature spaces, or diversified feature spaces that may have different distributions of features).

By providing probabilities or weights, the trained classifier is then able to decide a class for each input vector. Finally, the classification process is evaluated. The performance of the classifier can be measured based on different indicators [46]: precision, recall, accuracy, F-score, specificity, area under the curve (AUC), and error rate. These all are related to the actual classification task. However, other performance-oriented indicators can also be considered, such as CPU time for training, CPU time for testing, and memory allocated to the classification model [56].

Aside from the aforementioned challenges, there are also other sets of issues that are currently being investigated. These are:

- Issues related to cross-domain, cross topic and/or cross-genre datasets;
- Issues related to the specificity of the used language;
- Issues regarding the style change of authors when the writing environment changes from offline to online;
- The balanced or imbalanced nature of datasets.

Some examples which focus on these types of issues, alongside their solutions and/or findings, are presented next.

Participants in the Identification Task at PAN-2018 [9], investigated two types of classifications. The corpus consists of fan-fiction texts written in English, French, Italian, Polish, and Spanish, and a set of questions and answers on several topics in English. First, they addressed the cross-domain AA, finding that heterogeneous ensembles of simple classifiers and compression models outperformed more sophisticated approaches based on deep learning. Also, the set size is inversely correlated with attribution accuracy, especially for cases when more than 10 authors are considered. Second, they investigated the detection of style changes, where single-author and multi-author texts were distinguished. Techniques ranging from machine learning ensembles to deep learning with a rich set of features have been used to detect style changes, achieving the accuracy of up to nearly 90% over the entire dataset and several reaching 100%.

The issue of cross-topic confusion is addressed in [57] for AA. This problem arises when the training topic differs from the test topic. In such a scenario, the types of errors caused by the topic can be distinguished from the errors caused by the detection of the writing style. The findings show that classification is least likely to be affected by topic variations when parts of speech are considered as features.

The analysis conducted in [58] aimed to determine which approach, such as topic or style, is better for AA. The findings showed that online news, which have a wide variety of topics, are better classified using content-based features, while texts with less topical variation (e.g., legal judgments and movie reviews) benefit from using style-based features.

In [59] it is shown that syntax (e.g., sentence structure) helps AA on cross-genre texts, while additional lexical information (e.g., parts of speech such as nouns, verbs, adjectives, and adverbs) helps to classify cross-topic and single-domain texts. It is also shown that syntax-only models may not be efficient.

Language-specific issues (e.g., the complexity and structure of sentences) are addressed in [15] in relation to the Arabic language. Ensemble methods were used to improve the effectiveness of the AA task.

The authors of [60] propose solutions to address the many issues in AA (e.g., cross-domain, language specificity, writing environment) by introducing the concept of *stacked classifiers*, which are built from words, characters, parts of speech n-grams, syntactic dependencies, word embeddings, and more. This solution proposes that these *stacked classifiers* are dynamically included in the AA model according to the input.

Two different AA approaches called "writer-dependent" and "writer-independent" were addressed in [37]. In the first approach, they used a Support Vector Machine (SVM) to build a model for each author. The second approach combined a feature-based description with the concept of dissimilarity to determine whether a text is written by a particular author or not, thereby reducing the problem to a two-class problem. The tests were performed on texts written in Portuguese. For the first approach, 77 conjunctions and 94 adverbs were used to determine the authorship and the best accuracy results on the test set composed of 200 documents from 20 different authors were 83.2%. For the second approach, the same set of documents and conjunctions was used, obtaining the best result of 75.1% accuracy. In [38], along with conjunctions and adverbs, 50 verbs and 91 pronouns were added to improve the results obtained previously, achieving a 4% improvement in both "writer-dependent" and "writer-independent" approaches.

The challenges of variations in authors' style when the writing environment changes from traditional to online are addressed in [17]. These investigations consider changes in sentence length, word usage, readability, and frequency use of some parts of speech. The findings show that shorter sentences and words, as well as more adjectives and pronouns, are used online.

The authors of [61] proposed a feature extraction solution for AA. They investigated trigrams, bags of words, and most frequent terms in both balanced and imbalanced samples and showed with 79.68% accuracy that an author's writing style can be identified by using a single document.

2.4. Comparison

AA is a very important and currently intensively researched topic. However, the multitude of approaches makes it very difficult to have a unified view of the state-of-the-art results. In [10], authors highlight this challenge by noting significant differences in:

- Datasets
  - In terms of size: small (CCAT50, CMCC, Guardian10), medium (IMDb62, Blogs50), and large (PAN20, Gutenberg);
  - In terms of content: cross-topic ($\times_t$), cross-genre ($\times_g$), unique authors;
  - In terms of imbalance (imb): i.e., standard deviation of the number of documents per author;
  - In terms of topic confusion (as detailed in [57]).
- Performance metrics
  - In terms of type: accuracy, F1, c@1, recall, precision, macro-accuracy, AUC, R@8, and others;
  - In terms of computation: even for the same performance metrics there were different ways of computing them.
- Methods
  - In terms of the feature extraction method,
    * Feature-based: n-gram, summary statistics, co-occurrence graphs;
    * Embedding-based: char embedding, word embedding, transformers
    * Feature and embedding-based: BERT.

The work presented in [10] tries to address and "resolve" these differences, bringing everything to a common denominator, even when that meant recreating some results. To differentiate between different methods, authors of [10] grouped the results in 4 classes:

- Ngram: includes character n-grams, parts-of-speech and summary statistics as shown in [57,62–64];
- PPM: uses Prediction by Partial Matching (PPM) compression model to build a character-based model for each author, with works presented in [28,65];

- BERT: combines a BERT pre-trained language model with a dense layer for classification, as in [66];
- pALM: the per-Author Language Model (pALM), also using BERT as described in [67].

The results of the state of the art as presented in [10] are shown in Table 2.

Table 2. State of the art *macro-accuracy* of authorship attribution models. Information collected from [10] (Tables 1 and 3). *Name* is the name of the dataset; *No. docs* represents the number of documents in that dataset; *No. auth* represents the number of authors; *Content* indicates whether the documents are cross-topic ($\times_t$) or cross-genre ($\times_g$); *W/D* stands for *words per document*, representing the average length of documents; *imb* represents the *imbalance* of the dataset measured by the standard deviation of the number of documents per author.

Dataset						*Macro-Accuracy* (%) for Investigation Type			
Name	No. Docs	No. Auth	Content	W/D	Imb	Ngram	PPM	BERT	pALM
CCAT50	5000	50	-	506	0	76.68	69.36	65.72	63.36
CMCC	756	21	$\times_t$ $\times_g$	601	0	86.51	62.30	60.32	54.76
Guardian10	444	13	$\times_t$ $\times_g$	1052	6.7	100	86.28	84.23	66.67
IMDb62	62,000	62	-	349	2.6	98.81	95.90	98.80	-
Blogs50	66,000	50	-	122	553	72.28	72.16	74.95	-
PAN20	443,000	278,000	$\times_t$	3922	2.3	43.52	-	23.83	-
Gutenburg	29,000	4500	-	66,350	10.5	57.69	-	59.11	-

As can be seen in Table 2, the methods in the Ngram class generally work best. However, BERT-class methods can perform better on large training sets that are not cross-topic and/or cross-genre. The authors of [10] state that from their investigations it can be inferred that Ngram-class methods are preferred for datasets that have less than 50,000 words per author, while BERT-class methods should be preferred for datasets with over 100,000 words per author.

3. Proposed Dataset

The texts considered are Romanian stories, short stories, fairy tales, novels, articles, and sketches.

There are 400 such texts of different lengths, ranging from 91 to 39,195 words. Table 3 presents the averages and standard deviations of the number of words, unique words, and the ratio of words to unique words for each author. There are differences up to almost 7000 words between the average word counts (e.g., between Slavici and Oltean). For unique words, the difference between averages goes up to more than 1300 unique words (e.g., between Eminescu and Oltean). Even the ratio of total words to unique words is a significant difference between the authors (e.g., between Slavici and Oltean).

Eminescu and Slavici, the two authors with the largest averages also have large standard deviations for the number of words and the number of unique words. This means that their texts range from very short to very long. Gârleanu and Oltean have the shortest texts, as their average number of words and unique words and the corresponding standard deviations are the smallest.

There is also a correlation between the three groups of values (pertaining to the words, unique words, and the ratio between the two) that is to be expected as a larger or smaller number of words would contain a similar proportion of unique words or the ratio of the two, while the standard deviations of the ratio of total words to unique words tend to be more similar. However, Slavici has a very high ratio, which means that there are texts in which he repeats the same words more often, and in other texts, he does not. There is also a difference between Slavici and Eminescu here because even if they have similar word count average and unique word count average, their ratio differs. Eminescu has a similar representation in terms of ratio and standard deviation with his lifelong friend Creangă, which can mean that both may have similar tendencies in reusing words.

Table 3. Diversity of the considered dataset in terms of the length of the texts (i.e., number of words). *Author* is the author's name (the last name is in bold); *Average* is the mean number of words per text written by the corresponding author; *StdDev* is the standard deviation; *Average-Unique* is the mean number of unique words; *StdDev-Unique* is the standard deviation on unique words; *Average-Ratio* is the mean number of the ratio of total words to unique words; *StdDev-Ratio* is the standard deviation of the ratio of total words to unique words.

Author	Average	StdDev	Average-Unique	StdDev-Unique	Average-Ratio	StdDev-Ratio
Ion **Creangă**	3679.34	3633.42	1061.90	719.38	3.01	0.94
Barbu Ştefănescu **Delavrancea**	4166.39	3702.33	1421.34	948.41	2.66	0.58
Mihai **Eminescu**	5854.52	7858.89	1656.96	1716.08	2.92	0.87
Nicolae **Filimon**	2734.32	2589.72	1040.09	729.81	2.42	0.50
Emil **Gârleanu**	843.05	721.06	411.19	234.71	1.88	0.32
Petre **Ispirescu**	3302.80	1531.36	1017.73	340.37	3.10	0.49
Mihai **Oltean**	553.75	484.00	282.56	201.18	1.79	0.31
Emilia **Plugaru**	2253.88	2667.38	756.70	581.88	2.54	0.64
Liviu **Rebreanu**	2284.12	1971.88	889.70	550.92	2.36	0.44
Ioan **Slavici**	7531.54	8969.77	1520.42	1041.40	3.96	1.62

Table 4 shows the averages of the number of features that are contained in the texts corresponding to each author. The pattern depicted here is similar to that in Table 3, which is to be expected. However, standard deviations tend to be similar for all authors. These standard deviations are considerable in size, being on average as follows:

- 4.16 on the set of 56 features (i.e., the list of prepositions),
- 23.88 on the set of 415 features (i.e., the list of prepositions and adverbs),
- 25.38 on the set of 432 features (i.e., the list of prepositions, adverbs, and conjunctions).

This means that the frequency of feature occurrence differs even in the texts written by the same author.

Table 4. Diversity of the considered dataset in terms of the number of occurrences of the considered features in the texts. *Author* is the author's name (the last name is in bold); *Average-P* is the average number of the occurrence of the considered prepositions in the texts corresponding to each author; *StdDev-P* is the standard deviation for the occurrence of the prepositions; *Average-PA* is the average number of the occurrence of the considered prepositions and adverbs; *StdDev-PA* is the standard deviation of the number of the occurrence of the considered prepositions and adverbs; *Average-PAC* is the average number of the occurrence of the considered prepositions, adverbs, and conjunctions; *StdDev-PAC* is the standard deviation of the number of the occurrence of the considered prepositions, adverbs, and conjunctions.

Author	Average-P	StdDev-P	Average-PA	StdDev-PA	Average-PAC	StdDev-PAC
Ion **Creangă**	19.90	4.94	79.21	30.11	88.34	31.86
Barbu Ştefănescu **Delavrancea**	19.14	3.67	73.43	27.79	81.82	29.81
Mihai **Eminescu**	21.85	7.18	80.04	34.11	90.04	36.22
Nicolae **Filimon**	18.26	3.52	61.94	18.12	70.50	19.25
Emil **Gârleanu**	14.65	3.01	48.12	16.11	53.21	17.19
Petre **Ispirescu**	19.93	3.14	79.60	17.32	89.63	18.52
Mihai **Oltean**	11.88	3.82	33.16	17.51	37.69	18.96
Emilia **Plugaru**	16.13	3.61	69.83	22.62	77.48	23.58
Liviu **Rebreanu**	17.25	4.07	73.88	25.65	82.62	27.37
Ioan **Slavici**	21.29	4.72	96.08	29.48	105.87	31.09

The considered texts are collected from 4 websites and are written by 10 different authors, as shown in Table 5. The diversity of sources is relevant from a twofold perspective. First, especially for old texts, it is difficult to find or determine which is the original version.

Second, there may be differences between versions of the same text either because some words are no longer used or have changed their meaning, or because fragments of the text may be added or subtracted. For some authors, texts are sourced from multiple websites.

Table 5. List of authors (the author's last name is in bold), the number of texts considered for each author (total number is in bold), and their source (i.e., the website from which they were collected).

Author	No. of Texts	https://www.povesti.org	https://povesti-ro.weebly.com/	https://ro.wikisource.org/wiki/	https://www.povesti-pentru-copii.com/
Ion **Creangă**	**28**			4	24
Barbu Ştefănescu **Delavrancea**	**44**		2	28	14
Mihai **Eminescu**	**27**			21	6
Nicolae **Filimon**	**34**			31	3
Emil **Gârleanu**	**43**		34	9	
Petre **Ispirescu**	**40**		2	1	37
Mihai **Oltean**	**32**	32			
Emilia **Plugaru**	**40**				40
Liviu **Rebreanu**	**60**			60	
Ioan **Slavici**	**52**		3	39	10
TOTAL	**400**	32	41	193	134

The diversity of the texts is intentional because we wanted to emulate a more likely scenario where all these characteristics might not be controlled. This is because, for future texts to be tested on the trained models, the text length, the source, and the type of writing cannot be controlled or imposed.

To highlight the differences between the time frames of the periods in which the authors lived and wrote the considered texts, as well as the environment from which the texts were intended to be read, we gathered the information presented in Table 6. It can be seen that the considered texts were written in the time span of three centuries. This also brings an increased diversity between texts, since within such a large time span there have been significant developments in terms of language (e.g., diachronic developments), writing style relating to the desired reading medium (e.g., paper or online), topics (e.g., general concerns and concerns that relate to a particular time), and viewpoints (e.g., a particular worldview).

Table 6. List of authors, time spans of the periods in which the authors lived and wrote the considered texts and the medium from which the readers read their texts. *Author* is the author's name (the last name is in bold); *Life* is the lifetime of the author; *Publication* is the publication interval of the texts (note: the information presented here was not always easily accessible and some sources would contradict in terms of specific years, however, this information should be considered more as an indicative coordinate and should not be taken literally, the goal being that the literary texts be temporally framed in order to have a perspective on the period in which they were written/published); *Century* is a coarser temporal framing of the periods in which the texts were written; *Medium* is the environment from which most of the readers read the author's texts.

#	Author	Life	Publication	Century	Medium
0	Ion **Creangă**	1837–1889	1874–1898	19th	paper
1	Barbu Ştefănescu **Delavrancea**	1858–1918	1884–1909	19th–20th	paper
2	Mihai **Eminescu**	1850–1889	1872–1865	19th	paper
3	Nicolae **Filimon**	1819–1865	1857–1863	19th	paper
4	Emil **Gârleanu**	1878–1914	1907–1915	20th	paper
5	Petre **Ispirescu**	1830–1887	1882–1883	19th	paper
6	Mihai **Oltean**	1976–	2010–2022	21th	paper and online
7	Emilia **Plugaru**	1951–	2010–2017	21th	paper and online
8	Liviu **Rebreanu**	1885–1944	1908–1935	20th	paper
9	Ioan **Slavici**	1848–1925	1872–1920	19th–20th	paper

The diversity of the texts also pertains to the type of writing, i.e., stories, short stories, fairy tales, novels, articles, and sketches. Table 7 shows the distribution of these types of writing among the texts belonging to the 10 authors. The difference in the type of writing has an impact on the length of the texts (for example, a *novel* is considerably longer than a *short story*), genre (for example, *fairy tales* have more allegorical worlds that can require a specific style of writing), the topic (for example, an *article* may describe more mundane topics, requiring a different type of discourse compared to the other types of writing).

Table 7. List of authors and types of writing of the considered texts. *Author* is the author's name (the last name is in bold); *Article* * include, in addition to articles written for various newspapers and magazines, other types of writing that did not fit into the other categories, but relate to this category, such as *prose*, *essays*, and theatrical or musical *chronicles*. Total number of texts per type are in bold.

#	Author	Novel	Story	Short Story	Fairy Tale	*Article* *	Sketch
0	Ion **Creangă**	5	12	11			
1	Barbu Ştefănescu **Delavrancea**			37	7		
2	Mihai **Eminescu**	1	1	4	7	14	
3	Nicolae **Filimon**	6		5	3	20	
4	Emil **Gârleanu**			43			
5	Petre **Ispirescu**		1	1	38		
6	Mihai **Oltean**			32			
7	Emilia **Plugaru**		40				
8	Liviu **Rebreanu**		46				14
9	Ioan **Slavici**		14	38			
	TOTAL	**12**	**113**	**171**	**55**	**35**	**14**

Regarding the list of possible features, we selected as elements to identify the author of a text *inflexible parts of speech* (IPoS) (i.e., those that do not change their form in the context of communication): conjunctions, prepositions, interjections, and adverbs. Of these, we only considered those that were single-word and we removed the words that may represent other parts of speech, as some of them may have different functions depending on the context, and we did not use any syntactic or semantic processing of the text to carry out such an investigation.

We collected a list of 24 conjunctions that we checked on dexonline.ro (i.e., site that contains explanatory dictionaries of the Romanian language) not to be any other part of speech (not even among the inflexible ones). We also considered 3 short forms, thus arriving at a list of 27 conjunctions. The process of selecting prepositions was similar to that of selecting conjunctions, resulting in a list of 85 (including some short forms).

The lists of interjections and adverbs were taken from:

- https://ro.wiktionary.org/wiki/Categorie:Interjec%C8%9Bii_%C3%AEn_rom%C3%A2n%C4%83, accessed on 20 October 2022
- https://ro.wiktionary.org/wiki/Categorie:Adverbe_%C3%AEn_rom%C3%A2n%C4%83, accessed on 20 October 2022

To compile the lists of interjections and adverbs, we again considered only single-word ones and we eliminated words that may represent other parts of speech (e.g., proper nouns, nouns, adjectives, verbs), resulting in lists of 290 interjections and 670 adverbs.

The lists of the aforementioned IPoS also contain archaic forms in order to better identify the author. This is an important aspect that has to be taken into consideration (especially for our dataset which contains texts that were written over a time span of 3 centuries), as language is something that evolves and some words change as form and sometimes even as meaning or the way they are used.

From the lists corresponding to the considered IPoS features, we use only those that appear in the texts. Therefore, the actual lists of prepositions, adverbs, and conjunctions may be shorter. Details of the texts and the lists of inflexible parts of speech used can be found at reference [68].

4. Compared Methods

Below we present the methods we will use in our investigations.

4.1. Artificial Neural Networks

Artificial neural networks (ANN) is a machine learning method that applies the principle function approximation through learning by example (or based on provided training information) [69]. An ANN contains artificial neurons (or processing elements), organized in layers and connected by weighted arcs. The learning process takes place by adjusting the weights during the training process so that based on the input dataset the output outcome is obtained. Initially, these weights are chosen randomly.

The artificial neural structure is feedforward and has at least three layers: input, hidden (one or more), and output.

The experiments in this paper were performed using fast artificial neural network (FANN) [70] library. The error is RMSE. For the test set, the number of incorrectly classified items is also calculated.

4.2. Multi-Expression Programming

Multi-expression programming (MEP) is an evolutionary algorithm for generating computer programs. It can be applied to symbolic regression, time-series, and classification problems [71]. It is inspired by genetic programming [72] and uses three-address code [73] for the representation of programs.

MEP experiments use the MEPX software [74].

4.3. K-Nearest Neighbors

K-nearest neighbors (k-NN) [75–77] is a simple classification method based on the concept of instance-based learning [78]. It finds the k items, in the training set, that are closest to the test item and assigns the latter to the class that is most prevalent among these k items found.

The source code of k-NN used in this paper is written by us and is available at https://github.com/sanda-avram/ROST-source-code, (accessed on 8 November 2022) along other scripts and programs we wrote to perform the tests.

4.4. Support Vector Machine

A support vector machine (SVM) [79] is also a classification principle based on machine learning with the maximization (support) of separating distance/margin (vector). As in k-NN, SVM represents the items as points in a high-dimensional space and tries to separate them using a hyperplane. The particularity of SVM lies in the way in which such a hyperplane is selected, i.e., selecting the hyperplane that has the maximum distance to any item.

LIBSVM [80,81] is the support vector machine library that we used in our experiments. It supports classification, regression, and distribution estimation.

4.5. Decision Trees with C5.0

Classification can be completed by representing the acquired knowledge as decision trees [82]. A decision tree is a directed graph in which all nodes (except the root) have exactly one incoming edge. The root node has no incoming edge. All nodes that have outgoing edges are called internal (or test) nodes. All other nodes are called leaves (or decision) nodes. Such trees are built starting from the root by top–down inductive inference based on the values of the items in the training set. So, within each internal node, the instance space is divided into two or more sub-spaces based on the input attribute values.

An internal node may consider a single attribute. Each leaf is assigned to a class. Instances are classified by running them through the tree starting from the root to the leaves.

See5 and C5.0 [83] are data mining tools that produce classifiers expressed as either decision trees or rulesets, which we have used in our experiments.

5. Numerical Experiments

To prepare the dataset for the actual building of the classification model, the texts in the dataset were shuffled and divided into training (50%), validation (25%), and test (25%) sets, as detailed in Table 8. In cases where we only needed training and test sets, we concatenated the validation set to the training set. We reiterated the process (i.e., shuffle and split 50%–25%–25%) three times and, thus, obtained three different training–validation–test shuffles from the considered dataset.

Table 8. List of authors (the author's last name is in bold); the number of texts and their distribution on the training, validation, and test sets. The total number of texts per author, per set, and grand total are in bold.

#	Author	No. of Texts	TrainSet Size	ValidationSet Size	TestSet Size
0	Ion **Creangă**	**28**	14	7	7
1	Barbu Ştefănescu **Delavrancea**	**44**	22	11	11
2	Mihai **Eminescu**	**27**	15	6	6
3	Nicolae **Filimon**	**34**	18	8	8
4	Emil **Gârleanu**	**43**	23	10	10
5	Petre **Ispirescu**	**40**	20	10	10
6	Mihai **Oltean**	**32**	16	8	8
7	Emilia **Plugaru**	**40**	20	10	10
8	Liviu **Rebreanu**	**60**	30	15	15
9	Ioan **Slavici**	**52**	26	13	13
	TOTAL	**400**	**204**	**98**	**98**

Before building a numerical representation of the dataset as vectors of the frequency of occurrence of the considered features, we made a preliminary analysis to determine which of the inflexible parts of speech are more prevalent in our texts. Therefore, we counted the number of occurrences of each of them based on the lists described in Section 3. The findings are detailed in Table 9.

Table 9. The occurrence of inflexible parts of speech considered. *IPoS* stands for *Inflexible part of speech*; *No. of occurrence* is the total number of occurrences of the considered IPoS in all texts; *% from total words* represents the percentage corresponding to the *No. of occurrence* in terms of the total number of words in all texts (i.e., 1,342,133); *No. of files* represents the number of texts in which at least one word from the corresponding IPoS list appears; *Avg. per file* represents the *No. of occurrence* divided by the total number of texts/files (i.e., 400); and *No. of IPoS* represents the list length (i.e., the number of words) for each corresponding IPoS.

IPoS	No. of Occurrence	% from Total Words	No. of Files	Avg. per File	No. of IPoS
conjunctions	119,568	8.90	400	298.92	27
prepositions	176,733	13.16	400	441.83	85
interjections	6614	0.49	356	16.53	290
adverbs	127,811	9.52	400	319.52	670

Based on the data presented here, we decided not to consider interjections because they do not appear in all files (i.e., 44 files do not contain any interjections), and in the other files, their occurrence is much less compared to the rest of the IPoS considered. This investigation also allowed us to decide the order in which these IPoS will be considered in our tests. Thus, the order of investigation is prepositions, adverbs, and conjunctions.

Therefore, we would first consider only prepositions, then add adverbs to this list, and finally add conjunctions as well. The process of shuffling and splitting the texts into training–validation–test sets (described at the beginning of the current section, i.e., Section 5) was reiterated once more for each feature list considered. We, therefore, obtained different dataset representations, which we will refer further as described in Table 10. The last 3 entries (i.e., ROST-PC-1, ROST-PC-2, and ROST-PC-3) were used in a single experiment.

Table 10. Names used in the rest of the paper refer to the different dataset representations and their shuffles. Only the first 9 entries (with the *Designation* written in bold) were used for the entire set of investigations.

#	Designation	Features to Represent the Dataset	Shuffle
1	**ROST-P-1**	prepositions	#1
2	**ROST-P-2**	prepositions	#2
3	**ROST-P-3**	prepositions	#3
4	**ROST-PA-1**	prepositions and adverbs	#1
5	**ROST-PA-2**	prepositions and adverbs	#2
6	**ROST-PA-3**	prepositions and adverbs	#3
7	**ROST-PAC-1**	prepositions, adverbs and conjunctions	#1
8	**ROST-PAC-2**	prepositions, adverbs and conjunctions	#2
9	**ROST-PAC-3**	prepositions, adverbs and conjunctions	#3
10	ROST-PC-1	prepositions and conjunctions	#1
11	ROST-PC-2	prepositions and conjunctions	#2
12	ROST-PC-3	prepositions and conjunctions	#3

Correspondingly, we created different representations of the dataset as vectors of the frequency of occurrence of the considered feature lists. All these representations (i.e., training-validation-test sets) can be found as text files at reference [68]. These files contain feature-based numerical value representations for a different text on each line. On the last column of these files, are numbers from 0 to 9 corresponding to the author, as specified in the first columns of Tables 6–8.

5.1. Results

The parameter setting for all 5 methods are presented in Appendix A, while Appendix B contains some prerequisite tests.

Most results are presented in a tabular format. The percentages contained in the cells under the columns named *Best*, *Avg*, or *Error* may be highlighted using bold text or gray background. In these cases, the percentages in bold represent the best individual results (i.e., obtained by the respective method on any ROST-*-* in the dataset, out of the 9 representations mentioned above), while the gray-colored cells contain the best overall results (i.e., compared to all methods on that specific ROST-X-n representation of the dataset).

5.1.1. ANN

Results that showed that ANN is a good candidate to solve this kind of problem and prerequisite tests that determined the best ANN configuration (i.e., number of neurons on the hidden layer) for each dataset representation are detailed in Appendix B.1. The best values obtained for test errors and the number of neurons on the hidden layer for which these "bests" occurred are given in Table 11. These results show that the best test error rates were mainly generated by ANNs that have a number of neurons between 27 and 49. The best test error rate obtained with this method was 23.46% for ROST-PAC-3, while the best average was 36.93% for ROST-PAC-2.

Table 11. ANN results on the considered datasets. On each set, 30 runs are performed by ANNs with the hidden layer containing from 5 to 50 neurons. The number of incorrectly classified data is given as a percentage (the best results obtained by ANN on any ROST-*-* dataset representation are in bold). *Best* stands for the best solution (out of 30 runs on each of the 46 ANNs), *Avg* stands for *Average* (over 30 runs), *StdDev* stands for *Standard Deviation*, and *No. of neurons* stands for the number of neurons in the hidden layer of the ANN that produced the best solution. The best result obtained by ANN compared to all methods for a given ROST-X-n dataset representation is in a gray cell.

Dataset	Best	Avg	StdDev	No. of Neurons
ROST-P-1	61.22%	76.70%	6.30	46
ROST-P-2	60.20%	80.27%	10.58	36
ROST-P-3	57.14%	80.95%	10.30	28
ROST-PA-1	**24.48%**	45.03%	8.15	40
ROST-PA-2	24.48%	41.73%	5.78	45
ROST-PA-3	26.53%	47.82%	9.82	27
ROST-PAC-1	24.48%	38.16%	5.11	49
ROST-PAC-2	24.48%	**36.93%**	4.80	40
ROST-PAC-3	**23.46%**	37.21%	4.96	41

5.1.2. MEP

Results that showed that MEP can handle this type of problem are described in Appendix B.2.

We are interested in the generalization ability of the method. For this purpose, we performed full (30) runs on all datasets. The results, on the test sets, are given in Table 12.

Table 12. MEP results on the considered datasets. A total of 30 runs are performed. The number of incorrectly classified data is given as a percentage (the best results obtained by MEP on any ROST-*-* dataset representation are in bold). *Best* stands for the best solution (out of 30 runs), *Avg* stands for *Average* (over 30 runs) and *StdDev* stands for *Standard Deviation*. The best result obtained by MEP compared to all methods for a given ROST-X-n dataset representation is in a gray cell.

Dataset	Best	Avg	StdDev
ROST-P-1	54.08%	61.32%	4.11
ROST-P-2	52.04%	62.51%	4.46
ROST-P-3	48.97%	58.84%	4.16
ROST-PA-1	29.59%	36.49%	4.52
ROST-PA-2	**20.40%**	**27.95%**	3.87
ROST-PA-3	29.59%	39.93%	4.53
ROST-PAC-1	27.55%	33.84%	2.86
ROST-PAC-2	26.53%	34.89%	4.58
ROST-PAC-3	23.46%	34.38%	4.54

With this method, we obtained an overall "best" on all ROST-*-*, which is 20.40%, and also an overall "average" best with a value of 27.95%, both for ROST-PA-2.

One big problem is overfitting. The error on the training set is low (they are not given here, but sometimes are below 10%). However, on the validation and test sets the errors are much higher (2 or 3 times higher). This means that the model suffers from overfitting and has poor generalization ability. This is a known problem in machine learning and is usually corrected by providing more data (for instance more texts for an author).

5.1.3. k-NN

Preliminary tests and their results for determining the best value of k for each dataset representation are presented in Appendix B.3.

The best k-NN results are given in Table 13 with the corresponding value of k for which these "bests" were obtained. It can be seen that for all ROST-P-*, the values of k were higher (i.e., $k \geq 8$) than those for ROST-PA-* or ROST-PAC-* (i.e., $k \leq 4$). The best value obtained by this method was 29.59% for ROST-PAC-2 and ROST-PAC-3.

Table 13. k-NN results on the considered datasets. In total, 30 runs are performed with k varying with the run index. The number of incorrectly classified data is given as a percentage (the best results obtained by k-MM on any ROST-*-* dataset representation are in bold). *Best* stands for the best solution (out of the 30 runs), k stands for the value of k for which the best solution was obtained.

Dataset	Best	k
ROST-P-1	53.06%	8
ROST-P-2	54.08%	23
ROST-P-3	48.97%	11
ROST-PA-1	31.63%	1
ROST-PA-2	32.6%	1
ROST-PA-3	35.71%	1
ROST-PAC-1	33.67%	2
ROST-PAC-2	**29.59%**	1
ROST-PAC-3	**29.59%**	4

5.1.4. SVM

Prerequisite tests to determine the best kernel type and a good interval of values for the parameter *nu* are described in Appendix B.4, along with their results.

We ran tests for each kernel type and with *nu* varying from 0.1 to 1, as we saw in Figure A6 that for values less than 0.1, SVM is unlikely to produce the best results. The best results obtained are shown in Table 14.

Table 14. SVM results on the considered datasets. The number of incorrectly classified data is given as a percentage (the best results obtained by SVM on any ROST-*-* dataset representation are in bold). *Best* stands for the best test error rate (out of 30 runs with *nu* ranging from 0.001 to 1), and *nu* stands for the parameter specific to the selected type of SVM (i.e., nu-SVC). Results are given for each type of kernel that was used by the SVM. The best result obtained by SVM compared to all methods for a given ROST-X-n dataset representation is in a gray cell.

	Linear Kernel		**Polynomial Kernel**		**Radial Basis Kernel**		**Sigmoid Kernel**	
Dataset	**Best**	*nu*	**Best**	*nu*	**Best**	*nu*	**Best**	*nu*
ROST-P-1	43.87%	≥0.6	65.30%	0.5	59.18%	0.4	58.16%	0.4
ROST-P-2	55.10%	≥0.6	70.40%	0.2, 0.4	67.34%	0.4	68.37%	0.2, 0.4
ROST-P-3	43.87%	≥0.6	65.30%	0.5	59.18%	0.4	58.16%	0.4
ROST-PA-1	31.63%	0.5	51.02%	0.5	44.89%	0.3	45.91%	0.3
ROST-PA-2	26.53%	0.5	55.10%	≥0.6	41.89%	≥0.6	44.89%	≥0.6
ROST-PA-3	28.57%	0.4	54.08%	0.2, 0.3	51.02%	0.2	51.02%	0.2
ROST-PAC-1	**23.46%**	0.2	54.08%	0.2	50.00%	0.5	50.00%	0.5
ROST-PAC-2	24.48%	0.5	51.02%	≥0.6	39.79%	≥0.6	39.79%	≥0.6
ROST-PAC-3	26.53%	0.5	51.02%	0.4	41.83%	0.5	42.85%	0.5

As can be seen, the best values were obtained for values of parameter *nu* between 0.2 and 0.6 (where sometimes 0.6 is the smallest value of the set $\{0.6, 0.7, \ldots, 1\}$ for which the best test error was obtained). The best value obtained by this method was 23.46% for ROST-PAC-1, using the *linear kernel* and *nu* parameter value 0.2.

5.1.5. Decision Trees with C5.0

Advanced pruning options for optimizing the decision trees with C5.0 model and their results are presented in Appendix B.5. The best results were obtained by using $-m$ cases option, as detailed in Table 15.

Table 15. Decision tree results on the considered datasets. The number of incorrectly classified data is given as a percentage (the best results obtained by DT with C5.0 on any ROST-*-* dataset representation are in bold). *Error* stands for the test error rate, *Size* stands for the size of the decision tree required for that specific solution and *cases* stands for the threshold for which is decided to have two more that two branches at a specific branching point ($cases \in \{1, 2, \ldots, 30\}$). The best result obtained by DT with C5.0 compared to all methods for a given ROST-X-n dataset representation is in a gray cell.

Dataset	Error	Size	Cases
ROST-P-1	51.0%	18	8
ROST-P-2	51.0%	46	3
ROST-P-3	57.1%	99	1
ROST-PA-1	31.6%	13	12
ROST-PA-2	26.5%	57	1
ROST-PA-3	29.6%	31	3
ROST-PAC-1	28.6%	39	2
ROST-PAC-2	**24.5%**	12	14
ROST-PAC-3	26.5%	13	14

The best result obtained by this method was 24.5% on ROST-PAC-2, with $-m$ 14 option, on a decision tree of size 12. When no options were used, the size of the decision trees was considerably larger for ROST-P-* (i.e., $\geq$57) than those for ROST-PA-* and ROST-PAC-* (i.e., $\leq$39).

5.2. Comparison and Discussion

The findings of our investigations allow for a twofold perspective. The first perspective refers to the evaluation of the performance of the five investigated methods, as well as to the observation of the ability of the considered feature sets to better represent the dataset for successful classification. The other perspective is to place our results in the context of other state-of-the-art investigations in the field of author attribution.

5.2.1. Comparing the Internally Investigated Methods

From all the results presented above, upon consulting the tables containing the best test error rates, and especially the gray-colored cells (which contain the best results while comparing the methods amongst themselves) we can highlight the following:

- *ANN:*
  - Four best results for: ROST-PA-1, ROST-PA-3, ROST-PAC-2 and ROST-PAC-3 (see Table 11);
  - Best ANN 23.46% on ROST-PAC-3; best ANN average 36.93% on ROST-PAC-2;
  - Worst best **overall** 61.22% on ROST-P-1.
- *MEP:*
  - Two best results for ROST-PA-2 and ROST-PAC-3 (see Table 12);
  - Best **overall** 20.40% on ROST-PA-2; best **overall** average 27.95% on ROST-PA-2;
  - Worst best MEP 54.08% on ROST-P-1.
- *k-NN:*
  - Zero best results (see Table 13);
  - Best k-NN 29.59% on ROST-PAC-2 and ROST-PAC-3;
  - Worst k-NN 54.08% on ROST-P-2.
- *SVM:*
  - Four best results for: ROST-P-1, ROST-P-3, ROST-PAC-1 and ROST-PAC-2 (see Table 14);
  - Best SVM 23.44% on ROST-PAC-1;

- Worst SVM 52.10% on ROST-P-2.
- *Decision trees:*
  - Two best results for: ROST-P-2 and ROST-PAC-2 (see Table 15);
  - Best DT 24.5% on ROST-PAC-2;
  - Worst DT 57.10% on ROST-P-2.

Other notes from the results are:

- Best values for each method were obtained for ROST-PA-2 or ROST-PAC-*;
- The worst of these best results were obtained for ROST-P-1 or ROST-P-2;
- ANN and MEP suffer from overfitting. The training errors are significantly smaller than the test errors. This problem can only be solved by adding more data to the training set.

An overview of the best test results obtained by all five methods is given in Table 16.

Table 16. Top of methods on each shuffle of each dataset, based on the best results achieved by each method. The gray-colored box represents the overall best (i.e., for all datasets and with all methods).

Dataset	1st Place	2nd Place	3rd Place	4th Place	5th Place
ROST-P-1	**SVM** 43.87%	**DT** 51.0%	**k-NN** 53.06%	**MEP** 54.08%	**ANN** 61.22%
ROST-P-2	**DT** 51.0%	**MEP** 52.04%	**k-NN** 54.08%	**SVM** 55.10%	**ANN** 60.20%
ROST-P-3	**SVM** 43.87%	**k-NN,MEP** 48.97%		**DT,ANN** 57.14%	
ROST-PA-1	**ANN** 24.48%	**MEP** 29.59%	**SVM,DT,k-NN** 31.63%		
ROST-PA-2	**MEP** 20.40%	**ANN** 24.48%	**SVM,DT** 26.53%		**k-NN** 32.6%
ROST-PA-3	**ANN** 26.53%	**SVM** 28.57%	**MEP,DT** 29.59%		**k-NN** 35.71%
ROST-PAC-1	**SVM** 23.46%	**ANN** 24.48%	**MEP** 27.55%	**DT** 28.6%	**k-NN** 33.67%
ROST-PAC-2	**SVM,DT,ANN** 24.48%			**MEP** 26.53%	**k-NN** 29.59%
ROST-PAC-3	**MEP,ANN** 23.46%		**SVM,DT** 26.53%		**k-NN** 29.59%

ANN ranks last for all ROST-P-* and ranks 1st and 2nd for ROST-PA-* and ROST-PAC-*. MEP is either ranked 1st or ranked 2nd on all ROST-*-* with three exceptions, i.e., for ROST-P-1 and ROST-PAC-2 (at 4th place) and for ROST-PAC-1 (at 3rd place). k-NN performs better (i.e., 3rd and 2nd places) on ROST-P-*, and ranks last for ROST-PA-* and ROST-PAC-*. SVM is ranked 1st for ROST-P-* and ROST-PAC-* with two exceptions: for ROST-P-2 (ranked 4th) and for ROST-PAC-3 (on 3rd place). For ROST-PA-* SVM is in 3rd and 2nd places. Decision trees (DT) with C5.0 is mainly on the 3rd and 4th places, with three exceptions: for ROST-P-1 (on 2nd place), for ROST-P-2 (on 1st place), and for ROST-PAC-2 (on 1st place).

An overview of the average test results obtained by all five methods is given in Table 17. However, for ANN and MEP alone, we could generate different results with the same parameters, based on different starting *seed* values, with which we ran 30 different runs. For the other 3 methods, we used the best results obtained with a specific set of parameters (as in Table 16).

Comparing all 5 methods based on averages, SVM and DT take the lead as the two methods that share the 1st and 2nd places with two exceptions, i.e., for ROST-P-2 and ROST-P3 for which SVM and DT, respectively, rank 3rd. k-NN usually ranks 3rd, with four exceptions, when k-NN was ranked 2nd for ROST-P-2 and ROST-P-3, for ROST-PA-1 for which k-NN ranks 1st together with SVM and DT, and for ROST-PA-2 for which k-NN ranks 4th. MEP is generally ranked 4th with one exception, i.e., for ROST-PA-2 for which it ranks 3rd. ANN ranks last for all ROST-*-*.

For a better visual representation, we have plotted the results from Tables 16 and 17 in Figure 1.

Table 17. Top of methods on average results on each shuffle of each dataset. For k-NN, SVM, and DT we do not have 30 runs with the same parameters, so for these methods, the best values are presented here. The gray-colored box represents the overall best average (i.e., on all datasets and with all methods).

Dataset	1st Place	2nd Place	3rd Place	4th Place	5th Place
ROST-P-1	**SVM** 43.87%	**DT** 51.0%	**k-NN** 53.06%	**MEP** 61.32%	**ANN** 76.70%
ROST-P-2	**DT** 51.0%	**k-NN** 54.08%	**SVM** 55.10%	**MEP** 62.51%	**ANN** 80.27%
ROST-P-3	**SVM** 43.87%	**k-NN** 48.97%	**DT** 57.14%	**MEP** 58.84%	**ANN** 80.95%
ROST-PA-1	**SVM,DT,k-NN** 31.63%			**MEP** 36.49%	**ANN** 45.03%
ROST-PA-2	**SVM,DT** 26.53%		**MEP** 27.95%	**k-NN** 32.6%	**ANN** 41.73%
ROST-PA-3	**SVM** 28.57%	**DT** 29.59%	**k-NN** 35.71%	**MEP** 39.93%	**ANN** 47.82%
ROST-PAC-1	**SVM** 23.46%	**DT** 28.6%	**k-NN** 33.67%	**MEP** 33.84%	**ANN** 38.16%
ROST-PAC-2	**SVM,DT** 24.48%		**k-NN** 29.59%	**MEP** 34.89%	**ANN** 36.93%
ROST-PAC-3	**SVM,DT** 26.53%		**k-NN** 29.59%	**MEP** 34.38	**ANN** 37.21%

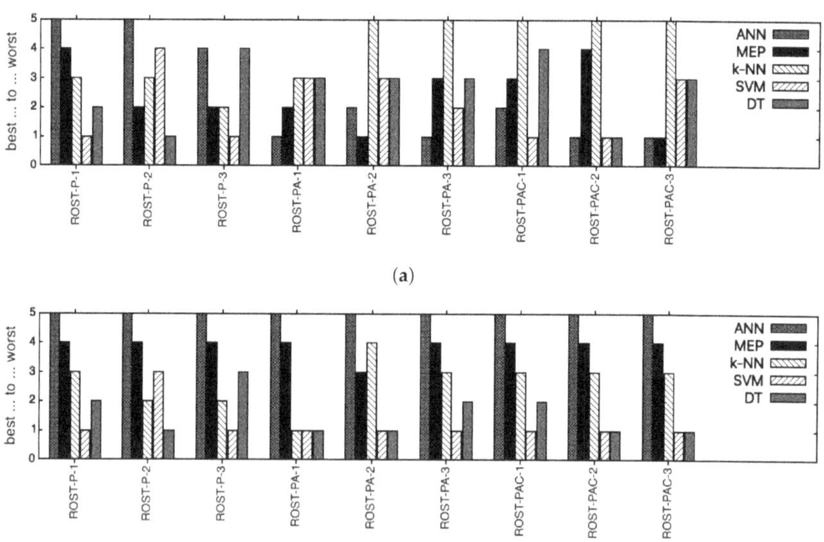

(**b**)

Figure 1. Top of methods on each shuffle of each dataset. Lower values are better. (**a**) Top of best results obtained by all methods (**b**) Top of average results, when applicable (i.e., over 30 runs for ANN and MEP).

We performed statistical tests to determine whether the results obtained by MEP and ANN are significantly different with a 95% confidence level. The tests were two-sample, equal variance, and two-tailed T-tests. The results are shown in Table 18.

Table 18. p-values obtained when comparing MEP and ANN results over 30 runs. *No. of neurons used by ANN on the hidden layer* represents the best-performing ANN structure on the specific ROST-*-*.

Dataset	p-Value (ANN vs. MEP Results)	No. of Neurons Used by ANN on the Hidden Layer
ROST-P-1	1.98×10^{-15}	46
ROST-P-2	4.23×10^{-11}	36
ROST-P-3	3.86×10^{-15}	28
ROST-PA-1	1.14×10^{-5}	40
ROST-PA-2	6.57×10^{-15}	45
ROST-PA-3	3.07×10^{-4}	27
ROST-PAC-1	2.47×10^{-4}	49
ROST-PAC-2	1.07×10^{-1}	40
ROST-PAC-3	2.80×10^{-2}	41

The p-values obtained show that the MEP and ANN test results are statistically significantly different for almost all ROST-*-* (i.e., $p < 0.05$) with one exception, i.e., for ROST-PAC-2 for which the differences are not statistically significant (i.e., $p = 0.107$).

Next, we wanted to see which feature set, out of the three we used, was the best for successful author attribution. Therefore, we plotted all best and best average results obtained with all methods (as presented in Tables 16 and 17) on all ROST-*-* and aggregated on the three datasets corresponding to the distinct feature lists, in Figure 2.

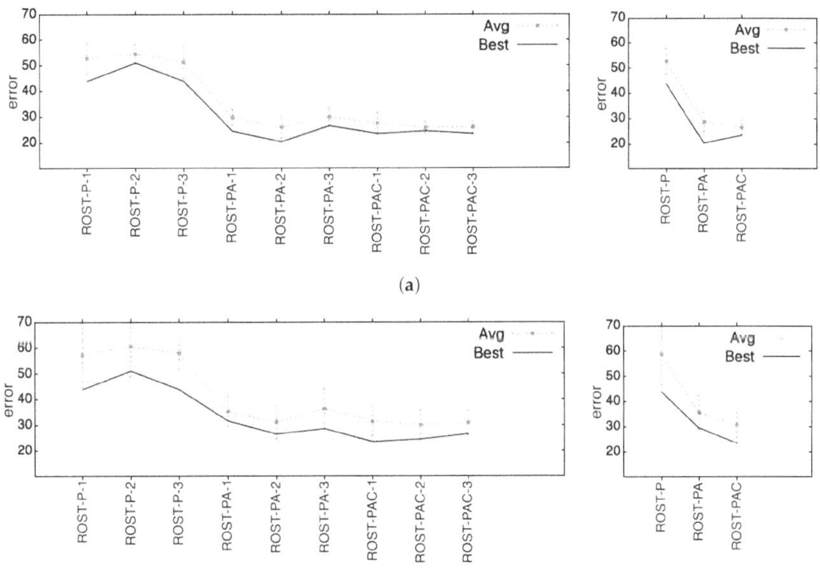

(a)

(b)

Figure 2. Results on the best solutions obtained on the considered datasets. The percentage of incorrectly classified data is plotted. *Best* stands for the best solution, *Avg* stands for *Average* and the *Standard Deviation* is represented by error bars. (**a**) *Best*, *Average* and *Standard Deviation* are computed on the values from Table 16; (**b**) *Best*, *Average*, and *Standard Deviation* are computed on the values given in Table 17.

Based on the results represented in Figure 2a (i.e., which considered only the best results, as detailed in Table 16) we can conclude that we obtained the best results on ROST-PA-* (i.e., corresponding to the 415 feature set, which contains prepositions and adverbs). However, using the average results, as shown in Figure 2b and detailed in Table 17 we infer that the best performance is obtained on ROST-PAC-* (i.e., corresponding to the 432-feature set, containing prepositions, adverbs, and conjunctions).

Another aspect worth mentioning based on the graphs presented in Figure 2 is related to the standard deviation (represented as error bars) between the results obtained by all methods considered on all considered datasets. Standard deviations are the smallest in Figure 2a, especially for ROST-PA-* and even more so for ROST-PAC-*. This means that the methods perform similarly on those datasets. For ROST-P-* and in Figure 2b, the standard deviations are larger, which means that there are bigger differences between the methods.

5.2.2. Comparisons with Solutions Presented in Related Work

To better evaluate our results and to better understand the discriminating power of the best performing method (i.e., MEP on ROST-PA-2), we also calculate the *macro-accuracy* (or *macro-average accuracy*). This metric allows us to compare our results with the results obtained by other methods on other datasets, as detailed in Table 2. For this, we considered the test for which we obtained our best result with MEP, with a test error rate of 20.40%. This means that 20 out of 98 tests were misclassified.

To perform all the necessary calculations, we used the *Accuracy evaluation* tool available at [84], build based on the paper [85]. By inputting the vector of *targets* (i.e., authors/classes that were the actual authors (i.e., correct classifications) of the test texts) and the vector of *outputs* (i.e., authors/classes identified by the algorithm as the authors of the test texts), we were first given a *Confusion value* of 0.2 and the *Confusion Matrix*, depicted in Table 19.

Table 19. *Confusion Matrix* (on the right side). Column headers and row headers (i.e., numbers from 0 to 9 that are written in bold) are the codes [1] given to our authors, as specified on the left side.

Code	Author		0	1	2	3	4	5	6	7	8	9
0	Ion **Creangă**	**0**	6	0	0	0	0	0	0	0	0	1
1	Barbu Ştefănescu **Delavrancea**	**1**	0	4	0	3	1	0	1	0	0	2
2	Mihai **Eminescu**	**2**	0	0	6	0	0	0	0	0	0	0
3	Nicolae **Filimon**	**3**	0	1	1	6	0	0	0	0	0	0
4	Emil **Gârleanu**	**4**	1	1	0	0	6	0	0	0	1	1
5	Petre **Ispirescu**	**5**	0	0	0	0	0	10	0	0	0	0
6	Mihai **Oltean**	**6**	0	0	0	0	0	0	8	0	0	0
7	Emilia **Plugaru**	**7**	0	1	0	0	1	0	0	8	0	0
8	Liviu **Rebreanu**	**8**	0	1	0	0	0	0	1	0	12	1
9	Ioan **Slavici**	**9**	0	0	0	0	0	0	0	0	1	12

[1] The authors' codes are the same as those specified in the first columns of Tables 6–8.

This matrix is a representation that highlights for each class/author the *true positives* (i.e., the number of cases in which an author was correctly identified as the author of the text), the *true negatives* (i.e., the number of cases where an author was correctly identified as not being the author of the text), the *false positives* (i.e., the number of cases in which an author was incorrectly identified as being the author of the text), the *false negatives* (i.e., the number of cases where an author was incorrectly identified as not being the author of the text). For binary classification, these four categories are easy to identify. However, in a multiclass classification, the *true positives* are contained in the main diagonal cells corresponding to each author, but the other three categories are distributed according to the actual authorship attribution made by the algorithm.

For each class/author, various metrics are calculated based on the confusion matrix. They are:

- *Precision*—the number of correctly attributed authors divided by the number of instances when the algorithm identified the attribution as correct;

- *Recall (Sensitivity)*—the number of correctly attributed authors divided by the number of test texts belonging to that author;
- *F-score*—a combination of the *Precision* and *Recall (Sensitivity)*.

Based on these individual values, the *Accuracy Evaluation Results* are calculated. The overall results are shown in Table 20.

Table 20. Accuracy evaluation Results. The macro-accuracy and corresponding macro-error are in bold.

Metric	Value (%)
Average Accuracy	**88.8401**
Error	**11.1599**
Precision (Micro)	79.9398
Recall (Micro)	97.251
F-score (Micro)	87.7498
Precision (Macro)	79.9398
Recall (Macro)	96.8525
F-score (Macro)	87.5871

Metrics marked with (Micro) are calculated by aggregating the contributions of all classes into the average metric. Thus, in a multiclass context, micro averages are preferred when there might be a class imbalance, as this method favors bigger classes. Metrics marked with (Macro) treat each class equally by averaging the individual metrics for each class.

Based on these results, we can state that the macro-accuracy obtained by MEP is 88.84%. We have 400 documents, and 10 authors in our dataset. The *content* of our texts is *cross-genre* (i.e., stories, short stories, fairy tales, novels, articles, and sketches) and *cross-topic* (as in different texts, different topics are covered). We also calculated an average number of words per document, which is 3355, and the *imbalance* (considered in [10] to be the standard deviation of the number of documents per author), which in our case is 10.45. Our type of investigation can be considered to be part of the Ngram class (this class and other investigation-type classes are presented in Section 2.4). Next, we recreated Table 2 (depicted in Section 2.4) while reordering the datasets based on their macro-accuracy results obtained by Ngram class methods in reverse order, and we have appropriately placed details of our own dataset and the macro-accuracy we achieved with MEP as shown above. This top is depicted in Table 21.

Table 21. State of the art *macro-accuracy* of authorship attribution models. Information collected from [10] (Tables 1 and 3). *Name* is the name of the dataset; *No.docs* represents the number of documents in that dataset, *No. auth* represents the number of authors; *Content* indicates whether the documents are cross-topic ($\times_t$) or cross-genre ($\times_g$); *W/D* stands for *words per documents*, being the average length of documents; *imb* represents the *imbalance* of the dataset as measured by the standard deviation of the number of documents per author.

Dataset						Investigation Type			
Name	**No. Docs**	**No. Auth**	**Content**	**W/D**	**Imb**	**Ngram**	**PPM**	**BERT**	**pALM**
Guardian10	444	13	$\times_t \times_g$	1052	6.7	100	86.28	84.23	66.67
IMDb62	62,000	62	–	349	2.6	98.81	95.90	98.80	–
ROST	400	10	$\times_t \times_g$	3355	10.45	88.84	–	–	–
CMCC	756	21	$\times_t \times_g$	601	0	86.51	62.30	60.32	54.76
CCAT50	5000	50	–	506	0	76.68	69.36	65.72	63.36
Blogs50	66,000	50	–	122	553	72.28	72.16	74.95	
PAN20	443,000	278,000	$\times_t$	3922	2.3	43.52		23.83	–
Gutenburg	28,000	4500		66,350	10.5	57.69	–	59.11	–

We would like to underline the large imbalance of our dataset compared with the first two datasets, the fact that we had fewer documents, and the fact that the average number of words in our texts, although higher, has a large standard deviation, as already shown in Table 3. Furthermore, as already presented in Section 3, our dataset is by design very heterogeneous from multiple perspectives which are not only in terms of content and size, but also the differences that pertain to the time periods of authors, the medium they wrote for (paper or online media), and the sources of the texts. Although all these aspects do not restrict the new test texts to certain characteristics (to be easily classified by the trained model), they make the classification problem even harder.

6. Conclusions and Further Work

In this paper, we introduced a new dataset of Romanian texts by different authors. This dataset is heterogeneous from multiple perspectives, such as the length of the texts, the sources from which they were collected, the time period in which the authors lived and wrote these texts, the intended reading medium (i.e., paper or online), and the type of writing (i.e., stories, short stories, fairy tales, novels, literary articles, and sketches). By choosing these very diverse texts we wanted to make sure that the new texts do not have to be restricted by these constraints. As features, we wanted to use the *inflexible parts of speech* (i.e., those that do not change their form in the context of communication): conjunctions, prepositions, interjections, and adverbs. After a closer investigation of their relevance to our dataset, we decided to use only prepositions, adverbs, and conjunctions, in that specific order, thus having three different feature lists of (1) 56 prepositions; (2) 415 prepositions and adverbs; and (3) 432 prepositions, adverbs, and conjunctions. Using these features, we constructed a numerical representation of our texts as vectors containing the frequencies of occurrence of the features in the considered texts, thus obtaining 3 distinct representations of our initial dataset. We divided the texts into training–validation–test sets of 50%–25%–25% ratios, while randomly shuffling them three times in order to have three randomly selected arrangements of texts in each set of training, validation, and testing.

To build our classifiers, we used five artificial intelligence techniques, namely artificial neural networks (ANN), multi-expression programming (MEP), k-nearest neighbor (k-NN), support vector machine (SVM), and decision trees (DT) with C5.0. We used the trained classifiers for authorship attribution on the texts selected for the test set. The best result we obtained was with MEP. By using this method, we obtained an overall "best" on all shuffles and all methods, which is of a 20.40% error rate.

Based on the results, we tried to determine which of the three distinct feature lists lead to the best performance. This inquiry was twofold. First, we considered the *best* results obtained by all methods. From this perspective, we achieved the best performance when using ROST-PA-* (i.e., the dataset with 415 features, which contains prepositions and adverbs). Second, we considered the *average* results over 30 different runs for ANN and MEP. These results indicate that the best performance was achieved when using ROST-PAC-* (i.e., the dataset with 432 features, which contains prepositions, adverbs, and conjunctions).

We also calculated the macro-accuracy for the best MEP result to compare it with other state-of-the-art methods on other datasets.

Given all the trained models that we obtained, the first future work is using ensemble decision. Additionally, determining whether multiple classifiers made the same error (i.e., attributing one text to the same incorrect author instead of the correct one) may mean that two authors have a similar style. This investigation can also go in the direction of detecting style similarities or grouping authors into style classes based on such similarities.

Extending our area of research is also how we would like to continue our investigations. We will not only fine-tune the current methods but also expand to the use of recurrent neural networks (RNN) and convolutional neural networks (CNN).

Regarding fine-tuning, we have already started an investigation using the top N most frequently used words in our corpus. Even though we have some preliminary results, this investigation is still a work in progress.

Using deep learning to fine-tune ANN is another direction we would like to tackle. We would also like to address overfitting and find solutions to mitigate this problem.

Linguistic analysis could help us as a complementary tool for detecting peculiarities that pertain to a specific author. For that, we will consider using long short-term memory (LSTM) architectures and pre-trained BERT models that are already available for Romanian. However, considering that a large section of our texts was written one or two centuries ago, we might need to further train BERT to be able to use it in our texts. That was one reason that we used inflexible parts of speech, as the impact of the diachronic developments of the language was greatly reduced.

We would also investigate the profile-based approach, where texts are treated cumulatively (per author) to build a *profile*, which is a representation of the author's style. Up to this point we have treated the training texts individually, an approach called *instance-based*.

In terms of moving towards other types of neural networks, we would like to achieve the initial idea from which this entire area of research was born, namely finding a "fingerprint" of an author. We already have some incipient ideas on how these instruments may help us in our endeavor, but these new directions are still in the very early stages for us.

Improving upon the dataset is also high on our priority list. We are considering adding new texts and new authors.

Author Contributions: Conceptualization, S.-M.A.; methodology, S.-M.A. and M.O.; software, S.-M.A. and M.O.; validation, S.-M.A. and M.O.; formal analysis, S.-M.A.; investigation, S.-M.A.; resources, S.-M.A.; data curation, S.-M.A.; writing—original draft preparation, S.-M.A.; writing—review and editing, S.-M.A. and M.O.; visualization, S.-M.A.; supervision, M.O.; project administration, S.-M.A.; funding acquisition, S.-M.A. All authors have read and agreed to the published version of the manuscript.

Funding: This research received no external funding.

Institutional Review Board Statement: Not applicable.

Informed Consent Statement: Not applicable.

Data Availability Statement: The proposed, used and analyzed dataset is available at https://www.kaggle.com/datasets/sandamariaavram/rost-romanian-stories-and-other-texts. The source code that we wrote to perform the tests are available at https://github.com/sanda-avram/ROST-source-code, accessed on 8 November 2022. The data presented in Tables 2 and 21 are openly available in [arXiv:2209.06869v2 https://arxiv.org/abs/2209.06869v2] at https://doi.org/10.48550/arXiv.2209.06869, accessed on 8 November 2022.

Acknowledgments. We thank Ludmila Jahn who helped with the English revision of the text.

Conflicts of Interest: The authors declare no conflict of interest.

Abbreviations

The following abbreviations are used in this manuscript:

AA	Authorship Attribution
ANN	Artificial Neural Networks
MPE	Multi Expression Programming
k-NN	k-Nearest Neighbour
SVM	Support Vector Machines
DT	Decision Trees
RMSE	Root Mean Square Error

FANN	Fast Artificial Neural Network
MEPX	Multi Expression Programming software
LIBSVM	Support Vector Machine library
C5.0	system for classifiers in the form of decision trees and rulesets
PoS	Part of Speech
IPoS	Inflexible Part of Speech
ROST	ROmanian Stories and other Texts
ROST-P-1	ROST dataset using prepositions as features, shuffle 1
ROST-P-2	ROST dataset using prepositions as features, shuffle 2
ROST-P-3	ROST dataset using prepositions as features, shuffle 3
ROST-P-*	ROST-P-1 and ROST-P-2 and ROST-P-3
ROST-PA-1	ROST dataset using prepositions and adverbs as features, shuffle 1
ROST-PA-2	ROST dataset using prepositions and adverbs as features, shuffle 2
ROST-PA-3	ROST dataset using prepositions and adverbs as features, shuffle 3
ROST-PA-*	ROST-PA-1 and ROST-PA-2 and ROST-PA-3
ROST-PAC-1	ROST dataset using prepositions, adverbs, and conjunctions as features, shuffle 1
ROST-PAC-2	ROST dataset using prepositions, adverbs, and conjunctions as features, shuffle 2
ROST-PAC-3	ROST dataset using prepositions, adverbs, and conjunctions as features, shuffle 3
ROST-PAC-*	ROST-PAC-1 and ROST-PAC-2 and ROST-PAC-3
ROST-PC-1	ROST dataset using prepositions and conjunctions as features, shuffle 1
ROST-PC-2	ROST dataset using prepositions and conjunctions as features, shuffle 2
ROST-PC-3	ROST dataset using prepositions and conjunctions as features, shuffle 3
ROST-*-*	ROST-P-* and ROST-PA-* and ROST-PAC-*
NLP	Natural Language Processing
BERT	Bidirectional Encoder Representations from Transformers
GPT	Generative Pre-trained Transformer
PPM	Prediction by Partial Matching
pALM	per-Author Language Model
AUC	Area Under the Curve
$\times_t$	cross-topic
$\times_g$	cross-genre
CCTA	Consumer Credit Trade Association

Appendix A. Parameter Settings

ANN parameters are presented in Table A1. We decided to use a fairly simple ANN architecture, using only 3 layers as we saw from the literature (e.g., [9]) that simple classifiers outperformed more sophisticated approaches based on deep learning in the case of cross-domain authorship attribution. We varied the number of neurons on the hidden layer to find a suitable ANN architecture for building our classification model.

Table A1. ANN parameters.

Parameter	Value
Activation function	SIGMOID
Maximum number of training epochs	500
Number of layers	3 (1 input, 1 hidden, and 1 output)
Number of neurons on hidden layer	from 5 to 50
Number of inputs	56, 415, 432 (corresponding to the considered sets)
Number of outputs	10 (corresponding to authors)
Error on training and validation	RMSE
Error on test	percent of incorrectly classified items
Desired error on validation	0.001

MEP parameters are detailed in Table A2. These parameters were obtained mostly through experimentation. We thought that small errors on the training set would also lead to small errors on the test set. However, we were wrong: the main problem we encountered was overfitting and poor generalization ability of the model. Thus, other sets of parameters can also generate similar results on the test set even if the training error will be higher.

Table A2. MEP parameters.

Parameter	Value
Subpopulation size	300
Number of subpopulations	25
Subpopulations architecture	ring
Migration rate	1 (per generation)
Chromosome length	200
Crossover probability	0.9
Mutation probability	0.01
Tournament size	2
Functions probability	0.4
Variables probability	0.5
Constants probability	0.1
Number of generations	1000
Mathematical functions	+,−,*, /, a<0?b:c, a<b?c:d
Number of constants	5
Constants initial interval	randomly generated over [0, 1]
Constants can evolve?	YES
Constants can evolve outside the initial interval?	YES
Constants delta	1

The k-NN considers only training and test data. Thus, we have training sets of 302 items, while the test contains 98 items. During the tests, we varied the value of *k* from 1 to 30. This is because we observed (as is depicted in Figure A1) that with higher values we would not obtain better results, as the results tend to deteriorate as the value of *k* increases. However, this depends on the number of features, as the results become bad faster for a consistent number (>100) of features, as for ROST-PC-*, compared to the evolution of the results for ROST-P-*, where the results do not deteriorate so fast by increasing the value of *k* in the case of a smaller number (<100) of features. To calculate the distance between the test value and the ones in the training set, we used Euclidean distance.

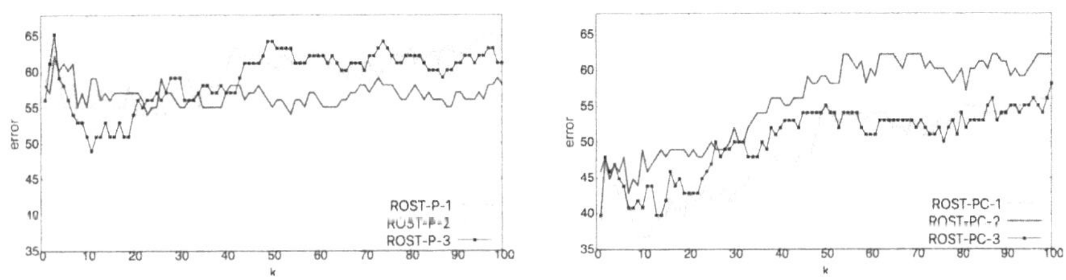

Figure A1. Evolution of error in k-NN for k values from 1 to 100.

Support vector machines also consider only training and test data. Therefore, the training sets consist of 302 items, while the test sets contain 98 items. We experimented with the *type of kernel* and *nu* parameters, selecting values that varied through all possible kernel types and values from 0.001 to 1 for *nu*. For the *type of kernel*, the best results were obtained for linear. For *nu* we had different values that gave better results depending on the dataset. However, even though we tried with values starting from 0.001, the best results were obtained for $nu \geq 0.2$. We also changed the seed for the random function with no effect on the results. The SVM parameters are given in Table A3.

Table A3. SVM parameters.

Parameter	Value
Type of SVM	nu-SVC
Type of kernel function	linear
Degree in kernel function	3
Gamma in kernel function	$1/num\_features$
Coef0 in kernel function	0
nu	from 0.1 to 1
Cache memory size in MB	100
Tolerance of termination criterion (*epsilon*)	0.001
Shrinking heuristics, 0 or 1	1
Whether to train an SVC model for probability estimates, 0 or 1	0

As with k-NN and SVM, the decision trees with the C5.0 algorithm also use only training and test data. Thus, there are 302 items in the training sets and 98 items in the tests. All considered features/attributes, which in our case are: prepositions, adverbs, and conjunctions, are set for the Decision Trees with C5.0 as "*continuous*" because they are numerical float values between 0 and 1 representing the frequency of occurrence in terms of the total number of words in the file in which they occur. For authors, we set explicit-defined discrete values from 0 to 9 for the 10 authors (as specified in the first columns of Tables 6–8). To improve our results, we experimented with advanced pruning options. These parameters along with others we used for decision trees with C5.0 are shown in Table A4. Apart from these parameters we also used the option $-I$ *seed*, to set the random seed, with $seed \in \{1, 2, \ldots, 9, 10, 20, \ldots, 100\}$, without any effect on the results.

Table A4. Parameters for decision trees with C5.0.

Parameter	Value
No. of attributes	57, 416, 433 (corresponding to the considered sets plus one more attribute for the author)
Global tree pruning	w and w/o (option $-g$)
Pruning confidence	option $-c$ CF, with $CF \in \{10, 20, \ldots, 100\}$
Minimum 2 branches for $\geq$ *cases*	option $-m$ *cases*, with $cases \in \{1, 2, \ldots, 30\}$

Appendix B. Prerequisite Tests and Results

Appendix B.1. ANN

As a prerequisite, we are interested in seeing how ANN evolves while training on the data. The ANN error evolution on a training set is shown in Figure A2.

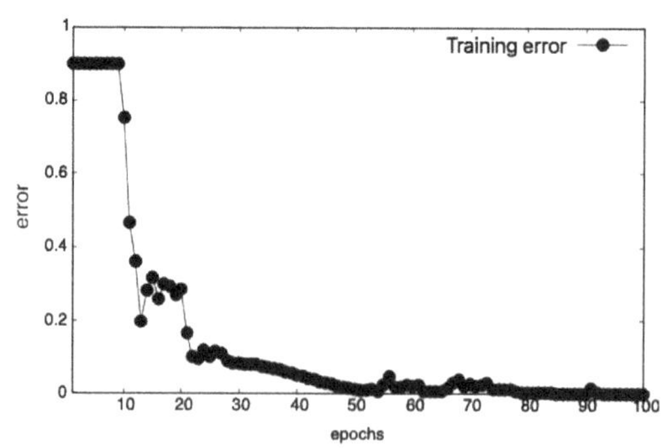

Figure A2. ANN error evolution on a training set.

It can be seen here that within 20 epochs, the training error drops below 0.1, while within 60 epochs, it reaches 0. Thus, ANN can be used to solve this kind of problem.

Next, we want to find a good value for the number of neurons on the hidden layer. In total, 30 runs were performed with the number of neurons (on the hidden layer) varying from 5 to 50.

The results for the 9 ROST-*-* are presented in Figure A3.

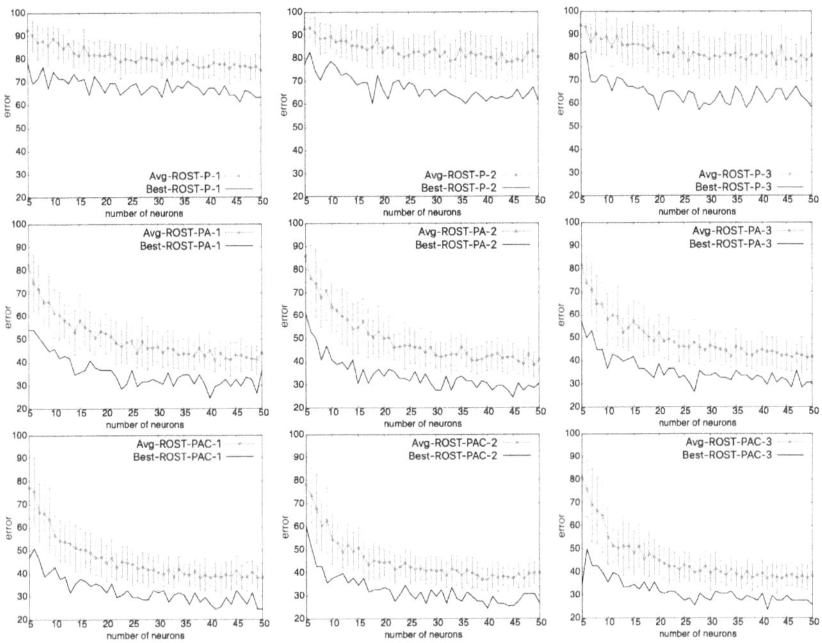

Figure A3. ANN results on the considered datasets. On each set, 30 runs are performed by ANNs with the hidden layer containing from 5 to 50 neurons. The percentage of incorrectly classified data is plotted. *Best* stands for the best solution (out of 30 runs), *Avg* stands for *Average* (over 30 runs), and the *Standard Deviation* is represented by error bars.

These graphics show that, using only 56 features (i.e., ROST-P-*) tests errors were very high, while with an increased number of features: i.e., 415 (i.e., ROST-PA-*) and 432 (i.e., ROST-PAC-*), respectively, test errors are significantly reduced. Moreover, it appears that the test error values tend to stabilize between 40 and 50 neurons on the hidden layer.

Appendix B.2. MEP

We are interested to see if MEP is able to discover a classifier and then to see how well it performs on new (test) data. The evolution of MEP error on a training set is shown in Figure A4. One can see that the error rapidly drops from over 65% to 15%. This means that MEP can handle this type of problem.

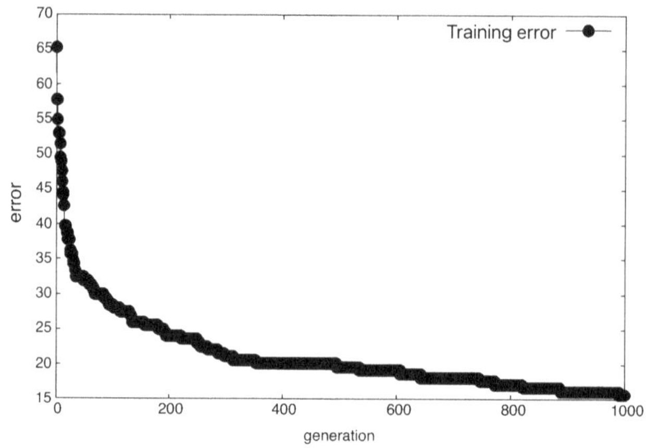

Figure A4. MEP error evolution on a training set.

Appendix B.3. K-NN

With k-NN we ran tests with k varying from 1 to 30. The results for all 9 ROST-*-* are plotted in Figure A5. It can be seen that the results for the 3 ROST-P-* have worst values than the values obtained for ROST-PA-* or ROST-PAC-*.

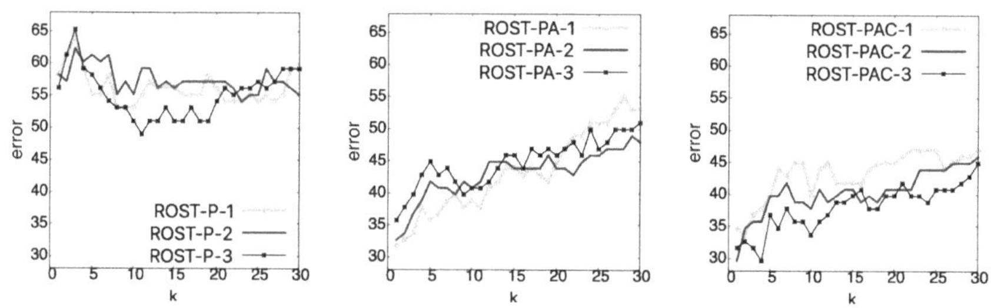

Figure A5. K-NN results on the considered datasets. In total, 30 runs are performed with *k* varying with the run index. The percentage of incorrectly classified data is plotted.

Appendix B.4. SVM

Initially, we tried to obtain the best kernel type for our tests, and as we have already read in the literature (e.g., in [37]) it seems that the *linear* type is the best for these types of problems (i.e., the classification for authorship attribution). We obtained significantly better results for this type as well. With this kernel type, we tried the find the best value for the *nu* parameter. Therefore, we run tests on all our ROST-*-* with *nu* values between 0.001 to 1. The results are shown in Figure A6.

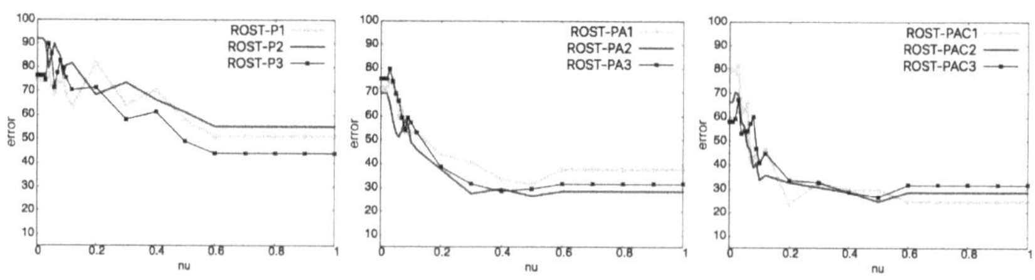

Figure A6. SVM results on the considered datasets. In total, 30 runs are performed with *nu* varying from 0.001 to 1. The percentage of incorrectly classified data is plotted.

Appendix B.5. DT

To optimize this method, we tried the advanced pruning options. For this we tried 3 options:

- $-g$, which disables the global tree pruning mechanism that prunes parts (of an initially large tree) that are predicted to have high error rates.
- $-c$ CF, changes the estimation of error rates. This affects the "severity of pruning". CF stands for *confidence level* and is a percentage. We chose values from 10 to 100 for the CF parameter.
- $-m$ *cases*, which influences the construction of the decision tree by having at least 2 branches at each branch point for which there are more than *cases* training items. The default value for *cases* is 2. We have selected values from 1 to 30 for the *cases* parameter.

The results obtained using decision trees with C5.0 are detailed in Table A5.

Table A5. Decision tree results on the considered datasets. The number of incorrectly classified data is given as a percentage. Result sets are grouped into columns of *Error*, *Size*, and sometimes a parameter. The first set of *Error*, *Size* columns represent the results obtained with no options. $-g$ stands for global tree pruning is disabled, $-c$ CF stands for setting the confidence level via the CF parameter, and $-m$ *cases* stands for controlling how the decision tree is built by using the *cases* parameter. *Error* stands for the test error rate, *Size* stands for the size of the decision tree required for that specific solution, CF stands for "confidence level" ($CF \in \{10, 20, \ldots, 100\}$), and *cases* stands for the threshold for which is decided to have two more that two branches at a specific branching point (*cases* $\in \{1, 2, \ldots, 30\}$).

			$-g$			$-c$ CF			$-m$ Cases	
Dataset	Error	Size	Error	Size	Error	Size	CF	Error	Size	Cases
ROST-P-1	58.2%	60	58.2%	60	58.2%	60	≥10	51.0%	18	8
ROST-P-2	53.1%	57	54.1%	61	53.1%	57	≥10	51.0%	46	3
ROST-P-3	69.4%	64	69.4%	64	69.4%	56	=10	57.1%	99	1
ROST-PA-1	35.7%	39	35.7%	42	35.7%	39	≥10	31.6%	13	12
ROST-PA-2	28.6%	38	27.6%	42	27.6%	43	>20	26.5%	57	1
ROST-PA-3	30.6%	38	30.6%	40	30.6%	38	≥10	29.6%	31	3
ROST-PAC-1	28.6%	39	28.6%	41	28.6%	39	≥10	28.6%	39	2
ROST-PAC-2	25.5%	37	25.5%	39	25.5%	37	≥10	24.5%	12	14
ROST-PAC-3	32.7%	38	33.7%	41	32.7%	38	≥10	26.5%	13	14

Using the $-g$ option, it can be seen that most of the trees have become larger (as expected since global tree pruning was disabled by this option). Changes in the results are marked in the table with the values in the boxes. However, most results remained the same, two worsened (i.e., for ROST-P-2 from 53.1% to 54.1% and for ROST-PAC-3 from 32.7% to 33.7%), while only one result improved (i.e., for ROST-PA-2 from 28.6% to 27.6%).

When using the $-c$ CF option, almost all results were similar to those obtained without using any option. The exceptions (marked with boxes), i.e., for ROST-PA-2 better results (i.e., 27.7% vs. 28.6% and the same as using the $-g$ option) were obtained by using a larger tree (i.e., 43 compared to 38; in this case larger than using the $-g$ option, which had a tree size of 42). In the case of ROST-P-3, only the tree size was optimized from 64 to 56 for $CF = 10$. For $CF > 20$, both the error and the tree size remained the same as without using any option, while for $CF = 20$, the tree size was slightly reduced (i.e., 63 from 64), but the error was higher (i.e., 70.4% from 69.4%).

Using the $-m$ cases option, we obtained improvements, as shown in Table A5. All error rates were improved, while the improvement in the tree size, although in some cases was significant (i.e., from 60 to 18, from 39 to 13, from 37 to 12, or from 38 to 14), in other cases the tree size increased or remained large (i.e., for ROST-P-3 from 64 to 99, for ROST-PA-2 from

38 to 58, and for ROST-PAC-1 it remained the same as when no option was used). For these three ROST-*-* mentioned above for which the tree size increased or remained large, the value of the *cases* parameter was very low (i.e., 1 or 2). For ROST-P-2 and ROST-PA-3, there is $cases = 3$ and the tree size did not change that much (i.e., from 38 to 31) and remained the same, respectively. For ROST-P-1, ROST-PA-1, ROST-PAC-2, and ROST-PA-3, $cases \geq 8$, and the three decision trees have greatly reduced in size to values ≤ 18.

To show the evolution of the error rates for the three datasets considered, we plotted the results of the decision trees obtained using C5.0 with the $-m$ option, with *cases* varying from 1 to 30. The results are shown in Figure A7.

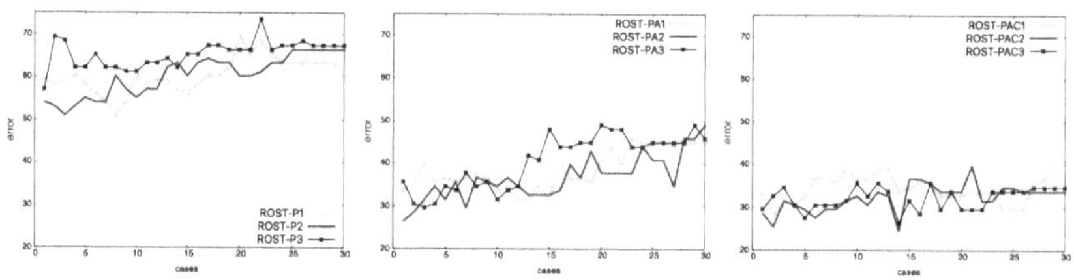

Figure A7. DT results on the considered datasets. In total, 30 runs are performed with the *cases* parameter (introduced by the $-m$ option) varying from 1 to 30. The percentage of incorrectly classified data is plotted.

References

1. de Oliveira, W.A., Jr.; Justino, E.; de Oliveira, L.S. Comparing compression models for authorship attribution. *Forensic Sci. Int.* **2013**, *228*, 100–104. [CrossRef]
2. Stamatatos, E.; Koppel, M. Plagiarism and authorship analysis: Introduction to the special issue. *Lang. Resour. Eval.* **2011**, *45*, 1–4. [CrossRef]
3. Koppel, M.; Schler, J.; Messeri, E. Authorship attribution in law enforcement scenarios. *NATO Secur. Through Sci. Ser. D Inf. Commun. Secur.* **2008**, *15*, 111.
4. Xu, J.M.; Zhu, X.; Bellmore, A. Fast learning for sentiment analysis on bullying. In Proceedings of the First International Workshop on Issues of Sentiment Discovery and Opinion Mining, Beijing, China, 12 August 2012; pp. 1–6.
5. Sinnott, R.; Wang, Z. Linking User Accounts across Social Media Platforms. In Proceedings of the 2021 IEEE/ACM 8th International Conference on Big Data Computing, Applications and Technologies (BDCAT'21), Leicester, UK, 6–9 December 2021; pp. 18–27.
6. Zhang, S. Authorship attribution and feature testing for short Chinese emails. *Int. J. Speech Lang. Law* **2016**, *23*, 71–97. [CrossRef]
7. Barbon, S.; Igawa, R.A.; Bogaz Zarpelão, B. Authorship verification applied to detection of compromised accounts on online social networks. *Multimed. Tools Appl.* **2017**, *76*, 3213–3233. [CrossRef]
8. Kestemont, M.; Manjavacas, E.; Markov, I.; Bevendorff, J.; Wiegmann, M.; Stamatatos, E.; Stein, B.; Potthast, M. Overview of the cross-domain authorship verification task at PAN 2021. In *CLEF (Working Notes)*; CEUR-WS: Bucharest, Romania, 21–24 September 2021.
9. Kestemont, M.; Tschuggnall, M.; Stamatatos, E.; Daelemans, W.; Specht, G.; Stein, B.; Potthast, M. Overview of the author identification task at PAN-2018: Cross-domain authorship attribution and style change detection. In *Working Notes Papers of the CLEF 2018 Evaluation Labs*; Cappellato, L., Ferro, N., Nie, J.Y., Soulier, L., Eds.; CLEF: Thessaloniki, Greece, 2018; Volume 2125; pp. 1–25.
10. Tyo, J.; Dhingra, B.; Lipton, Z.C. On the State of the Art in Authorship Attribution and Authorship Verification. *arXiv* **2022**, arXiv:2209.06869.
11. Barlas, G.; Stamatatos, E. A transfer learning approach to cross-domain authorship attribution. *Evol. Syst.* **2021**, *12*, 625–643. [CrossRef]
12. PAN Datasets. Available online: https://pan.webis.de/data.html?q=Attribution (accessed on 8 November 2022).
13. Tatman, R. Blog Authorship Corpus. Available online: https://www.kaggle.com/datasets/rtatman/blog-authorship-corpus (accessed on 8 November 2022).
14. Kestemont, M.; Stamatatos, E.; Manjavacas, E.; Daelemans, W.; Potthast, M.; Stein, B. *PAN19 Authorship Analysis: Cross-Domain Authorship Attribution*; 2019. https://doi.org/10.5281/zenodo.3530313 (accessed on 8 November 2022).
15. Al-Sarem, M.; Saeed, F.; Alsaeedi, A.; Boulila, W.; Al-Hadhrami, T. Ensemble methods for instance-based arabic language authorship attribution. *IEEE Access* **2020**, *8*, 17331–17345. [CrossRef]
16. AI, Twine. The Best Romanian Language Datasets of 2022. Available online: https://www.twine.net/blog/romanian-language-datasets/ (accessed on 8 November 2022).

17. Wang, H.; Riddell, A.; Juola, P. Mode effects' challenge to authorship attribution. In *Proceedings of the 16th Conference of the European Chapter of the Association for Computational Linguistics: Main Volume*; Association for Computational Linguistics: Punta Cana, Dominican Republic, 2021; pp. 1146–1155.
18. van Halteren, H.; Baayen, H.; Tweedie, F.; Haverkort, M.; Neijt, A. New Machine Learning Methods Demonstrate the Existence of a Human Stylome. *J. Quant. Linguist.* **2005**, *12*, 65–77. [CrossRef]
19. Gröndahl, T.; Asokan, N. Text analysis in adversarial settings: Does deception leave a stylistic trace? *ACM Comput. Surv. (CSUR)* **2019**, *52*, 45. [CrossRef]
20. Stamatatos, E. A survey of modern authorship attribution methods. *J. Am. Soc. Inf. Sci. Technol.* **2009**, *60*, 538–556. [CrossRef]
21. Sebastiani, F. Machine learning in automated text categorization. *ACM Comput. Surv. (CSUR)* **2002**, *34*, 1–47. [CrossRef]
22. Burrows, J.F. Word-patterns and story-shapes: The statistical analysis of narrative style. *Lit. Linguist. Comput.* **1987**, *2*, 61–70. [CrossRef]
23. Stamatatos, E. Authorship attribution based on feature set subspacing ensembles. *Int. J. Artif. Intell. Tools* **2006**, *15*, 823–838. [CrossRef]
24. Madigan, D.; Genkin, A.; Lewis, D.D.; Argamon, S.; Fradkin, D.; Ye, L. Author identification on the large scale. In Proceedings of the 2005 Meeting of the Classification Society of North America (CSNA), St. Louis, MO, USA, 8–12 June 2005.
25. Coyotl-Morales, R.M.; Villaseñor-Pineda, L.; Montes-y Gómez, M.; Rosso, P. Authorship attribution using word sequences. In *Iberoamerican Congress on Pattern Recognition*; Springer: Berlin/Heidelberg, Germany, 2006; pp. 844–853.
26. Sanderson, C.; Guenter, S. Short text authorship attribution via sequence kernels, Markov chains and author unmasking: An investigation. In Proceedings of the 2006 Conference on Empirical Methods in Natural Language Processing, Sydney, Australia, 22–23 July 2006; pp. 482–491.
27. Grieve, J. Quantitative authorship attribution: An evaluation of techniques. *Lit. Linguist. Comput.* **2007**, *22*, 251–270. [CrossRef]
28. Neal, T.; Sundararajan, K.; Fatima, A.; Yan, Y.; Xiang, Y.; Woodard, D. Surveying stylometry techniques and applications. *ACM Comput. Surv. (CSuR)* **2017**, *50*, 86. [CrossRef]
29. Zhang, C.; Wu, X.; Niu, Z.; Ding, W. Authorship identification from unstructured texts. *Knowl. Based Syst.* **2014**, *66*, 99–111. [CrossRef]
30. Forman, G. An extensive empirical study of feature selection metrics for text classification. *J. Mach. Learn. Res.* **2003**, *3*, 1289–1305.
31. Argamon, S.; Juola, P. Overview of the International Authorship Identification Competition at PAN-2011. In Proceedings of the Notebook Papers of CLEF 2011 Labs and Workshops, Amsterdam, The Netherlands, 19–22 September 2011.
32. Argamon, S.; Juola, P. *PAN11 Author Identification: Attribution*; CLEF 2011 Labs and Workshops, Notebook Papers; CLEF: Thessaloniki, Greece, 2011. [CrossRef]
33. Juola, P. An Overview of the Traditional Authorship Attribution Subtask. In Proceedings of the CLEF 2012 Evaluation Labs and Workshop—Working Notes Papers, Rome, Italy, 17–20 September 2012.
34. Kestemont, M.E.A. PAN18 Author Identification: Attribution. 2018. Available online: https://datasetsearch.research.google.com/search?query=pan18-authorship-attribution&docid=L2cvMTFsajRfZjZ6OQ%3D%3D/ (accessed on 7 November 2022).
35. Kestemont, M.; Stamatatos, E.; Manjavacas, E.; Daelemans, W.; Potthast, M.; Stein, B. Overview of the Cross-domain Authorship Attribution Task at PAN 2019. In *CLEF 2019 Labs and Workshops, Notebook Papers*; Cappellato, L., Ferro, N., Losada, D., Müller, H., Eds.; CLEF: Thessaloniki, Greece, 2019.
36. Kestemont, M.; Manjavacas, E.; Markov, I.; Bevendorff, J.; Wiegmann, M.; Stamatatos, E.; Potthast, M.; Stein, B. Overview of the Cross-Domain Authorship Verification Task at PAN 2020. In *CLEF 2020 Labs and Workshops, Notebook Papers*; Cappellato, L., Eickhoff, C., Ferro, N., Névéol, A., Eds.; CLEF: Thessaloniki, Greece, 2020.
37. Pavelec, D.; Oliveira, L.S.; Justino, E.J.; Batista, L.V. Using Conjunctions and Adverbs for Author Verification. *J. Univers. Comput. Sci.* **2008**, *14*, 2967–2981.
38. Varela, P.; Justino, E.; Oliveira, L.S. Verbs and pronouns for authorship attribution. In Proceedings of the 17th International Conference on Systems, Signals and Image Processing (IWSSIP 2010), Rio de Janeiro, Brazil, 17–19 June 2010; pp. 89–92.
39. Seroussi, Y.; Smyth, R.; Zukerman, I. Ghosts from the high court's past: Evidence from computational linguistics for Dixon ghosting for Mctiernan and rich. *Univ. N. S. W. Law J.* **2011**, *34*, 984–1005.
40. Seroussi, Y.; Zukerman, I.; Bohnert, F. Collaborative inference of sentiments from texts. In Proceedings of the International Conference on User Modeling, Adaptation, and Personalization, Manoa, HI, USA, 20–14 June 2010; Springer: Berlin/Heidelberg, Germany, 2010; pp. 195–206.
41. Seroussi, Y.; Bohnert, F.; Zukerman, I. Personalised rating prediction for new users using latent factor models. In Proceedings of the 22nd ACM Conference on Hypertext and Hypermedia, Eindhoven, The Netherlands, 6–9 June 2011; pp. 47–56.
42. Stamatatos, E. Author identification: Using text sampling to handle the class imbalance problem. *Inf. Process. Manag.* **2008**, *44*, 790–799. [CrossRef]
43. Stamatatos, E. On the robustness of authorship attribution based on character n-gram features. *JL Pol'y* **2012**, *21*, 421.
44. Schler, J.; Koppel, M.; Argamon, S.; Pennebaker, J.W. Effects of age and gender on blogging. In *AAAI Spring Symposium: Computational Approaches to Analyzing Weblogs*; AAAI Press: Menlo Park, CA, USA, 2006; Volume 6; pp. 199–205.
45. Goldstein, J.; Goodwin, K.; Sabin, R.; Winder, R. Creating and Using a Correlated Corpus to Glean Communicative Commonalities. In Proceedings of the Sixth International Conference on Language Resources and Evaluation (LREC'08), Marrakesh, Morocco, 28–30 May 2008.

46. Mirończuk, M.M.; Protasiewicz, J. A recent overview of the state-of-the-art elements of text classification. *Expert Syst. Appl.* **2018**, *106*, 36–54. [CrossRef]
47. Liu, B.; Xiao, Y.; Hao, Z. A selective multiple instance transfer learning method for text categorization problems. *Knowl. Based Syst.* **2018**, *141*, 178–187. [CrossRef]
48. Cunningham, P.; Cord, M.; Delany, S.J. Supervised learning. In *Machine Learning Techniques for Multimedia*; Springer: Berlin/Heidelberg, Germany, 2008; pp. 21–49.
49. Manning, C.D.; Raghavan, P.; Schutze, H. *Introduction to Information Retrieval*; Cambridge Univ. Press: Cambridge, UK, 2008, Ch. 20; pp. 405–416.
50. Mihalcea, R.; Radev, D. *Graph-Based Natural Language Processing and Information Retrieval*; Cambridge University Press: Cambridge, UK, 2011.
51. Altınel, B.; Ganiz, M.C.; Diri, B. Instance labeling in semi-supervised learning with meaning values of words. *Eng. Appl. Artif. Intell.* **2017**, *62*, 152–163. [CrossRef]
52. Lochter, J.V.; Zanetti, R.F.; Reller, D.; Almeida, T.A. Short text opinion detection using ensemble of classifiers and semantic indexing. *Expert Syst. Appl.* **2016**, *62*, 243–249. [CrossRef]
53. Hu, R.; Mac Namee, B.; Delany, S.J. Active learning for text classification with reusability. *Expert Syst. Appl.* **2016**, *45*, 438–449. [CrossRef]
54. Weiss, K.; Khoshgoftaar, T.M.; Wang, D. A survey of transfer learning. *J. Big Data* **2016**, *3*, 9. [CrossRef]
55. Zhao, J.; Xie, X.; Xu, X.; Sun, S. Multi-view learning overview: Recent progress and new challenges. *Inf. Fusion* **2017**, *38*, 43–54. [CrossRef]
56. Ali, R.; Lee, S.; Chung, T.C. Accurate multi-criteria decision making methodology for recommending machine learning algorithm. *Expert Syst. Appl.* **2017**, *71*, 257–278. [CrossRef]
57. Altakrori, M.; Cheung, J.C.K.; Fung, B.C.M. The Topic Confusion Task: A Novel Evaluation Scenario for Authorship Attribution. In *Findings of the Association for Computational Linguistics: EMNLP 2021*; Association for Computational Linguistics: Punta Cana, Dominican Republic, 2021; pp. 4242–4256. [CrossRef]
58. Sari, Y.; Stevenson, M.; Vlachos, A. Topic or style? Exploring the most useful features for authorship attribution. In Proceedings of the 27th International Conference on Computational Linguistics, Santa Fe, NM, USA, 20–26 August 2018; pp. 343–353.
59. Sundararajan, K.; Woodard, D. What represents "style" in authorship attribution? In Proceedings of the 27th International Conference on Computational Linguistics, Santa Fe, NM, USA, 20–26 August 2018; pp. 2814–2822.
60. Custódio, J.E.; Paraboni, I. Stacked authorship attribution of digital texts. *Expert Syst. Appl.* **2021**, *176*, 114866. [CrossRef]
61. González Brito, O.; Tapia Fabela, J.L.; Salas Hernández, S. New approach to feature extraction in authorship attribution. *Int. J. Comb. Optim. Probl. Inform.* **2021**, *12*, 87–97.
62. Murauer, B.; Specht, G. Developing a Benchmark for Reducing Data Bias in Authorship Attribution. In Proceedings of the 2nd Workshop on Evaluation and Comparison of NLP Systems, Punta Cana, Dominican Republic, 10–11 November 2021; Association for Computational Linguistics: Punta Cana, Dominican Republic, 2021; pp. 179–188. [CrossRef]
63. Bischoff, S.; Deckers, N.; Schliebs, M.; Thies, B.; Hagen, M.; Stamatatos, E.; Stein, B.; Potthast, M. The importance of suppressing domain style in authorship analysis. *arXiv* **2020**, arXiv:2005.14714.
64. Stamatatos, E. Masking topic-related information to enhance authorship attribution. *J. Assoc. Inf. Sci. Technol.* **2018**, *69*, 461–473. [CrossRef]
65. Halvani, O.; Graner, L. *Cross-Domain Authorship Attribution Based on Compression*; Working Notes of CLEF; Springer: Berlin/Heidelberg, Germany, 2018.
66. Fabien, M.; Villatoro-Tello, E.; Motlicek, P.; Parida, S. BertAA: BERT fine-tuning for Authorship Attribution. In Proceedings of the 17th International Conference on Natural Language Processing (ICON), Patna, India, 18–21 December 2020; NLP Association of India (NLPAI), Indian Institute of Technology Patna: Patna, India, 2020; pp. 127–137.
67. Barlas, G.; Stamatatos, E. Cross-domain authorship attribution using pre-trained language models. In *IFIP International Conference on Artificial Intelligence Applications and Innovations*; Springer: Berlin/Heidelberg, Germany, 2020; pp. 255–266.
68. Avram, S.M. ROST (ROmanian Stories and Other Texts). Available online: https://www.kaggle.com/datasets/sandamariaavram/rost-romanian-stories-and-other-texts (accessed on 8 November 2022).
69. Zurada, J.M. *Introduction to Artificial Neural Systems*; PWS Publishing Company: Boston, MA, USA, 1992.
70. Steffen, N. *Neural Networks Made Simple*; Fast Neural Network Library (Fann): Online Library, 2005; pp. 14–15.
71. Oltean, M. *Multi Expression Programming for Solving Classification Problems*; Technical Report; Research Square: Durham, NC, USA, 2022.
72. Koza, J. *Genetic Programming*; A Bradford Book; MIT Press: Cambridge, MA, USA, 1996.
73. Aho, A.V.; Sethi, R.; Ullman, J.D. *Compilers, Principles, Techniques, and Tools*; Addison-Wesley: Boston, MA, USA, 1986.
74. Oltean, M. MEPX Software. Available online: http://mepx.org/mepx_software.html (accessed on 8 November 2022).
75. Fix, E.; Hodges, J.J. *Discriminatory Analysis: Non-Parametric Discrimination: Consistency Properties*; Technical Report; USAF School of Aviation Medicine: Dayton, OH, USA, 1951.
76. Fix, E.; Hodges, J.J. *Discriminatory Analysis: Non-Parametric Discrimination: Small Sample Performance*; Technical Report; USAF School of Aviation Medicine: Dayton, OH, USA, 1952.
77. Altman, N.S. An introduction to kernel and nearest-neighbor nonparametric regression. *Am. Stat.* **1992**, *46*, 175–185.

78. Aha, D.W.; Kibler, D.; Albert, M.K. Instance-based learning algorithms. *Mach. Learn.* **1991**, *6*, 37–66. [CrossRef]
79. Boser, B.E.; Guyon, I.M.; Vapnik, V.N. A training algorithm for optimal margin classifiers. In Proceedings of the Fifth Annual Workshop on Computational Learning Theory, Pittsburgh, PA, USA, 27–29 July 1992; pp. 144–152.
80. Hsu, C.W.; Chang, C.C.; Lin, C.J. *A Practical Guide to Support Vector Classification*; Department of Computer Science and Information Engineering, University of National Taiwan: Taipei, Taiwan, 2003.
81. Chang, C.C.; Lin, C.J. LIBSVM: A library for support vector machines. *ACM Trans. Intell. Syst. Technol.* **2011**, *2*, 27. Available online: http://www.csie.ntu.edu.tw/~cjlin/libsvm (accessed on 3 November 2022). [CrossRef]
82. Quinlan, J.R. Induction of decision trees. *Mach. Learn.* **1986**, *1*, 81–106. [CrossRef]
83. RuleQuest. Data Mining Tools See5 and C5.0. Available online: https://www.rulequest.com/see5-info.html (accessed on 2 November 2022).
84. Pant, A.K. Accuracy Evaluation (A c++ Implementation for Calculating the Accuracy Metrics (Accuracy, Error Rate, Precision (Micro/Macro), Recall (Micro/Macro), Fscore (Micro/Macro)) for Classification Tasks). Available online: https://github.com/ashokpant/accuracy-evaluation-cpp (accessed on 29 October 2022).
85. Sokolova, M.; Lapalme, G. A systematic analysis of performance measures for classification tasks. *Inf. Process. Manag.* **2009**, *45*, 427–437. [CrossRef]

mathematics

Article

TwoViewDensityNet: Two-View Mammographic Breast Density Classification Based on Deep Convolutional Neural Network

Mariam Busaleh [1], Muhammad Hussain [1,*], Hatim A. Aboalsamh [1], Fazal-e-Amin [2] and Sarah A. Al Sultan [3]

[1] Department of Computer Science, College of Computer and Information Sciences, King Saud University, Riyadh 11451, Saudi Arabia
[2] Department of Software Engineering, College of Computer and Information Sciences, King Saud University, Riyadh 11543, Saudi Arabia
[3] Department of Radiology, College of Medicine, King Khalid University Hospital, King Saud University, Riyadh 12372, Saudi Arabia
* Correspondence: mhussain@ksu.edu.sa

Abstract: Dense breast tissue is a significant factor that increases the risk of breast cancer. Current mammographic density classification approaches are unable to provide enough classification accuracy. However, it remains a difficult problem to classify breast density. This paper proposes TwoViewDensityNet, an end-to-end deep learning-based method for mammographic breast density classification. The craniocaudal (CC) and mediolateral oblique (MLO) views of screening mammography provide two different views of each breast. As the two views are complementary, and dual-view-based methods have proven efficient, we use two views for breast classification. The loss function plays a key role in training a deep model; we employ the focal loss function because it focuses on learning hard cases. The method was thoroughly evaluated on two public datasets using 5-fold cross-validation, and it achieved an overall performance (F-score of 98.63%, AUC of 99.51%, accuracy of 95.83%) on DDSM and (F-score of 97.14%, AUC of 97.44%, accuracy of 96%) on the INbreast. The comparison shows that the TwoViewDensityNet outperforms the state-of-the-art methods for classifying breast density into BI-RADS class. It aids healthcare providers in providing patients with more accurate information and will help improve the diagnostic accuracy and reliability of mammographic breast density evaluation in clinical care.

Keywords: breast density classification; mammography; craniocaudal (CC) view; mediolateral oblique (MLO) view; BI-RADS; convolutional neural network (CNN); loss function

MSC: 68T07

Citation: Busaleh, M.; Hussain, M.; Aboalsamh, H.A.; Fazal-e-Amin; Al Sultan, S.A. TwoViewDensityNet: Two-View Mammographic Breast Density Classification Based on Deep Convolutional Neural Network. *Mathematics* **2022**, *10*, 4610. https://doi.org/10.3390/math10234610

Academic Editors: Adrian Sergiu Darabant and Diana-Laura Borza

Received: 27 October 2022
Accepted: 24 November 2022
Published: 5 December 2022

1. Introduction

Breast density is a significant risk factor for breast cancer because it indicates the proportion of fibroglandular tissue to fat tissue in the breast [1–4]. Breast tissue has varied X-ray attenuation qualities, resulting in a different mammographic density. Fat tissue is dark (radiolucent), while fibroglandular tissue is white (radiopaque) in appearance [5]. American College of Radiology (ACR) Breast Imaging Reporting and Data System (BI-RADS) results from the reporting system describe density levels [6]. According to the BI-RADS 5th edition, the distribution of parenchymal density based on the relative modulating factor hard negatives are the appearance of breast tissue is classified into four categories: BI-RADS I: fatty (0–25%), BI-RADSII: scattered density (26–50%), BI-RADSIII: heterogeneously dense (51–75%), BI-RADSIV: extremely dense (76–100%). Figure 1 presents examples of each type of BI-RADS mammogram from the Digital Database for Screening Mammography (DDSM). Mammographic breast density classification focuses significantly on breast cancer prevention and risk assessment in breast cancer studies. Many researchers in medical imaging recently applied deep-learning models to address this issue, although their performance is low and may not be for clinical application [7–10].

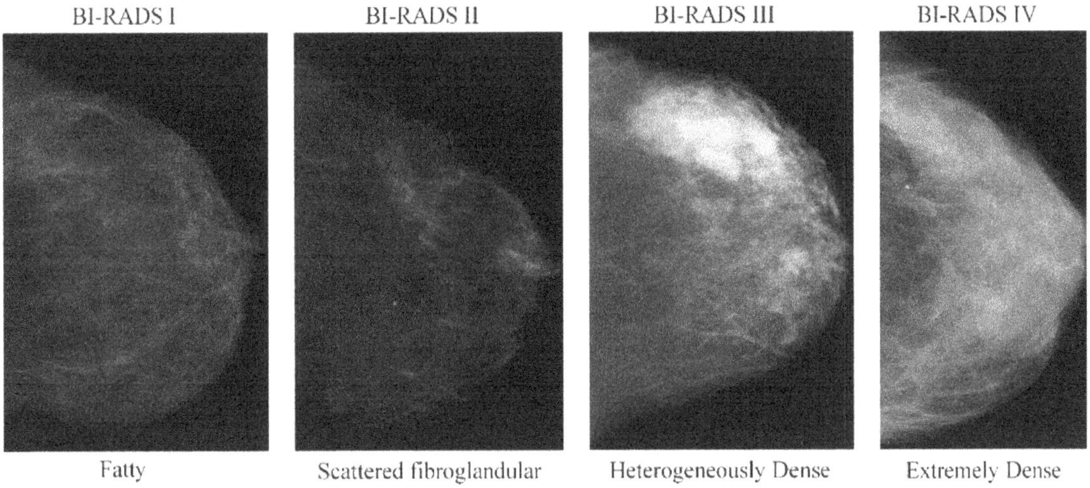

Figure 1. Examples of BI-RADS breast composition categories of breast density in increasing order of density from left to right [11].

The craniocaudal (CC) and mediolateral oblique (MLO) views of screening mammography provide distinct breast views. Due to the complementing characteristics of these two views, the dual view can be used for better performance because the dual-view strategy achieves a more promising performance than using a single view. We introduce a method for automatically classifying mammographic density from the two views that provide more information predicting breast cancer risk. The Digital Database for Screening Mammography (DDSM) dataset was used to test the system. The main contributions of this study can be summarized as follows:

- We proposed an end-to-end deep learning-based model—TwoViewDensityNet—for the classification of breast density using dual mammogram views, i.e., craniocaudal (CC) view and mediolateral oblique (MLO) view. It combines the CC and MLO views by leveraging the relationship between views and using a CNN as the backbone model. First, it extracts the complementary information from each view using a CNN model, fuses them using a concatenation layer, and finally, predicts the density class using an FC layer with SoftMax activation.
- We evaluated different preprocessing techniques to enhance the mammogram image before feeding it to the CNN model and found the one that is best suited for the proposed model.
- We employed different loss functions and their valuable characteristics to tackle the class-imbalance problem.

The remainder of this paper is organized as follows. Section 2 presents previous works related to breast density classification. Section 3 describes the proposed system of four BI-RADS categorizations. We present evaluation protocols in Section 4. Experimental results, as well as their interpretation and discussion, are presented in Section 5. Finally, we end up with the conclusions in Section 6.

2. Related Work

Many researchers have focused their attention on the challenge of classifying breast density into BI-RADS classifications. These approaches were tested with benchmark datasets such as the Digital Database for Screening Mammography (DDSM), INbreast, and

Private datasets. Several methods that use deep learning have been proposed, including single-view-based and multi-view-based, reviewed in the following sections. A summary of these studies in the recent literature is presented in Table 1.

Table 1. The comparison with different state-of-the-art methods for breast density classification.

References	Model	Dataset	ACC (%)	AUC (%)	F1-Score (%)
	Single View				
Li et al. [7] (2021)	ResNet50 + DC + CA (DC: dilated convolutions. CA:channel-wise attention)	Private	88.70	97.40	87.10
		INbreast	70	84.70	63.50
Jian et al. [14] (2020)	Inception-V4-SE- Attention	Private	92.17	-	-
	ResNeXt-SE-Attention and	Private	89.97		
	DenseNet-SE-Attention	Private	89.64		
Yi et al. [8] (2019)	ResNet-50	DDSM	68	-	-
Lehman et al. [10] (2019)	ResNet-18	Private	77	-	-
Gandomkar et al. [13] (2019)	Inception-V3	Private	83.33	-	77.50
Mohamed et al. [15] (2018)	AlexNet	Private	-	92	-
	Multi-View				
Zhao et al. [12] (2021)	BASCNet (ResNet) (Bilateral-view adaptive spatial and channel attention network)	DDSM	85.10	91.54	78.92
		INbreast	90.51	99.09	78.11
Li et al. [7] (2021)	ResNet50 + DC + CA (DC: dilated convolutions. CA: channel-wise attention)	Private	92.10	98.1	91.2
			92.50	98.2	91.7
			75.20	93.6	67.9
Timothy and Lakshman [16] (2020)	DualViewNet	CBISDDSM	-	89.70	-
Wu et al. [9] (2018)	VGG Net	Private	69.40	84.20	-

Li et al. [7] developed a CNN model based on dilated and attention-guided residual learning for the mammography density classification task. In addition, a multi-stream architecture was designed specifically to analyze multi-view mammograms. They achieved an accuracy of 88.7% and 70.0%, respectively. Yi et al. [8] developed deep convolutional neural networks (DCNNs) based on ResNet-50 to categorize two-dimensional mammography images, determine breast laterality, and assess breast tissue density. Their approach achieved 68% accuracy with breast density classification. Wu et al. [9] proposed a multi-view three-layer CNN to categorize breast density into the four density categories or superclasses (dense and non-dense), using all four mammography views as input. It gave an accuracy of 82.5% for superclasses and a macAUC (macro average) of 0.934 (Class 0: 0.971, Class 1: 0.859, C2: 0.905, and Class 3: 1) for the four-density classification. Lehman et al. [10] proposed deep learning based on ResNet-18 for dense and non-dense and BI-RADS density classification. They showed good agreement (kappa value = 77%) for four BI-RADS categorizations with radiologists in the test set. Zhao et al. [12] proposed a bilateral-view adaptive spatial and channel attention network (BASCNet) based on ResNet-50 as a backbone for fully automated breast density classification by integrating left and right breast information and adaptively capturing distinguishing features in space and channel dimensions. The method achieved accuracies of 85.10% and 90.51%. Gandomkar et al. [13] addressed the fine-tuning of the Inception-V3 model for the classification of breast density (i) fatty or dense, (ii) BI-RADS I, BI-RADS/II, and (iii) BI-RADS III/BI-RADS IV. The method achieved an accuracy of 83.33% and a Cohen's kappa of 0.775 for four BI-RADS categorizations. Jian et al. [14] developed an attention strategy in which the SE-Attention mechanism is combined with the CNN framework to classify four BI-RADS. This method achieved accuracies of 92.17%, 89.97%, 89.64%, and 89.20% for Inception-V4-SE- Attention, Inception-V4, ResNeXt, and DenseNet models, respectively. Mohamed et al. [15] designed an end-to-end

CNN model using improved AlexNet to classify breast density into BI-RADS categories. II and BI-RADS.III. The method achieved an AUC of 0.9421.

The preceding review of state-of-the-art approaches demonstrates that breast density classification requires additional research. All the methods discussed above use the cross-entropy function, which is often used for classification problems. We used different loss functions, such as focal and sum square error loss, to boost the CNN model's classification accuracy. Additionally, by utilizing different preprocessing approaches to improve the training data provided to the CNN, it is possible to learn various density features. The preceding review of state-of-the-art approaches demonstrates that breast density classification requires additional research. Unilateral mammography images may not contain enough information to accurately classify breast density [7,9,12]. The classification accuracy will be improved by incorporating image information from contralateral or multi-view mammography. Previous studies have based their criteria on multi-view (i.e., four views including left MLO, right MLO, left CC, right CC) or two-view (i.e., similar for two MLO-view or two CC-view). In addition, the training data provided to the CNN requirement of previous studies were based on input images of size 224 × 224, whereas we used input images of size 336 × 224 to accommodate the regular aspect ratio of mammograms.

Timothy and Lakshman [16] developed DualViewNet for density classification similar to our method. The proposed model classifies MLO and CC mammograms taken from the same breast. It gave an AUC of 89.70%. The main difference between this method and our approach is the architecture of the deep models. The method in [16] extracts features using convolutional layers of two deep models, concatenates them, and classifies them; As the features from the convolutional layers are concatenated directly, so the dimension of the feature space becomes very high, which leads to classification layer with a huge number of learnable parameters. It restricts the use of only the CNN models with a reduced number of parameters, such as MobileNetV2, to avoid overfitting. On the contrary, our method first extracts features using the convolutional layers of deep models, then reduces the dimension of the feature space using global average pooling (GAP) layers and concatenates them. In this way, the dimension of the feature space is significantly reduced, and the parameter complexity of the classification layer remains very low. It allows using any pretrained CNN model as a backbone avoiding the fear of overfitting. Moreover, we first extract the breast area, unlike the method in [16], to emphasize the breast density, not just color mapping to magma and resizing to 336 × 224.

3. Proposed Method

In mammography, two views, i.e., CC and MLO, of the ipsilateral breast (i.e., two-view analysis) and the corresponding views of the contralateral breast (i.e., bilateral analysis) are captured to analyze the breast for detecting possible abnormalities. Both views have a complementary relationship and reveal signs of an abnormality better than a single view. Various multi-view approaches were proposed to improve the detection of breast abnormal ities in mammograms. Multiple views of the right and left breasts in CC and MLO views are used to derive the information for these procedures. The ipsilateral analysis is based on combining the different projection views of the same breast, and bilateral analysis is based on combining the same projection view of the left and right breast [17–21]. This observation has been employed in different techniques for mass classification [22–24] and density classification. These studies reveal that multi-views result in better performance than a single view. Inspired by this, we propose a prediction model for breast density classification into four BI-RADS categories based on dual views, as shown in Figure 2. The proposed technique is an end-to-end deep learning-based model (we call it TwoViewDensityNet) that takes two views, i.e., two mammogram images of size 336 × 224 as input and predicts the label of the density type of the breast according to BI-RADS classification. It consists of two branches, one for each view. First, each branch preprocesses the corresponding view and extracts hierarchical features using a convolutional neural network (CNN) as a backbone model. The features from the two views are fused by the concatenation layer and passed to an FC layer, which serves as a classifier and yields the prediction label of the input mammographic views.

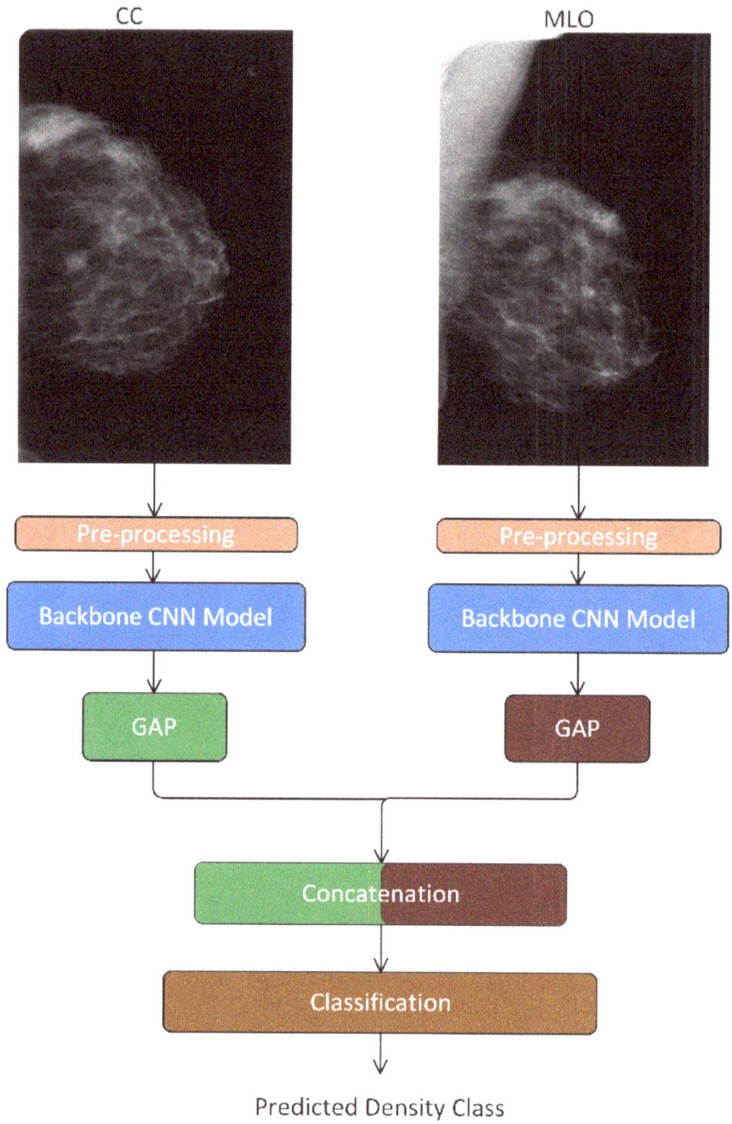

Figure 2. Proposed density classification system. GAP stands for global average pool.

The precise specification of this method relies on three important design decisions: (i) which preprocessing technique is suitable, (ii) which backbone CNN model is suited for this task, and (iii) which loss function helps to train the model so that it has good generalization. Each of these design decisions is discussed in detail in the following subsections.

3.1. Preprocessing

Breast tissue is crucial for discrimination between different breast density classes; it must be adequately separated from the background. Removing all artifacts from the image leaves only the breast tissue area for the model to learn from. In the first step, we used the threshold value 200 to generate a binary mask, where 0 (black) is the background pixel, and

1 (white) is the breast region, artifact, or noise pixel. Afterward, a morphological opening operator is applied to the binary image with a disk-type structuring element of size 9×9 to extract the breast tissue area; it is more prominent than any object; it is binarized as a single region. As a result, the most significant contours are retained, and the remainder is discarded. Then, we overlay this mask to eliminate mammography artifacts and keep only the breast tissue area. Then, the bounding box of the breast tissue is used to crop each view so that it mainly contains the breast tissue.

Furthermore, we use magma color mapping from 16-bit grayscale to 24-bit RGB, as used in [16]; it enhances the perceptual quality [25,26] of the fibroglandular tissue and fat tissue. In addition, it maps the gray-level mammogram image on an RGB image, which can be passed easily to pretrained CNN models, which are usually pretrained on RGB pictures from ImageNet [27]. Figure 3 illustrates the whole preprocessing process.

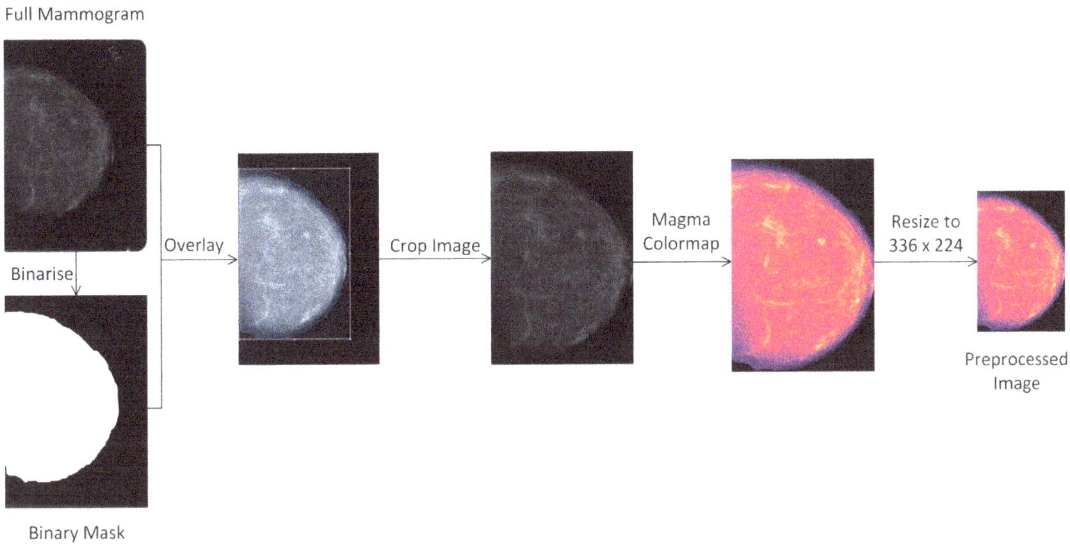

Figure 3. Preprocessing method for mammogram image.

3.2. Backbone Convolutional Neural Network (CNN) Model

The TwoViewDensityNet model employs two convolutional neural networks for feature extraction from each view. Greater depth in CNN models allows for extracting discriminative features, improving classification performance. Various widely used deep convolutional models, such as ResNet50 [28], EfficientNetb0 [29], and DenseNet201 [30], etc., can be exploited for feature extraction. We used ResNet-50 pretrained on ImageNet [27]; its architecture is based on residual learning, which allows increasing the depth of a CNN model that prevents the problem of gradient vanishing [31] and degradation [32,33].

3.3. Concatenation Layer

Different techniques combine the extracted deep features from the two views, such as concatenation and element-wise operations. In our proposed method, the features from the two views are fused by the concatenation layer. The output of the global average pooling (GAP) of ResNet-50 in the left branch is $x_1 = [\alpha_1, \alpha_2, \ldots, \alpha_{2048}]^T$, and the right branch is $x_2 = [\beta_1, \beta_2, \ldots, \beta_{2048}]^T$. To fuse features from both views, we concatenate them in x where $x = [\alpha_1, \alpha_2, \ldots, \alpha_{2048}, \beta_1, \beta_2, \ldots, \beta_{2048}]$.

3.4. Classification Layer

The last layer of the model is the classification layer; it is a fully connected layer with four output neurons to classify the input views into one of the four breast density categories; each neuron represents a different BI-RADS class. The output FC layer employs a SoftMax function as an activation function because it is the most commonly used activation function in the output layer; it converts the numerical output of a convolutional neural network to class-specific probability values. The predicted class of the input views is the one for which the posterior probability is maximum. The difference between the predicted class and the actual label is then calculated using a loss function at each training iteration.

3.5. Training the TwoViewDensityNet

The training of the network is an iterative process, and it depends on how accurately the error made by the network is measured, i.e., how the loss function is defined. First, we discuss the loss functions and then describe the optimization method used for training.

3.5.1. Loss Functions

The critical component of a deep-learning algorithm is the loss function; it indicates how much error a neural network makes in recognizing the input image. A sample's involvement in the optimization problem is measured using a loss function, which assigns a numerical value to each input instance, i.e., the loss. The model parameters are updated so that the loss is minimum. We adopt some well-known loss functions.

Weighted cross-entropy loss (WCE) [34].

Let K be the number of classes and N the number of training instances in a batch. Further, let y_{ni} be the predicted posterior probability of nth training example in the batch that belongs to i^{th} class, then the weighted cross-entropy loss function is calculated as follows in Equation (1):

$$Loss = -\frac{1}{N}\sum_{n=1}^{N}\sum_{i=1}^{K} w_i T_{ni} \ln y_{ni} \tag{1}$$

where T_{ni} is the true posterior probability of nth training example in the batch that belongs to an ith class (in one-hot encoding vector), and w_i is the prior of the ith class. Further, if the total batch size is N and the number of instances of the ith class is m_i, then $w_i = \frac{m_i}{N}$.

Focal loss (FL) [35].

Let K be the number of classes and N the number of training instances in a batch. Further, let y_{ni} be the predicted posterior probability of nth training example in the batch that it belongs to i^{th} class, then the focal loss function is calculated as follows in Equation (2):

$$Loss = -\frac{1}{N}\sum_{n=1}^{N}\sum_{i=1}^{K} T_{ni}\alpha(1-y_{ni})^{\gamma} \ln y_{ni} \tag{2}$$

where T_{ni} is the true posterior probability of nth training example in the batch that belongs to an ith class, and γ is the focusing parameter where $\gamma \epsilon [0, 0.5]$.

Sum square error loss (SSE) [36].

Let K be the number of classes and N the number of training instances in a batch. Further, let y_{ni} be the predicted posterior probability of the nth training example in the batch that belongs to the ith class, then the sum square error loss function is calculated as follows in Equation (3):

$$Loss = -\frac{1}{N}\sum_{n=1}^{N}\sum_{i=1}^{K} (y_{ni} - T_{ni})^2 \tag{3}$$

where T_{ni} is the true posterior probability of nth training example in the batch that belongs to an ith class.

3.5.2. Algorithms Used for Training

Fine-tuning involves various hyper-parameters: the optimization algorithm, learning rate, batch size, and the number of training epochs. We attempt different options to determine the best values of the hyperparameters. We tested three optimizers (Adam, SGD, and RMSprop), a learning rate between 1×10^{-4} and 1×10^{-2}, four batch sizes (16, 32, 64), and the number of epochs between 50 and 100. Early stopping is performed with patience of seven iterations to further reduce overfitting. Finally, we have decided on stochastic gradient descent (SGD) optimizers to fine-tune the models with a momentum of 0.9 and an initial learning rate of 1×10^{-4}. The training epoch is 50, and the batch size is 64; this would result in approximately 3–4 h of runtime.

3.5.3. Datasets

To verify the proposed system's efficiency and robustness, we employed two publicly available mammographic benchmark datasets:

Digital Database for Screening Mammography (DDSM) [11]. The DDSM database consists of 2620 mammography screening cases containing a total of 10,480 mammograms with a resolution of 4000 × 6000 pixels. Moreover, they are stored in portable gray map (PGM) format with 16 bits; every case includes two views of bilateral breasts craniocaudal (CC), mediolateral oblique (MLO), breast laterality (right vs. left), and Breast Imaging Reporting and Data System (BI-RADS) breast density (four categories: almost entirely fatty, scattered area of fibroglandular density, heterogeneously dense, and extremely dense). We selected two views of each breast density category, totaling 5406 images, and the image distribution over the four categories presented in Figure 4a. Five-fold cross-validation is used to train and test models. Figure 4b shows the data distribution for each fold.

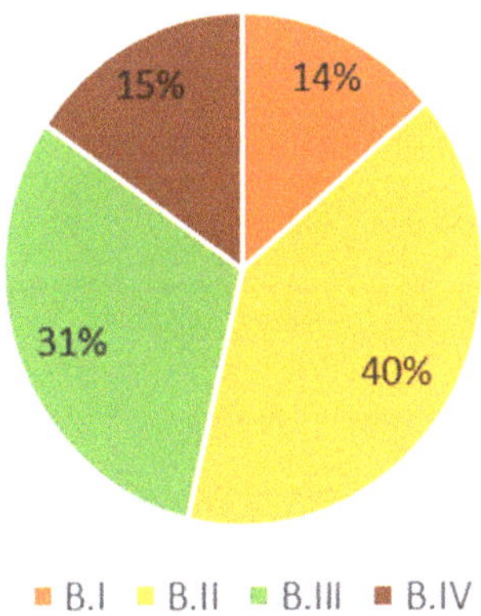

(a)

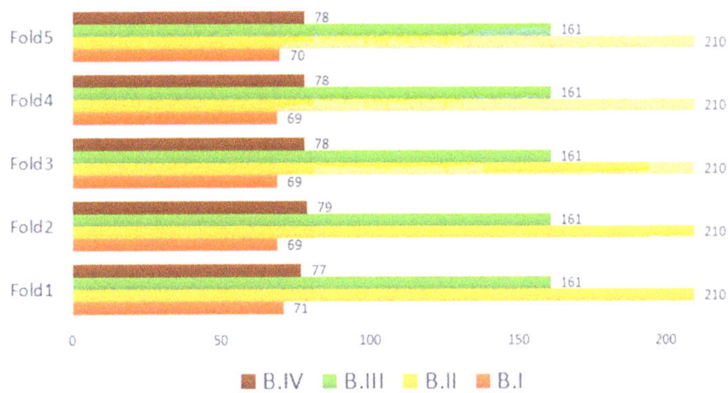

(b)

Figure 4. (**a**) Data distribution of the DDSM dataset over the four classes; (**b**) data distribution of the DDSM dataset for each fold.

INbreast [37] is taken from the Breast Centre at the University of Hospital de São João, Portugal. It contains 115 cases comprising digital images converted to DICOM format with a resolution of either 3328 × 4084 or 2560 × 3328 pixels. Each case includes both craniocaudal (CC) and mediolateral oblique (MLO) views and breast laterality (right vs. left) annotated with contour points of the ROIs. The density labels are annotated by radiologists as BI-RADS I, BI-RADS II, BI-RADS III, and BI-RADS IV. Out of the total number of BI-RADS categories, 136 belong to BI-RADS I, 147 to BI-RADS II, 99 to BI-RADS III, and 28 to BI-RADS IV. Furthermore, 5-fold cross-validation is used to train and test models.

3.5.4. Data Augmentation

Training a CNN model on a large number of training instances typically yields good results and high-performance values. Additionally, data imbalances may be alleviated with the use of augmentation techniques. To reproduce a large number of breast density variations in mammogram images, we used rotation (θ = 180°) and random horizontal and vertical flipping.

4. Evaluation Protocol

We randomly divided the data into a training set (80%), a validation set (10%), and a test set (10%) and used a 5-fold cross-validation technique to evaluate the proposed system. The cross-validation concept is based on partitioning the dataset into k equal-sized folds. Then, $k-1$ folds will be used to train and validate, with the remaining fold to test the classification models. The final result is calculated as the average of overall classes [38].

Using the confusion matrix in Table 2, a model's classification performance is evaluated primarily in terms of overall class accuracy (OCA), individual class accuracy (ICA), recall (RC), precision (PR), F1-score, Cohen's kappa [39–41]. The definitions of these performance measures are described with the help of Equations (4)–(8), as shown below:

$$\text{Overall Classification Accuracy (OCA.)} = \frac{\text{Correct predictions}}{\text{Total predictions}} \tag{4}$$

$$\text{Individual Classification Accuracy (ICA.)} = \frac{\text{Correct predictions belong to a specific class}}{\text{Total predictions belong to a specific class}} \tag{5}$$

$$\text{Precision} = \frac{\text{Tp}}{\text{TP} + \text{FP}}\ \text{Recall} = \frac{\text{Tp}}{\text{TP} + \text{FN}} \tag{6}$$

$$\text{F1 Score} = 2 \times \frac{\text{Precision} \times \text{Recall}}{\text{Precision} + \text{Recall}} \tag{7}$$

Table 2. Confusion matrix.

Confusion Matrix	Actual Positive	Actual Negative
Predicted Positive	TP [1]	FP [3]
Predicted Negative	FN [4]	TN [2]

[1] The number of true positives (TPs): the prediction was positive when the sample was malignant. [2] The number of true negatives (TNs): the prediction was negative when the sample was benign. [3] The number of false positives (FPs): the prediction was positive when the sample was benign. [4] The number of false negatives (FNs): the prediction was negative when the sample was malignant.

Cohen's kappa is calculated using the following:

$$\text{Kappa} = \frac{(P_o - P_e)}{(1 - P_e)}$$
$$P_e = \frac{(TP+FN)\times(TP+FP)+(FP+TN)\times(FN+TN)}{(TP+TN+FP+FN)^2};\ P_o = \frac{TP+TN}{TP+TN+FP+FN} \tag{8}$$

Additionally, the breast density classifier's performance was measured using the area under the ROC curve (AUC). The area under the receiver operating characteristic (AUC-ROC) curve is used to evaluate the effectiveness of classification problems with varying thresholds [42,43]. AUC is the separability measure, while ROC is a probability curve. It reveals the extent to which the model can differentiate between different types of data. The multiclass classifier considers the AUC between each class and all other classes (a one vs. all approach).

The system was implemented, and all experiments were performed in MATLAB R2021b version 9.11 with a deep-learning toolbox on AMD Ryzen Threadripper 3960X

24-core processor, 3.79 GHz, RAM 128 GB, and Nvidia graphics processing units (GPU) based in Santa Clara, CA, USA, GeForce RTX 3090 24 GB.

5. Experimental Results and Discussion

5.1. Ablation Study

This section conducts different ablation tests to validate the proposed system structure's efficiency.

5.1.1. Which Backbone Model?

The question of which CNN model to use as the system's backbone is emerging. The DDSM dataset was used to test three state-of-the-art CNN models. Based on the obtained results illustrated in Table 3, the selected backbone model for the breast density classification task was the ResNet-50. This decision was made because ResNet-50 outperformed other models in terms of overall classification accuracy. The variation in performance amongst the investigated CNN models can be attributable to the different design choices.

Table 3. The performance comparison on the DDSM dataset using different convolutional neural networks (CNN).

Model	Overall Classification Accuracy (OCA %)
ResNet 50 [28]	74.94
DenseNet201 [30]	69.58
EfficientNet b0 [29]	64.06

5.1.2. Which Preprocessing Operation?

Breast tissue characteristics in digital mammographic images will be more apparent after image enhancement, increasing the early breast cancer classification rate. A custom-tailored image processing technique will likely be needed to best display different image characteristics. Additionally, different breast density may benefit from specific algorithms and the performance disparities between the image preprocessing methods. As a result, we decided on magma color mapping, as presented in Table 4. An overview of different image preprocessing tasks is shown in Figure 5.

Table 4. The effect of preprocessing full mammograms on the DDSM test performance.

Model	Preprocessing	(OCA %)
ResNet50	Without	66.83
	Contrast-limited adaptive histogram equalization (CLAHE)	67.41
	Histogram equalization	65.23
	Magma color mapping	74.94

5.1.3. Single View or Dual View?

Comparing the results utilizing dual-view mammography inputs to those using single-view mammography input, it can be observed that the dual-view mammography inputs setting is beneficial to the density classification task, and improved statistics were obtained by all of the investigated models, including the backbone model ResNet50, as shown in Table 5.

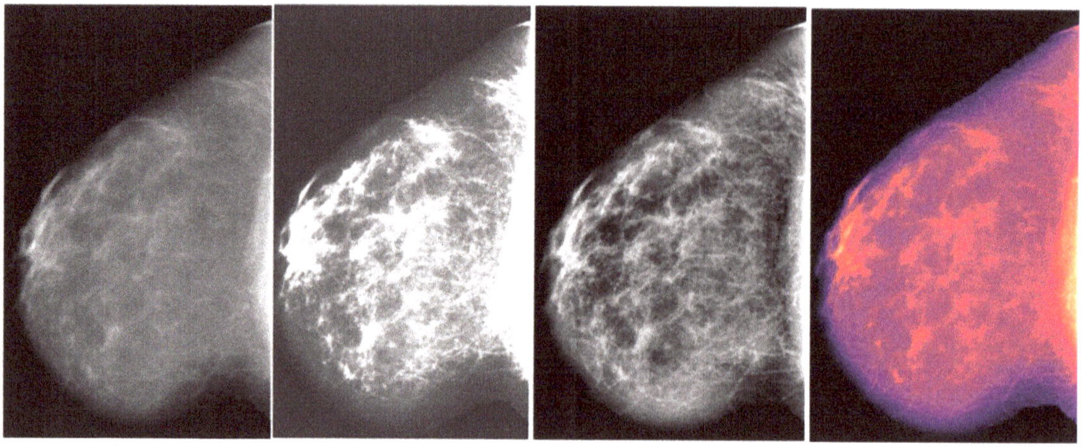

Figure 5. A comparison of the visual effects of different image preprocessing tasks.

Table 5. The effect of overall classification accuracy of the single view vs. dual View of the DDSM test.

Model	Overall Classification Accuracy (OCA %)
Single View	
ResNet 50	74.94
DenseNet201	69.58
EfficientNet b0	64.06
Dual View	
ResNet 50	91.36
DenseNet201	86.16
EfficientNet b0	73.97

5.1.4. Which Loss Function?

As mentioned in Section 3.5.1, We considered three loss functions: cross-entropy, focal, and SSE. We used the pretrained ResNet50 model as the backbone CNN model to test the effect of these loss functions. Figures 6 and 7 show the results of the three-loss function on the DDSM dataset. The focal loss function yields the best results in terms of all performance metrics because focal loss does this by decreasing the weight given to simple examples in the loss function, hence focusing on more hard examples. Table 6 shows the results. In Table 7, we provide the confusion matrix produced from the best experiment result to explore the classification behavior of the model.

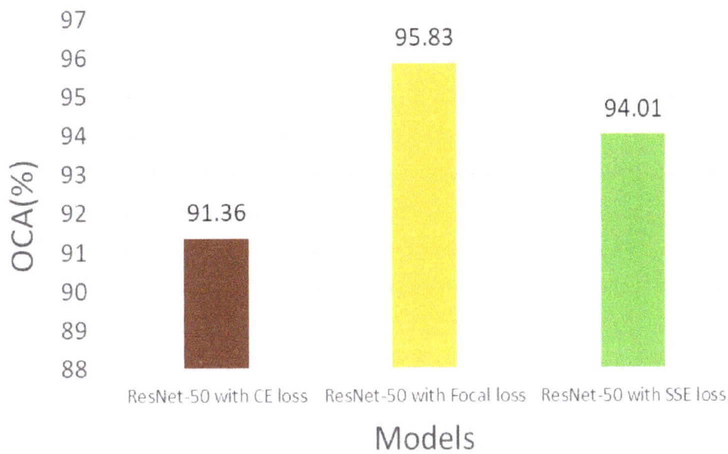

Figure 6. The effect of different loss functions of the DDSM test on overall classification accuracy.

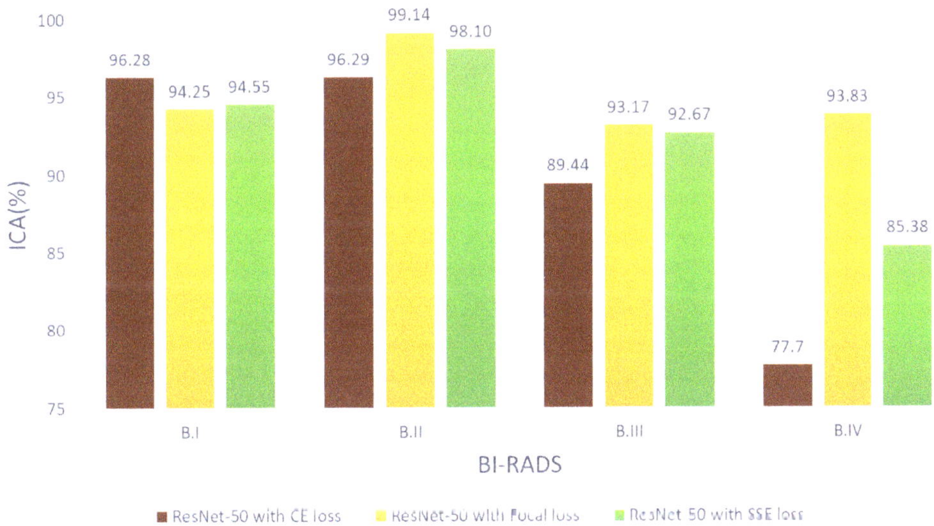

Figure 7. The effect of different loss functions of the DDSM test individual classification accuracy.

Table 6. The effect of different loss functions of the DDSM test.

Loss Function	OCA	IC_{B-I}	ICA_{B-II}	ICA_{B-III}	ICA_{B-IV}
ResNet-50 CE loss	91.36 ± 3.29	96.28 ± 3.29	96.29 ± 20	89.44 ± 2.10	77.70 ± 16.4
ResNet-50 focal loss	95.83 ± 3.63	94.25 ± 5.72	99.14 ± 0.98	93.17 ± 6.95	93.83 ± 5.86
ResNet-50 SSE loss	94.01 ± 3.61	94.55 ± 5.98	98.10 ± 1.17	92.67 ± 4.76	85.38 ± 9.96

Table 7. Confusion matrix of 5-folds of the best test (* OCA) and (** ICA).

Fold		Confusion Matrix Predicted				Accuracy (%)				
		B-I	**B-II**	**B-III**	**B-IV**	**OCA**	**IC$_{B-I}$**	**ICA$_{B-II}$**	**ICA$_{B-III}$**	**ICA$_{B-IV}$**
Fold 1	Actual B-I	63	8	0	0	94.03	88.73	98.10	93.17	89.61
	Actual B-II	4	206	0	0					
	Actual B-III	1	6	150	4					
	Actual B-IV	0	1	7	69					
Fold 2	Actual B-I	69	0	0	0	99.38	100	100	100	96.20
	Actual B-II	0	210	0	0					
	Actual B-III	0	0	161	0					
	Actual B-IV	0	1	2	76					
Fold 3	Actual B-I	61	8	0	0	91.89	88.41	98.10	88.20	85.90
	Actual B-II	4	206	0	0					
	Actual B-III	0	0	142	19					
	Actual B-IV	0	1	10	67					
Fold 4	Actual B-I	69	0	0	0	100	100	100	100	100
	Actual B-II	0	210	0	0					
	Actual B-III	0	0	161	0					
	Actual B-IV	0	0	0	78					
Fold 5	Actual B-I	66	4	0	0	93.83	94.29	99.52	84.47	97.44
	Actual B-II	1	209	0	0					
	Actual B-III	0	0	136	25					
	Actual B-IV	0	0	2	76					

* OCA: overall classification accuracy. ** ICA$_{BI-RADS}$: individual classification accuracy for BI-RADS (I, II, III, IV).

5.2. Comparison with State-of-the-Art Methods for Breast Density Classification

The method of Zhao et al. [12] has been introduced to compare related methods of the DDSM dataset with a four-view. The bilateral adaptive spatial and channel attention network (BASCNet) integrates the information of the left and right breasts. Li et al. [7] added dilated convolution and the channel attention mechanism to the ResNet network architecture with multi-view inputs (i.e., four-view, as well as two CC views or two MLO views of the left and right breasts). Wu et al. [9] used a VGG Net with four views as input. Our proposed method TwoViewDensityNet significantly outperforms the state-of-the-art methods since we used two views, CC and MLO, from the same breast.

Additionally, we applied different loss functions to improve performance accuracy. Our proposed method attained the highest accuracy of 95.83 on the DDSM, respectively, when TwoViewDensityNet used ResNet-50 as the backbone model with focal loss function; this is significantly higher than the existing methods. The findings were compared using a dual-view input. With a single-view input, it is evident that the dual-view input option is beneficial to the classification task and the ResNet50 backbone produced those improved metrics. Compared to Zhao et al. [12] on DDSM, our proposal outperformed w.r.t. all evaluation metrics, as presented in Table 8. To be precise, our model increased classification accuracy by 10% and 5% F1 score by 20% and 19% on the DDSM and INbreast, respectively, for dual-view inputs.

Table 8. The comparison with different state-of-the-art methods for breast density classification.

References	Model	Dataset	ACC (%)	AUC (%)	F1-score (%)	Kappa (%)
	Single View					
Li et al. [7], 2021	ResNet50 + DC + CA (DC: dilated convolutions. CA:channel-wise attention)	INbreast	70	84.70	63.50	-
Yi et al. [8], 2019	ResNet-50	DDSM	68	-	-	-
Lehman et al. [10], 2019	ResNet-18	INbreast	63.80	81.20	48.90	-
Gandomkar et al. [13], 2019	Inception-V3	INbreast	63.90	82.10	53.10	-
Mohamed et al. [15], 2018	AlexNet	INbreast	59.60	82	35.4	-
	Multi-View					
Zhao et al. [12], 2021	BASCNet (ResNet) (Bilateral-view adaptive spatial and channel attention network)	DDSM	85.10	91.54	78.92	-
		INbreast	90.51	99.09	78.11	-
Proposed system	TwoViewDensityNet	DDSM	95.83	99.51	98.63	94.37
		INbreast	96	97.44	97.14	94.31

5.3. Discussion

Utilizing the dual-view approach, we built and tested a system for classifying breast density tissue as B-I, B-II, B-III, or B-IV using the DDSM benchmark dataset as guidance. An end-to-end CNN model was utilized as the backbone model in the method. We combined the information from two views and learned which complementary information is essential in each view. When we fine-tune this backbone for left and right, each view's weight and complementary information are classified. Among the well-known CNN models, we investigated (ResNet-50, DenseNet-201, and Efficient-b0) and determined that ResNet-50 is the most suitable model for the system. That might be residual learning extracting global (high-level) features that effectively pay more attention to the semantics of fibroglandular tissue, which enables accurate discrimination of the four BI-RADS categories.

This study has some limitations. However, for the mammography dataset used in this study, the accessible images were limited, resulting in a severely uneven distribution across the four categories. Training a classification network with these datasets is quite difficult. Furthermore, breast density is a critical clinical characteristic used to determine a woman's risk of developing breast cancer. Our proposed system is well classified between non-dense breasts (fatty or scattered density) and dense breasts (heterogeneously dense or extremely dense). It is simple to differentiate between fatty and highly dense breasts in the clinical setting.

On the other hand, radiologists have difficulty visually and consistently distinguishing between the scatter density and heterogeneously dense categories [44]. According to our findings, the heterogeneously dense or extremely dense classification results are better than the fatty or scattered density; this might be because of the similar characteristic between fatty and heterogeneously dense or scattered density and extremely dense.

The performance of TwoViewDensityNet for the four BI-RADS classification tasks on the DDSM dataset is (F-score of 98.63%, AUC of 99.51%, accuracy of 95.83%) and the INbreast dataset is (F-score of 97.14%, AUC of 97.44%, accuracy of 96%).

6. Conclusions

We addressed the challenging problem of discriminating mammographic breast density and, by leveraging advances in deep learning, developed a system for this problem that leverages the complementary relationship between the craniocaudal (CC) and mediolateral oblique (MLO) views to improve the differentiation of BI-RADS class. We extensively tested the system on the benchmark datasets DDSM and INbreast and discovered that it outperforms the state-of-the-art approaches. ResNet-50 achieves better results as a backbone model for the system when focal loss is used for training. We will continue investigating deep-learning mammography models and develop more robust models. This would help radiologists enhance the current clinical breast density assessment. The proposed model can be used for other similar applications, which will be our future work.

Author Contributions: Conceptualization, M.B. and M.H.; Data curation, M.B. and S.A.A.S.; Formal analysis, M.B. and S.A.A.S.; Funding acquisition; Methodology, M.B., F.-e.-A. and M.H.; Project administration, F.-e.-A. and M.H.; Resources, F.-e.-A. and M.H.; Software, M.B.; Supervision, M.H. and H.A.A.; Validation, M.B.; Visualization, M.B.; Writing—original draft preparation, M.B.; Writing—review and editing, M.H. All authors have read and agreed to the published version of the manuscript.

Funding: The authors extend their appreciation to the Deputyship for Research & Innovation, Ministry of Education in Saudi Arabia for funding this research work through the project no. (IFKSURG-2-106).

Data Availability Statement: The DDSM dataset is available at: http://www.eng.usf.edu/cvprg/Mammography/Database.html (accessed on 25 November 2021).

Conflicts of Interest: The authors declare no conflict of interest.

References

1. Wolfe, J.N. Risk for breast cancer development determined by mammographic parenchymal pattern. *Cancer* **1976**, *37*, 2486–2492. [CrossRef] [PubMed]
2. Wolfe, J.N. Breast patterns as an index of risk for developing breast cancer. *Am. J. Roentgenol.* **1976**, *126*, 1130–1137. [CrossRef] [PubMed]
3. McCormack, V.A.; dos Santos Silva, I. Breast Density and Parenchymal Patterns as Markers of Breast Cancer Risk: A Meta-analysis. *Cancer Epidemiol. Biomark. Prev.* **2006**, *15*, 1159–1169. [CrossRef] [PubMed]
4. Nazari, S.S.; Mukherjee, P. An overview of mammographic density and its association with breast cancer. *Breast Cancer* **2018**, *25*, 259–267. [CrossRef] [PubMed]
5. Albeshan, S.M.; Hossain, S.Z.; Mackey, M.G.; Peat, J.K.; Al Tahan, F.M.; Brennan, P.C. Preliminary investigation of mammographic density among women in Riyadh: Association with breast cancer risk factors and implications for screening practices. *Clin. Imaging* **2019**, *54*, 138–147. [CrossRef]
6. American College of Radiology (ACR). *Illustrated Breast Imaging Reporting and Data System (BI-RADS)*; American College of Radiology: Reston, VA, USA, 2003.
7. Li, C.; Xu, J.; Liu, Q.; Zhou, Y.; Mou, L.; Pu, Z.; Xia, Y.; Zheng, H.; Wang, S. Multi-View Mammographic Density Classification by Dilated and Attention-Guided Residual Learning. *IEEE/ACM Trans. Comput. Biol. Bioinform.* **2020**, *18*, 1003–1013. [CrossRef]
8. Yi, P.H.; Lin, A.; Wei, J.; Yu, A.C.; Sair, H.I.; Hui, F.K.; Hager, G.D.; Harvey, S.C. Deep-Learning-Based Semantic Labeling for 2D Mammography and Comparison of Complexity for Machine Learning Tasks. *J. Digit. Imaging* **2019**, *32*, 565–570. [CrossRef]
9. Wu, N.; Geras, K.J.; Shen, Y.; Su, J.; Kim, S.G.; Kim, E.; Wolfson, S.; Moy, L.; Cho, K. Breast Density Classification with Deep Convolutional Neural Networks. In Proceedings of the 2018 IEEE International Conference on Acoustics, Speech and Signal Processing (ICASSP), Calgary, AB, Canada, 15–20 April 2018; pp. 6682–6686.
10. Lehman, C.D.; Yala, A.; Schuster, T.; Dontchos, B.; Bahl, M.; Swanson, K.; Barzilay, R. Mammographic Breast Density Assessment Using Deep Learning: Clinical Implementation. *Radiology* **2019**, *290*, 52–58. [CrossRef]
11. Heath, M.; Bowyer, K.; Kopans, D.; Kegelmeyer, P.; Moore, R.; Chang, K.; Munishkumaran, S. Current Status of the Digital Database for Screening Mammography. In *Digital Mammography*; Springer: Dordrecht, The Netherlands, 1998.
12. Zhao, W.; Wang, R.; Qi, Y.; Lou, M.; Wang, Y.; Yang, Y.; Deng, X.; Ma, Y. BASCNet: Bilateral adaptive spatial and channel attention network for breast density classification in the mammogram. *Biomed. Signal Process. Control.* **2021**, *70*, 103073. [CrossRef]
13. Gandomkar, Z.; Suleiman, M.E.; Demchig, D.; Brennan, P.C.; McEntee, M.F. BI-RADS Density Categorization Using Deep Neural Networks. In *Medical Imaging 2019: Image Perception, Observer Performance, and Technology Assessment*; SPIE: Bellingham, WA, USA, 2019.
14. Deng, J.; Ma, Y.; Li, D.A.; Zhao, J.; Liu, Y.; Zhang, H. Classification of breast density categories based on SE-Attention neural networks. *Comput. Methods Programs Biomed.* **2020**, *193*, 105489. [CrossRef]
15. Mohamed, A.A.; Berg, W.A.; Peng, H.; Luo, Y.; Jankowitz, R.C.; Wu, S. A deep learning method for classifying mammographic breast density categories. *Med. Phys.* **2017**, *45*, 314–321. [CrossRef] [PubMed]
16. Cogan, T.; Tamil, L.S. Deep Understanding of Breast Density Classification. In Proceedings of the 42nd Annual International Conference of the IEEE Engineering in Medicine & Biology Society (EMBC), Montreal, QC, Canada, 20–24 July 2020; pp. 1140–1143.
17. Jouirou, A.; Baâzaoui, A.; Barhoumi, W. Multi-view information fusion in mammograms: A comprehensive overview. *Inf. Fusion* **2019**, *52*, 308–321. [CrossRef]
18. Wilms, M.; Krüger, J.; Marx, M.; Ehrhardt, J.; Bischof, A.; Handels, H. Estimation of Corresponding Locations in Ipsilateral Mammograms: A Comparison of Different Methods. In *Medical Imaging 2015: Computer-Aided Diagnosis*; SPIE: Bellingham, WA, USA, 2015.

19. Ma, Y.; Peng, Y. Simultaneous detection and diagnosis of mammogram mass using bilateral analysis and soft label based metric learning. *Biocybern. Biomed. Eng.* **2022**, *42*, 215–232. [CrossRef]
20. Xian, J.; Wang, Z.; Cheng, K.-T.; Yang, X. Towards Robust Dual-View Transformation via Densifying Sparse Supervision for Mammography Lesion Matching. In Proceedings of the International Conference on Medical Image Computing and Computer-Assisted Intervention, Strasbourg, France, 27 September 2021.
21. Kowsalya, S.; Priyaa, D.S. An Adaptive Behavioral Learning Technique based Bilateral Asymmetry Detection in Mammogram Images. *Indian J. Sci. Technol.* **2016**, *9*, S1. [CrossRef]
22. Lyu, Q.; Namjoshi, S.V.; McTyre, E.; Topaloglu, U.; Barcus, R.; Chan, M.D.; Cramer, C.K.; Debinski, W.; Gurcan, M.N.; Lesser, G.J.; et al. A transformer-based deep learning approach for classifying brain metastases into primary organ sites using clinical whole brain MRI images. *Patterns* **2022**, 3, 100613. [CrossRef]
23. Dhungel, N.; Carneiro, G.; Bradley, A.P. Fully Automated Classification of Mammograms Using Deep Residual Neural Networks. In Proceedings of the IEEE 14th International Symposium on Biomedical Imaging (ISBI 2017), Melbourne, Australia, 18–21 April 2017; pp. 310–314.
24. Yi, D.; Sawyer, R.L.; Cohn, D.; Dunnmon, J.A.; Lam, C.K.; Xiao, X.; Rubin, D. Optimizing and Visualizing Deep Learning for Benign/Malignant Classification in Breast Tumors. *arXiv* **2017**, arXiv:1705.06362.
25. Cogan, T.; Cogan, M.; Tamil, L.S. RAMS: Remote and automatic mammogram screening. *Comput. Biol. Med.* **2019**, *107*, 18–29. [CrossRef]
26. MatPlotLib Perceptually Uniform Colormaps. Available online: https://www.mathworks.com/matlabcentral/fileexchange/62729-matplotlibperceptually-uniform-colormaps (accessed on 25 November 2021).
27. Russakovsky, O.; Deng, J.; Su, H.; Krause, J.; Satheesh, S.; Ma, S.; Huang, Z.; Karpathy, A.; Khosla, A.; Bernstein, M.; et al. ImageNet Large Scale Visual Recognition Challenge. *Int. J. Comput. Vis.* **2015**, *115*, 211–252. [CrossRef]
28. KHe, K.; Zhang, X.; Ren, S.; Sun, J. Deep Residual Learning for Image Recognition. In Proceedings of the 2016 IEEE Conference on Computer Vision and Pattern Recognition (CVPR), Las Vegas, NV, USA, 27–30 June 2016; pp. 770–778. [CrossRef]
29. Tan, M.; Le, Q.V. EfficientNet: Rethinking Model Scaling for Convolutional Neural Networks. In Proceedings of the International Conference on Machine Learning, Long Beach, CA, USA, 10–15 June 2019.
30. Huang, G.; Liu, Z.; Van Der Maaten, L.; Weinberger, K.Q. Densely Connected Convolutional Networks. In Proceedings of the 2017 IEEE Conference on Computer Vision and Pattern Recognition (CVPR), Honolulu, HI, USA, 21–26 July 2017; pp. 2261–2269.
31. Veit, A.; Wilber, M.J.; Belongie, S. Residual Networks Behave Like Ensembles of Relatively Shallow Networks. In Proceedings of the Advances in Neural Information Processing Systems 29, Barcelona, Spain, 5–10 December 2016; pp. 550–558.
32. Schmidhuber, J. Deep Learning in Neural Networks: An Overview. *Neural Netw.* **2015**, *61*, 85–117. [CrossRef]
33. Glorot, X.; Bengio, Y. Understanding the Difficulty of Training Deep Feedforward Neural Networks. In Proceedings of the 13th International Conference on Artificial Intelligence and Statistics (AISTATS), Sardinia, Italy, 13–15 May 2010; pp. 249–256.
34. De Boer, P.T.; Kroese, D.P.; Mannor, S.; Rubinstein, R.Y. A Tutorial on the Cross-Entropy Method. *Ann. Oper. Res.* **2005**, *134*, 19–67. [CrossRef]
35. Lin, T.Y.; Goyal, P.; Girshick, R.; He, K.; Dollár, P. Focal Loss for Dense Object Detection. In Proceedings of the IEEE Transactions on Pattern Analysis and Machine Intelligence, Venice, Italy, 22–29 October 2017.
36. Bosman, A.S.; Engelbrecht, A.; Helbig, M. Visualising basins of attraction for the cross-entropy and the squared error neural network loss functions. *Neurocomputing* **2020**, *400*, 113–136. [CrossRef]
37. Moreira, I.C.; Amaral, I.; Domingues, I.; Cardoso, A.; Cardoso, M.J.; Cardoso, J.S. Inbreast: Toward a full-field digital mammographic database. *Acad. Radiol.* **2012**, *19*, 236–248. [CrossRef] [PubMed]
38. Levin, E.; Fleisher, M. Accelerated learning in layered neural networks. *Complex Syst.* **1988**, *2*, 625–640.
39. Stone, M. Cross-validatory choice and assessment of statistical predictions. *J. R. Stat. Soc.* **1974**, 36, 111–147. [CrossRef]
40. Cetin, K.; Oktay, Y.; Sinan, A. Performance Analysis of Machine Learning Techniques in Intrusion Detection. In Proceedings of the 24th Signal Processing and Communication Application Conference (SIU), Zonguldak, Turkey, 16–19 May 2016; pp. 1473–1476.
41. Ranganathan, P.; Pramesh, C.S.; Aggarwal, R. Common pitfalls in statistical analysis: Measures of agreement. *Perspect. Clin. Res.* **2017**, *8*, 187–191. [CrossRef]
42. Hanley, J.A.; McNeil, B.J. The meaning and use of the area under a receiver operating characteristic (ROC) curve. *Radiology* **1982**, *143*, 29–36. [CrossRef]
43. Hoo, Z.H.; Candlish, J.; Teare, D. What is an ROC curve? *Emerg. Med. J.* **2017**, *34*, 357–359. [CrossRef]
44. Sprague, B.L.; Conant, E.F.; Onega, T.; Garcia, M.P.; Beaber, E.F.; Herschorn, S.D.; Lehman, C.D.; Tosteson, A.N.; Lacson, R.; Schnall, M.D.; et al. Variation in Mammographic Breast Density Assessments Among Radiologists in Clinical Practice: A Multicenter Observational Study. *Ann. Intern. Med.* **2016**, *165*, 457–464. [CrossRef]

mathematics MDPI

Article

Performance Analysis of Long Short-Term Memory Predictive Neural Networks on Time Series Data

Roland Bolboacă * and Piroska Haller

The Faculty of Engineering and Information Technology, George Emil Palade University of Medicine, Pharmacy, Science, and Technology of Târgu Mureş, 540139 Târgu Mureş, Romania; piroska.haller@umfst.ro
* Correspondence: roland.bolboaca@umfst.ro

Abstract: Long short-term memory neural networks have been proposed as a means of creating accurate models from large time series data originating from various fields. These models can further be utilized for prediction, control, or anomaly-detection algorithms. However, finding the optimal hyperparameters to maximize different performance criteria remains a challenge for both novice and experienced users. Hyperparameter optimization algorithms can often be a resource-intensive and time-consuming task, particularly when the impact of the hyperparameters on the performance of the neural network is not comprehended or known. Teacher forcing denotes a procedure that involves feeding the ground truth output from the previous time-step as input to the current time-step during training, while during testing feeding back the predicted values. This paper presents a comprehensive examination of the impact of hyperparameters on long short-term neural networks, with and without teacher forcing, on prediction performance. The study includes testing long short-term memory neural networks, with two variations of teacher forcing, in two prediction modes, using two configurations (i.e., multi-input single-output and multi-input multi-output) on a well-known chemical process simulation dataset. Furthermore, this paper demonstrates the applicability of a long short-term memory neural network with a modified teacher forcing approach in a process state monitoring system. Over 100,000 experiments were conducted with varying hyperparameters and in multiple neural network operation modes, revealing the direct impact of each tested hyperparameter on the training and testing procedures.

Keywords: long short-term memory (LSTM); recurrent neural network (RNN); teacher forcing; prediction; performance analysis; benchmarking; machine learning; Tennessee Eastman process; time series

MSC: 68T07; 68T09

Citation: Bolboacă, R.; Haller, P. Performance Analysis of Long Short-Term Memory Predictive Neural Networks on Time Series Data. *Mathematics* **2023**, *11*, 1432. https://doi.org/10.3390/math11061432

Academic Editors: Adrian Sergiu Darabant and Diana-Laura Borza

Received: 3 February 2023
Revised: 12 March 2023
Accepted: 14 March 2023
Published: 15 March 2023

1. Introduction

Machine learning algorithms, nowadays, are a "go-to" for solving a plethora of real-life problems in various domains, from healthcare [1], finance [2], and manufacturing [3] all the way to agriculture [4]. On a larger scale, machine learning can be regarded as an umbrella term incorporating a wide range of algorithms and models proposed for specific tasks, including medical diagnosis [5], predictive maintenance [6], text authorship attribution [7], human race recognition [8], and anomaly detection [9].

One specific subclass of machine learning includes neural networks. Since the first mention of artificial neurons almost 80 years ago [10], neural networks have constantly evolved and have been widely applied in numerous areas and domains, from economics [11] to medicine [12–14] to industrial domains [15]. Long short-term memory (LSTM) neural networks [16] are a special type of recurrent neural networks, initially proposed as a solution to the vanishing and exploding gradient problem. As predictors, LSTM neural networks are efficient in learning long- and short-term spatio-temporal dependencies in time series data. In the scientific literature, LSTMs have been proposed for prediction tasks on time series data in a multitude of papers [17–20]. Moreover, LSTMs have also been used for other task as well, such as text classification [21], phoneme classification [22], time series classification [19,23], electroencephalogram (EEG) classification [24], remaining useful life prediction [25], and sentiment analysis [26,27].

One major difficulty when working with neural networks is discovering the optimal hyperparameters [28] or the best-suited model for optimal performance. To this day, optimizing the hyperparameters involves finding the best values for specific datasets and for specific network architectures. Among the well-known optimization techniques, we find the grid search method [29], a blackbox hyperparameter optimization method involving finding the best values from a finite set. An alternative to grid search is random search [29], which involves randomly sampling hyperparameter values based on a search budget. Another popular optimization technique is Bayesian optimization [29], a technique that involves using a surrogate model to approximate a complex function and an acquisition function to determine the next point to evaluate. It operates through an iterative process, with the surrogate model and acquisition function being updated at each step.

The performance of neural networks has been analyzed by numerous researchers in diverse domains and on a multitude of datasets [30–39]. The classification and prediction performance of neural networks has been shown to be influenced by various factors, such as the architecture, the hyperparameters, and the dataset. While optimization techniques aid in discovering the best hyperparameters for such models, oftentimes an in-depth performance analysis is needed to observe and understand how different hyperparameters actually affect the functionality of the neural networks. Moreover, considering the high usability of neural networks by expert and novice users alike, oftentimes running an optimization algorithm (which can be time- and resource-consuming) is not enough without observing the model behavior.

This paper focuses on a prediction performance comparison between standard LSTMs and LSTMs trained with two variants of teacher forcing (TF) used for time series prediction in a process state monitoring system. The two variants of TF include the one proposed in [40] for anomaly-detection tasks (LSTMTF) and, as originally proposed in [41], for long-term forecasting (LSTMTFC).

By using an empirical approach, this paper analyzes the effects of different hyperparameters, such as the input sequence length, the number of time delays, the mini-batch size, the learning rate, and the number of hidden units, while training and testing the LSTM variants on time series data originating from an industrial process, namely, on the Tennessee Eastman process dataset [42,43]. Additionally, this paper also analyzes different neural network configurations, namely, multi-input single-output (MISO) and multi-input multi-output (MIMO) on two prediction modes, that is, many-to-many (M2M) and many-to-one (M2O). The performance analysis focuses on both the training and inference.

The prediction performance of different variants of LSTM was compared with the nonlinear auto-regressive neural networks with exogenous inputs (NARXNN). The authors of some large-scale studies, such as those in [30–32,35], performed thousands of experiments in this direction. For this study, approximately 100,000 neural networks were trained and tested using a wide range of hyperparameters, configurations, and prediction modes.

To the best of our knowledge, this is the first study focusing on time series prediction benchmarking of LSTM neural networks trained with TF compared to standard LSTMs. Furthermore, this paper also studies the exposure bias effect [44,45] for neural networks trained with TF in its original form. While exposure bias can affect the prediction performance of neural networks, we will also discuss the gained advantages of using LSTMs with TF for anomaly-detection tasks.

The remainder of the paper is organized as follows. Section 2 describes related studies, with special emphasis on concepts such as TF; the similarities between TF, NARXNN, and other recurrent neural networks; and hyperparameter optimization methods. The proposed approach is presented in Section 3. This is followed by Section 4, where the experimental assessment is presented. Section 5 describes the experimental results. Discussions, final remarks, and future work proposals are included in Section 6.

2. Related Work

An examination of the literature reveals a multitude of papers addressing the issues discussed throughout this paper. Thus, the related work section is split in three subsections. First, a background on teacher forcing is presented. Second, studies and benchmark papers on the topic of LSTM neural networks and recurrent neural networks (RNNs) are presented, addressing both predictive and classification tasks. Last, several highly cited hyperparameter optimization papers are investigated, while some proposed techniques from these papers are experimentally validated in the results section.

2.1. *Teacher Forcing Background*

We observed numerous similarities between LSTM with TF, Jordan neural networks [46], and NARXNN [35,47]. For a better understanding of the rest of this paper, the current section describes the similarities and differences between the previous terms as well as their applicability.

Recurrent neural networks, or RNNs, are neural networks that map sequence inputs to sequence outputs statefully. This means the output prediction depends not only on the input, but also on the hidden state of the system, which is updated as the sequence is processed over time [44,48,49]. Adding feedback loops to a feedforward neural network can be carried out using two fundamental approaches. The first approach is adding a feedback loop from the hidden layer to itself (or to the input layer); this resembles the Elman architecture, as originally proposed in [50]. Such an approach emphasizes, to a larger degree, the sequence of input values. The second approach is adding a feedback loop from the output layer to the input layer. This approach was first proposed in the Jordan neural network (JNN) architecture [46]. Compared to the Elman neural networks, this approach emphasizes the sequence of output values to a larger degree [48]. In the case of JNN, the previous output with only one time delay is fed back.

NARXNN denotes a special type of feedforward neural network where static back-propagation can be used for training, reducing the training phase time and resources compared to recurrent neural networks. One similarity between JNN and NARXNN is that both network architectures take exogenous variables as inputs, together with previous outputs as additional inputs. In the case of NARXNN, multiple time-steps from the output can be added as input. Additionally, NARXNN can take the exogenous variables as inputs with additional time delays (e.g., lags). NARXNNs are usually used in the engineering field for such tasks as dynamic system modeling, system identification, and particularly in the field of time series analysis.

TF was first proposed in [41], where the authors describe a training method that involves feeding back the current ground truth values as input in the subsequent time-steps. This way forces the neural network to remain as close as possible to the ground truth sequences. In recent years, several variants of TF have been proposed [51–55], most of them offering variations of this method for training recurrent neural networks (RNNs). In Goodfellow's book [44], TF was also introduced as a neural network training technique, applicable to recurrent neural networks that have output to hidden connections. This technique originates from the maximum likelihood criterion, where during the training phase, the neural network receives the ground truth value of the output as input at the next time-step.

Moreover, Goodfellow et al. in [44] state that TF is also applicable to models that have hidden-to-hidden connections as well. In this scenario, training is carried out using both TF and backpropagation through time (BPTT) [56–58].

TF has been applied in several domains for solving diverse problems [59–65] (in order of appearance). Apart from the original version of the algorithm, several variations have also been proposed, a large majority of them for training RNNs.

Toomarian et al. [59] patented, for NASA, a variant of TF for fast temporal neural learning applied in circular trajectory learning. The patent proposes a continuous form of TF that modifies the activation dynamics of additive neural networks, where rather than the actual value of the output variable, the error between the desired output and the actual output is fed back to the neural network in real time.

In the same direction of trajectory learning, Toomarian and Barhen [65] also proposed a methodology for supervised temporal learning in nonlinear neural networks. Their work incorporates TF and adjoint operators for fast circular trajectory learning. This version of TF is applied similarly to the one in [59] by feeding back the error between the actual and predicted value.

To avoid exposure bias when training models with TF, Taigman et al. [51] proposed a modification to the TF algorithm, where, during training the neural network does not take the previous observed value as input, but rather, an average between the observed value and the previous network outputs with the addition of random noise. Their solution is proposed as a text-to-speech method for mimicking voices from samples originating from the wild.

Moving towards the field of language modeling, we find the work of Drossos et al. [52]. Here, the authors propose a sound event detection recurrent neural network capable of learning language models. TF is applied here using a scheduled sampling approached, that is, during the training process, gradually, based on a probability, the observed values are replaced by the outputs of the model.

A multi-domain (e.g., language modeling, vocal synthesis, image, and handwriting generation) proposed solution using a generative adversarial network with a variation of TF is the work of Lamb et al. [66], namely, *Professor forcing*. Their approach entails training additional discriminators to differentiate free running from forced hidden states. This approach assures that the dynamic of the network will remain similar when using observed and freely sampled values during the training procedures.

Moving towards NARXNN-based proposed solutions, we find the work of Massaoudi et al. [55] with a photovoltaic power forecasting technique. Their solution encompasses a hybrid model consisting of an LSTM neural network and an NARXNN. The NARXNN gathers data and generates a residual error vector. This vector is then fed into an LSTM neural network as additional input, allowing the LSTM to produce both point-by-point and sequence forecasts. This combination of the NARXNN model and the LSTM allows for the generation of accurate and reliable forecasts.

A popular solution that highlights the similarities between neural networks with TF and NARXNN is Amazon's DeepAR [67]. DeepAR is a probabilistic forecasting technique that uses autoregressive RNNs to make predictions. It works by incorporating likelihoods and using nonlinear data transformation techniques, as learned by a neural network, to accurately forecast future outcomes. DeepAR is built upon an RNN where the input of the model consists of a combination of lagged target values and covariates. The model outputs either a point-by-point prediction with a standard loss function or a probabilistic prediction using the parameters of a probability density function (e.g., the mean and standard deviation value).

Other applications of NARXNN-based techniques, most of them in the energetic field, include: building temperature and energy forecasting [68,69], daily solar radiation prediction [70], load forecast for residential low-voltage distribution networks [71], hydrometeorological drought forecasting in hyper-arid climates [72], transformer oil-dissolved gas concentration prediction [73], electrical grid short-term load forecasting [74], lithium-ion battery state of health (SoH) estimation [75], and wind power prediction [76].

2.2. Neural Network Benchmarking Papers and Studies

Thomas Brueuel, from Google's research team, studied the behavior and performance of LSTM classifiers in [30]. This study analyses the behavior of LSTMs for different hyper-parameters, but also how the choice of non-linearities affects performance. Among the tested hyperparameters we find the learning rate, number of hidden units, and mini-batch size. The study focused on digit classification on two popular benchmarking datasets, namely, MNIST, which is an isolated digit handwriting classification dataset, and UW3, which is an OCR evaluation database. The results showed that the performance of LSTM classifiers mostly depends on learning rates, batching had little to no effect on performance, softmax training yielded better results compared to the least square training, and LSTMs without peephole connections obtained the best performance in comparison to LSTMs with peepholes.

Another large-scale study, on the performance of LSTM, is the work of Greff et al. [31]. Their study, named "LSTM: A search space odyssey", analyzed the performance of eight LSTM variants on three tasks: speech recognition, handwriting recognition, and polyphonic music modeling. The studied LSTM variants included *No input gate, No forget gate, No output gate, No input activation function, No output activation function, Coupled input and forget gate, No peepholes, and Full gate recurrence.* As for activation functions, the standard approach was followed, namely using the sigmoid and the hyperbolic tangent functions. The authors also studied the effects of hyperparameters on the performance of the neural networks, hyperparameters such as the hidden layer size, learning rate, momentum, and input noise. However, the hyperparamter effects were not tested on entire ranges of possible values, but rather using random searches in specific ranges. The findings of this study show that the learning rate had the largest effect on the experiments, followed by the hidden layer size, and an interesting finding showed that adding noise to the inputs decreased the performance and increased the training time. One unexpected result, as the authors state, was that momentum had no effect on the performance or the training time of any of the eight tested LSTM variants. One conclusion of the study reveals that the standard LSTM variant (i.e., VLSTM) performed equally well in comparison to the other tested variants.

In a more recent study, Siami-Namini et al. [32] analyzed the time series forecasting performance of unidirectional LSTMs and bidirectional LSTMS (BiLSTMs). The authors compared the performance of auto-regressive integrated moving average (ARIMA) models, LSTMs, and BiLSTMs in the context of predicting financial time series data. One interesting aspect of this research is the prediction performance when the time series data are learned in both directions (i.e., past-to-future and future-to-past). Their results showed that BiLSTM's training time was slower, but outperformed the unidirectional LSTM and ARIMA models in terms of prediction accuracy. Nonetheless, the authors provided no architectural or hyperparameter information about the tested neural networks, or whether the two architectures were trained and tested with the same set of hyperparameters.

Farzad et al. [33] examined the classification performance of LSTMs with various activation functions for the *forget, input*, and *output* gates. In their paper, the authors tested 23 activation functions for a Vanilla LSTM with a single hidden layer with various hidden units on three distinct datasets, namely, IMDB, Movie Review, and MNIST. Their results illustrate that on these three datasets, on average the less-known activations functions (e.g., Elliott, modified Elliott, and softsign) produced better results compared to the commonly used activation functions from the literature. Additionally, their results also show that activation functions with the range $[-0.5, 1.5]$ can produce better results and using a wider range for the codomain can yield a better performance.

In the direction of forecasting multivariate time series data, we find the work of Khodabakhsh et al. [34]. Here, the forecasting accuracy of an LSTM neural network was tested on a dataset originating from an industrial system, namely, a petrochemical plant. The authors measured the training time and the values of the loss function regarding the size of the hidden layers (two hidden layers were used). Moreover, the influence of the mini-batch size and number of features on the forecasting accuracy was also measured. Their results show that on this specific dataset, increasing the number of features yielded better results for all mini-batch sizes. Most of the training information and hyperparameter values are not mentioned, and it is not clear what features were used or how they were selected; the authors only mention that they increased the number of features.

Moving towards NARXNN performance analysis papers, we find the work of Menezes and Barreto [35]. This paper presents an empirical evaluation of long-term time series prediction performance of NARXNNs on two real-world datasets, namely, the chaotic laser time series and a variable-bit-rate video traffic time series. In this paper, two variants of NARXNN (i.e., series–parallel and parallel architectures) are compared with an Elman neural network [50] and a time delay neural network (TDNN) [36]. On the first dataset, their results show that, when running with the same configuration and using the standard gradient-based backpropagation algorithm, the NARXNN obtains better results than the TDNN and the Elman network. Similar results were obtained on the second dataset, where the variants of NARXNN outperformed both the TDNN and Elman networks when trained and tested with the same configuration. This paper, however, used fixed values for the hyperparameters for all experiments, without measuring the performance of the three neural networks on other values.

More recently, Kumar and Murugan [37] published another NARXNN performance analysis paper using various training functions. In this paper, various NARXNN architectures were trained and tested on the Bombay Stock Exchange (BSE100) closing stock index of the Indian stock market. As performance metrics, the authors used the mean square error (MSE) and the symmetric mean absolute percentage error (SMAPE), the complexity of the neural network with respect to the number of neurons in the hidden layer, the training time, and the convergence speed (measured in epochs). The results illustrate that resilient backpropagation and train one-step secant yielded better results in comparison with the other ten compared functions in terms of SMAPE and training time. The Levenberg Marquadrt method, however, outperformed all other training functions in terms of convergence speed and SMAPE. Conversely, the paper proposes the optimal number of neurons on the hidden layer for an improved prediction accuracy and reduced over-fitting. As previously mentioned for the other analyzed papers, the findings are only applicable to this specific dataset.

2.3. Neural Network Hyperparameter Optimization

A popular guide on hyperparameter optimization is the work of Yoshua Bengio [28]. In this paper, the author offers practical recommendations towards selecting the optimal hyperparameter values, in the context of backpropagated gradient and gradient-based optimization for large-scale and deep neural networks. Among the discussed hyperparameters, the author identifies the initial learning rate as the most important one, in most of the cases, with values in the range $(10^{-6}, 1)$, with the default value (e.g., 0.01) typically working for standard multi-layer neural networks. In terms of mini-batch size, the author identifies smaller values, even the default value of 32, to be efficient. As the author states, the impact of the mini-batch size should be mostly computational, affecting the training time and not the testing performance. This has been observed by other authors as well: Masters and Luschi in [77] experimentally proved that using smaller batch sizes, often as small as two, offers the best training stability and generalization performance. Moving on to the number of hidden units, in [28] the author proposes selecting the number of units to be larger than the input vector, as larger values would not affect the generalization performance but would require more computation power. For initialization, the author suggests that the biases can usually be initialized to zero and introduces several options for initializing the rest of the weights. The paper also describes two popular optimization techniques for searching the optimal hyperparameter values, namely, grid-search and random sampling.

In a different direction, Smith et al. in [38] proposed increasing the mini-batch size instead of decaying the learning rate. The authors tested their theory on two convolutional neural networks (i.e., Inception-ResNet-V2 and ResNet-50) on image classification tasks, namely, on the ImageNet dataset. Their results illustrate that in this scenario, on this dataset, they can achieve the same performance with reduced training time by increasing the mini-batch size.

Makoto et al. in [39] investigated several mini-batch creation strategies for neural machine translation models. This paper analysed mini-batch creation strategies such as sorting by length of source and target sentences. Their results suggest that the mini-batch size affects both the training speed and the accuracy of the model, with larger mini-batch sizes yielding better results.

While many papers are addressing the influence of different hyperparameters on the performance of neural networks, we believe one strong point of the current paper is an in-depth analysis and comparison of the performance of LSTMs trained with both TF and backpropagation through time. This study also tested using two variants of TF compared to standard LSTMs (i.e., VLSTMs) and to the classical TF approach. To the best of our knowledge, this is the first paper offering such a detailed analysis on LSTMTF, and on TF in general, on time series data.

3. Proposed Approach

The current section first offers a short overview of LSTMs and TF. Second, the configurations, hyperparameters, and prediction modes of the tested neural networks are described. Finally, this section introduces the performance evaluation metrics used in this paper, together with the feature-selection methods.

3.1. Long Short-Term Memory Neural Networks

This subsection concisely describes the concepts of LSTM with and without TF, together with the mathematical equations behind them.

The LSTM neural network can be defined as an enhanced version of an RNN, capable of capturing long- and short-term dependencies from data sequences, while also solving the exploding and vanishing gradient problem [78]. In this paper, the standard LSTM neural network will further be named Vanilla LSTM (VLSTM). The standard LSTM layers include LSTM units, as shown in Figure 1. These units take the current input vector, denoted as $X(t)$, together with the previous hidden state vector of the layer, further denoted as $h(t)$. The cell state vector, denoted as $C(t)$, is updated using three gates, namely, the input gate $I(t)$, the forget gate $f(t)$, and the output gate $o(t)$.

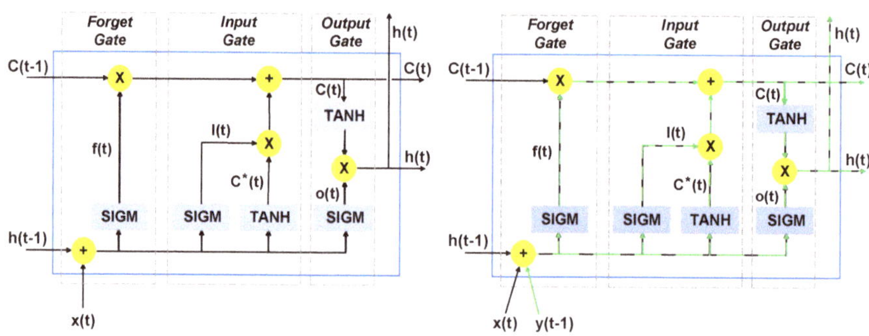

Figure 1. LSTM generic unit (**left**) together with an LSTM unit with teacher forcing (**right**). This figure originates from [40].

From an architectural point of view, these three gates can be viewed as three different layers included in the LSTM cell, where each gate regulates the information flow from and to the memory cell. The forget gate is responsible for determining what information is to be removed from the cell state, the input gate regulates what new information is to be stored in the cell state, and finally, the output gate controls the output of the LSTM unit, namely, the hidden state. At each time-step t, the hidden state vector $h(t)$ and the cell state vector $C(t)$ are transmitted to the next time-step $t+1$. Here, the hidden state also denotes the output of the LSTM unit at time t, and it represents the short-term memory of the unit, while the cell state $C(t)$ denotes the long-term memory.

The following equations describe the operations of the Vanilla LSTM units:

$$f(t) = sigm(\mathcal{W}_f X(t) + \mathcal{U}_f h(t-1) + b_f), \quad (1)$$

$$I(t) = sigm(\mathcal{W}_I X(t) + \mathcal{U}_I h(t-1) + b_I), \quad (2)$$

$$\overline{C}(t) = tanh(\mathcal{W}_C X(t-1) + \mathcal{U}_C h(t-1) + b_C), \quad (3)$$

$$C(t) = f(t) \cdot C(t-1) + I(t) \cdot \overline{C}(t), \quad (4)$$

$$o(t) = sigm(\mathcal{W}_o X(t) + \mathcal{U}_o h(t-1) + b_o), \quad (5)$$

$$h(t) = o(t) \cdot tanh(C(t)). \quad (6)$$

In Equations (1)–(6), $\mathcal{W}, \mathcal{U}$, and b denote the weight matrices for the inputs, outputs, hidden layer, and bias vector. In the same equations, $(\cdot)$ denotes the elementwise multiplication operation. The two activation functions are the sigmoid, denoted as $sigm$, and the hyperbolic tangent, denoted as $tanh$. The two activation functions are computed as follows:

$$\begin{aligned} sigm(x) &= \frac{1}{1+e^x}, \\ sigm(x) &\in (0,1), \end{aligned} \quad (7)$$

$$\begin{aligned} tanh(x) &= \frac{e^x - e^{-x}}{e^x + e^{-x}}, \\ tanh(x) &\in (-1,1). \end{aligned} \quad (8)$$

3.2. Long Short-Term Memory Networks with Teacher Forcing

Let $X(t)$, of size n, denote the input vector at time t, where $x_1(t), x_2(t), \ldots, x_n(t)$ represents the individual inputs (e.g., predictor variables) at time t. Let $y(t)$ be the ground truth value (i.e., the observed value) of the output variable (i.e., the response variable). In short, the LSTM represents a nonlinear function of the previous inputs and hidden states. As previously mentioned, applying the original version of TF involves altering the training procedures by adding, at each time-step, an extra input, which is the previous ground truth value $y(t-1)$. This extra input needs to be present during both training and inference. In the original version of TF, and in subsequent papers proposing modified versions of TF, it is assumed that this extra input or inputs (i.e., the previous ground truth value) is not available after training; thus, it is replaced by the previous predicted value, denoted as $\hat{y}(t-1)$ and computed on the output layer as follows:

$$\hat{y}(t-1) = \mathcal{W}_{\hat{y}} h(t-1) + b_{\hat{y}}. \quad (9)$$

In a process state monitoring system, the measured outputs are available [40]; thus, we proposed such a modification of the LSTM neural network for anomaly detection. In such a scenario, the extra input for the neural network is the previous ground truth value, denoted as $y(t-1)$.

As this paper analyses the performance of LSTMs with TF with the output variable fed back as input with multiple time delays, $Y(1:\tau)$ denotes the vector of output variables, with τ delays. Namely, if $Y(t-1) = (y_1(t-1), y_2(t-1), \ldots, y_m(t-1))$, where $y_1(t-1)$, $y_2(t-1), \ldots, y_m(t-1)$ denotes m output variables with one time delay, then $Y(1:\tau) = (y_1(t-1), y_1(t-2), \ldots, y_1(t-\tau), y_2(t-1), y_2(t-2), \ldots, y_2(t-\tau), \ldots, y_m(t-1), y_m(t-2), \ldots, y_m(t-\tau))$ denotes m output variables with τ time delays.

If we separate the input vector into the external inputs $X(t)$ and the previous ground truth value of the output variable $Y(1:\tau)$, the previous equations, from Section 3.1, can be rewritten as follows:

$$f(t) = sigm(\mathcal{W}_f^X X(t) + \mathcal{W}_f^Y Y(1:\tau) + \mathcal{U}_f h(t-1) + b_f), \tag{10}$$

$$I(t) = sigm(\mathcal{W}_I^X X(t) + \mathcal{W}_I^Y (1:\tau) + \mathcal{U}_I h(t-1) + b_I), \tag{11}$$

$$\overline{C}(t) = tanh(\mathcal{W}_C^X X(t-1) + \mathcal{W}_C^Y Y(1:\tau) + \mathcal{U}_C h(t-1) + b_C), \tag{12}$$

$$o(t) = sigm(\mathcal{W}_o^X X(t) + \mathcal{W}_o^Y Y(1:\tau) + \mathcal{U}_o h(t-1) + b_o). \tag{13}$$

These equations describe the forward pass during training for both LSTMTF and LSTMTFC, and the forward pass during inference for LSTMTF. For LSTMTFC, during inference, as the previous predicted values $\hat{Y}(1:\tau)$ with τ time delays are fed back as inputs to the current time-step, the equations become:

$$f(t) = sigm(\mathcal{W}_f^X X(t) + \mathcal{W}_f^{\hat{Y}} \hat{Y}(1:\tau) + \mathcal{U}_f h(t-1) + b_f), \tag{14}$$

$$I(t) = sigm(\mathcal{W}_I^X X(t) + \mathcal{W}_I^{\hat{Y}} \hat{Y}(1:\tau) + \mathcal{U}_I h(t-1) + b_I), \tag{15}$$

$$\overline{C}(t) = tanh(\mathcal{W}_C^X X(t-1) + \mathcal{W}_C^{\hat{Y}} \hat{Y}(1:\tau) + \mathcal{U}_C h(t-1) + b_C), \tag{16}$$

$$o(t) = sigm(\mathcal{W}_o^X X(t) + \mathcal{W}_o^{\hat{Y}} \hat{Y}(1:\tau) + \mathcal{U}_o h(t-1) + b_o). \tag{17}$$

TF, as applied to LSTMTF and LSTMTFC, does not introduce additional recurrent connections or weights from the output layer to the input layer; thus, the backwards propagation equations remain unchanged. Further details about BPTT and VLSTMs can be found in [56–58].

As described in [44], training models with the original version of TF can lead to poor prediction results, as during inference the model might be exposed to different data. This is referred to as exposure bias.

Exposure bias occurs when a machine learning model is not exposed to a diverse enough range of data during training. This can lead to poor performance and incorrect predictions when the model is used on data that do not match the characteristics of the training data. Essentially, exposure bias happens when the distribution of data seen by the model during training does not accurately reflect the distribution of data it will encounter in the real world.

Due to exposure bias, the LSTM's predictions can be unreliable and inaccurate when the previous predicted value is fed back as input during inference. However, feeding back the actual (i.e., observed) value, during both training and inference, is not possible if the observed values are no longer available after training. This issue was also highlighted by other researchers as well [45,45].

As LSTMTF feeds back the previous output ground truth value (i.e., observed value) during both training and inference, this phenomenon should be avoided in comparison to LSTMTFC. This holds under the assumption that the observed value is available during inference, as proposed in [40], in a process state monitoring system. In this scenario, any change in the previous values of the monitored variable should be reflected in the current output and subsequently in the prediction errors. This, in turn, would be advantageous when such a model is used for anomaly-detection tasks, by monitoring the change in the prediction errors of the model.

3.3. Neural Network Architectures and Prediction Modes

The performance and predictive capabilities of the three neural networks (i.e., VLSTM, LSTMTF, and LSTMTFC) are tested using two distinct configurations and in two operation modes.

First, in terms of the number of inputs and outputs, the neural networks are tested as multi-input single-output (MISO) and multi-input multi-output (MIMO). The MISO configuration involves predicting one variable using multiple input variables. Conversely, the MIMO configuration involves predicting multiple variables using multiple input variables.

Second, in terms of prediction modes, two approaches are followed, namely, M2O and M2M. In the case of M2O, the neural networks will take as input a sequence of X_n^t inputs; here, t denotes the number of time-steps (in other words, the length of the input sequence) and n denotes the number of input variables and will output only the final predicted value of the sequence. To exemplify, for every sequence of ten input values, the neural network will output the next value in the sequence.

In the case of M2M, the neural networks similarly take as input a sequence of X_n^t values and output another sequence of values of size t, the first prediction starting at $t_0 + 1$. Here, t_0 denotes the time of the first value in the input sequence.

To observe the influence of different hyperparameters on the training process and on the prediction capabilities, for all neural networks, in both MISO and MIMO configurations and in both M2O and M2M prediction modes, the following hyperparameters are analyzed:

- **Input Sequence Length (ISL)**: The input sequence length denotes the number of time-steps of the input variables fed to the neural network as a single sequence.
- **Teacher Forcing Lags (time-delays)**: For a given output variable, the number of lags denotes how many previous time-steps of said output variable will be fed back as input at the current time-step t. As previously mentioned, the number of lags is denoted as τ, where $\tau \geq 1$.
- **Mini-Batch Size (MBS)**: The mini-batch represents a subset of the training dataset used to evaluate the gradient of the loss function and update the weights of the model [77].
- **Learning Rate (LR)**: The learning rate is a hyperparameter that controls the rate of change for the weights after each optimization step. If the learning rate is too small, the model will learn slowly and training will take longer. If it is too high, the model may not find the optimal solution or may even diverge.
- **Number of Hidden Units (HU)**: The dimensionality of the LSTM hidden state. The hidden units represent the information that is retained by the layer from one time-step to the next, referred to as the hidden state.

The previous hyperparameters are divided into two categories: internal (LR, HU) and external (ISL, Lags, MBS) hyperparameters.

3.4. Performance Evaluation Metrics

To measure the performance, the following performance metrics are used:

1. **Training Convergence Time (epochs).** Convergence refers to the epoch at which the network's performance on the training data stops advancing. This often occurs after the network's weights and biases have been adjusted so that the network's output is as near to the desired output as feasible for a particular input. This value is computed by identifying the epoch after which the loss value does not increase or decrease by a percentage, further denoted as ϵ, for P consecutive epochs.
2. **Training Final Loss Value.** The final value of the training loss function after the maximum number of training epochs.
3. **Training Loss Mean Value.** The mean value of the training loss function, computed over all the training epochs.
4. **Testing Mean Absolute Error Value (MAE).**The mean average absolute error value computed on the testing set, as shown in Equation (18).

5. **Testing Error Standard Deviation Value.** The standard deviation of the absolute error computed on the testing set.

$$\mathrm{MAE} = \frac{1}{N}\sum_{i=1}^{N} |y_i - \hat{y}_i|, \tag{18}$$

In Equation (18), N denotes the total number of predictions and y_i and $\hat{y}_i$ denote the i-th observed and predicted value, respectively.

3.5. Feature Selection

The feature-selection methodology for the MISO configuration involves selecting the subgroup of inputs based on correlation coefficient scores computed between the selected output variable and the candidates for the input variables. Given one or more output variables, the Pearson correlation coefficient is computed. Next, from the list of possible input variables, those that exhibit the highest positive and negative coefficient scores are selected. This feature-selection methodology has been proposed and successfully applied in [40].

Let X denote the set of n available candidates for the input variables. Let Y denote the set containing the m selected output variables, where $Y = (y_1, y_2, \ldots, y_m)$. If we consider K to be the number of observations for each variable, then for a given input variable x and an output variable y, Pearsons's correlation coefficient is obtained using:

$$PC(x,y) = \frac{\sum_{j=1}^{K}(x_j - \overline{x})(y_j - \overline{y})}{\sqrt{\sum_{j=1}^{K}(x_j - \overline{x})^2}\sqrt{\sum_{j=1}^{K}(y_j - \overline{y})^2}}, \tag{19}$$

where $\overline{x}$ and $\overline{y}$ represent the average values of x and y, respectively.

For the MIMO configuration, all the available input candidates are selected, thus substantially increasing the complexity of the neural network and subsequently increasing the training involution. Nonetheless, the experimental assessment should reveal if this methodology yields better or worse results in comparison to the first proposed feature-selection method.

4. Experimental Assessment

This section describes the dataset used in the experimental assessment, the configurations, the hyperparameter values, and the performed experiments. The chosen dataset originates from a well-known, publicly available [43] benchmarking chemical process simulation, namely, the Tennessee Eastman process (TEP) [42]. This process has been proposed for various studies including plant-wide control strategy design, multivariate control, education, anomaly detection, and fault diagnosis.

The experimental assessment was performed in MATLAB R2022b running on a Lenovo Legion laptop with an AMD Ryzen 5 5600H CPU, 32 GB RAM DDR4, running Windows 10 PRO. The assessment results are showcased in the next chapter.

4.1. Dataset Description and Data Preprocessing

The Tennessee Eastman process (TEP), originally proposed by Downs and Vogel in 1992 [42], is a model of an industrial chemical process with the purpose of designing, researching, and assessing process control technologies. The TEP encompasses five major units, namely, the product condenser, the separator, the compressor, and the product stripper. As described in the original paper, the TEP outputs two liquid products and two byproducts from four input reactants. The chemical reactions are both irreversible and exothermic while the reaction rates are a function of temperature. In terms of reactant concentrations, the reactions are roughly first-order. The model described in the paper consists of 52 measurements (of which 41 are measurements for process variables together with 11 measurements for manipulated variables), and 20 fault types.

Now, the dataset selected for the experiments consists of four subsets, namely, fault-free training, fault-free testing, faulty testing, and faulty training. In this study, only the fault-free versions of the dataset were used (i.e., training and testing subsets), as only the prediction performance was analyzed and not the anomalous detection capabilities. The training subset consists of 500 simulations, each simulation having 500 observations, in total 250,000 observations. For each simulation, the variables were sampled every 3 min, while the simulation ran for 25 h in the case of the training subsets and for 48 h in the case of the testing subsets. The testing fault-free dataset consists of 500 simulations, each simulation having 960 observations, summing up to 480,000 data points. Each subset of the original dataset contains 55 columns. The complete list of variables is available in the original TEP paper [42]. Meanwhile, the datasets are publicly available for download [43]. For this study, a new subset was created for training by randomly selecting 10 simulations from the 500 available ones, the final training dataset containing 5000 observations, which equals 250 h of measurements.

In terms of preprocessing, the two datasets were normalized using the feature scaling method (i.e., bringing all values into the [0, 1] range), as shown in Equation (20).

$$\begin{aligned} x' &= \frac{x - x_{min}}{x_{max} - x_{min}}, \\ x' &\in [0, 1], \end{aligned} \tag{20}$$

where x' is the normalized value for a given feature x and x_{min}, x_{max} denote the minimum and maximum values of x, respectively. Furthermore, the scaling is performed independently for each feature. Both the training and testing set were normalized using the maximum and minimum values from the training set for each feature.

As there were no constant or duplicate columns, missing values, or obvious outliers, no further preprocessing was performed.

4.2. Neural Network Architectures

The neural networks are trained using the Adam optimizer [79]. Additionally, they contain one hidden layer, this way reducing their complexity, similarly to [80]. The experimental assessment should reveal if such reduced architectures can model the relationship between signals originating from industrial processes. As pointed out in [31,44], increasing the number of layers increases the complexity of the model (e.g., time and memory), while models with at least one hidden layer can represent an approximation of any function conditioned by the number of hidden units. A complete list of the selected inputs and outputs for both MISO and MIMO configurations is presented in Table 1.

Table 1. The list of selected inputs and outputs for the MISO and MIMO configurations. A detailed description of the variables can be found in the original TEP paper [42,43].

Configuration	Output Variables	Input Variables
MISO	Product Analysis F (Stream 11)	A Feed (stream 1) A and C Feed (Stream 4) Product Separator Pressure Stripper Pressure Stripper Temperature Stripper Steam Flow Reactor Cooling Water Outlet Temperature Reactor feed Analysis B Reactor feed Analysis E A feed flow (Stream 1) Reactor Cooling Water Flow
MIMO	Product Analysis F (Stream 11) Purge gas analysis (Stream 9)	All Continuous Process Measurements All Process Manipulated Variables

4.3. Experiments

The following subsection describes the performed experiments and measurements. These experiments were performed on the following neural networks, namely, VLSTM, LSTMTF, and LSTMTFC in both prediction modes, namely, many-to-many and many-to-one. The neural networks were tested in two configurations, namely, multi-input single-output (MISO), that is, multiple output variables and one input variable, and multi-input multi-output (MIMO), that is, multiple input and multiple output variables. Table 2 shows the complete list of fixed and varying hyperparameter values for the first three experiments. The selected hyperparameters for the fourth experiments are detailed in the text, in Section 4.3.4. For computing the training convergence time, the following values were selected: $\epsilon = 1\%$ and $P = 5$.

Table 2. The complete list of fixed and varying hyperparameter values for Experiments 1–3 for all the tested neural network architectures.

Experiment	Hidden Layers	Sequence Input Length	Hidden Units	Learning Rate	Mini-Batch Size	Epochs	Lags
1	1	[10, 500]	16	0.01	32	100	[1, 50]
2	1	40	16	0.01	[1, 128]	100	1
3	1	40	[1, 128]	[0.00001, 0.1]	32	100	1

4.3.1. Experiment 1

The first experiment measures the influence of the input sequence length and the number of lags (i.e., the number of time delays of the output variable that are fed back as input variables) on the performance of the LSTM architectures. Here, the networks are trained and tested with different values for both the sequence length and the number of lags. In this experiment, we used the same sequence length for training and testing.

4.3.2. Experiment 2

The second experiment focuses on measuring the influence of the mini-batch size on the overall performance of the LSTM neural networks. Similarly to the first experiment, most of the hyperparameters are fixed, and the networks are trained and tested with multiple mini-batch sizes.

4.3.3. Experiment 3

While the previous two experiments focused on external hyperparameters, we wanted to see how certain internal hyperparameters influence the performance of the analyzed neural networks. In this experiment, all the external hyperparameters are fixed while the networks are trained with varying learning rates and number of hidden units on the LSTM layer. Additionally, here, the training and testing times are compared between the MISO and MIMO configurations.

4.3.4. Experiment 4

As mentioned earlier, we observed some similarities between NARXNN and TF. In this experiment, the prediction performance of NARXNN is also analyzed. A NARXNN model is trained and tested on the same dataset using a series–parallel configuration and is tested in two configurations, namely, parallel and series–parallel. As for hyperparameters, the values chosen for this model are the following: 16 neurons on the hidden layer, the symmetric sigmoid transfer function for the hidden layer, one delay for the output feedback. Subsequently, the hyperparameters for the LSTM neural networks are as follows: an input sequence length of 40, 16 hidden units on the hidden layer, one delay for the output feedback, a mini-batch size of 16, 0.01 learning rate, and 100–1000 training epochs.

4.3.5. Experiment 5

The fifth experiment analyzes the performance of the models when using additional validation data during training. As mentioned in [44], the use of validation datasets during training can aid in avoiding model overfitting. Here, the authors state that, typically, the training dataset is split into two disjoint subsets, one for training and one for validation during training. Furthermore, the authors suggest using 80% of the training dataset for training and 20% for validation. In this experiment, the performance of the neural networks is analyzed using the same ranges as above for all the hyperparameters, with a lag value of one. Additionally, we use the early stopping method, which implies stopping the training procedures or saving and returning the best parameters once the validation error starts increasing [44].

5. Results

This section describes the experimental assessment results and is organized as follows: for each configuration (i.e., MISO, MIMO) and for each prediction mode (i.e., M2M, M2O), the results for each experiment for each of the three neural network architectures are presented in a side-by-side approach. For LSTMTF and LSTMTFC, as the training process is identical, there is only one figure with the loss values. Additionally, for the M2O prediction mode, as the neural networks output only the final value of the sequence (without the rest of the values in the sequence), LSTMTFC cannot be applied in this scenario; thus, only LSTMTF and VLSTM are showcased for the M2O prediction mode.

5.1. Multi-Input Single-Output Configuration

5.1.1. Experiment 1

For the first experiment, measuring the performance based on the input sequence length and on the number of lags, the entire training process, in terms of the loss values for the 100 training epochs, is presented in Figures 2 and 3.

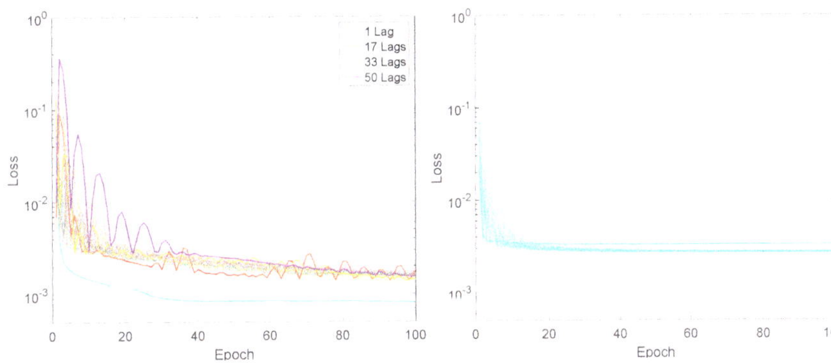

Figure 2. Illustration of the training loss for Experiment 1, LSTMTF (**left**) and VLSTM (**right**), using a many-to-many prediction mode. For each architecture, the lines with the same colors represent the loss for networks trained with the sequence length in the range [1:500]. The highlighted thick lines represent the training loss for a sequence length of 1.

In terms of final loss values, for the M2M prediction mode, after 100 training epochs, the values for LSTMTF were between 0.0008 and 0.0020 for input sequence lengths between 1 and 100 and between 0.0013 and 0.0022 for input sequence lengths between 100 and 500, with the final loss value increasing with the sequence length for sequence lengths in the range [1, 100]. In the case of VLSTM, the final loss values were higher for sequence lengths between 1 and 100, with values in the [0.0026, 0.0033] range, decreasing with the length of the input sequence. For sequence lengths in the [100, 500] the range of the final loss value was [0.0026, 0.0029].

Compared to the M2M prediction mode, for the M2O prediction mode, the final loss value decreased inversely proportional to the input sequence length for both architectures, from an average of 0.0025 for a sequence length of 10 to an average of 0.0005 for a sequence length of 500, for both LSTMTF and VLSTM.

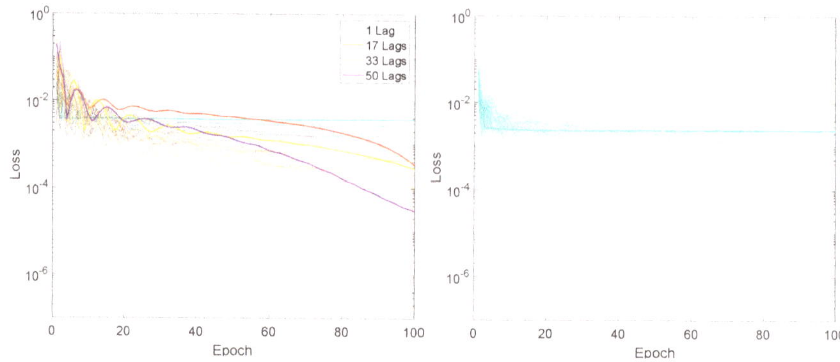

Figure 3. Illustration of the training loss for Experiment 1, LSTMTF (**left**) and VLSTM (**right**), using a many-to-one prediction mode. For each architecture, the lines with the same colors represent the loss for networks trained with the sequence length in the range [1:500]. The highlighted thick lines represent the training loss for a sequence length of 1.

For $\epsilon = 1\%$ and $P = 5$ epochs, the training convergence times for LSTMTF, in regard to the number of lags, can be seen in Table 3. Here, the minimum, average, and maximum values are shown for both prediction methods, computed for different numbers of lags. In the same table, it can be observed that for the M2M prediction mode, the minimum and average number of epochs until convergence increased from 86 for 1 lag to 97 for 50 lags. The maximum values for both prediction modes were equal to 100.

Similarly, in the M2O prediction mode, the average number of epochs increased from 65 for 1 lag to 87 for 50 lags, with overall smaller average values for M2O in comparison to M2M. In comparison to M2M, the minimum values for M2O were also smaller, ranging from 16 epochs when LSTMTF was trained with 1 lag to 41 in the case where LSTMTF was trained with 50 lags. As was the case for M2M, here, the maximum values were also equal to 100 for all experiments. Overall, the training convergence times, measured in epochs, for different sequence lengths were larger for LSTMTF compared to VLSTM, in both prediction modes; this is illustrated in Table 4.

Table 3. The training convergence time (epochs) for LSTMTF, computed with respect to the number of lags, for $\epsilon = 1\%$ and $P = 5$.

	Many-to-Many			Many-to-One		
	Min	**Avg**	**Max**	**Min**	**Avg**	**Max**
1 Lag	41	86	100	16	65	100
10 Lags	26	91	100	16	72	100
20 Lags	46	95	100	21	73	100
30 Lags	46	95	100	21	73	100
40 Lags	46	96	100	26	71	100
50 Lags	46	97	100	41	87	100

The loss average value for LSTMTF increased with the length of the input sequence for values between [1, 100] from 0.0013 to 0.0042, afterward remaining at an average of

0.0028 for sequence lengths between [101, 500] when trained with one lag. Overall, the loss average values increased for all sequence lengths with the addition of time delays, with an average of 0.004 for 10 lags, 0.005 for 20 lags, and 0.006 for 40 lags. In the case of VLSTM, no significant influence from the sequence length was observed on the average loss values.

Table 4. The average training convergence time (epochs) for LSTMTF and VLSTM, computed with respect to the input sequence length, for $\epsilon = 1\%$, $P = 5$, and 1 lag for LSTMTF.

	LSTMTF		VLSTM	
ISL	**Many-to-Many**	**Many-to-One**	**Many-to-Many**	**Many-to-One**
[10, 100]	70	83	32	38
[100, 200]	73	69	36	51
[200, 300]	86	82	44	57
[300, 400]	93	82	66	74
[400, 500]	90	86	80	79

In terms of final loss values, for M2M, after 100 training epochs, the values for LSTMTF were between 0.0008 and 0.0020 for input sequence lengths between 1 and 100 and between 0.0013 and 0.0022 for input sequence lengths between 100 and 500, the final loss value increasing with the sequence length for sequence lengths between [1, 100]. In the case of VLSTM, the final loss values were higher for sequence lengths between 1 and 100, with values in the [0.0026, 0.0033] range, decreasing with the length of the input sequence. For sequence lengths in the [100, 500] the range the final loss value was [0.0026, 0.0029].

Compared to the M2M prediction mode, for M2O the final loss value decreased inversely proportional to the input sequence length, for both architectures, from an average of 0.0025 for a sequence length of 10 to an average of 0.0005 for a sequence length of 500, for both LSTMTF and VLSTM.

The MAE computed with respect to the input sequence length and number of lags on the test set for the three architectures is illustrated in Figures 4 and 5.

In the case of M2M for LSTMTF, the best results were obtained for sequence lengths in the range of [1, 100] with the worst results for larger sequence lengths (in the range [400–500]). In the case of VLSTM, the MAE remained almost constant, in the range of [0.058, 0.061], for all sequence lengths. Conversely, LSTMFC obtained the worst results, 30 times larger than LSTMTF and 25 times larger than VLSTM.

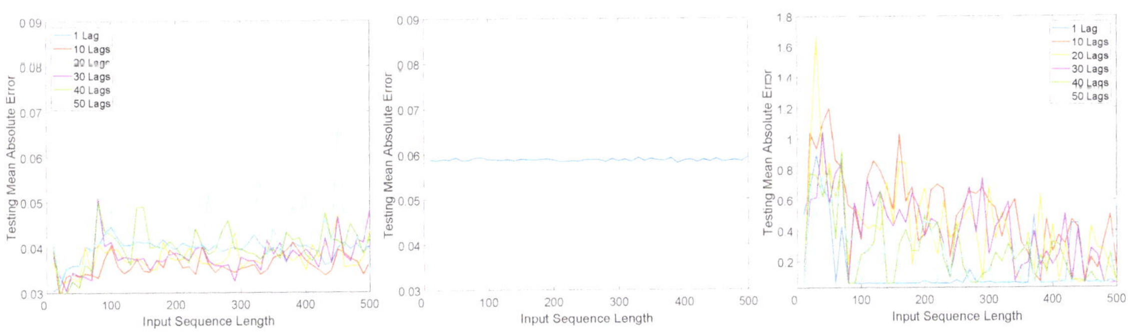

Figure 4. Illustration of the testing mean absolute error value for Experiment 1, LSTMTF (**left**), VLSTM (**middle**), and LSTMTFC (**right**), using a many-to-many prediction mode.

The same behavior was observed in terms of testing error standard deviation values, with values in the range of [0.037, 0.042] for LSTMTF for input sequence lengths in the range of [1, 100] and [0.0435, 0.046] for VLSTM for all input sequence lengths.

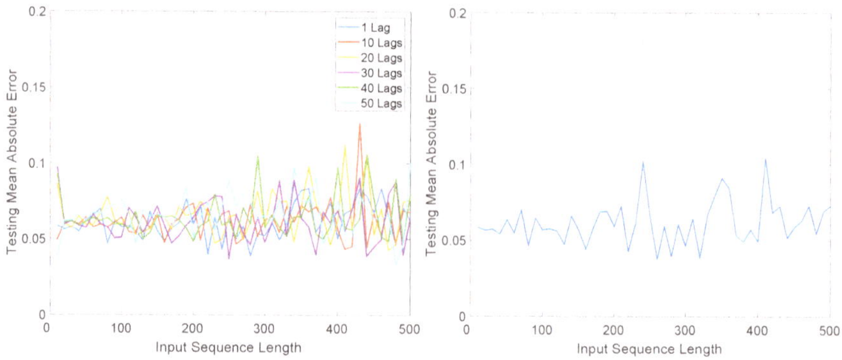

Figure 5. Illustration of the testing mean absolute error value for Experiment 1, LSTMTF (**left**) and VLSTM (**right**), using a many-to-one prediction mode.

In the case of M2O, LSTMTF and VLSTM obtained similar results, with a minimum value of 0.038 obtained by the LSTMTF with 50 time delays and a minimum of 0.038 obtained by VLSTM. As illustrated in Figure 5, the average of the testing MAE increased with the sequence length for the LSTMTF and VLSTM architectures.

Overall, in terms of the convergence time and MAE, for the first experiment, the results show that LSTMTF performed best with 1 lag and with an input sequence length in the range [1, 100] and showed no significant deviations with longer sequence lengths when using M2M mode, see Figure 4. In an M2O mode, however, increasing the input sequence length yielded the worst results outside the [1, 100] range, see Figure 5. The performance of the VLSTM in M2M mode was subtly affected by the input sequence length; however, the training convergence times increased with the sequence length. In the case of VLSTM in M2O mode, similarly to the case of LSTMTF, the MAE increased with the increasing sequence length. For LSTMTFC, the testing MAE was clearly influenced by the input sequence length, yielding the worst results for sequence lengths in the [1, 100] range.

5.1.2. Experiment 2

The training loss values for the second experiment based on different mini-batch sizes are illustrated in Figures 6 and 7. Additionally, the training convergence time for both architectures can be observed in Table 5.

Table 5. The training convergence time (epochs) for LSTMTF and VLSTM, computed with respect to the mini-batch size, for $\epsilon = 1\%$ and $P = 5$.

	LSTMTF		VLSTM	
MBS	**Many-to-Many**	**Many-to-One**	**Many-to-Many**	**Many-to-One**
2	100	46	12	66
8	51	31	16	41
16	86	41	41	32
32	100	51	46	56
64	86	56	51	56
128	100	56	51	57

The loss final value after 100 training epochs was smaller for mini-batch sizes between 2 and 32, with values in the range of [0.0007, 0.0018] for LSTMTF in an M2M prediction mode, while for mini-batch sizes between 32 and 128 the final values were in the [0.0013, 0.0023] range. In the case of M2O, for the same LSTMTF, the range of the final loss values was [0.0005, 0.0036] for mini-batch sizes between 2 and 32. For mini-batch sizes in the [32, 128] range, the final loss values were between 0.0014 and 0.0032. In the case of VLSTM, the final loss values for M2M were between 0.0022 and 0.0031 for mini-batch sizes between 2 and 32, and more constant in the [32, 128] mini-batch size range, with values between 0.0026 and 0.0028. Similarly to LSTMTF, for M2O, the range of the final loss values was [0.0001, 0.0023] for mini-batch sizes between 2 and 32 and between 0.0014 and 0.0019 for mini-batch sizes over 32.

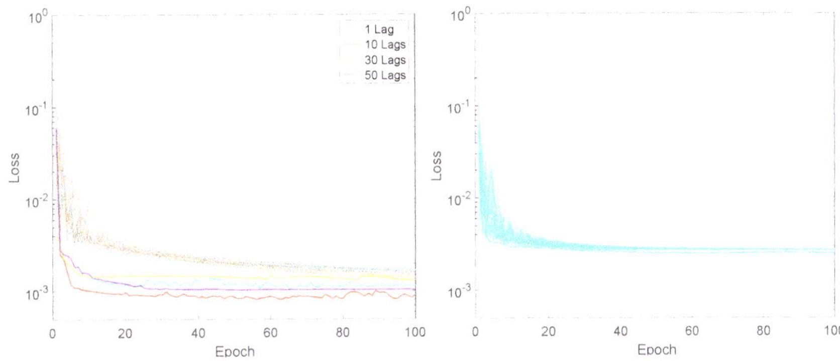

Figure 6. Illustration of the training loss for Experiment 2, LSTMTF (**left**) and VLSTM (**right**), using a many-to-many prediction mode. For each architecture, the lines with the same colors represent the loss for networks trained with mini-batch size in the [2:128] range. The highlighted thick lines represent the training loss for a mini-batch size of 2.

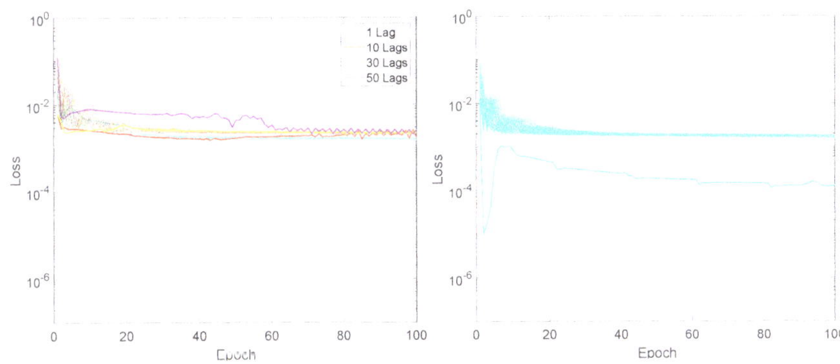

Figure 7. Illustration of the training loss for Experiment 2, LSTMTF (**left**) and VLSTM (**right**), using a many-to-one prediction mode. For each architecture, the lines with the same colors represent the loss for networks trained with the training mini-batch sizes in the [2:128] range. The highlighted thick lines represent the training loss for a mini-batch size of 2.

Moving on to the testing performance, Figures 8 and 9 illustrate the computed MAE for all architectures in both prediction modes. In Figure 8 it can be observed that overall the MAE is smaller for LSTMTF in an M2M prediction mode, for all mini-batch sizes, in comparison with the VLSTM. The best results were obtained by LSTMTF with mini-batch sizes in the range of [2, 32], with MAE values in the [0.030, 0.045] range, while the computed MAE for VLSTM was in the [0.058, 0.061] range for all mini-batch sizes. Similarly to the first experiment, the MAE for LSTMTFC was 50 times higher for mini-batch sizes in the [2, 32] range.

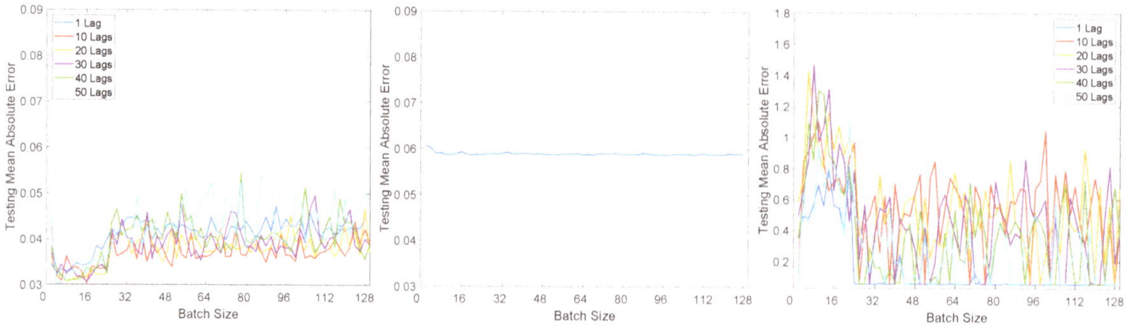

Figure 8. Illustration of the testing mean absolute error value for Experiment 2, LSTMTF (**left**), VLSTM (**middle**), and LSTMTFC (**right**), using a many-to-many prediction mode.

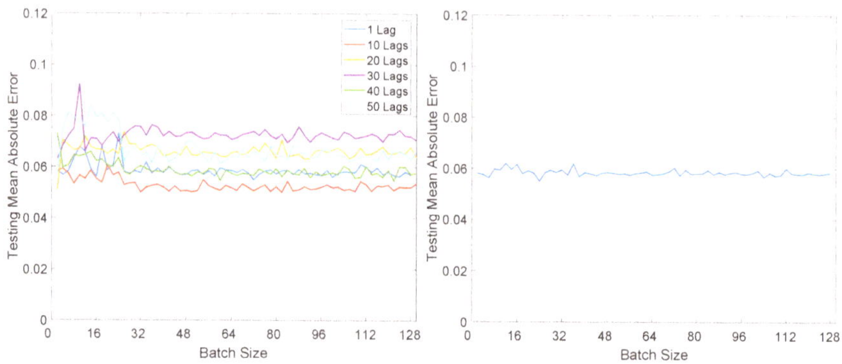

Figure 9. Illustration of the testing mean absolute error value for Experiment 2, LSTMTF (**left**) and VLSTM (**right**), using a many-to-one prediction mode.

Conversely, in the case of M2O, VLSTM outperformed LSTMTF in almost all experiments; this can be observed in Figure 9. The only exception here was the case of LSTMTF with 10 lags, where the testing MAE was in the range of [0.05, 0.06] in comparison to VLSTM, where the MAE was in the range of [0.055, 0.062].

Overall, for the second experiment, LSTMTF yielded the best results with mini-batch sizes in the [2, 32] range, while in the same mini-batch range LSTMTFC obtained the worst results, as illustrated in Figure 8. The performance of VLSTM, in both prediction modes, was influenced to a lesser extent by the mini-batch size, yielding constant results for all mini-batch sizes.

5.1.3. Experiment 3

In the third experiment, the neural networks were trained and tested with various learning rates and numbers of hidden units. The results, in terms of mean loss values, for both LSTMTF and VLSTM are illustrated in Figures 10 and 11. Additionally, the computed training convergence times with respect to the learning rate and to the number of hidden units are shown in Tables 6 and 7.

The final loss values for LSTMTF in an M2M prediction mode were in the [0.001, 0.003] range, with no significant changes based on the values of the learning rate. However, the number of hidden units had more of an influence on the final loss values, with values ranging from 0.0015 to 0.003 for hidden units between 2 and 16 and values ranging from 0.001 to 0.0012 for hidden units between 16 and 128, with small changes for hidden units in the [16, 128] range. The final loss values for VLSTM in an M2M prediction mode were in the [0.002, 0.003] range for all experiments, with no visible trend given by the values of the learning rate or the number of hidden units. For the M2O prediction mode, the results in terms of the final loss values for both LSTMTF and VLSTM were similar, in the [0.0001, 0.0004] range.

As for the mean loss values computed over all 100 training epochs, it can be observed in Figure 10 that in the case of LSTMTF and VLSTM in an M2M mode, the number of hidden units had an influence on the mean loss values, with higher values for hidden units in the [2, 16] range in comparison to the [32, 128] range. For the M2O mode, for both LSTMTF and VLSTM the influence of the number of hidden units was obvious for hidden units in the [2, 7] range, as can be observed in Figure 11.

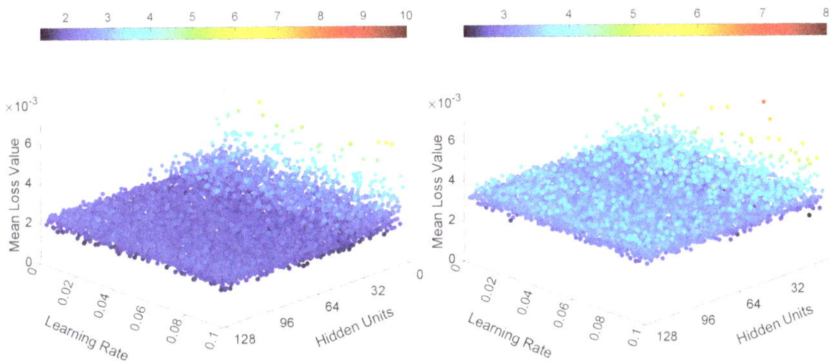

Figure 10. Illustration of the mean loss value for Experiment 3, LSTMTF (**left**) and VLSTM (**right**), using a many-to-many prediction mode.

As shown in Table 6, the average convergence time increased with the number of hidden units only in the case of LSTMTF in an M2O prediction mode. Here, the number of epochs increased from 38 for 2 hidden units to 47 for 128 hidden units. The remaining results for the average convergence time, for all architectures, are shown in the same table. By analyzing the results shown in Table 7, we observe that the learning rate had little to no influence on the training convergence time.

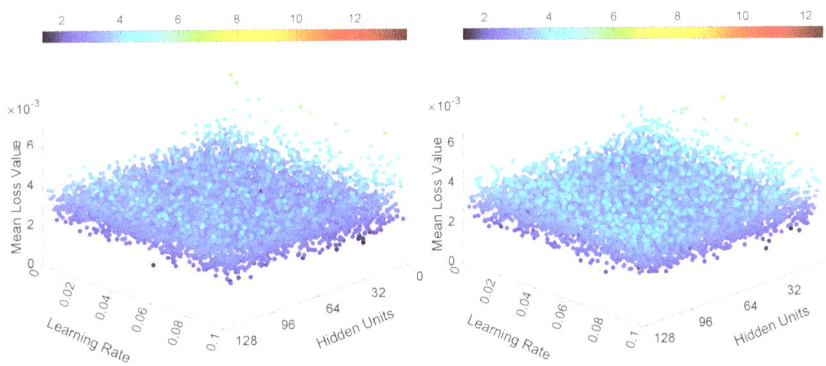

Figure 11. Illustration of the mean loss value for Experiment 3, LSTMTF (**left**) and VLSTM (**right**), using a many-to-one prediction mode.

Table 6. The training convergence time (epochs) for LSTMTF and VLSTM, computed with respect to the number of hidden units, for ϵ = 1% and P = 5.

	LSTMTF		VLSTM	
HU	**Many-to-Many**	**Many-to-One**	**Many-to-Many**	**Many-to-One**
2	81	38	30	38
8	73	40	25	44
16	76	43	24	43
32	79	47	22	44
64	77	44	22	42
128	58	47	23	47

Table 7. The training convergence time (epochs) for LSTMTF and VLSTM, computed with respect to the learning rate, for ϵ = 1% and P = 5.

	LSTMTF		VLSTM	
LR	**Many-to-Many**	**Many-to-One**	**Many-to-Many**	**Many-to-One**
[0.0001, 0.02]	71	46	23	45
[0.02, 0.04]	71	44	23	44
[0.04, 0.06]	71	44	23	44
[0.06, 0.08]	71	45	23	45
[0.08, 0.1]	71	44	23	44

The MAE computed on the testing dataset, for the third set of experiments, is illustrated in Figures 12 and 13. As can be seen in Figure 12, for LSTMTF in an M2M prediction mode, the learning rate had little influence over the testing MAE, and all the trained LSTMTF predicted similarly regardless of the learning rate values. In the same figure, the influence of the number of hidden units is visible, namely, hidden units in the [2, 16] range yielded larger values for the MAE, with values in the [0.04, 0.06] range. For 16 to 128 hidden units, the prediction MAE was in the [0.030, 0.036] range.

In the case of VLSTM, in an M2M prediction mode, it can be observed that the number of hidden units and learning rate influenced the testing MAE to a smaller degree, with the prediction MAE remaining in the [0.058, 0.061] range, in comparison to LSTMTF and LSTMTFC.

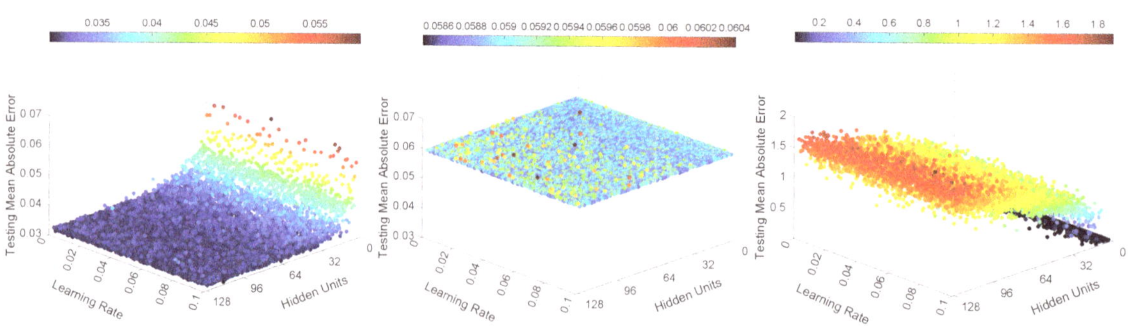

Figure 12. Illustration of the testing mean absolute error value for Experiment 3, LSTMTF (**left**), VLSTM (**middle**), and LSTMTFC (**right**), using a many-to-many prediction mode.

For LSTMTFC using an M2M prediction method, the number of hidden units seem to have an inverse influence compared to LSTMTF, namely, for hidden units in the [2, 16] range the prediction MAE was in the [0.04, 0.07] range. Conversely, for hidden units in the [16, 128] range, the prediction MAE was in the [0.08, 0.71] range, following an ascending trend in relation to the number of hidden units.

Figure 13 illustrates the M2O prediction mode. Here, the learning rate and number of hidden units had a smaller influence on the prediction MAE in comparison to M2M. In the same figure it can be observed that over all experiments, on average, the MAE was similar for both LSTMTF and VLSTM, with MAE values in the [0.055, 0.066] range. These results, in terms of MAE, for the M2O prediction mode, are consistent with the results for the first two experiments.

The testing error standard deviation values followed a similar trend as the testing MAE for all neural networks. For LSTMTF, in a, M2M prediction mode, the testing error standard deviation values for hidden units in the [0, 16] range were between 0.004 and 0.0045, while for hidden units between 16 and 128, the standard deviation values were between 0.0355 and 0.0358. For VLSTM, the standard deviation values were in the [0.044, 0.046] range. Finally, for LSTMTFC, the values for hidden units between 2 and 16 were in the [0.03, 0.1] range, while for 16 to 128 hidden units, the standard deviation values were between 0.1 to 0.59, increasing with the number of hidden units.

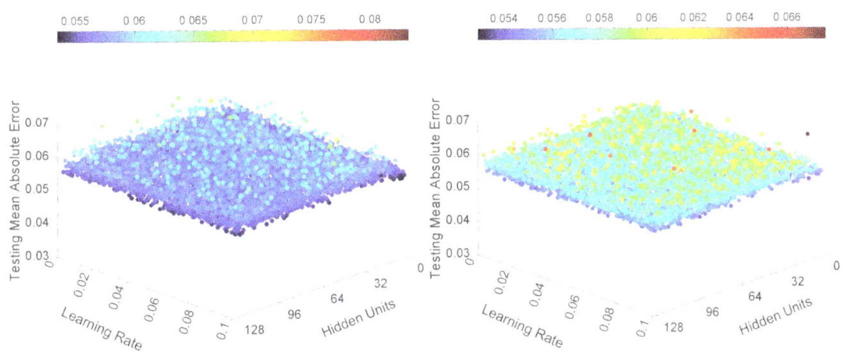

Figure 13. Illustration of the testing mean absolute error value for Experiment 3, LSTMTF (**left**) and VLSTM (**right**), using a many-to-one prediction mode.

Overall, for the third experiment, for all the tested LSTM variants, the learning rate had no significant influence on the testing MAE and on the training convergence time, as shown in Figure 12 and in Table 7. In terms of hidden units, for LSTMTF, the best results were obtained in the [16, 128] range, while for LSTMTFC the best results were obtained with hidden units in the [2, 16] range. VLSTM's performance was not significantly affected by the number of hidden units. In terms of convergence time, similar values were obtained for all LSTM variants with hidden units in the [2, 128] range, as illustrated in Table 6.

5.2. Multi-Input Multi-Output Configuration

5.2.1. Experiment 1

The evolution of the training loss values for the MIMO configuration for the first set of experiments, is illustrated in Figures 14 and 15. Here, the loss values over the 100 training epochs are similar to the MISO configuration for both LSTMTF and VLSTM.

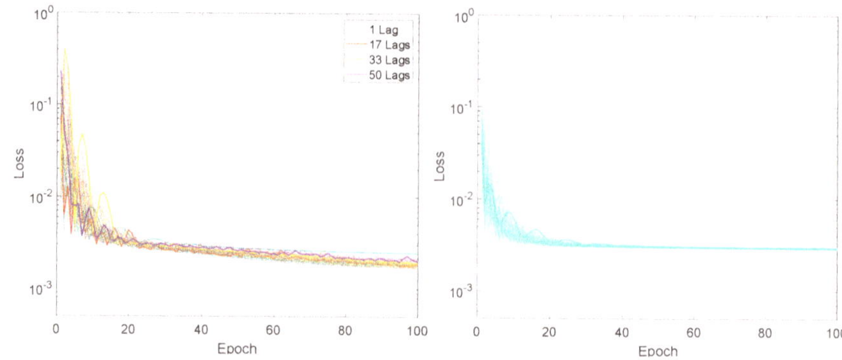

Figure 14. Illustration of the training loss for Experiment 1, LSTMTF (**left**) and VLSTM (**right**), using a many-to-many prediction mode. The highlighted thick lines represent the training loss for a mini-batch size of 2.

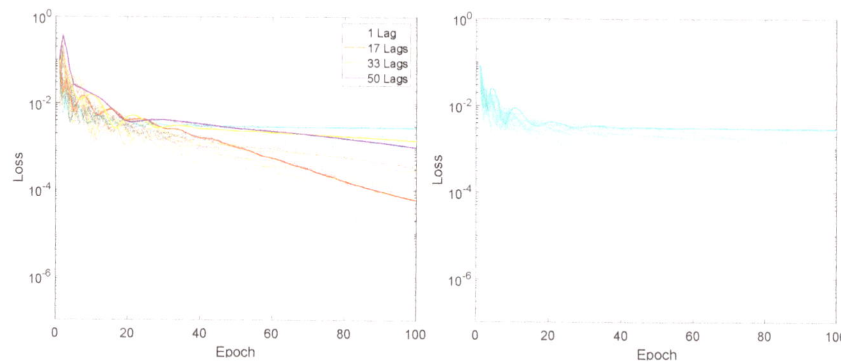

Figure 15. Illustration of the training loss for Experiment 1, LSTMTF (**left**) and VLSTM (**right**), using a many-to-one prediction mode. The highlighted thick lines represent the training loss for a mini-batch size of 2.

Figures 16 and 17 illustrate the testing prediction MAE for the MIMO configuration. Similarly to the results for the MISO configuration, here the testing MAE values of LSTMTF were in the [0.027, 0.040] range, and were smaller in comparison to the VLSTM MAE, which were in the [0,037, 0.038] range. These, however, were smaller compared to the MISO LSTMTF, where the MAE was in the [0.03, 0.06] range for all performed experiments. Another difference between MISO LSTMTF and MIMO LSTMTF is that the overall testing MAE values were larger for input sequence lengths in the range of [1, 100], as can be seen in Figure 16. The overall MAE was smaller for the MIMO configuration for all the tested models; for example, in the case of VLSTM the MAE decreased from [0.058, 0.061] to [0.038, 0.039].

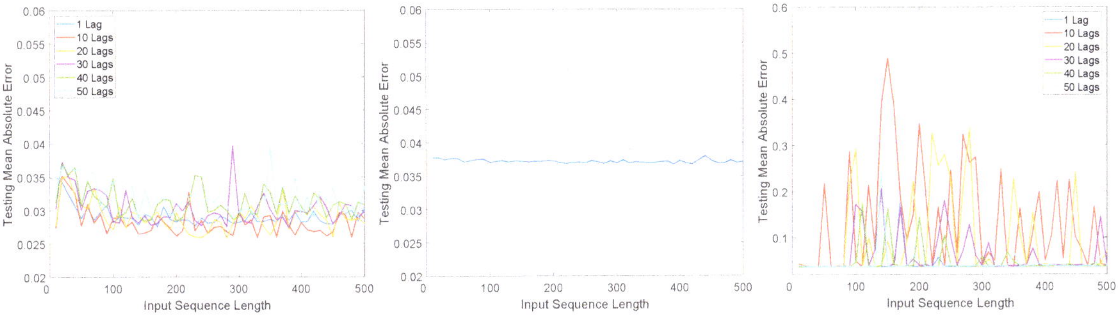

Figure 16. Illustration of the testing mean absolute error value for Experiment 1, LSTMTF (**left**), VLSTM (**middle**), and LSTMTFC (**right**), using a many-to-many prediction mode.

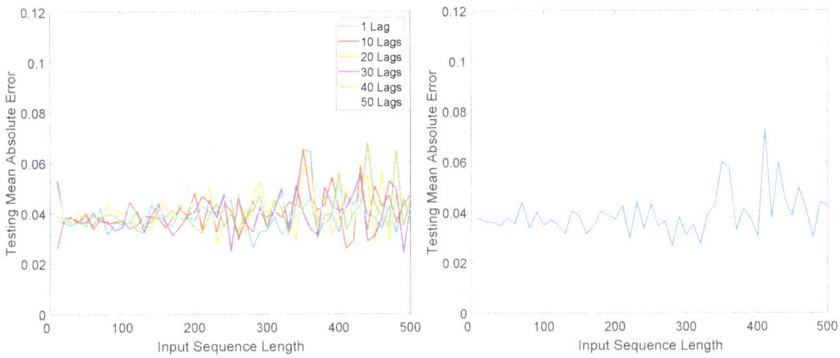

Figure 17. Illustration of the testing mean absolute error value for Experiment 1, LSTMTF (**left**) and VLSTM (**right**), using a many-to-one prediction mode.

5.2.2. Experiment 2

For the MIMO configuration, the results for the second set of experiments exhibit numerous similarities to the MISO configuration, both in the training loss values and in the prediction MAE. The training loss values are illustrated in Figures 18 and 19, while the prediction MAE is shown in Figures 20 and 21.

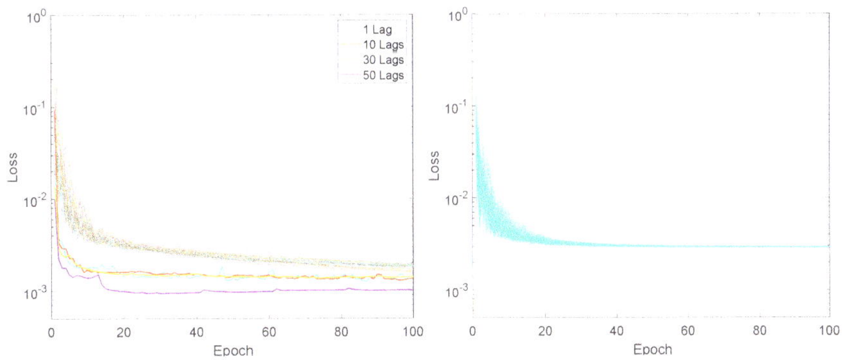

Figure 18. Illustration of the training loss for Experiment 2, LSTMTF (**left**) and VLSTM (**right**), using a many-to-many prediction mode.

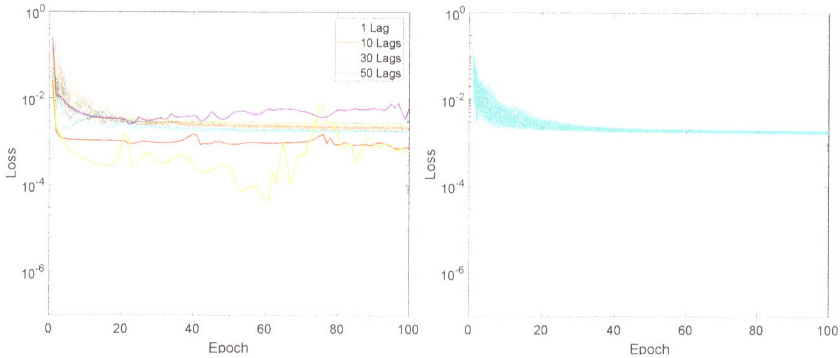

Figure 19. Illustration of the training loss for Experiment 2, LSTMTF (**left**) and VLSTM (**right**), using a many-to-one prediction mode.

Compared to the MISO configuration, here, the overall testing MAE for all three neural networks, namely, LSTMTF, LSTMTF, and VLSTM, running in both prediction modes, namely, M2M and M2O, has shown a decrease for all mini-batch sizes. This can be seen in Figures 8, 9, 20 and 21.

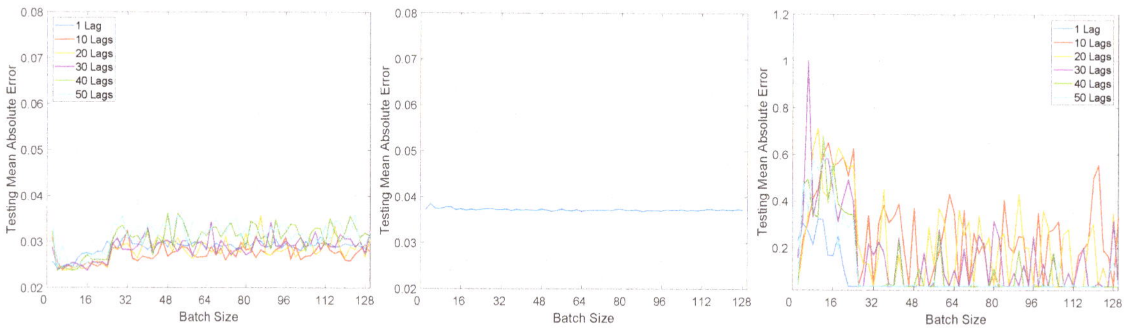

Figure 20. Illustration of the testing mean absolute error value for Experiment 2, LSTMTF (**left**), VLSTM (**middle**), and LSTMTFC (**right**), using a many-to-many prediction mode.

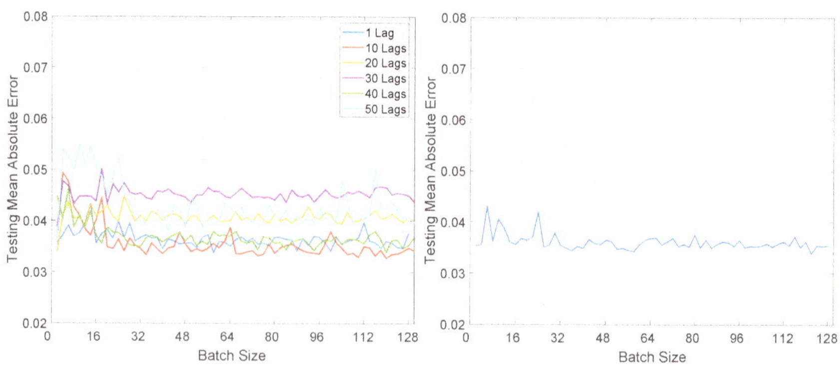

Figure 21. Illustration of the testing mean absolute error value for Experiment 2, LSTMTF (**left**) and VLSTM (**right**), using a many-to-one prediction mode.

The MAE values for M2M LSTMTF were in the [0.024, 0.036] range, for M2M VLSTM in the [0.07, 0.09] range, and for M2M LSTMTFC in the [0.05, 1] range, with smaller values for mini-batch sizes between 2 and 32. Similarly to the MISO configuration, for VLSTM in a MIMO configuration, the mini-batch size had no significant influence on the testing MAE.

5.2.3. Experiment 3

Figures 22 and 23 illustrate the mean loss values for the MIMO configuration for the third set of experiments. As shown in these two figures, the mean training loss values were smaller for LSTMTF compared to VLSTM. For LSTMTF the mean loss values were in the [0.0019, 0.026] range, while for VLSTM these values were in the [0.0019, 0.08] range. These differences are similar, in terms of value ranges, for both prediction modes.

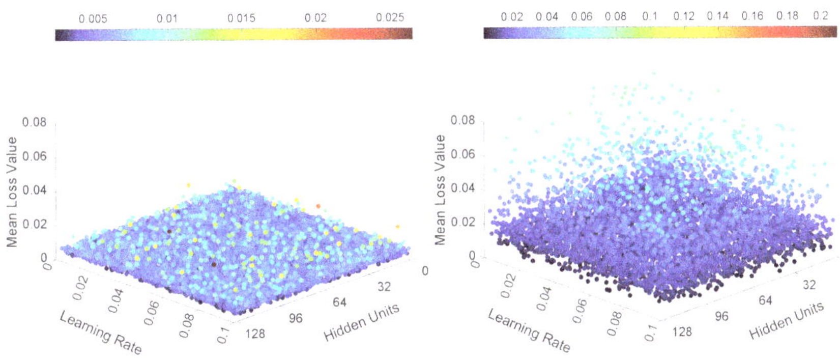

Figure 22. Illustration of the mean loss value for Experiment 3, LSTMTF (**left**) and VLSTM (**right**), using a many-to-many prediction mode.

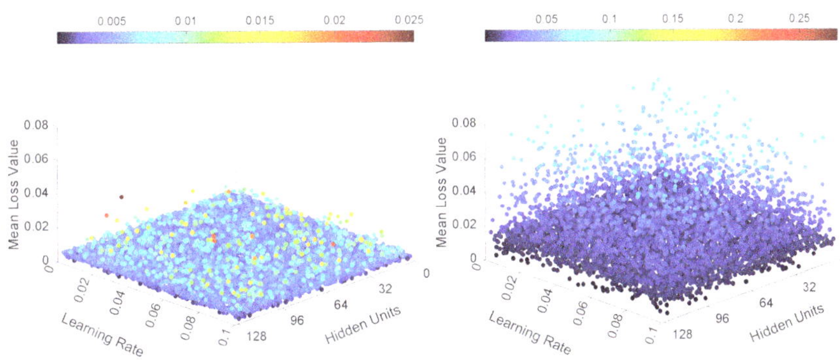

Figure 23. Illustration of the mean loss value for Experiment 3, LSTMTF (**left**) and VLSTM (**right**), using a many-to-one prediction mode.

The testing MAE is showcased in Figures 24 and 25. Similarly to the previous experiments, the behavior of the neural networks was similar to the MISO configuration, namely, the learning rate had no significant influence on the testing MAE. In the case of LSTMTF, the number of hidden units, in the [2, 16] range, yielded higher overall values for the MAE, while in the case of VLSTM the influence of the learning rate and the number of hidden units on the MAE was comparably smaller, as illustrated in the two figures.

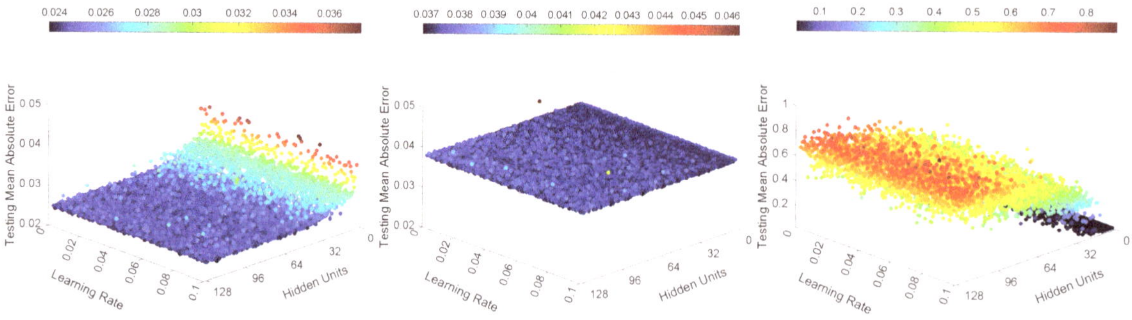

Figure 24. Illustration of the testing mean absolute error value for Experiment 3, LSTMTF (**left**), VLSTM (**middle**), and LSTMTFC (**right**), using a many-to-many prediction mode.

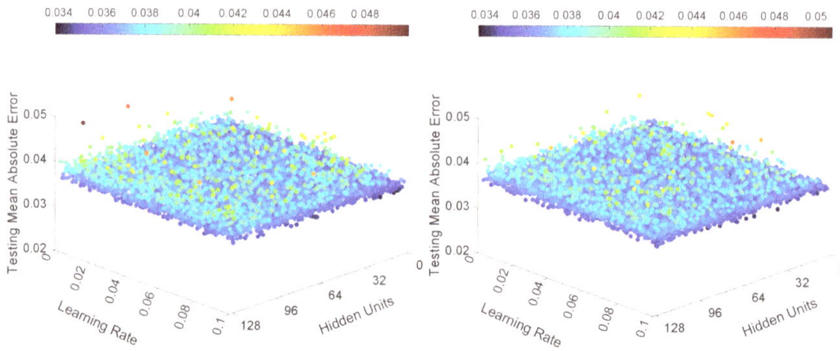

Figure 25. Illustration of the testing mean absolute error value for Experiment 3, LSTMTF (**left**) and VLSTM (**right**), using a many-to-one prediction mode.

The training and testing running times, measured in milliseconds, for the tested neural networks, on 50,000 data points, are shown in Table 8. As can be observed, the training time, when switching from the MISO to the MIMO configuration, increased on average by 21%, while the testing time increased on average by 28%.

Table 8. The actual training and testing times for 50,000 data points, measured in milliseconds, for LSTMTF and VLSTM.

	LSTMTF		VLSTM	
Time [ms]	**Many-to-Many**	**Many-to-One**	**Many-to-Many**	**Many-to-One**
MISO Training	1820	1831	1810	1870
MISO Testing	46.55	49.70	47.13	45.72
MIMO Training	2209	2294	2208	2236
MIMO Testing	57.27	63.08	60.74	61.71

5.2.4. Experiment 4

Figure 26 illustrates the results for Experiment 4. Here, the observed and the predicted values are shown for the MISO configuration using an M2M prediction mode for the three LSTM variants (i.e., LSTMTF, LSTMTFC, VLSTM) and for the two NARXNN variants (i.e., parallel and series–parallel).

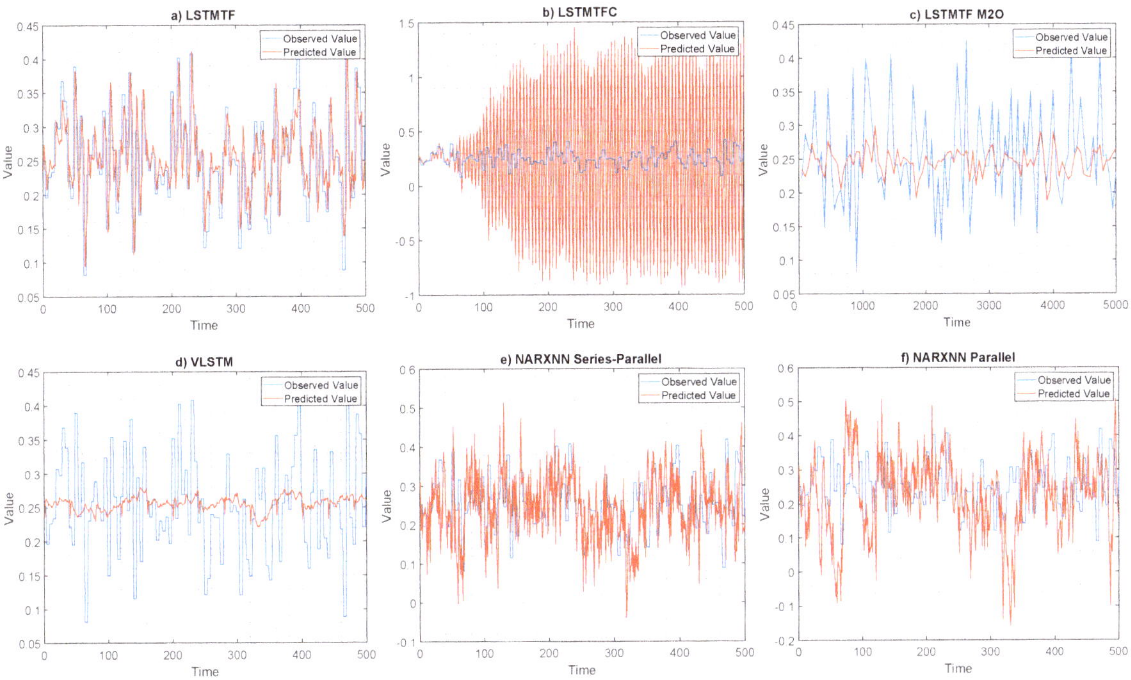

Figure 26. Illustration of the prediction performance for experiment 4. Subfigures (**a**,**b**,**d**–**f**) showcase the observed/predicted values on an entire cycle of 500 observations. Subfigure (**c**) showcases the observed/predicted values for LSTMTF using an M2O prediction mode for 5000 observations.

During training, the NARXNN models received the ground truth value of the output from the previous time-step as input for the next time-step. Similarly, during testing, the parallel architecture received the ground truth output value as input. In contrast, the series–parallel variant received the predicted value from the previous time-step as input for the next step during testing. These two operation modes are similar to LSTMTF and LSTMTFC.

As illustrated in Figure 26a, the LSTMTF's predicted values closely resemble the observed values, while for the LSTMTFC, Figure 26b, the prediction slowly deviates from the observed value, starting from the 60th time-step. These results further illustrate the exposure bias effect in the case of LSTMTFC.

In terms of MAE, for the testing dataset, the results are as follows (in increasing order) LSTMTF: 0.038, LSTMTF M2O: 0.054, VLSTM: 0.059, NARXNN Series–Parallel (1000 Epochs): 0.084, NARXNN Parallel (1000 epochs): 0.110, ARXNN Series–Parallel (100 Epochs): 0.113, NARXNN Parallel (100 epochs): 0.123, and LSTMTFC: 0.551.

5.2.5. Experiment 5

During the fifth experiment, the neural networks underwent training with a separate validation set that accounted for 20% of the original training set. The remaining 80% of observations were utilized for actual training purposes.

The results for the MISO configuration, in the case of LSTMTF using an M2M prediction mode, in regard to the sequence length, were as follows: for sequence lengths between 1 and 100 the MAE was in the [0.03, 0.045] range, increasing with the sequence length, and in the [0.04, 0.044] range for sequence lengths between 100 and 500, following a similar pattern as the results of Experiment 1. For the M2O prediction mode, the results were in the [0.052, 0.085] range, with the same pattern as the results of Experiment 1.

In the case of VLSTM, using an M2M mode, the MAE results were in the [0.058, 0.06] range, with no significant deviations in relation to the length of the input sequence. The results for the M2O prediction mode yielded MAE values in the [0.053, 0.14] range; the highest value of 0.14 was obtained for a sequence length of 470. LSTMTFC obtained similar results to those from Experiment 1, with large MAE values for sequence lengths between 1 and 100, with values up to 0.8, and values between 0.059 and 0.06 for larger sequence lengths.

While measuring the MAE for various mini-batch sizes (i.e., in the [2, 128] range), the following results were obtained: for LSTMTF using an M2M prediction mode, the MAE was in the [0.031, 0.053] range, while for the M2O mode it was in the [0.053, 0.06] range. The results followed a similar pattern to those of Experiment 2.

The VLSTM network obtained the following results: for the M2M prediction mode, the MAE was between 0.058 and 0.06, while for the M2O prediction mode, the MAE was between 0.052 and 0.058. Finally, LSTMTFC yielded MAE values between 0.04 and 0.065 for mini batch-sizes in the [2,32] range and MAE values in the [0.059, 0.25] range for mini-batch sizes above 32.

Moving on to the results for various numbers of hidden units and learning rates. LSTMTF using an M2M prediction mode obtained MAE values between 0.032 and 0.058; these values decreased inversely proportionally to the number of hidden units. Conversely, the same LSTMTF in an M2O prediction mode obtained MAE values in the [0.053, 0.063] range. Similarly to Experiment 3, there were no significant changes in the MAE with regard to the learning rate values.

In the same experiment, VLSTM using an M2M prediction mode obtained MAE values between 0.058 and 0.059 and MAE values between 0.053 and 0.063 when using an M2O prediction mode. The MAE values did not show significant fluctuations as the number of hidden units or learning rate values increased. Similarly to Experiment 3, LSTMTFC obtained better results for fewer hidden units, with an average of 0.06 MAE for 2 hidden units, over all learning rates. The MAE values increased with the number of hidden units, with the highest value of 1.69 obtained with 114 hidden units.

Regarding the input sequence length, the outcomes for the MIMO configuration were the following. LSTMTF in an M2M prediction mode produced MAE values between 0.024 and 0.028 while the M2O prediction mode yielded values between 0.03 and 0.06. The values for the M2M prediction mode were smaller in comparison to the ones from Experiment 1 while the values for the M2O prediction mode were larger.

VLSTM in a MIMO configuration yielded MAE values between 0.037 and 0.038 over all sequence lengths when used in an M2M prediction mode, and MAE values between 0.03 and 0.06 when used in an M2O prediction mode. The results for LSTMTFC yielded MAE values between 0.2 and 0.8. The largest MAE values between 0.47 and 0.8 were obtained for sequence lengths between 1 and 100.

When testing the performance, for various mini-batch sizes, using the MIMO configuration, the following results were obtained. LSTMTF in an M2M prediction mode yielded MAE values in the [0.023, 0.024] range for mini-batch sizes between 2 and 32 and between 0.024 and 0.032 for mini-batch sizes between 32 and 128. Here, the MAE displayed an upward trend with the increase in the mini-batch size. In the M2O prediction mode, the results for LSTMTF, in terms of MAE, were between 0.035 and 0.044.

The VLSTM using an M2M prediction mode yielded MAE values between 0.037 and 0.039 and, using an M2O prediction mode, MAE values between 0.035 and 0.038. LSTMTFC's prediction MAE results were in the [0.034, 0.77] range, with higher MAE values between 0.15 and 0.77 for mini-batch sizes between 2 and 64.

In the MIMO configuration, with regard to the number of hidden units and learning rate, the models obtained the following results. LSTMTF using an M2M prediction mode yielded MAE values in the [0.024, 0.036] range and, using an M2O prediction, the MAE values were in the [0.034, 0.041] range. The MAE in regard to the number of hidden units and learning rate values was similar to the results from MIMO Experiment 3. Here, with hidden units in the [2,16] range, the computed MAE was between 0.028 and 0.036. The MAE gradually decreased while increasing the number of hidden units.

In the case of M2M VLSTM, the range of the MAE was smaller with values between 0.037 and 0.038 with no visible effect from the number of hidden units or learning rate values. For VLSTM with an M2O approach, the MAE values were in the [0.034, 0.042] range for this experiment. Finally, LSTMTFC yielded MAE values between 0.04 and 0.25 for hidden units in the [2,16] range. In the [32,128] hidden unit range, the MAE for LSTMTFC was between 0.27 and 0.71, increasing with the number of hidden units. Similarly to the previous experiments, the change in the learning rate values had no visible impact on the prediction MAE.

6. Discussion, Conclusions, and Future Work

This paper offered an in-depth analysis of LSTM neural networks trained with and without teacher forcing. Teacher forcing was applied in two variants, with the actual (observed) value fed back as input during both training and testing, as proposed for anomaly-detection tasks (e.g., LSTMTF), and as originally proposed, with the predicted values fed back during testing (e.g., LSTMTFC). Additionally, the paper also introduced training and testing time measurements for the tested architectures.

The datasets used for the experimental assessment are publicly available, and originate from the well-known Tennessee Eastman chemical process simulation. The training and testing procedures were performed using a wide range of both internal and external hyperparameters, while the results were analyzed using various performance metrics. All the neural network architectures were tested in multiple configurations, namely, multi-input single-output and multi-input multi-output using two prediction modes: many-to-many and many-to-one. For reproducibility, all the tested neural network configurations, hyperparameters, and datasets were documented throughout this paper.

In both configurations, MISO and MIMO, the VLSTM (i.e., the standard LSTM without teacher forcing) obtained better results in terms of training convergence time for the M2M prediction method; however, in terms of prediction MAE, LSTMTF obtained better results. Out of the three neural networks, LSTMTFC obtained the worst results in terms of testing MAE using the M2M approach.

As pointed out by other researchers, feeding the observed value during training and the predicted value during testing may lead to unexpected and unreliable results reflected in the prediction values due to exposure bias. This behavior was observed and presented in the final experiment. The large differences between LSTMTF and LSTMTFC make the former a suitable candidate for anomaly-detection tasks, as proposed in [40], where any intervention in the process yields significant differences in the prediction error as the measured output is fed back, compared to LSTMTFC, where the prediction is fed back as additional input. Moreover, the ranges that yielded the best results, for all LSTM variants, were identified in the results section. In the case of M2O, the differences between the LSTMTF and VLSTM were not very significant in any of the performed experiments. While in this scenario, on this specific dataset, the overall results were better when using an M2M prediction mode, M2O modes might yield better results on other datasets and in different scenarios.

In every experimental scenario, there was a small decrease in the prediction error when switching from the MISO to the MIMO configuration on the same neural network type. However, the time taken for training and testing increased by 21% for training and 28% for testing when using the MIMO configuration. Overall, the input sequence length, mini-batch size, number of hidden units, and number of lags influenced the training and testing performance. Conversely, the learning rate's influence appeared to be smaller in all the experiments for all neural network architectures.

Experiment 5 yielded an intriguing outcome when utilizing the early stopping technique to train neural networks. The findings indicated that employing this approach did not result in any significant improvement in the MAE values across various scenarios or configurations. Nevertheless, despite the lack of a significant reduction in the prediction MAE, the comparable results to previous experiments suggest that neural networks can be trained with fewer data points and still perform similarly well for this dataset. It is important to note that in Experiment 5, only 80% of the original training set was used for training, with the remaining 20% serving as the validation set. Overall, for this set of experiments, LSTMTF generally outperformed the other models that were tested.

Among the performance metrics used in this paper, we included the MAE and the testing error standard deviation. These metrics can be useful, for example, in detection approaches such as the one in [40]. One potential alternative to using MAE as an evaluation metric is to consider the mean squared error (MSE) instead. Unlike MAE, which treats all errors equally, MSE gives greater weight to larger errors. This can be useful in situations where it is important to capture the magnitude of the error in the model's predictions.

As illustrated by the experimental results, the architecture of LSTMs can be significantly reduced, while still maintaining prediction performance. This was observed while using fewer features for the MISO architecture, while still obtaining similar results to the MIMO architecture. Moreover, by using TF, it was shown that the models can be trained with a reduced number of samples while using only one hidden layer and still outperform other models. The reduced architecture (i.e., number of inputs, one hidden layer, and number of hidden units) and the possibility of training models with fewer samples make such models suitable candidates for real-time operations and on resource-constrained devices.

As future work, we intend to further extend this research to include various other datasets originating from other industrial processes. One important possible future direction includes an in-depth analysis of the effects of missing measurements and variable sampling rates when dealing with time series data.

While this work presented an in-depth performance analysis of LSTMs, we intend to extend this work to include other models and on other prediction modes as well. An interesting architecture worth including in future work is the Encode-Decoder model, which operates differently from the models analyzed in this paper. Additionally, the results from this study, and from future extensions, can aid in developing new anomaly-detection, fault-detection, process control, and predictive maintenance techniques. Such methods could also be applied in other fields as well, for example, in healthcare monitoring and prediction.

Author Contributions: Conceptualization, R.B. and P.H.; methodology, R.B.; software, R.B.; validation, R.B. and P.H.; formal analysis, R.B.; investigation, R.B.; resources, R.B.; data curation, R.B. and P.H.; writing—original draft preparation, R.B.; writing—review and editing, R.B. and P.H.; visualization, R.B.; supervision, P.H.; project administration, R.B.; funding acquisition, R.B. All authors have read and agreed to the published version of the manuscript.

Funding: The article processing charge (APC) was funded by the Institution Organizing University Doctoral Studies (I.O.S.U.D.), the Doctoral School of Letters, Humanities and Applied Sciences, George Emil Palade University of Medicine, Pharmacy, Science, and Technology of Târgu Mureş, 540139 Târgu Mureş, Romania.

Data Availability Statement: The datasets used in this article are publicly available for download at: https://dataverse.harvard.edu/dataset.xhtml?persistentId=doi:10.7910/DVN/6C3JR1 (accessed on 1 February 2023). Furthermore, the paper containing the description of the datasets is available at [43].

Conflicts of Interest: The authors declare no conflict of interest.

Abbreviations

The following abbreviations are used in this manuscript:

HU	Number of Hidden Units
ISL	Input Sequence Length
JNN	Jordan Neural Network
LSTM	Long Short-term Memory Neural Network
LSTMTF	Long Short-term Memory Neural Network with Teacher Forcing as proposed in [40]
LSTMTFC	Long Short-term Memory Neural Network with the original Teacher Forcing algorithm
M2O	Many-to-One Prediction Mode
M2M	Many-to-Many Prediction Mode
MAE	Mean Absolute Error
MBS	Mini-Batch Size
MIMO	Multi Input Multi Output Configuration
MISO	Multi Input Single Output Configuration
MSE	Mean Squared Error
NARXNN	Nonlinear Auto-Regressive Neural Networks with eXogenous (external) inputs
RNN	Recurrent Neural Network
SMAPE	Symmetric Mean Absolute Percentage Error
SOH	State of Health
TEP	Tennessee Eastman Process
TF	Teacher Forcing
VLSTM	Vanilla Long Short-term Memory Neural Network

References

1. Shailaja, K.; Seetharamulu, B.; Jabbar, M. Machine learning in healthcare: A review. In Proceedings of the IEEE 2018 Second International Conference on Electronics, Communication and Aerospace Technology (ICECA), Coimbatore, India, 29–31 March 2018; pp. 910–914.
2. Dixon, M.F.; Halperin, I.; Bilokon, P. *Machine Learning in Finance*; Springer: Berlin/Heidelberg, Germany, 2020; Volume 1406.
3. Rai, R.; Tiwari, M.K.; Ivanov, D.; Dolgui, A. Machine learning in manufacturing and industry 4.0 applications. *Int. J. Prod. Res.* **2021**, *59*, 4773–4778. [CrossRef]
4. Liakos, K.G.; Busato, P.; Moshou, D.; Pearson, S.; Bochtis, D. Machine learning in agriculture: A review. *Sensors* **2018**, *18*, 2674. [CrossRef] [PubMed]
5. Călburean, P.A.; Grebenișan, P.; Nistor, I.A.; Pal, K.; Vacariu, V.; Drincal, R.K.; Țepes, O.; Bârlea, I.; Șuș, I.; Somkereki, C.; et al. Prediction of 3-year all-cause and cardiovascular cause mortality in a prospective percutaneous coronary intervention registry: Machine learning model outperforms conventional clinical risk scores. *Atherosclerosis* **2022**, *350*, 33–40. [CrossRef] [PubMed]
6. Carvalho, T.P.; Soares, F.A.; Vita, R.; Francisco, R.d.P.; Basto, J.P.; Alcalá, S.G. A systematic literature review of machine learning methods applied to predictive maintenance. *Comput. Ind. Eng.* **2019**, *137*, 106024. [CrossRef]
7. Avram, S.M.; Oltean, M. A Comparison of Several AI Techniques for Authorship Attribution on Romanian Texts. *Mathematics* **2022**, *10*, 4589. [CrossRef]
8. Darabant, A.S.; Borza, D.; Danescu, R. Recognizing human races through machine learning—A multi-network, multi-features study. *Mathematics* **2021**, *9*, 195. [CrossRef]
9. Nassif, A.B.; Talib, M.A.; Nasir, Q.; Dakalbab, F.M. Machine learning for anomaly detection: A systematic review. *IEEE Access* **2021**, *9*, 78658–78700. [CrossRef]
10. McCulloch, W.S.; Pitts, W. A logical calculus of the ideas immanent in nervous activity. *Bull. Math. Biophys.* **1943**, *5*, 115–133. [CrossRef]
11. Elmsili, B.; Outtaj, B. Artificial neural networks applications in economics and management research: An exploratory literature review. In Proceedings of the IEEE 2018 4th International Conference on Optimization and Applications (ICOA), Mohammedia, Morocco, 26–27 April 2018; pp. 1–6.
12. Haglin, J.M.; Jimenez, G.; Eltorai, A.E. Artificial neural networks in medicine. *Health Technol.* **2019**, *9*, 1–6. [CrossRef]
13. Ullah, A.; Malik, K.M.; Saudagar, A.K.J.; Khan, M.B.; Hasanat, M.H.A.; AlTameem, A.; AlKhathami, M.; Sajjad, M. COVID-19 Genome Sequence Analysis for New Variant Prediction and Generation. *Mathematics* **2022**, *10*, 4267. [CrossRef]
14. Abdel-Basset, M.; Hawash, H.; Alnowibet, K.A.; Mohamed, A.W.; Sallam, K.M. Interpretable Deep Learning for Discriminating Pneumonia from Lung Ultrasounds. *Mathematics* **2022**, *10*, 4153. [CrossRef]
15. Rodrigues, J.A.; Farinha, J.T.; Mendes, M.; Mateus, R.J.; Cardoso, A.J.M. Comparison of Different Features and Neural Networks for Predicting Industrial Paper Press Condition. *Energies* **2022**, *15*, 6308. [CrossRef]
16. Hochreiter, S.; Schmidhuber, J. Long short-term memory. *Neural Comput.* **1997**, *9*, 1735–1780. [CrossRef] [PubMed]

17. Gers, F.A.; Eck, D.; Schmidhuber, J. Applying LSTM to time series predictable through time-window approaches. In *Neural Nets WIRN Vietri-01*; Springer: Berlin/Heidelberg, Germany, 2002; pp. 193–200.
18. Siami-Namini, S.; Tavakoli, N.; Namin, A.S. A comparison of ARIMA and LSTM in forecasting time series. In Proceedings of the 2018 17th IEEE International Conference on Machine Learning and Applications (ICMLA), Orlando, FL, USA, 17–20 December 2018; pp. 1394–1401.
19. Karim, F.; Majumdar, S.; Darabi, H.; Chen, S. LSTM fully convolutional networks for time series classification. *IEEE Access* **2017**, *6*, 1662–1669. [CrossRef]
20. Sagheer, A.; Kotb, M. Time series forecasting of petroleum production using deep LSTM recurrent networks. *Neurocomputing* **2019**, *323*, 203–213. [CrossRef]
21. Zhou, C.; Sun, C.; Liu, Z.; Lau, F. A C-LSTM neural network for text classification. *arXiv* **2015**, arXiv:1511.08630.
22. Graves, A.; Fernández, S.; Schmidhuber, J. Bidirectional LSTM networks for improved phoneme classification and recognition. In *Proceedings of the International Conference on Artificial Neural Networks*; Springer: Berlin/Heidelberg, Germany, 2005; pp. 799–804.
23. Tan, H.X.; Aung, N.N.; Tian, J.; Chua, M.C.H.; Yang, Y.O. Time series classification using a modified LSTM approach from accelerometer-based data: A comparative study for gait cycle detection. *Gait Posture* **2019**, *74*, 128–134. [CrossRef]
24. Wang, P.; Jiang, A.; Liu, X.; Shang, J.; Zhang, L. LSTM-based EEG classification in motor imagery tasks. *IEEE Trans. Neural Syst. Rehabil. Eng.* **2018**, *26*, 2086–2095. [CrossRef]
25. Wang, X.; Huang, T.; Zhu, K.; Zhao, X. LSTM-Based Broad Learning System for Remaining Useful Life Prediction. *Mathematics* **2022**, *10*, 2066. [CrossRef]
26. Ma, Y.; Peng, H.; Khan, T.; Cambria, E.; Hussain, A. Sentic LSTM: A hybrid network for targeted aspect-based sentiment analysis. *Cogn. Comput.* **2018**, *10*, 639–650. [CrossRef]
27. Minaee, S.; Azimi, E.; Abdolrashidi, A. Deep-sentiment: Sentiment analysis using ensemble of cnn and bi-lstm models. *arXiv* **2019**, arXiv:1904.04206.
28. Bengio, Y. Practical recommendations for gradient-based training of deep architectures. In *Neural Networks: Tricks of the Trade*; Springer: Berlin/Heidelberg, Germany, 2012; pp. 437–478.
29. Feurer, M.; Hutter, F. Hyperparameter optimization. In *Automated Machine Learning*; Springer: Cham, Switzerland, 2019; pp. 3–33.
30. Breuel, T.M. Benchmarking of LSTM networks. *arXiv* **2015**, arXiv:1508.02774.
31. Greff, K.; Srivastava, R.K.; Koutník, J.; Steunebrink, B.R.; Schmidhuber, J. LSTM: A search space odyssey. *IEEE Trans. Neural Netw. Learn. Syst.* **2016**, *28*, 2222–2232. [CrossRef] [PubMed]
32. Siami-Namini, S.; Tavakoli, N.; Namin, A.S. The performance of LSTM and BiLSTM in forecasting time series. In Proceedings of the 2019 IEEE International Conference on Big Data (Big Data), Los Angeles, CA, USA, 9–12 December 2019; pp. 3285–3292.
33. Farzad, A.; Mashayekhi, H.; Hassanpour, H. A comparative performance analysis of different activation functions in LSTM networks for classification. *Neural Comput. Appl.* **2019**, *31*, 2507–2521. [CrossRef]
34. Khodabakhsh, A.; Ari, I.; Bakır, M.; Alagoz, S.M. Forecasting multivariate time-series data using LSTM and mini-batches. In *Proceedings of the 7th International Conference on Contemporary Issues in Data Science*; Springer: Berlin/Heidelberg, Germany, 2020; pp. 121–129.
35. Menezes, J.M.P., Jr.; Barreto, G.A. Long-term time series prediction with the NARX network: An empirical evaluation. *Neurocomputing* **2008**, *71*, 3335–3343. [CrossRef]
36. Principe, J.C.; Euliano, N.R.; Lefebvre, W.C. *Neural and Adaptive Systems: Fundamentals through Simulations with CD-ROM*; John Wiley & Sons, Inc.: Hoboken, NJ, USA, 1999.
37. Kumar, D.A.; Murugan, S. Performance analysis of NARX neural network backpropagation algorithm by various training functions for time series data. *Int. J. Data Sci.* **2018**, *3*, 308–325. [CrossRef]
38. Smith, S.L.; Kindermans, P.J.; Ying, C.; Le, Q.V. Don't decay the learning rate, increase the batch size. *arXiv* **2017**, arXiv:1711.00489.
39. Morishita, M.; Oda, Y.; Neubig, G.; Yoshino, K.; Sudoh, K.; Nakamura, S. An empirical study of mini-batch creation strategies for neural machine translation. *arXiv* **2017**, arXiv:1706.05765.
40. Bolboacă, R. Adaptive Ensemble Methods for Tampering Detection in Automotive Aftertreatment Systems. *IEEE Access* **2022**, *10*, 105497–105517. [CrossRef]
41. Williams, R.J.; Zipser, D. A learning algorithm for continually running fully recurrent neural networks. *Neural Comput.* **1989**, *1*, 270–280. [CrossRef]
42. Downs, J.J.; Vogel, E.F. A plant-wide industrial process control problem. *Comput. Chem. Eng.* **1993**, *17*, 245–255. [CrossRef]
43. Rieth, C.A.; Amsel, B.D.; Tran, R.; Cook, M.B. Additional Tennessee Eastman Process Simulation Data for Anomaly Detection Evaluation. *Harv. Dataverse* **2017**, *1*, 2017. [CrossRef]
44. Goodfellow, I.; Bengio, Y.; Courville, A. *Deep Learning*; MIT Press: Cambridge, MA, USA, 2016.
45. Schmidt, F. Generalization in generation: A closer look at exposure bias. *arXiv* **2019**, arXiv:1910.00292.
46. Jordan, M. Generic constraints on underspecified target trajectories. In *International Joint Conference on Neural Networks*; IEEE Press: New York, NY, USA, 1989; Volume 1, pp. 217–225. [CrossRef]
47. Lin, T.; Horne, B.G.; Tino, P.; Giles, C.L. Learning long-term dependencies in NARX recurrent neural networks. *IEEE Trans. Neural Netw.* **1996**, *7*, 1329–1338.
48. Medsker, L.; Jain, L.C. *Recurrent Neural Networks: Design and Applications*; CRC Press: Boca Raton, FL, USA, 1999.

49. Yu, Y.; Si, X.; Hu, C.; Zhang, J. A Review of Recurrent Neural Networks: LSTM Cells and Network Architectures. *Neural Comput.* **2019**, *31*, 1235–1270. [CrossRef] [PubMed]
50. Elman, J.L. Finding structure in time. *Cogn. Sci.* **1990**, *14*, 179–211. [CrossRef]
51. Taigman, Y.; Wolf, L.; Polyak, A.; Nachmani, E. Voiceloop: Voice fitting and synthesis via a phonological loop. *arXiv* **2017**, arXiv:1707.06588.
52. Drossos, K.; Gharib, S.; Magron, P.; Virtanen, T. Language modelling for sound event detection with teacher forcing and scheduled sampling. *arXiv* **2019**, arXiv:1907.08506.
53. Bengio, S.; Vinyals, O.; Jaitly, N.; Shazeer, N. Scheduled sampling for sequence prediction with recurrent neural networks. *Adv. Neural Inf. Process. Syst.* **2015**, *28*.
54. Loganathan, G.; Samarabandu, J.; Wang, X. Sequence to sequence pattern learning algorithm for real-time anomaly detection in network traffic. In Proceedings of the 2018 IEEE Canadian Conference on Electrical & Computer Engineering (CCECE), Quebec, QC, Canada, 13–16 May 2018; pp. 1–4.
55. Massaoudi, M.; Chihi, I.; Sidhom, L.; Trabelsi, M.; Refaat, S.S.; Abu-Rub, H.; Oueslati, F.S. An effective hybrid NARX-LSTM model for point and interval PV power forecasting. *IEEE Access* **2021**, *9*, 36571–36588. [CrossRef]
56. Werbos, P.J. Backpropagation through time: What it does and how to do it. *Proc. IEEE* **1990**, *78*, 1550–1560. [CrossRef]
57. Staudemeyer, R.C.; Morris, E.R. Understanding LSTM—A tutorial into long short-term memory recurrent neural networks. *arXivt* **2019**, arXiv:1909.09586.
58. Sherstinsky, A. Fundamentals of recurrent neural network (RNN) and long short-term memory (LSTM) network. *Phys. D Nonlinear Phenom.* **2020**, *404*, 132306. [CrossRef]
59. Toomarian, N.; Bahren, J. Fast Temporal Neural Learning Using Teacher Forcing. U.S. Patent No. 5,428,710, 27 June 1995.
60. Schrauwen, B.; Verstraeten, D.; Van Campenhout, J. An overview of reservoir computing: Theory, applications and implementations. In Proceedings of the 15th European Symposium on Artificial Neural Networks, Bruges, Belgium, 25–27 April 2007; pp. 471–482.
61. Qi, K.; Gong, Y.; Liu, X.; Liu, X.; Zheng, H.; Wang, S. Multi-task MR Imaging with Iterative Teacher Forcing and Re-weighted Deep Learning. *arXiv* **2020**, arXiv:2011.13614.
62. Goodman, S.; Ding, N.; Soricut, R. Teaforn: Teacher-forcing with n-grams. *arXiv* **2020**, arXiv:2010.03494.
63. Hao, Y.; Liu, Y.; Mou, L. Teacher Forcing Recovers Reward Functions for Text Generation. *arXiv* **2022**, arXiv:2210.08708.
64. Feng, Y.; Gu, S.; Guo, D.; Yang, Z.; Shao, C. Guiding teacher forcing with seer forcing for neural machine translation. *arXiv* **2021**, arXiv:2106.06751.
65. Toomarian, N.B.; Barhen, J. Learning a trajectory using adjoint functions and teacher forcing. *Neural Netw.* **1992**, *5*, 473–484. [CrossRef]
66. Lamb, A.M.; Alias Parth Goyal, A.G.; Zhang, Y.; Zhang, S.; Courville, A.C.; Bengio, Y. Professor forcing: A new algorithm for training recurrent networks. *Adv. Neural Inf. Process. Syst.* **2016**, *29*.
67. Salinas, D.; Flunkert, V.; Gasthaus, J.; Januschowski, T. DeepAR: Probabilistic forecasting with autoregressive recurrent networks. *Int. J. Forecast.* **2020**, *36*, 1181–1191. [CrossRef]
68. Delcroix, B.; Ny, J.L.; Bernier, M.; Azam, M.; Qu, B.; Venne, J.S. Autoregressive neural networks with exogenous variables for indoor temperature prediction in buildings. *Build. Simul.* **2021**, *14*, 165–178. [CrossRef]
69. Ruiz, L.G.B.; Cuéllar, M.P.; Calvo-Flores, M.D.; Jiménez, M.D.C.P. An Application of Non-Linear Autoregressive Neural Networks to Predict Energy Consumption in Public Buildings. *Energies* **2016**, *9*, 684. [CrossRef]
70. Boussaada, Z.; Curea, O.; Remaci, A.; Camblong, H.; Mrabet Bellaaj, N. A Nonlinear Autoregressive Exogenous (NARX) Neural Network Model for the Prediction of the Daily Direct Solar Radiation. *Energies* **2018**, *11*, 620. [CrossRef]
71. Bennett, C.; Stewart, R.A.; Lu, J. Autoregressive with Exogenous Variables and Neural Network Short-Term Load Forecast Models for Residential Low Voltage Distribution Networks. *Energies* **2014**, *7*, 2938–2960. [CrossRef]
72. Alsumaiei, A.A.; Alrashidi, M.S. Hydrometeorological Drought Forecasting in Hyper-Arid Climates Using Nonlinear Autoregressive Neural Networks. *Water* **2020**, *12*, 2611. [CrossRef]
73. Pereira, F.H.; Bezerra, F.E.; Junior, S.; Santos, J.; Chabu, I.; Souza, G.F.M.d.; Micerino, F.; Nabeta, S.I. Nonlinear Autoregressive Neural Network Models for Prediction of Transformer Oil-Dissolved Gas Concentrations. *Energies* **2018**, *11*, 1691. [CrossRef]
74. Buitrago, J.; Asfour, S. Short-Term Forecasting of Electric Loads Using Nonlinear Autoregressive Artificial Neural Networks with Exogenous Vector Inputs. *Energies* **2017**, *10*, 40. [CrossRef]
75. Ren, Z.; Du, C.; Ren, W. State of Health Estimation of Lithium-Ion Batteries Using a Multi-Feature-Extraction Strategy and PSO-NARXNN. *Batteries* **2023**, *9*, 7. [CrossRef]
76. Prasetyowati, A.; Sudibyo, H.; Sudiana, D. Wind Power Prediction by Using Wavelet Decomposition Mode Based NARX-Neural Network. In Proceedings of the 2017 International Conference on Computer Science and Artificial Intelligence, CSAI 2017, Jakarta, Indonesia, 5–7 December 2017; Association for Computing Machinery: New York, NY, USA, 2017; pp. 275–278. [CrossRef]
77. Masters, D.; Luschi, C. Revisiting small batch training for deep neural networks. *arXiv* **2018**, arXiv:1804.07612.
78. Hanin, B. Which Neural Net Architectures Give Rise to Exploding and Vanishing Gradients? In *Proceedings of the Advances in Neural Information Processing Systems*; Bengio, S., Wallach, H., Larochelle, H., Grauman, K., Cesa-Bianchi, N., Garnett, R., Eds.; Curran Associates, Inc.: New York, NY, USA, 2018; Volume 31.

79. Kingma, D.P.; Ba, J. Adam: A method for stochastic optimization. *arXiv* **2014**, arXiv:1412.6980.
80. Halpern-Wight, N.; Konstantinou, M.; Charalambides, A.G.; Reinders, A. Training and testing of a single-layer LSTM network for near-future solar forecasting. *Appl. Sci.* **2020**, *10*, 5873. [CrossRef]

mathematics

MDPI

Article

MelodyDiffusion: Chord-Conditioned Melody Generation Using a Transformer-Based Diffusion Model

Shuyu Li [1] and Yunsick Sung [2,*]

[1] Department of Multimedia Engineering, Graduate School, Dongguk University-Seoul, Seoul 04620, Republic of Korea
[2] Division of AI Software Convergence, Dongguk University-Seoul, Seoul 04620, Republic of Korea
* Correspondence: sung@dongguk.edu; Tel.: +82-2-2260-3338

Abstract: Artificial intelligence, particularly machine learning, has begun to permeate various real-world applications and is continually being explored in automatic music generation. The approaches to music generation can be broadly divided into two categories: rule-based and data-driven methods. Rule-based approaches rely on substantial prior knowledge and may struggle to handle large datasets, whereas data-driven approaches can solve these problems and have become increasingly popular. However, data-driven approaches still face challenges such as the difficulty of considering long-distance dependencies when handling discrete-sequence data and convergence during model training. Although the diffusion model has been introduced as a generative model to solve the convergence problem in generative adversarial networks, it has not yet been applied to discrete-sequence data. This paper proposes a transformer-based diffusion model known as MelodyDiffusion to handle discrete musical data and realize chord-conditioned melody generation. MelodyDiffusion replaces the U-nets used in traditional diffusion models with transformers to consider the long-distance dependencies using attention and parallel mechanisms. Moreover, a transformer-based encoder is designed to extract contextual information from chords as a condition to guide melody generation. MelodyDiffusion can automatically generate diverse melodies based on the provided chords in practical applications. The evaluation experiments, in which Hits@k was used as a metric to evaluate the restored melodies, demonstrate that the large-scale version of MelodyDiffusion achieves an accuracy of 72.41% (k = 1).

Keywords: melody generation; conditional generation; diffusion model; transformer

MSC: 68T99

Citation: Li, S.; Sung, Y. MelodyDiffusion: Chord-Conditioned Melody Generation Using a Transformer-Based Diffusion Model. *Mathematics* **2023**, *11*, 1915. https://doi.org/10.3390/math11081915

Academic Editors: Adrian Sergiu Darabant and Diana-Laura Borza

Received: 8 February 2023
Revised: 3 April 2023
Accepted: 17 April 2023
Published: 18 April 2023

1. Introduction

In recent years, significant advancements have been achieved in the automatic music generation field due to the development of machine learning, with numerous algorithms and techniques having been developed to produce high-quality original music [1,2]. Music generation methods can be broadly classified into rule-based and data-driven approaches.

Initially, owing to a lack of computational recourse and massive data support, rule-based approaches relying on predefined rules and constraints were used to generate music in various styles, such as classical, jazz, and pop music. These approaches often use musical knowledge representation systems to encode musical concepts and rules, such as tonality, rhythm, and harmony [3–6]. However, analyzing and encoding music theory into artificial features using rule-based approaches is difficult. Furthermore, even if rules are defined, it is challenging to apply them to other genres, styles, and instruments.

Data-driven approaches can utilize large amounts of data more efficiently than rule-based methods owing to the large increase in data volume. Data-driven approaches employ deep learning techniques to analyze and generate music based on datasets. Generative adversarial networks (GANs) have significantly advanced the music generation field. For example, continuous recurrent neural networks with adversarial training (C-RNN-GAN) [7], which are composed of long short-term memory (LSTM)-based generators and bidirectional LSTM-based discriminators, generates classical music by learning from a training dataset. SeqGAN [8] is another GAN-based model that uses reinforcement learning (RL) for sequential generation. It can be trained using data that consist of sequences of discrete tokens. SeqGAN models a generator using a stochastic policy in RL to bypass the generator differentiation problem and perform gradient policy updates directly. SeqGAN is specifically designed for sequence generation and can be trained on various data types. The goal of OR-GAN [9] is to improve the quality of the samples generated by SeqGAN. OR-GAN combines adversarial training with expert-based rewards and RL to generate samples that maintain information learned from data. In this manner, the sample diversity is retained, and the desired metrics are improved. The effectiveness of these approaches has been demonstrated in the generation of molecules encoded as text sequences and musical melodies. However, long-distance sequential data cannot be handled via these approaches owing to the backpropagation process through the time of the LSTM.

In addition to the combination of RNNs and GANs, MidiNet [10] generates music in the symbolic domain using a convolutional neural network (CNN)-based GAN model, allowing it to generate realistic symbolic music. The model incorporates a conditional mechanism to generate original melodies based on a chord sequence or via conditioning based on previously used melody bars. MuseGAN [11] is another GAN model based on CNNs that generates symbolic multitrack music. It includes the jamming, composer, and hybrid models, which are designed to address the unique challenges of music generation, such as its temporal nature and the interdependence of multiple tracks. Inco-GAN [12] is a type of polyphonic music that uses a CNN-based inception model for the conditional generation of polyphonic music that can be freely adjusted in terms of length. In addition, ChordGAN [13] is a chord-conditioned melody generation approach that uses a conditional GAN architecture and appropriate loss functions, similar to image-to-image translation algorithms. It can be used as a tool for musicians to learn compositional techniques for different styles using the same chords and automatically generate music.

Although the use of CNNs has improved the ability of models to extract local features, the issue of gradient vanishing that occurs when processing long-distance sequences has not been addressed. Moreover, balancing the generator and discriminator during dynamic learning is difficult, making it challenging to guarantee the convergence of the GANs during training.

The denoising diffusion probabilistic model (DDPM) [14] is a type of probabilistic generative model that includes the forward and reverse processes. A key benefit of DDPM is that it can be used to denoise data without explicit labels or supervision. This makes it particularly useful for denoising data in unsupervised learning, in which it is difficult or impossible to obtain labeled data. This model can help to address convergence issues in generative models and has achieved promising results in the generation of high-quality images. Moreover, the transformer module, which is used extensively in language modeling, allows the model to focus directly on all input words simultaneously and measure their importance using the attention mechanism. Thus, the model can efficiently capture the long-term dependencies and make more accurate predictions. Transformers also apply parallel processing, making them more efficient and faster to train than RNNs.

This paper proposes a method for chord-conditioned melody generation using a transformer-based diffusion model known as MelodyDiffusion. The following three modifications are made to the traditional diffusion model. First, in the forward process, the inputs of MelodyDiffusion are not continuous image-like data, but they are rather discrete sequences, and no pre-trained variational autoencoder (VAE) is required to map the discrete data to a continuous latent space. Second, in the reverse process, the U-nets of the traditional diffusion model are replaced with transformers, thereby enabling the model to handle discrete sequences and to consider long-distance dependencies. Finally, a transformer-based encoder is used to embed the conditions for guiding the reverse process, which allows for chord-conditioned music generation.

The main contributions of this paper are summarized as follows: (1) a novel diffusion model that operates directly on discrete data is designed, such that the diffusion model is not limited to image generation. (2) MelodyDiffusion uses transformers instead of U-nets to handle discrete sequences. Furthermore, a transformer-based encoder is developed to realize chord-conditioned melody generation. (3) The experiments reveal that MelodyDiffusion can generate diverse melodies based on the given chords.

2. Related Work

Researchers have started using transformers and diffusion models for music generation. Several representative approaches are described in the following subsections.

2.1. Transformer-Based Music Generation Approaches

As transformers are based on the attention mechanism, they offer more advantages than RNNs in processing sequential data. Some representative studies on the use of transformers for music generation are summarized as follows. CMT [15] is a chord-conditioned melody transformer model for generating K-pop melodies. The model produces the rhythm and pitch separately based on a given chord progression and is trained in two phases. This approach has exhibited promising results for chord-conditioned melody generation. MusicFrameworks [16] is a hierarchical music structure representation and multistep generative process for creating full-length melodies in a manner guided by long-term repetitive structure, chord, melodic contour, and rhythm constraints. The system organizes the full melody into sections and phrases. It generates a melody in each phrase by first generating the rhythm and basic melody using two separate transformer-based networks and then generating the melody in a way which is conditioned on the basic melody, rhythm, and chords. This approach allows for customization and variety by altering the chord, basic melody, and rhythm structures in the music framework. A music generation network based on transformers and guided by music theory has been proposed [17]. This network uses a transformer decoding block to learn the internal information of single-track music and cross-track transformers in order to learn the relationships among tracks involving different musical instruments. A reward network based on music theory is used to optimize network training and produce high-quality music. MELONS [18] is based on a graphical representation of music structure. It uses a multistep generation method with transformer-based networks to factor melody generation into the structure and structure-conditional melody generation. MRBERT [19] uses a pre-trained model that is based on the understanding of melody and rhythm to generate and fill in the melody and chords.

Therefore, in general, transformers have replaced RNNs in music generation tasks and achieved promising results.

2.2. Diffusion Model-Based Music Generation Approcaches

Owing to the remarkable achievements of diffusion models in image generation, researchers have attempted to apply them to waveform data, which are image-like, to accomplish music generation. The text-to-audio system has gained attention for its ability to synthesize general audio based on text descriptions. To address the issues of high computational costs and limited generation quality in previous studies, a diffusion-model-based text-to-audio system called AudioLDM [20] has been proposed. This system can learn continuous audio representations from contrastive language-audio pretraining latent spaces. By using pre-trained models, text embeddings can be used as conditions during sampling while audio mel-spectrogram embeddings are provided to train AudioLDM. Conversely, ERNIE-Music [21] is a diffusion model-based text-to-waveform method that uses lyrics in a textual format as input to control the music generation in waveform format. This is a multimodal generation approach that demonstrates the effective combination of discrete text data and continuous waveforms.

The above two approaches respectively represent music as mel-spectrograms and waveforms, which are continuous image-like data. However, music can also be represented as a discrete sequence composed of notes with specific durations, and transformers can be used to consider the long-distance dependencies between them. This not only extends the training data of diffusion models beyond audio-format music, but also allows for symbolic musical data to be used. A representative approach [22] was proposed for use to train diffusion models on symbolic music data by parameterizing the discrete domain in the continuous latent space of a pre-trained variational autoencoder. This research attempted to use a diffusion model with transformers to generate symbolic music. This enabled the models to generate sequences of latent embeddings through a reverse process and provided parallel generation with a fixed number of refinement steps. Similarly, in the latter work on scalable diffusion models with transformers [23], transformers were used as the main architecture for image generation, replacing U-nets. Furthermore, an autoencoder was used to embed the input into a continuous latent space.

However, the previous approach used a pre-trained biLSTM-based MusicVAE to map a discrete sequence onto a continuous latent space, as well as to decode a discrete sequence from the continuous latent space that is output by the diffusion model. In contrast, the method proposed herein aims to directly embed discrete sequences into the diffusion model, without requiring any intermediate process for conversion into continuous features. Furthermore, a transformer-based encoder is designed to extract contextual information from chords to realize chord-conditioned melody generation.

3. Chord-Conditioned Melody Generation Method

This paper proposes a method for chord-conditioned melody generation using a transformer-based diffusion model known as MelodyDiffusion. We first describe the representations of the melody and chords. Subsequently, we explain the structure and operation of the transformer-based diffusion model.

3.1. Date Representation

The music corpus OpenEWLD [24], which is a dataset consisting of lead sheets in XML format, is used during training. As illustrated in Figure 1, a piano roll is obtained from a lead sheet using the Python library pypianoroll. In the piano roll, each measure is divided into 40 parts. Therefore, each part is a 0.025 measure length; for example, "Duration: 0.25" indicates that a pitch takes up a 0.25 measure length. In a musical instrument digital interface, each pitch is defined with a unique index ranging from 0 to 127, thereby representing 128 types of pitches; for example, the index of "Pitch: C4" is 60. Thus, "Pitch: C4 Duration: 0.25" represents the sequence "60, 60, 60, 60, 0". It is worth noting that the end of this sequence is replaced with 0 given that the "offset" of the pitch must be clearly indicated. Supposing "Pitch: F4 Duration: 0.25" is followed by "Pitch: F4 Duration: 0.5", if the "offset" is not indicated, it will be difficult to distinguish these from "Pitch: F4 Duration: 0.75".

When a melody sequence is generated, the chord sequence can be obtained by simply supplementing the chord index in the corresponding position. A total of 446 chords have been detected and assigned an index in OpenEWLD, with the index 0 indicating "offset".

During training, eight consecutive measures are randomly extracted from any lead sheet in the dataset. The melody and chord sequences, both with a length of 320 (8×40), are obtained using the representation method described above.

3.2. Transformer-Based Diffusion Model

MelodyDiffusion includes forward and reverse processes. As shown in Figure 2, the forward process adds noise to the original melody based on time steps. The reverse process includes a denoising model and a pre-trained encoder, where the denoising model takes the noisy melody generated by the forward process as an input with which to eliminate the original melody. The pre-trained encoder extracts hidden features from the chords and is connected to the transformers in the denoising model through a cross-attention module to guide the denoising process. The forward and reverse processes are explained in more detail in the following sections.

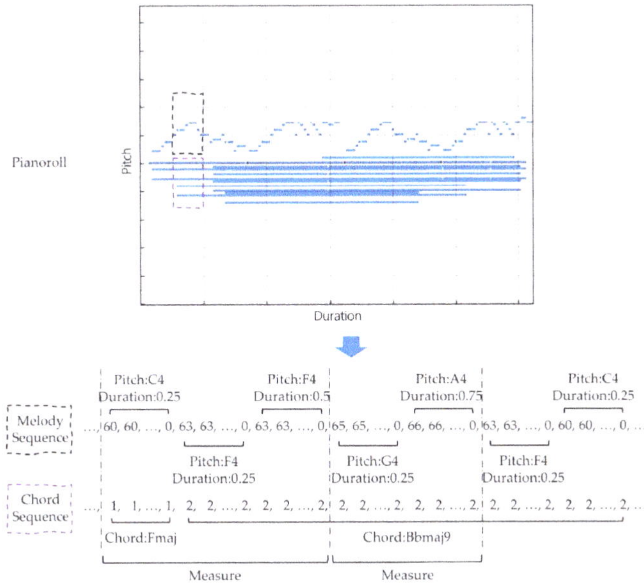

Figure 1. Example of melody and chord sequences converted from a piano roll. In the piano roll, a portion of the corresponding melody and chord were truncated. The black dotted box represents the truncated melody section, while the purple represents the truncated chord. The truncated melody and chord are converted to melody and chord sequences, with each segment between two dotted lines representing the length of one measure.

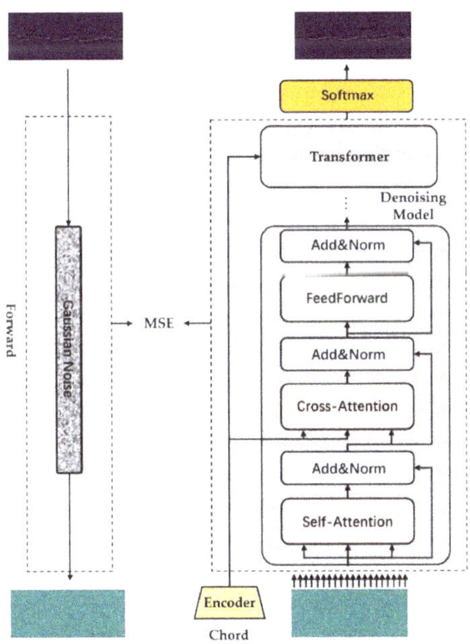

Figure 2. Model structure of MelodyDiffusion.

3.2.1. Notations

This section introduces the notation used in describing the forward and reverse processes, as shown in Table 1. In the forward process, time steps $t \in (1, T)$ are used to control adding the noise z on original melody x_0, where the noise z follows a Gaussian distribution. The reason for using Gaussian noise is that the noise must conform to a regular distribution, otherwise the diffusion model is unable predict it. Furthermore, Gaussian noise has been widely used in various diffusion models and has been proven to be effective. In addition, Gaussian noise has a wide range of applications and foundations in statistics and natural sciences; therefore, its use in diffusion models can better simulate real-world noise.

Table 1. Notations and their descriptions.

Notations	Description
t	Time steps
T	Max time step
z	Noise follows a Gaussian distribution
x_0	Original melody
$x_1, x_2, \ldots, x_t, \ldots, x_T$	Melodies with noise added based on time steps $t \in (1, T)$
β	Parameter that increases as time step t increases
$\epsilon_\theta(\cdot)$	Denoising model, where [1] θ represents the weights in the model
$\rho_\varphi(\cdot)$	Encoder, where [2] φ represents the weights in the encoder
$c_1, c_2, \ldots, c_n$	Chords that are input as the condition to the encoder
$h_1, h_2, \ldots, h_n$	Hidden features output by the encoder

[1,2] θ and φ represents the weights in $\epsilon_\theta(\cdot)$ and $\rho_\varphi(\cdot)$, and θ is updated during the training of the diffusion model, while φ is frozen.

$x_1, x_2, \ldots, x_t, \ldots, x_T$ represent noisy melodies with noise added based on different time steps t. β varies with t and serves as the parameter for controlling the level of noise added. ϵ_θ and ρ_θ represent the denoising model and encoder, respectively, in the reverse process. $c_1, c_2, \ldots, c_n$ represents the chords that are input as conditions to the encoder. $h_1, h_2, \ldots, h_n$ represents the hidden features output by the encoder.

3.2.2. Forward Process

The forward process follows the time steps 1 to T, recursively adds noise z to the original melody x_0, and saves the noising results of each time step, $x_1, x_2, \ldots, x_t, \ldots, x_T$. Noise is added to the melody at time step t using Equation (1), where β increases as t increases. Therefore, a larger t value indicates that more noise z is added to x_0.

$$x_t = \left(\sqrt{1-\beta_t}\right)x_{t-1} + \sqrt{\beta_t}z_t,\ t \in (1,\ T) \tag{1}$$

By recursively applying Equation (1), the noisy melody x_t at any time step t can be obtained based on the original melody x_0, as shown in Equation (2).

$$x_t = \left(\sqrt{1-\overline{\beta}_t}\right)x_0 + \sqrt{\overline{\beta}_t}z_t,\ t \in (1,\ T) \tag{2}$$

Specifically, each pitch in the melody sequence is embedded using one-hot encoding. As the pitch ranges from 1 to 128, the size of the one-hot encoded vector is 128. Subsequently, each vector undergoes noise processing, whereby the noise follows a Gaussian distribution and is controlled by the parameter β_t. Figure 3 presents the overall process of adding Gaussian noise to the melody sequences. A melody with a length of 320 is embedded into a 320×128 matrix through one-hot encoding. Thereafter, Gaussian noise of the same size as the one-hot encoded melody is generated. Finally, the Gaussian noise is added to the one-hot encoded melody using Equation (2) to obtain the noisy melody.

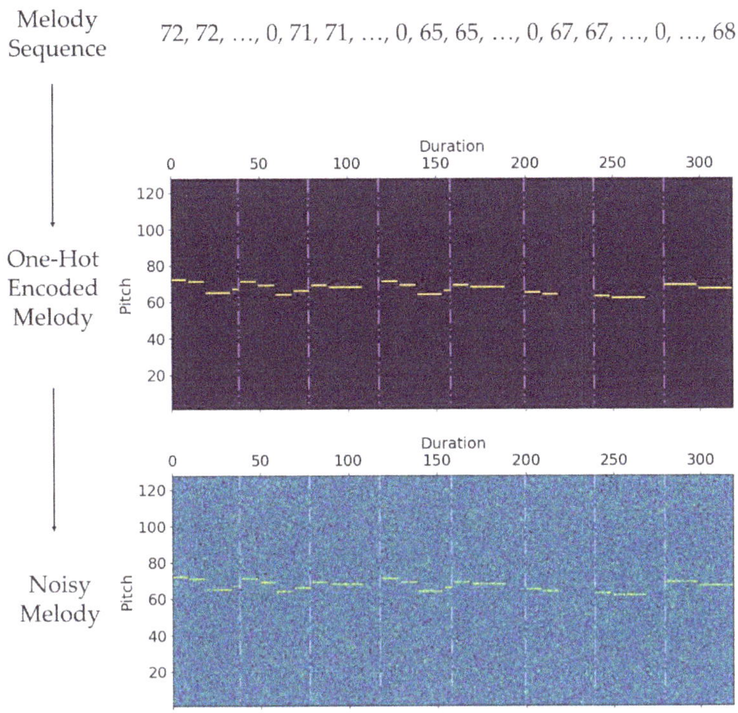

Figure 3. Adding Gaussian noise to the melody sequence.

3.2.3. Reverse Process

In the reverse process, the goal of denoising model ϵ_θ is to infer x_0 recursively from x_t. During the recursive process, Gaussian noise z'_t added to x_{t-1} is predicted based on x_t according to Equation (3). After z'_t is predicted, x'_{t-1} can be obtained easily by using Equation (4), which follows the inverse process of adding noise. Through training, x'_{t-1} gradually approximates the known x_{t-1} from the forward process. $\epsilon_\theta(\cdot)$ represents the denoising model. $\rho_\varphi(\cdot)$ represents the pre-trained encoder, which is composed of transformers using self-attention. It is differentiated from the denoising model $\epsilon_\theta(\cdot)$ given that is a pre-trained model which uses frozen weights during the training of the diffusion model. Moreover, c represents the chord sequence input to the encoder as a conditional input.

$$z'_t \propto \epsilon_\theta\left(\left(\sqrt{1-\bar{\beta}_t}\right)x_0 + \sqrt{\bar{\beta}_t}z_t,\ t\right)\rho_\varphi(c) \tag{3}$$

$$x_{t-1} \approx x'_{t-1} \propto \frac{1}{\sqrt{1-\beta_t}}\left(x_t - \frac{\beta_t}{\sqrt{\bar{\beta}_t}}z'_t\right) \tag{4}$$

Subsequently, the loss is calculated based on z'_t and z_t. In the reverse process, the noise z'_t is predicted based on x_t. In the forward process, the noise z_t added to x_{t-1} is known. The loss for updating the denoising model and encoder is obtained by calculating the difference between z'_t and z_t, and the loss function uses the mean squared error (MSE) as defined in Equation (5).

$$loss = \| z'_t - z_t \|^2 \tag{5}$$

As illustrated in Figure 2, the reverse process comprises two parts: the denoising model and a pre-trained encoder for inputting the chord information. The denoising model is composed of transformer blocks that use both self-attention and cross-attention mechanisms. The query, key, and value in the self-attention layer originate from the current input. Conversely, in the cross-attention layer, only the query originates from the previous layer, and the key and value are obtained through cross-attention. The structure of the encoder is similar to that of the denoising model, except that all cross-attention layers are replaced with self-attention layers. Its structure is similar to that of BERT [25], and it is pre-trained using the masked language modeling method [25]. The pre-training process is completed in advance. Specifically, chord sequences are randomly masked and fed into the encoder, which learns deeper representations in the process of recovering the masked parts

As shown in Figure 4, the denoising model is connected to the pre-trained layer through cross-attention. The pre-trained encoder receives the chord sequence $c_1, c_2, \ldots, c_n$ as an input and outputs the hidden features $h_1, h_2, \ldots, h_n$ of the contextual information. Subsequently, these hidden features are fed into each transformer in the denoising model via cross-attention.

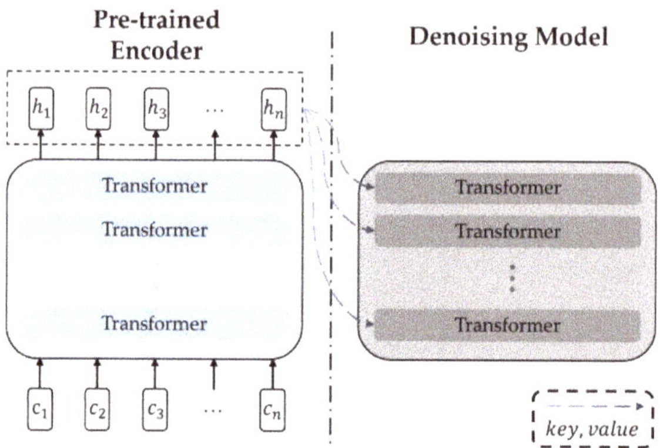

Figure 4. Pipeline of the conditioned-denoising in reverse process.

Algorithm 1 shows the training of MelodyDiffusion, while Algorithm 2 shows the method of sampling new melodies using Gaussian noise and conditional chords after the model has converged.

Algorithm 1 Training

repeat
$x_0 = f^{one-hot}(melody\ sequence)$
$c = chord\ sequence$
$t \in Uniform(\{1, \ldots, T\})$
$z_t \sim \mathcal{N}(0, \mathrm{I})$
Take gradient descent step on :
$\nabla_\theta \parallel \epsilon_\theta\left(\left(\sqrt{1-\bar{\beta}_t}\right)x_0 + \sqrt{\bar{\beta}_t}z_t,\ t\right)\rho_\varphi(c) - z_t \parallel^2$
until converged

Algorithm 2 Sampling

$x_T \sim \mathcal{N}(0, \mathrm{I})$
for t **in** $(1, \ldots, T)$:
$x'_{t-1} = \frac{1}{\sqrt{1-\beta_t}}\left(x_t - \frac{\beta_t}{\sqrt{\bar{\beta}_t}}z'_t\right)$
return x'_0

4. Experiments

Hits@k [26] was used as the metric with which to evaluate the quality of the generated melodies. Hits@k is a commonly used evaluation metric for the recommendation models and returns the top k results from the generated list, the latter being sorted by the softmax probability distribution. It represents the average percentage of rankings with a value lower than k in the generated samples. First, MelodyDiffusion-large was designed as a comparison to demonstrate the impact of changes in the hyperparameters of the transformer on the results. Second, "w/o encoder" was used for an ablation experiment. Here, "w/o encoder" represents MelodyDiffusion that did not use an encoder with chord conditions as an input. Finally, the stable diffusion model [27] was reproduced as a baseline, which is a conditional generative model based on U-nets. To adapt discrete data to the stable diffusion model, the input format was set to be slightly different from that of the transformer-based diffusion models.

4.1. Dateset

The Enhanced Wikifonia Leadsheet Dataset (EWLD) is a music lead sheet dataset. OpenEWLD [23] was used in the experiments reported in this paper. It was extracted from EWLD and only contained lead sheets in the public domain. Each lead sheet in OpenEWLD contains the melodies and chords that are required for training. These data were divided into 13,884 sample pairs consisting of eight measures for training and evaluation.

4.2. Experimental Environment

Table 2 lists the hyperparameters that were used during training in the forward process. Number of time steps signified that the maximum value for time step T was 500. β_{start} and β_{end} indicated that the minimum value for β_t in Equations (1) and (2) was 0.0001 and the maximum value was 0.02, with β increasing linearly over time t. The proposed method's models and the comparative models, which consisted of "w/o encoder", and stable diffusion model [27], used the same forward process in the experiment.

Table 2. Hyperparameters used in the forward process.

Hyperparameters	Values
Number of time steps T	500
Schedule of β_t	Linear
β_{start}	0.0001
β_{end}	0.02

Table 3 shows the hyperparameters of the encoder and denoising model in both the base and large versions of the MelodyDiffusion model. The hyperparameter settings of both the base and large versions were based on BERT-base and -large [25], which are types of transformer-based pre-trained model used for representation learning in natural language processing. In this paper, we attempted to use the transformer blocks of BERT as the main architecture of a diffusion model. The encoder and denoising model used the same structure, except that cross-attention was enabled in the denoising model.

Table 4 lists the hyperparameters used by the baseline model. The stable diffusion model was replicated as the baseline. The melody was added as one channel and input into the model in the form of a grayscale image. The model consisted of 12 blocks wherein 6 had functions of down-sampling and 6 had functions of up-sampling. Each block received hidden states extracted from the chords through cross attention from the encoder. The encoder used here was the same as the encoder used in MelodyDiffusion.

Table 3. Hyperparameters of encoder and denoising model in both the base and large versions of MelodyDiffusion.

Hyperparameters	MelodyDiff. (Base)	MelodyDiff. (Large)
Number of layers	12	24
Input size (Length; Embedded dimension)	320 × 128	320 × 128
Hidden size	768	1024
FFN inner hidden size	3072	4096
Attention heads	12	16
Attention head size	64	64

Table 4. Hyperparameters of the baseline model.

Hyperparameters	Stable Diffusion
Number of U-net blocks	12
Input size (Channel; Height; Width)	1 × 128 × 320
Output channel of blocks	128, 128, 256, 256, 512, 512

Table 5 displays the hyperparameters used in the training strategy, including global dropout to prevent overfitting, as well as parameters related to the optimizer AdamW and learning rate. A dropout value of 0.1 was globally used in the reverse process model. The AdamW optimizer was selected to update the model and its learning rate was set to 1×10^{-4}. The parameters relating to the optimizers, namely β_1 and β_2, were set to 0.9 and 0.98, respectively. The warm step, which indicates that the learning rate gradually increases from 0, reached its peak at 500 iterations and then decreased back to 0, following a cosine function.

Table 5. Hyperparameters of the training strategy.

Hyperparameters	Stable Diffusion
Dropout	0.1
AdamW ϵ (Learning rate)	1×10^{-4}
AdamW β_1	0.9
AdamW β_2	0.98
Warm steps	500
Schedule of the learning rate	cosine

4.3. Displays of Training

Figure 5 illustrates the melodies with added noise at different time steps during the forward process. In the original melody x_0, the melody was clearly defined. As the time step t increased to 100, the noisy melody x_{100} became increasingly difficult to recognize. When the time step t increased from 250 to 500, the melody became completely unrecognizable, and the measures were indistinguishable. This demonstrated that noise was gradually added during the forward process. As time steps increased, noise gradually dominated the melody, resulting in a gradual blurring until it became unrecognizable. This further confirms the importance of noise, which provides models with more creativity and diversity, resulting in the generation of more interesting melodies. In the MelodyDiffusion model, by randomly generating Gaussian noise distributions, different styles and qualities of melody generation results can be obtained.

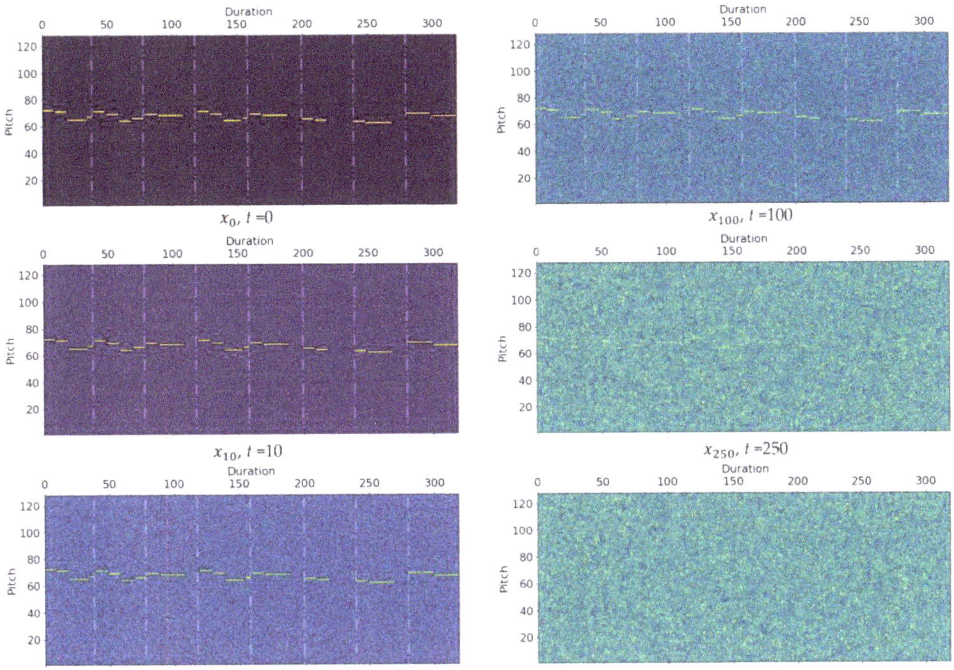

Figure 5. Examples of noise-added melodies at different time steps.

Figure 6 shows the change in MSE loss during the first 250 iterations of training for the MelodyDiffusion base and large models, as well as for the "w/o encoder" and the baseline stable diffusion models during the warm-up phase. Due to the larger number of parameters, the large model had a higher initial loss than the base model. In contrast to the transformer-based models, the stable diffusion model had a low initial loss given that it can predict the noise distribution based on local features by rapidly using convolution. However, as training continued, the transformer models began to excel at predicting noise on discrete data by considering the contextual information in both forward and backward directions. After 100 iterations, the MSE loss between the predicted noise and the actual noise distribution for all four models converged to approximately the same loss.

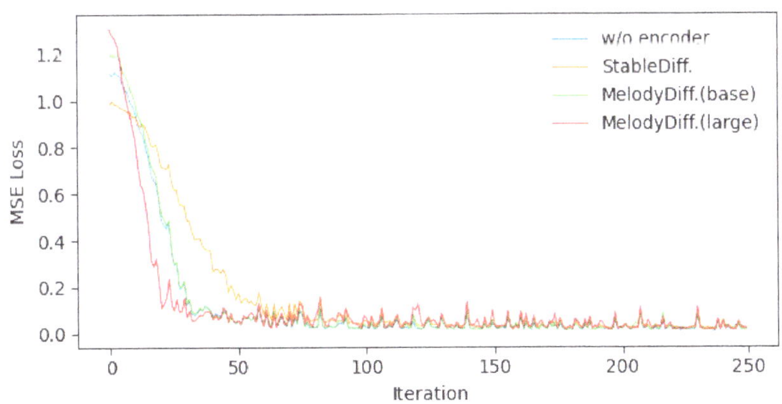

Figure 6. Change in MSE loss during training.

GANs can generate new samples based on noise. However, the goal of GANs is to restore the original sample x_0 from Gaussian noise distribution x_T, which is a challenging task. In contrast, MelodyDiffusion only infers x_{t-1} based on x_t. As shown in Figure 5, it is challenging to directly restore x_0 from x_{500}, making it difficult for the generator of a GAN to update based on the feedback from the discriminator. However, it is relatively easier to predict x_{499}. Furthermore, to make the model converge faster, the training method of the denoising diffusion implicit model (DDIM) [28] was used instead of the traditional DDPM. The reason DDIM was chosen is that the forward process of the diffusion model can include hundreds of steps, and as the DDPM based on Markov chains needs to traverse all time steps to generate a single sample. In DDIM, the forward process can be a non-Markov process and can be accelerated by subsampling.

4.4. Hits@k Evaluation Results

Table 6 presents the evaluation results of the generated melodies using Hist@k. In the restoration process of noisy melodies, which added Gaussian noise at time step T (T = 500) on the basis of the chords given, the reverse process was used to run T recursive denoising operations on the noisy melodies, and the probability distributions of the restored melodies were output through softmax. For Hist@k, k was set to 1, 3, 5, 10, and 20, and the average percentage of the pitch in the original melodies among the top k pitches in the softmax probability distribution was calculated. When k = 1, only the pitch with the highest probability in the softmax probability distribution was considered to evaluate the performance of the restoration, which was the key metric in this. The performance of the base version of MelodyDiffusion was slightly lower than that of the baseline stable diffusion model, being lower by 1.43%; meanwhile, the large version with a similar number of parameters had a performance which was 0.63% higher. However, the performance of the w/o encoder model, which did not use chords as auxiliaries, was worse than that of the other three conditional models. When k > 3, the Hist@k score of the stable diffusion model was higher than that of the MelodyDiffusion models. After analyzing the generated results, it was apparent that the section of the melody with significant changes in pitch affected the transformer's judgment in the restoration process given that it tended to make predictions based on contextual features. In contrast, the stable diffusion model, which utilized a CNN, could restore this section based on local features.

Table 6. Evaluation results of the generated melodies obtained using Hist@k.

	HITS@1 (%)	HITS@3 (%)	HITS@5 (%)	HITS@10 (%)	HITS@20 (%)
MelodyDiff. (base)	70.35	83.13	87.03	90.52	92.95
MelodyDiff. (large)	72.41	84.40	87.12	90.49	92.88
w/o encoder	66.78	80.99	86.98	89.66	91.87
StableDiff.	71.78	82.97	88.45	91.72	93.01

4.5. Comparison of Generated and Real Melodies

Figure 7 illustrates the generated melodies of the original melody (A) and those generated by the base (B) and large (C) versions of MelodyDiffusion, the stable diffusion model (D), and the w/o encoder (E). These melodies were generated by the models based on using random Gaussian noise as an input and utilizing the same chords as the condition (except for w/o encoder). The analysis of the results showed that all models could recognize the measures (with a duration of 40 for each measure). Second, there were obvious noise patterns in the background of (D); these occurred since the stable diffusion model, using CNN, could not eliminate interference based on contextual features. Finally, the three generated melodies in (E) were extremely similar, particularly in the case of the first two measures. This also indicated that the chords could provide diversity to the generated melodies.

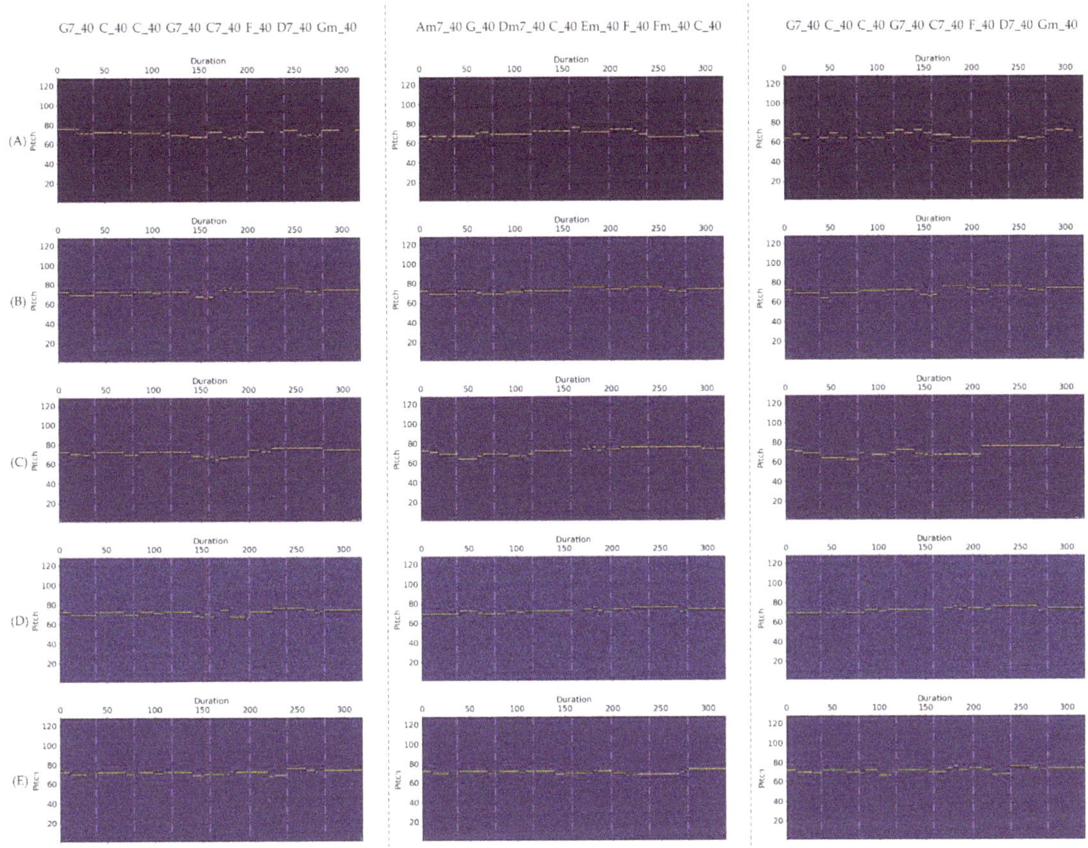

Figure 7. Visual comparison of the Softmax probability distribution of original and generated melodies. (**A**) Original melodies; (**B**) generated melodies based on the base version of MelodyDiffusion; (**C**) generated melodies based on the large version of MelodyDiffusion; (**D**) generated melodies based on the stable diffusion model; (**E**) generated melodies based on the w/o encoder system.

5. Conclusions

This paper proposed a chord-conditioned melody generation method using MelodyDiffusion, which is a diffusion model based on transformers. MelodyDiffusion consists of forward and reverse processes. In the forward process, Gaussian noise is added to melodies following the time step. In the reverse process, the noise is reduced through the denoising model, using the given chords as conditions. Following training, this model could effectively predict the noise distribution from noisy melodies. Hits@k was used as a metric to evaluate the generated melodies. The experimental results showed that the performance of the proposed method reached 70.35% and 72.41% (k = 1) for the base and large versions, respectively, in restoring noisy melodies, with the large version outperforming the baseline model (stable diffusion) by 0.63%. Additionally, the visual comparison showed that MelodyDiffusion could generate more diverse melodies under the condition of given chords compared to the unconditional diffusion model.

Currently, MelodyDiffusion can only generate monophonic melodies based on chords. Considering the practicality of polyphonic music composed of multiple instrument combinations, future research directions include identifying chords and melodies from polyphonic music, which mainly comprises multi-track polyphonic music, without distinguishing chords and melodies compared to datasets with paired chords and melodies.

Moreover, it is necessary to explore the application of MelodyDiffusion to other forms of musical data and generate polyphonic music containing multiple instruments based on these considerations are necessary.

Moreover, the diffusion model was originally proposed and used in the field of image generation; thus, although its main structure was replaced with transformers to handle discrete data with temporal properties in MelodyDiffusion, a limitation on the length of the generated samples exists. While increasing the processing length of transformers can generate longer samples, it also leads to higher training costs. A feasible approach is to guide the generation of subsequent melodies by treating previous melody patterns as conditional inputs, similar to what occurs in the conditioning of chord inputs.

Supplementary Materials: The following supporting information can be downloaded at: https://www.mdpi.com/article/10.3390/math11081915/s1, Demo S1: MIDI files generated by the MelodyDiffusion and MP3 files converted from them.

Author Contributions: Conceptualization, S.L. and Y.S.; methodology, S.L. and Y.S.; software, S.L. and Y.S.; validation, S.L. and Y.S.; writing-original draft, S.L.; writing—review & editing, Y.S. All authors have read and agreed to the published version of the manuscript.

Funding: This work was supported by the Ministry of Education of the Republic of Korea and the National Research Foundation of Korea (NRF-2021R1F1A1063466).

Data Availability Statement: Restrictions apply to the availability of these data. Data was obtained from https://github.com/00sapo/OpenEWLD and are available accessed on 1 October 2022. MIDI files generated by the MelodyDiffusion and MP3 files converted from them are available as Supplementary Materials.

Conflicts of Interest: The authors declare no conflict of interest.

References

1. Huang, C.A.; Vaswani, A.; Uszkoreit, J.; Shazeer, N.; Simon, I.; Hawthorne, C.; Dai, A.M.; Hoffman, M.D.; Dinculescu, M.; Eck, D. Music transformer: Generating Music with Long-term Structure. *arXiv* **2018**, arXiv:1809.04281.
2. Hawthorne, C.; Stasyuk, A.; Roberts, A.; Simon, I.; Huang, C.A.; Dieleman, S.; Elsen, E.; Engel, J.; Eck, D. Enabling Factorized Piano Music Modeling and Generation with the MAESTRO Dataset. *arXiv* **2018**, arXiv:1810.12247.
3. Salas, H.A.G.; Gelbukh, A.; Calvo, H.; Soria, F.G. Automatic Music Composition with Simple Probabilistic Generative Grammars. *Polibits* **2011**, *44*, 59–65. [CrossRef]
4. Alvaro, J.L.; Miranda, E.R.; Barros, B. Music Knowledge Analysis: Towards an Efficient Representation for Composition. In Proceedings of the 11th Conference of the Spanish Association for Artificial Intelligence (CAEPIA), Santiago de Compostela, Spain, 16–18 November 2005; pp. 331–341.
5. Akama, T. Controlling Symbolic Music Generation based on Concept Learning from Domain Knowledge. In Proceedings of the International Conference on Music Information Retrieval (ISMIR), Delft, The Netherlands, 4–8 November 2019; pp. 816–823.
6. Dubnov, S.; Assayag, G.; Lartillot, O.; Bejerano, G. Using Machine-Learning Methods for Musical Style Modeling. *Computer* **2003**, *36*, 73–80. [CrossRef]
7. Mogren, O. C-RNN-GAN: Continuous Recurrent Neural Networks with Adversarial Training. *arXiv* **2016**, arXiv:1611.09904.
8. Yu, L.; Zhang, W.; Wang, J.; Yu, Y. SeqGAN: Sequence Generative Adversarial Nets with Policy Gradient. In Proceedings of the 31st AAAI Conference on Artificial Intelligence, San Francisco, CA, USA, 4–9 February 2017; pp. 2852–2858.
9. Guimaraes, G.L.; Sanchez-Lengeling, B.; Outeiral, C.; Farias, P.L.C.; Aspuru-Guzik, A. Objective-Reinforced Generative Adversarial Networks (ORGAN) for Sequence Generation Models. *arXiv* **2017**, arXiv:1705.10843.
10. Yang, L.C.; Chou, S.Y.; Yang, Y.H. MidiNet: A Convolutional Generative Adversarial Network for Symbolic-domain Music Generation. *arXiv* **2017**, arXiv:1703.10847.
11. Dong, H.W.; Hsiao, W.Y.; Yang, L.C.; Yang, Y.H. MuseGan: Multi-Track Sequential Generative Adversarial Networks for Symbolic Music Generation and Accompaniment. In Proceedings of the 32nd AAAI Conference on Artificial Intelligence, New Orleans, LA, USA, 2–7 February 2018; pp. 34–41.
12. Li, S.; Sung, Y. INCO-GAN: Variable-length music generation method based on inception model-based conditional GAN. *Mathematics* **2021**, *9*, 387. [CrossRef]
13. Lu, C.; Dubnov, S. Chordgan: Symbolic Music Style Transfer with Chroma Feature Extraction. In Proceedings of the 2nd Conference on AI Music Creativity (AIMC), Online, 18–22 July 2021.
14. Ho, J.; Jain, A.; Abbeel, P. Denoising Diffusion Probabilistic Models. *Adv. Neural Inf. Proc. Syst.* **2020**, *33*, 6840–6851.
15. Choi, K.; Park, J.; Heo, W.; Jeon, S.; Park, J. Chord Conditioned Melody Generation with Transformer Based Decoders. *IEEE Access* **2021**, *9*, 42071–42080. [CrossRef]

16. Dai, S.; Jin, Z.; Gomes, C.; Dannenberg, R.B. Controllable Deep Melody Generation Via Hierarchical Music Structure Representation. *arXiv* **2021**, arXiv:2109.00663.
17. Jin, C.; Wang, T.; Li, X.; Tie, C.J.J.; Tie, Y.; Liu, S.; Yan, M.; Li, Y.; Wang, J.; Huang, S. A Transformer Generative Adversarial Network for Multi-Track Music Generation. *CAAI Trans. Intell. Technol.* **2022**, *7*, 369–380. [CrossRef]
18. Zou, Y.; Zou, P.; Zhao, Y.; Zhang, K.; Zhang, R.; Wang, X. MELONS: Generating Melody with Long-Term Structure Using Transformers and Structure Graph. In Proceedings of the International Conference on Acoustics, Speech and Signal Processing (ICASSP), Singapore, 23–27 May 2022; pp. 191–195.
19. Li, S.; Sung, Y. MRBERT: Pre-Training of Melody and Rhythm for Automatic Music Generation. *Mathematics* **2023**, *11*, 798. [CrossRef]
20. Liu, H.; Chen, Z.; Yuan, Y.; Mei, X.; Liu, X.; Mandic, D.; Wang, W.; Plumbley, M.D. AudioLDM: Text-to-Audio Generation with Latent Diffusion Models. *arXiv* **2023**, arXiv:2301.12503.
21. Zhu, P.; Pang, C.; Wang, S.; Chai, Y.; Sun, Y.; Tian, H.; Wu, H. ERNIE-Music: Text-to-Waveform Music Generation with Diffusion Models. *arXiv* **2023**, arXiv:2302.04456.
22. Mittal, G.; Engel, J.; Hawthorne, C.; Simon, I. Symbolic Music Generation with Diffusion Models. *arXiv* **2021**, arXiv:2103.16091.
23. Peebles, W.; Xie, S. Scalable Diffusion Models with Transformers. *arXiv* **2022**, arXiv:2212.09748.
24. Simonetta, F.; Carnovalini, F.; Orio, N.; Rodà, A. Symbolic Music Similarity through a Graph-Based Representation. In Proceedings of the Audio Mostly on Sound in Immersion and Emotion, North Wales, UK, 12–14 September 2018; pp. 1–7.
25. Devlin, J.; Chang, M.W.; Lee, K.; Toutanova, K. BERT: Pretraining of Deep Bidirectional Transformers for Language Understanding. *arXiv* **2018**, arXiv:1810.04805.
26. Zeng, M.; Tan, X.; Wang, R.; Ju, Z.; Qin, T.; Liu, T.Y. MusicBERT: Symbolic Music Understanding with Large-Scale Pre-Training. In Proceedings of the Findings of the Associations for Computational Linguistics: ACL-IJCNLP, Online, 1–6 August 2021; pp. 791–800.
27. Rombach, R.; Blattmann, A.; Lorenz, D.; Esser, P.; Ommer, B. High-Resolution Image Synthesis with Latent Diffusion Models. In Proceedings of the IEEE/CVF Conference on Computer Vision and Pattern Recognition (CVPR), New Orleans, LA, USA, 19–24 June 2022.
28. Song, J.; Meng, C.; Ermon, S. Denoising Diffusion Implicit Models. *arXiv* **2020**, arXiv:2010.02502.

mathematics

Article

A Semi-Federated Active Learning Framework for Unlabeled Online Network Data

Yuwen Zhou [1,2], Yuhan Hu [2,*], Jing Sun [1], Rui He [1] and Wenjie Kang [3]

1 College of Intelligence and Computing, Tianjin University, Tianjin 300350, China
2 Science and Technology on Information Systems Engineering Laboratory, Changsha 410073, China
3 Hunan Provincial Key Laboratory of Network Investigational Technology, Hunan Police Academy, Changsha 410125, China
* Correspondence: huyuhan16@nudt.edu.cn

Abstract: Federated Learning (FL) is a newly emerged federated optimization technique for distributed data in a federated network. The participants in FL that train the model locally are classified into client nodes. The server node assumes the responsibility to aggregate local models from client nodes without data moving. In this regard, FL is an ideal solution to protect data privacy at each node of the network. However, the raw data generated on each node are unlabeled, making it impossible for FL to apply these data directly to train a model. The large volume of data annotating work prevents FL from being widely applied in the real world, especially for online scenarios, where the data are generated continuously. Meanwhile, the data generated on different nodes tend to be differently distributed. It has been proved theoretically and experimentally that non-independent and identically distributed (non-IID) data harm the performance of FL. In this article, we design a semi-federated active learning (semi-FAL) framework to tackle the annotation and non-IID problems jointly. More specifically, the server node can provide (i) a pre-trained model to help each client node annotate the local data uniformly and (ii) an estimation of the global gradient to help correct the local gradient. The evaluation results demonstrate our semi-FAL framework can efficiently handle unlabeled online network data and achieves high accuracy and fast convergence.

Keywords: network data; federated learning; unlabeled data; heterogeneous data

MSC: 68T09

Citation: Zhou, Y.; Hu, Y.; Sun, J.; He, R.; Kang, W. A Semi-Federated Active Learning Framework for Unlabeled Online Network Data. *Mathematics* **2023**, *11*, 1972. https://doi.org/10.3390/math11081972

Academic Editors: Adrian Sergiu Darabant, Diana-Laura Borza and Catalin Stoean

Received: 22 March 2023
Revised: 12 April 2023
Accepted: 20 April 2023
Published: 21 April 2023

1. Introduction

Along with the explosion of data in devices and network terminals, an ever-increasing number of AI applications and services relying on these devices/terminals are emerging. Nevertheless, subject to laws on data privacy protection, the traditional centralized or decentralized training paradigm of the AI model is no longer feasible in many scenarios [1]. The phenomenon that devices/terminals are unwilling to share their private data which hinders the centralized training is called "data island". To this end, Federated Learning (FL) [2], a novel AI model training and inference framework, is promoted and introduced in many network edge intelligence applications, e.g., network anomaly detection [3] and internet traffic classification [4]. As an effective solution to deal with the "data island" problem and protect data privacy, FL aggregates various network nodes and uses their local parameters or gradient information. Therefore, it trains

a global model together without data moving and sharing. It is practical with respect to protecting data privacy.

In an FL application, the task is defined before learning begins, making FL a typical task-driven learning paradigm. Thus, as a task-driven approach [5], supervised learning is widely used to train a model with explicit functions in FL. For example, models for anomaly detection and attack classification in cybersecurity [6] are all trained via supervised learning.

Note that model training through supervised learning usually needs a large amount of labeled data, whereas data generated in most network nodes lack labels. Consequently, FL cannot be directly applied for secure model training with network data.

In previous work, efforts have been made to address the typical challenges of FL, i.e., communication efficiency, heterogeneous data, limited computation, incentive mechanism, etc. Unfortunately, almost all of the previous works have assumed that the local data of each node are perfectly ready to be used for training. Network data are unprocessed and unlabeled, while model training is completed via supervised learning with labeled data in most scenarios. Thus, it is impractical to execute model training directly with local unlabeled data.

Due to the particular characteristics of network data, we face several challenges when applying FL to network data. First, it is hard to label all the data (namely data annotation) in network applications. For those online network applications, e.g., network anomaly detection [3], data are constantly being generated, making accurate data annotation extremely costly. Thus, it is critical and challenging to minimize the cost of data annotation while maximizing the model benefit. Second, due to the independence of data annotation on each node, the annotated labels could be inconsistent, i.e., different labels may appear for the same data class. For example, in labeling the types of network attacks, the denial of service can be marked as "DoS" in a node, while "DDoS" is used as the label in another node. This issue could bring trouble to FL model training since the standard and uniform label is required for single-task model training. Nevertheless, besides the challenges of annotating data, non-IID data are another crucial challenge in FL, especially in scenarios where local data are unlabeled. As one of the basic technologies in the field of cyberspace security, internet traffic classification is also affected by non-IID data [4]. In addition, experimental studies in [7] show that even the existing state-of-the-art FL algorithms could not be optimal in all scenarios of non-IID data.

In summary, although FL learning could solve the "data island" problem and protect the privacy of data, it suffers from the gradient variance intensified by non-IID data. In addition, the pre-trained model and the global gradient estimation require the server to prepare the task-related data in advance. However, in reality, the local data are constantly generated and unable to be fully labeled, which deviates from the assumption of much state-of-art research. The above challenges have inspired us to design a new FL framework that could jointly address data annotation and non-IID issues. In this way, the new framework is expected to be used for network data. More specifically, we aim to answer the following significant questions in this work: (i) Is it possible to reduce the annotation workload by screening out the most crucial instances in current model training? (ii) Combined with data annotation, is there any way to address the issue caused by non-IID data during the federated optimization?

In this work, we pursue fast convergence of model training and high accuracy of model inference with unlabeled non-IID network data. The paper makes the following major contributions:

- To reduce the cost of data annotation, we introduce the idea of active learning [8] that a pre-trained model is used to test current unlabeled data and the instances with the wrong test result are selected to annotate manually. These manually annotated instances are used to train and update the pre-trained model.
- To eliminate the negative impact of non-IID data, we consider designing a gradient correction mechanism in which an unbiased estimation of the global gradient is used to correct the local gradient so that the gradient variance caused by non-IID data can be eliminated.
- Combining the advantages of active learning and FL, we design an accelerated **semi**-**f**ederated **a**ctive **l**earning (**semi-FAL**) optimization framework to handle the unlabeled and non-IID issues of local data using existing public historical data. The experiment result shows the higher accuracy, faster convergence and robustness of the proposed

framework semi-FAL compared with the other two typical federated learning frameworks.

The rest of the article is organized as follows. The following section reviews related literature. Next, the architecture design of semi-federated active learning is presented. Following that, operation details of semi-FAL are given. Then, the proposed architectures and mechanisms are evaluated in a case study. The discussion section compares our method with others. We also discuss future work in this section. The final section concludes the article.

2. Related Work

This section reviews existing solutions for training with unlabeled data in FL. Then, several representative methods are introduced to reduce the negative impact of heterogeneous data.

2.1. Solutions of Unlabeled Data Challenge

Data annotation is a practical challenge for the implementations of FL since the cost of annotation is generally high. Some studies have been conducted to find solutions for training with unlabeled data [9–11]. Federated Active Learning (F-AL) [9] is proposed to reduce the annotation cost through active learning and sample strategies. In F-AL, instances would be scored by an auxiliary model trained via FL and the instances with the highest scores would be annotated. Unsupervised learning is introduced in [10] and the federated of unsupervised learning method (FedUL) is proposed. In FedUL, the unlabeled client data are transformed into surrogate labeled data and the client model is modified to form a surrogate supervised FL task so that existing FL methods can be used. Dong et al. expected to make efficient use of distributed unlabeled medical data via a robust federated contrastive learning framework [11].

2.2. Solutions of Statistical Challenge

The statistical heterogeneity caused by non-IID data is a crucial factor, which impacts the practical application of FL. Currently, the performance of most FL algorithms can be better guaranteed with the IID data [2], while the convergence would be slowed down in non-IID settings [12]. A lot of studies have been conducted to tackle this issue [13–25]. These solutions are proposed from three aspects, i.e., local data, server setting and update rule. Zhao et al. expected to improve the local non-IID data by sharing a small subset dataset globally in [13]. Jeong et al. applied distillation and augmentation to improve the data distribution structure [14]. In addition, local batch normalization is also used to alleviate the feature shift caused by non-IID data in [16]. Instead of making an effort on local data, Xie et al. propose a multi-center FL framework where clients are divided into several groups according to the distribution of their local data [18]. In this multi-center framework, each center trains a global model. Since clients in the same group have similar distribution data, the global model trained in each center would not be heavily impacted by non-IID data. This multi-center FL framework applies a kind of clustering idea. Based on the clustering idea, more methods have been proposed, such as federated attentive message passing [21], the experience-driven control framework, FAVOR [22]. Moreover, some novel update rules have been designed to address the non-IID issue, such as SCAFFOLD [17], FedProto [19], FedPD [25], ASO-Fed [24]. In SCAFFOLD, control variates are used to reduce the impact of non-IID data. Instead of aggregating model parameters or gradients, FedProto transmits and aggregates prototypes. FedPD is designed from the primal-dual optimization perspective. An asynchronous update strategy is applied in ASO-Fed to tackle the heterogeneous issue.

All the above solutions are proposed under the assumption that local data have been annotated with the uniform rule, i.e., local data could be used to train the local and global models directly. However, data are often unlabeled after being generated in practice, especially in online scenarios. Motivated by the requirement to handle the challenges of data annotation and heterogeneous data together, we design an accelerated federated optimization framework, semi-FAL, for unlabeled data in the online network. In our semi-FAL, a server is expected to supply the pre-trained model and the global gradient estimation for clients. For this target, a task-driven federated network building architecture is designed to find a node with sufficient computing and data resources as the server from the global perspective. Focus on the local of each node in the federated network, the data-driven collaborative annotation and computation architecture is designed to address the data annotation and non-IID data issues. Then, we propose two-phase model training operations under the two designed architectures, respectively. In phase I, we strategically match the data of network nodes with the task, choosing an optimal node with task-related historical data and plenty of computing resources as the server and other nodes possessing task-related data to form a client set. Accordingly, a basic network of semi-FAL consists of a server node and several client nodes. In phase II, within the basic network formed in phase I, the server would provide a pre-trained model to help select crucial instances and clients would annotate these instances with the unified standard. In addition, an unbiased estimation of the global gradient would be computed and delivered by the server to clients to reduce the gradient variance caused by non-IID data.

3. Framework Design of Semi-Federated Active Learning

3.1. Framework Overview and Design Requirements

In the past decade, the scale of the network (e.g., IoT) has increased dramatically, resulting in massive network data. As the essential part of understanding, managing and operating modern wide-area, data-center and cellular networks [26], most of these data would be unlabeled and non-IID. To realize the effective use of these data, we design a novel FL framework to apply these unlabeled and non-IID data to train a model with fast convergence and high accuracy, as illustrated in Figure 1. Specifically, the framework could be divided into two phases: federated network building and collaborative learning. These two phases have their focus. The former focuses on selecting suitable nodes from the global network to construct the federated network. At the same time, the significant points of the latter are the operations on each node to realize the collaborative data annotation and model training with unlabeled non-IID data. In the design, some basic requirements need to be followed.

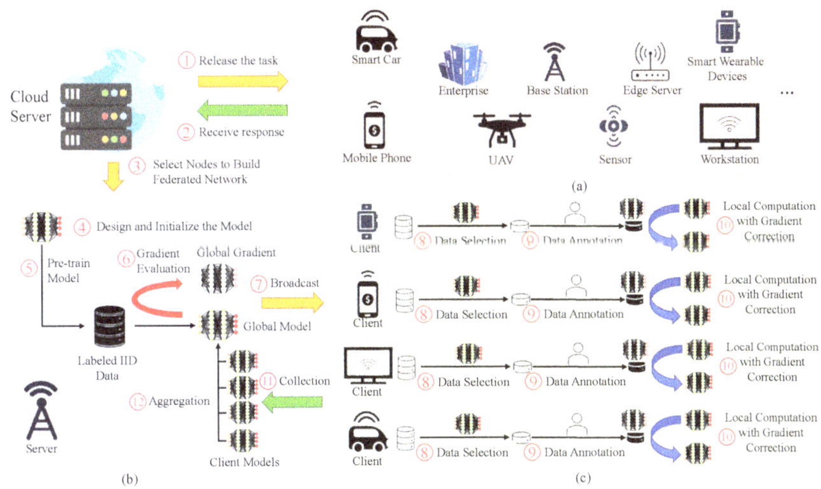

Figure 1. Semi-Federated Active Learning Framework: (**a**) task-driven servers and client selection; (**b**) server operation; (**c**) client operation.

- **Data Privacy Protection.** As the most critical point in data development and utilization, data privacy protection is the most important in our framework. To eliminate the risk of privacy leakage, the raw data of each network node would be only processed and used locally. Moreover, the model and the gradient transmitted between the server and the client would be encrypted.

- **Robustness for different data and models.** The models and data used to complete the task are different in different scenarios. Thus, the framework we designed needs to be able to deal with different datasets and models in various scenarios.

3.2. Global Perspective: Task-Driven Federated Network Building

Instead of randomly selecting a group of network nodes to build a federated network, we adopt a task-driven server and client selection strategy. Generally speaking, by releasing the task in the global network, we could receive the response from the target group where various network nodes would be contained, such as mobile phones, smart cars, enterprises, etc., as illustrated in Figure 1a. As the base of our semi-FAL, we would like to select a node having sufficiently idle computing resources and task-related labeled data to be the server of the federated network. Nodes with good infrastructures, such as enterprises, base stations and edge servers, usually have more computing resources than those primarily used to provide applications. In addition, data are produced constantly. For historical data, it is made to be a public dataset, deleted or stored in some nodes. For example, historical data that are related to the business would be accessible and found in an enterprise node. Thus, an optimal node with plenty of computing resources and historical data could be found among the target group as the server.

Note that the data stored in the server are expected to be labeled and IID so that the model pre-trained by the server could distinguish each class of data and the global gradient estimated by the server could be approximately unbiased. The IID data could be constructed via data augmentation [27], such as flipping, translation, rotation, etc. In some extreme scenarios, it may be hard to find a node with all data classes to construct an IID dataset. Multiple nodes could be selected as a server group to pre-train a model federatively. In addition, the performance of the pre-trained model would be limited since the data used are just historical data; that is, the pre-training model can only be used as a coarse-grained model to correctly identify the part of unlabeled data. In the following section, we disclose more details on how to use the data in the server to help the data annotation locally and to improve the performance of the final model. In this article, we name the task-driven server and client selection mechanism phase I operation toward the semi-FAL.

3.3. Local Perspective: Data-Driven Collaborative Annotation and Computation

As mentioned before, the server of our federated network would not just play a role in delivering, collecting and aggregating models but also supply some necessary computation with the data in the server to address the challenges of local unlabeled non-IID data. To reduce the cost of data annotation and improve the performance of the model effectively, we further design the collaborative annotation and computation architecture for FL. Specifically, a data-driven collaborative annotation and computation architecture is proposed to realize the unified annotation of local data and reduce the impact of non-IID data on model training. Note that data annotation and model training are interleaved so that this architecture would still be effective in online network settings.

The architecture and detailed design of a data annotation and training system in the server and the client are shown in Figure 1b and Figure 1c, respectively. The design includes two major components: the server and the client.

The Server: As the core of the federated network, the server would continue to undertake the same basic tasks as the server in general FL: global model design and initialization, global model broadcast, local model collection and local model aggregation. However, unlike the server in general FL, the server in our design possesses an IID dataset with labeled data. Thus, the initial model could be trained with this dataset before broadcasting the global model to the client. In addition, an unbiased estimation of the gradient for the current global model would be computed with the dataset. Then, this gradient would be delivered with the global model to the client together in each round. This global gradient would play a significant role in reducing the gradient variance caused by non-IID data.

The Client: The client nodes are usually the terminal devices that are closest to the users. The data of the client are often raw and produced constantly. To make use of the data, it is necessary to annotate them first. However, manual annotation is costly; that is, it would be unreasonable to annotate all the new data generated in each round manually. In addition, although the cost of automatic annotation via a trained model is low, the effect of annotation would be inferior. Thus, we draw on the idea of active learning. In each round of training, the global model is first used to test the local data and then the instances with wrong test results would be screened out to be annotated manually. After local data annotation, local training is ready to be executed.

With the support of the above data annotation and model training mechanism, FL could be executed with unlabeled and non-IID data. More details on the computing of semi-FAL are disclosed below. Specifically, we name the data-driven collaboration annotation and computation mechanism phase II operation toward the semi-FAL in this article.

4. Operations of Semi-Federated Active Learning

In this section, we first introduce relevant entities involved in the designed architectures and then present details about the aforementioned two key phases in achieving the semi-FAL.

4.1. Involved Entities

Cloud Server: A cloud server is selected to complete the overall coordination of the framework. As illustrated in Figure 1, the cloud server is mainly used to choose suitable nodes from the global network to build the federated network so that the training task can be completed. Additionally, the construction of the federated network would directly affect the total effect of the task with the network data.

Computation-intensive Nodes: The computation-intensive nodes mainly denote network nodes with a well constructed computing environment, such as base stations, edge servers and enterprises. In addition to sufficient computing resources, some historical data would be stored in these nodes. The above conditions fit our requirements for the server in our semi-FAL. Thus, these nodes are the primary candidates for the server in our federated network. The filtering of these nodes could be done through the feedback of nodes after releasing the task.

Terminal devices: Terminal devices are the main force of data generation and usually play the role of the client in a federated network. They are closest to users and the real environment of various applications. The model trained via FL or our semi-FAL would finally be deployed in terminal devices to supply the intelligent services. Thus, these nodes often have the most relevant data for target model training. However, data processing and model training are both energy intensive processes and the terminal device, especially mobile devices, tends to have limited battery storage. The quality of user experience (QoE) provided by the terminal device is determined by the service response and battery life of the device. Thus, to ensure a good QoE, the computations performed locally are preferably lightweight and fast so as not to occupy and consume too many computing and battery resources. A meaningful way to reduce the cost of model training with unlabeled data is that only the critical instances are selected to be annotated and used to train the local model.

4.2. Phase I: Establishment of Federated Network

Nodes Sets: To build a federated network for the current task, the first step is to identify all nodes that are willing and able to participate in the task. According to the actual conditions of these nodes and the requirements for the server in our semi-FAL, they could be divided into two sets: the server set dominated by computation-intensive nodes and the client set dominated by terminal devices. More factors, such as the connectivity with the other nodes, the cost to set this node as the server, etc., need to be considered for the server node. For the client node, whether it could provide the manual annotation of the data also needs to be considered.

Federated Network: A general federated network consists of a server and several clients. Given the above two sets of nodes for building the federated network, an optimal server node is expected to be selected to connect to as many client nodes as possible so that more network data can be used federatively to optimize the global model. Thus, the optimal server node would be selected from the server set through careful consideration of task-related data reserves, idle computing resources, communication resources and connectivity in the network.

Further Considerations: We also consider some practical constraints in building the federated network. First, historical data are rare in some emerging fields, so it is hard to find a node with plenty of computing and data resources as a server. At this point, we could find a node in the client set via some incentives to serve as a server. Second, the scale of the client is so large that a server is not enough to sustain the network. Our framework still works when multiple servers are involved in building the federated network.

4.3. Phase II: Collaborative Data Annotation and Model Training

As we make use of the historical data for the model pre-training, the discrimination accuracy of the model to fresh unlabeled data cannot be high. Therefore, in phase II, we leverage the local data to federatively optimize the global model via iterating data annotation, local training and global aggregation operations, thus further improving the inference accuracy of the model.

Data Annotation (Minimize the Annotation Cost): In each client, to reduce the manual annotation cost as much as possible, we need to find the critical instances for local training in each round. As illustrated in Figure 2a, the global model accepted by the client would be used to annotate local unlabeled data automatically at first. This process is equal to the model test; that is, input the unlabeled instance into the model and then output the label of the instance. After outputting the label of all local data, the owner of these data would determine whether these labels are correct. In this process, the data of the same label would be presented to the owner in the form of a batch so that the mislabeled data can be easily detected. These mislabeled instances are the critical instances in this round of training. Therefore, these instances would be selected and annotated manually as shown in Lines 5–6 of Algorithm 1. Furthermore, this process could be replaced by some intelligent methods, such as setting the probability thresholds of model output for a different label. Note that this would lead to the worse non-IID issue where only the key instances of each client are used to execute the local training. Thus, we design a gradient correction mechanism to reduce the negative impact of non-IID data.

Model Training (Reduce the Impact of Non-IID Data): The essence of model training is to continuously optimize model parameters to adapt to training instances. Thus, different distributed data would correspond to different optimization directions. In other words, non-IID data would cause gradient variance, which would make the model deviate from the global optimal. The essence of reducing the negative impact of non-IID data is to eliminate the gradient variance. Therefore, we design a novel gradient descent strategy as illustrated in Figure 2b. After completing the data annotation, for an arbitrary node j, a local gradient estimation g_j^* would be computed with the key instances and the global model. In each epoch of local training, the gradient descent could be formulated as the following:

$$w_{j,r+1} \leftarrow w_{j,r} - \eta_t(\nabla f(x_r, w_{j,r}) - g_j^* + \widetilde{g})$$

where $w_{j,r+1}$ denotes the local model in epoch $r+1$, η_t is the learning rate, f_j denotes the local loss function, x_r denotes the data instance and $\widetilde{g}$ is the global gradient estimation. Intuitively, we use the global gradient estimation $\widetilde{g}$ calculated in the server as the main body and the difference between the real, local gradient and the local gradient estimation $(\nabla f(x_r, w_{j,r}) - g_j^*)$ as the increment to update the local model as illustrated in Figure 2c.

The track in yellow is on behalf of the training process of local model $w_{j,r}$ toward $w_{j,r+1}$ in the general scenario. The grey line close to it denotes the local gradient estimation g_j^*. The red arrows between the two tracks are key updates for the local model. The dotted line in grey represents the global gradient estimation $\widetilde{g}$. The dotted line in blue is the direction of using the global gradient. The semi-FAL tries to add the difference (red arrows) to the global gradient to relieve the gradient variance and preserve the update feature of each client. Therefore, the local model $w_{j,r}$ is conducted to be $w_{j,r+1}$. In this way, the model in each client node would be optimized in a uniform direction so that no gradient variance would be generated. The update rule of global gradient $\widetilde{g}$ and other calculation details are given in Algorithm 1.

Algorithm 1 Semi-FAL: Semi-Federated Active Learning with Unlabeled Data

Input learning rate η_t for clients, learning rate α_t for server, model $\widetilde{w}$ and global gradient $\widetilde{g}$
for each iteration $t = 1, 2, \ldots, T$ **do**
  $S_t \leftarrow$ (sample a set of devices randomly)
  for each device $j \in S_t$ **in parallel do**
    $Y_j = \widetilde{w}(X_j)$
    $x_j^* \leftarrow$ (select the fault instances manually via Y_j)
    Picks x_j^* and computes the local gradient g_j^*
    $g_j^* = \nabla f(x_j^*, \widetilde{w})$
    $w_{j,1} = \widetilde{w}$
    for each local round $r = 1, 2, \ldots, R$ **do**
      $w_{j,r+1} \leftarrow w_{j,r} - \eta_t(\nabla f(x_r, w_{j,r}) - g_j^* + \widetilde{g})$
    end for
    $\Delta w_j = w_{j,R} - \widetilde{w}$
  end for
  server aggregation:
  $\widetilde{w} \leftarrow \widetilde{w} + \alpha_t \frac{1}{|S_t|} \sum_{j \in S_t} \Delta w_j$
  $\widetilde{g} = \widetilde{g} + \frac{1}{|S_t|} \sum_{j \in S_t} g_j^*$
end for

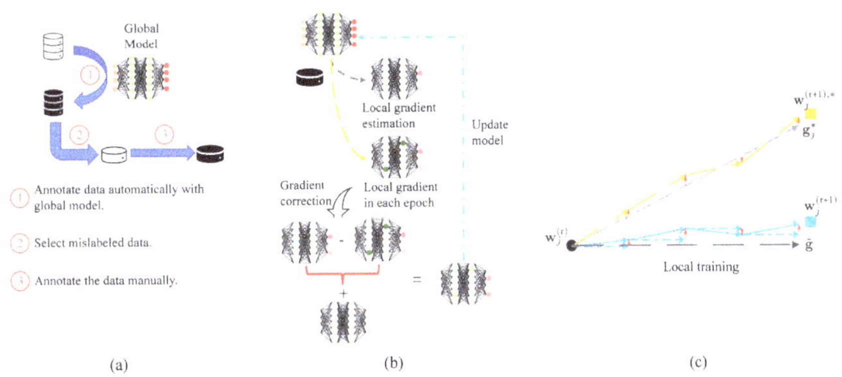

Figure 2. Detailed design of the collaborative data annotation and model training architecture in each client. (**a**) The annotation process of semi-FAL. The mislabeled data would be picked and labeled manually after being labeled by the model. (**b**) The model training process of semi-FAL. The semi-FAL uses gradient correction to direct the local gradient. (**c**) The update direction of local model.

Further Considerations: We further consider some practical considerations during the data annotation and the model training operations. Even if the semi-FAL could accelerate the process that experts label the new data, it still requires the expert to browse all labeled results generated via the model. Moreover, the framework needs to exchange information between the server node and client nodes. This might arouse the risk of being attacked. Security assurance and communication efficiency are essential to the implementation of FL in reality. To address these issues, we propose some ideas.

First, to ensure that each round of training could be completed quickly, the maximum amount of data to be annotated in each client should be determined by the local computing power. Second, as the model and the global gradient are delivered to the client, the cost of communication in our framework would be higher. Thus, the compression of the global model and the global gradient should be executed via lossless compression techniques, such as Sparse Ternary Compression [28] and Sparse Dithering [29], before broadcast. Third, due to the data of the server being historical data, as new data are generated, the global gradients calculated using the data of the server would be biased. Therefore, we could consider computing an unbiased global gradient estimation in a client node with IID data.

5. A Case Study

5.1. Experimental Setting

Scenario: In this case study, we consider completing online image classification tasks with a federated network consisting of 1 server and 100 clients. A small IID dataset is pre-deployed in the server to simulate the historical data and this dataset is labeled. For the client, we control the increase of the local data in each round and these data are unlabeled. To make the experiment more realistic, the data added to each client node in each round would match the distribution of the local historical data.

Datasets: We choose two classical image classification datasets, MNIST (http://yann.lecun.com/exdb/mnist/, accessed on 26 August 2022) and Fashion-MNIST (https://github.com/zalandoresearch/fashion-mnist, accessed on 26 August 2022), to evaluate the performance of our semi-FAL. MNIST is a handwritten digit dataset containing 60,000 training instances and 10,000 test instances. The Fashion-MNIST dataset consists of 60,000 28×28 greyscale images in 10 classes, with 6000 images per class. To investigate the robustness of our proposed framework for non-IID data, two data setting schemes are given: (1) IID setting: an equal amount of data is allocated to each client randomly. (2) Non-IID setting: to simulate non-IID data, the dataset is always divided and distributed to clients manually. In our design, the data are sorted via labels and then two classes of data are assigned to each client. Note that, to simulate the sequential data in an online network, we control the local data of each client increasing constantly.

Model: We design two models, logistic regression (LR) for MNIST and convolutional neural network (CNN) for Fashion-MNIST, in our experiments. Specifically, the CNN is designed with two 5×5 convolution layers (the first with 32 channels, the second with 64, each followed with 2×2 max pooling), a fully connected layer with 512 units and ReLu activation and a final softmax output layer (1,663,370 total parameters).

Benchmarks: We compare the performance of our semi-FAL with two typical FL frameworks, FedAvg [2] and SCAFFOLD (Stochastic Controlled Averaging algorithm) [17]. To ensure the fairness of the comparison, the pre-trained model is set as the initial model in each setting. Specifically, the model test accuracy from the following four settings is compared:

- Semi-FAL(UD): The model is trained with unlabeled data (UD) and local training is executed with the key instances.
- Semi-FAL(LD): The model is trained with labeled data (LD) and local training is executed with all local data.
- FedAvg: The model is trained with all local labeled data and local models are directly aggregated via weighted average without gradient correction.
- SCAFFOLD: The model is trained with all locally labeled data through SCAFFOLD. It uses a control variance to correct the 'client-drift' in its local updates.

5.2. Results and Analysis

Semi-FAL yields higher accuracy with benchmarks. Figure 3 summarizes the performance of semi-FAL compared with benchmarks. Figure 3a shows the result of applying different FL models using MNIST, LR. The four models using semi-FAL, no matter whether it is non-IID or IID and unlabeled data or labeled data, could obtain the highest accuracy after 100 iterations. Other contrast methods behave much worse than semi-FAL. The basic model FedAvg using non-IID data achieves the lowest accuracy. This means simply taking the average of the gradient generated from each client node might be inefficient when data are non-IID; more iterations should occur to increase the accuracy. Figure 3b is the result of using Fashion-MNIST, CNN also through 100 iterations. Under this scenario, all of the models behave relevantly unstably. Semi-FAL still obtains the best performance. Figure 3a,b both show that under the same model and dataset, the performance of the model trained via semi-FAL with unlabeled non-IID data is close to that of the model trained with unlabeled IID data. This strongly proves the effectiveness of the gradient correction mechanism in overcoming non-IID data issues.

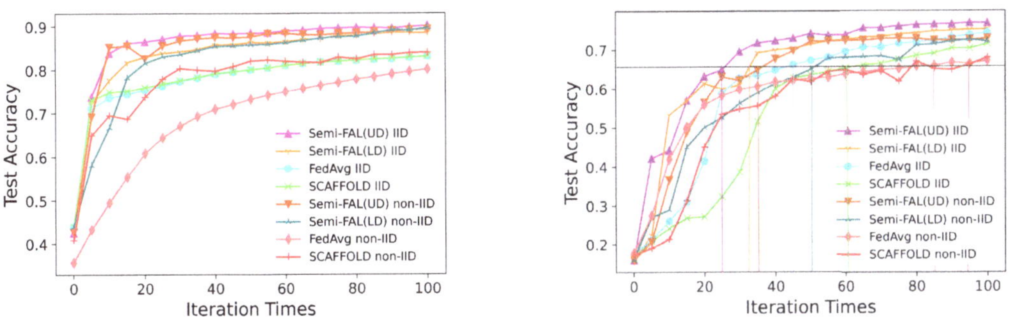

(**a**) *MNIST*, LR (**b**) *Fashion-MNIST*, CNN

Figure 3. The result of the case study: test accuracy vs. iteration rounds for the MNIST, LR and FEMNIST, CNN in IID and non-IID data settings.

Semi-FAL achieves faster convergence. In the MNIST, LR scenario, the semi-FAL(UD) using IID data could obtain high accuracy over 0.8 within 20 iterations but FedAvg and SCAFFOLD are unable to obtain the proximate performance even beyond 100 iterations. In the Fashion-MNIST, CNN scenario, the dotted lines show other methods need many more iterations than semi-FAL if they want to achieve accuracy at the same level. In addition, as is shown in the graph, the semi-FAL even performs better in unlabeled data than in labeled data scenarios. That is because semi-FAL could achieve faster convergence and high test accuracy with unlabeled data than with labeled data. The difference between these two settings is that a critical instance selection process would be executed before local training with unlabeled data and only the critical instances would be annotated and used to train the local model, while all labeled data would be used to train the model directly in the setting of labeled data. This scheme can select the most helpful instances for current global model training. In fact, this scheme can also be used in labeled data settings to accelerate the convergence of the model.

The performance of semi-FAL is robust to the model and data. We apply two different models, LR and CNN, and two different datasets, MNIST and Fashion-MNIST, to execute the empirical studies. The results in Figure 3 demonstrate that semi-FAL could achieve the best performance among all benchmarks under different model and data conditions. Note that, in all scenarios of our case study, the local data of each node are added constantly to simulate the online situation. Our semi-FAL is also robust to the online network data. However, it is shown that when applying MNIST, LR semi-FAL could achieve much higher accuracy than applying Fashion-MNIST, CNN after 100 iterations. This is common for all frameworks; the possible reason might be that the efficiency of the CNN is impacted by federated learning and needs more iterations to obtain higher accuracy. The results inspire us to do more research on applying semi-FAL to different models and datasets.

6. Discussion

In the experiments, we compared semi-FAL with two typical FL frameworks. The results show the efficiency of semi-FAL. There are seldom other methods that struggle to combine active learning and FL. Ref. [30] assumes the participating users are willing to share requested data between neighbor users. This puts emphasis on using active learning to select critical data that helps achieve balanced data distribution. However, if the requested data are sensitive, it would violate the principle of FL. Ref. [31] applies federated active learning on medical images. However, the goal of the work is to accelerate the training phase of federated learning but it ignores the impact of non-IID data. Furthermore, it only uses the extant active learning method and federated learning method, while semi-FAL designs a new method to solve the gradient variance. Ref. [32] also attaches importance to the application of federated active learning rather than the improvement of the method. Although ref. [33] touches upon the phenomenon of non-IID data, the authors do not solve it explicitly. Our semi-FAL is a universal framework that could be treated as the complement of these methods.

Future work. There are some possible constraints as discussed in Sections 4.2 and 4.3; we would try to solve them in the next step. In addition, We use typical datasets and models in the experiments while there are lots of new investigations that use deep learning methods to process complex images, e.g., [34]. We could do further research concerning applying semi-FAL on various different models and datasets to check its consistent efficiency. Through our investigation, we found that federal learning is applied to different scenarios: intrusion detection [33], network traffic prediction [4,35], etc. Our semi-FAL shows its superiority on the benchmarks, but its performance in the real environment is still unknown. The gap between reality and experiment is considerable. The predictable challenges derive from the inherent characteristics of FL and we should make further improvements in communication efficiency. In the future, we would use the proposed framework to solve practical problems in reality and test its robustness.

7. Conclusions

In this article, we propose the semi-federated active learning framework to realize accelerated federated optimization for online network data. It is an FL framework designed for training with unlabeled network data. The global model annotates the unlabeled local data automatically. The mislabeled data are viewed as critical instances and they are used to train the local model. The server would estimate the global gradient and use it to correct the local gradient to reduce the negative impact of non-IID data. Results from a case study demonstrate that semi-FAL is effective in dealing with the data annotation and non-IID data issues to realize the fast convergence and high accuracy of model training.

Author Contributions: Software, Y.H.; Writing—original draft, Y.Z.; Writing—review & editing, J.S. and R.H.; Project administration, W.K. All authors have read and agreed to the published version of the manuscript.

Funding: This research was funded by Excellent Youth funding of the Hunan Provincial Education Department [Grant No. 22B0938] and Hunan Province Legal Youth Research Project [Grant No. 22HNFX-D-004].

Data Availability Statement: The data supporting our reported results is open dataset. MNIST could be found in http://yann.lecun.com/exdb/mnist/, accessed on 21 March 2023, and Fashion-MNIST could be found in https://github.com/zalandoresearch/fashion-mnist, accessed on 21 March 2023.

Conflicts of Interest: The authors declare no conflict of interest.

References

1. Yang, Q.; Liu, Y.; Cheng, Y.; Kang, Y.; Chen, T.; Yu, H. Federated learning. *Synth. Lect. Artif. Intell. Mach. Learn.* **2019**, *13*, 1–207.
2. McMahan, B.; Moore, E.; Ramage, D.; Hampson, S.; Arcas, B.A. Communication-efficient learning of deep networks from decentralized data. In Proceedings of the Artificial Intelligence and Statistics, PMLR, Ft. Lauderdale, FL, USA, 20–22 April 2017; pp. 1273–1282.
3. Zhao, Y.; Wang, L.; Chen, J.; Teng, J. Network anomaly detection based on federated learning. *J. Beijing Univ. Chem. Technol. Nat. Sci.* **2021**, *48*, 92–99.
4. Mun, H.; Lee, Y. Internet traffic classification with federated learning. *Electronics* **2020**, *10*, 27. [CrossRef]
5. Sarker, I.H. Machine learning: Algorithms, real-world applications and research directions. *SN Comput. Sci.* **2021**, *2*, 1–21.
6. Alazab, M.; Swarna Priya, R.M.; Parimala, M.; Reddy, P.; Gadekallu, T.R.; Pham, Q.V. Federated learning for cybersecurity: Concepts, challenges and future directions. *IEEE Trans. Ind. Inform.* **2021**, *18*, 3501–3509. [CrossRef]
7. Li, Q.; Diao, Y.; Chen, Q.; He, B. Federated learning on non-iid data silos: An experimental study. *arXiv* **2021**, arXiv:2102.02079.
8. Settles, B. *Active Learning Literature Survey*; University of Wisconsin: Madison, WI, USA, 2009.
9. Ahn, J.H.; Kim, K.; Koh, J.; Li, Q. Federated Active Learning (F-AL): An Efficient Annotation Strategy for Federated Learning. *arXiv* **2022**, arXiv:2202.00195.
10. Lu, N.; Wang, Z.; Li, X.; Niu, G.; Dou, Q.; Sugiyama, M. Federated Learning from Only Unlabeled Data with Class-Conditional-Sharing Clients. *arXiv* **2022**, arXiv:2204.03304.
11. Dong, N.; Voiculescu, I. Federated contrastive learning for decentralized unlabeled medical images. In Proceedings of the International Conference on Medical Image Computing and Computer-Assisted Intervention, Strasbourg, France, 27 September–1 October 2021; Springer: Berlin/Heidelberg, Germany, 2021; pp. 378–387.
12. Li, X.; Huang, K.; Yang, W.; Wang, S.; Zhang, Z. On the convergence of fedavg on non-iid data. *arXiv* **2019**, arXiv:1907.02189.
13. Zhao, Y.; Li, M.; Lai, L.; Suda, N.; Civin, D.; Chandra, V. Federated learning with non-iid data. *arXiv* **2018**, arXiv:1806.00582.
14. Jeong, E.; Oh, S.; Kim, H.; Park, J.; Bennis, M.; Kim, S.L. Communication-Efficient On-Device Machine Learning: Federated Distillation and Augmentation under Non-IID Private Data. *arXiv* **2018**, arXiv:1811.11479v1.
15. Briggs, C.; Fan, Z.; Andras, P. Federated learning with hierarchical clustering of local updates to improve training on non-IID data. In Proceedings of the 2020 International Joint Conference on Neural Networks (IJCNN), Glasgow, UK, 19–24 July 2020; pp. 1–9.
16. Li, X.; Jiang, M.; Zhang, X.; Kamp, M.; Dou, Q. Fedbn: Federated learning on non-iid features via local batch normalization. *arXiv* **2021**, arXiv:2102.07623.
17. Karimireddy, S.P.; Kale, S.; Mohri, M.; Reddi, S.; Stich, S.; Suresh, A.T. Scaffold: Stochastic controlled averaging for federated learning. In Proceedings of the International Conference on Machine Learning, PMLR, Virtual, 13–18 July 2020; pp. 5132–5143.
18. Xie, M.; Long, G.; Shen, T.; Zhou, T.; Wang, X.; Jiang, J.; Zhang, C. Multi-center federated learning. *arXiv* **2021**, arXiv:2108.08647.
19. Tan, Y.; Long, G.; Liu, L.; Zhou, T.; Lu, Q.; Jiang, J.; Zhang, C. Fedproto: Federated prototype learning over heterogeneous devices. *arXiv* **2021**, arXiv:2105.00243.
20. Li, T.; Sahu, A.K.; Zaheer, M.; Sanjabi, M.; Talwalkar, A.; Smith, V. Federated optimization in heterogeneous networks. *Proc. Mach. Learn. Syst.* **2020**, *2*, 429–450.
21. Huang, Y.; Chu, L.; Zhou, Z.; Wang, L.; Liu, J.; Pei, J.; Zhang, Y. Personalized cross-silo federated learning on non-iid data. In Proceedings of the AAAI Conference on Artificial Intelligence, Virtual, 2–9 February 2021; Volume 35, pp. 7865–7873.
22. Wang, H.; Kaplan, Z.; Niu, D.; Li, B. Optimizing federated learning on non-iid data with reinforcement learning. In Proceedings of the IEEE INFOCOM 2020—IEEE Conference on Computer Communications, Virtual, 6–9 July 2020; pp. 1698–1707.
23. Shoham, N.; Avidor, T.; Keren, A.; Israel, N.; Benditkis, D.; Mor-Yosef, L.; Zeitak, I. Overcoming forgetting in federated learning on non-iid data. *arXiv* **2019**, arXiv:1910.07796.
24. Chen, Y.; Ning, Y.; Slawski, M.; Rangwala, H. Asynchronous online federated learning for edge devices with non-iid data. In Proceedings of the 2020 IEEE International Conference on Big Data (Big Data), IEEE, Virtual, 10–13 December 2020; pp. 15–24.
25. Zhang, X.; Hong, M.; Dhople, S.; Yin, W.; Liu, Y. Fedpd: A federated learning framework with optimal rates and adaptivity to non-iid data. *arXiv* **2020**, arXiv:2005.11418.
26. Warraich, E.; Shahbaz, M. Constructing the face of network data. In Proceedings of the SIGCOMM'21 Poster and Demo Sessions, Virtual, 23–27 August 2021; pp. 21–23.
27. Shorten, C.; Khoshgoftaar, T.M. A survey on image data augmentation for deep learning. *J. Big Data* **2019**, *6*, 1–48. [CrossRef]
28. Sattler, F.; Wiedemann, S.; Müller, K.R.; Samek, W. Robust and communication-efficient federated learning from non-iid data. *IEEE Trans. Neural Netw. Learn. Syst.* **2019**, *31*, 3400–3413. [CrossRef]
29. Albasyoni, A.; Safaryan, M.; Condat, L.; Richtárik, P. Optimal Gradient Compression for Distributed and Federated Learning. *arXiv* **2020**, arXiv:2010.03246.
30. Shullary, M.H.; Abdellatif, A.A.; Massoudn, Y. Energy-Efficient Active Federated Learning on Non-IID Data. In Proceedings of the 2022 IEEE 65th International Midwest Symposium on Circuits and Systems (MWSCAS), Online, 7–10 August 2022; pp. 1–4.
31. Deng, Z.; Yang, Y.; Suzuki, K.; Jin, Z. FedAL: An Federated Active Learning Framework for Efficient Labeling in Skin Lesion Analysis. In Proceedings of the 2022 IEEE International Conference on Systems, Man and Cybernetics (SMC), Prague, Czech Republic, 9–12 October 2022; pp. 1554–1559.
32. Ahmed, U.; Lin, J.C.W.; Srivastava, G. Semisupervised Federated Learning for Temporal News Hyperpatism Detection. *IEEE Trans. Comput. Soc. Syst.* **2023**, 1–12. [CrossRef]

33. Naeem, F.; Ali, M.; Kaddoum, G. Federated-Learning-Empowered Semi-Supervised Active Learning Framework for Intrusion Detection in ZSM. *IEEE Commun. Mag.* **2023**, *61*, 88–94. [CrossRef]
34. Elhanashi, A.; Lowe, D., Sr.; Saponara, S.; Moshfeghi, Y. Deep learning techniques to identify and classify COVID-19 abnormalities on chest X-ray images. In Proceedings of the Real-Time Image Processing and Deep Learning 2022, Orlando, FL, USA, 3–7 April 2022; Volume 12102, pp. 15–24.
35. Sanon, S.P.; Reddy, R.; Lipps, C.; Schotten, H.D. Secure Federated Learning: An Evaluation of Homomorphic Encrypted Network Traffic Prediction. In Proceedings of the 2023 IEEE 20th Consumer Communications & Networking Conference (CCNC), Las Vegas, NV, USA, 8–11 January 2023; pp. 1–6.

mathematics

MDPI

Article

Greenhouse Micro-Climate Prediction Based on Fixed Sensor Placements: A Machine Learning Approach

Oladayo S. Ajani [1], Member Joy Usigbe [1], Esther Aboyeji [1], Daniel Dooyum Uyeh [2], Yushin Ha [3,4], Tusan Park [4,5] and Rammohan Mallipeddi [1,*]

1 Department of Artificial Intelligence, Kyungpook National University, Daegu 37224, Republic of Korea; oladayosolomon@gmail.com (O.S.A.); usigbemember@gmail.com (M.J.U.); aboyejitolulopeesther@gmail.com (E.A.)
2 Department of Biosystems and Agricultural Engineering, Michigan State University, East Lansing, MI 48824, USA; uyehdooyum@gmail.com
3 Upland-Field Machinery Research Center, Kyungpook National University, Daegu 41566, Republic of Korea; yushin72@knu.ac.kr
4 Smart Agriculture Innovation Center, Kyungpook National University, Daegu 41566, Republic of Korea; tusan.park@knu.ac.kr
5 Department of Bio-Industrial Machinery Engineering, Kyungpook National University, Daegu 41566, Republic of Korea
* Correspondence: mallipeddi.ram@gmail.com

Abstract: Accurate measurement of micro-climates that include temperature and relative humidity is the bedrock of the control and management of plant life in protected cultivation systems. Hence, the use of a large number of sensors distributed within the greenhouse or mobile sensors that can be moved from one location to another has been proposed, which are both capital and labor-intensive. On the contrary, accurate measurement of micro-climates can be achieved through the identification of the optimal number of sensors and their optimal locations, whose measurements are representative of the micro-climate in the entire greenhouse. However, given the number of sensors, their optimal locations are proven to vary from time to time as the outdoor weather conditions change. Therefore, regularly shifting the sensors to their optimal locations with the change in outdoor conditions is cost-intensive and may not be appropriate. In this paper, a framework based on the dense neural network (DNN) is proposed to predict the measurements (temperature and humidity) corresponding to the optimal sensor locations, which vary relative to the outdoor weather, using the measurements from sensors whose locations are fixed. The employed framework demonstrates a very high correlation between the true and predicted values with an average coefficient value of 0.91 and 0.85 for both temperature and humidity, respectively. In other words, through a combination of the optimal number of fixed sensors and DNN architecture that performs multi-channel regression, we estimate the micro-climate of the greenhouse.

Keywords: greenhouse; temperature; relative humidity; optimal sensor locations; multi-channel regression; dense neural network

MSC: 68T20

Citation: Ajani, O.S.; Usigbe, M.J.; Aboyeji, E.; Uyeh, D.D.; Ha, Y.; Park, T.; Mallipeddi, R. Greenhouse Micro-Climate Prediction Based on Fixed Sensor Placements: A Machine Learning Approach. *Mathematics* **2023**, *11*, 3052. https://doi.org/10.3390/math11143052

Academic Editor: Huawen Liu

Received: 23 May 2023
Revised: 4 July 2023
Accepted: 7 July 2023
Published: 10 July 2023

1. Introduction

Agricultural products are crucial to the sustenance of humans and livestock. However, their production is faced with several challenges such as extreme weather conditions, soil erosion, pests, and disease outbreaks, which all have far-reaching effects on crop productivity and growth rate [1,2]. Protected cultivation systems such as greenhouses offer optimal production of agricultural products throughout the year by the appropriate control of micro- and macro-environments suitable for plant growth [3]. Furthermore, protected cultivation systems result in higher income compared to open-field cultivation as a result of their higher returns per unit area [4]. Hence, their adoption is increasing across continents [5]. Despite these benefits, the operation of greenhouses is non-linear in nature due to changing atmospheric conditions [6] and therefore requires intricate monitoring and control to obtain optimal yield. In other words, maintaining suitable temperature, which directly affects the humidity, is essential in greenhouse environmental control as these affect crop growth as well as quality and quantity [7–9]. Specifically, while effective temperature control improves plant growth and minimizes the energy consumed by the system, an appropriate relative humidity range is required to prevent fungal infection and control transpiration [10].

To facilitate monitoring and control in protected cultivation systems, the integration of different advanced sensing technologies becomes eminent [4,11,12]. Basically, sensors installed in greenhouses range from those used to monitor and control micro-climatic conditions such as temperature and relative humidity to soil-related parameters such as moisture, PH, and several others, which are vital for maintaining optimal conditions for favorable crop productivity and growth. In terms of micro-climates, previous studies have shown that monitoring and controlling the temperature and relative humidity within a greenhouse is complex and challenging due to drastic variations in daily and seasonal atmospheric conditions [13].

Generally, sensors are installed arbitrarily in protected systems based on factors such as grower resources, the size of the facility, and technical know-how [14]. Furthermore, in conventional settings, as many sensors as possible are usually installed to facilitate the necessary measurements. However, the use of multiple randomly/inappropriately placed sensors fails to provide measurements that are true estimates of greenhouse micro-climates. In addition, employing a large number of sensors results in large quantities of data that require efficient data management. In other words, the quality of information and consequently the estimation accuracy of micro-climates depend heavily on the number of sensors and their locations/placements. Therefore, optimizing the number of sensors and their locations, though a challenging task, is crucial as it forms the basis for accurate measurement of micro-climates and consequently optimal control of the cultivation system. Additionally, it reduces the overall operating cost of protected cultivation systems.

In the literature, methods have been proposed based on approximate models of partial differential equations (PDEs), such as the error covariance matrix of the Kalman filter or the finite difference method [15,16]. However, these methods were applied without any general systematic procedure to linear systems modeled based on a small number of sensors. Meanwhile, it is important to know that distributed processes, such as in protected cultivation systems, are intrinsically non-linear with infinite dimensions. Therefore, such methods are not appropriate for highly non-linear protected cultivation systems that feature high-dimensional representations. Consequently, different methods, such as genetic algorithms [17,18], Harris hawks optimization [19], the Fisher information matrix [20], the exponential-time exact algorithm [21], the system reliability criterion [22], and Bayesian optimization [23], have been proposed for optimal sensor placement in different application domains.

In terms of optimal sensor placement in protected cultivation systems (greenhouses), Yeon Lee et al. [14] proposed a combination of an error-based and entropy-based approach for the optimal location of temperature sensors. In the work, based on the reference temperature obtained by averaging the temperature data obtained from all the measurement locations, sensor locations with measurements statistically close to reference values were selected. Furthermore, the entropy method was used to realize locations that are greatly influenced by external environmental conditions. Based on these two methods, optimal sensor locations that provide representative data of the entire greenhouse condition, as well as understanding regions with high variations in temperature, were realized. In order to maximize the coverage area (a non-occlusion coverage scheme) in a vegetable-cultivating greenhouse, Wu et al. [24] proposed a hierarchical cooperative particle swarm optimization algorithm for directional sensor placement. Specifically, the decision variables were modeled in terms of the global effective coverage of each sensor and consequently the orientation angles of each sensor. The model demonstrated the capability to avoid occlusion between covered objects and also improved sensor utilization in general. However, the limitation of the aforementioned works is that their investigations were performed for a limited period of time and do not capture all the different planting seasons as well as different weather conditions. Recently, Uyeh et al. [25] proposed a reinforcement learning (RL)-based approach for optimal sensor location in greenhouses using a robust dataset that covers different planting seasons. From the analysis, it was evident that the optimal locations for temperature and relative humidity are different. Specifically, the RL-based model was able to rank the sensor locations based on their importance in estimating the greenhouse micro-climates, for each temperature and relative humidity. However, it was also reported that the ranking of sensor locations for effective measurement of greenhouse micro-climates varies during the different months of the year with the change in the external weather conditions.

Although the assertion that the optimal sensor locations change from month to month is intuitive and supported by a number of recent literature [26,27], the implication is that it would be required to move the sensors every month throughout the growing seasons or to have a huge number of sensors within the cultivation system. This need to relocate the sensors every month is tedious, expensive, and not ideal for a typical grower. Hence in this paper, based on the data collected from a greenhouse used to cultivate strawberries in [25], a framework based on the multi-channeled dense neural network (DNN) is proposed to be used to predict temperature and relative humidity values corresponding to the optimal sensor locations of each month without the need of moving the sensor from one location to another. Specifically, temperature and relative humidity values measured from the fixed locations (say the optimal locations of February) are used to predict the temperature and relative humidity values corresponding to the optimal locations of the other months referred to as target months (March, April, May, June, July, and October). The prediction of the temperature and relative humidity values corresponding to the optimal locations corresponding to the target month will help better estimate the micro-climates of the greenhouse. The effectiveness of the proposed model to predict temperature and relative humidity is demonstrated in terms of the resulting RMSE values. Furthermore, it is shown that the true and predicted sensor values are highly correlated based on Pearson's correlation coefficient. Overall the results obtained show that the proposed framework is efficient and applicable in predicting micro-climates within protected cultivation systems and also comes with the advantage of cost reduction.In addition, as the prediction is performed for each month using the same fixed locations, the proposed framework alleviates the issue related to shifting of the sensors with the change in the external weather conditions. In other words, the novel framework proposed in this paper becomes an initiative basis in the research community for modeling dynamic optimal sensor placement in cultivation systems based on fixed sensors. Finally, it is important to note that the choice of the multi-channel DNN employed in this work is motivated by its simplicity in terms of implementation and deployment since it is well suited to several low-precision hardware for deep learning compared to other variants.

The rest of this paper is organized as follows: In Section 2, a review of related works is presented. Section 3 gives a brief description of the dataset and the associated pre-processing stages. In Section 4, the proposed framework and the associated model are presented. Section 5 presented the results and discussions, and finally, in Section 6 conclusions and future works are highlighted.

2. Review of Related Works

The prediction of micro-climates in protected cultivation systems under different setups has been studied in the literature [9,28–30]. The prediction models often employed range from very basic deterministic models [28] to more advanced learning networks such as ANN [9], multi-layer perceptron neural network (MLP-NN) [29], and extreme learning machine (ELM) [30]. Although these works propose the use of learning or deterministic models for micro-climate predictions, most of them applied these models to achieve different goals. For example, the deterministic model proposed in [28] was aimed at predicting crop temperature from measured air temperature, air density, and other related sensor-measured environmental conditions. The authors argued that rather than the air temperature, the crop temperature is responsible for crop growth and development. In [31], a dynamic model based on energy and mass transport processes, such as the mechanism of conduction, convection, radiation, etc., was employed to realize a prediction model capable of predicting the temperature of air in plant communities. Although the use of such models is very dependent on the structure of the greenhouse model, the authors claimed that the proposed model can be extended for a general greenhouse micro-climate prediction model. In terms of the use of learning networks, Liu et al. [30] proposed the use of ELM for predicting temperature and relative humidity from historical samples of indoor temperature and humidity. In order words, the learning model is aimed at predicting current micro-climates based on previously sampled or measured micro-climates. This is beneficial in situations where the cost of continually measuring micro-climates in terms of energy and communication protocols is high and needs to be minimized. In [9,29], where MLP-NN and ANN were employed, respectively, the aim of the models was to predict indoor or internal micro-climates based on measured external micro-climates such as temperature, relative humidity, wind speed, etc. Although the aforementioned works have considered the prediction of micro-climates in the greenhouse setting, the aims of their predictions are different from ours, where we predict the measurements of micro-climates at varying optimal sensor locations using input data from fixed-placed sensors.

Generally, it can be observed that most of the aforementioned models are relatively not computationally expensive. This is because the choice of model or learning networks for such applications is usually motivated by the nature of the underlying data (real-valued vectors) and the need for quick prediction or low inference time. In a similar fashion, we employ a simple multi-channel learning model that extracts global features from all the input data, which are consequently fed into the channels' response for extracting local features corresponding to micro-climate measurements from different sensor locations.

3. Data Description and Pre-Processing

The dataset [25] employed in the current work contains sensor readings corresponding to internal temperature and relative humidity from 56 two-in-one sensors distributed within a greenhouse used to cultivate strawberries in Daegu, South Korea. The readings were collected for seven months (February, March, April, May, June, July and October). In [25], the same dataset was used to rank the sensor locations corresponding to each of the seven months. A more detailed description of the protected cultivation facility in terms of size and materials from which the data were collected, the type of sensors used, and how the 56 sensors were distributed within the greenhouse are provided in [25].

In Figure 1, the overall layout of the sensors in the considered greenhouse is provided. In addition, the sensor locations corresponding to temperature (T) and relative humidity (RH) corresponding to each month are ranked based on their ability to estimate the micro-climates of the greenhouse [25]. Due to space constraints, we only present the top 10 ranked sensor locations for each month in Table 1. A detailed ranking of the 56 sensors for each month can be found in [25].

In the current work, we assume that N_1 sensors are fixed at N_1 top-ranked locations (referred to as optimal locations) corresponding to the month of February, as shown in Table 1. It should be noted that the optimal locations corresponding to temperature and relative humidity are different. Therefore, the fixed sensor locations for measuring temperature and relative humidity would be different. By observing the measurements obtained at these fixed locations, the goal is to develop a model that can predict the measurements corresponding to the N_2 optimal locations of the target month (say March). By doing so, the micro-climates of the greenhouse in the month of March, the target month, is accurately estimated without shifting the locations of the sensors. In other words, one prediction model is developed corresponding to each target month (March, April, May, June, July, and October). Therefore, the prediction accuracy of the models determines the precision of micro-climates estimation.

Table 1. Locations of 10 top-ranked sensors corresponding to different months for temperature (T) and relative humidity (RH).

Rank	Optimal Locations													
	February		March		April		May		June		July		October	
	T	RH	T	RH	T	RH	T	RH	T	RH	T	RH	T	RH
1	E3	B4	G1	D6	A4	E4	D1	B2	E7	E2	B4	D3	A4	E4
2	F7	F5	C7	G6	E7	D2	B2	A3	C7	E6	D5	B6	E7	D2
3	D1	A1	B6	C4	F7	E3	F5	F6	F6	B2	G7	C3	F7	E3
4	D7	C1	A3	A2	A1	A2	C1	F7	D7	F7	G6	D6	A1	A2
5	E2	C5	D1	D3	E6	E6	D7	G6	G1	H3	E1	D7	E6	E6
6	C4	F2	E2	E6	D2	E5	A7	E3	E1	G6	E7	F5	D2	E5
7	H2	F3	D2	E1	F6	A4	C5	B4	G7	H1	D7	A3	F6	A4
8	E7	H5	B3	F4	G7	D3	F2	H1	B2	B1	G1	C2	G7	D3
9	G1	E2	C1	B4	G6	A5	F3	B1	A2	A6	F7	F4	G6	A5
10	E1	F1	E1	A5	D6	F2	A3	D7	E3	E4	A1	G3	D6	F2

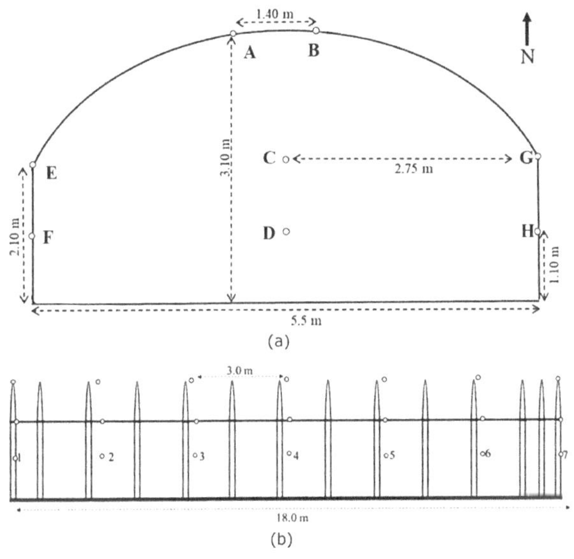

Figure 1. Layout of the 56 two-in-one sensors within the greenhouse: (**a**) Front view; (**b**) Side view.

Since the model is expected to predict the values corresponding to the sensors at the N_2 optimal locations in the target months based on measurements from February, it is important to ensure consistency in comparison across the various months. Therefore, considering that the number of days in February is less, the length of the entire data samples is limited to those available in the month of February. Furthermore, the rows with missing sensor values were removed across all corresponding input and target months.

In terms of implementing the learning networks, the datasets were divided into training, validation, and test sets. The training and test set consists of 80 percent and 20 percent of the entire data, respectively, and 20 percent of the training data were used as the validation set. In order words, the dataset was divided, with 64%, 16%, and 20% of the entire dataset used for training, validation, and testing, respectively. Table 2 provides a summary of the length of the training, test, and validation dataset. Furthermore, to ensure a faster convergence of the model, normalization of the input data based on the mean and standard deviation was performed. In the context of predicting sensor values, the input variable x is a N_1-dimensional vector comprising readings from N_1 temperature or relative humidity sensors for each case. The output y are N_2 real values corresponding to temperature or relative humidity values for the target months.

Table 2. Number of instances in train, validation, and test data.

Predicted Month	Temperature Data			Humidity Data		
	Train	Test	Validate	Train	Test	Validate
March	16,711	5223	4178	16,252	5080	4064
April	16,283	5089	4071	16,516	5162	4130
May	16,639	5200	4160	16,343	5108	4086
June	15,264	4771	3816	15,270	4772	3818
July	14,954	4674	3739	15,160	4738	3791
October	15,549	4860	3888	16,031	5010	4008

4. Methodology

4.1. Dense Neural Network (DNN)-Based Regression Model

Considering that the output is an N_2-dimensional vector where each element represents the sensor values corresponding to each of the N_2 optimal locations for the target month, a multi-channel DNN regression model is employed. In [32], a generalized approach to formalize any NN-based model can be found. In Figure 2, a generalized overview of the DNN architecture, where N_1 and N_2 are corresponding to the number of sensor locations considered at the input and output, respectively, is presented. Based on the target month, say March, the input to the networks is the temperature or relative humidity measurements taken at the N_1 optimal locations of February, which are considered as the fixed locations throughout the whole study. The input is passed through a series of 4 dense layers, namely, dense_0, dense_1 dense_2, and dense_3, as shown in Figure 2, which extract global features from all the N_1 input sensor values. These global features are then fed into N_2 different dense channels, the output of which represents the predicted sensor values corresponding to the N_2 optimal locations of the target month, March. Each of these N_2 dense channels helps extract the local features corresponding to each of the sensor locations. These dense channels consist of a single dense layer of 64 units with Relu activation functions and, consequently, a single-unit, dense layer as the output layer. Using the N_1 fixed locations, the learning model corresponding to each target month is trained for 200 epochs with a batch size of 64. The predicted values based on the proposed model are favorably compared with the real values corresponding to the target month in terms of the root mean square error (RMSE) and correlation coefficients.

4.2. Evaluation Metrics

To evaluate the proposed framework, we used two metrics, namely, root mean -squared error (RMSE) and Pearson's correlation coefficient (R), as expressed in Equations (1) and (2), respectively.

$$RMSE = \sqrt{\frac{1}{N}\sum_{j=1}^{N}(e_t)^2} \quad (1)$$

where N is the number of test samples and e_t is the error between the true and predicted sensor values.

$$R = \frac{\sum(x_i - \bar{x})(y_i - \bar{y})}{\sqrt{\sum(x_i - \bar{x})^2(y_i - \bar{y})^2}} \quad (2)$$

where x_i is the ith true sensor value, $\bar{x}$ is the mean of the true sensor values, y_i is the ith predicted sensor value, and $\bar{y}$ is the mean of the predicted sensor values.

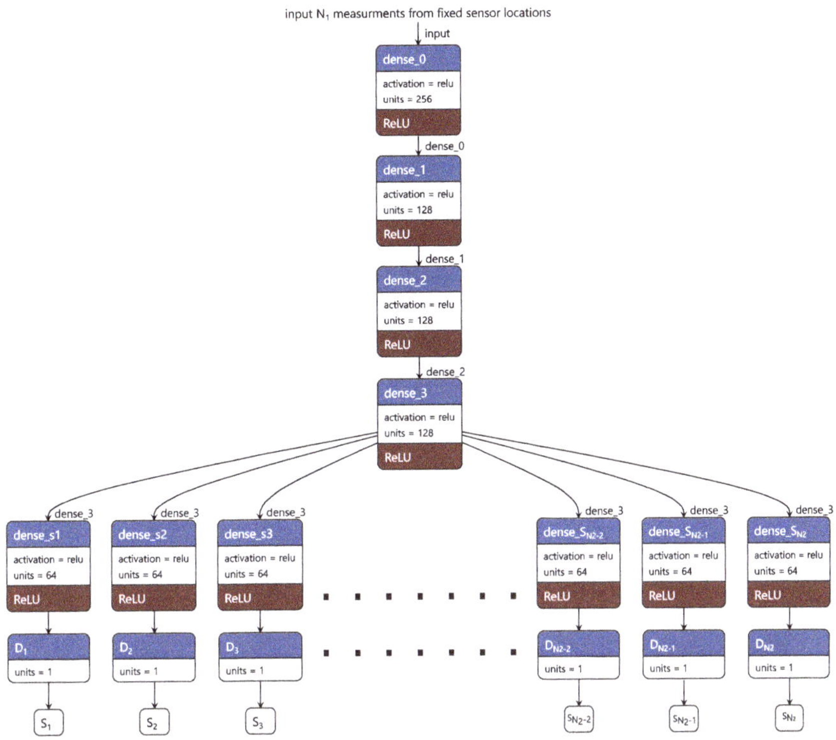

Figure 2. Architecture of proposed deep-neural-network-based multi-channel regression model for efficient micro-climate prediction using fixed sensor locations.

In addition, to evaluate the efficiency of the proposed framework, we provide RMSE values between the measured values (temperature and relative humidity) from the fixed sensor locations and the true measurements corresponding to the N_2 optimal sensors of the target month. In other words, we present the RMSE values, assuming that there exists no prediction model, as the one proposed in the current work. In addition, we present the percentage reduction in the RMSE values by comparing the RMSE values with and without the proposed DNN model.

5. Results and Discussion

The proposed model in this work was implemented and evaluated using Python and Keras installed on a computer with an Intel(R) Core(TM) i7, 2.60 GHz, 16 GB RAM, running Windows 10, 64-bit. The results from the experiments are presented in this section accordingly.

5.1. Temperature and Humidity Prediction RMSE

Based on different values of N_1 and N_2, the results of temperature prediction for all the six months are presented in Table 3 in terms of RMSE. Furthermore, the table includes the resulting RMSE of the sensor readings without the DNN model as well as the percentage error margin incurred with the DNN model compared with those without the DNN model. The resulting RMSE values, as presented in Table 3, is indicative that the error associated with the proposed DNN-based prediction of the temperature values from the optimal sensor locations in each month is significantly lower than those measured without the DNN model. Specifically, the proposed framework, which is based on the DNN model results in a 68.67% reduction in the average RMSE over all the five months compared to those obtained without the DNN model.

In [25], the optimal sensor locations were identified based on the ranking of all the 56 sensors distributed within the greenhouse. Consequently, $N_2 = 10$ sensors were selected. However, there was no clear analysis to justify why only $N_2 = 10$ sensors were selected as the optimal number of sensors. Since the DDN-based prediction of the greenhouse micro-climates is superior to those without the DNN model, we provide further analysis based on the DNN model. Specifically, to show the effect of using different numbers of input (N_1) and output (N_2) sensors, we present a graphical illustration of the percentage reduction in error incurred with the DNN model for N_1 = N_2 = 1, 5, 10, 15, and 20 for each month, respectively, in Figure 3. From the figure, it is clear from the error curves that the knee or saturation point is the N_1 = N_2 = 10 for all the months. This is because a drastic increase in error reduction is observed from N_1 = N_2 = 1 to N_1 = N_2 = 10. However, as the values of N_1 = $N_2 > 10$, the percentage improvement saturates. This might be because of the fact that adding more sensors may not provide any extra information that can help better estimate the micro-climates of the greenhouse. This validates the selection of 10 highly ranked sensors as optimal in [25].

In Table 4, the results of humidity prediction for all the associated months are presented in terms of RMSE. The table further includes the resulting RMSE of the sensor readings obtained without the DNN model. In terms of the RMSE, the results show that there is a 46.21% overall reduction in error of the predicted humidity values based on the DNN-based framework compared to those obtained without the DNN model. In addition, the percentage improvement in the measurement error of relative humidity follows a similar pattern to the temperature, as shown in Figure 3.

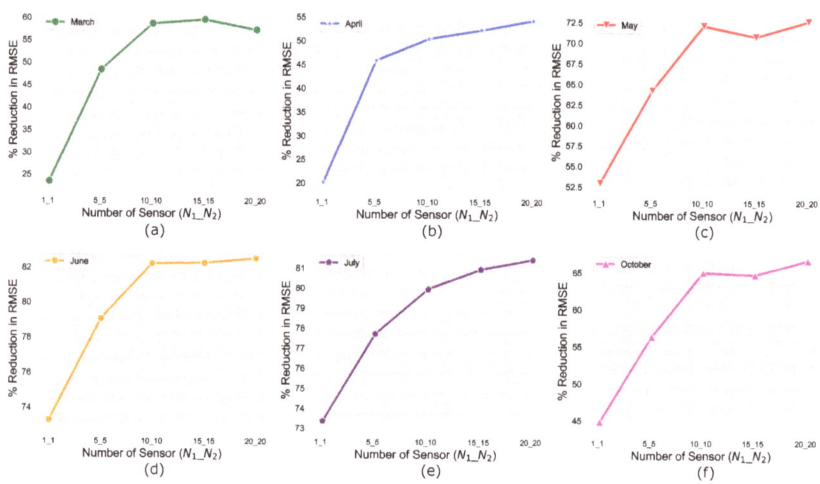

Figure 3. Percentage reduction in error corresponding to temperature measurement using different N_1 and N_2 for (**a**) March, (**b**) April, (**c**), May (**d**), June (**e**), July, and (**f**) October.

Table 3. Comparison of temperature prediction with and without DNN model in terms of RMSE for different values of N_1 and N_2.

Predicted Month	RMSE														
	$N_1 = 1, N_2 = 1$			$N_1 = 5, N_2 = 5$			$N_1 = 10, N_2 = 10$			$N_1 = 15, N_2 = 15$			$N_1 = 20, N_2 = 20$		
	DNN Model	W/O DNN Model	RMSE Reduction (%)	DNN Model	W/O DNN Model	RMSE Reduction (%)	DNN Model	W/O DNN Model	RMSE Reduction (%)	DNN Model	W/O DNN Model	RMSE Reduction (%)	DNN Model	W/O DNN Model	RMSE Reduction (%)
March	3.4313	4.486	23.5	2.2177	4.3059	48.49	1.7744	4.295	58.69	1.7274	4.27676	59.61	1.813	4.253	57.37
April	3.769	4.7207	20.16	2.8217	5.2158	45.9	2.4798	5.0001	50.41	2.3984	5.0265	52.28	2.2835	4.9931	54.27
May	4.879	10.3591	52.9	3.6129	10.0993	64.22	2.8061	10.051	72.08	2.9978	10.2512	70.76	2.8256	10.3058	72.58
June	4.5209	16.91844	73.28	3.4017	16.2493	79.06	2.9317	16.4949	82.23	2.8681	16.1764	82.26	2.8209	16.1334	82.52
July	3.555	13.3485	73.37	3.0707	13.7859	77.72	2.7632	13.7796	79.95	2.5978	13.6444	80.96	2.528	13.6213	81.44
October	3.9781	7.2066	44.8	3.2783	7.5076	56.33	2.6372	7.5388	65.01	2.6396	7.4724	64.68	2.4957	7.4801	66.64

Table 4. Comparison of relative humidity prediction with and without DNN model in terms of RMSE for different values of N_1 and N_2.

Predicted Month	RMSE														
	$N_1 = 1, N_2 = 1$			$N_1 = 5, N_2 = 5$			$N_1 = 10, N_2 = 10$			$N_1 = 15, N_2 = 15$			$N_1 = 20, N_2 = 20$		
	DNN Model	W/O DNN Model	RMSE Reduction (%)	DNN Model	W/O DNN Model	RMSE Reduction (%)	DNN Model	W/O DNN Model	RMSE Reduction (%)	DNN Model	W/O DNN Model	RMSE Reduction (%)	DNN Model	W/O DNN Model	RMSE Reduction (%)
March	14.2951	16.6314	14.05	12.013	16.1924	25.81	10.5982	16.1097	34.21	10.7687	16.13353	33.25	10.4168	16.0724	35.19
April	14.1778	22.7773	37.75	12.768	22.8833	44.2	13.0693	22.18422	41.09	10.5447	21.63	51.25	10.8462	21.8471	50.35
May	17.6504	26.2172	32.68	17.007[illegible]	26.8919	36.76	15.3399	26.9629	43.11	14.4252	26.359	45.27	13.81256	26.35056	47.82
June	15.5105	32.1841	51.81	14.020[illegible]	32.4554	56.8	13.6979	32.4173	57.75	13.28	32.1747	58.73	13.4313	32.08896	58.14
July	11.7474	24.05563	51.17	11.774[illegible]8	24.092	51.13	10.9207	24.2066	54.89	10.4535	23.9932	56.43	10.61337	23.9488	55.68
October	14.1119	23.4509	39.82	13.08[illegible]	23.126	43.4	12.363	23.1641	46.63	12.677	23.6228	46.34	12.6537	23.714	46.64

5.2. Correlation Coefficients

Correlation results based on Pearson's correlation coefficients between the real sensor value readings and predicted sensor value readings are shown in Table 5. From the table, it can be observed that the predicted sensor values are highly correlated with the true sensor values by an average correlation value of 0.91 and 0.85 for temperature and humidity, respectively. These average correlation values are comparable with those from the literature, where the correlation coefficients generally range between 0.977 to 0.980 and 0.825 to 0.967 for temperature and relative humidity, respectively [9,33].

Table 5. Performance comparison of proposed DNN framework for different N_1 and N_2 in terms of Pearson correlation coefficient.

Predicted Month	Correlation Coefficients									
	$N_1 = 1, N_2 = 1$		$N_1 = 5, N_2 = 5$		$N_1 = 10, N_2 = 10$		$N_1 = 15, N_2 = 15$		$N_1 = 20, N_2 = 20$	
	Temperature	Humidity	Temperature	Humidity	Temperature	Humidity	Temperature	Humidity	Temperature	Humidity
March	0.87	0.85	0.93	0.93	0.96	0.94	0.96	0.94	0.95	0.95
April	0.82	0.89	0.92	0.91	0.95	0.93	0.95	0.95	0.95	0.94
May	0.69	0.76	0.82	0.78	0.89	0.82	0.89	0.84	0.9	0.86
June	0.79	0.76	0.87	0.80	0.92	0.81	0.92	0.82	0.91	0.82
July	0.56	0.66	0.78	0.72	0.82	0.75	0.85	0.79	0.84	0.78
October	0.73	0.8	0.85	0.83	0.911	0.84	0.92	0.84	0.92	0.84

Furthermore, both temperature and humidity show a similar correlation trend, where the highest values of 0.95 and 0.94 are obtained in the month of March, while the lowest values of 0.82 and 0.75 are obtained in the month of July, respectively. This can be attributed to how the optimal sensor locations of March and July are distributed relative to the fixed sensor locations. In Figure 4, the fixed sensor locations (green) and optimal sensor locations of target months (March and July) are highlighted (glue) for both temperature and humidity to show the effect of the respective locations in the overall percentage of error reduction. In addition, the optimal locations of the target month (March and July) that overlap with some of the fixed locations are depicted in red.

As depicted in Figure 4a,b, the target months of March and July have four and five overlapping temperature sensor locations with respect to the fixed locations, respectively. Furthermore, as shown in the figure, the sensor locations of March compared to the fixed locations are closer, and for each of the fixed locations, there are also representative locations in March in the same region. However, in July, the sensor locations are much farther from those of the fixed locations when compared with those in March. Therefore, the proximity of the optimal sensor locations of the target month March with respect to the fixed locations resulted in a higher correlation compared to that of July.

Similarly, in terms of humidity, although both March and July have only one overlapping sensor location with fixed locations, as shown in Figure 4c,d, it is clear that the high correlation in March can be associated with the observation that the sensors are well distributed in regions close to the fixed locations. On the other hand, the sensor locations of July are simply packed in regions where none of the fixed sensors are located.

5.3. Effect of Number of Fixed Sensor Locations on the Prediction Accuracy of DNN Model

In the previous section, the analysis was conducted considering that the input and output dimensions, N_1 and N_2, respectively, are equal ($N_1 = N_2$). However, it would be interesting to investigate instances where $N_1 < N_2$ as this would help to facilitate decisions related to the trade-off between cost and accuracy of estimation. Specifically, the input dimension N_1 is directly related to cost, while the output dimension N is directly proportional to the accuracy of prediction, thus providing a better estimation of microclimates. In other words, since N_1 is the number of sensors that would be installed, as the number of N_1 sensors increases, the cost also increases. On the other hand, as the number of N_1 increases, the accuracy of prediction tends to increase until saturation is reached.

Table 6 summarizes the RMSE values for different combinations of the input and output number of sensors. From Table 6, we can observe that the prediction accuracy of the

DNN model, where the input of 10 sensors is provided is better compared to the prediction of the DNN model with only 5 input measurements. However, the prediction accuracy of the DNN model that employs five input measurements is better than the measurements taken from fixed sensors (or without the DNN model). In other words, it is intuitive that installing more sensors can help estimate the environment better, as clearly depicted in Figure 5, but it is expensive. Therefore, the best way is to use fewer sensors and use the model proposed so that the environment can be better estimated by predicting the values of the sensors at top preferred locations.

The above analysis was conducted with respect to the temperature measurement in the greenhouse. However, a similar observation was made with respect to the measurement of relative humidity in the greenhouse.

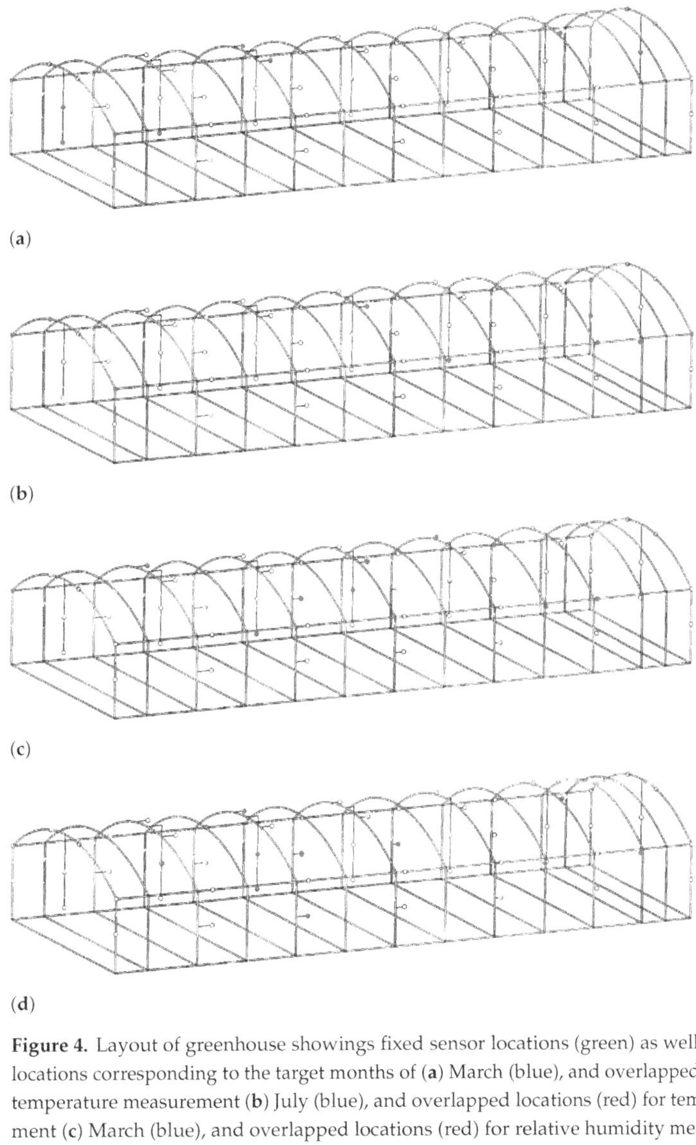

(a)

(b)

(c)

(d)

Figure 4. Layout of greenhouse showings fixed sensor locations (green) as well as optimal sensor locations corresponding to the target months of (**a**) March (blue), and overlapped locations (red) for temperature measurement (**b**) July (blue), and overlapped locations (red) for temperature measurement (**c**) March (blue), and overlapped locations (red) for relative humidity measurement (**d**) July (blue), and overlapped locations (red) for relative humidity measurement.

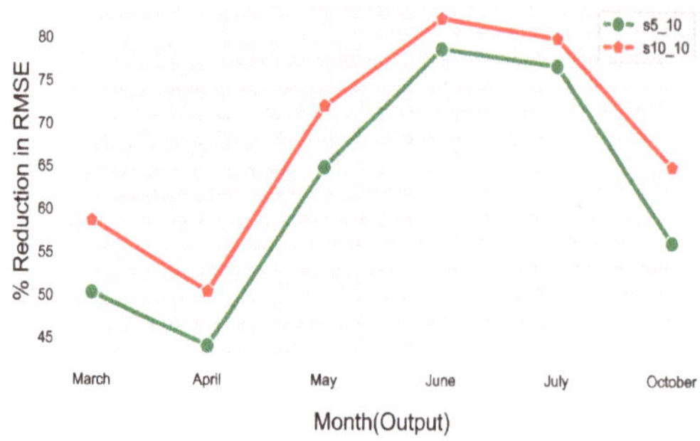

Figure 5. Effect of number of input sensors (N_1) on the prediction accuracy of temperature.

Table 6. Effect of number of sensors (N_1) on the temperature prediction accuracy of DNN model in terms of RMSE.

Predicted Month	RMSE		
	$N_1 = 5, N_2 = 10$	$N_1 = 10, N_2 = 10$	
	DNN Model	DNN Model	W/O DNN Model
March	2.1337	1.7744	4.295
April	2.811	2.4798	5.0001
May	3.5302	2.8061	10.051
June	3.5121	2.9317	16.4949
July	3.2077	2.7632	13.7796
October	3.305	2.6372	7.5388

6. Conclusions

In order to alleviate the need to move sensors from one dynamic optimal sensor location to another due to changes in the external weather condition, this study proposes a framework based on multi-channel dense neural network regression model for predicting micro-climates corresponding to changing sensor locations using measurements from fixed sensors. Results of micro-climate predictions obtained based on the proposed framework were comparable with the true sensor measurements corresponding to the dynamic sensor locations. Specifically, the proposed framework in terms of RMSE achieved a 68.67% reduction in error for temperature and 46.21% overall reduction in error for relative humidity compared with a setup without the proposed models. In terms of the Pearson correlation coefficient, the result showed a high correlation, with an average of 0.91 and 0.85 for temperature and relative humidity, respectively. The highest correlation values of 0.95 and 0.94 for temperature and relative humidity, respectively, obtained in the month of March and lowest values of 0.82 and 0.75 for temperature and relative humidity obtained in the month of July, can be explained as a result of the distance between the test month's (February) data and the respective predicted months. The deployment of the proposed framework would generally facilitate accurate monitoring and control of micro-climates in protected cultivation systems. Although the current work is limited to monthly variations of optimal sensor locations, investigating the proposed framework for intraday variations would be of interest in the future.

Author Contributions: Conceptualization, O.S.A. and R.M.; methodology, O.S.A. and R.M.; formal analysis, O.S.A., M.J.U., E.A. and R.M.; data curation, D.D.U., Y.H. and T.P.; writing—original draft preparation, O.S.A., M.J.U., E.A. and R.M.; writing—review and editing, O.S.A., M.J.U., E.A., D.D.U., Y.H., T.P. and R.M.; supervision, R.M. All authors have read and agreed to the published version of the manuscript.

Funding: This work was supported by the Basic Science Research Program through the National Research Foundation of Korea (NRF) funded by the Ministry of Education (2021R1I1A3049810) and the Korea Institute of Planning and Evaluation for Technology in Food, Agriculture, and Forestry

(IPET) through the Agriculture, Food and Rural Affairs Convergence Technologies Program for Educating Creative Global Leader, funded by the Ministry of Agriculture, Food and Rural Affairs (MAFRA) (320001-4), Republic of Korea.

Data Availability Statement: Not applicable.

Conflicts of Interest: The authors declare no conflict of interest.

References

1. Godde, C.; Mason-D'Croz, D.; Mayberry, D.; Thornton, P.; Herrero, M. Impacts of climate change on the livestock food supply chain; a review of the evidence. *Glob. Food Secur.* **2021**, *28*, 100488. [CrossRef] [PubMed]
2. Kumar, L.; Chhogyel, N.; Gopalakrishnan, T.; Hasan, M.K.; Jayasinghe, S.L.; Kariyawasam, C.S.; Kogo, B.K.; Ratnayake, S. Chapter 4—Climate change and future of agri-food production. In *Future Foods*; Bhat, R., Ed.; Academic Press: Cambridge, MA, USA, 2022; pp. 49–79. [CrossRef]
3. Reddy, P.P. *Sustainable Crop Protection under Protected Cultivation*; Springer: Singapore, 2016.
4. Zhang, W.; Xia Dou, Z.; He, P.; Ju, X.; Powlson, D.S.; Chadwick, D.R.; Norse, D.; Lu, Y.; Zhang, Y.; Wu, L.; et al. New technologies reduce greenhouse gas emissions from nitrogenous fertilizer in China. *Proc. Natl. Acad. Sci. USA* **2013**, *110*, 8375–8380. [CrossRef] [PubMed]
5. Research and Markets. Agricultural Films Market by Type (LLDPE, LDPE, Reclaim, EVA, HDPE), Application ((Greenhouse Films (Classic Greenhouse, Macro Tunnels), Silage Films (Silage Stretch Wraps), and Mulch Films (Transparent, Clear Mulches)), and Region—Global Forecast to 2028. 2022. Available online: https://www.marketsandmarkets.com/Market-Reports/agricultural-mulch-films-market-741.html. (accessed on 4 July 2022).
6. Zeng, S.; Hu, H.; Xu, L.; Li, G. Nonlinear Adaptive PID Control for Greenhouse Environment Based on RBF Network. *Sensors* **2012**, *12*, 5328–5348. [CrossRef] [PubMed]
7. Takahata, K.; Miura, H. Effects of Growth Period and Air Temperature on the Position of the Inflorescence on the Stem of Tomato Plants. *Hortic. J.* **2017**, *86*, 70–77. [CrossRef]
8. Syed, A.M.; Hachem, C. Review of Construction, Geometry, Heating, Ventilation, and Air-Conditioning, and Indoor Climate Requirements of Agricultural Greenhouses. *J. Biosyst. Eng.* **2019**, *23*, 18–27. [CrossRef]
9. Singh, V.K. Prediction of Greenhouse Micro-Climate Using Artificial Neural Network. *Appl. Ecol. Environ. Res.* **2017**, *15*, 767–778. [CrossRef]
10. Vox, G.; Teitel, M.; Pardossi, A.; Minuto, A.; Tinivella, F.; Schettini, E. Sustainable Greenhouse Systems. In *Sustainable Agriculture: Technology, Planning and Management*; Nova Science Publishers, Inc.: New York, NY, USA, 2010.
11. Harjunowibowo, D.; Ding, Y.; Omer, S.; Riffat, S. Recent Active Technologies of Greenhouse Systems—A Comprehensive Review. *Bulg. J. Agric. Sci.* **2018**, *24*, 158–170.
12. Bhujel, A.; Basak, J.K.; Khan, F.; Arulmozhi, E.; Jaihuni, M.; Sihalath, T.; Lee, D.; Park, J.; Kim, H.T. Sensor Systems for Greenhouse Microclimate Monitoring and Control: A Review. *J. Biosyst. Eng.* **2020**, *45*, 341–361. [CrossRef]
13. Fen-FangHe, C.M. Modeling greenhouse air humidity by means of artificial neural network and principal component analysis. *Comput. Eng. Agric.* **2010**, *71*, 9–23.
14. Yeon Lee, S.; Bok Lee, I.; Hyeon Yeo, U.; Woo Kim, R.; Gyu Kim, J. Optimal sensor placement for monitoring and controlling greenhouse internal environments. *Biosyst. Eng.* **2019**, *188*, 190–206. [CrossRef]
15. Kubrusly, C.S.; Malebranche, H. Sensors and controllers location in distributed systems—A survey. *Automatica* **1985**, *21*, 117–128. [CrossRef]
16. Alonso, A.A.; Kevrekidis, I.G.; Banga, J.R.; Frouzakis, C.E. Optimal sensor location and reduced order observer design for distributed process systems. *Comput. Chem. Eng.* **2004**, *28*, 27–35. [CrossRef]
17. Yi, T.; Li, H.; Gu, M. Optimal Sensor Placement for Health Monitoring of High-Rise Structure Based on Genetic Algorithm. *Math. Probl. Eng.* **2011**, *2011*, 395101. [CrossRef]
18. Liu, W.; Gao, W.; Sun, Y.; Xu, M. Optimal sensor placement for spatial lattice structure based on genetic algorithms. *J. Sound Vib.* **2008**, *317*, 175–189. [CrossRef]
19. Houssein, E.H.; Saad, M.R.; Hussain, K.; Zhu, W.; Shaban, H.; Hassaballah, M. Optimal Sink Node Placement in Large Scale Wireless Sensor Networks Based on Harris' Hawk Optimization Algorithm. *IEEE Access* **2020**, *8*, 19381–19397. [CrossRef]
20. Castro-Triguero, R.; Murugan, S.; Gallego, R.; Friswell, M.I. Robustness of optimal sensor placement under parametric uncertainty. *Mech. Syst. Signal Process.* **2013**, *41*, 268–287. [CrossRef]
21. Sun, Y.; Halgamuge, S. Minimum-Cost Heterogeneous Node Placement in Wireless Sensor Networks. *IEEE Access* **2019**, *7*, 14847–14858. [CrossRef]
22. Duan, R.; Lin, Y.; Feng, T. Optimal Sensor Placement Based on System Reliability Criterion Under Epistemic Uncertainty. *IEEE Access* **2018**, *6*, 57061–57072. [CrossRef]
23. Flynn, E.B.; Todd, M.D. A Bayesian approach to optimal sensor placement for structural health monitoring with application to active sensing. *Mech. Syst. Signal Process.* **2010**, *24*, 891–903. [CrossRef]
24. Wu, H.; Li, Q.; Zhu, H.; Han, X.; Li, Y.; Yang, B. Directional sensor placement in vegetable greenhouse for maximizing target coverage without occlusion. *Wirel. Netw.* **2020**, *26*, 4677–4687. [CrossRef]

25. Uyeh, D.D.; Bassey, B.I.; Mallipeddi, R.; Asem-Hiablie, S.; Amaizu, M.; Woo, S.; Ha, Y.S.; Park, T. A Reinforcement Learning Approach for Optimal Placement of Sensors in Protected Cultivation Systems. *IEEE Access* **2021**, *9*, 100781–100800. [CrossRef]
26. Ajani, O.S.; Aboyeji, E.; Mallipeddi, R.; Dooyum Uyeh, D.; Ha, Y.; Park, T. A genetic programming-based optimal sensor placement for greenhouse monitoring and control. *Front. Plant Sci.* **2023**, *14*, 1152036. [CrossRef] [PubMed]
27. Uyeh, D.D.; Iyiola, O.; Mallipeddi, R.; Asem-Hiablie, S.; Amaizu, M.; Ha, Y.; Park, T. Grid Search for Lowest Root Mean Squared Error in Predicting Optimal Sensor Location in Protected Cultivation Systems. *Front. Plant Sci.* **2022**, *13*, 920284. [CrossRef] [PubMed]
28. Körner, O.; Aaslyng, J.M.; Andreassen, A.U.; Holst, N. Microclimate Prediction for Dynamic Greenhouse Climate Control. *HortScience* **2007**, *42*, 272–279. [CrossRef]
29. Petrakis, T.; Kavga, A.; Thomopoulos, V.; Argiriou, A.A. Neural Network Model for Greenhouse Microclimate Predictions. *Agriculture* **2022**, *12*, 780. [CrossRef]
30. Liu, Q.; Jin, D.; Shen, J.; Fu, Z.; Linge, N. A WSN-based prediction model of microclimate in a greenhouse using extreme learning approaches. In Proceedings of the 2016 18th International Conference on Advanced Communication Technology (ICACT), PyeongChang, Republic of Korea, 31 January–3 February 2016; pp. 730–735. [CrossRef]
31. Singh, M.C.; Singh, J.; Singh, K. Development of a microclimate model for prediction of temperatures inside a naturally ventilated greenhouse under cucumber crop in soilless media. *Comput. Electron. Agric.* **2018**, *154*, 227–238. [CrossRef]
32. Bishop, C.M. *Pattern Recognition and Machine Learning*; Information Science and Statistics; Springer: Berlin/Heidelberg, Germany, 2006.
33. Chakir, S.; Bekraoui, A.; Zemmouri, E.M.; Majdoubi, H.; Mouqallid, M. Prediction of Olive Cuttings Greenhouse Microclimate Under Mediterranean Climate Using Artificial Neural Networks. In *Digital Technologies and Applications, Proceedings of the Digital Technologies and Applications, Fez, Morocco, 28–30 January 2022*; Motahhir, S., Bossoufi, B., Eds.; Springer: Cham, Switzerland, 2022; pp. 63–69.

mathematics

MDPI

Article

Global-Local Dynamic Adversarial Learning for Cross-Domain Sentiment Analysis

Juntao Lyu, Zheyuan Zhang, Shufeng Chen and Xiying Fan *

School of Computer and Communication Engineering, University of Science and Technology Beijing, Beijing 100083, China
* Correspondence: xiyingfan@ustb.edu.cn

Abstract: As one of the most widely used applications in domain adaption (DA), Cross-domain sentiment analysis (CDSA) aims to tackle the barrier of lacking in sentiment labeled data. Applying an adversarial network to DA to reduce the distribution discrepancy between source and target domains is a significant advance in CDSA. This adversarial DA paradigm utilizes a single global domain discriminator or a series of local domain discriminators to reduce marginal or conditional probability distribution discrepancies. In general, each discrepancy has a different effect on domain adaption. However, the existing CDSA algorithms ignore this point. Therefore, in this paper, we propose an effective, novel and unsupervised adversarial DA paradigm, Global-Local Dynamic Adversarial Learning (GLDAL). This paradigm is able to quantitively evaluate the weights of global distribution and every local distribution. We also study how to apply GLDAL to CDSA. As GLDAL can effectively reduce the distribution discrepancy between domains, it performs well in a series of CDSA experiments and achieves improvements in classification accuracy compared to similar methods. The effectiveness of each component is demonstrated through ablation experiments on different parts and a quantitative analysis of the dynamic factor. Overall, this approach achieves the desired DA effect with domain shifts.

Keywords: adversarial domain adaption; cross-domain sentiment analysis; global-local dynamic adversarial learning

MSC: 68T01

Citation: Lyu, J.; Zhang, Z.; Chen, S.; Fan, X. Global-Local Dynamic Adversarial Learning for Cross-Domain Sentiment Analysis. *Mathematics* **2023**, *11*, 3130. https://doi.org/10.3390/math11143130

Academic Editors: Adrian Sergiu Darabant and Diana-Laura Borza

Received: 21 May 2023
Revised: 4 July 2023
Accepted: 12 July 2023
Published: 15 July 2023

1. Introduction

Deep neural networks have led to impressive improvements in data mining. However, it is always time-consuming and expensive to acquire sufficient data, and especially to label them. The emergence of domain adaption [1] has significantly reduced the difficulty of labeling data and transferring knowledge between different domains. One of the most challenging problems in domain adaption is how to reduce or even eliminate the differences between the source domain and target domain [2]. In CDSA, these differences are reflected as domain discrepancies owing to the distinct expression of the reviewers' emotions from various domains [3]. In recent years, adversarial domain adaption [4] has been widely used to reduce different domains' distribution discrepancies. Most of them depend on either global domain discriminator to reduce marginal probability distribution discrepancy, or several local domain discriminators to reduce conditional probability distribution discrepancy. For example, DANN [4] only implements global adversarial adaption to align global distributions from different domains. Analogously, MADA [5] only utilizes a series of local domain discriminators to align subdomains. In true application scenarios, the global alignment and every single local alignment always contribute differently to the entire domain adaption. When two domains' marginal probability distributions are more dissimilar, it is obvious that global alignment plays a bigger role. Otherwise, local alignment is more important. Similarly, each local alignment makes different contributions to the total local alignment.

Due to the issues of domain transfer and concept drift, a sentiment classification model trained in one domain may not effectively generalize to other domains. The expressions of sentiment, viewpoints, and emotionally charged words evolve over time, making it challenging to maintain effective sentiment classification models across different domains. Therefore, employing domain adaptation methods can help reduce the drift of sentiment expression [6]. The main purpose of this study is to reduce the data distribution gap between the two emotion domains to enhance the generalization ability of cross-domain emotion classification data models. We want to achieve this goal by utilizing the global-domain discriminator and local-domain discriminator commonly used in traditional natural-language-processing text classifiers to minimize the difference between data margins and global distribution, thereby improving the generalization ability of cross-domain sentiment classification.

In this paper, we propose a novel domain adaption method GLOBAL–LOCAL DYNAMIC ADVERSARIAL LEARNING (GLDAL) for unsupervised adaption. GLDAL captures the multi-mode structure of data dynamically through adversarial learning. In CDSA, GLDAL is able to amplify the influence of the pivot words to learn domain-invariant features. The core components of GLDAL are the Global Dynamic Adversarial Factor (GDAF) and Local Dynamic Adversarial Factors (LDAF). The former has the ability to evaluate the relative significance of the marginal and conditional distributions both dynamically and quantitatively. Similarly, the latter plays the same role in the relationship between each conditional distribution. Therefore, GLDAL is able to improve the generalization of adversarial domain adaption.

In the following text, we detail the use of our proposed approach in deep neural network architectures, and experiment on popular sentiment classification datasets (SST, IMDB), where our proposed approach shows improvements compared to the previous state-of-the-art accuracy.

2. Related Work

2.1. Unsupervised Domain Adaption in Transfer Learning

Unsupervised domain adaptation (UDA) is an important branch of transfer learning. There are two main forms of UDA: traditional machine learning and deep learning. UDA based on traditional machine learning can be divided into two categories: (1) Subspace Alignment (SA) [7] and CORAL [8] use the subspace statistical characteristics to eliminate domain differences. (2) Distribution alignments TCA [9], JDA [10], BDA [11] and MEDA [12] are proposed to align the marginal probability distributions or conditional probability distributions between domains.

In the last few years, deep neural networks have been widely used in domain adaption [13–15]. Domain adversarial learning, as a branch of deep domain adaption, has been popular in recent years. The idea of adversarial learning comes from Generative Adversarial Networks (GAN) [16,17]. DANN [4] aligns the source and target distributions with only a single global domain discriminator. MADA [5] is able to execute the fine-grained alignment of different data distributions using multi-mode discriminators. DAAN [18] dynamically evaluates the relationship between the marginal and conditional distributions. Our GLDAL is also based on adversarial learning and global attention mechanism. By evaluating the relationship between every local subdomain and the relative importance of the marginal and conditional distributions, GLDAL significantly outperforms existing methods.

2.2. Cross-Domain Sentiment Analysis.

Sentiment analysis is also called opinion mining or tendency analysis. It is the process of analyzing and reasoning about subjective texts with emotions. Text representation is an important step in sentiment analysis. In recent years, the most representative work has been the BERT pre-trained model [19], Transformer-XL [20]. However, thegeneral sentiment analysis studies mentioned above only consider the performanc e in a single domain, ignoring the generalization ability, so cross-domain sentiment analysis has quickly become a research hotspot. BERT-DAAT [21] is a pre-trained model based on adversarial training methods that aims to provide the trained BERT with domain awareness. ADS-SAL [22] can dynamically learn an alignment weight for each word, so more important words will obtain higher alignment weights to achieve fine-grained adaptation.

3. Method

3.1. Problem Definition

In CDSA tasks about domain adaption, there are a source domain $D_s = \{x_s^i, y_s^i\}_{i=1}^{N_s}$ and a target domain $D_t = \{x_t^i\}_{i=1}^{N_t}$, where x_s and x_t is the set of sentences and y_s are the corresponding sentiment polarity labels. The goal of CDSA is to predict the target label $\hat{y}^t = \arg\max G_y(f(x_t))$ and minimize the target risk $\epsilon_t(G_y) = E_{(x_t,y_t)\sim\mathcal{D}_t}[G_y(f(x_t)) \neq y_t]$, where $G_y(\cdot)$ represents the Softmax output and $f(\cdot)$ refers to the feature representation.

3.2. Backbones for Cross-Domain Sentiment Analysis

3.2.1. Bidirectional Gate Recurrent Units with Attention

A Gate Recurrent Unit (GRU) with the attention mechanism [23] is an effective recurrent neural network for sentiment analysis. For a given n-dimensional input $(x_1, x_2, \ldots, x_n)$, the hidden layer of Bi-GRU outputs h_t at time t. The calculation process is as follows:

$$h_{f_t} = \sigma\left(W_{xh_f}x_t + W_{h_{fh_f}}h_{f_{t-1}} + b_{h_f}\right), h_{b_t} = \sigma\left(W_{xh_b}x_t + W_{h_bh_b}h_{b_{t-1}} + b_{h_b}\right), \tag{1}$$

$h_t = h_{f_t} \oplus h_{b_t}$, W is the weight matrix and b is the bias vector; σ is the activation function; h_{f_t} and h_{b_t} are the outputs of positive and negative GRU, respectively. $\oplus$ represents the element-wise summation. The simplification method is to construct a single vector c from the whole sequence, as follows:

$$e_t = Attention(h_t),\ \alpha_t = \frac{\exp(e_t)}{\sum_{k=1}^{T}\exp(e_k)},\ c = \sum_{t=1}^{T}\alpha_t h_t. \tag{2}$$

3.2.2. Capsule Neural Network Based on BERT

The BERT [19] model is a language model based on two-way Transformer. We directly use the feature representation of BERT as the word-embedding feature of the task and regard BERT as the upstream network. The Capsule Network [24] is composed of a group of neurons, which are used to represent the parameters of a specific type of object. We regard this network as a downstream network. The unique activation function ("squashing") is formulated as:

$$\mathbf{v}_j = \frac{\|\mathbf{s}_j\|^2}{1 + \|\mathbf{s}_j\|^2}\frac{\mathbf{s}_j}{\|\mathbf{s}_j\|}, \tag{3}$$

$\mathbf{s}_j$ is its total input and v_j is the output of capsule j . For capsule s_j, the input is determined by multiplying the output $u_i$of a capsule in the former layer by a weight matrix W_{ij} , c_{ij}, which are coefficients for coupling determined by the dynamic routing:

$$s_j = \sum_i c_{ij}\hat{u}_{j|i}, \quad \hat{u}_{j|i} = W_{ij}u_i. \tag{4}$$

3.3. Domain Adaption with Adversarial Learning

This adversarial training is like a game with two parts: feature extractor G_f and domain discriminator G_d. Through maximizing the loss of G_d, the parameters θ_f of G_f are trained while the parameters θ_d of G_d are trained by minimizing the loss of the domain discriminator. The total loss can be formalized as:

$$L\left(\theta_f, \theta_y, \theta_d\right) = \frac{1}{n_s} \sum_{\mathbf{x}_i \in \mathcal{D}_s} L_y\left(G_y\left(G_f(\mathbf{x}_i)\right), y_i\right) - \frac{\lambda}{n_s + n_t} \sum_{\mathbf{x}_i \in (\mathcal{D}_s \cup \mathcal{D}_t)} L_d\left(G_d\left(G_f(\mathbf{x}_i)\right), d_i\right), \tag{5}$$

Update the parameters of each part as the following equations:

$$\left(\hat{\theta}_f, \hat{\theta}_y\right) = \arg\min_{\theta_f, \theta_y} L\left(\theta_f, \theta_y, \theta_d\right), \; \left(\hat{\theta}_d\right) = \arg\max_{\theta_d} L\left(\theta_f, \theta_y, \theta_d\right) \tag{6}$$

Due to the adversarial relationship with parameter updating, the parameters $\theta_f, \theta_y, \theta_d$ will deliver a saddle point of Equation (6) after the training converges.

3.4. Global-Local Dynamic Adversarial Adaption Network

At present, the mainstream adversarial adaption methods reduce marginal or conditional probability distribution discrepancies. However, it is quite difficult to evaluate the importance of each contribution. Therefore, we should find a novel method that can *quantitatively* evaluate their importance and *dynamically* adjust the parameters of the neural network.

In this paper, we propose the GLOBAL–LOCAL DYNAMIC ADVERSARIAL LEARNING (GLDAL) shown in Figure 1 to make key improvements. GLDAL can effectively evaluate every single distribution's importance, aiming to better learn the domain-invariant features through adversarial learning. In GLDAL, the *Global* domain discriminator G_d and a series of *Local* domain discriminators G_d^u play a role in the domain adaption of marginal and conditional distributions, respectively. The most important innovation point is that we propose a novel, global-local dynamic training strategy using the *Global Dynamic Factor* ω and *Local Dynamic Factors* $\{\alpha_u\}_{u=1}^{U}$.

3.4.1. Label Classifier

The label classifier G_y (The blue part in Figure 1) in trained by samples from the source domain to implement label classification. The loss of G_y is formulated as:

$$L_y = \frac{1}{n_s} \sum_{\mathbf{x}_i \in \mathcal{D}_s} CrossEntropy\left(G_y\left(G_f(\mathbf{x}_i)\right), \mathbf{y}_i\right), \tag{7}$$

where $\mathbf{x}_i$, $\mathbf{y}_i$represents samples and their labels from the source domain; G_f is the feature extractor.

3.4.2. Global Domain Discriminator

Global domain discriminator G_d (The pink part in Figure 1) is wisely implemented to align the marginal probability distributions between two domains (source domain and target domain) in the feature space. We define the loss of global domain discriminator G_d as:

$$L_{global} = \frac{1}{n_s + n_t} \sum_{\mathbf{x}_i \in \mathcal{D}_s \cup \mathcal{D}_t} L_d\left(G_d\left(G_f(\mathbf{x}_i)\right), d_i\right). \tag{8}$$

In this formula, L_d represents the loss of domain discriminator. d_i is the domain label of the sample $\mathbf{x}_i$ and G_f is the feature extractor.

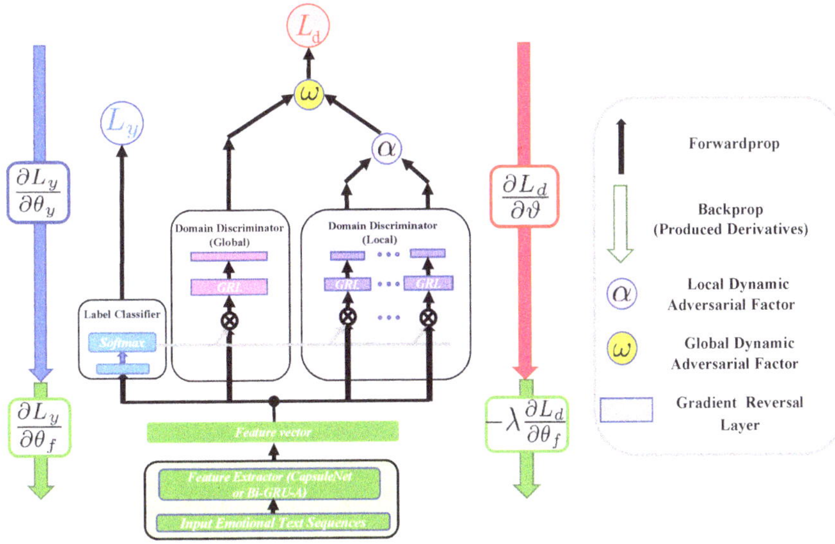

Figure 1. The architecture of the proposed GLOBAL–LOCAL DYNAMIC ADVERSARIAL LEARNING (GLDAL). First, input the Text Sequences into the Feature Extractor to obtain the feature vector distributed in the feature space. Next, there are two main loss functions, namely L_y and L_d. L_y is the classification loss. L_d is the loss combination of the global domain discriminator and local domain discriminators.

3.4.3. Local Domain Discriminator

The local domain discriminator G_d^u (The purple part in Figure 1) is composed of a series of U class-wise discriminators G_d^u; each is used to match the source domain and target domain data associated with class u. The output of the label classifier $\hat{\mathbf{y}}_i = G_y(\mathbf{x}_i)$ to each data point x_i is a probability distribution of the U classes. Therefore, we utilize the probability distribution $\hat{\mathbf{y}}_i$ to measure how many data points x_i should be attended to the U domain G_d^u. The loss function of the local domain discriminator is defined as:

$$L_{local} = \frac{1}{n_s + n_t} \sum_{u=1}^{U} \sum_{\mathbf{x}_i \in \mathcal{D}_s \cup \mathcal{D}_t} L_d^u \left(G_d^u \left(\hat{y}_i^u G_f(\mathbf{x}_i) \right), d_i \right), \tag{9}$$

3.5. *Global and Local Adversarial Factors*

In this part, we introduce how to quantitively evaluate the global distributions and each local distribution. Due to the adversarial characteristic, it is tricky to determine a concrete scheme. Generally, there are two straightforward ideas: Random Setting and Average Step Searching. The former randomly sets the value of dynamic factors and the latter picks the value of these factors with the same step size. For instance, if the scope of factor ω is [0, 1], the latter strategy will pick the value of ω = 0, 0.1, …, 0.9, 1.0 to perform training. However, both strategies are computation-consuming and time-consuming.

Therefore, in this paper, we propose two kinds of factors: global dynamic adversarial factorω and local dynamic adversarial factors $\{\alpha_u\}_{u=1}^{U}$ in order to dynamically and quantitively evaluate the importance of each distribution. This strategy has two significant advantages. Firstly, we utilize deep adversarial representations instead of shallow representations to learn these two kinds of factors, making GLDAL more robust. Secondly, every single dynamic factor is determined by the $\mathcal{SA}-distance$ (not hinge loss) of the discriminators, which is more efficient and convenient. In order to calculate the dynamic factors, we denote the global $\mathcal{SA}-distance$ of the global domain discriminator as:

$$d_{\mathcal{SA},g}(\mathcal{D}_s, \mathcal{D}_t) = 2\Big(1 - 2\Big(L_{global}\Big)\Big). \tag{10}$$

We also denote the local subdomain $\mathcal{SA}-distance$ as:

$$d_{\mathcal{SA},l}(\mathcal{D}_s^u, \mathcal{D}_t^u) = 2(1 - 2(L_{local}^u)). \tag{11}$$

These two kinds of distances can measure the distribution similarity of the source and target domain to some extent. $\mathcal{D}_s^u$ and $\mathcal{D}_t^u$ denote samples from class u, and L_{local}^u is the local subdomain discriminator loss over the class u.

3.5.1. The Global Dynamic Adversarial Factor ω

The global dynamic adversarial factor ω is used to calculate the weighted sum of global domain loss and local domain loss. ω is initialized as 1 in the first training epoch. After each training epoch, this factor ω can be estimated through global and local domain discriminators as:

$$\hat{\omega} = \frac{d_{\mathcal{SA},g}(\mathcal{D}_s, \mathcal{D}_t)}{d_{\mathcal{SA},g}(\mathcal{D}_s, \mathcal{D}_t) + \frac{1}{U}\sum_{u=1}^{U} d_{\mathcal{SA},l}(\mathcal{D}_s^u, \mathcal{D}_t^u)} \tag{12}$$

3.5.2. The Local Dynamic Adversarial Factors $\{\alpha_u\}_{u=1}^{U}$

The local domain loss L_{local} is composed of a series of local subdomain loss L_{local}^u by weighted summation. The local dynamic adversarial factors $\{\alpha_u\}_{u=1}^{U}$ act as coefficients in the weighted sum. The importance of the alignment of each subdomain is different, so we assign different weights to every subdomain. In general, if the difference between the source subdomain and the target subdomain regarding class u is larger, we should pay more attention to this subdomain, which is manifested by the fact that the weight of the alignment of this subdomain should be increased. Since $\mathcal{SA}-distance$ is an important parameter used to measure the similarity of the probability distributions of two subdomains $\mathcal{D}_s^u$ and $\mathcal{D}_t^u$, the parameter α_u can be estimated as:

$$\hat{\alpha}_u = \frac{\frac{1}{U}\sum_{u=1}^{U} d_{\mathcal{SA},l}(\mathcal{D}_s^u, \mathcal{D}_t^u)}{d_{\mathcal{SA},l}(\mathcal{D}_s^u, \mathcal{D}_t^u)}. \tag{13}$$

Each subdomain dynamic adversarial factor is initialized as 1 in the first training epoch. This factor-updating strategy follows the principle: If the $\mathcal{SA}-distance$ (Generally less than 0) between the subdomains about class u is larger, the weight for the alignment of subdomains about u will be greater. In this case, the domain discriminator G_d^u of the subdomain u can more easily discriminate the domain label information of the sample in the subdomain, which indicates that the difference between domains about class u is large. Therefore, we need to increase the proportion of L_{local}^u in the total local loss to ensure a better alignment effect about class u.

4. Experiments

In this section, we implement experiments to evaluate the proposed GLDAL against several previous state-of-the-art domain adaption methods. Our method GLDAL is validated on several popular standard datasets regarding cross-domain sentiment analysis. The training process is shown in Algorithm 1.

Algorithm 1 GLDAL

Input:
—samples $S = \{x_s^i, y_s^i\}_{i=1}^{N_s}$ and $T = \{x_t^i\}_{i=1}^{N_t}$, $\lambda, \mu, \omega, \{\alpha_u\}_{u=1}^{U}$

Output: Neural Network $\left\{G_y, G_f, G_d\right\}$

while stopping criterion is not meet **do**
  calculate the global domain loss L_{global_i}: Equation (8)
  calculate the global $\mathcal{SA}-distance$: Equation (10)
  acquire classification probability vector $\hat{y}_i$ from G_y: $\hat{y}_i \longleftarrow G_y\left(G_f(\mathbf{s}_i)\right)$
  calculate the sum of all local loss of sample s_i: Equation (9)
  calculate each local $\mathcal{SA}-distance$: Equation (11)
  if $s_i \in S$ **then**
    calculate the classification loss of: Equation (7)
  Backpropagation: $\Delta_\Theta \leftarrow \frac{\Delta L_{y_i}}{\Delta\Theta} - \lambda \frac{\Delta\left((1-\omega)L_{global}+\omega L_{local}\right)}{\Delta\Theta}$
  Update dynamic factor $\omega, \{\alpha_u\}_{u=1}^{U}$:
  $\hat{\omega}$: Equation (12), $\hat{\alpha}_u$: Equation (13)
return Output

4.1. Datasets

The Amazon Product Review dataset includes product reviews and metadata from Amazon; due to the uneven distribution of the samples, we set rating 0–1 as negative sentiment, 2–3 as medium and 5 as positive. We chose the following two datasets: Amazon reviews for clothing (**C**) and Amazon reviews for instant video (**I**).

SST-5 (**S5**), SST-2 (**S2**) are two versions of The Stanford Sentiment Treebank (SST); the former is (**S5**), with five categories (Very Positive, Positive, Neural, Negative), and the latter is (**S2**) with two categories (Positive, Negative).

IMDB (**IM**) is a review rating dataset for movie sentiment analysis, containing the same number of positive and negative sentiment samples. The COVID-19 Review dataset (**COR**) contains a sample of comments about COVID-19 and the corresponding sentiment scores (Very Positive, Positive, Neural, Negative). Tweet Review dataset **TR** contains daily comments and sentiment ratings scraped from tweets, with three categories (Positive, Neural, Negative).

We used these domain combinations and built six transfer learning tasks: (**C** $\rightarrow$ **TR**), (**TR** $\rightarrow$ **I**), (**COR** $\rightarrow$ **S5**), (**S5** $\rightarrow$ **COR**), (**IM** $\rightarrow$ **S2**), (**S2** $\rightarrow$ **IM**).

4.2. Baselines

Based on two previously mentioned backbones: **Bi-GRU-A** (Section 3.2.1) and **CapsuleNet** (Section 3.2.2),We compare our proposed GLOBAL-LOCAL DYNAMIC ADVERSARIAL LEARNING (GLDAL) with several state-of-the-art unsupervised deep do main adaption methods: **DDC** [25], **DaNN** [26], **DANN** [4], **D-CORAL** [15], **JAN** [27] **MADA** [5] and **DAAN** [18].

4.3. Implementation

We implement all methods on the PyTorch framework. For feature extractor backbones CapsuleNet and Bi-GRU-A, we fine-tune all word vectors and all attention layers and train the feature extraction layers with a learning rate of 10^{-5} and 10^{-4}, respectively. We use approximately 2–5 times the learning rate of the feature extractor to train the label classifier, and use 2–10 times the learning rate to train the local discriminator and global discriminator. The update of the important trade-off factor λ follows the **Warm Start** principles: $\lambda = \frac{2(hi-lo)}{1+\exp\left(-\frac{i}{N}\right)} - (hi-lo) + lo$. We set lo as 0, hi as 1, N as 100. Other hyperparameters are tuned via transfer cross-validation. The source code is available at https://github.com/killer2-1/GLDAL-for-CDSA (accessed on 20 May 2023).

4.4. Results

The classification accuracy (%) is shown in Tables 1 and 2. GLDAL outperforms all comparison methods on most CDSA tasks. It is also remarkable that our GLDAL has better effects than similar approaches such as DANN, MADA and DAAN. From the results, we can obtain some conclusions: (1) Generally, the methods based on adversarial learning (DANN, DAAN) perform better than non-adversarial learning methods (DaNN, DDC), which means that adversarial adaption is more effective. (2) Adversarial methods with an attention mechanism such as GLDAL achieves a better performance than DANN and MADA(no attention). (3) Compared with other methods, GLDAL outperforms almost all traditional comparison methods (DDC, DaNN, DANN) on most transfer tasks, which proves the proposed method is effective. For some of the more advanced methods, such as DAAN, GLDAL slightly outperforms these methods, which verifies our method's benefits.

Table 1. Accuracy (%) for unsupervised domain adaptation based on **Bi-GRU-A**(The bold stands for the best performance)

Method	C → TR	TR → I	COR → S5	S5 → COR	IM → S2	S2 → IM	AVG
Bi-GRU-A (No Transfer)	40.96	62.04	31.70	29.53	76.64	74.18	52.51
DDC	49.85	61.88	30.95	32.60	76.99	77.72	55.00
DaNN	45.35	63.65	31.31	32.00	78.46	78.40	54.86
DANN	49.01	65.98	32.84	33.53	80.81	78.82	56.83
D-CORAL	50.43	65.06	**33.78**	33.70	79.13	77.63	56.62
MADA	50.18	66.39	33.12	33.96	81.16	78.98	57.30
DAAN	50.69	66.05	33.09	34.08	80.99	79.02	57.32
GLDAL (Proposed Approach)	**51.25**	**66.53**	33.34	**34.12**	**81.34**	**79.16**	**57.62**

Table 2. Accuracy (%) of unsupervised domain adaptation based on **CapsuleNet**.

Method	C → TR	TR → I	COR → S5	S5 → COR	IM → S2	S2 → IM	AVG
CapsuleNet (No Transfer)	47.94	63.93	33.25	30.24	83.51	80.22	56.52
DDC	51.77	64.34	35.09	30.98	85.97	86.07	59.20
DaNN	50.16	66.56	34.15	31.49	85.45	86.14	58.99
DANN	53.55	67.72	35.21	34.45	86.11	85.60	60.44
D-CORAL	56.82	67.08	34.08	34.38	86.05	85.72	60.68
JAN	52.97	68.24	34.99	33.82	86.33	86.58	60.48
MADA	54.31	67.65	**35.79**	34.64	86.96	86.32	60.95
DAAN	54.76	68.78	34.96	34.24	**87.21**	86.50	61.08
GLDAL (Proposed Approach)	**56.97**	**68.92**	34.91	**35.07**	87.18	**86.83**	**61.64**

4.5. Effectiveness Analysis and Ablation Study

4.5.1. Analysis of the Importance of the Global Dynamic Adversarial Factor (GDAF) ω in GLDAL

In this section, the importance of GDAF ω in GLDAL is evaluated. The evaluation involves two key points: (1) Whether we should pay attention to the different effects of marginal and conditional probability in adverarial domain adaption. (2) The effectiveness of our evaluation for ω.

To illustrate the first point, we chose several transfer tasks and analyzed the results of GLDAL under different values of ω, as shown in in Figure 2. It is obvious that paying attention to the different effects of marginal and conditional distribution is important. The value of optimal ω varies on different tasks. This is because different feature representations are obtained under different ω.

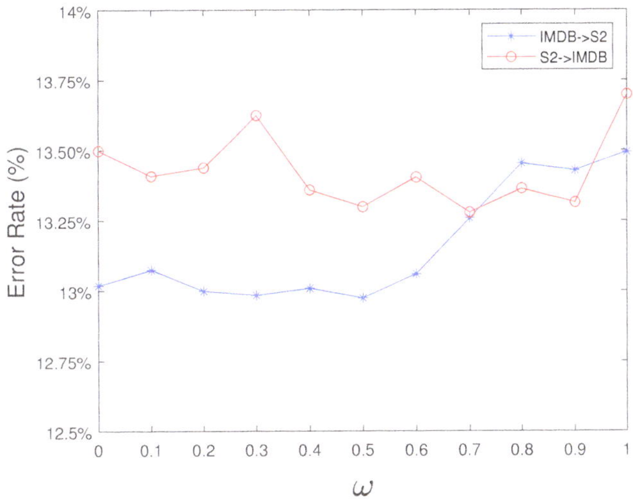

Figure 2. Performance of several tasks when searching $\omega \in [0, 1]$.

To illustrate the second point, we compared the accuracy of transfer tasks under different calculation methods for ω: Random Guessing, Average Searching (10 times) and our GLDAL. We also executed an ablation study with DANN ($\omega = 1$) and MADA ($\omega = 0$). Combining the results from Table 3, we can conclude that our method outperforms other four methods.

Table 3. Accuracy (%) for the effective analysis and ablation study of ω based on **CapsuleNet**.

Transfer Tasks	Average Search	Random Guessing	GLDAL	DANN ($\omega = 1$)	MADA ($\omega = 0$)
S2 $\rightarrow$ IM	86.15	86.52	86.83	85.60	86.32
S5 $\rightarrow$ COR	34.98	34.86	35.07	34.45	34.64
TR $\rightarrow$ I	67.73	68.25	68.92	67.72	67.65
AVG	62.95	63.21	63.61	62.60	62.87

4.5.2. Analysis of the Importance of the Local Dynamic Adversarial Factor (LDAF) $\{\alpha_u\}_{u=1}^{U}$ in GLDAL

In this section, based on the point oof whether we should pay attention to the different effect of each local subdomain, we analyze the importance of the local dynamic adversarial factor $\{\alpha_u\}_{u=1}^{U}$ in GLDAL. Like the analysis of ω, we also chose a series of tasks, and adopted the three methods shown below to conduct verification experiments: (1) A series of random number that are greater than 0, and the sum is fixed to U (RNSF); (2) DAAN (all LDAFs are fixed to 1); (3) Our GLDAL. We used $\mathcal{A}-distance$ [28] as a measure of cross-domain discrepancy. In general, the smaller the $\mathcal{A}-distance$, the better the domain adaption effect. The average results in each dataset are shown in Table 4.

Table 4. $\mathcal{A}-distance$ for all unsupervised domain adaptation tasks based on backbone **CapsuleNet** and **Bi-GRU-A**.

BackBone	RNSF	DAAN	GLDAL
CapsuleNet	0.988	0.952	0.925
Bi-GRU-A	1.053	1.007	0.978

5. Conclusions

In this paper, we proposed a novel GLOBAL–LOCAL DYNAMIC ADVERSARIAL LEARNING (GLDAL) for cross-domain sentiment analysis. Through quantitatively evaluating the relative importance of global distribution and all local distributions, GLDAL is able to dynamically adjust the learning weights of the global discriminator and local discriminators during training. This domain adaption strategy is based on the attention mechanism and has excellent effects on experimental tasks. As a general transfer learning strategy, GLDAL can also be applied to tasks in computer vision and the recommended system. In the future, we plan to extend GLDAL to more challenging transfer learning problems.

Author Contributions: Methodology, Z.Z. and X.F.; Resources, Z.Z.; Data curation, J.L. and S.C.; Writing—original draft, J.L.; Writing—review & editing, Z.Z.; Supervision, X.F. All authors have read and agreed to the published version of the manuscript.

Funding: This research received no external funding.

Data Availability Statement: There are the url links for our used dataset: IMDB: https://huggingface.co/datasets/imdb (accessed on 20 May 2023); SST: https://huggingface.co/datasets/sst2 (accessed on 20 May 2023); GloVe: https://nlp.stanford.edu/projects/glove/ (accessed on 20 May 2023); IMDB: https://huggingface.co/datasets/imdb (accessed on 20 May 2023).

Conflicts of Interest: The authors declare no conflict of interest.

References

1. Zhuang, F.; Qi, Z.; Duan, K.; Xi, D.; Zhu, Y.; Zhu, H.; Xiong, H.; He, Q. A Comprehensive Survey on Transfer Learning. *Proc. IEEE* **2021**, *109*, 43–76. [CrossRef]
2. Pan, S.J.; Yang, Q. A Survey on Transfer Learning. *IEEE Trans.* **2010**, *22*, 1345–1359. [CrossRef]
3. Gupta, B.; Awasthi, S.; Singh, P.; Ram, L.; Kumar, P.; Prasad, B.R.; Agarwal, S. Cross domain sentiment analysis using transfer learning. In Proceedings of the 2017 IEEE International Conference on Industrial and Information Systems (ICIIS), Peradeniya, Sri Lanka, 15–16 December 2017.
4. Ganin, Y.; Lempitsky, V.S. Unsupervised Domain Adaptation by Backpropagation. In Proceedings of the 32nd International Conference on Machine Learning, Lille, France, 6–11 July 2015; pp. 1180–1189.
5. Pei, Z.; Cao, Z.; Long, M.; Wang, J. Multi-Adversarial Domain Adaptation. In Proceedings of the AAAI Conference on Artificial Intelligence, New Orleans, LA, USA, 2–7 February 2018; pp. 3934–3941.
6. Zhang, M.; Li, X.; Wu, F. Moka-ADA: Adversarial domain adaptation with model-oriented knowledge adaptation for cross-domain sentiment analysis. *J. Supercomput.* **2023**, *79*, 13724–13743. [CrossRef]
7. Sun, B.; Saenko, K. Subspace Distribution Alignment for Unsupervised Domain Adaptation. In Proceedings of the 26th British Machine Vision Conference, Swansea, UK, 7–10 September 2015; pp. 24.1–24.10.
8. Sun, B.; Feng, J.; Saenko, K. Return of Frustratingly Easy Domain Adaptation. In Proceedings of the Thirtieth AAAI Conference on Artificial Intelligence, Phoenix, AZ, USA, 12–17 February 2016; pp. 2058–2065.
9. Pan, S.J.; Tsang, I.W.; Kwok, J.T.; Yang, Q. Domain Adaptation via Transfer Component Analysis. *IEEE Trans.* **2011**, *22*, 199–210. [CrossRef] [PubMed]
10. Long, M.; Wang, J.; Ding, G.; Sun, J.; Yu, P.S. Transfer Feature Learning with Joint Distribution Adaptation. In Proceedings of the IEEE International Conference on Computer Vision (ICCV), Sydney, Australia, 1–8 December 2013; pp. 2200–2207.
11. Wang, J.; Chen, Y.; Hao, S.; Feng, W.; Shen, Z. Balanced Distribution Adaptation for Transfer Learning. In Proceedings of the 2017 IEEE International Conference on Data Mining (ICDM), New Orleans, LA, USA, 18–21 November 2017.
12. Wang, J.; Feng, W.; Chen, Y.; Yu, H.; Huang, M.; Yu, P.S. Visual Domain Adaptation with Manifold Embedded Distribution Alignment. In Proceedings of the 26th ACM International Conference on Multimedia, Seoul, Republic of Korea, 22–26 October 2018; pp. 402–410.
13. Zhu, Y.; Zhuang, F.; Wang, J.; Chen, J.; Shi, Z.; Wu, W.; He, Q. Multi-representation adaptation network for cross-domain image classification. *Neural Netw.* **2019**, *119*, 214–221. [CrossRef] [PubMed]
14. Zhuang, F.; Cheng, X.; Luo, P.; Pan, S.J.; He, Q. Supervised Representation Learning: Transfer Learning with Deep Autoencoders. In Proceedings of the Twenty-Fourth International Joint Conference on Artificial Intelligence, Buenos Aires, Argentina, 25–31 July 2015; pp. 4119–4125.
15. Sun, B.; Saenko, K. Deep CORAL: Correlation Alignment for Deep Domain Adaptation. In Proceedings of the ECCV: European Conference on Computer Vision, Amsterdam, The Netherlands, 8–10 and 15–16 October 2016.
16. Goodfellow, I.J.; Pouget-Abadie, J.; Mirza, M.; Xu, B.; Warde-Farley, D.; Ozair, S.; Courville, A.C.; Bengio, Y. Generative Adversarial Nets. In Proceedings of the 52nd Annual Meeting of the Association for Computational Linguistics, Baltimore, ML, USA, 22–27 June 2014; pp. 2672–2680.

17. Durugkar, I.P.; Gemp, I.; Mahadevan, S. Generative Multi-Adversarial Networks. In Proceedings of the 5th International Conference on Learning Representations, ICLR 2017, Toulon, France, 24–26 April 2017.
18. Yu, C.; Wang, J.; Chen, Y.; Huang, M. Transfer Learning with Dynamic Adversarial Adaptation Network. In Proceedings of the 2019 IEEE International Conference on Data Mining (ICDM), Beijing, China, 8–11 November 2019; pp. 778–786.
19. Devlin, J.; Chang, M.; Lee, K.; Toutanova, K. BERT: Pre-training of Deep Bidirectional Transformers for Language Understanding. In Proceedings of the NAACL, Minneapolis, Minnesota, 2–7 June 2019; pp. 4171–4186.
20. Dai, Z.; Yang, Z.; Yang, Y.; Carbonell, J.G.; Le, Q.V.; Salakhutdinov, R. Transformer-XL: Attentive Language Models beyond a Fixed-Length Context. In Proceedings of the 57th Annual Meeting of the Association for Computational Linguistics, Florence, Italy, 28 July–2 August 2019; pp. 2978–2988.
21. Du, C.; Sun, H.; Wang, J.; Qi, Q.; Liao, J. Adversarial and Domain-Aware BERT for Cross-Domain Sentiment Analysis. In Proceedings of the 58th Annual Meeting of the Association for Computational Linguistics, Online, 5–10 July 2020; pp. 4019–4028.
22. Li, Z.; Li, X.; Wei, Y.; Bing, L.; Zhang, Y.; Yang, Q. Transferable End-to-End Aspect-based Sentiment Analysis with Selective Adversarial Learning. In Proceedings of the 2019 Conference on Empirical Methods in Natural Language Processing, Hong Kong, China, 3–7 November 2019; pp. 4589–4599.
23. Bahdanau, D.; Cho, K.; Bengio, Y. Neural Machine Translation by Jointly Learning to Align and Translate. In Proceedings of the 3rd International Conference on Learning Representations, ICLR 2015, San Diego, CA, USA, 7–9 May 2015.
24. Dong, Y.; Fu, Y.; Wang, L.; Chen, Y.; Dong, Y.; Li, J. A Sentiment Analysis Method of Capsule Network Based on BiLSTM. *IEEE Access* **2020**, *8*, 37014–37020. [CrossRef]
25. Tzeng, E.; Hoffman, J.; Zhang, N.; Saenko, K.; Darrell, T. Deep Domain Confusion: Maximizing for Domain Invariance. *arXiv* **2014**, arXiv:1412.3474 .
26. Ghifary, M.; Kleijn, W.B.; Zhang, M. Domain Adaptive Neural Networks for Object Recognition. In Proceedings of the 13th Pacific Rim International Conference on Artificial Intelligence, Gold Coast, QLD, Australia, 1–5 December 2014; pp. 898–904.
27. Long, M.; Zhu, H.; Wang, J.; Jordan, M.I. Deep Transfer Learning with Joint Adaptation Networks. In Proceedings of the 34th International Conference on Machine Learning, Sydney, NSW, Australia, 6–11 August 2017; pp. 2208–2217.
28. Ben-David, S.; Blitzer, J.; Crammer, K.; Pereira, F. Analysis of Representations for Domain Adaptation. In Proceedings of the Neural Information Processing Systems 19 (NIPS 2006), Vancouver, BC, Canada, 4–7 December 2006; Schölkopf, B., Platt, J.C.; Hofmann, T., Eds.; MIT Press: Cambridge, MA, USA,2006 ; pp. 137–144.

mathematics

MDPI

Article

BAE: Anomaly Detection Algorithm Based on Clustering and Autoencoder

Dongqi Wang, Mingshuo Nie and Dongming Chen *

Software College, Northeastern University, Shenyang 110169, China; wangdq@swc.neu.edu.cn (D.W.); niemingshuo@stumail.neu.edu.cn (M.N.)
* Correspondence: chendm@mail.neu.edu.cn

Abstract: In this paper, we propose an outlier-detection algorithm for detecting network traffic anomalies based on a clustering algorithm and an autoencoder model. The BIRCH clustering algorithm is employed as the pre-algorithm of the autoencoder to pre-classify datasets with complex data distribution characteristics, while the autoencoder model is used to detect outliers based on a threshold. The proposed BIRCH-Autoencoder (BAE) algorithm has been tested on four network security datasets, KDDCUP99, UNSW-NB15, CICIDS2017, and NSL-KDD, and compared with representative algorithms. The BAE algorithm achieved average F-scores of 96.160, 81.132, and 91.424 on the KDDCUP99, UNSW-NB15, and CICIDS2017 datasets, respectively. These experimental results demonstrate that the proposed approach can effectively and accurately detect anomalous data.

Keywords: pre-classification; BIRCH; Autoencoder; anomaly detection

MSC: 68W99

Citation: Wang, D.; Nie, M.; Chen, D. BAE: Anomaly Detection Algorithm Based on Clustering and Autoencoder. *Mathematics* **2023**, *11*, 3398. https://doi.org/10.3390/math11153398

Academic Editor: Faheim Sufi

Received: 29 June 2023
Revised: 18 July 2023
Accepted: 2 August 2023
Published: 3 August 2023

1. Introduction

In recent years, internet applications and services have become widely used. However, the open structure and lack of supervision of the internet have created a deteriorating network security environment, making it easier for attacks to occur. Hackers can have varied motivations, such as political, financial, or intellectual, which makes detection even more challenging [1]. Distributed Denial-of-Service (DDoS) is one such aggressive and threatening invasion of online servers that mainly has two attack methods [2]: one is sending packets to exploit software vulnerabilities of the target host, rendering it unable to provide service, and the other involves sending large amounts of useless network traffic to flood the target host with an attack on its service resources. This paper discusses flooding attacks as an anomaly-detection example in the following sections.

Autoencoder is a novel method based on anomaly detection, which can find the best subspace to capture the nonlinear correlation between features by using a neural network. In addition, it can effectively reduce the false positive rate. The Common Autoencoders include the Denoising Autoencoder (DAE) [3], Sparse Autoencoder (SAE) [4], Variational Autoencoder (VAE) [5], Stacked Convolutional Autoencoders (SCAE) [6], and so on. These different types of Autoencoders are widely used in the intrusion-detection field [7–9]. However, The traffic from different sources usually has different characteristics when an attack occurs. This traffic with different data distributions has a negative effect on training deep learning models. Most anomaly-detection models do not preprocess these data, but directly use them to detect abnormal traffic, which leads to defects in accuracy. In addition, the data used for anomaly detection is usually imbalanced, which also hinders the performance of anomaly-based detection, and there are few studies focusing on this question in the research community [1].

The contribution of this algorithm is to propose an anomaly-detection algorithm that can automatically pre-classify and independently detect anomalies based on the pre-classification results. The algorithm uses the BIRCH algorithm to pre-classify traffic and the Autoencoder technique to detect anomaly traffic. The experimental results obtained from analyzing real network traffic datasets show that the algorithm outperforms others in terms of detection performance.

The remaining parts of this paper are structured as follows. Section 2 introduces the application scenario of the algorithm proposed in this paper. Section 3 discuss the related research work on anomaly-detection methods. In Section 4, we introduce the process of data preprocessing, and the principle of BIRCH and Autoencoder are introduced in detail, with the idea of combining BIRCH with Autoencoder to detect traffic. In Section 5, we execute the experiments based on KDDCUP99, UNSW-NB15, CICIDS2017, and NSL-KDD to verify the proposed algorithm. We conclude our work in Section 6.

2. Application of Algorithm

Intrusion-detection systems usually rely on sufficient servers and bandwidth resources to defend against flooding attacks. And the poor interaction between detection and defense phases has always been a challenge because the packets' validity discrimination calculation has high time complexity and is difficult. At the same time, even if the detection system can filter out a certain proportion of attack traffic, how to guarantee the legal access of potential legitimate users to target systems or resources during the attack is still challenging.

When the protected host receives network traffic packets, the intrusion detection system can distinguish whether the intrusion occurs through the techniques of the packet regular filtering, the signature detection filtering of the packet stream, and the content-customized filtering of the packets. The output of these discrimination techniques is "quasi-legal" data composed of filtered packets. The proposed algorithm will execute anomaly detection on network packets during an attack. Because the legal data flow is far less than attacking data flow, the anomaly detection operation will be able to filter out the legal packets as outliers. And a "whitelist" will be established based on these selected packets' IP addresses to protect legal access to the system. This mechanism (see Figure 1) assumes that packets from the same legal sources are legal. The proposed intrusion-detection framework adopts the strategy of active-defense, which can reduce the requirement of the cooperation among detection and defense mechanisms and improve the compatibility of intrusion-detection methods in different network environments. In addition, the update mechanism based on "white list" can ensure the normal access of legitimate sources, thus ensuring the real-time monitoring of attacks and the communication requirements of legitimate users.

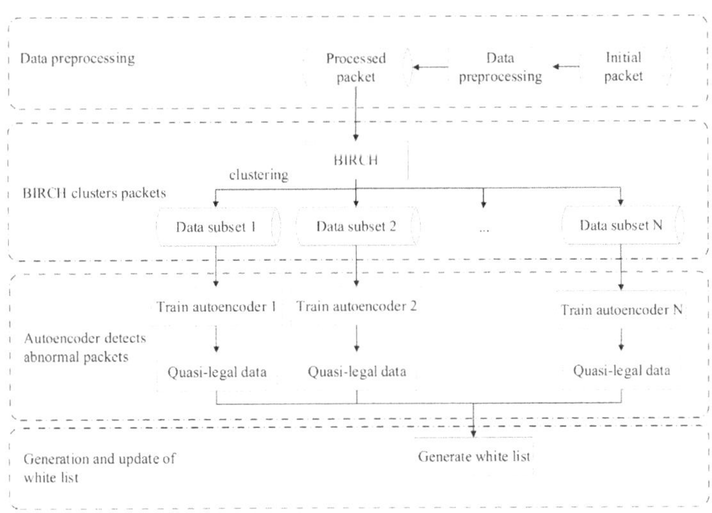

Figure 1. The framework of active-defense.

3. Related Works

Broadly speaking, traditional threshold-based DDoS detection methods are applications of anomaly detection. Anomaly detection represents the data by finding the correlation between data features and trying to map data to the optimal subspace. Through mapping, the process of data mapping to subspace, the data with a large reconstruction error is identified as abnormal data, comparing it to the majority of samples [8]. Principal Component Analysis (PCA) can be used for threshold-based outlier detection. Lakhina et al. [10] used the PCA algorithm to separate the high-dimensional space occupied by a set of network traffic measurements into disjoint subspaces corresponding to normal and anomaly network conditions and performed outlier detection on the subspaces. Yang et al. [11] and Zhu et al. [12] used different methods to detect anomalies by using reconstruction errors. In research history, Local Outlier Factor Algorithm (LOF) [13], PSO-BP [14], and the Intrusion-detection method using Online Sequence Extreme Learning Machine (OS-ELM) [15] have all used reconstruction error as the threshold for anomaly detection.

In practical applications, input features are typically nonlinear. Therefore, nonlinear methods, such as Autoencoders, are becoming a trending approach for analyzing network traffic data. To better capture the nonlinear correlation between features, Chen et al. [8] used a convolution Autoencoder with a smaller number of parameters to execute dimension reduction. Similarly, Shaikh et al. [16] proposed a deep learning framework for intrusion detection that utilized an Autoencoder and recurrent neural network (RNN). Fan et al. [17] proposed a dual automatic encoder (AnomalyDAE) framework for anomaly detection that captured the complex interactive information between the network structure and node attributes.

As deep learning advances, there are more and more algorithms and frameworks being developed to solve anomaly detection issues. Engly et al. [1] aimed to solve the issues of imbalanced data and ineffective features by using imbalance correction and feature selection. They conducted experiments on Random Forests, Neural Networks, and Gradient-Boosting Machines and found that the best detection performance could be achieved by an ensemble with two neural networks and a Gradient-Boosting Machine. Li et al. [18] focused on improving the detection accuracy of malicious nodes through an intrusion sensitivity-based trust management model and a supervised approach that employed machine learning techniques.

Autoencoder-based anomaly detection has also been applied to other fields. Azzalini et al. [19] proposed a minimally supervised method for detecting anomalies in autonomous robots using deep learning. Kolberg et al. [20] developed a novel presentation attack detection (PAD) method for fingerprint-based biometric authentication systems. Finally, Meng et al. attempted to develop a trust-based intrusion detection mechanism for a wireless sensor network (WSN) using Bayesian modeling.

As we can see, machine learning, particularly deep learning, has been extensively utilized in the field of anomaly-detection research. Researchers are currently exploring the use of different structural neural networks to satisfy specific data characteristics. Despite these efforts, most anomaly-detection methods still possess drawbacks with regards to false positives and inaccuracies.

4. Methods

4.1. Overall Framework of Proposed Method

This paper introduces an algorithm for detecting anomalies based on multiple thresholds. To determine the threshold for classifying traffic data as normal or anomalous, we train independent Autoencoders for each different network traffic, and each Autoencoder has its own unique threshold that depends on the specific classification result.

Since the performance of the threshold-based anomaly detection algorithm is greatly affected by the type of network traffic data used for model training [21], the data structure can impact anomaly detection, and changes in data distribution can decrease algorithm performance [22]. We propose the use of the BIRCH-Autoencoder (BAE) approach to pre-classify the training data and group network traffic packets with similar data structures. An Autoencoder is then trained for each subgroup, with the number of Autoencoders corresponding to the number of subgroups. This approach ensures that the models accurately describe the characteristics of network traffic and can handle complex data-distribution scenarios.

4.2. BIRCH for Data Pre-Classification

Balanced Iterative Reducing and Clustering Using Hierarchies (BIRCH) is an algorithm for clustering large datasets with limited memory resources [23], while minimizing the I/O cost by scanning datasets only once. BIRCH defines a cluster using Cluster Features (CFs) and represents the hierarchical architecture of clusters using a CF tree. This technique enables BIRCH to achieve fast and scalable clustering in large and even stream databases.

The CF and CF tree is the core methods of BIRCH. A CF is a triple-including clustering information, which is also additive. The definition of the additivity of CF is as follows:

Definition 1. *Suppose that $\{\vec{X_i}\}$ is the cluster of N d-dimensional data points, where i = 1, 2, . . ., N, the cluster's CF vector is defined as a triple: CF = (N, $\vec{LS}$, SS), where N is the number of data points, $\vec{LS}$ is the linear sum of the data points, i.e., $\sum_i^N \vec{X_i}$ and SS is the square sum of the N data points, i.e., $\sum_i^N \vec{X_i}^2$.*

Definition 2. *Suppose that $CF_1 = (N_1, \vec{LS_1}, SS_1)$ and $CF_2 = (N_2, \vec{LS_2}, SS_2)$ are the two disjoint clusters' CF vectors, which makes $CF_1 + CF_2 = (N_1 + N_2, \vec{LS_1} + \vec{LS_2}, SS_1 + SS_2)$.*

The use of CF in BIRCH offers two key advantages: it significantly reduces the amount of storage space needed for data and enables efficient calculations of all clustering decision indexes.

Definition 3. *Suppose that $\{\vec{X_i}\}$ is the cluster of N d-dimensional data points, where i = 1, 2, . . ., N, $\vec{X_0}$ is the centroid of the cluster, R is the radius of the cluster, and D is the diameter of the cluster, they are defined in Equations (1), (2) and (3), respectively.*

$$\vec{X_0} = \frac{\sum_i^N \vec{X_i}}{N} \tag{1}$$

$$R = \sqrt{\frac{\sum_i^N \left(\vec{X_i} - \vec{X_0}\right)^2}{N}} \tag{2}$$

$$D = \sqrt{\frac{\sum_i^N \sum_j^N \left(\vec{X_i} - \vec{X_j}\right)^2}{N(N-1)}} \tag{3}$$

The CF tree is a balanced tree with two parameters: branching factor B and threshold T. Each non-leaf node contains a maximum of B entries in the form of $\{CF_i, child_i\}$, where $i = 1, 2, \ldots, B$. The $child_i$ is a pointer to the i-th child node, and CF_i is the CF of the subcluster represented by this child node. A leaf node contains at most nL entries, each of the forms $\{CF_i\}$, where $i = 1, 2, \ldots, nL$. All entries in a leaf node must satisfy a threshold requirement. The size of the tree is determined by T, where the tree becomes smaller as T increases.

The BIRCH algorithm is employed as a pre-classification technique for the processed dataset prior to Autoencoder utilization. The number of clusters is specified to segment the processed dataset into distinct subsets based on unique clustering features, which are subsequently labeled with cluster tags for seamless Autoencoder anomaly detection.

4.3. Autoencoder for Anomaly Detection

The Autoencoder is a neural network algorithm that extracts hierarchical features from unlabeled data, aiming to reduce the dimensionality of high-dimensional input data. It achieves this by obtaining a low-dimensional vector representation of the original data and then reconstructing it back to the same dimension as the input data through the decoding process. This technique is useful for tasks, such as dimensionality reduction and data compression. An Autoencoder consists of the Encoder, Decoder, and Hidden Layer.

Definition 4. *Encoder. The Encoder is used for dimensionality reduction of high-dimensional features, which compresses the given input data to a specified dimension, which is equal to the number of neurons in the hidden layer.*

The mapping between coded input data x and implicit representation h is expressed by Equation (4).

$$h_i = f_\theta(x) = s\left(\sum_{j=1}^{n} W_{i,j}^{input} x_j + b_i^{input}\right) \quad (4)$$

x is the input vector. W represents the encoder weight matrix with size $m \times n$, and b is a bias vector of dimensionality m. s is a nonlinear activate function, generally a sigmoid logic function, and its expression is given in Equation (5).

$$y = s(x) = \frac{1}{1+e^{-x}} \quad (5)$$

Definition 5. *Decoder. the Decoder is used for data reconstruction, which can be regarded as the inverse process of the Encoder. The low-dimensional data representation of the hidden layer is decoded to the size of the original vector space.*

The mapping function of above decoder is given in Equation (6).

$$h_i' = g_{\theta'}(h) = s\left(\sum_{j=1}^{n} W_{i,j}^{hidden} h_j + b_i^{hidden}\right) \quad (6)$$

The process of training the Autoencoder is to find the minimum average reconstruction error on the given input data $\{x_1, x_2, \ldots, x_n\}$ and the output data $\{x_1', x_2', \ldots, x_n'\}$ reduced and reconstructed by the Autoencoder. This reconstruction error is defined by Equation (7).

$$L(x_i, x_i') = \sum_{j=1}^{d} (x_i - x_i')^2 \quad (7)$$

Specifically, the Autoencoder can compress the original input data and set the parameters and weights in the neural network according to the optimized reconstruction error. Ideally, this encoding will learn and describe the potential attributes of the input data. In this paper, the following functions (Equation (8)) are used to calculate the minimized average reconstruction error, and the L is the reconstruction error defined by Equation (7).

$$\theta^*, \theta'^* = \underset{\theta,\theta'}{\text{argmin}} \frac{1}{n} \sum_{i=1}^{n} L(x_i, x_i') = \underset{\theta,\theta'}{\text{argmin}} \frac{1}{n} \sum_{i=1}^{n} L(x_i, g_{\theta'}(f_\theta(x_i))) \quad (8)$$

After training the auto-encoder, the test data can be inputted into this model, and the anomaly data or normal data can be distinguished by the threshold division of the reconstruction error, as shown in Equation (9), where L is the reconstruction error defined by Equation (7). θ is the output error after inputting the test Packet into the outlier mining algorithm.

$$c(x_i) = \begin{cases} normal & L_i < \theta \\ abnormal & L_i > \theta \end{cases} \quad (9)$$

For datasets labeled with different cluster labels, train an Autoencoder for them, and use this Autoencoder to calculate the reconstruction error, which can be used to detect the attack data.

After training, the dataset for testing is used as the input of the model, and the reconstruction error is used as the anomaly score. When the calculation error of the dataset for testing is greater than the threshold, it is identified as anomaly data or normal data.

5. Experimental Analysis

In this section, Logistic Regression, SVM, and Decision Tree are compared to BAE, with the Autoencoder utilized for pre-classification to showcase the performance of various algorithms in the detection task. The Accuracy, Recall, Precision, and F-score are employed for the evaluation, and comparative experiments are conducted on four datasets: KDDCUP99 [24], UNSW-NB15 [25], CICIDS2017 [26], and NSL-KDD [27].

5.1. Datasets

In this paper, KDDCUP99, UNSW-NB15, CICIDS2017, and NSL-KDD are used for experiments. These datasets contain both up-to-date common attacks and typical attacks that happened in history. Three of the datasets (KDDCUP99, UNSW-NB15, and CICIDS2017) are unique, as they do not overlap. Somehow, the KDDCUP99 and NSL-KDD can be seen as different resolutions of the same set of data. Typically, intrusion-detection datasets are usually confidential to the public. In order for our model to acquire sufficient knowledge about abnormal network traffic, we have made every effort to gather a comprehensive collection of commonly used open-resource datasets. Here are some further details on the datasets:

- KDDCUP99: The safety audit dataset KDDCUP99 published by the IDS laboratory of Columbia University is compiled from the IDS dataset of MIT LL in 1998 [28]; here, we choose to use the 10% KDDCUP99 in our research [29].
- UNSW-NB15: The original network packet of the UNSW-NB15 dataset is a public security dataset, including normal network traffic data and network attack data created in the network-wide laboratory of the Australian Cyber Security Centre (ACCS) using the IXIA PerfectStorm tool.
- CICIDS 2017: the CICIDS 2017 dataset is a network security dataset released by the Canadian Institute for Cybersecurity (CIC) in 2018. It collects data of various network attacks through the mounted network terminal.
- NSL-KDD: NSL-KDD is a suggested dataset to solve some inherent problems of the KDDCUP99 dataset.

5.2. Experiments

The dataset originally consisted of non-normalized data that contained zeros or characters in both the important and secondary features. This directly impacted the calculation of the clustering features and the generation of the clustering feature tree in BIRCH. To address this issue, the Min-Max normalization technique [30] and One-hot methodology were employed in this paper.

Normalize the numerical data in the dataset, linearly transform the original data, and map the data between [0, 1]. The transformation function is given in Equation (10).

$$x' = \frac{x - \min(x)}{\max(x) - \min(x)} \tag{10}$$

For the character data in the dataset, the one-hot encoder is used to "binarize" the character data. Through the preprocessing of data, we can obtain a numerical and normalized dataset. At the same time, our research only focuses on DDoS attacks. Therefore, we select data with attack types of DDoS and DoS and Normal from different datasets and conduct subsequent experiments based on the data.

Firstly, the BIRCH is used to pre-classify all the data to obtain data subsets with different data characteristics, and these data subsets are used as new training data to be inputted into the corresponding Autoencoder model. In this paper, the Davies–Bouldin index (DBI) [31] is used to determine the number of clusters. This indicator is defined by Equation (11).

$$\mathrm{DBI} = \frac{1}{n}\sum_{i=1}^{n} \max_{i \neq i}\left(\frac{s_i + s_j}{d_{ij}}\right) \quad (11)$$

where s_i is the average distance from each point in the cluster i to the centroid of the cluster, d_{ij} is the distance between the centroid of the cluster i and the centroid of the cluster j, and n is the number of clusters.

The DBI index reflects the average degree of "similarity" among clusters. A DBI value closer to 0 indicates a more favorable clustering effect. In Figure 2, different cluster numbers were tested, and the DBI scores demonstrate that the optimal number of clusters for the KDDCUP99 dataset in this experiment is 4, while the UNSW-NB15 and CICIDS2017 datasets require 3 clusters. In all cases, a smaller DBI translates to a better clustering effect. Figure 3 illustrates the clustering effect diagram.

To demonstrate the impact of BIRCH on datasets with varied data distribution characteristics, this paper employs information entropy to depict the internal order degree of the datasets. The higher the level of order in a dataset, the lower its information entropy would be. The entropy values of the original datasets of KDDCUP99, UNSW-NB15, CICIDS2017, and NSL-KDD, without any prior classification, are 0.499, 0.576, 1.048, and 1.029, respectively. These values indicate that the original datasets have low levels of data order, which implies that they exhibit complex data distribution characteristics.

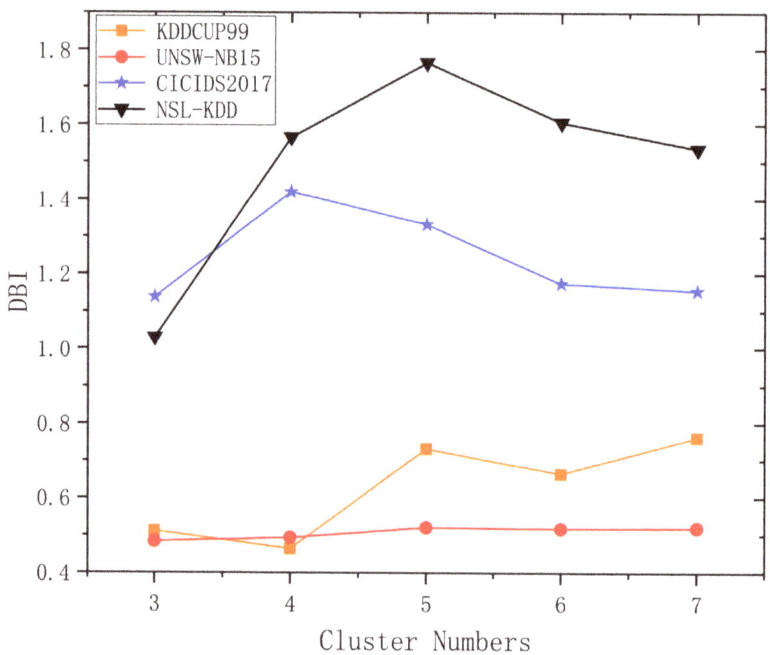

Figure 2. DBI under different cluster numbers in different datasets.

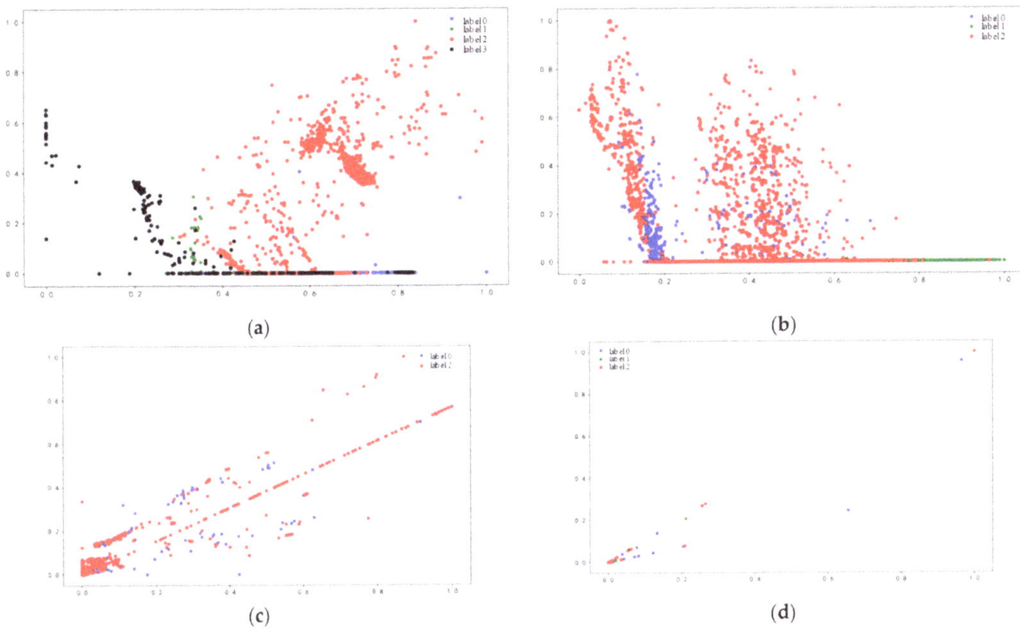

Figure 3. Scatter graph of clustering effect. Clustering effect of KDDCUP99. (**a**) UNSW-NB15; (**b**) CICIDS2017; (**c**) NSL-KDD; (**d**) datasets using BIRCH and PCA are used in dimensionality reduction.

After pre-classifying the datasets using BIRCH (see Figure 4), the information entropy of the different datasets decreases, which minimizes the impact of irregular data on anomaly detection. During the experiment, we observed that the information entropy of the data subset with cluster label 2 in the UNSW-NB15 dataset (0.683) and the data subset with cluster label 1 in the NSL-KDD dataset (1.037) was higher than that of the original dataset. By analyzing different types of data subsets based on information entropy, we found that subsets with significantly different quantities of normal and abnormal data tend to have lower information entropy. Conversely, subsets with different or roughly equal quantities of both types of data often have information entropy close to or greater than that of the original dataset. This is due to the calculation formula for information entropy. In our experiment, only two out of the thirteen data subsets had slightly higher information entropy compared to the original dataset. Therefore, the experimental results suggest that the BIRCH algorithm can improve the organization of data to some extent. Furthermore, in these two specific data subsets, the performance of anomaly detection was relatively better, indicating that the BIRCH algorithm excels in clustering data with similar characteristics, even though it may not accurately distinguish between different types of data during the clustering process.

In the training of the Autoencoder, the pre-classified subset is used as input data to train the Autoencoder. The Autoencoder is used to minimize the average reconstruction error. Using this reconstruction error, normal data and anomaly data can be classified.

In the testing of the Autoencoder, the test data is inputted into the Autoencoder, and the reconstruction error is used as the anomaly score. We stack two 8-layer convolution neural networks to build the Autoencoder and took a rectified linear unit (ReLU) activation function. The regularization coefficient of our L2 regularization is 10×10^{-5}. When the loss of data in the test set is greater than this threshold, it will be classified as normal data. Tables 1–4 show the experimental results based on different datasets. And Figures 5–7 show are the corresponding confusion matrices, which show more details on the experimental results.

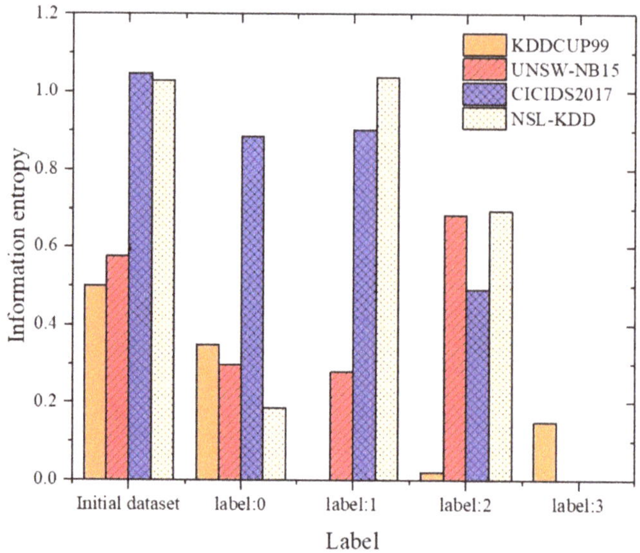

Figure 4. Information entropy of data subsets based on different datasets. KDDCUP99 (with label: i), UNSW-NB15 (with label: i), CICIDS2017 (with label: i), $i = 0, 1, 2\ldots$. This represents subsets of data with different cluster labels.

Table 1. Comparison of evaluation metrics of data subsets with different cluster labels. The metrics of subsets are averaged as the metrics of the whole dataset, which is compared with the traditional algorithm. BAE (with label: i), $i = 0, 1, 2, 3$ means that the BAE proposed in this paper is used to process the data subsets of different cluster labels of KDDCUP99.

Methods	Accuracy (%)	Recall (%)	Precision (%)	F-Score (%)
Logistic Regression	93.892	88.204	96.884	92.340
SVM	92.472	99.897	84.781	91.72
Decision Tree	95.302	99.929	89.933	94.668
Autoencoder	81.140	76.490	100.00	86.679
BAE (with label:0)	99.329	99.245	100.00	99.621
BAE (with label:1)	93.207	93.205	100.00	96.483
BAE (with label:2)	94.590	94.572	100.00	97.210
BAE (with label:3)	96.705	86.277	97.000	91.324
BAE (average)	95.958	93.325	99.250	96.160

Table 2. Results of each algorithm based on the UNSW-NB15 dataset. BAE (with label: i), $i = 0, 1, 2$ means that the BAE is used to process the subsets of different cluster labels of UNSW-NB15.

Methods	Accuracy (%)	Recall (%)	Precision (%)	F-Score (%)
Logistic Regression	89.516	80.438	62.031	70.046
SVM	90.755	70.117	69.492	69.803
Decision Tree	89.708	85.419	61.73	71.668
Auto-encoder	82.204	100.00	45.665	62.698
BAE (with label:0)	88.603	100.00	40.636	57.789
BAE (with label:1)	90.002	100.00	81.985	90.101
BAE (with label:2)	84.252	91.401	100.00	95.507
BAE (average)	87.619	97.137	74.207	81.132

Table 3. Results of each algorithm based on the CICIDS2017 dataset. BAE (with label: i), i = 0, 1, 2 means that the BAE is used to process the subsets of different cluster labels of CICIDS2017.

Methods	Accuracy (%)	Recall (%)	Precision (%)	F-Score (%)
Logistic Regression	89.888	95.499	88.204	91.707
SVM	88.312	89.537	90.406	89.969
Decision Tree	90.254	85.276	97.194	91.107
Auto-encoder	89.848	83.236	91.541	87.191
BAE (with label:0)	89.716	88.260	99.996	93.762
BAE (with label:1)	95.171	86.702	93.269	89.866
BAE (with label:2)	92.854	83.911	98.551	90.643
BAE (average)	92.580	86.291	97.272	91.424

Table 4. Results of each algorithm based on the NSL-KDD dataset. BAE (with label: i), i = 0, 1, 2 means that the BAE is used to process the subsets of different cluster labels of NSL-KDD.

Methods	Accuracy (%)	Recall (%)	Precision (%)	F-Score (%)
Logistic Regression	84.428	100.0	78.473	87.938
SVM	81.915	69.860	97.599	81.432
Decision Tree	92.932	89.494	97.872	93.496
Auto-encoder	74.421	83.864	64.486	72.910
BAE (with label:0)	95.160	96.561	98.457	97.499
BAE (with label:1)	86.838	82.958	100.0	90.685
BAE (with label:2)	81.644	84.639	70.977	77.208
BAE (average)	87.880	88.053	89.811	88.464

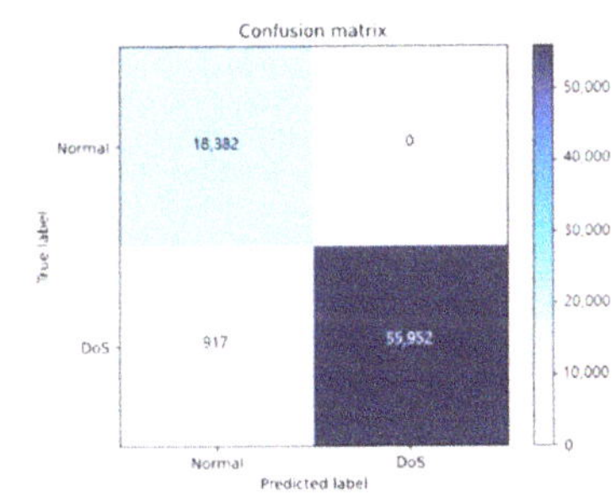

(a)

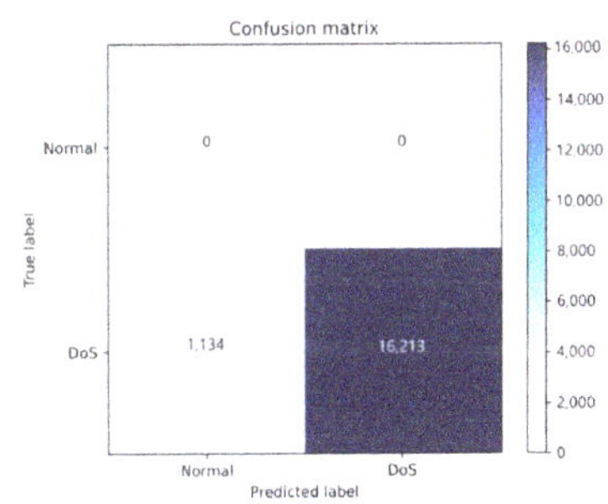

(b)

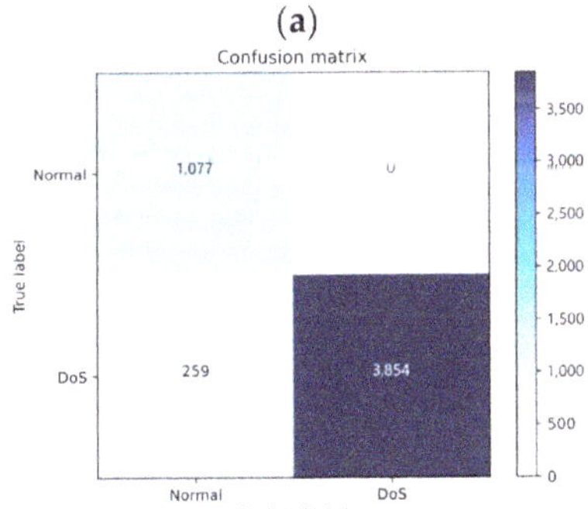

(c)

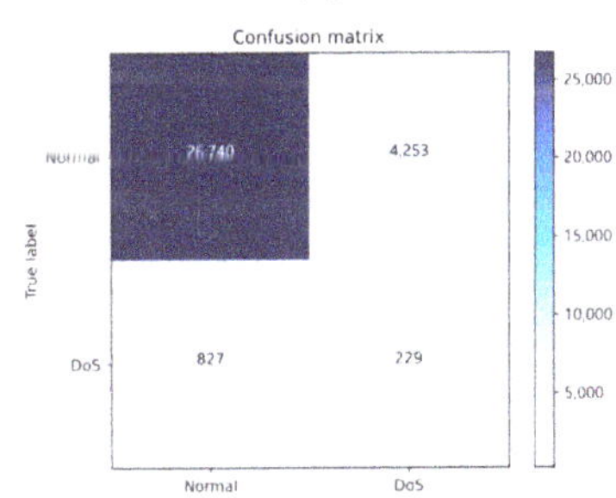

(d)

Figure 5. Confusion matrices of BAE algorithms' outcomes based on KDDCUP99. (**a**) label: 0; (**b**) label: 1; (**c**) label: 2; (**d**) label: 3.

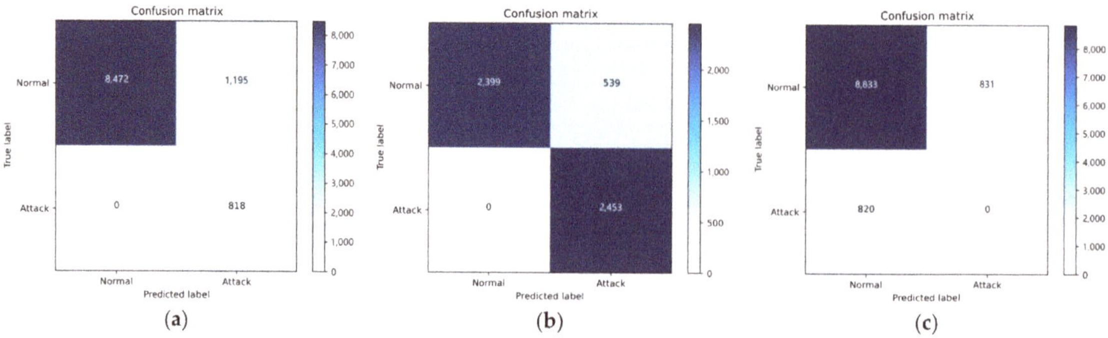

Figure 6. Confusion matrices of BAE algorithms' outcomes based on UNSW-NB15. (**a**) label: 0; (**b**) label: 1; (**c**) label: 2.

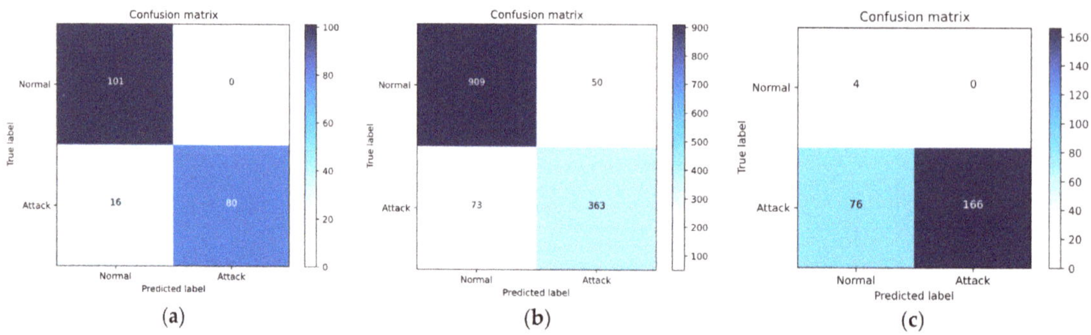

Figure 7. Confusion matrices of BAE algorithms' outcomes based on CICIDS2017. (**a**) label: 0; (**b**) label: 1; (**c**) label: 2.

In Table 1, the experimental results show that, compared with Logistic Regression, SVM, and Decision Tree, the BAE achieves better results in the accuracy, precision, and F-score. As we noticed, BAE's recall based on KDDCUP99 is 6% lower than SVM and the Decision Tree, but its accuracy and precision and F-score are much higher than SVM and the Decision Tree (up to 9%). For intrusion-detection tasks, informally, precision is the fraction of all detected anomalies that are real anomalies, whereas recall is the fraction of all real anomalies that are successfully detected. For real-world implementation, a higher false detection rate (low precision) will lead to poor user experience. Since BAE's average recall is more than 90%, we believe that trading a little bit recall for precision is a better choice. Compared with the Autoencoder without pre-classification, BAE has significantly improved the accuracy, recall rate, and F-score. The experimental results show that using BIRCH to pre-classify data can improve the evaluation indexes, and the architecture of BIRCH combined with the Autoencoder can obtain a better anomaly-detection effect. The experiments on the UNSW-NB15, CICIDS2017, and NSL-KDD also prove that the proposed method is effective. Using DBI to determine the optimal cluster number of UNSW-NB15, CICIDS2017, and NSL-KDD, values are all 3.

Results in Table 2 show that, compared with the logistic regression algorithm, SVM algorithm, and decision tree algorithm, the BAE algorithm performed slightly better in terms of the recall rate, precision rate, and F-score, but slightly worse in terms of accuracy. When comparing the experiments without pre-classification and directly using the proposed Autoencoder model in this paper with the experiments using pre-classification and the proposed Autoencoder model in this paper, the accuracy decreased by 5.415%, the precision rate decreased by 28.542%, and the F-score decreased by 18.434%.

Results in Table 3 show that the average accuracy of anomaly-detection experiments based on different data subsets is 92.580%. Compared with the logistic regression algorithm, SVM algorithm, and decision tree algorithm, the BAE algorithm performed better in terms of accuracy. When comparing the experiments with and without pre-classification using the proposed Autoencoder model in this paper, the accuracy decreased by 2.732%, the recall rate decreased by 3.055%, the precision rate decreased by 5.731%, and the F-score decreased by 4.233%.

In Tables 2–4, the experimental results demonstrate that BAE outperforms Logistic Regression, SVM, and the Decision Tree in terms of recall, precision, and F-score when processing UNSW-NB15, but slightly underperforms in accuracy. For CICIDS2017, BAE achieves higher accuracy. In NSL-KDD, BAE has a higher accuracy than Logistic Regression and SVM, but slightly lower accuracy than the Decision Tree. Across these four datasets, BAE achieves significant improvements in accuracy, precision, and F-score when compared to the Autoencoder without pre-classification. Also, as we can see from Figures 5–7, the confusion matrices maintain consistency with the corresponding experimental statistical results.

Based on the aforementioned results, BAE combined with BIRCH and the Autoencoder exhibits varying performance based on different datasets. However, overall, it results in better anomaly-detection outcomes.

6. Conclusions

In this work, we proposed an anomaly-detection algorithm called the BAE algorithm. BAE utilizes BIRCH as the pre-algorithm for the anomaly-detection algorithm based on the Autoencoder. BIRCH is effective in diminishing the impact of datasets with complex data distribution characteristics on the threshold for anomaly detection. Using DBI, the optimal cluster number for a data subset is selected based on the best clustering effect, and the corresponding Autoencoder is trained on the data subset outputted by BIRCH. The Autoencoder is often regarded as the core algorithm in intrusion-detection systems due to its potential to detect anomalous traffic. The model can compute the threshold by determining the disparity between input and output data and recognize legal and anomalous packets through the threshold. The proposed BAE algorithm has been validated experimentally using the KDDCUP99, UNSW-NB15, CICIDS2017, and NSL-KDD datasets. These experiments demonstrate the effective and accurate detection of anomalies in unlabeled data using the algorithm. In this research, optimizing the running efficiency of BAE was not a focus, and the computational complexity of the algorithm is not sufficiently low. In the future, we will put more effort into improving its running efficiency. Additionally, since BAE is a framework-like algorithm, alternative classic pre-classification algorithms can be used, and more advanced Autoencoders can be employed to replace the current one in order to achieve better performance.

Author Contributions: Conceptualization, D.W. and D.C.; methodology, D.W.; software, M.N.; validation, D.W. and D.C.; formal analysis, D.W. and M.N.; investigation, M.N.; resources, D.W.; data curation, M.N.; writing—original draft preparation, M.N.; writing—review and editing, D.W.; visualization, M.N.; supervision, D.C.; project administration, D.W.; funding acquisition, D.W. and D.C. All authors have read and agreed to the published version of the manuscript.

Funding: This work was supported in part by Science and Technology Plan Project of Liaoning Province (No. 2022-KF-11-04), in part by the Fundamental Research Funds for the Central Universities under Grant N2217002, in part by the Applied Basic Research Project of Liaoning Province under Grant 2023JH2/101300185, and in part by the Key Technologies Research and Development Program of Liaoning Province in China under Grant 2021JH1/10400079.

Data Availability Statement: All relevant data are within the manuscript.

Acknowledgments: We thank the anonymous reviewers for their careful reading and valuable comments, which were all valuable and helpful for revising and improving our paper, as well as for providing important guiding significance to our research.

Conflicts of Interest: The authors declare no conflict of interest.

References

1. Engly, A.H.; Larsen, A.R.; Meng, W. Evaluation of Anomaly-Based Intrusion Detection with Combined Imbalance Correction and Feature Selection. In Proceedings of the International Conference on Network and System Security, Melbourne, Australia, 25–27 November 2020; pp. 277–291.
2. Hussain, A.; Heidemann, J.; Papadopoulos, C. A framework for classifying denial of service attacks. In Proceedings of the 2003 Conference on Applications, Technologies, Architectures, and Protocols for Computer Communications, Karlsruhe, Germany, 25–29 August 2003; pp. 99–110.
3. Vincent, P.; Larochelle, H.; Lajoie, I.; Bengio, Y.; Manzagol, P.-A.; Bottou, L. Stacked denoising autoencoders: Learning useful representations in a deep network with a local denoising criterion. *J. Mach. Learn. Res.* **2010**, *11*, 3371–3408.
4. Al-Qatf, M.; Lasheng, Y.; Al-Habib, M.; Al-Sabahi, K. Deep learning approach combining sparse autoencoder with SVM for network intrusion detection. *IEEE Access* **2018**, *6*, 52843–52856. [CrossRef]
5. Kingma, D.P.; Welling, M. Auto-encoding variational bayes. *arXiv* **2013**, arXiv:1312.6114 2013.
6. Masci, J.; Meier, U.; Cireşan, D.; Schmidhuber, J. Stacked convolutional auto-encoders for hierarchical feature extraction. In *Lecture Notes in Computer Science, Proceedings of International Conference on Artificial Neural Networks, Espoo, Finland, 14–17 June 2011*; Springer: Berlin/Heidelberg, Germany, 2011; pp. 52–59.
7. Park, S.; Seo, S.; Kim, J. Network intrusion detection using stacked denoising autoencoder. *Adv. Sci. Lett.* **2017**, *23*, 9907–9911. [CrossRef]
8. Chen, Z.; Yeo, C.K.; Lee, B.S.; Lau, C.T. Autoencoder-based network anomaly detection. In Proceedings of the 2018 Wireless Telecommunications Symposium (WTS), Phoenix, AZ, USA, 17–20 April 2018; pp. 1–5.
9. Shone, N.; Ngoc, T.N.; Phai, V.D.; Shi, Q. A deep learning approach to network intrusion detection. *IEEE Trans. Emerg. Top. Comput. Intell.* **2018**, *2*, 41–50. [CrossRef]
10. Lakhina, A.; Crovella, M.; Diot, C. Diagnosing network-wide traffic anomalies. *ACM SIGCOMM Comput. Commun. Rev.* **2004**, *34*, 219–230. [CrossRef]
11. Yang, S.; Zhang, R.; Nie, F.; Li, X. Unsupervised feature selection based on reconstruction error minimization. In Proceedings of the ICASSP 2019–2019 IEEE International Conference on Acoustics, Speech and Signal Processing (ICASSP), Brighton, UK, 12–17 May 2019; pp. 2107–2111.
12. Zhu, Q.-H.; Yang, Y.-B. Subspace clustering via seeking neighbors with minimum reconstruction error. *Pattern Recognit. Lett.* **2018**, *115*, 66–73. [CrossRef]
13. Auskalnis, J.; Paulauskas, N.; Baskys, A. Application of local outlier factor algorithm to detect anomalies in computer network. *Elektron. Elektrotechnika* **2018**, *24*, 96–99. [CrossRef]
14. Shen, X.; Zhang, J. Research of intrusion detection based on the BP networks and the improved PSO algorithm. *Comput. Eng. Sci.* **2010**, *32*, 34–36.
15. Li, Y.; Qiu, R.; Jing, S. Intrusion detection system using Online Sequence Extreme Learning Machine (OS-ELM) in advanced metering infrastructure of smart grid. *PLoS ONE* **2018**, *13*, e0192216. [CrossRef] [PubMed]
16. Shaikh, R.A.; Shashikala, S. An Autoencoder and LSTM based Intrusion Detection approach against Denial of service attacks. In Proceedings of the 2019 1st International Conference on Advances in Information Technology (ICAIT), Chikmagalur, India, 24–27 July 2019; pp. 406–410.
17. Fan, H.; Zhang, F.; Li, Z. AnomalyDAE: Dual autoencoder for anomaly detection on attributed networks. In Proceedings of the ICASSP 2020—2020 IEEE International Conference on Acoustics, Speech and Signal Processing (ICASSP), Barcelona, Spain, 4–8 May 2020; pp. 5685–5689.
18. Li, W.; Meng, W.; Kwok, L.-F.; Horace, H. Enhancing collaborative intrusion detection networks against insider attacks using supervised intrusion sensitivity-based trust management model. *J. Netw. Comput. Appl.* **2017**, *77*, 135–145. [CrossRef]
19. Azzalini, D.; Bonali, L.; Amigoni, F. A Minimally Supervised Approach Based on Variational Autoencoders for Anomaly Detection in Autonomous Robots. *IEEE Robot. Autom. Lett.* **2021**, *6*, 2985–2992. [CrossRef]
20. Kolberg, J.; Grimmer, M.; Gomez-Barrero, M.; Busch, C. Anomaly detection with convolutional autoencoders for fingerprint presentation attack detection. *IEEE Trans. Biom. Behav. Identity Sci.* **2021**, *3*, 190–202. [CrossRef]
21. Tan, Z.; Jamdagni, A.; He, X.; Nanda, P.; Liu, R.P. A System for Denial-of-Service Attack Detection Based on Multivariate Correlation Analysis. *IEEE Trans. Parallel Distrib. Syst.* **2014**, *25*, 447–456. [CrossRef]
22. Maxion, R.A.; Tan, K.M. Benchmarking anomaly-based detection systems. In Proceedings of the International Conference on Dependable Systems and Networks, DSN, New York, NY, USA, 25–28 June 2000; pp. 623–630.
23. Zhang, T.; Ramakrishnan, R.; Livny, M. BIRCH: An efficient data clustering method for very large databases. *ACM Sigmod Rec.* **1996**, *25*, 103–114. [CrossRef]
24. Siddique, K.; Akhtar, Z.; Khan, F.A.; Kim, Y. KDD Cup 99 data sets: A perspective on the role of data sets in network intrusion detection research. *Computer* **2019**, *52*, 41–51. [CrossRef]
25. Moustafa, N.; Slay, J. UNSW-NB15: A comprehensive data set for network intrusion detection systems (UNSW-NB15 network data set). In Proceedings of the 2015 Military Communications and Information Systems Conference (MilCIS), Canberra, Australia, 10–12 November 2015; pp. 1–6.

26. Sharafaldin, I.; Lashkari, A.H.; Ghorbani, A.A. Toward generating a new intrusion detection dataset and intrusion traffic characterization. In Proceedings of the ICISSP, Funchal, Madeira, Portugal, 22–24 January 2018; pp. 108–116.
27. Revathi, S.; Malathi, A. A detailed analysis on NSL-KDD dataset using various machine learning techniques for intrusion detection. *Int. J. Eng. Res. Technol.* **2013**, *2*, 1848–1853.
28. Tavallaee, M.; Bagheri, E.; Lu, W.; Ghorbani, A.A. A detailed analysis of the KDD CUP 99 data set. In Proceedings of the IEEE International Conference on Computational Intelligence for Security & Defense Applications 2009, Ottawa, ON, Canada, 8–10 July 2009.
29. Datahub. Kddcup99. Available online: https://datahub.io/machine-learning/kddcup99 (accessed on 18 July 2023).
30. Ihsan, Z.; Idris, M.Y.; Abdullah, A.H. Attribute normalization techniques and performance of intrusion classifiers: A comparative analysis. *Life Sci. J.* **2013**, *10*, 2568–2576.
31. Davies, D.L.; Bouldin, D.W. A cluster separation measure. *IEEE Trans. Pattern Anal. Mach. Intell.* **1979**, *2*, 224–227. [CrossRef]

mathematics

MDPI

Article

Item Difficulty Prediction Using Item Text Features: Comparison of Predictive Performance across Machine-Learning Algorithms

Lubomír Štěpánek [1,2,*], Jana Dlouhá [1,3] and Patrícia Martinková [1,4]

1 Institute of Computer Science of the Czech Academy of Sciences, 182 07 Prague, Czech Republic; dlouha@cs.cas.cz (J.D.); martinkova@cs.cas.cz (P.M.)
2 First Faculty of Medicine, Charles University, 121 08 Prague, Czech Republic
3 Faculty of Arts, Charles University, 116 38 Prague, Czech Republic
4 Faculty of Education, Charles University, 110 00 Prague, Czech Republic
* Correspondence: lubomir.stepanek@cs.cas.cz

Abstract: This work presents a comparative analysis of various machine learning (ML) methods for predicting item difficulty in English reading comprehension tests using text features extracted from item wordings. A wide range of ML algorithms are employed within both the supervised regression and the classification tasks, including regularization methods, support vector machines, trees, random forests, back-propagation neural networks, and Naïve Bayes; moreover, the ML algorithms are compared to the performance of domain experts. Using f-fold cross-validation and considering the root mean square error (RMSE) as the performance metric, elastic net outperformed other approaches in a continuous item difficulty prediction. Within classifiers, random forests returned the highest extended predictive accuracy. We demonstrate that the ML algorithms implementing item text features can compete with predictions made by domain experts, and we suggest that they should be used to inform and improve these predictions, especially when item pre-testing is limited or unavailable. Future research is needed to study the performance of the ML algorithms using item text features on different item types and respondent populations.

Keywords: text-based item difficulty prediction; text features and item wording; machine learning; regularization methods; elastic net regression; support vector machines; regression and decision trees; random forests; neural networks; algorithm vs. domain expert's prediction performance

MSC: 62H12; 62H30; 68T50

Citation: Štěpánek, L.; Dlouhá, J.; Martinková, P. Item Difficulty Prediction Using Item Text Features: Comparison of Predictive Performance across Machine-Learning Algorithms. *Mathematics* **2023**, *11*, 4104. https://doi.org/10.3390/math11194104

Academic Editors: Huawen Liu, Gaige Wang and Ioannis G. Tsoulos

Received: 1 July 2023
Revised: 8 September 2023
Accepted: 22 September 2023
Published: 28 September 2023

1. Introduction

In educational assessment, the analysis of test items is crucial for designing reliable, valid and fair tests. Item difficulty, the most important item characteristic, is commonly estimated using classical test theory (CTT) and item response theory (IRT) models based on test-taker responses [1]; however, item pre-testing is not always possible, or it may be limited, e.g., due to security or legal reasons. In such situations, automated estimation of item difficulty based on their wording can inform test construction.

Various properties of text wording of a given test item determine how difficult the item is for a test-taker. The item text features, such as length, word frequencies related to established corpora, characteristics of linguistic similarities, and readability indices, can be used to predict item difficulty using machine learning (ML) algorithms. ML and natural language processing (NLP) are already used in different areas of education for automated essay or item scoring [2–4], automated item generation [5–9], data-driven intelligent tutoring systems [10], online proctoring and cheating detection [11–13], and in other situations [14–17]. In addition to commonly used methods such as linear regression or decision trees [18], regularization approaches and neural networks are sometimes used to estimate the item difficulty from item wording based on item features [19]. A wide range of ML algorithms has been used in this context in the past [18,20]. However, their predictive performance is usually not compared; moreover, ML algorithms are rarely compared to the performance of domain experts, which is crucial to determine to what extent the ML algorithms are capable of improving the predictive accuracy of human raters. This is an area of focus in the study.

To address this gap, we introduce a framework for predicting item difficulty using textual features from item wording. We assess the predictive accuracy of multiple ML methods, and we compare them with the predictions made by domain experts. The tools of choice for the prediction we apply on the item features are supervised ML regression methods, namely regularization techniques—such as the least absolute shrinkage and selection operator, ridge regression and elastic net regression—support vector machines, regression trees, random forests, and artificial neural networks with back-propagation [9,21]. We predict the item difficulty as a continuous dependent variable, as it would be returned from student response data. Furthermore, switching the same algorithms into a classification fashion, we predict the membership of each item in one of the predefined difficulty intervals. We assume that classification into one of a few item difficulty intervals could be easier and more accurate for the algorithms than predicting a precise difficulty point value. We hypothesize that ML algorithms are able to compete with human domain experts in predicting (or classifying) item difficulty and that they may further inform and improve the experts' predictions.

The paper proceeds as follows. We start by describing the data preparation needed for the implementation of ML algorithms on cognitive test items, including the text preprocessing and extraction of item features. We then describe the ML algorithms used in this study in Section 2, *Materials and Methods*. We briefly describe applied software, model architecture, algorithms' pre-setting, and tuning parameter values in Section 3, *Implementation*. Next, in Section 4, *Results*, we describe the results, namely the comparison of the accuracy of item difficulty predictions returned by different artificial ML algorithms and those performed by domain experts. Finally, we discuss the key findings in Section 5, *Discussion*, and offer some deductions in Section 6, *Conclusions*.

2. Materials and Methods

A description of a dataset we used for item difficulty prediction and of the applied ML algorithms we built on follows.

2.1. Dataset and Item Text Processing

For this study, we use item wordings from the English as a foreign language test administered over eight years (2016–2023) as a part of the Czech matura exam. We use items from reading comprehension sections containing multiple-choice items with a single-paragraph passage and four response options, denoted as Section 5. We also utilize a dataset of test-takers' answers for the calculation of difficulty for each item as described in more detail in the next section. Finally, item difficulty evaluation by domain experts comes from another (internal) dataset.

Item text wordings are extracted from portable document format-based files (with suffixes .pdf) using optical character recognition (OCR). Then, we apply the scraping methods employing empirical approaches such as regular expressions' masking, by which we obtain an unstructured text for each item's wording, split into item passage, item question, key option (the correct answer), and distractors (incorrect answers). Next, the text is tokenized, i.e., sentences are split into atomic parts (*tokens*), in this case, words. In the next step, stopwords and special characters are removed, and the tokens are lemmatized, i.e., they are transformed into their corresponding lemmas [22], as schematically indicated in Figure 1.

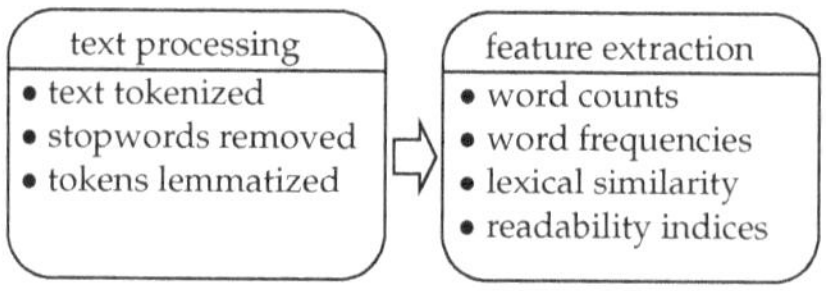

Figure 1. A scheme of text processing procedures and extraction of item text features.

Finally, item text features are derived [23]. We consider four types of item text features. Firstly, the *word counts* feature is easily calculated using lengths of vectors of item text tokens. Secondly, using The Corpus of Contemporary American English (COCA) [24,25], the *word frequencies* are assessed compared to usual frequencies of given words in ordinary language. Then, the *lexical similarity* is calculated using Euclidean and cosine metrics to describe how textually similar (or close) are vectors of tokens of item wording's different parts, e.g., how similar the item question and its key option, i.e., the correct answer, are, considering that their high lexical similarity may tend to make the item easier. Additionally, the lexical similarity between the key option and the distractors, i.e., incorrect answers, is calculated, considering that large dissimilarity can make the item easier. Lastly, we compute the *readability indices* depicting how easy-to-read and easy-to-understand the wording of the text is. In general, the readability indices usually follow formulae of the form

$$\text{readability index} = f\left(\boldsymbol{v}^T_{\text{word counts}}, \boldsymbol{v}^T_{\text{word frequencies}}, \boldsymbol{v}^T_{\text{word counts} \otimes \text{word frequencies}}\right),$$

where f is a function in an explicit form using a vector of absolute and relative counts of words and parts of speech of a given text $\boldsymbol{v}^T_{\text{word counts}}$, a vector of common or unique word's frequencies compared to everyday language, $\boldsymbol{v}^T_{\text{word frequencies}}$, and various combinations of previous two properties, $\boldsymbol{v}^T_{\text{word counts} \otimes \text{word frequencies}}$, as suggested by [26]. A more detailed explanation of individual item features derived using the above-described approaches is in Appendix A.

Eventually, using the above techniques, we derive more than 60 text features per item and list them into a structured dataset of size $n \times k$ so that each column represents one feature for each of n items, and each row contains a vector of all k features for a given item.

2.2. Item Difficulty Based on Student Responses

Having data from more than 50 thousand test-takers answering the items each year, we enrich the dataset of item text features constructed in the previous step by the item difficulty estimated using Rasch model [1] (p. 158), [27,28] from student responses. The Rasch model is relatively simple but can estimate item difficulty for each item; more complex models can describe other item parameters, such as item discrimination or item guessing, that are not of interest in this study. The Rasch models assumes that a test-taker with ability θ_p answers item i correctly with a probability

$$P(\text{test-taker with ability } \theta_p \text{ answers item } i \text{ correctly}) = \frac{e^{\theta_p - y_i}}{1 + e^{\theta_p - y_i}}, \tag{1}$$

where y_i is the difficulty Y of item i, that is of main interest in this study (thus the notation).

We use the conditional maximum likelihood method [1] (p. 165) to estimate difficulties for each item $i \in \{1, 2, \ldots, n\}$ based on the Rasch model (1). The conditional likelihood method accounts for the overall ability of the tested sample, which may differ each year; the item difficulty's estimate is proportional to a portion of incorrect answers to the item adjusted by a proportion of the total number of correct answers. As an output, we obtain a vector $(y_1, y_2, \ldots, y_n)^T$ of n values of item difficulty Y for each item. Note that estimates of item difficulty based on student responses are close to the true item difficulties when a representative and a sufficiently large sample of test-takers are available. This was the case in our study; however, such a respondent sample may not be available in all situations.

2.3. Machine Learning Algorithms

In this study, we compare the performance of several ML methods for predicting and classifying item difficulty. Let us define the regression and classification tasks more formally before describing the supervised regression and classification algorithms.

Assume we initially have $k \in \mathbb{N}$ item text features $X_1, X_2, \ldots, X_k$ and $(k+1)$-th variable Y, a dependent one, i.e., item difficulty, derived as indicated in the previous section. As an output of the Rasch model from Formula (1), the item difficulty Y is estimated as a continuous variable. The *regression task* algorithms predict a value y_i of the item difficulty Y for item i using values $x_{i,1}, x_{i,2}, \ldots, x_{i,k}$ of all item text features $X_1, X_2, \ldots, X_k$ as predictors.

However, for test construction, predicting an exact point value from an item difficulty continuum is unnecessary; test developers often rely on the item difficulty category, thus classifying item difficulty into only a few, e.g., five categories, is sufficient. Thus, we also implement the *classification task*. As the first step, the item difficulty Y is categorized, obtaining Y_c, so that it is split into $m \in \mathbb{N}$ disjunctive intervals $\{c_1, c_2, \ldots, c_m\}$ of the same size using appropriate quantiles. Thus, union $\bigcup_{\ell=1}^{m} c_\ell$ is a range of item difficulty variable Y, i.e.,

$$\bigcup_{\ell=1}^{m} c_\ell = \{\forall y \in \mathbb{R} : Y_{\min} \leq y \leq Y_{\max}\},$$

and intersection $\bigcap_{\ell=1}^{m} c_\ell$ is an empty set,

$$\bigcap_{\ell=1}^{m} c_\ell = \emptyset.$$

Then, within the classification task, item feature X_j, where $j \in \{1, 2, \ldots, k\}$, is treated as an independent variable for a classification model, which predicts the most-likely interval $c_\ell^* \in Y_c$ of the categorized item difficulty Y_c.

A flowchart of the regression task is in Figure 2; similarly, a classification task scheme is in Figure 3. Regardless of the regression or classification task, the predicted item difficulty values are compared to the 'true' ones as estimated using the Rasch model. To increase reproducibility as much as possible, algorithms are learned on training subsets, while point estimates of the predictive metrics are estimated on testing subsets. This is repeated several times to obtain a more robust estimate of the predictive performance, averaging all point estimates collected from individual iterations.

Domain experts estimate the item difficulty Y using their empirical knowledge in the field, and their item difficulty estimates Y might also be categorized to create Y_c. Thus, domain experts can be treated as "another" regression and "another" classification algorithm and their performance can be compared to the predictive and classification performance of ML algorithms. Many ML algorithms have both the regression and classification version [29], as we describe in more detail in the next section.

2.3.1. Regularization

Although regularization techniques could serve as regression algorithms, they also offer an option to select a subset of item features used for model building. Therefore, regularization methods enable *feature selection*, which helps reduce the problem's dimensionality with minimal loss of information.

LASSO (Least Absolute Shrinkage and Selection Operator) regression estimates a value y_i of item i's difficulty Y using least squares and L1 regularization-based coefficients $\beta_0, \beta_1, \ldots, \beta_k$ minimizing the following term,

$$\sum_{i=1}^{n} \left(y_i - \beta_0 - \sum_{j=1}^{k} \beta_j x_{i,j} \right)^2 + \lambda_{\text{LASSO}} \cdot \sum_{j=1}^{k} |\beta_j|, \quad (2)$$

where $x_{i,j}$ is a value of j-th feature of i-th item with $j \in \{1, 2, \ldots, k\}$ and $\lambda_{\text{LASSO}} > 0$ i a penalization term [30].

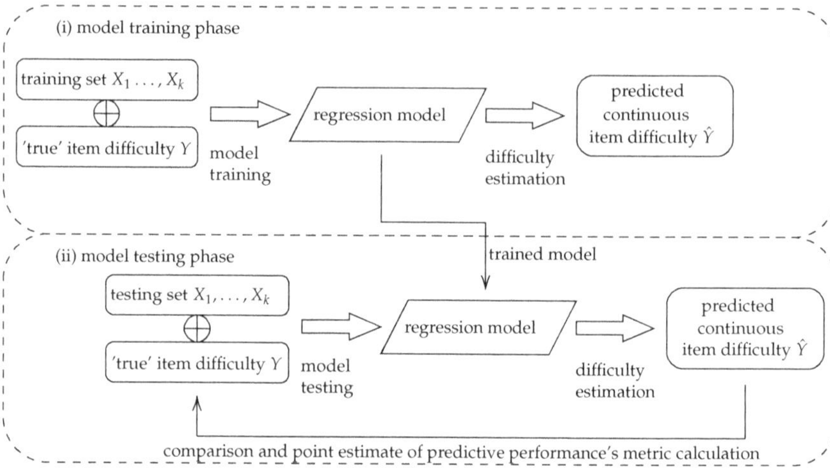

Figure 2. A flowchart of the regression task. The model is built using a training set, while item difficulty Y is predicted using a testing set. The training and testing phase are repeated several times within the cross-validation to increase the robustness and reproducibility of the predictive performance metric estimate. The 'true' item difficulty Y is in quotes since it is estimated from student response data rather than simulated.

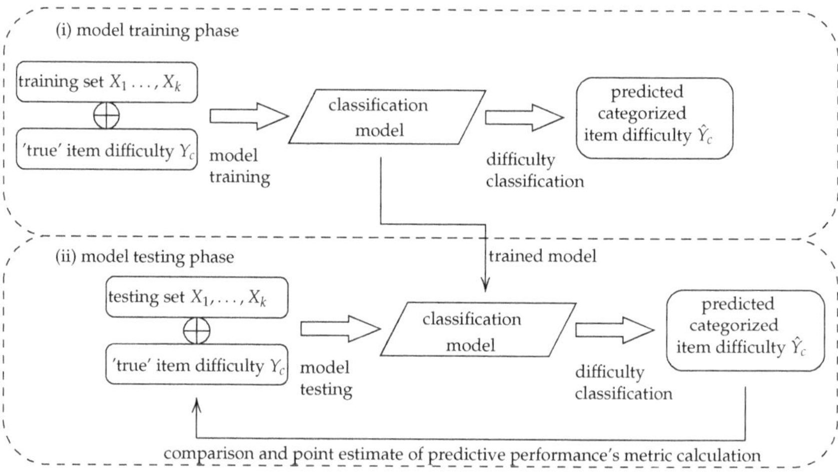

Figure 3. A flowchart of the classification task. The model is built using a training set, while item difficulty Y_c is classified using a testing set. The training and testing phase are repeated several times within the cross-validation to increase the robustness and reproducibility of the predictive performance metric estimate. The 'true' item difficulty category Y_c is in quotes since it is estimated from student response data rather than simulated.

Similarly, *ridge regression* uses L2 penalization and penalization term $\lambda_{\text{ridge}} > 0$ to minimize

$$\sum_{i=1}^{n} \left(y_i - \beta_0 - \sum_{j=1}^{k} \beta_j x_{i,j} \right)^2 + \lambda_{\text{ridge}} \cdot \sum_{j=1}^{k} \beta_j^2, \tag{3}$$

while item difficulty Y's value y_i is estimated for item i using its item text features $x_{i,j}$ with $j \in \{1, 2, \ldots, k\}$ [31].

Finally, *elastic net* regression combines both L1 and L2 penalization and minimizes the following function,

$$\sum_{i=1}^{n}\left(y_i - \beta_0 - \sum_{j=1}^{k}\beta_j x_{i,j}\right)^2 + \lambda_{\text{LASSO}} \cdot \sum_{j=1}^{k}|\beta_j| + \lambda_{\text{ridge}} \cdot \sum_{j=1}^{k}\beta_j^2 \tag{4}$$

to estimate item i's difficulty Y using its text features $x_{i,j}$, where $j \in \{1, 2, \ldots, k\}$. Assuming both penalizations, i.e., the L1 and L2 terms in Formula (4) are convex [32], elastic net usually reaches values of the function in Formula (4) as minimal as LASSO or ridge regression individually does, and, thus, performs at least as good as the previous two regularization algorithms [33].

Since Formulae (2)–(4) are minimized while coefficients $\beta_0, \beta_1, \ldots, \beta_k$ are estimated, the terms $\lambda_{\text{LASSO}} \sum_{j=1}^{k}|\beta_j|$, $\lambda_{\text{ridge}} \sum_{j=0}^{k}\beta_j^2$ are also minimized. Thus, if $\lambda_{\text{LASSO}} = 0$ or $\lambda_{\text{ridge}} = 0$, penalization terms in Formulae (2)–(4) are removed, and the functions in the formulae become ordinary least squares usual for multivariate linear regression. Otherwise, whenever is $\lambda_{\text{LASSO}} > 0$ and $\lambda_{\text{ridge}} > 0$, then, for β_j close to zero, such a coefficient tends to be shrunk towards zero, and, consequently, j-th item feature is removed from the model while $\hat{\beta}_j = 0$. Thus, regularization techniques could also work as feature selectors. LASSO is considered a better feature selector than ridge regression [34]. Intuitively, assuming j-th item feature X_j is likely to be removed from the model, so it is $0 < |\beta_j| < 1$, then also $0 \cdot |\beta_j| < |\beta_j| \cdot |\beta_j| < 1 \cdot |\beta_j|$ and, consequently, $\beta_j^2 < |\beta_j|$ $(\dagger)$. Whenever is $\lambda_{\text{ridge}} \cdot \beta_j$ or $\lambda_{\text{ridge}} \cdot \beta_j^2$ term large enough so that removing the j-th item feature X_j from the model would reduce the penalization term significantly, the j-th item feature is removed. Thus, for constant values of $\lambda_{\text{LASSO}} = \lambda_{\text{ridge}}$, due to $(\dagger)$, term $\lambda_{\text{ridge}} \cdot \beta_j^2$ in the ridge regression is not as large as term $\lambda_{\text{LASSO}} \cdot |\beta_j|$ in the LASSO, and, consequently, it is less likely that j-th item feature X_j is removed from the ridge regression model than from LASSO model, keeping the penalization levels the same for the two models.

2.3.2. Naïve Bayes Classifier

Naïve Bayes classifier classifies i-th item into the most likely class c_ℓ^* of item difficulty Y. The Bayes theorem assumes that a relationship between conditional probabilities $P(Y_i = c_l \mid \forall x_{i,j})$ and $P(\forall x_{i,j} \mid Y_i = c_\ell)$, where $\forall x_{i,j}$ term stands for a joint proposition $\{X_{i,1} = x_{i,1} \wedge X_{i,2} = x_{i,2} \wedge \cdots \wedge X_{i,k} = x_{i,k}\}$, is

$$P(Y_i = c_\ell \mid \forall x_{i,j}) = \frac{P(\forall x_{i,j} \mid Y_i = c_\ell)P(Y_i = c_\ell)}{P(\forall x_{i,j})}. \tag{5}$$

The non-conditional probabilities $P(Y_i = c_\ell)$ and $P(\forall x_{i,j})$ are constant for a given dataset [35] and can be easily estimated as

$$\hat{P}(Y_i = c_\ell) = \frac{1}{n}\sum_{i=1}^{n}\mathcal{I}(Y_i = c_\ell) \quad \text{and} \quad \hat{P}(\forall x_{i,j}) = \frac{1}{n \cdot k}\sum_{i=1}^{n}\sum_{j=1}^{k}\mathcal{I}(X_{i,j} = x_{i,j}), \tag{6}$$

where $\mathcal{I}(\mathcal{A})$ is an identifier function which is equal to 1 if and only if proposition A is true, otherwise it is equal to 0, i.e.,

$$\mathcal{I}(\mathcal{A}) = \begin{cases} 1, & \text{proposition } \mathcal{A} \text{ is true,} \\ 0, & \text{proposition } \mathcal{A} \text{ is false.} \end{cases} \tag{7}$$

Thus, proportion $\frac{P(Y_i = c_\ell)}{P(\forall x_{i,j})}$ is constant and Formula (5) can be rewritten as

$$P(Y_i = c_\ell \mid \forall x_{i,j}) \propto P(\forall x_{i,j}) \mid Y_i = c_\ell),$$

and as far as we assume classes $c_1, c_2, \ldots c_m$ are independent, we may also write

$$\begin{aligned} P(Y_i = c_\ell \mid \forall x_{i,j}) &\propto P(\forall x_{i,j} \mid Y_i = c_\ell) \propto \\ &\propto P(X_{i,1} = x_{i,1} \wedge X_{i,2} = x_{i,2} \wedge \cdots \wedge X_{i,k} = x_{i,k} \mid Y_i = c_\ell) \propto \\ &\propto \prod_{j=1}^{k} P(X_{i,j} = x_{i,j} \mid Y_i = c_\ell). \end{aligned}$$

With Naïve Bayes, item i is classified into interval c_ℓ^* so that

$$c_\ell^* = \underset{\ell \in \{1,2,\ldots,m\}}{\operatorname{argmax}} \left\{ P(Y_i = c_\ell \mid \forall x_{i,j}) \right\} = \underset{\ell \in \{1,2,\ldots,m\}}{\operatorname{argmax}} \left\{ \prod_{j=1}^{k} P(X_{i,j} = x_{i,j} \mid Y_i = c_\ell) \right\}.$$

For categorical item features X_j, probability $P(X_{i,j} = x_{i,j} \mid Y_i = c_\ell)$ is estimated similarly to Formula (6); for continuous variables X_j, it is estimated using cumulative version of normal distribution function, i.e., $\hat{P}(X_{i,j} = x_{i,j} \mid Y_i = c_\ell) = \Phi(x_{i,j} \pm \epsilon \mid Y_i = c_\ell)$ for small positive $\epsilon > 0$.

2.3.3. Support Vector Machines

Assuming the space of all item features $X_1 \times X_2 \times \cdots X_k$, *support vector machines* use a hyperplane to split the space into two disjunctive subspaces (of different classes). The splitting maximizes the margins, i.e., the distance between the two closest points, so that the first comes from one subspace (of the first class) while the latter comes from the second subspace (of the latter class). The hyperplane is orthogonal to the distance of the two closest points, assuming each subspace contains ideally observations of only one class; see Figure 4 for details. Assuming m classes, since one model of support vector machines can classify into only two classes, $\binom{m}{2}$ models in total are built [36].

Each model of support vector machines searches for a splitting hyperplane that follows a form of

$$\boldsymbol{w}^T \boldsymbol{x}_i - b = 0,$$

where $\boldsymbol{w}$ is a vector orthogonal to the splitting hyperplane, and b is maximally tolerated margin's width. Additionally, the two closest points from both subspaces are elements of mutually parallel hyperplanes (and also parallel to the splitting hyperplane), i.e., $\boldsymbol{w}^T \boldsymbol{x}_i - b > 0$ and $\boldsymbol{w}^T \boldsymbol{x}_i - b < 0$, respectively. Finally, the distance between the two closest points of different classes is $\left\{ \frac{2b}{\|\boldsymbol{w}\|} \right\}$, i.e., a width of both margins, and it should be maximized with respect to the existence of two distinguishable hyperplanes for two closest points of different classes, so that

$$\max \left\{ \frac{2b}{\|\boldsymbol{w}\|} \right\} \qquad \text{subject to} \qquad |\boldsymbol{w}^T \boldsymbol{x}_i - b| > 0,$$

where b as the tolerated margin width, i.e., a user's tuning parameter, is usually chosen as $b \geq 1$.

A kernel trick with various kernel functions is applied when the points that belong to different classes are not linearly separable. In principle, the universe of item features, $X_1 \times X_2 \times \cdots \times X_k$, is extended by new variables $U_1, U_2, \ldots$, that increase the universe dimensionality [37] and, eventually, after that, it becomes linearly separable as indicated in Figure 5.

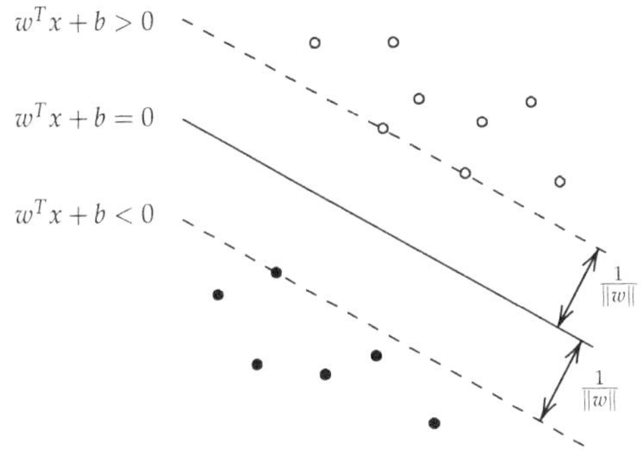

Figure 4. The margin between the hyperplane of the support vector machines (solid line) and the closest points of both subspaces (dashed lines) is maximized by the algorithm.

The classification of item i into difficulty Y's class c_i^* is then performed using a voting scheme, i.e., the class c_i^* is the one that the majority of all $\binom{m}{2}$ models votes for, i.e.,

$$c_i^* = \underset{\ell \in \{1,2,\dots,m\}}{\operatorname{argmax}} \left\{ \sum_{\mu=1}^{\binom{m}{2}} \mathcal{I}(\mu\text{-th model votes for class } \ell) \right\},$$

using the same mathematical notation and identifier function as defined in Formula (7).

When regression is applied, trivial (usually constant) models are built for each subspace of the space, divided by the splitting hyperplane. Therefore, averages of all coordinates of all observations belonging to a given subspace are calculated, representing the regression model of the given subspace.

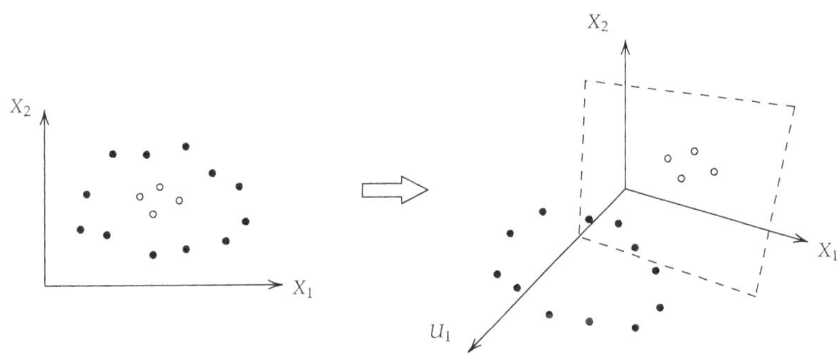

Figure 5. A visualization of the kernel trick's principle.

2.3.4. Regression and Classification Trees and Random Forests

Classification trees, also called *decision trees*, partition the dataset into subdatasets to contain ideally observations of only one class of item difficulty Y. The partitioning is performed successively from the original dataset by binary splitting; a given criterion is minimized within each dataset splitting. In other words, item features' universe $X_1 \times X_2 \times \cdots \times X_k$ is split into disjunctive orthogonal subspaces, including, if not all, then the vast majority of all points from one class of item difficulty Y. Each step of the dataset partitioning, i.e., splitting a parenting dataset into two new child subdatasets, enables the growth of a typical tree plot, dendrogram, by adding two new child branches; see Figure 6. The partitioning is applied multiple times until the dataset is split according to item difficulty Y classes' distribution [38].

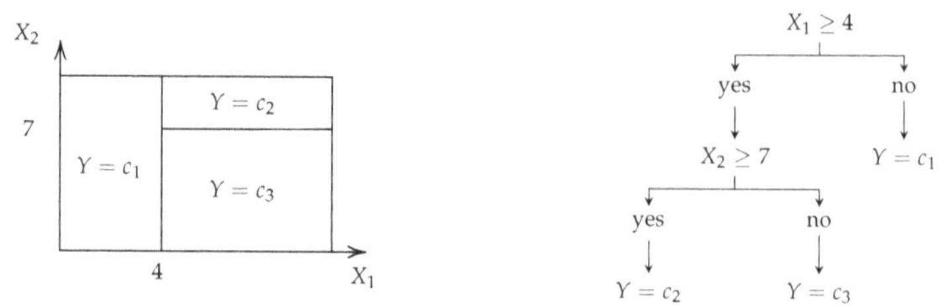

Figure 6. Linear splitting of the variables' space (on the **left**) and an appropriate tree representation (on the **right**).

Assuming $\rho_{\eta,\ell}$ is a proportion of observations of class c_ℓ in part of the dataset that defined by all node rules from root to node η, then $\rho_{\eta,\ell}$ should be maximized as much as possible using an impurity criterion $Q(\eta)$. The most often used impurity measures are the misclassification error,

$$Q(\eta) = 1 - \rho_{\eta,\ell}, \tag{8}$$

the Gini index,

$$Q(\eta) = \sum_{\ell=1}^{m} \rho_{\eta,\ell}(1 - \rho_{\eta,\ell}), \tag{9}$$

and the deviance, also called cross-entropy,

$$Q(\eta) = -\sum_{\ell=1}^{m} \rho_{\eta,\ell} \cdot \log \rho_{\eta,\ell}. \tag{10}$$

Obviously, the impurity measure $Q(\eta)$ is minimized in each dataset's partitioning since the lower the impurity measure is, the larger the proportion $\rho_{\eta,\ell}$ is. Trees tend to overfit the distribution of classes in the dataset; it means the tree growth is stopped no sooner than all leave nodes have the impurity criterion as minimized as possible. To avoid overfitting, various stopping criteria or pruning are applied [39].

Once the tree is grown, it enables to classify item i into difficulty Y's class c_ℓ^*, so that

$$c_\ell^* = \underset{\ell \in \{1,2,\dots,m\}}{\operatorname{argmax}} \left\{ \rho_{\text{leaf node determined by all node rules from root to the node, } \ell} \right\},$$

using the introduced notation and identifier function from Formula (7). Trivial (constant) models constructed for each subspace transform the classification trees into *regression trees* [40].

Multiple trees create a structure called *random forest*. Individual trees of a given random forest are mutually independent and different. This is ensured by applying only a subset of all item features pre-selected using a bootstrap for each new tree growing in a random forest. Finally, the classification or regression output of the random forest is determined by the voting scheme of individual trees [41], similarly as for the support vector machines: item i is classified into such a difficulty Y's class c_ℓ^* for which the majority of all trees in the random forest votes, i.e.,

$$c_\ell^* = \underset{\ell \in \{1,2,\dots,m\}}{\operatorname{argmax}} \left\{ \sum_{\tau \in \{\text{trees of random forest}\}} \mathcal{I}(\text{tree } \tau \text{ votes for class } \ell) \right\},$$

using the same mathematical notation as above.

2.3.5. Neural Networks

Neural networks are universal algorithms suitable for regression and classification tasks. An architecture of a neural network consists of a layer of input and output neuron(s) and several hidden layers so that each hidden layer consists of multiple neurons [42].

An example of the neuron is in Figure 7. On input of the neuron, there is a vector of signals from neurons of a previous layer, i.e., $\boldsymbol{z}_{l-1} = (z_{l-1,1}, z_{l-1,2}, \ldots)^T$, multiplied by a vector of weights $\boldsymbol{w}_{l-1} = (w_{l-1,1}, w_{l-1,2}, \ldots)^T$. If $l = 1$, the neurons of the first layer accept weighted signals from a vector of item i's features, $\boldsymbol{x}_i = (x_{i,1}, x_{i,2}, \ldots, x_{i,k})^T$. Weighted signals from $(l-1)$-th layer are summed up together with bias term b_l within Σ function, i.e.,

$$\Sigma = \boldsymbol{w}_{l-1} \cdot \boldsymbol{z}_{l-1} + b_l,$$

and proceeded to the σ function, which is an activating function, usually of the sigmoid form,

$$\sigma(\zeta) = \frac{1}{1 + e^{-\zeta}},$$

so that signal $y_{l,1}$ on output from the neuron of l-th layer is

$$y_{l,1} = \sigma(\Sigma + b_l) = \sigma(\boldsymbol{w}_{l-1} \cdot \boldsymbol{z}_{l-1} + b_l) = \frac{1}{1 + e^{-(\boldsymbol{w}_{l-1} \cdot \boldsymbol{z}_{l-1} + b_l)}},$$

which is finally transcended to the next, $(l+1)$-th layer. Vectors of weights, $\boldsymbol{w}_l = (w_{l,1}, w_{l,2}, \ldots)^T$ are adjusted within each iteration of so-called *backpropagation* when the weights are increased or decreased by small gradients to minimize the loss function, often implemented as L1 or L2 penalization [43].

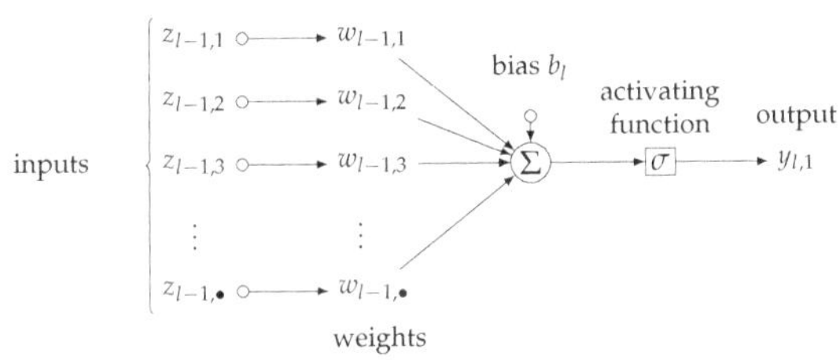

Figure 7. A scheme of one neuron in neural network.

In the regression framework, besides neurons in a hidden layer, we implement a single neuron in the output layer, returning continuous estimate $\hat{y}_i$ of item i's difficulty. In the classification framework, there are m output neurons representing classes $\{c_1, c_2, \ldots, c_m\}$ and we adopt voting for c_l^* in classifying network [44], as follows

$$c_\ell^* = \underset{\ell \in \{1,2,\ldots,m\}}{\operatorname{argmax}} \left\{ y_{\#\text{ of layers},\, \ell} \right\}.$$

2.3.6. Variable Importance Analysis

While the importance analysis is not a stand-alone algorithm for item difficulty (or its categorized variant) prediction, it enables us to evaluate how "important" a given variable is for a model, considering the predictive performance; in other words, how much poorer the model would predict if it lacked the given variable [45].

We apply two measures of variable importance; each variable, i.e., item feature, has its own value of the importance measure, considering a given dataset and model. Before we introduce the measures, we define the mean square error, MSE, as

$$\text{MSE}(\boldsymbol{y}, \hat{\boldsymbol{y}}) = \frac{1}{n} \sum_{i=1}^{n} (y_i - \hat{y}_i)^2, \tag{11}$$

for vectors $\boldsymbol{y} = (y_1, y_2, \ldots, y_n)^T$ and $\hat{\boldsymbol{y}} = (\hat{y}_1, \hat{y}_2, \ldots, \hat{y}_n)^T$ of observed and predicted difficulties of n items, respectively. The first importance measure is $\mathrm{MSE}_{\mathrm{increase}}(X_j)$, which is equal to an increase of mean square error of item difficulty prediction in such a model where values of the given item feature, X_j, are randomly permuted [45]. To be more specific, we firstly calculate mean square error $\mathrm{MSE}_{\{-\emptyset\}}$ of a full model with all original item features, then we compute mean square error $\mathrm{MSE}_{\{-j\}}$ of a model where item feature X_j has randomly shuffled values. Finally, $\mathrm{MSE}_{\mathrm{increase}}(X_j)$ is defined as

$$\mathrm{MSE}_{\mathrm{increase}}(X_j) = \frac{\mathrm{MSE}_{\{-j\}} - \mathrm{MSE}_{\{-\emptyset\}}}{\mathrm{MSE}_{\{-\emptyset\}}}. \quad (12)$$

The more important item feature X_j for adequate and accurate prediction of item difficulty, the larger the prediction error, measured using mean square error MSE, when the item feature X_j is missing in the model. Thus, the greater the value of $\mathrm{MSE}_{\mathrm{increase}}(X_j)$, the more important the item feature X_j for item difficulty prediction.

The second importance measure, node purity increase, $\mathrm{NodePurity}_{\mathrm{increase}}(X_j)$ is defined similarly. Once impurity metric $Q(\eta)$ is chosen, i.e., either misclassification error (8), Gini index (9) or deviance (10), the node purity increase, $\mathrm{NodePurity}_{\mathrm{increase}}(X_j)$, for item feature X_j is simply an increase of "1 minus impurity metric" term averaged over all leaf nodes if the item feature X_j is newly introduced into a new model [45]. Thus, having the averaged "1 − node impurity" term, $\overline{(1 - Q(\eta))}_{\{-j\}}$, of a tree model with all original item features except for item feature X_j, and averaged "1 − node impurity", $\overline{(1 - Q(\eta))}_{\{-\emptyset\}}$, of a model where item feature X_j is already included, the $\mathrm{NodePurity}_{\mathrm{increase}}(X_j)$ is then

$$\mathrm{NodePurity}_{\mathrm{increase}}(X_j) = \frac{\overline{(1 - Q(\eta))}_{\{-\emptyset\}} - \overline{(1 - Q(\eta))}_{\{-j\}}}{\overline{(1 - Q(\eta))}_{\{-j\}}}. \quad (13)$$

Again, the more important item feature X_j for the predictive model performance, the higher average "1 − node impurity" increase, i.e., the higher average purity increase we can expect once the item feature X_j is introduced into the model. Thus, the larger the value of $\mathrm{NodePurity}_{\mathrm{increase}}(X_j)$, the more important the item feature X_j for item difficulty prediction. According to some sources, e.g., [46], $\mathrm{MSE}_{\mathrm{increase}}(X_j)$ measure should be preferred to $\mathrm{NodePurity}_{\mathrm{increase}}(X_j)$, since the latter one is biased.

2.4. Evaluation of Algorithm Performance

Regression and classification tasks are evaluated using mutually different performance metrics. To obtain more robust estimates of the performance metrics, both regression and classification models are trained multiple times using various training sets, which enables us to average the metrics using all point estimates, collected one per each cross-validation iteration [47]; see Figures 2 and 3. We also compare an item difficulty prediction performance of the ML approaches with the performance of domain experts.

2.4.1. Evaluation of Regression Performance

The models within the regression task are evaluated and compared using root mean square error (RMSE), i.e.,

$$\mathrm{RMSE}(\boldsymbol{y}, \hat{\boldsymbol{y}}) = \sqrt{\frac{1}{n}\sum_{i=1}^{n}(y_i - \hat{y}_i)^2} \quad (14)$$

for vectors $\boldsymbol{y} = (y_1, y_2, \ldots, y_n)^T$ and $\hat{\boldsymbol{y}} = (\hat{y}_1, \hat{y}_2, \ldots, \hat{y}_n)^T$ of observed and predicted difficulties of n items, respectively. Obviously, inspecting Formulae (11) and (14), we obtain the following identity, $\mathrm{MSE}(\boldsymbol{y}, \hat{\boldsymbol{y}}) = \mathrm{RMSE}(\boldsymbol{y}, \hat{\boldsymbol{y}})^2$. Since RMSE indicates the significance of error between observed and predicted item difficulties, the lower RMSE indicates the better predictive performance of a given regression algorithm.

2.4.2. Evaluation of Classification Performance

Assuming there are m observed classes that are predicted using a classifier, we could calculate a number of cases $n_{u,v}$ when 'true' class c_u is predicted as class c_v, where $u \in \{1, 2, \ldots, m\}$ and $v \in \{1, 2, \ldots, m\}$. Listing these frequencies in a table, we obtain Table 1, called the *confusion matrix*.

Table 1. A confusion matrix for m observed, 'true' classes $Y_c \in \{c_1, c_2, \ldots, c_m\}$ (in rows) and m predicted classes $\hat{Y}_c \in \{c_1, c_2, \ldots, c_m\}$ (in columns).

		Predicted Class ($\hat{Y}_c$)			
		c_1	c_2	$\cdots$	c_m
'true' class (Y_c)	c_1	$n_{1,1}$	$n_{1,2}$	$\cdots$	$n_{1,m}$
	c_2	$n_{2,1}$	$n_{2,2}$	$\cdots$	$n_{2,m}$
	$\vdots$	$\vdots$	$\vdots$	$\ddots$	$\vdots$
	c_m	$n_{m,1}$	$n_{m,2}$	$\cdots$	$n_{m,m}$

The better and more accurate the classification is, the higher frequencies $n_{i,i}$ are aligned across the confusion matrix's principal diagonal. Thus, marking the confusion matrix as $\mathbf{C}$ and assuming vectors $\boldsymbol{y}_c$ of observed item difficulty classes and $\hat{\boldsymbol{y}}_c$ of predicted difficulty classes, we define *predictive accuracy* as the ratio of correctly classified items,

$$\begin{aligned} \text{predictive accuracy}(\boldsymbol{y}_c, \hat{\boldsymbol{y}}_c) &= \frac{1}{n}\sum_{i=1}^{n}\{\mathcal{I}(\hat{y}_{c,i} = c_\ell \wedge y_{c,i} = c_\ell)\} = \\ &= \frac{\operatorname{tr}\mathbf{C}}{\sum \mathbf{C}} = \frac{\sum_{u=1}^{m} n_{u,u}}{\sum_{u=1}^{m}\sum_{v=1}^{m} n_{u,v}}. \end{aligned} \tag{15}$$

The higher the predictive accuracy, the better and more accurate the classification is [48]. Each of m classes of item difficulty Y_c are of equal size in the dataset (classes are split using quantiles) (†). Assuming a classifier would predict difficulties $\boldsymbol{y}_c$ as vector $\hat{\boldsymbol{y}}_{c,r}$ as a random guessing algorithm, then an expected value of its predictive accuracy is

$$\begin{aligned} \mathbb{E}(\text{predictive accuracy}(\boldsymbol{y}_c, \hat{\boldsymbol{y}}_{c,r})) &= \sum_{\ell=1}^{m} P(\hat{Y}_c = c_\ell \mid Y_c = c_\ell) \cdot P(Y_c = c_\ell) \stackrel{(\dagger)}{=} \\ &\stackrel{(\dagger)}{=} \sum_{\ell=1}^{m} \frac{1}{m} \cdot \frac{1}{m} = \sum_{\ell=1}^{m} \frac{1}{m^2} = \frac{m}{m^2} = \frac{1}{m}. \end{aligned}$$

Values of predictive accuracy greater than $\frac{1}{m}$ indicate that a classifier performs better than a random guessing algorithm.

In practice, the very accurate prediction of a correct difficulty class is unnecessary. A prediction *close* enough to the correct difficulty class, i.e., the correct one or one class below or above the correct one, is still useful. Thus, we also measure the classifiers' performance using an *extended predictive accuracy*. The item i is evaluated as correctly classified if it is classified in the correct difficulty class $\hat{y}_{c,i} = y_{c,i} = c_\ell$, or one class higher if such a class exists, $\hat{y}_{c,i} = c_{\ell+1}$, or one class lower if such a class exists, $\hat{y}_{c,i} = c_{\ell-1}$, compared to the difficulty class estimated from student response data, thus

$$\text{extended predictive accuracy}(\boldsymbol{y}_c, \hat{\boldsymbol{y}}_c) = \frac{1}{n}\sum_{i=1}^{n}\{\mathcal{I}(\hat{y}_{c,i} \in \{c_{\ell-1}, c_\ell, c_{\ell+1}\} \wedge y_{c,i} = c_\ell)\}, \tag{16}$$

where $c_{\ell-1}$ is one class below c_ℓ, and $c_{\ell+1}$ is one class above c_ℓ, respectively, if it exists, and an empty set otherwise. Thus, a probability that a classifier in this sense correctly classifies category with subscript $\ell \in \{2, 3, \ldots, m-1\}$ is equal to $\frac{|\{\ell-1, \ell, \ell+1\}|}{m} = \frac{3}{m}$, while a probability that a classifier correctly classifies the first or last category with subscript

$\ell = 1$ or $\ell = m$ is equal to $\frac{|\{\ell,\ell+1\}|}{m} = \frac{2}{m}$ or $\frac{|\{\ell-1,\ell\}|}{m} = \frac{2}{m}$, respectively. Again, assumi a classifier would predict difficulties $\boldsymbol{y}_c$ as vector $\hat{\boldsymbol{y}}_{c,r}$ as a random guessing algorithm, th an expected value of its extended predictive accuracy is

$$\mathbb{E}(\text{extended predictive accuracy}(\boldsymbol{y}_c, \hat{\boldsymbol{y}}_{c,r})) =$$

$$= \sum_{\ell=1}^{m} P(\hat{Y}_c \in \{c_{\ell-1}, c_\ell, c_{\ell+1}\} \mid Y_c = c_\ell) \cdot P(Y_c = c_\ell) \stackrel{(\dagger)}{=}$$

$$\stackrel{(\dagger)}{=} \left(\frac{2}{m} + \underbrace{\frac{3}{m} + \cdots + \frac{3}{m}}_{(m-2)\text{-times}} + \frac{2}{m} \right) \cdot \frac{1}{m} = \frac{3m-2}{m^2}.$$

Thus, any values of extended predictive accuracy that are greater than $\frac{3m-2}{m^2}$ show th a classifier predicts better than a random guessing procedure.

2.4.3. Cross-Validation

To obtain more robust estimates, the performance metrics are re-estimated multip times within f-fold cross-validation, where $f \in \mathbb{N}$ and $f \geq 2$, using dataset splitting int training and testing subset of sizes of $\frac{f-1}{f}$ % and $\frac{1}{f}$ %, respectively, and then averaged [49 see Figure 8.

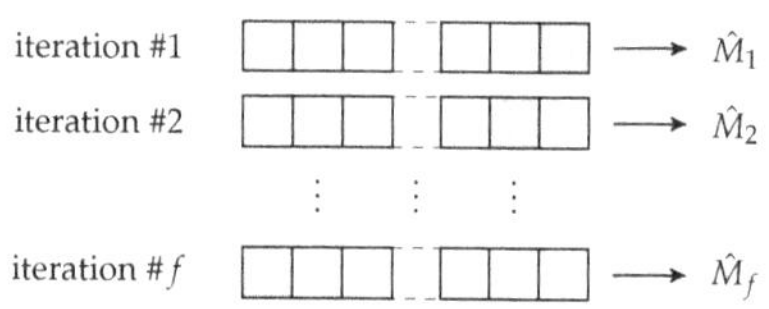

Figure 8. Within p-th iteration of f-fold cross-validation, where $p \in \{1, 2, \ldots, f\}$, $f > 1$ and $f \in \mathbb{N}$ a model is trained using the training set (colored in white) and tested using the test set (colored in grey), i.e., the $(f - p + 1)$-th of f equal-size parts, which the entire dataset was originally split into.

In particular, for even better comparison and integer-like sizes of both the training and testing subsets, it might be optimal to choose f as a divisor of sample size n; then the portions $\frac{f-1}{f}$ % and $\frac{1}{f}$ % for training and testing subsets, respectively, are of integer number sizes.

Assuming that p-th iteration of the f-fold cross-validation outputs point estimates of root mean square error, predictive or extended predictive accuracy $\hat{M}_p$, finally, we could average the estimates as

$$\bar{M} = \frac{1}{f} \sum_{p=1}^{f} \hat{M}_p,$$

to obtain a robust and unbiased estimate of $\hat{\mathbb{E}}(M) = \bar{M}$, i.e., the root mean square error, predictive or extended predictive accuracy [50], respectively.

2.4.4. Relationship between Model's Predictive Performance and a Number of Item Features in a Model

A value of the root mean square error, RMSE, following Formula (14) is *not* closely related to a number of item features considered within a model. Thus, model enrichment by any new extracted text item features could not necessarily improve predictive model performance. There are more details, formal derivation, and mathematical rationale of the relationship between the model predictive performance and the number of item features on model input in Online Supplement listed in Data Availability Statement at the end of the article.

3. Implementation

Text preprocessing and the entire analysis were implemented in statistical language and environment R [51]. For evaluation of the classification task, the continuous difficulty Y, estimated from student response data, of an original range $\langle -2.48, +1.63 \rangle$ was split into $m = 5$ disjunctive intervals, denoted $Y_c \in \{c_1, c_2, c_2, c_4, c_5\}$, of the same size using quintiles, specifically $\langle -2.48, -0.80 \rangle$, $\langle -0.80, -0.44 \rangle$, $\langle -0.44, +0.03 \rangle$, $\langle +0.03, +0.52 \rangle$, $\langle +0.52, +1.63 \rangle$, and labeled as {*very easy*, *easy*, *moderate*, *difficult*, *very difficult*}. Thus, regarding item difficulty, the dataset of item text wordings is well-balanced. While the final number of item features derived from their text wording is $k = 69$, the number of items is $n = 40$. Regarding the f-fold cross-validation, due to a straightforward advantage of whenever n is divisible by $f \geq 2$, we choose for $f = 20$. Thus, since $\frac{n}{f} = \frac{40}{20} = 2$, we applied a *leave-two-out cross-validation*.

Domain experts' evaluation of item difficulty originally uses an arbitrary scale of $\langle 1.0, 2.5 \rangle$. To make the experts' evaluation comparable with the outputs of classifiers, we split the experts' scale in the original logic the scale was designed, i.e., we consider $m = 5$ equidistant intervals over the range of $\langle 1.0, 2.5 \rangle$. Thus, we create $m = 5$ intervals of length 0.3 and name them also as {*very easy*, *easy*, *moderate*, *difficult*, *very difficult*}. Given the assumed Rasch model (1), the obtained 'true' item difficulty is on a logistic scale where very low and very high values are less common, yet possible. For this reason, we split the Rasch-based item difficulty using quantiles. The domain experts, on the other hand, naturally designed the difficulty evaluation scale in a linear fashion, which is our rationale for equidistant scale splitting.

The difficulty of items was estimated from student responses data using the Rasch model by the function `RM()` of `eRm` package [52]. Text preprocessing was performed using R package `quanteda` [53]. Regularization was implemented with a function `glmnet()` of `glmnet` package [54]. Naïve Bayes classifier and support vector machines were built using `naiveBayes()` and `svm()` functions of `e1071` package [55]. The radial kernel function was chosen for the kernel trick if applied. Classification and regression trees were enumerated by the function `rpart()` of `rpart` package [56]. Random forests' models were learned using function `randomForest()` from `randomForest` package [57], each time using 500 trees in a model, similarly as neural networks were modeled using `neuralnet()` function and `neuralnet` package [58]. The neural networks contain one hidden layer with the same number of neurons as item features on input.

4. Results

To assess the possibility and performance of item difficulty prediction from their textual wordings using ML methods, we applied the above-described methodology to the dataset of our interest. Firstly, we built supervised models of the regression task to estimate item difficulty as a continuous variable. There are outcomes of this approach more in detail in Table 2 presented using the root mean square errors (RMSE) for the $n = 40$ single-paragraph items, averaged over all $f = 20$ iterations of the f-fold cross-validation, across seven different regression algorithms and domain experts' estimates, too. The lower value of RMSE an algorithm outputs, the better accuracy and reliability its item difficulty estimate reaches.

A comparison of the algorithms highlights the varying performance levels between the models. Among the evaluated models, the regularization algorithms, i.e., LASSO regression, ridge regression, and elastic net, demonstrated superior performance by yielding the lowest RMSE value, indicating the highest accuracy and reliability. In particular, the elastic net returned the lowest RMSE of 0.666 among the regularization approaches (and, thus, among all models, too). Additionally, considering the data and model settings, the elastic net model outperformed domain experts in the continuous item difficulty prediction since domain experts reached an RMSE of 1.004. On the other hand, the regression trees and neural networks algorithm produced the highest RMSE value of about 0.978 and 0.971, respectively, suggesting less accuracy and reliability than the other models. The remaining algorithms displayed moderate performance levels. Meanwhile, regression trees and domain exper had higher but comparable RMSE values, further emphasizing the superior performance o the elastic net algorithm in this analysis. Since the domain experts evaluate item difficul mostly using numbers such as 1.0, 1.5, 2.0, 2.5 as described in Section 3, *Implementation*, the are a priori handicapped to estimate an exact point value of the item difficulty. Applyin Sheppard's correction [59], their RMSE as a measure following the logic of the secon moment is overestimated by a term of $\frac{\text{width of the interval between valid values}^2}{12} = \frac{0.5^2}{12} \approx 0.0$ However, in case all domain experts would systematically over- or under-estimate the tru item difficulty, their RMSE could be, in theory, overestimated by the width of the interva between valid values, thus, by 0.5.

Table 2. Values of root mean square error (RMSE) for seven regression algorithms and domai experts, respectively, estimating item difficulty as a continuous variable, calculated over $f = 2$ iterations of the f-fold cross-validation.

Regression Algorithm	Root Mean Square Error (RMSE)
LASSO regression	0.694
Ridge regression	0.719
Elastic net regression	0.666
Support vector machines	0.716
Regression trees	0.978
Random forests	0.719
Neural networks	0.971
Domain experts	1.004

Additionally, Table 3 presents the predictive and extended predictive accuracies of different classification algorithms, including Naïve Bayes classifier, support vector machines, classification trees, random forests, neural networks, and domain experts.

Table 3. Values of averaged predictive and extended predictive accuracies for five classification algorithms and domain experts, respectively, estimating item difficulty as a categorized variable, calculated over $f = 20$ iterations of the f-fold cross-validation.

Classification Algorithm	Predictive Accuracy	Extended Predictive Accuracy
Naïve Bayes classifier	0.175	0.425
Support vector machines	0.000	0.575
Classification trees	0.150	0.525
Random forests	0.325	0.650
Neural networks	0.225	0.550
Domain experts	0.225	0.650

Assuming that only an approximate match of a true and predicted category of item difficulty is sufficient for applications, we focus on extended predictive accuracy. From the ML algorithms, random forests output the highest extended predictive accuracy with a score of 0.650, while Naïve Bayes classifier showed the lowest extended predictive accuracy, achieving a score of only 0.425. Domain experts achieved a superior accuracy of 0.650, indicating their important role in the classification of item difficulty.

For a better understanding of individual classifiers' predictive capacity, we plot the confusion matrices for each algorithm (see Figure 9), where each row represents numbers of items in each of the observed classes, while each column represents numbers of items in each of the difficulty classes predicted by the algorithm. The numbers in cells of the confusion matrices are summations over all iterations of the f-fold cross-validation. Overall, the results suggest that the ML algorithms could benefit from further improvement to accurately classify items in all classes of difficulty, especially in the middle classes, i.e., from *easy* to *difficult*. The domain experts did not use the highest category, *very difficult* much for these items; this may be caused by the fact that the test is in general easy and especially this type of item may appear simple compared to exercises from high school textbooks.

Tables 4 and 5 present the variable importance analysis of different item text features applied in our model for item difficulty prediction and classification. While Table 4 uses $MSE_{increase}$ metric, Table 5 utilizes $NodePurity_{increase}$ metric of variable importance. Both measures are reported in Tables 4 and 5 as an average $\pm$ standard deviation based on $f = 20$ point estimates from all iterations of f-fold cross-validation. The $MSE_{increase}$ as a metric of an item feature's importance operates with mean square error (MSE), which is a squared value of RMSE; it is more suitable for regression models and prediction of item difficulty as a continuous variable. Whereas $NodePurity_{increase}$ as a metric of item feature's importance calculates impurity of leaf nodes when classifying into a category of item difficulty; thus, it performs better in the classification of item difficulty. Both measures can provide valuable insights into feature importance; however, they may result in different rankings as they capture distinct aspects of model prediction performance. By considering both metrics, we can comprehensively understand item feature importance and make informed decisions for analysis and interpretation.

According to Table 4, the number of all characters in item wording seems to be the most crucial feature for item difficulty, with $MSE_{increase}$ of $5.912 \pm 0.0.673$, followed by the word length's standard deviation (in characters) with $MSE_{increase}$ about 4.845 ± 0.799. Various features such as readability indices, indices of similarity or portion of shared words between item passage, distractors, item question or key option, as well as longest and average word length in item wording, follow, with $MSE_{increase}$ between about 0.900 and 3.500.

In Table 5, the same two features seem to determine the classification of item difficulty the most—the word length's standard deviation (in characters) with $NodePurity_{increase}$ about 1.644 ± 0.121, and the number of all characters in item wording with $NodePurity_{increase}$ of 1.455 ± 0.137. Additionally, some of the readability indices, numbers of monosyllabic and rare words, or similarity between different parts of item wording are important for correct item difficulty prediction, returning $NodePurity_{increase}$ in an interval of 0.030–0.080.

A detailed explanation of individual item features listed in Tables 4 and 5 is in Appendix A. Note that although we sorted the item features in decreasing order according to the importance measures in Tables 4 and 5, the intervals for importance measures' mean values, indicated by $\pm$ standard deviation terms, overlap between various item features. Thus, the importance analysis is only illustrative.

Table 6 provides a summary of elastic net regression's model following Formula (4) that minimized the root mean square error, RMSE, with $\hat{\lambda}_{LASSO} \approx 1$ and $\hat{\lambda}_{ridge} \approx 0$. While most item features were removed by shrinking their coefficients towards zero, the item features listed in Table 6 are those that remained in the model. Compared to the item features' importance analysis, the elastic net model could tell us not only which item features are essential for the final model but also what is the approximate direction of a relationship between the features and item difficulty. The elastic net model suggests that a larger total number of characters in item text wording increases item difficulty ($\hat{\beta} = 0.002 > 0$), and that greater Dalle-Chall and FOG readability indices also make the item more difficult ($\hat{\beta} = 0.004 > 0$ and $\hat{\beta} = 0.026 > 0$, respectively). In addition to this, an increased standard deviation of word lengths within item wording ($\hat{\beta} = 0.809 \gg 0$) and an average sentence length (words) in distractors ($\hat{\beta} = 0.002 \gg 0$) increase item difficulty as well as does the greater proportion of common words in the passage and distractors ($\hat{\beta} = 0.630 \gg 0$) (the passage and distractors–common $words_1$ is a proportion of a number of common words in the item passage also found in the wording of distractors, to a number of all words in the item passage).

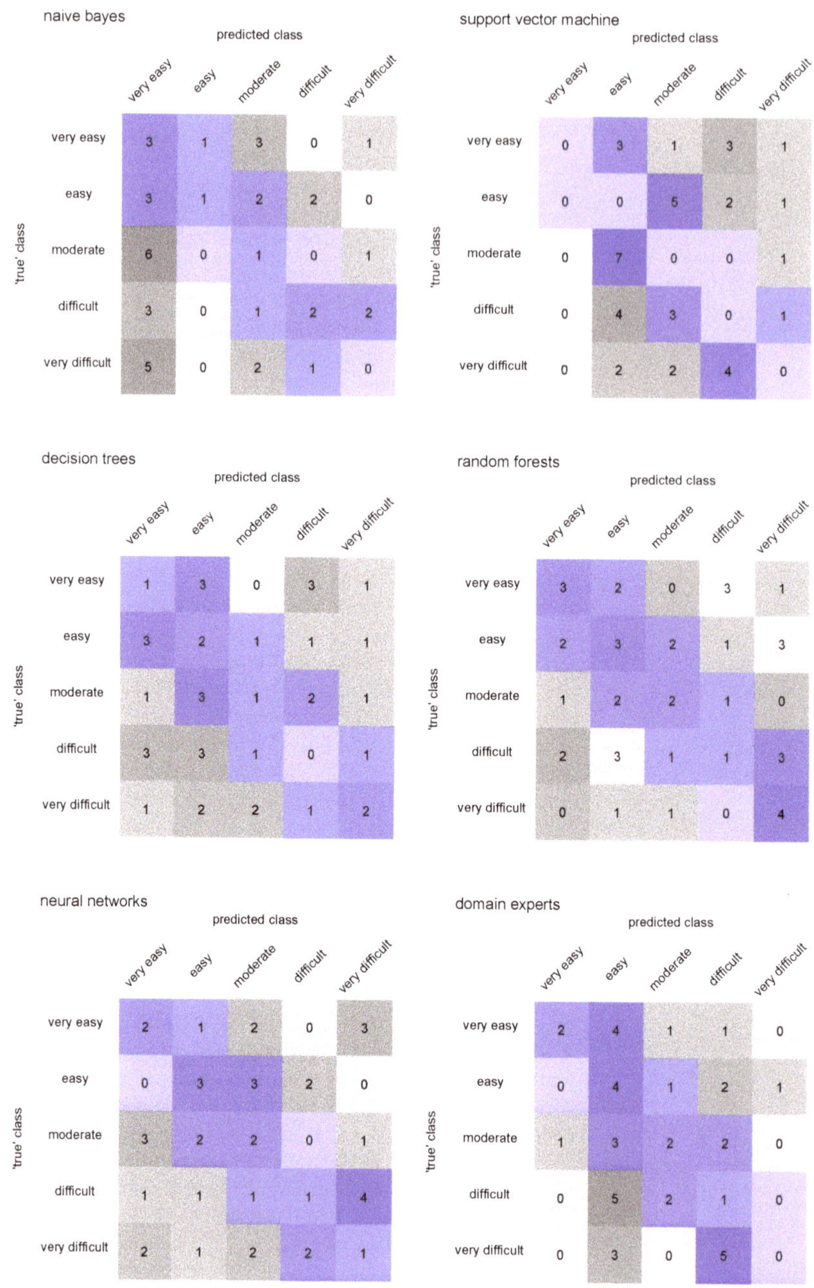

Figure 9. Summative confusion matrices for five classification algorithms and domain experts, respectively. For each algorithm, within each iteration of the f-fold cross-validation, a partial confusion matrix was calculated from training $\frac{1}{f}$ fraction of the dataset, and the resulting f confusion matrices were combined into one final summative confusion matrix, which is displayed. The blue color indicates cells considered for calculating the extended predictive accuracy.

Table 4. Top twenty item features with the highest value of importance for item difficulty prediction, measured using $MSE_{increase}$. The $MSE_{increase}$ measure is reported as an average $\pm$ standard deviation based on $f = 20$ point estimates from all iterations of f-fold cross-validation. A detailed explanation of individual item features listed in the table is in Appendix A. The abbreviation COCA stands for The Corpus of Contemporary American English, DF matrix for document-feature matrix.

Item Feature	$MSE_{increase}$
Number of characters	5.912 ± 0.673
Word length's standard deviation (characters)	4.845 ± 0.799
Passage and distractors–word2vec similarity	3.521 ± 0.823
Text readability–Traenkle-Bailer index	3.385 ± 0.767
Question and key item–word2vec similarity	2.447 ± 0.956
Distractors–average sentence length (words)	2.385 ± 0.838
Key option and distractors–number of features from a DF matrix	2.225 ± 0.697
Distractors–average word length (characters)	1.689 ± 0.827
Distractors–average word length (characters)	1.689 ± 0.827
Text readability–SMOG index	1.680 ± 0.790
Question and key option–number of features from a DF matrix	1.655 ± 0.807
Item passage and distractors–common words$_1$	1.570 ± 0.832
Passage and key option–word2vec similarity	1.409 ± 0.979
Text readability–FOG index	1.355 ± 1.143
Question and passage–euclidean distance	1.341 ± 0.784
Average word length (characters)	1.322 ± 0.972
Passage and key option–euclidean distance	1.266 ± 0.997
Passage and distractors–euclidean distance	1.072 ± 1.218
Item passage and distractors–cosine similarity	1.018 ± 0.933
Question and distractors–euclidean distance	0.937 ± 0.927

Table 5. Top twenty item features with the highest value of importance for item difficulty prediction, measured using $NodePurity_{increase}$. The $NodePurity_{increase}$ measure is reported as an average $\pm$ standard deviation based on $f = 20$ point estimates from all iterations of f-fold cross-validation. A detailed explanation of individual item features listed in the table is in Appendix A. The abbreviation CEFR stands for The Common European Framework of Reference for Languages, DF matrix for document-feature matrix.

Item Feature	$NodePurity_{increase}$
Word length's standard deviation (characters)	1.644 ± 0.121
Number of characters	1.455 ± 0.137
Text readability–Traenkle-Bailer index	1.214 ± 0.118
Question and key item–word2vec similarity	0.820 ± 0.103
Passage and distractors–word2vec similarity	0.819 ± 0.097
Passage and distractors–euclidean distance	0.806 ± 0.128
Item passage and distractors–common words$_1$	0.707 ± 0.099
Distractors–average word length (characters)	0.684 ± 0.153
Distractors–average word length (characters)	0.684 ± 0.153
Question and passage–number of features from a DF matrix	0.674 ± 0.063
Text readability–FOG index	0.631 ± 0.101
Text readability–Dale-Chall index	0.620 ± 0.095
Text readability–SMOG index	0.537 ± 0.067
Distractors–average sentence length (words)	0.514 ± 0.089
Key option and distractors–number of features from a DF matrix	0.508 ± 0.099
Item passage and distractors–cosine similarity	0.499 ± 0.087
Average word length (characters)	0.478 ± 0.068
Question and passage–euclidean distance	0.463 ± 0.083
Average sentence length (words)	0.458 ± 0.062
Passage and key option–euclidean distance	0.431 ± 0.047

Table 6. Coefficients of elastic net regression's model that minimizes RMSE with $\hat{\lambda}_{\text{LASSO}} \approx 1$ an $\hat{\lambda}_{\text{ridge}} \approx 0$.

Item Feature	**Coefficient**
(intercept)	−3.808
Number of characters	0.002
Word length's standard deviation (characters)	0.809
Distractors–average sentence length (words)	0.002
Dale-Chall index	0.004
FOG index	0.026
Passage and distractors–common words$_1$	0.630
Key option and distractors–word2vec similarity	0.023

Finally, considering Table 6, increased word2vec similarity between key option and distractors is associated with a higher item difficulty ($\hat{\beta} = 0.023 > 0$) (the key option and distractors–word2vec similarity is a similarity of the key option and distractors of the item wording based on word2vec algorithms, where vectors of tokens for both parts are generated and the similarity between them is captured from the context). These features were also detected as important by the importance analysis.

An example of a decision tree, estimating categorized item difficulty as an interval is in Figure 10. The tree in the figure uses various item features such as the word length's standard deviation (in characters), frequency of uncommon words–according to COCA corpus, item passage and key option–common words$_1$, key option and distractors–number of features from a document-feature matrix, distractors–average sentence length (in words), passage and distractors–word2vec similarity, and number of all characters in item wording. An interpretation is possible and relatively straightforward–in general, if the item's words vary significantly in their lengths, the frequency of uncommon words is high, the proportion of words common for key option and distractors is low enough, item passage and distractors are dissimilar enough, or the item wording is long enough, then the item's difficulty is relatively high.

More specifically, if the word length's standard deviation (in characters) is not lower than 2.3, then the item's difficulty is *difficult* (in $\langle +0.03, +0.52)$) or *very difficult* (in $\langle +0.52, +1.63)$). Otherwise, when the frequency of uncommon words–according to COCA corpus is lower than 0.26, the item's difficulty could be *easy* (in $\langle -0.80, -0.44)$) or *difficult* (in $\langle +0.03, +0.52)$), according to the common words$_1$ among the item passage and key option. Conditional on the previous rules, whenever the number of features from a document-feature matrix of key option and distractors, i.e., a number of common words both in item key option and distractors, is less than 15, the item's difficulty is *very easy* (in $\langle -2.48, -0.80)$) *easy* (in $\langle -0.80, -0.44)$), or could be *difficult* (in in $\langle +0.03, +0.52)$) for the number of characters at least 1062. If the word2vec similarity between passage and distractors is lower than 0.79, then the item difficulty is *moderate* (in $\langle -0.44, +0.03)$). Otherwise, the item difficulty depends on the number of characters in the item wording–usually, if the difficulty could be one of two different difficulty classes, a lower character number in item wording tends to classify the item into the easier class, as we can see in the last-but-one nodes in the tree in Figure 10.

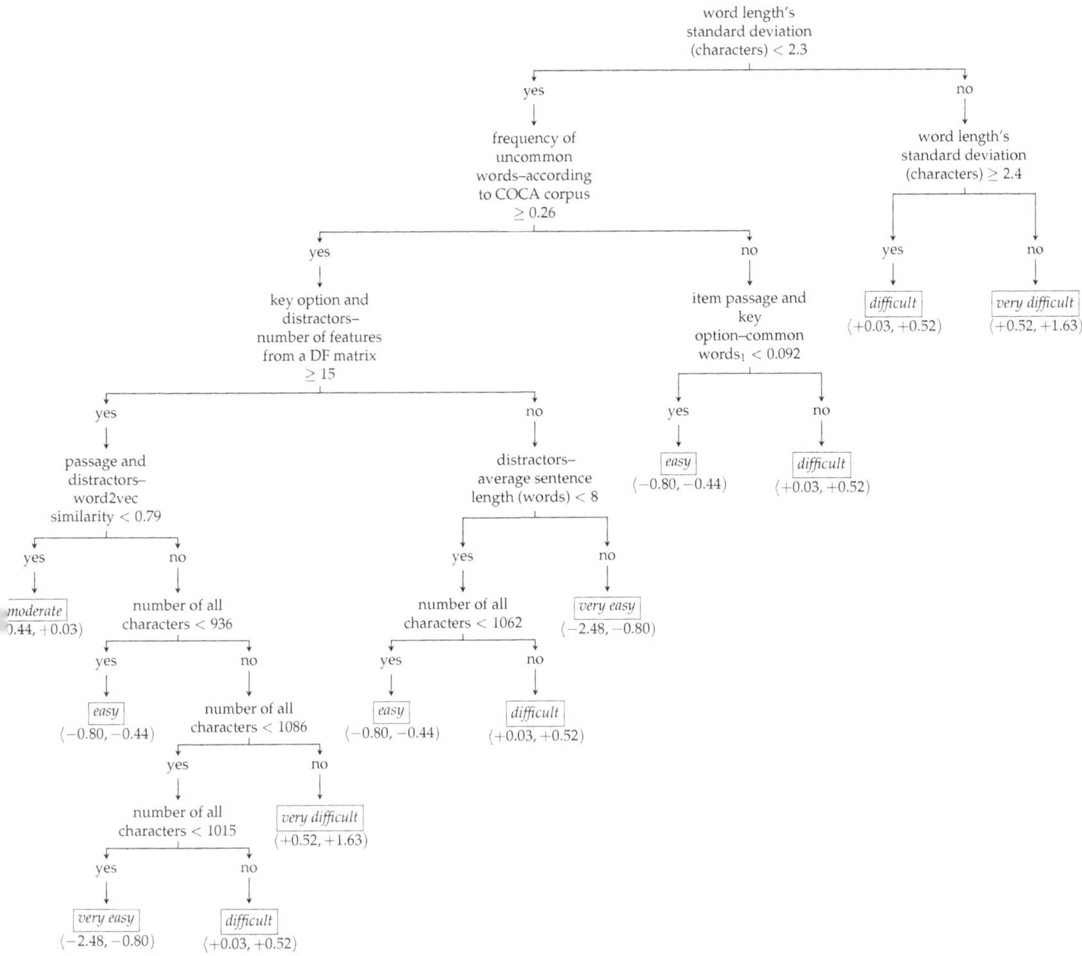

Figure 10. An example of a decision tree classifying the categorized item difficulty into a difficulty class (and an appropriate interval).

5. Discussion

In this work, we provided a framework for predicting the difficulty of cognitive test items from their wording. We extracted various text features from English reading comprehension items and employed a number of ML algorithms. Our work is unique in that it compares a wide range of ML algorithms, both for regression and classification tasks, as well as in relating the predictions to those of domain experts. We also provide reproducible R code, which can be used and built on in future studies. The prediction of item difficulty using item text features may save time and resources needed for pre-testing and may help especially in situations when pre-testing is limited or not feasible. ML prediction of item difficulty presented in this work has the potential to be more precise than domain experts, and if not fully replacing domain experts, it may be used to guide and improve their predictions, as well as any imprecise estimates coming from pre-testing based on small or less representative samples.

Among all regression task algorithms, regularization approaches seemed to overcome others, similar to [60,61]. This is expectable given that the amount of data included in the training subset was relatively low. All ML algorithms outperformed domain experts in this task, although the domain experts are handicapped by not using a continuous scale, as mentioned in Section 4. To govern the accuracy-precision trade-off towar higher accuracy [62], we also considered the task of classifying the item difficulty into or a few categories. Domain experts slightly outperformed ML algorithms in the accuracy difficulty classification when the task was to classify the item difficulty into five categori From the ML algorithms, the random forests predicted with the highest extended predicti accuracy and performed almost as well as domain experts. We suppose that random fores could return the best predictive performance since this algorithm is a priori ensemble embedding multiple decision trees.

It is hard to compare our results to those of other studies, given that different stu ies train ML algorithms on data which may differ in the topic, the number of availab items, variability of item content and difficulty, as well as used difficulty scale or dif culty distribution among various parts of the scale. Benedetto et al. in [63] applied M techniques on multiple true-false questions from CloudAcademy to predict the questio difficulty and received RMSE about 0.700–0.900 for random forests, decision trees, suppo vector machines, and linear regression. In another paper, Benedetto et al. [64] introduce an R2DE model for newly generated items and automatically predicted their difficult originating from interval $\langle -5, +5 \rangle$ with RMSE of 0.823, which is approximately comp rable to our results, i.e., RMSE of 0.668 (elastic net) on item difficulty coming from a interval $\langle -2.48, +1.63 \rangle$. Using word embedding and support vector machine with th radial kernel, Ehara in [65] reported RMSE about 3.632 for item difficulty prediction o English vocabulary tests with a pre-estimated difficulty range in $\langle -2, +4 \rangle$; since our datase if of similar difficulty range, we received better performance for item difficulty predictio in case of support vector machines—an RMSE of 0.716. Lee et al. in [66] predicted iten difficulty for C-tests, i.e., tests where the second part of every second word is missin and should be fulfilled by a test-taker, and reached an RMSE of 0.240 using advance architectures of support vector machines and neural networks. Regarding the adaptiv scenarios, Pandarova et al. in [67] predicted the difficulty of cued gap-filling items usin common item features and several ridge regression models and obtained an RMSE of 0.77 Qiu et al. in [68] trained a document-enhanced attention-based neural network on dat from medical online education websites in China to predict the correct-answer ratio (ir the range of 0 to 1) and output RMSE of 0.131. They also compared the approach with support vector machines-based prediction, yielding an RMSE of about 0.172, which is considering their difficulty range $\langle 0, 1 \rangle$, comparable with our results. Ha et al. in [69], anc Xue et al. in [70] published, besides response times, prediction of item difficulty using medical datasets based on correct-answer ratios (i.e., difficulty in a range of 0 to 1) and employing various ML methods and transfer learning, resulting in an RMSE in the range of 0.200–0.300. Similar approaches and results as Ha et al. in [69] are also reported by Yaneva et al. in [71]. Yin et al. in [72] proposed a new text-embedded and hierarchical pre-trained model QuesNet for item representation, that is able to predict item difficulty ranged in the interval 0–1, with an RMSE of 0.253. Several studies went deeper into item difficulty classification rather than continuous prediction. Hsu et al. in [73] predicted item difficulty (of five levels, i.e., *very easy*, *easy*, *moderate*, *difficult*, *very difficult*) in social studies tests using semantic spaces and word embedding techniques, by which they reached accuracy about 0.350 and extended accuracy about 0.780. Similar to our study, they also found that semantic similarity between an item stem and the options strongly impacts item difficulty. One year later, Lin et al. in [74] remade the analysis by Hsu and applied long short-term memory on the same problem and datasets; they received an accuracy of 0.370 and extended accuracy of 0.840. Compared with the above-mentioned studies, our analysis is limited by the number of items available for training the ML algorithms, as well as by the relatively low and homogeneous item difficulty related to the level of the exam, which was set to B1 according to the Common European Framework of Reference for Languages (CEFR) standard.

This study opens several paths for further research. One possible path to improving the algorithms presented here is to extend or improve the extracted item text features while keeping in mind that simply boosting a number of item features would not necessarily improve model predictive performance; see Section 2.4.4. We focused on text content rather than context within the item difficulty prediction using their text wording. In our case, various readability indices and indices of similarity between individual parts of item text wording seemed to be important for the difficulty prediction, similarly to [73]. Additionally, considering the elastic net summary, the standard deviation of item words' length (in characters) was of significant importance. The contentual features are easier to extract, while they may reduce information encoded in the textual wording significantly [75]. Further research may consider also incorporating contextual analysis, which, however, also requires extensive samples of textual data [76]. Other future paths include tuning the settings of the involved ML algorithms or even including further ML methods.

Involving a wider range of training datasets is another possible path to follow. Our work focused on predicting item difficulty in the reading comprehension section of the English language test; however, the possible usage of the methods presented here is much wider. Similar methods may find their use in the prediction of item difficulty in other knowledge tests [69,70,77], or to provide a better understanding of the rating of the quality of grant proposals [78,79] when a text complementing numerical ratings is available. Text analysis and ML methods may provide a deeper insight into item-level differences in responding and explain so-called differential item functioning (DIF) [80–82] or item-level between-group differences in change after treatment (differential item functioning in change, DIF-C) [83]. Given the increasing computational power, we expect more research implementing textual data analysis will complement the analysis of rating data in the future.

6. Conclusions

To conclude, the text analysis of item wording may be useful for the prediction of item difficulty, especially when item pre-testing is limited or not available. Machine learning algorithms, particularly regularization or random forests, may be able to inform and improve item difficulty estimates of the domain experts. Future studies should consider more complex and deeper text analysis, including context analysis, as well as other ML methods, and method tuning to even further improve the performance of the item difficulty prediction.

Author Contributions: Conceptualization, L.Š., J.D. and P.M.; Data curation, L.Š., J.D. and P.M.; Formal analysis, L.Š., J.D. and P.M.; Funding acquisition, P.M.; Investigation, L.Š., J.D. and P.M.; Methodology, L.Š., J.D. and P.M.; Project administration, P.M.; Resources, L.Š., J.D. and P.M.; Software, L.Š., J.D. and P.M.; Supervision, P.M.; Validation, L.Š., J.D. and P.M.; Visualization, L.Š.; Writing—original draft, L.Š., J.D. and P.M.; Writing—review & editing, L.Š., J.D. and P.M. All authors have read and agreed to the published version of the manuscript.

Funding: The study was supported by the Czech Science Foundation Grant Number 21-03658S, by the institutional support RVO 67985807, and by the Charles University programme Progres Q15 "Life course, lifestyle and quality of life from the perspective of individual adaptation and the relationship of the actors and institutions".

Data Availability Statement: Data, source code for the ML analysis, and further supplementary material are available at OSF platform at https://osf.io/nzfgk/ (accessed on 27 September 2023). Original data with item wordings are available at https://data.cermat.cz/ (in Czech) (accessed on 30 March 2023).

Acknowledgments: The authors thank the Centre for Evaluation of Educational Achievement for sharing insights on item difficulty evaluation and for data of preliminary difficulty predictions by domain experts. We also thank anonymous reviewers and Eva Potužníková for suggestions to previous versions of the manuscript and Filip Martinek for assistance with software computations.

Conflicts of Interest: The authors declare no conflict of interest. The funders had no role in the design of the study; in the collection, analyses, or interpretation of data; in the writing of the manuscript, or in the decision to publish the results.

Appendix A

In this part of the appendix, we describe selected item features and their definitior in more detail, particularly those listed in Tables 4 and 5. The wording of an item usuall consists of the following parts: an item passage, a question, a key option, and distractor The item passage is an introductory text of varying length that mentions important term or definitions asked in the following item question or describes the item's context. The ite question is followed by a permutation of a key option, i.e., a correct answer, and severa distractors, i.e., incorrect answers. In summary below, we mark any of the item wordin part as $\{\mathcal{A}\}$,

$$\{\mathcal{A}\} \in \{\text{item passage, question, key option, distractors}\},$$

and any pair of the item wording parts as $\{\mathcal{A} \text{ and } \mathcal{B}\}$,

$$\begin{aligned}\{\mathcal{A} \text{ and } \mathcal{B}\} \in \{&\text{key option and distractors,}\\ &\text{item passage and distractors,}\\ &\text{item passage and key option,}\\ &\text{question and distractors,}\\ &\text{question and key option,}\\ &\text{item passage and question}\}.\end{aligned}$$

Each item feature is either a characteristic of an entire item text wording (i.e., there is one numerical value of the item feature for the item) or of each item wording part (i.e. there is one numerical value for each wording part), or a pair of item wording parts. In case the item feature is a numerical characteristic of part $\mathcal{A}$ of the item wording, or pair of parts $\{\mathcal{A} \text{ and } \mathcal{B}\}$ of the item wording, it is indicated below using $\{\mathcal{A}\}$: "item feature label", or $\{\mathcal{A} \text{ and } \mathcal{B}\}$: "item feature label" notation, respectively.

Item Feature	Description or Definition of the Item Feature
number of characters	Total number of characters in a text of the item wording.
$\{\mathcal{A}\}$–number of characters	Total number of characters in a text of part $\mathcal{A}$ of the item wording.
number of tokens	Total number of unique tokens, i.e., words in a text of the item wording.
$\{\mathcal{A}\}$–number of tokens	Total number of unique tokens, i.e., words in a text of part $\mathcal{A}$ of the item wording.
number of monosyllabic words	Number of monosyllabic words, i.e., words with only one syllable in a text of the item wording.
$\{\mathcal{A}\}$–number of monosyllabic words	Number of monosyllabic words, i.e., words with only one syllable in a text of part $\mathcal{A}$ of the item wording.
number of multi-syllable words	Number of multi-syllable words, i.e., words with more than three syllables in a text of the item wording.
$\{\mathcal{A}\}$–number of multi-syllable words	Number of multi-syllable words, i.e., words with more than three syllables in a text of part $\mathcal{A}$ of the item wording.
average word length (characters)	Average number of characters in words in a text of the item wording.
$\{\mathcal{A}\}$–average word length (characters)	Average number of characters in words in a text of part $\mathcal{A}$ of the item wording.
longest word length (characters)	Number of characters contained by the longest word in a text of the item wording.

A}–longest word length (characters)	Number of characters contained by the longest word in a text of part $\mathcal{A}$ of the item wording.
verage sentence length (words)	Average number of words in sentences in a text of the item wording.
A}–average sentence length (words)	Average number of words in sentences in a text of part $\mathcal{A}$ of the item wording.
vord length's standard deviation (characters)	Standard deviation of a number of characters in words in a text of the item wording.
A}–word length's standard deviation (characters)	Standard deviation of a number of characters in words in a text of part $\mathcal{A}$ of the item wording.
number of uncommon words, according to COCA corpus	Number of words in a text of the item wording that appear *uncommonly* as defined in COCA (Corpus of Contemporary American English) corpus.
number of rare words, according to COCA corpus	Number of words in a text of the item wording that appear *rarely* as defined in COCA (Corpus of Contemporary American English) corpus.
frequency of the A1 words (CEFR)	Frequency of words in a text of the item wording at A1 level in CEFR (Common European Framework of Reference for Languages) scale.
frequency of the B2–C2 words (CEFR)	Frequency of words in a text of the item wording at B2–C2 levels in CEFR (Common European Framework of Reference for Languages) scale.
number of footnotes (hints) in the item	Total number of footnotes or hints in a text of the item wording.
Dale-Chall index	The readability score of a text of the item wording based on Dale-Chall readability formula. Dale-Chall readability formula follows, $$\text{Dale-Chall index} = \left(95 \cdot \frac{n_{\text{difficult}}}{n_w}\right) - (0.69 \cdot \overline{w}),$$ where $n_{\text{difficult}}$ is a number of words not included in Dale-Chall list of 3000 familiar words, n_w is a total number of words in a text of the item wording, and $\overline{w}$ is a value computed as a number of words divided by a number of sentences, i.e., it is an average number of words per a sentence [84]. The greater is a value of Dale-Chall index for a given text, the more difficult is to read the text.
FOG index	The readability score of a text of the item wording based on Gunning's Fog Index. The formula is $$\text{FOG index} = 0.4 \cdot \left(\overline{w} + 100 \cdot \frac{n_{\text{words with} \geq 3 \text{ syllables}}}{n_w}\right),$$ where, again, $\overline{w}$ is a value computed as a number of words divided by a number of sentences, i.e., it is an average number of words per a sentence, n_w is a total number of words in a text of the item wording, and $n_{\text{words with} \geq 3 \text{ syllables}}$ is a number of words with three or more syllables in a text of the item wording [85]. If the average length of a sentence or the number of words with three or more syllables in a text increases, the FOG index increases, too.

SMOG index	The readability score of a text of the item wording based o Simple Measure of Gobbledygook (SMOG) index, so $$\text{SMOG index} = 1.043 \cdot \sqrt{n_{\text{words with} \geq 3 \text{ syllables}} \cdot \left(\frac{30}{n_s}\right)} + 3.129$$ where $n_{\text{words with} \geq 3 \text{ syllables}}$ is a number of words with three o more syllables in a text of the item wording and n_s is a number o sentences in a text of the item wording [86]. Whenever the terr $\frac{\sqrt{n_{\text{words with} \geq 3 \text{ syllables}}}}{n_s}$ increases, i.e., the square root of a number o words with three or more syllables per a sentence, readability increases in difficulty and the SMOG index increases.
Traenkle-Bailer index	The readability score of a text of the item wording based on Traenkle-Bailer index (mostly used in German-speaking countries) is calculated as $$\text{T-B index} = 224.68 - (79.83 \cdot \bar{c}) - (12.24 \cdot \bar{w}) - \left(129.29 \cdot \frac{n_{\text{prep}}}{n_w}\right)$$ where $\bar{c}$ is an average number of characters per a word, $\bar{w}$ is an average number of words per a sentence, n_{prep} is a number of prepositions and n_w is a total number of words in a text of the item wording [87]. Traenkle-Bailer index decreases, if the average number of characters per a word, average number of words per a sentence, or average number of prepositions per a word increases.
$\{\mathcal{A}$ and $\mathcal{B}\}$–euclidean distance	Let us assume two textual parts of item wording, $\mathcal{A}$ and $\mathcal{B}$, so that a union of their tokens has a length $l \in \mathbb{N}$. Additionally, let us assume two vectors of the same length l, i.e., $\boldsymbol{t}_{\mathcal{A}} = (t_{\mathcal{A},1}, t_{\mathcal{A},2}, \ldots, t_{\mathcal{A},l})^T$ and $\boldsymbol{t}_{\mathcal{B}} = (t_{\mathcal{B},1}, t_{\mathcal{B},2}, \ldots, t_{\mathcal{B},l})^T$, where $t_{\mathcal{A},i} = 1$ (or $t_{\mathcal{B},i} = 1$) if and only if text $\mathcal{A}$ (text $\mathcal{B}$) contains token i, otherwise is $t_{\mathcal{A},i} = 0$ (or $t_{\mathcal{B},i} = 0$), for $\forall i \in \{1, 2, \ldots, l\}$. The euclidean distance between the parts $\mathcal{A}$ and $\mathcal{B}$ is $$d(\mathcal{A}, \mathcal{B}) = \sqrt{\sum_{i=1}^{l} (t_{\mathcal{A},i} - t_{\mathcal{B},i})^2}.$$ The more similar the parts $\mathcal{A}$ and $\mathcal{B}$ of the item wording are, the lower the value of euclidean distance $d(\mathcal{A}, \mathcal{B})$ is.
$\{\mathcal{A}$ and $\mathcal{B}\}$–cosine similarity	Again, let us assume two textual parts of item wording, $\mathcal{A}$ and $\mathcal{B}$, so that a union of their tokens has a length $l \in \mathbb{N}$. Additionally, let us assume two vectors of the same length l, i.e., $\boldsymbol{t}_{\mathcal{A}} = (t_{\mathcal{A},1}, t_{\mathcal{A},2}, \ldots, t_{\mathcal{A},l})^T$ and $\boldsymbol{t}_{\mathcal{B}} = (t_{\mathcal{B},1}, t_{\mathcal{B},2}, \ldots, t_{\mathcal{B},l})^T$, where $t_{\mathcal{A},i} = 1$ (or $t_{\mathcal{B},i} = 1$) if and only if text $\mathcal{A}$ (text $\mathcal{B}$) contains token i, otherwise is $t_{\mathcal{A},i} = 0$ (or $t_{\mathcal{B},i} = 0$), for $\forall i \in \{1, 2, \ldots, l\}$. The cosine similarity between the parts $\mathcal{A}$ and $\mathcal{B}$ is $$\cos(\mathcal{A}, \mathcal{B}) = \frac{\boldsymbol{t}_{\mathcal{A}} \cdot \boldsymbol{t}_{\mathcal{B}}}{\Vert\boldsymbol{t}_{\mathcal{A}}\Vert \, \Vert\boldsymbol{t}_{\mathcal{B}}\Vert} = \frac{\sum_{i=1}^{l} t_{\mathcal{A},i} \cdot t_{\mathcal{B},i}}{\sqrt{\sum_{i=1}^{l} t_{\mathcal{A},i}^2} \cdot \sqrt{\sum_{i=1}^{l} t_{\mathcal{B},i}^2}}$$ The more similar the parts $\mathcal{A}$ and $\mathcal{B}$ of the item wording are, the higher the value of cosine similarity $\cos(\mathcal{A}, \mathcal{B})$ is.

$\{\mathcal{A}$ and $\mathcal{B}\}$–word2vec similarity	Similarity of parts $\mathcal{A}$ and $\mathcal{B}$ of the item wording based on word2vec algorithms. Vectors of tokens for each part $\mathcal{A}$ and $\mathcal{B}$ are generated, and the similarity between them is captured from the context [88]. Thus, text parts with similar context end up with similar vectors and high word2vec similarity.
$\{\mathcal{A}$ and $\mathcal{B}\}$–common words$_1$	Proportion of common words from a text of part $\mathcal{A}$ found in a text of part $\mathcal{B}$ of the item wording. Let us assume two textual parts of item wording, $\mathcal{A}$ and $\mathcal{B}$, so that a union of their tokens, called also *document-feature matrix* has a length $l \in \mathbb{N}$. Additionally, let us assume two vectors of the same length l, i.e., $\boldsymbol{t}_{\mathcal{A}} = (t_{\mathcal{A},1}, t_{\mathcal{A},2}, \dots, t_{\mathcal{A},l})^T$ and $\boldsymbol{t}_{\mathcal{B}} = (t_{\mathcal{B},1}, t_{\mathcal{B},2}, \dots, t_{\mathcal{B},l})^T$, where $t_{\mathcal{A},i} = 1$ (or $t_{\mathcal{B},i} = 1$) if and only if text $\mathcal{A}$ (text $\mathcal{B}$) contains token i, otherwise is $t_{\mathcal{A},i} = 0$ (or $t_{\mathcal{B},i} = 0$), for $\forall i \in \{1,2,\dots,l\}$. Then the $\{\mathcal{A}$ and $\mathcal{B}\}$–common words$_1$ is $$\{\mathcal{A} \text{ and } \mathcal{B}\}\text{–common words}_1 = \frac{\boldsymbol{t}_{\mathcal{A}} \cdot \boldsymbol{t}_{\mathcal{B}}}{\lVert \boldsymbol{t}_{\mathcal{A}} \rVert^2} = \frac{\sum_{i=1}^{l} t_{\mathcal{A},i} \cdot t_{\mathcal{B},i}}{\sum_{i=1}^{l} t_{\mathcal{A},i}^2} = = \frac{\sum_{i=1}^{l} t_{\mathcal{A},i} \cdot t_{\mathcal{B},i}}{\sum_{i=1}^{l} t_{\mathcal{A},i}}.$$
$\{\mathcal{A}$ and $\mathcal{B}\}$–common words$_2$	Proportion of common words from a text of part $\mathcal{B}$ found in a text of part $\mathcal{A}$ of the item wording. Let us assume two textual parts of item wording, $\mathcal{A}$ and $\mathcal{B}$, so that a union of their tokens, called also *document-feature matrix* has a length $l \in \mathbb{N}$. Additionally, let us assume two vectors of the same length l, i.e., $\boldsymbol{t}_{\mathcal{A}} = (t_{\mathcal{A},1}, t_{\mathcal{A},2}, \dots, t_{\mathcal{A},l})^T$ and $\boldsymbol{t}_{\mathcal{B}} = (t_{\mathcal{B},1}, t_{\mathcal{B},2}, \dots, t_{\mathcal{B},l})^T$, where $t_{\mathcal{A},i} = 1$ (or $t_{\mathcal{B},i} = 1$) if and only if text $\mathcal{A}$ (text $\mathcal{B}$) contains token i, otherwise is $t_{\mathcal{A},i} = 0$ (or $t_{\mathcal{B},i} = 0$), for $\forall i \in \{1,2,\dots,l\}$. Then the $\{\mathcal{A}$ and $\mathcal{B}\}$–common words$_2$ is $$\{\mathcal{A} \text{ and } \mathcal{B}\}\text{–common words}_2 = \frac{\boldsymbol{t}_{\mathcal{A}} \cdot \boldsymbol{t}_{\mathcal{B}}}{\lVert \boldsymbol{t}_{\mathcal{B}} \rVert^2} = \frac{\sum_{i=1}^{l} t_{\mathcal{A},i} \cdot t_{\mathcal{B},i}}{\sum_{i=1}^{l} t_{\mathcal{B},i}^2} = = \frac{\sum_{i=1}^{l} t_{\mathcal{A},i} \cdot t_{\mathcal{B},i}}{\sum_{i=1}^{l} t_{\mathcal{B},i}}.$$
$\{\mathcal{A}$ and $\mathcal{B}\}$–number of features from a document-feature (DF) matrix	Let us assume two textual parts of item wording, $\mathcal{A}$ and $\mathcal{B}$, so that a union of their tokens, called also *document-feature matrix* (abbreviated as DF matrix) has a length $l \in \mathbb{N}$. Additionally, let us assume two vectors of the same length l, i.e., $\boldsymbol{t}_{\mathcal{A}} = (t_{\mathcal{A},1}, t_{\mathcal{A},2}, \dots, t_{\mathcal{A},l})^T$ and $\boldsymbol{t}_{\mathcal{B}} = (t_{\mathcal{B},1}, t_{\mathcal{B},2}, \dots, t_{\mathcal{B},l})^T$, where $t_{\mathcal{A},i} = 1$ (or $t_{\mathcal{B},i} = 1$) if and only if text $\mathcal{A}$ (text $\mathcal{B}$) contains token i, otherwise is $t_{\mathcal{A},i} = 0$ (or $t_{\mathcal{B},i} = 0$), for $\forall i \in \{1,2,\dots,l\}$. The number of features from a document-feature matrix for the parts $\mathcal{A}$ and $\mathcal{B}$ is equal to $$\lVert \boldsymbol{t}_{\mathcal{A}} \rVert^2 + \lVert \boldsymbol{t}_{\mathcal{B}} \rVert^2 = \sum_{i=1}^{l} t_{\mathcal{A},i}^2 + \sum_{i=1}^{l} t_{\mathcal{B},i}^2 = \sum_{i=1}^{l} t_{\mathcal{A},i} + \sum_{i=1}^{l} t_{\mathcal{B},i}.$$ Obviously, since $\forall i \in \{1,2,\dots,l\}$ is either $t_{\mathcal{A},i} = 1$, or $t_{\mathcal{B},i} = 1$, or $t_{\mathcal{A},i} = t_{\mathcal{B},i} = 1$, it is also $$l \leq \lVert \boldsymbol{t}_{\mathcal{A}} \rVert^2 + \lVert \boldsymbol{t}_{\mathcal{B}} \rVert^2 = \sum_{i=1}^{l} t_{\mathcal{A},i}^2 + \sum_{i=1}^{l} t_{\mathcal{B},i}^2 = \sum_{i=1}^{l} t_{\mathcal{A},i} + \sum_{i=1}^{l} t_{\mathcal{B},i} \leq 2l.$$

References

1. Martinková, P.; Hladká, A. *Computational Aspects of Psychometric Methods: With R*; CRC Press: Boca Raton, FL, USA, 2023.
2. Kumar, V.; Boulanger, D. Explainable Automated Essay Scoring: Deep Learning Really Has Pedagogical Value. *Front. Educ.* **202** *5*, 572367.
3. Amorim, E.; Cançado, M.; Veloso, A. Automated Essay Scoring in the Presence of Biased Ratings. In Proceedings of the 201 Conference of the North American Chapter of the Association for Computational Linguistics: Human Language Technologie New Orleans, LA, USA, 1–6 June 2018; Association for Computational Linguistics: New Orleans, LA, USA, 2018; 1 (Long Papers pp. 229–237.
4. Tashu, T.M.; Maurya, C.K.; Horvath, T. Deep Learning Architecture for Automatic Essay Scoring. *arXiv* **2022**, arXiv:2206.0823 [CrossRef]
5. Flor, M.; Hao, J. *Text Mining and Automated Scoring*; Springer International Publishing: Cham, Switzerland, 2021; pp. 245–26 [CrossRef]
6. Attali, Y.; Runge, A.; LaFlair, G.T.; Yancey, K.; Goodwin, S.; Park, Y.; Davier, A.A.v. The interactive reading task: Transformer-base automatic item generation. *Front. Artif. Intell.* **2022**, *5*, 903077. [CrossRef]
7. Gierl, M.J.; Lai, H.; Turner, S.R. Using automatic item generation to create multiple-choice test items. *Med. Educ.* **2012**, *46*, 757–76 [CrossRef]
8. Du, X.; Shao, J.; Cardie, C. Learning to Ask: Neural Question Generation for Reading Comprehension. In Proceedings of the 55th Annual Meeting of the Association for Computational Linguistics (Volume 1: Long Papers), Vancouver, BC, Canada, 30 July– August 2017; Association for Computational Linguistics: Vancouver, Canada, 2017; pp. 1342–1352. [CrossRef]
9. Settles, B.; T LaFlair, G.; Hagiwara, M. Machine learning–driven language assessment. *Trans. Assoc. Comput. Linguist.* **2020** *8*, 247–263. [CrossRef]
10. Kochmar, E.; Vu, D.D.; Belfer, R.; Gupta, V.; Serban, I.V.; Pineau, J. Automated Data-Driven Generation of Personalized Pedagogical Interventions in Intelligent Tutoring Systems. *Int. J. Artif. Intell. Educ.* **2022**, *32*, 323–349. [CrossRef]
11. Gopalakrishnan, K.; Dhiyaneshwaran, N.; Yugesh, P. Online proctoring system using image processing and machine learning *Int. J. Health Sci.* **2022**, *6*, 891–899. [CrossRef]
12. Kaddoura, S.; Popescu, D.E.; Hemanth, J.D. A systematic review on machine learning models for online learning and examination systems. *PeerJ Comput. Sci.* **2022**, *8*, e986. [CrossRef]
13. Kamalov, F.; Sulieman, H.; Santandreu Calonge, D. Machine learning based approach to exam cheating detection. *PLoS ONE* **2021**, *16*, e0254340. [CrossRef]
14. von Davier, M.; Tyack, L.; Khorramdel, L. Scoring Graphical Responses in TIMSS 2019 Using Artificial Neural Networks. *Educ. Psychol. Meas.* **2023**, *83*, 556–585.
15. von Davier, M.; Tyack, L.; Khorramdel, L. Automated Scoring of Graphical Open-Ended Responses Using Artificial Neural Networks. *arXiv* **2022**, arXiv:2201.01783. [CrossRef]
16. von Davier, A.A.; Mislevy, R.J.; Hao, J. (Eds.) *Computational Psychometrics: New Methodologies for a New Generation of Digital Learning and Assessment: With Examples in R and Python*; Methodology of Educational Measurement and Assessment; Springer International Publishing: Cham, Switzerland, 2021. [CrossRef]
17. Hvitfeldt, E.; Silge, J. *Supervised Machine Learning for Text Analysis in R*; Chapman and Hall/CRC: Boca Raton, FL, USA, 2021.
18. Ferrara, S.; Steedle, J.T.; Frantz, R.S. Response demands of reading comprehension test items: A review of item difficulty modeling studies. *Appl. Meas. Educ.* **2022**, *35*, 237–253. [CrossRef]
19. Belov, D.I. Predicting Item Characteristic Curve (ICC) Using a Softmax Classifier. In *Proceedings of the Annual Meeting of the Psychometric Society*; Springer: Cham, Switzerland, 2022; pp. 171–184. [CrossRef]
20. AlKhuzaey, S.; Grasso, F.; Payne, T.R.; Tamma, V. A systematic review of data-driven approaches to item difficulty prediction. In *Lecture Notes in Computer Science*; Lecture notes in computer science; Springer International Publishing: Cham, Switzerland, 2021; pp. 29–41.
21. James, G.; Witten, D.; Hastie, T.; Tibshirani, R. *An Introduction to Statistical Learning*; Springer: New York, NY, USA, 2021.
22. Jurafsky, D. *Speech and Language Processing: An Introduction to Natural Language Processing, Computational Linguistics, and Speech Recognition*; Pearson Prentice Hall: Upper Saddle River, NJ, USA, 2009.
23. Chomsky, N. Three models for the description of language. *IEEE Trans. Inf. Theory* **1956**, *2*, 113–124. [CrossRef]
24. Davies, M. The Corpus of Contemporary American English (COCA). 2008. Available online: http://corpus.byu.edu/coca/ (accessed on 29 June 2023).
25. Davies, M. Most Frequent 100,000 Word Forms in English (Based on Data from the COCA Corpus). 2011. Available online: https://www.wordfrequency.info/ (accessed on 29 June 2023).
26. Tonelli, S.; Tran Manh, K.; Pianta, E. Making Readability Indices Readable. In *Proceedings of the First Workshop on Predicting and Improving Text Readability for Target Reader Populations*; Association for Computational Linguistics: Montréal, QC, Canada, 2012; pp. 40–48.
27. Rasch, G. *Probabilistic Models for Some Intelligence and Attainment Tests*; The University of Chicago Press: Chicago, IL, USA, 1993.
28. Debelak, R.; Strobl, C.; Zeigenfuse, M.D. *An introduction to the Rasch Model with Examples in R*; CRC Press: Boca Raton, FL, USA, 2022.
29. Alpaydin, E. *Introduction to Machine Learning*; MIT Press: Cambridge, MA, USA, 2010.

30. Tibshirani, R. Regression Shrinkage and Selection Via the Lasso. *J. R. Stat. Soc. Ser. (Methodol.)* **1996**, *58*, 267–288. [CrossRef]
31. Hoerl, A.E.; Kennard, R.W. Ridge Regression: Biased Estimation for Nonorthogonal Problems. *Technometrics* **1970**, *12*, 55–67. [CrossRef]
32. Tuia, D.; Flamary, R.; Barlaud, M. To be or not to be convex? A study on regularization in hyperspectral image classification. In Proceedings of the 2015 IEEE International Geoscience and Remote Sensing Symposium (IGARSS), Milan, Italy, 26–31 July 2015; IEEE: Piscataway, NJ, USA, 2015. [CrossRef]
33. Zou, H.; Hastie, T. Regularization and Variable Selection Via the Elastic Net. *J. R. Stat. Soc. Ser. Stat. Methodol.* **2005**, *67*, 301–320. [CrossRef]
34. Fan, J.; Li, R. Comment: Feature Screening and Variable Selection via Iterative Ridge Regression. *Technometrics* **2020**, *62*, 434–437. [CrossRef]
35. Friedman, N.; Geiger, D.; Goldszmidt, M. Bayesian Network Classifiers. *Mach. Learn.* **1997**, *29*, 131–163. [CrossRef]
36. Cortes, C.; Vapnik, V. Support-vector networks. *Mach. Learn.* **1995**, *20*, 273–297. [CrossRef]
37. Schölkopf, B. The Kernel Trick for Distances. In Proceedings of the 13th International Conference on Neural Information Processing Systems (NIPS'00), Hong Kong, China, 3–6 October 2006; MIT Press: Cambridge, MA, USA, 2000; pp. 283–289.
38. Gray, N.A.B. Capturing knowledge through top-down induction of decision trees. *IEEE Expert* **1990**, *5*, 41–50. [CrossRef]
39. Breslow, L.A.; Aha, D.W. Simplifying decision trees: A survey. *Knowl. Eng. Rev.* **1997**, *12*, 1–40. [CrossRef]
40. Rutkowski, L.; Jaworski, M.; Pietruczuk, L.; Duda, P. The CART Decision Tree for Mining Data Streams. *Inf. Sci.* **2014**, *266*, 1–15. [CrossRef]
41. Breiman, L. *Classification and Regression Trees*; Chapman & Hall: New York, NY, USA, 1993.
42. McCulloch, W.S.; Pitts, W. A logical calculus of the ideas immanent in nervous activity. *Bull. Math. Biophys.* **1943**, *5*, 115–133. [CrossRef]
43. Rojas, R. The Backpropagation Algorithm. In *Neural Networks*; Springer: Berlin/Heidelberg, Germany, 1996; pp. 149–182. [CrossRef]
44. Mishra, M.; Srivastava, M. A view of Artificial Neural Network. In Proceedings of the 2014 International Conference on Advances in Engineering & Technology Research (ICAETR-2014), Unnao, Kanpur, India, 1–2 August 2014; IEEE: Piscataway, NJ, USA, 2014. [CrossRef]
45. Hastie, T.; Tibshirani, R.; Friedman, J. *The Elements of Statistical Learning*; Springer: New York, NY, USA, 2009. [CrossRef]
46. Altmann, A.; Toloşi, L.; Sander, O.; Lengauer, T. Permutation importance: A corrected feature importance measure. *Bioinformatics* **2010**, *26*, 1340–1347. [CrossRef] [PubMed]
47. Powers, D.M.W. Evaluation: From precision, recall and F-measure to ROC, informedness, markedness and correlation. *arXiv* **2020**, arXiv:2010.16061.
48. Provost, F.J.; Fawcett, T.; Kohavi, R. The Case against Accuracy Estimation for Comparing Induction Algorithms. In Proceedings of the Fifteenth International Conference on Machine Learning (ICML '98), Madison, WI, USA, 24–27 July 1998; Morgan Kaufmann Publishers Inc.: San Francisco, CA, USA, 1998; pp. 445–453.
49. Moore, A.W.; Lee, M.S. Efficient algorithms for minimizing cross validation error. In Proceedings of the 11th International Conference on Machine Learning, New Brunswick, NJ, USA, 10–13 July 1994; Morgan Kaufmann: Burlington, MA, USA, 1994; pp. 190–198.
50. Kohavi, R. A Study of Cross-Validation and Bootstrap for Accuracy Estimation and Model Selection. In Proceedings of the 14th International Joint Conference on Artificial Intelligence–Volume 2 (IJCAI'95), Montréal, QC, Canada, 20–25 August 1995; Morgan Kaufmann Publishers Inc.: San Francisco, CA, USA, 1995; pp. 1137–1143.
51. R Core Team. *R: A Language and Environment for Statistical Computing*; R Core Team: Vienna, Austria, 2021.
52. Mair, P.; Hatzinger, R.; Maier, M.J.; Rusch, T.; Debelak, R. eRm: Extended Rasch Modeling. 2021. Available online: https://cran.r-project.org/web/packages/eRm/index.html (accessed on 29 June 2023).
53. Benoit, K.; Watanabe, K.; Wang, H.; Nulty, P.; Obeng, A.; Müller, S.; Matsuo, A. Quanteda: An R Package for the Quantitative Analysis of Textual Data. *J. Open Source Softw.* **2018**, *3*, 774. [CrossRef]
54. Friedman, J.; Tibshirani, R.; Hastie, T. Regularization Paths for Generalized Linear Models via Coordinate Descent. *J. Stat. Softw.* **2010**, *33*, 1–22. [CrossRef]
55. Meyer, D.; Dimitriadou, E.; Hornik, K.; Weingessel, A.; Leisch, F. e1071: Misc Functions of the Department of Statistics, Probability Theory Group (Formerly: E1071), TU Wien. 2023. R Package Version 1.7-13. Available online: https://rdrr.io/rforge/e1071/ (accessed on 29 June 2023).
56. Therneau, T.; Atkinson, B. rpart: Recursive Partitioning and Regression Trees, 2022. R Package Version 4.1.19. Available online: https://cogns.northwestern.edu/cbmg/LiawAndWiener2002.pdf (accessed on 29 June 2023).
57. Liaw, A.; Wiener, M. Classification and Regression by Random Forest. *R News* **2002**, 2, 18–22.
58. Fritsch, S.; Guenther, F.; Wright, M.N. *neuralnet: Training of Neural Networks*, 2019. R Package Version 1.44.2. Available online: https://journal.r-project.org/archive/2010/RJ-2010-006/RJ-2010-006.pdf (accessed on 29 June 2023).
59. Craig, C.C. A Note on Sheppard's Corrections. *Ann. Math. Stat.* **1941**, *12*, 339–345. [CrossRef]
60. Chen, J.; de Hoogh, K.; Gulliver, J.; Hoffmann, B.; Hertel, O.; Ketzel, M.; Bauwelinck, M.; van Donkelaar, A.; Hvidtfeldt, U.A.; Katsouyanni, K.; et al. A comparison of linear regression, regularization, and machine learning algorithms to develop Europe-wide spatial models of fine particles and nitrogen dioxide. *Environ. Int.* **2019**, *130*, 104934. [CrossRef]

61. Dong, Y.; Zhou, S.; Xing, L.; Chen, Y.; Ren, Z.; Dong, Y.; Zhang, X. Deep learning methods may not outperform other machi learning methods on analyzing genomic studies. *Front. Genet.* **2022**, *13*, 992070. [CrossRef]
62. Su, J.; Fraser, N.J.; Gambardella, G.; Blott, M.; Durelli, G.; Thomas, D.B.; Leong, P.; Cheung, P.Y.K. Accuracy to Throughp Trade-offs for Reduced Precision Neural Networks on Reconfigurable Logic. *arXiv* **2018**, arXiv:1807.10577. [CrossRef]
63. Benedetto, L.; Cappelli, A.; Turrin, R.; Cremonesi, P. Introducing a Framework to Assess Newly Created Questions with Natu Language Processing. In *Lecture Notes in Computer Science*; Springer International Publishing: Cham, Switzerland, 2020; pp. 43– [CrossRef]
64. Benedetto, L.; Cappelli, A.; Turrin, R.; Cremonesi, P. R2DE: A NLP approach to estimating IRT parameters of newly generat questions. In *Proceedings of the Tenth International Conference on Learning Analytics & Knowledge*; ACM: New York, NY, USA, 20. [CrossRef]
65. Ehara, Y. Building an English Vocabulary Knowledge Dataset of Japanese English-as-a-Second-Language Learners Usi Crowdsourcing. In Proceedings of the Eleventh International Conference on Language Resources and Evaluation (LREC 201 Miyazaki, Japan, 7–12 May 2018; European Language Resources Association (ELRA): Miyazaki, Japan, 2018.
66. Lee, J.U.; Schwan, E.; Meyer, C.M. Manipulating the Difficulty of C-Tests. In Proceedings of the 57th Annual Meeting of t Association for Computational Linguistics, Florence, Italy, 28 July–2 August 2019; Association for Computational Linguisti Florence, Italy, 2019; pp. 360–370. [CrossRef]
67. Pandarova, I.; Schmidt, T.; Hartig, J.; Boubekki, A.; Jones, R.D.; Brefeld, U. Predicting the Difficulty of Exercise Items for Dynam Difficulty Adaptation in Adaptive Language Tutoring. *Int. J. Artif. Intell. Educ.* **2019**, *29*, 342–367. [CrossRef]
68. Qiu, Z.; Wu, X.; Fan, W. Question Difficulty Prediction for Multiple Choice Problems in Medical Exams. In Proceedings of t 28th ACM International Conference on Information and Knowledge Management, Beijing, China, 3–7 November 2019; AC New York, NY, USA, 2019.
69. Ha, L.A.; Yaneva, V.; Baldwin, P.; Mee, J. Predicting the Difficulty of Multiple Choice Questions in a High-stakes Medical Exa In Proceedings of the Fourteenth Workshop on Innovative Use of NLP for Building Educational Applications, Florence, Italy, August 2019; Association for Computational Linguistics: Florence, Italy, 2019; pp. 11–20. [CrossRef]
70. Xue, K.; Yaneva, V.; Runyon, C.; Baldwin, P. Predicting the Difficulty and Response Time of Multiple Choice Questions Usin Transfer Learning. In Proceedings of the Fifteenth Workshop on Innovative Use of NLP for Building Educational Application Online, 10 July 2020; Association for Computational Linguistics: Seattle, WA, USA, 2020; pp. 193–197. [CrossRef]
71. Yaneva, V.; Ha, L.A.; Baldwin, P.; Mee, J. Predicting Item Survival for Multiple Choice Questions in a High-Stakes Medical Exa In Proceedings of the Twelfth Language Resources and Evaluation Conference,Marseille, France, 11–16 May 2020; Europea Language Resources Association: Marseille, France, 2020; pp. 6812–6818.
72. Yin, Y.; Liu, Q.; Huang, Z.; Chen, E.; Tong, W.; Wang, S.; Su, Y. QuesNet. In Proceedings of the 25th ACM SIGKDD Internationa Conference on Knowledge Discovery & Data Mining, Anchorage, AK, USA, 4–8 August 2019; ACM: New York, NY, USA, 201
73. Hsu, F.Y.; Lee, H.M.; Chang, T.H.; Sung, Y.T. Automated estimation of item difficulty for multiple-choice tests: An application o word embedding techniques. *Inf. Process. Manag.* **2018**, *54*, 969–984. [CrossRef]
74. Lin, L.H.; Chang, T.H.; Hsu, F.Y. Automated Prediction of Item Difficulty in Reading Comprehension Using Long Short-Ter Memory. In Proceedings of the 2019 International Conference on Asian Language Processing (IALP), Shanghai, China, 15–1 November 2019; IEEE: Piscataway, NJ, USA, 2019.
75. McTavish, D.G.; Pirro, E.B. Contextual content analysis. *Qual. Quant.* **1990**, *24*, 245–265. [CrossRef]
76. Stipak, B.; Hensler, C. Statistical Inference in Contextual Analysis. *Am. J. Political Sci.* **1982**, *26*, 151. [CrossRef]
77. Martinková, P.; Štěpánek, L.; Drabinová, A.; Houdek, J.; Vejražka, M.; Štuka, Č. Semi-real-time analyses of item characteristics fo medical school admission tests. In Proceedings of the 2017 Federated Conference on Computer Science and Information Systems Prague, Czech Republic, 3–6 September 2017; IEEE: Piscataway, NJ, USA, 2017.
78. Erosheva, E.A.; Martinková, P.; Lee, C.J. When zero may not be zero: A cautionary note on the use of inter-rater reliability in evaluating grant peer review. *J. R. Stat. Soc. Ser. (Stat. Soc.)* **2021**, *184*, 904–919. [CrossRef]
79. Van den Besselaar, P.; Sandström, U.; Schiffbaenker, H. Studying grant decision-making: A linguistic analysis of review reports *Scientometrics* **2018**, *117*, 313–329. [CrossRef]
80. Penfield, R.D.; Camilli, G. Differential item functioning and item bias. In *Psychometrics*; Rao, C.R., Sinharay, S., Eds.; Handbook of Statistics; Elsevier: Amsterdam, The Netherlands, 2006; Volume 26, pp. 125–167. [CrossRef]
81. Martinková, P.; Drabinová, A.; Liaw, Y.L.; Sanders, E.A.; McFarland, J.L.; Price, R.M. Checking equity: Why differential item functioning analysis should be a routine part of developing conceptual assessments. *CBE-Life Sci. Educ.* **2017**, *16*, rm2. [CrossRef]
82. Hladká, A.; Martinková, P. difNLR: Generalized Logistic Regression Models for DIF and DDF Detection. *R J.* **2020**, *12*, 300–323. [CrossRef]
83. Martinková, P.; Hladká, A.; Potužníková, E. Is academic tracking related to gains in learning competence? Using propensity score matching and differential item change functioning analysis for better understanding of tracking implications. *Learn. Instr.* **2020**, *66*, 101286. [CrossRef]
84. Chall, J.S.; Dale, E. *Readability REVISITED: The New Dale-Chall Readability Formula*; Brookline Books: Cambridge, MA, USA, 1995.
85. Gunning, R. *The Technique of Clear Writing*; McGraw-Hill: New York, NY, USA, 1952.
86. McLaughlin, G.H. SMOG Grading: A New Readability Formula. *J. Read.* **1969**, *12*, 639–646.

7. Tränkle, U.; Bailer, H. Kreuzvalidierung und Neuberechnung von Lesbarkeitsformeln für die deutsche Sprache. *Zeitschrift für Entwicklungspsychologie und Pädagogische Psychologie* **1984**, *16*, 231–244.
8. Mikolov, T.; Chen, K.; Corrado, G.; Dean, J. Efficient Estimation of Word Representations in Vector Space. *arXiv* **2013**. arXiv:1301.3781.

mathematics

MDPI

Article

Predictive Prompts with Joint Training of Large Language Models for Explainable Recommendation

Ching-Sheng Lin [1,*], Chung-Nan Tsai [2], Shao-Tang Su [1], Jung-Sing Jwo [1,3], Cheng-Hsiung Lee [1] and Xin Wang [4]

1 Master Program of Digital Innovation, Tunghai University, Taichung 40704, Taiwan
2 Lam Research Japan GK, Kanagawa 222-0033, Japan
3 Department of Computer Science, Tunghai University, Taichung 40704, Taiwan
4 Department of Epidemiology and Biostatistics, University at Albany School of Public Health, State Universit of New York, Rensselaer, NY 12144, USA
* Correspondence: cslin612@thu.edu.tw

Abstract: Large language models have recently gained popularity in various applications due to thei ability to generate natural text for complex tasks. Recommendation systems, one of the frequentl studied research topics, can be further improved using the capabilities of large language models t track and understand user behaviors and preferences. In this research, we aim to build reliable anc transparent recommendation system by generating human-readable explanations to help users obtair better insights into the recommended items and gain more trust. We propose a learning scheme tc jointly train the rating prediction task and explanation generation task. The rating prediction task learns the predictive representation from the input of user and item vectors. Subsequently, inspired by the recent success of prompt engineering, these predictive representations are served as predictive prompts, which are soft embeddings, to elicit and steer any knowledge behind language models for the explanation generation task. Empirical studies show that the proposed approach achieves competitive results compared with other existing baselines on the public English TripAdvisor dataset of explainable recommendations.

Keywords: large language models; recommendation systems; human-readable explanations; rating prediction task; explanation generation task; prompt engineering; predictive prompt

MSC: 94A16

Citation: Lin, C.-S.; Tsai, C.-N.; Su, S.-T.; Jwo, J.-S.; Lee, C.-H.; Wang, X. Predictive Prompts with Joint Training of Large Language Models for Explainable Recommendation. *Mathematics* **2023**, *11*, 4230. https://doi.org/10.3390/math11204230

Academic Editors: Adrian Sergiu Darabant and Diana-Laura Borza

Received: 23 August 2023
Revised: 22 September 2023
Accepted: 4 October 2023
Published: 10 October 2023

1. Introduction

Recommendation systems have been widely adapted in various applications including e-commerce sites, social media usages, and content platforms to address the information overload [1]. The recommendation engines help in predicting the right items to the customer based on the histories of other similar users, the attributes of users and items, and the customer's explicit or implicit personal preferences. There are two major approaches to solve this research problem where Collaborative Filtering (CF) assumes people who share similar past preferences will likely have similar preferences in the future and Content-Based Filtering (CBF) suggests items to users based on the similarity comparison between users' preferences and items' characteristics [2].

However, traditional recommendation techniques have less interaction with users to discover their real-time requirements, resulting in inaccurate predictions and causing a bad user experience. To overcome these challenges, conversational recommendation systems have emerged as a promising alternative which enables users to interact with the recommendation agents through natural language dialogue. This natural and intuitive interaction mode not only provides an avenue to better understand customers' needs but also offers a better user experience [3]. With the recent advancement and popularity of conversational agents (especially the game-changer, ChatGPT), conversational AIs are able to communicate with users on a broad range of topics like never before [4]. Figure 1 demonstrates a conversational recommendation system between a user and an agent for multiple turns shown in black text. Although a massive amount of recommendation algorithms are powerful enough to generate accurate recommendations, most of them fail to produce explanations for their recommendations and lack transparency.

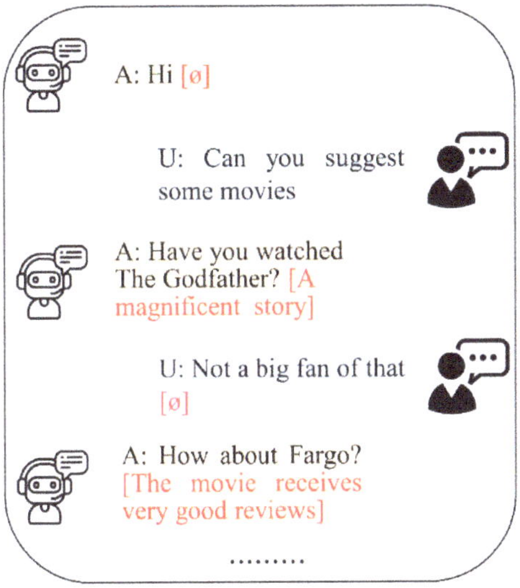

Figure 1. A dialogue example of an explainable recommendation system.

There is a general agreement that both accuracy and explainability are crucial aspects for the evaluation of recommendation systems [5,6]. Applying text explanations to the recommended items would increase user trust as well as help users easily make decisions and boost user satisfaction. Hence, more and more research efforts have been devoted to improving the recommendation and enhancing the explanations for the non-explainable black box recommender systems [7]. The red text in Figure 1 illustrates the explanations of the recommendation system.

Most recently, large-scale pre-trained language models (PLMs) have been the focus of mainstream media and achieved outstanding performance in various natural language processing tasks [8]. The main reason that PLMs have taken the Internet by storm is due to their easy adoption. GPT series models trained to predict the next word in an autoregressive process have gained the most attention and instigated a training paradigm shift from pre-training and fine-tuning to prompt learning [9].

Since PLMs are usually trained on large corpora and are difficult to optimize for small training data, it is important to develop an approach to efficiently exploit and influence PLMs' output. Prompt-based learning is an emerging solution by automatically generating prompts in order to adopt PLMs to perform downstream tasks [10]. In this paper, we take user id and item id as the input to generate explanations for the recommendations by leveraging the PLMs. The proposed learning scheme jointly trains the rating prediction task and explanation generation task. The rating prediction task learns the predictive representation from the input of user and item vectors. Subsequently, these predictive representations are served as predictive prompts, which are soft embeddings, to elicit and steer any knowledge behind language models for the explanation generation task. Compared with the hard prompts which have to rely on human experts to design templates and are difficult to optimize, soft prompts could be directly fine-tuned using data from downstream tasks and possess more representation ability. Unlike the traditional joint training strategy which mainly optimizes multiple tasks simultaneously, our end-to-end joint model also explicitly incorporates features extracted from one task into the other ta for the purpose of the interaction between tasks.

The key contributions of our proposed approach are two-fold:

- We propose a joint training scheme to predict the recommendation rating and produ explanations of the recommendation based on the prompt learning. The predicti prompts are taken from the predictive representations learned in the rating predictic task, and fed into PLMs to generate output text.
- Experiments are conducted on the TripAdvisor dataset to verify the effectiveness of o approach on both rating prediction task and explanation generation task. The resul show that our method is not only capable of generating suitable explanations but al achieves promising performance comparable with other state-of-the-art algorithn in terms of Root Mean Square Error (RMSE) and Mean Absolute Error (MAE) for th rating prediction task.

The rest of this paper is structured as follows. In Section 2, several research fielc and paradigms related to the works of this paper are reviewed. In Section 3, an in-dept discussion of our joint model is provided and discussed. In Section 4, empirical studie are performed on the public dataset to examine the effectiveness and further analyze th results of the proposed model. In the last section, we make some conclusions and briefl present some possible future investigations.

2. Related Work

Since our proposed model is a joint training framework to predict the recommer dation rating and generate explanations of the recommendation based on the predictiv prompts using language models, we review three related research directions including th recommendation system, pre-trained language models and prompt learning in this sectio

2.1. Recommendation Systems

Since the earliest recommendation algorithm in the 1990s, this research field ha always been actively investigated by both industry and academia [11]. Content-basec filtering recommendation algorithms have improved their performance by operating or embedding representations compared to the traditional feature-engineering approache such as Bag-of-Words and TF-IDF [12]. Collaborative filtering is another popular technique in recommender systems to predict user interests by analyzing the behaviors and opinions of similar users. Since graph neural networks (GNNs) have facilitated the representatior learning in recent years, the Graph Matching-based Collaborative Filtering model (GMCF considers two types of attribute interactions where inner interactions independently operate on either user-specific or item-specific attributes, and cross interactions further integrate the interdependent relationships between user-specific and item-specific attributes [13]. A recommendation system based on sentiment analysis and matrix factorization (SAMF) was proposed to address data sparsity and credibility. It combines topic models, matrix factorization and deep learning to enhance recommendation accuracy [14].

Compared to traditional recommender systems, the conversational recommendation system provides a human-like interaction that enables users to receive personalized recommendations which are highly relevant to their needs and truly beneficial for their decision making [15]. To address the cold-start users and static model issues, the ConTS model is designed to dynamically ask users to provide their favorite attributes of the item and then make rational recommendations [16]. The EAR model is proposed to estimate the user preference over items (Estimation stage), learn a reinforced dialogue policy on multi-round conversational recommendations (Action stage), and update the learning model based on users' feedback (Reflection stage) [17].

As the explanation in the recommendation systems is becoming more and more important, a Deep Explicit Attentive Multi-View Learning Model (DEAML) adopts a knowledge graph to produce explanations, and applies an attentive multi-view learning model for solving the rating prediction problem [5]. To leverage the user interaction in the recommendation system, a multitask learning framework is used to simultaneously train the recommendation task, explanation generation, and user feedback incorporation [6].

2.2. Pre-Trained Language Models

The Transformer architecture is an encoder–decoder structure with self-attention mechanism to learn long-range representation that was initially applied to natural language processing tasks and has been widely extended to various domains [18]. It often follows the self-supervised pre-training strategy and enables fast adaptation to downstream tasks. Based on the pre-training mechanism, there are three variants of structures including Transformer encoders, Transformer decoders and full Transformers with encoder–decoders [19].

The objective of the Transformer encoder framework aims to predict hidden text using a bidirectional Transformer encoder. BERT which is pre-trained on Masked Language Model (MLM) and Next Sentence Prediction (NSP) is one of the most remarkable models in this category that achieves state-of-the-art performances on many NLP tasks [20]. The Transformer decoder framework employs an autoregressive generation by predicting the next text conditioned on the past sequence. GPT series models apply left-to-right unidirectional modeling to pre-train on large scale corpus and allow in-context learning without fine-tuning the original model parameters [21,22]. The Transformer encoder–decoder architecture is a sequence-to-sequence learning model where the encoder masks several fragments and the decoder manages to recover these hidden sections. BookGPT guides language models to predict user ratings textually for book recommendation tasks where the output format is based on predefined templates [23]. Generative recommendation (GenRec) is a recommendation system that leverages large language models to directly generate recommended items, instead of using traditional ranking-based approaches by calculating the rating score for each candidate item [24].

2.3. Prompt Learning

Prompt-based learning aims at learning or developing suitable and effective representations that can elicit the large PLMs to carry out the given task or solve the specific problem. This new paradigm of learning has achieved a lot of success in diverse NLP tasks because of its adaptability and capability.

Automated prompt engineering can be classified into discrete prompts and continuous prompts [10]. Discrete prompts work on searching natural language text and appending these text as prompts to reformulate the downstream task. For example, to perform the sentiment analysis of the given sentence "I like the game very much", a possible discrete prompt could be like "The game is" and the PLMs would be leveraged to predict a next token for determining the sentiment of the sentence [25]. LAPAQA generates discrete prompts by extracting the text located between the input and output from large text corpora [26]. Continuous prompts, in contrast to the discrete prompting method which requires human-understandable text, enable the model to learn from the continuous vector space of the underlying PLMs. Prefix-Tuning is a novel technique to guide the PLMs towards the designated task where task-specific vectors are prepended to the input sequence as prefixes [9]. In the prompt-based news recommendation (PBNR) approach, news recommendation is considered as a text-to-text language task, taking into account users' past reading behaviors. During model training, both ranking loss and language generation loss are integrated [27]. A Prompt Learning for News Recommendation (Prompt4NR) framework changes the prediction task from determining if a user would click on a candidate news article into a cloze-style mask-prediction task with various prompt templates [28].

3. Proposed Method

The objective of this paper is to recommend item i to user u and provide a comprehensive explanation simultaneously. Our network model to address the explainable recommendation problem is a joint training framework based on prompt-based learning for the large language model and is depicted in Figure 2. There are two major components in our system. The first component is a deep neural network used to predict a recommendation score from a given user–item pair (left-hand side of Figure 2). The second component utilizes the latent representation learned from the first component as the predictive prompts feeding them into a large PLM to generate explanations (right-hand side of Figure 2).

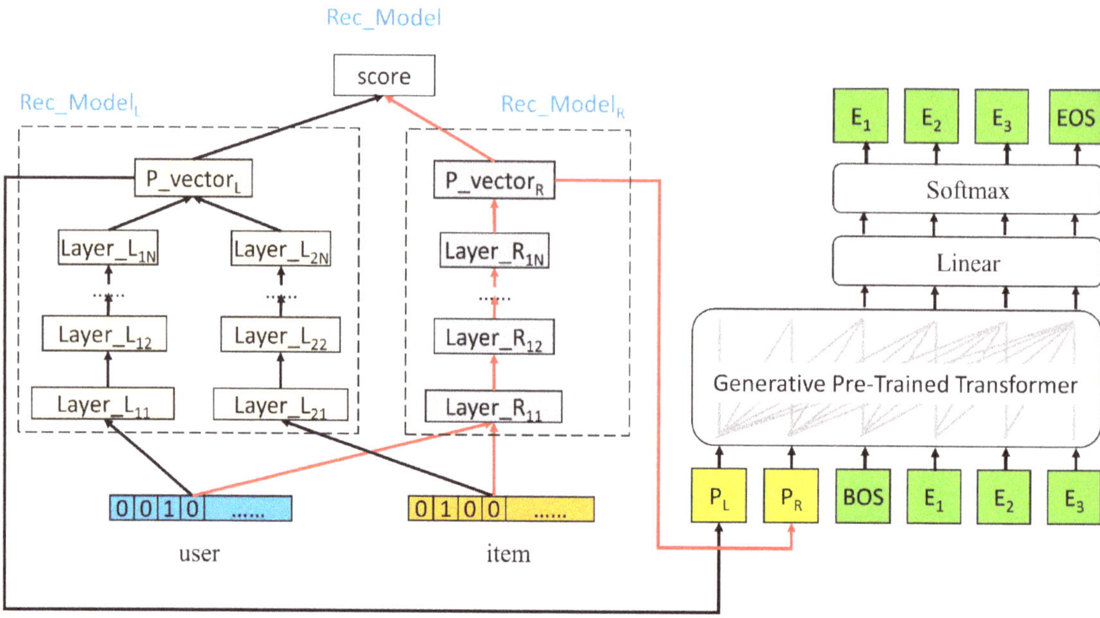

Figure 2. The architecture of prompt-based explainable recommendation model.

3.1. Prompt-Based Explainable Recommendation Architecture

In this research, we address the problem of explainable recommendation by proposing a joint model for recommendation score prediction and explainable text generation, exploiting the dependencies between these two tasks to enhance the performance compared to independent models. Joint training is a frequently employed approach when closely related tasks can be trained simultaneously and share similar datasets. In the context of neural network models, as these tasks share specific model layers, it promotes the model to acquire more universally applicable representations, thereby maximizing its generalization performance across all tasks. The recommendation score prediction is based on Collaborative Filtering of fusion learning [29]. Once the score has been established, the predictive vectors obtained during the learning process are leveraged with the use of pre-trained language models, which provide the rich information derived from large training corpus, to generate explanations.

Inspired from the DeepCF [29], our recommendation model (Rec_Model) contains two branches of deep network where one is Rec_Model$_L$ to learn the representation and the other is Rec_Model$_R$ to learn the match function (left-hand side of Figure 2). Unlike DeepCF which takes user ratings and item ratings as inputs, Rec_Model directly uses IDs of users and items. The Rec_Model$_L$ consists of two subnetworks represented by Layer_L$_{1n}$ and Layer_L$_{2n}$, respectively. The input of Layer_L$_{11}$ is the user id and the input of Layer_L$_{21}$ is the item id. By combining the last layers Layer_L$_{1N}$ and Layer_L$_{2N}$, the final representation is P_vector$_L$. Regarding the structure of Rec_Model$_R$, the concatenation of the user id and item id is passed into the $Layer\_R_{11}$ and is processed through multiple layers to form the final representation P_vector_R. The Rec_Model_L can be formulated as:

$$\begin{aligned} X_j^{L_1} &= a\left(X_{j-1}^{L_1} W^{L_1}\right) \\ X_j^{L_2} &= a\left(X_{j-1}^{L_2} W^{L_2}\right) \\ P\_vector_L &= X^{L1} \odot X^{L2} \end{aligned} \tag{1}$$

where W^{L_1} and $X_j^{L_1}$ define the weight matrix and input of the j-th layer, respectively. $a(\cdot)$ denotes the activation function to learn more complex representation. The same notations are applied to the subnetwork $Layer\_L_{2n}$ as well. Subsequently, the element-wise product is employed to the outputs of two subnetworks to yield P_vector_L. Meanwhile, the formulation of Rec_Model_R is described below:

$$\begin{aligned} X_j^{R_1} &= a\left(X_{j-1}^{R_1} W^{R_1}\right) \\ P\_vector_R &= X^{R1} \end{aligned} \tag{2}$$

where W^{R_1} and $X_j^{R_1}$ are the weight matrix and input of the j-th layer. The final X^{R1} is symbolized by P_vector_R. Given the outputs of two branches, we combine them and make the prediction score as follows:

$$\hat{s}_{u,i} = a\left(W^F \begin{bmatrix} P\_vector_L \\ P\_vector_R \end{bmatrix}\right) \tag{3}$$

where W^F is the weight matrix and $\hat{s}_{u,i}$ is the prediction score of the recommendation.

After the recommendation process has finished, we propose a prompt learning method to elicit the knowledge behind the pre-trained language models for the explanation generation task (right-hand side of Figure 2). In this part, P_vector_L and P_vector_R are served as predictive prompts represented by P_L and P_R to trigger the explanation words and GPT-2 is used as the pre-trained language generation model. We made extensive use of the GPT2 libraries created by the HuggingFace community. These libraries provide a wide range of robust deep learning tools and efficiently integrate with the PyTorch framework. GPT2 has been trained on large amount of data and significantly demonstrated remarkable performance across many natural language processing tasks. During the training phase, the prompts with explanation words (e_j) are fed into GPT-2 to obtain the encoding X^E. Then, X^E is passed through a linear layer with softmax activation to generate a probability distribution over the full vocabulary. The formulation can be expressed as

$$d_j = \mathrm{softmax}\left(X^E W^E\right) \tag{4}$$

where d_j is the probability distribution and W^E is the weight matrix.

3.2. Learning Process

During the training stage, to learn the recommendation score prediction module, we set the loss function using mean square error as:

$$Loss_R = \frac{1}{|Tr|} \sum \left(\hat{s}_{u,i} - s_{u,i}\right)^2 \tag{5}$$

where $s_{u,I}$ is the ground-truth recommendation score and $|Tr|$ denotes the size of training samples. To learn the explanation generation, we choose negative log-likelihood as the loss function, which is defined below:

$$Loss_E = \frac{1}{|Tr|} \sum \frac{1}{|Exp|} \sum -\log d_j^{e_j} \tag{6}$$

where |Exp| denotes the number of explanation words. To jointly model both recomme dation score prediction and explanations, we combine two tasks into a multi-task learni architecture and formulate the loss function as:

$$\text{Loss}_\text{T} = \min_{\theta}(\text{Loss}_\text{R} + \alpha \text{Loss}_\text{E}) \quad (7)$$

where α is the weighted parameter to balance two terms.

In the inference phase, initially, we use the predictive prompts with a special wo BOS as the input. The autoregressive process takes the input, runs through the explanati generation network, selects a word based on the generated word probability distributi over the vocabulary and appends the selected word to the end of the input to form the ne input. Then, the autoregressive process is repeated until a special generated word EOS produced [30].

Algorithm 1 demonstrates the training procedure of our proposed model.

Algorithm 1: Prompt-Based Explainable Recommendation Model.

Input: The training dataset D {User (U), Item (I), Explanation (E)}
Output: θ for all the trainable weights in the model

1: Randomly initialize θ
2: **repeat**:
3:   **for** each mini-batch {u, i, e} in D:
4:     Calculate P_vector_L and P_vector_R to obtain $\hat{s}_{u,i}$
5:     Compute the Loss_R in Equation (5)
6:     Calculate d_j based on the expression of Equation (4)
7:     Compute the Loss_E in Equation (6)
8:     Compute the Loss_T in Equation (7)
9:     Update the weight θ to minimize the Loss_T
10:   **end for**
11: **until** convergence:

4. Experiments and Results

In this section, we develop empirical studies to assess the proposed method in recom mendation and explanation tasks. The flow of the experiments includes data-processing training, testing and ablation studies. The data are described and divided into differen sets for the evaluation (Section 4.1). We train the model for baselines and our approac with training set, subsequently evaluating the performance of each model in terms o the evaluation criterion (Section 4.2) with separate test data after the training procedure (Section 4.3). The ablation studies are conducted to examine the impact and importance o each component in our model (Section 4.4).

4.1. Dataset

The source used for evaluating our model is the TripAdvisor dataset which contains 9765 users, 6280 items and 320,023 reviews. The ground-truth explanations are those sentences from reviews. Similar to the prior research settings [31,32], the training, validation, and testing sets are divided in an 8:1:1 ratio, resulting in 256,017 training samples, 32,003 validation samples and 32,003 testing samples, respectively. Sample data can be seen in Figure 3.


```
{'user': 1, 'item': 0, 'rating': 5, 'text': 'we had to wait for the room to be ready and we good a free up grade as a compensation'},
{'user': 53, 'item': 0, 'rating': 4, 'text': 'the pool was really high up and has an amazing view'},
{'user': 56, 'item': 0, 'rating': 5, 'text': 'the pool is just fabulous'},
{'user': 58, 'item': 0, 'rating': 5, 'text': 'the gym is set up high to give you stunning views of hong kong harbour while you work'},
```


Figure 3. Sample data.

4.2. Evaluation Criterion

To assess the overall performance of our proposed solution automatically, both the recommendation task and explanation generation need to be evaluated. Regarding the measurement of recommendation module, we employ two popular metrics, Root Mean Square Error (RMSE) and Mean Absolute Error (MAE) [11]. For the generation of explanations, we adopt BLEU (Bilingual Evaluation Understudy) [33] and ROUGE (Recall-Oriented Understudy for Gisting Evaluation) [34] as two evaluation indicators.

ROUGE-N Precision calculates the ratio of the number of N-grams in the system results that also appear in the reference results, divided by the total number of N-grams in the system results. ROUGE-N Recall measures the proportion of N-grams in the reference results that are also found in the system results, divided by the total number of N-grams in the reference results. ROUGE-N F-score is the harmonic mean of ROUGE-N Precision and ROUGE-N Recall. In this research, we report ROUGE-1 F-score (ROUGE1-F) and ROUGE-2 F-score (ROUGE2-F). The BLEU score automatically evaluates sentence generation quality by calculating n-gram precision between system outputs and reference results, while also incorporating a brevity penalty (BP) to avoid excessively brief sentences. We use Bleu-1 and Bleu-4 scores to assess the quality and fluency of generated explanations. It is worth to note that although BLEU and ROUGE scores are typical and standard metrics for evaluation, focusing only on the lexical overlap between system-generated and human-written answers may be biased. Adapting these two metrics to better correlate lexical overlap with the human judgment is an important future research direction.

4.3. Experimental Performances

To validate the efficacy, our proposed method is compared with several state-of-the-art models as the baselines:

- Att2Seq [35]: This method is an attention-enhanced attribute-to-sequence network and is initially proposed to create product reviews. The model uses the user ID, product ID, and rating as attributes.
- NRT [36]: Unlike reviews which are lengthy and time consuming, tips are very succinct insights to capture user experience with only a few words in E-commerce sites. This paper uses multi-task learning framework to predict product ratings and generate tips where the rating prediction is based on a multi-layer perceptron network and tip generation is a sequence decoder model. The input of this model consists of user id and item id.
- PEPLER-MF [32]: PEPLER is a personalized prompt-based learning for explainable recommendation using pre-trained language models based on user and item IDs. PEPLER-MF uses Matrix Factorization (MF) for the recommendation rating score prediction by the user and item embeddings. The explanations are produced with the aid of pre-trained language models.
- PEPLER-MLP [32]: This method is another variant of PEPLER. The major difference is that this model trains a Multi-Layer Perceptron (MLP) to estimate the rating scores.

The experimental comparison is operated in the environment of a Windows 10 OS, utilizing an Intel Core i9 central processing unit (CPU) with 128 GB of memory, and a GPU NVIDIA GeForce RTX 3090 with a memory size of 24 GB. We adjust the hyper-parameters empirically to ensure the training quality and the hyper-parameter settings can be seen in Table 1.

According to the comparison results displayed in Table 2 where the first two baselines (Att2Seq and NRT) are directly obtained from the relevant papers and the results of the rest (PEPLER-MF and PEPLER-MLP) are generated by the provided source codes of those papers, we achieve the highest scores with respect to BLEU-1, ROUGE1-F, ROUGE2-F and MAE, demonstrating the capability to make appropriate recommendations and create acceptable explanations. Regarding the performance of recommendation task measured in RMSE and MAE, in addition to PEPLER-MF, most methods exhibit similar performances aligned with the prior research findings [37]. Our method receives high scores on BLEU-1 but lacks consistent improvements on higher-order BLEU and ROUGE scores. Since GPT2 a generation-based language model, it may produce synonyms or paraphrases of referenc text, which have similar or identical semantic content but receive lower ROUGE and BLE scores. Combining automated metrics and human evaluation to assess the performanc of a generation-based language model comprehensively is very important and is wort further investigation.

Table 1. Hyper-parameter configuration.

Parameter	Value
batch size	128
epoch	10
P_vector$_L$ size	768
P_vector$_R$ size	768
layers N in Rec_Model	2
learning rate	0.00075

Table 2. Comparative assessment of all competing methods on TripAdvisor dataset.

	BLEU-1	BLEU-4	ROUGE1-F	ROUGE2-F	RMSE	MAE
Att2Seq	15.20%	0.96%	16.38%	2.19%	-	-
NRT	13.76%	0.80%	15.58%	1.68%	**0.790**	0.610
PEPLER-MF	15.94%	**1.14**%	16.38%	2.14%	1.574	1.341
PEPLER-MLP	15.91%	1.03%	16.39%	2.13%	0.799	0.612
Our Model	**16.45**%	1.10%	**16.71**%	**2.24**%	0.795	**0.607**

In Table 3, we additionally list various examples, including the ground truth (Ground truth_X) and the generated explanations (Generation_X), to demonstrate our results. From what we can see, the polarity of each generated explanation aligns with the ground truth. However, there is still significant potential for improvement in context generation. As observed in example 5, although the sentiment of the explanation is correct, the subjects are not accurately described. Incorporating more information of users and items could be an avenue to direct the language model's generation.

Table 3. Five example outputs produced by our model and the corresponding ground truths.

Ground truth_1: location was good and was close to many restaurants
Generation_1: the hotel is located in a great location
Ground truth_2: pool area is good though
Generation_2 the pool is great and the staff are very helpful
Ground truth_3: the bed is very comfortable and the bath room is great
Generation_3 the bed was very comfortable and the bathroom was clean and modern
Ground truth_4: i enjoyed the front desk staff
Generation_4 the front desk staff was very helpful

Table 3. *Cont.*

Ground truth_5: gym also very small and with an odd smell
Generation_5 the room was very small and the bathroom was very small

4.4. Ablation Studies

To validate the applicability of our suggestions, we execute ablation studies on the TripAdvisor dataset to explore the advantages of our methodology and quantify the impact of each critical module. Referring to the findings presented in Table 4, removing either P_vector_L or P_vector_R leads to performance degradation in terms of all evaluation metrics. Hence, we are confident that our approach can significantly improve the performance of explainable recommendation by jointly learning the recommendation module and explanation generation.

Table 4. Ablation experimental results.

	BLEU-1	BLEU-4	ROUGE1-F	ROUGE2-F	RMSE	MAE
Our Model	16.45%	1.10%	16.71%	2.24%	0.795	0.607
$-P\_vector_L$	15.89%	1.03%	16.43%	2.14%	0.796	0.611
$-P\_vector_R$	15.81%	1.03%	16.41%	2.17%	0.798	0.612

5. Conclusions

In this work, we propose a prompt-based method to address the explainable recommendation system with the leverage of pre-trained language models. To optimize both recommendation correctness and explanation generation simultaneously, we apply a multi-task learning strategy. We perform experimental studies on the TripAdvisor dataset and yield satisfactory results in terms of BLEU-1, ROUGE1-F, ROUGE2-F and MAE. The direction of adopting predictive prompts in pre-trained language models provides a promising alternative to produce reasonable recommendation explanations.

Our future work is to expand upon this paper by focusing on the following areas. First, as the current approach only uses the embeddings learned from the rating task as predictive prompts, we will investigate more predictive prompts for explanation generation such as the item descriptions and users' preferences. Second, the research of recommendation systems is still an evolving field [38] and we intend to delve further into more advanced recommendation models. With the increasing quality of recommendation accuracy, we expect to enhance both recommendation performance and explanation generation at once. Third, the current language model is based on GPT-2 and we will explore other knowledge enhanced pre-trained language models to improve the explanation generation [39].

Author Contributions: Supervision, J.-S.J.; methodology, C.-S.L. and C.-H.L.; investigation, C.-S.L., C.-N.T. and S.-T.S.; writing—review and editing, C.-S.L. and X.W. All authors have read and agreed to the published version of the manuscript.

Funding: This work is financially supported by the National Science and Technology Council (NSTC) of Taiwan under Grant 112-2221-E-029 -019 -.

Data Availability Statement: TripAdvisor datasets can be found https://github.com/lileipisces/PEPLER (accessed on 13 March 2023).

Conflicts of Interest: The authors declare no conflict of interest.

References

1. Kumar, P.; Thakur, R.S. Recommendation system techniques and related issues: A survey. *Int. J. Inf. Technol.* **2018**, *10*, 495–5 [CrossRef]
2. Barkan, O.; Koenigstein, N.; Yogev, E.; Katz, O. CB2CF: A neural multiview content-to-collaborative filtering model for complete cold item recommendations. In Proceedings of the 13th ACM Conference on Recommender Systems, Copenhagen Denma 16–20 September 2019; pp. 228–236.
3. Liu, Z.; Wang, H.; Niu, Z.; Wu, H.; Che, W.; Liu, T. Towards Conversational Recommendation over Multi-Type Dialo In Proceedings of the 58th Annual Meeting of the Association-for-Computational-Linguistics (ACL), Online, 5–10 July 20 pp. 1036–1049.
4. Van Dis, E.A.; Bollen, J.; Zuidema, W.; van Rooij, R.; Bockting, C.L. ChatGPT: Five priorities for research. *Nature* **2023**, *614*, 224–2 [CrossRef] [PubMed]
5. Gao, J.; Wang, X.; Wang, Y.; Xie, X. Explainable recommendation through attentive multi-view learning. In Proceedings of t AAAI Conference on Artificial Intelligence, Honolulu, HI, USA, 27 January–1 February 2019; Volume 33, pp. 3622–3629.
6. Chen, Z.; Wang, X.; Xie, X.; Parsana, M.; Soni, A.; Ao, X.; Chen, E. Towards explainable conversational recommendation. Proceedings of the Twenty-Ninth International Conference on International Joint Conferences on Artificial Intelligence, Yokohar Japan, 7–15 January 2021; pp. 2994–3000.
7. Alshammari, M.; Nasraoui, O.; Sanders, S. Mining semantic knowledge graphs to add explainability to black box recommend systems. *IEEE Access* **2019**, *7*, 110563–110579. [CrossRef]
8. Zhang, S.; Roller, S.; Goyal, N.; Artetxe, M.; Chen, M.; Chen, S.; Dewan, C.; Diab, M.; Li, X.; Zettlemoyer, L.; et al. Opt: Ope pre-trained transformer language models. *arXiv* **2022**, arXiv:2205.01068.
9. Li, X.L.; Liang, P. Prefix-Tuning: Optimizing Continuous Prompts for Generation. In Proceedings of the 59th Annual Meetin of the Association for Computational Linguistics and the 11th International Joint Conference on Natural Language Processin Online, 1–6 August 2021; Volume 1, pp. 4582–4597.
10. Liu, P.; Yuan, W.; Fu, J.; Jiang, Z.; Hayashi, H.; Neubig, G. Pre-train, prompt, and predict: A systematic survey of promptin methods in natural language processing. *ACM Comput. Surv.* **2023**, *55*, 1–35. [CrossRef]
11. Ko, H.; Lee, S.; Park, Y.; Choi, A. A survey of recommendation systems: Recommendation models, techniques, and applicatio fields. *Electronics* **2022**, *11*, 141. [CrossRef]
12. Chen, K.; Liang, B.; Ma, X.; Gu, M. Learning audio embeddings with user listening data for content-based music recommendatio In Proceedings of the ICASSP 2021–2021 IEEE International Conference on Acoustics, Speech and Signal Processing (ICASSP Toronto, Canada, 6–11 June 2021; pp. 3015–3019.
13. Su, Y.; Zhang, R.; MErfani, S.; Gan, J. Neural graph matching based collaborative filtering. In Proceedings of the 44th Internationa ACM SIGIR Conference on Research and Development in Information Retrieval, Online, 11–15 July 2021; pp. 849–858.
14. Liu, N.; Zhao, J. Recommendation system based on deep sentiment analysis and matrix factorization. *IEEE Access* **2023**, *1* 16994–17001. [CrossRef]
15. Radlinski, F.; Boutilier, C.; Ramachandran, D.; Vendrov, I. Subjective attributes in conversational recommendation system Challenges and opportunities. In Proceedings of the AAAI Conference on Artificial Intelligence, Online, 22 February–1 Marcl 2022; Volume 36, pp. 12287–12293.
16. Li, S.; Lei, W.; Wu, Q.; He, X.; Jiang, P.; Chua, T.S. Seamlessly unifying attributes and items: Conversational recommendation fo cold-start users. *ACM Trans. Inf. Syst.* **2021**, *39*, 1–29. [CrossRef]
17. Lei, W.; He, X.; Miao, Y.; Wu, Q.; Hong, R.; Kan, M.Y.; Chua, T.S. Estimation-action-reflection: Towards deep interaction betweer conversational and recommender systems. In Proceedings of the 13th International Conference on Web Search and Data Mining Online, 10–13 July 2020; pp. 304–312.
18. Vaswani, A.; Shazeer, N.; Parmar, N.; Uszkoreit, J.; Jones, L.; Gomez, A.N.; Kaiser, Ł.; Polosukhin, I. Attention is all you need. *Adv Neural Inf. Process. Syst.* **2017**, *30*. [CrossRef]
19. Wang, H.; Li, J.; Wu, H.; Hovy, E.; Sun, Y. Pre-Trained Language Models and Their Applications. *Engineering* **2022**, *25*, 51–65 [CrossRef]
20. Devlin, J.; Chang, M.-W.; Lee, K.; Toutanova, K. BERT: Pre-training of Deep Bidirectional Transformers for Language Understanding. In Proceedings of the NAACL-HLT, Minneapolis, MN, USA, 2–7 June 2019; pp. 4171–4186.
21. Radford, A.; Wu, J.; Child, R.; Luan, D.; Amodei, D.; Sutskever, I. Language models are unsupervised multitask learners. *OpenAI Blog* **2019**, *1*, 9.
22. Brown, T.; Mann, B.; Ryder, N.; Subbiah, M.; Kaplan, J.D.; Dhariwal, P.; Neelakantan, A.; Shyam, P.; Sastry, G.; Askell, A. Language models are few-shot learners. *Adv. Neural Inf. Process. Syst.* **2020**, *33*, 1877–1901.
23. Zhiyuli, A.; Chen, Y.; Zhang, X.; Liang, X. BookGPT: A General Framework for Book Recommendation Empowered by Large Language Model. *arXiv* **2023**, arXiv:2305.15673.
24. Ji, J.; Li, Z.; Xu, S.; Hua, W.; Ge, Y.; Tan, J.; Zhang, Y. Genrec: Large language model for generative recommendation. *arXiv* **2023**, arXiv:2307.
25. Cai, X.; Xu, H.; Xu, S.; Zhang, Y. BadPrompt: Backdoor Attacks on Continuous Prompts. *Adv. Neural Inf. Process. Syst.* **2022**, *35*, 37068–37080.

26. Jiang, Z.; Xu, F.F.; Araki, J.; Neubig, G. How can we know what language models know? *Trans. Assoc. Comput. Linguist.* **2020**, *8*, 423–438. [CrossRef]
27. Li, X.; Zhang, Y.; Malthouse, E.C. PBNR: Prompt-based News Recommender System. *arXiv* **2023**, arXiv:2304.07862.
28. Zhang, Z.; Wang, B. Prompt learning for news recommendation. *arXiv* **2023**, arXiv:2304.05263.
29. Deng, Z.H.; Huang, L.; Wang, C.D.; Lai, J.H.; Philip, S.Y. Deepcf: A unified framework of representation learning and matching function learning in recommender system. In Proceedings of the AAAI Conference on Artificial Intelligence, Honolulu, HI, USA, 27 January–1 February 2019; Volume 33, pp. 61–68.
30. He, T.; Tan, X.; Xia, Y.; He, D.; Qin, T.; Chen, Z.; Liu, T.Y. Layer-wise coordination between encoder and decoder for neural machine translation. *Adv. Neural Inf. Process. Syst.* **2018**, *31*. Available online: https://api.semanticscholar.org/CorpusID:54088698 (accessed on 9 October 2023).
31. Geng, S.; Fu, Z.; Ge, Y.; Li, L.; De Melo, G.; Zhang, Y. Improving personalized explanation generation through visualization. In Proceedings of the 60th Annual Meeting of the Association for Computational Linguistics, Dublin, Ireland, 22–27 May 2022; Volume 1, pp. 244–255.
32. Li, L.; Zhang, Y.; Chen, L. Personalized prompt learning for explainable recommendation. *ACM Trans. Inf. Syst.* **2023**, *41*, 1–26. [CrossRef]
33. Papineni, K.; Roukos, S.; Ward, T.; Zhu, W.J. Bleu: A method for automatic evaluation of machine translation. In Proceedings of the 40th Annual Meeting of the Association for Computational Linguistics, Philadelphia, PA, USA, 7–12 July 2002; pp. 311–318.
34. Lin, C.Y. Rouge: A package for automatic evaluation of summaries. In *Text Summarization Branches Out*; Association for Computational Linguistics: Barcelona, Spain, 2004; pp. 74–81.
35. Dong, L.; Huang, S.; Wei, F.; Lapata, M.; Zhou, M.; Xu, K. Learning to generate product reviews from attributes. In Proceedings of the 15th Conference of the European Chapter of the Association for Computational Linguistics, Valencia, Spain, 3–7 April 2017; Volume 1, pp. 623–632.
36. Li, P.; Wang, Z.; Ren, Z.; Bing, L.; Lam, W. Neural rating regression with abstractive tips generation for recommendation. In Proceedings of the 40th International ACM SIGIR Conference on Research and Development in Information Retrieval, Tokyo, Japan, 7–11 August 2017; pp. 345–354.
37. Li, L.; Zhang, Y.; Chen, L. Personalized Transformer for Explainable Recommendation. In Proceedings of the 59th Annual Meeting of the Association for Computational Linguistics and the 11th International Joint Conference on Natural Language Processing, Bangkok, Thailand, 1–6 August 2021; Volume 1.
38. Gao, C.; Zheng, Y.; Li, N.; Li, Y.; Qin, Y.; Piao, J.; Quan, Y.; Chang, J.; Jin, D.; He, X.; et al. A survey of graph neural networks for recommender systems: Challenges, methods, and directions. *ACM Trans. Recomm. Syst.* **2023**, *1*, 1–51. [CrossRef]
39. Hu, L.; Liu, Z.; Zhao, Z.; Hou, L.; Nie, L.; Li, J. A Survey of Knowledge Enhanced Pre-Trained Language Models. *IEEE Trans. Knowl. Data Eng.* **2023**, 1–19. [CrossRef]

mathematics

MDPI

Article

Investigating Effective Geometric Transformation for Image Augmentation to Improve Static Hand Gestures with a Pre-Trained Convolutional Neural Network

Baiti-Ahmad Awaluddin [1,2], Chun-Tang Chao [1] and Juing-Shian Chiou [1,*]

1 Department of Electrical Engineering, Southern Taiwan University of Science and Technology, 1, Nan-Tai St., Yongkang District, Tainan 71005, Taiwan; da82b207@stust.edu.tw (B.-A.A.); tang@stust.edu.tw (C.-T.C.)
2 Department of Electronics Engineering Education, Universitas Negeri Yogyakarta, Yogyakarta 55281, Indonesia
* Correspondence: jschiou@stust.edu.tw; Tel.: +886-916-221-152; Fax: +886-6-3010-069

Abstract: Hand gesture recognition (HGR) is a challenging and fascinating research topic in computer vision with numerous daily life applications. In HGR, computers aim to identify and classify hand gestures. The limited diversity of the dataset used in HGR is due to the limited number of hand gesture demonstrators, acquisition environments, and hand pose variations despite previous efforts. Geometric image augmentations are commonly used to address these limitations. These augmentations include scaling, translation, rotation, flipping, and image shearing. However, research has yet to focus on identifying the best geometric transformations for augmenting the HGR dataset. This study employed three commonly utilized pre-trained models for image classification tasks, namely ResNet50, MobileNetV2, and InceptionV3. The system's performance was evaluated on five static HGR datasets: DLSI, HG14, ArabicASL, MU HandImages ASL, and Sebastian Marcell. The experimental results demonstrate that many geometric transformations are unnecessary for HGR image augmentation. Image shearing and horizontal flipping are the most influential transformations for augmenting the HGR dataset and achieving better classification performance. Moreover, ResNet50 outperforms MobileNetV2 and InceptionV3 for static HGR.

Keywords: hand gesture recognition; image augmentation; geometric transformation; ResNet; MobileNet; inception; static datasets

MSC: 68T07

Citation: Awaluddin, B.-A.; Chao, C.-T.; Chiou, J.-S. Investigating Effective Geometric Transformation for Image Augmentation to Improve Static Hand Gestures with a Pre-Trained Convolutional Neural Network. *Mathematics* **2023**, *11*, 4783. https://doi.org/10.3390/math11234783

Academic Editors: Adrian Sergiu Darabant, Diana-Laura Borza and Faheim Sufi

Received: 21 October 2023
Revised: 20 November 2023
Accepted: 24 November 2023
Published: 27 November 2023

1. Introduction

Interacting with computers using hand gestures can provide users with a natural and intuitive interface. As a result, much research has focused on developing more accurate and effective hand gesture recognition (HGR) methods and applying them in various contexts. Hand gestures are currently utilized in multiple applications, such as games [1,2], virtual and augmented reality [3–5], assisted living [6,7], and cognitive development evaluation [8]. In addition, hand gesture recognition has gained significant interest in several industries, including human–robot interaction in manufacturing [9–11] and autonomous vehicle control [12,13]. With the recent growth of HGR, there is an increasing demand for more advanced and robust methods to meet the requirements of various applications.

Despite the remarkable success of deep neural networks in HGR [14,15], there are still significant challenges in this research area. The complexity of hand gestures and differences in hand size are just two factors that can affect the performance of recognition algorithms. The training of deep neural networks with insufficient data can lead to overfitting or failure to learn a high-performance model. Various training schemes, including dropout layers and data augmentation techniques [16], have been proposed to address this challenge.

Data augmentation is a popular technique for increasing the size of a dataset and addressing the problem of insufficient data [17,18]. Various approaches to image-based data augmentation exist, encompassing geometric transformations, color manipulations, random occlusion, and methods grounded in deep learning, such as Generative Adversarial Networks (GANs) [18]. Among these, geometric transformations—comprising image scaling, rotation, translation, shearing, and flipping—stand out as one of the most prevalent approaches. These operations are crucial in expanding the sample pool for training deep neural networks, balancing dataset sizes, and enhancing overall efficiency [19].

Geometric transformations have been extensively applied in hand gesture recognition (HGR) studies to augment datasets effectively. For example, in Ref. [20], geometric augmentation demonstrated a noteworthy enhancement, improving CNN performance by up to 5%. Another study focusing on HGR, utilizing capsule networks, showcased improved results when combined with geometric augmentation involving rotation and translation operations [21]. Similarly, Ref. [22] used an adapted CNN and image translation (both vertically and horizontally) to augment original data, resulting in a notable 4% boost in classification accuracy. Moreover, Ref. [23] utilized random scaling and horizontal/vertical translation to increase the diversity of training data for HGR applications.

The integration of color transformations with geometric transformations has notably enhanced the performance of HGR systems. Color transformations involve histogram equalization, contrast or brightness enhancement, white balancing, sharpening, and blurring [24]. For instance, in Ref. [25], combining the shearing transformation with sigmoid and gamma correction augmented the original images, resulting in a 5% improvement in accuracy.

In their research, Taylor and Nicthe [26] highlighted the effectiveness of data augmentation methods in enhancing the classification task performance of CNNs. Specifically, their evaluation of various data augmentation schemes using a relatively simple CNN architecture showed that geometric augmentation methods outperformed photometric methods when training on a coarse-grained dataset, and these findings underscore the importance of augmenting coarse-grained training datasets using transformations that alter the geometry of images rather than focusing solely on lighting and color modifications.

GANs can be utilized for data augmentation [27,28] by training them to generate new synthetic data. GANs face challenges due to the potential for mode collapse, non-convergence, and oscillatory behavior [29,30]. There are differences between synthetic data, which are artificially created without using actual datasets, and the term "augmented data", which involves generating additional training data through modifications or transformations to the primary data. The primary objective of augmented data is to expand the diversity of the training set, prevent overfitting, and enhance the model's generalization capacity to previously unseen data. Data augmentation techniques can be applied to various data types, including images, text, and audio. On the other hand, augmented data provide significant advantages in improving the performance of deep learning models across various applications, such as object detection, image classification, image recognition, natural language understanding, semantic segmentation, and more [31]. This method has enhanced the efficiency and outcomes of deep learning models by generating new and diverse training examples for datasets. Moreover, the use of augmented data can also reduce operational costs related to the collection and labeling of data for deep learning models [28]. Deep learning models often require time-consuming and expensive operations for data collection and labeling.

Numerous studies demonstrate the superiority of geometric transformations over other methods. Furthermore, when aiming for generalization, a model capable of recognizing new datasets is essential. A CNN model requires sufficient depth, trained on large datasets, which demands substantial computational resources. Hence, an alternative is needed, and that comes in the form of using pre-existing models. These models have been trained beforehand with ample resources and can be applied to new datasets—a process known as transfer learning. There are numerous available CNN models that can be utilized. In this study, three pre-trained CNN models are employed for static ha gesture recognition (HGR) tasks, namely ResNet50, MobileNetV2, and InceptionV3, c sen for their outstanding performance [32]. Therefore, this paper aims to address t following objectives:

1. Investigate whether using as many augmentations as possible on geometric transf mations or focusing on a subset of the most effective geometric transformations yiel better results in improving model performance.
2. Identify augmentation methods within geometric transformations that yield the hig est accuracy rates in enhancing CNN performance, which is achieved through systematic analysis. This involves a thorough examination of various geometric tra formations, assessing their impact on the model's accuracy. The selection process based on rigorous experimentation and quantitative evaluation, ensuring that t chosen augmentation methods contribute significantly to the improved performan of Convolutional Neural Networks (CNNs) in the context of static hand gestu recognition. The effectiveness is substantiated by comparative analyses and statistic measures, providing a robust foundation for the identified augmentation methods.
3. Compare the performance of three pre-trained models, ResNet50, MobileNetV2, an InceptionV3, in the classification of static hand gestures (HGRs). The evaluation these three models is conducted to assess their ability to classify static hand gesture providing crucial insights for further development in this field.
4. This research undertakes an evaluation of the accuracy of pre-trained neural network for image classification. Section 2 describes research methodology. Section 3 describe the dataset, image augmentation, geometric transformations, CNN theory, and pr trained neural networks (ResNet, MobileNet, and Inception). Section 4 presents th experimental setup, dataset preparation, and results using single and combined neur networks. Section 5 analyzes the performance of each pre-trained neural network an discusses the impact of image augmentation and geometric transformations on mod accuracy. Additionally, we explore implications and future research opportunities i this area. Finally, Section 6 summarizes important findings, highlights our research' significance, and outlines future directions, including developing an image augmen tation framework for static hand gesture recognition based on pre-trained ResNet5 models that combine multiple geometric transformations with color modifications.

2. Research Methodology

In this research, the steps to determine the best geometric transformation for imag augmentation to improve recognition accuracy in hand gesture recognition (HGR) tasks an compare the performance of the pre-trained CNN models (ResNet50, MobileNetV2, and InceptionV3) are executed through a structured methodological approach. An illustration o the steps in the research methodology can be found in Figure 1. The researchers formulate the following research objectives:

1. Investigation of the necessity of employing geometric transformations for image augmentation in CNN-based HGR tasks;
2. Exploration of the optimal geometric transformation based on CNNs for image aug- mentation in HGR tasks;
3. Determining the most effective pre-trained CNN model (ResNet50, MobileNetV2, or Inceptionv3) for HGR tasks.

Firstly, diverse datasets, such as HG14, DLSI, MU HandImages ASL, Sebastian Marcel, and ArASL2018, were collected to encompass as many HGR contexts as possible. The next step involves the application of transfer learning to pre-trained models, namely ResNet50, MobileNetV2, and InceptionV3, to comprehend complex hand gesture features.

Evaluation is conducted in two main aspects, namely the effectiveness of image augmentation and the performance of pre-trained models, using accuracy metrics during transfer learning. Geometric transformations, such as scaling, rotation, translation, shearing, and flipping, are explored in the augmentation evaluation. At the same time, the performance of pre-trained models is measured by comparing ResNet50, MobileNetV2, and InceptionV3 in classifying HGR datasets.

This research evaluates results and presents in-depth conclusions based on experimental findings. Overall, these methodological steps form a comprehensive framework to understand the role of image augmentation and CNN models in improving the accuracy of HGR systems. By implementation programming using Python 3.6.13, particularly with TensorFlow support, a solid technical foundation is provided, ensuring efficiency and optimal performance in conducting this experiment.

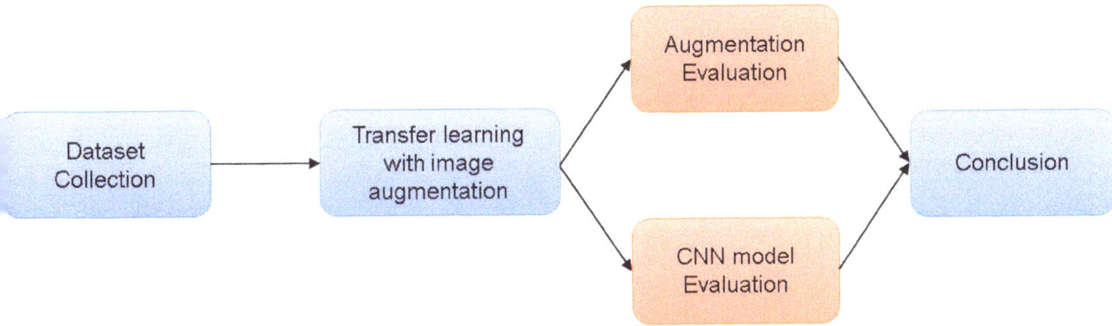

Figure 1. Overview of the research methodology employed in this study.

3. Material

3.1. Dataset

This research utilized five publicly available datasets for HGR: HG14, DLSI, MU HandImages ASL, Sebastian Marcel Static Hand Gestures, and ArASL2018. These datasets were selected to comprehensively evaluate the most suitable geometric transformation for augmenting the HGR dataset. Each dataset possessed unique characteristics such as gesture categories, image background, image size, and color channels. ArabicSL was the most extensive dataset, containing 54,049 images divided into 32 classes, while MU HandImages ASL was the smallest, with only 2425 images divided into 26 classes.

3.1.1. Hand Gesture 14 (HG14) Dataset

Guler et al. [33] created the Hand Gestures 14 (HG14) dataset, containing 14 hand gestures suitable for hand interaction and application control in augmented reality. The dataset includes 14,000 photos with RGB channels and a size of 256 $\times$ 256 pixels. Each image has a simple and uniformly colored background, as shown in Figure 2 [33].

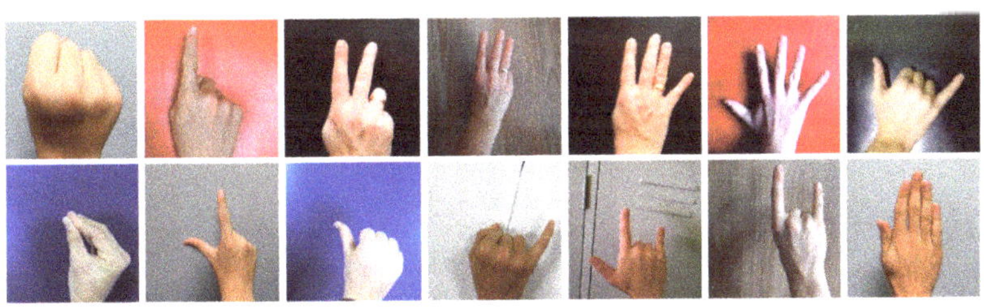

Figure 2. Sample images from the HG14 dataset showcasing the 14 distinct hand gestures.

3.1.2. DLSI (Department de Llenguatges Sistemes Informàtics) Dataset

Alashhab et al. [34] created the DLSI (Department de Llenguatges Sistemes Informàtics) dataset to recognize gestures for visually impaired people. Various smartphone cameras captured indoor and outdoor scenes under realistic conditions. The dataset comprises

12,064 frames divided into 6 gestures, each normalized to 224 × 224 pixels. Figure 3 [3 shows the sample images.

Figure 3. Sample images of the six different hand gestures are included in the DLSI dataset.

3.1.3. Massey University HandImages ASL Dataset

The dataset MU HandImages ASL was created by Barczak et al. at Massey University (MU), New Zealand. It contains 2425 images from 5 individuals, with each hand pose captured in a room with varying lighting conditions and a green screen background. The dataset consists of 26 classes representing standard American Sign Language (ASL) gestures, with black background images and varying pixel sizes depending on the hand pose's shape Figure 4 [34] shows some sample images from this dataset.

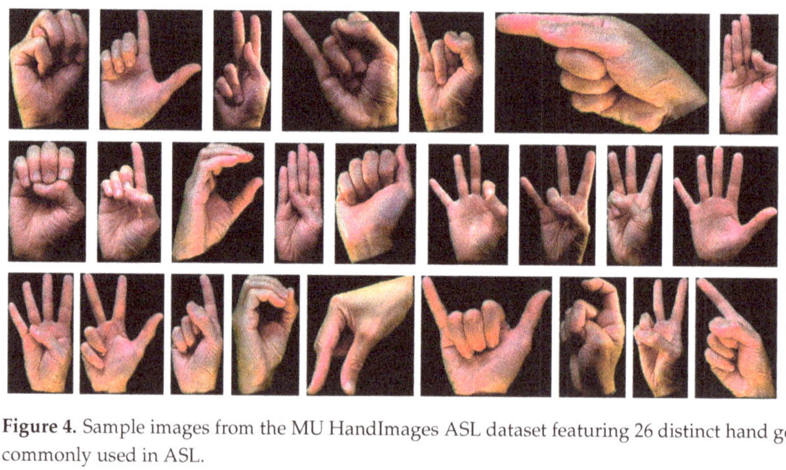

Figure 4. Sample images from the MU HandImages ASL dataset featuring 26 distinct hand gestures commonly used in ASL.

3.1.4. Sebastian Marcel Static Hand Gesture Dataset

The Sebastian Marcel Static Hand Gesture Dataset was used as the training set for developing a neural network model to recognize hand postures in images. Hand gestures were segmented using space discretization based on face location and body anthropometry. The dataset includes six hand postures (a, b, c, point, five, v) demonstrated by ten individuals captured in uniform and complex backgrounds with varying image sizes, depending on the hand gesture. Figure 5 [34] shows some sample images from this dataset.

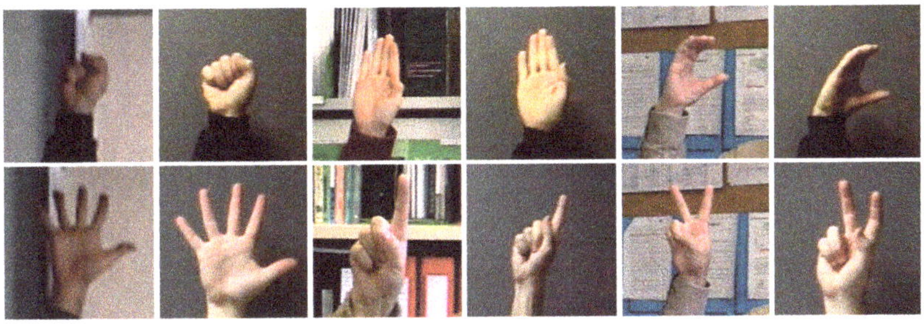

Figure 5. Sample images from the Sebastian Marcel Static Hand Gesture Dataset featuring six distinct hand gestures demonstrated by ten individuals.

3.1.5. ArASL2018 Dataset

The ArASL2018 (Arabic Alphabet Sign Language 2018) dataset [35] includes 54,049 grayscale images of 32 hand poses representing the Arabic Alphabet Sign Language. Hand gestures were captured from 40 individuals across different age groups under uniform backgrounds and good lighting conditions. Some image preprocessing was performed to remove noise and center the hand object in the image. Figure 6 [35] shows some sample images from this dataset.

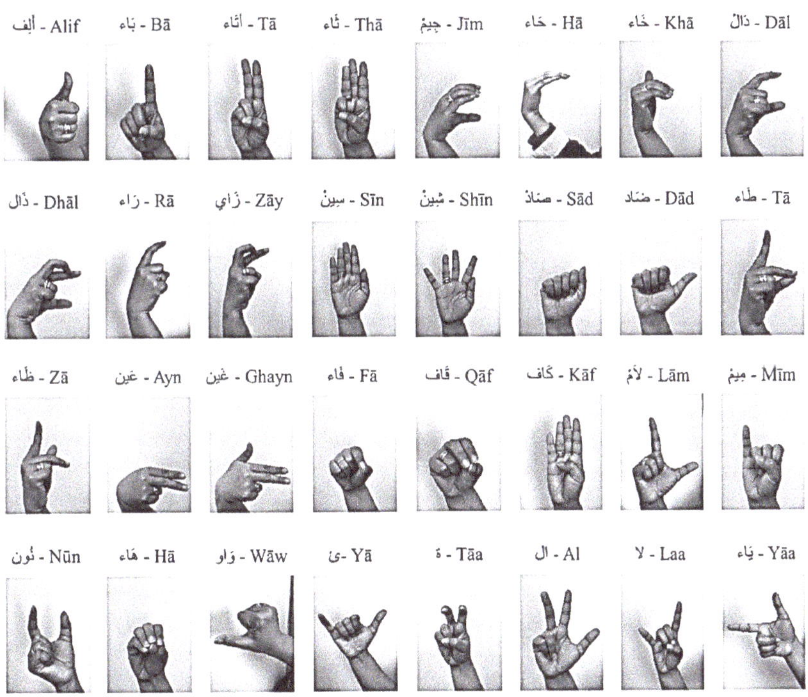

Figure 6. Sample images from the ArASL2018 dataset featuring 32 distinct hand poses representing Arabic Sign Language.

3.2. *Image Augmentation*

Image augmentation is a technique to avoid overfitting in neural network traini by transforming the original data or image using specific techniques [18]. Geomet transformations such as scaling, rotation, translation (shifting), shearing, and flipping c augment image data. These transformations can produce new images from the origin ones, helping to generalize the knowledge learned by classifiers, such as neural networ

Traditional image augmentation involves storing the augmented data on disk alor side the original data, resulting in increased storage requirements, especially for lar datasets. An alternative approach called "on-the-fly" augmentation was proposed to a dress this issue [18]. This approach performs augmentation during training rather th storing augmented images in storage, leading to better knowledge generalization becau it produces new data/images in every training epoch. This work used the on-the-fly au mentation strategy to achieve better performance in hand gesture recognition. The flow on-the-fly augmentation is illustrated in Figure 7.

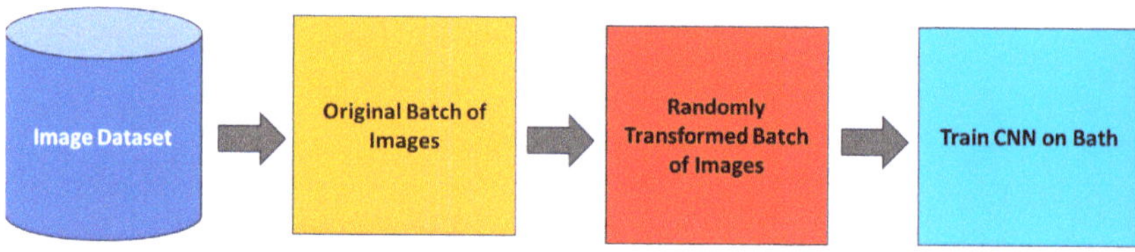

Figure 7. Illustration of the "on-the-fly" image augmentation approach.

As shown in Figure 7, the original image dataset is divided into small batches. Eac batch undergoes random geometric transformations before being used for training a m chine learning or deep learning algorithm. This technique produces different augmente images in each batch and epoch, allowing for better knowledge generalization.

3.3. *Geometric Transformation*

This work evaluated all geometric transformations to determine the most suitable fo the HGR task. However, it should be noted that certain transformations, such as invertin may not be ideal for specific image types, such as digit images, which can confuse th numbers 6 and 9.

3.3.1. Image Scaling

Image scaling resizes an input image to a larger or smaller size using a scale facto Equations (1) [36] and (2) [36] can be used to perform image scaling, where (x, y) are the coordinates of a pixel in the original image, (x', y') are the coordinates of the pixel in the scaled image, and s_x and s_y are the scale factors for the rows and columns of the image respectively.

$$x' = x \cdot s_x \quad (1)$$

$$y' = y \cdot s_y \quad (2)$$

Interpolation can be used to smooth the edges of the object in the scaled image and maintain the aspect ratio when $s_x = s_y$. Image scaling improves model performance and robustness to input size variations. When an image is scaled up, it is cropped to its original size, while for scaling down, the original size is maintained with space filled using the nearest pixel neighbor technique. Figure 8 shows a sample of a scaled image.

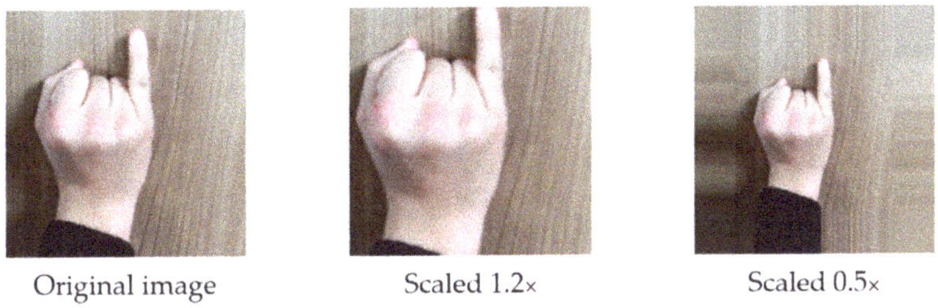

Figure 8. Samples of scaled images using nearest neighbor interpolation.

3.3.2. Image Rotation

Image rotation is a common data augmentation technique in computer vision tasks and involves rotating an image by a certain angle (typically 0 to 360 degrees) to create additional training data. Equations (3) [37] and (4) [37] perform image rotation using (x,y) as the original pixel coordinates and (x',y') as the corresponding pixel coordinates in the rotated image. The rotation angle in radians is represented by θ, and (cx, cy) are the image center coordinates.

$$x' = (x - cx)\cos\theta - (y - cy)\sin\theta + cx \tag{3}$$

$$y' = (x - cx)\sin\theta + (y - cy)\cos\theta + cy \tag{4}$$

Similar to image scaling, image rotation may result in blank areas that need to be filled using interpolation techniques, such as the nearest pixel technique used in this work. Figure 9 provides a sample of image rotation using the nearest pixel technique to interpolate the blank areas around the rotated image.

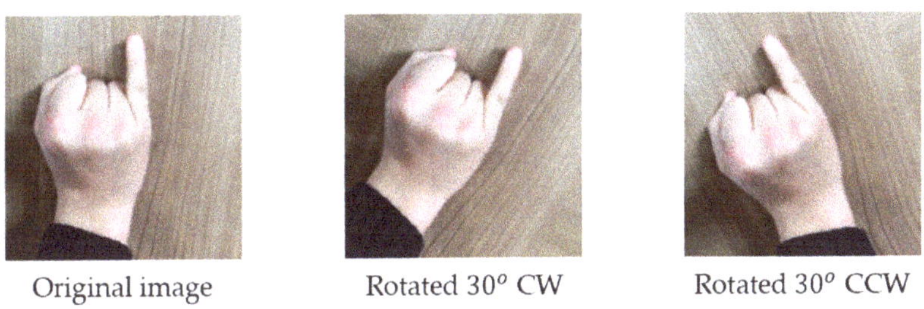

Figure 9. Sample of image rotation with nearest pixel interpolation.

3.3.3. Image Translation

Image translation shifts an image along the x-axis and y-axis by a certain number of pixels to create additional training data, improving model robustness to position variations. Equations (5) [38] and (6) [38] are used for x-axis and y-axis translation, respectively, where (x,y) are the coordinates of a pixel in the original image, (x',y') are the coordinates of the corresponding pixel in the translated image, and (dx, dy) are the translation offsets.

$$x' = x + dx \tag{5}$$

$$y' = y + dy \tag{6}$$

The nearest pixel interpolation technique also fills blank areas in the translated images. Figure 10 shows a sample of a translated image.

Original image Shifted -20% vertically Shifted 30% horizontally

Figure 10. Sample of the translated image using nearest pixel interpolation.

3.3.4. Image Shearing

Image shearing is a technique that skews an image along the x-axis and y-axis by shifting each row or column of pixels by a certain amount based on its y-coordinate or x-coordinate, respectively. This technique helps handle input images captured from different perspectives or angles. Shearing an image along the x-axis and y-axis can be achieved using Equations (7) [39] and (8) [39], where (x,y) are the coordinates of a pixel in the original image, (x',y') are the coordinates of the corresponding pixel in the sheared image, and shx and shy are the shear factors along the x-axis and y-axis, respectively.

$$x' = x + shx \times y \tag{7}$$

$$y' = y + shy \times x \tag{8}$$

Nearest pixel neighbor interpolation is applied to fill the blank area in the sheared images. Figure 11 provides a sample of the sheared image using nearest pixel interpolation.

Original image Sheared 20% Sheared -20%

Figure 11. Sample of the sheared image with nearest pixel interpolation.

3.3.5. Image Flipping

Image flipping reverses the left and right sides of the image. For HGR, only horizontal flipping is used. The formula for horizontal flipping is provided in Equation (9) [40], where (x,y) are the coordinates of a pixel in the original image, x' is the corresponding pixel index in the flipped image, and W is the width of the image.

$$x' = (W - 1) - x \tag{9}$$

To flip the entire image, each row of pixels is reversed from left to right. No interpolation is needed for flipping an image horizontally. Figure 12 shows a sample of horizontally flipped images.

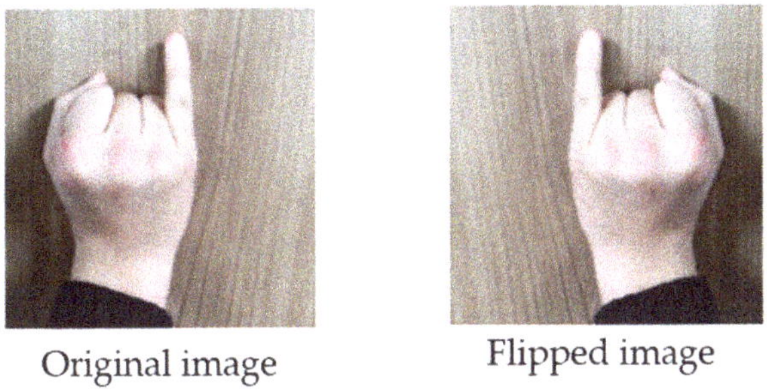

Figure 12. Sample of horizontally flipped image.

3.4. Convolutional Neural Networks (CNNs)

Deep learning (DL) has various architectures, one of which is Convolutional Neural Networks (CNNs), which are known for their effectiveness in image recognition compared to traditional machine learning approaches [41]. The basic idea of the CNN is the technique of image convolution, which combines an input matrix and a kernel matrix to produce a third matrix that represents how one matrix is modified by the other.

A CNN architecture generally consists of two parts: feature extraction and classification [42], as depicted in Figure 13. The feature extraction part applies image convolution to the input image to produce a series of feature maps. These features are then used in the classification part to classify the label of the input image.

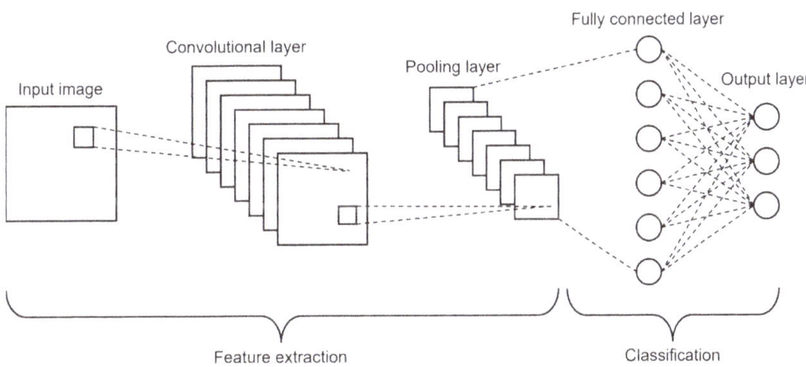

Figure 13. CNN architecture with feature extraction and classification parts.

A CNN applies convolution to produce a set of feature maps. Each filter can detect specific patterns from the input image, such as edges, lines, or corners. The output of the convolutional layer is passed through a non-linear activation function, such as ReLUs (Rectified Linear Units), to introduce non-linearity and learn complex representations of the input image. The ReLU function is defined in Equation (10) [43]:

$$f(x) = max(0, x) \tag{10}$$

ReLUs (Rectified Linear Units) are an activation function introduced by [44] and have a strong biological and mathematical underpinning. In 2011, they were demonstrated to further improve the training of deep neural networks. They work by thresholding values at 0, i.e., $f(x) = max(0, x)$. Simply put, they output 0 when $x < 0$, and conversely, they output a linear function when $x \geq 0$.

The pooling layer is used after the convolutional layer to reduce the dimensionality of the feature maps and introduce translational invariance. Max pooling takes the maximum value within a local neighborhood, and average pooling calculates the average value.

Fully connected layers perform a classification task by mapping the previous laye output to a set of output classes. The network adjusts its weights and biases throu a backpropagation algorithm to minimize a loss function that measures the differen between the predicted and true output during training.

3.5. *Pre-Trained Neural Networks*

To be effective, a CNN model should be sufficiently deep (deep CNN) and train on large amounts of data to learn various patterns from the dataset [45]. Training a CN requires a powerful machine with a dedicated Graphics Processing Unit (GPU) for paral computation and ample memory to store the dataset and CNN parameters during trainir Therefore, researchers have developed pre-trained CNN models on large public datase such as ImageNet or Microsoft COCO [46]. These pre-trained models can be used to build CNN-based system for image classification and can be retrained for custom cases using ne datasets. This process, called transfer learning, enables pre-trained models to be trained less time and use less computational power. This work uses three pre-trained CNN mode for static hand gesture recognition (HGR) tasks, ResNet50, MobileNetV2, and InceptionV due to their excellent performance, as reported in [32].

3.5.1. ResNet50

ResNet50 is a pre-trained CNN model proposed by Microsoft Research in 2015 [41]. uses Residual Network architecture to solve the problem of vanishing gradients in dee learning. The Residual Network contains residual connections, which add the input of layer to its output, creating a shortcut connection. Figure 14 shows that the network ca skip over layers that might not contribute much to the output.

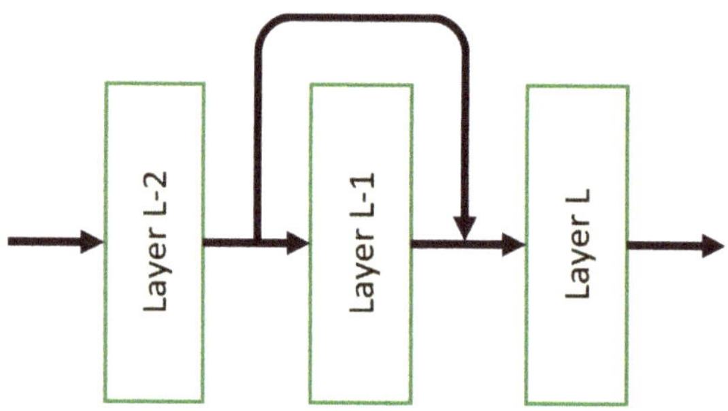

Figure 14. Illustration of a residual connection with the input of layer L-1 added to its output.

The ResNet50 architecture comprises 50 layers, including 49 convolutional layers and 1 fully connected layer, and is divided into 5 convolutional stages. Each stage contains severa residual blocks, as shown in Figure 15. The first stage consists of a single convolutional layer that performs a 7×7 convolution with a stride of 2, followed by a max pooling layer with a pool size of 3×3 and a stride of 2. The subsequent stages contain three, four, six and three residual blocks, each with three convolutional layers using a combination of $1 \times 1, 3 \times 3$, and 1×1 convolutions, batch normalization, and ReLU activation. The output of the fifth convolutional stage is processed by a global average pooling layer that averages the feature maps across the spatial dimensions. The resulting output is passed through a fully connected layer with 1000 output units corresponding to the number of classes in the ImageNet dataset.

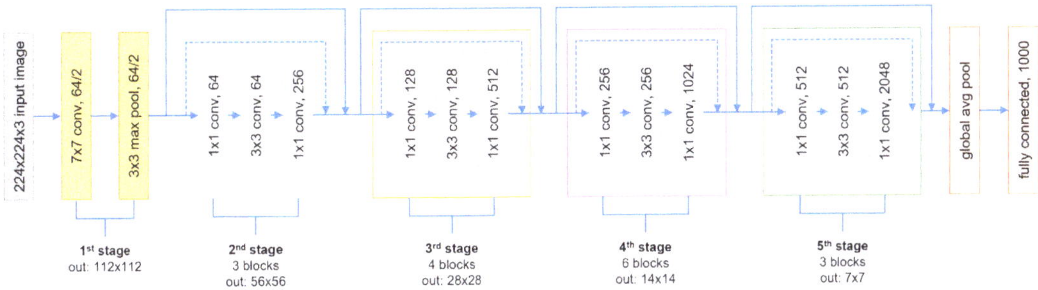

Figure 15. ResNet50 architecture with 49 convolutional layers and 1 fully connected layer.

3.5.2. MobileNetV2

MobileNetV2 is a CNN model proposed by Google in 2018 as an efficient alternative to deep neural networks for deployment on mobile and embedded devices [47]. It uses depthwise separable convolutions, which split the convolution operation into a depthwise convolution and a pointwise convolution, significantly reducing computational complexity and memory usage. MobileNetV2 also introduces several new features that improve its performance while maintaining efficiency. Figure 16 illustrates the working of depthwise separable convolutions.

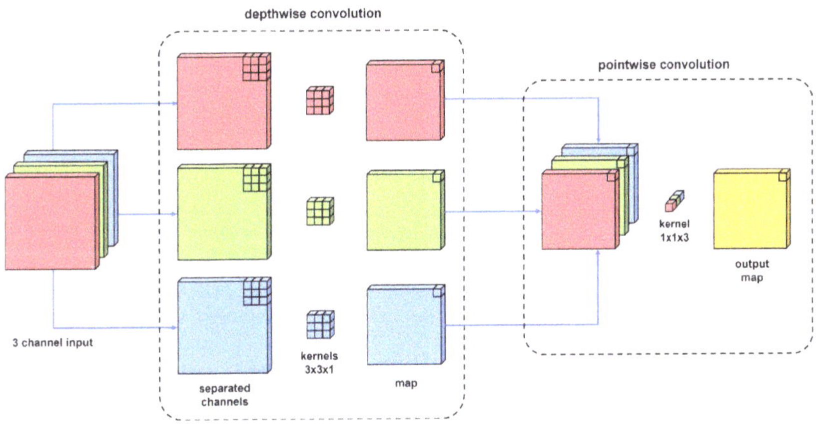

Figure 16. Illustration of depthwise separable convolutions showing the depthwise convolution and pointwise convolution.

The architecture of MobileNetV2 can be divided into three parts: the stem, the body, and the head. The stem has a single convolutional layer that performs a 3×3 convolution with a stride of 2, followed by batch normalization and a non-linear activation function. The body contains a series of inverted residual blocks, each with a depthwise separable convolution, a linear bottleneck, and batch normalization with a non-linear activation function. The MobileNetV2 architecture includes a linear bottleneck that enhances the network's representational power while keeping its computational cost low. The architecture's head consists of a global average pooling layer, a 1×1 convolutional layer, and a fully connected layer that uses a SoftMax activation function. Figure 17 provides a visual representation of the MobileNetV2 architecture.

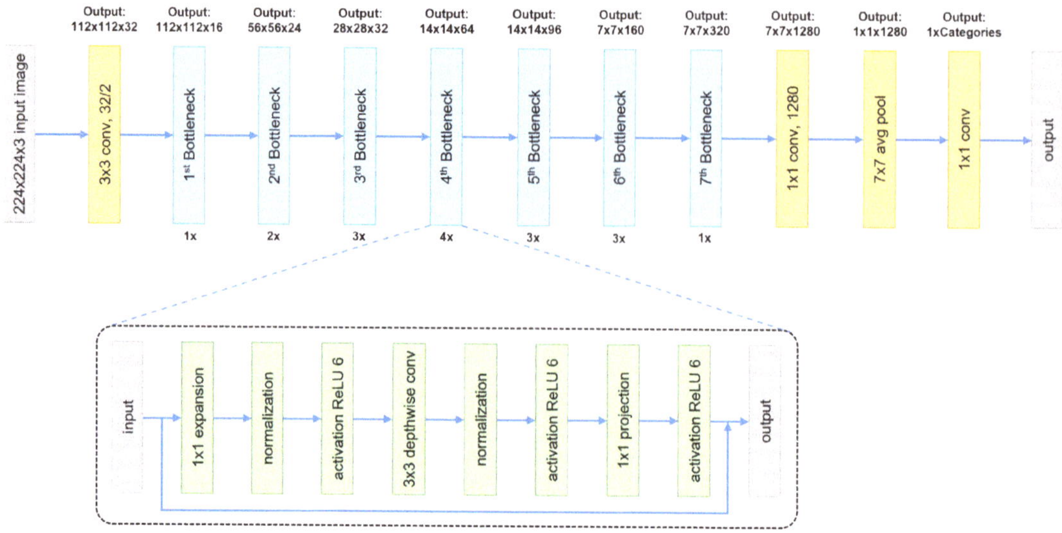

Figure 17. MobileNetV2 architecture with 17 bottleneck layers.

3.5.3. InceptionV3

InceptionV3 is a pre-trained CNN architecture introduced by Google in 2015 [48,49]. It uses multiple filters of different sizes in parallel at each stage of the network to capture features at multiple resolutions and scales, increasing the ability to recognize objects of different sizes and shapes. InceptionV3 also uses factorization to reduce the computational cost of the convolutional layers for more efficient performance. The architecture can be divided into the stem, inception modules, and classification layers [48]. The stem processes the input image and extracts low-level features, while the inception modules perform most of the computation. Each inception module consists of several parallel convolutional layers of different sizes combined using concatenation. Each module's output passes through a factorization layer, reducing feature map channels. A global average pooling layer, followed by a fully connected layer with SoftMax activation, produces the network's final output. The architecture of InceptionV3 is illustrated in Figure 18.

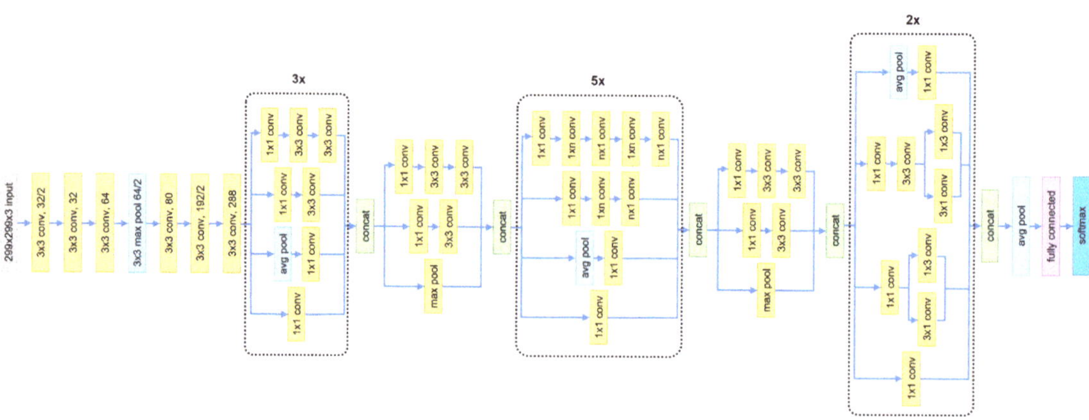

Figure 18. InceptionV3 CNN architecture.

3.6. Programming Tools

In this research using the Python programming language, especially TensorFlow2.6.2, the ImageDataGenerator command serves as a key tool to enhance the performance of models in hand gesture recognition (HGR) tasks. This experiment utilizes each dataset, establishing a solid foundation. By applying transfer learning to pre-trained models, like ResNet50, MobileNetV2, and InceptionV3, the models can comprehend complex features of hand gestures.

The official TensorFlow documentation [50] explains that the ImageDataGenerator plays a central role in image augmentation, exploring geometric transformations like scaling, rotation, translation, shearing, and flipping. The use of commands such as "fit" to calculate internal statistics and "flow" to dynamically generate batches of images creates an efficient and adaptive experimental environment [50]. In TensorFlow, the ImageDataGenerator provides various parameters to control augmentation, such as scaling, rotation, and flipping. The official TensorFlow documentation offers examples of usage and recommended methods. For example:

```
"'python
from tensorflow.keras.preprocessing.image import ImageDataGenerator

# Creating an instance of ImageDataGenerator with augmentation parameters
datagen = ImageDataGenerator(
rotation_range = 20,
width_shift_range = 0.2,
height_shift_range = 0.2,
shear_range = 0.2,
zoom_range = 0.2,
horizontal_flip = True,
fill_mode = 'nearest'
)

# Calculating internal statistics (fit) - assuming x_train is the image data
datagen.fit(x_train)

# Generating batches of images dynamically using flow
generated_images = datagen.flow(x_train, batch_size = 32)
'''
```

Experiments are conducted by trying each pre-trained model on different datasets, with the application of individual and combined augmentations. This structured approach provides a deep understanding of the impact of augmentation on model performance across various datasets. The official TensorFlow documentation, including code examples and parameters, serves as the primary reference source to detail the usage of the ImageDataGenerator and strengthen the experimental framework.

4. Results

4.1. Experimental Setup

This study aims to determine the optimal geometric transformation for image augmentation on the HGR dataset to improve classifier accuracy. To achieve this, it employed an "on-the-fly" augmentation strategy and defined several parameters for random geometric transformations, as shown in Table 1. Each transformation function was applied individually during the training phase of the deep learning algorithm, and the process was repeated three times to ensure consistent performance.

Table 1. Parameter settings for geometric transformations used in image augmentation.

Geometric Transformation	Direction	Parameter Setting
Scaling	Horizontal and vertical	[−20%, 20%]
Rotation	CW and CCW	[−30°, 30°]
Translation	Horizontal and vertical	[−20%, 20%]
Shearing	Horizontal	[−20°, 20°]
Flipping	Horizontal	[True, False]

Transfer learning uses ImageNet pre-trained weights as the initial network's weights the experiment to avoid complex and high computation during learning. The optimizati of weights only occurs in the classification layer of the pre-trained model to optimi the networks in the fully connected layers. Adaptive Moment Estimation (ADAM), a optimization algorithm, is employed to enhance the training process and avoid gradie vanishing during training [51]. The pre-trained network is retrained for 50 epochs wi a batch size of 32. To maintain the ImageNet pre-trained weights, network training performed by freezing all the layers in the feature extraction part. The performance of th networks is evaluated using the "accuracy" metric.

The experiment uses Python programming language with several libraries, such a TensorFlow, Matplotlib, and NumPy, on a personal computer with the specifications liste in Table 2.

Table 2. Hardware and software specifications for the experiment.

Hardware/Software	Specification
Processor (CPU)	Intel Core i5-9300H @2.40 GHz
Memory (RAM)	32 GB DDR4
Graphics Processing Unit (GPU)	Nvidia GTX 1660 Ti—6GB vRAM
Operating system	Windows 11
Python version	3.6.13
Cuda/CuDNN version	11.0/8.0

4.2. Dataset Preparation

In this study, we used five publicly available datasets of HGR, as described in Section 2 These datasets were used to evaluate the effectiveness of various experiment scenarios, as summarized in Table 3. To train our networks, we randomly split each dataset into three parts for training, evaluation, and testing, respectively, with a distribution of 60:20:20. To augment the training data, we used the ImageDataGenerator module TensorFlow [50]. It is important to note that only the training data were augmented.

Table 3. Specification of datasets used for the experiment.

Dataset	Number of Data	Number of Classes	Images Size	Image Background
DLSI	12,064	6	224 × 224	complex
HG14	14,000	14	256 × 256	uniform
MU HandImages ASL	2425	26	vary	uniform
Sebastian Marcel	5531	6	vary	uniform and complex
ArASL2018	54,049	32	64 × 64	uniform

In this work, it was observed that specific parameters in the HGR dataset could impact the classification performance, such as input size and image background. As shown in Table 3, each dataset had different sizes, so all input images were resized to a uniform size of 224 × 224 pixels with three color channels (RGB) commonly used in pre-trained CNN models like VGG, ResNet, and Inception.

The image background was classified as uniform or complex based on the dominance of a single color or simple texture versus multiple colors, textures, or objects. While a uniform background is easier to recognize and more accurate, it may not represent real-life scenarios. Conversely, a complex background may be more challenging to recognize but is more representative of real-life situations. Using HGR datasets with uniform and complex backgrounds, we could analyze the impact of geometric-based augmentation on background variations.

4.3. Experimental Results

The experiments were conducted based on the scenarios explained in the previous section, which are divided into two parts. The first part involves a single augmentation experiment to observe which geometric augmentation (scaling, rotation, translation, shearing, and flipping) can lead to the best performance. The second part involves a combined augmentation experiment to observe whether image augmentation using all five geometric transformations produces better performance than a single one. As the datasets have a different number of classes and are balanced; the only performance metric used is accuracy.

4.3.1. Results on Single Augmentation

The first experiment involved using a pre-trained ResNet50 model that was retrained on the five HGR datasets. Each input image was augmented using the ImageDataGenerator module from the TensorFlow library before being fed into the pre-trained model for learning. Overall, ResNet50 performed very well for all datasets and geometric transformations, achieving accuracies of over 95% for almost all experiment scenarios. Specifically, ResNet50 achieved the highest accuracy when using the DLSI and HG14 datasets, with average accuracies of 97.67% and 97.47%, respectively, for all geometric transformations. This result is surprising because the DLSI dataset has a complex image background. On the other hand, the lowest accuracy was obtained when using the Sebastian Marcel dataset, with an average accuracy of 94.98%. The performance of ResNet50 on all datasets is summarized in Table 4.

Table 4. Classification accuracy results of geometric image augmentation using ResNet50 architecture.

Dataset	Geometric Transformations—Accuracy (%)					Dataset Average Accuracy (%)
	Scaling	Rotation	Translation	Shearing	Flipping	
DLSI	97.86	97.37	97.47	97.86	97.77	**97.67**
HG14	97.07	97.46	98.32	97.18	97.32	**97.47**
MU HandImages ASL	95.14	97.26	96.05	97.26	97.57	**96.66**
ArASL2018	96.61	94.66	96.04	97.26	97.15	**96.34**
Sebastian Marcel	93.60	95.07	96.06	94.58	95.57	**94.98**
Geometric Avg. Accuracy (%)	**96.06**	**96.36**	**96.79**	**96.83**	**97.08**	

Based on the results presented in Table 4, horizontal flipping achieved the highest accuracy among the five geometric transformations, with an average accuracy of 97.08%. Furthermore, image shearing and translation produced better results than scaling and rotation.

Moving on to the second experiment, as shown in Table 5, MobileNetV2 performed worse than ResNet50 for all datasets. The MU HandImage ASL dataset achieved the highest accuracy among all datasets, with significant differences from the other datasets of up to 38%. However, MobileNetV2 performed poorly in classifying the DLSI dataset with a complex image background. Unlike ResNet50, shearing transformation produced the best results for all datasets, with an overall accuracy of 78.85%, followed by horizontal flipping, with an average accuracy of 74.72%.

Table 5. Results of geometric image augmentation on the MobileNetV2 architecture.

Dataset	Geometric Transformations—Accuracy (%)					Dataset Average Accuracy (%)
	Scaling	Rotation	Translation	Shearing	Flipping	
DLSI	73.63	73.78	69.96	79.79	76.66	**74.76**
HG14	59.18	57.75	59.00	65.18	60.39	**60.30**
MU HandImages ASL	92.40	90.88	91.49	95.74	95.74	**93.25**
ArASL2018	69.21	59.53	63.83	84.09	74.79	**70.29**
Sebastian Marcel	65.52	61.08	63.05	69.46	66.01	**65.02**
Geometric Avg. Accuracy (%)	**71.99**	**68.60**	**69.47**	**78.85**	**74.72**	

Table 6 shows the results of using the InceptionV3 architecture for geometric imag augmentation. Similar to MobileNetV2, the MU HandImage ASL dataset achieved th highest accuracy. The shearing operation resulted in the highest accuracy compared to othe geometric transformations for all datasets. However, InceptionV3 struggled to recogniz the hand gestures in the HG14 dataset, which had the lowest accuracy. This is surprisin because HG14 uses a uniform background in each image, and the difference in accurac compared to other datasets is significant.

Table 6. Results of geometric image augmentation on the InceptionV3 architecture.

Dataset	Geometric Transformations—Accuracy (%)					Dataset Average Accuracy (%)
	Scaling	Rotation	Translation	Shearing	Flipping	
DLSI	67.28	65.44	60.92	71.70	69.27	**66.92**
HG14	48.57	41.54	39.43	49.11	40.25	**43.78**
MU HandImages ASL	89.06	86.63	82.67	94.22	89.06	**84.34**
ArASL2018	82.93	76.75	67.33	85.75	74.37	**70.47**
Sebastian Marcel	70.94	73.89	67.49	74.38	72.41	**74.07**
Geometric Avg. Accuracy (%)	**71.76**	**68.85**	**63.57**	**75.03**	**69.07**	

4.3.2. Results of Combined Augmentation

This study performed experiments to compare the performance of pre-trained models trained with single and combined geometric transformations. The same experimental setup as before was used with three repetitions for each dataset to ensure consistency of model performance. Table 7 shows that single augmentation yielded better results than combined augmentation for every pre-trained model. The most significant decreases in accuracy were observed in MobileNetV2 and InceptionV3, which experienced drops of 11.54% and 18.00%, respectively. The worst accuracy was obtained for HG14 and ArASL2018 datasets when using MobileNetV2 and InceptionV3 with combined augmentation, with an accuracy below 50%. However, MU HandImages ASL maintained good accuracy for each pre-trained model using single or combined augmentation.

Table 7. Comparison of accuracies between single and combined augmentation methods.

Dataset	ResNet50 (%)		MobileNetV2 (%)		InceptionV3 (%)	
	Single	Combined	Single	Combined	Single	Combined
DLSI	97.67	97.96	74.76	65.29	66.92	52.09
HG14	97.47	96.61	60.30	48.86	43.78	28.82
MU HandImages ASL	96.66	93.62	93.25	94.22	84.34	76.60
ArASL2018	96.34	92.41	70.29	39.38	70.47	18.47
Sebastian Marcel	94.98	95.57	65.02	58.13	74.07	74.38
Avg. Accuracy (%)	**96.62**	**95.23**	**72.72**	**61.18**	**67.92**	**50.07**

5. Discussion

The experimental discussion in this research presents noteworthy findings that can serve as a foundation for further research and development in hand gesture recognition (HGR). Analyzing the documented experimental results in Sections 4–6 reveals that image shearing holds the most significant influence on the classification accuracy among the five geometric transformations used for image augmentation. It is noteworthy that despite the accuracy value of image shearing in ResNet50 being lower compared to the flipping transformation, MobileNet, and Inception, in contrast, it achieved the highest accuracy values.

This observed significance can be attributed to the technical aspects of image shearing, wherein its ability to handle variations in object perspective and other specific characteristics renders it a crucial augmentation technique for enhancing the accuracy of hand gesture recognition models.

The implication of these findings is that constructing a classification model capable of effectively managing variations in object perspective is crucial for achieving high accuracy in HGR. Furthermore, image flipping emerges as the second most influential geometric transformation for the HGR task, as evidenced by the relatively higher accuracy observed in both image shearing and flipping, as indicated in Figure 21. This underscores the importance of developing an HGR model that can adeptly handle both variations in object perspective and the reflection of gestures by the right or left hand. It is noteworthy that while image scaling can impact classification accuracy, its effect is comparatively lower than image shearing and flipping.

The use of image rotation as an augmentation method in hand gesture recognition (HGR) datasets is generally applicable, but its effectiveness depends on the types of gestures present in the dataset. Some gestures may require hand position rotation to differentiate between distinct signs. For instance, in the MU HandImage ASL (Massey dataset), the gesture for the letter "i" is nearly identical to the letter "j", and the gesture for the letter "z" is identical to the number "1", as shown in Figure 19. In such cases, it is advisable to carefully consider the use of image rotation or even exclude it from augmentation operations to avoid introducing ambiguity into the dataset.

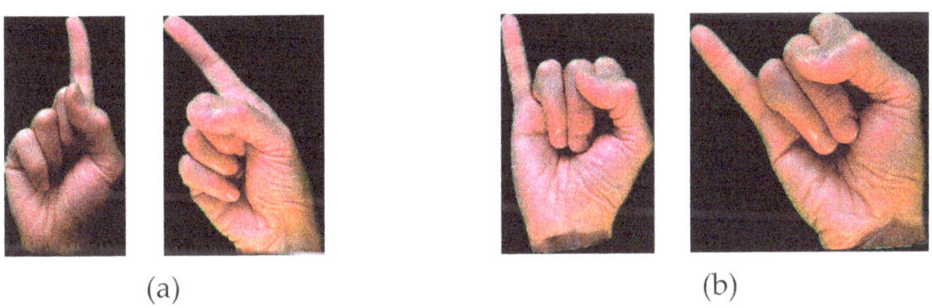

Figure 19. The identical gestures between the number "1" and the letter "z" shown in (**a**) and the letters "i" and "j" shown in (**b**) in the MU HandImage ASL dataset are only distinguished by hand position. Therefore, rotation can be excluded from the augmentation operations.

Similar to rotation, Figure 20 illustrates that image translation, particularly in the HG14 dataset, can produce ambiguously augmented data, such as in the HG14 dataset, where the horizontal translation of gesture number "6" may be identical to gesture number "9". Similarly, gesture number "11" may be highly like gesture number "12" when shifted to the left. To handle this issue, translation can be excluded from augmentation, or the range of translation can be limited.

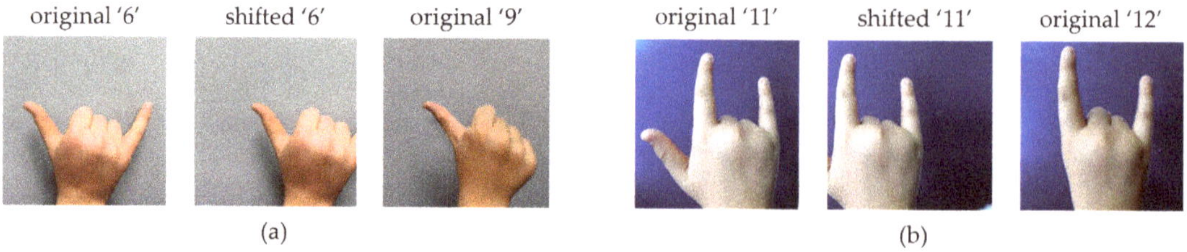

Figure 20. Similar hand gestures in the HG14 dataset due to translational transformation: (**a**) "6" a "9" and (**b**) "11" and "12".

Figure 21 provides additional insights, confirming that image shearing and flippi are effective techniques for augmenting static hand gesture recognition (HGR) datase This effectiveness holds true across diverse datasets and pre-trained models. While i age scaling is a viable option, Figure 22 highlights a cautionary note—using an excessi number of transformations can lead to overly complex images, potentially causing miscl sification. Consequently, a more practical approach for image augmentation in HGR tas using Convolutional Neural Networks (CNNs) may involve combining two geometr transformations.

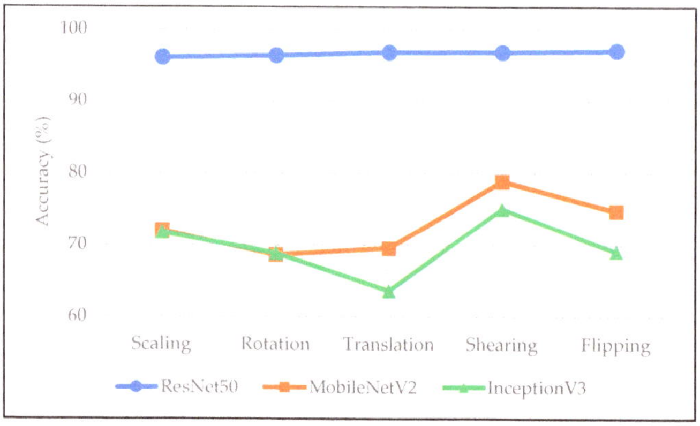

Figure 21. Comparison of classification accuracy among different geometric transformations usin different pre-trained models.

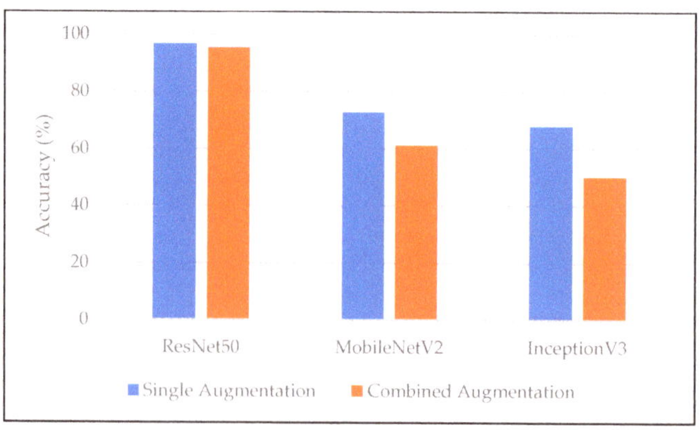

Figure 22. Comparison of classification performance between single and combined geometric augmentations on different pre-trained models.

This experiment reveals that ResNet50 outperforms MobileNetV2 and InceptionV3 in static HGR datasets. Figure 22 demonstrates the superior performance of ResNet50, a popular CNN architecture, compared to MobileNetV2 and InceptionV3. The notable advantages of ResNet50, including its less complex network that demands less computing power and memory, have significant practical implications for real-world applications. In the development of hand gesture recognition applications for devices with limited computational resources, choosing ResNet50 can result in faster and more energy-efficient models. This is particularly crucial in scenarios such as mobile devices, where optimizing resource usage is paramount for a seamless user experience.

6. Conclusions

Based on the results of the experiments conducted for static hand gesture recognition using Convolutional Neural Network (CNN) models, several conclusions can be drawn to guide the development of more efficient methods for this task.

Firstly, in the context of geometric transformations, it was found that the use of shearing and flipping had the most significant impact on improving the model's accuracy. These transformations help the model better cope with variations in object perspectives, indicating that building a classification model capable of handling changes in viewpoint is a crucial aspect of static hand gesture recognition.

Secondly, in choosing a CNN model, ResNet50 consistently proved to outperform MobileNetV2 and InceptionV3. Although ResNet50 may require more computational power, the advantage of high-accuracy results suggests its importance in selecting a model for this task.

However, the conclusions also highlight that overly complex geometric transformations can harm the model's performance, especially for MobileNetV2 and InceptionV3. Excessive geometric transformations may involve using too many types of transformations, making the model struggle to understand actual patterns, as each training example experiences significant variation. Therefore, a balance is needed between performance improvement and real-world representation by selecting transformations suitable for the dataset's characteristics.

Moreover, future research may consider color modifications in addition to geometric transformations. Further understanding of how to optimize image augmentation methods, including color variations, can significantly contribute to improving model performance, especially in situations where color variations may affect image interpretation.

As a direction for future research, this study can be expanded by combining multiplex geometric transformations with color modifications, creating a more holistic and effective image augmentation framework. Additionally, further exploration can be conducted in situations where there is a lack of data or significant variation between datasets. Integration with transfer learning techniques and the development of more complex models can also be an interesting focus of research. Thus, this study provides a foundation for further exploration in enhancing the efficiency and effectiveness of static hand gesture recognition using a CNN-based approach.

Author Contributions: Conceptualization, B.-A.A.; methodology, B.-A.A.; software, B.-A.A.; validation, B.-A.A. and C.-T.C.; formal analysis, B.-A.A.; investigation, B.-A.A.; resources, B.-A.A.; data curation, B.-A.A.; writing—original draft preparation, B.-A.A.; writing—review and editing, B.-A.A. and C.-T.C.; visualization, B.-A.A.; supervision, C.-T.C. and J.-S.C.; project administration, J.-S.C.; funding acquisition, J.-S.C. All authors have read and agreed to the published version of the manuscript.

Funding: This research was funded by the National Science and Technology Council, Taiwan grant number NSTC 112-2221-E-218-017.

Institutional Review Board Statement: Not applicable.

Informed Consent Statement: Not applicable.

Data Availability Statement: All datasets in this work can be accessed through the link provided Section 2.

Conflicts of Interest: The authors declare no conflict of interest.

References

1. Lee, C.; Kim, J.; Cho, S.; Kim, J.; Yoo, J.; Kwon, S. Development of Real-Time Hand Gesture Recognition for Tabletop Holograph Display Interaction Using Azure Kinect. *Sensors* **2020**, *20*, 4566. [CrossRef]
2. Ekneling, S.; Sonestedt, T.; Georgiadis, A.; Yousefi, S.; Chana, J. Magestro: Gamification of the Data Collection Process f Development of the Hand Gesture Recognition Technology. In Proceedings of the 2018 IEEE International Symposium on Mixe and Augmented Reality Adjunct (ISMAR-Adjunct), Munich, Germany, 16–20 October 2018; pp. 417–418.
3. Bai, Z.; Wang, L.; Zhou, S.; Cao, Y.; Liu, Y.; Zhang, J. Fast Recognition Method of Football Robot's Graphics From the V Perspective. *IEEE Access* **2020**, *8*, 161472–161479. [CrossRef]
4. Nooruddin, N.; Dembani, R.; Maitlo, N. HGR: Hand-Gesture-Recognition Based Text Input Method for AR/VR Wearable Device In Proceedings of the 2020 IEEE International Conference on Systems, Man, and Cybernetics (SMC), Toronto, ON, Canada, 11–1 October 2020; pp. 744–751.
5. Zhao, J.; An, R.; Xu, R.; Lin, B. Comparing Hand Gestures and a Gamepad Interface for Locomotion in Virtual Environments. *In J. Hum.-Comput. Stud.* **2022**, *166*, 102868. [CrossRef]
6. Mezari, A.; Maglogiannis, I. An Easily Customized Gesture Recognizer for Assisted Living Using Commodity Mobile Device *J. Healthc. Eng.* **2018**, *2018*, 3180652. [CrossRef] [PubMed]
7. Roberge, A.; Bouchard, B.; Maître, J.; Gaboury, S. Hand Gestures Identification for Fine-Grained Human Activity Recognition i Smart Homes. In *Procedia Computer Science*; Elsevier B.V.: Amsterdam, The Netherlands; Liara Laboratory, University of Quebe Chicoutimi 555 Boul. Universite: Saguenay, QC, Canada, 2022; Volume 201, pp. 32–39.
8. Huang, X.; Hu, S.; Guo, Q. Multi-Object Recognition Based on Improved YOLOv4. In Proceedings of the 2021 CAA Symposiu on Fault Detection, Supervision, and Safety for Technical Processes (SAFEPROCESS), Chengdu, China, 17–18 December 202 pp. 1–4.
9. Kaczmarek, W.; Panasiuk, J.; Borys, S.; Banach, P. Industrial Robot Control by Means of Gestures and Voice Commands in Off-Lin and On-Line Mode. *Sensors* **2020**, *20*, 6358. [CrossRef]
10. Neto, P.; Simão, M.; Mendes, N.; Safeea, M. Gesture-Based Human-Robot Interaction for Human Assistance in Manufacturing *Int. J. Adv. Manuf. Technol.* **2019**, *101*, 119–135. [CrossRef]
11. Ding, I.-J.; Su, J.-L. Designs of Human–Robot Interaction Using Depth Sensor-Based Hand Gesture Communication for Smar Material-Handling Robot Operations. *Proc. Inst. Mech. Eng. Part B J. Eng. Manuf.* **2023**, *237*, 392–413. [CrossRef]
12. Young, G.; Milne, H.; Griffiths, D.; Padfield, E.; Blenkinsopp, R.; Georgiou, O. Designing Mid-Air Haptic Gesture Controlled Use Interfaces for Cars. *Proc. ACM Hum.-Comput. Interact.* **2020**, *4*, 1–23. [CrossRef]
13. Qian, X.; Ju, W.; Sirkin, D.M. Aladdin's Magic Carpet: Navigation by in-Air Static Hand Gesture in Autonomous Vehicles. *Int. J Hum.–Comput. Interact.* **2020**, *36*, 1912–1927. [CrossRef]
14. Devineau, G.; Moutarde, F.; Xi, W.; Yang, J. Deep Learning for Hand Gesture Recognition on Skeletal Data. In Proceedings of the 2018 13th IEEE International Conference on Automatic Face & Gesture Recognition (FG 2018), Xi'an, China, 15–19 May 2018; pp 106–113.
15. Wang, J.; Liu, T.; Wang, X. Human Hand Gesture Recognition with Convolutional Neural Networks for K-12 Double-Teachers Instruction Mode Classroom. *Infrared Phys. Technol.* **2020**, *111*, 103464. [CrossRef]
16. Khoh, W.H.; Pang, Y.H.; Teoh, A.B.J.; Ooi, S.Y. In-Air Hand Gesture Signature Using Transfer Learning and Its Forgery Attack. *Appl. Soft Comput.* **2021**, *113*, 108033. [CrossRef]
17. Khosla, C.; Saini, B.S. Enhancing Performance of Deep Learning Models with Different Data Augmentation Techniques: A Survey. In Proceedings of the 2020 International Conference on Intelligent Engineering and Management (ICIEM), London, UK, 17–19 June 2020; pp. 79–85.
18. Shorten, C.; Khoshgoftaar, T.M. A Survey on Image Data Augmentation for Deep Learning. *J. Big Data* **2019**, *6*, 60. [CrossRef]
19. Kalaivani, S.; Asha, N.; Gayathri, A. Geometric Transformations-Based Medical Image Augmentation. In *GANs for Data Augmentation in Healthcare*; Solanki, A., Naved, M., Eds.; Springer International Publishing: Cham, Switzerland, 2023; pp. 133–141, ISBN 978-3-031-43204-0.
20. Islam, M.Z.; Hossain, M.S.; ul Islam, R.; Andersson, K. Static Hand Gesture Recognition Using Convolutional Neural Network with Data Augmentation. In Proceedings of the 2019 Joint 8th International Conference on Informatics, Electronics & Vision (ICIEV) and 2019 3rd International Conference on Imaging, Vision & Pattern Recognition (icIVPR), Spokane, WA, USA, 30 May–2 June 2019; pp. 324–329.
21. Bousbai, K.; Merah, M. Hand Gesture Recognition Using Capabilities of Capsule Network and Data Augmentation. In Proceedings of the 2022 7th International Conference on Image and Signal Processing and their Applications (ISPA), Mostaganem, Algeria, 8–9 May 2022; pp. 1–5.

22. Alani, A.A.; Cosma, G.; Taherkhani, A.; McGinnity, T.M. Hand Gesture Recognition Using an Adapted Convolutional Neural Network with Data Augmentation. In Proceedings of the 2018 4th International Conference on Information Management (ICIM), Oxford, UK, 25–27 May 2018; pp. 5–12.
23. Zhou, W.; Chen, K. A Lightweight Hand Gesture Recognition in Complex Backgrounds. *Displays* **2022**, *74*, 102226. [CrossRef]
24. Galdran, A.; Alvarez-Gila, A.; Meyer, M.I.; Saratxaga, C.L.; Araújo, T.; Garrote, E.; Aresta, G.; Costa, P.; Mendonça, A.M.; Campilho, A. Data-Driven Color Augmentation Techniques for Deep Skin Image Analysis. *arXiv* **2017**, arXiv:1703.03702.
25. Tan, Y.S.; Lim, K.M.; Lee, C.P. Hand Gesture Recognition via Enhanced Densely Connected Convolutional Neural Network. *Expert Syst. Appl.* **2021**, *175*, 114797. [CrossRef]
26. Taylor, L.; Nitschke, G. Improving Deep Learning with Generic Data Augmentation. In Proceedings of the 2018 IEEE Symposium Series on Computational Intelligence (SSCI), Bangalore, India, 18–21 November 2018; pp. 1542–1547.
27. Motamed, S.; Rogalla, P.; Khalvati, F. Data Augmentation Using Generative Adversarial Networks (GANs) for GAN-Based Detection of Pneumonia and COVID-19 in Chest X-Ray Images. *Inform. Med. Unlocked* **2021**, *27*, 100779. [CrossRef] [PubMed]
28. Rajeev, C.; Natarajan, K. Data Augmentation in Classifying Chest Radiograph Images (CXR) Using DCGAN-CNN. In *GANs for Data Augmentation in Healthcare*; Solanki, A., Naved, M., Eds.; Springer International Publishing: Cham, Switzerland, 2023; pp. 91–110. ISBN 978-3-031-43204-0.
29. Farahanipad, F.; Rezaei, M.; Nasr, M.S.; Kamangar, F.; Athitsos, V. A Survey on GAN-Based Data Augmentation for Hand Pose Estimation Problem. *Technologies* **2022**, *10*, 43. [CrossRef]
30. Saxena, D.; Cao, J. Generative Adversarial Networks (GANs): Challenges, Solutions, and Future Directions. *ACM Comput. Surv. CSUR* **2021**, *54*, 1–42. [CrossRef]
31. Ciano, G.; Andreini, P.; Mazzierli, T.; Bianchini, M.; Scarselli, F. A Multi-Stage GAN for Multi-Organ Chest X-Ray Image Generation and Segmentation. *Mathematics* **2021**, *9*, 2896. [CrossRef]
32. Avianto, D.; Harjoko, A.; Afiahayati. CNN-Based Classification for Highly Similar Vehicle Model Using Multi-Task Learning. *J. Imaging* **2022**, *8*, 293. [CrossRef]
33. Güler, O.; Yücedağ, İ. Hand Gesture Recognition from 2D Images by Using Convolutional Capsule Neural Networks. *Arab. J. Sci. Eng.* **2022**, *47*, 1211–1225. [CrossRef]
34. Alashhab, S.; Gallego, A.J.; Lozano, M.Á. Efficient Gesture Recognition for the Assistance of Visually Impaired People Using Multi-Head Neural Networks. *Eng. Appl. Artif. Intell.* **2022**, *114*, 105188. [CrossRef]
35. Latif, G.; Mohammad, N.; Alghazo, J.; AlKhalaf, R.; AlKhalaf, R. ArASL: Arabic Alphabets Sign Language Dataset. *Data Brief* **2019**, *23*, 103777. [CrossRef] [PubMed]
36. Lecture—Image Processing: Geometric Operations—Scaling | WueCampus. Available online: https://wuecampus.uni-wuerzburg.de/moodle/mod/book/view.php?id=958001&chapterid=10072 (accessed on 17 November 2023).
37. Lecture—Image Processing: Geometric Operations—Rotation | WueCampus. Available online: https://wuecampus.uni-wuerzburg.de/moodle/mod/book/view.php?id=958001&chapterid=10071 (accessed on 17 November 2023).
38. Lecture—Image Processing: Geometric Operations—Translation | WueCampus. Available online: https://wuecampus.uni-wuerzburg.de/moodle/mod/book/view.php?id=958001&chapterid=10067 (accessed on 17 November 2023).
39. Shearing in 2D Graphics. GeeksforGeeks 2020. Available online: https://www.geeksforgeeks.org/shearing-in-2d-graphics/ (accessed on 17 November 2023).
40. Lecture—Image Processing: Geometric Operations—Mirroring | WueCampus. Available online: https://wuecampus.uni-wuerzburg.de/moodle/mod/book/view.php?id=958001&chapterid=10073 (accessed on 17 November 2023).
41. He, K.; Zhang, X.; Ren, S.; Sun, J. Deep Residual Learning for Image Recognition. In Proceedings of the 2016 IEEE Conference on Computer Vision and Pattern Recognition (CVPR), Las Vegas, NV, USA, 27–30 June 2016; pp. 770–778.
42. Phung, V.H.; Rhee, E.J. A High-Accuracy Model Average Ensemble of Convolutional Neural Networks for Classification of Cloud Image Patches on Small Datasets. *Appl. Sci.* **2019**, *9*, 4500. [CrossRef]
43. Agarap, A.F. Deep Learning Using Rectified Linear Units (ReLU). *arXiv* **2019**, arXiv:1803.08375.
44. Hahnloser, R.H.R.; Sarpeshkar, R.; Mahowald, M.A.; Douglas, R.J.; Seung, H.S. Digital Selection and Analogue Amplification Coexist in a Cortex-Inspired Silicon Circuit. *Nature* **2000**, *405*, 947–951. [CrossRef]
45. Alzubaidi, L.; Zhang, J.; Humaidi, A.J.; Al-Dujaili, A.; Duan, Y.; Al-Shamma, O.; Santamaría, J.; Fadhel, M.A.; Al-Amidie, M.; Farhan, L. Review of Deep Learning: Concepts, CNN Architectures, Challenges, Applications, Future Directions. *J. Big Data* **2021**, *8*, 53. [CrossRef]
46. Subburaj, S.; Murugavalli, S. Survey on Sign Language Recognition in Context of Vision-Based and Deep Learning. *Meas. Sens.* **2022**, *23*, 100385. [CrossRef]
47. Sandler, M.; Howard, A.; Zhu, M.; Zhmoginov, A.; Chen, L.-C. MobileNetV2: Inverted Residuals and Linear Bottlenecks. In Proceedings of the 2018 IEEE/CVF Conference on Computer Vision and Pattern Recognition, Salt Lake City, UT, USA, 18–23 June 2018; pp. 4510–4520.
48. Szegedy, C.; Vanhoucke, V.; Ioffe, S.; Shlens, J.; Wojna, Z. Rethinking the Inception Architecture for Computer Vision. In Proceedings of the 2016 IEEE Conference on Computer Vision and Pattern Recognition (CVPR), Las Vegas, NV, USA, 27–30 June 2016; pp. 2818–2826.

49. Szegedy, C.; Liu, W.; Jia, Y.; Sermanet, P.; Reed, S.; Anguelov, D.; Erhan, D.; Vanhoucke, V.; Rabinovich, A. Going Deeper w Convolutions. In Proceedings of the 2015 IEEE Conference on Computer Vision and Pattern Recognition (CVPR), Boston, M USA, 7–12 June 2015; pp. 1–9.
50. Tf.Keras.Preprocessing.Image.ImageDataGenerator | TensorFlow v2.14.0. Available online: https://www.tensorflow.org/a docs/python/tf/keras/preprocessing/image/ImageDataGenerator (accessed on 13 November 2023).
51. Kingma, D.P.; Ba, J. Adam: A Method for Stochastic Optimization. *arXiv* **2017**, arXiv:1412.6980.

mathematics

MDPI

ticle

.utomated Classification of Agricultural Species through arallel Artificial Multiple Intelligence System–Ensemble)eep Learning

eartisak Sriprateep [1], Surajet Khonjun [2,*], Paulina Golinska-Dawson [3], Rapeepan Pitakaso [2], Peerawat Luesak [4], ıanatkij Srichok [2], Somphop Chiaranai [2], Sarayut Gonwirat [5] and Budsaba Buakum [6]

1 Manufacturing and Materials Research Unit (MMR), Department of Manufacturing Engineering, Faculty of Engineering, Maha Sarakham University, Maha Sarakham 44150, Thailand; keartisak.s@msu.ac.th
2 Artificial Intelligence Optimization SMART Laboratory, Industrial Engineering Department, Faculty of Engineering, Ubon Ratchathani University, Ubon Ratchathani 34190, Thailand; rapeepan.p@ubu.ac.th (R.P.); thanatkij.s@ubu.ac.th (T.S.); somphop.ch.64@ubu.ac.th (S.C.)
3 Institute of Logistics, Poznan University of Technology, Jacka Rychlewskiego 2 Street, 60-965 Poznan, Poland; paulina.golinska@put.poznan.pl
4 Department of Industrial Engineering, Faculty of Engineering, Rajamangala University of Technology Lanna, Chiang Rai 57120, Thailand; peerawat@rmutl.ac.th
5 Department of Computer Engineering and Automation, Kalasin University, Kalasin 46000, Thailand; sarayut.go@ksu.ac.th
6 Department of Horticulture, Faculty of Agriculture, Ubon Ratchathani University, Ubon Ratchathani 34190, Thailand; budsaba.b@ubu.ac.th
* Correspondence: surajet.k@ubu.ac.th

Abstract: The classification of certain agricultural species poses a formidable challenge due to their inherent resemblance and the absence of dependable visual discriminators. The accurate identification of these plants holds substantial importance in industries such as cosmetics, pharmaceuticals, and herbal medicine, where the optimization of essential compound yields and product quality is paramount. In response to this challenge, we have devised an automated classification system based on deep learning principles, designed to achieve precision and efficiency in species classification. Our approach leverages a diverse dataset encompassing various cultivars and employs the Parallel Artificial Multiple Intelligence System–Ensemble Deep Learning model (P-AMIS-E). This model integrates ensemble image segmentation techniques, including U-Net and Mask-R-CNN, alongside image augmentation and convolutional neural network (CNN) architectures such as SqueezeNet, ShuffleNetv2 1.0x, MobileNetV3, and InceptionV1. The culmination of these elements results in the P-AMIS-E model, enhanced by an Artificial Multiple Intelligence System (AMIS) for decision fusion, ultimately achieving an impressive accuracy rate of 98.41%. This accuracy notably surpasses the performance of existing methods, such as ResNet-101 and Xception, which attain 93.74% accuracy on the testing dataset. Moreover, when applied to an unseen dataset, the P-AMIS-E model demonstrates a substantial advantage, yielding accuracy rates ranging from 4.45% to 31.16% higher than those of the compared methods. It is worth highlighting that our heterogeneous ensemble approach consistently outperforms both single large models and homogeneous ensemble methods, achieving an average improvement of 13.45%. This paper provides a case study focused on the Centella Asiatica Urban (CAU) cultivar to exemplify the practical application of our approach. By integrating image segmentation, augmentation, and decision fusion, we have significantly enhanced accuracy and efficiency. This research holds theoretical implications for the advancement of deep learning techniques in image classification tasks while also offering practical benefits for industries reliant on precise species identification.

Keywords: Centella Asiatica; linn; urban; ensemble deep learning; image segmentation; image enhancement; medicinal plants; traditional medicine; pharmaceuticals

:itation: Sriprateep, K.; Khonjun, S.; ;olinska-Dawson, P.; Pitakaso, R.; .uesak, P.; Srichok, T.; Chiaranai, S.; ;onwirat, S.; Buakum, B. Automated :lassification of Agricultural Species hrough Parallel Artificial Multiple ntelligence System–Ensemble Deep Learning. *Mathematics* **2024**, *12*, 351. ıttps://doi.org/10.3390/ math12020351

Academic Editor: Alessandro Niccolai

Received: 20 December 2023
Revised: 15 January 2024
Accepted: 20 January 2024
Published: 22 January 2024

MSC: 68T07

1. Introduction

The Centella Asiatica Urban (CAU) cultivar holds paramount significance with the realms of agriculture and pharmaceutics, owing to its heterogeneous characteristi and specialized cultivation prerequisites. Particularly in regions like Thailand, a myria of CAU cultivars exhibit diverse levels of resilience to pests and diseases, coupled wi variations in the concentration of vital compounds. Such variability necessitates be-spok cultivation practices to maximize the yield of these essential compounds and to ensure th highest standard of product quality. This underscores the critical need for an accurate an precise classification of CAU cultivars, thereby providing a compelling rationale for ou research [1,2].

Historically, the domain of automated plant classification has been predominantl centered around disease detection and the identification of general species, employin methodologies such as Multi-Layer Perceptron (MLP), the k-Nearest Neighbor (k-NN algorithm, and stacked autoencoders. While these approaches have proven efficacious i certain scenarios, they are notably deficient in their capacity to accurately classify specifi cultivars such as CAU. This limitation primarily stems from their inability to discern th intricate nuances and complex attributes that are unique to various CAU cultivars, resultin in inefficiencies and inaccuracies in classification processes [3,4].

In an endeavor to surmount these challenges, our research introduces the innovativ Parallel-Artificial Multiple Intelligence System-Ensemble (P-AMIS-E) model, a cutting-edge deep learning-based classification system. The P-AMIS-E model adeptly amalgamates an array of ensemble image segmentation techniques, including U-Net and Mask R-CNN with image augmentation and diverse Convolutional Neural Network (CNN) architectures This synergy enhances the accuracy and efficiency of classification, enabling a more detailed and nuanced analysis of the unique characteristics inherent to CAU cultivars [5–7].

In an endeavor to surmount these challenges, our research introduces the innovative Parallel Artificial Multiple Intelligence System–Ensemble (P-AMIS-E) model, a cutting-edge deep-learning-based classification system. The P-AMIS-E model adeptly amalgamates an array of ensemble image segmentation techniques, including U-Net and Mask R-CNN with image augmentation and diverse convolutional neural network (CNN) architectures. This synergy enhances the accuracy and efficiency of classification, enabling a more detailed and nuanced analysis of the unique characteristics inherent to CAU cultivars [8].

This study introduces the Parallel-Artificial Multiple Intelligence System-Ensemble Deep Learning model (P-AMIS-E), marking a significant advancement in the field of agricultural species classification, specifically targeting the complex identification of Centella Asiatica Urban (CAU) cultivars. The P-AMIS-E model's novelty lies in its unique blend of cutting-edge deep learning techniques, which include:

1. We present the Ensemble of Convolutional Neural Network (CNN) Architectures: Integrating various CNN architectures like SqueezeNet, ShuffleNetv2 1.0x, MobileNetV3, and InceptionV1, our model robustly tackles the intricacies in cultivar classification while minimizing overfitting.
2. Advanced Image Segmentation Techniques: Employing a combination of U-net and Mask-R-CNN segmentation methods, the model achieves a precise and detailed analysis of CAU cultivars, enhancing classification accuracy.
3. Innovative Use of an Artificial Multiple Intelligence System (AMIS): The adaptation of AMIS for decision fusion in the P-AMIS-E model optimizes the classification accuracy.
4. Practical and Theoretical Implications: The model has significant implications for the agricultural and pharmaceutical industries, where precise species identification is key. Additionally, it contributes to the theoretical advancement of deep learning in image classification, setting new standards for real-world applications.

These contributions underscore the study's importance in bridging the gap in automated plant classification, particularly for complex cultivars like CAU, and advancing deep learning methodologies in practical and theoretical domains.

The structure of the article is meticulously organized as follows: Section 2 delves into the related literature, Section 3 elucidates the research methodology employed, Section 4 delineates the computational results obtained, Section 5 engages in a comprehensive discussion of the research findings, and finally, Section 6 culminates with the conclusion and offers perspectives on future research directions.

2. Related Literature

In this section, we endeavor to compartmentalize the literature review into three distinct components: (1) an examination of the rationale behind the classification of the CAU cultivar, (2) a comprehensive assessment of the deep learning methodologies employed in the classification of plant science data, and (3) an in-depth analysis of the decision fusion strategies utilized in ensemble-based deep learning models.

2.1. Cultivar Differentiation in CAU

Accurate cultivar differentiation in Centella Asiatica (Linn.) Urban (CAU) holds critical significance for several compelling reasons. First, it serves as the foundation for distinguishing various species within the *Centella* genus, such as *Centella cordifolia* and *Centella erecta*, which exhibit distinct morphological and genetic characteristics [1]. This differentiation enables a deeper exploration of the chemical composition and pharmacological properties unique to each species. Variations in the triterpene glycosides, phenolics, and antioxidant capacity among different *Centella* species have been documented [2]. Understanding these differences is pivotal for medicinal development and the formulation of herbal products.

Furthermore, precise cultivar differentiation plays a pivotal role in the authentic identification of CAU. In Indian systems of medicine, CAU is renowned for its memory-enhancing and nervine-disorder-treating properties [9,10]. Ensuring the authenticity of CAU cultivars is crucial for advancing scientific research, medicinal development, and quality control standards in the herbal product industry.

The impact of cultivar differentiation in CAU extends to the realm of quality control in medical product manufacturing. Distinct CAU cultivars have been found to exhibit variations in macroscopic and histomorpho-diagnostic profiles, as well as the triterpenoid content and yield. These variations have implications for the pharmacognostic characterization and regulatory aspects of quality control measures for crude drugs. Additionally, the choice of cultivar can influence the biotechnological production of centellosides, the bioactive compounds in CAU. Research has demonstrated that polyploidy induction can enhance the medicinal value of CAU, resulting in higher yields and triterpenoid contents [11]. Hence, a comprehensive understanding of cultivar differentiation in CAU is indispensable for ensuring the consistent and high-quality production of medicinal products derived from this plant [12,13].

Moreover, CAU cultivars have exhibited phenotypic plasticity, enabling them to thrive in diverse environmental conditions [14]. Extensive studies have shed light on the plant's growth behavior, revealing that certain soil types, such as sandy and humus soil, are conducive to rapid propagation [15]. Additionally, challenges related to weed growth, with *Cyperus rotundus* L. being a prominent weed species in *Centella* plantations, have been identified [1]. The remarkable adaptability of CAU to varying environmental conditions has made it a valuable asset in ethnomedicinal healthcare systems [16]. Furthermore, the germination of CAU seeds has been linked to the color of the pericarp, indicating different stages of seed development [17]. In summary, the cultivation and growth of CAU are influenced by a multitude of factors, encompassing the soil type, weed control, and seed development stage.

Distinguishing among different CAU cultivars based solely on their appearance presents a complex and challenging endeavor [18]. Experts face difficulties owing to morphological similarities, inconsistent phenotypic expressions, natural hybridization eve regional naming variations, and the absence of standardized identification systems [Addressing these challenges necessitates collaborative efforts among botanists, hortic turists, geneticists, and traditional practitioners in developing comprehensive databa and analytical tools. By doing so, experts can overcome these obstacles and contribute the preservation and advancement of CAU cultivation and utilization. The developm of a rapid and accurate CAU cultivar classification system may prove indispensable overcoming these challenges, offering significant benefits to the agricultural commun particularly in the realm of CAU classification.

2.2. Deep Learning Models for Plant Image Classification

Deep learning methodologies have revolutionized the field of plant sciences, part ularly in automated image classification. These advanced techniques have significant enhanced plant classification systems, providing precise tools for identifying and categ rizing plant diseases. This progress has had a positive impact on crop productivity ar quality. Among the standout models are convolutional neural networks (CNNs), MnasN SqueezeNet, and ShuffleNetv2. These models have shown exceptional performance image classification, especially in detecting plant diseases.

Building on these advancements, recent methods, like the one introduced by Ch et al., 2022 [20], have taken a leap forward. Their study unveils the Dual-Path Mixe Domain Residual Threshold Network (DP-MRTN), a novel approach for bearing fau diagnosis in noisy environments. This model skillfully combines channel and spatial atte tion mechanisms, a residual structure, a soft threshold function, and dilated convolutio This synergy allows the network to effectively select crucial features without the need fo separate denoising algorithms. The DP-MRTN method has been proven to significant enhance the accuracy of fault diagnosis in noisy conditions, achieving over 99% accuracy i various noise scenarios. It surpasses traditional deep learning techniques, offering a mo robust solution for monitoring mechanical equipment in challenging environments.

However, despite these successes, there is still a research gap in applying model like Augmented MnasNet, SqueezeNet, and ShuffleNetv2 to CAU cultivar classificatio To bridge this gap, ensemble deep learning techniques have come to the forefront as promising approach. These techniques improve accuracy, mitigate overfitting, and increas robustness. Moreover, the integration of metaheuristic algorithms such as differential evo lution, particle swarm optimization, and genetic algorithms into decision fusion strategie is poised to further boost the effectiveness of ensemble models.

Our study focuses on developing an ensemble deep learning classification model by harmonizing efficient CNN architectures with advanced image segmentation method and metaheuristic-based decision fusion strategies. This approach aims to significantly improve accuracy and reliability in CAU cultivar classification, thus bridging the existing research gap. The diverse characteristics and cultivation requirements of the Centella Asiatica (Linn.) Urban (CAU) cultivar make it an ideal case study. In Thailand, the varying resistance of CAU cultivars to diseases and pests, along with differences in essentia compound concentrations, necessitates tailored cultivation techniques for an optimal yield and product quality [16,21,22]. Additionally, the divergence in agronomic traits among CAU cultivars based on their growth region emphasizes the need for rapid and precise classification to inform cultivation practices [17,23,24].

Deep learning models have exhibited impressive performances across various plant image classification domains, including disease identification and flower species recogni tion [25]. Notably, models like VGG-Net and the Inception module excel in plant disease identification, while techniques like 3-D CNN and CNN with ConvLSTM layers have enhanced plant accession classification through the integration of spatial and temporal data for improved accuracy [26]. DenseNet121 has also proved effective in accurately classifying flower species [27]. These studies collectively underscore the effectiveness of deep learning models in plant image classification, often achieving accuracy rates exceeding 94%.

Among the standout models in plant classification research are MnasNet, SqueezeNet, and ShuffleNetV2. These models have demonstrated their prowess in various applications. For instance, SqueezeNet achieved a remarkable 96% accuracy rate in citrus fruit disease classification, and ShuffleNetV2 demonstrated efficient low-power image classification for edge computing [28,29]. Furthermore, Patil utilized a support vector machine (SVM) classifier in combination with various features for plant identification, achieving an overall accuracy of 78% [30]. Additionally, Heredia explored the application of deep learning models like ResNet50 in large-scale biodiversity monitoring, noting substantial accuracy improvements over existing methods [31,32].

MnasNet, SqueezeNet, and ShuffleNetv2 each offer unique advantages in plant classification. MnasNet, being a lightweight neural network, achieves a high accuracy with a minimal computational cost [33]. SqueezeNet, another compact model, excels in rapid image processing on edge devices while maintaining a high accuracy. ShuffleNetv2, known for its multihop lightwave network, leverages optical interconnection to enhance rapid packet communication, thus reducing fiber cabling congestion and enabling modular growth [34,35]. These models exemplify the potential of efficient and effective deep learning models across various applications, including computer vision and natural language processing.

Ensemble deep learning models play a critical role in improving disease detection and pest recognition accuracy in plant classification by combining the strengths of multiple models for enhanced generalization [36–39]. Deep ensemble models, which merge deep learning with ensemble learning, exhibit remarkable generalization performance, holding great potential for transforming plant recognition systems. Deep ensemble neural networks (DENNs) have even surpassed state-of-the-art pre-trained models in plant disease detection [39]. Additionally, model compression techniques, such as pruning and quantization, have successfully reduced the computational demands of deep learning models in plant seedling classification without significant accuracy loss [40]. Despite the advantages and high accuracy of models like MnasNet, SqueezeNet, and ShuffleNetv2, the application of ensemble deep learning in these contexts remains an underexplored area of research. Our study aims to develop a CAU cultivar classification system by harnessing ensemble deep learning with these models, ultimately advancing plant classification and contributing to the development of robust plant recognition systems.

In addition to deep learning models, preprocessing techniques such as image segmentation and augmentation play a crucial role in plant classification systems. Methods like U-Net and R-Net segmentation have found successful application in various plant science contexts [41]. For example, 3D U-Net has been used to segment root and soil volumes in MRI scans, enhancing the signal-to-noise ratio and resolution. Another study leveraged a U-Net-based CNN for segmenting root images from rhizotrons, yielding strong correlations with manual annotations. Additionally, an EncU-Net model, based on U-Net architecture, achieved over 90% success in lesion segmentation in dermoscopic images, demonstrating the efficacy of these segmentation methods in plant science [16].

2.3. Decision Fusion Strategy in Ensemble Deep Learning

In ensemble deep learning, decision fusion strategies play a pivotal role in enhancing the generalization performance by combining the decisions of multiple models. These strategies encompass static fusion and dynamic fusion methods. Static fusion assumes uniform capabilities among agents or disregards agents with subpar performance, whereas dynamic fusion adapts to the competence of each base agent on test states. A dynamic fusion method for deep reinforcement learning, for instance, measures base agent performance on validation states and adjusts agent weights based on their performance and similarity to new states [42]. Decision-level fusion methods have found applications in diverse domains, including COVID-19 patient health prediction through calibrated ensemble classifiers employing a soft voting technique [43]. In target recognition tasks, an ensemble-learning-based information fusion model has improved the recognition abilities of distributed sensors [44]. Ensemble learning frameworks have also enhanced cooperati spectrum sensing in cognitive radio systems, utilizing convolutional neural networks a fusion strategies for global decision making [45].

Metaheuristic techniques like swarm intelligence (SI) and evolutionary computi (EC) have effectively optimized deep neural networks (DNNs) in various tasks [46]. Th excel in generating optimal hyperparameters and structures for DNNs when dealing wi extensive datasets [47]. Ensemble learning has further been applied to enhance sentime analysis [48], text classification [49], and epileptic seizure prediction [50]. For instan a stacking ensemble approach boosted accuracy in sentiment analysis by leveraging t strengths of different deep models.

Artificial multiple intelligences systems (AMISs) were initially proposed by Pitaka et al. [8] to streamline the agricultural product flow from Thailand to neighboring countri Subsequently, an AMIS was employed to determine optimal weights for ensemble dee learning models in classifying various medical images [51,52]. Recently, an AMIS w utilized to optimize ensemble classification models in two stages, combining differe image segmentation methods and CNN architectures. This double ensemble model outp formed traditional fusion methods like unweighted averages and majority voting, yieldi outstanding accuracy.

In this research, AMIS will combine two segmentation methods and three CN architectures for CAU cultivar classification. However, modifications are required, as th original AMIS used in [53] cannot be directly applied. New improvement methods ar introduced, and adjustments to the probability function for selecting improvement metho will be made.

3. Research Methods

The proposed research entails the creation and deployment of an automated classif cation system for CAU species utilizing the parallel AMIS ensemble model (P-AMIS-E Initially, diverse CAU species will be collected and photographed to constitute the trainin and testing datasets. Subsequently, the P-AMIS-E model will be developed, trained, an tested on this dataset, aiming to enhance species classification accuracy and efficiency whil minimizing manual intervention. The model's performance will be assessed and analyze in subsequent sections of this paper.

3.1. Dataset Preparation

The Centella Asiatica Urban (CAU) specimens were gathered from diverse productio sources. The study encompassed five distinct CAU cultivars, specifically Rayong, Cha choengsao, Nakhon Pathom, Ubon Ratchathani, and Prachin Buri. Each of these cultivars underwent uniform cultivation conditions and care procedures for a duration of 12 weeks Fresh leaf samples from all cultivars were meticulously collected and photographed against a white background to ensure consistency.

The dataset was subsequently partitioned into two subsets: CALU-1 and CALU-2. The CALU-1 dataset served as the training and testing set for the model, while the CALU-2 dataset remained unseen and was reserved for validation purposes. The total number of images present in both datasets is detailed in Table 1.

Table 1. Detail of the datasets in CALU-1 and CALU-2.

	CALU-1										CALU-2									
	CM	**NP**	**NR**	**NS**	**NT**	**NB**	**PB**	**RB**	**SK**	**UB**	**CM**	**NP**	**NR**	**NS**	**NT**	**NB**	**PB**	**RB**	**SK**	**UB**
Training set	1005	1089	1000	1000	1007	1000	1056	1056	1090	1000	-	-	-	-	-	-	-	-	-	-
Testing set	504	504	500	500	505	570	506	594	539	500	500	502	500	541	528	500	575	594	568	500
Total	1509	1593	1500	1500	1512	1570	1562	1650	1629	1500	500	502	500	541	528	500	575	594	568	500

Note: Chiang Mai: (CM), Nakhon Pathom: (NP), Nakhon Ratchasima: (NR), Nakhon Si Thammarat: (NS), Narathiwat: (NT), Nonthaburi: (NB), Prachin Buri: (PB), Ratchaburi: (RB), Songkhla: (SK), Ubon Ratchathani; (UB).

Based on the data presented in Table 1, CALU-1 was split into two subsets, namely, the train dataset (80%) and the test dataset (20%). The CALU-1 dataset contained a total of 3240 images, whereas CALU-2 consisted of 3591 images and was only utilized to evaluate the effectiveness of the proposed method. Examples of all five types of *Centella asiatica* (L.) Urban from both datasets are shown in Figure 1.

Figure 1. Example of all types of *Centella asiatica* (L.) urban from both datasets.

3.2. Develop the P-AMIS-E

The development of the P-AMIS-E comprised four steps: (1) image augmentation, (2) the ensemble of two types of image segmentation, (3) the ensemble of various types of CNN architectures, and (4) the application of AMIS as the decision fusion strategy. The workflow diagram of the P-AMIS-E is shown in Figure 2.

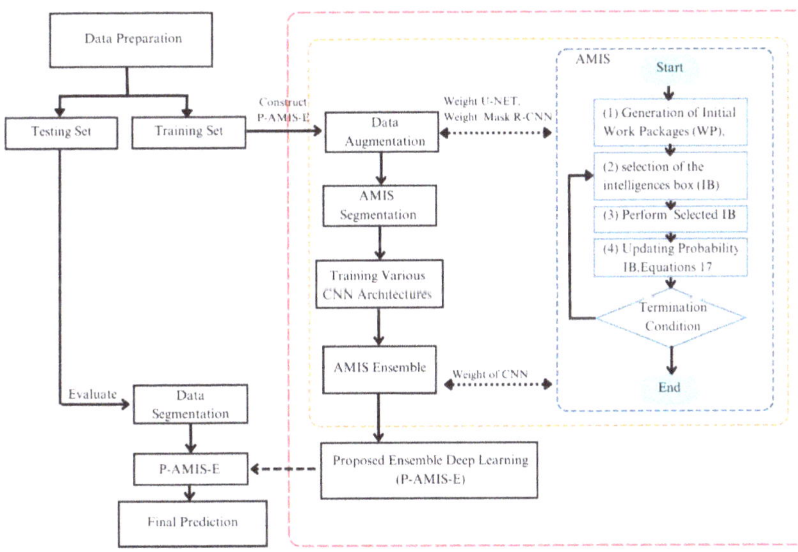

Figure 2. Workflow diagram of the proposed method.

In accordance with Figure 2, the proposed methodology was initiated by inputting the training images into the image segmentation methods. Subsequently, the training images underwent processing within the 'ensemble image segmentation procedure'. During this stage, the Adaptive Metaheuristic-based Image Segmentation (AMIS) served as the decision fusion strategy for the proposed model. Following this step in the diagram, the ima were input into the ensemble convolutional neural network (CNN) model, culminating the final prediction. For the testing dataset, the images were directed straight to the im segmentation procedure, utilizing the model previously trained on the training datase predict the ultimate class of each image. To elucidate the proposed algorithm, we provid stepwise explanation in the following subsections.

3.2.1. Image Augmentation

To enhance the performance of an automated classification model for CAU specie variety of image augmentation techniques were employed, including rotation (at angles 90, 180, and 270 degrees), flipping (both horizontally and vertically), zooming at differe scales, cropping to focus on specific plant parts, adding Gaussian noise for varying pi intensity and lighting condition simulation, color jitter for random adjustments in brig ness, contrast, saturation, and hue, and shearing to skew the original images and impro perspective recognition.

Through the application of these augmentation techniques, the diversity of the traini dataset was increased, leading to the improved performance of the classification mod The augmented dataset was then utilized to train the model, resulting in high accuracy a robustness in recognizing CAU species [54–56].

3.2.2. Image Segmentation

This study employed two image segmentation methods, U-Net and Mask R-CNN, segment the important features of the CAU's leaf. U-Net was chosen for leaf segmentati due to its suitability for images with limited training data, particularly in medical ima analysis [57,58]. The U-Net architecture consists of an encoder network and a decod network connected by a bottleneck layer. The encoder network captures contextual i formation, while the decoder network generates the segmentation mask. U-Net has bee successful in various image segmentation tasks, including the segmentation of organs, t mors, and blood vessels in medical imaging, and other segmentation tasks such as satelli and microscopy image segmentation. The success of U-Net is attributed to several factor including the use of skip connections that recover spatial information, its relative lig weight and efficiency, and its adaptability to different segmentation tasks and datasets.

Mask R-CNN is a state-of-the-art deep learning algorithm that performs object de tection and instance segmentation simultaneously. It extends Faster R-CNN by adding parallel branch for predicting segmentation masks. Mask R-CNN outputs a set of boundin boxes, class labels, and segmentation masks to precisely segment objects at the pixel leve A small convolutional neural network produces the mask for each region proposal ger erated by the object detection branch [59,60]. Mask R-CNN's versatility and effectivenes make it useful in various computer vision applications, such as autonomous vehicle medical image analysis, and robotics, as it performs both object detection and instanc segmentation simultaneously.

The segmentation of images of the CAU's leaf will be conducted through the utiliza tion of two distinct methodologies: U-Net and Mask-R-CNN. Subsequently, the outcome derived from these two approaches will be amalgamated to yield a unified solution, em ploying an Artificial Multiple Intelligence System (AMIS). The framework depicting the ensemble segmentation is visually depicted in Figure 3.

The proposed approach involves the integration of two diverse image segmentation methods, namely, U-Net and Mask-R-CNN, to form a unified solution. This fusion will be achieved through the optimization of weights assigned to the outcomes obtained from U-Net and Mask-R-CNN networks.

$$Z = \sum_{i=1}^{I} W_i Y_i \quad (1)$$

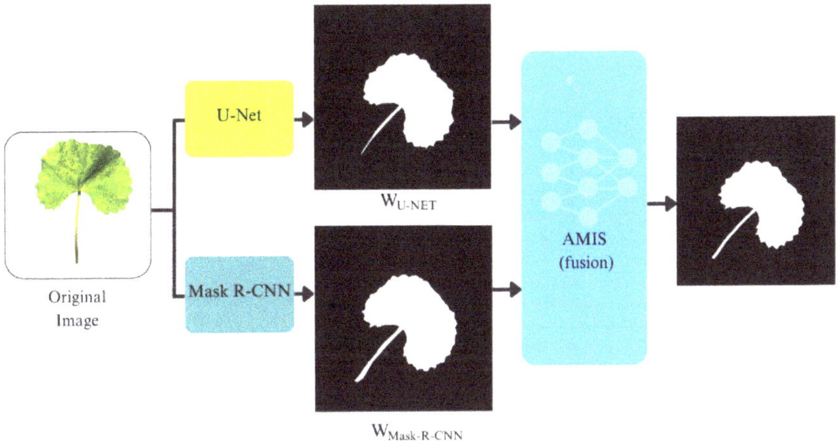

Figure 3. AMIS-ensemble segmentation.

The segmentation solution is formulated through the utilization of Equation (1), where Y_i represents the outcome derived from segmentation method I, W_i denotes the weight assigned to each method obtained from the AMIS, and Z represents the ultimate predictive value of the AMIS-ensemble segmentation. The AMIS algorithm will be explained in Section 3.2.4.

3.2.3. Ensemble the CNN Models

To establish an Automated Classification model for CAU species based on a convolutional neural network (CNN) architecture, it is imperative to choose a suitable model that encompasses precision and efficiency. In this investigation, we explore a series of compact yet impactful CNN architectures as candidates for this purpose.

We elaborate on our innovative ensemble Convolutional Neural Network (CNN) model, specifically engineered for the classification of the Centella Asiatica Urban (CAU) cultivar. A key aspect of this model is its adherence to a strict size constraint, remaining under 80 MB to facilitate deployment in fast-response environments. This is achieved through the integration of a series of lightweight yet proficient CNN architectures within an ensemble framework.

The ensemble configuration encompasses an ensemble of nine distinct neural network architectures, comprising four instances of SqueezeNet models, each approximately 5 MB in size, three ShuffleNetv2 1.0x models, with an individual model size of approximately 6 MB, one Inception v1 model, occupying an approximate space of 20 MB, and three MobileNetV3 models, each weighing approximately 6 MB. In aggregate, the ensemble model consumes a total storage space of 77 MB. The selection of these models was grounded in their efficiency and capacity to conduct a nuanced analysis of the input data, which, in the context of our research, encompasses diverse imagery of CAU cultivars. For more comprehensive details regarding these architectural choices, refer to references [61–64].

Central to our ensemble model is the application of an Artificial Multiple Intelligence System (AMIS) in the decision fusion layer. This innovative strategy leverages the strengths of each model in the ensemble, utilizing AMIS to intelligently integrate their individual predictions. The AMIS approach in the decision fusion layer assesses the outputs from the SqueezeNet, ShuffleNetv2, Inception v1, and MobileNetV3 models, considering each model's confidence and accuracy to formulate a final classification decision.

The diagram (Figure 4) depicts this ensemble architecture, illustrating the individual data processing paths of the CNN models and their convergence at the AMIS-based decision fusion layer. This layer is the linchpin of our ensemble model, where the combined intelligence and analytical power of the individual models are synthesized to achieve optimal balance between accuracy and computational efficiency.

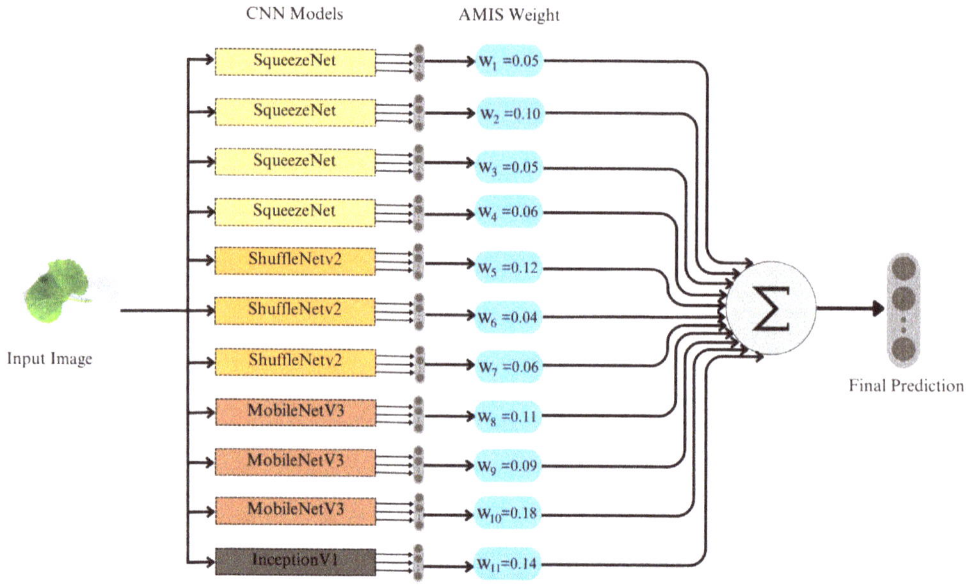

Figure 4. Proposed ensemble architecture.

Through the AMIS in the decision fusion layer, our ensemble model not only ensures a comprehensive and nuanced analysis of CAU cultivars but also maintains the agility and responsiveness essential for real-time classification applications. This unique integration of multiple CNN architectures with the AMIS-driven decision fusion represents a significant advancement in agricultural species classification, particularly in environments where the speed and model size are critical constraints.

This refined approach to decision fusion within our ensemble model exemplifies the practical application of advanced AI techniques in agricultural settings. It marks a significant step forward in addressing the challenges of accurate CAU cultivar classification while adhering to the constraints of fast-response applications and model efficiency.

To test the effectiveness of the proposed model, we will compare the method with the homogenous SqueezeNet, the ShuffleNetv2 1.0x model, and MobileNetV3 and the state-of-the-art single model which has a size of 80–120 MB, ResNet-101 (102 MB) [65], Xception (88 MB) [66], NASNet-A Mobile (84 MB) [67], and MobileNetV3-Large (113 MB) [64] to be fairly compared to the proposed model. Details of the proposed and compared methods are shown in Table 2.

According to the data presented in Table 2, our proposed model will undergo a comparative analysis with diverse methodologies, encompassing both individual large models and homogeneous ensemble models, with model sizes ranging from 80 to 113 MB. To facilitate a fair comparison, all methods will be re-implemented based on the conceptual frameworks provided in the references. Subsequently, comprehensive testing of these methods will be conducted on the established dataset.

Table 2. List of the proposed method's details.

Methods	Number of CNNs	Homogenous (Ho)/Heterogenous (He)/ Single Model (Single)	Total Size
esNet-101 [65]	1	Single	102
ception [66]	1	Single	88
ASNet-A Mobile [67]	1	Single	84
obileNetV3-Large [64]	1	Single	113
queezeNet [61]	16	Homogenous	80
huffleNetv2 1.0x [62]	14	Homogenous	84
obileNetV3 [64]	14	Homogenous	84
nceptionV1 [63]	4	Homogenous	80
roposed Methods	11	Heterogenous	77

3.2.4. Parallel-AMIS-Ensemble Model (P-AMIS-E)

AMIS decision fusion strategies will be used in two parts of the proposed model parallelly. Figure 5 demonstrates the parallel-AMIS-ensemble model used in this study.

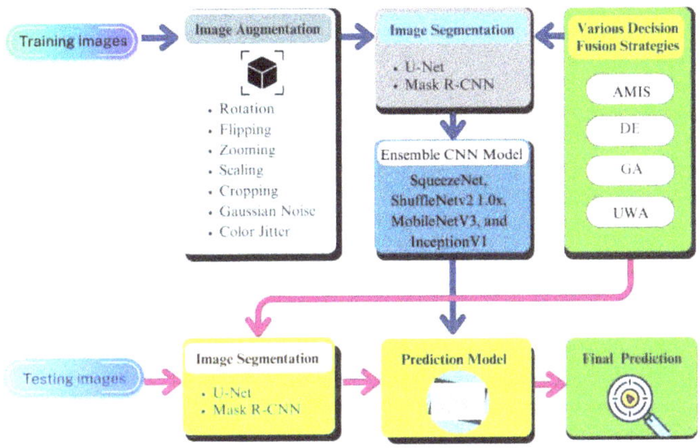

Figure 5. Framework of P-AMIS-E.

Figure 5 demonstrates the synergistic application of U-Net and Mask R-CNN for the segmentation of Centella Asiatica Urban (CAU) leaf imagery. U-Net's encoder–decoder architecture is particularly adept at processing images with sparse data, a scenario prevalent in medical image analysis. Characterized by skip connections, U-Net's design adeptly recovers spatial information, thereby augmenting its efficiency and versatility across a spectrum of segmentation tasks. Complementing U-Net, Mask R-CNN, an advanced iteration of Faster R-CNN, incorporates a parallel branch dedicated to predicting segmentation masks alongside object detection. This results in meticulously detailed pixel-level segmentation, encompassing bounding boxes, class labels, and masks, all produced by a succinct convolutional network. Mask R-CNN's bifunctional capability renders it a highly adaptable tool in a variety of contexts, including autonomous vehicles, medical imaging, and robotics.

The fusion of U-Net and Mask R-CNN, as depicted in Figure 5, capitalizes on the distinct strengths of each method, culminating in a comprehensive solution adept at navigating the intricacies of CAU leaf segmentation. The integration process utilizes an Artificial Multiple Intelligence System (AMIS) to merge the results from both segmentation techniques, thereby significantly enhancing the precision of cultivar classification.

In the P-AMIS-E model, the journey begins with the initial image, intended to discern various CAU cultivars. This image is subjected to dual segmentation techniques—U-Net and Mask-R-CNN—whose outputs are subsequently unified within the AMIS ensemble framework. Following segmentation, geometric image augmentation is applied, prep ing the segmented images for analysis by four distinct CNN architectures: SqueezeN ShuffleNetv2 1.0x, MobileNetV3, and InceptionV1.

Each CNN architecture contributes a unique perspective, yielding four separate p dictions in every iteration. The P-AMIS-E model synthesizes these individual insights i a singular, cohesive prediction using the AMIS framework. Thus, the Parallel-Artific Multiple-Intelligence System-Ensemble (P-AMIS-E) model emerges as the culmination this intricate and multifaceted approach, standing as a testament to the power of integra artificial intelligence in the realm of plant cultivar classification.

The AMIS framework consists of four key stages, namely, (1) the generation of init work packages (WP), (2) the selection of the intelligences box (IB) by the WP, (3) t performance of the improvement procedure utilizing the selected IB, (4) updating heurist information, and (5) the iterative repetition of steps (2) to (4) until the termination conditio are satisfied.

In our investigation, we have adopted a customized adaptation of the Artificial Mu ple Intelligence Systems (AMIS) as the favored technique for decision fusion, effective employed in both image segmentation and the integration of Convolutional Neural N work (CNN) architectures. The conceptual foundation of AMIS was originally put forth Pitakaso et al. [8]. This study builds upon the AMIS model proposed by the aforemention author, which was designed to optimize the transborder agricultural production logis network in the north-eastern region of Thailand.

The AMIS framework consists of a coherent sequence of five steps, encompassing the generation of the initial set of work packages (WPs), (2) the selection of the preferr intelligent box (IB) by the WPs, (3) the implementation of the improvement method by th WPs using the selected IB, (4) the updating of heuristics information, and (5) the iterati execution of steps (2) through (4) until the predefined termination conditions are met.

The utilization of AMIS shall be applied to ascertain the most favorable weightir scheme for amalgamating dissimilar solution types acquired from a variety of segmentatio methods and architectures. This specific approach will be juxtaposed with alternati decision fusion strategies—notably, the unweighted average model (UWM), along wi the adapted differential evolution algorithm (DE) proposed by Kabanikhin [68], and th modified Genetic algorithm (GA) proposed by S. Yang & Collings [69]. By employin this comparative analysis, we aim to discern the efficacy and superiority of AMIS i enhancing the fusion of diverse solutions, thereby contributing to advancements in th field of segmentation methodologies and architectural integration.

The unweighted average model (UWA) is characterized by its equitable distribution c weight across each prediction value (Y_{ij}), where 'i' denotes the CNN label and 'j' indicate the prediction class, a representation applicable to segmented image classes, denoted by or 1. The fusion process of the UWA is governed by Equation (2), while AMIS, DE, and G employ Equation (3) to compute the final weight. Here, Y_{ij} signifies the predicted value c CNN 'i' for class 'j' prior to the application of both equations.

Subsequently, upon merging multiple CNN results, V_j is utilized to categorize clas 'j', with each CNN 'i' assigned a weight (W_i) based on the total number of CNNs o segmentation methods (I) and the number of classes (J). This methodology ensures comprehensive and systematic approach to determining the final weights and achieving a effective fusion of diverse CNN outputs, thereby contributing to the enhanced classificatio performance and segmentation results in our study.

$$V_j = \frac{\sum_{i=1}^{I} Y_{ij}}{I} \quad (2)$$

$$V_j = \sum_{i=1}^{I} W_i Y_{ij} \quad (3)$$

In this investigation, AMIS, DE, and GA were employed to ascertain the optima value of W_i in the given scenario. The unweighted average decision fusion strategy (UWA presents a straightforward and computationally efficient approach for integrating ensemble deep learning models. UWA distributes equal weights to each CNN, which facilitates the ease of implementation and interpretation. However, UWA's limitation lies in its lack of optimization capabilities, impeding its ability to finely tune the ensemble performance.

On the other hand, Differential Evolution (DE) exhibits robust global search capabilities, rendering it suitable for addressing intricate optimization problems, particularly those characterized by noisy landscapes. DE adapts adeptly to multimodal search spaces; nevertheless, it may converge at a slower pace and necessitate greater memory resources due to its population-based approach.

In contrast, the Genetic Algorithm (GA) strikes a harmonious balance between exploration and exploitation, enabling faster convergence. Nonetheless, GA's performance may be sensitive to parameter settings, and it may encounter challenges in highly complex landscapes. Each of these methods, with their unique strengths and limitations, contributes to the diversification of decision fusion approaches, offering valuable insights into optimizing ensemble performance for deep learning models. AMIS can be explained stepwise as follows.

Generate the Initial Work Package

In this section, we undertake the generation of WPs at random, where each WP is characterized by dimensions of 1 × D, with 'D' representing the number of image segmentation methods or the CNN architectures under consideration. To initiate this process, we employ a real number for the first track, uniformly and randomly generated within the interval of 0 and 1, as governed by Equation (4).

$$X_{ki1} = U(0,1) \tag{4}$$

Within this context, the notation X_{ki1} pertains to the specific value within WP 'k' at element 'i' during the first iteration. Here, 'i' denotes the count of available CNN/segmented methods, while 'k' signifies the predetermined number of WPs. Moreover, alongside the primary set of WPs, two supplementary sets, denoted as the best work package (BWP) and random work package (RWP), were also stochastically generated during the initial iteration.

$$BWP_{ki1} = U(0,1) \tag{5}$$

$$RWP_{ki1} = U(0,1) \tag{6}$$

Within the provided context, BWP_{kit} denotes the set comprising the best solutions acquired from the initial iteration up to iteration 't', whereas RWP_{kit} is a randomly selected set determined by a specific formula. During the inaugural iteration, both BWP_{kit} and RWP_{kit} were generated randomly utilizing Equations (5) and (6), respectively. Subsequently, Equation (7) was employed to update X_{kit}, whereby the value of X_{kit} in iteration 't + 1' is derived from the value of X_{kit} in iteration 't', employing a selected Improvement Box (IB) operator. For instance, an illustrative track with D = 5 is as follows: {0.11, 0.28, 0.19, 0.94, 0.75}. This WP's value will undergo recalculation to obtain the value of W_i, entailing further steps in the iterative process.

$$P_{ki} = \frac{X_{ki}}{\sum_{i=1}^{i} X_{ki}} \tag{7}$$

Equation (8) has been adapted to address the variability arising from the presence of 'k' number of WPs. To this end, C_{kj} is employed for classifying class 'j' based on WP 'k', while P_{ki} represents the weight associated with the CNN/segmentation method 'i' utilizing values from WP 'k'.

$$C_{kj} = \sum_{i=1}^{I} P_{ki} Y_{ij} \tag{8}$$

Perform WP Improvement Procedures

The work packages (WPs) undergo iterative execution, wherein the enhancement solutions is achieved through the application of intelligence boxes (IBs). In this study, v adopt a selection of IBs, specifically differential evolution (DE)-inspired variants, name DEI-I, DEI-II, and DEI-III, along with additional methods, such as random crossover (RC single-bit mutation inspired (SMI), SWAP, restart (RT), and scaling factors (SF). Each these methods is incorporated using formulaic expressions, as provided in Equations (through (16), respectively. These IBs collectively contribute to the systematic improveme of solutions, thereby enhancing the efficacy of our approach in the research domain.

$$X_{kit} = X_{r1it-1} + F1(X_{r2it-1} - X_{r3it-1}) \quad ($$

$$X_{kit} = X_{r1it-1} + F1(X_{r2it-1} - X_{r3it-1}) + F2(X_{r4it-1} - X_{r5it-1}) \quad (1$$

$$X_{kit} = X_{r1it-1} + F1\left(B_i^{gbest} - X_{rit-1}\right) + F2(X_{r2it-1} - X_{r3it-1}) \quad (1$$

$$X_{kit} = \begin{cases} X_{kit-1} & if\ R_{ki} \leq CR \\ R_{kit-1} & otherwise \end{cases} \quad (1$$

$$X_{kit} = \begin{cases} X_{kit-1} & if\ R_{ki} \leq CR \\ X_{r1it-1} & otherwise \end{cases} \quad (1$$

$$X_{kit} = B_i^{gbest} + F1(X_{r1it-1} - X_{rit-1}) + F2(X_{r2it-1} - X_{r3it-1}) \quad (14$$

$$X_{kit} = R_{ki} \quad (15$$

$$X_{kit} = \begin{cases} X_{kit-1} & if\ R_{ki} \leq CR \\ R_{ki}X_{kit-1} & otherwise \end{cases} \quad (16$$

The set of randomly selected work packages, denoted as r1, r2, r3, r4, and r5, excludes work package 'k'. Furthermore, R_{kit} represents a randomly generated numbe corresponding to work package 'k' at position 'i' during iteration 'k', and R_{ki} denotes random number corresponding to work package 'k' at position 'i'. The crossover rate (CR is set to 0.7, determining the frequency of crossover operations during the simulation.

The notation B_i^{gbest} designates the best work package found thus far in the simulation These defined parameters and notations play pivotal roles in facilitating the comprehensive exploration and optimization of work packages during the simulation process.

In the process of IB selection, each WP has the liberty to choose an IB in the curren iteration, without being bound by the IB chosen in the last or prior iterations. However, the likelihood of selecting each IB may vary, being either reduced or increased based on the quality of solutions generated using that particular IB. The probability function governing the selection of IB 'b' in iteration 't' is described by Equation (17). Within this equation when the parameter 'F' is assigned a value of 0.4, 'A_{bt}' denotes the average solution quality derived from all tracks that have hitherto chosen IB 'b', iteration 't'. A_{t-1}^{best} signifies the average solution quality of tracks that have previously selected the 'best' information bit which is determined by its highest average accuracy. ρ denotes the constant number which is set to "20". Additionally, 'N_{bt-1}' represents the count of tracks that have selected IB 'p up to the current iteration. The parameter 'I_{bt-1}' increases by 1 if IB 'b' contains the best work package, 'B_i^{gbest}', otherwise it remains unchanged. The constant parameter 'K' has been set to 30, and Q is defined as the constant number which is set to 100. It is noteworthy that all predefined parameters have been meticulously established through the preliminary tests conducted during the course of this research, ensuring their appropriateness for the optimization process.

$$P_{bt} = \frac{FN_{bt-1} + (1-F)A_{bt-1} + KI_{bt-1} + \rho\frac{Q}{|A_{bt-1} - A_{t-1}^{best}|}}{\sum_{b=1}^{B} FN_{bt-1} + (1-F)A_{bt-1} + KI_{bt-1} + \rho\frac{Q}{|A_{bt-1} - A_{t-1}^{best}|}} \quad (17)$$

Equation (17) serves as a probability function that guides the selection of 'IB', denoted as 'b', during iteration 't'. This equation derives from four distinct components, each drawing from historical data related to the performance of various 'IBs'. These components collectively inform the likelihood of selecting 'IB' 'b' based on its past performance.

The first component quantifies how frequently 'IB' 'b' has been chosen in previous iterations. This metric reflects the popularity of 'IB' 'b' among the selection process and implies that more frequently selected 'IBs' might have the potential to yield superior solutions. The second component in Equation (17) calculates the average value of the 'objective function' associated with 'IB' 'b'. This component provides insights into the typical performance level of 'IB' 'b'.

The third component counts the instances where 'IB' 'b' has consistently outperformed all other 'IBs' in the same iteration. This highlights 'IB' 'b's ability to consistently find the best solutions. The final component considers the difference between the average solution value of 'IB' 'b' and the 'best IB'. It introduces an additional dimension to the evaluation process.

Once these components are combined in Equation (17) to compute the probability of selecting 'IB' 'b', a roulette wheel selection method will be employed for the subsequent step. This roulette wheel selection ensures that 'WP' (Worker Package) selects 'IB' based on their respective probabilities. Higher probabilities will correspond to a greater chance of selection, favoring 'IBs' that have consistently demonstrated superior performance in comparison to others. In summary, Equation (17) and the roulette wheel selection method work in tandem to choose the most promising 'IB' based on their historical performance, fostering a dynamic and adaptive selection process.

In each iteration, it is imperative to update the values of several parameters in response to the prevailing conditions. These essential factors encompass R_{ki}, R_{kit}, N_{bt}, A_{bt}, B_i^{gbest}, and I_{bt-1}. Subsequently, the selection of IB, the performance on the selected IB, and the updating of the probability of the IB are executed iteratively until a specified termination condition is satisfied, such as a predetermined computational time limit or a prescribed number of iterations. This iterative process ensures the progressive refinement and convergence of the algorithm, ultimately leading to the attainment of reliable and optimized results within the specified constraints.

3.3. *Performance Measurement Matric and the Comparison Methods*

Performance metrics play a pivotal role in assessing the efficacy of deep learning models, providing valuable insights into their performance on specific tasks and guiding informed decisions for researchers and practitioners. Notably, accuracy stands as a fundamental metric, measuring the proportion of correctly classified instances relative to the total dataset size and offering an overarching measure of correctness. In Section 3.2.4, we will undertake a comprehensive performance evaluation, comparing the efficacy of all individual models and homogeneous ensemble models. Additionally, we will implement the Vision Transformer (ViT) approach, as presented by [70], to provide a benchmark for assessing the performance of our proposed model.

In parallel, precision endeavors to minimize false positives by gauging the ratio of true positive predictions to the total predicted positive instances. Conversely, the recall, synonymous with sensitivity or the true positive rate, proves indispensable when reducing false negatives, capturing the ratio of true positive predictions to the total actual positive instances. The contribution to model evaluation includes the F1-score, which effectively balances precision and recall, especially when handling imbalanced class distributi The calculations for the accuracy, precision, recall, and F1 score can be calculated us Equations (18)–(21).

$$Accuracy = \frac{n_{TP} + n_{TN}}{n_{TP} + n_{PN} + n_{FP} + n_{FN}} \quad ($$

$$Precision = \frac{n_{TP}}{n_{TP} + n_{FP}} \quad ($$

$$Recall = \frac{n_{TP}}{n_{TP} + n_{FN}} \quad ($$

$$\text{F1} - \text{score} = \frac{2n_{TP}}{2n_{TP} + n_{FP} + n_{FN}} \quad (:$$

where n_{TP} is the number of true positives, n_{TN} is the number of true negatives, n_{FP} is t number of false positives, and n_{FN} is the number of false negatives.

In addition to accuracy, the area under the receiver operating characteristic (RO curve (AUC) is a crucial performance metric, especially for binary classification tas The ROC curve illustrates the trade-off between the true positive rate and false positi rate, with the AUC representing the area under this curve. Higher AUC values in cate a superior model performance, making it a valuable tool for comparing differe models. These metrics together provide a comprehensive understanding of the strengt and weaknesses of the deep learning model, which is essential for model selection aı optimization. The function used to calculate 'AUC' in our experiment can be fouı at 'https://scikit-learn.org/stable/modules/geneated/sklearn.merics.roc_auc_score.htr Accepted date (15 January 2024).

This study sets forth to explore the efficacy of two decision fusion strategies: th "unweighted average" (UWA) approach, which uniformly amalgamates individual cla sifier outputs [52], and a tailored artificial multiple intelligence system (AMIS) [8]. AM incorporates the differential evolution algorithm (DE) [51], and genetic algorithm (GA) [5 to optimize the weights assigned to each classifier, seeking to enhance the performance the ensemble classifier.

In summary, the proposed method can be condensed into algorithmic form, as depicte in Algorithm 1.

Algorithm 1: Construction of the Parallel-Artificial Multiple Intelligence System-Ensemble Deep Learning model (P-AMIS-E)

Input: Image training set, list the number of each type of CNN architecture.

Step (1) Generate new images with data augmentation on the training set, including the method: rotation, flipping, zooming, cropping,
Gaussian noise, shearing lighting simulation, brightness, contrast, saturation, and hue.

Step (2) Construct the AMIS-ensemble segmentation.

- Training U-Net and Mask-R-CNN networks.
- Optimize U-net and Mask-R-CNN weights using AMIS in Algorithm 1, whose objective is to minimize segmentation loss.

Step (3) Segment images in Step (1) using AMIS-ensemble segmentation in Step (2).

Step (4) Construct and train each CNN in the list, and number each type of CNN architecture with a segmented image set in Step (3).

Step (5) Construct the AMIS-ensemble CNN.

- Predict the CNN output $\left(Y_{kj}\right)$, with the CNN index k and class j, of all CNNs in Step (4) from the input segmented image set in Step (3).
- Optimize CNN weights using AMIS, whose objective is to maximize the accuracy rate on the prediction output Y_{kj} of all CNNs.

Output: AMIS-ensemble CNN with an optimal weight.

The analysis will utilize Gradient-weighted Class Activation Mapping (Grad-CAM) to elucidate the decision-making process of the AI across different classes within the classification model. Grad-CAM, a technique enhancing the transparency of convolutional neural network-based models, achieves this by visualizing essential input regions for predicting specific classes. The method employs gradients originating from the target concept, like a classification class, within the final convolutional layer to create a coarse localization map that highlights significant image areas for concept prediction. Regarding the computation of neuron importance weights α_k^c, we define $f_k(x, y)$ as the activation of unit '*k*' in the last convolutional layer at spatial location (x, y). We calculate the gradient of the score for class '*c*' (prior to softmax), denoted as y^c, with respect to these features f_k. The gradient undergoes global-average pooling over width and height dimensions (indexed by x and y) to obtain α_k^c, as determined by Equation (22).

$$\alpha_k^c = \frac{1}{Z}\sum_x \sum_y \frac{\partial y^c}{\partial f_k(x, y)} \quad (22)$$

Let Z denote the number of pixels in the feature map and $\frac{\partial y^c}{\partial f_k(x,y)}$ represent the gradient. Concerning the Grad-CAM heatmap $L_{Grad-CAM}^c$, it is derived as a weighted summation of feature maps, subsequently subjected to a ReLU activation, as outlined in Equation (23). The incorporation of ReLU activation ensures the visualization of features that positively impact the class of interest while disregarding negative contributions.

$$L_{Grad-CAM}^c = ReLU\left(\sum_k \alpha_k^c f_k\right) \quad (23)$$

Visualization involves normalizing the heatmap $L_{Grad-CAM}^c$, which is subsequently superimposed onto the input image. This visualization approach reveals the crucial regions within the input image that are instrumental in predicting class '*c*'. The utilization of Grad-CAM enables the acquisition of a visual elucidation for the convolutional neural network's decision-making process, emphasizing the distinctive image areas employed by the model in class identification.

4. Computational Result

In this investigation, two distinct computing resources were harnessed to facilitate the development and testing of our algorithm. During the training phase, we availed the computational capabilities of Google Collaboratory, which granted access to an NVIDIA Tesla V100 boasting 16 GB of RAM and commensurate specifications. This arrangement proved instrumental in training our model on a robust computing resource, well equipped to manage the taxing computational requirements inherent to our algorithm.

For the evaluation of the proposed model's performance, we conducted simulations on a separate computing system, equipped with two Intel Xeon-2.30GHz CPUs, 52 GB of RAM, and a Tesla K80 GPU with 16 GB of GPU RAM. The meticulous selection of this computing system was based on its ability to proficiently handle the computational demands entailed by our simulation process, thus affording us the opportunity to meticulously assess the model's performance. By leveraging these two distinct and high-performance computing platforms, we attained the precision and dependability required to achieve accurate and reliable outcomes throughout our study. The algorithmic and model parameter configurations are presented within Table 3 for reference.

Table 3. Model parameter configurations.

CNN Hyperparameters		Metaheuristics (GA, DE, and AMIS) Hyperparameters	
Number of CNN epochs of a single model	100	Number of populations (NWP)	100
Number of CNN epochs in an ensemble	30	Number of iterations (G)	100
CNN optimizer	Adam	Crossover rate of DE and AMIS (CR)	0.3
Learning rate	0.0001	Mutation rate of DE	0.07
Batch size	32	First Scaling Factor of DE (F) and AMIS (F_1)	1.67
Image size	331 × 331	Second Scaling Factor of AMIS (F_2)	1.2

The experimentation phase was partitioned into three distinct groups, with the experimental framework visually depicted in Figure 6. In the initial group, various combinations of the proposed methods were rigorously tested to ascertain the optimal performing combination. Subsequently, the second group undertook a comprehensive evaluation of our proposed method, in contrast to state-of-the-art approaches, utilizing the best combination of methods identified in the initial group while focusing on the CALU-1 dataset.

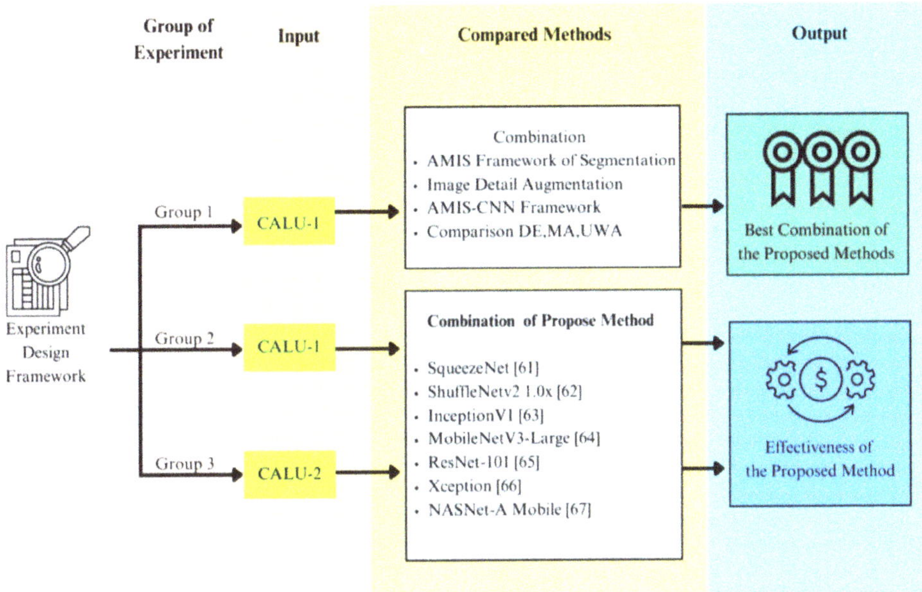

Figure 6. Experimental design framework.

To gauge the efficacy and generalizability of the proposed method, the third group assessed its performance on an unseen dataset, CALU-2. This methodological division allowed for a systematic and meticulous evaluation of the proposed approach while also facilitating a rigorous comparison with existing state-of-the-art methods.

The illustrative framework depicted in Figure 6 served as a clear roadmap for guiding the experiment's progression, enabling the achievement of reliable and reproducible results. By adopting this well-structured experimental design, we could confidently examine the efficacy of our proposed method and draw meaningful comparisons with the existing state-of-the-art techniques.

4.1. Unveiling the Optimal Combination of Diverse Model Configurations

As delineated in our research methodology, we leveraged two distinct image segmentation methods—specifically, the Mask R-CNN and U-Net methods, along with an ensemble of these two methods, achieved through four decision fusion strategies: the unweighted average (UWA), differential evolution algorithm (DE), genetic algorithm (GA), and modified artificial multiple intelligence system (AMIS). Additionally, we incorporated one type of image augmentation method into the experimentation. Consequently, the entire experimentation encompassed a total of 32 distinct experimental configurations, meticulously summarized in Table 4.

Table 4. The design of an experiment to reveal the best combination of the model's elements.

No.	Segmentation				Augmentation		Decision Fusion Strategies			
	No Segmentation	Mask R-CNN	U-Net	Ensemble Segmentation	No Augmentation	With Augmentation	AMIS	DE	GA	UW
1	✓	-	-	-	✓	-	✓	-	-	-
2	✓	-	-	-	✓	-	-	✓	-	-
3	✓	-	-	-	✓	-	-	-	✓	
4	✓	-	-	-	✓	-	-	-	-	✓
5	✓	-	-	-	-	✓	✓	-	-	-
6	✓	-	-	-	-	✓	-	✓	-	-
7	✓	-	-	-	-	✓	-	-	✓	-
8	✓	-	-	-	-	✓	-	-	-	✓
9	-	✓	-	-	✓	-	✓	-	-	-
10	-	✓	-	-	✓	-	-	✓	-	-
11	-	✓	-	-	✓	-	-	-	✓	-
12	-	✓	-	-	✓	-	-	-	-	✓
13	-	✓	-	-	-	✓	✓	-	-	-
14	-	✓	-	-	-	✓	-	✓	-	-
15	-	✓	-	-	-	✓	-	-	✓	-
16	-	✓	-	-	-	✓	-	-	-	✓
17	-	-	✓	-	✓	-	✓	-	-	-
18	-	-	✓	-	✓	-	-	✓	-	-
19	-	-	✓	-	✓	-	-	-	✓	-
20	-	-	✓	-	✓	-	-	-	-	✓
21	-	-	✓	-	-	✓	✓	-	-	-
22	-	-	✓	-	-	✓	-	✓	-	-
23	-	-	✓	-	-	✓	-	-	✓	
24	-	-	✓	-	-	✓	-	-	-	✓
25	-	-	-	✓	✓	-	✓	-	-	-
26	-	-	-	✓	✓	-	-	✓	-	-
27	-	-	-	✓	✓	-	-	-	✓	-
28	-	-	-	✓	✓	-	-	-	-	✓
29	-	-	-	✓	-	✓	✓	-	-	-
30	-	-	-	✓	-	✓	-	✓	-	-
31	-	-	-	✓	-	✓	-	-	✓	-
32	-	-	-	✓	-	✓	-	-	-	✓

Then, we use CALU-1 to test the effectiveness of the proposed model and reveal th best combination of the various elements of the proposed model; the computational resu is shown in Table 5. When comparing different methods of classification, it is essenti to carefully select performance measures that align with the goals and requirements o the study. While the choice of performance measures may vary depending on the specifi application, several commonly used measures are available for evaluating the classificatio performance. These measures include the accuracy, precision, recall, F1 score, and RO curve and AUC. Accuracy represents the proportion of correctly classified instances, whil precision measures the proportion of true positives among all positive predictions. Recal on the other hand, represents the proportion of true positives among all actual positiv instances. The F1 score combines precision and recall into a single measure that provide a balanced evaluation of both metrics. Finally, the ROC curve and AUC are measures o the trade-off between the true positive rate and false positive rate at various threshold The result of 12 experiments is shown in Table 5, and the conclusion of the benefit of usin different elements of the proposed method is shown in Table 6.

The findings from our experimental study, as presented in Table 6, reveal that th ensemble segmentation method, incorporating both Mask R-CNN and U-Net, demonstrate a notably higher accuracy compared to models that omit segmentation. The improvemen in accuracy is by an average of 13.69% and 10.98% when compared to models employin Mask R-CNN and U-Net individually, respectively. Additionally, the results align with Precision, Recall, F1-Score, and AUC as evaluation metrics.

Table 5. Result of the tested run for CALU-1.

No.	Accuracy	Precision	Recall	F1-Score	AUC
1	82.14	82.40	82.40	82.81	82.15
2	82.79	81.64	81.61	81.96	80.88
3	81.75	81.33	80.35	80.21	80.43
4	79.29	79.65	79.57	79.57	79.45
5	83.25	83.42	83.70	83.69	83.22
6	84.59	83.68	83.71	84.52	84.65
7	82.16	82.17	82.35	83.68	83.23
8	80.48	80.14	80.10	80.95	80.45
9	85.88	85.25	85.97	85.48	85.82
10	83.55	83.75	83.52	83.43	83.97
11	82.51	81.56	82.73	82.73	82.76
12	83.78	80.18	83.64	83.47	82.31
13	86.14	84.40	86.40	86.81	86.15
14	84.79	84.64	84.61	84.96	84.88
15	81.75	81.33	80.35	80.21	81.43
16	82.29	81.65	81.57	98.57	81.45
17	88.25	88.42	88.70	88.69	88.22
18	85.59	85.68	85.71	85.52	85.65
19	84.16	84.17	84.35	84.68	85.23
20	83.48	83.14	83.10	83.95	83.45
21	89.88	89.25	89.97	89.48	89.82
22	87.55	87.75	87.52	87.43	87.97
23	86.51	86.56	86.73	86.73	86.76
24	84.78	84.18	84.64	84.47	84.31
25	93.14	93.40	93.40	93.81	93.15
26	90.79	90.64	90.61	90.96	90.88
27	90.35	90.33	90.35	90.21	89.43
28	88.29	88.65	88.57	88.57	88.45
29	98.54	98.57	98.71	98.83	98.95
30	96.91	96.62	96.48	96.52	96.21
31	94.16	94.17	94.35	94.68	95.15
32	92.48	92.14	92.10	92.95	92.42

Table 6. Conclusion of the benefit of using different elements of the proposed methods.

No.	Segmentation				Augmentation		Decision Fusion Strategies			
	No Segmentation	Mask R-CNN	U-Net	Ensemble	No Augmentation	With Augmentation	AMIS	DE	GA	UWA
Accuracy	82.06	83.84	86.28	93.08	85.36	87.27	88.40	87.07	85.42	84.36
Precision	81.80	82.85	86.14	93.07	85.01	86.92	88.14	86.80	85.20	83.72
Recall	81.72	83.60	86.34	93.07	85.29	87.08	88.65	86.72	85.20	84.16
F1-score	82.17	85.71	86.37	93.32	85.38	88.41	88.70	86.91	85.39	86.56
AUC	81.81	83.60	86.43	93.08	85.14	87.32	88.44	86.89	85.55	84.04

Furthermore, the computational analysis shows that models with image augmentation yield a superior quality by 2.54% compared to those without it. Among the decision fusion strategies utilized, AMIS stands out with a higher quality, outperforming DE, GA, and UWA by average margins of 1.83%, 3.65%, and 4.62%, respectively.

As a result, the most optimal combination of models comprises ensemble segmentation, image augmentation, and the adoption of AMIS as the decision fusion strategy. This model will serve as the benchmark to compare against state-of-the-art methods in the subsequent section.

4.2. A Comparative Analysis of the Proposed Model against State-of-the-Art Methods Using th CALU-1 Dataset

The experimental dataset employed in this study is denoted as CALU-1, consisti of a total of 15,525 images. The dataset was meticulously partitioned into two distir groups: 10,303 images were allocated for the training procedure, while the remaini 5222 images were earmarked for testing both the proposed models and the compar methods. To assess the performance of the models comprehensively, essential performan metrics such as the AUC, precision, accuracy, recall, and F1-score were employed. T results of this comprehensive evaluation are succinctly presented in Table 7.

Table 7. Comparative performance analysis of diverse methodologies on the CALU-1 dataset.

Methods	Accuracy	Precision	Recall	F1-Score	AUC
ViT [70]	91.32	89.19	90.48	90.85	91.52
ResNet-101 [65]	88.38	84.19	86.29	87.42	89.01
Xception [66]	89.27	88.40	89.89	88.72	90.29
NASNet-A Mobile [67]	91.63	91.83	89.74	90.21	91.96
MobileNetV3-Large [64]	92.51	92.17	90.97	91.35	91.38
SqueezeNet [61]	93.21	93.37	94.13	93.73	94.41
ShuffleNetv2 1.0x [62]	94.36	93.73	94.09	94.27	94.83
MobileNetV3 [64]	94.72	93.96	94.64	94.93	95.97
InceptionV1 [63]	95.05	94.18	94.79	95.48	95.99
Proposed Methods	98.41	97.82	97.99	99.61	98.39

Table 7 presents the comprehensive performance evaluation of various deep learnin methods on the CALU-1 dataset, utilizing five essential performance metrics: Accurac Precision, Recall, F1-score, and AUC (Area Under the Curve). Each row in the tabl corresponds to a specific deep learning architecture, while the columns represent th respective performance metric values for each method.

Among the evaluated methods are well-established architectures such as ViT, ResNe 101, Xception, NASNet-A Mobile, MobileNetV3-Large, SqueezeNet, ShuffleNetv2 1.0 MobileNetV3, and InceptionV1. Additionally, the table incorporates the results of th proposed methods, which were designed and tested during the present study.

Upon the analysis of the results, noteworthy observations emerged. First and foremos the proposed methods demonstrate superior performance across all performance metric surpassing all other architectures in the evaluation. With an accuracy of 98.41%, th proposed methods achieve an impressive level of correct classification. Moreover, thei precision of 97.82% indicates a highly effective ability to minimize false positive prediction

Further, the recall rate of 97.99% highlights the proposed methods' proficiency in cap turing actual positive instances accurately. The proposed methods also achieve a remarkabl F1-score of 99.61%, signifying an exceptional balance between precisior and recall.

Finally, the proposed methods exhibit an outstanding AUC value of 98.39%, showcas ing their excellent discriminative power and overall performance in comparison to other state-of-the-art methods. These results robustly validate the efficacy and superiority of the proposed methods for image segmentation tasks on the CALU-1 dataset, emphasizing their significance in advancing the field of deep learning and image analysis.

4.3. Comparative Analysis of the Proposed Model against State-of-the-Art Methods Using the Unseen CALU-2 Dataset

All proposed methods have been tested with CALU-2, which is the unseen dataset that has 5308 images. The result of the experiment is shown in Table 8.

Table 8. Result of the classification model using CALU-2.

Methods	Number of CNNs	Homogenous (Ho)/Heterogenous (He)/ Single Model (Single)	Total Size	Training Time (Minutes)	Testing Time (Second/ Image)	Accuracy	Precision	Recall	F1-Score	AUC
T [70]	1	Single		-	-	90.24	89.53	88.48	89.01	90.45
sNet-101 [65]	1	Single	102	62.48	0.83	88.7	84.6	85.8	87.9	89.5
eption [66]	1	Single	88	47.59	0.48	90.1	88.1	90.7	88.8	89.7
ASNet-A Mobile [67]	1	Single	84	45.32	0.49	92.6	92.1	89.8	89.7	91.8
obileNetV3-Large [64]	1	Single	113	67.55	1.34	92.6	92.6	90.8	91.4	91.7
ueezeNet [61]	1	Single	5	5.44	0.10	76.2	75.9	75.5	75.8	76.9
uffleNetv2 1.0x [62]	1	Single	6	5.98	0.12	76.8	76.8	76.2	77.1	77.3
obileNetV3 [64]	1	Single	6	6.01	0.13	75.1	74.8	75.6	74.9	75.6
ceptionV1 [63]	1	Single	20	15.7	0.20	79.4	78.9	79.2	79.1	79.8
ueezeNet [61]	16	Homogenous	80	39.03	0.44	92.8	93.6	94.1	93.5	93.9
uffleNetv2 1.0x [62]	14	Homogenous	84	44.19	0.48	94.2	93.9	94.1	94.6	94.8
obileNetV3 [64]	14	Homogenous	84	43.95	0.47	94.1	94.7	95.3	95.3	95.5
ceptionV1 [63]	4	Homogenous	80	37.58	0.44	94.3	94.8	95.5	95.6	95.7
oposed Methods	11	Heterogenous	77	34.59	0.34	98.5	97.5	97.4	99.0	97.7

Table 8 provides a comprehensive comparison of various deep learning models, evaluating their performance metrics on the CALU-2 dataset. These models fall into three categories: single models, homogeneous ensembles, and our proposed heterogeneous ensemble.

Starting with the single models, ViT, ResNet-101, Xception, NASNet-A Mobile, and MobileNetV3-Large are notable for their substantial sizes, ranging from 84 MB to 113 MB. They exhibit commendable accuracy, scoring between 88.7% and 92.6%. However, their training times are significantly high, particularly ResNet-101, which takes 62.48 min. The testing time per image varies from 0.48 to 1.34 s, with Mo-bileNetV3-Large being the fastest. While these single models offer respectable accuracy, their size and extensive training times may constrain their applicability.

Turning to SqueezeNet, ShuffleNetv2 1.0x, MobileNetV3, and InceptionV1, we encounter a diverse set of single models, characterized by their relatively lightweight sizes (ranging from 5 MB to 20 MB). These models, despite their compactness, achieve competitive accuracy scores, all surpassing the 75% mark. Notably, they present trade-offs between accuracy and computational efficiency. For instance, SqueezeNet delivers 76.2% accuracy, alongside a remarkably brief 5.44 min of training time and a swift 0.10 s of testing per image. In contrast, InceptionV1 achieves the highest single-model accuracy at 79.4%. However, it necessitates a longer training period (15.7 min) and 0.20 s for image testing. These single models cater to various application requirements, allowing users to choose the optimal trade-off between accuracy and computational resources.

Transitioning to the homogeneous ensemble models, which include SqueezeNet, ShuffleNetv2 1.0x, MobileNetV3, and InceptionV1, we notice their unification of models of the same type. These homogeneous ensembles collectively achieve remarkable accuracy, averaging around 94%. This accuracy surge represents a significant improvement over their individual single models, highlighting the advantages of ensemble learning. However, this gain in accuracy coincides with lengthier training periods, ranging from 37.58 to 44.19 min—substantially longer than those of single models. Nevertheless, the testing times remain relatively efficient, ranging from 0.44 to 0.48 s per image. These homogeneous ensembles excel in scenarios prioritizing maximum accuracy, even at the expense of increased training times.

In contrast, our proposed heterogeneous ensemble method, which amalgamates diverse models, including SqueezeNet, ShuffleNetv2 1.0x, MobileNetV3, and InceptionV1, emerges with an outstanding accuracy of 98.5%. Notably, this remarkable accuracy is attained with significantly shorter training durations, as low as 34.59 min, alongside efficient testing times of 0.34 s per image. This underscores the potency of leveraging diverse model architectures within ensemble learning. The proposed heterogeneous ensemble not only outperforms homogeneous ensembles in terms of accuracy but also maintains efficiency in both training and testing.

In summary, our proposed heterogeneous ensemble method excels in terms of accur and computational efficiency when compared to both single models and homogene ensembles. This underscores the advantage of harnessing diverse model architectu to achieve exceptional accuracy while optimizing computational resources, making compelling approach for image classification tasks, such as CAU cultivar classification

To conduct a thorough analysis of 'explainable AI', we will utilize Figure 7a,b a Figure 8 to showcase the confusion matrix and the Heatmap GradCAM for both the CA 1 and CALU-2 datasets. This approach aims to provide insights into the decision-mak processes of artificial intelligence.

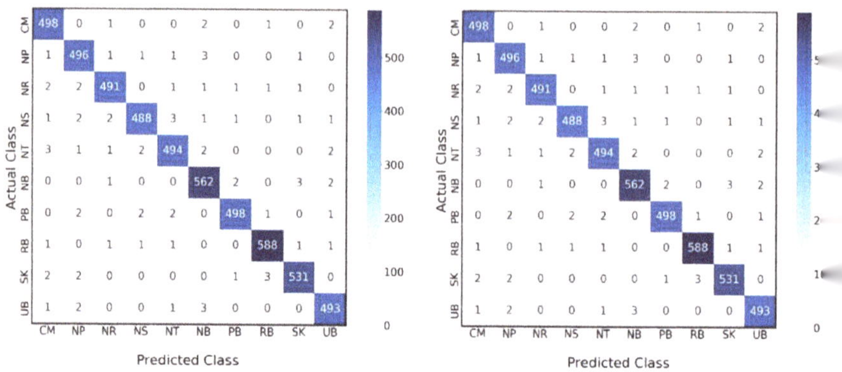

(a) (b)

Figure 7. Confusion matrices for the classification of agricultural cultivars across various regions Thailand using the models CALU-1 (**a**) and CALU-2 (**b**). The horizontal axis represents the predict classifications, and the vertical axis represents the actual classifications, with the regions denoted t the following abbreviations: CM (Chiang Mai), NP (Nakhon Pathom), NR (Nakhon Ratchasima), N (Nakhon Si Thammarat), NT (Narathiwat), NB (Nonthaburi), PB (Prachin Buri), RB (Ratchaburi), S (Songkhla), and UB (Ubon Ratchathani). The number within each cell reflects the count of predictio made by the respective model for each actual-predicted pair, with the main diagonal showing th number of correct predictions per region.

Figure 7 presents the confusion matrices for two distinct models, CALU-1 and CALU- applied to the classification of various regions based on their unique agricultural cult vars. The axes of each matrix represent the predicted classes (horizontal axis) and th actual classes (vertical axis) corresponding to different regions in Thailand. Each entr in the matrices denotes the number of instances that a region's cultivar, represented b its abbreviation, was predicted to be of a certain class versus its true class. The diagona cells, highlighted by the greater numbers, indicate the number of correct predictions fo each region, where the model's prediction aligns with the actual class. Off-diagonal cell represent misclassifications, where the predicted class does not match the actual class. Th regions are denoted by their initials: CM for Chiang Mai, NP for Nakhon Pathom, NR fo Nakhon Ratchasima, NS for Nakhon Si Thammarat, NT for Narathiwat, NB for Nonthabur PB for Prachin Buri, RB for Ratchaburi, SK for Songkhla, and UB for Ubon Ratchathan The matrices offer a visual and quantitative analysis of the model's performance acros different regional cultivars, with a clear emphasis on the model's accuracy and areas wher the classification performance could be improved.

Figure 8. The Heatmap GradCam of leaf classification employing the proposed model.

Figure 7a,b illustrates the confusion matrix obtained from the proposed model's classification outcomes. It is evident that the Ubon Ratchathani cultivar exhibits the highest accuracy when compared to other cultivars from CALU-1 and CALU-2. However, the Narathiwat cultivar demonstrates the highest degree of misclassification for CALU-1 and CALU-2. This can be attributed to the fact that the Narathiwat Cultivar shares leaf characteristics that closely resemble those of other cultivars such as NP, NB, and PB. Notably, the discrepancies primarily arise from subtle variations in size and certain aspects of outward appearance among these cultivars.

To elucidate the underlying reasons for the variations in accuracy across different cu vars, a meticulous analysis is warranted. In this regard, the Heatmap GradCAM techniq serves as an insightful tool for expounding upon the distinctive classification outcomes. evidenced in Figure 8, the GradCAM visualization sheds light on the discriminative regio exploited by the AI model when categorizing diverse leaf types within varying cultiva It becomes apparent that the Ubon Ratchathani cultivar is predominantly assessed bas on features situated toward the center of the leaf's surface. In contrast, the Prachin Bu cultivar places greater reliance on attributes located along the leaf's periphery. This relian on distinct regions is notably prevalent among certain cultivars where the curvature of t leaf's edge diverges, prompting a strategic shift in classification emphasis. Furthermore, t classification decision-making process is notably influenced by the leaf's size, as evidenc by the conspicuously reddened regions depicted in the heatmap. This characteristic is mc pronounced in cultivars boasting larger leaf dimensions, including CM, NP, and NR.

In the next experiment, we will test the datasets CALU-1 and CALU-2 by splitting t datasets into k-folds to validate the datasets. We will use three and five folds of the te datasets and test for the result obtained from using different groups of trained datase The results are shown in Table 9.

Table 9. K-fold validation result using three and five as the k of the datasets CALU-1 and CALU-2

	CALU-1									
	3-cv					5-cv				
Methods	Accuracy	Precision	Recall	F1-Score	AUC	Accuracy	Precision	Recall	F1-Score	AUC
ViT [70]	91.19 ± 1.57	89.01 ± 2.39	90.13 ± 0.99	91.04 ± 1.23	92.02 ± 1.61	91.32 ± 1.24	89.19 ± 1.45	90.48 ± 1.02	90.85 ± 1.24	91.52 ± 2.49
ResNet-101 [65]	81.49 ± 2.73	83.04 ± 1.96	83.73 ± 1.84	86.24 ± 2.40	88.18 ± 1.44	82.38 ± 2.18	83.99 ± 2.39	84.59 ± 2.57	86.53 ± 1.77	88.41 ± 0.85
Xception [66]	82.95 ± 1.05	86.39 ± 1.83	87.39 ± 1.68	87.19 ± 2.19	89.22 ± 1.05	82.27 ± 1.47	87.18 ± 2.31	88.45 ± 1.49	87.69 ± 1.84	89.37 ± 0.34
NASNet-A Mobile [67]	87.83 ± 1.86	89.15 ± 2.17	88.12 ± 1.06	88.05 ± 1.83	89.29 ± 1.82	88.33 ± 1.49	90.42 ± 2.09	88.38 ± 1.35	88.78 ± 1.48	89.84 ± 0.93
MobileNetV3-Large [64]	89.24 ± 1.32	90.86 ± 1.19	89.07 ± 2.51	89.48 ± 1.78	89.94 ± 1.01	90.18 ± 0.87	91.03 ± 1.56	89.42 ± 1.58	90.37 ± 1.31	90.68 ± 1.19
SqueezeNet [61]	91.49 ± 1.93	91.83 ± 1.68	91.92 ± 1.94	92.03 ± 1.51	92.38 ± 2.49	92.05 ± 1.31	92.15 ± 1.39	92.63 ± 1.61	92.59 ± 0.93	93.15 ± 1.43
ShuffleNetv2 1.0x [62]	92.84 ± 2.01	92.16 ± 1.15	92.14 ± 1.53	92.58 ± 1.58	92.75 ± 2.18	93.36 ± 2.18	92.54 ± 1.42	92.89 ± 1.14	93.18 ± 0.58	93.41 ± 0.84
MobileNetV3 [64]	93.81 ± 1.19	91.85 ± 2.12	93.08 ± 1.74	92.71 ± 1.06	94.19 ± 1.42	94.34 ± 1.34	92.09 ± 1.90	93.62 ± 0.98	93.32 ± 1.31	95.03 ± 2.44
InceptionV1 [63]	93.75 ± 1.58	93.11 ± 1.11	93.27 ± 1.85	93.72 ± 2.49	93.93 ± 1.86	94.18 ± 1.74	93.74 ± 1.35	93.88 ± 1.19	94.46 ± 1.58	95.27 ± 1.31
Proposed Methods	93.46 ± 1.04	97.20 ± 0.58	96.74 ± 0.69	97.89 ± 1.31	98.15 ± 0.47	97.47 ± 1.31	97.43 ± 1.31	97.10 ± 0.84	98.31 ± 0.74	98.83 ± 0.84

	CALU-2									
	3-cv					5-cv				
Methods	Accuracy	Precision	Recall	F1-Score	AUC	Accuracy	Precision	Recall	F1-Score	AUC
ViT [70]	89.31 ± 1.14	88.48 ± 1.95	89.11 ± 1.27	88.30 ± 1.64	89.94 ± 1.38	90.15 ± 1.65	88.94 ± 1.96	88.23 ± 1.87	89.01 ± 1.48	90.45 ± 1.76
ResNet-101 [65]	80.98 ± 1.84	82.76 ± 2.14	83.18 ± 1.73	85.78 ± 1.83	87.11 ± 1.91	82.08 ± 2.04	83.41 ± 1.58	83.81 ± 1.93	86.31 ± 1.96	87.59 ± 1.28
Xception [66]	82.47 ± 1.27	86.19 ± 1.18	87.01 ± 1.18	86.39 ± 1.91	88.35 ± 1.18	81.89 ± 1.97	86.84 ± 2.19	88.19 ± 1.01	87.54 ± 2.14	88.93 ± 1.92
NASNet-A Mobile [67]	86.81 ± 1.53	89.28 ± 2.05	87.27 ± 1.84	87.74 ± 1.19	88.38 ± 1.79	87.18 ± 1.63	90.07 ± 1.17	88.07 ± 1.28	88.18 ± 2.16	89.04 ± 0.84
MobileNetV3-Large [64]	89.07 ± 1.94	90.21 ± 1.57	88.41 ± 2.01	88.79 ± 1.28	89.15 ± 1.93	89.49 ± 1.58	90.68 ± 2.48	89.28 ± 1.84	90.25 ± 1.96	90.18 ± 1.48
SqueezeNet [61]	91.04 ± 1.18	91.43 ± 1.18	91.26 ± 1.93	91.48 ± 1.11	92.08 ± 2.00	91.79 ± 1.08	91.82 ± 0.58	92.17 ± 1.93	92.05 ± 1.15	92.76 ± 1.92
ShuffleNetv2 1.0x [62]	92.18 ± 1.85	91.78 ± 1.05	91.68 ± 1.27	92.06 ± 1.96	92.01 ± 1.84	92.85 ± 2.00	92.14 ± 1.05	92.53 ± 1.08	93.01 ± 1.39	93.06 ± 1.53
MobileNetV3 [64]	93.29 ± 1.53	91.04 ± 2.08	92.37 ± 1.86	92.51 ± 1.79	93.75 ± 1.48	94.09 ± 1.18	91.30 ± 1.88	93.08 ± 1.34	93.15 ± 1.88	95.88 ± 1.92
InceptionV1 [63]	93.18 ± 1.57	92.16 ± 1.89	92.83 ± 1.19	93.04 ± 2.04	93.41 ± 1.19	94.01 ± 1.31	93.08 ± 1.19	93.14 ± 1.83	94.19 ± 2.93	95.08 ± 2.90
Proposed Methods	93.21 ± 1.81	96.81 ± 0.85	96.06 ± 0.94	97.18 ± 1.15	97.41 ± 0.97	97.14 ± 1.04	97.11 ± 1.08	96.47 ± 0.76	98.14 ± 1.15	98.48 ± 0.63

Upon scrutinizing the performance of the "Proposed Methods" in relation to alternative methodologies across the CALU-1 and CALU-2 datasets, several salient observations come to light. Concerning accuracy, the "Proposed Methods" consistently provide competitive outcomes. In CALU-1, their achievements manifest as accuracy rates of 93.21% and 97.14% through the utilization of threefold and fivefold cross-validation paradigms, correspondingly. These figures situate the "Proposed Methods" in close juxtaposition to distinguished techniques such as "MobileNetV3" and "InceptionV1." This ability to achieve a competitive accuracy is also shown in CALU-2, thereby corroborating the robustness of the proposed approach.

Advancing to the realm of precision, the "Proposed Methods" perpetually transcend their counterparts. Within CALU-1, they yield precision metrics of 96.81% and 97.11% in conjunction with threefold and fivefold cross-validation sequences, individually. Evident here is their significant ability to accurately discern positive instances. These successful outcomes also reflect those of CALU-2, where the "Proposed Methods" exhibit precision metrics of 96.81% and 97.11%.

Delving into the domain of recall, the "Proposed Methods" exhibit commendable results across both datasets. For CALU-1, their recall achieves maximum values of 96.06% and 96.47% by virtue of threefold and fivefold cross-validation regimes, respectively. This ability to identify positive instances is in accordance with the results observed for CALU-2, where the recall rates reached 96.06% and 96.47%.

Additionally, the "Proposed Methods" exhibit effective results in terms of precision and recall, achieving elevated F1-scores. For CALU-1, F1-scores of 97.18% and 98.14% (for threefold and fivefold, respectively) demonstrate their ability to achieve a symbiotic balance among these dual metrics. This is also reflected in the F1-scores found for CALU-2, achieving values of 97.18% and 98.14%.

In terms of discerning between the categorical classes, the "Proposed Methods" demonstrate consistent AUC values. This indicates their ability to discern between positive and negative instances. With AUC values reaching 97.41% and 98.48% for the threefold and fivefold cross-validation modalities within CALU-1, and similar values also being found for CALU-2, the superiority of the proposed approach is demonstrated.

Furthermore, the resilience exhibited by the "Proposed Methods" across both datasets is palpable, as evidenced by their meager standard deviations. These serve to uphold the premise of a dependable and consistent comportment of the model.

In a contextual juxtaposition of threefold and fivefold cross-validation, a discernible constant trend ensues. While both methodologies render commendable performances, the dominion of fivefold cross-validation precipitates marginally elevated precision, recall, F1-Score, and AUC values. This underscores the enhanced capability imparted by a greater multitude of folds in encapsulating subtle intricacies and affording a more granular evaluation of the model's performance.

In the ensuing experimental phase, we shall undertake an assessment of the proposed model's performance, employing a dataset amalgamated from CALU-1 and CALU-2. Notably, these datasets deviate from the conventional white background, introducing a degree of environmental heterogeneity. The principal objective of this experiment resides in gauging the robustness of the aforementioned model across a spectrum of diverse scenarios.

Furthermore, our investigation will extend to the exploration of variance within the standard fusion strategies. Specifically, we will juxtapose the conventional majority voting and unweighted averaging approaches with our novel AMIS fusion technique. The dataset under consideration comprises a total of 343 images representing class CM, 340 images for NP, 338 images for NR, 346 images for NS, 350 images for NT, 339 images for NB, 350 images for PB, 351 images for RB, 355 images for SK, and 351 images for UB. It is noteworthy that all of these images feature backgrounds that deviate from the standard white backdrop. In aggregate, our dataset comprises 3463 images, which collectively constitute the testing dataset denoted as CALU-3G.

This dataset is herein referred to as CALU-3G for the sake of clarity and reference. Subsequently, the computational results derived from this evaluation are presented in

Table 10. These results will be subject to further analysis and serve as a basis for compara[illegible] assessment.

Table 10. Performance Evaluation of the Proposed Model on the CALU-3G Dataset.

Methods	Accuracy	Precision	Recall	F1-Score	AUC
ViT [70]	90.1	89.5	88.4	88.9	90.4
ResNet-101 [65]	88.6	84.6	85.7	87.7	89.3
Xception [66]	90.1	87.9	90.6	88.7	89.7
NASNet-A Mobile [67]	92.5	92.0	89.7	89.7	91.7
MobileNetV3-Large [64]	92.5	92.5	90.7	91.4	91.7
SqueezeNet [61]	76.2	75.7	75.5	75.8	76.9
ShuffleNetv2 1.0x [62]	76.7	76.7	76.1	77.0	77.3
MobileNetV3 [64]	75.0	74.7	75.4	74.9	75.5
InceptionV1 [63]	79.3	78.8	79.2	78.9	79.7
SqueezeNet [61]	92.8	93.4	94.1	93.5	93.7
ShuffleNetv2 1.0x [62]	94.1	93.9	94.1	94.6	94.6
MobileNetV3 [64]	94.0	94.5	95.2	95.2	95.4
InceptionV1 [63]	94.2	94.7	95.5	95.5	95.5
Proposed Methods (Majority Voting)	94.3	94.8	95.8	95.8	95.2
Proposed Methods (Unweighted Average)	94.3	94.7	95.6	95.5	94.9
Proposed Methods (AMIS)	98.4	97.5	97.2	98.8	97.6

The analysis of the performance evaluation results on the CALU-3G dataset, as pr[illegible]sented in Table 10, offers significant insights into the model's efficacy in classifying Cente[illegible] Asiatica Urban (CAU) cultivars against varying backgrounds. Notably, the CALU-3[illegible] dataset, composed solely of images with normal (non-white) backgrounds, presents a mo[illegible] challenging classification environment compared to the CALU-1 and CALU-2 datase[illegible] which included both white and normal backgrounds. This complexity in the CALU-3[illegible] dataset is likely due to the increased background noise and variation, potentially impactir[illegible] the models' ability to accurately identify relevant features.

Upon comparing the models' performance across these datasets, it becomes evide[illegible] that the proposed models demonstrate a robust adaptability to background variatior[illegible] However, the superior performance metrics observed in the CALU-3G dataset indica[illegible] an enhanced ability of the models to handle more complex, real-world scenarios, wher[illegible] background noise is prevalent. This robustness is crucial for practical applications i[illegible] agricultural species classification, where diverse environmental conditions are the norm[illegible]

Further, examining the impact of different decision fusion strategies in the propose[illegible] model sheds light on their relative effectiveness. The strategies employed include majorit[illegible] voting, unweighted average, and AMIS (Artificial Multiple Intelligence System). Th[illegible] performance of majority voting and unweighted average strategies on the CALU-3[illegible] dataset is remarkably similar across key metrics like accuracy, precision, recall, F1-scor[illegible] and AUC. This similarity could suggest a balanced contribution from each model in th[illegible] ensemble, leading to comparable outcomes for these fusion methods.

In contrast, the AMIS strategy significantly outperforms the other strategies, achievin[illegible] notable improvements in all performance metrics, including a remarkable accuracy of 98.4[illegible] and an F1-score of 98.8%. This superior performance can be attributed to AMIS's dynami[illegible] optimization of weights based on individual model performances, enabling a more effectiv[illegible] integration of outputs. The marked improvement with AMIS highlights its capability t[illegible] handle complex datasets like CALU-3G, reinforcing the value of advanced decision fusio[illegible] techniques in agricultural species classification, especially under challenging conditions.

In conclusion, the analysis underscores the importance of considering backgroun[illegible] variability in model development and the efficacy of sophisticated decision fusion strategie[illegible] like AMIS in enhancing classification performance in complex scenarios.

5. Discussion

In the ensuing section, we shall expound upon the rationale underpinning the juxtaposition of our findings with extant research and methodologies. The ensuing discourse will be delineated across three dimensions, namely, (1) progressions in the automated differentiation of *Centella asiatica* (L.) urban cultivars to augment agricultural practices and facilitate the quality control of medicinal products; (2) an evaluative examination aimed at the augmentation of *Centella asiatica* (L.) urban cultivar classification through the implementation of a parallel-AMIS-ensemble model; and (3) a comparative analysis of decision fusion strategies within the purview of metaheuristic optimization.

5.1. Advancements in the Automated Cultivar Differentiation of Centella asiatica *(L.) Urban for Enhanced Agricultural Practices and Medicinal Product Quality Control*

Studies by Novianti [17] and Raj [23] have identified variations in agronomic traits among *Centella asiatica* (L.) Urban (CAU) cultivars based on their growth regions, resulting in diverse shapes and attributes, potentially leading to varying essential substances. However, the expert differentiation of CAU cultivars remains challenging, with misclassification risking improper treatment cultivations and compromising the quality control of medical product production [21,22]. To address this gap, the research aims to develop an automated CAU cultivar classification system with high precision, achieving an impressive 98.41 percent accuracy.

The proposed model for automated cultivar differentiation in CAU yields highly promising results, surpassing existing methods in the literature by a significant margin [4–7]. Its efficacy and robustness are evident in the swift processing time of only 0.34 s per image, enabling the accurate identification of CAU cultivars. This expeditious and accurate classification empowers farmers to promptly adjust treatment cultivations, optimizing the plant production yield and ensuring superior essential compound yields and product quality [21,22].

The main finding of this research lies in the successful development of an automated CAU cultivar classification system with remarkable accuracy and efficiency. Precisely predicting cultivar types with 98.41 percent accuracy represents a significant advancement in plant classification. This underscores the potential of deep learning techniques, particularly the proposed ensemble of convolutional neural networks, for solving complex classification tasks in plant sciences. The application of this model can revolutionize CAU cultivar identification, leading to enhanced agricultural practices and consistent medicinal product manufacturing.

Academically, this research contributes to botanical classification and taxonomy by accurately differentiating CAU cultivars, enriching the understanding of genetic diversity and morphological characteristics within the Centella genus. Additionally, advancements in pharmacology are evident through in-depth studies of the chemical composition and pharmacological properties of different CAU species, benefiting medicinal development and herbal product formulation.

From a policy perspective, the high accuracy and efficiency of the proposed model hold immense value for pharmaceutical and agricultural industries. Quality control in medicinal product manufacturing can be greatly enhanced through precise cultivar differentiation, ensuring the consistent and high-quality production of medicinal products derived from CAU. This preserves the integrity of traditional medicine and strengthens healthcare systems. Moreover, in agriculture, the automated classification system empowers farmers to optimize plant production yields through precise cultivar identification, resulting in improved agricultural practices.

The research underscores the potential of deep learning models, such as convolutional neural networks, in addressing complex challenges in plant sciences. Policymakers in the agricultural and healthcare sectors can promote the adoption of automated systems to enhance productivity, sustainability, and quality assurance in herb production and medicinal product manufacturing. Ultimately, this research paves the way for advancements in agricultural practices and medical product quality control, presenting valuable implicatic for both academia and policy-making domains.

5.2. Enhancing CAU Cultivar Classification through the Parallel-AMIS-Ensemble Model: A Comparative Study

In this research, a novel approach, the parallel-AMIS-ensemble model, was p posed to handle the CAU cultivar classification system. The model incorporates tv segmentation methods, U-Net and Mask-R-CNN, and four distinct CNN architectur namely, SqueezeNet, ShuffleNetv2 1.0x, MobileNetV3, and InceptionV1, to form the e semble CNN model. The computational results demonstrate a remarkable classificati accuracy of 98.41%. Notably, the ensemble image segmentation method and the e semble CNN architectures contributed significantly to 13.69% and 4.62% increases accuracy, respectively.

The main finding of this study is the successful implementation of the parallel-AM ensemble model for CAU cultivar classification, achieving an impressive accuracy 98.41%. This result surpasses existing approaches in the literature, such as the VGGN and Inception module, 3-D CNN, CNN with ConvLSTM layers, DenseNet121, SVM, ar ResNet50, which exhibited accuracies ranging from 78% to 96% [25–27,29,31,32]. Th superiority of the proposed model is evident, with a considerable 5.32% to 23.08% accura improvement compared to the existing methods. The use of parallel-AMIS-ensemb significantly enhances the solution quality for CAU cultivar classification, showcasing i potential for addressing complex problems in plant sciences.

The academic implications of this research lie in the advancement of automate cultivar classification using the parallel-AMIS-ensemble model. By incorporating multip segmentation methods and CNN architectures, the proposed model represents a significar step forward in image-based plant classification tasks. This approach can be applied nc only to CAU cultivar classification but also to other similar problems in plant science contributing to the broader field of botanical classification and taxonomy.

From a policy perspective, the successful implementation of the parallel-AMIS-ensemb model has practical implications for the agriculture and pharmaceutical industries. In agr culture, accurate cultivar classification empowers farmers with valuable insights int plant growth and optimal treatment practices. The increased accuracy of the propose model ensures more precise cultivation treatments, enhancing agricultural productivit and sustainable crop management.

In the pharmaceutical industry, precise cultivar classification is crucial for medicina product manufacturing and quality control. The high accuracy of the parallel-AMIS ensemble model ensures the consistent and reliable production of medicinal product derived from CAU, supporting the integrity of traditional medicine and enhancing health care systems.

This research contributes to the advancement of automated cultivar classification and highlights the potential of ensemble models in addressing complex challenges in plant sciences. Policymakers in the agricultural and healthcare sectors can leverage the insights from this research to promote the adoption of advanced technologies and automated systems, fostering productivity, sustainability, and quality assurance in herb production and medicinal product manufacturing.

The employment of large models in deep learning, particularly in the context of agricultural species classification, presents a juxtaposition of computational complexity and enhanced performance. While these models, including the Parallel-Artificial Multiple Intelligence System-Ensemble (P-AMIS-E) utilized in our study, offer superior accuracy and sophisticated capabilities, their size and complexity warrant a thorough consideration of their impact on the research.

First, large models typically require substantial computational resources for training and inference. This demand can pose challenges in terms of accessibility and feasibility, particularly in resource-constrained environments. In our study, while the P-AMIS-E model demonstrates high accuracy in classifying the Centella Asiatica Urban (CAU) cultivar, it inherently necessitates significant computational power, a factor that could limit its applicability in settings with limited technical infrastructure.

Moreover, the complexity of large models can also affect their interpretability and transparency. As these models become more intricate, understanding the rationale behind their decisions becomes increasingly challenging. This lack of transparency can be a crucial factor in fields where explainability is essential, such as in medical or pharmaceutical applications. In our research, we acknowledge this complexity and advocate for ongoing efforts to enhance the interpretability of such models without compromising their performance.

Despite these challenges, the benefits of large models in achieving high accuracy and handling complex tasks are undeniable. The P-AMIS-E model's capability to accurately classify the CAU cultivar is a testament to the effectiveness of these models in handling nuanced and detailed tasks, which smaller models might not handle as efficiently. This effectiveness is particularly vital in the context of our research, where precision in classification directly influences the quality and efficacy of products in the cosmetics, pharmaceutical, and herbal medicine industries.

In conclusion, while the use of large models in our research offers significant advantages in terms of accuracy and capability, it is crucial to balance these benefits with considerations of computational demand, interpretability, and practical applicability. Future research directions might include optimizing these large models to reduce their computational footprint while maintaining their accuracy or developing hybrid approaches that combine the strengths of both large and smaller models.

5.3. A Comparative Study of Decision Fusion Strategies in Metaheuristic Optimization

Besides the use of ensemble image segmentation and the ensemble CNN's architectures, one of the key successes of the P-AMIS-E is the decision fusion strategy, which is used to combine different entities together to obtain the solution for the prediction model.

In our experimental results, AMIS exhibited superior performance compared to other decision fusion strategies, including DE (Differential Evolution), GA (Genetic Algorithm), and UAW (Unweighted Average), in terms of solution quality. AMIS achieved a maximum improvement of 4.62% over the mentioned methods. This significant enhancement can be attributed to AMIS's effective improvement method, which incorporates a diverse range of heuristics and metaheuristics. As a result, AMIS demonstrates both exploration and exploitation search behavior, enabling it to explore wider solution spaces and conduct intensive searches in specific scenarios. Additionally, AMIS incorporates a restart procedure, allowing it to escape from local optima when necessary [51–53].

The main finding of this research is the clear superiority of AMIS as a decision fusion strategy compared to simpler methods proposed in the literature, such as majority voting, swarm intelligences, and unweighted average [42,44–46]. AMIS's comprehensive set of heuristics and metaheuristics equips it with the ability to seek better solutions effectively. Through extensive experimentation, AMIS consistently outperforms other approaches, highlighting its potential as a highly effective decision fusion strategy.

From an academic perspective, this research contributes to the advancement of decision fusion strategies, particularly with the introduction of AMIS. The integration of diverse heuristics and metaheuristics enriches the field of metaheuristic optimization, enhancing the capabilities of such strategies in tackling complex problem spaces and achieving better solutions. This study provides valuable insights for researchers and practitioners involved in optimization and computational intelligence domains.

On a policy level, the superior performance of AMIS in terms of solution quality has practical implications for various industries. The adoption of AMIS as a decision fusion strategy can lead to improved outcomes in real-world applications. Policymakers in sectors reliant on optimization processes, such as supply chain management, logistics, and resource allocation, can consider implementing AMIS to enhance decision-making processes and achieve more efficient and effective solutions.

5.4. Key Contributions of the P-AMIS-E Model

Our research makes several pivotal contributions to the field of agricultural spec classification, particularly in the context of using deep learning methodologies. Th contributions are multifaceted, addressing both theoretical advancements and practi applications.

Innovative Integration of Deep Learning Techniques: At the core of our contributi is the development of the Parallel-Artificial Multiple Intelligence System-Ensemble AMIS-E) model. This model uniquely combines advanced image segmentation meth (U-net, Mask-R-CNN) with a variety of CNN architectures (SqueezeNet, ShuffleNe 1.0x, MobileNetV3, InceptionV1). This integration allows for the nuanced processing visual data, crucial for distinguishing between species with highly similar appearan The model's ability to analyze subtle visual differences provides a significant leap forwa from traditional classification methods.

Enhanced Accuracy and Efficiency in Classification: Our model achieves a remarka classification accuracy of 98.41%, which is a notable improvement over existing mod such as ResNet-101 and Xception, which have an accuracy of 93.74%. This heighten accuracy is crucial in fields such as pharmaceuticals, cosmetics, and herbal medicine, wh the precise identification of species directly impacts product quality and efficacy.

Effective Use of Limited Data: Addressing the common challenge of data scarcity agricultural contexts, our model efficiently utilizes image augmentation techniques. Th approach allows the model to train effectively on smaller datasets, overcoming a significa barrier faced by many existing classification systems.

Adaptability and Robustness through AMIS Decision Fusion: The use of AMIS de sion fusion in our model enhances its adaptability to different species and environmen conditions. This robustness is particularly advantageous for agricultural applicatio where variability is a constant.

Balancing Computational Efficiency with Accuracy: We have optimized the P-AM E model to ensure that it remains computationally efficient without compromising c accuracy. This optimization makes the model accessible and practical for use in vario settings, including those with limited computational resources.

Theoretical and Practical Implications: Theoretically, our study advances the und standing of how deep learning techniques can be effectively applied to image classificati tasks in agriculture. Practically, it offers a tool that can be directly employed in industri that rely on accurate species identification, thereby having a tangible impact on the quali of products and services in these sectors.

In summary, our research contributes to the field of agricultural species classificati by providing an advanced, accurate, and adaptable model. The P-AMIS-E model represen a significant advancement in the application of deep learning techniques to real-worl challenges in agriculture. These contributions are expected to have a lasting impact o both the academic study of machine learning in agriculture and its practical application i related industries.

5.5. Advantages of the Model and Research Limitations

First, the uniqueness of our approach lies in the integration of advanced deep learnin techniques, specifically designed for the complex task of classifying agricultural specie like the Centella Asiatica Urban (CAU) cultivar. While classification problems in machin learning are indeed common, the challenge intensifies when dealing with highly simila species, where conventional classification models often fall short. Our method, employin the Parallel-Artificial Multiple Intelligence System-Ensemble (P-AMIS-E) model, offers nuanced solution that is tailored to address these specific challenges.

One of the key advantages of our approach is its remarkable accuracy, which at 98.41% is significantly higher than that achieved by traditional models such as ResNet-101 an Xception, which stand at 93.74%. This heightened accuracy is crucial in industries suc as pharmaceuticals and cosmetics, where the precise identification of species has direct implications for product quality and efficacy.

Furthermore, our method demonstrates an enhanced ability to process and classify images with limited data availability, a common hurdle in agricultural classification. The use of ensemble image segmentation techniques, like U-Net and Mask R-CNN, alongside a range of CNN architectures, contributes to this improved performance. By leveraging these advanced techniques, our model effectively addresses the limitations of data scarcity often encountered in this domain.

Additionally, the incorporation of the AMIS decision fusion strategy in the P-AMIS-E model is a novel aspect of our study. This strategy synergistically combines the outputs of various deep learning models, resulting in a more robust and reliable classification system. This integrated approach is particularly beneficial in handling the variability and complexity inherent in species like the CAU cultivar.

Our research offers a sophisticated solution to a complex classification problem, characterized by high accuracy, efficiency in handling limited data scenarios, and robustness through an innovative ensemble approach. These attributes distinguish our study within the realm of classification problems, particularly in the context of agricultural species classification. We believe that these enhancements and the specific focus on CAU cultivar classification significantly contribute to both the theoretical and practical advancements in this field.

A critical examination of existing agricultural species classification models reveals several limitations that our research addresses. Traditional models often falter in differentiating species with similar visual features, leading to classification inaccuracies, particularly in closely related cultivars. Another significant challenge is the dependence on large datasets for training, which is impractical in many agricultural contexts. Additionally, the rigidity of conventional systems limits their adaptability to diverse species and environmental conditions. Lastly, the high computational demands of advanced models pose restrictions in resource-limited settings.

Our study introduces the Parallel-Artificial Multiple Intelligence System-Ensemble (P-AMIS-E) model as a solution to these prevalent issues. The P-AMIS-E model's integration of U-net and Mask-R-CNN for image segmentation, combined with various CNN architectures, enables it to accurately classify species with closely resembling features. This model overcomes the data limitation challenge by effectively utilizing image augmentation techniques, allowing for efficient learning from limited datasets. Furthermore, the incorporation of ensemble learning and AMIS decision fusion enhances the model's adaptability and robustness, making it versatile across different agricultural scenarios. Importantly, we have optimized the model to balance computational efficiency with accuracy, ensuring its applicability in diverse settings, including those with constrained computational resources. Through these innovations, our research not only advances the theoretical framework of deep learning in image classification tasks but also provides practical solutions to the agricultural industry's need for precise species identification.

6. Conclusions and Outlook

In this research, we developed an innovative method for the precise differentiation and categorization of plant species, with a particular focus on herbs and plants exhibiting multiple varieties. These plant varieties possess distinct characteristics, varying quantities of essential compounds, and divergent cultivation requirements. The accurate and precise classification of plant varieties plays a pivotal role in optimizing cultivation, production planning, and quality control processes, ultimately enhancing efficiency in product development and management.

The classification of Centella Asiatica Urban (CAU) cultivars presents a formidable challenge due to the striking similarity between species and the absence of reliable visual features for differentiation. This challenge assumes paramount importance in industries such as pharmaceuticals, cosmetics, and herbal medicine, where precise species identification is vital to ensuring product quality and safety. To address this intricate task, conducted comprehensive research aimed at developing an automated classification s tem grounded in deep learning techniques capable of accurately and efficiently classifyi CAU species.

Our research methodology entailed the assembly of a diverse and extensive data comprising Centella Asiatica Urban (CAU) cultivars. Subsequently, we constructed a robu automated classification system employing the Parallel Artificial Multiple Intelligen System–Ensemble Deep Learning model (P-AMIS-E). This sophisticated model integrat ensemble image segmentation techniques, specifically U-Net and Mask-R-CNN, alongsi image augmentation and an ensemble of convolutional neural network (CNN) architectur including SqueezeNet, ShuffleNetv2 1.0x, MobileNetV3, and InceptionV1. The hallma of our model was its utilization of the Artificial Multiple Intelligence System (AMIS) as decision fusion strategy, significantly augmenting the accuracy and efficiency.

Our results are emblematic of the model's remarkable performance. The P-AMIS model achieved an astounding accuracy rate of 98.41%, signifying a substantial advanc ment compared to state-of-the-art methods. Notably, existing methods such as ResNet-1(Xception, NASNet-A Mobile, and MobileNetV3-Large attained an accuracy rate of 93.74 on the testing dataset. Moreover, the P-AMIS-E model exhibited a substantial advanta when applied to an unseen dataset, yielding accuracy rates ranging from 4.45% to 31.16 higher than those achieved by the compared methods.

In summary, our research introduces a pioneering approach to the precise classificatic of plant species, with a particular emphasis on CAU cultivars. The integration of ensemb image segmentation techniques, image augmentation, and decision fusion within the dee learning framework has yielded remarkable improvements in accuracy and efficienc These findings carry profound implications for the evolution of deep learning technique in the realm of image classification. We recommend further exploration of the potential c ensemble deep learning models, coupled with continued investigations into the optima amalgamation of image segmentation, image augmentation, and decision fusion strategie Additionally, expanding the dataset to encompass a broader range of CAU species an exploring the potential of transfer learning to enhance the model's performance on nev species represent promising avenues for future research.

Author Contributions: K.S.: conceptualization, methodology. B.B.: validation. P.G.-D.: forma analysis, writing the original draft. S.G.: software. R.P.: supervision, writing—review and edi ing. T.S. and S.C.: resources. P.L.: conceptualization. S.K.: funding acquisition, conceptualizatior writing—review and editing. All authors have read and agreed to the published version c the manuscript.

Funding: This research project was financially supported by Mahasarakham University.

Data Availability Statement: Data will be made available on request.

Conflicts of Interest: The authors declare no conflicts of interest.

References

1. Susanti, D.; Safrina, D.; Wijaya, N.R. Weed's Vegetation Analysis of Centella (*Centella asiatica* L. Urban) Plantations. *Caraka Tani J. Sustain. Agric.* **2021**, *36*, 110. [CrossRef]
2. Jamil, S.S.; Nizami, Q.; Salam, M. *Centella asiatica* (Linn.) Urban—A Review. *CSIR* **2007**, *6*, 158–170.
3. Prabavathi, S.; Kanmani, P. Plant Leaf Disease Detection and Classification Using Optimized CNN Model. *IJRTE* **2021**, *9*, 233–238. [CrossRef]
4. Yang, M.-M.; Nayeem, A.; Shen, L.-L. Plant Classification Based on Stacked Autoencoder. In Proceedings of the 2017 IEEE 2nd Information Technology, Networking, Electronic and Automation Control Conference (ITNEC), Chengdu, China, 15–17 December 2017; IEEE: Piscataway, NJ, USA, 2017; pp. 1082–1086.
5. Chen, J.; Yin, H.; Zhang, D. A Self-Adaptive Classification Method for Plant Disease Detection Using GMDH-Logistic Model. *Sustain. Comput. Inform. Syst.* **2020**, *28*, 100415. [CrossRef]
6. Pacifico, L.D.S.; Macario, V.; Oliveira, J.F.L. Plant Classification Using Artificial Neural Networks. In Proceedings of the 2018 International Joint Conference on Neural Networks (IJCNN), Rio de Janeiro, Brazil, 8–13 July 2018; IEEE: Piscataway, NJ, USA, 2018; pp. 1–6.

Britto, L.F.S.; Pacifico, L.D.S. Plant Classification Using Weighted K-NN Variants. In Proceedings of the Anais do XV Encontro Nacional de Inteligência Artificial e Computacional (ENIAC 2018), São Paulo, Brazil, 22–25 October 2018; Sociedade Brasileira de Computação—SBC: Porto Alegre, Brazil, 2018; pp. 58–69.

Pitakaso, R.; Nanthasamroeng, N.; Srichok, T.; Khonjun, S.; Weerayuth, N.; Kotmongkol, T.; Pornprasert, P.; Pranet, K. A Novel Artificial Multiple Intelligence System (AMIS) for Agricultural Product Transborder Logistics Network Design in the Greater Mekong Subregion (GMS). *Computation* **2022**, *10*, 126. [CrossRef]

Chandrika, U.G.; Prasad Kumara, P.A.A.S. Chapter Four—Gotu Kola (*Centella asiatica*): Nutritional Properties and Plausible Health Benefits. *Adv. Food Nutr. Res.* **2015**, *76*, 125–157. [CrossRef]

Shin, H.Y.; Kim, H.; Jung, S.; Jeong, E.-J.; Lee, K.-H.; Bae, Y.-J.; Suh, H.J.; Jang, K.-I.; Yu, K.-W. Interrelationship Between Secondary Metabolites and Antioxidant Capacities of *Centella asiatica* Using Bivariate and Multivariate Correlation Analyses. *Appl. Biol. Chem.* **2021**, *64*, 82. [CrossRef]

Sudhakaran, M.V. Botanical Pharmacognosy of *Centella asiatica* (Linn.) Urban. *Pharmacogn. J.* **2017**, *9*, 546–558. [CrossRef]

Prasad, A.; Mathur, A.; Mathur, A. Advances and Emerging Research Trends for Modulation of Centelloside Biosynthesis in *Centella asiatica* (L.) Urban—A Review. *Ind. Crops Prod.* **2019**, *141*, 111768. [CrossRef]

Thong-on, W.; Arimatsu, P.; Pitiporn, S.; Soonthornchareonnon, N.; Prathanturarug, S. Field Evaluation of in Vitro-Induced Tetraploid and Diploid *Centella asiatica* (L.) Urban. *J. Nat. Med.* **2014**, *68*, 267–273. [CrossRef] [PubMed]

Devkota, A.; Jha, P.K. Phenotypic Plasticity of *Centella asiatica* (L.) Urb. Growing in Different Habitats of Nepal. *Trop. Plant Res.* **2019**, *6*, 1–7. [CrossRef]

Patel, D. Growth Pattern Study on *Centella asiatica* (L.) Urban in Herbal Garden. *Int. J. Herb. Med.* **2015**, *3*, 9–12.

Biswas, D.; Mandal, S.; Chatterjee Saha, S.; Tudu, C.K.; Nandy, S.; Batiha, G.E.; Shekhawat, M.S.; Pandey, D.K.; Dey, A. Ethnobotany, Phytochemistry, Pharmacology, and Toxicity of *Centella asiatica* (L.) Urban: A Comprehensive Review. *Phytother. Res.* **2021**, *35*, 6624–6654. [CrossRef]

Novianti, C.; Purbaningsih, S.; Salamah, A. The Effect of Different Pericarp Color on Seed Germination of *Centella asiatica* (L.) Urban. *AIP Conf. Proc.* **2016**, *1729*, 020064.

Alqahtani, A.; Cho, J.-L.; Wong, K.H.; Li, K.M.; Razmovski-Naumovski, V.; Li, G.Q. Differentiation of Three Centella Species in Australia as Inferred from Morphological Characteristics, ISSR Molecular Fingerprinting and Phytochemical Composition. *Front. Plant Sci.* **2017**, *8*, 1980. [CrossRef]

Singh, J.; Singh Sangwan, R.; Gupta, S.; Saxena, S.; Sangwan, N.S. Profiling of Triterpenoid Saponin Content Variation in Different Chemotypic Accessions of *Centella asiatica* L. *Plant Genet. Resour.* **2015**, *13*, 176–179. [CrossRef]

Chen, Y.; Zhang, D.; Zhang, H.; Wang, Q.-G. Dual-Path Mixed-Domain Residual Threshold Networks for Bearing Fault Diagnosis. *IEEE Trans. Ind. Electron.* **2022**, *69*, 13462–13472. [CrossRef]

Azizi, M.M.F.; Lau, H.Y.; Abu-Bakar, N. Integration of Advanced Technologies for Plant Variety and Cultivar Identification. *J. Biosci.* **2021**, *46*, 91. [CrossRef]

Legner, N.; Meinen, C.; Rauber, R. Root Differentiation of Agricultural Plant Cultivars and Proveniences Using FTIR Spectroscopy. *Front. Plant Sci.* **2018**, *9*, 748. [CrossRef]

Raj, T.L.; Vanila, D.; Ganthi, S. Comparative Pharmacognostical Studies on Genuine, Commercial and Adulterant Samples of *Centella asiatica* (L.) Urban. *Res. Rev. J. Pharmacol.* **2013**, *3*, 6–9.

Srivastava, S.; Verma, S.; Gupta, A.; Rajan, S.; Rawat, A. Studies on Chemotypic Variation in *Centella asiatica* (L.) Urban from Nilgiri Range of India. *J. Planar Chromatogr. Mod. TLC* **2014**, *27*, 454–459. [CrossRef]

5. Bhargavi, D.; Narayana, C.L.; Ramana, K.V. Plant Disease Identification by Using Deep Learning Models. *J. Emerg. Technol. Innov. Res.* **2021**, *8*, b150–b157.

Smetanin, A.; Uzhinskiy, A.; Ososkov, G.; Goncharov, P.; Nechaevskiy, A. Deep Learning Methods for the Plant Disease Detection Platform. *AIP Conf. Proc.* **2021**, *2377*, 060006.

7. Barbedo, J.G.A. Deep Learning Applied to Plant Pathology: The Problem of Data Representativeness. *Trop. Plant Pathol.* **2021**, *47*, 85–94. [CrossRef]

3. Khan, E.; Rehman, M.Z.U.; Ahmed, F.; Khan, M.A. Classification of Diseases in Citrus Fruits Using SqueezeNet. In Proceedings of the 2021 International Conference on Applied and Engineering Mathematics (ICAEM), Taxila, Pakistan, 30–31 August 2021; IEEE: Piscataway, NJ, USA, 2021; pp. 67–72.

9. Ran, H.; Wen, S.; Wang, S.; Cao, Y.; Zhou, P.; Huang, T. Memristor-Based Edge Computing of ShuffleNetV2 for Image Classification. *IEEE Trans. Comput.-Aided Des. Integr. Circuits Syst.* **2021**, *40*, 1701–1710. [CrossRef]

0. Imanov, E.; Alzouhbi, A.K. Machine Learning Comparative Analysis for Plant Classification. In Proceedings of the 13th International Conference on Theory and Application of Fuzzy Systems and Soft Computing—ICAFS-2018, Warsaw, Poland, 27–28 August 2018; Aliev, R.A., Kacprzyk, J., Pedrycz, W., Jamshidi, M., Sadikoglu, F.M., Eds.; Springer International Publishing: Cham, Switzerland, 2019; Volume 896, pp. 586–593.

1. Nandyal, S.; Patil, B.; Pattanshetty, A. Plant Classification Using SVM Classifier. In Proceedings of the Third International Conference on Computational Intelligence and Information Technology (CIIT 2013), Mumbai, India, 18–19 October 2013; Institution of Engineering and Technology: Stevenage, UK, 2013; pp. 519–523.

32. Xu, Z.; Hu, J.; Zheng, K.; Yan, L.; Wang, C.; Zhou, X. Fusion Shuffle Light Detector. In Proceedings of the 2021 16th Internatic Conference on Computer Science & Education (ICCSE), Lancaster, UK, 17–21 August 2021; IEEE: Piscataway, NJ, USA, 2 pp. 718–721.
33. Liu, Y.; Li, Z.; Chen, X.; Gong, G.; Lu, H. Improving the Accuracy of SqueezeNet with Negligible Extra Computational Cost Proceedings of the 2020 International Conference on High Performance Big Data and Intelligent Systems (HPBD&IS), Shenz China, 23 May 2020; IEEE: Piscataway, NJ, USA, 2022; pp. 1–6.
34. Karol, M.J. Optical Interconnection Using ShuffleNet Multihop Networks in Multi-Connected Ring Topologies. In Proceeding the Symposium proceedings on Communications Architectures and Protocols, Stanford, CA, USA, 16–18 August 1988; AC New York, NY, USA, 1988; pp. 25–34.
35. Yang, M.; Ma, T.; Tian, Q.; Tian, Y.; Al-Dhelaan, A.; Al-Dhelaan, M. Aggregated Squeeze-and-Excitation Transformations Densely Connected Convolutional Networks. *Vis. Comput.* **2022**, *38*, 2661–2674. [CrossRef]
36. Keh, S.S. Semi-Supervised Noisy Student Pre-Training on EfficientNet Architectures for Plant Pathology Classification. *ar* **2020**, arXiv:2012.00332.
37. Khanramaki, M.; Askari Asli-Ardeh, E.; Kozegar, E. Citrus Pests Classification Using an Ensemble of Deep Learning Mod *Comput. Electron. Agric.* **2021**, *186*, 106192. [CrossRef]
38. Mokeev, V. An Ensemble of Learning Machine Models for Plant Recognition. In Proceedings of the Analysis of Images, Soc Networks and Texts, Kazan, Russia, 17–19 July 2019; Van Der Aalst, W.M.P., Batagelj, V., Ignatov, D.I., Khachay, M., Kusko V., Kutuzov, A., Kuznetsov, S.O., Lomazova, I.A., Loukachevitch, N., Napoli, A., et al., Eds.; Springer International Publishi Cham, Switzerland, 2020; Volume 1086, pp. 256–262.
39. Vallabhajosyula, S.; Sistla, V.; Kolli, V.K.K. Transfer Learning-Based Deep Ensemble Neural Network for Plant Leaf Dise Detection. *J. Plant Dis. Prot.* **2022**, *129*, 545–558. [CrossRef]
40. Fountsop, A.N.; Ebongue Kedieng Fendji, J.L.; Atemkeng, M. Deep Learning Models Compression for Agricultural Plants. *Ap Sci.* **2020**, *10*, 6866. [CrossRef]
41. Javaid, A.; Gurmet, R.; Sharma, N. *Centella asiatica* (L.) Urban: A Predominantly Self-Pollinated Herbal Perennial Plant of Fam Apiaceae. *Vegetos Int. J. Plant Res. Biotechnol.* **2018**, *31*, 53. [CrossRef]
42. Ganaie, M.A.; Hu, M.; Tanveer, M.; Suganthan, P.N. Ensemble Deep Learning: A Review. *Eng. Appl. Artif. Intell.* **2022**, *115*, 1051 [CrossRef]
43. Chan, P.P.K.; Xiao, M.; Qin, X.; Kees, N. Dynamic Fusion for Ensemble of Deep Q-Network. *Int. J. Mach. Learn. Cybern.* **2021**, 1031–1040. [CrossRef]
44. Gumaei, A.; Ismail, W.N.; Rafiul Hassan, M.; Hassan, M.M.; Mohamed, E.; Alelaiwi, A.; Fortino, G. A Decision-Level Fusic Method for COVID-19 Patient Health Prediction. *Big Data Res.* **2022**, *27*, 100287. [CrossRef]
45. Xu, J.; Li, L.; Ji, M. Ensemble Learning Based Multi-Source Information Fusion. In Proceedings of the 2019 Internation Conference on Image and Video Processing, and Artificial Intelligence, Shanghai, China, 23–25 November 2019; Su, R., Ed.; SP Bellingham, WA, USA, 2019; p. 81.
46. Mohammed, A.; Kora, R. An Effective Ensemble Deep Learning Framework for Text Classification. *J. King Saud Univ. Comput. I Sci.* **2022**, *34*, 8825–8837. [CrossRef]
47. Mohammadi, A.; Shaverizade, A. Ensemble Deep Learning for Aspect-Based Sentiment Analysis. *IJNAA* **2021**, *12*, 29–3 [CrossRef]
48. Salal, Y.K.; Abdullaev, S.M. Deep Learning Based Ensemble Approach to Predict Student Academic Performance: Case Stuc In Proceedings of the 2020 3rd International Conference on Intelligent Sustainable Systems (ICISS), Thoothukudi, India, 3- December 2020; IEEE: Piscataway, NJ, USA, 2020; pp. 191–198.
49. Abd Elaziz, M.; Dahou, A.; Abualigah, L.; Yu, L.; Alshinwan, M.; Khasawneh, A.M.; Lu, S. Advanced Metaheuristic Optimizatic Techniques in Applications of Deep Neural Networks: A Review. *Neural Comput. Appl.* **2021**, *33*, 14079–14099. [CrossRef]
50. Muhammad Usman, S.; Khalid, S.; Bashir, S. A Deep Learning Based Ensemble Learning Method for Epileptic Seizure Predictio *Comput. Biol. Med.* **2021**, *136*, 104710. [CrossRef]
51. Prasitpuriprecha, C.; Jantama, S.S.; Preeprem, T.; Pitakaso, R.; Srichok, T.; Khonjun, S.; Weerayuth, N.; Gonwirat, S.; Enkvetchaku P.; Kaewta, C.; et al. Drug-Resistant Tuberculosis Treatment Recommendation, and Multi-Class Tuberculosis Detection an Classification Using Ensemble Deep Learning-Based System. *Pharmaceuticals* **2022**, *16*, 13. [CrossRef]
52. Prasitpuriprecha, C.; Pitakaso, R.; Gonwirat, S.; Enkvetchakul, P.; Preeprem, T.; Jantama, S.S.; Kaewta, C.; Weerayuth, N.; Srichol T.; Khonjun, S.; et al. Embedded AMIS-Deep Learning with Dialog-Based Object Query System for Multi-Class Tuberculosis Dru Response Classification. *Diagnostics* **2022**, *12*, 2980. [CrossRef]
53. Sethanan, K.; Pitakaso, R.; Srichok, T.; Khonjun, S.; Thannipat, P.; Wanram, S.; Boonmee, C.; Gonwirat, S.; Enkvetchakul, F Kaewta, C. Double AMIS-Ensemble Deep Learning for Skin Cancer Classification Expert Systems with Applications. *Expert Sys Appl.* **2023**, *234*, 121047. [CrossRef]
54. Alomar, K.; Aysel, H.I.; Cai, X. Data Augmentation in Classification and Segmentation: A Survey and New Strategies. *J. Imagin* **2023**, *9*, 46. [CrossRef] [PubMed]
55. Altalak, M.; Ammad Uddin, M.; Alajmi, A.; Rizg, A. Smart Agriculture Applications Using Deep Learning Technologies: A Survey. *Appl. Sci.* **2022**, *12*, 5919. [CrossRef]

Yang, M.; Ding, S. Algorithm for Appearance Simulation of Plant Diseases Based on Symptom Classification. *Front. Plant Sci.* **2022**, *13*, 935157. [CrossRef] [PubMed]

Ronneberger, O.; Fischer, P.; Brox, T. U-Net: Convolutional Networks for Biomedical Image Segmentation. In Proceedings of the Medical Image Computing and Computer-Assisted Intervention–MICCAI 2015: 18th International Conference, Munich, Germany, 5–9 October 2015; pp. 234–241.

Zhang, S.; Zhang, C. Modified U-Net for Plant Diseased Leaf Image Segmentation. *Comput. Electron. Agric.* **2023**, *204*, 107511. [CrossRef]

He, K.; Gkioxari, G.; Dollar, P.; Girshick, R. Mask R-CNN. In Proceedings of the 2017 IEEE International Conference on Computer Vision (ICCV), Venice, Italy, 22–29 October 2017; IEEE: Piscataway, NJ, USA, 2017; pp. 2980–2988.

Mu, X.; He, L.; Heinemann, P.; Schupp, J.; Karkee, M. Mask R-CNN Based Apple Flower Detection and King Flower Identification for Precision Pollination. *Smart Agric. Technol.* **2023**, *4*, 100151. [CrossRef]

Li, M.; He, L.; Lei, C.; Gong, Y. Fine-Grained Image Classification Model Based on Improved SqueezeNet. In Proceedings of the 2021 IEEE 5th Advanced Information Technology, Electronic and Automation Control Conference (IAEAC), Chongqing, China, 12–14 March 2021; IEEE: Piscataway, NJ, USA, 2021; pp. 393–399.

Ghosh, S.; Mondal, M.J.; Sen, S.; Chatterjee, S.; Kar Roy, N.; Patnaik, S. A Novel Approach to Detect and Classify Fruits Using ShuffleNet V2. In Proceedings of the 2020 IEEE Applied Signal Processing Conference (ASPCON), Kolkata, India, 7–9 October 2020; IEEE: Piscataway, NJ, USA, 2020; pp. 163–167.

. Ozsariyildiz, S.; Tolman, F. First Experiences with an Inception Support Modeller for the Building and Construction Industry. In Proceedings of the Eighth International Conference on Durability of Building Materials and Components, Vancouver, BC, Canada, 30 May–3 June 1999; pp. 2234–2245.

. Hussain, A.; Barua, B.; Osman, A.; Abozariba, R.; Asyhari, A.T. Performance of MobileNetV3 Transfer Learning on Handheld Device-Based Real-Time Tree Species Identification. In Proceedings of the 2021 26th International Conference on Automation and Computing (ICAC), Portsmouth, UK, 2–4 September 2021; IEEE: Piscataway, NJ, USA, 2021; pp. 1–6.

. Ghosal, P.; Nandanwar, L.; Kanchan, S.; Bhadra, A.; Chakraborty, J.; Nandi, D. Brain Tumor Classification Using ResNet-101 Based Squeeze and Excitation Deep Neural Network. In Proceedings of the 2019 Second International Conference on Advanced Computational and Communication Paradigms (ICACCP), Gangtok, India, 25–28 February 2019; IEEE: Piscataway, NJ, USA, 2019; pp. 1–6.

. Zhang, Y.; Liao, J.; Ran, M.; Li, X.; Wang, S.; Liu, L. ST-Xception: A Depthwise Separable Convolution Network for Military Sign Language Recognition. In Proceedings of the 2020 IEEE International Conference on Systems, Man, and Cybernetics (SMC), Toronto, ON, Canada, 11–14 October 2020; IEEE: Piscataway, NJ, USA, 2020; pp. 3200–3205.

7. Cakmak, M.; Tenekeci, M.E. Melanoma Detection from Dermoscopy Images Using Nasnet Mobile with Transfer Learning. In Proceedings of the 2021 29th Signal Processing and Communications Applications Conference (SIU), Istanbul, Turkey, 9–11 June 2021; IEEE: Piscataway, NJ, USA, 2021; pp. 1–4.

8. Kabanikhin, S.; Krivorotko, O.; Bektemessov, Z.; Bektemessov, M.; Zhang, S. Differential Evolution Algorithm of Solving an Inverse Problem for the Spatial Solow Mathematical Model. *J. Inverse Ill-Posed Probl.* **2020**, *28*, 761–774. [CrossRef]

9. Yang, S.; Collings, P.J. The Genetic Algorithm: Using Biology to Compute Liquid Crystal Director Configurations. *Crystals* **2020**, *10*, 1041. [CrossRef]

0. Fu, X.; Ma, Q.; Yang, F.; Zhang, C.; Zhao, X.; Chang, F.; Han, L. Crop Pest Image Recognition Based on the Improved ViT Method. *Inf. Process. Agric.* 2023, *in press*. [CrossRef]

mathematics MDPI

Article

Code Comments: A Way of Identifying Similarities in the Source Code

Rares Folea * and Emil Slusanschi

Department of Computer Science and Engineering, Faculty for Automatic Control and Computers, National University of Science and Technology Politehnica Bucharest, Splaiul Independentei 313, Sector 6, 060042 Bucharest, Romania; emil.slusanschi@cs.pub.ro
* Correspondence: rares.folea@stud.acs.upb.ro

Abstract: This study investigates whether analyzing the code comments available in the sour code can effectively reveal functional similarities within software. The authors explore how bo machine-readable comments (such as linter instructions) and human-readable comments (in natu language) can contribute towards measuring the code similarity. For the former, the work is relyi on computing the cosine similarity over the one-hot encoded representation of the machine-readab comments, while for the latter, the focus is on detecting similarities in English comments, usi threshold-based computations against the similarity measurements obtained using models based Levenshtein distances (for form-based matches), Word2Vec (for contextual word representation as well as deep learning models, such as Sentence Transformers or Universal Sentence Encoder (f semantic similarity). For evaluation, this research has analyzed the similarities between differe source code versions of the open-source code editor, VSCode, based on existing ESlint-specif directives, as well as applying natural language processing techniques on incremental releases Kubernetes, an open-source system for automating containerized application management. Th experiments outlines the potential for detecting code similarities solely based on comments, an observations indicate that models like Universal Sentence Encoder are providing a favorable balanc between recall and precision. This research is integrated into Project Martial, an open-source proje for automatic assistance in detecting plagiarism in software.

Keywords: code similarity; linter analysis; comments analysis; software plagiarism; plagiaris detection; universal sentence encoder

MSC: 68T20

Citation: Folea, R.; Slusanschi, E. Code Comments: A Way of Identifying Similarities in the Source Code. *Mathematics* **2024**, *12*, 1073. https://doi.org/10.3390/math12071073

Academic Editor: Stelios D. Georgiou

Received: 20 February 2024
Revised: 17 March 2024
Accepted: 26 March 2024
Published: 2 April 2024

1. Introduction

The research aims to expand automated methods for detecting software code similarities, designing tools that facilitate collaboration between human experts and software. This will support informed plagiarism decisions through an interactive process where the broader context of the code, including comments and coding style, is automatically analyzed. To this end, this research introduces two novel models for identifying code similarities based solely on source code comments: one targeting machine-readable comments and the other focusing on human-readable comments.

There are several methods that have been used for detecting software code similarities, with the most common being *fingerprint-based* techniques [1–4], which aim to create distinctive *"signatures"* of code sections, allowing for automatic comparison. The main downside of these is that they lack the ability to fully explain flagged similarities, thus necessitating in-depth human review. *Software birthmarks* aim to address these limitations by extracting more robust identifying features and can work on both source code [4–7] and binary code [6,8–10]. Advanced birthmark techniques may incorporate machine learning to improve accuracy in complex programs. Finally, *code embeddings*-based solutions are another promising technique, as they are able to capture semantic meaning, as well as enabling similarity detection based on functionality. While these have primarily been applied to source code [11–13], they hold potential for binary code [14] analysis as well.

Ultimately, even if these techniques offer varying degrees of automation and explainability, human judgment remains essential for determining true plagiarism [15,16]. The current research focuses solely on the detection part of code similarities.

This paper continues with Section 2, which aims to classify and analyze comments in code, based on the target audience. Section 3 underscores the importance of comments as part of software development, and Section 4 proposes a formal method to represent comments within the source code as multisets, allowing analysis of comment structures within their local context. Later, Section 5 investigates whether code comments alone can reveal similarities between programs. It demonstrates how to analyze machine-readable comments, to detect similarities across different releases, with examples from ESLint instructions available in VSCode, and it explores the successful application of natural language processing techniques to human-readable comments, highlighting the superior balance of recall and precision achieved by the Universal Sentence Encoder [17] model. Section 6 discusses the implementation of the techniques in Project Martial, an open-source project for detecting software plagiarism. Section 7 discusses the interpretation of the results presented in this paper and finally, Section 8 summarizes the contributions of this paper, draws some conclusions and outlines potential future research directions.

2. Classification of Comments

Donald Knuth concluded in [18] that *computer programming is an art*, because it *applies accumulated knowledge to the world*, which *requires skill and ingenuity, and especially because it produces objects of beauty*. Such a powerful statement uplifts the merits of software developers but comes with a not-so-obvious pitfall when viewing software in the context of continuous development with contributions from a set of ever-changing engineers. In order to help the readers and reviewers comprehend the structure and purpose of the code, developers would provide lasting explanations, in the form of code comments, to the main program's source code. Programming languages all agreed on the importance of providing such mechanisms, and for pioneer programming languages such as Fortran, the convention was that any line beginning with either the C character or an * in the first column is a comment. The Fortran basics guide states that *well-written comments are crucial to program readability*. Even in assembly languages, comments have been introduced to allow the developers explain, in a human-readable statement, the outcome. In x86 assembly, comments are usually denoted by the use of the semicolon (;) symbol, but variations also allow for shell-like (#) or C-like (//, /*) structures.

While often perceived as elements irrelevant to the computer, comments were historically only dropped from automatic analysis due to language specification limitations. For example, in early Fortran, when punch cards were prevalent, a comment character in the first column would designate the entire card as a comment, causing the execution to completely ignore it.

Kernighan and Ritchie reinforced this notion in their influential book [19] describing C specifications, which stated that *any characters between /* and */ are ignored by the compiler; they may be used freely to make a program easier to understand*. An example of a grammar implementation of this statement is presented in the appendix, Code Listing A.1.

Predictably, programming languages and software development technologies have evolved, introducing new complexities and requirements. Consequently, "*code comments*" have gained significance in various stages of the life-cycle of a program, moving beyond their traditionally overlooked role. For instance, in some languages including Python, specifying a custom encoding requires adding a special comment line at the very beginning of the file, as illustrated in Code Listing A.2. Another example, presented in Code Listing A.3, covers operating system directives, but there are also cases where code comments, while not directly affecting program execution or interpretation, provide guidance for external analysis tools, such as instructions for linters (Code Listings A.4 and A.5) or static analy (Code Listing A.6). Nonetheless, they can also provide hints, instructing compiler interpreters to alter the behavior of the program.

Therefore, even if the primary use of comments was and remains to indicate expla tions for software engineers that are reviewing existing codebases, there are quite a exceptional cases where it is reasonable for commentaries to be designed in a way they are machine-readable, in order to allow actions to be automatically performed, various systems.

Moreover, there are other machine-readable expressions, besides comment stateme that do not directly influence the functionality of the executable code. Pragma stateme within libraries or languages are an example; they modify the binary only if the comp supports them. Consider OpenMP: if the compiler does not support its pragmas, tl are discarded, ensuring the resulting binary still functions as intended (Code Listing A While analyzing such pragmas could potentially assist in determining code similarit that analysis is outside of the scope of this paper.

3. Statistics on Open-Source Projects

Because open-source projects promote transparency, by releasing the source co within a project, they are a good source of analysis, as opposed to proprietary softwa provided in binary format, where past traces of comments have already been eliminat This paper analyzed the evolution of the commentary in code, for notable open-sour projects, such as, but not limited to, Kubernetes [20] (Go), Visual Studio Code (TypeScri and Linux [21] (C). Table 1 summarizes quantitative data for all the analyzed projec with the ratio of total lines of comments to code varying anywhere between 8% and 2 across different projects, but the percentages increases even further if the reporting switch towards counting the total number of characters (between 16% and 33%) or words (betwe 21% and 43%), that are contained in the comments against the total corpus.

Table 1. Quantitative analysis of comment distribution for various open-source projects (includi projects written in Go, TypeScript, Java, C and C++), employing code analysis tools to measu comment density, length and the ratio of English words (defined as words composed entirely alphabetical characters from the English alphabet).

Project (Main Programming Language)	Total Lines of Comments | Code (Ratio)	Total Number of Single- | Multi- Line Comments	Number of Comments Chars (RATIO)	Number of Comments Words (Ratio)	Number of English Words | Total Number of Words Based on Alphabet
kubernetes-1.1.1 (Go)	167k | 780k (21.51%)	84k | 2k	8.2M (32.24%)	972k (35.53%)	831k | 900k (92.34%)
VSCode-1.1.0 (TS)	64k | 474k (13.52%)	12k | 16k	3.6M (21.48%)	452k (27.33%)	410k | 426k (96.11%)
VSCode-1.40.0 (TS)	66k | 704k (9.49%)	24k | 13k	3.6M (14.55%)	387k (16.62%)	336k | 353k (95.36%)
VSCode-1.78.0 (TS)	109k | 1.2M (8.92%)	44k | 20k	6.1M (12.98%)	656k (15.44%)	572k | 600k (95.41%)
docker-cli-24.0.0 (Go)	166k | 780k (21.33%)	87k | 461	7.4M (28.56%)	983k (32.36%)	655k | 725k (90.37%)
guava-32.0.0 (Java)	175k | 804k (21.84%)	24k | 20k	8.9M (31.56%)	1.1M (42.95%)	1.0M | 1.1M (95.47%)
moby-24.0.0 (Go)	278k | 1.7M (16.38%)	201k | 1.8k	13.8M (26.28%)	1.8M (29.85%)	1.4M | 1.5M (92.66%)
elasticsearch-8.1.0 (Java)	304k | 3.0M (9.90%)	73k | 48k	18.4M (14.08%)	2.1M (23.91%)	1.9M | 2.0M (95.37%)
tensorflow-2.13.0 (C++)	333k | 2.5M (13.00%)	224k | 49k	16.9M (16.86%)	2.1M (26.42%)	1.8M | 1.9M (95.16%)
linux-3.0 (C)	1.1M | 10.9M (10.20%)	42k | 695k	62.8M (21.10%)	8.3M (26.11%)	6.9M | 7.4M (93.62%)
linux-4.0 (C)	1.3M | 14.3M (9.53%)	31k | 819k	76.3M (19.75%)	10.3M (25.05%)	8.6M | 9.2M (93.69%)
linux-5.0 (C)	1.6M | 18.5M (8.88%)	46k | 970k	92.1M (18.37%)	12.4M (23.70%)	10.3M | 11.1M (93.44%)
linux-6.0 (C)	1.7M | 22.4M (8.00%)	80k | 1M	101M (16.61%)	13.5M (21.64%)	11.2M | 12.0M (92.98%)

Kubernetes v1.1.1 was released in 2015, and in January 2023, v1.26.1 has been release Figure 1 presents the ratio of comments w.r.t. the total lines of code. Between these version comments have been ranging between 15% and 25% of the total number of lines in th source code, peaking to about 1.5M of lines of comments (out of a total of 5.5M) in th last analysed release. Even if the proportion of comments to total lines of code fluctuate within consecutive versions, the overall long-term trend is ascendant, which could indicat an increased emphasis on code readability, maintainability, or collaboration within th Kubernetes development community. If the investigation is char-wise (counting the ratio of characters appearing in comments against the total number of characters appearing in the source code) or word-wise (counting the ratio of space-separated words) focused, the percentages are even bigger; 35% for chars and 41% for the words. Figure 2 captures the evolution of these percentages against different versions of Kubernetes. Moreover, these data suggest a clear upward trend in the use of code comments within large-scale open-source projects, with both the relative and absolute amounts of comment words increasing over time, and indicate that comments are becoming essential tools for navigating and comprehending the complexities of large-scale open-source projects to make the source code more accessible and understandable.

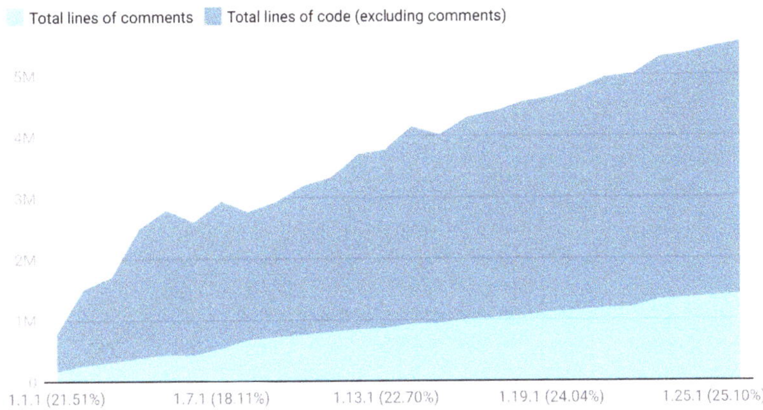

Figure 1. The evolution of the total number of lines of comments and lines of code across different versions of Kubernetes. In parentheses, it is captured the proportion of lines of comments within the total source code corpus. This analysis spans roughly 10 years of continuous development, between the first release in 2013 and the first available release from 2023. Kubernetes releases currently happen approximately three times per year. The ratio trend over time is important because commenting practices within the Kubernetes project might have changed over time, converging towards the idea of offering insights into the maintainability, collaboration dynamics and code readability within this complex open-source system.

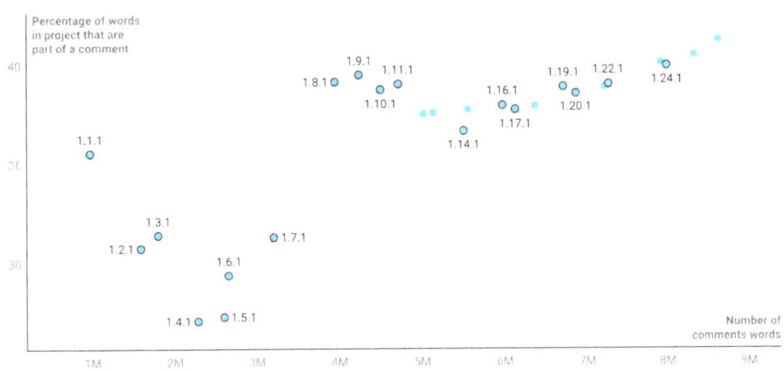

Figure 2. This figure shows the percentage of words in different Kubernetes versions that are part of comments out of the total corpus. These data offer insights into how commenting practices evolve within large-scale open-source software projects, showing an increasing trend in the amount of words part of comments out of the total corpus, across releases, as well as an ever increasing trend in the absolute number of comment words.

4. Formalizing Code Comments Analysis

Let $\mathscr{A}$ be the text representation of the source code. By $\mathcal{C}$ it is denoted the set of blocks of comments from $\mathscr{A}$. All single-line comments are mapped to an element o For languages that support multi-line comments, for simplicity, multi-line blocks are a modelled as a single element of $\mathcal{C}$.

An important statement is that $\mathcal{C}$ is finite. Given that all source codes are finite sets instructions of the programming language, $\mathscr{A}$ is also finite. As $\mathcal{C}$ is built exclusively a subset of $\mathscr{A}$, $\mathcal{C}$ is also finite.

Let $\mathscr{C} = (\mathcal{C}, m)$ be the multiset of **all blocks of comments** from $\mathscr{A}$, where $m($ provides the multiplicity of the element c_i in $\mathscr{A}$. The multiset representation helps capturing the count of duplicated comments.

There is one aspect that is yet not covered, regarding the fact that a logical comme may not spawn over one single line. One proposal would be to aim to concatenate multip line-independent comments when performing the analysis.

Let $\mathcal{C}^* = \{\overline{c_{i_1} c_{i_2} \ldots c_{i_k}} \mid c_{i_1} c_{i_2} \ldots c_{i_k} \in \mathcal{C}, i_x \neq i_y, \forall x \neq y\}$, and denote by $\mathscr{C}^* = (\mathcal{C}^*, m$ the multiset of **all concatenated blocks of comments** from $\mathscr{A}$, where $m^*(\overline{c_{i_1} c_{i_2} \ldots c_{i_k}})$ $m(c_{i_1}) \cdot m(c_{i_2}) \cdot \ldots \cdot m(c_{i_k})$.

While $\mathscr{C}^*$ provides the most extensive set to search in, it is impractical to analy all possible concatenations, as the cardinality grows over powers rule. To allow room f a meaningful analysis, the cardinality of this set can be reduced by analyzing multi-li comments based on their locality.

Let the function $line(c_i)$ return a set of lines where comment c_i was found in and let $\mathcal{C}^+ = \{\overline{c_{i_1} c_{i_2} \ldots c_{i_k}} \mid \exists l_{i_1} \in line(c_{i_1}), l_{i_2} \in line(c_{i_2}), l_{i_k} \in line(c_{i_k}), l_{i_z} < l_{i_t} \forall z$ $t, c_{i_1} c_{i_2} \ldots c_{i_k} \in \mathcal{C}, i_x \neq i_y, \forall x \neq y, \nexists c_q \in \mathcal{C}, q \notin i_j, \nexists l_q \in line(c_q) s.t.\ l_{i_z} < l_q < l_{i_t}\}$, an denote by $\mathscr{C}^+ = (\mathcal{C}^+, m^+)$ the multiset of all **locally concatenated blocks of commen** from $\mathscr{A}$. It is important to note that m^+ exists, and it is equal to the total number of possib combinations of $l_{i_j}, j \in \overline{1 \ldots k}$.

In practice, the cardinality of $\mathcal{C}^+$ is a scaling issue for automatic detection, so let th subset $\mathcal{C}_r^+$ be defined, with the additional constraint from $\mathcal{C}^+$ that allows for maximur r single line comments concatenation, i.e., any element $\overline{c_{i_1} c_{i_2} \ldots c_{i_k}} \in \mathcal{C}_r^+$ must have k r. Likewise, let $\mathscr{C}_r^+ = (\mathcal{C}_r^+, m_r^+)$ be the multiset of all **locally concatenated blocks o comments of maximum length of** r from $\mathscr{A}$ and m_r^+ be the total number of possib combinations of $l_{i_j}, j \in \overline{1 \ldots k}$.

By convention, $\mathscr{C}_\infty^+ = \mathscr{C}^+$.

An important note to make is that, for any given finite $\mathscr{A}$, $\mathcal{C}^+$ will also be finite.

To prove this, let $r_0 = \sum_{i=1}^{|\mathcal{C}^+|} m(r_i)$. Therefore, the set $\mathscr{C}_{r_0}^+$ will contain the maximun possible length concatenation of comments, $\overline{c_{i_1} c_{i_2} \ldots c_{i_{r_0}}}$, this set representing the concaten tion of all comments from the source code. Therefore, $\forall r_x \geq r_0, \mathscr{C}_{r_x}^+ = \mathscr{C}_{r_0}^+$ and $\mathscr{C}^+ = \mathscr{C}_{r_0}^+$

Modeling Repetitive Comments

Because duplicated comments are a frequent phenomenon in code (Code Listing A. presents such an example), a worthwhile analysis would investigate the necessity o both repetition detection and locality context searching for code similarity analysis. This property will be explicitly used in subsequent sections related to the investigation o machine-readable comments, where the multiplicity of lint comments has a key role in computing the similarity.

To address situations where duplicate comments appear in different locations and to better capture the importance of locality context, the model requires an extension for repetitive comments.

The multiplicity is covered in the model via the multiplicity function m_r^+ of the multiset $(\mathcal{C}_r^+, m_r^+)$. Code Listing A.8 demonstrates how seemingly isolated single-line comments, when considered together, form a cohesive explanation requiring locality context for accurate analysis.

Locality context searching will be enforced in the models via the r-parameter of $\mathscr{C}_r^+$. Due to computational constraints, the research will only focus on $\mathscr{C}_r^+$, with a finite r. To pick an appropriate value of r, the authors have empirically evaluated the capabilities of detecting similarities with respect to r. Choosing a finite smaller value for r makes the approach prone to missing true positives, as well as not defending against willful changes between the analyzed versions. An improvement can be made if more computational resources are available by increasing the value of r, or using $\mathscr{C}_\infty^+$. The proposed models runs two main algorithms: one algorithm is optional and it is only applied for *generating the embeddings* for models that need one, such as transformers and sentence encoders, and the other algorithm is mandatory and it process the comments (or their associated embeddings) from different sources, one pair at a time. The complexity of the former algorithm grows linearly with r, while the latter algorithm is quadratic in r. Figure 3 presents some practical results, which outline the two dependencies of these algorithms with respect to the increase in r.

Choosing this particular value was, in this research, based on empirical tests on Kubernetes releases, where $r = 6$ was considered to be the right trade-off. For any $r \geq 6$, the numbers of similarities identified remained constant, and large chunks of similar comments identified were also covered by analyzing subsets. When evaluating the model, the increase from $r = 1$ to $r = 3$ led to several more matches, but the the growth from $r = 3$ to $r = 6$ slowed considerably. Because the only downside of choosing a larger value for r is the increase in the computational expense, it is recommended to adopt a value that fits the available physical resources, as well as potential time constraints of the application. Please consult Figure 3 for the performance implications associated with choosing $r = 6$, for the scenario analysed in this paper.

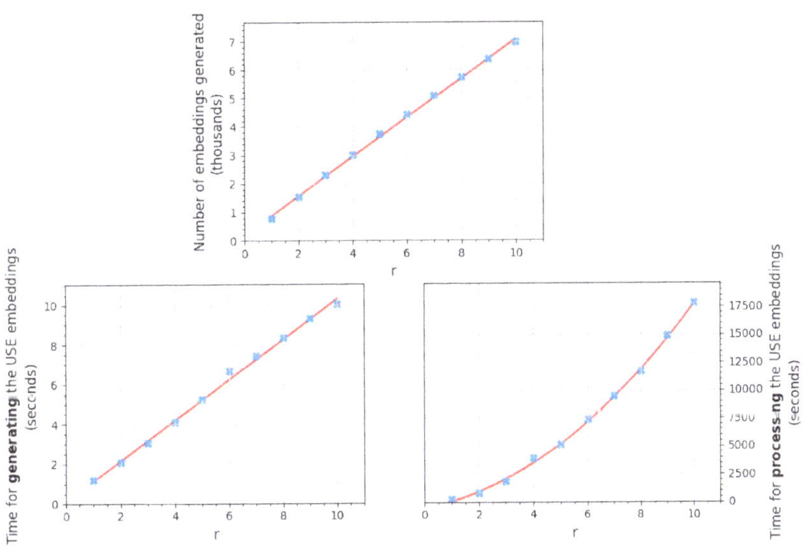

Figure 3. The performance of the Universal Sentence Encoder, when tested against different values of r, based on a subset of Kubernetes v1.2.1 and v1.3.1 code, analyzing a corpus of 6000 lines of code.

5. Analyzing Code Similarity

Sections 2 and 3 have emphasized the importance of comments to any non-trivial software project and, given their relevance, this research investigates if whether analyzing the comments from a source code can provide sufficient information to perform relevant measurements of code similarity. The presented approach would involve combining natural language processing techniques with the analysis of comment structure and their placement

within the code. This paper will separately treat machine- and human-readable comm
in the next two subsections.

5.1. Machine-Readable Comments

In order to validate whether machine-readable comments may help in measuring c
similarity to some degree, the research presents the evolution of ESlint [22] traces for
VSCode Project [23]. It is worth noting that because currently VScode releases hap
monthly, with the notable exception that there is no release in December, this provi
plenty of resources to analyse.

Figure 4 captures a subset of ESlint-identified issues in the VSCode Project, wh
some similarities between incremental versions of this software will be analysed.
analyzing the similarity for a particular use case, $\mathscr{C}_1^+$ suffices for identifying all the ES
suppressions.

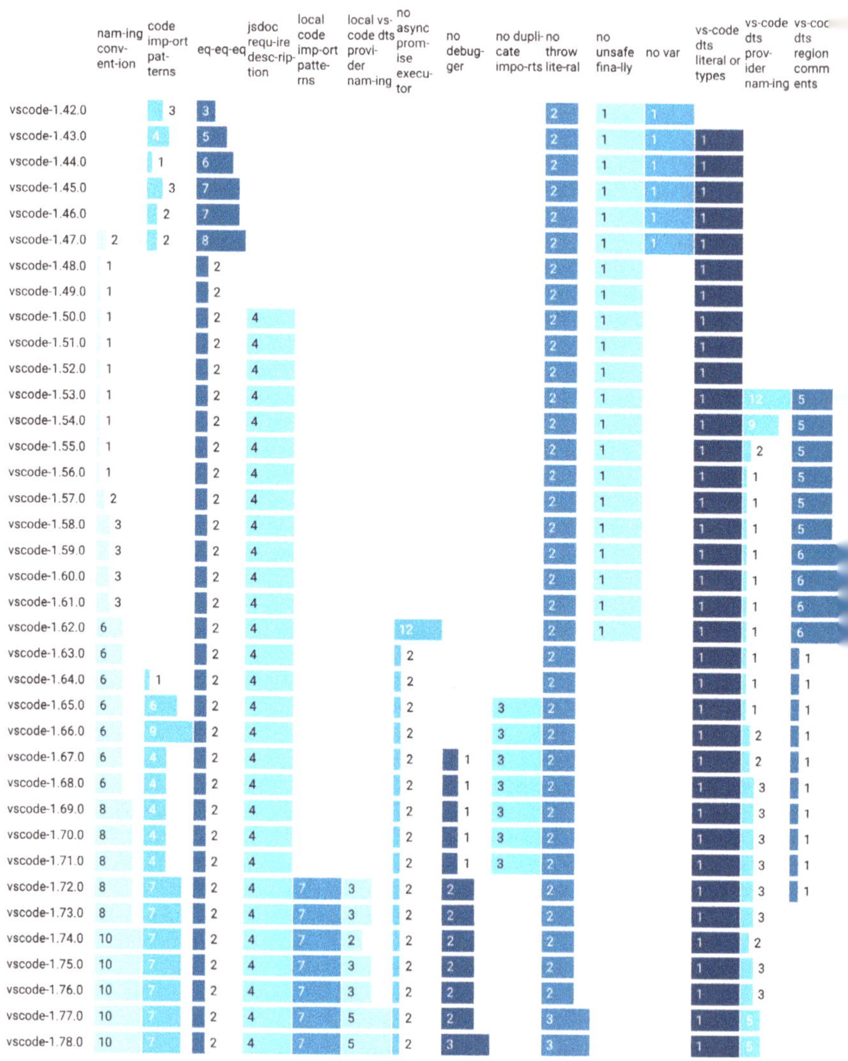

Figure 4. Subset of ESlint issues signaled on incremental VSCode versions, later than 1.42. Version
prior to this had no ESlint suppressing expressions.

Let $\mathcal{L}$ be the set of all lint overrides identified in $\mathscr{A}$. $\forall l \in \mathcal{L}\ \exists c_i \in C_1^+$, such that l appears in c_i. The occurrences of l are tracked by modeling the multiset $\mathscr{L} = (\mathcal{L}, m_l)$, where $m_l = \sum m(c_i) \forall i$, such that l appears in $c_i, c_i \in \mathscr{C}_1^+ = (C_1^+, m)$.

In order to compute a metric that captures the similarity of the two algorithms, defined by $\mathscr{A}_1$ and $\mathscr{A}_2$, based on the linter findings, the research uses the cosine similarity. Let $\mathscr{L}_1$ and $\mathscr{L}_2$ be the multisets that describe the lint overrides identified in $\mathscr{A}_1$ and $\mathscr{A}_2$ and let $\mathscr{L} = \mathscr{L}_1 \bigcup \mathscr{L}_2$. The method attaches to each algorithm $\mathscr{A}$ a vector embedding $v_{\mathscr{A}}$ that corresponds to the hot-encoding of the set of lint issues present in an $\mathscr{A}$, weighted by their occurrence.

$v_{\mathscr{A}} = [\bigcup m^{\#}(l_i)],\ \forall l_i \in \mathscr{L}$, where

$$m^{\#}(l_i) = \begin{cases} 0, & l_i \notin \mathscr{L}_{\mathscr{A}} \\ m(l_i), & l_i \in \mathscr{L}_{\mathscr{A}} \end{cases}$$

Figure 5 presents the results of computing the cosine-based similarity based on ESlint suppressions in various VSCode releases by computing the value $\cos(\theta) = \dfrac{v_{\mathscr{A}_1} \cdot v_{\mathscr{A}_2}}{\|v_{\mathscr{A}_1}\|_2 \|v_{\mathscr{A}_2}\|_2}$. This score contains more linter issues (27) than the ones presented in Figure 4 (a subset of 15 linter issues).

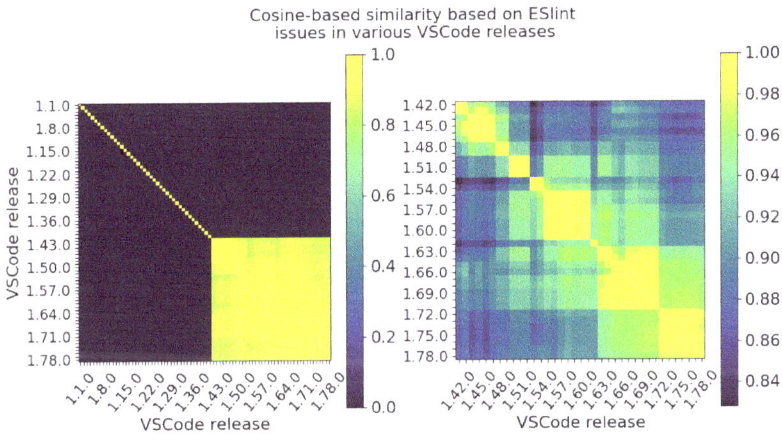

Figure 5. Similarity calculation based on ESlint data for various releases of VSCode. In the left heatmap, all the VScode releases are being presented, ranging from: 1.1 -> 1.78, and on the right, only a relevant subset of analyzed versions with ESlint reported issues are captured, versions: 1.42 -> 1.78. By convention, let $\cos(\theta) = 1$ if $\mathscr{A}_1 = \mathscr{A}_2$. The left image presents a limitation of the current model (for versions 1.1 -> 1.41) in the absence of machine-readable comments, for which the model is not able to produce meaningful similarity detection, while the right heatmap outlines cases where the model performs well and is able to create a relevant similarity measurement.

Of particular note are the similarity scores presented in Figure 5 are built entirely based on the cosine similarity of the resulting one-hot encodings obtained from the data available in Figure 4, and each square in the heatmap obtained in Figure 5 corresponds to the cosine similarity between the vectors available in the latter. For example, as the vectors defining the lint issues in VSCode versions v1.48 and v1.49 are equal, their cosine similarity score will be 1 and, therefore, matched with the highest intensity square in the heat-map.

It is worth mentioning that the closer the versions are, in general, the higher the similarity observed by this algorithm. Comparing v1.42 with v1.43, the similarity score obtained is around 0.991, while v1.42 with v1.44, the similarity is 0.947. Finally, v1.42 with v1.77 yields a similarity score of 0.867. The similarity is, however, not described by a strictly monotonic function. For example, v1.42 with v1.78 yields a similarity score of 0.870, grea than the one obtained against v1.77.

Please note that earlier than v1.42, there were no lint issues in the code of VSCode, $v_{\mathscr{A}}$ is a nil-vector and, therefore, cosine similarity is nil for each comparison. This resea therefore excludes versions below v1.42 from the analysis, for which the current meth does not provide any meaningful inputs. This is a known limitation of this model moc which is irrelevant for similarity analysis for any two source codes that lack machi readable comments.

5.2. *Human Comments*

Because the intend is to leverage established natural language processing technologi for computing code similarity through comment analysis, as a prerequisite, the resear aims to evaluate the applicability of such techniques to code comments. by analyzing t percentage of actual English words found within comments. To approximate whethe word belongs to the English lexicon, it will be cross-referenced against the `nltk`'s corpus words, `enchant`'s `US_en` dictionary and `wordnet`'s corpus.

Figure 6 shows that for Kubernetes, between 91 and 93 percent of all the alpha (contai only a–z letters) words from comments are words belonging to the English lexicon. Son coding style guides may actually enforce the proper use of grammar and vocabulary in t code-base. For example, the Google Style Guide for writing code in languages such as C+ Go or Java state that *comments that are complete sentences should be capitalized and punctuat like standard English sentences* [24] and *comments should be as readable as narrative text, wi proper capitalization and punctuation* [25].

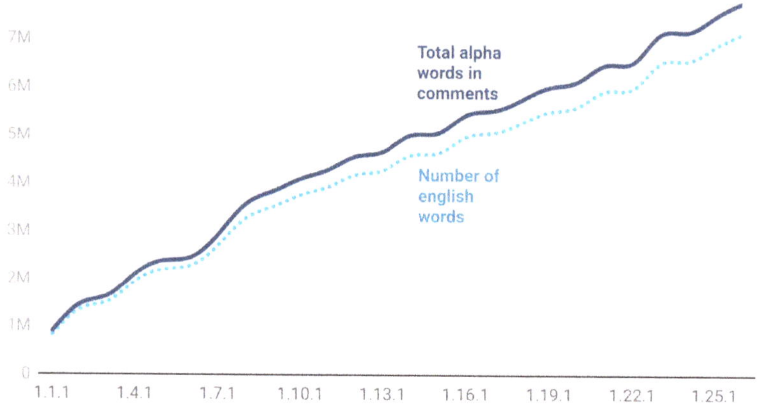

Figure 6. The evolution of the number of English identified words against the total number o alphabetical comment words identified in different versions of Kubernetes.

English dominates open-source software development as the most frequently usec human-readable language. This simplifies the analysis, as understanding the percentage of meaningful English words provides a close approximation of the total percentage o words belonging to the lexicon of a human-spoken language. This concept is illustrated ir Listing A.10. However, comments might not always adhere strictly to natural language syntax, even when intended to convey meaning similar to spoken language, which may be a limitation of the presented solution. In Listing A.11, even if the name of the flag is not part of any lexicon, it is easier for humans to understand the meaning of that value.

To analyze the similarity between two algorithms, defined by $\mathscr{A}_1$ and $\mathscr{A}_2$, the model will investigate $\mathscr{C}^+_{6_1} = (C^+_{6_1}, m^+_{6_1})$ and $\mathscr{C}^+_{6_2} = (C^+_{6_2}, m^+_{6_2})$, the multiset containing locally concatenated blocks of comments of maximum length of 6 from $\mathscr{A}_1$ and $\mathscr{A}_2$. The models are detecting similarities in code comments by computing a similarity function $s(c_1, c_2) \in [0,1]$

against each two elements of these sets and a threshold value $t \in (0,1]$. If $s(c_1, c_2) \geq t$, the model considers c_1, c_2 to have a similarity and labels the pair accordingly.

There are trade-offs in choosing an appropriate value of t. At limit cases, $t \to 0$ will make all comments look similar, while $t \to 1$ will enforce that only exact comments are labeled with similarities.

The choice of similarity function is crucial to this approach. Since obtaining definitively similar code samples is challenging [26], this study constructs the analysis dataset using incremental versions of the same program. The assumption is that recent versions represent a high degree of similarity. To validate whether comments can indicate similarity between different releases, this model is evaluated against the evolution of comments in various Kubernetes versions. The research explores a wide range of techniques: from basic string matching and fuzzy matching with **rapidfuzz** [27], to advanced NLP approaches. These include cosine similarity calculations based on **word2vec** embeddings [28], as well as models based on *deep contextualized of word representations*, which aim to create vector embeddings from the code comments.

A Levenshtein-based similarity function will typically provide higher precision scores but will be prone not to detect changes of form without substance, while a contextualized word representation may be able to generalize for more complex cases but is at risk of triggering false positives. More details backing up this statement will be available in Sections 7 and 8.

It is important to consider that the model treats consecutive comments as potentially connected and analyzes them accordingly (up to r). In reality, they could be related, or they may not be related at all. That is not a limitation of the approach, because if the model matches the entire group as similar, with a distinct group of consecutive comments obtained from the analyzed source, related or not locally, they result in a similarity that is worth analyzing. In the context of plagiarism detection, as per the argument of [15], *"after specific sections of the programs have been flagged as similar, it shouldn't matter whether the questionable code was initially uncovered by software or by a person"* and that *"the argument for plagiarism should stand on its own"*.

Another consideration in choosing the optimal model is the associated complexity of the method. In Table 2, it is presented the total time required to perform the two tasks (generating and processing the similarities) on a dataset of over 12 thousands lines of Go code. The total time of the analysis is the sum of these intervals. Simpler models like Word2Vec are faster for both generating and processing embeddings, while more complex models (such as ELMo or RoBERTa) are computationally demanding. The Universal Sentence Encoder demonstrates significant efficiency in embedding generation but incurs a longer computational cost during the subsequent processing stage. Levenshtein-based models are notable outliers in the presented table, as their extremely good performance in terms of speed, but come with the trade-off of missing broader semantic understanding.

Table 2. Time statistics (obtained on a 2.3 GHz Dual-Core Intel Core i5 processor) for generating and processing embeddings on over 12,000 Go lines, obtained from a subset of Kubernetes v1.2.1 and v1.3.1 and v1.25.1 repositories. The Levenshtein-based models require no prior work for generating embeddings, and the processing step simply involves evaluating the text-based similarity of the two analyzed comments.

Model	Generating Embeddings	Computing Similarities
Levenshtein	n/a	39 s
Word2Vec	32 s	1 m 44 s
ELMo	12 h 14 m	1 h 57 m
RoBERTa	28 m 48 s	1 h 58 m
Universal Sentence Encoder	6 s	2 h 12 m

For analyzing the performance of the models, the authors have compared the predictions of similarity of the models against a human-labeled dataset obtained from over 12,000 lines of Go code from the source code of Kubernetes *"/pkg/api"* directories versions v1 (April, 2016), v1.3.1 (July 2016) and v1.25.1 (September 2021). The dataset contains 3 comments, and the ground truth contains 49573 identified similarities between pair comments (including 3594 identity similarities). This dataset has a big class imbalance: total number of *'not similar'* matches on the code comments is nearly *6 million*, compa to *'similar'* classes, which are on the order of *50 thousands*. As a result, to obtain the m reliable assessment of the model's performance, in this analysis the evaluation based on F1-Score will be prioritize. This is because a high F1-Score indicates the model perfor well in both minimizing both false positives and false negatives, even if the datase unbalanced.

The performance of the models on this dataset is also summarized in Table 3 by eva ating the models using precision, recall and F1-Score as metrics. It also computes the ma and weighted average, as well as the accuracy. The model based on the Universal Sente Encoder seems to achieve the best quantitative results, maintaining a good balance betw precision and recall on the analyzed Kubernetes-based test dataset described above.

Table 3. A performance comparison of different models tested against around 35 thousand comme from three versions of Kubernetes source code. The presence of numerous trivial similarity examp within the dataset, such as identical or nearly identical comments, can lead to artificially infla performance metrics, even for relatively simplistic models. Optimizing for the long tail provide more realistic measure of a model's capabilities in real-world code analysis. The ELMo-based mo is being ignored when computing the most appropriate model for optimizing a certain metric becau of the low F1-Score.

Model	Metric	Precision	Recall	F1-Score
Levenshtein	not similar	0.99823	**0.99999**	0.99912
	similar	**0.99979**	0.77115	0.87071
	macro avg	0.99901	0.88557	0.93491
	weighted avg	0.99824	0.99824	0.99813
	accuracy			0.99824
Word2Vec	not similar	**0.99996**	0.99923	0.99959
	similar	0.90861	**0.99469**	0.94970
	macro avg	0.95428	**0.99696**	0.97465
	weighted avg	0.99926	0.99919	0.99921
	accuracy			0.99919
ELMo [1]	not similar	0.99999	0.46312	0.63306
	similar	0.01420	0.99984	0.02800
	macro avg	0.50710	0.73148	0.33053
	weighted avg	0.99243	0.46724	0.62841
	accuracy			0.46724
RoBERTa	not similar	0.99832	0.99871	0.99852
	similar	0.82492	0.78297	0.80339
	macro avg	0.91162	0.89084	0.90096
	weighted avg	0.99699	0.99706	0.99702
	accuracy			0.99706
USE	not similar	0.99986	0.99998	**0.99992**
	similar	0.99856	0.98162	**0.99002**
	macro avg	**0.99921**	0.99081	**0.99497**
	weighted avg	**0.99985**	**0.99985**	**0.99985**
	accuracy			**0.99985**

[1] The ELMo model is not taken into account for optimizing a certain metric because of the low overall F1-score.

Because the dataset contains many comments that are either identical or have very minor changes across consecutive versions, even simple models will easily identify them as similar. This artificially inflates accuracy, precision and recall. It is therefore critical to optimize the long tail of misses in the data presented in Table 3, as spotting trivial similarities is far less valuable than pinpointing the more subtle similarities that require a deeper understanding of the natural language used.

5.2.1. Levenshtein-Based Models

Rapidfuzz [27] is an implementation of an approximate string matching algorithm, which aims to only approximately find strings that match a given pattern based on *Levenshtein distance*. While matches in this approach are high quality and clear indications on similarity [29–31], produced by making a variety of minor changes of inserting, deleting or substituting words, the method has a low hit rate [32] on more advanced cases, where structural changes are involved.

The results seem to be of high quality due to the number of false positive matches being minimal compared to other methods. For high values of t, the number of false positive matches is almost nonexistent (for $t = 1$, only exact matching will be performed). Some qualitative examples are described in Appendix B.1, *in Examples B1 towards B6*. However, overall, the match perspective is bounded in identifying true positives. It works really well in identifying form changes, such as typos, refactoring or (almost) duplicated code comments.

5.2.2. Word2Vec-Based Models

Spacy's approach to computing similarity involves assigning each word a vector representation derived from a pre-trained model. This model has been trained on large corpora using the Word2Vec technique [28], enabling the creation of contextual embeddings. To calculate the similarity between full sentences, Spacy averages the word embeddings and computes the cosine difference. While generally useful [33], this method can yield unexpected results. False positives may arise due to the *"canceling out"* effect within the averaged embeddings or from the model misinterpreting similarities between unrelated words.

This method can identify the very vast majority of similarities that Levenshtein-based models can, as seen in Appendix B.2, *example B7*, but it can also find more complex sequence paraphrases, as seen in *examples B8 and B9*. *Examples B10 and B11* capture more cases, including complete rephrases and rewording of the original statements. *Example B12* is a debatable case if the similarity is correctly identified by the current model. While the two comments refer to similar things (bind addresses, IP addresses, 0.0.0.0, servers and serving), it is rather difficult to state their exact similarity, even for a human expert.

5.2.3. ELMo-Based Models

ELMo [34] is a model that computes the embeddings from the states of a two-layer bi-directional language model [35]. In practice, running the *ELMo*-based model for large projects is expensive computationally. The risk of false positives can be addressed either by increasing the value of t, or by human judgement. Even when performing the detection with a very high value for the threshold ($t = 0.98$), in the presented experiments, the model identified a really high number of false positive matches, consequently leading to inefficiency.

The suitability of ELMo-based models for this specific task appears questionable. Analysis of the examples reveals shortcomings, as presented by the qualitative analysis on the examples from Appendix B.3. The only similarity in *example B13* is that both comments reference the same GenericAPIServer, but the context in which it is referenced appears to be completely different (*creation* | *usage* of IP). *Examples B14–B16* seem completely unrelated, and the matches are not particularly helpful in helping the manual labor involved by the operators.

5.2.4. Sentence Transformers

In the research, the authors have used the RoBERTa [36] model implementation fr the SentenceTransformers framework, which is a BERT [37]-based model to create emb dings from text, as developed in [38]. These neural networks use Siamese structures convert semantically meaningful embeddings from sentences. Given the output emb dings generated from $\mathscr{C}_6^+$, the research computed the cosine similarity and chose $t = 0.$ for the experiments. Overall, the quality of the matches is pretty high.

As shown in *examples B17–B19* from Appendix B.4, the model has thus proven go capabilities of identifying similarities, as it can identify pretty well changes in the phras as well as similar meaning within multiple different statements.

5.2.5. Universal Sentence Encoder

The Universal Sentence Encoder [17] is yet another model that the authors ha selected for evaluating for encoding sentences into embedding vectors. The model (ava able online, open-source, at: https://tfhub.dev/google/universal-sentence-encoder/ accessed on 16 March 2024) has been trained with a deep averaging network encoder [3 Similar to the Sentence Transformers model, the use of the Universal Sentence Encod seems to provide a better balance concerning the ratio of true to false positives than th rest of the analyzed methods. *Examples B20–B22*, referenced in Appendix B.5, show sever qualitative similarities identified by the model.

Qualitatively, the most notable misclassifications of this model, which are not observe in simpler methods such as Levenshtein or Word2vec models, happens in commen that contain numerical values. For example, between Kubernetes v1.2.1 and v1.25.1, change observed around the code-base is that "*Copyright 2016*" comments got replaced b "*Copyright 2021*". The model fails to identify in many cases such similarities, as exemplifie in *example B23*.

This paper evaluated the performance of the algorithm for multiple values of r an summarized the results in Figure 3. According to the results displayed, the generatio part of the embeddings is very fast for this particular model, as it can generate more tha 700 embeddings per second on a 2.3 GHz Dual-Core Intel Core i5 processor, and the tim efficacy grows linearly with larger inputs. In terms of the processing, as mentioned i Section 4, the performance is quadratic because the required number of evaluations i quadratic in the total number of embeddings, and practical experiments have observe that, on the same architecture, it executes about 2800 similarity evaluations per second.

6. Implementation Details and Reproducibility

The techniques presented in this paper have been incorporated into Project Martia an open-source initiative for automated software plagiarism detection (source code avai able at https://github.com/raresraf/project-martial, accessed on 16 March 2024). Th implementation includes a user interface that visually highlights potentially similar cod sections, as identified by the similarity functions described within the presented model The authors acknowledge the valuable insights provided by the work in [35] for the analysi of human-readable comments, as well as the detailed implementation details that hav been provided.

The natural language processing components of the models are being implemented in Python, utilizing libraries such as scikit-learn and Matplotlib for the presentation of the data and frameworks such as TensorFlow and PyTorch for importing, loading and running the transformer-based models presented in this paper. A review of the dependencies used for the processing of human-based comments can be consulted within the project-martia code, under the comments drivers from the "*modules/*".

For syntactic and semantic code parsing, the software stack uses ANTLR (ANother Tool for Language Recognition), a parser generator that uses a top-down LL-based algorithm for parsing.

The data presented in Table 1 and in Figures 1, 2 and 6 are reproducible using the modules associated with the project-martial code, under *"grammars/"*. The data presented in Figures 4 and 5 are reproducible using the modules under *"parsers/"*. The raw data numbers are also available under *"dataset/"*. Figure 3 is reproducible running the executables provided under *"scripts/"*.

For the plots, Figures 1, 2, 5 and 6 are built using datawrapper, an online data visualization product. Figures 3 and 5 are generated using the Matplotlib library.

The web-based user interface is developed in TypeScript, providing a responsive and intuitive experience for code review. Figure 7 illustrates how the software highlights potentially similar comments identified, aiding users in identifying areas of interest for code similarity. For a review of the implementation, please consult the resources under *ui/*.

The back-end server is built in Python, using the Flask framework, which is capable of serving API requests over HTTP, and the source code is accessible in the root directory of the project, under *main.py*.

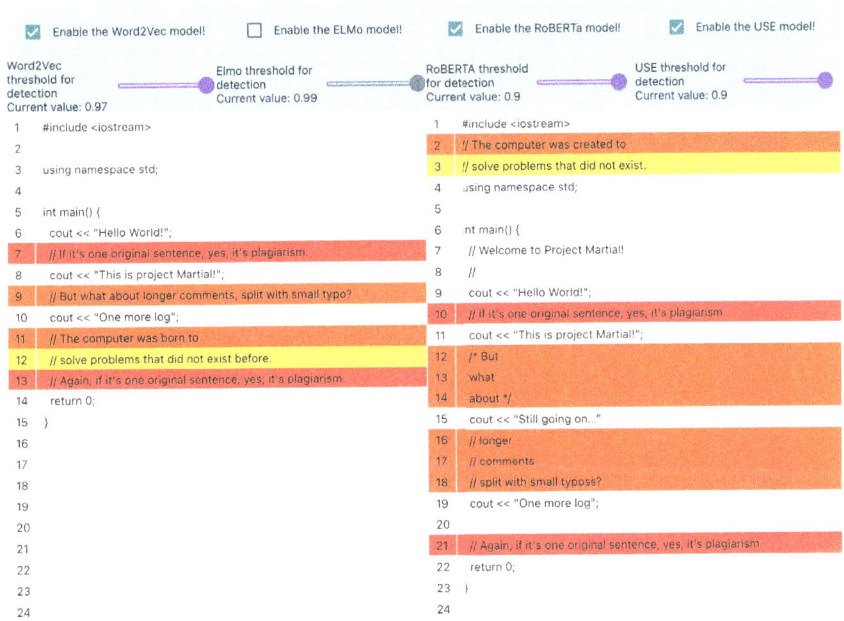

Figure 7. The web-based interface of Project Martial, highlighting potentially similar comments to visually guide users towards areas where code similarities might exist.

7. Discussion

For the proposed solutions, this research observed that Levenshtein-based models offer excellent precision but may miss broader semantic similarities, while contextualized word embeddings such as Word2Vec or Universal Sentence Encoders perform better by capturing some of these complexities. However, these models might have some more false positives than Levenshtein-based, which minimizes almost to zero this metric.

The dataset used for evaluation was extracted from a subset of three Kubernetes versions, accumulating over 12 thousands lines of code and around 50 thousands identified similarities in comments. The best (Based on the F1-Score achieved on the dataset presented in this paper, from collected commentaries from three Kubernetes versions) model was based on the Universal Sentence Encoder [17], achieving a strong balance between precision and recall, but it showed some limitations when operating with sentences containing numerical values.

In addition, the Universal Sentence Encoder-based model stands out with effic embedding generation, though processing of the embeddings is slower, due to thei creased size. As expected, simpler models such as Levenshtein- and Word2Vec-based significantly faster (see Table 2). Due to their still good performance, Word2Vec-ba models can provide feasible alternatives to Universal Sentence Encoders, as they only u fraction of the computational power required to run the analysis.

8. Conclusions and Future Work

This study aimed to develop practical methods for detecting code similarities analyzing various types of software comments, and the results confirm the valuable cor bution of comments in revealing code similarities.

Machine-readable comments (like ESlint directives) proved surprisingly effect when using techniques like cosine similarity and one-hot encoding, while the investigat of human-readable English comments demonstrated the power of semantic similar models (Sentence Transformers, Universal Sentence Encoder) over form-based matchi techniques (Levenshtein-based approaches). The former model can be classified in collection of *software birthmarks* approaches, while the latter is an *embedding-based* mode

The research, performed on a diverse set of open-source projects, confirms the predc inance of English in open-source code comments, making NLP methods highly applical However, a further area of research can be analyzing the potential deviations from strict r ural language syntax, which should be considered when analyzing non-machine-readal comments, as this case exists in software projects, as pointed out in Table 1 and Figure The quantitative analysis of comment distribution has been captured in Table 1 for vario open-source projects (including projects written in Go, TypeScript, Java, C and C++), ai ing to uncover language-specific commenting practices, readability trends and potent correlations with project maturity.

Integrating this research into Project Martial adds practical value by enhancing t capabilities of software plagiarism detection tools. The two proposed models are used an ensemble manner, meaning that their predictions are combined in the score of similari to achieve a more accurate and robust outcome.

As future work, it would be useful to extend this analysis beyond the analyzed datase of Kubernetes and VSCode repositories in order to capture a larger variety of softwa languages and project types. This assesses the wider applicability of comment-base similarity detection, as well as performing further human-assisted validations, on th utility of these tools, to make the right trade-offs between precision and recall while fir tuning the parameters. Nonetheless, as the state-of-the-art pre-trained language mode improve, it becomes possible to update detectors to generate more sophisticated sentenc level representations for similarity checks than the capabilities of the current models.

Additionally, future work could explore the fine-tuning of models like RoBERTa other Sentence Transformers on large-scale code comment datasets. This fine-tuning ha the potential to improve the models' sensitivity to the nuances of programming languag and domain-specific terminology often found in comments.

Finally, the model's reliance on comments presents a clear limitation, hindering i use on code-bases which have minimal documentation or for which comments have bee intentionally removed. Future research, as part of the development of Project Martial, wi investigate hybrid approaches that synergistically combine comment-based analysis wit structural code analysis techniques. This would provide a more robust similarity detectio solution applicable to a wider range of software.

Author Contributions: Conceptualization: R.F. and E.S.; Methodology: R.F. and E.S.; Software: R.F Validation: R.F. and E.S.; Writing: R.F. and E.S. All authors have read and agreed to the publishe version of the manuscript.

Funding: This research received no external funding.

Data Availability Statement: All the datasets used and the experiment code are available online at https://github.com/raresraf/project-martial, accessed on 16 March 2024.

Conflicts of Interest: The authors declare no conflicts of interest.

Appendix A. Code Listings: Classification Model

This appendix contains relevant code listings that offer detailed examples illustrating the context in which certain statements in the paper are made.

Listing A.1. This language specification of the C programming language is exemplified by the ANTLR's implementation of the language grammar in the open-source examples [39]. Skip statements instruct the lexer to discard a given token, implying that a skipped lexer rule cannot be later used in a parser rules.

```
BlockComment: '/*' .*? '*/' -> skip;
LineComment: '//' [\r\n]* -> skip;
```

Listing A.2. To support the Greek alphabet in a python program, the cp869 codec may be used. This is indicated to the interpreter by specifying a first-line comment.

```
# -*- coding: cp869 -*-
```

Listing A.3. A well-known method for making scripts directly executable is the UNIX 'shebang' line. For example, this "comment" line appears at the start of a Python script and indicates what interpreter should be used (in this case, version 3.9). Python interpreters themselves will ignore the shebang line since it is not relevant to the code's logic, but it provides valuable information to the operating system in order to be able to launch it in execution.

```
#!/usr/bin/env python3.9
```

Listing A.4. pylint is a tool specific for Python. In order to enable or disable a message for a particular module, a comment-like statement should be added.

```
# pylint: disable=wildcard-import, method-hidden, line-too-long
```

Listing A.5. For TypeScript, the disabling of the type checking for a source file may be accomplished with a two-line comment.

```
// ESlint-disable-next-line @typescript-ESlint/ban-ts-comment
// @ts-nocheck
```

Listing A.6. Cppcheck is a static analysis tool that checks C/C++ code for various err and style issues, including potential buffer access out-of-bounds errors. This comment t Cppcheck to ignore the "bufferAccessOutOfBounds" warning on the line of code wh this comment appears.

```
// cppcheck-suppress bufferAccessOutOfBounds

array[index] = value; // This line might trigger the warning
```

Listing A.7. An OpenMP example that showcases the "pragma omp parallel for" synt a core OpenMP directive. It instructs the compiler to create a parallel region where t following for loop will be executed by multiple threads. In the absence of parallel supp for a given architecture, the directive will simply be ignored, and the program will be ab to (correctly) proceed and execute the statements in a serial manner.

```
int sum = 0;
#pragma omp parallel for reduction(+:sum)
for (int i = 0; i < N; i++) {
    sum += a[i];
}
```

Listing A.8. Sample (Kubernetes) comment that needs to be analyzed in context to captu the correct meaning. Individually reading and interpreting single lines of comments is n enough for a complete understanding. For example, comment line 4 has no standalon meaning, but in context, it connects the first three blocks, as well as with the fifth line comment.

```
// teststale checks the staleness of a test binary. go test -c builds a test
// binary but it does no staleness check. In other words, every time one runs
// go test -c, it compiles the test packages and links the binary even when
// nothing has changed. This program helps to mitigate that problem by allowing
// to check the staleness of a given test package and its binary.
```

Listing A.9. Example (Kubernetes) of situations where duplicated comments may occur

```
// In host_config.go.
type Resources struct {
  ...
  // Kernel memory limit (in bytes)
  KernelMemory int64 `json:"kernel_memory"`
  ...
}

// In cgroup_unix.go.
type Resources struct {
  // Applicable to UNIX platforms
  ...
  KernelMemory          int64          // Kernel memory limit (in bytes)
  ...
}
```

Listing A.10. Sample comment from Kubernetes project, written in compliant English grammar.

```
'ackage leaderelection implements leader election of a set of endpoints.
't uses an annotation in the endpoints object to store the record of the election state.
This implementation does not guarantee that only one client is acting as a leader (a.k.a. fencing).
A client observes timestamps captured locally to infer the state of the leader election.
```

Listing A.11. Example for Linux Kernel where a comment is used to point the reader from the hexadecimal number 0x00400000 to the EXT4_EOFBLOCKS_FL flag. ext4 is pointing to the Linux journaling file system (fourth extended filesystem) and EOFBLOCKS is indicating the number of blocks allocated beyond the end-of-file (EOF). This is how the EXT4_EOFBLOCKS_FL block can have a natural language equivalent, while at first glance, it was not composed of parts from lexicon.

```
0x00400000 /* EXT4_EOFBLOCKS_FL */
```

Appendix B. Code Listings: Qualitative Analysis

This appendix section presents a qualitative analysis of comments identified as similar using the proposed models. To provide context, examples of similar comments are included, along with an in-depth discussion of their characteristics in Section 5.

Appendix B.1. Qualitative Analysis of the Identified Similarities for the Levenshtein-Based Model

This section contains some sample similarities, identified in comment snippets between releases Kubernetes 1.2.1 and 1.3.1, using a similarity score with the matching threshold $t = 0.97$ and a Levenshtein-based model:

Example B1

Copyright 2015 The Kubernetes Authors All rights reserved

Copyright 2016 The Kubernetes Authors All rights reserved

Example B2

For maximal backwards compatibility if no subnets are tagged it will fallback to the current subnet

For maximal backwards compatibility if no subnets are tagged it will fallback to the current subnet

Example B3

Canonicalize returns the canonical form of q and its suffix see comment on Quantity

CanonicalizeBytes returns the canonical form of q and its suffix see comment on Quantity

Example B4

May also be set in SecurityContext If set in both SecurityContext and

May also be set in PodSecurityContext If set in both SecurityContext and

Example B5

If the affinity requirements specified by this field are not met at

If the anti-affinity requirements specified by this field are not met at

Example B6

URISchemeHTTP means that the scheme used will be http

URISchemeHTTPS means that the scheme used will be https

Appendix B.2. Qualitative Analysis of the Identified Similarities for the Word2vec-Based Mod

This section identifies comments sections with high similarity scores between relea Kubernetes 1.2.1 and 1.3.1 using Spacy's word2vec-based similarity score with a thresh of $t = 0.97$:

Example B7

InstanceID returns the cloud provider ID of the specified instance

ExternalID returns the cloud provider ID of the specified instance deprecated

Example B8

Produces a path that etcd understands to the resource by combining the namespace in the context with the given prefix

Produces a path that etcd understands to the root of the resource by combining the namespace in the context with the giv prefix

Example B9

Because in release 11 apisextensionsv1beta1 returns response with empty APIVersion we use StripVersionNegotiatedSerializer

Because in release 11 api returns response with empty APIVersion we use StripVersionNegotiatedSerializer to keep the respon backwards

Example B10

Scans all managed zones to return the GCE PD Prefer getDiskByName if the zone can be established

zone can be provided to specify the zone for the PD if empty all managed zones will be searched

Example B11

leaseDuration is the duration that nonleader candidates will wait after observing a leadership renewal until attempting t acquire leadership of a led but unrenewed leader slot This is effectively the maximum duration that a leader can be stoppe before it is replaced by another candidate This is only applicable if leader election is enabled

renewDeadline is the interval between attempts by the acting master to renew a leadership slot before it stops leading This mus be less than or equal to the lease duration This is only applicable if leader election is enabled

Example B12

healthzBindAddress is the IP address for the health check server to serve on defaulting to 127.0.0.1 set to 0.0.0.0 for all interface

bindAddress is the IP address for the proxy server to serve on set to 0.0.0.0

Appendix B.3. Qualitative Analysis of the Identified Similarities for the ELMo-Based Model

This appendix presents several qualitative examples of identified comments similarities between releases Kubernetes 1.2.1 and 1.3.1 using an ELMo-based model with a very high threshold value ($t = 0.98$).

Example B13

Select the first valid IP from ServiceClusterIPRange to use as the GenericAPIServer service IP

New returns a new instance of GenericAPIServer from the given config

Example B14

is because the forwarding rule is used as the indicator that the load

what its IP address is if it exists and any error we encountered

Example B15

Map storing information about all groups to be exposed in discovery response

Used to customize default proxy dialtls options

Example B16

Unless required by applicable law or agreed to in writing software

EnsureLoadBalancer creates a new load balancer name or updates the existing one Returns the status of the balancer

Appendix B.4. Qualitative Analysis of the Identified Similarities for the RoBERTa-Based Model

The RoBERTa-based model detected comment sections with high similarity scores between Kubernetes releases 1.2.1 and 1.3.1. These findings are presented in this section.

Example B17

a mustache is an eligible helper if

a mustache is definitely a helper if it is an eligible helper and

Example B18

target average CPU utilization represented as a percentage of requested CPU over all the pods

current average CPU utilization over all pods represented as a percentage of requested CPU

Example B19

Available represents the storage space available bytes for the Volume For Volumes that share a filesystem with the host eg emptydir hostpath this is the available

Capacity represents the total capacity bytes of the volumes underlying storage For Volumes that share a filesystem with the host eg emptydir hostpath this is the size of the underlying storage

Appendix B.5. Qualitative Analysis of the Identified Similarities for the Universal Sentence Encoder-Based Model

This section presents some qualitative analysis on comments exhibiting high similarity scores between Kubernetes releases 1.2.1 and 1.3.1, as detected by the Universal Sentence Encoder-based model.

Example B20

This is a simple passthrough of the ELB client interface which allows for testing

This is a simple passthrough of the Autoscaling client interface which allows for testing

Example B21

so this implementation always returns nil false

LoadBalancer always returns nil false in this implementation

Example B22

Returns resources allocated to system cgroups in the machine

SystemCgroupsLimit returns resources allocated to system cgroups in the machine

While the quantitative analysis shows that this model performs well, qualitatively, common misclassification that this model encounters when needing to handle numeric values can be observed. The example presented below was not observed by the model as potential similarity:

Example B23

Copyright 2016 The Kubernetes Authors.

Copyright 2021 The Kubernetes Authors.

References

1. Schleimer, S.; Wilkerson, D.S.; Aiken, A. Winnowing: Local algorithms for document fingerprinting. In Proceedings of the 20(ACM SIGMOD International Conference on Management of Data, San Diego, CA, USA, 10–12 June 2003; pp. 76–85.
2. Chilowicz, M.; Duris, E.; Roussel, G. Syntax tree fingerprinting for source code similarity detection. In Proceedings of the 20C IEEE 17th International Conference on Program Comprehension, Vancouver, BC, Canada, 17–19 May 2009; pp. 243–247.
3. Narayanan, S.; Simi, S. Source code plagiarism detection and performance analysis using fingerprint based distance measu method. In Proceedings of the 2012 7th International Conference on Computer Science & Education (ICCSE), Melbourne, VI(Australia, 14–17 July 2012; pp. 1065–1068.
4. Cesare, S.; Xiang, Y. *Software Similarity and Classification*; Springer: Cham, Switzerland, 2012.
5. Myles, G.; Collberg, C. K-gram based software birthmarks. In Proceedings of the 2005 ACM symposium on Applied Computin Santa Fe, NM, USA, 13–17 May 2005; pp. 314–318.
6. Tian, Z.; Zheng, Q.; Liu, T.; Fan, M.; Zhuang, E.; Yang, Z. Software Plagiarism Detection with Birthmarks Based on Dynamic Ke Instruction Sequences. *IEEE Trans. Softw. Eng.* **2015**, *41*, 1217–1235. [CrossRef]
7. Myles, G.; Collberg, C. Detecting software theft via whole program path birthmarks. In Proceedings of the Information Security 7th International Conference, ISC 2004, Palo Alto, CA, USA, 27–29 September 2004; Proceedings 7; Springer: Cham, Switzerlanc 2004; pp. 404–415.
8. Ullah, F.; Wang, J.; Farhan, M.; Habib, M.; Khalid, S. Software plagiarism detection in multiprogramming languages usin machine learning approach. *Concurr. Comput. Pract. Exp.* **2021**, *33*, e5000. [CrossRef]
9. Lu, B.; Liu, F.; Ge, X.; Liu, B.; Luo, X. A software birthmark based on dynamic opcode n-gram. In Proceedings of the Internationa Conference on Semantic Computing (ICSC 2007), Irvine, CA, USA, 17–19 September 2007; pp. 37–44.
10. Tian, Z.; Wang, Q.; Gao, C.; Chen, L.; Wu, D. Plagiarism detection of multi-threaded programs via siamese neural networks. *IEEE Access* **2020**, *8*, 160802–160814. [CrossRef]
11. Chen, Z.; Monperrus, M. A literature study of embeddings on source code. *arXiv* **2019**, arXiv:1904.03061.
12. Alon, U.; Brody, S.; Levy, O.; Yahav, E. code2seq: Generating sequences from structured representations of code. *arXiv* **2018**, arXiv:1808.01400.
13. Alon, U.; Zilberstein, M.; Levy, O.; Yahav, E. code2vec: Learning distributed representations of code. *Proc. ACM Program. Lang* **2019**, *3*, 1–29. [CrossRef]
14. Folea, R.; Iacob, R.; Slusanschi, E.; Rebedea, T. Complexity-Based Code Embeddings. In *Proceedings of the International Conference on Computational Collective Intelligence*; Springer: Cham, Switzerland, 2023; pp. 256–269.
15. Plagiarism Detection. Available online: https://theory.stanford.edu/~aiken/moss/ (accessed on 23 September 2023).

Wahle, J.P.; Ruas, T.; Kirstein, F.; Gipp, B. How large language models are transforming machine-paraphrased plagiarism. *arXiv* **2022**, arXiv:2210.03568.

Cer, D.; Yang, Y.; Kong, S.y.; Hua, N.; Limtiaco, N.; John, R.S.; Constant, N.; Guajardo-Cespedes, M.; Yuan, S.; Tar, C.; et al. Universal sentence encoder. *arXiv* **2018**, arXiv:1803.11175.

Knuth, D.E. *The Art of Computer Programming*; Pearson Education: London, UK, 1997; Volume 3.

Kernighan, B.W.; Ritchie, D.M. *The C PROGRAMMING Language*; Prentice hall: London, UK, 1988.

Burns, B.; Grant, B.; Oppenheimer, D.; Brewer, E.; Wilkes, J. Borg, omega, and kubernetes. *Commun. ACM* **2016**, *59*, 50–57. [CrossRef]

Torvalds, L. The linux edge. *Commun. ACM* **1999**, *42*, 38–39. [CrossRef]

Find and Fix Problems in Your JavaScript Code—ESLint—Pluggable JavaScript Linter. Available online: https://eslint.org/ (accessed on 27 October 2023).

Visual Studio Code—Code Editing. Redefined. Available online: https://code.visualstudio.com/ (accessed on 27 October 2023).

styleguide | Style Guides for Google-Originated Open-SOURCE Projects. Available online: https://google.github.io/styleguide/go/decisions (accessed on 26 March 2023).

Google C++ Style Guide. Available online: https://google.github.io/styleguide/cppguide.html (accessed on 26 March 2023).

Chae, D.K.; Ha, J.; Kim, S.W.; Kang, B.; Im, E.G. Software plagiarism detection: A graph-based approach. In Proceedings of the 22nd ACM International Conference on Information & Knowledge Management, San Francisco, CA, USA, 27 October–1 November 2013; pp. 1577–1580.

rapidfuzz · PyPI. Available online: https://pypi.org/project/rapidfuzz/ (accessed on 8 December 2023).

Mikolov, T.; Chen, K.; Corrado, G.; Dean, J. Efficient estimation of word representations in vector space. *arXiv* **2013**, arXiv:1301.3781.

Su, Z.; Ahn, B.R.; Eom, K.Y.; Kang, M.K.; Kim, J.P.; Kim, M.K. Plagiarism detection using the Levenshtein distance and Smith-Waterman algorithm. In Proceedings of the 2008 3rd International Conference on Innovative Computing Information and Control, Dalian, China, 18–20 June 2008; p. 569.

Scerbakov, N.; Schukin, A.; Sabinin, O. Plagiarism detection in SQL student assignments. In *Proceedings of the Teaching and Learning in a Digital World: Proceedings of the 20th International Conference on Interactive Collaborative Learning—Volume 2*; Springer: Cham, Switzerland, 2018; pp. 110–115.

Soyusiawaty, D.; Rahmawanto, F. Similarity Detector on the Student Assignment Document Using Levenshtein Distance Method. In Proceedings of the 2018 International Seminar on Research of Information Technology and Intelligent Systems (ISRITI), Yogyakarta, Indonesia, 21–22 November 2018; pp. 656–661. [CrossRef]

Greenhill, S.J. Levenshtein distances fail to identify language relationships accurately. *Comput. Linguist.* **2011**, *37*, 689–698. [CrossRef]

Stan, A.I.; Truică, C.O.; Apostol, E.S. SimpLex: A lexical text simplification architecture. *Neural Comput. Appl.* **2023**, *35*, 6265–6280.

Sarzynska-Wawer, J.; Wawer, A.; Pawlak, A.; Szymanowska, J.; Stefaniak, I.; Jarkiewicz, M.; Okruszek, L. Detecting formal thought disorder by deep contextualized word representations. *Psychiatry Res.* **2021**, *304*, 114135. [CrossRef] [PubMed]

Ultimate Guide to Text Similarity with Python—NewsCatcher. Available online: https://www.newscatcherapi.com/blog/ultimate-guide-to-text-similarity-with-python (accessed on 16 September 2023).

Liu, Y.; Ott, M.; Goyal, N.; Du, J.; Joshi, M.; Chen, D.; Levy, O.; Lewis, M.; Zettlemoyer, L.; Stoyanov, V. Roberta: A robustly optimized bert pretraining approach. *arXiv* **2019**, arXiv:1907.11692.

Devlin, J.; Chang, M.W.; Lee, K.; Toutanova, K. Bert: Pre-training of deep bidirectional transformers for language understanding. *arXiv* **2018**, arXiv:1810.04805.

Reimers, N.; Gurevych, I. Sentence-bert: Sentence embeddings using siamese bert-networks. *arXiv* **2019**, arXiv:1908.10084.

Parr, T. The definitive ANTLR 4 reference. In *The Definitive ANTLR 4 Reference. Sample Grammars*; Torrosa: Barcelona, Spain, 2013. Available online: https://github.com/antlr/grammars-v4 (accessed on 23 September 2023).

MDPI
St. Alban-Anlage 66
4052 Basel
Switzerland
www.mdpi.com

Mathematics Editorial Office
E-mail: mathematics@mdpi.com
www.mdpi.com/journal/mathematics

www.ingramcontent.com/pod-product-compliance
Lightning Source LLC
Chambersburg PA
CBHW061501220926
51850CB00004B/140
* 9 7 8 3 7 2 5 8 1 0 6 7 3 *